THE OXFORD HANDBOOK OF

BIBLICAL STUDIES

THE OXFORD HANDBOOK OF

BIBLICAL STUDIES

Edited by

J. W. ROGERSON

and

JUDITH M. LIEU

OXFORD
UNIVERSITY PRESS

OXFORD
UNIVERSITY PRESS

Great Clarendon Street, Oxford OX2 6DP

Oxford University Press is a department of the University of Oxford.
It furthers the University's objective of excellence in research, scholarship,
and education by publishing worldwide in

Oxford New York

Auckland Cape Town Dar es Salaam Hong Kong Karachi
Kuala Lumpur Madrid Melbourne Mexico City Nairobi
New Delhi Shanghai Taipei Toronto

With offices in

Argentina Austria Brazil Chile Czech Republic France Greece
Guatemala Hungary Italy Japan Poland Portugal Singapore
South Korea Switzerland Thailand Turkey Ukraine Vietnam

Oxford is a registered trade mark of Oxford University Press
in the UK and in certain other countries

Published in the United States
by Oxford University Press Inc., New York

© Oxford University Press 2006

The moral rights of the authors have been asserted
Database right Oxford University Press (maker)

First published 2006

Library of Congress Cataloging-in-Publication Data

The Oxford handbook of biblical studies / edited by J.W. Rogerson and Judith M. Lieu
p. cm.
Includes index.
ISBN-13: 978-0-19-925425-5 (alk. paper)
ISBN-10: 0-19-925425-7 (alk. paper)
1. Bible–Criticism, interpretation, etc. I. Rogerson, J. W. (John William), 1935- II. Lieu, Judith.
BS511.3.094 2006
220.6–dc22
2005030685

Typeset by SPI Publisher Services, Pondicherry, India
Printed in Great Britain on acid-free paper by Antony Rowe Ltd., Chippenham, Wiltshire

ISBN 0–19–925425–7   978–0–19–925425–5

1 3 5 7 9 10 8 6 4 2

CONTENTS

Part I   On the Discipline

SECTION 1. HISTORY OF THE DISCIPLINE IN THE LAST SEVENTY YEARS

SECTION 2. THE IMPACT OF OTHER DISCIPLINES UPON BIBLICAL SCHOLARSHIP

Part II Languages, Translation, and Textual Transmission of the Bible

Part III Historical and Social Study of the Bible

SECTION 1. BACKGROUND AND CONTEXT

Part IV The Composition of the Bible

Part V Methods in Biblical Scholarship

LIST OF CONTRIBUTORS

John R. Bartlett is Emeritus Professor of Pastoral Studies at Trinity College, Dublin.

J. N. Birdsall was Professor of New Testament, University of Birmingham, now deceased.

Walter Brueggemann is Professor of Old Testament, Columbia Theological Seminary, Decatur, Georgia.

Richard A. Burridge is Dean of King's College London.

John M. Court is Honorary Senior Research Fellow in Biblical Studies at the University of Kent.

Eryl W. Davies is Reader in Old Testament at the University of Wales, Bangor.

Philip Davies is Emeritus Professor of Biblical Studies at the University of Sheffield.

Katharine J. Dell is Senior Lecturer in Old Testament at the University of Cambridge.

James D. G. Dunn is Lightfoot Professor Emeritus of Divinity at the University of Durham.

John Elwolde is Translation Consultant to the United Bible Societies.

Craig A. Evans is Payzant Distinguished Professor of New Testament at Acadia Divinity College, Nova Scotia.

Johannes P. Floss is Emeritus Professor of Old Testament at the University of Aachen.

Lester L. Grabbe is Professor of Hebrew Bible and Early Judaism at the University of Hull.

Erich S. Gruen is Gladys Rehard Wood Professor of History and Classics at the University of California, Berkeley.

Harriet A. Harris is Chaplain at Wadham College, Oxford.

Robert Hayward is Professor of Hebrew at the University of Durham.

Catherine Hezser is Reader in Middle Eastern Religions at the School of Oriental and African Studies, London.

Bernd Janowski is Professor of Old Testament at the University of Tübingen.

Kenneth Kitchen is Emeritus Professor of Egyptology at the University of Liverpool.

Michael A. Knibb is Samuel Davidson Professor Emeritus of Old Testament Studies at King's College London.

Reinhard G. Kratz is Professor of Old Testament at the University of Göttingen.

W. G. Lambert is Emeritus Professor of Assyriology at the University of Birmingham.

Judith M. Lieu is Professor of New Testament at King's College London.

Lee Martin McDonald is President and Professor of New Testament Studies at Acadia Divinity School, Nova Scotia.

Jonathan Magonet is Professor and Principal at Leo Baeck College, London.

Alan Millard is Rankin Professor Emeritus of Hebrew and Ancient Semitic Languages at the University of Liverpool.

Margaret M. Mitchell is Associate Professor of New Testament at the University of Chicago Divinity School.

Robert Morgan is a former Reader in Theology at the University of Oxford.

Gerard J. Norton is a former Reader at the University of Birmingham.

Stanley E. Porter is President, Dean and Professor of New Testament at McMaster Divinity College, Hamilton, Ontario.

Peter Richardson is Emeritus Professor of Religion at the University of Toronto.

J. W. Rogerson is Emeritus Professor of Biblical Studies at the University of Sheffield.

Deborah W. Rooke is Lecturer in Old Testament Studies at King's College London.

Christopher Rowland is Professor of Exegesis of Holy Scripture at the University of Oxford.

Alison Salvesen is University Research Lecturer in Jewish Bible Versions at the University of Oxford.

Arie Van der Kooij is Professor of Old Testament at the University of Leiden.

Marie-Theres Wacker is Professor of Old Testament and Women's Research at the University of Münster.

Gordon Wenham is at Trinity College Bristol, and was formerly Professor of Old Testament at the University of Gloucestershire.

Keith W. Whitelam is Professor of Biblical Studies at the University of Sheffield.

LIST OF ABBREVIATIONS

AB	Anchor Bible
ABD	*Anchor Bible Dictionary*
AGAJU	Arbeiten zur Geschichte des antiken Judentums und des Urchristentums
ANRW	Aufstieg und Niedergang der römischen Welt
AP	A. Cowley, *Aramaic Papyri of the Fifth Century B.C.* (Oxford: Clarendon Press, 1923; repr. Osnabrück: Otto Zeller, 1967)
APOT	*Apocrypha and Pseudepigrapha of the Old Testament*
ATD	Das Alte Testament Deutsch
ATSAT	Arbeiten zu Text und Sprache im Alten Testament
BA	*Biblical Archaeologist*
BARev	*Biblical Archaeology Review*
BEvTh	Beiträge zur evangelischen Theologie
BGU	*Aegyptische Urkunden aus dem Königlichen Museen zu Berlin, Griechische Urkunden*
BHK	Biblia Hebraica, edited by R. Kittel. Stuttgart, various editions
BHQ	Biblia Hebraica Quinta
BHS	Biblia Hebraica Stuttgartensia, edited by K. Elliger and W. Rudolph. Stuttgart, 1983
BIOSCS	*Bulletin of the International Organization for Septuagint and Cognate Studies*
BIS	Biblical Interpretation Series
BJRL	*Bulletin of the John Rylands University of Manchester Library*
BJS	Brown Judaic Studies
BM	E. G. Kraeling, *The Brooklyn Museum Aramaic Papyri* (New Haven: Yale University Press, 1953)
BWANT	Beiträge zur Wissenschaft vom Alten und Neuen Testament
BZ	*Biblische Zeitschrift*
BZAW	Beihefte zur Zeitschrift für die alttestamentliche Wissenschaft
BZNW	Beihefte zur Zeitschrift für die neutestamentliche Wissenschaft
CBQ	*Catholic Biblical Quarterly*
CBQ MS	*Catholic Biblical Quarterly*, Monograph Series
CEJL	Commentaries on Early Jewish Literature
CIJ	*Corpus inscriptionum iudaicarum*

CIL	*Corpus inscriptionum latinarum*
COS	Cambridge Oriental Series
CPI	*Corpus papyrorum iudaicarum*
CQ	Classical Quarterly
CRINT	Compendium rerum iudaicarum ad Novum Testamentum
CSCT	Columbia Studies in the Classical Tradition
DJD	Discoveries in the Judaean Desert
EAEHL	*Encyclopedia of Archaeological Excavations in the Holy Land*
EKL	*Evangelisches Kirchenlexikon*, 3rd edn.
EQ	*Evangelical Quarterly*
ET	*Expository Times*
ETL	Ephemerides theologicae Lovanienses
EvTh	*Evangelische Theologie*
FOTL	Forms of the Old Testament Literature
FRLANT	Forschungen zur Religion und Literatur des Alten und Neuen Testaments
GAT	Grundrisse zum Alten Testament
HAR	*Hebrew Annual Review*
HAT	Handbuch zum Alten Testament
HdO	Handbuch der Orientalistik
HSM	Harvard Semitic Monographs
HTR	*Harvard Theological Review*
HUBP	Hebrew University Bible Project
HUCA	*Hebrew Union College Annual*
IEJ	*Israel Exploration Journal*
ILS	*Inscriptiones latinae selectae*
JBL	*Journal of Biblical Literature*
JBR	*Journal of Bible and Religion*
JBTh	*Jahrbücher für biblische Theologie*
JJS	*Journal of Jewish Studies*
JR	*Journal of Religion*
JRS	*Journal of Roman Studies*
JSHRZ	Jüdische Schriften aus hellenistisch-römischer Zeit
JSJ	*Journal for the Study of Judaism*
JSJSup	*Journal for the Study of Judaism*, Supplement Series
JSNT	*Journal for the Study of the New Testament*
JSNTS.S	*Journal for the Study of the New Testament*, Supplement Series
JSOT	*Journal for the Study of the Old Testament*
JSOTS.S	*Journal for the Study of the Old Testament*, Supplement Series
JSP	*Journal for the Study of the Pseudepigrapha*
JSS	*Journal of Semitic Studies*
JTS	*Journal of Theological Studies*

LCL	Loeb Classical Library
LSJ	H. G. Liddell, R. Scott, and H. S. Jones, *A Greek–English Lexicon*, 9th edn. with revised supplement, Oxford, 1996
LThK	*Lexikon für Theologie und Kirche*, 3rd edn.
NB	*New Blackfriars*
NEA	*Near Eastern Archaeology*
NT	*Novum Testamentum*
NT Supp	*Novum Testamentum* Supplements
NTOA	Novum testamentum et orbis antiquus
NTS	*New Testament Studies*
NTTS	New Testament Tools and Studies
OBO	Orbis biblicus et orientalis
OBT	Overtures to Biblical Theology
OEANE	*Oxford Encyclopedia of the Ancient Near East*
OGIS	*Orientis graeci inscriptiones selectae* (ed. W. Dittenberger, 2 vols., Leipzig, 1903–5)
OTP	*Old Testament Pseudepigrapha*
OTL	Old Testament Library
OTS	Oudtestamentische Studiën
PEQ	*Palestine Exploration Quarterly*
RB	*Revue Biblique*
RevQ	*Revue de Qumran*
RGG	*Religion in Geschichte und Gegenwart*, 4th edn.
SBL	Society of Biblical Literature
SBL DS	Society of Biblical Literature, Dissertation Series
SBL SCS	Society of Biblical Literature, Septuagint and Cognate Studies
SBLMS	Society of Biblical Literature Monograph Series
SBLTT	Society of Biblical Literature Texts and Translations
SBT	Studies in Biblical Theology
SEG	*Supplementum epigraphicum graecum*
SFSJH	South Florida Studies in Jewish History
SHR	Studies in the History of Religions
SJLA	Studies in Judaism in Late Antiquity
SJT	*Scottish Journal of Theology*
SNTSMS	Society of New Testament Studies Monograph Series
SPB	Studia Postbiblica
STDJ	Studies on the Texts of the Desert of Judah
SVT	Supplements to *Vetus Testamentum*
TAD	Bezalel Porten and Ada Yardeni, *Textbook of Aramaic Documents from Ancient Egypt*, i–iv, Hebrew University, Department of the History of the Jewish People, Texts and Studies for Students; Jerusalem: Hebrew University, 1986–99

ThLZ	*Theologische Literaturzeitung*
ThPQ	*Theologisch-praktische Quartalschrift*
TLS	*Times Literary Supplement*
TRE	*Theologische Realenzyklopädie*
TSAJ	Texte und Studien zum antiken Judentum
TUAT	Texte zur Umwelt des Alten Testaments, ed. O. Kaiser. Gütersloher Verlagshaus Gerd Mohn: Gütersloh 1982–1997, Supplement 2001
VigChrSupp	Supplements to *Vigiliae Christianae*
VT	*Vetus Testamentum*
VuF	*Verkündigung und Forschung*
WMANT	Wissenschaftliche Monographien zum Alten und Neuen Testament
WUNT	Wissenschaftliche Untersuchungen zum Neuen Testament
ZNW	*Zeitschrift für die neutestamentliche Wissenschaft*

PREFACE

What is (or should it be are? but we shall stay with the singular) Biblical Studies? Is it a watered-down version of theology with the doctrinal parts omitted? Is it like Religious Studies, but concentrating on Judaism and Christianity? The answer is that Biblical Studies is a collection of various, and in some cases independent, disciplines clustering around a collection of texts known as the Bible whose precise limits (those of the Bible) are still a matter of disagreement among various branches of the Christian churches. These disciplines range from Archaeology, Egyptology, and Assyriology through Textual Criticism, Linguistics, History, and Sociology, to Literary Theory, Feminism, and Theology, to name only some. That these disciplines should have come to be connected with the study of the Bible results from the unique position that the Bible (however understood) has occupied in Western history, art, and culture for some 2,000 years. No comparable collection of texts has been subjected to such sustained critical examination and elucidation over such a long period of time. The present Handbook aims to indicate to readers the current state of scholarship associated with the Bible.

On the assumption that readers will concentrate upon particular chapters that interest or concern them, rather than attempt to read the Handbook from beginning to end, no attempt has been made by the editors to harmonize the contributions. Anyone who does succeed in reading it from beginning to end will notice that there is occasionally some overlap of material, not to mention differences of opinion among the contributors. Also, it will be noticeable that English-speaking contributors from North America seem to read a different set of books from those in Britain, while contributors from Germany concentrate primarily on German-speaking scholarship (an exception is the essay on feminism). These differences are representative of the state of scholarship, which has become so technical and specialized that even scholars working in a comparatively small area cannot hope to master the secondary literature produced by experts working in different countries and languages. However, in the view of the editors, the diversity that becomes apparent in the Handbook is a reliable guide to the present state of Biblical Studies.

The Handbook has taken longer to reach its final form than the editors originally envisaged. In several cases, contributors had to withdraw for personal reasons, and in one case, that of Dr Ian MacDonald, who agreed to write the chapter on ethics, his sad death before he had been able to complete the work meant that another contributor had to be sought at short notice. Also, Professor J. N. Birdsall died before his article went to press. The editors wish to record their gratitude both to those colleagues who met the original deadlines and who then had to wait longer than expected for the collection to be completed, and those who stepped in at short notice to fill unanticipated gaps.

The four essays from German colleagues have been translated by John Rogerson and approved and amended by the contributors. In the case of the highly technical essay by Johannes Floss, additional help was given by two colleagues in Aachen, Professor P. G. Meyer and Dr. P. H. Marsden. John Rogerson is also grateful to his niece Rhianna Fulford, who provided help with scanning, typing, indexing, and formatting.

Judith Lieu

J. W. Rogerson

PART I

ON THE DISCIPLINE

HISTORY OF THE DISCIPLINE IN THE LAST SEVENTY YEARS

CHAPTER 1

OLD TESTAMENT

J. W. ROGERSON

ALL divisions of time are arbitrary, if not conventional, and this is certainly true of any attempt to divide Old Testament scholarship into neat periods of time. Seventy years ago the discipline was still reacting in various ways to the theory of the history of Israelite religion and sacrifice and the theory of how and when the Old Testament had been composed that had received classical expression fifty years earlier in J. Wellhausen's *Prolegomena* (1883). In Germany the discipline was also having to face the determined attempts of the 'German Christian' movement to banish the study of Hebrew and the Old Testament from universities and the use of the Old Testament from Christian worship. However, the ending of the Second World War initiated a period of consolidation with strongly marked theological interests, until the emergence, in the late 1960s, of new methodologies including structuralism, literature criticism, feminist and liberation theology, deconstruction, and canonical criticism. The present essay will therefore be divided into three main sections: 1. Up to 1945; 2. From 1945 to 1970; 3. From 1970. Even so, these divisions will not provide hard and fast periods which avoid overlap and repetition.

1. UP TO 1945

The position stated classically by Wellhausen (although it can also be found with different emphases in Robertson Smith (1881) and Abraham Kuenen (1874–5) divided the history of Israelite religion into three periods. The first, that of the period of the Judges and the early monarchy (twelfth to eighth centuries BCE), was characterized by many local sanctuaries. There was no centrally organized priesthood or ritual, and there were family or city-based communal occasions of worship (Judg. 21: 19, 1 Sam. 9: 11–14; 20: 18–29) as well as celebrations at harvest times. These conditions were represented in the sources of the Pentateuch designated as J and E (because they *mainly* used the divine names Jahweh and Elohim respectively) as well as in Judges and the books of Samuel. Under the influence of the eighth-century prophets and their demand for exclusive loyalty to God backed by social justice, the composition of Deuteronomy (D) in the seventh century initiated a reformation in the reign of Josiah around 622, which closed the local sanctuaries and made Jerusalem the sole legitimate place of sacrifice. This second period ended with the destruction of Jerusalem and its temple by the Babylonians in 587 and the resulting period of exile. The third period was that of the restoration after 540, when the temple was eventually rebuilt (*c.*515) and when the Priestly (P) and ritual portions of the Pentateuch were composed. An implication of this position was that little could be known of the history of Israel before the rise of the monarchy in the late eleventh century, and that most of what was attributed to Moses was the projection back into earlier times of what were essentially the rituals of the post-exilic period.

Leaving aside the attempts that were made to vindicate the account of Israel's religion that were derived from a straightforward non-critical reading of the text (i.e. the traditional view), scholarship reacted in several ways to the position outlined by Wellhausen. These can be characterized as literary, archaeological, and anthropological, although these categories are not exact.

(a) Literary Responses

These took two forms. On the one hand were the attempts of scholars such as Budde and Eissfeldt to extend the tracing of the Pentateuchal sources J and E into the books of Joshua, Judges, and 1 Samuel, or to refine the analysis by the discovery of new sources such as Eissfeldt's 'L' source (Eissfeldt 1922). The other approach, associated particularly with the work of Gunkel (1901–10), took the sources for granted and enquired after the form and origin of the units from which they were composed. This led to the form-critical investigation of the sources in one of its senses (see Chapter 34 below).

(b) Archaeological Responses

These took various forms: cultural, religious, and historical. The cultural responses were based upon the discovery of Assyrian and Babylonian texts which resembled the biblical accounts of creation and flood and the laws of Exodus 21–4. They illuminated the cultural context of ancient Israel and disclosed the history, religion, and culture of ancient Mesopotamia as never before. One conclusion that was drawn from these discoveries was that everything that was thought to be unique to the Old Testament was, in fact, derived from Babylon (Delitzsch 1901–2). This view, as later developed by Delitzsch (1921), would provide ammunition for 'German Christian' attempts to discredit the Old Testament. In a different direction, the similarities between the religions of Mesopotamia and Israel stimulated the formation of the 'history of religions school', a group of scholars originally based in Göttingen who, without relinquishing their commitment to the Old Testament as scripture, were concerned to trace the emergence of Israel's faith within the wider cultural background (Klatt 1969). There was a similar development in New Testament scholarship (see Chapter 2 below). Particular attention was paid to the Babylonian roots of Israelite apocalyptic and eschatology, and a concrete working out of these general ideas led, in Scandinavian and British scholarship, to theories about how sacral kingship in ancient Israel had played a vital role in forming beliefs about the universal kingship of the God of Israel and of messianic expectations (Volz 1912; Mowinckel 1922; Hooke 1935). Drawing upon reconstructions of the Babylonian new year festival, biblical scholars reconstructed an annual ceremony in ancient Israel in which the king played a crucial role. He underwent ritual humiliation and death before being restored to life and participating in a sacred marriage.

These ceremonies ensured the prosperity of the community for the coming year. They were reconstructed mainly from the psalms (thus reversing the post-exilic dates to which most of them had been previously assigned by critical scholarship), but it was believed that the creation story of Genesis 1 was also used in the rituals, rituals which ultimately looked beyond the immediate future to an eschatological consummation of God's universal rule.

The historical response took two forms. The excavation work of W. F. Albright and his students had the aim of confirming the historicity of the biblical record in opposition to negative conclusions about what could be known of Israel's history prior to the period of the Judges, conclusions that went back through Wellhausen to the early nineteenth century. Albright believed that he had found evidence for the conquest of Canaan as related in the book of Joshua, and that other discoveries confirmed the claim in Genesis that the Hebrew ancestors (Abraham, Isaac, and Jacob) had migrated from northern Mesopotamia some time in the first half of the second millennium. His book *From the Stone Age to Christianity* (1940) presented what was in fact a vindication of the biblical account of Israel's history, with a decisive role being attributed to Moses in founding Israel's distinctive faith. With some modification, Albright's position continued to be advocated by his pupils G. E. Wright (1957) and J. Bright until (in the case of Bright) the 1980s (Bright 1981). German scholars such as G. Schumacher and E. Sellin were also pioneers in Palestinian archaeology, but a distinctive contribution to biblical geography and history was made by the researches on the ground by A. Alt and M. Noth. While broadly accepting the Wellhausen synthesis, they refined it in several directions. Alt's essay 'The God of the Fathers' (1929) identified the religion of Abraham and the Ancestors with a type of religion deduced from (much later) Nabataean sources in which the phrase 'the God of X' (X being a person) indicated a loose bond between an individual and the god in whose honour that individual had founded a cult. Noth's researches into the period of the Judges (1930) led him to conclude that prior to the monarchy Israel had been an amphictyony: that is, a tribal league centred upon a specific sanctuary, whose members had a common religion, mutual obligations, and basic laws. Noth traced the material common to the presumed Pentateuchal sources J and E to the tradition held by the members of the amphictyony. The researches of Alt and Noth had the effect of providing a more positive picture of Israel before the monarchy. On another matter they were in direct opposition to Albright, holding that there had been no Israelite conquest of Canaan, but, rather, a gradual process of settlement. Noth's commentary on Joshua (1938) argued that its stories of conquest were largely aetiological: that is, folk stories generated long after the event to explain the history of particular sites. Noth's researches into the composition of the Pentateuch (1948) also led him into direct conflict with Albright, with the conclusion that virtually nothing could be known about Moses.

Anthropological responses to the Wellhausen synthesis developed the implication of his work: namely, that there had been a steady development or evolution of Israelite belief from polytheism, through henotheism, to monotheism. Using the method known as the doctrine of survivals (i.e. reference to customs thought to be 'primitive') and comparing them with features of other cultures, especially the cultures of modern so-called primitive peoples, scholars such as Oesterley and Robinson (1930) found references in the Old Testament to animism (the worship of spirits believed to reside in trees or springs) and polytheism, in accounting for the development of Israel's faith.

(c) The German Church Struggle

The 'German Christians', a movement closely allied to the National Socialism of Adolf Hitler, expressed their anti-Semitism by targeting the Old Testament, among other things identified as Jewish (Scholder 1977–85; Weber 2000). The view that there was something distinctive and German about German Christianity had been argued well before the rise of Hitler by Artur Bonus (1914). It was then taken up by 'German Christians' and combined with views such as those of Delitzsch to maintain that the Old Testament had no place in Christianity or its worship. It is difficult from the vantage-point of hindsight to appreciate the pressures under which Old Testament scholars in Germany were placed, pressures that included boycotts and sit-ins by 'German Christian' students, and pressures exerted by university administrations that were required to execute government policies after 1933 (Scherffig 1989–94). While some, such as G. von Rad, became members of the Confessing Church in opposition to National Socialism, others succumbed to the pressures, while others carried on as best as they could in the circumstances. Outright theological opposition came from the Swiss scholar Vischer in his *The Witness of the Old Testament to Christ* (1934–42), which sought to identify the implicit presence of Christ in Old Testament narratives in support of his view that the Old Testament was not only indispensable to the church, but the book without which it was impossible to understand the New Testament.

(d) Other Theological Responses

If Vischer's work can be seen as a response to the situation created by the 'German Christian' movement, the remarkable number of other Old Testament theologies that appeared in German in the 1930s were more of a response to the 'dialectical theology' of the 1920s. This latter movement, associated particularly with the Swiss theologian Karl Barth, was a direct challenge to the 'liberal' theology presumed to be allied to the practice of historical criticism. It claimed that a distinction should be made between what could be gained by historical research and what was revealed to faith, and it stressed that faith was concerned centrally with life. These claims posed fundamental questions for scholars who were writing about the theology of the Old Testament. If an Old Testament theology was simply an account of the beliefs that ancient Israelites had held at different times in their history, it failed the test of enabling modern believers to gain from the Old Testament those aspects of revelation that would help them to live the life of faith. If, on the other hand, all the emphasis was placed upon the revelatory element, there was a danger that the knowledge gained from historical criticism would at best be ignored and at worst be regarded as irrelevant. Walter Eichrodt (1933–9), Ernst Sellin (1933), and Ludwig Köhler (1935) sought to bridge this divide by organizing their theological work around key institutions or ideas that described the relationship between God and his people, rather than abstract truths or doctrines that were unrelated to life. The historical-critical dimension was retained by examining how the divine–human relationship had manifested itself at different periods and in different ways. The dimension of revelation was safeguarded by the claim that it was precisely in and through the historical processes of Israel's existence that God's character and will were disclosed. Even so, the desired synthesis could not be achieved without an element of subjective interpretation. Eichrodt chose the institution of the covenant as the organizing principle of his investigations, while for Sellin and Köhler the guiding ideas were those of the holiness of God and the lordship of God, respectively. In Britain a distinctive contribution to the discussion was made by H. W. Robinson who, in publications from as early as 1905, had argued that the Israelite experience of reality was different from that of modern Western humans. This approach was a variation on the use of anthropology, because it drew upon studies of 'primitive' peoples and their alleged psychology, and argued that it was precisely because of an awareness of reality different from that of moderns that ancient Israelites were able to perceive the divine in the events of nature and history. Robinson was only partly able to work this out in a theology of the Old Testament before his death (Robinson 1946), but the legacy of his view of ancient Hebrew psychology lasted well into the following period.

2. 1945 TO 1970

This period will be dealt with under four main headings: the discovery of the Dead Sea Scrolls, the biblical theology movement, Old Testament theology, and the debate about the history of Israel.

(a) The Dead Sea Scrolls

The news which reached the scholarly world in the late 1940s to the effect that significant quantities of ancient Hebrew and Aramaic manuscripts had been discovered in caves near the north-west end of the Dead Sea was completely unexpected. It had the effect of diverting a considerable number of Old Testament scholars away from what they had been doing to devoting their whole attention to the new discoveries. The fact that the discoveries were to affect the study of sectarian Judaism and the New Testament rather more than the Old Testament did not prevent Old Testament specialists from entering the fray and contributing to theories about the origin and beliefs of the group generally believed to have written the sectarian documents in the hundred years or so before the beginning of the Common Era (see Cross 1958). It is noteworthy that Old Testament scholars from Germany became less involved in these discussions than their Anglo-Saxon or other Continental colleagues. Perhaps this was an indication of the much stronger commitment to Old Testament interpretation by German-speaking scholars than by their colleagues elsewhere. The immediate gain for Old Testament scholarship was confined to the field of textual criticism, the importance of the discoveries lying in the fact that the Hebrew fragments were about 1,000 years older than those on which scholarly editions of the Hebrew Bible were based. The seventh edition of the *Biblia Hebraica* edited by R. Kittel (1951) included variant readings from the Isaiah manuscript (IQIs^a) and the Habakkuk scroll, and some of these were reflected in the Revised Standard Version translation of the Bible (1952). However, scholars would have to wait for many years before all the biblical fragments were published. Early theories about the textual transmission of the Old Testament based upon the discoveries posited three main centres of textual production: Alexandria (the Septuagint and some Qumran manuscripts), Palestinian (the Samaritan Pentateuch and some Qumran manuscripts), and Babylonian (the Masoretic Text). However, this did not explain why more than one text type was found at Qumran, and later research modified this view.

(b) Biblical Theology

The term 'biblical theology' is ambiguous (it can mean either the theology contained in the Bible or a theology in accordance with what the Bible contains; see Ebeling 1963); it has been applied to various movements within biblical scholarship from the late eighteenth century; and it presupposes the unity of the Old and New Testaments (see, generally, Barr 1999). In the present section the term will be used to describe the Old Testament aspect of a movement that was prominent especially, although not exclusively, in English-speaking scholarship in roughly the period 1945 to 1960, although it had its roots in earlier scholarship (for the New Testament aspect see Chapter 2 below). It was an attempt to harness the results of historical-critical study of the Bible to the theological and social needs of the churches in the immediate post-war period, and it did so by claiming that Hebrew psychology and the Hebrew language possessed certain unique features that made them suitable vehicles for divine revelation. At the level of psychology (in a very broad sense), the Hebrews possessed an awareness of history and historical processes not shared by their neighbours, for whom reality was more closely perceived in relation to the recurring cycles of nature. With regard to language, Hebrew was said to be a dynamic, verb and action-orientated language, in opposition to Greek, which was characterized as more static and noun-orientated. Biblical theology could thus accommodate the results of the history-of-religions approach by using the latter as a foil to the Old Testament. These results demonstrated the uniqueness of the Hebrew conception of reality. Historical criticism was important precisely because it investigated and corroborated the historical events through which God had acted to reveal himself. The roots of the claims made about the distinctive Hebrew way of perceiving reality went back to works such as those of Pederson (1926–40) and H. W. Robinson (1936), but they were given classical expression in two books by G. E. Wright, *The Old Testament against its Environment* (1950) and *God who Acts: Biblical Theology as Recital* (1952). In Britain the movement found expression in studies of the biblical view of man (*sic*) and of work (Ryder Smith 1951) and in *A Theological Word Book of the Bible* (1950) edited by A. Richardson. The assumption behind these exercises was that the impact of divine revelation upon Hebrew experience left thought forms and linguistic features which could be systematized by means of word studies. It was taken for granted that because Hebrew thought and language had been uniquely formed by contact with the divine, the results gained from the studies of the thought forms and language would be normative for Christian attempts to understand the world and to shape its future.

The biblical theology movement failed because of its dependence upon flawed linguistic methods (Barr 1961) and outdated theories of social anthropology (see Rogerson 1974 and 1978). Its view that Israelites perceived history in ways different from their neighbours was also challenged (Albrektson 1967). The fundamental concern that inspired the movement, however, that of how to harness historical criticism to the needs of theology and of faith communities, would be taken up later by one of its critics, B. S. Childs.

(c) Old Testament Theology

The years 1957–60 saw the publication of one of the most important and influential Old Testament theologies of the twentieth century, that of Gerhard von Rad. It was both a masterly synthesis of much research by many scholars that had preceded it and possessed an originality that anticipated later developments, even if those developments went off in different directions than those indicated by von Rad. To the question 'What is the subject-matter of an Old Testament theology?', the answer was simple. It was Israel's confessions of its belief that God had chosen and sustained the people, as contained in the literary traditions of the Old Testament. How had God chosen and made himself known to Israel? Initially, in many ways, in various places, and at different times to individuals and to groups. These encounters had been recorded in various ways: in cult legends, aetiologies, poems, songs, and sagas. The encounters continued by units being combined into greater literary wholes. This was not merely a literary exercise. It had its setting in cultic celebrations at which the stories of God's dealings with Israel were recounted, and at which this history and thus the divine encounter were experienced anew, as something present and actual. In time, the literary traditions became the Pentateuchal sources J and E, and the period between their completion and the composition of Deuteronomy and the Deuteronomistic History beginning in the late seventh century was bridged by the prophets. These did not generally retell the histories of God's dealings with Israel, but rather looked forward to what God was about to do, for judgement or salvation. The Babylonian exile in the sixth century caused a major disruption, which was interpreted by the Deuteronomistic Historians in terms of reluctance of the people to obey God's commandments. Von Rad was uncertain about the origins of the Priestly traditions, noting their lack of reference to the house of David. This suggested that while, after the exile, they came to represent the practice of ritual and priesthood in the Jerusalem sanctuary, they did not necessarily originate in Jerusalem.

Two matters central to von Rad's position were his view of what could be known about the history of Israel prior to the period of the Judges, and how Israel's view of its history, as expressed in the Old Testament, was to be related to a scholarly, 'objective' reconstruction of that history. Von Rad accepted the researches of Alt and Noth, especially the latter's view that the principal themes of the story of God's dealings with Israel—the promise of land to the Ancestors (Abraham, Isaac, and Jacob), the exodus from Egypt, the law giving at Sinai, and the occupation of Canaan—had been developed separately and were not originally connected with each other. Their fusion was part of the creative process of building the tradition, assisted by cultic celebrations. The fact that stories about Moses were present in several of the themes—for example, the exodus and the Sinai law giving—suggested to Noth that the presence of Moses in the traditions was a later development in the process of tradition building, a conclusion that von Rad seemed to accept. At any rate, his view was that the events in which God had disclosed himself were beyond recovery by historians, which also meant that nothing could be known historically about personages such as Abraham. One reason for this, according to von Rad, was that until the sixth century when the Deuteronomistic History was composed, the only way in which occurrences could be described in Israel was by means of *Dichtung*—a German word normally translated 'fiction', but which in von Rad's usage seems to have indicated not falsification, but a poetic, creative, and imaginative account of happenings that expressed their inner meanings. Another reason was that personages such as Abraham were personifications of groups and their experiences, as well as being individuals whose names had been remembered.

Important for von Rad's view of how the traditions had coalesced into the connected stories of the sources J and E was the tribal league or amphictyony, proposed by Noth (1930). This association of Israelite tribes in the period of the Judges was the melting-pot which enabled the isolated experiences of different groups to become the property of the whole people. What God had done for one group or individual he had done for all. Von Rad's view of Israel's history from the period of the monarchy was less controversial, except that he believed that a new spirit, a kind of enlightenment, had emerged in the reign of Solomon. This affected the way in which the older traditions were now read, and resulted in there being no new perceptions of God's dealings with the people until the rise of the eighth-century prophets. In the post-exilic period Israel withdrew from its confession of God's dealings with the people in its history, to a position dominated by obedience to the law.

What was the place within an Old Testament theology of Israel's history as reconstructed by scholarly research? The answer was none. This did not mean that von Rad ignored it; it contributed vitally to his view of how and when the historical traditions had been formed. But it was the way in which Israel had chosen to link together the disparate accounts of God's workings that was of prime theological importance. No less important were the ways in which the tradition contradicted itself: for example, in the attitudes to monarchy expressed in 1 Samuel 8–10. What this amounted to was a rehabilitation, for theological purposes, of the Old Testament's own picture of its history, a picture which critical scholarship in the previous 150 years had so painstakingly taken apart and reassembled in a totally different form. Space considerations preclude any further description of von Rad's consequent treatment of the themes and institutions central to Israel's understanding of God's dealings with the people.

The achievement of von Rad lay in the way in which he was able to combine the results of historical research and literary, form-critical, and redaction studies of Old Testament texts to produce a theology centred upon divine–human encounter. This meant that it was not an intellectual account of what Israelites had believed, but a portrayal of dynamic and changing processes in which encounter with God was renewed, as received traditions were interpreted and reinterpreted in the face of concrete situations. In at least two ways von Rad anticipated things to come, although they would take forms of which he would hardly have approved. On the one hand, his insistence on the priority of Israel's own ways of constructing its traditions anticipated at the later canonical criticism, while his rehabilitation of the Old Testament's own picture of its history was not far from 'final form' approaches to the biblical text.

(d) Histories of Israel

The publication of the histories of Israel by Noth (1950) and Bright (1960) summed up and brought into direct conflict the tendencies noted above in German and American scholarship. While Bright accepted some of Noth's positions—for example, that Israel was a tribal confederacy in the period of the Judges—and took full account of developments in source and literary criticism, his history was essentially a nuanced and sensitive treatment of the picture presented in the Bible itself, from the time of the Patriarchs to the Maccabean Revolt. For Bright, the Patriarchs were recognizable historical personages; the exodus from Egypt could be dated to the thirteenth century; all the major lines of Israel's religion could be traced back to Moses, 'the great founder of Israel' (Bright 1960: 132); and while the conquest of Canaan under Joshua was not unequivocally endorsed by archaeological discoveries, it could 'be regarded as certain that a violent irruption into the land took place late in the thirteenth century' (Bright 1960: 120). Noth's history began, not with the Patriarchs, but with the origins of the tribes and their existence in Canaan as a tribal confederacy. The Old Testament accounts of the Patriarchs, the exodus, and the Sinai law giving were treated as traditions of the tribal league, whose main value was the information they provided about the beliefs of the tribes. The events that they presupposed were not easily accessible, and in any case were anachronistically ascribed to all Israel, whereas 'Israel' had come into being as a tribal league only in Canaan. In the case of the occupation of Canaan, this was a complex process of peaceful settlement, probably bound up with larger migrations of peoples such as the Aramean wanderings. The destruction of cities identified by Albright and Bright as evidence for the biblical account of the conquest were to be ascribed to the inter-city feuds known from the Amarna Letters of the thirteenth century and to the upheavals consequent upon the invasion of the Sea Peoples around 1200 BCE (Noth 1950: 79–80). From the time of Saul onwards, there was little for the two histories to disagree on, except that Noth's history went as far as the Bar Kochba Revolt in the early second century CE.

3. FROM 1970

Introduction

The most striking feature of the past thirty-five years has been the way in which Old Testament studies have embraced new disciplines. Until the 1960s the historical-critical method was the only 'respectable' academic way of approaching the text, even if 'conservative' scholars disputed its results by arguing, for example, that they were based upon too superficial a knowledge of the ancient Near East. Beginning in the 1960s, methods influenced by linguistic and anthropological structuralism began to be applied to the Old Testament, not least by experts in those fields such as Barthes (in Barthes et al. 1971) and Leach (1966). Around the same time Old

Testament scholars influenced by literary 'New Criticism' began to look at texts as pieces of literature. A further development was that liberation theologians and feminist scholars began to produce important studies of Old Testament texts, and as all these approaches begin to make headway in the discipline, they were enlarged to include such things as reader-response criticism, deconstruction, and psychological ways of reading texts influenced by theorists such as Foucault and Lacan. 'Post-modernism' became a further factor, with its insistence on the lack of master narratives by which to understand and characterize reality. Amid all this, historical criticism developed new insights and techniques, sometimes in dialogue with the newer methodologies. There was a new awareness of the importance of the history of the discipline (see Smend 1989). The study of social anthropology led to a questioning of many of the older assumptions about Hebrew mentality (Rogerson 1978), while the application of sociology to biblical narratives—in fact, an extension and refinement of form-critical work begun by Gunkel and Gressmann—yielded new information about Israelite society. A revival of interest in Old Testament ethics and in the contribution of biblical texts to understanding contemporary problems produced notable studies by Walter Brueggemann (1977). A significant development in the area of theology was initiated by Childs's canonical criticism, while in the area of the history of Israel new techniques and developments in archaeology produced a sharp polarization between scholars described as maximalist or minimalist in regard to what could be known about ancient Israel's history. In the field of traditional literary criticism of the Old Testament, as opposed to the newer literature criticism, there was a marked tendency to date everything a good deal later than had previously been the case. The formative period, ironically that about which scholarship was less well informed than some earlier periods, was seen to be the Persian period of the late sixth to the late fourth centuries BCE. Also within more traditional Old Testament studies the rise of the so-called Richter school called for a new level of technical expertise in the handling of ancient Hebrew texts based upon modern linguistics (see Chapter 34 below). The ground that needs to be covered in the remainder of this chapter is immense and will necessitate treatment that is highly selective and brief. The sections that follow will deal with literary approaches, anthropology and sociology, feminist and liberation interpretations, ethics, theology, archaeology and history, and traditional literary criticism.

(a) Literary Approaches

Although the first essays in literary interpretation of the Old Testament were published in the 1970s, the impetus for the approach has been taken to be

E. Auerbach's *Mimesis*, published in German in 1946 and in English translation in 1968. *Mimesis* is, to quote the book's subtitle, about 'the representation of reality in Western literature', and Auerbach illustrated this on the basis of European literature extending over many centuries, but also including, in the first chapter, Homer and the Bible. *Mimesis* showed that the Bible could be treated 'like any other book' when it came to asking how its stories sought to represent reality, and this opened the way to pioneering studies such as that by Good on irony in the Old Testament (1965), Licht on story-telling in the Bible (1978), and Bar-Efrat on narrative art in the Bible (1979 in Hebrew, 1989 in English). Also in the 1970s Gros Louis, Ackerman, and Warshaw edited a two-volume work on *Literary Interpretations of Biblical Narratives* (1974), and Robert Alter published some of the essays that would form the basis for his influential *The Art of Biblical Narrative* (1981). The 1980s saw the appearance of Adele Berlin's *Poetics and Interpretation of Biblical Narrative* (1983) and *The Literary Guide to the Bible* edited by Alter and Kermode (1987). Many of the contributors to the latter would make distinguished contributions to the field in their own right. Through these and other works, Old Testament studies became familiar with chiastic structures, the formal structuring of plots and narratives, and concepts such as 'point of view' and implied author. Where these studies differed from what had gone before was in taking the final form of the text to be a literary whole. Whereas source criticism would look to apparent contradictions in a text to indicate the work of redactors who had combined disparate sources, literature criticism would accommodate these features to literary devices that contributed dramatic or other effects. There was, indeed, a tendency in literature criticism to regard the possibility of accommodating apparent discrepancies in the text to literary explanations, as proof against the older source criticism. Reader-response criticism, strongly influenced by the work of Fish (1980), focused attention upon reading and readers, and the interests and assumptions that they brought to the text, while deconstruction, influenced by Derrida (1967), looked for contradictions in texts, not in order to identify sources but to show how texts can often undermine themselves by contradictory statements. Acceptance of the view that interpretation is profoundly affected by the assumptions brought by readers to texts (a point clearly proved by work on the history of biblical interpretation) can also be turned back upon texts themselves. If readers have interests, so do texts (and their authors if they can be identified), and this leads to ideological criticism, to the attempt to identify class, gender, and power interests that have affected the production of texts (see Barr 2000). The many 'readings' of Old Testament texts that have been produced by attention to the interests of the texts and their interpreters, as well as to their literary structures and devices, have greatly enriched the discipline. They have also often disregarded attempts to make literature criticism 'scientific' (see below, section g).

(b) Anthropology and Sociology

As noted above, anthropology and sociology in the forms of investigation of the social settings of units of tradition were well established in Old Testament studies. From the late 1960s scholars using these methods were influenced, among other things, by the descriptions of contemporary tribal peoples by Evans-Pritchard and his associates (Evans-Pritchard 1937, 1956, 1965; Lienhardt 1961), by American cultural anthropologists such as Service (1962), and by the structural anthropology of Lévi-Strauss, whose monumental volumes on myth stimulated new thinking in this area (Lévi-Strauss 1964–71; Kirk 1970). This led to a re-evaluation of many ideas about Hebrew mentality (Rogerson 1974, 1978) and to a work on Israelite history and religion that made a great impact, Gottwald's *The Tribes of Yahweh* (1978). Gottwald developed an idea first proposed by Mendenhall (1962), that the Israelite occupation of Canaan had been an internal revolt of peasants against the city-states. Gottwald proposed that the revolt produced an egalitarian society, which in turn engendered belief in YHWH as a God of liberation. Subsequent history, with the rise of the monarchy, represented a failure to maintain this ideal. Based upon extensive anthropological and sociological research, Gottwald's book owed something to the Civil Rights Movement of the 1960s in America. In Germany, the student unrest and demonstrations of 1968–9 also influenced a generation of scholars, who determined to see Israelite history in terms of social attempts to achieve justice. An influential anthropological book was Sigrist's *Regulierte Anarchie* (1967), an attempt to describe segmentary societies which lacked a central governing authority. Crüsemann's *Der Widerstand gegen das Königtum* (1978) drew upon Sigrist to describe Israelite history as a struggle between egalitarian and power-based centralizing principles. The fact that a concern for civil rights and social justice affected these developments did not invalidate them. These concerns merely shifted attention to a study of 'class' and other conflicts that existed in ancient Israelite society. In the work of Brueggemann a series of studies and commentaries created a link between social concerns and problems as presented in the Old Testament, and the similar problems facing today's world, thus providing insights for theology and ethics. Among social problems dealt with by this newer sociological research was the impact of the exile upon those who experienced it (D. L. Smith 1989) and the development of social 'classes' in the post-exilic period (Kippenberg 1982).

(c) Feminist and Liberation Interpretations

Already in the work of Gottwald and Crüsemann there was a strong element of liberation, and this was both anticipated and developed in works stemming from the liberation theologians of Latin America, most notably Gutiérrez's *A Theology of Liberation* (1974). Liberation theologians questioned the right of Western-based academics in secure employment to be the sole guardians of biblical interpretation, and claimed that they, too, working among the oppressed peoples of their continent, had a right to be heard. Feminist theologians made a similar point, noting that biblical interpretation had been an almost entirely male preserve, and claiming the right to expose the patriarchal biases of the Old Testament, its silencing of women's voices, and the way in which the interpretation of the Bible over the centuries had contributed to the oppression of women. Both approaches drew upon a variety of methods. Historical-critical and sociological methods illuminated the social position of women and of oppressed groups in ancient Israel, while the newer literary methods, especially in feminist interpretation, made 'readings' from a feminist perspective possible. Liberationists paid particular attention to the story of the Exodus and to the preaching of social justice by the prophets. Feminists concentrated upon texts which had been used to justify the subordination of women, such as Genesis 1–3. They also concentrated upon notable women in the Old Testament and the Apocrypha. Attention to the history of interpretation from a feminist angle led to a history of cultural studies, and especially to the way in which male artists had represented women in portrayals of incidents in the Old Testament and the Apocrypha. For some liberationists and feminists the Old Testament was 'irredeemable' so much did it represent class and male interests (Mosala 1989 and Daly 1973). The purpose of research was to remedy these deficiencies. Others found ways of using the Old Testament in the interests of women and the church (Trible 1978). The accusation by Jewish feminists that to condemn the Old Testament as irredeemably patriarchal was a form of anti-Judaism was taken particular seriously in Germany, and attempts were made to develop a form of feminist interpretation that was sensitive to this issue (Schottroff and Wacker 1995).

(d) Ethics

Having been something of a Cinderella subject in Old Testament studies, ethics has assumed a more central position, especially through the work of Barton in Britain and Otto in Germany. The latter's *Theologische Ethik* (1994) concentrated upon the legal traditions of the Old Testament, comparing them with other legal texts from the ancient Near East in order to show their distinctiveness, a distinctiveness stemming from Israelite belief in God as being in solidarity with his people, and especially with the oppressed and disadvantaged. Barton (2003) has studied prophetic texts, especially Amos, and has suggested ways of handling narrative texts. The work of Birch (1991) is also essentially a narrative approach, while, from a conservative angle, W. C. Kaiser (1983) has adopted a more propositional and apologetic stance. Old Testament ethical teaching can, according to Kaiser, be defended as revelations of God's will. C. J. H. Wright's approach from a conservative angle (1995) is more subtle, and seeks to present Israelite society by contrast with the society of Israel's neighbours, as containing examples to be emulated.

(e) Theology

A main point of contention has been whether it is possible to write a theology of the Old Testament, as opposed to a history of Israelite religion (Albertz 1992) or a description of *theologies* contained in the Old Testament (Gerstenberger 2001). This has not prevented Westermann (1978), Preuß (1991–2), O. Kaiser (1993–2003), Brueggemann (1997), and Rendtorff (1999–2001) from producing theologies, and the discussion has repeated some of the issues aired in the 1920s in the famous article by Eissfeldt (1926). The matter is complicated, of course, by the much greater diversity of possible methodical approaches to Old Testament interpretation, and it becomes imperative for authors to identify the interests in terms of which they attempt a theology. The main development to be mentioned here is that of the canonical approach announced by Childs in 1977 and developed in other works (Childs 1979). Canonical criticism is an attempt to harness historical criticism to the interests of faith communities by claiming that a canonical process can be discerned in the way in which Old Testament traditions were shaped into their final form in order to become scripture. The discernment of this process enables priorities to be established which can then be used by modern scholars to undertake theological interpretation of biblical texts in accordance with the intentions of the redactors who deliberately and consciously produced sacred texts, i.e. scripture. While Childs's approach has aroused opposition, defence, and modification, it has raised fundamental questions about how and why the Old Testament reached its present form, and whether the answers to these questions are in any way mandatory for interpreters, especially those who belong to communities for whom the Old Testament is 'scripture'.

(f) Archaeology and History

The refinement of archaeological methods over the past forty years has produced a new picture of the history of ancient Israel that has major implications for the story of the Old Testament. Large-scale surveys of whole areas and the plotting of settlements have largely replaced the old practice of excavating individual prominent sites. It has become clear that the areas of Trans-Jordan known as Ammon,

Moab, and Edom did not become small 'states' until the ninth century BCE (Bienkowski 1992), and that the same is probably true of the area occupied by the northern kingdom, Israel. Judah lagged behind and did not become a 'state' until the eighth century (Jamieson-Drake 1991). The implications of these findings for the picture of the reigns of David and Solomon have divided scholars sharply into 'maximalists' and 'minimalists'. The former maintain that it is still possible to use archaeology to support the biblical picture of an occupation of Canaan by Israelites in the late thirteenth century (albeit a more peaceful one than is implied by the book of Joshua), followed by the gradual emergence of a nation ruled by David and Solomon and their successors in the divided kingdoms (Mazar 1990). The 'minimalists' argue that the archaeological picture should have priority, and that the biblical picture of the 'empires' of David and Solomon has no basis in fact (see Davies 1992). There seems to be general agreement that the Israelite settlement in Canaan was largely peaceful, and not even the 'maximalists' attempt to recover the periods of the Patriarchs and Moses and the exodus. There is general agreement that the main outlines of the narratives of the divided monarchy in the books of Kings are to a greater extent in accordance with what can be checked from extra-biblical—i.e. Egyptian, Assyrian, Babylonian, and Persian— records. The debate is currently in full flight, and only time will tell how it is resolved. A major development in archaeology has been the work of Keel and his associates in collecting and classifying the artistic representations on seals, amulets, and other items (Keel and Uehlinger 1992). This has shed enormous light upon the popular religion of ancient Israel, and has provided rich material for any history of religion(s) in the area.

(g) Literary Criticism

Two trends can be noted here. The first is a tendency to date Old Testament sources much later than was previously done, with the J source being assigned to the post-exilic period (van Seters 1975, 1983), the composition of parts of Isaiah 1–39 being placed in Hellenistic times (O. Kaiser 1973), and the psalms being dated to post-exilic times (Gerstenberger 1988). Studies of the prophetic books have emphasized the role of prophetic 'schools' in the transmission and redaction of the works, while the composition of the narrative parts of the Pentateuch and former prophets (Joshua to 2 Kings) have indicated continuous processes of supplementation and redaction (Kratz 2000). The other trend, discussed more fully in Chapter 34 below, has been the attempt by Richter (1971) and his associates to introduce precision and rigour into literary criticism by generating morphemic transcriptions of the Hebrew and Aramaic of the Old Testament, and by applying linguistic analyses of a highly technical nature.

Conclusion

Much has changed since 1970. Looking back to the work of Noth and von Rad, few would agree today that there was an Israelite amphictyony or tribal league in the period of the Judges which was the catalyst for the fusion of disparate elements of tradition into a coherent story. Whereas Noth and von Rad saw the reign of Solomon as the likely period in which Israel's literature began to flourish, the more likely period is now thought to be that of Hezekiah at the end of the eighth century. New ways of viewing the history, sociology, and religion of ancient Israel have had to compete with the arrival of new methods, as well as the investigation of the Old Testament from new standpoints, such as feminism and liberation theology. At the same time there has been a renewed interest in Old Testament ethics, and in how Old Testament texts can speak to today's world. The resultant picture is that of a discipline full of vigour, offering many new challenges and possibilities.

BIBLIOGRAPHY

ALBERTZ, R. 1992. *Religionsgeschichte Israels in alttestamentlicher Zeit.* Göttingen: Vandenhoeck & Ruprecht.

ALBREKTSON, B. 1967. *History and the Gods.* Lund: Gleerup.

ALBRIGHT, W. F. 1940. *From the Stone Age to Christianity: Monotheism and the Historical Process.* Baltimore: Johns Hopkins University Press.

ALT, A. 1929. *Der Gott der Väter.* BWANT. Stuttgart: Kohlhammer. Reprinted in *Kleine Schriften*, i. Munich: C. H. Beck, 1957, 1–78. ET in *Essays on Old Testament History and Religion.* Oxford: Blackwell, 1966.

ALTER, R. 1981. *The Art of Biblical Narrative.* London: George Allen & Unwin.

—— and KERMODE, F., eds. 1987. *The Literary Guide to the Bible.* London: Collins.

AUERBACH, E. 1953. *Mimesis: The Representation of Reality in Western Literature.* Princeton: Princeton University Press.

BAR-EFRAT, S. 1989. *Narrative Art in the Bible.* Sheffield: Almond Press.

BARR, J. 1961. *The Semantics of Biblical Language.* Oxford: Oxford University Press.

—— 1999. *The Concept of Biblical Theology: An Old Testament Perspective.* London: SCM Press.

—— 2000. *History and Ideology in the Old Testament: Biblical Studies at the End of a Millennium.* Oxford: Oxford University Press.

BARTHES, R. *et al.* 1971. *Analyse structural et exégèse biblique: essais d'interprétation.* Neuchâtel: de la Chaux et Niestlé.

BARTON, J. 2003. *Understanding Old Testament Ethics: Approaches and Explorations.* Louisville, Ky.: Westminster/John Knox Press.

BERLIN, A. 1983. *Poetics and Interpretation of Biblical Narrative.* Sheffield: Almond Press.

BIENKOWSKI, P. 1992. *Early Eden and Moab: The Beginning of the Iron Age in Southern Jordan.* Sheffield Archaeological Monographs 7. Sheffield: J. R. Collis.

BIRCH, B.C. 1991. *Let Justice Roll Down: The Old Testament, Ethics, and Christian Life.* Louisville, Ky.: Westminster/John Knox Press.

BONUS, A. 1914. *Zur Germanisierung des Christentums.* Jena, 1911.

BRIGHT, J. 1960. *A History of Israel.* London: SCM Press. 3rd edn. 1981.

BRUEGGEMANN, W. 1977. *The Land as Gift: Promise and Challenge in Biblical Faith.* Philadelphia: Fortress Press.

—— (1997). *Theology of the Old Testament: Testimony, Dispute, Advocacy.* Minneapolis: Fortress Press.

CHILDS, B. S. 1979. *Introduction to the Old Testament as Scripture.* London: SCM Press.

CROSS, F. M. 1958. *The Ancient Library of Qumran and Modern Biblical Studies.* London: Gerald Duckworth & Co.

CRÜSEMANN, F. 1978. *Der Widerstand gegen das Königtum: die antiköniglichen Texte des Alten Testaments und der Kampf um den Frühen Israelitischen Staat.* WMANT 49. Neu-kirchen: Neukirchener Verlag.

DALY, M. 1973. *Beyond God the Father: Toward a Philosophy of Women's Liberation.* Boston: Beacon Press; repr. 1985.

DAVIES, P. R. 1992. 'In Search of "Ancient Israel" '. JSOTS.S 148. Sheffield: Sheffield Academic Press.

DELITZSCH, F. 1903. *Babel and Bible.* London: Williams & Norgate.

—— 1921. *Die Grosse Täuschung.* Stuttgart: Deutsche Verlagsanstalt.

DERRIDA, J. 1967. *L'Écriture et la différence.* Paris: Éditions du Seuil.

EBELING, G. 1963. 'The Significance of the Historical Critical Method for Church and Theology in Protestantism'. In *Word and Faith*, London: SCM Press, 17–61.

EICHRODT, W. 1933–9. *Theologie des Alten Testaments*, 3 vols. Leipzig: J. C. Hinrichs.

EISSFELDT, O. 1922. *Hexateuch-Synopse: Die Erzählung des fünf Bucher Moses und des Buches Josa mit dem Anfanger des Richterbuches.* Leipzig: J. C. Hinrichs.

—— 1926. 'Israelitisch-jüdische Religionsgeschichte und alttestamentliche Theologie'. *Zeitschrift für die alttestamentliche Wissenschaft*, 44: 1–12.

EVANS-PRITCHARD, E. E. 1937. *Witchcraft, Oracles and Magic among the Azande.* Oxford: Clarendon Press.

—— 1940. *The Nuer: A Description of the Modes of Livelihood and Political Institutions of a Nilotic People.* Oxford: Clarendon Press.

—— 1956. *Nuer Religion.* Oxford: Clarendon Press.

—— 1965. *Theories of Primitive Religion.* Oxford: Clarendon Press.

FISH, S. 1980. *Is there a Text in the Class?* Cambridge, Mass.: Harvard University Press.

GERSTENBERGER, E. S. 1988. *Psalms Part 1, with an Introduction to Cultic Poetry.* FOTL 14. Grand Rapids, Mich. Eerdmans.

—— 2001. *Theologien im Alten Testament: Pluralität und Synkretismus alttestamentlichen Gottesglaubens.* Stuttgart: Kohlhammer. ET: *Theologies in the Old Testament.* London: T. & T. Clark International, 2002.

GOOD, E. M. 1965. *Irony in the Old Testament.* Philadelphia: Westminster Press.

GOTTWALD, N. K. 1979. *The Tribes of Yahweh: A Sociology of the Religion of Liberated Israel, 1250–1050 B.C.E.* Maryknoll, NY: Orbis Books.

GROS LOUIS, K. R. et al. 1974. *Literary Interpretations of Biblical Narratives.* Nashville: Abingdon Press.

GUNKEL, H. 1901; 1902; 1910. *Genesis.* GAT. Göttingen: Vandenhoeck & Ruprecht.

GUTIÉRREZ, G. 1974. *A Theology of Liberation.* London: SCM Press.

HOOKE, S. H. 1935. *The Labyrinth: Further Studies in the Relation between Myth and Ritual in the Ancient World*. London: SPCK.

JAMIESON-DRAKE, D. W. 1991. *Scribes and Schools in Monarchic Judah: A Socio-Archaeological Approach*. SWBA 9. Sheffield: Sheffield Academic Press.

KAISER, O. 1973. *Der Prophet Jesaja Kapitel 13–39*. ATD 18. Göttingen: Vandenhoeck & Ruprecht.

—— 1993–2003. *Der Gott des Alten Testaments*. Göttingen: Vandenhoeck & Ruprecht.

KAISER, W. C. jun. 1983. *Toward Old Testament Ethics*. Grand Rapids, Mich.: Academie Books.

KEEL, O., and UEHLINGER, C. 1992. *Göttinen, Götter und Gottessymbole: Neue Erkenntnisse zur Religionsgeschichte Kanaans und Israels aufgrund bislang unerschlossener ikonographischer Quellen*. QD 134. Friburg: Herder.

KIPPENBERG, H. G. 1982. *Religion und Klassenbildung im Antiken Judäa: Eine religionssoziologische Studie zum Verhältnis von Tradition und Gesellschaftliche Entwicklung*, 2nd edn. Göttingen: Vandenhoeck & Ruprecht.

KIRK, G. S. 1970. *Myth: Its Meaning and Functions in Ancient and Other Cultures*. Cambridge: Cambridge University Press; Berkeley and Los Angeles: University of California Press.

KITTEL, R. 1937. *Biblia Hebraica*. Stuttgart: Priviligierte Württembergische Bibelanstalt; 7th edn. 1951.

KLATT, W. 1969. *Hermann Gunkel: Zu seinel Theologie der Religionsgeschichte und zur Entstehung der Formgeschichtlichen Methode*. FRLANT 100. Göttingen: Vandenhoeck & Ruprecht.

KÖHLER, L. 1935. *Theologie des Alten Testaments*. Tübingen: J. C. B. Mohr.

KRATZ, R. G. 2000. *Die Komposition der historischen Bücher des Alten Testaments*. Göttingen: Vandenhoeck & Ruprecht.

KUENEN, A. 1874–5. *The Religion of Israel to the Fall of the Jewish State*, 3 vols. London.

LEACH, E. 1966. 'The Legitimacy of Solomon'. *European Journal of Sociology*, 7: 58–101. Reprinted in *Genesis as Myth and other Essays*, London: Jonathan Cape, 1969, 25–83.

LÉVI-STRAUSS, C. 1964–71. *Mythologique*, 4 vols. Paris: Plon.

LICHT, J. 1978. *Storytelling in the Bible*. Jerusalem: Magnes, The Hebrew University.

LIENHARDT, G. 1961. *Divinity and Experience: The Religion of the Dinka*. Oxford: Clarendon Press.

MAZAR, A. 1990. *Archaeology of the Land of the Bible, 10,000–586 B.C.E.* New York: Doubleday.

MENDENHALL, G. E. 1962. 'The Hebrew Conquest of Palestine'. *BA* 25: 66–87.

MOSALA, I. J. 1989. *Biblical Hermeneutics and Black Theology in South Africa*. Grand Rapids, Mich.: Eerdmans.

MOWINCKEL, S. 1922. *Psalmenstudien*, ii: *Das Thronbesteigungsfest Jahwähs und der Ursprung der Eschatalogie*. Oslo: Skrifter utgitt av Det Norske Videnskaps-Akademi.

NOTH, M. 1930. *Das System der Zwölf Stämme Israels*. Stuttgart:

—— 1938. *Das Buch Josua*. HAT I, 7. Tübingen: Mohr Siebeck.

—— 1948. *Überlieferungsgeschichte des Pentateuch*. Stuttgart: Kohlhammer. ET: *A History of Pentateuchal Traditions*. Englewood Cliffs, NJ: Prentice-Hall, 1972.

—— 1950. *Geschichte Israels*. Göttingen: Vandenhoeck & Ruprecht.

OESTERLEY, W. O. E., and ROBINSON, T. H. 1930. *Hebrew Religion: Its Origin and Development*. London: SPCK.

OTTO, E. 1994. *Theologische Ethik des Alten Testaments*. Stuttgart: Kohlhammer.

PEDERSEN, J. 1926–40. *Israel: Its Life and Culture*, 4 vols. London: Oxford University Press; Copenhagen: Branner Og Korch.

PREUß, H. D. 1991–2. *Theologie des Alten Testaments*. Stuttgart: Verlag W. Kohlhammer.

RAD, G. von. 1957–60. *Theologie des Alten Testaments*. Munich: Chr. Kaiser Verlag.

RENDTORFF, R. 1999–2001. *Theologie des Alten Testaments: Ein kanonischer Entwurf*. Neukirchen-Vluyn: Neukirchener Verlag.

RICHARDSON, A., ed. 1950. *A Theological Word Book of the Bible*. London: SCM Press.

RICHTER, W. 1971. *Exegese als Literaturwissenschaft: Entwurf einer alttestmentlichen Literaturtheorie und Methodologie*. Göttingen: Vandenhoeck & Ruprecht.

ROBINSON, H. W. 1936. 'The Hebrew Conception of Corporate Personality'. In P. Volz *et al.*, eds., *Werden und Wesen des Alten Testaments*. BZAW 66. Berlin: Töpelman, 49–62.

—— 1946. *Inspiration and Revelation in the Old Testament*. Oxford: Clarendon Press.

ROGERSON, J. W. 1974. *Myth in Old Testament Interpretation*. Berlin: De Gruyter.

—— 1978. *Anthropology and the Old Testament*. Oxford: Blackwell; reprint Sheffield: JSOT Press, 1984.

SCHERFFIG, W. 1989–94. *Junge Theologen im 'Dritten Reich': Dokumente, Briefe, Erfahrungen*. Neukirchen: Neukirchener Verlag.

SCHOLDER, K. 2000. *Die Kirchen und das Dritte Reich*, 2 vols. Munich: Propyläen Taschenbuch.

SCHOTTROFF, L., and WACKER, M.-T., eds. 1995. *Von der Wurzel getragen: Deutschsprachige christlich-feministische Exegese in Auseinandersetzung mit Antijudaismus*. Leiden: E. J. Brill.

SELLIN, E. 1933. *Alttestamentliche Theologie auf religionsgeschichtlicher Grundlage*. Leipzig: Quelle & Meyer.

SERVICE, E. R. 1962. *Primitive Social Organisation: An Evolutionary Perspective*. New York: Random House.

SETERS, G. VAN. 1975. *Abraham in History and Tradition*. New Haven and London: Yale University Press.

—— 1983. *In Search of History: Historiography in the Ancient World and the Origins of Biblical History*. New Haven and London: Yale University Press.

SIGRIST, C. 1967. *Regulierte Anarchie: Untersuchungen zum Fehlen und zur Entstehung politischer Herrschaft in segmentären Gesellschaften Afrikas*. Frankfurt am Main: Syndikat.

SMEND, R. 1989. *Deutsche Alttestamentler in Drei Jahrhunderten*. Göttingen: Vandenhoeck & Ruprecht.

—— 1991. *Epochen der Biblekritik*. Munich: Kaiser Verlag.

SMITH, C. R. 1951. *The Bible Doctrine of Man*. London: Epworth Press.

SMITH, D. L. 1989. *The Religion of the Landless: The Social Context of the Babylonian Exile*. Bloomington, Ind.: Meyer Stone Books.

SMITH, W. R. 1881. *The Old Testament in the Jewish Church: Twelve Lectures on Biblical Criticism*. Edinburgh.

TRIBLE, P. 1978. *God and the Rhetoric of Sexuality*. Philadelphia: Fortress Press.

VISCHER, W. 1934–42. *Das Christuszeugnis des Alten Testaments*. Zürich: A. G. Zollikon.

VOLZ, P. 1912. *Das Neujahrfest Jahwehs*. Tübingen: Mohr.

WEBER, C. 2000. *Altes Testament und völkische Frage: Der biblische Volksbegriff in der alttestamentlichen Wissenschaft der nationalsozialistischen Zeit, dargestellt am Beispiel von Johannes Hempel*. Tübingen: Mohr Siebeck.

WELLHAUSEN, J. 1983. *Prolegomena zur Geschichte Israels.* Berlin: W. de Gruyter.

WESTERMANN, C. 1978. *Theologie des Alten Testaments in Grundzügen.* Göttingen: Vandenhoeck & Ruprecht.

WRIGHT, C. J. H. 1995. *Walking in the Ways of the Lord: The Ethical Authority of the Old Testament.* Leicester: Apollos.

WRIGHT, G. E. 1950. *The Old Testament against its Environment.* SBT 2 London: SCM Press.

—— 1952. *God who Acts: Biblical Theology as Recital.* SBT 8. London: SCM Press.

—— 1957. *Biblical Archaeology.* Philadelphia: Westminster Press; London: Gerald Duckworth & Co.

CHAPTER 2

NEW TESTAMENT

ROBERT MORGAN

There are biblical echoes in the choice of a seventy-year span, and it embraces some living scholars' memories, but the politically dreadful 1930s provide no dramatic markers for periodizing biblical studies. They offer instead a few echoes of the more vibrant preceding decade and of the golden century of New Testament historical criticism, from F. C. Baur in 1831 on the divisions in Corinth, to Walter Bauer in 1934 on *Orthodoxy and Heresy in Early Christianity*. Both those monographs emphasized the theological diversity in early Christianity uncovered by historical research, whereas the neo-Reformation biblical interpreters of the 1920s combined their form criticism with a unifying theological understanding of revelation. Our topic is the New Testament scholarship which built on that critical heritage, while being partly moved by those theological impulses, from the times of destruction and rebuilding in Europe to a new political, economic, and cultural hegemony in the globally threatened present day.[1]

---

[1] The 200 years of critical study which stand behind these seventy years may best be pondered with the help of W. G. Kümmel, *The New Testament: The History of the Investigation of its Problems* (1957; ET: London: SCM Press, 1973), and W. Baird, *History of New Testament Research*, i and ii (Minneapolis: Fortress Press, 1992, 2003). Both end where this survey begins. For a fuller account of twentieth-century research, see W. Horbury's article in *A Century of Theological and Religious Studies in Britain*, ed. E. Nicholson (Oxford: Oxford University Press, 2004). Information on individual scholars can be found in John H. Hayes, *Dictionary of Biblical Interpretation* (Nashville: Abingdon Press, 1999), and Donald K. McKim, *Historical Handbook of Major Biblical Interpreters* (Downers Grove, Ill.: Inter-Varsity Press, 1998). J. K. Riches, *A Century of New Testament Study* (Cambridge: Lutterworth, 1993), and *The New Testament and its Modern Interpreters*, ed. E. J. Epp and G. W. MacRae (Philadelphia: Fortress Press, 1989) also provide good overviews. The most recent survey is *The Face of New Testament Studies*, ed. S. McKnight *et al.* (Grand Rapids, Mich.: Baker Academic; Leicester: Apollos, 2004).

The still quite large German theological faculties depend on their close relationship with the state-sponsored churches (Protestant and Roman Catholic), and even aside from this a responsibility for ministerial training has sustained substantial continuity throughout our seventy years. Scholarly longevity, the conservatism often associated with biblical theology, and the traditional character of biblical commentaries (widely considered the biblical scholar's primary publishing obligation and multiplying exponentially since the Second World War) have also made for continuity, but three scholarly generations differ sufficiently to be labelled (from an English-speaking perspective) as times of continuation (1935–62), transition (1960s and 1970s), and innovation (1980–2005). The changing social, political, and economic environments are reflected in a tendency towards cautious theological synthesis in our first generation; theological radicalism, internationalism, and ecumenism in the second; and a new pluralism, including some retreat from or repudiation of theology, in the third.

1. CONTINUITIES

The influence of our own beliefs, values, and location on our historical perspectives may be acknowledged at the outset by prioritizing the gospels and starting this survey with a local landmark scarcely visible from across the Atlantic, much less from across the North Sea: R. H. Lightfoot's Bampton Lectures in Oxford on *History and Interpretation in the Gospels* (1935). Anglican divinity has usually been concerned more with the Word made flesh than with the Word proclaimed, and, side-tracked by controversy with the eighteenth-century deists and their intellectual progeny, with the gospels as reliable historical records. Lutherans prioritize the apostle Paul, but in Britain Paul has often been read through Lucan spectacles, as perhaps the New Testament canon intends, and has been seen as secondary to the four gospels.

Lightfoot caused a minor stir in England with his concluding echo of Job 26: 14 that the gospels 'yield us little more than the whisper of his voice; we trace in them but the outskirts of his ways' (p. 225). His sympathetic accounts of Wrede, *The Messianic Secret in the Gospels* (1901), of Wellhausen's gospel commentaries and *Einleitung* (1903–5), and of the *Formgeschichte* which had become prominent in Germany since the First World War, contrasted sharply with Sanday's 'regrettable' (p. 17) condemnation of Wrede back in 1907, and even with Vincent Taylor's domestication of form criticism in *The Formation of the Gospel Tradition* (1933). The form critics' history-of-traditions approach to the Old and New Testaments had been pioneered at the start of the century by Bultmann's direct and indirect mentors from the history of religion(s) school. After the Second World War it led to redaction criticism and came to dominate twentieth-century gospel criticism, providing the methodological basis for the scepticism of most late twentieth-century historical Jesus research.

Outside Germany the sceptical implications of form criticism were temporarily resisted until in 1963 Lightfoot's pupil D. E. Nineham published a popular commentary on Mark which introduced students to the changing landscape. In the same year, Bultmann's form-critical classic on *The History of the Synoptic Tradition* (1921, 2nd edn. 1931) appeared in English. More sceptical than Martin Dibelius's *From Tradition to Gospel* (1919, translated in the USA in 1934), it initiated a decade of translations that ended fifty years of limited contact between the two language-zones. This increasing acceptance of German methods and results was facilitated by the new interest in historical Jesus research among Bultmann's pupils, most attractively represented by G. Bornkamm's *Jesus of Nazareth* (1956, ET 1960). Right from the start of our period (*The Eucharistic Words of Jesus* first appeared in 1935), J. Jeremias's less sceptical conclusions and theological endorsement of historical Jesus research promised traffic across the North Sea. His classic work, *The Parables of Jesus* (1947, ET 1954, 2nd edn. 1963), continued, and corrected C. H. Dodd's account of Jesus' teaching; but it was not until 1966 that N. Perrin ('the Wredestrasse becomes the Hauptstrasse') could acknowledge a wider assimilation of history-of-traditions assumptions.

By then, close international contact among biblical scholars was normal. Back in 1935 Lightfoot's lectures were unusual in their promotion of form criticism, and innovative in developing composition criticism and (like Wrede) anticipating redaction criticism. This final refinement of history-of-traditions research was pioneered mainly by Bultmann's pupils after the Second World War, and some of the same scholars broke with their teacher in addressing 'the problem of the historical Jesus'. That was the title of the 1953 lecture of E. Käsemann said by J. M. Robinson to inaugurate 'a new quest', but better seen as a new phase in the ongoing project.

All these developments had roots in the beginnings of the modern discipline. D. F. Strauss's *Life of Jesus* (1835, ET 1846, repr. 1973) had illuminated the history of the gospel traditions, and F. C. Baur had both highlighted the theological differences between the evangelists (1844–7) and also reaffirmed the theological necessity of historical Jesus research. Critical study of the synoptic gospels since 1935 has thus focused on the three lines of enquiry pioneered by Strauss and Baur: (*a*) the finished literary products and their authors and original audiences (Baur's 'tendency criticism', the redaction criticism of Bornkamm, Marxsen, and Conzelmann, and newer literary approaches); (*b*) the early traditions transmitted by the synoptic evangelists (form criticism and its predecessors); and (*c*) the quest for the historical figure of Jesus, understood in his Palestinian Jewish environment, after a long concealment in theologically coloured gospel traditions.

Today the third of these enquiries again excites most interest, but writing during the German theological reaction against liberal life-of-Jesus research (1921–53), Lightfoot reported on the second and said most about the first. His 'eight Divinity Lecture Sermons' scarcely needed (p. 9) to recap the source criticism by which liberal theologians in nineteenth-century Germany had sought to reconstruct the 'historical Jesus' following Strauss's demolition of the gospel history. This work was continued in the Oxford seminar of William Sanday, leading to B. H. Streeter's *The Four Gospels* (1924). Its well-grounded conviction about the priority of Mark was later further strengthened through this providing the source-critical base for some convincing accounts of Matthew's and Luke's 'redaction' of Mark. The revival by W. R. Farmer in 1964 of an alternative, the 'Griesbach hypothesis' of Matthean priority and a supposed use of Matthew and Luke by Mark (a view pioneered by H. Owen in 1764), has found little support. Sometimes labelled 'The Two-Gospel Hypothesis', to distinguish it from the 'two-source hypothesis' of Mark and Q being used by Matthew and Luke, it is a reminder that all proposed solutions to 'the synoptic problem' (the literary relationships between these three gospels) are only hypotheses.

The proto-Luke hypothesis (that there had been an earlier version of Luke not based on or using Mark) was advocated by Streeter and Vincent Taylor in the 1920s, but has also found little support. The second (Q) plank of the two-source hypothesis, however, has gone from strength to hypothetical strength, thanks partly to the rediscovery at Nag Hammadi in 1945 of a 'sayings gospel', the complete (114 sayings) Gospel of Thomas (published in 1959). An intelligent minority still dispenses with Q, arguing that Luke knew Matthew as well as his main source Mark. If Luke knew Matthew, and also had independent access to some of Matthew's traditions, a more modest form of Q (mini-Q) would be implied.

More important by far are the meanings of these texts and the broader trends affecting their interpretation. The richest fruit of the late nineteenth-century flowering of history-of-religions research on Judaism was the rediscovery of eschatology. This topic dominated twentieth-century scholarship, and was re-inforced by the discovery of the Dead Sea Scrolls in 1947. Since then, further study of early Judaism and a fresh recognition of the largely Jewish character of the New Testament itself have become characteristic marks of its critical investigation in our period, dwarfing recent challenges to this historical paradigm.

Lightfoot's lecture-sermons provide reminders of what preceded our period and pointers to some of what followed, but the seventy years from 1935 can be better epitomized by comparing and contrasting two of his greater close contemporaries. The North Welsh Congregationalist C. H. Dodd (1884–1973) had already published *The Meaning of Paul for Today* (1920), *The Authority of the Bible* (1928), and *The Epistle to the Romans* (1932) before our starting-point in 1935, the year in which *The Parables of the Kingdom* and *The Bible and the Greeks* appeared. The Marburg professor Rudolf Bultmann (1884–1976), a personal student of Gunkel, J. Weiss, and Heitmüller from the history of religion(s) school and a close follower of Wrede and Bousset from the same group, had summed up a generation of gospel criticism in *The History of the Synoptic Tradition* (1921, 2nd edn. 1931). He had then (influenced by Karl Barth and Gogarten) changed his idiom, while remaining fairly close to his doctrine teacher W. Herrmann (1846–1922). His determination to combine his liberal critical heritage and that proto-existentialist piety with Barth's dialectical theology and its assessment of the 1920s cultural mood can best be seen in the collections of essays, *Faith and Understanding*, i (1933, ET 1969), *Existence and Faith* (Eng. edn. S. M. Ogden, 1961, essays from 1917 to 1957), and in the introduction to his *Jesus and the Word* (1926, ET 1934). In the 1940s and 1950s Bultmann became a controversial figure in conservative church circles for wanting to 'demythologize' the New Testament, interpreting (away) its mythological material, especially its futurist eschatology and apocalyptic language, in existentialist terms, as well as for his historical scepticism; but today his theological seriousness is admired by conservatives and liberals alike, even as they disagree with many of his historical and hermeneutical proposals.

Dodd's search for a unifying synthesis was programmatically announced in his Cambridge inaugural lecture on *The Present Task in New Testament Studies* (1936). The kerygma identified in *The Apostolic Preaching and its Developments* (1936) was developed in subsequent publications, including *According to the Scriptures* (1952) on 'The sub-structure of New Testament theology'. But the finest twentieth-century synthesis was Bultmann's *Theology of the New Testament* (vol. i 1948, ET 1951; vol. ii 1953, ET 1955). Its central plank remains among the church's most creative interpretations of Paul's theology. Both scholars were also form critics, though of a very different ilk, and both used Paul's word 'kerygma', though in rather different ways. And in the 1930s both were working on what were to be their greatest books, both on the Fourth Gospel. F. C. Baur's claim a century earlier that John is the climax of New Testament theology can find support in Bultmann's Meyer Commentary (1941, ET 1971) and in Dodd's *The Interpretation of the Fourth Gospel* (1953).

The main difference between the British and the German masters is visible even in the title of Dodd's further work, *Historical Tradition in the Fourth Gospel* (1963), but their similarities are also illuminating. Both aimed to interpret the New Testament in ways that are historically responsible, and sensitive to religious language, but also under the presupposition (as Bultmann put it in *Theology of the New Testament*, ii. 251) 'that they have something to say to the present'. Both interpretations of the Johannine theology also posited a history-of-religions context which included Hellenistic and Palestinian Judaism, and yet neither now seems satisfactory in this respect, because both underestimated the probably sectarian Jewish setting of this gospel. The turn, or return, of New Testament scholarship in the second half of the twentieth century to Judaism, including sectarian Judaism, marks its distance today from these two representative figures.

If Bultmann's work has lasted better than Dodd's, one reason is its stronger engagement with modern (Continental) philosophy and systematic theology. Like

Bultmann, Dodd also reinterpreted New Testament eschatology to weaken its futurist fantasies, and he also had some outstanding disciples, including C. F. D. Moule, W. D. Davies, G. B. Caird, T. F. Glasson, and J. A. T. Robinson, but Bultmann's demythologizing and existential interpretation inspired two generations of future professors and clergy to do their theology as scriptural interpretation. Only E. C. Hoskyns (who at Cambridge inspired A. M. Ramsey, C. F. Evans, and C. K. Barrett, among others) might have had that kind of wider impact, but he died prematurely in 1937, his commentary on John unfinished. It was edited by F. N. Davey and published in 1940.

The difference between England and Germany at that time lay less in the quality of historical and exegetical research (though the size of the German faculties has always made for a difference in quantity) than in the depth of hermeneutical penetration. Dodd's concerns were reflected in some mid-century discussions of 'the authority of the Bible' that saw a need for new foundations, but that discussion looked dated by 1960. By contrast, Bultmann's hermeneutical programme was then still in its prime, bitterly attacked by traditionalists but criticized and developed by his eminent pupils and by his more radical disciple, Herbert Braun. It is still a point of reference for theologically committed interpretation of the New Testament today.

Most New Testament study in the first of our three generations was church-related in that many leading scholars were Protestant clergy with preaching responsibilities, and most European undergraduates were preparing for the ordained ministry or to teach Christianity in schools. In North America most biblical research was done in Protestant seminaries, some attached to great universities, but still church-related. These scholars were alive to the distance between the ancient texts and the modern world, but were in different ways aiming to bridge it. In Germany and Switzerland it was (and still is) self-evident that New Testament professors in theological faculties are *Theologen*, educated in systematic and practical as well as historical and philosophical theology. That explains the hermeneutical sophistication of some German New Testament theologians who built theological and philosophical reflection into their historical and exegetical study of the Bible.

A religious community requires interpretations of its scriptures which are both credible and speak of God. They must accordingly be true to the authors and texts, both in their historical contexts and in their aim to speak of God. That requires modern historical study, but this does not normally speak of God—hence the hermeneutical requirement to combine historical exegesis and reconstruction with a theology, i.e. contemporary talk of God. The alternatives are for biblical scholarship to repudiate the hermeneutical task and not speak responsibly of God, or to argue that historical research itself can do this. The 'biblical theology' movement of the 1940s and 1950s underestimated the historical and cultural distance between the Bible and modern believers, but its religious motivations were shared by most biblical teachers—conservative, liberal, and radical. Several of its critics were theologically as well as historically sophisticated, and New Testament theology was often seen as the crown of the discipline, or the goal towards which all other New Testament studies were pointing. Theology guided and beckoned the discipline, even though comparatively few complete New Testament theologies were published.

The strong religious interest present in much of the best New Testament scholarship throughout our period was as evident in the German endorsement of form criticism as in the initial repudiation in Britain of its sceptical implications. The new approach saw the early church transmitting Jesus traditions orally in order to communicate its faith. That corresponds to what Christians are always bound to do, and this strong ecclesiological dimension to the new gospel criticism excited even Anglicans, who were more interested in church tradition, ministry, and sacraments than in the sermon-related 'forms' identified by Dibelius, or the didactic and controversial emphases of Bultmann. In Germany New Testament interpretation influenced by the neo-Reformation dialectical theology of the 1920s dovetailed with form criticism (and with the Luther renaissance) in its emphasis on the kerygma, or Word of God preached, addressing humans and changing their self-understanding. Historical exegesis and reconstruction were pursued as before, but historical knowledge was here subordinated to theological interpretations of the texts, and 'the Word' rather than history was seen as the key to human speaking of God's self-revelation in Christ.

Cultural and theological reactions against the optimism of Protestant liberalism with its idealist metaphysics of history were inevitable after the First World War. Ignited by the genius of Barth, theologies of the Word sustained German and Swiss Protestantism for fifty years. But biblical scholarship was not ready to abandon its historical-critical paradigm, least of all in Germany, where its roots were strongest and already bearing fruit internationally, and later in German and American Roman Catholicism. It is a measure of Bultmann's success in harnessing the best historical scholarship of his liberal teachers to the new theological agendas of Barth and Gogarten that later attacks on his synthesis came more from theological than from exegetical disagreements. Even his loyal if rebellious pupil Ernst Käsemann (1906–98), who questioned his exegesis at many points while sharing his hermeneutical programme, was guided by theological considerations. Käsemann's conception of early Christian 'apocalyptic', for example, by which he meant futurist, dualist, and cosmic *eschatology*, was driven by a religious, theological, and even political imperative to criticize Bultmann's relative neglect of Christian hope and the struggle for social change, rather than by fresh study of the literary genre 'apocalypse'.

Bultmann's existentialist theology, articulated through his interpretation of Paul and especially John, was an attempt to solve the hermeneutical problem of speaking of God with and through these texts. It had already been challenged by Oscar Cullmann's retrieval in *Christ and Time* (1946, ET 1951) of the nineteenth-century theological idea of 'salvation history' to solve the same problem. Cullmann thought that this idea expressed the New Testament's understanding of the revelation of God in Jesus Christ, 'the centre of time'. Conzelmann showed its value in clarifying *The Theology of St Luke* (German: *Die Mitte der Zeit*, 1956, ET 1960), and Käsemann admitted its (subordinate) role in Paul's theology, but they both shared Bultmann's disapproval of finding revelation in historical events. L. Goppelt's *Typos* (1939) and posthumous *Theology of the New Testament* (1975–6, ET 1981–2) and W. G. Küm- mel's *Promise and Fulfilment* (1945, 2nd edn. 1953, ET 1957) appealed to 'salvation history' to root theology in the historical events of the Bible, but despite some initial enthusiasm in the biblical theology movement, Cullmann's theological programme persuaded few. His *Salvation in History* (1965, ET 1967) came too late to halt the Bultmannian 'victory in Europe' and in parts of the United States.

A more powerful attack on Bultmann's contraction of history to the present experience of history, and eschatology to the present moment of decision, was launched in the late 1950s by W. Pannenberg and a group of his colleagues in Heidelberg. Inspired more by Hegel than Heidegger, and rejecting any idea of a special history (salvation history) alongside the real stuff, they saw 'universal history' as the best framework for speaking of God. Despite the participation of U. Wilckens, whose *Theologie des Neuen Testaments* later (2002–) gave due weight to the history of Jesus and the resurrection appearances, and their appeal to a notion of apocalyptic as disclosing in advance a revelation which could not be manifest before the end of history, this theological movement made little impact on New Testament scholarship. Pannenberg's view of the resurrection as a historical event was rejected by Bultmannians almost as vehemently as they had rejected W. Künneth's revival of nineteenth-century conservative talk of 'salvation facts' in *The Theology of the Resurrection* (1933, 4th edn. 1951, ET 1965).

Pannenberg's theological reflection on real history and nature coincided with the decline of existentialism, and together with Moltmann's *Theology of Hope* (1965, ET 1967) contributed to the partial eclipse of Bultmann's hermeneutics around 1970. Pannenberg built his traditional German association of New Testament and sys- tematic theology into a vision of history which, like that of Baur and Troeltsch, was more open to theological interpretations than the more positivistic attitudes of most biblical scholars, but he did this as a systematic theologian. The Bultman- nians' hermeneutically informed attempts to do modern Christian theology as New Testament theology was by 1970 losing its power to set the agenda and direction of biblical scholarship.

The religious motivation and orientation of most biblical study in this period is visible even in the lexicographical research of Kittel's *Theological Dictionary of the New Testament* (10 vols., 1932–73, ET 1964–76). The dedication of the first volume to Schlatter and the importance of the earlier volumes for the biblical theology movement hint at roots in H. Cremer's *Biblico-Theological Lexicon* (1874, 4th edn. 1886, ET 1878, 2nd edn. 1895), in which linguistic expertise supported traditional theological positions. A conservative and edifying tendency is more overtly present in the more compact (3 vols.) *Theologisches Begriffslexikon* (1967–71, ET with revisions and additions: *Dictionary of New Testament Theology*, ed. C. Brown, 1975) and the French Dominican C. Spicq's *Theological Lexicon* (3 vols., 1978, ET 1994). The papyri had seemed to imply that the Greek of the New Testament was simply the common Greek of the day (*koinē*), but further attention to its Septuagint background showed how it also drew on a particular Jewish theological vocabulary. Some biblical theologians' misuse of etymology was exposed by J. Barr in *The Semantics of Biblical Language* (1961), and Kittel's dictionary was not immune, but the path from language to theology which so excited Hoskyns and his pupils still has much to teach a linguistically less educated generation. H. Balz and G. Schneider, eds., *Exegetical Dictionary of the New Testament* (3 vols., 1980–3, ET 1990–3) maintains this invaluable tradition.

Other lexical and grammatical works in our period also have roots in both liberalism and pietism. Walter Bauer's now standard *Greek–German Lexicon of the New Testament* (2nd edn. 1928, landmark 4th edn 1952, 6th edn. 1988) was developed from E. Preuschen's original attempt (1896, ET 1898, 2nd. edn. 1905) to take account of the new knowledge of Hellenistic Greek gained from the papyri. It became a *Greek–English Lexicon* in 1957, embarrassingly labelled after its translators, Arndt and Gingrich. The 1979 revision is commonly called BAGD (Bauer, Arndt, Gingrich, Danker). Similarly, a standard *Grammar of New Testament Greek* by F. Blass and A. Debrunner was the fourth edition (1913) of Blass's 1896 work. It was revised in 1947, and by F. Rehkopf in 1976 for its fourteenth edition. The English translation by R. Funk (1961) is based on the tenth (1959) edition. J. H. Moulton, *A Grammar of New Testament Greek* (vol. i, 1906) was continued with W. F. Howard in 1919–29 (vol. ii) and by N. Turner in 1963 (vol. iii). The Southern Baptist A. T. Robertson died in 1934, but his classic, *A Grammar of the Greek New Testament in the Light of Historical Research* (1914) and also *A Shorter Grammar of the Greek New Testament* (1908) remained standard works. As these examples suggest, and J. H. Moulton and G. Milligan, *The Vocabulary of the Greek Testament* (1930) and A. Deissmann's earlier works confirm, our period is one of ongoing conversations (e.g. C. F. D. Moule, *An Idiom Book of New Testament Greek*, 1959) and minor improvements rather than major advances in lexicography and grammar, despite the impact of modern linguistics—e.g. in a lexicon based on semantic domains by J. P. Louw and E. A. Nida (1988). New materials continue to become available, as may be seen in G. H. R. Horsley, ed., *New Documents Illustrating Early Christianity: A Review of the Greek Inscriptions and Papyri published in 1978* (5 vols., 1981–9), and the notion of a 'Jewish Greek' is still alive, but few go much further than admitting the influence of the Septuagint.

The many papyri discovered in the rubbish heaps of Egypt in the late nineteenth century included fragments of the New Testament from the second and third centuries, i.e. earlier than the best fourth-century uncials (manuscripts in capital letters), the codices Sinaiticus and Vaticanus. New commentaries and new editions of older ones incorporated the minor textual alterations suggested by these discoveries, among them the Chester Beatty and the Bodmer papyri. Fuller details were included in constant revisions of editions of the Greek New Testament, notably the United Bible Society's 1965 text, revised in 1975 (3rd edn.) to correspond to the 26th edition of Nestle-Aland (1979). B. M. Metzger, ed., *A Textual Commentary on the Greek New Testament* (1991) discusses some of the committee decisions reached by majority votes. G. D. Kilpatrick and his pupil J. K. Elliott pressed for a more eclectic approach to choosing between various readings, asking what best fits the particular context and the author's style.

The papyri also evidence the preference of the early Christians for the codex over the scrolls used for Jewish scriptures, and this has led to new suggestions about the emergence of a New Testament canon in the second century, with the beginnings of this collection possibly going back to the end of the first century. In *The First Edition of the New Testament* (1996, ET 2000) David Trobisch denies that the canonical status of the New Testament collection resulted from a long and complicated process. He argues that a mid-second-century 'first edition' was challenged, but was already a collection, and already Christian scripture. This discussion takes us close to the end of our seventy years, but it uses the new manuscript evidence to continue a debate associated above all with von Harnack, and with H. von Campenhausen, *The Formation of the Christian Bible* (1968, ET 1972).

New English translations of the Bible have also multiplied since 1935, but whereas the Revised Version of 1884 owed its importance to enormous advances in textual criticism and lexicography, and the twentieth century saw modest gains in both, changes in the English language and the desire to communicate more effectively account more for the further work. The main landmarks are the Revised Standard Version (New Testament 1946, revised 1952; NRSV 1989) and the New English Bible (New Testament 1961; REB 1989).

2. TRANSITIONS

Our divisions are admittedly arbitrary. It is no more possible to interpret the 1960s and 1970s without constant reference to what preceded them than it was the 1930s and 1950s. On the other hand, no European who lived through the Second World War and its aftermath will deny that the 1960s were different. This change was reflected as sharply in theology as in other culture-critical disciplines, because theology is a part of its religious tradition and community, and the latter a part of society. Biblical scholarship includes essential tasks whose social and theological implications are minimal, but the subject-matter of the Bible and the religious motivation of most readers constantly draws alert students into the wider cultural debate.

Subdividing our seventy years at around 1962 places the American 'biblical theology movement' and its European stimuli (Barth, Eichrodt, Kittel, Cullmann, for example) in the generation of theological syntheses. But that movement was scarcely affected by the New Testament theology of Bultmann, whose followers were still at the height of their powers in the 1960s and still advancing his project of kerygmatic theology and radical historical criticism. The 'transitions' made by German Protestant scholarship at this time included the export and increasing influence of its earlier classics. Translations into English of both old and new German scholarly works affected teaching, and the development of Roman Catholic biblical scholarship following the Second Vatican Council (1962–5) and the expansion of North American scholarship made this transitional period the seedbed of more dramatic changes in the discipline. Some roots of the Roman Catholic revival can be traced in the encyclical *Divino Afflante Spiritu* (1943) and in the Dominican École biblique et archéologique founded by Lagrange in Jerusalem in 1890 (and so named in 1920) which had survived the lamentable persecution of Modernists. The emergence in the 1960s of leaders such as H. Schürmann, R. Schnackenburg, A. Vögtle, R. E. Brown, and J. A. Fitzmyer (all Roman Catholic priests deeply rooted in their tradition) showed that the best Protestant scholarship could now be assimilated by loyal Catholic churchmen without much difficulty. That list shows too that the American expansion now included Roman Catholic, as well as Protestant and Jewish, scholars.

Within German New Testament theology the major debates on the question of the historical Jesus, the interpretation of Pauline and Johannine theology, the development of early Christianity from (perhaps) apocalyptic beginnings to (so-called) early Catholicism, and the canon were initially conducted most sharply within the dominant Bultmann school. In the 1960s these debates were greatly enlarged by the participation of other countries and by German Roman Catholic contributions. Academic New Testament studies were now more visibly international and inter-confessional, not only because ecumenical agencies encouraged this (as they had long done), but because scholars could now afford to travel, attend more conferences, and buy more foreign books. International scholarly friendships which a few had fostered before and after the First World War, now became normal. On one religious border cultivated sporadically at least since Justin, though often with polemical intent, these friendships became even more significant.

A few Christian scholars ever since Origen have learned Hebrew and Judaism from rabbis (C. K. Barrett studying rabbinics with H. Loewe is a modern example), and in Europe around 1900 this collaboration was growing. In the United States, and especially since the Second World War, it has flourished. The study of Second

Temple and rabbinic Judaism in Germany by such giants as Schürer, Schlatter, Bousset, and Billerbeck had failed to end the shameful history of Western anti-Semitism to which the churches have contributed, but the emigration of some Jewish scholars sowed the seeds of a better future. Among them, David Daube attended Dodd's Cambridge seminar and later published *The New Testament and Rabbinic Judaism* (1956), having co-edited the Dodd Festschrift in 1955 with his friend, Dodd's pupil and fellow Welshman, W. D. Davies, the author of *Paul and Rabbinic Judaism* (1948).

Well before the 1960s, this represents the beginning of a major transition. Davies's book adumbrates the work of his student E. P. Sanders, whose *Paul and Palestinian Judaism* appeared in 1977. This goes behind Dodd's (1932), Barrett's (1957), and Käsemann's (1973) Protestant commentaries on Romans, W. L. Knox's books on Paul (1925, 1939), and Bultmann's, Conzelmann's, and Bornkamm's (1969, ET 1971) various accounts of Paul's theology, back to Albert Schweitzer's emphasis on participation in Christ. Sanders's book was more influential than his teacher's. Whereas the culture had by 1964 caught up, and Davies's later work, *The Setting of the Sermon on the Mount* (1964), which related Matthew's gospel to developments in post-70 Judaism, became a landmark, his earlier book remained somewhat on the margins, together with the Jewish scholar H. J. Schoeps' *Paul* (1959, ET 1961) and J. Munck's *Paul and the Salvation of Mankind* (1954, ET 1959), a major Danish critique of the main lines of early Christian history and theology laid down in 1831 by F. C. Baur. In the 1950s the major influence was Bultmann, whose classic presentation of Paul's recognizably biblical (i.e. fundamentally Jewish) theology in a Lutheran and existentialist mould, had also appeared in 1948 (ET 1951).

In 1948 the Dead Sea Scrolls, having been discovered only a year earlier, had yet to make their impact. Thirty years after that discovery it was Sanders's 400 pages on Judaism, taking up and documenting G. F. Moore's devastating thesis in 'Christian writers on Judaism' (*HTR* 14 (1921), 197–254) rather than his Schweitzerian Paul which changed the shape of Pauline studies. It did so by denying that Judaism was a legalistic religion of merit and works righteousness. This account of early Judaism, based on an intimate knowledge of the Tannaitic literature, the Dead Sea Scrolls, and the Apocrypha and Pseudepigrapha, was followed by *Paul, the Law and the Jewish People* (1983), which gave the historical Paul a sharper profile. Its alternative to 'the Lutheran Paul' was partly anticipated by K. Stendahl's provocative essay on 'Paul and the Introspective Conscience of the West' (1963) and independently reinforced by H. Räisänen, *Paul and the Law* (also 1983) and F. Watson, *Paul, Judaism, and the Gentiles* (1986, but written in 1983). This 'new perspective' is now embedded in such widely read commentaries and textbooks as J. D. G. Dunn on Romans (1988) and Galatians (1993) and *The Theology of Paul the Apostle* (1998), but the subsequent debate, best followed in S. Westerholm, *Perspectives Old and New on Paul* (2004), suggests, without belittling Sanders's achievement, that the heart of the apostle's religion and theology is more profoundly understood and appreciated in the modern German and Swiss tradition with its vital roots in Augustine, Luther, and Calvin.

Interpretations of Paul in which solid historical exegesis has reinforced Reformation theological perspectives have thus been modified by a new emphasis on the historical context of Paul's argument for justification by faith alone in his defence of his law-free Gentile mission. The shift of emphasis should not be exaggerated. Influential Pauline scholars barely affected by Sanders, such as N. A. Dahl, C. K. Barrett, J. L. Martyn, U. Wilckens, L. E. Keck, J. C. Beker, C. Roetzel, M. D. Hooker, and J. Becker all have deep theological roots in the Reformation tradition. But here too there is movement as some of them follow G. Howard, R. B. Hays, L. T. Johnson, and S. K. Williams in taking Paul's rare (seven times) phrase 'faith of Jesus' (or Christ) to mean Jesus' own faith (or faithfulness unto death), rather than Paul's more typical 'faith *in* Christ'. This exegetical adjustment makes the historical memory of Jesus more significant for Paul (and so for some modern theology) than it was in the conception of Bultmann and his followers.

The interpretation of Paul is the weather-vane of New Testament scholarship because here theologians have strong meat and historians strong evidence. Ancient history is not the only frame of reference in which the New Testament can be studied, but since the 1830s this has increasingly provided context, methods, and goals, even during periods of reaction against historicism. Christian identity depends on, and theology and preaching draw from, the gospels and Paul. They therefore need biblical scholarship to clarify the faith intentions of these ancient texts and authors. However, the necessary development of a historical perspective brought with it non-theological readings which described their first-century religion without relating this to contemporary Christianity, even implicitly. The hermeneutical problem could be left to theologians, while biblical scholars did their proper linguistic, literary, and historical work. This programme, enunciated by Wrede in 1897, and differently in the Chicago school of the early twentieth century, gained ground as the balance between historical and hermeneutical interests shifted in the 1970s. Disembodied ideas and their linguistic backgrounds seemed less interesting than life in society. The history of theology is a part of the history of religion, and that is social history. Ideas were to be understood (and perhaps explained) in their social contexts. The shift was to social history, now interpreted by sociological theory, and the relative richness of data about Paul and the communities he addressed in the 50s made the seven undoubtedly authentic epistles one major field for this new emphasis.

An even more important field for the new approaches was historical Jesus research, where again a recognizable historical figure was influential in a recognizable social context. Here the evidence is less reliable, because the primary sources stand at some remove from the events they relate. New questions with which to interrogate the evidence can elicit fresh knowledge, but more evidence to interrogate is especially welcome, and the context of Jesus' activity has been explored in different ways. The contributions of archaeology and epigraphy, though less helpful than in Old Testament studies, have been eagerly sifted. Where interest in ideas declines, the architecture of house-churches, synagogues, Herod's palace, and topography assume a new importance.

Social history is demanded by the nature of the New Testament material, but the 'sociological turn' in some historical criticism of Old and New Testaments also reflected wider social, cultural, and educational shifts in Europe and North America at the end of the 1960s. Classical form critics had not pursued the sociological aspects of their theory that literary forms had their 'setting in the life' of the early church. Käsemann's conviction that Johannine Christianity was sectarian had not encouraged him to analyse the texts with tools from the social sciences. But interest in the Jewish sect responsible for the scrolls at Qumran would soon invite fresh attention to Ernst Troeltsch's typology of sects, and this would prove suggestive for historical Jesus research and for the earliest phases of the church, as well as in Johannine studies. Historical and sociological hypotheses about Christian origins were stimulated by a better understanding of Judaism and a more sophisticated understanding of sectarianism. The new social location of some American biblical studies in university departments of religion was also encouraging new relationships with the social sciences and with Jewish studies. A new generation of scholars was asking new questions.

In North America John Gager's *Kingdom and Community* (1975) applied Festinger's theory of cognitive dissonance and Coser's account of the functions of social conflict to interpret early Christianity as a millenarian movement, but his allowing analogies from other societies to compensate for the scarcity of empirical data from the ancient world was generally rejected. Several scholars used Bryan Wilson's analysis of sects in their discussion of the messianic sect. A little earlier in Germany Gerd Theissen's pioneering studies of the synoptic tradition and Paul drew on sociological theory to set the historical and textual data in a new light, pressing questions first raised before 1914 but left undeveloped during the theological revival of the 1920s and its afterglow. His sophisticated methodological discussions and historical probes were later collected in English as *The Social Setting of Pauline Christianity* (1982), *Social Reality and the Early Christians* (1992), and *The Gospels in Context* (1992). His work and that of J. H. Schütz in *Paul and the Anatomy of Apostolic Authority* (1975) among others was drawn on by Wayne Meeks in *The First Urban Christians* (1983), the representative and standard work on 'the social world of the apostle Paul' (subtitle). Meeks has articulated this change of sensibility in studies of *The Moral World of the First Christians* (1986) and *The Origins of Christian Morality* (1993). His essays from 1972 to 2002 collected (with 'Reflections on an Era') as *In Search of the Early Christians* (2002) include his celebrated essay on 'The Man from Heaven in Johannine Sectarianism' (1972) which highlighted the interdisciplinary potential of this development.

Others have taken social-scientific approaches further. B. Malina followed *The New Testament World: Insights from Cultural Anthropology* (1981, rev. 1993) with *Biblical Social Values and their Meaning* (1993, with J. J. Pilch) and a series of 'social science commentaries'. J. H. Elliott pioneered 'a sociological exegesis of 1 Peter, its situation and strategy' in *A Home for the Homeless* (1981), and in Britain P. F. Esler has more recently continued the work of this group in studies of Galatians (1998) and Romans (2003) following an earlier 'socio-redactional' monograph on Luke–Acts (1987) and works on social-scientific modelling. Examples from North America could be multiplied, but the way this trend has continued to develop over thirty years can best be illustrated by comparing Gerd Theissen's pioneering 'sociology of the Jesus movement', *The First Followers of Jesus* (1977, ET 1978), with its expansion to four times its length in 2004 (ET 2006), or with E. W. and W. Stegemann, *The Jesus Movement: A Social History of its First Century* (1995, ET 1999), which focuses on the economic and social conditions of those early Jewish-Christian sectarian communities.

The combination of sociological questioning and a better understanding of Judaism is most evident in the historical Jesus research of our third period, but special mention should be made of studies of the Johannine community. J. L. Martyn's *History and Theology in the Fourth Gospel* (1968), relating the history of the community and origins of the gospel to developments in Judaism after 70 CE, as W. D. Davies had done for Matthew in *The Setting of the Sermon on the Mount* (1964), was a turning point in America barely recognized in continental Europe. R. E. Brown's Anchor Bible commentary on John (vol. i, 1964; vol. ii, 1969) and *The Community of the Beloved Disciple* (1979) also reconstructed (also hypothetically) the history of the community, and W. Meeks dug deeply into its Jewish messianic background in *The Prophet-King* (1967). D. Rensberger, *Johannine Faith and Liberating Community* (1988; in Britain: *Overcoming the World*, 1989) shows what fresh light can be thrown on this history from sociological perspectives.

The psychology of religion has yielded far less than sociological theory, despite the advocacy of Theissen in *Psychological Aspects of Pauline Theology* (1983, ET 1987) and some more recent work on social psychology. Clinical data are not available from the ancient world, but biblical symbols can be interpreted with the help of various discourses. Works such as R. Scroggs, *Paul for a New Day* (1977), R. Hamerton-Kelly, *God the Father* (1979)—a taboo theme for some—and D. A. Via, *Self-Deception and Wholeness in Paul and Matthew* (1990), as well as the varied works of W. Wink all draw on psychology, and perhaps deserve more attention than they have yet received.

The change of sensibility associated with the social sciences can be seen most clearly in liberation and feminist theology. Both are more closely related to practice than most biblical scholarship, and both began to affect biblical studies during this transitional period. E. S. Fiorenza, *In Memory of Her* (1982), is the landmark, even if her advocacy of advocacy has not been widely accepted in academic circles, and some of her proposals are hard to justify historically and exegetically. Feminist interpretation of the Bible has been more successful when proposed in the framework of the modern literary approaches to the Bible which flourished in our third period. The application of structuralism to the parables and other narratives in the 1970s gave only a hint of this impending major and variegated shift in some biblical scholarship.

3. INNOVATIONS

Despite the sub-head, the first thing to say about this third period (1980–2005) is: more of the same. Commentaries and monographs multiplied, the study of the ancient world advanced, contextualizing the New Testament better in its Hellenistic environment; textual criticism occupied its own niche, new translations were produced, and newly available texts (especially those rejected by the church) excited the media. *The Anchor Bible Dictionary* (6 vols., 1992) sums up much of the twentieth century's work, and renewed interest in the history of the discipline has already been signalled by our initial footnote. *The Apocryphal Old Testament* (ed. H. F. D. Sparks, 1984), *The Old Testament Pseudepigrapha* (2 vols., ed. J. H. Charlesworth, 1983–5), and an edition of the Qumran texts are never far from the New Testament student's desk. Wrede's 1897 call for a 'history of early Christian religion and theology' has been echoed by H. Räisänen, *Beyond New Testament Theology* (1990, 2nd edn. 2000), and answered by H. Koester (1980, ET 1982), W. Schmithals (1994, ET 1997), and K. Berger (1994). Wrede's insistence on tracing developments into the second century has been splendidly vindicated by P. Lampe, *From Paul to Valentinus* (2003) and C. E. Hill, *The Johannine Corpus in the Early Church* (2004), and in Christology by L. Hurtado, *Lord Jesus Christ* (2003), challenging W. Bousset's *Kyrios Christos* (1913, 2nd edn. 1921; ET 1970). Introductions to the New Testament, most notably by L. T. Johnson (1986, 2nd edn. 1999), U. Schnelle (1998), R. E. Brown (1997), and more recently P. Achtemeier, J. B. Green and M. M. Thompson (2001), D. Burkett (2002), G. Theissen (2002, ET 2003), and C. Holladay (2005), inevitably cover much of the same ground as earlier textbooks, though the shortage of non-German New Testament theologies has led 'introductions' to absorb much of that genre. Several New Testament theologies have been published since 1990, among them those of H. Hübner (1990–5), P. Stuhlmacher (1992–9; ET 2006), J. Gnilka (1994), G. Strecker (1996, ET 2000), W. Thüsing (2nd edn. 1996–9), F. Hahn (2002), U. Wilckens (2002–), and I. H. Marshall (2004). Further works on Jewish messianism, e.g. J. J. Collins, *The*

Scepter and the Star (1995), and W. Horbury, *Jewish Messianism and the Cult of Christ* (1998), have illuminated the foundations of Christology, and these have been surveyed by J. D. G. Dunn (1980, 2nd edn. 1989), M. de Jonge (1988), F. Matera (1999), C. Tuckett (2001), and L. Hurtado (2003). In the study of Paul 'much more of the same' includes experiment on a solid scholarly base: e.g. D. B. Martin, *The Corinthian Body* (1995), and T. Engberg-Pedersen, *Paul and the Stoics* (2000), and significant Jewish contributions by A. F. Segal, *Paul the Convert* (1990), and D. Boyarin, *A Radical Jew* (1994).

None of this is mere repetition, and some of it is innovatory, but it is progress along familiar lines, enriched by the developments already noted, the road widened by an upsurge in academic publishing and some media interest. This is clearest in historical Jesus research, where, since 1985, R. Funk's 'Jesus seminar' has gained a hearing for a minor reaction against the twentieth-century consensus that eschatology provides the key to understanding Jesus historically. That theory, advanced by J. Weiss in *Jesus' Proclamation of the Kingdom of God* (1892, ET 1971) and popularized by Albert Schweitzer, *The Quest of the Historical Jesus* (1906, ET 1910, rev. 2000), has dominated the study of Christian origins, but its intertestamental Jewish roots became less prominent as the New Testament was interpreted theologically. A new phase in historical Jesus research became apparent as the intensive new study of early Judaism brought with it a fresh emphasis on Jesus' Jewishness. This was signalled by the Qumran specialist Geza Vermes in *Jesus the Jew* (1973). His title and non-theological perspective were significant, but his main contribution to Jesus research lay in reviving a nineteenth-century argument that Jesus' Aramaic phrase 'son of man' was not an eschatological title (that came later) but a circumlocution referring to himself, 'a man'. The linguistic debate continues, but many now doubt whether the apocalyptic meaning from Dan. 7: 13 goes back to Jesus himself.

The full impact of modern Jewish studies and a shift from the theological perspectives of G. Bornkamm and of J. Jeremias, *New Testament Theology, i: The Proclamation of Jesus* (1971), became apparent in E. P. Sanders, *Jesus and Judaism* (1985), *Jewish Law from Jesus to the Mishnah* (1990), and *The Historical Figure of Jesus* (1993). In Germany much earlier, Martin Hengel had preceded his monumental *Judaism and Hellenism* (1969, ET 1974) with a sparkling monograph on *The Charismatic Leader and his Followers* (1968, ET 1981), showing that a deep knowledge of Judaism was not incompatible with a passionate theological interest in Jesus. The same can be said of Gerd Theissen's writings on Jesus, from his popular narrative *The Shadow of the Galilean* (1986, ET 1987) to his standard textbook (with A. Merz), *The Historical Jesus* (1996, ET 1998) and (with D. Winter) his methodological study, *The Quest for the Plausible Jesus* (1997, ET 2002).

A similar theological and hermeneutical interest is evident in some English-language writing on Jesus, notably B. F. Meyer, *The Aims of Jesus* (1979), A. E. Harvey, *Jesus and the Constraints of History* (1982), M. J. Borg, *Jesus: A New Vision*

(1988), J. P. Meier, *A Marginal Jew* (1991–), B. Chilton, *Pure Kingdom: Jesus' Vision of God* (1996), N. T. Wright, *Jesus and the Victory of God* (1996), L. E. Keck, *Who is Jesus?* (2000), and J. D. G. Dunn, *Jesus Remembered* (2003). Elsewhere the connection of Jesus research with Christian theology has sometimes been repudiated and often left implicit. The religious and social potential of such portraits as R. A. Horsley, *Jesus and the Spiral of Violence* (1987), Dale Allison, *Jesus of Nazareth, Millenarian Prophet* (1998), and J. D. Crossan, *The Historical Jesus: The Life of a Mediterranean Jewish Peasant* (1991) is undeniable, but these historical reconstructions contain little explicit hermeneutical reflection.

As some of these titles indicate, an increase in knowledge of Palestinian Judaism from archaeology and intensive study of Jewish texts has brought not more certainty about Jesus, but more possible Jewish contexts in which to place this Galilean holy man (Vermes), charismatic (Hengel), eschatological prophet (Sanders), rabbi (Chilton), pharisee (H. Falk), revolutionary (S. G. F. Brandon), social reformer (Horsley), peasant (Crossan), or cynic (B. Mack and F. G. Downing). Perhaps Jesus fits neatly into none of these categories. How his central theme, the kingdom of God, was intended remains disputed, and with it how eschatology and ethics are related in his teaching. Whether he called himself a/the son of man and what he may have meant by it still depends on which of the sayings attributed to him are considered authentic. Why exactly he was executed remains debated: for example, in J. D. Crossan, *Who Killed Jesus?* (1995), a (polemical) response to R. E. Brown's monumental *The Death of the Messiah* (1994). Crossan's subtitle, 'Exploring the Roots of Anti-Semitism in the Gospel Story of the Death of Jesus', reflects a persistent concern in New Testament research since W. D. Davies on Paul and P. Winter's *On the Trial of Jesus* (1961) to neutralize its anti-Jewish potential.

The distinctive feature of this new phase of historical Jesus research is its renewed effort to situate him in his Galilean context and reduced emphasis upon history-of-traditions analysis of individual sayings to determine the earliest strata and decide which may go back to Jesus. That work, however, continues, especially in the study of Q, where attempts have been made to detect an earlier, non-eschatological wisdom layer going back to Jesus. J. S. Kloppenborg, *The Formation of Q: Trajectories in Ancient Wisdom Collections* (1987), has in this way given (hypothetical) support to non-eschatological accounts of Jesus, such as those of J. D. Crossan and B. L. Mack. This theory has also found support in *The Gospel of Thomas*, which provides a possibly independent version of a few synoptic sayings and parables; but the non-eschatological character of this Gnostic text is more probably a reflection of its author's own viewpoint. The ongoing debate confirms that neither the study of early Judaism nor careful analysis of the gospel traditions should be neglected. It also confirms that while few certainties are available, the range of credible reconstructions is neither damaging to nor necessarily supportive of orthodox Christianity. One might suggest that the ongoing process of historical research is more important for theology than its disputed results.

Several recent books about 'the historical Jesus' have paid little attention to John's gospel, while acknowledging that it contains some reliable historical evidence. That is because its method is apparently to communicate the religious meaning of Jesus by the composition of new discourses rather than by reporting his actual words. One may ask whether John renders Jesus' intention correctly, but if answers cannot be verified historically, this is a question for New Testament theology rather than historical Jesus research. A main focus of Johannine study has accordingly been on these finished compositions, but scholars have continued to investigate possible sources. Thus J. Ashton's magisterial *Understanding the Fourth Gospel* (1991) discusses Bultmann's hypothetical 'signs source', promoted by R. T. Fortna to *The Gospel of Signs* (1970), and correlates this with the history of the Johannine community in its relation to the synagogue, but is primarily interested in the gospel's main theological themes. A recent (2001) collection of essays, *Jesus in Johannine Tradition*, edited by R. T. Fortna and T. Thatcher, explores the gospel's prehistory, and twenty-five contributions to a Leuven conference volume on *Anti-Judaism and the Fourth Gospel* (2001) signal a flashpoint; but most recent monographs, such as C. R. Koester, *Symbolism in the Fourth Gospel* (1995), and M. M. Thompson, *The God of the Gospel of John* (2001), concentrate on the literary character and theology of the gospel.

Jewish studies, sociological enquiry, and responses to anti-Semitism have combined in a similar way in the study of Matthew's gospel, where the evidence is clear, and in Luke–Acts, where it is not, and also in writing on the book of Revelation. The debate about Jamnia and Palestinian Judaism following the Jewish War (CE 66–73) has advanced since W. D. Davies (1964) and J. L. Martyn (1968), but the relationship of Matthew to its synagogue neighbour is as clear as that of John to the parent religion. A. J. Saldarini saw Matthew and his community as 'deviant Jews' in a collection of cross-disciplinary essays edited by D. L. Balch on the *Social History of the Matthean Community* (1991), and in *Matthew's Christian-Jewish Community* (1994) developed the similar thesis of J. A. Overman, *Matthew's Gospel and Formative Judaism* (1990). This was taken further by D. C. Sim, *The Gospel of Matthew and Christian Judaism* (1998). After nearly fifty years since the Second World War the redaction criticism classically represented by G. Bornkamm, G. Barth, and H. J. Held, *Tradition and Interpretation in Matthew* (1960, ET 1963), and by G. Strecker, *Der Weg der Gerechtigkeit* (1962), was thus complemented in the 1990s by a new centre of interest. As in historical Jesus research, some found envisioning the broader religious scene exciting, while others, such as G. N. Stanton in *A Gospel for a New People* (1992), have effectively defended and developed more traditional positions.

Despite being by far the largest work in the New Testament, the origins of Luke–Acts (many now treat this as a single literary work; it at least projects a unified theological conception) are less clear than its purposes (cf. Luke 1: 1–4) and the author's evident enthusiasm for Paul and his Gentile mission. Against the consensus that Luke was a Gentile or a 'godfearer', some have argued that he was Jewish, especially J. Jervell in a series of essays since 1962, and D. L. Tiede, *Prophecy and History in Luke–Acts* (1980). J. T. Sanders and J. B. Tyson claim that Luke is anti-Jewish, whereas the collection edited by D. P. Moessner on *Jesus and the Heritage of Israel* (1999) takes a positive view. The 'Context Group' led by B. Malina, J. H. Elliott, and J. J. Pilch continued its productions with *The Social World of Luke– Acts* in 1991, and feminist interpreters such as T. K. Seim, *The Double Message: Patterns of Gender in Luke–Acts* (1994), have found much to criticize in this author whose presentation of women characters had generally met with approval. Here, as in Matthean studies, the research inaugurated by Conzelmann's redaction criticism and summed up in Fitzmyer's Anchor Bible Commentary (vol. i, 1981; vol. ii, 1985) has been enriched by new concerns.

A more seismic shift away from history-of-traditions approaches has been not to sociological and contextual studies but to modern literary analyses of the biblical narratives. The best-known examples in Lucan studies are by C. H. Talbert, R. C. Tannehill, L. T. Johnson, and J. B. Tyson; yet here, where the evangelist's theological purposes are historical as well as narrative, historical studies have unsurprisingly remained the most common. It has been in the study of Mark, where redaction criticism could make little secure progress in the absence of the evangelist's sources, and sociological probes such as H. C. Kee, *Community of the New Age* (1977), were constrained by lack of evidence, that literary studies of the existing text have proved most popular. From J. Dewey, *Markan Public Debate* (1980), D. Rhoads and D. Michie, *Mark as Story* (1982), R. M. Fowler, *Loaves and Fishes* (1981) and *Let the Reader Understand* (1991), M. A. Tolbert, *Sowing the Gospel* (1989), to several studies of J. R. Donahue, A. Stock, and E. S. Malbon, new literary approaches have here proved at least as valuable as the more traditional approaches powerfully represented by M. Hengel, H. Räisänen, and E. Best. The balance is neatly struck (seven literary articles, six historical) in W. R. Telford's indispensable *The Inter- pretation of Mark* (2nd edn. 1995). The best political and liberationist studies of Mark, C. Myers, *Binding the Strong Man* (1988), and R. A. Horsley, *Hearing the Whole Story* (2001), have a literary as well as a sociological dimension.

Several students of N. Perrin (1921–76) in Chicago worked on Mark, most building literary approaches on to historical criticism. The most inviting area for purely literary analyses was parable research, in which Dan O. Via, *The Parables: Their Literary and Existential Dimension* (1967), had advanced the American literary study of the gospels pioneered by Amos Wilder and William Beardslee. In Johannine studies, A. Culpepper, *Anatomy of the Fourth Gospel* (1983), attended to the literary design of the text, and F. J. Moloney wrote a narrative critical commentary on the gospel (1993–8).

As his title indicates, Via's work was theological as well as literary, but structur- alist approaches to the parables and several narratological approaches to the gospels moved further from theology than earlier historical studies. Among the surveys, Stephen Moore's *Literary Criticism and the Gospels* (1989) stands out for its theoretical brilliance and hints of post-modern perversity. Like A. Thiselton's more wide-ranging *New Horizons in Hermeneutics* (1992) and the various contributions to theological hermeneutics by H. Weder, F. Watson, and S. Fowl, it shows that 'modern literary approaches' cover a wide spectrum, in which only some dovetail with theological interests. One question posed for those who read the Bible as scripture concerns textual indeterminacy. For scripture to provide a *norm* for Christian faith and life, the intention of the texts remains crucial, but read as a *source* of faith and devotion, scripture, like other literary texts, constantly generates fresh insights unknown to the author, and here 'pre-critical' typological and allegorical interpretations are sometimes suggestive. In Germany Luther's exegesis has regularly attracted the attention of theologians, but work in the history of New Testament interpretation prior to the eighteenth century has been done largely by historians and students of English literature. The newly expanding study of the Bible's reception history by exegetes such as C. Rowland and J. L. Kovacs is therefore welcome. It is not a substitute for the basic task of historical exegesis, which requires linguistic and historical as well as literary skills, but a source of further insights. Its potential is clearest in the Evangelisch-Katholisch Kommentar series, especially U. Luz on Matthew (1985–2002, ET 1990–); see also his *Matthew in History* (1994). Three commentary series in English have recently picked up this baton: the Ancient Christian Commentary on Scripture (1998–), the Blackwell Bible Commentaries (2003–), and most notably *The Church's Bible* (2004–) which translates substantial portions of the Fathers.

Modern literary approaches have thrown less light on the epistles. Historical exegesis guided by and stimulating historical hypotheses remains dominant here, but a lonely structuralist furrow has been ploughed by D. Patte. N. R. Petersen has integrated historical, literary, and social-scientific perspectives to interpret Paul's narrative world in *Rediscovering Paul* (1985), and ancient epistolography, forms, and genres have been further studied. An ancient line of literary enquiry has been reopened with the recent re-emergence of rhetorical criticism. H. D. Betz's Hermeneia Commentary on Galatians (1979) remains its most consistent application to a complete text, and his student and successor Margaret Mitchell has shown what this approach can achieve with her monograph on 1 Corinthians, *Paul and the Rhetoric of Reconciliation* (1991). Rhetoric was such a pervasive factor in Hellenistic education and culture that one might expect more, but it remains a question how deeply any of the New Testament authors were inculturated into it. D. E. Aune, *The Westminster Dictionary of New Testament and Early Christian Literature and Rhetoric* (2003), provides an invaluable resource.

The ways in which literary approaches can fruitfully be combined with historical exegesis and reconstruction could be illustrated from many authors and standard topics. One example is R. B. Hays's contribution to the use of the Old Testament in the New, *Echoes of Scripture in the Letters of Paul* (1989). The search for inter-textual echoes has become so common in secular literary criticism that its blossoming in biblical studies is no surprise.

Hays's earlier monograph on *The Faith of Jesus Christ* (1983, 2nd edn. 2001) had identified an underlying narrative substructure, the story of Jesus, as a generating feature of Paul's theology, and his subsequent masterpiece *The Moral Vision of the New Testament* (1996) brought a literary sensitivity to the hermeneutical task. Comparing this with the theological ethics of an older generation, e.g. E. Lohse and W. Schrage, or the anti-theological thrust of J. T. Sanders (1975), indicates one ecclesial direction in which this central concern can be pursued, alongside the more secular social history (informed by anthropology) advanced by Meeks. Similar to Hays's combination of historical, literary, and contemporary perspectives in New Testament ethics is W. Countryman, *Dirt, Greed and Sex* (1988).

The early Christian prophet responsible for the Book of Revelation has challenged the ingenuity of literary scholars. The recent upsurge of interest in this text on the edge of the canon owes much to the millennium. Much has been written about it from literary, social-historical, sociological, liberationist, and reception-historical perspectives. The visual and imaginative dimensions of this text must be taken seriously, on account of both the damage and the inspiration its reception has wrought.

If Revelation is one text lately to have emerged from the shadows into which it was cast by the Greek Fathers and the magisterial Reformers, another is the Epistle of James. Luther's negative judgement on it was a reflection of his own agenda, and the fact that this text is in the canon invites New Testament scholars and requires New Testament theologians to engage with it. As a possible route into the now largely lost history of Christian Judaism, it appealed to the Jewish Qumran specialist R. Eisenman, whose eccentric but remarkable *James the Brother of Jesus* (1997) provoked several more conventional accounts of this key figure. The serious moral content of this writing perhaps makes more immediate sense today than the more profound theological arguments of St Paul. Some reaction against Paul's immense prestige since Origen and Augustine, some loss of confidence regarding the identity of Christianity, and some determination not to allow such considerations to interfere with the free play of and with literary texts are changing the shape of some New Testament syllabuses.

These remarks are themselves indicative of a new pluralism in biblical studies, extending far beyond the Western church and university scene sampled selectively here. The wider world offers a variety of perspectives beyond the liberation theology which has most impressed Western interpreters. Christian theologians will have their own ideas about what kinds of biblical study are most appropriate in their own varied contexts, but they cannot object to others doing other things with these public texts, and must surely celebrate their partnership with Jewish scholars in studying their Jewish-born Lord, his least and greatest apostle, and some unknown but highly influential messianic Jewish and perhaps Gentile writers.

The plurality of interpretations is an even greater challenge to Christian identity than the historical diversity perceived within the canon earlier in our period. In the 1960s the 'canon' was labelled a 'problem' by some theologians, and a 'canon within a canon' was occasionally proposed. In the 1980s equally deliberate theological aims were pursued on a more conservative and even biblicist track in the 'canonical criticism' of B. S. Childs. But however valid a concentration on the (more or less) 'final form of the text' is for some literary and theological purposes, Christian theology is committed by its appeal to God in Jesus to raise historical questions, and that means also to go behind the relevant texts. However, the new emphasis on textuality and the newer emphasis on the reader are also of interest to religious readers of the Bible. Reader-response approaches, for example, have points of contact with kerygmatic theology, and both can serve the claim echoed in the appropriate formula at the end of liturgical readings of scripture: 'Hear the Word of the Lord' (in the witness of the text to God in Christ). That other approaches to these texts are also possible is but a part of life's rich tapestry.

THE IMPACT OF OTHER DISCIPLINES UPON BIBLICAL SCHOLARSHIP

CHAPTER 3

ARCHAEOLOGY

JOHN R. BARTLETT

This article examines archaeology's impact on biblical scholarship, especially over the last two centuries. It describes the Christian pilgrims, explorers, travellers, map-makers, and military surveyors, who prepared the way for the archaeologists. The article focuses on twentieth-century archaeology in Palestine/Israel, demonstrating archaeology's growing independence as a discipline and its effect on modern understanding of the Bible's presentation of history.

EARLY INTEREST IN BIBLICAL SITES

The Hebrew scriptures themselves do not show much interest in archaeological matters, but there is a revealing statement in Josh. 8: 28: 'So Joshua burned Ai, and made it for ever a heap of ruins, as it is to this day.' The author apparently knew the ruins, and associated them, rightly or wrongly, with the work of Joshua. The Babylonian kings Nebuchadnezzar (605–562 BCE) and Nabonidus (556–539 BCE) are reported to have had antiquarian interests; Nabonidus excavated temples at Ur, Uruk, and Agade, and found a foundation-stone laid by Narram-Sin (c.2350 BCE). However, we do not hear of any other archaeological interest in ancient sites until early Christian pilgrims began to try to identify sites associated with the birth, ministry, death, and resurrection of Jesus. If the discovery of the true cross, credited to Helena, mother of the emperor Constantine, on her pilgrimage to Jerusalem in

326–7, is a pious legend (see Hunt 1982: 38–42), the observations of the Bordeaux pilgrim in 333 are precise and reveal an enquiring mind, ready to distinguish between the Jericho of Joshua and the Jericho of Jesus (Wilkinson 1971: 160–1). In the same period Eusebius, bishop of Caesarea, c.260–339, produced a gazetteer of biblical place-names known as the *Onomasticon* (Klostermann 1904; Freeman-Grenville, Chapman, and Taylor 2003), which certainly witnesses to a more than pietistic interest. The Spanish nun Egeria, travelling c.381–5, was primarily concerned with holy places and holy people, but she was observant, especially about the landscape and places through which she travelled. The sixth-century mosaic map of the Holy Land in the church at Madeba was designed to educate Christian pilgrims; it drew not only on place-names from the gospels and the Old Testament, and on Eusebius's *Onomasticon*, but also on knowledge of the Roman road system, and on first-hand knowledge of sixth-century Palestinian cities. Later travellers leaving informative accounts included Theodosius (sixth century), Bishop Arculf (seventh century), Bishop Willibald of Eichstätt (educated in Hampshire, eighth century), and the monk Bernard from Mont St Michel (ninth century) (conveniently collected in Wright 1848, repr. 1968). In the tenth century it was an Islamic scholar, Mukaddasi, who explored Palestine and wrote a description of Jerusalem (985). Through the eleventh century Palestine was virtually closed to Christian travellers until the Crusades reopened it; travel accounts were written by, among others, the English pilgrim Saewulf (1102), Theoderich (1172), Nachmanides (the Spanish rabbi Moshe ben Nachman, 1267). However, though travellers were observant, and sometimes curious, there was little or no understanding of scientific study of the past and its material remains, because 'the limits of human research and speculation concerning human nature had been fixed by divine ordinance embodied in the tradition of the Church. Curiosity (*curiositas*), the attempt to push the bounds of knowledge further, was associated with an heretical spirit' (Frend 1996: 8).

TRAVELLERS AND MAPS

The era of the Crusades led to new interest in Palestine, revealed in travellers' and chroniclers' accounts, and especially in the development of maps of Palestine (cf. especially the Matthew Paris map of 1252, and the Sanuto and Vesconti map of 1320, and that of the English traveller William Wey in 1462; see Nebenzahl 1986). The first printed atlas was the *Geographia* of the second-century Claudius Ptolemaeus (Rome 1478, Ulm 1482 and 1486), which included Nicolas Germanus's version of

Ptolemy's original *Quarta tabula Asiae*; alongside it in the Ulm editions appeared a much fuller, fifteenth-century *Tabula Moderna Terrae Sanctae* (Dilke 1985: 162). Ptolemy's scientific work was foundational until surveying by triangulation and the exact calculation of longitude were achieved in the seventeenth century, though individual travellers contributed to improvements in detail. The maps published by sixteenth-century map-makers like Gerardus Mercator, Abraham Ortelius, and Christian von Adrichom, and works of biblical scholarship like Thomas Fuller's *A Pisgah-sight of Palestine* (1650) and Adrian Reland's *Palestina ex monumentis veteribus illustrata* (1714) were an important prerequisite to the work of seventeenth- to eighteenth-century scholarly travellers. Such travellers included Pietro della Valle, who in 1650–8 travelled widely in the Near East, correctly identifying Ur with Tell el-Mukayyar; Henry Maundrell (1665–1701), whose *Journey from Aleppo to Jerusalem* (1703) is observant and illustrated with drawings and plans; and Bishop Richard Pococke (1704–65), who published *A Description of the East and Some Other Countries* (1745). Robert Wood (1717–71), by his accurate reports and architectural drawings of the ruins of Palmyra (1753), and Baalbek (1757) set new standards for future Near Eastern archaeologists.

Surveying and Site Identification

Traditional learning had been challenged by the development of science from the days of Galileo, but it was only in the nineteenth century that biblical scholarship in particular began to open up to increasing archaeological, geographical, and historical discoveries. Professional scientific mapping of Palestine began with Pierre Jacotin, who mapped the coastal plain and lower Galilee for Napoleon in 1799, though apparently not by triangulation; this was first used in a survey of Palestine and Syria by a British military survey in 1840–1 (Jones 1973). This achievement was soon overshadowed by the surveying of Jerusalem (1865), Sinai (1868–9), and western Palestine (1871–7) by British army engineers under the aegis of the Palestine Exploration Fund (founded in 1865). (A Survey of eastern Palestine was begun in 1872, but was abandoned for political reasons after several months' work.) Just before the 1840–1 survey, the American professor Edward Robinson (1794–1863), with his former student Eli Smith, then a missionary in Beirut, travelled throughout Palestine (1838–9, and again in 1852) to locate places mentioned in the Bible. He worked from the Arabic place-names, which, he argued, preserved cognates to the ancient Semitic biblical names (though on geographical grounds Robinson correctly declined to identify Lachish with Um Lakis; *Biblical Researches*, ii. 388–9). 'On

May 4 and 5 he travelled north of Jerusalem and on the basis of Arabic place-names established nine identifications with biblical places: Anathoth, Geba, Rimmon, Michmash, Bethel, Ophrah, Beeroth, Gibeon and Mizpah. Of these only the identification of Beeroth has proved to be uncertain' (de Geus 1980: 65). Robinson did not recognize, however, that the 'tells' of the Palestinian plain were the remains of ancient cities, so could not identify Lachish with Tell ed-Duweir. Albrecht Alt (1883–1956) famously commented that 'in Robinson's footnotes are forever buried the errors of many generations' (Alt 1939: 374). Robinson and Smith's *Biblical Researches* (1841 and 1856) remains an essential reference work. The researches of Robinson and the Survey of Western Palestine between them laid the foundations for all subsequent archaeological work and much biblical historical scholarship.

FOUNDING OF ARCHAEOLOGICAL SOCIETIES

Nineteenth-century Palestine and its surrounding region were of growing public interest. Petra had been rediscovered for Europeans by J. L. Burkhardt (1784–1817) in 1812, and well illustrated by L de Laborde (1830), and then by the artists David Roberts (in Palestine 1838–9) and W. H. Bartlett (in Palestine 1841–4). The River Jordan and the Dead Sea had been explored in 1848 by an American naval lieutenant, W. F. Lynch. The development of Sunday schools, the church-goer's interest in the Bible, the general growth of education, the arrival of Cook's Tours, coupled with cheaper printing technology, all fed the interest. Steamships and railways opened tourist routes for the wealthier classes, while politicians and businessmen dreamed of a land route to India via the Levant. The foundation of the Palestine Exploration Fund (1865), whose aim was the scientific investigation of 'the Archaeology, Geography, Geology and Natural History of Palestine', met a growing intellectual interest, and through its journal, the *Palestine Exploration Fund Quarterly Statement*, presented the results of continuing exploration and excavation to its subscribers. The British School of Archaeology in Jerusalem, modelled on similar schools in Rome and Athens, was founded in 1912, with an offshoot in Amman in 1978. Similar societies appeared elsewhere: the first institute of the American Schools of Oriental Research was founded in Jerusalem in 1900, soon followed by its *Bulletin*. Also in Jerusalem, the French Dominicans established the École biblique et archéologique in 1890, with their journal, the *Revue biblique*, in 1892. In Germany, the Deutscher Verein für Erforschung Palästinas, with its periodical *Zeitschrift des deutschen Palästina-Vereins*, was founded in 1877, and the Deutsches evangelisches Institut für Altertumswissenschaft des Heiligen Landes, with its *Palästina-Jahrbuch*, appeared in 1900. In Israel, the Israel Exploration Society (formerly the Jewish Palestine Exploration Society, founded in 1914) launched the *Israel Exploration Journal* in 1951. All these societies have had an enormous impact on the world of biblical scholarship.

Discoveries in Egypt and Mesopotamia

What made a real impact on the nineteenth-century public imagination was the series of astonishing discoveries made in Egypt and Mesopotamia. Scholarly study of Egypt began seriously with Napoleon's expedition in 1799, and advanced with the discovery of the Rosetta Stone in 1799 and the decipherment of the Egyptian hieroglyphics by Jean François Champollion in 1822. Academic work continued through scholars like S. Birch and R. S. Poole at the British Museum, and the French Gaston Maspero and Mariette Pasha. In 1882 was founded the Egypt Exploration Society, which led to excavation at El-Amarna, where in 1887 a peasant woman unearthed an archive of over 300 clay tablets bearing cuneiform inscriptions (James 1982: 95). These fourteenth-century BCE 'Amarna Letters', written to the ruling Pharaoh by local rulers in Canaan, with their references to the military activities in Palestine of the *habiru*, who sounded suspiciously like the Hebrews, influenced biblical scholars' discussion of the date of the exodus from the 1890s to the 1960s, when it was finally accepted that neither the equation of 'Hebrew' with *habiru* nor the nature of the exodus story was as simple as had previously been thought (cf. Coote 1990: 33–93; Na'aman 1992).

Ancient Mesopotamia yielded even more sensational material. In 1843–4 the Frenchman Emile Botta excavated the ancient Dur Sharrukin ('city of Sargon', now Khorsabad in Iraq), and found pictorial reliefs from the walls of Sargon II's palace, which were promptly exhibited in Paris; later a pair of human-headed winged bulls (now in the Louvre) were found flanking the city gate. (Later, between 1929 and 1935, a Chicago Oriental Institute expedition found a list of Assyrian kings from earliest times to 748 BCE.) In 1846–51 the British scholar Austen Henry Layard excavated Sennacherib's palace at Nineveh, revealing the stone reliefs, now in the British Museum, depicting Sennacherib's siege of biblical Lachish. Layard's assistant, Hormuzd Rassam, subsequently found Ashurbanipal's library of 24,000 cuneiform tablets; the cuneiform script of the Assyrian, Babylonian, and Old Persian records was deciphered by G. F. Grotefend, H. C. Rawlinson, Edward Hincks, and Jules Oppert. Among Ashurbanipal's tablets George Smith in 1872 discovered the Babylonian story of the Flood (by remarkable good fortune in 1873 recovering the missing portions in Nineveh itself). (Leonard Woolley's claim in 1929 to have 'discovered the Flood' while excavating at Ur turned out to be less important, the stratum in question being either a wind-borne dune or the deposit of one of many local floods.) Attempts were made to excavate Babylon by Layard, Oppert, and Rawlinson, but the most important excavation was that of R. Koldewey (1899–1914), which revealed the Babylon of Nebuchadnezzar II and its Ishtar Gate. Particularly exciting for biblical scholars was the discovery and decipherment of the annals and records of the ninth- to seventh-century Assyrian kings, and of the Babylonian Chronicle which covered, with some serious gaps, the years 626–539 BCE. References in these to kings of Israel and Judah broadly corroborated the sequence given in the biblical 2 Kings (cf. Grabbe 1997: 24–6). In the following century came the discovery and decipherment of Hittite records in Turkey (1911–13), of second millennium BCE archives at Nuzi in Iraq (1925–31) and at Mari in Syria (from 1934), and of Canaanite documents at Ras Shamra on the Syrian coast (1929). Such discoveries set the Bible in a much wider context and changed the way in which scholars and others saw ancient Israel and its literature and religion; the controversial *Babel und Bibel* (1902–3) by F. Delitzsch (1850–1922) argued that Old Testament religion was heavily dependent on the Babylonian culture. This went too far; subsequent scholars have tended to derive Israelite religion from its Canaanite context. Clearly, however, Egypt and Mesopotamia were not the only influences upon ancient Israel; Arabia, the Aegean, and Anatolia also played their part.

ARCHAEOLOGY IN PALESTINE AND ISRAEL, 1863–2000

The first archaeological excavations in Palestine were F. de Saulcy's investigation of the 'Tombs of the Kings' (in fact, the family tomb of a first-century CE convert to Judaism, Queen Helena of Adiabene) in 1863, and Charles Warren's shaft and tunnel exploration of Herod's temple's foundations (1867–8) and minor excavations at Jericho (1868). For the next twenty years the Palestine Exploration Fund concentrated on surveying the land—the Survey of Western Palestine, 1871–80; Eastern Palestine, 1881–2; the Wadi Arabah, 1883–4. The discovery of the Mesha stele (or Moabite Stone) in 1868 led to further archaeological exploration of Jordan by the American Palestine Exploration Society (1873, 1875–7) and by G. Schumacher for the Palestine Exploration Fund and the Deutsche Palästina-Vereins (1884–6), and later by R. E. Brunnow and A. Domaszewski (1897–8) and A. Musil (1900–6).

Major excavation in Palestine began under Flinders Petrie at Tell el-Hesi in 1890 (Moorey 1991: 28–9; Drower 1985: 159–63), which Petrie selected largely because he identified it with biblical Lachish. Petrie started on the eastern side of the tell, where the wadi had cut into it, exposing the strata. Pottery and artefacts from each level were noted separately; 'here for the first time the relationship of the pottery to the stratigraphy of the site was recorded' (Drower 1985: 160–1). The pottery sequence thus secured could be used to date similar strata elsewhere, and the stratified discovery of Egyptian inscriptions or royal scarabs allowed cross-linkage with the accepted Egyptian chronology. Later, similar linkages could be made with Assyrian chronology. Petrie's stratigraphy at Tell el-Hesi, though not uncriticized (see Wheeler 1956: 29–34; Davies 1988: 49), provided the methodological basis for the next century's archaeology in Palestine. Petrie erred, however, in identifying Tell el-Hesi with biblical Lachish, thus imposing the biblical history of Lachish on the archaeological evidence of the wrong site (Lachish is generally identified with Tell ed-Duweir). However, excavations now followed at sites chosen for their biblical importance: R. A. S. Macalister excavated at Gezer (1902–8) and Jerusalem (1923–4); G. A. Reisner excavated Samaria (1908–10); E. Sellin and C. Watzinger excavated Jericho (1907–9); C. S. Fisher (1921–3) and A. Rowe (1924–9) excavated at Bethshean, and C. S. Fisher (1925–7) initiated the University of Chicago expedition to Megiddo, which lasted until 1939. Meanwhile, in 1922 W. F. Albright excavated Tell el-Ful (identified by Robinson as King Saul's capital at Gibeah) before moving to Tell Beit Mirsim (1926–32), then wrongly identified as biblical Debir. The 1930s saw enormous archaeological activity in Palestine, with excavations at Tell en-Nasbeh (biblical Mizpah) (W. F. Bade, 1926–35), Bethshemesh (E. Grant, 1938–9), Samaria (J. W. Crowfoot, 1931–5), Jericho (J. Garstang, 1930–6), Et-Tell (biblical Ai) (J. M. Krause, 1933–5), Tell ed-Duweir (Lachish) (J. Starkey, 1933–8), and Tell el-Kheleifeh (wrongly identified with Ezion-Geber) (N. Glueck, 1938–40).

Archaeological work was largely suspended during the Second World War and the formation of the state of Israel in 1948, but afterwards work resumed at important sites, including Tell el-Far'ah North (biblical Tirzah) (R. de Vaux, 1946–60), El-Jib (Gibeon) (J. B. Pritchard, 1956–63), Ramat Rahel (Beth-hakkerem) (A. Aharoni, 1954–62), Tell Balata (Shechem) (G. E. Wright, 1956–63), Hazor, Masada, and again Megiddo (Y. Yadin, 1955–8, 1963–5, and 1970–1), Jericho and Jerusalem (K. M. Kenyon, 1953–8, 1961–7), Arad (R. Amiran, 1962–78), Et-Tell (Ai) (J. Calloway, 1964–9), Tel Dan (A. Biran, 1966–99), Beersheba (A. Aharoni, 1969–75), Tell Hesban (Heshbon) (S. Horn, 1968–78), Tell ed-Duweir/Tel Lakish (D. Ussishkin, 1972–87), Buseirah (Bozrah in Edom) (C.-M. Bennett, 1973–9), Tel Dor (E. Stern, 1980–96), Jerusalem (Y. Shiloh, 1978–88), Tel Miqne (Ekron) (T. Dothan and S. Gitin, 1983–90, 1993–6), Ascalon (L. E. Stager, 1985–), Tel Beit Shean (A. Mazar, 1989–91), Hazor (Amnon Ben-Tor, 1990–), Tel Beth Shemesh (S. Bunimovitz, Z. Lederman, and R. Kletter, 1990–2000).

BIBLICAL AND ARCHAEOLOGICAL SYNTHESIS

Petrie's pioneering pottery chronology was improved by the American scholar W. F. Albright, who at Tell Beit Mirsim (1926–32) developed a new and generally accepted Palestinian ceramic index. Albright, a linguistic and archaeological polymath, became the dominant authority in biblical and archaeological study for several decades. He produced an archaeological and biblical synthesis that supported the essential historicity of the biblical picture of the patriarchal age, exodus, conquest, Judges' period, and early monarchy (Albright 1940, 1949). This synthesis, an alternative to the radical revision of the biblical tradition associated with such scholars as Wellhausen, Kuenen, and Robertson Smith, influenced a generation of American scholars; George Ernest Wright's *Biblical Archaeology* (1957, 1962) and John Bright's *A History of Israel* (1960) became standard and influential student textbooks for several decades. This synthesis was popular also among Israeli scholars (cf. the work of Yadin at Hazor); in discussing Israeli archaeologists, A. Mazar noted (1988: 127) that 'Quite naturally, every opportunity is taken to relate archaeological evidence to the biblical text'. But the Albrightian model attracted increasing criticism from both archaeologists and biblical scholars.

In Britain, biblical and archaeological disciplines remained separate. Archaeologists like J. Crowfoot, J. Garstang, J. Starkey, and K. M. Kenyon were not biblical scholars. Kenyon applied Wheeler's methods to the excavation of Jericho and Jerusalem, developing what became known as the 'Wheeler–Kenyon' technique. This used the trench method but refined it by meticulous observation and recording of the statigraphy; Kenyon checked the statigraphy by preserving the baulk and drawing the vertical section as a record of what had been dug (Moorey 1979; 1981: 28–30). Kenyon's excavation at Jericho (1952–9) re-dated Garstang's 'double wall' by a thousand years from the Late Bronze to the Early Bronze Age, and disproved the existence of any but the smallest settlement at Jericho in the fourteenth to thirteenth century BCE, thus completely undermining the traditional view of the dating of the exodus (in the fifteenth century BCE) and of the conquest of Canaan. The only ruined city walls visible to the author of Joshua were those of the Middle Bronze Age, destroyed in the sixteenth century BCE (see Kenyon 1957: 256–62; Bartlett 1982: 96–8, 106). Kenyon's excavations at Jerusalem (1961–7), followed by those of Y. Shiloh (1978–85), revealed above the spring on the south-eastern hill massive terraces of stone-walled compartments filled with rubble; these were perhaps the foundation for a citadel above, and perhaps belong to the fourteenth to thirteenth centuries BCE. Very little evidence was found on the south-eastern hill for the twelfth to eleventh centuries BCE Jerusalem, or for the tenth-century BCE buildings credited to Solomon by the Deuteronomistic History—a palace (1 Kgs. 7: 1), 'the House of the Forest of Lebanon' (1 Kgs. 7: 2), 'the hall of pillars'

(1 Kgs. 7: 6), 'the hall of judgment', a house for Pharaoh's daughter, and the 'millo' (1 Kgs. 7: 6–8, 9: 24) (all in addition to his temple, which was probably on the site of Herod's later temple). Kenyon thought that these were located in the neck of land between the Temple platform and the former town on the south-east hill (Kenyon 1974: 128), but that Roman quarrying had destroyed all evidence (p. 118). Kenyon was more positive about Solomonic Jerusalem than her archaeological evidence allowed, being unconsciously influenced by the biblical picture. Nevertheless, her work prepared the way for later, more minimalist approaches.

REVISION OF BIBLICAL HISTORY: GENESIS AND EXODUS

Since Albright's time, archaeological and biblical scholarship has seriously revised the previously accepted picture of biblical history. Attempts to identify Abraham's family migration with a supposed westward Amorite migration at the collapse of the Early Bronze Age c.2100–1800 BCE, or to explain personal names, marriage customs, or laws of property by reference to fifteenth century Nuzi or Mari documents have failed to convince. Abraham's life-style is no longer seen as reflecting Intermediate Early Bronze/Middle Bronze bedouin, or donkey carava-neers trading between Mesopotamia and Egypt, or tent-dwellers living alongside Middle Bronze Age cities in Canaan; rather, with its references to Philistines and Aramaeans, Ammonites, Moabites, and Edomites, Ishmael and his descendants Kedar, Nebaioth, and Tema, Assyria and its cities of Nineveh and Calah, camel caravans and spices, Genesis reflects the first millennium world of the Assyrian empire. With its emphasis on the southern centres of Hebron and (Jeru)salem (Gen. 14: 18) and the northern centres of Bethel and Shechem, the Abraham story reveals knowledge of the kingdoms of Israel and Judah (cf. Gen. 49: 8–12, 22–6), in its present form probably deriving from Judah's *floruit* in the seventh century BCE. The exodus story also suffers from a lack of firm archaeological support. While the biblical Pithom, Raamses (Exod. 1: 11), and Succoth (Exod. 12: 37; Num. 33: 5), can be associated with names from the thirteenth century or the New Kingdom (Migdol, 'fortress', Exod. 14: 1, is a name which might belong to any period), and though a thirteenth-century Egyptian text mentions the entry of *shasu* tribes from Edom to Egypt, via *Tjkw* (= Succoth?) to *Pr-Itm* (Pithom), there is no mention in Egyptian records, archives, or inscriptions, of any Israelite presence in Egypt or of irregular Israelite departure from it; nor is there archaeological evidence of an

Israelite sojourn in Sinai. The 'Apiru ('fugitives', 'refugees') of the fourteenth-century BCE Amarna Letters and elsewhere cannot easily be identified with the later biblical Hebrews (Na'aman 1992). The earliest Egyptian reference to Israel, from the late thirteenth-century Merneptah stele, mentions the destruction of a group of people called Israel apparently already existing in the land of Canaan. Finkelstein and Silberman (2001: 68–71; cf. Dever 2003: 18–19) therefore date the exodus story in its present form to seventh-century Judah, when places like Kadesh-barnea and Ezion-geber were active (as they were not in the thirteenth century), and sees it as reflecting late seventh- or early sixth-century conflict between Judah and Egypt (cf. 2 Kgs. 23: 29).

REVISION OF BIBLICAL HISTORY: CONQUEST OR SETTLEMENT?

Until recently, discussion of the Israelite 'conquest' and 'settlement' has been based more on literary-historical analysis than on archaeological evidence. Recently, however, archaeological concerns and techniques have changed. The development of surveys alongside excavations, the use of radio-carbon dating, geological, botanical, and faunal analysis, chemical study of the provenance of pottery and other items, all assisted by new computer technology, have allowed archaeologists to study ancient technologies, survival strategies, agricultural production, nomadic pastoralism, population growth, settlement patterns, road systems, regional and urban economies, the development of trade, religious behaviour, and indeed the internal development of societies (for a survey see Levy 1995), and recently 'ethno-archaeology' (see NEA 63 (2000): 1–2). These approaches now affect scholarly understanding of the origins of Israel.

In 1925 and 1939 A. Alt developed his thesis of a gradual 'peaceful infiltration' or sedentarization of Canaan by individual tribes, in a way analogous to semi-nomadic transhumance. He was supported by A. Aharoni, who saw examples of this in Iron Age I settlements in Upper Galilee (the tribes of Naphtali and Asher) and in the Beersheba valley (the tribe of Simeon). In 1962 G. Mendenhall developed a new approach; there was no immigration by any external group, but rather the energizing and unifying of the country people against the Canaanite city-states as the Late Bronze Age collapsed; in this the adoption of Yahwism played an important part. In 1979 N. Gottwald developed this thesis, arguing that Israel's tribes developed from socially disadvantaged rural Canaanites, reacting under socio-economic pressures against wealthy landowners, and seeking a new egalitarianism in the hill country. Settlement there was made possible by new technical developments: the use of iron tools, the excavation and plastering of cisterns to collect water, and the terracing of the hillsides to grow vines and olives. W. G. Dever, though dismissing the importance of Yahwism in this process, supported the idea of the indigenous development of early Israel by pointing to the new development of some 300 Early Iron I sites in the hill country (Dever 1997). He saw these as 'proto-Israelite', representing the first settlements of the ancestors of biblical Israel. Dever argued on the basis of the 'Isbet Sartah abecedary that their script derived from the Canaanite tradition (1997: 34, 45). These settlers were 'displaced Canaanites' (cf. Ezek. 16: 2–3); their pottery was 'standard, domestic Canaanite-style pottery, long at home everywhere in western Palestine'. 'This pottery displays no "foreign element", no Egyptian reminiscences, and it is certainly not anything that one could connect with a "nomadic lifestyle" ' (Dever 1997: 29). Here Dever challenged Finkelstein, who, noting that the layout of the earlier sites—an oval of connected rooms enclosing a courtyard—suggested the traditional tent encampment of pastoral nomads, and argued that the people of these unfortified hilltop villages were originally pastoralists from the desert fringe, settling in the hills in order to survive when grain production in the lowlands declined at the collapse of the Late Bronze Age cities—for pastoral nomads needed grain and traded it for their meat and milk (Finkelstein and Silberman 2001: 105–18; cf. Finkelstein 1988). Formerly, archaeologists identified these hilltop village people as Israelites by their use of four-room houses and collared-rim storage jars, and the absence of pig-bones, but such features are no longer accepted as certain proofs of ethnicity (cf. Finkelstein and Silberman 2001: 118–20; Hesse and Wapnish 1997); these village people Dever has now identified as 'proto-Israelites', apparent ancestors of the later Israelite occupants of the land.

Thus the traditional picture of Israel's 'conquest' of Canaan has been dramatically revised as a result of archaeological excavation and survey in the hill country. The evidence from Canaanite cities, formerly used to support the conquest theory, no longer works; certain cities named in the conquest narratives—Jericho, Ai, Heshbon, and Arad—were not Late Bronze Age cities. The kingdom of Edom, mentioned as an obstacle to Israel's migration in Num. 20: 14–21, did not yet exist, as was shown by the excavations of Bennett at Umm el-Biyarah, Tafileh, and Busayra and the surveys of B. McDonald (Bartlett 1989: 67–82). The destruction of Bethel and Tell Beit Mirsim (no longer identified with Debir of Josh. 10: 18 f.) at the end of the thirteenth century and of Lachish in the mid-twelfth century can no longer be confidently assigned on archaeological grounds to the Israelites, according to the Merneptah Stele virtually destroyed by the Egyptians. The picture drawn from the book of Joshua of Israel's organized military conquest of Canaan has been abandoned (Dever 2003: 23–74).

REVISION OF BIBLICAL HISTORY: SOLOMON'S KINGDOM AND THE MONARCHIC PERIOD

Archaeology has also impacted heavily on the biblical picture of David and Solomon and the early history of Israel and Judah. The Bible presents David as a king who defeated the Philistines, the Syrians, the Ammonites, the Moabites, and the Edomites, so preparing the ground for the kingdom of Solomon, whose power was respected from Egypt to Syria, and whose buildings included not only a great temple, a palace, government buildings, the *millo*, and a wall in Jerusalem (1 Kings 6–8, 9: 15) but also the cities of Hazor, Megiddo, and Gezer and other sites, and cities for stores, for chariots, and for horsemen (1 Kgs. 9: 15–18). Repeated excavation has found virtually nothing definitely ascribable to either David or Solomon at Jerusalem, but a reference to the 'house of David' on a stele of the Aramaean king Hazael at Tel Dan (Biran and Naveh 1993: 81–98; Lemaire 1998) (and perhaps a similar reference on the Mesha Stele a little earlier; Lemaire 1994: 30–7) at least confirmed the existence and reputation of the Davidic dynasty in the late ninth century BCE. Excavations at Hazor, Megiddo, and Gezer revealed similar six-chambered gates and associated casemate city walls which were dated to the tenth century BCE and credited to Solomon (Yadin 1977: 853–4), thus confirming the accepted picture of Solomon's power; at Megiddo there were also two ashlar-built palaces originally credited to Solomon (cf. Ussishkin 1973). Dever (2001: 132) argues firmly from the pottery evidence for a tenth-century Solomonic date for the Gezer gateway (and so by implication for the other gates). However, this dating for the Gezer gateway is based on the unsustainable assumption that it was destroyed by Shoshenq I of Egypt c.925 BCE (see James 2002: 177), and the dating of the gateways, walls, and palaces of Megiddo and Hazor has recently been revised downward to the Omride period of the ninth century by comparison with the structures and pottery evidence of Jezreel and Samaria (Finkelstein and Silberman 2001: 186–90, 340–4). If correct, these findings seriously challenge the biblical picture of a powerful Solomonic kingdom, and strongly support the Assyrian evidence for the political importance of the house of Omri in Israel.

However, archaeology has expanded the biblical picture as well as challenged it. For example, 2 Kgs. 18: 14 notes the presence of Sennacherib, king of Assyria, at Lachish, but pointedly ignores the destruction of Lachish in 701 BCE after a siege dramatically revealed both by Assyrian reliefs at Nineveh and by Ussishkin's excavations at Tell ed-Duweir (Ussishkin 1982: 1997). Excavation has certainly done much to illuminate the life of the Iron Age kingdoms of Israel and Judah, revealing military forts, small villages, city walls and gates, siege warfare, water systems, palaces, houses, tombs, temples, shrines, and their contents—pottery, metal ware, farming tools, weapons, official and personal seals, weights, ostraca and inscriptions, figurines, cultic objects, textiles, jewellery and ornaments, food-stuffs, and so on (see King and Stager 2001). Dever has demonstrated (2001: 144–57) that the details of the Solomonic temple presented in 2 Kings 6–8 can be illustrated and corroborated from excavated *realia* (though not from the temple site itself), and has similarly illustrated other cultic activity and popular religion in Israel and Judah from archaeological data (2001: 174–9; cf. also King and Stager 2001: 319–81). The view that the Israelites were strongly monotheistic has been challenged by archaeological evidence suggesting that Israel's religion was to some extent plural-istic, notably the inscriptions from Kuntillet 'Ajrud and Khirbet el-Qom, which Dever (1990: 144–5) interprets as meaning that Yahweh had the Canaanite goddess Asherah as consort (*contra* Mayes 1997: 61–4; on the cult of Asherah in Israel see Hadley 2000). Important evidence for Iron Age cult in ancient Israel comes from the Iron II strata at Tel Dan (cf. 1 Kgs. 12: 25–31), with a *bamah* (high place, sanctuary), *masseboth* (standing stones), a room with an altar and a sceptre head buried below it, incense shovels, and a jar for ashes.

PERSIAN AND HELLENISTIC PERIODS

Much attention has been paid in recent decades to the archaeology of the Persian and Hellenistic periods (conventionally 539–63 BCE). Most of the evidence comes from sites along the coastal strip and plains—Tel Akko, Tell Abu Hawam, Shiq-mona, Tel Megadim, Tel Dor, Jaffa, Yavneh-Yam, Ashkelon, Gaza, Tell Jemmeh, Lachish, and Marisa. Trade is visible in the increasing use of weights, coins, and pottery imports (especially Attic pottery) (Stern 1995), and industrial activity such as dyeing, weaving, and pressing wine and olive oil. The cities—e.g. Tell Abu Hawam, Shiqmona, Tel Megadim, Dor, and Marisa—began to exhibit the Hellen-istic style of town planning. At Dor the fortifications developed in the third century BCE from the Phoenician to the Greek style (see Stern 1995). The hill country, however, remained agricultural and poorer (Berlin 1997: 4). Third-century agricul-tural trade with Egypt, in slaves, grain, and oil, is evidenced in the Zenon papyri (the archive of an official of Ptolemy II's finance minister Apollonius); the bilingual ostracon from Kh. el-Qom dated 277 BCE tells of money-lenders operating in both Greek and Aramaic; by 200 BCE a royal official near Bethshean could set up a public inscription in Greek. The Sidonian colony of Marisa bred pigeons and made olive oil, and buried its dead in splendidly painted Hellenistic tombs. The general picture of third-century life in Palestine is well illustrated by Eccles. 2: 4–8. The archaeological evidence (for a convenient summary see Berlin 1997) has vividly underlined the changing nature of society in third- to second-century Palestine, as it moved from Persian control to the new Hellenistic world of the Ptolemies and Seleucids, and ultimately to the autonomous rule of the Hasmonaean kingdom via the Maccabees. One of the best indicators of this development is the description of the Maccabees' family tomb built by Simon c.140 BCE, with its pyramids, columns, memorial armour, and carved ships (1 Macc. 13: 27–30), though no remains have been found.

ARCHAEOLOGY AND THE HERODIAN PERIOD

When linking archaeology and 'the Bible', most writers have concentrated on the Old Testament/Hebrew scriptures. Early discoveries impacted more upon the ancient Near East and the history of Israel than upon the life of Jesus and his early followers. The archaeology of Roman Palestine and the early church concerned classical rather than biblical scholars. This situation changed with the advent of the State of Israel, whose archaeologists had little interest in the early development of Christianity, but much interest in Hellenistic, Herodian, and Roman Palestine, and in the archaeology of early Judaism, especially that of early synagogues. First-century CE synagogues were excavated at Gamala (cf. Josephus, BJ 4. 1), at Masada, and perhaps at Magdala. Knowledge of first-century Jerusalem has been enhanced by Kenyon's work in the 1960s, B. Mazar's excavations on the Temple Mount (Haram al-Sharif) (Mazar and Mazar 1989), and Avigad's work in the Jewish Quarter (Avigad 1984). Excavations at Jericho by the American School of Oriental Research in the 1950s and 1960s, followed by the Hebrew University expedition under E. Netzer, revealed surprisingly sophisticated and luxurious Hasmonaean and Herodian palaces on the banks of the Wadi Qelt; other Herodian palaces were excavated at Masada and Herodium. Yadin's dramatic excavations at Masada (1963–5) demonstrated the development of the Herodian palaces, the Zealot occupation, and the Roman siege and destruction of the site. Excavation of Caesarea has been nearly continuous from the 1950s to the present, covering all periods of its history, but revealing especially the Herodian harbour and city, including a theatre, a temple platform, *horrea* vaults, and a grid system of streets (Levine and Netzer 1986; Holum et al. 1988; Holum 1997). In Galilee Sepphoris was excavated jointly by Duke University and the Hebrew University of Jerusalem (1985–94) under E. Meyers, E. Netzer, and C. Meyers; some evidence of the Hellenistic and Herodian periods was found. Josephus says that Herod Antipas 'fortified Sepphoris to be the ornament [perhaps militarily] of all Galilee, and called it Autocratoris [suggesting both its autonomy and its loyalty to Augustus]' (*Ant.* 18. 27), but apart from the remains of a villa and several ritual baths (*mikvaot*) not much has survived to reveal the city's importance apart from the theatre, whose precise date is uncertain (Strange 1992; Meyers and Meyers 1997). Sepphoris is near Nazareth, and its influence on Jesus and his upbringing has been much discussed. Also important is the Late Hellenistic and Roman country villa of Tel Anafa (excavated 1968–73, 1978–86, under the direction of S. Weinberg and S. Herbert); in its Hellenistic phase it seems to have been associated with Tyre, but in its first-century CE Roman phase more closely with Galilee and Caesarea Philippi (in the territory of Herod Philip) (Weinberg 1971; Herbert 1991, 1997). South of Palestine, the kingdom and especially the architecture of Nabataea have been investigated (Wenning 1987; McKenzie 1990); McKenzie has recently reinvestigated the first-century temple at et-Tannur first excavated by Glueck (Glueck 1966; Roche 1997; McKenzie *et al.* 2002).

What has emerged from this work is the enormous extent of Herod's building programme in Palestine (not to mention his contribution abroad) (for full details see Roller 1998; Chancey and Porter 2001). Famously, Herod rebuilt the Jerusalem Temple, extending the older precinct (the join is visible in the east wall 32m north of the south-east corner) by huge in-fills and supporting walls, spanning the Tyropoeon valley on the west with a new staircase, and building broad stairways and two new entrances on the south side. (The size of the stones, some up to 10m long, is noted in Mark 13: 1 and parallels.) Herod built a huge palace for himself at Jerusalem on a podium 330 × 130m, the western and northern palaces on Masada, three palaces or large residential villas with audience halls, peristyle courts, gardens, and baths with hypocausts and hollow walls (tubulation) in the Wadi Qelt near Jericho, a palace fortress at Machaerus, east of the Dead Sea, a palace mausoleum at Herodium, west of it, a prison fortress Hyrkania, south of Jerusalem, the palace-fortress of Antonia in Jerusalem, three towers (Hippikos, Phasael, and Mariamme) in Jerusalem, border fortresses in Judaea (Arad, Aroer, Beersheba, Tel Ira), above Jericho (Doq and Kypros), in the Jordan valley (Alexandreion), in Peraia (Herodeion, later replaced by Livias), and in Galilee (Gaba). He built or rebuilt cities at Anthedon (renaming it Agrippias) near Gaza, Phasaelis, Esebonitis (biblical Heshbon), Sebaste (Samaria), Antipatris, possibly Sepphoris, and Caesarea with its port. He built temples to Augustus at Sebaste, Caesarea, and Paneion, and an enclosure round the patriarchal tombs at Hebron (perhaps hinted at by Jesus in Luke 11: 48), and a similar enclosure at Mamre nearby. He built amphitheatres at Caesarea, Jericho, and Jerusalem, theatres at Caesarea, Jerusalem, and perhaps at Sebaste and Jericho also, hippodromes at Jericho and Jerusalem, stadia probably at Jericho and Sebaste, and gymnasia in Syria but not within his own kingdom. Throughout Herod used Roman rather than Greek architectural technology and building techniques, including *opus reticulatum*, marble decoration, mosaics, and mural painting on plaster. He was particularly interested in hydraulic engineering, creating a sewage system at Caesarea, and various aqueducts and pools for his palaces. Apart from the reference in Mark 13: 1, and the hint in Luke 11: 48, the New Testament is regrettably silent on Herod's works. St Paul might have been aware of Herod's overseas contribution at Antioch, Damascus, and Athens.

Herod's sons continued the work. The ethnarch Archelaos built a new city, Archelais, near Jericho; Antipas, tetrarch of Galilee, founded Tiberias (John 6: 23) in honour of the emperor Tiberius, with a magnificent palace (did Jesus have this in mind in Matt. 11: 8?), a synagogue, and a stadium (not excavated), and refounded Sepphoris as Autocratoris, perhaps building its theatre. Philip, tetrarch of Peraia, founded Caesarea Philippi (Mark 8: 27 and par.), honouring both Caesar and himself, near Paneion. He refounded Bethsaida as Julias, naming it after the emperor's wife, whose image he put on his coins. Bethsaida was the city of the disciples Peter, Andrew, and Philip (John 1: 44; see also Mark 8: 22, Luke 9: 10, 10: 13). Peter and Andrew were fishermen, and one house excavated from the Hellenistic/Early Roman levels at Bethsaida contained a fishing hook, lead weights, and a curved needle for net mending (Arav 1991). From the Sea of Galilee itself was excavated (1985) a first-century carvel-built boat 8.2m long (Wachsmann 1986–7).

Excavation has revealed many details of first-century life. The 'Burnt House' in Jerusalem vividly illustrates the Roman destruction of Jerusalem in 70 CE; in the debris were found stone jars, cups, and bowls meeting the demands of Jewish purification law (cf. John 2: 6; cf. also Mark 7: 3–4). Ritual baths (*miqvaot*) at Sepphoris, Masada, and elsewhere illustrate the contemporary Jewish concern for ritual cleanliness. Hundreds of stone ossuaries witness to funerary practice; some bear the names and occupations of the person whose bones they preserved. The names, in Hebrew, Aramaic, or Greek, include many names well known from the Bible. One such ossuary bore the name of 'Alexander son of Simon' in Greek, with 'Alexander of Cyrene' in Aramaic (cf. Mark 15: 21, Simon of Cyrene, the father of Alexander); another, with 'Yehosep son of *qyp*'' brings to mind the high priest Caiaphas (McKane 1997). Coins (in the gospels the silver *denarius* of Mark 13: 15; the copper *as*, or *assarion*, one-sixteenth of a *denarius*, of Matt. 10: 29; the *quadrans*, one-quarter of an *as*, cf. Matt. 5: 26; and the *lepton*, half of a *quadrans*, the widow's mite, Mark 12: 42, Luke 12: 59) give useful information about the Hasmonaean and the Herodian rulers, and of Roman administration (see Betlyon 1992). One form of the *denarius* minted by Mark Antony *c*.31 CE shows the eagle (a symbol of Roman power) between two military standards. Herod's erection of an eagle over the temple entrance caused a riot, as did Pontius Pilate's introduction in 26 CE of Roman military standards, with their images of the emperor, into Jerusalem (Jos. *BJ* 2. 169–74; *Ant.* 18. 55–9). Such coins may explain Jesus' saying in Matt. 24: 28/ Luke 17: 37 (Kreitzer 1996: 58–68). Well-known inscriptions illustrating Hellenistic and Roman Palestine include the fragment at Caesarea recording the building by Pontius Pilatus, Prefect of Judaea, of a shrine for the emperor Tiberius, and two

Greek copies of the inscription written warning Gentiles not to proceed beyond the barrier into the inner temple on pain of death. Outside Palestine, a broken inscription excavated in Delphi in Greece in 1905 which mentioned the proconsul L. Iunius Gallio (cf. Acts 18: 12), who was in office either summer 50–1 or 51–2, has become the fixed point from which the chronology of Paul's life is calculated. J. Murphy-O'Connor (1983) has imaginatively used the plan of a first-century Roman villa at Corinth to illustrate the church community, and the church in Aquila and Prisca's house (1 Cor. 16: 19) in Corinth. Rom. 16: 4 suggests a similar 'house-church' in Rome, but there is no archaeological evidence for it. The identification of Hellenistic houses beneath the fourth-century *domus ecclesiae* and the fifth-century octagonal church in Capernaum with the original home of Peter is based largely on the tradition preserved by Egeria (381–4) and the indication of *graffiti* and pottery that from the mid-first century the room was put to public rather than private use.

SUMMARY

Archaeological findings have radically changed modern scholarly presentation of early Israel, for archaeological evidence has virtually replaced the non-contemporary biblical account for the early period. The Bible is no longer the lens through which the archaeologist interprets the evidence, and biblical scholars have reappraised the value of the biblical texts for the reconstruction of Israel's history (for a discussion of recent 'minimalism' among biblical historians see Bartlett 2004). The New Testament period is shorter in span, and its authors are closer to their subject, the gospel writers being two or at most three generations after Jesus. In this field, archaeology has illuminated the details rather than corrected the framework. The exception is the discovery at Qumran and the writings associated with it, which has added a new dimension to our knowledge of Jewish sectarian belief and practice in late Second Temple period, and offered new scope to textual critics. Qumran will be examined in a separate section. It is fair to note that in the last half-century, archaeology has ceased to be concerned with defending the essential historicity of the biblical story, but has sometimes been used for modern political ends, to the equal dismay of its scholarly practitioners.

Suggested reading

For a good introduction to archaeology and biblical studies from 1890 to 1990, see Moorey 1991. Studies of American, British, French, German, and Israeli archaeologists can be found in J. F. Drinkard, G. L. Mattingly and J. M. Miller, eds., *Benchmarks in Time and Culture: An Introduction to the History and Methodology of Syro-Palestinian Archaeology* (Atlanta: Scholars Press, 1988). A useful general introduction is J. C. H. Laughlin, *Archaeology and the Bible* (London and New York: Routledge, 2000). Details of individual sites can be found in *The New Encyclopedia of Archaeological Excavations in the Holy Land*, ed. E. Stern (Jerusalem, 1993), *OEANE* and *ABD*.

Bibliography

Albright, W. F. 1940. *From the Stone Age to Christianity*. Baltimore: Johns Hopkins University Press.

—— 1949. *The Archaeology of Palestine*. Harmondsworth: Penguin.

Alt, A. 1939. 'Edward Robinson on the Identification of Biblical Sites'. *JBL* 58: 365–72.

Arav, R. 1991. 'Bethsaida, 1989'. *IEJ* 41: 184–5.

Avigad, N. 1984. *Discovering Jerusalem*. Oxford: Blackwell.

Bartlett, J. R. 1982. *Jericho*. Cities of the Biblical World. Guildford: Lutterworth.

—— 1989. *The Bible: Faith and Evidence*. London: British Museum Publications.

—— 1997. 'What has Archaeology to do with the Bible—or vice versa?' In J. R. Bartlett, ed., *Archaeology and Biblical Interpretation*, London and New York: Routledge, 1–19.

—— 2004. 'Between Scylla and Charybdis: The problem of Israelite Historiography'. In C. McCarthy and J. F. Healey, eds., *Biblical and Near Eastern Essays: Studies in Honour of Kevin J. Cathcart*, JSOTS. S 375 (Sheffield: Sheffield Academic Press), 180–94.

Berlin, A. M. 1997. 'Between Large Forces: Palestine in the Hellenistic period'. *BA* 60/1: 2–51.

Betlyon, J. W. 1992. 'Coinage'. *ABD* i. 1076–89.

Biran, A., and Naveh, J. 1993. 'An Aramaic Stele Fragment from Tel Dan'. *IEJ* 43/8: 1–98.

Bright, J. 1960. *A History of Israel*. London: SCM Press.

Chancey, M., and Porter, A. 2001. 'The Archaeology of Roman Palestine'. *NEA* 64/4: 164–203.

Coote, R. B. 1990. *Early Israel: A New Horizon*. Minneapolis: Fortress Press.

Davies, G. I. 1988. 'British Archaeologists'. In J. F. Drinkard Jr, G. L. Mattingly, and J. M. Miller, eds., *Benchmarks in Time and Culture*, Atlanta: Scholars Press, 37–62.

De Geus, C. H. J. 1980. 'Idumaea'. *Jaarbericht van het vooraziatisch-egyptisch genootschap 'Ex Oriente Lux'*, 26: 53–74.

Dever, W. G. 1990. *Recent Archaeological Studies and Biblical Research*. Seattle and London: University of Washington Press.

—— 1997. 'Archaeology and the Emergence of Israel'. In J. R. Bartlett, ed., *Archaeology and Biblical Interpretation*, London & New York: Routledge, 20–50.

—— 2001. *What Did the Biblical Writers Know and When did they Know it?* Grand Rapids, Mich.: Eerdmans.

—— 2003. *Who Were the Early Israelites and Where did they Come From?* Grand Rapids, Mich.: Eerdmans.

DILKE, O. A. W. 1985. *Greek and Roman Maps.* Baltimore and London: Johns Hopkins University Press.

DROWER, M. S. 1985. *Flinders Petrie: A Life in Archaeology.* London: Gollancz.

FINKELSTEIN, I. 1988. *The Archaeology of the Israelite Settlement.* Jerusalem: Israel Exploration Society.

—— and SILBERMAN, N. A. 2001. *The Bible Unearthed.* New York: Free Press (Simon & Schuster).

FREEMAN-GRENVILLE, G. S. P., CHAPMAN, R. L., III, and TAYLOR, J. E. 2003. *The Onomasticon by Eusebius of Caesarea.* Jerusalem: Carta.

FREND, W. H. C. 1996. *The Archaeology of Early Christianity.* London: Geoffrey Chapman.

GLUECK, N. 1966. *Deities and Dolphins.* London: Cassell.

GRABBE, L. L. 1997. 'Are Historians of Ancient Palestine Fellow Creatures—or Different Animals?' In L. L. Grabbe, ed., *Can a 'History of Israel' be Written?*, JSOTS.S 245, Sheffield: Sheffield Academic Press, 19–36.

HADLEY, J. M. 2000. *The Cult of Asherah in Ancient Israel and Judah: Evidence for a Hebrew Goddess,* University of Cambridge Oriental Publications 57. Cambridge: Cambridge University Press.

HAYES, J. H., and MILLER, J. M. 1977. *Israelite and Judaean History.* London: SCM Press.

HERBERT, S. C. 1997. 'Anafa, Tel'. In *OEANE* i. 117–18.

HESSE, B. and WAPNISH, P. 1997. 'Can Pig Remains be Used for Ethnic Diagnosis in the Ancient Near East?' In N. A. Silberman and D. Small, eds., *The Archaeology of Israel: Constructing the Past, Interpreting the Present,* JSOTS.S 237, Sheffield: Sheffield Academic Press, 238–70.

HOLUM, K. G. 1997. 'Caesarea'. *OEANE* i. 399–404.

—— HOHLFELDER, R. L., BULL, R. G., and RABAN, A. 1988. *King Herod's Dream: Caesarea on the Sea.* New York: W. W. Norton.

HUNT, F. D. 1982. *Holy Land Pilgrimage in the Later Roman Empire AD 312–460.* Oxford: Clarendon Press.

JAMES, P. 2002. Review of W. G. Dever, *What did the Biblical Writers Know and When did they Know it? PEQ* 134/2: 176–8.

JAMES, T. G. H., ed. 1982. *Excavating in Egypt: The Egypt Exploration Society 1882–1982.* London: British Museum Publications.

JONES, Y. 1973. 'British Military Surveys of Palestine and Syria 1840–1841'. *Cartographic Journal* 10/1: 29–41.

KENYON, K. M. 1939. 'Excavation Methods in Palestine'. *PEQ* 71: 29–40.

—— 1957. *Digging up Jericho.* London: Benn.

—— 1974. *Digging up Jerusalem.* London: Benn.

KING, P. J., and STAGER, L. E. 2001. *Life in Biblical Israel.* Louisville, Ky., and London: Westminster/John Knox Press.

KLOSTERMANN, E. 1904. Eusebius: *Das Onomastikon der biblischen Orstnamen.* Die griechischen christlichen Schriftsteller der ersten drei Jahrhunderte: Eusebius III. 1. Leipzig: J. C. Hinrichs.

KREITZER, L. J. 1996. *Striking New Images: Roman Imperial Coinage and the New Testament World*. JSNTS.S 134. Sheffield: Sheffield Academic Press.

LEMAIRE, A. 1994. ' "House of David" Restored in Moabite Inscription'. *BARev* 20/3: 30–7.

——— 1998. 'The Tel Dan Stela as a Piece of Royal Historiography'. *JSOT* 81: 3–14.

LEVINE, L. I., and NETZER, E. 1986. *Excavations at Caesarea Maritima, 1975, 1976, 1979: Final Report*. Qedem 21. Jerusalem.

LEVY, T. E., ed. 1995. *The Archaeology of Society in the Holy Land*. London: Leicester University Press.

MCKANE, B. 1997. 'Ossuary'. *OEANE* iv. 187–8.

MCKENZIE, J. M. 1990. *The Architecture of Petra*. Oxford: Oxford University Press for the British Academy, The British School of Archaeology in Jerusalem, and the British Institute in Amman for Archaeology and History.

MCKENZIE, J. S., GIBSON, S., and REEVES, A. T. 2002. 'Reconstruction of the Nabataean Temple Complex at Khirbet et-Tannur'. *PEQ* 134/1: 44–83.

MAYES, A. D. H. 1997. 'Kuntillet 'Ajrud and the History of Israelite religion'. In J. R. Bartlett, ed., *Archaeology and Biblical Interpretation*, London and New York: Routledge, 51–66.

MAZAR, A. 1988. 'Israeli Archaeologists'. In J. F. Drinkard, G. L. Mattingly, and J. M. Miller, eds., *Benchmarks in Time and Culture*, Atlanta: Scholars Press, 109–28.

MAZAR, B., and MAZAR, E. 1989. *Excavations in the South of the Temple Mount*. Qedem 29. Jerusalem: Hebrew University of Jerusalem.

MEYERS, C. L., and MEYERS, E. M. 1997. 'Sepphoris'. In *OEANE* iv. 527–36.

MOOREY, R. 1979. 'Kathleen Kenyon and Palestinian Archaeology'. *PEQ* 111: 3–10.

——— 1981. *Excavation in Palestine*. Guildford: Lutterworth Press.

——— 1991. *A Century of Biblical Archaeology*. Cambridge: Lutterworth Press.

MURPHY-O'CONNOR, J. 1983. *St Paul's Corinth: Texts and Archaeology*. Wilmington, Del.: Glazier.

NA'AMAN, N. 1992. 'Amarna Letters'. *ABD* i. 174–81.

NEBENZAHL, K. 1986. *Maps of the Holy Land*. New York: Abbeville Press.

ROBINSON, E., and SMITH, E. 1841. *Biblical Researches in Palestine, Mount Sinai and Arabia Petraea: A Journal of Travels in the Year 1838 by E. Robinson and E. Smith Undertaken in Reference to Biblical Geography*, 3 vols. London: Murray.

——— ——— 1856. *Biblical Researches in Palestine and the Adjacent Regions: A Journal of Travels in the Years 1838 and 1852 by E. Robinson, E. Smith and Others*. London: Murray.

ROCHE, M.-J. 1997. 'Tannur, Khirbet et-'. In OEANE 153–5.

ROLLER, D. W. 1998. *The Building Programme of Herod the Great*. Berkeley: University of California Press.

STERN, E. 1995. 'Between Persia and Greece: Trade, Administration and Warfare in the Persian and Hellenistic Periods'. In T. E. Levy, ed., *The Archaeology of Society in the Holy Land*, London: Leicester University Press, 432–45.

STRANGE, J. F. 1992. 'Six Campaigns at Sepphoris: The University of South Florida Excavations, 1983–1989'. In L. I. Levine, ed., *The Galilee in Late Antiquity*, New York; Jerusalem: Jewish Theological Seminary of America, 339–55.

USSISHKIN, D. 1973. 'King Solomon's Palaces'. *BA* 36: 78–105.

——— 1982. *The Conquest of Lachish by Sennacherib*. Tel Aviv: Tel Aviv University Institute of Archaeology.

——— 1997. 'Lachish'. *OEANE* iii. 3 17–23.

WACHSMANN, S. 1986–7. 'The Excavation of the Kinneret Boat'. *Bulletin of the Anglo-Israel Archaeological Society*, 6: 50–2.

WEINBERG, S. S. 1971. 'Tel Anafa: The Hellenistic town', *IEJ* 21: 86–109.

WENNING, R. 1987. *Die Nabatäer: Denkmäler und Geschichte*. Novum Testamentum et Orbis Antiquus 3. Göttingen: Vandenhoeck & Ruprecht.

WHEELER, M. 1956. *Archaeology from the Earth*. Harmondsworth: Penguin.

WILKINSON, J. 1971. *Egeria's Travels*. London: SPCK.

WRIGHT, G. E. 1957, 1962. *Biblical Archaeology*. London: Duckworth.

WRIGHT, T., ed. 1848. *Early Travels in Palestine*. New York: Ktav, repr. 1968.

YADIN, Y. 1977. 'Megiddo'. EAEHL iii. 830–56.

CHAPTER 4

ANCIENT NEAR EASTERN STUDIES: MESOPOTAMIA

W. G. LAMBERT

The idea that understanding of the Hebrew Bible can be helped by study of other ancient Near Eastern documents is nothing new. In the Hellenistic age there was a fascination on the part of some Greek speakers with the great antiquity claimed for the Egyptians and Babylonians, and some learned Jews became aware that the Babylonians had traditions related to the earlier chapters of Genesis, and a history which in part ran parallel to their own. Since these Jews had no direct access to cuneiform texts, they had to depend on Babylonian writers who wrote in Greek, and Berossus from the first half of the third century BCE was the main, and perhaps only genuine one. Thus in the mid-second century BCE Eupolemus, one of the Maccabean envoys to Rome, wrote a work in Greek stating that Babylon was the first city to be settled after the Flood, an item occurring in Berossus, but not in the Bible. Josephus, in the later first century CE, several times quotes Berossus explicitly by name to confirm or elaborate things in the Bible. Later Christian patristic writers followed his example. However, with the destruction of the library of Alexandria, the rise of Islam, and the arrival of the Middle Ages, the works of Berossus—even in the summaries used by the patristic writers—and other similar works were lost, and remain so. Some interest in these matters continued, and a culmination can be seen in the work of I. P. Cory, *Ancient Fragments of the*

Phoenician, Chaldaean, Egyptian, Tyrian, Carthaginian, Indian, Persian, and other Writers; with an Introducory Dissertation: and an Inquiry into the Philosophy and Trinity of the Ancients (London, best edition = the second, 1832).

By Cory's time a renewed and intensified interest in these matters resulted from, first, exploration and then excavation of sites known from the Bible, especially at first in Assyria. In the hundred years *c.*1740–1840 a succession of European travellers issued reports on their travels, and from 1840 onwards the digging began, and has continued to the present time. At first the techniques of excavation were by modern standards very crude, but they were often successful in extracting objects from the ground, and, where practicable, the objects were then removed to European museums. Mistakes were sometimes made in the interpretation of this work. For example, one of the first major digs was at an Assyrian mound by P. É. Botta, the results of which appeared in the massive folio volumes entitled *Monument de Ninive* (Paris, 1849), but the mound was not in fact ancient Nineveh, but Dur-Sharruken, a new city built by Sargon II of Assyria, the king mentioned in the Bible in Isa. 20: 1. Over the last 150 years archaeological techniques have been much improved, and study of the results has been very much refined, so that materials recovered can be used with some confidence in Old Testament study.

Material remains and physical objects have their uses. For example, the far from lucid accounts of the building of Solomon's temple in Kings and Chronicles can be illuminated from the remains of similar temples excavated at other places in Palestine and Syria. The allusions to seals and sealing in the Hebrew Bible become clearer when ancient seals and clay objects with sealings are known. Ancient art, in contrast, is still a dangerous subject. Very little indeed has survived from the Holy Land itself. So to provide illustrations in popular or even learned books on the Old Testament there is a custom of reproducing pictures of statues or reliefs with captions which may be totally false, or lacking any evidence whatsoever. Of course there are exceptions. The Assyrian palace relief showing Sennacherib's assault on Lachish is confirmed by the palace in which it was found and by captions on the reliefs. But seven-headed monsters and gods pursuing miscellaneous monsters usually cannot be identified for certain.

Here our concern is primarily with written remains of all kinds, which can be much more explicit than uninscribed objects. Ancient Mesopotamia has yielded tens of thousands of clay tablets with cuneiform inscriptions, apart from monumental stone inscriptions and inscriptions on other media. Palestine and Syria, by contrast, have yielded comparatively little inscriptional material, partly because much was written on papyrus and leather, which has not survived, partly because they were less rich than their Mesopotamian neighbours and so produced less written material.

The old alphabetic script which the Israelites shared with the Phoenicians, Ammonites, Moabites, and Edomites has not been a problem. It changed after the exile into the so-called square script still used for modern Hebrew. Knowledge of cuneiform, in contrast, was lost early in the Christian era, so it had to be deciphered, which took place slowly over the nineteenth century CE. The script began as a pictographic and symbol script c.3000 BCE and developed in various centres in Mesopotamia, west Iran, and Anatolia, so that the whole gamut is vast and very complicated. There are hundreds of signs for whole words, syllables, vowels, and to mark things in the script, but no signs for consonants. The results of decipherment are impressive, since the following languages are now understood to a more or less degree.

Sumerian   This was used in the far south of Mesopotamia, the area nearest the Gulf, for the millennium c.3000–2000 BCE, and was kept on by the Babylonians as a language of learning up to the Parthian era.

Akkadian   This is the language closest to biblical Hebrew, Semitic, though written in an entirely different script. The oldest form, now called Old Akkadian, is known from c.2500–2000 BCE, after which it divides into two main dialects: Babylonian and Assyrian, both known to us from c.2000 BCE onwards. Assyrian died out soon after the fall of Assyria in 612 BCE, but Babylonian continued in use, at least in Babylon itself among a few families, up to the first century CE.

Elamite   The language of south-west Iran, known to us from c.2300–300 BCE, but not fully understood.

Hurrian   The language of the Hurrians (Biblical 'Horites'), who are first known c.2200 BCE and spread with their language c.1500 BCE from Kurdistan and north-east Mesopotamia to Syria and the east Mediterranean, but then merged into the local populations and so disappeared as an ethnic group by 1100 BCE. Their language is not yet fully understood, and it is difficult to form a reliable estimate of their cultural impact on the relevant areas. It is best seen in religious archives of the Hittites.

Urartian   Urartu, biblical Ararat, was not a mountain, but the mountainous area of later Armenia. The Urartians are known to us c.900–650 BCE, and their language is closely related to Hurrian, but has no other known cognates. They formed a unified kingdom, and their royal inscriptions can be translated with some assurance.

Hittite   The people lived in Anatolia, and their language, an Indo-European one, is attested c.1700–1200 BCE. At certain times they formed a powerful empire, but eventually disappeared. Their language is well understood, and another Indo-European language, Luvian, attested in Anatolia contemporary with Hittite, survived the demise of that people and, written in a hieroglyphic script, was used by north Syrian states c.1000–700 BCE. Good progress has been made in understanding it.

Persian   Old Persian, written in a specially devised cuneiform script of only forty-three signs, was the official language of the Persian empire, known to us c.550–330 BCE, and is well understood.

What, then, is the result of this recovery of documents for understanding the Old Testament? Essentially, the Old Testament can now be set in its original context. It is a collection of diverse texts assembled by a religious community to help in conserving and promoting their faith. It is only incidentally that they tell us about the larger world from which this corpus survived, and in so far as its authors were not sympathetic to other cultures and ideologies, we cannot expect to find systematic information about their neighbours. For us it is a question of how the ancient Israelites preserved their traditional texts and beliefs when other ancient Near Eastern nations did not, and information about these other nations is thus of primary importance. Also, it is easy for us to misinterpret the ancient Hebrew writings from our own very different intellectual world. Familiarity with the thought of the other ancient Near Eastern peoples can give us a better perspective on that of the Israelites.

To proceed, I shall give first an example of the finding of a Babylonian text which has obvious relevance and attracted much popular attention at the time, but which raised questions which could not be adequately answered at the time. Then a general survey of the whole field will be offered.

British-promoted excavations at the true Nineveh, the large site across the Tigris from modern Mosul, uncovered the remains of the palace of Ashurbanipal, the last great Assyrian king, in a series of digs about the middle of the nineteenth century CE. This king had assembled a large library of cuneiform tablets, many of which were recovered and taken to the British museum. Here work on decipherment began, and George Smith succeeded in piecing together, among other texts, a Babylonian version of the biblical flood story, including the sending out of birds from the ark as the waters were subsiding. This was announced to a meeting of the Society of Biblical Archaeology in 1872 and received much learned and popular attention. The serious questions raised were when this text was composed, from what materials, and how it is related to the account in Genesis. In 1872 knowledge was insufficient to address these questions seriously, but today the issues can be defined, even if definitive answers still cannot be given.

This field is now a vast one, but most of the extra-biblical evidence is still from Babylonia and Assyria. Despite the finding of the Moabite Stone with its version of a period of the history of the northern Israelite kingdom in the nineteenth century CE and the finding in the twentieth century CE of the Ugaritic clay tablets (c.1400–1300 BCE) with, among other things, extensive Baal myths; the plaster inscription from Tell Deir 'Alla (in Jordan) about Balaam, a figure hitherto known only from the narrative of Numbers 22–4 and later biblical allusions; the very fragmentary stele from Tell Dan mentioning 'the house of David'; and by now hundreds of Hebrew bullae with impressions of seals of persons known from the books of Kings or their servants, the sad fact is how little has been recovered from Syria/Palestine with direct biblical relevance.

HISTORY (1): UP TO THE FLOOD

The Israelite faith was, much more than other ancient Near Eastern religions, tied up with history. The Hebrew Bible begins with creation and proceeds in a straight line in what the Israelites conceived as history—with diversions—to the Babylonian captivity. Some additional books take the story down to the return from the Babylonian captivity. For us it is a matter of concern how historical in our sense of the word these narratives are. The first nine chapters of Genesis—from creation to the Flood—have Mesopotamian parallels. The two accounts of creation—the first in seven days, the second, the Garden of Eden—bear no close relationship to other creation myths, though the first contains some elements, such as beginning from earth and water, found elsewhere in the ancient Near East and beyond. After the accounts of creation, Adam, the first man, heads a line of ten long-lived patriarchs, culminating in the Flood. The Sumerian King List, known from copies c.2100–1600 BCE, in some copies begins with from eight to ten long-reigning kings following the institution of kingship by the gods, and culminating in the Flood. This antediluvian section was originally a separate list, lacking in a late third-millennium copy (c.2100–2000 BCE) and from some early second-millennium copies. However, the form with the prefixed antediluvian section became the norm, and was copied out so that we know it from a late Assyrian copy (c.750–650 BCE) and in Greek from Berossus, a Babylonian priest c.300 BCE. The post-diluvian kings were originally Sumerian rulers, but as the list was copied out over the centuries, the Babylonian kings were added on until at least the earlier part of first millennium BCE. There is one literary version of the Flood in Sumerian, and two major ones in Babylonian, the Atra-hasis Epic, and Tablet XI of the Gilgamesh Epic. Atra-hasis in known from copies c.1700 BCE, long before the earliest possible date for Genesis, so priority in time seems to rest on the Mesopotamian side, where floods are an annual occurrence.

It would appear that the Hebrew author or authors used traditions of Mesopotamian origin in the early chapters of Genesis, but produced something very different in detail. The Sumero-Babylonian list is of kings, not necessarily father and son in succession, while Genesis offers a genealogy leading eventually to the Hebrew monarchy of David and his line. For this too there is a parallel of Mesopotamian origin. A Babylonian tablet with ritual content invokes all the ancestors of Ammi-ṣaduqa, great-great-grandson of Hammurabi, king of Babylon in the seventeenth century BCE. A total of twenty-eight ancestors is given, the last nine being the well-known kings of the First Dynasty of Babylon, the earlier ones not so far identifiable as historical figures. The First Dynasty of Babylon were Amorites, part of a migration down the Euphrates c.2000 BCE. No documents in the Amorite language survive, but thousands of personal names are known, from which it appears that Amorite was a kind of primitive Hebrew. Part of this traditional ancestry of the kings of Babylon also survives in the Assyrian King List, a document first attested in the thirteenth century BCE, but regularly updated until the closing days of the Assyrian power. The information it contains after c.1500 BCE is generally reliable, but the earlier material is a garbled hotchpotch. The section which parallels some of Hammurabi's ancestors is in fact the ancestry of Shamshi-Adad I, king of Assyria c.1800 BCE, and he was not an Assyrian by descent, but an Amorite who had imposed himself on the Assyrians by force of arms. Thus the Amorites in Mesopotamia in the eighteenth and seventeenth centuries BCE had rulers who professed to be descended from a long traditional ancestry, and this is what is combined with the Sumero-Babylonian tradition of long-reigning kings before the Flood in Genesis.

HISTORY (II):
THE FLOOD TO THE EXODUS

Little light from the ancient Near East falls on this period (Egypt is not included), though a case has been made that some personal names, such as Jacob and Benjamin, have Amorite parallels, and that a number of archaic and poetic Hebrew terms are paralleled in Amorite as known from the Mari documents, from the site on the Euphrates close to the modern Iraqi–Syrian border. In general the case is well made, but the material is not restricted to this one section of the Hebrew Bible, and its impact is more on the meaning of particular words than on the whole narrative. But the period of the settlement in the promised land and of the judges and the early monarchy—even the great King Solomon—so far lack corroboration or amplification from non-biblical sources.

HISTORY (III): THE DIVIDED MONARCHY
AND THE EXILE

Only as the Assyrians expanded westwards from their homeland in the area of modern Mosul in the ninth and eighth centuries BCE did they come into contact with the biblical world and give us independent evidence. The Assyrian documentation is extremely important, for two reasons. First, their royal inscriptions increased in length and historical detail as they became more powerful and took over more territory. Some such inscriptions even offer year-by-year detailed records, and they all date from the reign of the ruler whose exploits are being described. Though they are official documents of the king for his glorification, with appropriate caution they can be used as reliable sources. The rare outright defeats are not recorded as such, and in some reigns there was editorial rearrangement for clarity of presentation, but on the whole they offer reliable fact. Secondly, the Assyrian documents of the first millennium BCE provide us with a reliable chronology. Events were dated by a state officer called a *līmu*, who held office for one year only, and the king himself held this office in the first or second year of his reign. Lists of these officers were compiled for purely practical purposes, though some copies also add a brief note giving the most important event of each year as indicated by the *līmu*'s name. One such note is of a solar eclipse in a given month which ties down the whole sequence with modern time-reckoning. There are rare scribal errors in these lists, but one or two years at the most is involved. Also there are Assyrian king lists giving the names of the kings and their years of reign, probably extracted from the lists of *līmu* officers, but providing further valuable material for reconstruction of the history of the period. On these bases it is possible to reconstruct a more or less exact sequence of events from *c.*900 to 612 BCE, when the Assyrian empire fell.

Israel became involved in Assyrian history from the time of King Ahab onwards, and while there are some problems in reconciling the two sources, Assyrian and Hebrew, much is made clearer by the extra-biblical material. For example, deporting populations, which the Assyrians did to the northern Hebrew kingdom, was a normal practice. The Assyrians lacked any civil administration to hold down conquered peoples, so they switched populations around to deprive them of patriotic spirit as they were forced to settle in new environments.

The Assyrian empire fell to Medes and Babylonians, but the latter succeeded the Assyrians as the great power in the ancient Near East. Unfortunately, their royal inscriptions contain very little history, and they had no system of annual *līmu* officers. However, since they dated events by year of the reigning king, king lists were compiled for practical reasons, but no complete lists for the late Babylonian empire have survived. Annalistic chronicles were composed with events briefly recorded, but while these are generally reliable and important, only part of the period is covered by what has survived. The very day on which Jerusalem fell to Nebuchadnezzar is recorded in one of these chronicles. Despite this lack of complete records, a fair amount of this period can be reconstructed historically, and it provides a clearer perspective on both historical and prophetic books of the Old Testament, though the period was quite short: 612–539 BCE. The Babylonian captivity began in this period.

History (iv): The Return from Exile

The Persians put an end to the late Babylonian empire, and took its place, from 539 to 331 BCE. From royal sources we are not better informed than from the late Babylonian kings: royal inscriptions survive, but are not informative for us. The tradition of Babylonian chronicles continued, and when they survive, they offer concise but reliable information. Greek writers also survive, but their historical material is often suspect or clearly wrong. However, an outline history of the period is possible, and that puts in clearer perspective the Hebrew books from or alluding to this period. Dates for kings' reigns are again sure and precise.

Law

The first five books of the Bible are called 'Law' (*torah*) in Hebrew, but only parts of the second to the fifth can strictly claim that title. Modern study generally recognizes different strata of law from differing periods. The earliest is the so-called Book of the Covenant (Exodus 21–3); a later Deuteronomic code is contained in the book of that name; and the latest, the so-called Priestly legislation is scattered through Exodus, Leviticus, and Numbers. Laws and legal matter survive from other ancient Near Eastern nations, mostly from Mesopotamia and in cuneiform. What can be called 'codes', though some quibble at the term, are the following:

(i)   Sumerian, from Ur-Nammu or Shulgi, kings of Ur, *c.*2100–2050 BCE
(ii)   Sumerian, from Lipit-Ishtar of Isin, *c.*1930 BCE
(iii) Babylonian, from the town of Eshnunna, *c.*1770 BCE

(iv)   Babylonian, from Hammurabi of Babylon, *c*.1750 BCE
(v)   Hittite, *c*.1650–1500 BCE
(vi)   Assyrian, *c*.1300–1100 BCE

There is a tradition within these codes. Laws are copied from the earlier into the later, often with more explicit wording or other amplification. The length of the codes also usually increases with passage of time, Hammurabi's being the longest of the surviving ones. The Assyrian was apparently much longer still, but little remains. In addition to the codes, kings also promulgated legal decrees for particular economic purposes—for example, by cancelling certain types of debt. Examples are known from Uru-inimgina of Lagash (Sumerian, *c*.2400 BCE) and from various Mesopotamian kings (in Babylonian) *c*.2000–1500 BCE. Finally, thousands of court case records survive from *c*.2100–1600 especially, showing how justice was in fact dispensed.

Some striking points emerge from this material. First, the court records show that generally no particular attention was paid to the existing local code. A bench of magistrates decided each case on its merits, guided by their collective wisdom and accumulated experience. Some laws, in Hammurabi's code especially, are totally impracticable, and could not be enforced. Further, no code is known from otherwise well-documented late Babylonian times. Hammurabi's laws were copied out by scribes as a library text for study by scholars, but not for lawyers. In short, the codes did not provide the rules for everyday life. Secondly, the legal edicts appear to have been formulated for immediate enforcement, but not for perpetuity. If needed, another edict could be issued a few years later.

Biblical laws can be compared only with the Mesopotamian codes of *c*.2100–1700 BCE, though details of the Hittite and Assyrian codes are also relevant. Their statuses raise questions, of course, about the status of biblical laws in Israel, but do not provide answers. Generally the biblical law is much more concerned with religious life and duties than what we would consider forensic. But comparisons do yield conclusions. The Book of the Covenant is closest to the Mesopotamian codes. Deuteronomy and the Priestly material are more remote. An example: laws nos. 53–5 of the Eshnunna code deal with the goring ox and parallel Exod. 21: 28–32, and in part they are identically worded. Here the Book of the Covenant is clearly based on Near Eastern traditions. But only Hammurabi's laws nos. 196–203 lay down the *lex talionis* ('eye for eye, tooth for tooth'); previous codes prescribe fines for bodily injury. Hammurabi was an Amorite, and the *lex talionis* is more suited to desert life than urban life with courts and magistrates. Presumably both Hammurabi and the Book of the Covenant depend on the same Amorite custom.

Legal documents from Nuzi (*c*.1450–1400 BCE, near Kirkuk, with much Hurrian influence) have been pressed as illustrating patriarchal society, but the case has been exaggerated. The archives of Mari (c.1800 BCE, on the Euphrates close to the modern Iraqi–Syrian border) have also been pressed for revealing an Amorite society with parallels to the patriarchal narratives. There is more that is valid here, but in the linguistic rather than legal sphere.

LITERATURE

For the latter part of the nineteenth century and the first half of the twentieth century CE, Old Testament scholarship was much occupied with the Graf–Wellhausen analysis of the Pentateuch. These two scholars claimed that it was compiled from four main pre-existing sources, three of which had been put together by a 'scissors and paste' method into a single account. That the principle was legitimate did not need justification, since a comparison of Samuel–Kings in the current Hebrew Bible with Chronicles proves that ancient authors did often compile from pre-existing sources in this way. But having only the final form of the text, one may justifiably ask whether such conclusions can be sure, except in very clear cases. Recovery of ancient Near Eastern literature has further confirmed this conclusion. The Babylonian Gilgamesh Epic is based on a free retelling of two surviving Sumerian Gilgamesh epics combined with other, no longer surviving material, into a dramatic literary whole c.1700 BCE. This composite epic was then passed down the centuries in substantially variant forms until in the first millennium BCE one edition became standard and mostly ousted all other recensions. Unlike the Pentateuch, this Gilgamesh tradition can be tapped at various stages in its development, and the two Sumerian epics are preserved, one in two very different recensions. Comparison of different copies of Sumerian incantations and Babylonian translations of them also reveals modifications creeping into the wording in a manner quite like the hair-splitting analyses of even single sentences in the Hebrew Bible proposed by scholars in the wake of Wellhausen. But often the changes in the incantations could never be guessed without the existence of the variant copies.

Items of wording as well as literary techniques are also shared by the Old Testament and other ancient Near Eastern literature. In 1 Sam. 9: 8 and 16: 9 men in addressing King David refer to themselves as 'a dead dog'. Exactly the same self-deprecatory expression is used in neo-Babylonian and neo-Assyrian letters to the Assyrian king. One could dismiss this as a common phrase on everyone's lips, but there was of course much oral literature in circulation too. An example of a whole

Gilgamesh Old Babylonian Vorderasiatisches Museum + British Museum, iii. 6–14	Ecclesiastes 9: 7–9
As for you, Gilgamesh, let your belly be full, day and night ever rejoice, every day have pleasure.	Go, eat your food with rejoicing. drink your wine with a happy heart, for God has already accepted your deeds.
Day and night dance and make merry.	
Let your garments be clean, Wash your head, bathe in water, Look at the little one who holds your hand,	Let your garments be white on every occasion, do not spare the oil on your head.
Let your spouse have constant pleasure in your bosom.	Enjoy life with the woman you love all the days of your futility
This is the task of [mankind.]	which God has given you under the sun.

topos shared occurs in the Old Babylonian Gilgamesh Epic (*c*.1700 BCE) and Ecclesiastes (a post-exilic composition):

The similarities here are too great to be explained as coincidence, and the vast priority in time on the Babylonian side means that Ecclesiastes has depended on a tradition, written or oral, of long standing in the ancient Near East.

Still another literary matter is Hebrew composition in styles previously known elsewhere in the ancient Near East. The best example is Daniel 11, which presents a mass of detailed history in the form of predictions with names of people and places omitted or obscured. Previous Hebrew prophets also predicted the future, but never in such detailed annalistic form. There was, however, a Babylonian genre of this kind that was still being produced at the end of the Persian empire, and most probably the author of Daniel knew of it and took it over for his own purposes.

RELIGION

This is certainly a key topic, which could occupy a big book, so little more than a few hints can be given here. Plenty of Sumerian, Babylonian, and Hittite hymns and prayers survive, in which phraseology and sentiments similar to those of the biblical psalms can be found. Hebrew sacrificial terminology was also employed by the Phoenicians, and the Classical Greeks had a similar regimen. The biblical proverbs are often similar to those of other ancient Near Eastern cultures. What is different is the conception of the divine. The polytheism of most of the ancient Near East expressed very well their conception of the physical universe as controlled by a host of independent superhuman powers. Israelite monotheism is distinct. Claims for Egyptian monotheism under Akhnaton, also a kind of Babylonian monotheism in some first-millennium BCE theological texts have been taken into account, also the fairly common view that Israelite monotheism arose only in the Babylonian captivity; before then, it was rather a henotheism. There may be some truth in these points, save for Akhnaton; but Israelite religion had the advantages in the concept of one all-powerful God. There was no longer a whole pantheon of often divided and squabbling gods in control of the universe. Thus moral standards in Israel have an intensity not found in Mesopotamia. Gilgamesh, as quoted above, is urged to a pure hedonism. Ecclesiastes advises to enjoy the pleasures of life without forgetting God. The Israelite God works in history with consistency to a predetermined goal. Sumerian and Babylonian gods intervene in human affairs only *ad hoc* and often whimsically.

The recovery of knowledge of the ancient Near East during the last 150 years has made possible a realistic assessment of the relative character of ancient Israel.

BIBLIOGRAPHY

Introduction

Eupolemus
LAMBERT, W. G. 1978. *The Background of Jewish Apocalyptic: Ethel M. Wood Lecture 1977.* London: Athlone Press.

Berossus
BURSTEIN, S. M. 1978. *the babyloniaca of berossus: sources and monographs,* sources from the ancient near east i. 5. Malibu, Calif.: Undena.

Travellers, early excavation, and decipherment
ROGERS, R. W. 1901. *A History of Babylonia and Assyria,* 2nd edn. New York: Eaton and Mains, i. 1–253.

History (i)

Sumerian King List
EDZARD, D. O. 1980–3. 'Königslisten und Chroniken, A. Sumerisch'. In *Reallexikon der Assyriologie,* vi. 77–84.

STEINKELLER, P. 2003. 'An Ur III Manuscript of the Sumerian King List'. In W. Sallaberger, K. Volk, and A. Zgoll, eds., *Literatur, Politik und Recht in Mesopotamien*, Wiesbaden: Harrassowitz, 267–92.

Sumerian flood story

CIVIL, M. 1969. In Lambert and Millard (1969), 138–45, 167–72.

Atra-hasis Epic

LAMBERT, W. G., and MILLARD, A. R. 1969. *Atra-ḥasīs: The Babylonian Story of the Flood*. Oxford: Clarendon Press; repr. Winona Lake, Ind.: Eisenbrauns, 1999.

Gilgamesh Epic

GEORGE, A. R. 2003. *The Babylonian Gilgamesh Epic*. Oxford: Oxford University Press.

Ancestors of Ammi-ṣaduqa

CHARPIN, D., and DURAND, J.-M. 1986. 'Fils de Sim'al: Les Origines tribales des rois de Mari'. *Revue d'Assyriologie*, 80: 141–83.

FINKELSTEIN, J. J. 1966. 'The Genealogy of the Hammurapi Dynasty'. *Journal of Cuneiform Studies*, 20: 95–118.

Assyrian King List

GRAYSON, A. K. 1980–3. 'Königslisten und Chroniken, B, Akkadisch, § 3.9 King List 9. Assyrian King List'. In *Reallexikon der Assyriologie*, vi: 101–16.

History (ii)

Mari and the Amorites

FLEMING, D. E. 1998. 'Mari and the Possibilities of Biblical Memory'. *Revue d'Assyriologie*, 92: 41–78.

MALAMAT, A. 1989. *Mari and the Early Israelite Experience*, Schweich Lectures 1984. Oxford: Oxford University Press.

SASSON, J. M. 1998. 'About "Mari and the Bible" '. *Revue d'Assyriologie*, 92: 97–123.

History (iii) a: Assyrian royal inscriptions

General Survey

LAMBERT, W. G. 2004. 'Mesopotanian Sources and Pre-exilic Israel'. In J. Day, ed., *In Search of Pre-exilic Israel*, London and New York: Continuum, 352–65.

Editions with translations

GRAYSON, A. K. 1996. *Assyrian Rulers of the Early First Millennium BC*, ii: *858–745 BC*. The Royal Inscriptions of Mesopotamia, Assyrian periods, 3. Toronto, Buffalo, and London: University of Toronto Press.

TADMOR, H. 1994. *The Inscriptions of Tiglath-pileser III King of Assyria*. Jerusalem: Israel Academy of Sciences and Humanities.

Translations of relevant excerpts with brief notes

BORGER, R. 1984. In O. Kaiser, *Texte aus der Umwelt des Alten Testaments*, i, Gütersloh: Gerd Mohn, 354–410.

Excerpts edited with full discussion
KUAN, J. K. 1995. *Neo-Assyrian Historical Inscriptions and Syria-Palestine*. Jian Dao Dissertation Series 1, Bible and Literature 1. Hong Kong: Alliance Bible Seminary.

History (iii) b: Assyrian līmu lists
MILLARD, A. 1994. *The Eponyms of the Assyrian Empire, 910–612 BC*. State Archives of Assyria Studies ii. Helsinki: The Neo-Assyrian Text Corpus Project.

History (iii) c: Babylonian Chronicles
GRAYSON, A. K. 1975. *Assyrian and Babylonian Chronicles*. Texts from Cuneiform Sources V. Locust Valley, NY: J. J. Augustin.

Law
Translations of the codes with brief notes
ROTH, M. T. 1995. *Law Collections from Mesopotamia and Asia Minor*. Writings from the Ancient World, Society of Biblical Literature, 6. Atlanta: Scholars Press.

Edition of edicts with full discussion
KRAUS, F. R. 1984. *Königliche Verfügungen in altbabylonischer Zeit*. Studia et Documenta ad Iura Orientis Antiqui Pertinentia, II. Leiden: Brill.

Late use of Hammurabi's laws
LAMBERT, W. G. 1989. 'The Laws of Hammurabi in the First Millennium'. In M. Lebeau and P. Talon, eds., *Reflets des deux fleuves*, Akkadica, supp. VI, Leuven: Peeters, 95–8.

Nuzi customs
EICHLER, B. L. 1989. 'Nuzi and the Bible: A Retrospective'. In H. Behrens, D. Loding, and M. T. Roth, eds., *DUMU-E₂-DUB-BA-A: Studies in Honor of Åke W. Sjöberg*, Occasional Publications of the Samuel Noah Kramer Fund, 11, Philadelphia: University Museum, Philadelphia, 107–19.

Literature
Gilgamesh Epic: see above under *History (i)*.
Variant incantations, Sumerian and Babylonian
LAMBERT, W. G. 1974. 'Dingir.šà.dib.ba Incantations'. *Journal of Near Eastern Studies*, 35: 267–322.

The phrase 'dead dog' Hebrew in 2 Sam. 9: 8 and 16: 9; Babylonian and Assyrian
OPPENHEIM, A. L., *et al.* 1971. *The Assyrian Dictionary of the Oriental Institute of the University of Chicago*, viii K. Chicago: Oriental Institute, Chicago. 72 b.

Daniel 11
LAMBERT, W. G. 1978. Work listed above under 'Eupolemus', 7–17.

Religion

Babylonian monotheism

LAMBERT, W. G. 1975. 'The Historical Development of the Mesopotamian Pantheon: A Study in Sophisticated Polytheism'. In H. Goedicke and J. J. Roberts, eds., *Unity and Diversity: Essays in the History, Literature, and Religion of the Ancient Near East*, Baltimore and London: Johns Hopkins University Press, 191–200.

CHAPTER 5

ANCIENT NEAR EASTERN STUDIES: EGYPT

KENNETH KITCHEN

1. INTRODUCTION: BEGINNINGS

Before 1800, no accurate first-hand knowledge of Egypt's ancient remains was available to compare with biblical mentions of that land and its ancient civilization. During the nineteenth century, detailed pioneering exploration of Egypt and Nubia led to extensive recording and major publications of the visible monuments and inscriptions, while decipherment of ancient Egypt's hieroglyphic and other scripts, along with their language, finally opened the way towards recovering three millennia of history, literature, and social organization, including religious belief and practice. During the last third of the nineteenth century, excavations added further materials. Different countries had different objectives. Thus, the French went for monumental temple sites (Deir el-Bahri, Abydos, Karnak, the Ptolemaic temples), while the Germans began systematic clearance of unexplored pyramids and their complexes, and the city of the 'heretic' pharaoh Akhnaton, first explored by Petrie. In Victorian Britain, much popular interest focused on possible connections with the Bible, and especially on its 'Egyptian' themes such as the exodus. So, the Egypt Exploration Fund of that time initially undertook pioneering excavations at east Delta sites, looking for evidence of such biblical places as Raamses, Pithom, Succoth, Tanis, Goshen, and so on. The vast ruins of Tanis were unmistakable, with masses of stonework derived from temples of the Ramesses kings and of later rulers; so, the site of Hebrew Zoan = Egyptian Djaᶜan(et) = Greek Tanis was assured. Likewise at Bubastis = Egyptian Pi-Bast = Hebrew Pi-Beseth. However, the other places proved elusive, and also (thanks to the primitive archaeological techniques of that time) such sites as Tell el-Maskhuta produced very limited Egyptian monuments for much labour, and very little trace of either the Hebrews or other Semites. Petrie was slightly more 'successful', biblically, in his discovery of the victory stela of Merneptah (naming Israel) in 1896, but not in his attempts to identify further Delta sites such as Tell er-Retaba.

Therefore, with the start of the twentieth century, the interests of the Fund (now, Egypt Exploration Society) and other such agencies shifted to much more prom-ising sites of purely Egyptological interest, with invaluable results for that discipline down to the present day. No firm identifications could be made for (e.g.) Pithom or Succoth, while disputes over rival identifications for Raamses raged for decades, down to the 1970s, when very modern work at Khataana-Qantir and Tell el-Dab'a by Bietak and Pusch finally confirmed the 1930s/1940s views of Hamza and Habachi, fixing Raamses (strictly, Egyptian Pi-Ramesse) and the Hyksos centre Avaris respectively at these two neighbouring sites (cf. Bietak 1975: 189–98 for Avaris and 199–220 for Pi-Ramesse). The often colourful scenes of Egyptian life in tomb-chapels of the Middle and New Kingdoms (c.2000–1070 BCE) were much used to illustrate the Egyptian episodes of the Joseph and exodus narratives from the mid-nineteenth century onwards. The impact of the last half-century of Egyptology covers several themes.

2. EGYPTOLOGY AND THE TRADITIONS OF EARLY HEBREW ANTIQUITY (PATRIARCHS AND EXODUS)

2.1. Patriarchal Traditions

Abraham reputedly flirted only briefly with Egypt (Gen. 12: 10–20), but almost one-quarter of Genesis (37, 39–50) is devoted to the fortunes of his putative descendants Jacob and Joseph in Egypt. Features in this 'Joseph narrative' have often been compared with data from ancient Egyptian sources, but rarely at length. Vergote

(1959) dealt with eight major subjects, using linguistic data and pictorial background, finding many specific examples of real knowledge of Egyptian conditions. His end result was to posit a basic narrative originating in the Ramesside period (the thirteenth century BCE), with even a Moses, becoming the supposed J source, while other elements came in later with the putative E source of biblical scholarship. Then Redford (1970) gave a wider but more sceptical view of the narrative, concentrating more on literary structure; he viewed it as a 'novella' first composed in the later fifth century BCE, showing more limited knowledge of Egypt than Vergote had claimed. However, despite much of great value in this work, his scepticism proved, on closer examination, to be largely misplaced on both philological and other grounds (Kitchen 1973a), leaving open the possibility of an original early family tradition reformulated in the thirteenth century and reaching its final form in the first millennium.

2.2. The Exodus Tradition

In recent decades, the date and nature of the emergence of 'early Israel' (or even 'proto-Israel') has been intensely debated. In that context, the reality or otherwise of the Hebrew exodus from Egypt has likewise been subjected to assessments varying widely from pure fiction to substantial historicity. Being fully occupied with Egypt's rich civilization through its 3,000 years, most Egyptologists are not concerned with biblical studies. But here also, reactions to the exodus narratives have varied greatly. On the pessimistic side, one may cite Redford (1987: 150; 1992: 412–13; 1997: 63), who viewed the exodus narrative as largely folklore (1997), possibly relating to a group of pastoralists who visited Egypt, then left as part of the expulsion of the Hyksos (1987; 1992—a view going back in part to Manetho and Josephus!) The present narratives would belong to the seventh to fourth centuries BCE (1987: 149; cf. 1992: 414; 'Saito-Persian', likewise 1997: 63), in terms of content. But mediating views need to be noticed too. Also in 1987, Bietak pointed out features concerning the exodus locations in Egypt that clearly contradicted the Redford view, in that the name Raamses does not require an initial Pi- as in Egyptian (pointed out by Gardiner and Helck long since), and that local geographical/textual data set Pithom at Tell er-Retaba, not Tell el-Maskhuta, while Ramesside remains in these locations rule out an exclusively late, Saito-Persian date for such details in the narrative (Bietak 1987: 168–70). In turn, like Bietak, Yurco (1997) was able to point out features in the exodus accounts that go in part with Ramesside origins and Saito-Persian retouches (Yurco 1997: 50). Going further, very recent advances in the archaeology of the East Delta have clarified the sequences of some of its Ramesside and Late Period sites, showing local shifts as time went on (Hoffmeier 1997: *passim*), while more thorough studies of textual and longer-known archaeological data clearly show a Ramesside-epoch element and further definitely 'Nilotic' features in the exodus narratives (Kitchen 1998*b*; Kitchen 2003*b*: 297–324, 351–5, 367–9). Thus, an actual event (but with several thousand, not two million people!) in the thirteenth century BCE from the East Delta would be feasible, followed by some record and traditions, incorporated into their present covenantal/legal context later, with some retouches in the first millennium BCE. So at least three overall viewpoints can be seen at present in Egyptology: near-total scepticism, a cautious middle-of-the-road approach citing data overlooked by the sceptics, and a more positive evaluation, based on newer evidence and fuller study of older data.

2.3. Epochs of the 'United Monarchy' and its Fall

Here, we reach the period of Egypt's twenty-first and twenty-second dynasties coeval with the reigns of David and Solomon as reported in Samuel, Kings, and Chronicles. Interest here has focused on the pharaoh reputed to have given a daughter in marriage to Solomon after capturing Gezer (1 Kgs. 3: 1; 9: 16, 24), and on the hostile campaign of King Shishak of Egypt after Solomon's death (1 Kgs. 14: 25–6), besides possible cultural links (cf. sect. 2.5 below). There is good reason to believe that the division of the Hebrew kingdom occurred *c.*930 BCE (Galil 1996, and earlier Thiele 1986), setting Solomon at *c.*970–930. Likewise, there are solid reasons for calculating Egyptian dates back from 664 BCE (date of the effective change from the twenty-fifth to twenty-sixth dynasties) to close on 945 BCE for the change-over from the twenty-first to the twenty-second dynasty. The last king of the twenty-first dynasty (Tyetkheperure Psusennes II) reigned between thirteen and fifteen years, such that his predecessor Siamun (reigning nineteen years, within *c.*979/977–960/958) overlapped the earlier years of Solomon. Thus 'the pharaoh that smote Gezer' and married off a daughter to Solomon would have to have been Siamun, simply as a matter of practical chronology (for full data, see Kitchen 1973*b*). So far, Siamun is the only king of his line to display a formal scene of military triumph in a monumental context, which fits well his probable military role here. Also, the scepticism of some (e.g. Redford 1992: 311) about a late period pharaoh giving a daughter in marriage abroad (usually on the basis of Amenophis III's refusal to do this 400 years before!) is disproved both by his granddaughter's willingness to become a wife to foreign royalty at Tutankhamun's death, and by the known examples of such royal daughter marriages to commoners and foreigners precisely in the tenth to eighth centuries BCE (cf. Kitchen 2003*a*: 118–21).

The Shishak who despoiled the kingdoms of Rehoboam of Judah and of Jeroboam of Israel in the former's fifth year, *c.*925 BCE, is universally admitted by all competent scholars to have been the Shoshenq I (*c.*945–924 BCE), founder of the twenty-second dynasty, well-attested in the contemporary Egyptian monumental sources. And of all the known kings Shoshenq (I–VII), he is the only one who exhibits a whole series of monuments attesting to a campaign in Palestine, and datable by these monuments (stela, at Silsila, year 21) to c.925 BCE. Of these the most important is his famous list of Palestinian place-names, known from direct comparison with over fifty earlier lists of c.1500–1150 BCE to have been one of the most original, first-hand, and authentic such lists of the entire series, and it covers Shoshenq I's actions both in Judah and in Israel as far north as Megiddo, where part of a stela of his was found. Attempts to limit his campaign solely to Judah (e.g. Wilson 2001, based on only a few of this type of list and scene) are misplaced; cf. full studies, e.g. by Kitchen 1973*b*: 432–47 (plus 294–302, 575–6), and Kitchen 2001. This document is an invaluable resource, and even its prefatory rhetorical text is unique in this series (see details in Kitchen 1999: 433–40).

It is commonplace to dismiss the reports of the wealth of Solomon as mere romantic fiction. But as soon as Shoshenq I returned home from his Palestinian campaign, he launched immense and costly building projects on a scale never witnessed since the palmy imperial days of Ramesses II, and rivalling Ramesses III. These included the huge forecourt of the Temple of Amun at Karnak in Thebes (biggest of its kind) with a major gateway and the famous triumphal relief and list, a similar undertaking for the Temple of Ptah at Memphis, and an entire temple (and second relief and list) at El-Hiba well south of Memphis. Then, immediately after the death of Shoshenq I (Shishak), his successor Osorkon I went on a spending spree which remains unparalleled in its generosity (nearly 400 tons of gold and silver bullion) to the temples and cults of Egypt at this or any other period, and all within the first four years of his reign. Clearly, all this expenditure by Shoshenq and Osorkon may have stemmed from several sources: e.g. increased trade, or use of accumulated resources from the state treasury. But if so, why did Shoshenq I in particular wait twenty years before doing this? It would seem reasonable to suggest that he had indeed also stripped out whatever David and Solomon had garnered in their capital, and added this to the resources used for the new dynasty's delayed capital expenditures (cf. Kitchen 1973*b*: 301–4).

2.4. Egypt, Israel, and Judah, c.900–586 BCE

Little more than a century after the death of Shoshenq I, under far less able kings, the political unity of Egypt began to break up. From c.818 BCE, in the early years of Shoshenq III, Pedubast I set up a rival and parallel dynasty (the twenty-third on later reckoning), splitting Egypt's kingship. Then, during the eighth century BCE, other local kinglets arose in northern and central Upper Egypt at Heracleopolis and Hermopolis, while local princedoms of Libyan chiefs usurped authority all over the

Delta, retaining their powers down to the early seventh century BCE, even under the twenty-fifth dynasty from Kush (Nubia); see the maps in Kitchen 1973*b*: 346, 401, figs. 4 and 7 respectively. Thus, by the later eighth century, the ongoing kings of the parallel twenty-second and twenty-third dynasties reigned in all the splendour of their forebears, especially the twenty-second at Tanis, but as mere shadow rulers in terms of political power.

This was the situation in 725 BCE, when Hoshea of Israel rebelled against paying tribute to Assyria, and unwisely sought help by sending to 'So, King of Egypt' (2 Kgs. 17: 4). At that time, the nearest Egyptian ruler was indeed the reigning king of the twenty-second dynasty, who was then Osorkon IV, attested during the invasion of Piye ('Piankhy') from Kush in 728 BCE, and still there down to 716 BCE, as the [U]shilkanni of Sargon II. His bases in Tanis and Bubastis were impressive, but he had not inherited the vaster power of those who had built them up a century before, and so could afford Hoshea no help. From time to time, attempts have been made to amend the Hebrew reference as if intending to be read as 'to Sais, [to] the king of Egypt' (thus, by Goedicke 1963, copied by others since). This is without merit. It is needless in terms of the presence of Osorkon IV as closest neighbour to Palestine, and because the town of Sais was a mere backwater in 725 BCE, far distant from Canaan's shores, ruled only by local Libyan chiefs, Osorkon and Tefnakht I, who had no known relations abroad; and the Hebrew 'So' and the Egyptian for Sais do not properly correspond, unless arbitrarily emended. Again, the abbreviation of late period Egyptian kings' names does occur periodically, despite occasional statements to the contrary. So we are better off staying with the attested king Osorkon IV here, for many good reasons (given by Kitchen 1973*b*: 372–5, 551–2, and pp. xxxiv–xxxix; and Kitchen 2003*b*: 15–16 and 67 n. 24).

Rather more controversy has long attended the presence of 'Tirhakah king of Kush' in Palestine as ally of Hezekiah of Judah against Sennacherib of Assyria in 701 BCE. It is known that his twenty-six-year reign in Egypt began in 690 BCE, as it immediately preceded the accessions of Tanutamun (twenty-fifth dynasty) in the south and of Psamtek I (twenty-sixth dynasty) in the north in 664 BCE. Therefore, his appearance leading an Egypto-Nubian force in Palestine in 701 BCE was long condemned as erroneous. However, two factors speak against too facile an assumption along these lines. First, the narratives in 2 Kings and Isaiah as we have them did not reach their present form before 681 BCE, for both of them record the death of Sennacherib (2 Kgs. 19: 37; Isa. 37: 38), which happened in that year. By that time, Tirhaqah (better, Taharqa) had indeed been ruler of Egypt as well as Kush for almost a decade, of course (from 690). Thus, the narrator was (in 681) calling him 'king' as his then-current title. Support for this usage comes from Taharqa's own texts. When summoned north by Shabako, then reigning as king in Egypt, Taharqa on a stela of his own reign calls himself 'His Majesty' also, of a period when he was not yet king of Egypt. Such usage is universal, down to our own times—e.g. we would readily say, 'Queen Elizabeth II was born in 1926', as we live during her reign—but she was, of course only a princess at that time (see Kitchen 1973*b*: 157–61, 383–6, 552–4, and pp. xxxix–xlii). Secondly, the discovery of an Assyrian text at Tang-i Var in Iran mentions Shapataka, King/Ruler of Nubia/Kush ('Meluhha') in 706 BCE at latest. This item points to a probability, barely considered hitherto: namely, that the kings of Kush found it impossible to rule over the entire 2,000-mile length of both Egypt and Nubia from Memphis in northern Egypt. Therefore, they split this immense north–south domain into two: a senior king ruling at Memphis in Egypt, and his adjutant (and future successor) ruling Kush from Napata there. This was precisely what the New Kingdom pharaohs had done, centuries before, for the same reason of administrative necessity. Thus, it would appear that when Shabako took over Egypt in 715 BCE, he appointed Shebitku (Assyrian 'Shapataka') as his co-ruler in Kush, whether entitled 'King' or not. Then, when in 702 BCE Shebitku succeeded Shabako as king in Egypt, he appointed Taharqa in 702 as ruler of Kush in turn—which is what we have (for 701) in Kings and Isaiah. Thereafter, when Taharqa succeeded Shebitku as king in Egypt in 690, he would have appointed Tanutamun as ruler in Kush. Doubtless, Tanuta-mun would have followed this practice also—but the Assyrians expelled him promptly in 663 from Egypt back into Nubia, hence he was restricted permanently to the rule of Kush (Nubia) itself, and the dual arrangement lapsed. Some such dual arrangement was foreseen by Redford (1999: 60), and this writer (Kitchen 2003*b*: 16, 67 n. 25). Thus the biblical phrase is in fact more closely accurate than anyone had suspected—in 701, Taharqa was indeed ruler of Kush, but not yet of Egypt. The mentions of Necho II and of Hophra (abbreviation for [Wa]hibre) are long recognized, and therefore call for no special comment; they are well tied into the overall historical picture as derived from Assyrian, neo-Babylonian, Egyptian, and later Greek sources.

2.5. Egypt and Hebrew Poetry and Wisdom Literature

The forms and content of Hebrew poetry have long been studied and compared with those of the lush poetry of Syrian Ugarit and with that of Akkadian in Mesopotamia. Egypt too offers three millennia of comparable poetry; all these regions shared many formal features but kept their own emphases in wording and content. Egyptian and Hebrew hymns and psalms were compared and contrasted at length by Barucq (1962); a clear, brief exposition of poetical norms found in Egyptian (as elsewhere) and representative poetry of all kinds are given in Kitchen 1999. The Song of Songs has often been compared to Egyptian lyric poetry, latterly by Fox (1985) (fuller translations in Kitchen 1999).

Instructional and other wisdom literature was shared all across the biblical world. The instruction by Amenemope (*c*.1200 BCE) was claimed to be the original of parts of Proverbs; but in many cases, the concepts thus compared prove to have been drawn from older common stock, so a direct relationship is open to some question (see Ruffle 1977). Thus, riches fly away like geese in Amenemope X: 4–5 (Lichtheim in Hallo and Younger 1997: 18), while in Proverbs 23: 5 they fly off like an eagle. But already, 700 years before either, riches are like the sparrows that cannot settle (Sumerian Proverb Collection I: 18; Gordon 1959: 50)! Thus, both Amenemope and Proverbs drew upon a long-current common concept, not here upon each other. All such instructional writers were compilers rather than inventors; Solomon equates 'words of the wise' with 'what I teach' (Prov. 22: 17), and again (24: 23) 'further words of the wise'. Thus Amenemope and other such earlier 'sayings of the wise' could have been utilized, one way or another, in Proverbs. In format, of forty known instructional texts (half of these being Egyptian), roughly half each in all the cultures involved follow either the simple framework of title plus main text, consisting of a series of observations or injunctions, or else the fuller one of title, a prologue (always either exhortation or biographical), and then the main text. This formal history through three millennia (including Proverbs) was established by Kitchen (1979), doubted by Weeks (1994), and then shown to be strictly factual by Kitchen 1998a. Attempts have been made to link Ecclesiastes with the cynical component in Egyptian harpers' songs, but the affinity here is weaker, and other Near-Eastern sources afford equally good parallels. Biblical Job and the secular Egyptian 'Eloquent Peasant' both protest over misfortune.

Suggested Reading

Among the following, the essays in Ahituv and Oren 1998 give a sampling of diverse opinions on early Israel (and Egypt's possible role), plus Hoffmeier 1997. Redford 1992 provides the more sceptical viewpoint on Israel and Egypt at all periods, while Kitchen 2003b includes a more positive assessment in a wider context. The basic textbook on later Egypt is Kitchen 1973b, while Dever and Gitin 2003 provide a wide series of essays on that period (Iron Age) with archaeological emphases.

Bibliography

Ahituv, S., and Oren, E. D., eds. 1998. *The Origin of Early Israel: Current Debate, Biblical, Historical and Archaeological Perspectives.* Beer-Sheva, 12. Beer-Sheva: Ben-Gurion University of the Negev Press; London: University College London.

Barucq, A. 1962. *L'Expression de la louange divine et de la prière dans la Bible et en Égypte.* Cairo: Institut Français d'Archéologie Orientale.

BIETAK, M. 1975. *Tell el-Dab'a II*. Vienna: Akademie der Wissenschaften.

—— 1987. 'Comments on the "Exodus" '. In Rainey 1987: 163–71.

DEVER, W. G., and GITIN, S., eds. 2003. *Symbiosis, Symbolism and the Power of the Past*. Winona Lake, Ind.: Eisenbrauns.

FOX, M. V. 1985. *The Song of Songs and the Ancient Egyptian Love Songs*. Madison: University of Wisconsin Press.

FRERICHS, E. S., and LESKO, L. H., eds. 1997. *Exodus: The Egyptian Evidence*. Winona Lake, Ind.: Eisenbrauns.

GALIL, G. 1996. *The Chronology of the Kings of Israel and Judah*. Leiden: E. J. Brill.

GOEDICKE, H. 1963. 'The End of "So, King of Egypt" '. *Bulletin of the American Schools of Oriental Research*, no. 171: 64–6.

GORDON, E. I. 1959. *Sumerian Proverbs*. Philadelphia: University Museum.

HALLO, W. W., and YOUNGER, K. L. 1997. *The Context of Scripture*, i. Leiden: E. J. Brill.

HOFFMEIER, J. K. 1997. *Israel in Egypt: The Evidence for the Authenticity of the Exodus Tradition*. New York and Oxford: Oxford University Press.

HORNUNG, E., and KEEL, O., eds. 1979. *Studien zu altägyptischen Lebenslehren*. Orbis Biblicus et Orientalis, 28. Freiburg: Universitätsverlag Freiburg; Göttingen: Vandenhoeck & Ruprecht.

KITCHEN, K. A. 1973a. Review of D. B. Redford, *A Study of the Biblical Story of Joseph*. *Oriens Antiquus*, 12: 233–42.

—— 1973b. *The Third Intermediate Period in Egypt (1100–650 BC)*. Warminster: Aris & Phillips. 2nd edn. 1986, rev. 2nd edn. 1996.

—— 1979. 'The Basic Literary Forms and Formulations of Ancient Instructional Writings in Egypt and Western Asia'. In Hornung and Keel 1979: 235–82.

—— 1998a. 'Biblical Instructional Wisdom: The Decisive Voice of the Ancient Near East'. In Lubetski *et al.* 1998: 346–63.

—— 1998b. 'Egyptians and Hebrews, from Ra'amses to Jericho'. In Ahituv and Oren 1998: 65–131.

—— 1999. *Poetry of Ancient Egypt*. Jonsered: P. Åströms Förlag.

—— 2001. 'The Shoshenqs of Egypt and Palestine'. *JSOT* 93: 3–12.

—— 2003a. 'Egyptian Interventions in the Levant in Iron Age II'. In Dever and Gitin 2003: 113–32.

—— 2003b. *On the Reliability of the Old Testament*. Grand Rapids, Mich.: Eerdmans.

LUBETSKI, M., GOTTLIEB, C., and KELLER, S., eds. 1998. *Boundaries of the Ancient Near-Eastern World: A Tribute to Cyrus H. Gordon*. JSOTS.S 273. Sheffield: Sheffield Academic Press.

RAINEY, A. F., ed. 1987. *Egypt, Israel, Sinai: Archaeological and Historical Relationships in the Biblical Period*. Tel Aviv: University of Tel Aviv Press.

REDFORD, D. B. 1970. *A Study of the Biblical Story of Joseph (Genesis 37–50)*. Supplements to *VT*, 20. Leiden: E. J. Brill.

—— 1987. 'An Egyptological Perspective on the Exodus Narrative'. In Rainey 1987: 137–61.

—— 1992. *Egypt, Canaan and Israel in Ancient Times*. Princeton: Princeton Univerity Press.

—— 1997. 'Observations on the Sojourn of the Bene-Israel'. In Frerichs and Lesko 1997: 57–66.

—— 1999. 'A Note on the Chronology of Dynasty 25 and the Inscription of Sargon II at Tang-i Var'. *Orientalia*, n.s. 68: 58–60.

RUFFLE, J. 1977. 'The Teaching of Amenemope and its Connection with the Book of Proverbs. *Tyndale Bulletin*, 28: 29–68.

THIELE, E. R. 1986. *The Mysterious Numbers of the Hebrew Kings*, 3rd edn. Grand Rapids, Mich.: Eerdmans.

VERGOTE, J. 1959. *Joseph en Égypte: Genèse chap. 37–50 à la lumière des études égyptologiques récentes*. Louvain: Publications Universitaires.

WEEKS, S. 1994. *Early Israelite Wisdom*. Oxford: Clarendon Press.

WILSON, K. A. 2001. *The Campaign of Pharaoh Shoshenq I into Palestine*. Ann Arbor: UMI.

YURCO, F. J. 1997. 'Merneptah's Canaanite Campaign and Israel's Origins'. In Frerichs and Lesko 1997: 27–55.

CHAPTER 6

QUMRAN STUDIES

PHILIP DAVIES

The importance of the scrolls from Qumran for understanding the Hebrew Bible is fairly wide-ranging and has in some respects been underestimated. If 'revolution-ize' is too strong a term, the Dead Sea Scrolls have undoubtedly provoked biblical scholarship into completely new ways of thinking about the manner in which the biblical literature originated and was, transmitted, interpreted, and canonized. In the areas of text and canon, much has been learned, and a good deal of discussion generated; in respect of Hebrew linguistics, the nature and variety of Qumran Hebrew has also been much debated, though with rather less acknowledged impact on other aspects of biblical studies. Even less, perhaps, has it been appreciated how the discovery of an ancient Jewish library itself can help us in modelling the formation and history of the biblical literature within similar scribal communities.

Another far-reaching and widely felt implication of the Scrolls for study of the Hebrew Bible, however, is for our understanding of early Judaism. The de-scription which the Qumran manuscripts offers us of a self-consciously 'elect' group, deriving from their reading of the scriptures a system of Jewish belief critical of the current religious and political leadership, and sustained by a segregated life-style, obliges us to recognize the variety of beliefs, practices, and controversies that comprise Second Temple Judaism. But what has not been generally deduced from this realization is that the scriptures themselves, in the closed canon and fixed text in which the rabbis transmitted it, do not offer a normative or even balanced account of the official religious discourse of ancient Judaism. Rather, it seems that the official scriptural canon, and the meaning and application of much of its contents, were a source of contention among Jews.

We shall look first at Qumran evidence for the 'Bible' itself relating to the emergence of a scriptural canon and the textual characteristics of its components;

then at the way in which the Qumran literature 'extends' scripture through re-writing and interpretation; and finally we shall consider the broader issues raised by the Scrolls about the nature and function of the Jewish scriptures.

CANONS AND CANON FORMATION

What are loosely termed the Qumran 'biblical' manuscripts comprise about 25 per cent of the total (about 220 out of nearly 900). However, the adjective 'biblical' with reference to Qumran manuscripts is strictly incorrect, since not only were there no 'bibles' at that time (second century BCE to first century CE), but very probably no fixed ('closed') canon of writings, or at least not one universally accepted. A number of religiously authoritative writings were, however, recognized and interpreted by the authors of the Scrolls, so that we can correctly speak of 'scriptures', and certainly of scrolls and scroll collections that would have formed an 'open' canon of writings that were regarded as definitive of Judaism—that is, of Judaism as understood by their readers; and while most of these scriptures were so regarded by all Jews, some were recognized as such only by certain Jewish groups. Among the Qumran scrolls, we can identify with some certainty both categories, but we cannot be certain of the criteria for canonical status, or of the boundaries between 'canonical' and 'non-canonical'; without a fixed canon, in fact, such boundaries were probably blurred (probably more so than in modern Protestant Bibles with their 'Apocrypha').

We cannot, then, assume that the 'scriptures' of the writers and owners of the Qumran scrolls were confined to books belonging to the Masoretic canon (the Protestant 'Old Testament'). Manuscripts of Tobit, ben Sira, various texts related to the figure of Enoch, *Jubilees*, and the *Letter of Jeremiah*, many of them still included in certain modern Christian Bibles, were also found at Qumran. In addition, it is not unlikely that such works as the *Community Rule* (S), the *Damascus Document* (D), or the *Temple Scroll* were accorded a canonical status of some kind by one or more Jewish groups. (That recently authored works could achieve a canonical status is shown by the example of the book of Daniel.)

But our main interest here is not in the 'Qumran canon' but in the Hebrew canon that eventually formed the rabbinic scriptures and (in a slightly different format) the Christian 'Old Testament'. The Hebrew Bible is divided into three categories: law, prophets, and writings, and we find some evidence of this division in the Scrolls. In the *Community Rule* (1QS) 1: 3, for example, we read 'as he [God] commanded by the hand of Moses and all His servants the prophets', with a similar conjunction of 'Moses' and 'the prophets' in other texts also. The 'law of Moses' would have comprised the books of the Torah (the Pentateuch), and among the Scrolls are fragments of three manuscripts that appear to have contained at least two consecutive Torah books, suggesting perhaps that the whole Torah may sometimes have been written on one scroll, as in later Jewish practice. The scriptures referred to as 'prophets', however, may have included books later classified as among the 'Writings' (or even not represented in the Masoretic canon at all); Daniel and Psalms, for instance, were probably treated in this way, for David is explicitly named in one text (11QCompDav) as a 'prophet', and certain Psalm passages are interpreted in Qumran commentaries called *pesharim* as predictions. In this, the Scrolls in fact partly reflect the evidence of the New Testament and of the first-century CE Jewish historian Josephus, who in his *Against Apion* includes the 'history' books and Daniel among the writings of 'prophets'. However, such a division was not necessarily definitive: in the *Halakhic Letter* (4QMMT) C11 we read: '. . . the book of Moses and the books of the prophets and of David and [the deeds of] each succeeding generation', which may suggest that, along with the Psalms, some 'historical' books, perhaps those later designated the 'Former Prophets', were recognized, by this Scroll's authors at least, as a distinct category of scriptures.

Can we deduce more precisely what writings at Qumran would have been deemed 'scriptural' and what a 'scriptural' status would have entailed? It is impossible to be very sure. If the popularity of certain writings is a clue, then we have the following works in more than ten copies at Qumran: Torah (except Numbers); Psalms, Isaiah, *Jubilees*, Enoch, S (*Community Rule*), and D (*Damascus Document*). Can we suggest that the text of canonized scrolls was less subject to variety, more 'stable'? No: Genesis and Leviticus display for the most part only slight textual variation, but Exodus and Numbers are each represented in two different versions, while Deuteronomy (with the largest number of copies) has the most fluid text of all the Mosaic books. The 'prophetic' texts show rather less stability than the Torah (as well as the Masoretic edition, the Septuagint edition of Jeremiah is also represented in its Hebrew form). There seems therefore no evidence of a concern generally to fix the texts of works regarded as scriptural (see further below). The degree of divergence in the text of any work may point, rather, to the length of period of transmission (and thus may help determine the age of composition, though this cannot be applied as a crude measure).

The use of the citation formula 'as it is written' has been suggested by several scholars as a mark of canonical status. Such formulae occur about seventy times, with reference to all the books of the Mosaic canon and also to select books within the Masoretic categories of 'Former Prophets' (Joshua, Samuel) and 'Latter Prophets' (Isaiah, Ezekiel, Hosea, Amos, Micah, Zechariah, and Malachi); also to Psalms and Proverbs. But the texts that contain such citations are actually rather few (D, S, 4QFlorilegium, 4QTestimonia, 11QMelchizedek, and 1QMilhamah), and there is also at least one such citation of a book that is *not* in the Masoretic canon

(*Damascus Document* (D) 4. 15 of a statement of Levi, son of Jacob). More significantly, the number of allusions to supposedly scriptural books *without* the use of a citation formula is also very large, and CD 16. 3–4 refers the reader to the Book of Jubilees in a way that suggests that it may have had scriptural authority. The author's predilection, the genre of the text in which the citation occurs, and perhaps the function of the citation may explain the use of a formula rather than some overt 'canonical' status.

Can we, finally, determine from the Qumran evidence works that all Jews recognized as canonical, as distinct from those so regarded only by certain groups? The use of some texts in argument with other Jews is a possible clue. Since Qumran scriptures, as we have seen, probably included works not so viewed in other Jewish communities or sects (for example, the Samaritans and Sadducees apparently regarded only the Pentateuch/Torah as canon), disputes with others could only be based on texts deemed 'scriptural' by all, or at least by those opponents who were being challenged. Of the Qumran texts possibly directed polemically to outsiders, however, only the *Damascus Document* (in part) and the *Halakhic Letter* clearly qualify. What is interesting, however, is that several prophetic books are frequently cited in D, alongside Torah. Does this tell us that Jews generally accepted these prophetic books as part of their 'canon'? Or do we infer only that those engaged by the polemics (probably Pharisees) did?

There is one interesting case in which we can see a scriptural canon in the process of being compiled. The scroll of Psalms from Cave 11 has excited particular interest because its contents (corresponding roughly to Psalms 101 onwards in the MT Psalter) parallels the MT order only approximately, and it appends some additional psalms at the end (including Psalm 151, preserved in the Septuagint). Other Psalms scrolls at Qumran have different arrangements. Thus, while *a* Psalm collection was perhaps among the scriptures of most Jews, there was perhaps no universally agreed list of contents or order, at least for the last two sections (Psalms 90 onwards).

We can therefore conclude that the notion of a scriptural canon was shared at Qumran with other Jews, and that the core of this canon included Torah, prophets, and Davidic compositions. But we cannot infer a fixed or closed canon, or confine its contents to those books included in the Hebrew Bible.

Text and Textual Criticism

Before the discovery of the Dead Sea Scrolls, our oldest Hebrew biblical manuscripts were medieval. Now, that date has been put back a millennium; we have copies of all the books now in the Jewish scriptures, except for Nehemiah and Esther; and in nearly every case we have multiple copies. While nearly all of these are written in the 'square script' of the period, a few manuscripts of Pentateuchal books use the archaic alphabet that it replaced somewhere around the neo-Babylonian or early Persian periods (sixth to fifth century BCE).

The manner in which what in retrospect we loosely term 'biblical' scrolls were transmitted, revised, glossed, and commented on suggests that our modern reverence for a canonical text as verbally sacrosanct does not apply to the writers of the Qumran scrolls. We do have, in most cases, multiple copies of each book (mostly in fragments); and here we encounter our first surprise: no two copies are exactly the same. Often the differences are minor, but sometimes not. Sometimes certain readings follow the Septuagint rather than the Masoretic Text, and indeed, we also find, as well as five manuscripts of the book of Jeremiah close to the canonized Hebrew Text, one, perhaps two, corresponding to the rather different edition represented by the Septuagint. In one remarkable case we have an entire passage now missing from 1 Samuel 10, probably accidentally lost from the canonized texts but preserved in one Qumran manuscript (4QSam^a) and now restored at v. 27 in the NRSV.

Is there any kind of pattern in the diversity of texts at Qumran? It was thought until quite recently that three local 'families' of texts, underlying the Masoretic Text (Babylonia), the Septuagint (Egypt), and a 'Palestinian' one (the Samaritan biblical text) could be identified. But the range of variation is too wide for this explanation. Although about 40 per cent of these 'biblical' manuscripts are fairly close to the Masoretic Text, a further 25 per cent show no systematic agreement with any of the three 'families'. One group (a further 25 per cent) is distinguished also by its use of fuller spellings, characteristic of many non-'biblical' Qumran manuscripts, and also by numerous errors and corrections. Some general conclusions to be drawn are as follows. (1) Many biblical books existed in differing textual versions from early on, and it is impossible (perhaps even inappropriate) to try to reconstruct an 'original' version—the original goal of many textual critics. (2) The owners of the Scrolls (and almost certainly other Jews as well) exhibited no great concern for a single authoritative text of these books. However, there is a possible qualification to this last conclusion: the text form finally fixed for each book (the Masoretic Text) was clearly widely adopted during the first century CE; the Qumran manuscripts may indicate that even in the preceding century this text form was predominating, though not in a single invariable wording.

LANGUAGE

The majority of the Scrolls are written in Hebrew, but exhibit various kinds. Naturally, the 'biblical' manuscripts reflect both standard classical Hebrew and the 'Late Biblical Hebrew' characteristic of Chronicles, Ezra, Nehemiah, and

Qoheleth. But there are also texts composed in what is often termed 'Qumran Hebrew'—for example, the *Community Rule* and *War Scroll*, while the Copper Scroll and the *Halakhic Letter* are closer to what we know later as 'rabbinic' or 'Mishnaic' Hebrew. In addition, the *Damascus Document* is written in a style imitative of classical biblical Hebrew.

How do we account for the variety? Was Qumran Hebrew a living Judaean dialect, or a purely literary language? In either case, is it to be seen as transitional between biblical and rabbinic Hebrew? To these questions there is no agreed answer, but there are clearly implications for those who wish to date biblical texts by means of linguistic criteria. It is now thought possible that Hebrew did not entirely give way to Aramaic during the Second Temple period; that linguistic variation may have a class or regional basis rather than a purely chronological one; and that a tradition of writing in classical Hebrew persisted well into the Graeco-Roman period. At any rate, the clear evidence of different forms of Hebrew written contemporaneously raises the same possibility for earlier periods also, thus complicating any linguistic criteria for dating biblical writings.

Text and Interpretation as a Continuum

As has often been remarked, virtually *all* of the Qumran texts are to some extent derived from, or inspired by, scripture. The Qumran scrolls also demonstrate the way in which scriptural texts interpret each other and even develop themselves through a kind of 'internal' interpretation (see Fishbane 1985). The formal separation of 'text' and 'commentary' with which moderns are familiar does not readily apply to the period before both canon and text were fixed. Before this act of 'freezing' the canon's form and content, biblical texts were not merely copied and recopied, but in the copying process were also adapted, enlarged, and edited, as a kind of ongoing interpretative exercise. At Qumran we find this process extended beyond the texts themselves to embrace paraphrased books and passages, excerpts, forming a continuum with the biblical manuscripts themselves. Compositions like the *Damascus Document* or the *Hodayoth* offer another model: they are so permeated with scriptural language that quotation, allusion, and paraphrase are often impossible to disentangle.

Quite apart from three targums (two on Job, one on Leviticus), we have as examples of 'rewritten Bible' the *Genesis Apocryphon* and *Jubilees*, 4Q123 and 4Q364–7; excerpted passages comprise not only *tefillin* and *mezuzoth* but other anthologies, such as 4QTestimonia or 4Q252. Some of these join texts to form a kind of theme or plot, and include a linking commentary (4QFlorilegium, 11QMelchizedek, 4Q364–7). There are also numerous other paraphrases, halakoth (religious laws) consisting of reordered biblical laws (11QTemple, 4QOrdinances); at the other end of the spectrum are texts or passages that are permeated with scriptural language and allusions without making explicit citations. Finally, there are also formal commentaries (i.e. *pesharim*), in which scriptural text and comment are separated. We are clearly dealing with authors who were not only familiar with the scriptural texts, but had inherited and developed a variety of ways in which these texts were presented, represented, interpreted, and applied, and undoubtedly the ways in which scriptures were used here represent a wider pattern of Jewish hermeneutics.

Schools, Archives, Libraries

It has long been recognized that the contents of the Hebrew Bible were composed, edited, and transmitted within communities of literate individuals, mostly employed in the service of court or temple. These 'scribes' (or 'wise': *sopherim* or *hakamim*) were the public 'intellectuals' of their societies, responsible for the creation and preservation of *literary* documentation, such as annals, myths, laws, liturgies, oracular collections, and whatever else served the functioning of the state apparatus. Such scribal communities almost certainly centred their activities in schools, which served as a matrix for both teaching and 'research'; and for both purposes libraries were indispensable. The scrolls in these libraries were both the resource and the product of the activity of such schools.

But until the discovery of the Qumran scrolls, physical evidence of the literary activity of such communities was lacking. Indeed, we cannot be sure whether the Qumran scrolls represent the library of a single community (and whether such a community was in fact based at Qumran), or a collection of libraries stored for safe keeping in a remote location. But the contents correspond perfectly to what we would expect a learned community to possess, copy, and compose: documents that belonged to what we might call the national 'canon' alongside those of more relevance to the particular character of the community/communities. The existence of multiple copies also shows us simultaneous signs of ongoing editing; and so, while we can only speculate about or infer biblical sources and 'redactions', in the Scrolls we can see this process taking place. Different manuscripts of, for example, the *Community Rule* and the *War Scroll* illustrate how these texts went through several editions, and perhaps never achieved any 'definitive' form. As a model for the process by which the biblical literature took its shape, the Qumran library or libraries and the associated communities provide a very important resource.

IDEOLOGICAL CONFLICT AND THE HEBREW BIBLE

It is common to refer to the writers of the Qumran scrolls as 'sectarians'; but this term implies a kind of normativity beyond the boundaries of this 'sect'. If, of course, the sect is identified with 'Essenes', as is common, then the writers were no more (or less) sectarian than Sadducees or Pharisees, whom Josephus describes in the same terms. The Qumran scrolls in fact show us how a core of basic concepts was consistently read and interpreted in the light of the values of a group that saw itself as the true continuation of the real, historical 'Israel'. (We can see a parallel process in the New Testament.)

The modern scholar can perceive, however, that the Qumran writings do not draw exclusively on categories and ideas prominent in the Hebrew Bible. Alongside the 'law of Moses' and the writings of the prophets, we find religious traditions from elsewhere, and in particular from the books of Enoch. This dependence has led some scholars to speak even of an 'Enochic Judaism' from which the writers of the Scrolls were descended. In this 'Judaism', emphasis rests on the figure of Enoch and the divine wisdom he received, from his heavenly journey, his understanding of astrology and meteorology, and his knowledge of the past and future. The books of Enoch (better known to us as I or 'Ethiopic' Enoch, but now known at Qumran as four or five separate compositions, originally in Hebrew) provide the Qumran authors with a myth of fallen angels as the origin of evil, a 'solar' calendar of 364 days, not of twelve lunar months (about 354 days), a tradition of a final judgement of all creation, and an interest in the names, identity, and function of numerous heavenly beings. In particular, 'Enochic Judaism' espouses a pessimistic view of Israel's history, one of almost continuous evil and rebellion, from which only the elect will be released at the end of time.

Against this 'sectarian' view, should the literature of the Hebrew Bible be seen as a more universal, 'normative' canon? To an extent, perhaps: but there is also evidence that many of these Enochic traditions have been suppressed, especially in the book of Genesis, where Enoch himself and the story of the angelic fall are brutally truncated. The belief that Israel's sin and punishment continue also surfaces in Daniel 9, and the angelic origin of sin in the ritual of the scapegoat (Leviticus 16) 'for Azazel' (one of the names of the leader of the fallen angels). The large number of texts at Qumran in which Genesis is 'rewritten' show a concern to revise its view of the origin and nature of sin as disobedience to God's commands, and refocus attention on its heavenly origin and the final judgement that will remove it for ever, just as the Flood once destroyed the offspring and the followers of the fallen angels.

The influence of Enoch traditions is evident also in the New Testament and early Christianity (Satan is one such instance, the fallen angel, the 'Belial' of the Qumran scrolls), and we are forced to ask whether it is correct to regard the Hebrew Bible as a reliable or normative source for 'Jewish belief' prior to the fall of the Temple in 70 CE. Two considerations (among others) prompt this suspicion. First, the view prevailing before the discoveries at Qumran of a 'normative' and relatively homogeneous Judaism during the Second Temple period has now been abandoned, largely thanks to the Scrolls, which clearly betray a set of ideological conflicts that seem to have fairly ancient origins. Many passages in the prophetic literature (especially in Malachi, Zechariah, and Isaiah 56–66) that express protest against the rulers and priests of Jerusalem may well represent organized or identifiable groups, possibly connected with antecedents of the movement(s) that generated the Qumran scrolls. Second, the canonical view, often repeated in modern histories of Israel, that there was a 'restoration' of a 'remnant' under the Persians is challenged throughout the Scrolls, which see their present time as still one of 'exile' and reject the legitimacy of the priesthood, the Temple, and indeed of the rest of 'Israel'. It follows that we must consider the Hebrew Bible itself as implicated in the conflicts that still engaged most Palestinian Jews at the end of the Second Temple period, and consider the act of fixing the canon and text in the light of such disputes. The relative insignificance of Enoch and Enochic traditions in Genesis, for example, may indicate a deliberate suppression of tradition that we know from other sources to have been prominent in Second Temple Judaism. The Scrolls, in other words, permit us to ask more pointedly about the social and political context in which the Hebrew Bible was formed from a once more varied set of canonized writings within Judaism.

BIBLIOGRAPHY

CAMPBELL, J. G. 2002. *Deciphering the Dead Sea Scrolls*, 2nd edn. Oxford: Blackwell.

DAVIES, P. R., BROOKE, G. J., and CALLAWAY, P. R. 2002. *The Complete World of the Dead Sea Scrolls*. London: Thames and Hudson.

—— 2003. 'Biblical Interpretation in the Dead Sea Scrolls'. In A. J. Hauser and D. F. Watson, eds., *A History of Biblical Interpretation*, Grand Rapids, Mich.: Eerdmans, 144–66.

FISHBANE, M. 1985. *Biblical Interpretation in Ancient Israel*. Oxford: Clarendon Press.

QIMRON, E. 2000. 'The Nature of DSS Hebrew and its Relation to BH and MH.' In T. Muraoka and J. F. Elwolde, eds., *Diggers at the Well: Proceedings of a Third International Symposium on the Hebrew of the Dead Sea Scrolls and Ben Sira*, Leiden: Brill, 232–44.

VANDERKAM, J. C. 1994. *The Dead Sea Scrolls Today*. Grand Rapids, Mich.: Eerdmans; London: SPCK.

CHAPTER 7

STUDY OF THE GRAECO-ROMAN WORLD

PETER RICHARDSON

1. INTRODUCTION

Classical language, rhetoric, philosophy, and culture have had a continuing impact on study of the Bible since antiquity. When Tertullian (c.160–225 CE) asked, 'What has Athens to do with Jerusalem?', he anticipated the ambivalent relationship between the classical and biblical worlds. Though he had a good classical education and used its tools, he was suspicious of their effect on scripture. The rise of formal biblical scholarship during the Renaissance set the study of the Bible firmly and naturally within the humanist and intellectual context of the study of the Graeco-Roman world. The development of critical biblical studies in the nineteenth and early twentieth centuries triggered another major leap in the importance of classical study upon biblical studies, for virtually all scholars of theology and biblical studies then had deep classical roots. Greek and Roman languages, literatures, and histories directly and indirectly informed the study of the Bible. The influence of those worlds on biblical studies declined in the mid-twentieth century as the balance shifted from the study of theology to the study of religion. In recent years, new approaches to the study of the Bible have prompted a vigorous return to investigations of the riches of Greece and Rome.

2. Language, Literature, and Rhetoric

Language

The earliest and most direct influence of classical studies was the study of Greek. No monument to that influence is more visible than the great lexicon known as Liddell, Scott, Jones (LSJ). It was the cumulative result of three centuries of gathering and publishing documents, preparing accurate critical editions, studying the language's grammar, syntax, and semantic principles. Biblical scholars produced their own tools alongside these works, focused on the *Koinē* ('common') Greek, which underlies the New Testament, such as Moulton and Milligan's *Vocabulary of the Greek New Testament* (as it is usually known). The standard lexicon has come to be Walter Bauer's revision of Erwin Preuschen's German work, turned into English and fully revised by Arndt and Gingrich and, more recently, Danker (2000). LSJ's monumental work, however, remains a fundamental resource for the Greek language.

Along with Moulton and Milligan, Adolf Deissman (1927) in Germany demonstrated that *Koinē* Greek had its own integrity and character, and should not be seen either as 'barbaric' or as 'Holy Spirit' Greek. *Koinē* was the language of Alexander and his army, as it was of trade and commerce; it was the everyday language of Greek speakers around and within Palestine, in coastal cities and the Decapolis, and it was common even in Jerusalem burial inscriptions. It was the language of the early Christian world, the New Testament, much of the intertestamental literature, and several early translations of the Hebrew Bible (the Septuagint, and later, Aquila, Theodotion, and Symmachus).

By comparison, the influence of the study of Latin on biblical studies has been more limited. The use of Latin was largely confined to Rome, Italy, the western Mediterranean, and North Africa; it had only a small foothold in the Levant, where Beirut was one of the few eastern Roman colonies to use Latin in inscriptions. Latin's influence has been felt in three less significant areas: first, as a language into which the Bible was translated early on (Old Latin, Jerome, and the Vulgate); second, as the language of many early Christian exegetical and expository works, particularly from North Africa (Tertullian and Cyprian, for example); and third, as the language of the Roman church and Roman bishops, beginning in the late second century CE.

Literature

The study of classical literature has shed light on the understanding of biblical authors' methods, goals, structures, allusions, models, and influences. Though the categories usually used of biblical literature do not coincide with classical categories, the study of literary genres has been increasingly influential in the last two generations. Letters, histories, novels, biographies, and apologies have attracted substantial attention from scholars of Christian origins, who have explicitly acknowledged their obligations to the earlier classical work. For example, study of the form and function of Paul's letters could not have developed so quickly without earlier work on ancient Greek letters. Even though the question of genres in Greek and Latin literature is a still controversial topic, biblical scholars seem to make genre distinctions more comfortably than their colleagues.

Rhetoric

Greek and Latin rhetoric—the art of public speaking—has been profitably applied to the study of both Old and New Testaments, especially in the last two decades, though its roots are earlier. Most influential have been rhetorical works, especially handbooks, of Aristotle, Dionysius, Quintillian, and Cicero. The study of rhetoric has been used effectively to understand the composition of many kinds of early Christian literature, especially letters, homilies, and their sub-units. Different types of rhetoric (forensic, deliberative, demonstrative) have been used as templates for various pieces of literature, and the different sections of a speech (exordium, statement of facts, proof, refutation, for example) have become influential in the study of similar forms within biblical literature. Students of rhetoric in the ancient world made declamations in various literary forms (*chreia* or moral anecdote, *mythos* or fable, *gnōmē* or pithy maxim, for example), which have also been utilized in interpreting biblical forms.

3. HISTORY, POLITICS, LAW, AND ECONOMY

History

Since biblical literature is inextricably bound up with history, classical literature's parallel interests have naturally been applied to biblical history. The histories intersect, so the connections between the disciplines have been strong, making it impossible to work on biblical history without at the same time being familiar with the questions, methods, and conclusions of classical historians. The Bible is rather laconic in providing a chronologically clear framework; the study of biblical history, particularly from the Persian period on, depends substantially on a framework supplied by Greek and Roman historians and refined by classical scholars. Historians such as Herodotus (Persian period), Quintus Curtius Rufus (Alexandrian period), Appian (Civil Wars), Suetonius and Tacitus (early Imperial period) are vitally important for biblical history.

Relevant to biblical study are such matters as Greek city-states, Greek expansionism, Alexander and his conquests, the Diadochoi and the subsequent empires that impinge on the biblical regions (especially the Seleucids and Ptolemies), the rise of Rome and Roman expansion, Roman civil unrest and strife, Imperial developments from Augustus onwards, provincial acquisitions, Rome's dealings with Parthia and other states in the region. Classical investigations into Roman borders and boundaries (*limēs*), the roles and organization of the army, and persons who appear within biblical history have also influenced the course of biblical studies.

Josephus is a special case, studied by both classicists and biblical scholars. He wrote about Judaism as a Jew (under the patronage of Vespasian, Titus, and Domitian) but within a Roman Imperial setting, drawing on Roman, Greek, and Jewish authorities. In many cases, we owe what we know about Jewish events and dates and even people, especially in the first century BCE and the first century CE, to Josephus. Some points of intersection are of considerable significance for the Bible: the Hasmonaean Revolt and its aftermath, the careers of the various members of the Herodian dynasty, the census under Quirinius, and the Jewish Revolt, to mention just a few. While Josephus is only tangentially within the purview of classical scholars, partly because his writings were preserved by the early church, his work is fundamentally important for the history of the relevant periods, not to mention other issues such as Roman Imperial administration, biography, apologies, historiography, and hermeneutics.

Civic and Political Institutions

Classical analyses of Greek and Roman civic organization and institutions are directly relevant to the related institutional features of biblical life: studies of the *polis* ('city') and the forms it took in the East, on the one hand, and the importance of the *colonia* ('colony'), on the other. This is true of the provincial organizations of Persian, Seleucid, and Ptolemaic empires, and also of Roman provincial institutions. Since biblical events took place within the context of the Graeco-Roman world, the comparative materials which classicists bring to bear on events and issues are often essential for adequate understandings. For example, the division of Herod's kingdom and the subsequent alterations in that tripartite arrangement, the situation at the time of Jesus' execution, and the events leading up to the Jewish Revolt ultimately depend on knowing about the Roman political system in a minor province such as Judaea.

The large-scale organization of Graeco-Roman society (slavery, social status, roles of women) as well as its small-scale features (imported cults, roles and significance of healing centres) has formed the bedrock of similar studies by biblical scholars. Local voluntary associations, for example, have become important in studies of the organization of Jewish and Christian communities, especially in regions outside Palestine/Judaea.

Economy and Trade

The central and long-recognized importance of trade and commerce in the early Roman period took time to seep into biblical studies. It has influenced interpretations of the rise of Christianity and developments within Judaism in the same periods. The Augustan *pax romana* opened up or modified trade and transportation routes, which in turn affected the Jewish state and its neighbours, especially under Herod the Great, for whom development of the economy was important. When Christianity was emerging from Judaism, its earliest expansionary moves were to cities and regions that were developing as commercial centres and that had significant Jewish communities, such as Caesarea Maritima, Antioch, Ephesus, Corinth, and Alexandria. An appreciation of the dynamic growth of Judaism and Christianity—and their interplay—depends in part on how the economy was organized, trade encouraged, and professions incorporated into the local economies.

Law

Biblical studies of law (*torah, nomos*), whether Jewish or Christian, are less directly dependent upon classical scholarship than might be true of other sub-areas treated in this chapter. While Greek and Roman law are compared for the light they shed on each other, they have not much influenced the study of *Torah*. Discussions of biblical law, within both Israelite and Second Temple Judaism, have tended to be cast, understandably, within the context of other ancient Near Eastern bodies of law. Ancient writers on Judaism's law within the context of Roman culture, such as Philo and Josephus (both in a Diaspora context), have shown a considerable concern for understanding that *Torah* within a Roman or Greek context. Legal studies in the early rabbinic period, when the *Mishnah* and *Tosefta* were compiled, have tended to be less concerned with this issue.

Nevertheless, specific aspects of Roman law have had a direct bearing on interpretation of biblical literature. Given that one of the prime duties of public officials was maintenance of public order, the application of their powers could be extensive. How did they exercise their powers with respect to individuals and groups? What criminal procedures were used? What were the rights of citizens and resident aliens? What limitations were there on penal practices? How were criminals executed? In some cases, understanding Roman law results in calling into question the accuracy of early Christian accounts. Representative issues include the degree to which Rome gave Judaism, especially in the Diaspora, special status, as Josephus claims; the legal position of Christianity in the Roman state; the extent of Roman persecution of fledgling Christianity; the grounds on which Christians were executed; the frequency of 'martyrdoms'; and public attitudes to 'games' in the amphitheatres of the Roman world.

4. Philosophy and Religion

Philosophy

Studies of Greek and Roman philosophical schools shed light on biblical intellectual developments. Since philosophy is enquiry into the principles of reality and its ultimacy, it was natural for Jews such as Philo to refer to Judaism as philosophy. Josephus likened Jewish groups to philosophical schools, a tendency that still continues. Paul was compared to Stoics long ago; the most recent in a long line is a comparison of the early Jesus movement with Cynicism. It is common to depend on the formative philosophical studies of classical scholars to provide the insights against which the relevant biblical material is examined. Some documents of Judaism and Christianity can be fruitfully understood within a framework provided by the philosophical schools and their literary products: in the early Christian period, with Cynic–Stoic materials, with Middle Platonism, and with Neoplatonism.

Religion

Greek religion, and Roman religion following its lead, was tolerant of worship of a wide range of deities, including deities foreign to Graeco-Roman cultures, such as Isis or Mithra or the God of Israel. Worship of the Olympian deities did not ordinarily create much sense of a personal relationship with the god, though study of Greek and Roman religion has clarified the wide range of attachments possible. Except in general ways, investigation of Olympian religion has not influenced understandings of biblical religion very deeply. Three subsets of issues, however, have had a strong impact on biblical scholarship: mystery religions, new religions, and ruler cults. Ruler cults were particularly strong in the Greek East, in settings such as Macedonia, Persia, Pergamon, the Seleucid empire, and the Ptolemaic empire. Their features and challenges are essential elements in the interpretation of the Bible, influencing study of Hellenistic civilization in the Levant, perceived threats to the worship of Judaism, the rise of synagogues in Egypt, the setting of Paul, and the early church's spread. The Roman Imperial cult—worship of the Emperor alongside the goddess Roma, which Augustus allowed albeit without enthusiasm—advanced vigorously in areas where early Christianity first spread. It represented an important choice that early Christians had to make. Among the earliest competitors of belief in Jesus were such new religions as the worship of Mithra from Iran and the worship of Isis from Egypt, along with others such as Cybele from Phrygia in Asia Minor. Classical scholars have provided stunning amounts of detail in the last quarter-century, and some features of their cultic practices have had important effects on the conceptualizing of early Christianity. The cults of Dionysos and Demeter (and Kore) were ancient mystery religions with long histories and deep attractiveness. They have been less effectively examined and applied to the Bible, partly because their initiation rites were so important, and there were such severe penalties for revealing their secrets that almost no information has come down about their activities. All three sub-fields—mystery religions, new religions, and Imperial religion—had footholds in Palestine: Samaria/Sebaste, Sepphoris, Beth Shean, Caesarea Maritima, and Panias.

Oracles, Miracles, and Magic

Oracular cult sites, particularly those associated with Apollo (e.g. Delphi, Klaros, Didyma), offered more personalized ways of hearing the god's voice and applying it in one's own personal circumstances. Numerous inscriptions at the various sites have provided insight into just how important socially and politically and religiously oracles were. The same is true of healing activities associated with cult sites dedicated especially to Asklepios; again, inscriptions and artefacts show the deeply held convictions with which worshippers came to an Asklepieion and recorded their thanks for healing received. These too might be found in Palestine for example, in Kedesh and in Jerusalem. Someone who could influence healing, through magic spells or incantations or secret symbols, was, in the Graeco-Roman world, often thought of as a holy man, *theios anēr*, a directly relevant ancient religious model for interpreting Jesus and Paul, or even Moses.

Greek and Roman religion has had a substantial impact on the ways in which both Judaism and Christianity have been viewed, including such aspects as initiation, salvation, resurrection, healing, prophecy, dream interpretation, communal life, worship, settings for worship, and many more.

5. SCIENCE AND GEOGRAPHY

With colonization, trade, travel, and exploration came a curiosity about the world, which had a substantial impact in the literature of both Greece and Rome. Homer, Hesiod, Scylax, Hecataeus, Pythias, and others, gave rise to a mathematically based understanding of a spherical world that contrasted sharply with the prevailing biblical view, but which was absorbed into Roman views of their domination of the Mediterranean world. This was one aspect of diverse scientific interests, such as water management, military implements, materials and methods of construction, astronomy, botany, anatomy, medicine, physics, and so on.

Though Graeco-Roman scientific work has not affected study of the Bible as much as it might, one group of writers is important for illuminating the biblical world: Strabo, Pliny the Elder, Pliny the Younger, and Pausanias. Pausanias's descriptions of sites in Greece and elsewhere have—in conjunction with archaeological investiga-tions—transformed scholars' approach to cities, such as Corinth or Athens. Strabo's accounts of the lands, cities, and peoples of Asia, Syria, Arabia, among others, have been called the world's first ethnographic writings. His accounts—sometimes enli-vened with ethnographic tidbits—of the living habits of small groups have sharpened the reading of other sources, not least the Bible. By contrast, Pliny the Elder was most concerned with the natural world, providing a mine of information about ancient materials, plants, and animals. His nephew, Pliny the Younger, largely bypassed the natural history interests of his more learned uncle, but he has left a collection of literary letters that reveal much about Roman society.

6. CULTURE, ANTHROPOLOGY, ARCHITECTURE, AND ARCHAEOLOGY

Material Culture and Archaeology

Study of Greek and Roman antiquities, and the collecting of those antiquities, began before similar biblical activity. Works of art were collected: first sculpture and then painting, pottery, and architecture. In some notorious cases, zeal for collecting resulted in large structures or parts of structures (the Elgin Marbles, Pergamon's Altar of Zeus) being removed to European museums. Subsequent archaeological investigations into the material culture of Rome, Greece, Cyprus, the Ionian coastline of Asia Minor, and the Levant has since proceeded along lines more or less parallel to Near Eastern or biblical research. From the vast accumulation of classical data has come a good grasp of urban and rural developments, religious and social life, housing, entertainment, infrastructure, and civic organization. Particular benefits have accrued in examining the immediate contexts of Paul and other early Christians in the regions around the Aegean Sea and in Italy and Rome, but they include other areas, such as Syria, Italy, and North Africa. Biblical scholars working with material culture draw extensively from related classical evidence and the questions that prompt the accumulation of that evidence. In many areas of investigation—housing forms, temples, painting and sculpture, pottery, for example—Graeco-Roman analyses pre-dated equivalent biblical analyses.

Investigations of specific cities—Rome, Ephesus, Pergamon, Miletus, Priene, Corinth, Athens, all are relevant—are models for similar investigations of biblical sites, though only rarely have biblical cities become as well understood. That said, it should be noted that rural agrarian towns and villages have attracted more serious attention in the biblical field than the classical.

Papyri and Inscriptions

The data accumulated in collections of epigraphic texts (inscriptions written on stone or metal or pottery) that have emerged from excavations and chance finds in the Graeco-Roman world have changed modern understandings of ancient society. Immensely useful collections of inscriptions and papyri have altered our views of ancient patronage, civic life, contracts, treaties, death and burial, roads and travel, military affairs, and numerous other details of daily life, religion, business, and government. While the earliest collections of such materials long pre-date the modern period (Josephus already included such material in his works), the advances from the Renaissance on have been immense. Collections include:

- *Aegyptische Urkunden aus den Königlichen Museen zu Berlin, Griechische Urkunden* (*BGU*).
- *Corpus inscriptionum latinarum* (*CIL*)
- *Corpus inscriptionum iudaicarum* (*CIJ*)
- *Corpus papyrorum iudaicarum* (*CPJ*)
- *Inscriptiones latinae selectae* (*ILS*)
- *Orientis graeci inscriptiones selectae* (*OGIS*)
- *Supplementum epigraphicum graecum* (*SEG*)

Papyrology, which studies texts written on papyrus, and sometimes related materials such as parchment and wood, has emerged from work in the arid regions of Egypt and the Near East, where papyri documents sometimes survive (the earliest

Greek papyrus from Egypt was excavated from the Villa dei Pisoni at Herculaneum in 1752–4). Like epigraphs, papyri reflect the concerns of daily life: contracts, private letters, wills, receipts, contracts, lawsuits, petitions, and the like. The Oxyrhynchus papyri are the most famous Graeco-Roman papyri bearing directly on biblical studies, with fragments of biblical and extra-canonical works. Other collections, such as the Nag Hammadi documents, which reflect the life and practices of a gnostic group in Egypt, or the Dead Sea Scrolls, which reflect a monastic group at Qumran, are usually the province of Near Eastern and biblical scholars. The techniques of investigation and interpretation, however, are common to both.

Architecture

The major monuments of Greece and Rome reflect their cultures directly. Their study has helped to give built form to biblical periods and cultures, not only where they naturally impinge on one another, such as in the Decapolis or coastal cities that envelop Palestine, but in details and decorative influences. Interpreting religion or urban life or burial practices in Judaism or early Christianity depends upon related studies in the Graeco-Roman world. Synagogue developments, for example, can best be understood through examining buildings for voluntary associations. The Temple in Jerusalem may be viewed against the background of Roman *stoas*, basilicas, and *temenoi*. Gymnasia (as in Jerusalem in the Seleucid period) or baths (in the early Roman period) cannot be appreciated apart from the prototypical Graeco-Roman institutions. Such building types as the stadium, hippodrome, theatre, and *xystos* were introduced into Jewish areas thought to be inimical to such developments, sometimes with relatively little conflict.

Greek and Roman urban design was influential, particularly such developments as the gridiron plan. Some features, such as colonnaded streets, began in the Levant and were exported to the wider Mediterranean world. When the influences were being felt most publicly and strongly (first century BCE to second century CE), they came from Rome. Markets, *nymphaea*, streets, and public buildings all had Roman roots. These Graeco-Roman approaches influenced even local design at the level of small villages.

Culture and Society

Other features of the Graeco-Roman world, involving work and trades, travel, commerce, inns, and other accommodations, have been more extensively studied than their counterparts in biblical society. Studies of literacy in the biblical world likewise draw on studies of Graeco-Roman literacy. Other important Mediterranean social markers depend on Greek and Roman studies: roles of women and the variations in those roles; honour and shame in matters of family life, sexuality, and gender relations; marriage, divorce, infanticide, and education; social status and patronal relations, including slaves, freedmen, and citizens; dress and clothing; brigandage, piracy, revolution, and resistance to imposed authority. The list of influential cultural features and their study is long. It is not the case that classical scholars were always active first, but it is clear that the impact of studies of the Graeco-Roman world is deep and growing deeper. The biblical world was a part of a much larger Mediterranean world that was dominated by the civilizations of Greece and Rome. The importance of its study for biblical studies has increased, not diminished.

7. CONCLUSION

Examinations of the Graeco-Roman and biblical worlds have a symbiotic relationship with each other. They cannot be conducted in isolation. Classical scholars often work with texts and languages rooted in the Levant, while biblical scholars work in the languages and cultures of Greece and Rome, using the tools and the refined questions that have naturally emerged. The study of the Graeco-Roman world's impact on biblical studies is stronger at the beginning of the twenty-first century than it has been for a century, though the linguistic and literary tools for appreciating that impact, regrettably, have diminished in importance within biblical studies.

SUGGESTED READING

Among recent works that have applied the resources of the Graeco-Roman world to biblical study from a variety of perspectives are the following.

BALCH, D. 1989. *The New Testament in its Social Environment*. Philadelphia: Westminster/ John Knox.
HORSLEY, R. A. 1997. *Paul and Empire: Religion and Power in Roman Imperial Society*. Harrisburg, Pa.: Trinity.
JEFFERS, J. S. 1999. *The Greco-Roman World of the New Testament Era*. Downers Grove, Ill.: InterVarsity Press.

KENNEDY, G. 1972. *The Art of Rhetoric in the Roman World*. Princeton: Princeton University Press.

LINTOTT, A. 1993. *Imperium Romanum, Politics and Administration*. London and New York: Routledge.

MACMULLEN, R. 1974. *Roman Social Relations*. New Haven: Yale University Press.

MILLAR, F. 1993. *The Roman Near East, 31 BC–AD 337*. Cambridge, Mass.: Harvard University Press.

PRICE, S. R. F. 1984. *Rituals and Power: The Roman Imperial Cult in Asia Minor*. Cambridge: Cambridge University Press.

RICHARDSON, P. 1999. *Herod, King of the Jews and Friend of the Romans*. Minneapolis: Fortress.

BIBLIOGRAPHY

BAUER, W., ARNDT, W. F., and GINGRICH, F. W. 2000 [1957]. *A Greek–English Lexicon of the New Testament and Other Early Christian Literature*, rev. F. W. Danker. Chicago: University of Chicago Press.

BGU: 1895–1912, *Aegyptische Urkunden aus den Königlichen Museen zu Berlin, Griechische Urkunden*, Berlin: Weidman (CIJ).

CIL: 1862– . *Corpus inscriptionum latinarum*. Berlin.

CIJ: FREY, J. B. 1936–52. *Corpus inscriptionum iudaicarum*. Vatican City: Pontificio istituto di archeologia cristiana.

CPJ: TCHERIKOVER, VICTOR A. 1957–64. *Corpus papyrorum iudaicarum*. Cambridge, Mass.: Harvard University Press.

DEISSMAN, ADOLF. 1927. *Light from the Ancient East: The New Testament Illustrated by Recently Discovered Texts of the Graeco-Roman World*. London: Hodder & Stoughton.

ILS: DESSAU, H. 1892–1916. *Inscriptiones latinae selectae*. Berlin.

LIDDELL, H. G., SCOTT, R., and JONES, H. S. 1940 [1843]. *A Greek–English Lexicon*. Oxford: Clarendon Press, numerous editions.

MOULTON, J. H., and MILLIGAN, G. 1914–30 [1949]. *Vocabulary of the Greek New Testament Illustrated from the Papyri and other Non-literary Sources*. Repr. Grand Rapids, Mich.: Eerdmans.

OGIS: DITTENBERGER, W. 1903–5. *Orientis graeci inscriptiones selectae*. Leipzig: Herzel.

SEG: 1923– . *Supplementum epigraphicum graecum*, Lugduni Batavorum apud A. W. Sijthoff. Leiden: J. J. E. Hondius.

CHAPTER 8

DIASPORA AND RABBINIC JUDAISM

CATHERINE HEZSER

The study of the history, literature, and religious beliefs and practices of ancient Jews in the Land of Israel and the Diaspora provides the proper background and context for the study of the later books of the Hebrew Bible, the Apocrypha and Pseudepigrapha, and the New Testament writings. From the time of the Babylonian exile, and especially from Hellenistic times onwards, a vibrant Jewish Diaspora existed alongside the Jewish community in the Land of Israel (see Barclay 1996; Rutgers 1995 and 1998; Isaac and Oppenheimer 1996). During the time of the Second Temple (520 BCE to 70 CE) and throughout rabbinic times Israel nevertheless remained the centre of world Jewry (cf. Gafni 1997). The books of the Hebrew Bible and the Apocrypha and Pseudepigrapha were written by Jews who lived in the Diaspora or the Land of Israel; the books of the New Testament were written by Jewish and Gentile Christians in various Diaspora locations which also had Jewish communities. Thus the direct experience of Jewish life or the indirect knowledge of and interaction with Jews would have had an impact on the literature which the biblical authors created.

The significance and canonization of the Hebrew Bible was crucial for the development of both rabbinic Judaism and early Christianity. In the first centuries CE both of these movements emerged as inheritors and interpreters of the biblical tradition. Their partly similar and partly different interpretations led to analogous phenomena as well as to disputes, animosities, and competition. Besides the Bible, the Graeco-Roman cultural tradition had a major impact on both rabbinic Judaism and early Christianity. Again, similarities as well as differences in the respective adaptation of this tradition can be observed. Since both ancient Judaism and early Christianity were influenced by the Bible on the one hand and by Graeco-Roman culture on the other, analogies in the usage of certain literary forms and artistic symbols, in the development of institutions and offices, and the evolution of prayer and liturgy occurred.

These analogies have to be examined in their respective historical, literary, and cultural contexts. They may be due to partly similar, yet also partly different, adaptations of earlier biblical and/or Graeco-Roman prototypes rather than to direct influence of Diaspora or rabbinic Judaism on early Christianity, or vice versa. The critical examination of the partly similar and partly different ways in which early Judaism and Christianity evolved out of their common biblical heritage and Hellenistic and Roman cultural environment constitutes a challenge and opportunity for scholars today.

1. The Significance of the Torah in Ancient Judaism

From the time after the Babylonian exile onwards, and especially in Second Temple times, written ancestral traditions, which were eventually collected and canonized as the Torah, Writings, and Prophets which make up the Hebrew Bible (Tanakh), increasingly gained in importance as holy scriptures and symbols of Jewish identity. One may assume that even those Jews who were illiterate or barely literate and could not read and study the Torah themselves had a notion of the Torah as part of their national religious heritage. This notion did not turn ancient Jews into a 'textual community' or warrant calling Judaism a 'religion of the book'. Only a small minority of male experts were able to read and interpret the Holy Scriptures. Nevertheless, the sacred writings would form the core of Jewish ideology in the late Second Temple period, on which the various Jewish groups would base their claims of religious truth and authority (see Baumgarten 1997; Cohen 1987). With the Torah's increase in significance, the role of the various Torah experts expanded as well.

One may assume that in Second Temple times the Temple scribes who were responsible for the writing and maintenance of the holy scrolls were seen, and considered themselves, to be experts in Torah interpretation. In addition, the group of the Pharisees emerged, who emphasized the significance of Torah study along-side Temple worship as a means of democratizing the Jewish religion. The sources about the scribes and Pharisees transmitted in the New Testament, Josephus's writings, and rabbinic literature are sparse, biased, and partly contradictory, so that a clear picture of these groups cannot be gained any more, but their dedication to the Torah is obvious (see Schäfer 1991). Once the ancestral traditions had gained a broad symbolic and ideological value amongst the masses, religious and political leaders could use them to gain and maintain their power. Not only the Pharisees, but also the leaders of the rebel movements in the First Jewish Revolt, were aware of the high value of the Torah in people's consciousness and tried to legitimize their actions by presenting themselves as defenders of the holy books (see Thatcher 1998: 134–6). Roman officials' destruction of Torah scrolls led to mass riots and popular opposition to the Roman occupation of the land (cf. Josephus, BJ. 2. 12. 2).

Although many of the early post-70 rabbis may have been of Pharisaic origin, the rabbinic movement was not the direct continuation of Pharisaism (see Cohen 1984: 36–42). It was not a sect which distinguished itself from other, competitive groupings within Jewish society, but a network of geographically dispersed, like-minded Torah scholars who tried to convince their co-religionists of the truth and validity of their teachings and practice. Rabbis did not function as formal communal leaders with institutional authority. They should rather be seen as informal teachers, legal experts, and moral advisors, whose authority was based on their personal Torah knowledge and skills of persuasion (see Hezser 1997: 185–239). They saw themselves as an intellectual élite and claimed a monopoly on the interpretation of the holy writings and their application to everyday life situations. One of the characteristics of rabbinic teaching in general, and midrash exegesis in particular, is the pluralism of diverse interpretations and derivations based on the basic indeterminacy of the biblical text (see Handelman 1982; Faur 1986).

The biblical canon was not fixed by rabbis at Yavneh, as is traditionally assumed (see Lewis 1964; Schäfer 1975; Stemberger 1977; Beckwith 1988; Leiman 1991). This traditional assumption is usually connected with the belief that rabbis developed a Jewish orthodoxy which declared certain beliefs and practices canonical and tried to exclude heretics from its midst. The notion of a rabbinic orthodoxy which held synods and councils is entirely inappropriate for antiquity, however, and did not develop before the Middle Ages. The canonization of the Hebrew Bible must rather be seen as a gradual process which started in the post-exilic and Hellenistic period and continued into the Middle Ages until the first printed editions were made (see Veltri 1990: 214–15). In the first centuries CE rabbis seem to have agreed upon the sanctity of the five books of the Torah and a number of other writings, but some biblical books continued to be seen as controversial, and no agreement was reached on them (e.g. Song of Songs, Qoheleth, Esther). The phenomenon that midrashic commentaries datable to tannaitic (70–200 CE) and amoraic times (third to fifth century CE) exist for the books of the Pentateuch only indicates that rabbis held the Torah, i.e. the five books of Moses, in much higher esteem than the other biblical writings, and based their teachings on them.

2. THE GRAECO-ROMAN CULTURAL CONTEXT

From Hellenistic times onwards, Judaism in both the Land of Israel and the Diaspora developed in an environment which was heavily influenced by Graeco-Roman culture and adapted to it in various ways. From the time of Alexander the Great's conquest of Palestine and other parts of the Near East onwards (332–1 BCE), Jews were exposed to Hellenistic material culture, literature, cultic practices, education, administration, morality, and ideas. There was no unanimous rejection or acceptance of the 'foreign' culture by the Jewish community at large. One rather has to reckon with a very variegated selection and adaptation of particular elements by individual Jews, families, and the residents of a particular place. In the past, scholars have sometimes tried to minimize the impact of Graeco-Roman culture on Judaism (see Feldman 1993). Others have shown that Jews and Judaism in both the land of Israel and the Diaspora were thoroughly Hellenized, and that the difference was only a gradual one (see Bickerman 1988; Hengel 1991; Goodman 1998; Gruen 2002).

Martin Hengel has presented the Jewish encounter with Hellenism as the basis and background for the development of early Christianity. Certain ideas and elements associated with early Christianity were already part and parcel of Hellenistic Judaism before Christianity emerged. Whereas Hengel's notion of Hellenistic Judaism's influence on early Christianity is valid and constructive, his stark contrast between the universalism and liberalism present in Hellenistic Judaism and its successor, early Christianity, on the one hand, and the allegedly exclusivist and narrow-minded Pharisaic-rabbinic Judaism of Roman Palestine, on the other, is not. Hengel argues, for example, that the 'profound transformation' of Palestinian Judaism in the Hellenistic era did not affect the 'hardened' stance of Hasidic, Pharisaic, and rabbinic Judaism which focused on Torah observance only. Christianity is presented as the 'new force which burst the framework of a nationalistic legalism which had grown too narrow with its prophetic and eschatological appeal' (1991: 309). Hengel's depiction of rabbinic Judaism must be seen as a caricature, which is not based on a close reading and understanding of the rabbinic sources themselves.

Rabbinic literature shows that the rabbis of the first five centuries were constantly exposed to and challenged by the dominant Graeco-Roman culture (see Alexander 1990 and the studies collected in Schäfer 1998 and 2002 and Schäfer and Hezser 2000). They did not live in a separate enclave which left them entirely unaffected by what was happening in society at large; rather, they participated in and constantly interacted with their more or less Hellenized Jewish and non-Jewish contemporaries. This interaction has left many traces in rabbinic sources. Rabbis used Graeco-Roman loan-words and literary forms (see Lieberman 1962 and 1965). Their legal thinking resembled that of Roman jurists in many regards (see Hezser

1998 and 2003). They discussed the religious permissibility of visits to Roman theatres and bathhouses and were aware of the widespread usage of pagan art (see Jacobs 1998 *a, b,* and 2000; Neusner 1991). Some rabbis were in favour of giving their children a Greek education (see Hezser 2001: 90–4). The very phenomenon of the sage resembled the role and function of the pagan holy man and Graeco-Roman philosopher in many regards (see Fischel 1973: p. xii; Hezser 2000: 162–6). In the following, these analogies will be elucidated in more detail.

3. LITERARY ANALOGIES

One consequence of the shared biblical and Graeco-Roman context of rabbinic Judaism and early Christianity are certain literary forms which appear in both rabbinic literature and the New Testament and have been adapted by the two communities in partly similar and partly different ways. Before describing these literary forms, it is necessary to stress, however, that the larger literary genres found in the two corpora differ from each other considerably. No biographical narratives like the gospels, which focus on one particular teacher, are to be found amongst rabbinic documents. In striking contrast to the focus on and elevation of one particular sage, rabbinic documents present rabbis as basically indistinctive from each other, suppressing individual traits. The editors, who remain anonymous themselves, try to give the impression of the rabbinic movement as a democratic and pluralistic community of Torah experts who all have the same status and whose legal opinions and biblical interpretations are all equally valid. Rabbinic literature is therefore characterized by what can be called inter-subjectivity, in contrast to the emphasis on individual personages and authors in early Christian writing.

Similarly, no commentaries written by individual rabbis, comparable to those written by the Christian church fathers, exist. Rabbinic midrashic works are skillfully constructed collections of multiple alternative and partly contradictory interpretations attributed to many different rabbis or transmitted anonymously (see Porton 1979; Boyarin 1990; Stern 1996). Nevertheless, comparisons with Christian Bible exegesis are possible (see Visotzky 1995).

Other characteristics of rabbinic literature are the unsystematic presentation of the material and the lack of narrative and thematic development. Although Talmudic *sugyot* (thematic units) and midrashic homilies evince a certain internal logic and coherence, they do not develop their subject in a systematic way. The meaning of the argumentation often reveals itself to the initiated scholar only; that is, it presupposes a broad knowledge of both the Torah and rabbinic tradition. Therefore we must assume that rabbinic literature was school literature, meant for further discussion amongst rabbinic scholars and students, rather than popular literature written for a broad and more or less uneducated public.

Despite these differences with regard to the genres of rabbinic and Christian writings, analogies in the usage of smaller literary forms, which may have had their origins in oral transmission, exist. One such form was the *chreia*, or *apophthegma*, which was particularly suited to express the views of the sage and to present him as a model which others could emulate (see Fischel 1968; Porton 1981; Avery-Peck 1993; Hezser 1996). It consists of a narrative introduction and culminates in a poignant saying which reveals the difference between the sage and mainstream society. Such stories were first told about Graeco-Roman philosophers and later about Jesus, rabbis, and desert monks. They were transmitted by these sages' students and meant to commemorate them as models of practical and moral wisdom.

Another literary form which appears in both the gospels and New Testament writings is the parable. Particularly common in both philosophical and rabbinic writings, especially midrash, are the so-called king parables in which the king stands for God (see Ziegler 1903). In the parables of the gospels the king has usually been replaced by a householder. The images and details of the parables are usually taken from everyday life, not only the royal court but also the world of the slave, peasant, and day labourer (see Hezser 1996). In their midrashic context parables are used to illustrate the biblical verses which frame them (see Stern 1991). Prior to their inclusion in the literary genre midrash, these parables, like the parables of the gospels, seem to have been transmitted orally, however, without a biblical verse or an interpretation. The listener had to determine their meaning for him or herself by applying their message to the specific context, the *Sitz im Leben*, in which they were told.

Other literary forms which are shared by the New Testament and rabbinic writings are the wise (moral or legal) saying, the list, the *exemplum*, and the anecdote. All of these forms also appear in (Stoic) philosophical texts, and it is likely that they were common forms used by both philosophers and Jewish and Christian religious teachers in antiquity (cf. Fischel 1977). Their particular adaptation in both rabbinic Judaism and early Christianity deserves further study. Unfortunately, no form history of rabbinic literature exists, yet all of these and possibly other, not yet detected literary forms need to be studied carefully with regard to their transmission and redaction history (see Hezser 2000).

4. INSTITUTIONS AND OFFICES

The form and development of institutions and offices in ancient Judaism and the early church provides the background and context in which biblical and rabbinic literature was created. During Second Temple times the institution of the Jerusalem

Temple stood at the centre of Jewish religious life, and its priestly hierarchy (high priest, ordinary priests, Levites) had official authority in cultic and sometimes also political matters. Scribes attached to the Temple seem to have fulfilled various administrative functions in addition to writing religious texts and secular documents (see Demsky and Bar-Ilan 1988). A special school for the training of scribes may have been attached to the Temple (see p. 14). One may assume that these scribes were the ones who were most familiar with the texts of the ancestral tradition. They would produce copies of biblical manuscripts, preserve the scrolls in the Temple precincts, and also serve as experts in reading and interpreting them.

After the destruction of the Temple in 70 CE, rabbis set themselves up as religious experts and promoted Torah study and observance as the most important religious activity. Although status differences existed amongst rabbis, the rabbis were not organized hierarchically, but rather formed a loose network of colleague-friends who supported but also competed with each other (see Hezser 1997: 255–306). Each rabbi had a circle of close students, who lived with him and served him in various ways, and a broader and more detached set of sympathizers who valued his counsel in religious and everyday life matters. Rabbis' main functions were those of teachers, on the one hand, and legal (halakhic) advisors, on the other. They were concerned with applying the biblical tradition to everyday life situations, to sanctify the ordinary and to serve the holy in the here and now.

From the time of R. Yehudah ha-Nasi at the end of the second century CE onwards, the patriarch seems to have emerged as *primus inter pares* amongst rabbis (see Jacobs 1995). We may assume that his position was based on his reputation as a Torah expert, his family background, wealth, and good connections amongst high-ranking Jews and Romans. He was not officially recognized by the Romans until the fifth century, shortly before the institution came to its end. He does not seem to have been the president of a central court (sanhedrin) or academy, for whose existence after 70 CE no convincing evidence exists (see Goodblatt 1994: 232–76). One rather has to reckon with many local study rooms or houses and informal courts associated with the patriarch as well as with various rabbis. Accordingly, the rabbinic movement was not centralized, but should be imagined as an informal network of colleague-friends, resident in a variety of Galilean and coastal cities, towns, and villages (see Hezser 1997: 157–84).

Due to the nature of the evidence, the question of rabbis' and the patriarch's actual influence on the religious life of their fellow Jews cannot be answered any more. Scholarly opinions range from the traditional, no longer valid maximalist view of rabbis as authoritative leaders of local Jewish communities with the patriarch at the top of the rabbinic hierarchy (see e.g. Safrai 1974: 378; Avi-Yonah 1976; Alon 1989: 467) to the minimalist view of rabbis as an insignificant intellectual élite at the margins of Jewish society (Schwartz 2001). Since rabbis did not possess any institutional authority, their power must have been based on their ability to persuade: they won adherents amongst those who valued Torah piety and saw the individual rabbi as an incorporation of the Torah as the word of God. Since rabbis' authority was both role-related and personal, some rabbis would have had more adherents than others. The percentage of 'rabbinic' Jews in Jewish society of the first centuries remains unknown, though. No rabbis are known to have existed in the Diaspora, and Palestinian rabbis' sphere of influence would have been more or less limited to Roman Palestine.

Due to our almost complete lack of Jewish literary sources from Diaspora Judaism in the first centuries CE and the scant archaeological fieldwork done so far, our knowledge of the social and religious life of those communities is based mostly on inscriptions and funerary architecture. Most of the evidence stems from late ancient Rome, where a Jewish community existed from the first century BCE onwards. On the basis of funerary remains and artistic production, the interaction between Jews and non-Jews can be determined (see Rutgers 1995). The main literary source produced by (a) Roman Jew(s) of the fourth century CE is the *Collatio Legum Mosaicarum et Romanarum*, a systematic juxtaposition of biblical (mostly Exodus and Deuteronomy) and Roman law (see Rutgers 1998: 235–78). This collection seems to have been created to emphasize the primacy of Mosaic law and to show that it was fully compatible with Roman jurists' ordinances.

5. PRAYER AND LITURGY

In both early Judaism and Christianity a religious service developed in which the public reading of the Torah formed an important part. This service was not necessarily linked to the existence of synagogues and churches, for which archaeo-logical evidence is sparse before the fourth century CE (see Levine 2000). It could take place in multi-functional assembly houses or even in private dwellings, as the literary references to the so-called house-churches in the letters of Paul attest. This custom may have developed initially in the Diaspora, at some distance from the Jerusalem Temple. The earliest epigraphical and archaeological evidence for syn-agogues stems from Egypt and other Diaspora locations in Hellenistic times. The gospels, Josephus, and the Theodotus inscription suggest that Torah reading in a public setting also took place in Roman Palestine before the destruction of the Temple, but it may not have been widespread at that time.

As already pointed out, Torah study and observance became the central focus of Jewish identity only after 70 CE. But even then, some time may have elapsed until public Torah reading and prayer services became a widespread practice. Both the literary and the archaeological evidence converge in late antiquity. Rabbinic sources from the third to fifth centuries attest to the existence of Jewish elementary schools, whose main function was to teach boys to read from the Torah (see Hezser 2001: 49–54); that is, to increase the pool of possible Torah readers at a time when the literacy rate amongst adults was very low. For approximately the same period of time, the archaeological evidence for synagogue buildings increases dramatically. Late antique synagogues were lavish buildings with artistic decorations which formed the religious centres of the Jewish communities (on ancient Jewish art see Hachlili 1988 and 1998). The very fact of the emergence of the synagogue as the local Jewish religious centre in late antiquity, as well as the synagogue's architectural style and features, may have been influenced by the building of churches in Byzantine Palestine (see Schwartz 2001; Milson 2002).

The synagogue service with its focus on Torah reading, translation (*targum*), and interpretation, on the one hand, and communal prayer, on the other, developed gradually and did not reach a fixed form until the Middle Ages (see Hoffmann 1979). In the first centuries CE rabbis agreed about the central significance of the Shema‘ and the Amidah (the so-called Eighteen Benedictions), but the exact wording of the Amidah was still disputed, as was the wording of many other benedictions and prayer formulas. One may assume that each local congregation developed its own liturgy, with its own versions of the prayers. Greek-speaking congregations may even have recited some prayers—and read the Torah?—in Greek, although rabbis were opposed to these practices. Since rabbis were not the leaders of synagogues in antiquity, their influence on the development of the liturgy remains uncertain. Disputes in rabbinic literature may reflect the variations in local practice rather than the rabbis' influence on it.

6. The Question of Contacts and Influence

The Hebrew Bible constituted the basis on which both rabbinic Judaism and early Christianity claimed their legitimacy. Both the rabbis and early Christian leaders saw themselves as the legitimate interpreters of the Bible and claimed a monopoly on their respective interpretations. In rabbinic midrash a multiplicity of interpretations of each biblical verse stand side by side. Sometimes similarities with Christian Bible interpretations are observable, or rabbinic reactions to and contradictions of the 'wrong' Christian view (see Visotzky 1995). The extent to which rabbis were familiar with Christian Bible interpretation is impossible to specify, though. Some Christian views may have reached them indirectly, through hearsay, rather than being based on their own readings (the extent to which rabbis were able to read Greek is equally uncertain) or contacts with Christian scholars.

The tendency nowadays is away from the positivistic search for direct influences of one text on another, to view the development of ancient Judaism and Christianity in the context of the multicultural realm in which ancient Jews and Christians lived in the Near East and the ancient Mediterranean world, especially in cosmopolitan cities. Whether a particular Christian text actually influenced a particular rabbinic utterance, or vice versa, cannot be fully determined; nor is it of great relevance. What is much more interesting and important is to investigate the ways in which both Jewish and Christian exegesis participated in ancient hermeneutics at large, both where similar solutions were reached and where one tradition differed from the other. If this approach is applied consistently, the characteristics of ancient Jewish and Christian Bible interpretation and adaptation will become clearer. At the same time, the boundaries between the two traditions will become more blurred, and many analogies emerge.

Suggested Reading

Various issues relating to the writing, canonization, transmission, and interpretation of the Hebrew Bible in ancient Judaism are dealt with in Mulder (1988). A general historical introduction to ancient Judaism in Hellenistic and Roman times is provided by Schäfer (1995). Goodman (2000) and Schwartz (2001) are more specific studies of Jewish society under Roman rule. For a concise and historically informed introduction to rabbinic literature, see Stemberger (1996). Other introductory works on ancient Judaism which provide a broad overview for the student and non-specialist alike are Cohen (1987) and Schiffman (1991). The social structure of the rabbinic movement in Roman Palestine has been analysed by Hezser (1997), while Jewish communities in the Diaspora are the subject of Rutgers' (1995 and 1998) and Barclay's (1996) works. The literary form midrash has been introduced by Porton (1979), and Boyarin (1990) and Stern (1996) have studied its characteristics on the basis of post-modern literary theories. A comparison between rabbinic and Christian exegesis is to be found in Visotzky (1995), while the Graeco-Roman context of ancient Judaism in general, and rabbinic literature in particular, is elucidated in the articles collected in Goodman (1998), Schäfer (1998 and 2002) and Schäfer and Hezser (2000).

BIBLIOGRAPHY

ALEXANDER, P. 1990. 'Quid Athenis et Hierosolymis?' In P. R. Davis and R. T. White, eds., *A Tribute to Geza Vermes: Essays on Jewish and Christian Literature and History*, Sheffield: Sheffield Academic Press, 101–24.

ALON, G. 1989. *The Jews in Their Land in the Talmudic Age (70–640 CE)*, 3rd edn. Cambridge, Mass.: Harvard University Press.

AVERY-PECK, A. J. 1993. 'Classifying Early Rabbinic Pronouncement Stories'. *SBL Seminar Papers*, 223–44.

AVI-YONAH, M. 1976. *The Jews of Palestine: Political History from the Bar Kokhba War to the Arab Conquest*. New York: Schocken Books.

BARCLAY, J. M. G. 1996. *Jews in the Mediterranean Disapora: From Alexander to Trajan (323 BCE–117 CE)*. Edinburgh: T. & T. Clark.

BAUMGARTEN, A. 1997. *The Flourishing of Jewish Sects in the Maccabean Era: An Interpretation*. Leiden: Brill.

BECKWITH, R. T. 1988. 'The Formation of the Hebrew Bible'. In Mulder 1988: 39–86.

BICKERMAN, E. J. 1988. *The Jews in the Greek Age*. Cambridge, Mass.: Harvard University Press.

BOYARIN, D. 1990. *Intertextuality and the Reading of Midrash*. Bloomington, Ind.: University of Indiana Press.

COHEN, S. J. D. 1984. 'The Significance of Yavneh: Pharisees, Rabbis, and the End of Jewish Sectarianism'. *HUCA* 55: 27–53.

—— 1987. *From the Maccabees to the Mishnah*. Philadelphia: Westminster Press.

DEMSKY, A., and BAR-ILAN, M. 1988. 'Writing in Ancient Israel and Early Judaism, Part One: The Biblical Period'. In Mulder 1988: 1–20.

FAUR, J. 1986. *Golden Doves with Silver Dots: Semiotics and Textuality in Rabbinic Tradition*. Bloomington, Ind.: University of Indiana Press.

FELDMAN, L. H. 1993. *Jew and Gentile in the Ancient World: Attitudes and Interactions from Alexander to Justinian*. Princeton: Princeton University Press.

FISCHEL, H. A. 1968. 'Studies in Cynicism and the Ancient Near East: The Transformation of a Chria'. In J. Neusner, ed., *Religions in Antiquity: Essays in Memory of Erwin Ramsdell Goodenough*, Leiden: Brill, 372–411.

—— 1973. *Rabbinic Literature and Greco-Roman Philosophy: A Study of Epicurea and Rhetorica in Early Midrashic Writings*. Leiden: Brill.

—— ed. 1977. *Essays in Greco-Roman and Related Talmudic Literature*. New York: Ktav Publishing House.

GAFNI, I. M. 1997. *Land, Center and Diaspora: Jewish Constructs in Late Antiquity*. Sheffield: Sheffield Academic Press.

GOODBLATT, D. 1994. *The Monarchic Principle: Studies in Jewish Self-Government in Antiquity*. Tübingen: Mohr-Siebeck.

GOODMAN, M., ed. 1998. *Jews in a Graeco-Roman World*. Oxford: Clarendon Press; New York: Oxford University Press.

—— 2000. *State and Society in Roman Galilee, A.D. 132–212*, 2nd edn. London and Portland, Ore.: Vallentine Mitchell.

GRUEN, E. S. 2002. *Diaspora: Jews Amidst Greeks and Romans*. Cambridge, Mass.: Harvard University Press.

HACHLILI, R. 1988. *Ancient Jewish Art and Archaeology in the Land of Israel*. Leiden: Brill.

—— 1998. *Ancient Jewish Art and Archaeology in the Diaspora*. Leiden: Brill.

HANDELMAN, S. A. 1982. *The Slayers of Moses: The Emergence of Rabbinic Interpretation in Modern Literary Criticism*. Albany, NY: State University of New York Press.

HENGEL, M. 1991. *Judaism and Hellenism: Studies in their Encounter in Palestine during the Early Hellenistic Period*, 2 vols. in one, 2nd edn. Minneapolis: Fortress Press.

HEZSER, C. 1996. 'Die Verwendung der hellenistischen Gattung Chrie im frühen Christentum und Judentum'. *JSJ* 27: 371–439.

—— 1997. *The Social Structure of the Rabbinic Movement in Roman Palestine*. Tübingen: Mohr-Siebeck.

—— 1998. 'The Codification of Legal Knowledge in Late Antiquity: The Talmud Yerushalmi and Roman Law Codes'. In Schäfer, ed., 1998: 581–641.

—— 2000. 'Interfaces between Rabbinic Literature and Graeco-Roman Philosophy'. In Schäfer and Hezser 2000: 161–87.

—— 2001. *Jewish Literacy in Roman Palestine*. Tübingen: Mohr-Siebeck.

—— ed. 2003. *Rabbinic Law in its Roman and Near Eastern Context*. Tübingen: Mohr-Siebeck.

HOFFMAN, L. A. 1979. *The Canonization of the Synagogue Service*. Notre Dame, Ind., and London: University of Notre Dame Press.

ISAAC, B., and OPPENHEIMER, A., eds. 1996. *Studies on the Jewish Diaspora in the Hellenistic and Roman Periods*. Tel Aviv: Ramot Publishing.

JACOBS, M. 1995. *Die Institution des iudischen Patriarchen: Eine quellen- und traditionskritische Studie zur Geschichte der Juden in der Spätantike*. Tübingen: Mohr-Siebeck.

—— 1998*a*. 'Römische Thermenkultur im Spiegel des Talmud Yerushalmi'. In Schäfer 1998: 219–311.

—— 1998*b*. 'Theatres and Performances as Reflected in the Talmud Yerushalmi'. In Schäfer 1998: 327–47.

—— 2000. 'Pagane Tempel in Palestina—rabbinische Aussagen im Vergleich mit archaeologischen Funden'. In Schäfer and Hezser 2000: ii. 139–59.

LEIMAN, S. Z. 1991. *The Canonization of Hebrew Scripture: The Talmudic and Midrashic Evidence*, 2nd edn. New Haven: Connecticut Academy of Arts and Sciences.

LEVINE, L. I. 2000. *The Ancient Synagogue: The First Thousand Years*. New Haven and London: Yale University Press.

LEWIS, J. P. 1964. 'What Do We Mean by Yavneh?' *JBR* 32: 125–32.

LIEBERMAN, S. 1962. *Hellenism in Jewish Palestine*, 2nd edn. New York: Jewish Theological Seminary of America.

—— 1965. *Greek in Jewish Palestine*, 2nd edn. New York: Jewish Theological Seminary of America.

MILSON, D. W. 2002. 'Aspects of the Impact of Christian Art on Synagogues in Byzantine Palestine'. Doctoral thesis, Oxford University.

MULDER, M. J., ed. 1988. *Mikra. Text. Translation, Reading, and Interpretation of the Hebrew Bible in Ancient Judaism and Early Christianity*. Assen and Philadelphia: Fortress Press.

NEUSNER, J. 1991. *Symbol and Theology in Early Judaism*. Minneapolis: Fortress Press.

PORTON, G. G. 1979. 'Midrash: Palestinian Jews and the Hebrew Bible in the Graeco-Roman Period'. *ANRW* II. 19. 2: 103–38.

—— 1981. 'The Pronouncement Story in Tannaitic Literature: A Review of Bultmann's Theory'. *Semeia* 20: 81–99.

RUTGERS, L. V. 1995. *The Jews in Late Ancient Rome: Evidence of Cultural Interaction in the Roman Diaspora*. Leiden: Brill.

—— 1998. *The Hidden Heritage of Diaspora Judaism*, 2nd edn. Leiden: Brill.

SAFRAI, S. 1974. 'Jewish Self-Government'. In S. Safrai and M. Stem, *The Jewish People in the First Century*, CRINT 1.1, Assen: Van Gorcum, 377–419.

SCHÄFER, P. 1975. 'Die sogenannte Synode von Jabne: Zur Trennung von Juden und Christen im ersten/zweiten Jh. n. Chr'. *Judaica* 31: 54–64.

—— 1991. 'Der vorrabbinische Pharisäismus'. In M. Hengel and U. Heckel, eds., *Paulus und das antike Judentum*, Tübingen: Mohr-Siebeck, 125–72.

—— 1995. *The History of the Jews in Antiquity*. Luxembourg: Harwood Academic Publishers.

—— ed. 1998. *The Talmud Yerushalmi and Graeco-Roman Culture*, i. Tübingen: Mohr-Siebeck.

—— ed. 2002. *The Talmud Yerushalmi and Graeco-Roman Culture*, iii. Tübingen: Mohr-Siebeck.

—— and HEZSER, C., eds. 2000. *The Talmud Yerushalmi and Graeco-Roman Culture*, ii. Tübingen: Mohr-Siebeck.

SCHIFFMAN, L. H. 1991. *From Text to Tradition: A History of Second Temple and Rabbinic Judaism*. Hoboken, NJ: Ktav Publishing House.

SCHWARTZ, S. 2001. *Imperialism and Jewish Society, 200 B.C.E. to 640 C.E.* Princeton: Princeton University Press.

STEMBERGER, G. 1977. 'Die sogenannte "Synode von Jabne" und das frühe Christentum'. *Kairos*, 19: 14–21.

—— 1996. *Introduction to the Talmud and Midrash*, 2nd edn. Edinburgh: T. & T. Clark.

STERN, D. 1991. *Parables in Midrash: Narrative and Exegesis in Rabbinic Literature*. Cambridge: Cambridge University Press.

—— 1996. *Midrash and Theory: Ancient Jewish Exegesis and Contemporary Literary Studies*. Evanston, Ill.: Northwestern University Press.

THATCHER, T. 1998. 'Literacy, Textual Communities, and Josephus' *Jewish War*'. *JSJ* 29: 123–42.

VELTRI, G. 1990. 'Zur traditionsgeschichtlichen Entwicklung des Bewusstseins von einem Kanon: Die Yavneh-Frage'. *JSJ* 21: 210–26.

VISOTZKY, B. L. 1995. *Fathers of the World: Essays in Rabbinic and Patristic Literatures*. Tübingen: Mohr-Siebeck.

ZIEGLER, I. 1903. *Die Konigsgleichnisse des Midrasch beleuchtet durch die römische Kaiserzeit*. Breslau: Schlesische Verlagsanstalt v. S. Schottlaender.

PART II

LANGUAGES, TRANSLATION, AND TEXTUAL TRANSMISSION OF THE BIBLE

CHAPTER 9

LANGUAGE AND TRANSLATION OF THE OLD TESTAMENT

JOHN ELWOLDE

INTRODUCTION

After a brief linguistic sketch of the Hebrew and Aramaic of the Bible (see also Elwolde, forthcoming; McCarter 2004; Creason 2004), this article focuses on the inherent difficulty of ascertaining meaning in the Hebrew Bible (or, in the Christian tradition, the Old Testament, without the deutero-canonical, or apocryphal, books), from both a textual and a linguistic perspective. In order to make this topic accessible to non-specialists, most of the examples employed relate to vocabulary and phraseology. The lens through which the issue will be viewed is mainly that of translations, in particular the most important of the ancient versions, the Old Greek (more loosely, the Septuagint, or LXX, much of which was completed in the late third and second centuries BCE (see Conybeare and Stock 2001 [1905]; Jobes and Silva 2000)), but also other ancient versions and modern translations. The difficulties of translating from Hebrew into other languages, because of differences in the ways that languages (and speakers of those languages) structure the world, will only occasionally be referred to. Accessible presentations of the kind of issues encountered may be found in Clark and Hatton 2004 and other items in the same series.

BIBLICAL HEBREW AND ARAMAIC:
LINGUISTIC OVERVIEW

Although the Bible contains material that is diverse in genre, date, and provenance, from after the Exile up to the early Middle Ages this diverse material underwent a process of standardization that gave it a strong veneer of linguistic unity. As for texts actually composed during this post-exilic period, there is evidence both for ignorance of Hebrew and for the encroachment of Aramaic on spoken and literary usage (see Neh. 8, 8, 13: 24, and contrast with 2 Kgs. 18: 26–8). Post-exilic texts seem to reflect the more or less artificial employment of the pre-exilic 'classical' literary language, which no longer existed as a spoken medium, as well as influence from a vernacular dialect of Hebrew, from the north of the country, which would eventually find its literary expression in the 'rabbinic Hebrew' of the Mishnah (see Pérez Fernández 1997). However, before the Exile it is reasonable to assume that the Hebrew found in the Bible flourished as a literary language, and there is no positive evidence to suggest that the spoken language was significantly different, at least in the southern kingdom. A language somewhat different from that found in this 'classical Hebrew' of pre-exilic prose texts is seen in the remnants of the Bible's earliest, poetic literature. This poetry is usually thought to represent a northern literary idiom that reflects contact with the language and literature of Israel's Canaanite antecedents and Aramaic-speaking neighbours (see Hadas-Lebel 1995).

The alphabet familiar to us as 'Hebrew' is in fact the Aramaic script, used for writing Hebrew after the Exile. A form of the older Hebrew script, found in many Hebrew inscriptions from the pre-exilic period, was retained by the Samaritans. It also continued to be used occasionally, for example, at Qumran in some biblical manuscripts and for writing the divine name, and at the time of the Bar Kochba Revolt (132–5 CE) on coins signalling a hoped-for return to former glory. Hebrew (and Aramaic) is read from right to left and employs twenty-two letters for the representation of up to twenty-nine consonants. In order to ensure that a reader does not confuse, for example, *dabar* ('word') with *dibber* ('he spoke') or *deber* ('plague'), small marks, or 'points' to indicate vowels and other phonetic information are added to this purely consonantal writing system. In the system of 'pointing' found in the Tiberian Masoretic Text (see below), nine basic vowel signs, each one on its own or in combination with another vowel sign or a consonant, represent fourteen or fifteen different vowels.

The basic (or 'dictionary') form of most Hebrew words tends to be either mono- or bi-syllabic, with the stress generally falling on the final syllable, at least in the Tiberian system. Hebrew nouns and adjectives do not employ case-endings (for nominative, accusative, or genitive), although there are two genders, unmarked (masculine) and marked (feminine). Typical 'feminine' markers for nouns and adjectives are -a or -et in the singular and -ot (as against 'masculine' -im) in the plural.

Verbless sentences, in which a subject and complement are simply juxtaposed, without the verb 'to be', are common, as are verbs expressing states of being: 'be big', 'be old', etc. Central elements of the Hebrew verb system include the 'perfect', which states that such-and-such an action has taken place (typically, rendered by past forms in English) and the 'imperfect', where the focus is on the unfolding of the action or process denoted (typically rendered in English by present, future, conditional, or subjunctive forms). There are also two additional conjugations, traditionally called waw-consecutives. The best-known feature of these forms is that, broadly speaking, the conjugation that looks most like the 'imperfect' functions as though it were a 'perfect', and vice versa. In general, the use of the different forms of the Hebrew verb is dictated not by considerations of time but by often subtle constraints of word order and of previous choices in the verbal system. A series of 'derived conjugations', in which the basic form of a verb is modified by the addition of prefixes, duplication of consonants, or changes of vowels, allows Hebrew to express regular modifications of meaning (passive, reflexive, reciprocal, causative, intensive, etc.): e.g. šabar (simple conjugation) ('he broke'); šubbar (passive-intensive) ('he was shattered'). Hebrew has a variety of conjunctions, although it also frequently employs simple co-ordination of clauses with we- ('and') instead of using subordinate clauses. English clauses of the type 'when he does' are typically construed in Hebrew as 'in (or "as") his doing'. See Joüon 1993; Lambdin 1973.

Aramaic and Hebrew are not mutually intelligible dialects, but separate languages, each with a wealth of literary and spoken traditions that go well beyond the evidence of the Bible (see Beyer 1986; Fitzmyer 1979; Sáenz-Badillos 1993). However, contact between the Hebrew and Aramaic languages and their speakers dates from the very beginnings of Israel's history (see Gen. 31: 47; Deut. 26: 5) and continued through the intertestamental period and beyond (see Lemaire 1988). Many words in the Aramaic portions of the Bible (Dan. 2: 4–7: 28; Ezra 4: 8–6: 18; 7: 12–26) have recognizable cognates in the Hebrew sections, and there are numerous Aramaisms in biblical Hebrew (and Hebraisms in biblical Aramaic). Obvious features that distinguish biblical Aramaic from Hebrew include Aramaic's use of a suffixed— rather than prefixed—definite article, e.g. bayt-a ('the house') (Hebrew hab-bayit), the object marker le- (rarely yat) rather than Hebrew 'et, di ('which, that, because') (Hebrew 'ašer), man 'who?' (Hebrew mi), la 'no, not' (Hebrew lo), and 'itay 'there is' (Hebrew yeš). See Rosenthal 1995.

THE HEBREW BIBLE AND THE MASORETIC TEXT

We often speak of 'the Hebrew text of the Bible', as though there were one Bible and one Hebrew text. Both assumptions are problematic. Against the notion of 'one Bible', we only need to remind ourselves of the use of deutero-canonical books by the Roman Catholic and Eastern Rite churches, preceded by Hellenistic Jews and by the Dead Sea Scrolls community, where the 'apocryphal' or 'pseudepigraphic' works of Sirach (Ecclesiasticus), Tobit, *1 Enoch*, and *Jubilees* are attested in their original Hebrew and/or Aramaic forms. As for 'the Hebrew text', the evidence of the Dead Sea Scrolls and the LXX is that a variety of Hebrew text traditions existed prior to 70 CE (see Tov 2001; Abegg, Flint, and Ulrich 1999). In short, the picture we have of Judaism from the third century BCE to the first century CE is that of diversity—in beliefs and practice, in canon, and in text.

After 70 CE, one text became overwhelmingly dominant in Judaism (and, especially after the Reformation, in Christianity). That text underlies the so-called Masoretic Text (MT), found today in standard editions of the Hebrew Bible. 'Masorete' may be understood as 'tradent' or 'one who hands down' the biblical text. Individual Masoretes were associated with one of the various Masoretic 'schools' or traditions that were active from the sixth to the tenth century CE.

The MT is the result of the fixing, by Masoretes, of the consonantal text into a particular linguistic shape through the 'pointing' of the text with this secondary information. Pointing denotes the overlaying of marks on the consonantal text in order accurately to represent its liturgical recitation, grammatical structure, and pronunciation (see Yeivin 1980). It is obvious that once the exact linguistic shape is thus fixed, so also, to a large extent, is the interpretation of the text. The Masoretes also incorporated into biblical manuscripts the *masorah*, a detailed system of notes relating to the text, mainly of a statistical-linguistic nature (see Kelley, Mynatt, and Crawford 1998). The Masoretic tradition that became by far the most important was associated with the town of Tiberias. Because all Masoretic manuscripts, Tiberian or other, rely in principle on the same consonantal text, differences among later biblical manuscripts and, ultimately, printed editions are relatively minor.

That consonantal text (or one very similar to it) preceded the start of Masoretic activity by up to eight centuries, as evidenced by the existence of biblical texts among the Dead Sea Scrolls that vary very little from the MT. This text, which we shall call for convenience 'MT precursor', can be compared and contrasted with other ancient consonantal texts that display some degree of substantive difference from it. In some cases, these different Hebrew texts are directly available to us: for example, the Samaritan Pentateuch and those biblical manuscripts from the Dead Sea Scrolls that differ from MT precursor. MT precursor can also be compared with the hypothetical *Vorlage* (underlying Hebrew text) of the LXX or other ancient versions (obtained by 'retroverting' or back-translating into Hebrew).

In practice, when biblical scholars or Bible translators speak of 'the Hebrew text', they mean in general the Tiberian MT, although they will rather often diverge from it in respect of boundaries between clauses and (somewhat less) in the vocalization of words. Here, then, scholars might be said to have returned to MT precursor. Less frequent, but hardly uncommon, is the adoption of a reading (extant or retroverted) that differs even from that text. For example, if we combine the footnotes referring to the Dead Sea Scrolls in NRSV, REB, CEV, and NIV, we find that in some 135 different verses (the majority being from 1 and 2 Samuel and Isaiah) evidence from the Scrolls has been utilized.

CHANGES FROM (POINTED) MT TO (UNPOINTED) MT PRECURSOR

If a translator or interpreter approaches the text in its consonantal form only, the opportunities for readings of the text other than those established in MT are multiplied. For example, at Gen. 47: 31, the form *mṭh*, vocalized in MT as *miṭṭa* ('couch') is interpreted by LXX as *maṭe* ('staff'). At the close of Exod. 5: 16, there is a difficult sequence, vocalized in MT as *weḥaṭat 'ammeka* ('You are unjust to your own people') (NRSV; cf. LXX). However, unvocalized the sequence is open to interpretation as: '(this is) the sin of your people' or 'your people have sinned' or even 'the sin is with you' (reading, with Symmachus, whose Greek translation appeared between 150 and 250 CE (see Salvesen 1991), the preposition *'im* ('with') for the noun *'am* ('people')).

According to the Masoretic accents, Prov. 26: 17 reads, literally, 'one who seizes the ears of a dog is a passer-by who becomes angry over a dispute that is not his'. However, many modern translations effectively change this word division and interpret *'ober* ('one passing') (hence 'passer-by') as modifying 'dog': 'one who seizes the ears of a passing dog is one who becomes angry...'. A well-known ancient example of this phenomenon relates to Isa. 40: 3, where the LXX, followed by the New Testament, understands 'A voice crying in the wilderness, "Prepare..."' whereas the Masoretic punctuation as well as the parallelism of the verse supports interpretation as 'A voice crying, "In the wilderness prepare..."'.

Elsewhere, the redistribution of text can cross the boundaries of the Masoretic verse division. (It should be borne in mind here that early Hebrew manuscripts, from Qumran and elsewhere, do not make any obvious mark between verses even though they clearly do mark a space between different sections of text, which broadly correspond to those found in Masoretic Manuscripts.) For example, at Hos. 4: 11 we read in MT that various activities 'take (away) the heart'. The next verse then reads 'My people consult...'. However, LXX takes 'my people' with the 'heart' of the preceding verse, and then reads the verb of v. 12 without an explicit subject: '...take away the heart of my people. They consult...'. Even within the words of MT (rather than between them), a different division of the text is sometimes argued to yield a 'better' sense. For example, at Jer. 8: 4, we have a difficult text that appears to say 'will they fall and not arise; will he return and not return (*'im yašub welo' yašub*)?' Following the lead of LXX, most translations extract sense from this by interpreting the repeated verb in two slightly different senses, 'turn away' and 'turn back'. However, the Masoretic notes (*masorah*) to this passage offer a different solution (not, of course, necessarily the correct one): namely, to redistribute the consonants and to read *'im yašubu lo' yašub* ('if they turn (away) he will not turn (away))'.

Such rereadings of the consonantal text have been part of mainstream Jewish interpretation. A striking example is provided by the great eleventh-century exegete Rashi, on Gen. 1: 1. Rashi points out that the first word of the Bible, *berešit*, is most naturally taken to mean 'at the beginning of'. But with the following word, *br'*, pointed in MT as *bara* '(God) created', *berešit* has to be taken as 'in the beginning' (without 'of') in order to yield any grammatical sense ('in the beginning God created...'). To resolve this dilemma, Rashi suggests reading the second word not as *bara* but as *bero* '(God's) creating of'. With this slight modification towards expected grammar, the beginning of the Bible may be read as 'At the beginning of God's creating of the heavens and the earth, when the earth was..., God said...' (cf. NJPS). Short of Rashi's solution, there really is no way out of the impasse—one must either slip quickly by the grammar, as most translations (including LXX) and John 1: 1 do, or invoke 'hidden' senses of the *be-* or the *rešit*, as many early Jewish and Christian interpretations do.

DIFFERENCES BETWEEN MT AND NON-MASORETIC TRADITIONS

MT itself will occasionally incorporate what might be an ancient textual variant (not merely a re-pointing) that has been rejected by the Masoretes. For example, at Gen. 38: 14 the Masoretes reject the reading *whw' lw' ntnh* ('and he did not give her'), followed by LXX and Theodotion (mid-second-century CE translator into Greek) and impose *why' lw' ntnh* ('and she was not given'), followed by Aquila (early second-century CE translator into Greek), Symmachus (see above), the Samaritan Pentateuch, and Targum Onqelos (an Aramaic explanatory translation undertaken between the first and fifth centuries CE). At Judg. 18: 30, the earliest form of the Hebrew text probably read 'Moses', but to this name an extra, raised, consonant has been added (and different vowels overlaid) so as to give 'Manasseh', a more appropriate candidate for the ancestor of a priest of a non-Jerusalemite cult! (Manuscripts of LXX vary between the two readings; the Vulgate (Latin translation or revision completed in the fifth century CE) has 'Moses'.)

Other substantive variations between MT precursor and different ancient Hebrew text traditions include the following features. A significantly different word may be used at a given place, for example 'the sixth day' as the one on which God finished the work of creation (Gen. 2: 2) in the Samaritan Pentateuch and the *Vorlage* of LXX and Peshitta (Syriac translation perhaps dating mainly from the first and second centuries CE) instead of 'the seventh day' of MT (and Vulgate), or Mt Gerizim as the mountain on which the tablets of the law were to be placed, according to the Samaritan Pentateuch, as against Mt Ebal in MT (Deut. 27: 4). Additional words may be found—for example, those that Cain said to Abel before they went out into the field (Gen. 4: 8), which are supplied in the Samaritan Pentateuch ('let us go out into the field'), LXX, Vulgate, and Peshitta, but which are not found in MT, the Dead Sea Scrolls, or in Targum Onqelos. Another example is the word 'light' as the object of the 'suffering servant's' sight at Isa. 53: 11, in both Isaiah scrolls from Qumran.

A much larger-scale addition to MT is represented by, for example, 1 Sam. 11: 1. Here LXX includes the words 'And it happened after about a month' not found in MT. Much more dramatically, 4QSam[a] has not only these words (in Hebrew) but also, before them, a quite lengthy description of the conflict between Nahash and the people of Gad and Reuben, an account that tallies with the one transmitted by Josephus. NRSV adds the text from 4QSam[a].

Other major differences include the significantly shorter versions of Job and Jeremiah found in LXX. In the case of Jeremiah (where LXX and MT also have substantially different orderings of the text), the Qumran biblical manuscripts represent both longer and shorter versions. The Dead Sea Scrolls (as, to a certain extent, the LXX) display differences, with respect to MT, in the order and content of the Psalms. The LXX has longer versions of (or additional material in), for example, Esther and Daniel, as well as entire books that have no counterpart in MT, even though some of these, such as Sirach (Ecclesiasticus) and Tobit, have been found in their original Hebrew (or Aramaic) versions at Qumran and elsewhere.

ASCERTAINING 'EARLIER' READINGS

Of course, aside from such major differences it is almost impossible to be certain at any point that a version (Greek, Latin, Syriac) did not read what MT now has but modified it in some way, consciously or by accident and for any one or more of a number of reasons. The same broadly applies to small-scale substantive differences in other Hebrew texts (Qumran, Samaritan). But what we can say is that Hebrew text traditions other than the tradition represented by MT existed in the third century BCE to the first century CE. However, it should be emphasized that by and large where they share the same material (i.e. outside of the cases represented by Job, Jeremiah, and the deutero-canonical/apocryphal books) there is a very high degree of correspondence between these texts and the consonantal text of MT.

We can never be absolutely certain about which is the 'earlier' text in any given instance. As a possible example of where LXX might reflect a form of the text prior to MT (or MT precursor), see Ps. 75: 6 (EVV 5), where MT reads *tedabberu besawwa'r 'ataq* ('you (are not to) speak with a neck impudence'). However, LXX has 'do not speak against God unrighteousness', where (leaving aside the difference between 'impudence' and 'unrighteousness') it seems clear that the translator has read a text that instead of *sw'r*, which could only be vocalized as *saww'ar* ('neck'), had *swr*, which could be vocalized either as *sawwar* ('neck') (i.e. a variant spelling of *saww'ar*) or as *sur* ('rock'), interpreted by LXX as a title for God. It seems likely here that LXX (here followed by REB) represents an earlier form of the text, with *swr*, to which the tradition represented by MT has inserted an aleph (') in order to ensure a 'neck' reading over a 'rock' one.

On the other hand, at the end of Hos. 14: 3 (EVV 2) MT reads literally 'and we will repay bulls, our lip', which appears to mean 'we will offer in sacrifice words (of praise, thanksgiving) instead of, or alongside, animals', a sentiment consistent with the beginning of the verse: 'take with you words and return to Y'. But LXX (followed by NRSV) has 'and we will repay the fruit of our lips', which seems to reflect a reading of the text not as *parim śepatenu (prym śptnw)* but as *peri miśśepotenu* ('fruit from our lips') *(pry mśptnw)* or (invoking the use of 'enclitic mem') *peri-m śepotenu* ('fruit of our lips'). However, it is far from clear that LXX has preserved a more original reading here. Instead, it is possible that the translator simply misread the Hebrew text, perhaps under the influence of the expression 'fruit of the lips', which occurs in Hebrew and Greek Jewish sources later than the Hebrew Bible, but is not attested (elsewhere) within it.

A more certain example of a mistake in LXX is at Gen. 18: 12, where the LXX translator seems to have read *'dnh* not, as in MT, as *'edna* ('(sexual) pleasure') but as *'adena* ('thus far'), found at Eccles. 4: 2. The form *'adena* almost certainly derives from a variety of the Hebrew language other than that represented by pre-exilic, 'classical' prose. Its use at Gen. 18: 12 is one indication of the influence on the

Greek translators of more or less colloquial and dialectal, 'post-classical', forms of Hebrew as well as by Aramaic, which was probably more familiar to them than Hebrew of any kind. This Aramaic influence is reflected in some LXX transliterations of the Hebrew text, based on Aramaic rather than Hebrew (e.g. *pascha* ('Passover'), *sabbata* ('Sabbath')), and occasionally a Greek translator has understood a Hebrew word as though it were Aramaic. For example, at Isa. 9: 4 (EVV 5), in a difficult text, *bedamim* has been understood not as 'with blood' but (as in Aramaic) as 'in compensation'. Studies of the techniques of the LXX translators include Olofsson 1990; Beck 2000; Sollamo and Sipilä 2001.

In various biblical passages, it has been argued that the present text of MT is the result of confusion in the transition from the earlier, Hebrew script to the later, Aramaic one (see above). For example, at Ps. 137: 5, 'if I forget you, Jerusalem, my right hand will forget' has been emended to '... I will forget my right hand' by pointing to the similarity between the third person feminine prefix (taw, *t*) in the older alphabet and the first person one (aleph, ') in the Aramaic alphabet. Similarly, 1 Sam. 24: 11, 'and he said to kill you, but she had pity upon you' has been resolved by the same device, '... but I had mercy upon you', in this case supported by LXX. It has also been claimed that MT precursor (or its predecessor) incorporated a number of abbreviations. For example, at Deut. 32: 35, MT reads 'to me [*ly*] is vengeance, and repaying at the time their foot slips'. However, here LXX has 'on the day of vengeance', a reading that seems to reflect Hebrew *lywm*, which is precisely what we find in the Samaritan Pentateuch, in parallelism with *l't* ('at the time') (cf. REB, CEV). On the other hand, at Judg. 19: 18 LXX has 'my house', and many modern translations (and Nova Vulgata (a recent papally authorized revision of the Vulgate intended to represent scholarly editions of the Hebrew and Greek texts of the Bible)) assume that *bet yhwh* ('house of Y') in MT is the result of an early misunderstanding of the first person possessive suffix (*beti* (*byty*) ('my house')) as an abbreviation for the tetragrammaton.

For relatively accessible presentations of text-critical matters, such as those presented above, see Barthélemy *et al.* 1976–80; Hognesius 2003; de Waard 2003; see also Schenker 2004.

Corrupt, or Difficult, Texts

Sequences in MT from which no acceptable sense, from a purely linguistic perspective, can be squeezed are rare indeed. On the other hand, there are not a few passages that, although formally coherent, are counter-intuitive or inconsistent with the rest of the text itself or with our knowledge or expectations of the world. For example at the end of 2 Sam. 4: 10, we read *'ašer leṭitti lo bešora* ('which was for my giving him good news'). This sequence, while by no means incomprehensible, seems out of place in context. The simplest remedy would seem to be to assume a confusion of the yodh (*y*) of *ltty* (*leṭitti*) and the waw (*w*) of *lw* (*lo*), which are frequently difficult to distinguish, for example in the Dead Sea Scrolls, and to assume an original *leṭitto li* ('...for his giving me...'). At 1 Sam. 13: 8, *lammo'ed 'ašer šemu'el* ('at the appointment which was Samuel'), although grammatical, lacks obvious meaning. Here, the least intrusive solution (although not necessarily the correct one) is to revocalize *'ašer* ('that, which') as *'iššer* ('he had blessed'), i.e. 'at the appointment Samuel had blessed' (cf. Vulgate); alternatively, various manuscripts of MT read *'ašer sam šemu'el* ('which Samuel had placed'), suggesting that *sam* might have been omitted by mistake at some point due to confusion with the *šem-* of *šemu'el*. At 1 Sam. 13: 1, MT says that Saul was 'a year old' when he became king. The Vulgate renders literally, but LXX lacks the entire verse (which contains another significant difficulty), and modern English versions almost unanimously insert an ellipsis marker: 'Saul was...years old when he became king' (NJPS). Here, short of following ancient interpreters in claiming that the text means that Saul was as naïve as a one-year-old, acceptance of textual corruption in MT or its precursor appears inevitable. However, in such instances, even where there is an alternative Hebrew text tradition or versional evidence that appears to give a 'better' reading, we should also be aware of the possibility that the alternative tradition was faced with the same text as we have in MT but 'improved' it in some way.

PROBLEMS OF COHERENCE
AND CONSISTENCY

In the preceding examples, a degree of incongruity was immediately obvious. However, in other cases the problem of linguistic or logical coherence arises only within a somewhat larger context than that of the sentence or verse. For example, Gen. 3: 21 speaks of God making for Adam and Eve 'tunics of skin', although the slaughter of animals, at least for food, had not yet been sanctioned (cf. Gen. 1: 29; 9: 2–4). Early translators and interpreters saw a problem here and solved it in various ways. A lexical solution was to see in the Hebrew *'or* ('skin') an equivalent of *'or* ('light'); i.e. God covered them with light (cf. Targum Onqelos: *lebušin diqar* ('garments of honour')). A lexico-grammatical solution was to interpret the skin as belonging to Adam and Eve, not to an animal, and to understand the genitive ('of') construction as conveying the sense of 'for', i.e. 'tunics for their bodies'. A third solution might be called referential: the text was retained in its regular sense, but the skin was taken to be that of the serpent, which periodically sheds its skin.

Whereas Gen. 3: 21 seems to point to a lacuna in our information, Gen. 2: 17 shows two apparent inconsistencies. The first concerns the addressee. In MT it is clearly Adam alone who is spoken to (as Eve had not yet been sculpted): 'you shall not eat...; when you eat...you will die', with singular forms throughout. However, LXX, probably with an eye to Eve's reporting of the same words at Gen. 3: 3, switches from singular 'you' in v. 16 to the plural in v. 17. Gen. 2: 17 conceals another problem of inconsistency, in that quite plainly neither Adam nor Eve fell down dead on the day they ate from the forbidden tree. In connection with this verse we can see in the translation of Symmachus how a translator can be at one point more faithful to the text (more 'literal') and at another more interpretative. Unlike LXX, Symmachus renders 'you shall not eat' (etc.) as a singular, in line with the Hebrew; however, later in the verse, perturbed like many by the apparent non-fulfilment of the punishment stated, Symmachus does not, like LXX, render quite literally, but adds a modifying interpretation: 'you will become mortal'. It is, of course, not entirely impossible that this was the meaning intended by the Hebrew (and this interpretation is broadly followed in ancient times by, for example, Targum Pseudo-Jonathan, and in modern times by, among others, REB). However, we should note that although the translator has tried to make sense of the text and to help the reader, in presenting one particular interpretation that crystallizes his own exegetical and theological insight into the passage he has removed from the reader the possibility of reaching a different conclusion (albeit one that the translator might regard as erroneous).

INSUFFICIENT INFORMATION

A different kind of problem is faced when we understand the immediate meaning of a word or a sequence of words, but do not possess sufficient information, either from the literary context in which it appears or from our knowledge of the world of the author, to decide exactly to what it refers. For example, at Deut. 32: 36, *'azelat yad* (literally '(their) hand has gone'), although it seems clear that the 'hand' is figurative of strength or power, the combination of the fact that the verb *'azal* can mean both 'come' and 'go' and that the possessor of the 'hand' is not specified means that it is unclear whether the 'going of the hand' refers to the draining away of Israelite power (as is normally assumed), or, as Targum Onqelos and Rashi interpret, the progress of enemy strength.

At Job 31: 27, literally, 'and my hand has kissed my mouth', even when we move past the curious image of the mouth receiving rather than giving a kiss, we are really no wiser as to what is being referred to here (beyond the action described). From the context provided, it is likely that some kind of idolatrous gesture is intended, but we do not have sufficient access to the cultural world of the author of Job to go much beyond this. Moreover, only the most attentive of readers or listeners is likely to make the association, through context, with idolatry, so translations have a choice of effectively leaving the reader in the dark or incorporating information that the original readers or listeners might have had in their minds: cf. TEV: 'honour them by kissing my hand in reverence to them'.

In some cases, even when we have a reasonably extended section of text, we cannot be quite sure of what the real thrust of the piece is. For example, at Mal. 2: 10–16, although unfaithfulness is clearly being addressed and marital imagery is clearly employed, it is far from evident that what is being specifically denounced is intermarriage of Israelite men with foreign women (and the concomitant divorcing of their Israelite wives), priestly betrayal of the covenant with Levi, or introduction of non-Yahwistic elements into the cult. Part of the problem here is that terms that have a clear application in one context can be used, by extension, or figuratively, in other quite different ones (see Ogden 1988).

Words of Ambiguous or Uncertain Reference

Related to the preceding problem is the fact that frequently a word will have two or more quite distinct senses, and on some occasions it is difficult to decide which is the most appropriate one. A case in point is the verb *qana*, which generally means 'to take possession of' or, more specifically, 'to buy', but occasionally signifies 'to create' (a meaning associated with the cognate verb in, for example, Ugaritic). This meaning has been seen at Gen. 4: 1; 14: 19, 22; Deut. 32: 6; Ps. 139: 13, and Prov. 8: 22. Of particular interest here are the first passage and the last one. In the case of the last passage there is clearly an enormous theological difference between wisdom being 'acquired' by God, as a prerequisite of his creative activity (in which case wisdom clearly existed, alongside God, before creation; cf. Job 28: 23–7), and its being 'created' by him, in which case the absolute sovereignty of God is maintained.

Against this background we should probably understand the LXX's choice of the verb *ktizo* ('establish, create') here (and in a dependent passage at Sir. 1: 9).

At Gen. 4: 1, *qaniti 'iš 'et yhwh*, the issue of what *qana* means (did Eve acquire a man or create one?) is complicated by uncertainty about the meaning of the particle *'et*. One line of interpretation takes *'et* to be the object marker; cf. Targum Pseudo-Jonathan (completed after the seventh century CE): 'I acquired a man, an angel of Y' (in allusion to Cain's demonic paternity). In general, though, the preposition *'et* is understood here, not in the usual sense, 'with', but 'by means of', 'with the help of', a sense which, however, is only rarely attested (cf. e.g. Judg. 8: 7). Attempting to conserve the more usual sense of prepositional *'et*, Rashi, basing himself on an earlier tradition, interprets as 'I have become a partner with God in creation' (as against the earlier creation of Adam and Eve by God alone). The interpretative tradition also reflects doubt about the identity of the 'man' (*'iš*). He is generally taken to be Eve's son, Cain, but outside this context the term would more naturally be expected to refer to her husband, Adam. Hence, an early tradition interprets as 'behold, I (re)gain my husband through Y'. Here, then, we have an example of a recurrent basic issue in translation: namely, how to understand an ambiguous or difficult word when an equal amount of uncertainty is attached to the other words that we need to be able to understand in order to provide an interpretation, through context, of the first word!

REFERENCE, CONNOTATION, AND FOCUS

Even when a word appears to have just one, quite concrete meaning, it is frequently difficult precisely to identify the referent. For example, at Lev. 11: 22, what exactly are the four types of creature mentioned? We assume that all are, loosely speaking, 'locusts', of one kind or another, because the first item (*'arbe*) and the last one (*ḥaḡaḇ*) are well attested elsewhere in the Bible, apparently in this sense. But the other two words (*sol'am* and *ḥargol*) occur only in this verse. And even for the first two, our scientific identification is, ultimately, conjectural. In principle, all these uncertainties have to be faced before we start to think about translating the meanings we have decided upon into a language whose speakers have very limited experience of such creatures or languages which make less or more fine distinctions than Hebrew did (which has an additional five words referring to such insects!) To give another example, it is not certain whether the animals caught by Samson at Judg. 15: 4 were foxes, jackals, or a different creature. In the case of 'behemoth' (in form apparently the plural of *behema* ('beast')) at Job 40: 15, even though the next four verses provide a description, translations are divided about the reference and the best way to present it to readers—contrast 'the chief of beasts, the crocodile' (REB), 'the hippopotamus' (CEV), 'beasts' (LXX), 'Behemoth' (Vulgate, NRSV, NJB, NJPS), 'the monster Behemoth' (TEV).

And once we determine what kind of animal we believe to have been signified in the Hebrew text, in many cases we also have to consider what associations such words (and referents) gave rise to in the minds of Hebrew-speakers (as reflected, for example, in the Bible's use of simile and metaphor) and whether these associations are shared by the culture of those who will use the translation. It is clear, for example, that the number 40 in the Bible has a particular associative load that is difficult to determine and even harder to transmit to another language in a natural way. Or, from a different area of life, what similarity is there in fact or in social perception between a biblical priest *(kohen)* and a priest in a Roman Catholic, or an Orthodox, or a Protestant receptor community? More fundamentally, should we render the office of Melchizedek, Micaiah's priest, Eli, and the priests of the Jerusalem Temple all by the same term, just because Hebrew does?

Colour terminology (see Brenner 1983) is another example of how complex it is to ascertain referential and associative meanings and then to convey these into another language. The basic problem is that words for apparently the same colour in different languages can cover a significantly different range of the same light spectrum. Sensitivity to this phenomenon must affect our understanding and rendering of, for example, the description of the first horse in Zech. 1: 8; 6: 2 (JPS, NEB: 'bay'; NRSV, TEV, NJB: 'red'), depending on whether we interpret the Hebrew colour term *'adom* as basically 'earth-coloured' (cf. *'adama* ('earth')), i.e. nearer to 'brown' (cf. the description of David in 1 Sam. 16: 12 or of the lover in Song 5: 10), or, as traditionally, nearer to 'red' (perhaps 'blood-coloured'; cf. *dam* ('blood')). But then, in the case of the Zechariah passage there is also a different, more exegetical, element that enters our consideration: do we believe that the choice of colour is deliberately surreal (a *red* horse) because of the nature of the vision or because 'red' has some special symbolic value. In this connection, we should note that the connotations of colour terms in Hebrew do not necessarily correspond with those in other languages. For example, in view of the description of the lover at Song 5: 11, it is quite possible that at 1: 5 'black' is a positive term (as LXX, NRSV: 'I am black *and* beautiful', REB, TEV), not negative (as Vulgate, NJB: 'I am black, *but* lovely', NJPS, CEV).

Kinship terms also represent a complex area. A simple example is Hebrew *'ah*, which can denote not only a male sibling ('brother') but also a nephew, a cousin, or another quite close male relative, and, very often, a 'fellow tribesman' or 'compatriot'. After unravelling what exactly *'ah* does refer to in a particular biblical text, the translator can then sometimes be faced with significant perceptual mismatches between Hebrew and the receptor language—for example, if the receptor language has two complementary terms, one for 'younger brother', another for 'older brother'. For a translator, having to make such a referential distinction on each occasion is sometimes not only difficult but also theologically problematic (in the New Testament, when dealing with the 'brothers' of Jesus, for example).

Terms for emotions are also notoriously difficult. At Gen. 4: 5, what does the Hebrew, literally 'and it became heated for Cain', really mean? In LXX Cain is grieved, in Symmachus he feels angry, in Targum Onqelos he feels strongly.

In the same way that the precise reference of a word can shift from one text (or context) to another, so can its associative or connotative value. For example, outside Proverbs, NRSV consistently renders the adjective and verb from the Hebrew root *'rm* negatively, as '(be) crafty', '(show) craftiness', or '(be) cunning'. However, in Proverbs it always renders the same set of words positively, as '(be) prudent', '(show) prudence', or, more commonly, '(be) clever'. Similar remarks apply to the corresponding noun, *orma*: 'treachery' (Exod. 21: 14), 'cunning' (Josh. 9: 4); but 'shrewdness' (Prov. 1: 4), 'prudence' (Prov. 8: 5, 12). NRSV (which is not alone in its choices here) might be correct in reserving the positive usage for Proverbs, but the fact that this positive usage is so well attested might also lead us to consider whether the statement about the serpent in Gen. 3: 1 was actually intended to be as negative as many translations take it to be or whether it simply reflected, more neutrally, ancient folk conceptions about the wisdom and immortality of the serpent (cf. LXX: *fronimos* ('wise'; NJPS: 'shrewd')).

Not infrequently, the associative value of a word is more important in a given text than its actual reference: for example, in the use of 'dog' at 1 Sam. 24: 15; 2 Sam. 9: 8, etc. Somewhat similarly, in words without a high associative value, the function of a particular referent rather than its form can be the most salient feature expressed by the Hebrew text. This distinction between form and function might underlie some of the renderings of the Hebrew *'ohel* ('tent') by the Greek words *oikos* and *oikia* (which normally translate the Hebrew *bayit* ('house')). For example, at Gen. 24: 67, in MT Isaac takes Rebekah into his mother's tent, but in LXX into her house; at Gen. 31: 33, Laban goes searching tent to tent in MT, but house to house in LXX; at Lev. 14: 8 the cleansed 'leper' has to leave his tent (MT)/house (LXX) and stay outside the encampment. Although exegetical motives might sometimes stand behind these changes, in others it seems likely that the LXX translators have used *oikos/oikia* as 'home', focusing on the function of the tent rather than on its form.

Failure to identify the primary semantic focus of a word in a particular passage can lead to distorted and even perverse renderings. For example, at Prov. 5: 7 (also discussed below), it is almost certain that the focus of the word *zara* (in MT) 'strange woman' is on the woman's 'foreignness'. That foreignness is either with regard to the kin group to which the author and reader belongs (in which case here the 'foreign woman', whether in a lawful or in an illicit relationship with an Israelite reader, is a potential risk to the reader's fidelity to his traditional religion) or with regard to the (male) reader himself (in which case the sense of *zara* is a woman, be she married, single, and/or foreign, who is legally 'unavailable' to the reader). On either reading, the focus of *zara* is on the relationship of the author or reader to the woman, not on the character, moral or other, of that woman.

This focus is well captured by NJPS's 'forbidden woman' (TEV's 'another man's wife' is too specific). LXX, which has *gune porne* ('a woman, a prostitute'), might reflect a text that read *išša zona*, or simply *zona* (*znh*), for *zara* (*zrh*), but it is difficult to justify the *meretrix* ('prostitute') of the Vulgate, 'adulteress' of REB and NJB, 'immoral woman' of CEV, or the especially remarkable 'loose woman' of NRSV, which is not so much a translation as a radical transculturation!

Effectively, these renderings represent in differing degrees the imposition of the translator's social background and moral judgements on a text that shares neither of these. Note in particular NJB, which, in addition to its choice of 'adulteress', also renders the neutral 'smooth' by the pejorative 'unctuous' later in the verse. We are sharply reminded that translation can never escape being an exercise in the ideological seizure of a text. The translator and his or her interior and exterior world always stand between the reader or hearer of a translation and the original text, and, in effect, guide the reader's interpretation (at every level) of that text. For introductory surveys of linguistic, and especially, semantic issues in biblical interpretation, see Barr 1961; Sawyer 1972; Silva 1995; for problems in the transfer of meaning to receptor languages, see Larson 1998.

Figurative Language

Language is pervaded by semantic extensions and figurative usages of a more or less striking character (see Bullinger 1898; Gibson 1998; Caird 1980). But what was immediately recognized as figurative in the culture that produced the source text may not be so apprehended by those who have access to that text only through non-mother-tongue knowledge of its language or through a translation. For example, at Ps. 24: 4 the point of 'one innocent of palms and pure of heart' is lost without the understanding (if necessary, incorporated in the translation) that the body parts here are metonymous for the actions and thoughts associated with them—CEV's 'Only those who do right for the right reasons' is commendably adventurous here. In Jer. 47: 5, 'baldness has come to Gaza', there is both metonymy, i.e. baldness for the sense of mourning expressed by shaving the head, and synecdoche, of a place for the people living there, both well expressed by TEV: 'Great sorrow has come to the people of Gaza'. Just as a place can stand for its people, so can part of a place stand for the whole, as in Gen. 22: 17, 'and your seed will inherit the gate of your enemies' (i.e. their city), and Ruth 4: 10, 'and the name of the deceased will not be cut off... from the gate of his place' (i.e. from his native city). LXX has 'cities' in the first verse (like Targum Onqelos) and 'the tribe of his people' in the second.

On many occasions, however, the existence of a figurative usage is not so clear. At Isa. 52: 7, 'how beautiful on the mountains are the feet of a messenger', it is unlikely that the aesthetic impact of the messenger's feet is really in primary focus here, but rather what they stand for: the messenger's footsteps (NJPS), his coming (TEV), or the messenger himself (CEV). Sometimes, our blindness to figurative language is caused by our culturally, or theologically, conditioned impressions of the context in which it occurs. For example, it is possible that 'the knowledge of good and evil' at Gen. 2: 17 and 3: 5 does not focus on moral issues at all, but is rather a merismus for 'complete knowledge' (compare the parallelism at 2 Sam. 14: 17, 20) or, less radically, that 'good' and 'evil' refer to what is advantageous or disadvantageous.

On other occasions, that a figure is being used is not in doubt, but we cannot be sure quite what its primary focus is. For example, at Prov. 25: 15, 'a soft tongue will break a bone', it is clear from the preceding statement, 'with patience (literally "length of anger") a judge will be persuaded', that metaphorical language is intended. The problem is whether the primary focus of the metaphor is basically that of patience (in keeping with the first statement), or whether, as commonly, the word for 'tongue' is used metonymously for 'speech', in which case the point of the overall figure is that 'gentle talk can... overcome any problem' (CEV). Or compare the LXX rendering of 'uncircumcised of lips' at Exod. 6: 12 (*alogos* (literally 'wordless')) with that of v. 30 (*ischnophonos* ('withered of sound')). In the case of Deut. 34: 5, 'and Moses died there... at the mouth of ['al pi] Y', most translations, ancient and modern, interpret 'mouth' as metonymous for 'command, word'. However, a segment of the Jewish interpretative tradition (e.g. Targum Pseudo-Jonathan, Talmud, and Rashi) understands 'al pi to mean 'by a kiss (from Y)'. Moreover, some biblical metaphors are especially rich or polyvalent. For example, in the case of 'dust', it is frequently difficult to decide where the primary focus of its use in a particular passage lies: on mortality, lowliness, unfruitfulness, or some other feature.

At Prov. 5: 3 (already discussed, above), the Hebrew translates literally as 'for the lips of a (female) stranger drip honey and her palate is smoother than oil'. Now, given that in the Bible both lips and palate can function by metonymy for speech, which in turn can be called 'smooth', that is, 'flattering', it is likely that the primary image here is one of seductive talk. However, in recognizing this (and expressing it in translation), it is important not to lose sight of the evidently erotic tenor of the figure as a whole, although this is precisely what happens when (as in NRSV or CEV), 'lips' and 'palate' are translated as 'words', 'speech', etc. On the other hand, TEV has over-focused on the erotic imagery, 'The lips of another man's wife may be as sweet as honey and her kisses as smooth as olive oil', and has lost sight of the main point. In this case the safest course would seem to be, as NJPS, to translate literally and to leave it to the reader to discern, aided by context (and perhaps notes), the interplay of images.

Focusing on the salient point of an image can also lead translators to alter, for the sake of naturalness in the receptor language, some element in the original figure, so long as that modification does not affect the overall thrust of the figure. For example, at Prov. 27: 16 the LXX speaks of seizing the tail of a dog rather than, as in Hebrew, its ears (although here the change might also be for alliteration: *kraton kerkou kunos* ('seizing a tail of a dog'); less likely is a difference in the *Vorlage*: *bznb* ('by the tail of') for MT *b'zny* ('by the ears of')).

A modern translation will often clarify, or decode, a figurative usage, if it is felt that readers will not readily comprehend it. Some precedents are already found in the ancient versions. For example, at Isa. 9: 13 (EVV 14) the Hebrew reads 'head and tail, palm branch and reed' (NRSV), which LXX interprets as 'head and tail, great and small', leaving the first figure as it was but interpreting the second one. The Vulgate adopts the same approach, but 'clarifies' differently, *caput et caudam incurvantem et refrenantem* ('head and tail, the one that bends and the one that holds back'), an interesting illustration of the danger inherent in 'explaining' a metaphor, because, as already indicated, we can never be quite sure that the writer was focusing on one aspect (LXX: status) or another (Vulgate: flexibility).

Moreover, in this matter, as in almost every other in connection with translation, it is often difficult to see where linguistic assistance ends and interpretative imposition begins. An uncomplicated example is Deut. 8: 9, 'a land whose stones are iron', where Symmachus adds an 'as (iron)'. One cannot help but think that here the translator was being more pedantic than helpful! At Exod. 19: 4, where God says that he carried Israel 'on eagles' wings', CEV, as an aid to the secularized reader, renders 'just as a mighty eagle'. LXX and Symmachus, obviously aware of the literal untruthfulness of the Hebrew statement, also inserted a *hos(ei)* ('as, as though'), thus ensuring that the original sequence would be understood figuratively. However, the Greek translators' decision here probably derived less from any supposed linguistic difficulty than from a perceived danger of a materialistic, idolatrous understanding of God. Similarly, in Deuteronomy 32 (the Song of Moses), the Hebrew word *ṣur* ('rock') occurs eight times, once with literal reference, five times in reference to Y, and twice in reference to other gods. The repeated usage and the context mean that the figurative reference is clear, and so modern versions tend to translate literally, leaving it to the reader to decode the metaphor. In view of this, it is likely that LXX's rendering of *ṣur* in reference to God as *theos* ('God') is intended less to clarify a difficult metaphor as to avoid any wording that might be conducive to idolatry. Similar comments probably apply to Targum Onqelos's rendering of *ṣur* as *taqqip̄* ('strong (one)') and *teqop̄* ('strength'). Compare as well the LXX's eradication of pagan allusions at Deut. 32: 24, where the parallel Hebrew terms *rešep̄* and *qeṭeb* (at least the first of which is also found as the name of a Canaanite deity) are 'demythologized' by being rendered as 'birds' and 'destruction'. Within MT itself we see a further stage in this kind of process in the treatment of the name of the god Baal, which is replaced by the dysphemism *bošet* ('shame') on various occasions (especially in the names 'Ishbosheth' and 'Mephibosheth' in 2 Samuel as against 'Eshbaal' and 'Meribbaal' in 1 Chronicles; see also Jer. 3: 24 and Hos. 9: 10). Although this alteration is reflected in both Masoretic and non-Masoretic (LXX, 4QSamᵃ) traditions, it seems to have been stronger in the Masoretic one—see Jer. 11: 13, where MT has 'you placed altars to shame, altars to offer incense to Baal', but LXX lacks 'altars to shame'.

Also attested are euphemistic changes, or toning down of language, for example in connection with sex. Thus, the Masoretes replace the verb *šagal* (Deut. 28: 30; Isa. 13: 16; Jer. 3: 2; Zech. 14: 2), apparently 'rape, treat as prostitute', with the phonetically similar *šakab*, apparently, 'bed, lay'. LXX reflects the same sensitivities, rendering 'have' in the first two instances and 'defile' in the second two. In Deuteronomy, the Samaritan Pentateuch has the modest 'will lie with her', and Targum Onqelos, 'will accommodate her' (in some manuscripts). At Judg. 19: 2, the MT appears to say that the Levite's concubine 'prostituted herself [*zana* (*znh*)] against him', i.e. had sex with another man, but manuscripts of LXX say either that she was angry (*zanah* [*znḥ*], or perhaps *zana* in a different sense) with him or, as the Vulgate, that she left him ('*azab*). If MT's reading is original here, then LXX (or its *Vorlage*) would appear to be an attempt to soften the candour of the sexual imagery preserved by MT.

In other cases, figurative, and non-figurative, language may be interpreted in the service of the translator's contemporary religious situation. Thus, for example, at Num. 24: 17, LXX renders Hebrew 'star' literally, but 'staff' (*šebet* perhaps originally in this context 'comet') by 'man', probably in allusion to a messianic figure. However, in the later Targum Onqelos, the messianic reference is more obvious: 'star' is 'king' and 'staff' is 'messiah'. In connection with LXX's rendering of 'tent' in MT by 'house' (see above), some of the passages might represent a type of exegeticizing interpretation in which the conditions of early Israel are 'updated' to those of the translators' Jewish contemporaries; a striking example is Gen. 25: 27, where for MT '*ohalim* ('tents') the LXX has *oikia* ('a house'), and Targum Onqelos has *bet 'ulpana* ('a house of instruction'), thus providing from its interpretation of the text an ancient precedent for the study houses of the targumist's time. Renderings that are explicitly conditioned by ideology can be used not just to guide the beliefs of the receptor community, but also to defend it against the claims of rival belief systems sharing the same text. Against this background may be seen the replacement by the later Greek translators, Aquila and Theodotion, of LXX's *parthenos* ('virgin') in the messianic text (for early Christians) Isa. 7: 14 by *neanis* ('young woman'). Most scholars would agree that this is a more accurate rendering of the Hebrew ('*alma*), but the improvement in translation was probably driven primarily by ideological factors.

GRAMMATICAL AND STYLISTIC FEATURES

Because of its more technical character, we have hardly touched upon the topic of syntax, or the way in which clauses and sentences are combined into particular arrangements (see Waltke and O'Connor 1990). One word-order feature that can be seen quite easily and that has an obvious impact on translation is ellipsis, where certain elements are omitted but need to be supplied, implicitly in order to yield (what we assume to be) the intended meaning. The basic problem here is one of recognizing an ellipsis when it occurs. The following two texts are among the otherwise rather obscure passages that might be illuminated by such recognition. At Mic. 7: 3, the Hebrew text seems to read literally: 'the officer asks and the judge for recompense'. Here, the interpretation is eased by assuming an ellipsis, 'the official and the judge each asks for recompense' (as NRSV) or 'the official asks, and the judge decrees, for recompense', a double ellipsis. A double ellipsis has also been identified at 1 Sam. 16: 7, which reads literally 'for not that which humankind sees', where for sense to be obtained (without emending the text) the words 'God sees' need to be provided.

In the following example, it is not so much ellipsis as a curious arrangement of the text that might be at issue. At Exod. 19: 13, the Hebrew reads 'for it is indeed to be stoned or shot with arrows, whether beast or man, it shall not live'. Here, it is possible that a chiastic arrangement was intended, with the stoning reserved for the man and the shooting for the beast. Compare Matt. 7: 6, where it is probably the dogs and not the pigs that attack (cf. TEV, CEV).

In fact, parallelistic arrangements, especially 'envelope' (*inclusio*) and chiastic structures are extremely common in the Bible, not just as a more or less conscious device in poetry (see Watson 1984; Zogbo and Wendland 2000), but also in prose. Note, for example, 'all' at the beginning and end of Gen. 9: 3, 'in booths' at the beginning and end of Lev. 23: 42, 'like him' at the beginning and end of 2 Kgs. 23: 25, and the (almost perfect) chiastic structure at Isa. 6: 10: 'fatten heart...ears harden...eyes seal...see with eyes...with ears hear...heart understands'.

CONCLUDING REMARKS

The examples presented in this article represent but a tiny fraction of the problems that face any interpreter or translator of the Hebrew Bible. It is as though he or she is constantly walking on shifting sands, with neither the text itself nor the meaning expressed by the elements of that text secure. And when a translator or interpreter finds that a passage, or a verse, or a clause, or a word is easy to work out, we must suspect that this is merely a reflection of the superficial nature of their knowledge of the language or of the culture and society that gave rise to the text. Even in modern language translation, a translator can never be fully sure of what the author meant, just as he or she can never control the meaning that a reader will attribute to the translation. On the one hand, language is essentially malleable, and one can do pretty much what one likes with words. An insult in one context can be a term of endearment in another. On the other hand, there is an essential discontinuity between what one person means and what another understands. Something intended by a speaker as a mild reproach can cause unintended pain to an interlocutor. If such insecurity and dissonance are inherent in intra-language spoken communication, how much more so when that language is abstracted from a specific social interaction and put down in writing. The written text, although purporting to express meaning, actually presents the reader with a bewildering array of uncertainties, many of which would have been resolved in face-to-face spoken communication. An author can control his or her words and can intend them to express such-and-such an idea, but he or she cannot control the meaningfulness (or lack of it) those words will have for any particular reader or listener, let alone for a translator, who, in effect, creates a new text, a kind of fantasia on the original. Just as the original text stands between its author and even those who share that author's culture (including language), beckoning and yet bewildering, so the translator stands between even this illusory communion of meaning and a new set of readers who may be far removed in time, place, and culture from the original author. For the readers of the translation, the only communion of meaning to which they can aspire is that which obtains between them and the translator. The original text, the society in which it was produced, and the intentions of its author are even further beyond their reach than they were for the translator. If a translator, albeit more by chance than on the basis of secure knowledge, does not distort too greatly the emotive impact and the information content intended by the original author, a good job may be said to have been done. However, if a reader is really interested in the meaning of the text, then a translation can only be a first stage, a set of signposts, often unwittingly misleading, which should be supplemented by detailed study of a variety of commentaries and other tools, which give access to the social, material, and conceptual worlds of the Bible, and, ideally, by study of the biblical languages themselves.

BIBLIOGRAPHY

ABEGG, MARTIN, FLINT, PETER, and ULRICH, EUGENE 1999 *The Dead Sea Scrolls Bible: The Oldest Known Bible, Translated and with Commentary.* Edinburgh: T. & T. Clark.

BAASTEN, M. F. J., and VAN PEURSEN, W. Th., eds. 2003. *Hamlet on a Hill: Semitic and Greek Studies Presented to Professor T. Muraoka on the Occasion of his Sixty-Fifth Birthday.* Orientalia Lovaniensia Analecta, 118. Leuven: Peeters.

BARR, J. 1961. *The Semantics of Biblical Language.* London: SCM Press.

BARTHÉLMY, D. *et al.* 1976–80. *Preliminary and Interim Report on the Hebrew Old Testament Text Project,* i [Pentateuch]. London: United Bible Societies. ii: *Historical Books.* Stuttgart: United Bible Societies, 1976. iii: *Poetical Books.* Stuttgart: United Bible Societies, 1977. iv–v: *Prophetical Books I–II.* New York: United Bible Societies, 1979–80.

BATALDEN, S., CANN, K., and DEAN, J., eds. 2004. *Sowing the Word: The Cultural Impact of the British and Foreign Bible Society 1804–2004.* Sheffield: Sheffield Phoenix Press.

BECK, J. 2000. *Translators as Storytellers: A Study in Septuagint Translation Technique.* New York: Peter Lang.

BEYER, K. 1986. *The Aramaic Language: Its Distribution and Subdivisions,* trans. J. F. Healey. Göttingen: Vandenhoeck & Ruprecht.

BRENNER, A. 1983. *Colour Terms in the Old Testament.* JSOTS.S 21. Sheffield: JSOT Press.

—— and VAN HENTEN, J. W., eds. 2002. *Bible Translation on the Threshold of the Twenty-First Century: Translation, Reception, Culture and Religion.* JSOTS.S 353. Sheffield: Sheffield Academic Press.

BULLINGER, E. W. 1898. *Figures of Speech Used in the Bible, Explained and Illustrated.* London: Eyre and Spottiswoode; repr. Grand Rapids, Mich.: Baker Book House, 1968.

CAIRD, G. B. 1980. *The Language and Imagery of the Bible.* Studies in Theology. London: Duckworth.

CLARK, D. J., and HATTON, HOWARD 2002. *A Handbook on Haggai, Zechariah, and Malachi.* UBS Handbook Series. New York: United Bible Societies.

CONYBEARE, F. C., and STOCK, St. GEORGE 2001. *Grammar of Septuagint Greek: With Selected Readings, Vocabularies, and Updated Indexes.* Peabody, Mass.: Hendrickson Publishers, Inc.; orig. pub. Boston: Ginn and Company, 1905.

CREASON, S. 2004. 'Aramaic'. In Roger D. Woodard, ed., *The Cambridge Encyclopedia of the World's Ancient Languages,* Cambridge: Cambridge University Press, 391–426.

ELWOLDE, J. F. 'Hebrew and Aramaic Grammar and Lexicography' and 'Hebrew and Aramaic Languages'. In Stanley E. Porter, ed., *Dictionary of Biblical Interpretation and Criticism,* London: Routledge, forthcoming.

FITZMYER, J. A. 1979. 'The Phases of the Aramaic Language'. In *A Wandering Aramean: Collected Aramaic Essays,* SBLMS, 25. Missoula, Mont.: Scholars Press, 57–84.

GIBSON, J. C. L. 1998. *Language and Imagery in the Old Testament.* London: SPCK.

HADAS-LEBEL, M. 1995. *Histoire de la Langue Hébraïque: des Origines à l'Époque de la Mishna,* 4th edn. Collection de la Revue des Études Juives, 21. Paris and Leuven: E. Peeters.

HOGNESIUS, K. 2003. *The Text of 2 Chronicles 1–16: A Critical Edition with Textual Commentary.* Coniectanea Biblica Old Testament Series, 51. Stockholm: Almqvist & Wiksell International.

HORBURY, W., ed. 1999. *Hebrew Study from Ezra to Ben-Yehuda.* Edinburgh: T. & T. Clark.

JOBES, K. H., and SILVA, MOISÉS 2000. *Invitation to the Septuagint.* Grand Rapids, Mich.: Baker Academic.

JOÜON, P. 1993. *A Grammar of Biblical Hebrew,* corrected rev. edn., trans. and ed. T. Muraoka. Subsidia Biblica, 14. 1–2; Roma: Editrice Pontificio Istituto Biblico.

KALTNER, J. and MCKENZIE, STEVEN L., eds. 2002. *Beyond Babel: A Handbook for Biblical Hebrew and Related Languages*. Society of Biblical Literature Resources for Biblical Study, 42. Atlanta: Society of Biblical Literature.

KELLEY, P. H., MYNATT, DANIEL S., and CRAWFORD, TIMOTHY G. 1998. *The Masorah of Biblica Hebraica Stuttgartensia: Introduction and Annotated Glossary*. Grand Rapids, Mich.: William B. Eerdman Publishing Company.

KNOBLOCH, F. W. ed. 2002. *Biblical Translation in Context*. Studies and Texts in Jewish History and Culture, 10. Bethesda, Md.: University Press of Maryland.

LAMBDIN, T. O. 1973. *Introduction to Biblical Hebrew*. London: Darton, Longman, and Todd.

LARSON, M. L. 1998. *Meaning-Based Translation: A Guide to Cross-Language Equivalence*, 2nd edn. Lanham, Md: University Press of America.

LEMAIRE, A. 1988. 'Aramaic Literature and Hebrew: Contacts and Influences in the First Millennium B. C. E.'. In Moshe Bar-Asher, ed., *Proceedings of the Ninth World Congress of Jewish Studies, Jerusalem, August 4–12, 1985; Panel Sessions: Hebrew and Aramaic*, Jerusalem: World Union of Jewish Studies, 9–24.

MCCARTER, P. K. 2004. 'Hebrew'. In Roger D. Woodard, ed., *The Cambridge Encyclopedia of the World's Ancient Languages*, Cambridge: Cambridge University Press, 319–64.

MAYES, A. D. H., ed. 2000. *Text in Context: Essays by Members of the Society for Old Testament Study*. Oxford: Oxford University Press.

METZGER, B. M. 2001. *The Bible in Translation: Ancient and English Versions*. Grand Rapids, Mich.: Baker Academic.

NOSS, PHILIP A., ed. 2002. *Current Trends in Scripture Translation*. UBS Bulletin, 194/5. Reading: United Bible Societies.

La Nouvelle Bible Segond, Édition d'Étude (Alliance Biblique Universelle, 2002).

OGDEN, G. S. 1988. 'The Use of Figurative Language in Malachi 2.10–16'. *Bible Translator*, 39: 223–30.

OLOFSSON, S. 1990. *The LXX Version: A Guide to the Translation Technique of the Septuagint*. Coniectanea Biblica, Old Testament Series, 30. Stockholm: Almqvist & Wicksell International.

PÉREZ FERNÁNDEZ, M. 1997. *An Introductory Grammar of Rabbinic Hebrew*, trans. J. F. Elwolde. Leiden: E. J. Brill.

ROSENTHAL, F. 1995. *A Grammar of Biblical Aramaic*, 6th rev. edn. Porta Linguarum Orientalium, n.s. 5. Wiesbaden: Otto Harrasowitz.

SÁENZ-BADILLOS, Á. 1993. *A History of the Hebrew Language*, trans. J. F. Elwolde. Cambridge: Cambridge University Press.

SALVESEN, A. 1991. *Symmachus in the Pentateuch*. Journal of Semitic Studies Monograph, 15. Manchester: The Victoria University of Manchester.

SAWYER, J. F. A. 1972. *Semantics in Biblical Research: New Methods of Defining Hebrew Words for Salvation*. Studies in Biblical Theology, 2nd ser. 24. London: SCM Press.

SCHENKER, A., ed. 2004. *The Earliest Text of the Hebrew Bible: The Relationship between the Masoretic Text and the Hebrew Base of the Septuagint Reconsidered*. Septuagint and Cognate Studies Series, 52. Leiden: E. J. Brill.

SILVA, M. 1995. *Biblical Words and their Meaning: An Introduction to Lexical Semantics*, rev. edn. Grand Rapids, Mich.: Zondervan.

SOLLAMO, R., and SIPILÄ, SEPPO, eds. 2001. *Helsinki Perspectives on the Translation Technique of the Septuagint*. Publications of the Finnish Exegetical Society, 82. Helsinki: The Finnish Exegetical Society; Göttingen: Vandenhoeck & Ruprecht.

Tov, E. 2001. *Textual Criticism of the Hebrew Bible*, 2nd edn. Minneapolis: Fortress Press; Assen: Van Gorcum.

De Waard, J. 2003. *A Handbook on Jeremiah*. Textual Criticism and the Translator, 2. Winona Lake, Ind.: Eisenbrauns.

Waltke, B. K., and O'Connor, M. 1990. *An Introduction to Biblical Hebrew Syntax*. Winona Lake, Ind.: Eisenbrauns.

Watson, W. G. E. 1984. *Classical Hebrew Poetry: A Guide to its Techniques*. JSOTS.S 94. Sheffield: JSOT Press.

Wilt, T., ed. 2003. *Bible Translation: Frames of Reference*. Manchester: St. Jerome Publishing.

Wright, B. G. 1989. *No Small Difference: Sirach's Relationship to Its Hebrew Parent Text*. SBL SCS 26. Atlanta: Scholars Press.

Yeivin, I. 1980. *Introduction to the Tiberian Masorah*, trans. and ed. E. J. Revell. Society of Biblical Literature Masoretic Studies, 5. N.p.: Scholars Press and International Organization for Masoretic Studies.

Zogbo, L., and Wendland, Ernst R. 2000. *Hebrew Poetry in the Bible: A Guide for Understanding and for Translating*. UBS Helps for Translators. New York: United Bible Societies.

CHAPTER 10

LANGUAGE, TRANSLATION, VERSIONS, AND TEXT OF THE APOCRYPHA

MICHAEL A. KNIBB

INTRODUCTION

The meaning of the term 'Apocrypha', as discussed later in this volume in the chapter 'The Growth of the Apocrypha' (Chapter 29), is ambiguous in both early Christian and modern usage. Here it is perhaps sufficient to state that the present essay is intended to cover the apocryphal and deutero-canonical books included in the NRSV, and that the term 'Apocrypha' is used with this specific meaning. As in the later chapter, reference will also be made to the *Book of Enoch* (*1 Enoch*) because it, like the *Book of Jubilees*, is regarded as canonical by the Ethiopian Church.

The writings of the Apocrypha have in common the fact that although none belong in the Hebrew Bible, they all, with the exception of 2 Esdras, are included in manuscripts of the Greek Bible. However, the appearance of homogeneity that this suggests disguises the fact that while some of these writings were composed in

Greek, others were composed in Hebrew or Aramaic and were translated into Greek as part of the wider process by which the books of the Hebrew Bible were translated into Greek, and for similar reasons. So far as the Apocrypha is concerned, it is possible from the point of view of language of composition to distinguish three main groups of writings. (1) Works whose Greek style shows that they were composed in Greek: additions B and E to the Book of Esther, Wisdom of Solomon, 2 Maccabees, 3 Maccabees, 2 Esdras 1–2, 15–16, 4 Maccabees, and probably the Prayer of Manasseh. (2) Works for which the discovery of Hebrew or Aramaic manuscripts of their texts—particularly, but not only, as part of the discoveries at Qumran—has confirmed the view that they were composed in one or other of these languages: Tobit, Ecclesiasticus, and Psalm 151. (3) Works for which composition in Hebrew or Aramaic seems very probable, or is at least suspected, even though we lack textual proof of this: Judith, the additions to the Book of Esther (except for additions B and E), Baruch, the Letter of Jeremiah, the additions to the Greek Book of Daniel, 1 Maccabees, and 1 Esdras. In addition, 2 Esdras 3–14 was also probably composed in Hebrew, but neither the original Hebrew nor the Greek translation of this have survived, and we are dependent on the evidence of the versions made from the Greek, particularly the Latin version.

The discovery of Aramaic manuscripts of *1 Enoch* at Qumran has confirmed the view that this work, or at least the major part of it, was composed in Aramaic. In addition to these Aramaic fragments of *1 Enoch*, portions of the Greek translation have also survived, but for the book as a whole we are dependent on the Ethiopic version.

The fragments of four Aramaic manuscripts and one Hebrew manuscript of Tobit found in Cave 4 at Qumran are clearly of great importance for the text of this book, and the same is true of the Hebrew psalm manuscript from Qumran Cave 11 that includes Psalm 151, and of the fragments of a number of Hebrew manuscripts of Ecclesiasticus, of which some were found in the store-room of a Cairo synagogue, one at Masada, and two at Qumran (see further below). But even for these writings, the Greek text is of primary importance, and this is all the more true for the remaining writings of the Apocrypha except for 2 Esdras. Study of the text of the Apocrypha thus forms part of Septuagintal studies (for introductions to the Septuagint, see Swete 1914; Jellicoe 1968; Dorival, Harl, and Munnich 1988; Jobes and Silva 2000; Fernández Marcos 2000; Siegert 2001, 2003; Dines 2004).

As in the case of the translation of the books of the Hebrew Bible, there are three types of witness to the Greek text: (1) Greek manuscripts and papyri; (2) the versions; (3) quotations in early Christian writings. For what follows it should be pointed out that while *Esdras a* of the Septuagint is 1 Esdras of the Apocrypha, *Esdras b* of the Septuagint gives the Greek translation of Ezra–Nehemiah, and is not the same as 2 Esdras of the Apocrypha.

GREEK MANUSCRIPTS AND PAPYRI

The most important witnesses for the recovery of the earliest accessible form of the Greek text are the four major uncial codices: Codex Vaticanus (B), Codex Sinaiticus (S (ℵ in Swete, see below)), Codex Alexandrinus (A), and Codex Venetus (V). (Descriptions of these are given in Swete 1914: 122–32; Jellicoe 1968: 175–88, 197–9.) Within these codices there is some variation in the position of individual historical, poetic, and prophetic books, and in the relative order of the groups of poetic and prophetic books (see the lists in Swete 1914: 201–2); but Tobit and Judith are placed after Esther or Daniel; Wisdom and Ecclesiasticus are grouped with the Wisdom books; Baruch and the Letter of Jeremiah follow Jeremiah; 1–4 Maccabees, which were not included in B, are grouped with Esdras a–b, Esther, Tobit, and Judith, or (in V) with Daniel, Tobit, Judith; 1 Esdras (Esdras a) normally follows Paraleipomena; the Prayer of Manasseh is included in the Odes and in A is grouped with the Psalms and the wisdom books (the Odes are not present in B or S or in the surviving portions of V); and Psalm 151 follows Psalm 150.

It was primarily the four uncials B, S (ℵ), A, and V, and in particular the first three of these, that were used by Swete (1887–94) and Rahlfs (1935) for their editions of the Septuagint. But whereas the former for the most part used B for his text and gave the variants of the other manuscripts in the textual apparatus, Rahlfs provided a critical text, and it is this edition that is the more useful. For serious study of the Greek text of the books of the Apocrypha, the individual volumes of the Göttingen Septuagint, where available, are indispensable.

The relatively small number of other uncials (which are normally identified by capital letters) tend to be of lesser importance, and the same is also true of the much larger number of miniscules (identified by numbers). However, while many of the latter support one or other of the three major uncials (B, S, and A), others are important because they are representative of the Origenic (Hexaplaric) recension or of the Lucianic recension (also known as the Antiochene or Antiochian recension). The former is represented, for example, by 88 (the Chigi manuscript), which contains Jeremiah, Daniel, Ezekiel, and Isaiah, and 253, which contains the wisdom books; the latter is represented, for example, by 248, which contains the wisdom books plus Esdras a and b, Esther, Tobit, and Judith, and 637, which contains the wisdom books.

The papyri are of importance for the recovery of the earliest accessible form of the Greek text, but for the most part only quite small fragments of the books of the Apocrypha have survived.

THE EARLY VERSIONS

The writings of the Apocrypha, like the writings of the Old and New Testaments and as part of the same process, were translated in the early centuries of the Christian Era into a number of languages, to meet the needs of the areas and countries that had recently been converted to Christianity (for the Syriac version as a partial exception, see below). These early versions were in almost all cases made from the Greek, and include the following: Syriac, Latin, Coptic, Armenian, Ethiopic, Arabic. The versions vary considerably in character—for example, in the extent to which they are literal or free—and are of considerable interest in their own right; but, with the exception of 2 Esdras and 1 *Enoch*, they are of secondary importance in comparison with the Greek for the text of the writings of the Apocrypha. Some brief comments follow on the Syriac, Latin, and Ethiopic versions; for the Coptic, Armenian, and Arabic, see the articles by Mills (1992), Alexanian (1992), and Jellicoe (1968: 266–8) respectively.

Syriac Versions

The precise date and place of origin of the Peshitta version—the standard Syriac version (Syr)—of the Old Testament and of the Apocrypha are unknown. There is, however, good evidence to suggest that the books of the Old Testament were translated into Syriac from a Hebrew original, and it has recently been argued that the translation was made by Jews in Edessa who subsequently converted to Christianity and took their translation with them (Weitzman 1999: 206–62). The translation of the books of the Apocrypha, with the exception of Ecclesiasticus, was made from the Greek, most probably by Christians, and the Syriac translation of the Old Testament and Apocrypha as a whole was preserved and transmitted by Christians. The fact that the Old Syriac Gospels, which are dated to about 200, in some quotations of Old Testament passages follow the Syriac Old Testament suggests that the translation of most of the books of the Old Testament was completed by the end of the second century; the translation of the books of the Apocrypha is likely to have followed soon after.

The use of the term 'Peshitta' for the Syriac version is not attested before the ninth century; the word means 'simple', and was used of this version to distinguish it from the Syro-Hexapla of the Old Testament (see below) and the Harklean version of the New. For the text of the Syriac version, see the individual volumes of the Leiden edition; and for introductions, see Brock 1992; Weitzman 1999.

The Peshitta version of the Syriac is to be distinguished from the Syro-Hexapla (Syh). This provides a very literal translation into Syriac of the text of the fifth column of Origen's Hexapla, which was intended to bring the Septuagint translation into line with the Hebrew. The translation was undertaken by Paul of Tella in the early seventh century in a monastery near Alexandria, and was made at the request of the Syrian Orthodox patriarch, Athanasius. The Syro-Hexapla is a very important witness of the Hexaplaric text, and some manuscripts preserve the Hexaplaric signs.

Latin Versions

The translation of the Greek Bible into Latin derives from North Africa, and dates back to as early as the second century, although it is likely that the translation, like the Septuagint itself, was made book by book over a period of time. As use of the translation spread, it was subject to successive revision on the basis of Greek witnesses different from those used by the original translators, and manuscripts of this version, as well as quotations from it by the Latin Fathers, reveal many differences. The name *Vetus Latina*, or Old Latin (La), given to this version covers the variety of revised texts represented by the manuscripts and quotations.

It was in response to the variety of Latin texts in circulation that Jerome, who worked under the patronage of Pope Damasus, undertook his work of revision. He began with the gospels and the Psalter, but then in Bethlehem after 387 he revised a number of books of the Old Testament on the basis of Greek manuscripts with a Hexaplaric text (and in the process prepared the second of his three translations of the Psalter). Finally, in the last decade of the fourth century and the first decade of the fifth he prepared a Latin translation of the Old Testament from the Hebrew text. This version was not immediately accepted as authoritative, and for a time merely added to the revisions of the Latin text in circulation. But over the following centuries Jerome's translation gained in authority, and it is essentially his translation that from the sixteenth century has been known as the Vulgate. However, Jerome was concerned only with the books that belonged in the Hebrew canon, and as far as the Apocrypha is concerned, he translated only Tobit, Judith, and the additions to Esther and Daniel; the translations of the other books of the Apocrypha that are to be found in manuscripts of the Vulgate remain essentially the Old Latin.

A major critical edition of the Old Latin is in the process of being published by the Vetus Latina Institute at Beuron (B. Fischer and colleagues), and one of the Vulgate has been issued by the Benedictines of San Girolamo in Rome (H. Quentin and colleagues, 1926–95). An excellent edition of the latter with an abridged apparatus was published by R. Weber in two volumes (1969; later editions have been issued in a single volume). For an introduction, see Bogaert 1992.

Ethiopic Version

The translation of the books of the Greek Bible into Geez—that is, classical Ethiopic (Aeth)—was made during the fifth and sixth century, and followed a century or so after the adoption of Christianity by the Aksumite ruler Ezana in the middle of the fourth century. However, it is important to recognize that although the translation dates back to the fifth or sixth century, almost all the extant manuscripts date from the fifteenth century or later, and that only a very small number date from the fourteenth century, much less from before then. The translation was made from the Greek, but in the case of the books of the Old Testament the text was revised in the fourteenth century on the basis of Arabic or Syro-Arabic texts, and in the latter part of the fifteenth century, or later, on the basis of the Hebrew. But for a book such as 1 *Enoch*, while earlier and later forms of the text can clearly be distinguished, it is not clear how far the revision was textually based. For an introduction, see Knibb (1999).

QUOTATIONS

Quotations from the books of the Apocrypha—and Pseudepigrapha—do occur in early Christian writings, and may be of importance in providing a witness to early forms of the Greek and of the Old Latin. The relevant authors are discussed in the introductions to each book in the volumes of the Göttingen edition of the Septuagint, and the evidence is given in the textual apparatus in each volume.

TRANSLATIONS AND INTRODUCTIONS

In addition to the translations of the books of the Apocrypha in the NRSV and in other editions of the Bible that include the Apocrypha, translations are to be found in the editions of the Apocrypha and Pseudepigrapha edited by Charles (1913) and Charlesworth (1983, 1985). Similar collections have been published in other languages: for example, in German, in the series *Jüdische Schriften aus hellenistisch-römischer Zeit*, edited by Kummel, Habicht, Kaiser, Plöger, and Schreiner (1973–).

These all contain information concerning the text and versions of each book. The *Introduction* by Denis (2000) is the most up-to-date and detailed work to deal with the text and versions of the books of the Apocrypha, but the Introduction by deSilva (2002) also contains helpful information.

TEXTS COMPOSED IN GREEK

The Wisdom of Solomon

The evidence for the view that Wisdom was composed in Greek is overwhelming. The fact that the author quotes from the Septuagint version of the Old Testament already makes composition in Greek extremely likely (cf. e.g. 2: 12 and Isa. 3: 10; 11: 22 and Isa. 40: 15; 16: 22 and Exod. 9: 24; Holmes 1913: 524–5). The text is written in a good Greek style, and shows none of the characteristics of translation Greek. The author does adapt his style to the point that he makes use of *parallelismus membrorum*, which is a characteristic feature of Hebrew verse, but he also employs 'the features of florid Greek rhetorical prose' (Reese 1970: 25–6). The book makes use of a full range of Hellenistic stylistic devices (Reese 1970: 25–31; Winston 1979: 14–17), and both the book as a whole and the sections of which it is composed deploy literary genres familiar from Hellenistic rhetorical texts. The smaller literary genres include the diatribe (1: 1–6: 11 + 6: 17–20; 11: 15–15: 19), the 'problem' genre (6: 12–16 + 6: 21–10: 21), and the comparison (*synkrisis*; 11: 1–14 + 16: 1–19: 22), and the book itself represents an example of the protreptic genre (*logos protrepticos*; Reese 1970: 90–121). Above all, the author's vocabulary points very strongly to composition in Greek. He uses 335 words, almost 20 per cent of a total vocabulary of 1,734 different words, that do not occur in any other canonical book of the Septuagint; but of these, many, as Reese (1970: 3–25) has demonstrated, are characteristic of Hellenistic religious, philosophical, ethical, and psychological vocabulary. In the light of this evidence, few scholars have argued for composition in Hebrew or Aramaic and translation into Greek, and such suggestions as have been made, such as Zimmermann's view (1966–7) that Wisdom was composed in Aramaic, have found little acceptance.

The Greek text of Wisdom was edited for the Göttingen edition by Ziegler (1962). He based his edition primarily on B and S, which he believed to be related, and A, and he argued that readings attested by B-S and A, and supported by the majority of the miniscules, had an undisputed claim to be placed in the text, but that their unique readings were in almost all cases secondary (Ziegler 1962: 61–2;

Winston 1979: 64–6). Ziegler also discusses the versions of Wisdom, and records their evidence in his apparatus. The *Vetus Latina* dates from the second half of the second century, and is of particular importance, because it is based on Greek manuscripts earlier than any still extant (Ziegler 1962: 16–17). The *Vetus Latina* text of Wisdom has been edited in the Beuron edition by Thiele (1977–85). The Christian character of the Syriac version of Wisdom is discussed by Drijvers (1986), and the text has been edited in the Leiden edition by Emerton and Lane (1979). For the other versions, see Ziegler's edition.

Other Texts Composed in Greek

The same kind of considerations that apply to Wisdom also apply to the other texts that were undoubtedly composed in Greek. Here it must suffice to refer to the Bibliography for references to text editions and studies of 2 Maccabees, 3 Maccabees, and 4 Maccabees. Brief comments on additions B and E to Esther and on 2 Esdras 1–2, 15–16, will be included in the appropriate place below. Comment on the Prayer of Manasseh follows here.

The Prayer of Manasseh   Although probably of an earlier origin, the oldest form of the Prayer of Manasseh in existence is that contained in the Church Order known as the *Didascalia*. It occurs in the context of a narrative concerning Manasseh in which passages from 2 Kings 21 and 2 Chronicles 33 are interwoven with a number of additions; the story of Manasseh serves, together with other examples drawn from Scripture, to illustrate the theme of God's mercy towards sinners who repent. The *Didascalia* was composed in Greek, probably in the first half of the third century, and is thought to derive from Syria. The Greek text of the *Didascalia* is lost, but there is a Syriac translation in existence, and the Greek text itself was incorporated in the *Apostolic Constitutions*. This collection of ecclesiastical laws dates from the latter part of the fourth century, and almost certainly comes from Syria. The Greek text of the *Apostolic Constitutions* survives, and there is also a Syriac translation.

The Prayer of Manasseh is also included in the Septuagint, and it is possible that the text was taken from the *Apostolic Constitutions*. It occurs in the Septuagint in the Odes, a collection, appended to the Psalter, of fifteen psalms used in the liturgy that were, with the exception of the Prayer and the Morning Hymn, all taken from the books of the Old and the New Testament. The Odes are not present in B and S, but they do occur in A and in T (Codex Turicensis), in miniscule manuscripts, and in manuscripts of the Vulgate. The Göttingen edition of the Odes, is based primarily on A, T, and 55, and includes in the apparatus for the Prayer of Manasseh the evidence of the Vulgate and of the text in the *Apostolic Constitutions* (Rahlfs 1931: 78–80, 361–3). Translations of the Prayer have generally been based on the Greek, but Charlesworth (1985) has based his translation on the Syriac text as edited by Baars and Schneider (1972) from a combination of the evidence of manuscripts of the Peshitta and that of manuscripts of the *Didascalia.*

The brevity of the Prayer makes it difficult to determine with any certainty whether the text was composed in Greek or in Hebrew or Aramaic (Ryle 1913: 614–15; Charlesworth 1985: 625–7). However, the style and language, and the use of phrases derived from the Septuagint, point strongly to the view that the Prayer was composed in Greek (Denis 2000: i. 678–9).

A Hebrew 'Psalm of Manasseh' does occur in a collection of non-canonical psalms found at Qumran (4Q381 33), but this bears no relation to the Greek Prayer of Manasseh beyond the basic theme of confession of sin (Schuller 1998: 122–3).

Texts Composed in Hebrew or Aramaic

Tobit

The occurrence of Semitisms in the Greek text of Tobit led older scholars to suspect that the work had been composed in Hebrew or Aramaic (cf. Pfeiffer 1949: 272–3), and these suspicions were confirmed by the discovery of fragments of four Aramaic manuscripts (4Q196–9) and one Hebrew manuscript (4Q200) of Tobit at Qumran. The Aramaic and the Hebrew forms of the text from Qumran agree in general with one form of the Greek text, but the relationship between the different strands of the textual tradition is complex. Helpful accounts of the textual evidence available and of the relationship between the different forms of the text are given by Fitzmyer 1995*a*; 1995*b*: 1–5; Otzen 2002: 60–5.

The four Aramaic manuscripts from Qumran cover approximately 20 per cent of the text of Tobit (with some overlap), and the Hebrew manuscript covers approximately 6 per cent (with some overlap with the Aramaic). The four Aramaic manuscripts differ among themselves, and the Hebrew is not a translation of the text of any of the Aramaic manuscripts. However, it is probable that the Hebrew text has been translated from an Aramaic text, and that the original story was composed in Aramaic (Fitzmyer 1995*a*: 669–72; Moore 1996: 33–9; Otzen 2002: 61).

The Greek text exists in three different forms: a short recension (GrI) represented by B, A, V, papyrus 990, and most miniscules; a long recension (GrII) represented by S, papyrus 910, and miniscule 319; and an intermediate recension

(GrIII) represented by 106 and 107. In the past there was a tendency to favour the short recension, and to regard the long recension, which is more strongly marked by Semitisms than the short one, as an expanded version of this; but the position has been reversed by the discoveries at Qumran. According to Fitzmyer, although the Greek is not a direct translation of either the Aramaic or the Hebrew, 'both the Aramaic and the Hebrew form of the Tobit story found at Qumran agree in general with the long recension of the book' (Fitzmyer 1995b: 2). It now seems most likely that GrI is a shortened version of GrII, and thus, whereas the RSV is based on the short recension, the NRSV is based on the long recension. GrIII, the intermediate recension, is related to GrII—and within that tradition is closer to the Old Latin (see below) than to S—but has taken over some elements from GrI (Hanhart 1983: 33). The Göttingen edition (Hanhart) prints the long and short forms of the Greek text separately.

The manuscripts of the Old Latin represent different types of text, but, as noted previously, the Old Latin is an important early witness to the Greek text. The Old Latin of Tobit is closely affiliated to GrII, and provides help in filling gaps in S and in throwing light on corrupt passages in GrII. Unfortunately, there is no modern edition of the text, but one is being prepared by the Vetus Latina Institute at Beuron.

In his preface to the Vulgate translation of Tobit, Jerome states that an expert in Aramaic and Hebrew translated an Aramaic text of Tobit into Hebrew for him, and that from this oral Hebrew version he dictated his Latin translation to a secretary in one day. It is clear, however, that Jerome also made use of the existing Old Latin text, even though the Vulgate translation represents a considerable abridgement of the Old Latin and belongs to the short recension (Fitzmyer 1995a: 657–60).

The other versions are of secondary importance. There are also a medieval Aramaic version and various Hebrew versions of Tobit in existence, but these were translated from the Greek and the Latin version.

Sirach

It has always been known that the Greek version of the Wisdom of Jesus Son of Sirach (Ecclesiasticus) was a translation of a work composed in Hebrew, because the author's grandson states this explicitly in the Prologue to his translation of his grandfather's book. But, apart from some quotations in rabbinic writings, the Hebrew text was lost until, at the end of the nineteenth century, substantial remains of four manuscripts of the Hebrew were discovered in the Genizah, a store-room for discarded manuscripts, of a synagogue in Cairo. Further leaves of these and other manuscripts were subsequently identified amongst the fragments recovered from the Genizah, and the remains of six manuscripts (A–F) are now known, of which three are represented only by a single leaf. The manuscripts date from the eleventh or twelfth century, although C, a florilegium, may be older (E has not been dated). In addition, two small fragments of the Hebrew of Sir. 6: 14–15, 20–31, were discovered in Cave 2 at Qumran (2Q18), and the Hebrew of Sir. 51: 13–20, 30b, is preserved in the Psalms Scroll from Cave 11 (11QPs^a). Finally, the major part of the Hebrew of Sir. 39: 27–44: 17 was discovered at Masada. The Masada manuscript dates from the first half of the first century BCE, 2Q18 from the second half of the first century BCE, and 11QPs^a from the first half of the first century CE. In total, the ancient and the medieval manuscripts now provide the Hebrew original of some two-thirds of the text known from the Greek. There is some overlap both amongst the Cairo manuscripts and between Cairo manuscript B and the Masada manu-script, and it was the basic identity of the text of manuscript B with that of the Masada manuscript that finally resolved the doubts about the authenticity of the Cairo manuscripts that had been expressed by some scholars. Information about the Hebrew manuscripts is given by Beentjes in his edition of all the Hebrew material (1997; cf. Skehan and Di Lella 1987: 51–62). Beentjes has subsequently published a list of corrections to his 1997 edition (Beentjes 2002).

The Greek text exists in two forms: the original Greek translation (GrI) repre-sented by B, S, and A, and by many miniscules, and an expanded form of this (GrII), which contains some 300 cola not found in GrI. This expanded text is not a new and independent translation, but represents rather the outcome of a series of revisions of GrI on the basis of the Hebrew; the manuscripts of GrII transmit the GrI text, but expand this as seemed necessary in the light of the Hebrew. However, no single manuscript represents GrII as such, but additions characteristic of GrII are to be found in representatives of the Origenic recension (particularly 253-Syh) and the Lucianic recension (e.g. 248, the best-known witness of GrII), and in the Old Latin (see below); the manuscripts do not contain all the additional material, but only a selection (Ziegler 1965: 70, 73–5). Ziegler's edition in the Göttingen series prints the GrII additions in smaller type in the body of the Greek text. The NRSV, which is based on GrI, but has sometimes followed the Hebrew where it appears to offer a better text, and occasionally the Syriac or the Old Latin, normally gives the GrII additions in the footnotes.

Study of the Cairo Genizah manuscripts A, B, and C has shown that two recensions (HI and HII) are also present in the Hebrew, in that these manuscripts contain some ninety additions to the original text, some of which are comparable to the additions found in GrII (see e.g. 3: 25; 11: 15–16; 16: 15–16, which are all attested by HII, GrII, and the Syriac (see below)). The additions in GrII go back ultimately to a revision or revisions of GrI on the basis of Hebrew manuscripts representative of HII (cf. Ziegler 1965: 83–4; Skehan and Di Lella 1987: 57–9).

As noted, the Old Latin is an important source for GrII. It contains some of the additions that are to be found in the Origenic and Lucianic recensions, but it also contains additions that are no longer attested in Greek, but are doubtless based on a Greek original (Ziegler 1965: 74). An edition is being published by Thiele (1987–). Of the other versions, the Syriac is the most important. It contains a number of additions of the type found in HII and GrII. In contrast to the other books of the Apocrypha, the translation was based on the Hebrew, and may have been made by Jews. But if the translation was made by Jews, it was certainly revised by Christians at an early stage, and there is good evidence for the view that the basic Syriac version, including at least some of its Christian features, was in existence by at least the end of the third century (Owens 1989). It has been argued by Winter (1977) that the original translation was produced by Ebionites no later than the early part of the fourth century, and was revised by orthodox Christians in the latter part of that century; but there is no evidence in the translation for views that could be described as distinctively Ebionite. An edition of the most important manuscript of the Syriac version (Milan, Ambrosian Library, MS B. 21 Inferiore, known as 7a1), together with Spanish and English translations, has been published by Calduch-Benages, Ferrer, and Liesen (2003).

Psalm 151

The Psalms Scroll from Cave 11 contained the Hebrew text not only of Sir. 51: 13–20, 30b, but also of a number of other texts that do not form part of the Hebrew Bible, including that of Psalm 151 (11QPs^a XXVIII) and of two other apocryphal psalms (see below). The Hebrew text was unknown before the discovery of 11QPs^a, but in the light of its evidence it appears that the Greek text of Psalm 151 is an abbreviated conflation of what were two psalms in the Hebrew: 151A and 151B. The complete text of Ps. 151A is preserved in 11QPs^a XXVIII, but only the fragmentary remains of the first two lines of Ps. 151B. For the text, see Sanders 1965: 49, 53–64.

The Greek text of Psalm 151 follows directly after that of Psalm 150 in manuscripts of the Greek Psalter, but in the superscription it is said to be 'outside the number': that is, outside the 150 psalms of which the canonical Psalter consists in both the Greek Bible and the Hebrew, albeit by different combinations and divisions of psalms. It may be observed that there has been a debate as to whether 11QPs^a was regarded at Qumran as a true scriptural Psalter or as a secondary collection based on Psalms 1–150 in their traditional Hebrew form; for a summary and assessment, see Flint 1997: 7–9, 202–27. The Greek text of Psalm 151 is included by Rahlfs (1931) in his edition of the Psalms and Odes.

Psalm 151 is also preserved in versions dependent on the Greek, including the Old Latin and the Syriac. Of these, the Syriac should be mentioned separately, in that Psalm 151 occurs in Syriac as the first of a group of five Syriac psalms, the existence of which was first noted in the eighteenth century. The Psalms Scroll from Cave 11 contains the Hebrew text of the second and third Syriac psalms (= Pss. 154, 155;

11QPs^a XVIII, XXIV) in addition to that of Psalm 151. However, whereas the Syriac version of Psalm 151 was made from the Greek (Sanders 1965: 54; Denis 2000: i. 528; Wigtill 1983), Syriac psalms 152–5 appear to be based on a Hebrew text. The Syriac text was edited by Baars (1972).

1 Enoch

The Ethiopic *Book of Enoch*, which represents the most extensive form of the book that we possess, consists of five sections or booklets: the *Book of Watchers*, the *Parables*, the *Astronomical Book*, the *Book of Dreams*, and the *Epistle of Enoch*. The discovery of the fragments of eleven Aramaic manuscripts of *1 Enoch* in Cave 4 at Qumran confirmed the view that four at least of these sections were composed in Aramaic, and it is likely that the *Parables*, the only section of which no fragments have been found at Qumran, was also composed in Aramaic or, if not, in Hebrew. But it is clear that there were significant differences between the form in which the Enoch traditions existed at Qumran and the book as it existed in its most developed form in Ethiopic. For an overview of the textual evidence, see Knibb 2001; Nicklesburg 2001: 9–20; Knibb 2002.

Four of the Aramaic manuscripts (4QEnastr^{a-d} ar (4Q208–11)) contain only material related to the *Astronomical Book* of the Ethiopic (*1 En.* 72–82). The Aramaic fragments belong, on the one hand, to a synchronistic calendar of the phases of the moon, which has no precise parallel in *1 En.* 72–82, but is perhaps summarized in *1 En.* 73: 4–8 and 74: 3–9, and on the other, to material corresponding to *1 En.* 76–9 and 82. The oldest of the manuscripts (4Q208), which dates back to the late third or early second century BCE, contains only fragments of the synchronistic calendar, and it is only in 4Q209, from the early years of the first century CE, that we have fragments of both types of material. The Ethiopic version of the *Astronomical Book* represents a radical abridgement and recasting of the book in its Aramaic form, and in the case of chapters 72–5, it remains open to question how far the Ethiopic provides evidence of the book as it existed at the time of its original composition.

The fragments of the remaining seven manuscripts (4QEn^{a-g} ar (4Q201–2, 204–7, 212)) belong to parts of the *Book of Watchers*, the *Book of Dreams*, and the *Epistle*. The fragments of 4Q201, which dates from the first half of the second century BCE, but is thought to have been copied from an older—possibly much older—manuscript, belong only to the *Book of Watchers*, and it appears that 4Q201 contained only this section of *1 Enoch*. It appears likely also that 4Q202, from the middle of the second century BCE, contained only the *Book of Watchers*, and that 4Q212, from the middle or latter part of the first century BCE, contained only the *Epistle*, although this last point has been questioned. 4Q207, which dates from the third quarter of the second century BCE, consists of only a small fragment belonging to the *Book of Dreams*. However, the fragments of 4Q204, from the last third of the first century BCE, belong to the *Book of Watchers*, the *Book of Dreams*, and the *Epistle*, and thus attest the existence at Qumran of a corpus of Enochic writings in a single manuscript—but a corpus which did not include the *Astronomical Book*, much less the *Parables*. (Milik 1976: 310 argued that the Enochic *Book of Giants* was copied in the same manuscript between the *Book of Watchers* and the *Book of Dreams*, but this now seems unlikely.) 4Q205 and 4Q206—the former of the same age as 4Q204, the latter from the first half of the first century BCE—both contain fragments belonging to the *Book of Watchers* and the *Book of Dreams*, but it appears that they too contained in addition the *Epistle*. The date of 4Q204 confirms the existence of a tripartite corpus of Enochic writings by at least the end of the first century BCE, and it was probably in existence for some time before then, but it remains unknown when more precisely the corpus was formed. For the text of the Aramaic fragments, see Milik 1976; Stuckenbruck 2000; Tigchelaar and García Martínez 2000).

The Aramaic Enochic writings were translated into Greek, and it is likely that it was at the Greek stage, rather than the Ethiopic, that the *Astronomical Book* was abridged and considerably revised, and that it and the *Parables* were successively inserted into the Enochic corpus to produce the book familiar from the Ethiopic version. However, we have no precise information about the circumstances in which the translation of the Enochic traditions into Greek was undertaken, or whether all the parts of the corpus were translated at once, although this is probably unlikely. Barr, from his study of the Greek translation in comparison with the Aramaic original, has suggested that the translation 'belonged to the same general stage and stratum of translation as the LXX translation of Daniel' (1979: 191). It has been suggested that some tiny papyrus fragments of Greek manuscripts from Qumran Cave 7 (7Q4, 8, 11–14) belong to a Greek translation of the *Epistle*, but the fragments are too small for this to be certain; for references, see Knibb 2001: 401.

The Greek text is preserved only partially, and the two most substantial portions of text to have survived are contained in the Akhmim manuscript and the Chester Beatty–Michigan papyrus. The former, which dates from the sixth or perhaps the end of the fifth century, contains incomplete copies of two different manuscripts of the *Book of Watchers*; the latter, from the fourth century, contains an incomplete version of the *Epistle*; in both cases a number of other, Christian writings were copied in the same manuscript. The Greek text of the *Book of Watchers* and the *Epistle* in these witnesses is broadly similar to that from which the Ethiopic version was made. Brief extracts from the *Book of Watchers* in the *Chronicle* of Syncellus, dating from the early ninth century, provide a slightly different form of the Greek text. Other evidence for the Greek text of 1 *Enoch* is confined to a few fragments and a relatively small number of quotations (including that of 1 *En.* 1: 9 in Jude 14). For the text of all the Greek material, see Black 1970; and for an introduction, see Denis 2000: i. 104–21.

The Ethiopic version of *1 Enoch* provides the only clear evidence for the existence of an Enochic 'pentateuch'; but, as indicated, it seems probable that already at the Greek stage the book had acquired its fivefold form. The Ethiopic translation was made from the Greek version, probably in the fifth or sixth century, but the oldest manuscripts of the book that we possess date from the fifteenth century, and the majority are from the seventeenth or eighteenth century. The manuscripts provide two different forms of the text, an older and a younger. The latter is a revision of the former, but it should be observed that the oldest accessible form of the Ethiopic version of *1 Enoch* that we possess dates back only to the fifteenth century. For an edition and translation, see Knibb 1978; and for a translation, see Nickelsburg and VanderKam 2004.

TEXTS PROBABLY COMPOSED IN HEBREW OR ARAMAIC

2 Esdras

The work entitled 2 Esdras in the Apocrypha is included in the Slavonic Bible as 3 Esdras and in the Appendix to the Vulgate as 4 Esdras, but, as noted previously, does not survive in Greek. It is composite in origin. The main part, which consists of chapters 3–14 and is more commonly known as 4 Ezra, is a Jewish apocalypse and dates from towards the end of the first century CE. Chapters 1–2 (known as 5 Ezra) and chapters 15–16 (known as 6 Ezra) are Christian supplements, and date from the second and third centuries respectively (cf. Knibb 1979: 76–8, 110, 183–4). The complete work (chapters 1–16) survives only in a Latin translation (and in some versions dependent on a late form of the Latin), but translations of chapters 3–14 (4 Ezra) also exist in Syriac, Ethiopic, Georgian, Arabic (in two different forms), Armenian, and in a fragment of a Coptic version—all directly dependent on a Greek version (see below)—as well as in a number of versions dependent on the Latin and in a third Arabic version dependent on the Syriac. A very clear overview of all the textual evidence for 2 Esdras 3–14 (4 Ezra) is given by Stone (1990: 1–11; cf. Denis 2000*a*: i. 828–46), and what follows is primarily concerned with this part of 2 Esdras.

Although it has been disputed, it is now universally accepted that the versions of 4 Ezra are all directly or indirectly dependent on a now lost Greek version. That such a Greek text did once exist is clear both on the grounds of general probabil-ity—the analogy provided by the textual histories of the other apocryphal books—and from the fact that there are in existence a small number of quotations from the Greek (for the text of these, see Denis 1970; cf. Denis 2000a: i. 828–31). Further confirmation of the existence of such a Greek text has been provided by the analysis by Mussies of Graecisms in the Latin version (1974). However, it is also clear that the Greek text that lay behind the versions was itself a translation from a Semitic original. It has been argued that 4 Ezra was written in Aramaic, but in the light of the number of Hebraisms that are still discernible in the Latin text, it is generally accepted that the language of composition was Hebrew, albeit a Hebrew subject to Aramaic influence; see the list of Hebraisms given by Violet 1924: pp. xxxi–xxxix; cf. Stone 1990: 10–11; Klijn 1983: 9–11.

The most important of the versions that were translated directly from the Greek divide into two groups: on the one hand the Latin and the Syriac, on the other the Georgian, the Ethiopic, and the fragment of the Coptic. Of these it is generally the case that it is the first group, and in particular the Latin, that is the most important, and it is on the Latin, as edited by Weber (1969: ii. 1931–74), that the NRSV translation was primarily based, although account was also taken of the other versions that are directly dependent on the Greek. Apart from Weber, important editions of the Latin text were published by Bensly (1895) and Violet (1910); the most recent edition is that of Klijn (1983). The manuscripts of the Latin version were divided by James (in the Introduction to Bensly's edition (1895: pp. xxi–xxii)) into two families or recensions, one French, the other Spanish, and for 4 Ezra the French family normally represents the more original form of the text (cf. Violet 1910: p. xxiv). There are a significant number of quotations in the Latin Fathers, in particular in the writings of Ambrose; see the list in Violet 1910: pp. xliv–xlvi; cf. Klijn 1983: 93–7.

The Syriac text has been edited by Bidawid (1973) for the Leiden edition on the basis of the only complete manuscript known to exist. However, a complete Arabic version based on the Syriac is now also known (Stone 1990: 6). For the remaining versions, it may be noted that Violet's edition of the Latin text (1910) was accom-panied by translations in parallel columns of the other major versions directly dependent on the Greek (Syriac, Ethiopic, Arabic (in two forms), and Armenian). This work has now largely been superseded by that of Klijn (1992), which provides a German translation of the Latin text and, in an apparatus under the translation, the variants of the three most important versions (Syriac, Ethiopic, and Georgian) in German translation.

5 Ezra and 6 Ezra survive only in Latin, and in some versions dependent on a late form of the Latin. There is good evidence that 6 Ezra was composed in Greek—and a fourth-century papyrus fragment of the Greek text of 15: 57–9 does survive—but although it is probable that 5 Ezra was composed in Greek, composition in Latin cannot be excluded (see Bergren 1990: 306–8; 1998: 17–18; Wolter 2001:

784–5, 828–9). There are significant differences between the French and Spanish recensions of these two books, including the fact that in the former the three works occur in the order 5 Ezra, 4 Ezra, 6 Ezra, in the latter in the order 4 Ezra, 6 Ezra, 5 Ezra. For 6 Ezra the French recension is more original than the Spanish, but for 5 Ezra the Spanish recension is older, and the French represents an inner-versional improvement of this (see Bergren 1990: 207–11; 1998: 89–92; Wolter 2001: 773–4; cf. already James in Bensly 1895: pp. lxxvii–lxxviii). However, in 5 Ezra the differences between the two recensions are such that Wolter gives translations of both in parallel columns. For the Latin text of 5 and 6 Ezra, see Bensly 1895: 83–92; Bergren 1990: 335–99; 1998: 161–225.

Denis (2000b: i. 870–1), with reference to Basset (1899), states that 5 and 6 Ezra both exist in Ethiopic, but this is not so; the translations given by Basset (1899: 114–39), to which Denis refers, are explicitly said to be of the Latin version (cf. also Basset 1899: 6, 18).

OTHER TEXTS PROBABLY COMPOSED IN HEBREW OR ARAMAIC

The presence of Semitisms in the Greek texts of the books not so far discussed (Judith, the additions to Esther (except for additions B and E), Baruch, the Letter of Jeremiah, the additions to the Greek Book of Daniel, 1 Maccabees, 1 Esdras) has led to the view that each of these was also composed in Hebrew or Aramaic, even though we lack textual proof of this of the kind available, for example, in the case of Tobit. However, apart from very brief comment on three of these writings, it must suffice here to refer to the Bibliography for references to text editions and studies.

The Additions to the Book of Esther

The Greek translation of Esther differs from the Hebrew in a number of respects, including the addition of six passages that are not present in the Hebrew. These additions were placed by Jerome at the end of his Latin translation of the book (cf. Weber 1969: i. 724–30) and were included as a block in the Apocrypha of the AV and RV without the rest of the text. The NRSV, like other recent translations, gives a translation of the complete Greek text of Esther with the additions included in their correct place in the narrative. The presence of Semitisms in the Greek text of additions A, C, D, and F has led to the view that these additions were composed in Hebrew or Aramaic (cf. Moore 1973; 1977: 155), but in view of their florid and rhetorical style it seems clear that additions B and E were composed in Greek.

The Additions to the Greek Book of Daniel

The Greek translation of Daniel, in a way similar to that of Esther, differs from the Hebrew and Aramaic text in a number of respects, including the addition of three passages that are not in the Hebrew or Aramaic: the Prayer of Azariah and the Song of the Three Jews; Susanna; and Bel and the Dragon. The Greek text of the additions, like that of the canonical book itself, exists in two forms: the Old Greek, or Septuagint, represented by papyrus 967, from the beginning of the third century, miniscule 88, and the Syrohexaplar; and the version attributed to Theodotion, represented by virtually all the other manuscripts and witnesses; for an overview of the textual evidence, see Moore 1977: 30–4, 52–3, 92, 129; Collins 1993: 2–12. Papyrus 967, as a pre-Hexaplaric witness to the Old Greek, represents a very important addition to the evidence of 88 and Syh, which were both subject to Hexaplaric influence, and for this reason the revised edition of Ziegler's original 1954 Göttingen edition by Munnich (1999), which takes full account of 967, is indispensable for the study of the Book of Daniel and the additions. In the revised edition the Old Greek and the Theodotionic text are given on facing pages. However, it was the Theodotonic text that was adopted by the Church, and it is this text that forms the basis of the NRSV translation of the additions.

In all the witnesses the Prayer of Azariah and the Song of the Three Jews are inserted in chapter 3 after verse 23, but the position of Susanna and of Bel and the Dragon varies: in 967 the order is Daniel, Bel and the Dragon, Susanna; in 88 and Syh, Daniel, Susanna, Bel and the Dragon; in the Theodotionic version, Susanna, Daniel, Bel and the Dragon. The story of Susanna in both the Old Greek and in Theodotion serves to explain how Daniel came to prominence and was thus an appropriate figure to be trained at the court of Nebuchadnezzar (Dan. 1), and the placing of the story before the book in Theodotion is in accordance with this understanding (Knibb 2001: i. 27–8). The Vulgate largely follows the Theodotionic version, but adopts the order Daniel, Susanna, Bel and the Dragon, and it is this order that is followed in the NRSV and in other English translations.

It is widely accepted that the additions, with the possible exception of the prose material in 3: 24–5, 46–50, were composed in a Semitic language, probably Hebrew (cf. e.g. Moore 1977: 5–6, 25–6, 44–9, 81–4, 119–20; Collins 1993: 199, 202–5, 410–11, 427–8).

1 Esdras

The difficulty with 1 Esdras is to know whether it is a fragment of a translation of a more original form of the biblical account of the restoration under Ezra, in which the story of the three young men has been interpolated, perhaps at the Greek stage, or whether it should be regarded as a new compilation or composition based on Chronicles, Ezra, and Nehemiah; for representatives of the two views, see, for example, Pohlmann (1970, 1980) and Williamson (1977: 12–36; 1996). However, it seems most likely that 1 Esdras should be regarded as a new composition, and thus Talshir, for example, has recently argued that 1 Esdras was based on a section of Chronicles–Ezra–Nehemiah, and that the book 'was created for the purpose of retelling the history of the Restoration in such a way that it revolved around the Story of the Three Youths and its hero Zerubbabel' (1999: 106). Talshir has argued that the story of the three young men was composed in Aramaic, and in any case it seems likely that the whole book is a translation of a Semitic original.

Suggested Reading

The Introduction by deSilva (2002) contains much helpful information concerning the topics covered in this essay, but the only book to deal directly, and in detail, with these topics is the two-volume work in French by Denis *et al.* (2000). Otherwise the various introductions to the Septuagint provide a good deal of relevant background information: for example, Dines 2004, Fernández Marcos 2000, or, in French, Dorival, Harl, and Munnich 1988. Full details of all these books are given below.

Bibliography

General

ALEXANIAN, J. M. 1992. 'Armenian Versions'. *ABD* vi. 805–8.

BOGAERT, P.-M. 1992. 'Latin Versions'. *ABD* vi. 799–803.

BROCK, S. P. 1992. 'Syriac Versions'. *ABD* vi. 794–9.

CHARLES, R. H., ed. 1913. *The Apocrypha and Pseudepigrapha of the Old Testament in English*, 2 vols. Oxford: Clarendon Press.

CHARLESWORTH, J. H., ed. 1983, 1985. *The Old Testament Pseudepigrapha*, 2 vols. Garden City, NY: Doubleday.

DENIS, A.-M. et collaborateurs avec le concours de J.-C. Haelewyck. 2000. *Introduction à la littérature religieuse judéo-hellénistique*, 2 vols. Turnhout: Brepols.

DE SILVA, D. A. 2002. *Introducing the Apocrypha: Message, Context, and Significance*. Grand Rapids, Mich.: Baker Academic.

DINES, J. 2004. *The Septuagint*. Understanding the Bible and its World. London and New York: T. & T. Clark (Continuum).

DORIVAL, G., HARL, M., and MUNNICH, O. 1988. *La Bible grecque des Septante: Du judaïsme hellénistique au christianisme ancien*. Initiations au christianisme ancien. Paris: Les Éditions du Cerf, 2nd edn. 1994.

FERNÁNDEZ MARCOS, N. 2000. *The Septuagint in Context: Introduction to the Greek Version of the Bible*, trans. W. G. E. Watson. Leiden and Boston: Brill.

JELLICOE, S. 1968. *The Septuagint and Modern Study*. Oxford: Clarendon Press.

JOBES, K. H., and SILVA, M. 2000. *Invitation to the Septuagint*. Grand Rapids, Mich.: Baker Academic; Carlisle: Paternoster.

KNIBB, M. A. 1999. *Translating the Bible: The Ethiopic Version of the Old Testament*. The Schweich Lectures of the British Academy, 1995. Oxford: Oxford University Press for the British Academy.

KUMMEL, W. G., HABICHT, C., KAISER, O., PLÖGER, O., and SCHREINER, J., eds. (1973–). *Jüdische Schriften aus hellenistisch-römischer Zeit*, 6 vols. Gütersloh: Gütersloher Verlagshaus Gerd Mohn.

MILLS, W. E. 1992. 'Coptic Versions'. *ABD* vi. 803.

QUENTIN, H. *et al.* eds. 1926–95. *Biblia Sacra iuxta Latinam Vulgatam versionem ad codicum fidem iussu Pauli PP. VI cura et studio monachorum abbatiae pontificiae Sancti Hieronymi in urbe ordinis Sancti Benedicti edita*, 18 vols. Rome: Vatican Press.

RAHLFS, A. 1935. *Septuaginta, id est Vetus Testamentum graece iuxta LXX Interpretes*, 2 vols. Stuttgart: Privilegierte Württembergische Bibelanstalt.

SIEGERT, F. 2001. *Zwischen Hebräischer Bibel und Altem Testament: Eine Einführung in die Septuaginta*. Münster, Hamburg, and London: Lit Verlag.

—— 2003. *Register zur 'Einführung in die Septuaginta'. Mit einem Kapitel zur Wirkungsgeschichte*. Münster, Hamburg, and London: Lit Verlag.

SWETE, H. B. 1887–94. *The Old Testament in Greek according to the Septuagint*, 3 vols. Cambridge: Cambridge University Press.

—— 1914. *An Introduction to the Old Testament in Greek*, rev. R. R. Ottley. Cambridge: Cambridge University Press.

WEBER, R. 1969. *Biblia Sacra iuxta Vulgatam Versionem*, 2 vols. Stuttgart: Würtembergische Bibelanstalt, 4th edn. 1994 (later editions in one volume).

WEITZMAN, M. P. 1999. *The Syriac Version of the Old Testament: An Introduction*. University of Cambridge Oriental Publications, 56. Cambridge: Cambridge University Press.

The books of the Apocrypha are listed below in the order in which they occur in the NRSV.

Tobit

FITZMYER, J. A. 1995*a*. 'The Aramaic and Hebrew Fragments of Tobit from Qumran Cave 4'. *CBQ* 57, 655–75.

—— 1995*b*. 'Tobit'. In M. Broshi *et al.*, eds., *Qumran Cave 4.XIV. Parabiblical Texts, Part 2*, DJD 19, Oxford: Clarendon Press, 1–76.

HANHART, R. 1983. *Tobit*. Septuaginta. Vetus Testamentum Graecum Auctoritate Academiae Scientiarum Gottingensis editum VIII, 5. Göttingen: Vandenhoeck & Ruprecht.

MOORE, C. A. 1996. *Tobit*. AB 40A. New York: Doubleday.

OTZEN, B. 2002. *Tobit and Judith*. Guides to the Apocrypha and Pseudepigrapha. London and New York: Sheffield Academic Press (Continuum).

PFEIFFER, R. H. 1949. *History of New Testament Times with an Introduction to the Apocrypha*. London: Adam & Charles Black.

Judith

HANHART, R. 1979. *Judith*. Septuaginta. Vetus Testamentum Graecum Auctoritate Academiae Scientiarum Gottingensis editum VIII, 4. Göttingen: Vandenhoeck & Ruprecht.

MOORE, C. A. 1985. *Judith*. AB 40. New York: Doubleday.

OTZEN, B. 2002. *Tobit and Judith*. Guides to the Apocrypha and Pseudepigrapha. London and New York: Sheffield Academic Press (Continuum).

The Additions to the Book of Esther

HANHART, R. 1966. *Esther*. Septuaginta. Vetus Testamentum Graecum Auctoritate Academiae Scientiarum Gottingensis editum VIII, 3. Göttingen: Vandenhoeck & Ruprecht, 2nd edn. 1983.

MOORE, C. A. 1973. 'On the Origin of the LXX Additions to the Book of Esther'. *JBL* 92, 382–93.

—— 1977. *Daniel, Esther and Jeremiah: The Additions*. AB 44. New York: Doubleday.

WEBER, R. 1969. *Biblia Sacra iuxta Vulgatam Versionem* (see above), i. 712–30. 4th edn. 1994.

The Wisdom of Solomon

DRIJVERS, H. J. W. 1986. 'The Peshitta of *Sapientia Salomonis*'. In H. L. J. Vanstiphout *et al.*, eds., *Scripta Signa Vocis: Studies about Scripts, Scriptures, Scribes and Language in the Near East presented to J. H. Hospers*, Groningen: Egbert Forsten, 15–30.

EMERTON, J. A., and LANE, D. J. 1979. 'The Wisdom of Solomon'. In *The Old Testament in Syriac according to the Peshitta Version*, Part II, fascicle 5, Leiden: Brill.

HOLMES, S. 1913. The Wisdom of Solomon. In *APOT* i. 518–68.

REESE, J. M. 1970. *Hellenistic Influence on the Book of Wisdom and its Consequences*. Analecta Biblica, 41. Rome: Biblical Institute Press.

THIELE, W. 1977–85. *Vetus Latina: Die Reste der altlateinischen Bibel nach Petrus Sabatier neu gesammelt und herausgegeben von der Erzabtei Beuron*, vol. xi.1: *Sapientia Salomonis*. Freiburg: Verlag Herder.

WINSTON, D. 1979. *The Wisdom of Solomon*. AB 43. Garden City, NY: Doubleday.

ZIEGLER, J., ed. 1962. *Sapientia Salomonis*. Septuaginta. Vetus Testamentum Graecum Auctoritate Academiae Scientiarum Gottingensis editum XII, 1. Göttingen: Vandenhoeck & Ruprecht, 2nd edn. 1980.

ZIMMERMANN, F. 1966–7. 'The Book of Wisdom: Its Language and Character', *Jewish Quarterly Review*, n.s. 57: 1–27, 101–35.

Ecclesiasticus

BEENTJES, P. C. 1997. *The Book of Ben Sira in Hebrew: A Text Edition of All Extant Hebrew Manuscripts and a Synopsis of All Parallel Hebrew Ben Sira Texts*. SVT 68. Leiden, New York, and Cologne: Brill.

BEENTJES, P. C. 2002. 'Errata et Corrigenda'. In R. Egger-Wenzel, ed., *Ben Sira's God: Proceedings of the International Ben Sira Conference, Durham, Ushaw College 2001*, BZAW 321, Berlin: de Gruyter, 375–7.

CALDUCH-BENAGES, N., FERRER, J. and LIESEN, J. 2003. *La Sabiduria del Escriba (The Wisdom of the Scribe)*. Biblioteca Midrásica, 26. Estella (Navarra): Editorial Verbo Divino.

OWENS, R. J. 1989. 'The Early Syriac Text of Ben Sira in the Demonstrations of Aphrahat'. *JSS*, 34: 39–75.

SKEHAN, P. W., and DI LELLA, A. A. 1987. *The Wisdom of Ben Sira*. AB 39. New York: Doubleday.

THIELE, W. 1987– . *Vetus Latina: Die Reste der altlateinischen Bibel nach Petrus Sabatier neu gesammelt und herausgegeben von der Erzabtei Beuron*, vol. xi.2: *Sirach (Ecclesiasticus)*. Freiburg: Verlag Herder.

WINTER, M. M. 1977. 'The Origins of Ben Sira in Syriac'. *VT* 27: 237–53, 494–507.

ZIEGLER, J., ed. 1965. *Sapientia Iesu Filii Sirach*. Septuaginta. Vetus Testamentum Graecum Auctoritate Academiae Scientiarum Gottingensis editum XII, 2. Göttingen: Vandenhoeck & Ruprecht, 2nd edn. 1980.

Baruch and the Letter of Jeremiah

MOORE, C. A. 1977. *Daniel, Esther and Jeremiah: The Additions*. AB 44. New York: Doubleday.

ZIEGLER, J. 1957. *Ieremias. Baruch. Threni. Epistula Ieremiae*. Septuaginta. Vetus Testamentum Graecum Auctoritate Academiae Scientiarum Gottingensis editum XV. Göttingen: Vandenhoeck & Ruprecht, 2nd edn. 1976.

The Additions to the Greek Book of Daniel

COLLINS, J. J. 1993. *Daniel: A Commentary on the Book of Daniel*. Hermeneia. Minneapolis: Fortress Press.

KNIBB, M. A. 2001. 'The Book of Daniel in its Context'. In J. J. Collins and P. W. Flint, eds., *The Book of Daniel: Composition and Reception*, SVT 83, 2 vols., Leiden, Boston, and Cologne: Brill, i. 16–35.

MOORE, C. A. 1977. *Daniel, Esther and Jeremiah: The Additions*. AB 44. New York: Doubleday.

ZIEGLER, J. 1954. *Susanna. Daniel. Bel et Draco*. 2nd edn. rev. O. Munnich. Septuaginta. Vetus Testamentum Graecum Auctoritate Academiae Scientiarum Gottingensis editum XVI, 2. Göttingen: Vandenhoeck & Ruprecht, 1999.

1 Maccabees

BARTLETT, J. R. 1998. *1 Maccabees*. Guides to the Apocrypha and Pseudepigrapha. Sheffield: Sheffield Academic Press.

GOLDSTEIN, J. A. 1976. *1 Maccabees*. AB 41. New York: Doubleday.

KAPPLER, W. 1936. *Maccabaeorum liber I*. Septuaginta. Vetus Testamentum Graecum Auctoritate Academiae Scientiarum Gottingensis editum IX, 1. Göttingen: Vandenhoeck & Ruprecht, 3rd edn. 1990.

2 Maccabees

GOLDSTEIN, J. A. 1983. *II Maccabees*. AB 41A. New York: Doubleday.

HANHART, R. 1959. *Maccabaeorum liber II*. Septuaginta. Vetus Testamentum Graecum Auctoritate Academiae Scientiarum Gottingensis editum IX, 2. Göttingen: Vandenhoeck & Ruprecht, 2nd edn. 1976.

1 Esdras

HANHART, R. 1974. *Esdrae liber I*. Septuaginta. Vetus Testamentum Graecum Auctoritate Academiae Scientiarum Gottingensis editum VIII, 1. Göttingen: Vandenhoeck & Ruprecht, 2nd edn. 1991.

POHLMANN, K.-F. 1970. *Studien zum dritten Esra: Ein Beitrag zur Frage nach dem ursprunglichen Schluss des chronistischen Geschichtswerks*. FRLANT 104. Göttingen: Vandenhoek & Ruprecht.

—— 1980. '3. Esra-Buch'. JSHRZ i. 5. 375–426.

TALSHIR, Z. 1999. *1 Esdras from Origin to Translation*. SBL SCS 47. Atlanta: Society of Biblical Literature.

WILLIAMSON, H. G. M. 1977. *Israel in the Books of Chronicles*. Cambridge: Cambridge University Press.

—— 1996. 'The Problem with First Esdras'. In J. Barton and D. J. Reimer, eds., *After the Exile: Essays in Honour of Rex Mason*, Macon, Ga.: Mercer University Press, 201–16.

The Prayer of Manasseh

BAARS, W., and SCHNEIDER, H. 1972. 'Prayer of Manasseh'. In *The Old Testament in Syriac according to the Peshitta Version*, part IV, fascicle 6, Leiden: Brill.

CHARLESWORTH, J. H. 1985. 'Prayer of Manasseh'. *OTP* ii. 625–37.

DENIS, A.-M. 2000. 'La Prière de Manassé, sa captivité et sa délivrance'. In *Introduction*, i. 659–79.

RAHLFS, A. 1931. *Psalmi cum Odis*. Septuaginta. Vetus Testamentum Graecum Auctoritate Academiae Scientiarum Gottingensis editum X. Göttingen: Vandenhoeck & Ruprecht, 3rd edn. 1975.

RYLE, H. E. 1913. 'The Prayer of Manasseh'. *APOT* i. 612–24.

SCHULLER, E. 1998. '381. 4QNon-Canonical Psalms B'. In E. Eshel *et al.*, eds., *Qumran Cave 4.VI: Poetical and Liturgical Texts, Part 1*, DJD 11, Oxford: Clarendon Press, 87–172.

Psalm 151

BAARS, W. 1972. 'Apocryphal Psalms'. In *The Old Testament in Syriac according to the Peshitta Version*, Part IV, fascicle 6, Leiden: Brill.

DENIS, A.-M. 2000. 'Les Psaumes de Salomon, autres psaumes non bibliques et la littérature salomonienne'. In *Introduction*, i. 507–46, esp. 526–30.

FLINT, P. W. 1997. *The Dead Sea Psalms Scrolls and the Book of Psalms*. STDJ 17. Leiden, New York, and Cologne: Brill.

RAHLFS A. 1931. *Psalmi cum Odis*, 3rd edn. 1975. See above under Prayer of Manasseh.

SANDERS, J. A. 1965. *The Psalms Scroll of Qumrân Cave 11 (11QPs^a)*. DJD 4. Oxford: Clarendon Press.

WIGTILL, D. N. 1983. 'The Sequence of the Translations of Apocryphal Psalm 151'. *RevQ* 11, 3: 401–7.

3 Maccabees

DENIS, A.-M. 2000. 'Le Livre 3 des Machabées'. In *Introduction*, i. 547–59, esp. 554–5, 559.

HADAS, M. 1953. *The Third and Fourth Books of Maccabees*. Jewish Apocryphal Literature, 3. New York: Harper & Brothers for the Dropsie College.

HANHART, R. 1960. *Maccabaeorum liber III*. Septuaginta. Vetus Testamentum Graecum Auctoritate Academiae Scientiarum Gottingensis editum IX, 3. Göttingen: Vandenhoeck & Ruprecht, 2nd edn. 1980.

2 Esdras

BASSET, R. 1899. *Les Apocryphes éthiopiens traduits en Français*, ix: *Apocalypse d'Esdras*. Paris: Bibliothèque de la Haute Science.

BENSLY, R. L., with an introduction by M. R. James. 1895. *The Fourth Book of Ezra*. Texts and Studies III, 2. Cambridge: Cambridge University Press.

BERGREN, T. A. 1990. *Fifth Ezra: The Text, Origin and Early History*. SBL SCS 25. Atlanta: Scholars Press.

—— 1998. *Sixth Ezra: The Text and Origin*. New York and Oxford: Oxford University Press.

BIDAWID, R. J. 1973. '4 Esdras'. In *The Old Testament in Syriac according to the Peshitta Version*, Part IV, fascicle 3, Leiden: Brill.

DENIS, A. M. 1970. *Apocalypsis Esdrae Quarta*. In M. Black, *Apocalypsis Henochi graece*. A.-M. Denis, *Fragmenta pseudepigraphorum quae supersunt graeca*, Pseudepigrapha Veteris Testamenti Graece, III, Leiden: Brill, 130–2.

—— 2000a. 'L'Apocalypse 4 Esdras'. In *Introduction*, i. 815–53.

—— 2000b. 'L'Apocalypse greque d'Esdras, la vision du bienheureux Esdras et les écrits au titres parallèles'. In *Introduction*, i. 855–76, esp. 870–2.

KLIJN, A. F. J. 1983. *Der Lateinische Text der Apokalypse des Esra*. Texte und Untersuchungen der altchristlichen Literatur, 131. Berlin: Akademie-Verlag.

—— 1992. *Die Esra-Apokalypse (IV. Esra)*. Die griechischen christlichen Schriftsteller der ersten drei Jahrhunderte. Berlin: Akademie Verlag.

KNIBB, M. A. 1979. *Commentary on 2 Esdras*. In R. J. Coggins and M. A. Knibb, *The First and Second Books of Esdras*, The Cambridge Bible Commentary on the New English Bible, Cambridge: Cambridge University Press.

MUSSIES G. 1974. 'When Do Graecisms Prove that a Latin Text Is a Translation?' In *Vruchten van de Uithof: Studies opgedragen aan Dr H. A. Brongers*, Utrecht: Theologisch Instituut, 100–19.

STONE, M. E. 1990. *Fourth Ezra: A Commentary on the Book of Fourth Ezra*. Hermeneia. Minneapolis: Fortress Press.

VIOLET, B. 1910. *Die Esra-Apokalypse (IV. Esra)*, Erster Teil: *Die Überlieferung*. Die griechischen christlichen Schriftsteller der ersten drei Jahrhunderte. Leipzig: J. C. Hinrichs'sche Buchhandlung.

—— 1924. *Die Apokalypsen des Esra und des Baruch in deutscher Gestalt*. Die griechischen christlichen Schriftsteller der ersten drei Jahrhunderte. Leipzig: J. C. Hinrichs'sche Buchhandlung.

WEBER, R. 1969. *Biblia Sacra iuxta Vulgatam Versionem* (see above), 1931–74. 4th edn. 1994.

WOLTER, M. 2001. '5. Esra-Buch, 6. Esra-Buch'. *JSHRZ* iii, 7. 765–880.

4 Maccabees

DENIS, A.-M. 2000. 'Le Livre 4 des Machabées'. In *Introduction*, i. 561–73, esp. 567–9.

HADAS, M. 1953. *The Third and Fourth Books of Maccabees*, Jewish Apocryphal Literature, 3. New York: Harper & Brothers for the Dropsie College.

KLAUCK, H.-J. 1989. '4. Makkabäerbuch'. *JSHRZ* iii, 6. 645–764, esp. 678–80.

RAHLFS, A. 1935. In *Septuaginta* i. 1157–84.

1 Enoch

BARR, J. 1978–9. 'Aramaic-Greek Notes on the Book of Enoch'. *JSS* 23 (1978): 184–98; 24 (1979): 179–92.

BLACK, M. 1970. *Apocalypsis Henochi graece*. In M. Black, *Apocalypsis Henochi graece*. A.-M. Denis, *Fragmenta pseudepigraphorum quae supersunt graeca*, Pseudepigrapha Veteris Testamenti Graece, III, Leiden: Brill, 1–44.

DENIS, A.-M. 2000. 'Le Livre d'Hénoch (Éthiopen)'. In *Introduction*, i. 59–144, esp. 100–33.

KNIBB, M. A. in consultation with E. Ullendorff. 1978. *The Ethiopic Book of Enoch: A New Edition in the Light of the Aramaic Dead Sea Fragments*, 2 vols. Oxford: Clarendon Press.

—— 2001. 'Christian Adoption and Transmission of Jewish Pseudepigrapha: The Case of *1 Enoch*'. *JSJ* 32: 396–415.

—— 2002. 'Interpreting the *Book of Enoch*: Reflections on a Recently Published Commentary'. *JSJ* 33: 437–50.

MILIK, J. T. 1976. *The Books of Enoch: Aramaic Fragments of Qumrân Cave 4*. Oxford: Clarendon Press.

NICKELSBURG, G. W. E. 2001. *1 Enoch 1: A Commentary on the Book of Enoch, Chapters 1–36, 81–108*. Hermeneia. Minneapolis: Fortress Press.

—— and VANDERKAM, J. C. 2004. *1 Enoch: A New Translation*. Minneapolis: Fortress Press.

STUCKENBRUCK, L. 2000. '201. 2–8. 4QEnoch[a] ar'. In S. J. Pfann *et al.*, eds., *Qumran Cave 4.XXVI: Cryptic Texts and Miscellanea, Part 1*, DJD 36, Oxford: Clarendon Press, 3–7.

TIGCHELAAR, E. J. C., and GARCÍA MARTÍNEZ, F. 2000. '208–209. 4QAstronomical Enoch[a–b] ar'. In S. J. Pfann *et al.*, eds., *Qumran Cave 4.XXVI* (as above), 95–171.

CHAPTER 11

LANGUAGE AND TRANSLATION OF THE NEW TESTAMENT

STANLEY E. PORTER

The language and translation of the New Testament are two closely related issues. One addresses the question of the nature and background of the language in which the New Testament was written by its original authors, and the other addresses the varied and ongoing responses to this text by those who for various reasons have found it necessary to read the New Testament in languages other than the original. I will here discuss the issues surrounding the Greek of the New Testament, with reference to theories regarding other languages that may have played a part in the linguistic milieu of the New Testament. Then I will discuss issues surrounding the rise of modern translations, especially those into English.

1. THE LANGUAGE OF THE NEW TESTAMENT—GREEK

Whereas the Old Testament was written mostly in Hebrew, with some portions in Aramaic, the New Testament was, apart from a few individual words (e.g. Mark 5:

41, 7: 34, 15: 34//Matt. 27: 46), written virtually entirely in a form of ancient Greek. This much has long been recognized by scholars and others alike. However, there have been a number of issues surrounding this Greek of the New Testament. These include: (a) the nature of this Greek, (b) the use of Greek in the early church and possibly by Jesus and his followers, (c) the characteristics of this Greek, and (d) recent innovations in the study of the Greek of the New Testament.

a. The Nature of the Greek of the New Testament

Classical philology dedicated itself to studying the best examples of literary Greek produced by the most distinguished Greek stylists. When these same scholars and others turned to the Greek of the New Testament, it was clear that the Greek that they were reading was recognizably similar in many ways, but in many ways also quite different. The periodic (intricate and involved) sentences of classical Greek were noticeably missing in New Testament Greek (exceptions would include Luke 1: 1–4 and arguably some parts of Hebrews), being replaced by a much more straightforward and linear or paratactic style; some of the linguistic forms that distinguished some of the best authors were missing (for example, the optative mood or the dual number); and the vocabulary was restricted in scope (there are only a little over 5,000 different words used in the New Testament), among other features. As a result, when biblical scholars especially (who often in the past were classically trained) turned their attention to the Greek of the New Testament, they had to explain how it was that a Greek text could be so culturally important and convey such deep theological truths while being written in what appeared to be an inferior form of Greek—certainly not a form of Greek that could rival the style of writers such as Thucydides, the great tragedians, or even Plato. As a result, there were a number of explanations put forward to explain the nature of this Greek.

The first theory was that the Greek of the New Testament was a special form of Greek, called by various names, such as 'biblical Greek', 'Jewish or Christian Greek', 'ecclesiastical Greek', 'synagogue Greek', or even a divinely inspired Greek (so-called Holy Ghost Greek). This position, advocated by some in the eighteenth and even late into the nineteenth century (such as Friedrich Blass 1898), and revived again in the twentieth century, tried to come to terms with the powerful impact of the New Testament while not having a suitable linguistic point of comparison. Their explanation was that the elevated thought demanded some form of elevated language, even if it did not appear to be elevated in comparison with other forms of Greek.

With the discovery of quantities of Greek documentary papyri in the sands of Egypt near the end of the nineteenth century and well into the twentieth, however, the situation changed dramatically. Suddenly there was a wealth of evidence that the Greek of the New Testament did not stand alone, but, so it was argued by such scholars as Adolf Deissmann (e.g. in Porter 1991: 39–59) and James Hope Moulton (e.g. in Porter 1991: 60–97), was part and parcel of the Greek used throughout the Graeco-Roman world. To use the language of more recent discussion, it reflected one of the registers of usage of the Graeco-Roman world. Deissmann and Moulton, among others, undertook in their publications to show at various points where items of New Testament Greek lexis and syntax were to be paralleled in the Greek papyri from Egypt. Some questioned whether the examples from Egypt were suitable parallels, themselves having possibly been influenced by Semitic languages, but, as Teodorsson (1977: 25–35) so ably makes the point, there are no other types of Greek to be found in Egypt, or elsewhere, from this time.

The deaths of Deissmann and Moulton left discussion open for a backlash against their ideas and a resurgence of a form of Semitic language hypothesis, usually focusing upon Aramaic, although it has been argued that Hebrew was in use in Palestine during this time. The enduring Semitic hypothesis has taken a number of different forms, from arguing that the New Testament reflects Semitic language because in many places it is a direct, theological translation from Aramaic (Charles Torrey in Porter 1991: 98–111), to the more widespread and persistent belief that the New Testament is directly dependent upon an original Aramaic stratum. Earlier forms of this hypothesis failed adequately to support their retroversions into Aramaic (recently revived by Maurice Casey 1998), although more moderate forms of the hypothesis have continued to identify the possible influence of Aramaic upon the Greek of the New Testament (e.g. Matthew Black in Porter 1991: 112–25 and Joseph Fitzmyer, e.g. in Porter 1991: 126–62).

More recently, two earlier theories have been revived. Gehman (e.g. in Porter 1991: 163–73), Turner (e.g. in Porter 1991: 174–90), and most recently Walser (2001), are each identified with attempts to revive the notion that the Greek of the New Testament constitutes a special form of Greek. They believe that this was a special dialect of Greek used in the synagogue and early church, which is reflected in grammatical peculiarities of the Greek of the New Testament. There has also been a revival of Deissmann's and Moulton's belief that the Greek of the New Testament was reflective of at least some of the dialects or registers of Greek in use throughout the Mediterranean area in the first century (such as Moises Silva e.g. in Porter 1991: 174–90, Lars Rydbeck e.g. in Porter 1991: 205–26, and Stanley Porter 1989, 1996). Much of the most recent discussion has occurred within the growing recognition that first-century Palestine was heavily multilingual.

Progress on the issue of the nature of the Greek of the New Testament seems to focus now upon differentiation of registers or dialects of usage, with recognition that particular registers may well have local or even personal characteristics (e.g. see Porter 2000c).

b. The Use of Greek in the Early Church, and Even by Jesus

The question of the type of language found in the New Testament is closely related to the question of the language of the early church, and even of Jesus and his closest followers. By the time of the emergence of the books of the New Testament, and the Apostolic Fathers in the late first and early second centuries, it is clear that Greek was the language of the Christian church. This comes as a surprise to many, who cannot imagine peasants as being able to use Greek. This stereotype is based upon a number of misunderstandings, however. These include a failure to realize the integration and Hellenization of the Mediterranean world certainly from the time of Alexander on (if not before), enhanced by the conquests of the Roman Empire, the importance of a lingua franca for economic survival within such a world, the linguistic competence of the early Christians, such as Paul and even James (see Johnson 1995), and the diverse socio-economic nature of the early church as it quickly spread outside Palestine, among others.

If it is granted that, at least by the time of writing of the New Testament books, Greek was a major language of the early church, and the conclusion seems undeniable, then the question becomes whether Jesus himself and his disciples may have spoken Greek. Aramaic was the predominant language of the Jewish people ever since their return from exile in the fourth century BCE, and Aramaic continued to be widely used, especially in Palestine by Jews. The development of the Targumic tradition—Aramaic paraphrases or translations of the Hebrew Scriptures—probably constitutes evidence that Aramaic, rather than Hebrew, became the language of communication and religion for a significant number of Jews, at least within Palestine. Nevertheless, there remains dispute over the earliness and relevance of the Targumic tradition for study of the New Testament.

The question of the language(s) of Jews outside Palestine, however, is often neglected, but proves illuminating. The translation of the Hebrew Scriptures into Greek—what has come to be called the Septuagint (or sometimes in its earliest form, the Old Greek)—beginning in the third century BCE in Egypt and continuing up to the Christian era, indicates that Greek became an important language not only for communication but also for the religion of the Jews. The situation in Egypt is probably reflective of the situation elsewhere in the Graeco-Roman/Mediterranean world, such that even Palestine was influenced by the use of Greek for religious purposes, as is evidenced by the discovery of a variety of Greek documents, such as apocryphal Greek manuscripts and a number of Greek manuscripts of the Hebrew Scriptures as well as other Greek documents, even among the Dead Sea documents (e.g. Minor Prophets Scroll, Bar Kokhba letters, Babatha archive). Thus, there is substantial evidence to establish that the vast majority of the Jews of the time, who lived outside of Palestine, used Greek as their primary language, even if they also spoke a local language or Aramaic.

In discussing the languages in use in Palestine itself, and hence the potential language of Jesus, there are three possibilities. There is substantial textual and epigraphical evidence to establish that Aramaic was widely used in Palestine by Jews of the time. This evidence includes the biblical books of Daniel and Ezra, non-canonical books such as 1 Enoch, and a range of inscriptional, ossuary, epistolary, papyrological, and other literary evidence. It is highly likely that the Gospels, when they record Jesus using Aramaic, are citing the original wording that he uttered and offering a translation for readers who knew Greek but not Aramaic, rather than suggesting that Jesus spoke Greek and used the occasional Aramaic word.

A more highly contentious issue is the amount of Hebrew used in Palestine at the time. As already noted above, it appears that few outside Palestine knew Hebrew, apart possibly from those in some restricted religious contexts. There is even serious question about how widespread knowledge of Hebrew was in Palestine, including questions about its use in the synagogue. It has been argued on occasion that a form of Mishnaic Hebrew was in use, as confirmed by Judaean Desert documents, such as the Hebrew Bar Kokhba letters, as well as ossuary, numismatic, and literary evidence. Some have even argued that, while Aramaic was the language of the upper social level, Hebrew was the language of the lower social levels. Nevertheless, if Hebrew was used at all, its usage was probably not widespread, and the number of Hebrew inscriptions found in Palestine is small.

There is even more controversy over whether Jesus and his disciples spoke Greek. It is fairly easy to establish that in Galilee in particular Greek was widespread, especially by those who engaged in commercial enterprises. The same is true, although probably to a slightly lesser extent, in Judaea. Besides the evidence offered above concerning the lingua franca of the Roman Empire, there is the evidence from the Gospels (see below), literary evidence, and a diversity of epigraphic evidence. The last includes several key letters from the time of Bar Kokhba (c.132–5 CE) that attest to the fact that it was at times easier to find someone who could write in Greek than who could do so in a Semitic language—and these letters come from the Jewish revolutionaries themselves.

Although there are some who deny that Jesus spoke any language other than Aramaic, there is a growing number of scholars who recognize that Jesus certainly spoke Aramaic but probably also spoke Greek on occasion. Most scholars do not wish to attempt to identify such episodes, even if they recognize it as possible that Jesus did speak Greek. A few scholars have been willing to try to identify such episodes. The criteria for identification might well include the plausibility of Greek being used in the particular context. For those episodes where Greek is presumed, the use of independent accounts is helpful in establishing what may well have been said on the occasion. Those passages that have been identified as possible instances where Jesus conversed in Greek with others are the following (see Porter 2000a, 2003):

1. John 12: 20–8, where the Greeks approach Jesus (but Jesus is not recorded as saying anything);
2. Luke 17: 11–14, the healing of the Samaritan leper;
3. John 4: 4–26, Jesus' conversation with the Samaritan woman;
4. Matt. 8: 5–13//John 4: 46–54, Jesus' conversation with the centurion or commander;
5. Mark 2: 13–14//Matt. 9: 9//Luke 5: 27–8, Jesus' calling of Levi/Matthew;
6. Mark 7: 25–30//Matt. 15: 21–8, Jesus' conversation with the Syrophoenician or Canaanite woman;
7. Mark 12: 13–17//Matt. 22: 16–22//Luke 20: 20–6, Jesus' conversation with the Pharisees and Herodians over the Roman coin;
8. Mark 8: 27–30//Matt. 16: 13–20//Luke 9: 18–21, Jesus' conversation with his disciples at Caesarea Philippi;
9. Mark 15: 2–5//Matt. 27: 11–14//Luke 23: 2–4//John 18: 29–38, Jesus' trial before Pilate.

These possible instances have been arranged in order of increasing probability. The first is an episode where it is plausible that Greek was used, but provides no possible wording. The second and third are found in only a single episode, where multiple independent attestation cannot be established. Instances 4–8 depend upon the independence of the accounts, but have both the presumption of Greek being used in the context and the possibility of independent accounts attesting to this fact. The last instance has the greatest degree of probability and likelihood that Greek was spoken; since all four Gospels record the same basic event and specifically the wording of Jesus, there is a high likelihood of independence in the Gospel traditions, there is no interpreter recorded as being present, and there is very little chance that Pilate would have spoken Aramaic. In fact, it is plausible that on this basis we have the very words of Jesus in Greek in this episode.

At the very least, this discussion indicates that it is highly probable that Jesus was himself multilingual, knowing Aramaic and Greek, and possibly Hebrew (Luke 4: 16–30), even if we cannot establish with certainty the language of a given episode, especially where the question of Greek is involved.

c. Characteristics of New Testament Greek

The language that the New Testament was written in is a form of Hellenistic Greek. Hellenistic Greek was the lingua franca of the Graeco-Roman world, and became so after the conquests of Alexander the Great in the fourth century BCE. Although a number of indigenous languages continued to be used in various regions—such as Aramaic in Palestine, but also various other local languages in Asia Minor (e.g. Phrygian)—Greek became the language of commerce, administration, and even government. Numerous multilingual inscriptions from the Hellenistic and Graeco-Roman periods, as well as references in literary authors and the record of communication throughout the empire by means of letter, make clear that the common language was Greek.

The history of the development of the Greek language is an intriguing one, and of relevance for describing the Greek of the New Testament. Although Linear A has yet to be deciphered, it has been established that the language of the Myceneans was a form of early Greek, reflected in their script, called Linear B. When the Mycenean age closed abruptly in the thirteenth century BCE or so, the Greek territory fell into what is often called a dark age. It emerged again from this dark age in the ninth century BCE. This is often referred to as 'the period of the dialects', and includes the Archaic and Classical literary periods. It is called 'the period of the dialects' because there were a number of different local dialects used by the Greek city-states. Scholars are undecided as to whether they came about through a series of migrations or invasions, or whether they came about as local developments of linguistic tendencies already found in those areas (see Horrocks 1997: 7–15). The major three dialects were West Greek, Attic-Ionic, and Boeotian, with many scholars now adding a fourth, Arcado-Cyprian. These languages were recognizably similar in most regards and were appropriately given the label Greek, although there were distinctive regional peculiarities in terms of morphology, syntax, and vocabulary (e.g. the use of *an* versus *ke* as the conditional particle). Most importantly, there were differences in pronunciation that perpetuated divisions among the dialects.

The Attic form of the Ionic dialect gained in significance due to the literary, cultural, and economic power of the city of Athens. As a result, the Attic dialect came to be established as the literary standard, and it is the dialect in which much of the literature of Classical Greece is preserved. Attic also came to be the language that was used for administrative purposes. This form of Greek is what Horrocks calls 'Great Attic' (1997: 27–31), due to its widespread significance and usage. As a result, there were a number of changes that took place in the language as it was regularized in terms of the other dialects and more widespread usage. Many of these features (e.g. the use of -σσ rather than -ττ characteristic of Attic Greek, and the loss of the dual number) are ones that were carried into the Greek of the Hellenistic period, and hence into the Greek of the New Testament. This process of Attic forming the basis of the administrative as well as literary language of the Classical Greek world then became more widespread with the conquests of the Greek mainland by Philip II of Macedon, Alexander the Great's father, and then with the conquests of Alexander himself (who was educated by Aristotle, and who shared his father's reverence for things Greek).

There have been a number of opinions regarding the nature of the development of the Greek of the Hellenistic world, and more particularly of the Greek of the New Testament. Some scholars have maintained that the Greek of the Hellenistic world was an amalgamation of features of the various Greek dialects, and that each of them contributed in recognizable ways to this linguistic hybrid. This theory is not so widely held in recent research, which indicates that the basis of the common Greek of the Hellenistic period—a virtually dialectless form of language in widespread use for administration and even literature, consistent in linguistic structure, even if subject to regional pronunciation differences (Palmer 1980: 189–90)—is the Great Attic of the Classical period. This form of a common Greek language, based mostly upon the Attic form of the Ionic dialect, became the common Greek, or Koine, of the Hellenistic world, and was widely disseminated, initially through sporadic trade, but especially by Alexander and his conquests from 330 to 320 BCE. This process of dissemination by soldiers, merchants, and bureaucrats moved Greek further from its language base, and, as a result, a process of simplification and systematization took place. With the establishment of the Greek kingdoms after Alexander's death—the kingdoms of the Diadochi included Greece, Asia Minor, Ptolemaic Egypt, and Seleucid Syria—the cultural milieu of Greek domination continued, even if local languages survived. The evidence for this is seen especially in the Greek documentary papyri from Egypt, along with those from Palestine. Greek was clearly the second language of a huge number of people—but it was the first language for many as well.

As a result, Greek was forced to become a suitable tool for the range of communication contexts in which it was utilized. The result was register adaptation according to need and circumstances. There was even an effort in the second century CE to rebel against the widespread use of Greek in forms that did not match the supposed standards set by Classical usage. This so-called Atticistic movement tried to impose the characteristics of the earlier period, and resulted in introducing instances of artificial Greek usage that hyper-corrected to Attic norms (e.g. in use of the optative mood in some writers). These register differentiations can be distinguished along the following lines (Porter 1989b: 153):

vulgar usage—found in many documentary papyri;
non-literary usage—official and documentary papyri, scientific and related texts, inscriptions, and some more popular philosophers, such as Epictetus;
literary usage—historians and philosophers of the Graeco-Roman era, such as Philo, Josephus, Polybius, Arrian;
Atticism—Plutarch and Lucian, among others.

Some of the noticeable features of Hellenistic Greek include the following:

paratactic style and word order was utilized more than periodic style;
the subtleties of classical pitch accent were replaced by stress accent;
vowel reduction occurred as itacism (the tendency toward the use of the *i* sound) occurred;
the personal endings of verbs and nouns were simplified and regularized;

the final *nu* was used more frequently;

prepositions were used increasingly with the accusative case;

certain particles fell out of use;

the older *mi* verb forms were regularized with *omega* forms;

sigmatic aorist verbal tense-forms tended to replace non-sigmatic forms;

a little later the perfect tense-form came under pressure;

the optative mood virtually disappeared (except in certain Atticistic writers, where it was often used unnaturally) under pressure from the subjunctive mood;

the middle voice began to be restricted in usage;

the subjunctive with *hina* began to replace the infinitive to indicate purpose and result clauses;

the dative case eventually disappeared under pressure from the accusative;

and verbal periphrasis increased in frequency.

Many of these features, as well as others, continued to develop in subsequent periods, and can be witnessed in the Greek of the Church Fathers and later the Byzantine period.

d. Recent Innovations in the Study of the Greek of the New Testament

The greatest innovation in recent study of the Greek of the New Testament is the utilization of modern linguistic methodologies for the study of this ancient language (see Porter 1989a). Traditionally, the Greek of the New Testament has been studied according to the canons of classical philology, which (as noted above) has resulted in some of the confusion and misunderstanding regarding the language. Modem linguistic methodologies have, for the most part, been developed for the study of modern languages, especially English. The result has been resistance to their use, especially since their employment requires development and modification of the methods so as to be suitable for application to Greek. Despite the efforts of some to resist such efforts, there have been a number of recent methodological innovations and resultant conclusions in the study of the Greek of the New Testament. Several can be mentioned here, if only briefly (see Porter 1997, 2000d).

1. Verbal Structure   Analysis of the Greek verbal structure has developed from one that was time-based (well into the nineteenth century; Winer 1882) to one that was based on the purported objective kind of action (*Aktionsart*; late nineteenth into the twentieth century; Moulton 1908) to one that was based upon realizing the subjective perspective of the speaker or writer (aspect; twentieth and twenty-first centuries; Porter 1989b, Fanning 1990, McKay 1994, Decker 2001, Porter and

O'Donnell 2001). As a result of recent research, fewer and fewer scholars are arguing for the time-based nature of the tense-forms in Greek, even in the indicative mood. Scholars for the last 100 years have increasingly realized that the non-indicative moods (e.g. the subjunctive, optative, imperative, as well as participle and infinitive) do not indicate time by the selection of tense-form. In some ways, this makes the Greek verbal structure more like, rather than unlike, the Hebrew verbal structure (incidentally, this calls into question some of the unwarranted disjunctions drawn between Greek and Hebrew, and their respective mindsets, on the basis of language). Most Western European languages are quite heavily time-oriented in their verbal system, unlike some Eastern/Oriental languages, and Greek in this regard relies upon contextual indicators, including genre and temporal and discourse indicators, rather than verbal morphology (the so-called tense-forms of the verbs) to determine the time of an event. Instead, the selection by an author or speaker (the choice is often sub- or un-conscious) of a particular tense-form indicates the author's perspective on the action. The full exegetical implications of these findings have not yet been realized, as it is only recently that commentaries on the Greek texts of the New Testament are being written that try to appropriate these insights into Greek verbal structure (see e.g. Gundry 1993). However, more and more exegetes are noting that the verbal tense-forms in Greek are used to indicate the author's perspective on the action, and to shape the discourse in its communicative function.

2. Case and Frame Analysis   Case and frame analysis are related in recent research in Greek, since they are both concerned with what are often called semantic cases. The traditional category for discussing cases in Greek is in terms of morphological case-forms: that is, the cases that are indicated by the endings on words, including the nominative, accusative, genitive, and dative (and sometimes the vocative) cases. As noted above, there were some changes in the formal case systems in Hellenistic Greek, which finally resulted in the disappearance of the dative case and an increase in occurrence of the accusative case. Recent case and frame analysis, however, is not concerned with formal cases but with the underlying semantic functions that are represented by various cases. As a result, there have been a number of analyses of the semantic cases of New Testament writers. Simon Wong (1997) in his analysis of case in Paul defines the following: agent, experiencer, patient, complement, reference, benefactive, locative, source, goal, path, instrument, comitative, manner, and measure. Frame analysis in recent New Testament study (pioneered by Paul Danove 2001) focuses upon what is called valency: that is, the number of places that a verb can take (one, two, or three). These places are then correlated with semantic cases. The result of such efforts is to develop a lexicon of the Greek of the New Testament that analyses verbs, and verbal elements, in terms of their valency and semantic frames.

3. Written Texts and Literacy Studies   The analysis of ancient languages, including ancient Greek, is limited to the textual remains, whether these are in the form of scraps of papyri of documentary texts or extended literary texts such as Thucydides. In the application of modern linguistic methodology—most often developed in terms of the spoken forms of modern languages—the fact that such methods must be applied to written texts has not been fully appreciated. There are two major points to notice here that are being taken into account in recent research. One is that the literary remains are inherently skewed, because many of the documents that have survived from the ancient world have survived only as a result of chance and caprice, others because of interest, and others because of the limitations of literacy (see Harris 1989). Therefore, there is nothing that guarantees that the remains that we have for examination are at all representative of the texts that were being generated in the ancient world. In fact, we know that there were huge numbers of works written in the ancient world that have disappeared without any trace being found so far. There is also the problem that even if we were to have all of the written texts from the ancient world, we would still not have any of the spoken texts, since these have literally disappeared into the air in a pre-recording device era. However, the second point to note is that recent research has made clear that it is unwise to overemphasize the differences between spoken and written language. In the past, much research drew firm distinctions between the two, whereas more recent research has indicated that written and spoken forms of languages fall along a continuum (Biber 1988). The entire range of the continuum needs to be explored, and in some ways is represented by the various authors and books of the New Testament.

4. Register Analysis   Whereas dialect analysis is concerned with the permanent differences in languages, such as differences in spelling, syntax, and pronunciation, register analysis is concerned with the non-permanent differences. Register in fact is used in a variety of ways to describe differences in usage of a language, without wishing to draw the kinds of firm lines of distinction that are often implied by the use of the notion of dialect. To be more precise in terms of our analysis here, register is concerned with analysis of the features of language that resulted from a particular context of situation. Recent studies of register in terms of the Greek of the New Testament have made advances in analysing the various features of the Greek used in the New Testament in terms of the ideas that are being conveyed, the people who are involved in the interaction, and the medium by which the communication takes place. As a result, one can analyse a book such as Mark's Gospel and note a number of features of that book that are different from, say, one of Paul's letters. The medium might be similar—that is, a written document—but in the original context an oral reading was probably expected, certainly for Paul's letters. The people involved are quite different, however. One of the recent questions in Gospel research is whether the formally anonymous Gospels were written primarily with a particular church in mind, or whether they were written from the start with a much wider audience envisioned, or some place in between (see Bauckham 1998). Paul's letters, by contrast, were written by the apostle himself, perhaps with some help or accompaniment, for a specific church or group of churches in a specific city or region. The ideational level is highly contrastive between the Gospel of Mark and a Pauline letter. The biographical structure of the Gospel is quite different from the occasional and theological nature of the Pauline letters (for contrasting examples, see Porter 2000*b*, 2000*e* on Mark, and Porter and O'Donnell 2000 on Romans).

5. Discourse Analysis and Corpus-Based Studies   Discourse analysis, or sometimes (better?) called text linguistics, has taken modern linguistics to a new and potentially much more productive level of analysis. What distinguishes discourse analysis is attention to an entire discourse. Traditionally, much modern linguistic research confined analysis to small linguistic units, such as the word or sentence. Discourse analysis appreciates the fact that language, when it is used, is not used simply in terms of individual words or sentences, but as entire discourses. These entire discourses set the parameters for the consequent analysis. Discourse analysis, originally derived from conversational analysis, has been applied in an intense way to the study of written texts. Approaches to the material include both top-down and bottom-up analyses. Top-down analyses begin with the shape of the discourse (register or genre) and proceed to analyse the increasingly smaller parts that make up the discourse. Bottom-up analysis begins with smaller units and assembles the discourse from these smaller units. Discourse analysis has found that there is usually an abundance of data to be analysed. This has resulted in studies that concentrate on various dimensions of the discourse, such as discourse boundaries, cohesion (the linguistic elements that create a unified discourse) and coherence (the ideational elements that create comprehension), and focus and prominence. Reed (1997) provides an interesting instance of how use of discourse analysis can address not only issues of recent provenance but ones of long standing, such as the literary integrity of Philippians. Studies of discourse analysis—as well as other areas of Greek language study—are also benefiting greatly from advances in corpus linguistics (see O'Donnell 1999 and forthcoming). Corpus linguistics is less a method than an approach that believes that observations regarding language should be based upon study of as large a corpus of texts as possible. In many ways, the New Testament comprises a representative corpus for study of Greek, but efforts are under way to develop a larger corpus of Hellenistic texts for study. Machine-readable and retrievable formats have increased the possibilities of utilizing such resources.

These are only some of the issues being discussed at the forefront of recent New Testament Greek study. There are other issues that have been introduced and will no doubt attract further attention in the future. It is fair to say that, despite a lengthy history of study, there is still much more to be learned from close examination of the Greek of the New Testament, especially as innovative methods are developed and refined.

2. The Translation of the New Testament

The New Testament has probably been translated more than any other book, ancient or modern. The history of the translation of the New Testament provides a fascinating account of how various individuals and groups of people have understood this text. Most translations have come about because of the inability to read the original Greek, and, as a result, the translations themselves have in many, if not most, instances come to be given the same kind of sacred status that the original has had—in effect, if not in fact. The issues discussed here focus upon the English translations and include: (a) the textual basis of modern translations, (b) issues in translational theory, and (c) modern translations of the Bible into English.

a. The Textual Basis of Modern Translations

There has been a significant shift in the textual basis of the translations of the Greek New Testament (see Porter 2001a for fuller treatment). The Catholic versions, even until recently, were based upon the Latin Vulgate. Those translations that utilized the original Greek, however, still faced a number of issues regarding the text. The Renaissance rediscovery of classical learning, and the advent of movable type printing, provided the impetus to publish the Greek text of the New Testament. In a race with the appearance of Cardinal Ximenes' Complutensian New Testament (printed in 1514 but not issued until around 1522), Erasmus published his Greek New Testament in 1516 (second edition 1519, and a further three editions). This text was based mainly on two late Byzantine manuscripts (supplemented by three or four others, dating to around the twelfth century), with some portions of Revelation retroverted from Latin because of the limitations of his manuscripts. The preface to the second edition of the Elzevirs' printing of a Greek New Testament in 1633 (resembling that of Erasmus but based on one of Beza from 1565) contained reference to the text as the one that was 'received' by all. This *Textus Receptus* was used by New Testament Greek scholarship until the nineteenth century, when publication of the major early codexes (fourth and fifth centuries), and discovery of the Greek papyri (not fully appreciated until the twentieth century, however), shifted the textual basis of New Testament scholarship toward the Alexandrian tradition. Constantin Tischendorf established the importance of these recent textual findings, issuing eight editions of the Greek New Testament, especially utilizing in the eighth edition his recently discovered Codex Sinaiticus (1869). B. F. Westcott and F. J. A. Hort, however, became probably the most well-known systematizers of the principles of textual criticism, when they published their Greek New Testament and principles of textual criticism in 1881—a system still used widely in creating today's eclectic text: that is, one that collates a number of manuscripts, rather than relying exclusively on one. Nevertheless, they relied heavily upon the codexes Sinaiticus and Vaticanus, against which readings in other manuscripts were assessed. In 1898, Eberhard Nestle created a completely eclectic text by collating the readings in Westcott and Hort's, Tischendorf's, and at first Richard Weymouth's and later Bernhard Weiss's editions, the basis of the current Nestle–Aland New Testament (27th edition, Aland 1993). In the early 1960s, in an effort to provide a Greek text for Bible translators, Eugene Nida instigated the American Bible Society's Greek New Testament project. That edition, although originally independent, is now the same text as the Nestle–Aland text since its 26th edition (1979) and the third edition of the UBS text, which itself has reached four editions (1966, 1968, 1975 corr. 1983, 1993).

A number of texts have formed the bases of other versions of the Bible discussed below. We do not have the exact text that was used for the Authorized Version (or King James Bible), but a reconstructed text was issued by F. H. A. Scrivener in 1881 as part of the revisions for the Revised Version, and was thought by him to reflect the fifth edition of Beza's text, published in 1598 (others have thought it reflects an edition published by Stephanus in 1550). Organizations such as the Trinitarian Bible Society have continued to keep editions of the *Textus Receptus* in print. An edition of the majority text, relying upon the Byzantine textual tradition and in many ways resembling the *Textus Receptus*, has been issued by Zane Hodges and A. L. Farstad (1982). The text of Hermann von Soden (1913) was used by Moffatt for his translation (the only major version to follow von Soden). Richard Weymouth published the Greek text that he translated (1886), which was based upon a collation of the major published editions available in the nineteenth century, including those that followed the *Textus Receptus* and the Alexandrian textual tradition. R. V. G. Tasker in 1964 published the eclectic Greek text followed by the New English Bible, with appended notes regarding variant readings.

Since the time of the Revised Version, there has been a definite rejection of the *Textus Receptus* as the basis of modern English translations, and the acceptance of the Alexandrian textual tradition in the form of various eclectic texts, especially that of Nestle–Aland. With the number of complete or nearly complete early codexes, such as Sinaiticus and Vaticanus, however, it would be possible for New Testament scholars to use a single manuscript as their textual basis. Early complete New Testament manuscripts are much closer to the time of writing than are later eclectic texts (and even the single text Hebrew manuscripts used in Old Testament study). One advantage of using a single manuscript is that it represents an actual text that was utilized historically and transmitted within a faith community, unlike the modern eclectic text, which is a product of nineteenth- and twentieth-century scholarship, not that of an ancient church.

b. Issues in Translational Theory

The ancients themselves were familiar with the issue of translation—although in the West this usually meant translation of ancient documents into Greek. The Septuagint, the most important and largest translation project of the ancient Western world, no doubt came about because most ancient Jews, especially those in Egypt, did not know Hebrew. There were probably also non-Jews who wished to read the Hebrew Scriptures, but they did not know, nor were willing to learn, ancient Hebrew. As a result of such situations, a number of ancient writers, such as Cicero, reflected upon translation. However, there was no consistent ancient theory of translation. Instead, one discovers a range of approaches among ancient translations—even the Septuagint includes a number of translational styles, moving (interestingly enough) from a more fluid and literary translation in the Pentateuch to increasingly more literalistic translation in later books (on these issues, see Porter 2001*a*, 2001*b*, 2005).

1. Formal and Dynamic Equivalence   Most translation in the ancient world, as well as into modern times, followed what has come to be called literalistic or formal equivalence translation—even though a number of earlier translators were not slavish in their renderings. Formal or literalistic translation, represented in such translations as the Authorized Version, the Revised Standard Version in English, and the English Standard Version, is characterized by what is claimed to be a close following of the original text, a consistency in the translation of individual words, word order that reflects the original, and even an archaic type of language that maintains the biblical sound of the tradition.

In the middle of last century, Nida began systematizing a new approach to biblical translation. In his major works (1964; Nida and Taber 1976; De Waard and Nida 1986), Nida developed his dynamic or, now, functional, equivalence translational principles. Rejecting theories regarding the specialness of the Greek of the New Testament, Nida endorses the notion that the Greek reflects the common language of the Mediterranean world of the time. He believes that there was mutual understanding between users and receivers, governed by the speaker's intention. It is the distinctive characteristics of each language, however, that create the problems for translation, since these features demand that the content be preserved even if the incidentals, such as form, must be changed. Nevertheless, he endorses the notion that what can be said in one language can be said in another.

As a consequence, Nida developed his now well-known theory of kernel sentences in relation to the source—message—receptor structure of language. He also utilizes the notions of surface and underlying kernel sentences, in which similar surface structures do not necessarily mean that the underlying kernels are the same. As a result, the translator must analyse the surface construction in the source language and render this into its kernel, and then transfer this to the receptor language, and render it in the surface structure. The example that Nida utilizes is Mark 1: 4, and the phrase that John preached 'a baptism of repentance for the forgiveness of sins'. This phrase consists of five 'basic kernels' and their proposed relations: (1) 'John preached X' (X stands for the entire indirect discourse), (2) 'John baptizes the people', (3) 'The people repent', (4) 'God forgives X', (5) 'the people sin'. Nida then offers two means of rendering the phrase—'I will baptize you' or 'You will receive baptism', for languages that do not have passive formations, and 'John preached, "Repent and be baptized, so that God will forgive the evil you have done" ', for those that do.

Several criticisms have been raised against Nida's theory—although much translation theory, at least in biblical studies, continues to look to Nida for guidance. The first concerns his kernel-based theoretical model (Porter 1999). Nida's model has not kept pace with developments in the Chomskyan-influenced linguistic world, but continues to reflect a model similar to Chomsky's early phrase-structure model (Chomsky 1957). This model has been superseded in the eyes of many. There are also doubts as to whether there is any method by which recovery of meaning at the deep structure is possible. Further questions have been raised about the relationship between the Chomskyan theory and the applied translational theory of Nida. The example of Mark 1: 4, an attempt to bridge this gap, has been criticized for lack of precision.

A second criticism concerns functional equivalence itself. There is the question of whether functional equivalence is a goal that can be attained, and if so, whether it is desirable to attempt to do so (Van Leeuwen 2001). Rather than run the risk of distortion of the message of the original, it has been argued that features of the original should be preserved, especially when there are not direct equivalences between the original and receptor languages. It is only when these features are maintained that an equivalent effect can be maintained.

The third criticism concerns common language translation. The question has been raised as to whether, especially in English, the same principles of translation should be utilized for a culture in which the Bible is being rendered into a language receiving the Bible for the first time (Ryken 2002). This is a criticism of restricting oneself to a single translation, rather than being a criticism of dynamic equivalence translation itself. The notion of a common language translation, however, would appear to have its rightful place in the increasingly diverse cultural world in which English is the world language.

There are a number of other models of translation that have been, or are being, developed (see the essays in Wilt 2003). These include discourse-based models, the application of relevance theory, and the use of systemic linguistics, to name a few. In many ways, however, each of these more recent developments reflects or responds to the underlying principles of dynamic equivalence translation theory as pioneered by Nida.

2. Gender and Language Issues   One of the most highly contentious issues in recent discussion of Bible translation is how to render gendered language in a gender-free, gender-neutral, or gender-inclusive way. These grammatical issues impinge on the larger issue of the male orientation of the biblical world, and how one might address that through translation (individual translations are discussed further below).

The New Revised Standard Version and the Revised English Bible were the first major Bibles to be published as gender-sensitive Bibles (the New Jerusalem Bible made some attempt to address the issue). The appearance of the New Revised Standard Version, more so than the Revised English Bible, caused little reaction focused on their gender-inclusive language. The attempt to introduce in North America a New International Version reflecting gender-free language was not so successful. Such a Bible was published in the United Kingdom (1995), but a concurrent attempt in the United States brought a reaction that resulted in the publisher withdrawing this revised version (see Strauss 1998, Carson 1998, and Poythress and Grudem 2000). Then, in 2001, the publisher decided to publish the TNIV New Testament, amid a predictable amount of furore but an equal, if not larger, attempt by the publisher to justify the venture by marshalling the opinions of supporters and orchestrating mass distributions of these New Testaments.

The immediate issue stems from the linguistic questions involved—even if there are underlying (and sometimes unspoken) theological issues. Greek has grammatical gender: that is, certain kinds of words that appear with a designation of gender (e.g. masculine, feminine, or neuter). This gender often follows natural gender, but not always (e.g. 'woman' is feminine, but 'child' is neuter). In ancient times, if there was a single male in an audience of women, reference to the group would require a masculine word-form. An example is use of the Greek masculine word 'brethren' when speaking to a group of Christians that might include numerous women. Further, there are certain words that are used to speak of representative individuals (e.g. 'someone'), and these words are gendered also. There is the further question of how one speaks of God—and here the theological issues confront the linguistic. The word for 'God' in the Greek New Testament is grammatically masculine, so grammatical reference is made with masculine pronouns. Grammatically, concord of a masculine noun and masculine pronoun may be required, but recent theological discussion has raised the question of the gender of God, and whether it is now advisable to speak of God being masculine *or* feminine, or masculine *and* feminine, or whether these terms are even relevant at all.

Gender-inclusive Bibles have attempted to overcome some of these difficulties by adopting a number of contextually sensitive translational features. For example, in some contexts the word 'they' can be used to indicate male and female participants, while in others 'brothers and sisters' might be more appropriate; or the word 'humanity' or 'humankind' can be used for generic 'man'. Not all problems can be solved so easily, however. Besides the problem with God mentioned above, there is the problem of Jesus Christ, who is clearly depicted in the New Testament as both a man and the saviour of humankind. For many, it is not an issue that Jesus is still referred to as a man, so long as his being the Christ is seen not to be gender-based. This raises further issues related to some of the earliest Christological controversies of the Church, regarding the human and divine natures of Jesus Christ and their interrelationships. Further difficulty is created by the title that Jesus often uses of himself, 'son of man', with its twofold gendered reference. One soon realizes that tension can often be created between the gendered basis of the original language and attempts to eradicate such reference in modern English.

3. Cultural Issues   The modern Bible translation movement is closely linked with the modern missionary movement, so it is inevitable that issues regarding cultural imperialism are raised regarding translation. It has been argued recently, for example, that the kind of translation programme reflected by Nida imposes a cultural hegemony of the receptor language over the source language (Venuti 1995). This is caused by the fact that the translation, meant to be fully comprehensible in the receptor language, neglects both the context and the content of the source text. Venuti has argued for restraining 'the ethnocentric violence of translation' (p. 20), which, he believes, exerts control over the translated text. He believes that Nida's translational model domesticates the text in the process of creating fluent translations. As a result, differences in language and culture are sublimated to the influence of the receptor language. Venuti argues for a foreignizing translation that, while not free from its own cultural political agendas, 'resists dominant target-language cultural values so as to signify the linguistic and cultural difference of the foreign text' (p. 23).

It is probably not fair to chastise Nida and his fellow Bible translators for being culturally insensitive. Nevertheless, some important insights should be appreciated from the cultural critique of modern translational practice. One is that all translational theory—even that of those who criticize dynamic equivalence—is theory-laden, even (or especially?) for those who claim that they are trying to produce an especially accurate translation. However, while the cultural critique of translation has validity in our pluriform world, the critique is also objecting to much more than simply the particularities of modem Bible translation. There is what appears to be a cultural and religious disagreement between Nida and his objectors. The objection is to the particular Christian orientation of those involved in Bible translation world-wide. At the end of the day, one's response may be governed by one's agreement with the theological position of those involved in Bible translation.

c. Modern Translations of the Bible into English

Modern vernacular translations have often reflected the theological climate of the times, besides proving to be important linguistically (for more detail, see Ewert 1983; Porter 2001a). For a number of languages, such as German (Luther's Bible of 1522), a significant translation has been instrumental in fixing the modern form of the language. English had a number of important translations, such as those by Tyndale (1526) and Coverdale (1535), and the Bibles that preceded the Authorized Version (AV) or King James Bible (Great Bible 1539, Geneva Bible 1560, Bishops' Bible 1568)—all of which were drawn upon in various ways by those who translated the AV (1611). This Bible established itself as pre-eminent from the second half of the seventeenth until into the twentieth century.

Before the twentieth century, there had been a number of individual translations, such as by Wesley (1775), but the AV held sway. However, in the light of the efforts of individual scholars and new manuscript discoveries, the need for a revision of the AV was known. The formation in 1870 of a committee to oversee the revision of the AV created huge interest in new versions. As a result, there were more Bibles translated into English in the twentieth century than during any other period in history.

The translation that paved the way for most of these translations was the Revised Version. The committee formed in 1870 in England, which had representation by various denominations, and was shadowed by an American committee, sought to bring the Revised Version into line with recently discovered ancient manuscripts, to correct errors, and to clarify inconsistencies and ambiguous wording—all without unnecessarily changing the AV. The New Testament appeared in 1881 (Old Testament 1885, Apocrypha 1895). Despite large sales, the conservative revision committee was seen to have failed. Excluding those disappointed that favourite texts were now excluded (e.g. John 5: 3–4; Acts 8: 37; 1 John 5: 7; the Westcott and Hort edition, being developed, was followed), the most important shortcoming was its inelegant

English style, especially in the New Testament, because of an attempt to render each Greek word with the same English word, a practice not followed in the AV. The American counterpart, the American Standard Version (1901), bolder than its English counterpart in eliminating archaisms, was more popular. This failed attempt helped to set the stage for more, rather than fewer, modern translations in the twentieth century.

In the history of translation, one of the noteworthy tensions has been between versions produced by individuals and those by committees, of which there have been numbers by each. Once the need for a more up-to-date English version had been illustrated by the failed Revised Version, a number of individuals in the first half of the twentieth century produced their own versions. Motivated by differing circumstances, these individuals produced a number of credible and well-received translations. The success of the personal translations then gave renewed impetus to committee translations, which dominated translation in the second half of the twentieth century.

Even after considerable passing of time, several personal translations still merit comment. Weymouth's (1903)—the result of his having worked with other translation projects, his classical expertise, and his work in textual criticism (see above)—was published as a supplement to other versions as a contemporary English translation. The Scottish pastor and scholar James Moffatt published two translations—The *Historical New Testament* (1901) and his better-known New Translation (New Testament 1913, Old Testament 1924, combined version 1926). Moffatt, an innovative translator, wished to overcome the archaisms of the AV and reflect what he considered the most important linguistic advances. This led to the major criticisms of the translation, especially his using Old Testament source criticism and von Soden's Greek text.

The first American English personal translation of lasting value was made by Edgar J. Goodspeed. Goodspeed, a New Testament scholar with interest in the recently discovered Greek papyri, wished to produce a translation in American English suitable for public use. The New Testament of his An American Translation (1923) was written in a smooth American English, evidencing much detailed knowledge of the Greek text (Old Testament by J. M. P. Smith 1927, combined edition 1931). Goodspeed's teaching at the University of Chicago, considered by many a theologically liberal institution, and his wording that differed from the AV (though more accurate), resulted in much criticism of the translation.

Catholics during this time continued to use the Douai–Rheims translation of the Vulgate (New Testament 1582, Old Testament 1609–10, revised in the eighteenth century by Richard Challoner; reprinted numerous times in the nineteenth century). A revision of this translation was thought necessary, and the British Catholic scholar and man of letters Ronald Knox completed his revision of the New Testament in 1945 (Old Testament 1949). His attempt to render the language of the Vulgate into what a native English-speaker would say was commendable; but, since 1943, and especially after Vatican II, Catholic scholars were allowed and even encouraged to utilize the original languages, so his version is anachronistic.

From his work with British youth during the Second World War, J. B. Phillips wanted to communicate the Bible to those who did not understand biblical English. He produced a translation that reflected spoken English, translating the original in a smooth, flowing, and understandable language. Beginning with his Letters to Young Churches (1947), which included Paul's letters, Hebrews, and the catholic epistles (with a laudatory preface by C. S. Lewis), and following on with other parts (Gospels in 1952, Acts in 1955, and Revelation in 1957), Phillips issued his entire New Testament in 1958. Phillips produced a revised edition in 1972, based upon the United Bible Societies' Greek New Testament, rather than his earlier use of Westcott and Hort. Many consider Phillips's translation to reflect high literary sensitivity, although most probably consider it too paraphrastic.

Other personal translations of the New Testament worth noting, including those produced in the second half of the twentieth century, include Gerrit Verkuyl's Berkeley Version (New Testament 1945, entire Bible 1959); that of the Jewish scholar Hugh Schonfield, the first Jewish translator of the New Testament into English (1955); the classical scholar E. V. Rieu's Penguin Gospels (1952), and his son C. H. Rieu's Acts of the Apostles (1957); that of the classical scholar Richmond Lattimore (Gospels 1962, Acts and Letters 1982); the paraphrase of the American Standard Version by Kenneth Taylor in his Living Bible (1971); and the Presbyterian minister Eugene Peterson's *The Message: The New Testament in Contemporary Language* (1993; entire Bible 2002). A revision of the Living Bible, using the Hebrew and Greek texts, has been published as the New Living Translation (1996). The translation of the New Testament in 1966 of the Today's English Version, which became the New Testament portion of the Good News Bible (1976), was done by essentially one person, Robert Bratcher (but this was never promoted as a personal translation) (see below).

These personal translations all represent significant achievements in the history of Bible translation. These translators had to overcome the resistance to creating any translation other than the AV in English-speaking circles, and did so by a combination of phenomenal learning and wise judgement in deciding how to render words and phrases into language understandable by their audiences. Without these individual efforts, the history of Bible translation would certainly be much impoverished.

The second half of the twentieth century was dominated by group translational projects. Such projects were undoubtedly slow in developing in the first half of the century on account of the failure of the Revised Version and the continuing admiration, even veneration, of the AV. A noteworthy exception (if it can be said to be so) is the Twentieth Century New Testament, a version by a small group of twenty ministers and laymen (none of them scholars) in 1902. The translators, concerned that the Bible be understood by readers in their own language as they use it, organized the New Testament in chronological order.

There are two committee-made translations created in the English-speaking world in the second half of the twentieth century that stand out above the rest. One is the Revised Standard Version, itself a revision of the American Standard Version. The International Council of Religious Education (later the National Council of the Churches of Christ in the USA) was given the copyright of the American Standard Version, and in 1937 set up a committee with broad denominational representation to oversee its revision. The translation was meant to preserve the AV where possible, but to take into consideration recent biblical scholarship, including textual criticism, and render this into a form of English that could be used for both public and private reading. The New Testament essentially used an eclectic text based on Nestle's Greek New Testament (16th (1936) and 17th (1941) editions). The Revised Standard Version returned to the AV's practice of rendering the same word by differing English words. The Revised Standard Version met with mixed reactions when the New Testament was published in 1946 (both Testaments 1952). For over twenty-five years, until the New International Version was published, it was the predominant English version. Among many revisions, in 1974 a project was started that resulted in the New Revised Standard Version with gender-neutral language (1989). The sometimes vitriolic negative reaction to the Revised Standard Version would seem quaint if it were not that similar kinds of reactions still confront translations (see above on the TNIV). There were accusations that theological truths had been lost in the translation. In many circles, the consensus is that the Revised Standard Version and now the New Revised Standard Version in most ways accomplished their purpose.

In Britain, the New English Bible attempted to be a completely new translation, rather than simply a revision of a previous translation. C. H. Dodd, and later G. R. Driver, headed a committee set up in 1947 to produce such a translation meant to have a timeless quality that avoided both archaisms and modernisms, did not preserve the language of former versions, and was written so that it could be used for reading aloud (New Testament 1961, complete Bible with Apocrypha 1970). However, it was criticized for not finding the right stylistic level—some thought that it had gone beyond what the average intelligent reader could understand, while others thought that it was rather too prosaic in its phrasing and expression. The New English Bible never caught on in North America. A revision, published in 1989 as the Revised English Bible, utilized inclusive gender (see above).

At about the same time in Britain, Roman Catholics undertook an English version directly from the original Hebrew and Greek, rather than from the Latin Vulgate. English-speaking Catholic scholars, including J. R. R. Tolkien, taking their model and inspiration (as well as the textual notes), from the French translation La Bible de Jerusalem (1956), produced their own rendering of the Hebrew and Greek (checked against the French version), publishing the Jerusalem Bible in 1966. The Jerusalem Bible, without the encumbrance of residual AV English still found in the Revised Standard Version, was designed especially as a study Bible. Revised and reissued as the New Jerusalem Bible in 1985, some have thought that its revisions are more literalistic than the earlier version. In the United States, the equivalent Catholic translation was the New American Bible. Originally the Confraternity Bible, this version took a long time to appear in its final form, due to changing policy on translation by the Roman Catholic Church. The New Testament, first translated from the Vulgate, was issued in 1941 (the Old Testament from the Hebrew in 1969). Retranslation of the New Testament from Greek delayed issuing of the entire Bible until 1970. The version has maintained some traditional Bible translation language, while utilizing some of the developments of the twentieth century, such as rendering the same word by differing English words depending upon context.

In the United States at about the same time, several other significant and lasting Bible translation projects were under way. A conservative foundation undertook publication of a new version of the Bible, out of concern that the virtues of the American Standard Version were being lost in the spate of translations since 1901. The New American Standard Bible was published with the New Testament in 1963 (entire Bible 1971, revised 1995). This version has proved highly useful for students of the original languages, because of the literalness of the translation, but it is far from fluid modern English.

The second, the translation of the Good News Bible, or Today's English Version, was the brain-child of Nida, and exemplifies his dynamic or functional equivalence translation theory (see above). As a result, technical and biblical language are avoided, expressing the text in short sentences utilizing limited vocabulary. Sponsored by the American Bible Society, the New Testament was translated from the United Bible Societies' Greek New Testament by Robert Bratcher, and appeared as *Good News for Modern Man: The New Testament in Today's English Version* (1966, with subsequent editions; entire Good News Bible 1976, with Apocrypha 1979; now known as the Good News Translation). This translation has been widely used by those for whom English is not their first language, and as an aid in rendering the Bible into languages for which the Bible is the first written document—although many castigated it because of what they perceived as theological deficiencies. Reflecting the same translational tradition, but with more attention to its place at the end of a process beginning with the AV, is the Contemporary English Version. Utilizing the latest Greek texts (UBS Greek New Testament, third and fourth editions, 1975 and 1993), this translation utilizes dynamic or functional equivalence, while also wishing to be seen as a translation that preserves the virtues of the AV in its literary style. The Contemporary English Version (currently under revision) was published in 1995, and aroused the same kind of negative response as did the Good News Bible.

Along with the Revised Standard Version, the most significant American translation to date is the New International Version. Growing out of a concern of some American denominations to find a general purpose Bible in contemporary English (they rejected the Revised Standard Version), the New International Version committee, set up in 1965, brought together scholars from not only the United States but other English-speaking countries, such as Canada, Great Britain, Australia, and New Zealand—hence its name. In many ways a conservative alternative to the Revised Standard Version, the New International Version used a text very similar to that of the standard eclectic Greek New Testament, and was published in 1973 (entire Bible 1978). A gender-neutral version, Today's New International Version, has recently been published to great fanfare (New Testament 2001; entire Bible 2005), as noted above. At times the NIV/TNIV is colloquial and unstilted, while at other times it retains biblical language. Not as dependent upon the tradition of the AV as the Revised Standard Version, the NIV/TNIV is generally consistent in its renderings of gender-neutral language.

This survey will close with reference to three further translations, which perhaps reflect the diversity now present in English translations. Not unexpectedly, Bible translation has not escaped the desire to be technologically up-to-date. The result has been a number of translations that are now available in a variety of machine-readable forms, including availability on the internet and on CD-roms. Whereas most of these translations are electronic forms of previously made translations, one translation, the NET Bible (New English Translation), has been developed in both print and electronic form from the start (1996 and following). This translation seems to follow a modified form of dynamic equivalence. Distinctives of this translation are its availability for free distribution through the net and its publication with extensive and insightful notes, which comment on a range of issues from language to theology. By contrast, the English Standard Version (2001) is a conscious attempt to pull back from dynamic equivalence translation and produce what the publisher describes as an 'essentially literal' translation based on the Revised Standard Version. More specifically, in the area of gendered language, the translation endorses the use of 'he' on the basis of how the pronouns are used in the original language and as consistent with its literalistic approach. In some ways, this makes it surprising that they also endorse for the most part the use of the eclectic text of Nestle–Aland and the United Bible Societies. The Holman Christian Standard Bible (2000) attempts to hold a mediating position. Rejecting both formal equivalence and dynamic equivalence, the Holman Bible contends that it follows a principle of optimal equivalence: that is, being literal where possible and dynamic where necessary, so as to optimize meaning. In other words, as the twenty-first century gets under way, there are translations of the Bible that represent the range of translational methodologies, as well as availing themselves of the latest in technology to package the modern form of the ancient text.

BIBLIOGRAPHY

ALAND, B. *et al.* 1993. *Nestle–Aland Novum Testamentum Graece.* Stuttgart: Deutsche Bibelgesellschaft.

BAUCKHAM, R., ed. 1998. *The Gospels for All Christians: Rethinking the Gospel Audiences.* Grand Rapids, Mich.: Eerdmans.

BIBER, D. 1988. *Variation across Speech and Writing.* Cambridge: Cambridge University Press.

BLASS, F. 1898. *Philology of the Gospels.* London: Macmillan.

CARSON, D. A. 1998. *The Inclusive Language Debate: A Plea for Realism.* Grand Rapids, Mich.: Baker.

CASEY, M. 1998. *Aramaic Sources of Mark's Gospel.* Cambridge: Cambridge University Press.

CHOMSKY, N. 1957. *Syntactic Structures.* The Hague: Mouton.

DANOVE, P. 2001. *Linguistics and Exegesis in the Gospel of Mark: Applications of a Case Frame Analysis and Lexicon.* Sheffield: Sheffield Academic Press.

DECKER, R. J. 2001. *Temporal Deixis of the Greek Verb in the Gospel of Mark with Reference to Verbal Aspect.* New York: Lang.

DE WAARD, J., and NIDA, E. A. 1986. *From One Language to Another: Functional Equivalence in Bible Translating.* Nashville: Nelson.

EWERT, D. 1983. *From Ancient Tablets to Modern Translations: A General Introduction to the Bible.* Grand Rapids, Mich.: Zondervan.

FANNING, B. M. 1990. *Verbal Aspect in New Testament Greek.* Oxford: Clarendon Press.

GUNDRY, R. H. 1993. *Mark: A Commentary on his Apology for the Cross.* Grand Rapids, Mich.: Eerdmans.

HARRIS, W. V. 1989. *Ancient Literacy.* Cambridge, Mass.: Harvard University Press.

HODGES, Z., and FARSTAD, A. L. 1982. *The Greek New Testament According to the Majority Text.* Nashville: Nelson.

HORROCKS, G. 1997. *Greek: A History of the Language and its Speakers.* London: Longman.

JOHNSON, L. T. 1995. *The Letter of James.* New York: Doubleday.

MCKAY, K. L. 1994. *A New Syntax of the Verb in New Testament Greek.* New York: Lang.

MOULTON, J. H. 1908. *Prolegomena to A Grammar of New Testament Greek.* Edinburgh: T. & T. Clark.

NESTLE, E. 1898. *Novum Testamentum Graece.* Württemburg: Württemburgische Bibelanstalt.

NIDA, E. A. 1964. *Toward a Science of Translating.* Leiden: Brill.

—— and TABER, C. 1976. *The Theory and Practice of Translation.* Leiden: Brill.

O'DONNELL, M. B. 1999. 'The Use of Annotated Corpora for New Testament Discourse Analysis: A Survey of Current Practice and Future Prospects'. In S. E. Porter and J. T. Reed, eds., *Discourse Analysis and the New Testament: Approaches and Results,* Sheffield: Sheffield Academic Press, 71–117.

—— forthcoming. *Corpus Linguistics and the Greek of the New Testament.* Sheffield: Sheffield Phoenix Press.

PALMER, L. R. 1980. *The Greek Language.* London: Faber & Faber.

PORTER, S. E. 1989*a*. 'Studying Ancient Languages from a Modern Linguistic Perspective: Essential Terms and Terminology'. *Filología Neotestamentaria,* 2.4: 147–72.

—— 1989*b*. *Verbal Aspect in the Greek of the New Testament, with Reference to Tense and Mood.* New York: Lang.

—— ed. 1991. *The Language of the New Testament: Classic Essays*. Sheffield: JSOT Press.

—— 1996. *Studies in the Greek New Testament: Theory and Practice*. New York: Lang.

—— 1997. 'The Greek Language of the New Testament'. In S. E. Porter, ed., *Handbook to Exegesis of the New Testament*, Leiden: Brill, 99–130.

—— 1999. 'Mark 1.4, Baptism and Translation'. In S. E. Porter and A. R. Cross, eds., *Baptism, the New Testament and the Church: Historical and Contemporary Studies in Honour of R.E.O. White*, Sheffield: Sheffield Academic Press, 81–98.

—— 2000*a*. *The Criteria for Authenticity in Historical-Jesus Research: Previous Discussion and New Proposals*. Sheffield: Sheffield Academic Press.

—— 2000*b*. 'Dialect and Register in the Greek of the New Testament: Theory'. In M. D. Carroll R., ed., *Rethinking Contexts, Rereading Texts: Contributions from the Social Sciences to Biblical Interpretation*, Sheffield: Sheffield Academic Press, 190–208.

—— ed. 2000*c*. *Diglossia and Other Topics in New Testament Linguistics*. Sheffield: Sheffield Academic Press.

—— 2000*d*. 'Greek of the New Testament'. In C. A. Evans and S. E. Porter, eds., *Dictionary of New Testament Background*, Downers Grove, Ill.: InterVarsity Press, 426–35.

—— 2000*e*. 'Register in the Greek of the New Testament: Application with Reference to Mark's Gospel'. In M. D. Carroll R., ed., *Rethinking Contexts, Rereading Texts: Contributions from the Social Sciences to Biblical Interpretation*, Sheffield: Sheffield Academic Press, 209–29.

—— 2001*a*. 'Modern Translations'. In J. Rogerson, ed., *The Oxford Illustrated History of the Bible*, Oxford: Oxford University Press, 134–61.

—— 2001*b*. 'Some Issues in Modern Translation Theory and Study of the Greek New Testament'. *Currents in Research: Biblical Studies*, 9: 350–82.

—— 2003. 'Luke 17.11–19 and the Criteria for Authenticity Revisited'. *Journal for the Study of the Historical Jesus*, 1.2: 201–24.

—— 2005. 'Eugene Nida and Translation'. *The Bible Translator*, 56.1: 8–19.

—— and O'DONNELL, M. B. 2000. 'Semantics and Patterns of Argumentation in the Book of Romans: Definitions, Proposals, Data and Experiments'. In Porter 2000*c*: 154–204.

—— —— 2001. 'The Greek Verbal Network Viewed from a Probabilistic Standpoint: An Exercise in Hallidayan Linguistics'. *Filología Neotestamentaria*, 14: 3–41.

POYTHRESS, V. S., and GRUDEM, W. A. 2000. *The Gender-Neutral Bible Controversy: Muting the Masculinity of God's Words*. Nashville: Broadman and Holman.

REED, J. T. 1997. *A Discourse Analysis of Philippians: Method and Rhetoric in the Debate over Literary Integrity*. Sheffield: Sheffield Academic Press.

RYKEN, L. 2002. *The Word of God in English: Criteria for Excellence in Bible Translation*. Wheaton, Ill.: Crossway.

SCRIVENER, F. H. A. 1881. *The New Testament in Greek According to the Text Followed in the Authorised Version Together with the Variations Adopted in the Revised Version*. Cambridge: Cambridge University Press.

STRAUSS, M. L. 1998. *Distorting Scripture? The Challenge of Bible Translation and Gender Accuracy*. Downers Grove, Ill.: InterVarsity Press.

TASKER, R. V. G. 1964. *The Greek New Testament*. Oxford: Oxford University Press; Cambridge: Cambridge University Press.

TEODORSSON, S.-T. 1977. *The Phonology of Ptolemaic Koine*. Gothenburg: Acta Universitatis Gothoburgensis.

TISCHENDORF, C. 1869–72. *Novum Testamentum Graece*, 8th edn. Leipzig: Giesecke & Devrient.

VAN LEEUWEN, R. C. 2001. 'On Bible Translation and Hermeneutics'. In C. Bartholomew, C. Green and K. Möller, eds., *After Pentecost: Language and Biblical Interpretation*, Carlisle: Paternoster, 284–311.

VENUTI, L. 1995. *The Translator's Invisibility: A History of Translation*. London: Routledge.

VON SODEN, H. 1913. *Die Schriften des Neuen Testaments in ihrer ältesten erreichbaren Textgestalt hergestellt auf Grund ihrer Textgeschichte*, Part 2: *Text mit Apparat*. Göttingen: Vandenhoeck & Ruprecht.

WALSER, G. 2001. *The Greek of the Ancient Synagogue: An Investigation on the Greek of the Septuagint, Pseudepigrapha and the New Testament*. Stockholm: Almqvist & Wiksell.

WESTCOTT, B. F., and HORT, F. J. A. 1881. *The New Testament in the Original Greek*, 2 vols. Cambridge: Macmillan.

WEYMOUTH, R. F. 1886. *The Resultant Greek Testament*. London: James Clarke.

WILT, T., ed. 2003. *Bible Translation: Frames of Reference*. Manchester: St Jerome.

WINER, G. B. 1882. *A Treatise on the Grammar of New Testament Greek Regarded as a Sure Basis for New Testament Exegesis*, trans. W. F. Moulton. Edinburgh: T. & T. Clark.

WONG, S. S. M. 1997. *A Classification of Semantic Case-Relations in the Pauline Epistles*. New York: Lang.

CHAPTER 12

ANCIENT VERSIONS AND TEXTUAL TRANSMISSION OF THE OLD TESTAMENT

GERARD J. NORTON

INTRODUCTION

This essay will first give a schematic outline of the history of the Hebrew text in four stages. The elements that readers will meet in modern editions of that text are then presented. These modern editions find a common focus in the great Tiberian manuscripts of about 1000 CE linked with the name of ben Asher. These manuscripts are presented in conjunction with the editions. The possibility of finding variant Hebrew traditions in manuscripts from after that date is discussed, and largely rejected. The discernment of differing traditions in witnesses from before 1000 CE is discussed with reference to the ancient versions and the manuscript traditions from Qumran.

OUTLINE HISTORY OF THE TEXT

In the first stage the 'original texts' of individual books of the Old Testament were composed in different generations, and in different historical circumstances. In the case of some books (e.g. the prophet Isaiah) there may have been long initial periods of oral transmission. The commitment of a book to writing may also have been a long process that itself had many stages. The book of Daniel is something of an extreme case, because of the unusually brief period between its composition and its commitment to writing as indicated by the earliest fragments we possess of the book. At the other extreme lie books such as Isaiah, that may have circulated in several varying forms for centuries before our earliest witnesses to that text. The history of the text of the Hebrew Bible in a pre-canonical stage must be considered book by book and development by development. 'It must remain, for the time being within the realm of conjecture' (Goshen-Gottstein 1965: L[12]). It quickly encounters the same problems as a history of the people of Israel and Judah. The data on which we could base such a history of the first stage of the text are problematic. It is not possible to discuss them here.

A second stage (although not strictly speaking a chronological or developmental stage, because it is defined by accidents of survival rather than any developments in the text) may tentatively be identified as the earliest text or texts to which we have access through direct and indirect witnesses. The more significant of these witnesses will be discussed below. Goshen-Gottstein (1965) considered that this period began about 300 BCE.

In the third stage, one of these forms is chosen as the definitive form for tradition in Jewish contexts, and is now termed the proto-Masoretic. The nature of this choice is unclear, but it seems most likely that the text adopted was already held in high esteem by a dominant Jewish group of the time, probably the Pharisees. Alternative forms—termed extra-Masoretic or non-Masoretic—sometimes fall into disuse, whether by suppression or neglect. One or other of these may have been the textual basis for translation into Greek or another language in the first or second stages. The proto-Masoretic form is consonantal (although some consonants indicate vowels). Subsequent translations from Hebrew are made from this proto-Masoretic text. Great efforts are made to transmit this text faithfully, with the addition over the centuries of elements that conserve the pronunciation, reading, and writing details.

The fourth stage represented in modern editions is the fully developed Masoretic text based on the manuscripts produced by the ben Asher family of Masoretes at Tiberias in the ninth and tenth centuries. This forms the basis for modern editions of the Hebrew text. After this period there were no further developments of the Hebrew text itself. The task changes to the conservation, reproduction, and interpretation of the text, which was seen to have been perfected by the Masoretes of Tiberias.

This four-stage description is loosely based on that adopted by the Hebrew Old Testament Text Project of the United Bible Societies (Barthélemy *et al.* 1980, final report Barthélemy 1982, 1986, 1992), as well as that articulated by M. H. Goshen-Gottstein in his introduction to the sample edition of the book of Isaiah for the Hebrew University Bible Project (1965). A history of the text that builds on a hypothetical reconstruction of the process of composition is soon lost in speculation. In what follows we consider the material primarily in relation to stages two to four, and in function of the editions and sources available to the reader.

MODERN EDITIONS OF THE HEBREW TEXT

Diplomatic or Eclectic?

Most modern editions of the Hebrew Bible are 'diplomatic'. This means that they are based on a single manuscript or printed source, whether that is the Aleppo Codex, the Leningrad Codex, or the 1525 edition of ben Hayyim. The decision to publish 'diplomatic' editions of single manuscripts calls for the reader to be active in interpreting the critical apparatus. The alternative to a diplomatic edition is an eclectic edition, where the text as printed draws on many manuscripts to give the oldest text in the view of the editors. This is the method of most New Testament editions. Eclectic editions are also the preferred option in classical Greek and Latin text editions. These have generated an expectation in the European and American tradition that a similar option will be taken in the Hebrew Biblical text. For the present that is not possible.

The diplomatic option in respect of the Hebrew Bible text recognizes that the search for an original text may be futile, but that we are editing fine examples of a stable tradition which may have had several alternative forms at an earlier stage, perhaps even to the earliest attested texts. In a sense the process of composition ended with the Masoretic Text.

ELEMENTS OF A MODERN EDITION

Modern editions are concerned with three principal, interrelated elements of the text: (a) consonants and how they are laid out on the page, (b) vocalization and cantillation, (c) Masorah (magna and parva). In addition to these three, a critical edition adds one or more apparatus (d), usually at the bottom of the page. This apparatus gives alternative readings, sometimes evaluates them, and where the edition is diplomatic, indicates whether (in the editor's view) these readings are to be preferred to those of the base text.

a. Consonants and How They are Laid Out on the Page

The consonants are by far the oldest of the text elements, and define the text. For some texts, such as Exodus 15 and Deuteronomy 32, a particular layout is traditional. In books traditionally held to be prose (all but Proverbs, Job, and Psalms) there is a double system of paragraphing, represented rather inadequately in many editions by gaps and letters. This representation problem is largely a consequence of the broader column width adopted in the editions by comparison with manuscripts. Poetic books (Proverbs, Job, and Psalms) in the Tiberian manuscripts have a gap in most lines, but the placing of these gaps is not significant for the sense of the lines. It is possible that an earlier system of poetic layout in some texts similar to that of Exodus 15 has been lost in response to a need to economize space linked with the change from separate scrolls to comprehensive book form (codex) (Yeivin 1969).

b. Vocalization and Cantillation

The biblical text was never a purely consonantal text, but was always a read text. As the centuries passed, it was considered necessary that the reading tradition be noted along with the consonants. The person who wrote the consonantal element of a manuscript was not necessarily or even usually the same person who wrote the vocalization and other elements of the text. The full development known as Tiberian found in medieval manuscripts and modern editions was probably linked with the Karaites, a rigorist Jewish group who came to prominence in the eighth century, and were remarkable for their rejection of sources of authority other than the Bible.

Other systems of vowel notation were developed, and these are linked with Palestinian and Babylonian groups. Although largely lost, or at least forgotten in Europe, they came back into prominence with the discovery of the Cairo Geniza in the late nineteenth century, and the studies of S. Schechter, P. Kahle, and A. Sperber. Study of these fragments, even when they were not extensive, has indicated that various parallel systems were worked on until the Tiberian system was developed, and indeed after that. With hindsight, dominance by the comprehensive Tiberian system seems inevitable. Yet the existence of fine manuscripts such as the Reuchlin written in about 1105 CE show that alternative pointing systems continued to be used (Sperber 1956). The Babylonian tradition of pointing seems to have been used in the Yemen until the twelfth and thirteenth centuries. The region subsequently developed its own tradition under the influence of Tiberian pointing (Würthwein 1995: 23; Barthélemy 1992: p. xxxii). Our evidence is incomplete. The endorsement by Maimonides (1135–1204 CE) of the Torah arrangement of a Ben Asher manuscript both attested and furthered the acceptance of this tradition as a whole.

Other elements indicate how Hebrew words might have been pronounced before the Tiberian system of notation was developed. These include transliterations of words (technical terms, place-names, etc.) in ancient Latin and Greek translations and commentaries. Fragments of a transliteration into Greek of the whole Hebrew Bible used in the Hexapla of Origen (prepared in about 240 CE) also help. Each source has its own problems, including the phonetic system of the receptor language and its capacity to express the Hebrew sounds. A clear appreciation of the relationship of the ancient sources to the Tiberian system of pronunciation has yet to be given.

Closely associated with the vowel points which preserved pronunciation, a system of cantillation or accents was developed in the Tiberian tradition. This preserved a tradition of reading the text with word groupings, cadence, sense units, and intonation. At times the rhythms of chant seem to have superseded those of syntax. Perhaps because of this, editions and translations of the Hebrew Bible in Christian contexts have not tended to pay this element sufficient attention. Yet the accent and vowel systems are interconnected. Where the cantillation indicates that two words are to be read closely together, or in disjuncted fashion, the vowel pointing is affected.

The antiquity of the vowel system has been a matter of recurrent controversy, linked with the names of Levita, Buxtorf, Capellus, and Simon, and more generally with Reformation controversies in the Western Church. More recently, the issue of the authority of the vowel points has arisen in the context of textual emendations based on modern philology.

Qere-Kethib 'read-written'

The vocalization system does not always tally with the consonants transmitted. An extreme instance of this is provided by the instances where there are words which are written and not pronounced at all (Jer. 51: 3; Ruth 3: 12), and other instances where we have the vowels to be pronounced, but no consonants to go with them (2 Sam. 18: 20; Ruth 3: 5). Despite several passionately advanced theories, no satisfactory explanation has been given for these phenomena. Perhaps they record a reading tradition that was close to but not identical with the consonantal text transmitted by the Tiberian Masoretes. If this is so, they inspire confidence in the vocalization system as a whole, showing that it was not an *ad hoc* innovatory measure inspired by the best the scribes could make of the consonantal text as they worked through it, but was itself a transmitted tradition. (Gordis 1937, 1981; Tov 1992)

c. The Masorah

This called attention to particular features of the text. Its principal function seems to have been to help readers and copyists to read and transmit the text accurately. There are three principal elements of the Masorah.

In the manuscript, a small circle over or between key words draws attention to a marginal note, called the small Masorah (Masorah parva). This tends to be brief, and frequently records the number of times a particular form occurs in a given context, or gives a brief note about that form. So, for example, if there is a note that a word occurs twice, once with final *h* and once without final *h*, the reader and copyist are alerted not to confuse the two forms. It is possible that some of these notes are an expression of a desire to preserve a particular form of the text in the face of known variants. The Masorah parva also indicates the consonants or vowels that would go with the incongruent vocalization noted in the paragraph above on Qere-Kethib.

The great Masorah (Masorah magna) was written in the upper and lower margins of the manuscript. It normally begins with the consonants of the reference word(s) in the text, and the marginal note of the small Masorah. It then makes explicit the information about other instances given as a number in the small Masorah. The texts referred to are identified by a word or sequence of words unique to the context of each. Until the numbering of verses (Pagnini 1527) and the publication of concordances based on this numbering, this was the only way to refer to particular verses. The list is not necessarily found at the place corresponding to the first element in the list. A list is sometimes, but not usually, repeated where an element within it occurs. A concordance of the repeated lists is found in the work of Weil (1971) mentioned below.

The final Masorah (Masorah finalis) is found at the end of a book, or group of books, or even a manuscript. This final Masorah of a book is often brief, and notes matters such as the number of words in that book and the mid-point of the book. The Masorah found at the end of the section or of the manuscript can be very complex and contain various lists and arrangements of lists.

The history of the compilation of these Masoretic notes and lists is unclear. They are not uniform from manuscript to manuscript, but they seem to be related. Conflicts are found between the evidence given in the small Masorah and that of the great Masorah, and again between the observations of either Masorah and the biblical text. Editions of the Bible based on a single Tiberian manuscript have fewer such conflicts than editions in the tradition of Ben Hayyim, but their frequency even in these manuscripts shows that the data of the Masorah have an independent composition and transmission history (Ginsburg 1880–95; Weil 1971; Yeivin 1980).

It is worth noting in conclusion that all of the elements added to the consonantal text (vowels, accents, Masorah) were intended to conserve the traditional biblical text. They did not innovate.

d. The Apparatus of an Edition

This is compiled by the editor of the text, and can be in one or more registers. Traditionally, it presents one or more alternative readings to that presented in the main text. Because of the lack of pre-1000 CE readings available in Hebrew, the critical apparatus of Hebrew Bibles has tended to rely heavily on readings obtained by retroversion from ancient translations, and on conjectural suggestions. These have little or no link with surviving ancient Hebrew readings, but are based on the editor's knowledge of the Hebrew language, sometimes bolstered by a confidence that an inspired text must conform to the grammatical standards of the editor. Some such conjectural readings have been transmitted from edition to edition with ever increasing status. The eighteenth-century edition of C. F. Houbigant was particularly influential here. Both retroversion and conjecture have been widely discussed in recent years, following important treatments of relevant issues by Goshen-Gottstein (1963), Barr (1968) Albrektson (1981) Tov (1981), and Gibson (1981). On the issue of conjectures and the authority granted them in the modern period, the reflections of A. E. Housman (1922) were seminal, even though expressed in the context of classical texts.

From 1947 onwards, a great number of new biblical manuscripts became available (see below and Chapter 6 on Qumran). Some seem to confirm conjectures previously ventured, but the issue is rarely as simple as that. The work of weighing and assessing the Qumran readings, and integrating them with the readings retroverted from the versions has only begun. The process by which this is done will be considered in Chapter 33 on textual criticism. Closer study shows that in many editions of the Hebrew Bible, the ancient versions have principally been brought to bear when there is a perceived difficulty of some sort with the Hebrew text. This has led to an undervaluation of the role of these texts in the history of the communities for which they were made.

MANUSCRIPTS AND EDITIONS
OF THE HEBREW BIBLE

Editions in the Tiberian Tradition

Edition Based on the Aleppo Codex

At the Hebrew University of Jerusalem, a major project is under way to edit the text of the Aleppo Codex of 925 CE (Goshen-Gottstein 1976). This manuscript entered the scholarly domain only after the almost complete destruction of its Torah (Pentateuch) section in 1948. Ironically, it was the layout of the sections and songs of the Torah that Maimonides had singled out in his model codex. Could the Aleppo Codex ever be definitively identified as this codex? On the basis of the survival of Deuteronomy 32, this codex is identified by the editor as the one produced by Aaron ben Asher and favoured by Maimonides. With this splendid manuscript as base, this Hebrew University Bible Project (HUBP) was planned to 'present *in toto* the known data concerning the biblical text, its variants and its development' (Goshen-Gottstein 1965: [7]). There are four registers of apparatus, dealing with (i) the ancient versions; (ii) the scrolls from the Judaean Desert (The Dead Sea Scrolls) and the rabbinic literature; (iii) medieval Bible manuscripts (after 800 CE); (iv) spelling, vowels, and accents as compared with a few pre-selected manuscripts close in tradition to the Aleppo Codex. The use of such registers is a useful way to present the material, but makes heavy demands on the reader following a variant through several periods. Here, as in other diplomatic editions, the reader of the apparatus is urged to use the information given as stimulus to look at more complete presentations of the sources cited (Goshen-Gottstein 1965: [19]).

To date, the volumes on Isaiah (1975), Jeremiah (1997), and Ezekiel (2004) have appeared, and the text of the Minor Prophets is in preparation. An ancillary journal *Textus* discusses sources and issues relating to the edition.

Editions Based on the Leningrad Codex

This codex of the whole Hebrew Bible is in the second Firkovich collection in the Russian National Library in St Petersburg. We have no indication of its provenance before its sale to the library by the Karaite manuscript dealer A. Firkovich in 1876. It seems to have been written in 1008 CE. It is the oldest complete Hebrew Bible extant. It is a fine representative of the ben Asher tradition, although, unlike the incomplete Aleppo Codex, it can have no claim to having been written by Aaron ben Asher himself. In fact, one of the notes at the end of the manuscript indicates that it was corrected according to others prepared by Aaron ben Mosheh ben Asher. The influential German scholar Rudolf Kittel was swayed by Paul Kahle to abandon the text then traditional, and to adopt the Leningrad Codex as the base for the third edition of the *Biblia Hebraica* which he edited with other scholars. Kahle later noted that he and Kittel had hoped to be able to replace the Leningrad with the Aleppo Codex (which was at that time complete), but that it was not possible to obtain a copy ('Prolegomena' to third edition of *Biblia Hebraica* (BHK), p. 111). For this edition, Kahle edited the Masoretic Text as well as the Masorah parva and the brief Masorah finalis for each book and section. Kittel (who died in 1929) and other editors prepared the critical apparatus. The text was laid out as a single broad column on the page. Passages judged by the editors to be poetic were laid out in verse lines, following the perceived principles of Hebrew prosody, but with little attention to the Masoretic punctuation.

The fourth in the *Biblia Hebraica* series, *Biblia Hebraica Stuttgartensia* (BHS), had the same basic text, albeit with a different, if no less arbitrary layout. The Masorah parva was hugely reworked by Gerard Weil, and no longer reproduces that of the Leningrad manuscript. The text volume contains references to a correspondingly reworked Masorah magna published as a separate volume by Weil (1971). This volume gives the Masoretic lists in numbered sequence according to where they first occur in the manuscript. Weil died before he could complete a projected commentary on palaeographical and philological aspects, and a third volume on aspects of the Masorah parva, especially where it is independent of the Masorah magna.

Biblia Hebraica Quinta (BHQ), the fifth in the series, is in preparation by an international and inter-confessional group chaired by Prof. A. Schenker of Fribourg, Switzerland. It will contain the text and all the Masorah as given in the manuscript, and not as systematized by Weil. The apparatus of this edition will differ from previous editions, in that it will try to present the weight of the evidence of all of the available witnesses, and it will often give an indication of the nature of the relationship the editor perceives between the variants indicated and the preferred text. This risks being perceived as too controlling, but the implicit judgements of previous editions were more difficult to engage with and were no less controlling because less explicit. A companion volume will help the reader to interpret and appreciate this intricate system, as well as explain options taken in the critical apparatus. Extensive guidelines furnished to the editors and a review process prior to publication are intended to ensure a minimum of disparity in editorial approach from book to book. The first fascicle appeared in 2004 (Schenker 2004), and progress is now expected to be rapid. Other published editions of the main text of the Leningrad Codex, without the Masorah, include those of A. Dothan (1973, 2001), *Biblia Hebraica Leningradensia*. A facsimile edition was published under the general editorship of D. N. Freedman in 1998. The text of Codex Leningrad is becoming widely diffused.

Editions Based on Other Manuscripts

These include that edited by N. H. Snaith, based primarily on the first hand of MS Or 2626–8 of the British Library. Although based on different manuscripts, the text is very close to that of BHK and BHS. The 1524–5 second Rabbinic Bible printed by Daniel Bomberg in Venice (Goshen-Gottstein 1972), although itself probably an eclectic text, has proved a single source for many editions of the Bible. This was prepared by Jacob ben Hayyim, and is distinguished from the first Rabbinic Bible of 1516/17 by the inclusion of the Masorah. The sources for this text are not clear, but they seem to have included one or more manuscripts in the ben Asher tradition represented by Aleppo and Leningrad. This text of Ben Hayyim is still influential today, occupying a position in Jewish tradition sometimes seen as analogous to that of the *Textus Receptus* in New Testament studies. This term should be used with caution in the context of the Hebrew Bible. It was used by Kittel for the first two editions of *Biblia Hebraica*. The edition produced by Ginsburg for the British and Foreign Bible Society (and published posthumously in 1926) is an example of persistent dependence on the second Rabbinic Bible. In this case collations are added from seventy biblical manuscripts and nineteen editions prior to 1525. These added little to the value of the edition. Tov (1992: 78) considers the following to be the most prominent non-critical editions or series of editions: J. Buxtorf (1611), J. Athias (1661), J. Leusden (2nd edn. 1667), D. E. Jablonski (1669), E. van der Hooght (1701), J. D. Michaelis (1720), A. Hahn (1831), E. F. C. Rosenmüller (1834), M. H. Letteris (1852), and M. Koren (1966). Other important Tiberian manuscripts are available for sections of the Bible. Preliminary lists and descriptions may be found in Yeivin (1980), and a more technical description in Beit Arié, Sirat, and Glatzer (1997). The Ancient Biblical Manuscript Centre of Claremont, California, has been instrumental in making copies of ancient biblical manuscripts available to the scholarly world.

Non-Tiberian Traditions

*Traditions Later than 1000 CE other than those Worked
on by Tiberian Masoretes*

The eighteenth-century collations of the consonantal text published by Kennicott (1776–80) and de Rossi (1784–8) showed that there was no reason to suppose the existence of any significantly variant Hebrew textual tradition among medieval manuscripts or early editions preserved in Europe. Their magnificent publications (if particularly inaccurate in the case of Kennicott) serve only to demonstrate the insignificance of the data therein. This was shown by Davidson (1839) and affirmed by Goshen-Gottstein (1966). There is no point in emending an earlier text by reference to a later one when there is little possibility that the later reading comes from an independent tradition. This is true no matter how convenient that later reading may be, or how well it may tally with retroversions from versional readings. The most such coincidences can do is to show how a difficulty in the text is resolved similarly but independently by different sources. The reading is, as Barthélemy (1992: p. ccxvi) put it 'in the air'.

Traditions Earlier than 1000 CE other than those Worked on by ben Asher

Essentially there are two areas of study: the evidence from ancient translations, and the Hebrew texts from Qumran and surrounding areas.

We must first note the relevance for our discussion of the physical form (scroll or codex) in which the ancient witnesses were transmitted. The scroll form is older than the codex. Early scrolls most frequently contained only a single book. Different forms of a book could coexist on different scrolls. A codex, however, joined particular forms of texts in sequence. The origins of the texts might lie in scrolls of differing age and provenance, but once the texts were joined in a codex, they tended to be copied together and to be weighed or assessed together, as though they were a unity of similar age and provenance. The modern critic has to weigh the characteristics of each translation unit. The care with which a manuscript is executed is not an index of the antiquity of its readings. Groups of books, such as the Pentateuch, or Prophets, reached book form before whole Bibles. Christians opted for the codex form from early days (Roberts and Skeat 1983). The oldest codices we have that probably once contained the whole Old and New Testaments (called Pandects) are codices Vaticanus and Alexandrinus, and they are Christian manuscripts written in Greek. Perhaps it is true to say that Christians had a vested interest in having Old and New Testaments in a single volume, whereas the Jewish tradition distinguished between Torah, Prophets, and Writings, and of course did not deal with the Christian New Testament. Among Jews, the scroll remains normative for liturgical use. For the Pentateuch these scrolls are unadorned with vowel signs or marginal notes.

The first codex ever made (as distinct from the oldest surviving codex) to contain the whole of the Hebrew Bible may well be the Aleppo Codex of 925 CE mentioned above (so claimed Goshen-Gottstein 1963, and in the introduction to the facsimile edition, 1976).

The codex or book form was not bound by regulations affecting the scroll form, and so could be innovative in aspects of the text. The enterprise to contain the whole of the Hebrew Bible in a single codex may have led to an experimental readjustment of column width. This may have been particularly significant in the layout of poetical books. The Hebrew codices as we have them do not show the extreme differences in quality of text between section and section, book and book that we find, for example in the Greek Codex Vaticanus. Rather, they seem to be the product of an integrated, harmonious process. The notes transmitted in the margins of the Hebrew codex often refer to the whole Hebrew Old Testament as a unity.

a. Translations before 1000 CE

We treat the translations first, because to the present they have been of more influence in discussions of the Hebrew Bible text, and because for many books of the Old Testament they still present a more complete Bible text than that available from other sources.

While maintaining that the Hebrew text had been copied faithfully from earliest times, successive generations have been aware of differences between the Hebrew text and the ancient translations. This is particularly evident in the Septuagint. If the Jews were not to accuse the (fellow Jewish) translators of bad faith or incompetence, and so devalue the translation texts, some explanation had to be found. Jewish tradition suggested that changes had been made deliberately by the translators (Tov 1984). This may have links with the traditional lists of 'emendations of the scribes', or *tiqqune sopherim* (McCarthy 1981). These acknowledge the existence of places where the Hebrew text was altered, while implicitly making the case that this only happened in a limited number of known cases.

The differences between the transmitted Hebrew text and the texts of ancient translations became particularly obvious in Europe with the publication of the great Polyglot Bibles of the sixteenth and seventeenth centuries (Schenker 1994). These were more than stunning exercises in typography. By giving close literal Latin translations of the Hebrew and of its versions, they made people aware of the differences between them. This was the case, even though not all the Latin translations in question were made specially for the Polyglot Bibles, and in any case all of them were far removed in time and culture from the Vulgate. None the less, in some ways this is the ideal presentation of the Hebrew Bible and the ancient versions. Respecting the integrity of each text and the community it was identified with, it allowed comparison of whole traditions rather than isolated readings. Perhaps the wonders of the computer age and hypertext can enable us to dream again of such a project.

Biblical translation has always been a controversial (ad)venture, perhaps because Jewish tradition is itself so conscious of the care taken to transmit a fixed text exactly (Brock 1972). Although translation was undertaken first, and most significantly, within Judaism itself, the use of translations of the Hebrew Bible as sacred texts was soon a feature of Christianity as it expanded in a Greek- and Latin-speaking world. None the less, Christianity rarely lost the sense that great authority lay with a particular fixed Hebrew text of Jewish tradition, received in translation by Christians. There is an essential difference between this 'original' text, on the one hand, even when translated, and para-texts such as paraphrases or commentaries, on the other hand. Occasionally, as in the correspondence between Augustine and Jerome in the fourth century CE, we can detect some nervousness about leaving the discernment of the sense of Scripture in the hands of those rare Christians who could read Hebrew.

The translations with which we are concerned in this chapter were made from Hebrew texts that were earlier than the Tiberian Masoretic Text. These Hebrew texts contained only the consonantal element of the text with slight separation of the words. There would have been a tradition of reading this text, but we are unsure how consistently that was transmitted or how well it is represented by the Tiberian vocalization system (see above).

By applying the rules of language and logic, it is often possible to suggest what Hebrew text may underlie a given translation. This 'retroversion' is a very uncertain process. The linguistic constraints and usages of the relevant languages have to be considered, as do the intentions, consistency, and skills of the translator. These are discussed elsewhere in this volume. The accuracy of such a retroversion will be greater if the translation in question tended to be literal, consistent, and to treat small units at a time (Barr 1979). Even with the most literal ancient translations, one has to allow that retroversion gives us only an approximate idea of the underlying Hebrew text (the *Vorlage*).

In speaking about the ancient versions made from a Hebrew text, it is common practice to describe their characteristics with reference to the Masoretic/proto-Masoretic text. Critical editions try to find the earliest form of each text, recognizing that various vectors may have been influential in their transmission (e.g. to bring the translation closer to a respected Hebrew text, or to make the translation more acceptable on a cultural, literary, or linguistic level to the recipient community).

It is reasonable to question the justification for characterizing ancient versions by comparing the text of the version in question with a Hebrew text for which we have direct attestation only from a date much later than the making of the version, or even that version's earliest witnesses. The premiss on which such comparisons are based is that the Hebrew consonantal text and reading tradition have been transmitted faithfully, and that they represent those which provided the base text (*Vorlage*) of the ancient translation. Alternatively, some argue that the Hebrew text represents a common standard against which translations are characterized, whether or not it is the base text (*Vorlage*) from which the translation was made.

The ancient versions which were made before this form of text was selected for exclusive transmission were not necessarily made all at the same time or from the same Hebrew textual tradition, or from that Hebrew text selected to become the proto-Masoretic text. In some cases, such as Jeremiah, that seems unlikely. Absolute judgements are not necessarily helpful. The relationship between the ancient translation and the Masoretic Text can vary in certain particulars, or from section to section of a book.

When this retroverted Hebrew text differs from the Masoretic Text, we have to ask whether these differences were the result of an initiative of the translator, or a feature of the transmission process of the text in question. Did they perhaps reflect a different Hebrew text? If so, in what way was this related to the Hebrew text as transmitted in the Hebrew (Masoretic) tradition? (Tov 1993). The decision as to which variant reading can be judged to be the source of another, and therefore older, is a matter for textual criticism, and will be discussed elsewhere in this volume.

We do not have the original texts of translations made in antiquity. Each translation had its own history, determined by the needs and concerns of the community. The extent of the differences between Hebrew authoritative (proto-Masoretic) text and any translation text varied from translation to translation and from book or translation section to book or translation section. The communities transmitting translation texts did not necessarily attach the same importance to precision and exactitude as did the transmitters of the Hebrew texts. The process of determining the earliest extant reading or set of readings for each translation is no less considerable than the determination of the oldest extant Hebrew text.

Communities which did not have ready access to the Hebrew text show a common tendency to boost the status of their translation by ascribing special solemnity to the manner in which the translation was made, the texts from which it was made, or to the figures to whom it is attributed.

The Greek Old Testament (Septuagint, Old Greek)

The Greek translation of the Pentateuch seems to have originated in Alexandria in the third century BCE, or possibly later. Embellished accounts are given by Pseudo-Aristeas, Philo, and Josephus. These stories relate principally to the translation of the Pentateuch. They serve to buttress the prestige of the Greek translation by affirming that it was made at the scholarly city of Alexandria in an organized fashion by royal decree from the best manuscripts in Jerusalem by the most competent translators, and that the finished translation was protected from piecemeal emendations. Philo adds elements of miraculous divine inspiration for the translation. In Christian tradition this aura of inspiration spread from the translation of the Pentateuch to the Greek translation of all of the books considered canonical. In reality, we know little about the place, dates, and circumstances of many of the translations into Greek (Harl, Dorival, and Munnich 1994).

The Septuagint Project at Göttingen has produced the most comprehensive edition of the Septuagint to date, grouping the manuscripts according to type, and providing ancillary studies where necessary. The work inevitably varies slightly from editor to editor in a project of such magnitude and long duration. This has been forestalled to some extent by having a single editor (J. W. Wevers) edit the whole of the Pentateuch, and another (J. Ziegler) the whole of the major and minor Prophets. This has been reviewed twice at a forty-year interval by Barthélemy (1953; 1992: pp. cxvii–cxxxviii). The Göttingen project is soon to end. The most striking unfinished task is probably a second edition of the Psalter, the 1931 edition of which by A. Rahlfs was seen to be problematic, but remote preparations have been made (Aejmelaeus and Quast 2000).

The two-volume edition of the Septuagint published by A. Rahlfs in 1935 is more widely quoted, but the user needs to be aware that the judgements there may not be the same as those of the larger Göttingen edition which was based on wider evidence, and considered material that came to light after 1935.

The Septuagint translations were all made initially by Jews for the use of Jews. Many Christian communities felt that the Greek translations of their Old Testament should therefore be acknowledged by the Jews as bearing authority. By the time the Gospels were written, there was a plurality of Greek Old Testament texts in circulation, and these related in different ways to a single Hebrew text considered increasingly authoritative among the Jews. Which was the authentic Greek representative of the Hebrew text? Alteration of these Greek translations to make them a closer representative of the Hebrew text that dominated after the disastrous revolts of the first centuries CE was for long linked with the texts subsequently incorporated by Origen (185–253?) into the Hexapla, his great columnar comparison of Hebrew and Greek texts. Greek scrolls of the Minor Prophets discovered in the Judaean Desert led D. Barthélemy (1963) to posit that the work of emendation of the texts to make them more literal translations of a prestigious Hebrew text must be almost as old as the Greek translations themselves. This also implies that the emergence of a particular Hebrew text as dominant precedes the events of 70 and 135 CE. In the first centuries of the Common Era, the status of these Greek texts seems to have declined among the Jews, although they may have continued in minority use until the fall of Constantinople (de Lange 1996). Christians, however, relied greatly on the Greek texts, but had to deal with a confusing multiplicity. Origen tried to collate the principal Greek texts of his day in such a way that a single Greek text could be prepared that would be a secure reference point for Christians in dialogue with Jews. Because Origen's multi-columned text looked to the proto-Masoretic Hebrew for its organization and as the point of reference for the annotations of the Greek Bible that was subsequently prepared, his legacy has not been a particularly happy one for those who wish to work with pre-Origenian forms of the Septuagint, or forms of the Hebrew text other than the proto-Masoretic. Only pre-Origenian forms of the Septuagint can give us an indication of how the Hebrew from which the Septuagint was translated differed from the proto-Masoretic text.

The Göttingen project has produced eclectic texts that represent, in the editors' judgement, the Old Greek. In Madrid, part of the great research enterprise into the history of the text has produced editions of the Antiochian text, a tradition of the Old Greek that largely escaped the influence of the Hexapla (Fernández Marcos and Busto Saiz 1989, 1992, 1996).

Many questions concerning the proto-Masoretic text and its pronunciation could be solved if the first two columns of the Hexapla had been conserved to a greater extent. Although a few fragments of copies of parts of the Hexapla have survived, none includes the Hebrew column, presumably because of the practical difficulty for scribes unfamiliar with Hebrew. Over 125 years after the collection of Field (1875), work is beginning on a new collection of Hexaplaric fragments (Salvesen 1998).

In Christian tradition the Greek translation has been a rich source of theological reflection. Undervalued for many years, during which it was seen primarily as a tool in the study of the Hebrew Bible, the Septuagint is now once again the focus of fruitful study both in its own right, and together with its daughter versions in a context of Christian patristic studies. After many years without adequate translations into modern languages, several projects of translation and commentary are now afoot (Pietersma 1997, 2000; Harl 1998; Cacciari and Tampellini 1998; Kreuzer 2001). Useful modern introductions are increasing awareness of these important texts (Harl, Dorival, and Munnich 1994; Jobes and Silva 2000; Dines 2004).

Aramaic Targums

The dating of the surviving targums is controversial and complex. None the less, the discovery of targums at Qumran proves beyond question the antiquity of the phenomenon of translation of biblical texts into Aramaic, even if their relation to the previously known targums is not clear. The targums now extant may represent only a fraction of those of antiquity. These are the principal surviving targums.

Targums to the Pentateuch
Targum of Onqelos contains the whole Pentateuch. It was probably produced in Palestine, but is known as the Babylonian Targum. Targum of Pseudo-Jonathan contains most of the Pentateuch. It is a complex text, related to other texts, but having a great deal of material proper to itself. Some of these elements may go back to 100 BCE. The Fragment Targum covers sections of varying length, sometimes quite brief, of the Pentateuch. The Palestinian Targum, long presumed lost apart from some fragments, was found to have survived at Rome in a unique manuscript, Codex Neofiti I, published towards the end of the twentieth century (Diez Macho 1968–79). The dating of the text is controversial, but is not necessarily after the beginning of the Common Era.

Targums to the Former Prophets (Joshua, Judges, Samuel–Kings) and Later Prophets (Isaiah, Jeremiah, Ezekiel, Minor Prophets)
Targum Jonathan to the Prophets was probably produced in Palestine, even though it was well known in Babylon, where it seems to have been edited.

Targums to the Writings
These targums have not yet been studied in the same depth as the targums to the other parts of Scripture. They are generally supposed to be late compositions of individuals. In this they differ from the complex compositions identified with Jonathan and Onkelos (McNamara 1972).

The differences between the Aramaic targums and the Hebrew text are not the same as the differences between the Greek Old Testament and the Hebrew text. Targums are not best considered simply as translations of the Old Testament text.

Perhaps this difference in perspective is best explained by reference to the function of the respective texts. Whereas in Jewish liturgy, the targum seems to have accompanied the Hebrew reading as interpretation as well as translation, the Greek text seems to have been read on its own in the place of the Hebrew text in Greek-speaking Jewish communities (Norton 1994). Freed from this responsibility of being the 'sacred text', the targum is loosely linked to the Hebrew text. At times its interpretative additions or expansions tell us little about the Hebrew text. At other times, they can show us how they have understood an ambiguous Hebrew text, or which Hebrew text was read when variants exist. These can also be of interest to those who study the background to the New Testament writings. A modern English translation project is nearing completion (McNamara 1987–). (See also the article 'Targum' in the *Supplément au Dictionnaire de la Bible*.)

Latin Translations

Among ancient Latin translations of the Old Testament we distinguish crudely between the Old Latin and the Vulgate.

The Old Latin

No single date, place, or initiative of translation can be ascribed to the translation of the Old Latin from the Septuagint. It is usually identified with Latin-speaking communities in northern (Roman) Africa and southern Gaul. The differences between circulated texts seem to be a matter of constant revision rather than of multiple translations, but there may well have been more than a single translation. The Old Latin is a daughter translation of the Septuagint, and although of great interest as a witness to that text, is of only secondary interest to those focused on the Hebrew text.

For those concerned with the reception and interpretation of the Old Testament in the Latin Church, the Old Latin text remains crucial, despite its idiosyncrasies. It was the text commented on by Christian theologians and commentators of the Latin language until the eighth or ninth centuries. An edition of the Vetus *Latina*, begun in 1949, and initially edited by B. Fischer, is proceeding slowly, but will eventually replace the eighteenth-century edition of Sabatier.

The Vulgate

The text in question has been known by this name since the sixteenth century. It is linked to St Jerome (d. 420 CE), but is not simply to be identified with his translations. The Latin Bible in one volume (pandect) as promulgated in the University of Paris in the thirteenth century was largely composed, in its Old Testament section, of the translations of Jerome from the Hebrew. This may be explained by the authority linked with an original commission by Pope Damasus after 382 CE, as well as Jerome's own prestige as a Christian scholar who had mastered Hebrew. The most striking exception in this collection was the Psalter, which was an earlier translation made by Jerome from the Greek. This may reflect the liturgy of the court of Charlemagne, which led Alcuin (d. 804) to choose it for early codices. A critical edition of Jerome's translations of the old Testament has been completed by the Benedictine Abbey of St Jerome in Rome (1926–95). A smaller two-volume edition published at Stuttgart is also useful (Weber 1994). This is quite distinct from the *Nova Vulgata* of 1979, which is a revision of Jerome's text on the basis of the ancient versions intended for contemporary use by the Roman Catholic Church.

In Roman Catholic studies, the authority given to the Vulgate by the first session of the Council of Trent in 1546 has frequently been misunderstood. It has more to do with canon and with a source for dogmatic teaching than with identification of any particular Latin text. In fact, a new edition of the Vulgate was badly needed at the time. Pope Sixtus V published an edition in 1590. This was hurriedly altered and reissued under Clement VIII in 1592. This very confusion demonstrates that no single text was given final authority by the Council. English translations of the Catholic Vulgate are widely available, if somewhat dated in language. Contemporary Roman Catholic Bible texts used in the liturgy and teaching are based on the Hebrew (and Aramaic and Greek where appropriate) texts of the Old Testament.

The Syriac Version and the Hebrew Old Testament

Although several forms of the Old Testament are found in Syriac, only that termed the 'Peshitta' is a direct witness to an underlying Hebrew. It was made book by book over a long period in the first centuries CE. Some books seem to indicate a Christian context, while others are thought to be most probably Jewish, on the basis of links with the targum tradition. Perhaps the divisions between the two backgrounds should not be drawn too tightly. (Weitzman (1999) envisages a marginal Jewish community that eventually embraced Christianity.) This is the form of Syriac Bible still in use in the Syriac churches. The Peshitta Institute in Leiden has published a diplomatic edition of Manuscript 7a1. This Milan manuscript was published by Ceriani in 1876. As with all diplomatic editions, it is important to consult the apparatus for early evidence that may be preferable to the reading of the base manuscript. In the Peshitta the earliest form of the translations seems to have been the closest to the Hebrew text. This was successively revised to provide a more stylistically polished Syriac text that sometimes, however, presents pseudo-variants if retroverted to Hebrew. Interpretation of this feature has been a problem in editions of the Hebrew Bible. Other forms of the Syriac Old Testament are not helpful as witnesses to the Hebrew text, as they are relatively late and based on Origen's revision of the Septuagint on the basis of the Hexapla (Syrohexapla, seventh century) or the Septuagint (Syrolucianic, sixth century), or a combination of pre-existing Syriac texts and Antiochian Greek texts (Jacob of Edessa, eighth century).

b. Hebrew Witnesses pre-1000: A Twentieth-century Upheaval

This, then, was the situation with regard to the Hebrew Bible in the first half of the twentieth century: as well as the traditionally authoritative text derived from that of the early sixteenth-century rabbinic Bibles, increasing authority was being given to the Aleppo and Leningrad codices. All of these represented the Tiberian school of vocalization of the ben Asher family. Other codices of the Pentateuch or Prophets of this Tiberian tradition also survived from the eighth to the tenth centuries (Yeivin 1980; Beit Arie, Sirat, and Glatzer 1997).

i.   The Cairo Geniza

Other Hebrew evidence, such as that from the Cairo Geniza (Kahle 1947, 1959), was fragmentary, and was more useful in establishing the history of the transmission of the text than the edition of the text itself. The non-Tiberain vocalization systems have been noted above.

ii.   The Samaritan Pentateuch

The seventeenth century saw the discovery of a Samaritan Hebrew manuscript of the Pentateuch written in 1345. This differed in what were then calculated as about 7,000 respects from the rabbinic Bible, but agreed with the Septuagint Pentateuch in about 1,900 of these. (The calculations would today be done on the basis of different texts, so these figures are not sound.) The excitement largely evaporated in the wake of a magisterial study by Gesenius published in 1815. This study dismissed the Samaritan Pentateuch and the source text of the Septuagint as both being derived from a common popular text inferior to the Jerusalem text which was the ancestor of the Masoretic Text. P. Kahle (1915, 1950) was perhaps the strongest counterbalancing voice. In this as in other areas he advanced a theory of a number of textual forms coexisting before a particular form was chosen as normative. It was not a question of one form being better or worse than another, but of a multiplicity of forms coexisting. When Kahle published (1947), the Samaritan Pentateuch was isolated as a variant Hebrew witness, and so it was hard to decide the matter one way or the other. The manuscript tradition of the Samaritan Pentateuch itself was relatively lean, and all manuscripts seemed to relate to a single standardized text. The perceived links with the Septuagint were not sufficient to ensure the Samaritan tradition a context, or even a date of origin, for the origins of the Septuagint were themselves very controversial. Subsequent discoveries at Qumran, as well as a reappraisal of the evidence, have indicated that the Samaritan Pentateuch is an early and widespread development of the Hebrew text, but independent of the proto-Masoretic text (Salmon 1951; Würthwein 1995: 46–7).

Perhaps because of a combination of the controversy about its worth and the difficulty in obtaining access to the relatively few old manuscripts of the Samaritan Pentateuch that exist, the problematic edition of A. F. von Gall (1914–18) has not yet been replaced. Tal (1994) produced a diplomatic edition of MS 6 of the Nablus synagogue.

iii.   The Nash Papyrus

This document, discovered in Egypt in 1902, continues to deserve mention in a survey such as this because for fifty years it was the oldest known fragment of a biblical text. It contains a text of the Ten Commandments that is a combination of the texts of Exod. 20: 2–17 and Deut. 5: 6–21 as well as the Shema of Deut. 6: 4 f. Although these are biblical texts, their combination in this papyrus fragment indicates that they are not derived from a biblical manuscript, but from some related text (e.g. prayers, teaching). It can be dated with some confidence to the last centuries BCE.

iv.   Qumran

The discoveries at Qumran and the surrounding area from 1947 are treated in greater depth elsewhere in this volume. Controversies over dating and authenticity were eventually resolved. The Hebrew Bible texts seemed lost for a while in the various controversies centred on the discovery of documents outside the Hebrew Bible and their consequences for the identity of the community, and the history of Judaism and Christianity. Yet, these apparently humdrum biblical texts with their tiny variants are of great importance for all who study the biblical text. Not the least important aspect is their dating. These manuscripts linked with Qumran were all written before 70 CE. Other manuscripts, from nearby Wadi Murabba'at, linked with the Bar Kochba Revolt, could not have been written after 135 CE. The official publications of these documents are in the Oxford Discoveries in the Judaean Desert series. A microfiche edition of photographs of the scrolls is also available (Tov 1993a), as are many ancillary studies of particular manuscripts.

Until the discoveries at Qumran, there was little evidence that non-proto-Masoretic consonantal texts existed in Hebrew, apart from the controversial Samaritan Pentateuch. Most apparent variants presented by the ancient versions could be attributed to the initiative of the translator or the transmission process. Others presumed that these readings gave a text earlier than (and therefore superior to) the Tiberian Masoretic Text, simply because it differed from it and came from an ancient source, albeit by retroversion. This is well seen in the apparatus to editions and in commentaries on the text.

Although some complete biblical books, and fragments of many books, or of a number of copies of these books have been found at Qumran, nothing remotely comparable to a 'complete Hebrew Bible' has been found there. The texts were written on scrolls. With a few possible exceptions, each scroll contained only one biblical book. Many Hebrew texts are clearly the ancestors of our Masoretic Bible.

However, there are other texts of the same books existing at the same time that are different from them. Some of these differences evoke the text from which the Septuagint may have been translated, and others relate to the Samaritan Pentateuch, but the relationship is complicated (Tov 1992, 1993b).

The texts from Qumran give us a new picture of the history of the biblical text. Yet if textual plurality in Hebrew lies behind the differences found in the ancient translations, more questions arise. If the different textual forms found at Qumran were not ancestors of the present Hebrew text, but were more like relatives by a collateral line, how then should these variants be used in an edition of the Hebrew text? Literary, canonical, and textual criticism intertwine. How should an edition present such evidence? Fortunately I do not have to answer all these questions here. The point, however, is that the preparation of an edition requires a working model of the history of the text and clear goals if it is to weigh the data appropriately. The discovery of the plurality of textual traditions which seem to have preceded the choice of a single consonantal tradition as authoritative did not automatically confirm the existence of all putative Hebrew variants previously proposed on the basis of retroversion from ancient versions. The translation factors already identified before the Qumran finds (e.g. difficulties of retroversion, constraints of the receptor language, theological and cultural factors, errors of scribe or copyist) must still be taken into account. None the less, the discoveries at Qumran and their confirmation of the existence of textual plurality in the Hebrew biblical text gave consideration of these factors a broader context. A word of caution is in order. Even though many texts have been found at Qumran, we still do not have all of the texts that were extant (even at Qumran) at the time when the translations were being made. Neither do we know how representative these texts are of the kinds of texts that would have been conserved in other Jewish communities, or even in Jerusalem.

If at Qumran we find no apparent difference in status granted to texts which are the ancestors of the Masoretic Texts and those which are not, then it is reasonable to conclude that, at Qumran at least, the canonical discussion about whether one form was to be transmitted and others suppressed had not been resolved by 70 CE. It seems, therefore, to be later than the early days of Christianity. This raises questions about how the authority of the group or community that chose one text of a biblical book rather than another, and was responsible for its subsequent authority, is to be recognized by groups (e.g. Christians) who were already in the process of breaking away from Judaism before that decision was taken. Similarly, the decision of the same authoritative context that a book was or was not to be considered privileged (canonical) is not necessarily to be accepted by other groups (e.g. Christians). The book of Sirach is a case in point. Many Christian denominations accept Sirach as canonical, despite a clear option among the Jewish communities and post-Reformation communities of the Latin Church to exclude it from the canon of Tanakh.

Many factors indicate that the group at Qumran were reactionary, isolated, and conservative. The rise of prestige (authority?) of a particular text form may have been more evident in Jerusalem or other centres, especially if it was linked with one of the groups other than the Essenes. We have no manuscript group comparable to Qumran to confirm this, but one piece of evidence indicates that this may have been the case. The text of the Greek translation of the Hebrew Bible (the Septuagint, LXX) seems to have begun a process of revision towards a more literal representation of the form eventually adopted as proto-Masoretic at a very early stage (Barthélemy 1963). This certainly implies that in certain circles at least this form of the text enjoyed such prestige that it was important for the users of a Greek translation to be identified with it if they were to be taken seriously.

On the basis of the limited evidence provided at Wadi Murabba'at, south of Qumran, an argument can be made that at some stage between the year 70 and the year 135, the multiplicity of text forms was abandoned, and one particular form of a Hebrew text was adopted for future use. This hangs on the finding of a Hebrew scroll of the Minor Prophets that was itself close to the proto-Masoretic text type, and indeed shows further corrections towards that type. Other fragments have been found there, but they are too small or too damaged to be read. It is argued that once the proto-Masoretic books dominated, variant forms of these books (and even whole books, such as 1 Enoch), were no longer copied, or more probably were suppressed in Jewish tradition. Such an authoritative decision has often been linked with a meeting in Jamnia at the end of the first century CE, but this solution may be no more accurate than the earlier attributions to Ezra and the Great Synagogue. The issue of canon is considered elsewhere in this volume (Chapter 43). Here we will limit ourselves to a note that the argument based on the proto-Masoretic form found at Murabba'at depends on a single scroll. The logical basis for the conclusions suggested would be much stronger if a number of scrolls of the proto-Masoretic group were found.

CONCLUSION

I have chosen to discuss the text of the Hebrew Bible in an order that respects that in which people access the data that we have. Although I have not touched on the process of composition of the text, and I believe it unlikely that much headway can be made in regard to specific texts, work is under way in the area of the social milieux in which the texts may have been composed (Lemaire 1981; Davies 1998).

SUGGESTED READING

More chronologically structured histories of the text can be found in Mulder 1988; D. Norton 1993; *The Cambridge History*, 1963, 1969, 1970; Barthélemy 1982: *1–*114; 1986: *1–*81; 1992: pp. i–ccxlii), and Trebolle Barrera 1998.

BIBLIOGRAPHY

ACKROYD, P. R., and EVANS, C. F. 1970. *From the Beginnings to Jerome.* Cambridge History of the Bible, i. Cambridge: Cambridge University Press.

AEJMELAEUS, A., and QUAST, U., eds. 2000. *Der Septuaginta-Psalter und seine Töchterüber-setzungen: Symposium in Göttingen 1997.* Mitteilungen der Septuaginta-Unternehmens, 24. Göttingen: Vandenhoeck & Ruprecht.

ALBREKTSON, B. 1981. 'Difficilior lectio probabilior: Remembering all the way'. *OTS* 21: 5–18.

BARR, J. 1968. *Comparative Philology and the Text of the Old Testament.* Oxford: Oxford University Press.

—— 1979. *The Typology of Literalism in Ancient Biblical Translations.* Mitteilungen des Septuaginta-Unternehmens, 15. Göttingen: Vandenhoeck & Ruprecht.

BARTHÉLEMY, D. 1953. Review of Ziegler, *Ezekiel* in the Göttingen Septuagint. *RB* 60: 606–10

—— 1963. *Les Devanciers d'Aquila: Première publication intégrale du texte des fragments du Dodekapropheton trouvés dans le desert de Juda.* SVT 10. Leiden: Brill.

—— 1978. *Études d'histoire du texte de l'A.T.* OBO 21. Fribourg-Suisse: Editions Universi-taires; Göttingen: Vandenhoeck & Ruprecht.

—— 1982, 1986, 1992. *Critique Textuelle de l'Ancien Testament.* OBO 50/1/2/3. Fribourg-Suisse: Editions Universitaires; Göttingen: Vandenhoeck & Ruprecht.

—— HULST, A. R., LOHFINK, N., MCHARDY, W. D., RÜGER, H. P., and SANDERS, J. A. 1973–80. *Preliminary and Interim Report on the Hebrew Old Testament Text Project,* 5 vols. New York: United Bible Societies.

BEIT ARIÉ, M., SIRAT, C., and GLATZER, M. 1997. *Codices hebraicis litteris exarati quo tempore scripti fuerint exhibentes,* Tome 1: *jusqu' 1020.* Monumenta Palaeographia Medii Aevi, Series Hebraica, 1 Turnhout: Brepols.

Bénédictine Abbey of St Jerome. 1926–95. *Biblia Sacra iuxta latinam vulgatam versionem,* 18 vols. Rome: Vatican.

BROCK, S. P. 1972. 'The Phenomenon of the Septuagint'. In *The Witness of Tradition,* OTS 17. Leiden: Brill, 1–36.

CACCIARI, A., and TAMPELLINI, S. 1998. 'La Bibbia dei Settanta'. *BIOSCS* 31: 36–8.

Cambridge History of the Bible. See Ackroyd and Evans 1970; Lampe 1969; Greenslade 1963.

CERIANI, A. M. 1876. *Translatio Syra Pescitto Veteris Testamenti ex codice Ambrosiano sec. fere VI photolithographice edita.* Milan: della Croce.

DAVIDSON, S. 1839. *Lectures in Biblical Criticism.* Edinburgh: T. & T. Clark.

DAVIES, P. R. 1998. *The Canonization of the Hebrew Scriptures.* Library of Ancient Israel. Nashville: Westminster/John Knox.

DIEZ MACHO, A. 1968–79. *Neophyti I: Targum Palestinese MS de la Biblioteca Vaticana*, 6 vols. Madrid and Barcelona: Consejo Superior de Investigaciones Cientificas.

DINES, J. M. 2004. *The Septuagint*, ed. M. A. Knibb. London and New York: T. & T. Clark.

DOTHAN, A. 1973. *Torah, Nevi'im u-Khetuvim*. Tel Aviv: Huts'ah 'Edi.

—— 2001. *Biblia Hebraica Leningradensia*. Peabody, Mass.: Hendrickson.

ELLIGER, K., and RUDOLPH, W. 1977. *Biblia Hebraica Stuttgartensia*. Stuttgart: Deutsche Bibelgesellschaft.

FERNÁNDEZ-MARCOS, N. 1998. *Introducción a las versiones griegas de la Biblia*. Madrid: Consejo Superior de Investigaciones Cientificas.

—— and BUSTO SAIZ, J. R. 1989, 1992, 1996. *El Texto Antioqueno de la biblia griega*. Madrid: Instituto de filologia del Consejo Superior de Investigaciones Cientificas.

FIELD, F. 1875. *Origenis Hexaplorum quae Supersunt*, 2 vols. Oxford: Clarendon Press.

FISCHER, B. 1949– . *Vetus Latina: Die Reste der altlateinischen Bibel nach Petrus Sabatier neu gesammelt und herausgegeben von Erzabtei Beuron*. Freiburg: Herder.

FREEDMAN, D. N., ed. 1998. *The Leningrad Codex: A Facsimile Edition*. Grand Rapids, Mich.: Eerdmans; Leiden: Brill.

GALL, A. F. von. 1914–18. *Der hebräische Pentateuch der Samaritaner*. Giessen: Töpelmann.

GESENIUS, G. 1815. *De pentateuchi samaritani origine, indole et auctoritate commentario philologico-critica*. Halle: Libreria Rengerianae.

GIBSON, A. 1981. *Biblical Semantic Logic: A Premilinary Analysis*. Sheffield: Sheffield Academic Press, 2nd edn. 2001

GINSBURG, C. D. 1880–1905. *The Masorah Compiled from Manuscripts Alphabetically and Lexically Arranged*, 6 vols. London.

—— 1926. *The Pentateuch, The Earlier Prophets, The Later Prophets, The Writings Diligently Revised According to the Massorah and the Earlier Editions with the Various Readings from Mss and the Ancient Versions*. London: British and Foreign Bible Society.

GORDIS, R. 1937, 1981. *The Biblical Text in the Making*. New York: KTAV.

GOSHEN-GOTTSTEIN, M. H. 1963a, 'Theory and Practice of Textual Criticism: The Text-critical Use of the Septuagint'. *Textus*, 3: 130–58.

—— 1963b. 'The Rise of the Tiberian Bible Text'. In A. Altmann, ed., *Biblical and other Studies*, Cambridge, Mass.: Harvard University Press, 79–122; repr. in S. Z. Leiman, ed., *The Canon and Masorah of the Hebrew Bible: An Introductory Reader*, New York: KTAV, 1974.

—— 1965. *The Book of Isaiah, Sample Edition with Introduction*. HUBP. Jerusalem: Magnes Press.

—— 1966. 'Hebrew Biblical Manuscripts: Their History and their Place in the HUBP Edition'. *Biblica*, 48: 243–90.

—— ed. 1972. *Biblia Rabbinica: A Reprint of the 1525 Venice Edition*. Jerusalem: Makor.

—— ed. 1976. *The Aleppo Codex, Provided with Massoretic Notes and Pointed by Aaron ben Asher, the Text Considered Authoritative by Maimonides*. Jerusalem: Magnes Press.

—— and TALMON, S., eds. 2004. *The Book of Ezekiel*. HUBP. Jerusalem: Magnes Press.

GREENSLADE, S. L. 1963. *The West from the Reformation to the Present Day*. Cambridge History of the Bible, iii. Cambridge: Cambridge University Press.

HARL, M. 1986– . *La Bible d'Alexandrie*. Paris: Cerf.

—— 1998. 'La Bible d'Alexandrie'. *BIOSCS* 31: 31–5.

—— DORIVAL, G., and MUNNICH, O. 1994. *La Bible Grecque des Septante: du judaisme hellénistique au christianisme ancien*. Paris: Cerf/Centre National de la Recherche Scientifique. Hebrew University Bible Project. 1965.

HOUBIGANT, C. F. 1753. *Biblia Hebraica cum notis criticis et versione latina*. Paris.

HOUSMAN, A. E. 1922. 'The Application of Thought to Textual Criticism'. *Proceedings of the Classical Association*, 18: 67 ff.; repr. in *idem, Selected Prose*, ed. John Carter, Cambridge: Cambridge University Press, 1961, 131–50.

JOBES, K. H., and SILVA, M. 2000. *Invitation to the Septuagint*. Grand Rapids, Mich.: Baker.

KAHLE, P. 1915. 'Untersuchungen zur Geschichte des Pentateuchtextes', *Theologische Studien und Kritiken*, 88: 399–439.

—— 1947, 1959. *The Cairo Geniza*. Oxford: Blackwell.

—— 1950. 'Zur Aussprache des Hebräischen bei den Samaritanern'. In *Festschrift Alfred Bertholet*, Tübingen: Mohr, 281–6.

KELLEY, P. H., Mynatt, D. S., and Crawford, T. G. *The Masorah of Biblia Hebraica Stuttgartensia: Introduction and Annotated Glossary*. Grand Rapids, Mich. and Cambridge: Eerdmans.

KENNICOTT, B. 1776, 1780. *Vetus Testamentum Hebraicum cum variis lectionibus*. Oxford.

KITTEL, R. (ed.) 1905. *Biblia Hebraica*. Leipzig: J. C. Hinrichs; 2nd edn. 1913.

—— 1937. *Biblia Hebraica*. Stuttgart: Würtembergische Bibelanstalt.

KREUZER, S. 2001. 'A German Translation of the Septuagint'. *BIOSCS* 34: 40–6.

LAMPE, G. W. H. 1969. *The West from the Fathers to the Reformation*. Cambridge History of the Bible, ii. Cambridge: Cambridge University Press.

LANGE, N. DE 1996. *Greek Jewish Texts from the Cairo Genizah*. TSAJ 51. Tübingen: J. C. B. Mohr (Paul Siebeck).

LE DÉAUT, R. 2002. 'Targum'. In *Supplément au Dictionnaire de la Bible*, Paris: Letonzey & Ané, xiii. 1*–344*.

LEMAIRE, A. 1981. *Les Écoles et la Formation de la Bible dans l'ancien Israel*. OBO 39. Fribourg-Suisse: Editions Universitaires; Göttingen: Vandenhoeck & Ruprecht.

LIPSCHÜTZ, L. 1962. 'Mishael ben Uzziel's Treatise on the Differences between ben Asher and ben Naphthali'. *Textus*, 2: 1–57.

McCARTHY, C. 1981. *The Tiqqune Sopherim*. OBO 36. Fribourg-Suisse: Editions Universitaires; Göttingen: Vandenhoeck & Ruprecht.

McNAMARA, M. 1972. *Targum and Testament: Aramaic Paraphrases of the Hebrew Bible: A Light on the New Testament*. Shannon: Irish University Press.

—— (project director) 1987– . *The Aramaic Bible: The Targums*. Wilmington, Del.: M. Glazier.

MULDER, M. 1988. 'The Transmission of the Biblical Text'. In *Mikra: Text, Translation, Reading and Interpretation of the Hebrew Bible in Ancient Judaism and Early Christianity*, CRINT 2/1, Assen: van Gorcum; Philadelphia: Fortress, 87–135.

NORTON, D. 1993. *A History of the Bible as Literature*, 2 vols., i: *From Antiquity to 1700*; ii: *From 1700 to the Present Day*. Cambridge: Cambridge University Press.

NORTON, G. 1994. 'Jews, Greeks, and the Hexapla of Origen'. In D. R. G. Beattie and M. J. McNamara, eds., *The Aramaic Bible: Targums in their Historical Context*, JSOTS.S 166: 400–19.

Nova Vulgata Bibliorum Sacrorum editio. 1979. Rome: Vatican.

PAGNINI, S. 1527. *Biblia . . . nova translatio*. Lyons.

PIETERSMA, A. 1998. 'A New English Translation of the Septuagint'. In IX Congress of the International Organization for Septuagint and Cognate Studies, Atlanta: Scholars Press.

—— 2000. *A New English Translation of the Septuagint and the Other Greek Translations Traditionally Included under that Title: The Psalms*. New York and Oxford: Oxford University Press.

RAHLFS, A. 1931. *Psalmi cum Odis*. Göttingen: Vandenhoeck & Ruprecht.

RAHLFS, A. 1935. *Septuaginta, id est Vetus Testamentum graece iuxta LXX interpretes*, 2 vols. Stuttgart: Privilegierte Würtembergische Bibelanstalt.

ROBERTS, C. H., and SKEAT, T. C. 1983. *The Birth of the Codex*. London: Oxford University Press.

ROSSI, J. B. DE 1784–8. *Variae lectiones Veteris Testamenti*, 4 vols. Parma.

SABATIER, P. 1743. *Bibliorum sacrorum latinae versiones antiquae seu Vetus Latina*, 2 vols. Rheims.

SALVESEN, A., ed. 1998. *Origen's Hexapla and Fragments*. TSAJ 5. Tübingen: J. C. B. Mohr (Paul Siebeck).

SCHENKER, A. 1994. 'Der alttestamentliche Text in den vier grossen Polyglottenbibeln nach dem heutigen Stand der Forschung'. *Theologische Revue* 90, 177–88.

—— et al. 2004. *Biblia Hebraica Quinta: Fascicle 18: General Introduction and Megilloth*. Stuttgart: Deutsche Bibelgesellschaft.

SNAITH, N. H. 1958. *Hebrew Bible*. London: British and Foreign Bible Society.

SPERBER, A. 1956. *Codex Reuchlinianus*. The Pre-Masoretic Bible. Corpus Codicum Hebraicorum Mediiaevi II. Copenhagen: Munksgaard.

TAL, A. 1994. *The Samaritan Pentateuch Edited According to Ms 6 (C) of the Shekhem Synagogue*. Tel Aviv: Chaim Rosenberg School of Jewish Studies.

TALMON, S. 1951. 'The Samaritan Pentateuch'. *JJS* 2: 140–50.

—— RABIN, C., and TOV, E. 1997. *The Book of Jeremiah*. The Hebrew University Bible. Jerusalem: Magnes Press.

TOV, E. 1981. *The Text-critical Use of the Septuagint in Biblical Research*. Jerusalem Biblical Studies 3. Jerusalem: Simor.

—— 1984. 'The Rabbinic Tradition Concerning the "Alterations" Inserted into the Greek Pentateuch and their Relation to the Original Text of the LXX'. *JSJ* 15: 65–89.

—— 1992. *Textual Criticism of the Hebrew Bible*. Minneapolis: Fortress; Assen and Maastricht: Van Gorcum.

—— 1993a. *The Dead Sea Scrolls on Microfiche: A Comprehensive Facsimile Edition of the Texts from the Judaean Desert*. Leiden: Brill.

—— 1993b. 'Some Reflections on the Hebrew Texts from which the Septuagint was Translated'. *Journal of Northwest Semitic Languages*, 19: 107–22.

TREBOLLE BARRERA, J. 1998. *The Jewish Bible and the Christian Bible: An Introduction to the History of the Bible*. Leiden: Brill; Grand Rapids, Mich.: Eerdmans.

WEBER, R. 1969. *Biblia Sacra iuxta Vulgatam Versionem*, 2 vols. Stuttgart: German Bible Society; 4th edn. 1994.

WEIL, F. 1971. *Massorah Gedolah*. Rome: Pontificium Institutum Biblicum; Stuttgart: Societas biblica Virtembergensis.

WEITZMAN, M. 1999. *The Syriac Version of the Old Testament*. University of Cambridge Oriental Publications. Cambridge: Cambridge University Press.

WÜRTHWEIN, E. 1995. *The Text of the Old Testament*, 2nd English edn., trans. Erroll F. Rhodes. Grand Rapids, Mich.: Eerdmans.

YEIVIN, I. 1969. 'The Division into Sections in the Psalms'. *Textus*, 7: 76–102.

—— 1980. *Introduction to the Tiberian Masorah*, ed. E. J. Revell. SBL Masoretic Studies, 5. Missoula, Mo.: Scholars Press.

CHAPTER 13

TEXTUAL TRANSMISSION AND VERSIONS OF THE NEW TESTAMENT

J. N. BIRDSALL

No doubts may be entertained that the documents gathered into the collection which we call the scriptures of the New Testament are from the earliest years of the Christian movement, and most if not all from the first century of the Christian era. Traces of those documents are encountered in manuscript remains of the second century, in identifiable allusions and quotations by writers of the second century and increasingly of later centuries, and in early translations traceable to the second and third centuries (Latin, Syriac, and Coptic). If we take a late second-century writer, Irenaeus of Lyons, as a fixed point, we shall find in his work the main outlines of the later canon: that is, the accepted list of authoritative books. In verbatim quotation we shall find considerable evidence of the wording known uniformly at that point in subsequent years, but also of a number of variations of wording from standard editions which a proportion of later manuscripts present. His evidence is preceded historically by a more slender body of textual material and allusive reference in earlier second-century Christian writers. But from before about 150 CE we have little direct evidence of the spread or use of the New Testament books, and it is largely fragmentary or conveyed by implication.

To trace the earliest stages of the transmission of the New Testament documents, then, is a species of prehistory or archaeology. We need to use data largely from the documents themselves, and the specimens will be items to which attention has been drawn by those who seek to trace the growth and composition of the canonical books and to comment upon their meaning. These specimens will often not be patient of being dealt with by strictly text-critical methods, but will be simply interpreted as indications of what might be revealed if a significant sample of extensive text from this early period (say 50 to 150 CE) became available.

The scenarios differ according to the parts of the canon under investigation. It has frequently been attempted to link the composition of each of the gospels with a specific locality within which that gospel was current from its earliest period of existence. This hypothesis has carried the implication that for some unspecified period each gospel was the sole literary source of knowledge of Jesus in the church for which it was initially written or in the adjacent region. Recently voices have been heard urging that early circulation of each gospel within the whole Christian body should be envisaged, so that there would have been earlier interaction of written materials within the whole Christian body.

Either construct might provide an explanation of variants in the later text when the notion and entity of the 'fourfold gospel' made its appearance. Since the former model has been the background of discussion whenever this period and its data have been debated, we confine ourselves to the newly proposed possibility of an early period when gospels were in closer contact than we have hitherto assumed. For my own part, I should indicate that I consider the data to show that St John's Gospel maintained its isolation for a longer period than was the case with the three 'synoptic gospels'. This would not have produced different effects in terms of textual criticism, but the time occupied by the creation of variants would have been longer in the case of John than of the others. This would be one factor in the contrasts between that gospel and the others.

Two or three phenomena immediately suggest themselves as more readily explained within a setting of fairly early parallel existence of three or four gospels. First, in several early quotations of or allusions to the teaching of Jesus in early Christian writings, such as the apostolic fathers and others, the text of sayings is found to present harmonization of parallel passages. Existence of separate documents side by side shortly after their composition would give ready occasion for this to come about by accident or design, memory playing its part. Second, in the same setting, we find centos made up of excerpts from different gospels as well as from sources not later included in the canonical four. Such could be created easily in a setting where, in addition to oral traditions, the written gospels had already spread widely. Third, it is sometimes the case that sayings or narrative statements in which literal rendering from a Semitic source has been perceived have a variant more in line with Greek idiom or style. These variants may exist side by side in documents which appear from later evidence to be contemporary in their earliest attestation. The background to this is more easily envisaged in a setting of multiplicity of gospel copies, where one strain would retain the Semitizing form (probably nearer to the original) while another would bear the mark of early correction.

Fourth, we can find in all gospels variations of wording and addition of words which seem to have had only a short early life span as part of a gospel text, although their echoes may ring through many centuries. We should be particularly mindful of these variant readings, since they could well be original to the autograph and later eased away, if there seemed to be some possible lack of accuracy or inclination to inaccurate teaching in them. Perhaps the piercing of the side of Jesus before his expiry known in St Matthew's Gospel in an ancient and influential text family but absent in the rest might be an instance of this. Another ancient variant is an addition regarding the appearance of fire upon the Jordan after the baptism of Jesus. This is known over a wide geographical range, and persists in East and West for many centuries, especially in harmonies of the gospels. The corrupting influence of harmonization could eventually happen whether at first only one gospel was known or when there was early contact between gospels, but its frequent and widespread appearance might more easily stem from very early comparison and exchange of different gospels. In Mark 10: 11, 12, we find in a few witnesses (Greek, Syriac, and Georgian) a form of prohibition of divorce in which the clause regarding the woman precedes that regarding the man. This appears to lie behind the allusion to this element of the Lord's teaching cited by Paul in 1 Cor. 7: 10, 11, but has been transformed in the other synoptic gospels to a 'man first' order.

We are not dealing with gospels alone. The letters of which most of the rest of the New Testament is composed would have circulated. In the case of Paul's letters, a recent hypothesis proposes that some of them were edited very early to form a corpus (Gamble 1977). We know in any event that letters were sent to churches other than their first, named recipients. Striking evidence here, attested in some manuscripts, is the absence of the phrases 'in Rome' and 'in Ephesus' in the opening verses of the respective epistles. The manuscripts which attest these are not the same in the two epistles. The many variations of text which often appear to spring from the complex style of the apostle may sometimes have arisen in the different churches which had become the recipients of a collection of his letters. The complexity of some sections is such that one speculates that distinct sets of attempted clarification have become tangled in transmission. We know far less about the letters attributed to other Christian leaders. The prophecy of John, the Apocalypse, has a structure which suggests that it was sent as a missive to a group of churches. The consequent dispersal of seven copies of the original to these recipients could have been the beginning of variation within the text, although there has been no testing yet of such a suggestion.

Acts presents us with very complex variation of its text in the earliest witnesses. Some scholars have stressed that this account of the expansion of the early church is a second volume of which the first is the Gospel according to St Luke. Perhaps the variation within the Gospel should be more closely associated with that of Acts and examined to discover if any tendencies may be observed differing in style by contrast with the other gospels. This was done in the past by Friedrich Blass (1895) and Theodor Zahn (1909). The more recent suggestion of W. E. Strange (1992) that the differences in Acts might be derived from intermediate forms of the work, each emanating from the same author, could be extended to see if it could be used to explain textual variation in Luke. Concentration on the Codex Bezae as representative of one strain of the text of Acts is misleading. That manuscript is of importance, but is idiosyncratic in a number of ways. Complex though the evidence is, we must, in discussing shared variants of the Codex Bezae, lay as much or more stress on Greek minuscule manuscripts, sometimes quite late in date, on the versions, especially Latin, Syriac, and Coptic, and on the quotations of early Latin Fathers and of Irenaeus. We may often find earlier strata there than in Bezae. This is so throughout the gospels too.

This discussion has taken us willy-nilly into the second century. In the concluding remarks of the preceding paragraph, it also shows an aspect of research on that century: namely, the constant encounter with fragmentary evidence and the necessity to extrapolate from evidence dated in later centuries back to probabilities of the earlier time. We have Greek manuscripts of the second century, but many are very fragmented, and none is full, though stretches of text can be studied. The Greek-writing fathers and other authors quote rarely. Their evidence has shown itself patient of interpretations both affirmatory and sceptical, largely dependent on presuppositions of the investigators and the fashions of their generations. Justin has gospel quotations, with the complicating factor that harmonization of the synoptics often shows itself. If the Gospel of John was known to him or to his predecessors, it was in some remote fashion which did not commend the text to quotation. Two early Christian thinkers and writers, soon rejected as unrepresentative of normative Christian belief, were very active in editions of other parts of the canon: Marcion and Tatian. Marcion produced editions of the Pauline letters and the Gospel of Luke, with severe editing based on his theology. Tatian produced a harmony of the four gospels, which is traceable in Syriac and other languages of Eastern Christianity and in Latin and the later languages of Western Europe. It is still debated whether he composed his work in a Greek form. The influence of Marcion and Tatian may be observed not only in the traces of the works they edited (i.e. Luke and the Pauline letters in Marcion's case, the four gospels in Tatian's) but in the whole body of biblical manuscripts: there is still ongoing detailed debate and a vast bibliography.

We find ourselves on more secure ground later in the century in the work of Irenaeus, bishop of Lyons. Originally from Smyrna, he was priest and later bishop to the considerable Greek immigrant population in Gaul. His main surviving work is directed against the Gnostic teachers who were active there. This five-book treatise *Against Heresies* (*Adversus Haereses*) survives as a whole in Latin, a translation probably made in the third century. Its trustworthiness has been shown from substantial Greek fragments and from a very literal translation of its two last books into Armenian. He quotes richly from the gospels, the Pauline letters, and the book of Revelation, while Acts and the Catholic epistles are far from unrepresented. From Revelation he quotes in accordance with the manuscripts which Joseph Schmid's (1955–6) work has shown to preserve the most reliable form of the text. The affiliation of the text quoted by him from all the rest of the New Testament is often in accord with the text traditionally termed 'the Western Text' (Klijn 1949). This term is a misnomer now, but was coined when the main witness to it, Greek witness apart, was the Old Latin version; over two centuries, considerable support in Syriac and Coptic has also been found. The Codex Bezae mentioned above remains the most striking Greek witness for the gospels and Acts. It contains Greek and Latin text on facing pages, and is of late fourth- or early fifth-century origin. It was probably produced in the East, a strong case having been made most recently for Beirut: some weighty opinion nevertheless still maintains Western origin in a Latin-speaking area. The unique readings of the Codex Bezae should not be taken as typical of the 'Western Text' without further support.

The first versions or translations were made in the second century. The Latin first appears in the province of Africa, where in the ninth decade of the second century the martyrs of Scillium carried gospels and Pauline letters. Tertullian, writing at the time, appears to know a Latin version, although he often translates for himself. The harmony of Tatian is the probable form in which the gospel reached the Syriac-speaking area (from the Mediterranean coast through Mesopotamia into what is now Iran and Central Asia). The fourfold 'separated' gospels in Syriac were probably created from the harmony text following a Greek model. By the time of Ephrem the Syrian (c.280–370) both are in use, but the harmony still dominates. Its traces are still discernible as late as the thirteenth century. In Egypt, Coptic versions seem to have been slower in appearing, perhaps because Christianity established itself first in the urban centres where Greek was spoken.

Moving from the late second century into the third, we enter a period of consolidation in all areas of the life of the church. In the field of text, there appears a text which in recent discussion has been called 'Alexandrian' since the main attestation of its use and existence is in the quotations made by Alexandrian and other Egyptian writers. The third-century father Origen is especially significant in this respect. Some extensive gospel texts on papyrus in the Bodmer collection and the great majuscule manuscripts (formerly termed 'uncials')—namely, Sinaiticus, Vaticanus, and Ephraimi Rescriptus—attest this text. It shows qualities which derive from the scholarship developed in Alexandria and other centres for the preservation of earlier Greek literature. It reveals a careful inclination to preserve the earliest attainable text even in the face of changes in language and in fashionable standards of style. At the same time, it is on its guard against expansion, innovation, and banality. Over 100 years ago, Westcott and Hort (1881) gave to it the misleading title of 'Neutral'. This suggests that it has no faults, which is not so. But if they sought to say that as a rule it rejected various kinds of corruption and retained vividness of expression, they stated the truth.

Study of the quotations of Origen at first suggested that he used such a text in Alexandria but a different one after his move to Caesarea c.230 CE. There thus arose, other factors also playing their part, the theory of 'local texts'. This postulated that the texts of the New Testament in a number of different locations diverged spontaneously. While this may be so where the texts in question were the earliest in the region, e.g. especially translations into another language, it does not apply to the phenomena which the study of Origen brought to the fore. Further study showed that both in Alexandria and in Caesarea two different gospel texts were available to him, and both these texts appear to be the product of deliberate editorial activity. He himself, however, is certainly not to be considered an editor who formed and promulgated such a text. From an assertion in his commentary on Matthew, we are made aware that he would not have dared to deal with the text of scripture in this way.

An important study of Origen's knowledge of and attitude to variations of text was made some years ago by B. M. Metzger (1968). From this, a number of interesting and significant points are to be derived: first, that he knew a number of variant readings in different parts of the New Testament; second, that he always discussed all the variants at a particular place, even if sometimes expressing preference for one or another. On occasion, but by no means regularly, he suggested the influence of scribal error. Third, it is clear from the details which he gives of the distribution of variants in his day, that readings which he knew may now be unknown to us from our data, or that those which he spoke of as the regular text may be exceptional to us or transmitted only in the ancient transla-tions. His critical preference may be for readings in these categories. These things highlight that our data are preserved haphazardly, and our picture of the textual *status quo* of those early centuries may be thereby severely skewed in places, a fact we easily overlook.

The text identified in some of Origen's works written at Caesarea was initially called (inevitably) the 'Caesarean text'. But many difficulties have revealed them-selves over the years which have eroded the willingness of scholars to agree that here we have a unified text. Rather, we have a process in which the critical principle of choice and amalgamation is taking place over a long period of time. In the 'Caesarean' text, readings of the Alexandrian text have a significant place, but readings of the so-called Western text are equally abundant. There is also some independent revision of style. Thus we may say that it is a process, rather than a text, its differing attestations being moments or phases of the process. Some would see in it the signs of a process which eventually, a century or two later, issued in the earliest form of the Byzantine text.

During this period and into the years after Origen's death, stretching from the early third century into the early years of the fourth, we may perceive side by side throughout the Roman world, which was the central theatre of the development of the church, two significant experiences of the church. First, it is a church under intense persecution, the response of the authorities to its increasing growth. Origen died after torture. His successor at Caesarea, Pamphilus, died a martyr. We still possess evidence of his faithful work collating and correcting manuscripts while he was in prison. Colophons contemporary with the work reveal this. Sometimes the later church historian and commentator Eusebius visited Pamphilus and others in prison and shared in this last labour of love. For the second feature to be seen side by side with this is the church's increasing assimilation of learning and its robust encounter with the world, intellectual as well as moral and spiritual. This happened both in the Empire but also in the East beyond its bounds, under Persian or local rulers.

The spread of the faith and its intellectual defence, tested and tried in these two arenas, was the church's own primary task. The response of the wider church to this was that leaders of the churches outside the Empire and their younger scholars came to centres such as Caesarea and Antioch, studying there and assimilating the methods of precision in the biblical pursuits of the day. It is against this background that we may regard the new wave of translations. There was revision of the Latin in the West attested by writers of the third century in Europe, termed thus 'the European Latin'. There are daughter versions of the earliest Syriac, pre-eminently the Armenian. The Armenian nation was brought into the church by the conversion of its king in the late third or early fourth century. It was given their own alphabet about a century later. This was the work of Mesrop-Mashtotz, and led to the translation of the Bible made from Syriac. In the fifth century, revision was made from Greek manuscripts. It is this later rendering alone that has survived in manuscripts, the earlier being accessible only by reconstruction from quotation and allusion.

Two other Christian cultures developed in the Caucasus, Armenia being a prime point for launching the evangelization. These are the cultures of Georgia and of the Caucasian Albania. Initial testimony was given in Georgia in the fourth century by Nino, an Armenian slave-woman. We have biblical manuscripts, albeit fragmentary, from the fifth century. These, and the witness of the earliest Georgian martyr, the queen Shushanik (martyred 17 October, 476), show the existence in Georgian translation of the gospels, the Pauline epistles, the Psalms, and some other parts of the Old Testament. Liturgy, hagiography, and homiletic materials are also known. This rich flowering of a whole sacred literature may be ascribed conjecturally not simply to translators in the homeland but to Georgian members of the monastic community in Palestine. Armenian sources lie behind much of this, but there was also awareness of the Greek. From this perhaps springs the fact that for the gospels we have two related yet distinct recensions. In our earliest fragments, however, we find the text of some manuscripts moving from blocks of one recension to blocks of the other. In quotations, vocabulary from either source may sometimes be mingled. But for Acts and the epistles, we have only one primary recension. The Revelation of John was not translated until the tenth century.

Until very recently, the language of the Christian Albanians and its alphabet were almost entirely unknown apart from some inscriptions and a late manuscript in Armenian depicting the alphabet. (Their culture was extinguished by waves of Muslim occupation.) But in recent new discoveries at St Catherine's Monastery on Mount Sinai, two palimpsests have come to light, the underwriting of which reveals a lectionary in the Albanian language. When it is more accessible, we shall learn much.

Another ancient language which was provided with an alphabet for biblical translation is Gothic, the oldest Germanic language known to us. It is extant now only in the manuscript remains of the biblical version and a fragmentary commentary on the Gospel of St John. The Goths had entered the Roman Empire by the third century, and Christianity had already been planted amongst them by that time. A Christian Goth named Wulfila was ordained bishop in the fourth century. As part of his ministry, he devised an alphabet and translated the New Testament and some few parts of the Old. The version migrated westwards with its readers, and was linked with the history of both Visigoths and Ostrogoths. Coming into contact with the Latin version, it interacted with it. The basic Greek from which the original translation was made was an early form of the Byzantine text, but its later history in contact with the Latin has made it a version sometimes difficult to interpret.

All this expansion of the church and development of texts and translations was in train during the period of persecutions before the accession of Constantine (308 CE). This led to the end of persecution and to the status of *religio licita* being granted to the church. The church could now devote yet more energy both to evangelization and to biblical scholarship. The latter also intensified as the quest for the definition of the faith grew, giving rise to dispute and schism. From within the literature generated in this context, we begin to gain a far denser knowledge of the textual form of scripture. We also perceive a new textual form emerging, new vehicles for the use of scripture in Christian worship, and in the manuscripts which survive from the succeeding centuries we find more complex presentations of the scriptural documents, for study or for worship.

The 'new textual form' here referred to has already made an appearance in our survey; it is 'the Byzantine text'. This began to make its appearance in the fourth century. One of its earliest witnesses is the Freer Codex, housed in Washington DC, named from its donor, Charles Freer. It is a fifth-century text of the four gospels (Sanders 1912a, b). Its text of Matthew and Luke is referred to here; its other gospels present texts with other affiliations. Change of text is not uncommon. It shows that different manuscripts were present in the scriptorium from which the manuscript comes, used probably haphazardly as exemplars as the copying proceeded. A number of definite statements about the Byantine text's origin and attestation have been made in the past. But they need to be modified, or perhaps rejected. They include that Lucian, a scholar and martyr of Antioch, was its editor. But secure evidence is lacking, as careful studies by Metzger (1963) and Zuntz (1953) have revealed. Another is that the first Christian writer to make general use of that text was the great bishop and preacher of Antioch and of Constantinople, John Chrysostom. But when we seek to examine this, we find, first, that the text of his homilies is not yet certainly fixed, and so not a sound basis for conclusions; and second, that where soundings have been taken, it is only an approximation of the Byzantine text that is revealed. But of the existence of this text in many manuscripts dating from between the fourth and the fifteenth century, there is no doubt.

We see the Byzantine text appearing in strength in or about the fifth century and becoming dominant in the Greek Empire from about the tenth century. It has been most thoroughly studied by the early twentieth-century scholar Hermann von Soden (1902–13). There were a number of faults in his whole work, which was an edition of the New Testament. This led at first to neglect of his analyses, but subsequently several have proved to have much of value. His work on the Byzantine text is such a case. He found that over the thousand years of its growth and dominance three main varieties can be discerned within it, and some minor ones. A late form was used by the early editors of the printed Greek New Testament in the sixteenth century. It thus dominated devotion and learning for three centuries after that, in the guise of the Greek text called *Textus Receptus* by one of its publishers. This means 'accepted text', and suggested that it was definitive. It is generally rendered 'Received Text', not quite correctly. It is still in some quarters defended as original. Examination of the Byzantine text reveals it as an edited text which would have had its beginnings in the period just prior to the 'Peace of the Church'. Its tendency, when contrasted with other texts of that period, is frequently to prefer polished variations differing in style from the wording of other groups but with little distinction in sense. One factor in this would have been to commend the Christian scriptures to the educated classes.

A useful aid to perceiving this, as I have found, is an edition of the Greek New Testament in that sixteenth-century form edited by the conservative scholar F. H. A. Scrivener in 1881. In this are highlighted points at which the 'Received Text' (i.e. the sixteenth-century imprint) was implicitly altered by the Committee which revised the English 'Authorized Version' in 1881. These alterations were occasioned by the revisers' acceptance of the text edited by Westcott and Hort, who preferred the 'Alexandrian' text. A study of these highlighted readings (i.e. the basis of alteration by the revisers) clearly reveals the main motivations of the creators of the Byzantine text.

Along with those created for such stylistic reasons are other instances: for example, frequent conflations which have the effect of preserving two prior readings, sometimes with tautology. Another feature is the retention or adoption of readings deriving from the Western text. Günther Zuntz has laid stress on the importance of these in his study *The Text of the Epistles* (1953) (a masterpiece which all should study). He emphasizes that readings shared by Western and Byzantine texts (even when the Western witness is not preserved in Greek, but only in a version) must be ancient, and hence, although often unacceptable, should necessarily be examined in any assessment of the total significance of the textual data. There are further readings preserved which are clearly erroneous. One which I have been able to examine appears to be the debris of a primitive mistake.

At Matt. 13:55, the name *Ioannes* appears in the list of the brothers of Jesus following *Iakobos* (that is, in place of forms of *Ioseph*). This seems to be an error arising from the familiar and frequent collocation elsewhere of 'James and John'. It is found in various different manuscript texts. Amongst these are the Codex Sinaiticus (linked with Caesarea and the scholar and martyr Pamphilus), the Codex Bezae, full of ancient material but still as enigmatic as ever, about nine other manuscripts with the older form of writing, and a bevy of later ones with important traces of early text. It is not surprising to find attestation too in Origen—namely, in his Commentary on John—and it must antedate the earliest of these. (As a further sidelight on Origen, we should note that this is one quotation of three from this same verse in this commentary. The others read a form of Joseph!) The influence of this weighty tradition for *Ioannes* must have continued, as, according to von Soden's analyses, the earliest form of the Byzantine text has the reading, although it did not survive to be included in the printed text. With its wide attestation would also harmonize the further fact that the majority of lectionaries read *Ioannes* here. It is a hard decision whether it is an error of an early scribe or a slip of the author (as the conservative scholar Theodor Zahn (1909) thought), yet it almost 'made it' into the 'Received Text'!

The notion of variation in the text of scripture has caused considerable unease over the past centuries, ever since more and more manuscripts became known, and variant readings of greater and greater moment were revealed. The changes are ascribed by those alarmed at their recognition to deliberate alteration with the intent to dilute the content of the statement of the Christian faith in its fulness. These fears still lie behind the conservative effort to publish a text based not on the earliest manuscripts but on the majority of manuscripts, most of which come from the latest centuries before the invention of printing (Robinson and Pierpont 1991). In the later twentieth century, we have seen another criticism levelled by scholars of radical inclination, who discern in the very texts which modern critical scholarship has established, changes at a very early stage, even before the fourth century CE. These are analysed as showing the traces of constant effort to ensure that no opinion, especially about the natures or person of Jesus Christ, judged erroneous and heretical in the controversies of those days, should have apparent foundation or purchase in the wording of scriptural passages (Ehrman 1993). Any passages falling under this judgement have been changed. While my judgement is that the classical statement of the case is an overstatement, this factor was certainly present, as has long been known to at least some textual critics, myself amongst them.

What, in conclusion, do we make of the situation from our survey of the data? Has scripture been handed down by 'bogeymen' intent on 'corruption' (a technical term much misunderstood and recently intentionally misused)? This is not my perception. The transmission of scripture has been the work of those who were primarily Christians, and must be seen in the context of their concern for the clear and true statement of the faith. They did their best to preserve the text, but saw the task in part as ensuring too that its message was comprehended. They could also make mistakes, and these were not always completely removed. It is the effects of the desire for absolute clarity, and especially for expressions which left no room for erroneous interpretation, considered useful in their day, which are today seen by a majority as hindrances to our perception of the pristine documents. However, many variant readings are early, some being errors, but others indicative of early tradition or exegesis. There is much valuable data latent in the critical apparatus as well as in the text of our modern critical editions.

Suggested Reading

Birdsall, J. N. 1970. 'The New Testament'. In P. R. Ackroyd and C. F. Evans, eds., *The Cambridge History of the Bible*, Cambridge: Cambridge University Press, i. 308–77.

Bibliography

Bauckham, R., ed. 1998. *The Gospels for All Christians*. Grand Rapids, Mich.: Eerdmans; Edinburgh: T. & T. Clark.

Birdsall, J. N. 1961. 'The Text of the Revelation of Saint John (the work of Josef Schmid)'. *EQ* 33: 228–38.

—— 1992 'The Recent History of New Testament Textual Criticism (from Westcott and Hort, 1881, to the present)'. In ANRW Pt.2. 26. 100–91.

Blass, F. 1895. *Acta apostolorum editio philologica*. Göttingen: Dandenhoed & Ruprecht.

—— 1896. *Acta apostolorum secundum formam quae videtur Romanam*. Leipzig.

Bruce, F. F. 1963. *The Books and the Parchments*, 3rd. edn. Basingstoke: Pickering & Inglis.

Clark, A. C. 1933. *The Acts of the Apostles: A Critical Edition*. Oxford: Clarendon Press.

Ehrman, B. D. 1993. *The Orthodox Corruption of Scripture*. New York and Oxford: Oxford University Press.

EHRMAN, B. D., and HOLMES, MICHAEL W., eds. 1994. *The Text of the New Testament in Contemporary Research. Essays on the Status Questionis.* Studies and Documents, 46. Grand Rapids, Mich.: Eerdmans.

GAMBLE, H. Y. 1977. *The Textual History of the Letter to the Romans.* Studies and Documents, 42. Grand Rapids, Mich.: Eerdmans.

GRANT, R. M. 1970/1. *Augustus to Constantine.* New York and London: Collins.

—— 1988. *Greek Apologists of the Second Century.* Philadelphia: Westminster/John Knox.

HATCH, W. H. P. 1939. *The Principal Uncial Manuscripts of the New Testament.* Chicago: University of Chicago Press.

—— 1951. *Facsimiles and Descriptions of Minuscule Manuscripts of the New Testament.* Cambridge, Mass.: Harvard University Press.

KENYON, F. 1958. *Our Bible and the Ancient Manuscripts,* new rev. edn. by A. W. Adams. London: Eyre & Spottiswoode.

KLIJN, A. F. J. 1949. *A Survey of the Researches into the Western Text of the Four Gospels and Acts.* Utrecht: Kemink and Zoon.

LAKE, K. 1928. *The Text of the New Testament,* 6th edn. by Silva New. London: Rivingtons.

—— and LAKE, S. 1938/48. *An Introduction to the New Testament.* London: Christophers.

METZGER, B. M. 1963. 'The Lucianic Recension of the Greek Bible'. In *The History of New Testament Textual Criticism,* Leiden: Brill, 1–41.

—— 1968. 'Explicit References in the Works of Origen to Variant Readings in New Testament Manuscripts'. In *Historical and Literary Studies: Pagan, Jewish, and Christian,* Leiden: Brill, 88–103.

MUSURILLO, H. 1972. *The Acts of the Christian Martyrs.* Oxford: Clarendon Press.

REYNOLDS, L. C., and WILSON, N. G. 1991. *Scribes and Scholars: A Guide to the Transmission of Greek and Latin Literature,* 3rd edn. Oxford: Oxford University Press.

ROPES, J. H. 1926. *The Beginnings of Christianity,* iii: *The Text of Acts,* ed. F. J. Foakes Jackson and Kirsopp Lake. London: Macmillan.

SANDAY, W., and Turner, C. H., eds. 1923. *Nouum Testamentum Sancti Irenaei.* Old Latin Biblical Texts 7. Oxford: Clarendon Press.

SANDERS, H. A. 1912a. *The New Testament Manuscripts in the Freer Collection.* New York: Macmillan.

—— 1912b. *Facsimile of the Washington Manuscript of the Four Gospels in the Freer Collection.* Ann Arbor: University of Michigan Press.

SCHMID, J. 1955–6. *Studien zur Geschichte des griechischen Apokalypse-Textes.* Munich: K. Zink.

SCRIVENER, F. A. 1881. *The New Testament in the Original Greek, according to the Text Followed in the Authorised Version, together with the Variations Adopted in the Revised Version.* Cambridge: The University Press.

SODEN, H. VON, ed. 1902–13. *Die Schriften des Neuen Testaments in ihrer ältesten erreichbaren Textgestalt hergestellt auf Grund ihrer Textgeschichte,* 4 vols. Göttingen: Vandenhoeck & Ruprecht.

STRANGE, W. A. 1992. *The Problem of the Text of Acts.* SNTS MS 71. Cambridge: Cambridge University Press.

STREETER, B. H. 1950. *The Four Gospels,* rev. edn. London: Macmillan.

WESTCOTT, B. F., and HORT, F. J. A. 1881. *The New Testament in the Original Greek.* London: Macmillan. 2nd edn. 1890.

WILSON, N. G. 1996. *Scholars of Byzantium*, rev. edn. London: Duckworth.

ZAHN, T. 1909. *Introduction to the New Testament*. Edinburgh: ET.

—— 1916. *Die Urausgabe der Apostelgeschichte des Lucas*. Forschungen zur Geschichte des neutestamentlichen Kanons und der altkirchen Literatur, 9. Leipzig and Berlin.

ZUNTZ, G. 1953. *The Text of the Epistles*. Schweich Lectures 1946. London: Oxford University Press for the British Academy.

PART III

HISTORICAL AND SOCIAL STUDY OF THE BIBLE

BACKGROUND AND CONTEXT

INTRODUCTION: GENERAL PROBLEMS OF STUDYING THE TEXT OF THE BIBLE IN ORDER TO RECONSTRUCT HISTORY AND SOCIAL BACKGROUND

KEITH W. WHITELAM

INTRODUCTION

It would seem a matter of common sense that any reconstruction of the history of ancient Israel, or of particular aspects of Israelite society, should rely heavily upon the Bible for the majority of its information. Charles Foster Kent, in the opening volume of his influential *A History of the Hebrew People*, one of the standard works of American biblical scholarship at the end of the nineteenth century, described the Bible as 'the text book of Old Testament history' (Kent 1896: 4).[1] It is a view that has been restated recently with considerable force in Provan, Long, and Longman's *A Biblical History of Israel*, where they claim that 'in principle no *better* avenue of access to ancient Israel's past is available', and that not to depend heavily upon the Bible in the presentation of the history of Israel is irrational (Provan, Long, and Longman 2003: 98–9). However, careful reflection on these issues reveals that this matter is not nearly as straightforward as the appeal to common sense or rationality suggests.[2]

Many scholars share the view that the Hebrew Bible offers the best, or the only, avenue to access Israel's past. Yet our standard histories of ancient Israel are a curious mixture of part prolegomena, part commentary on the biblical text, and part historical reconstruction. They are not narrative histories—synthetic treatments describing, analysing, and explaining the historical process—such as John Keay's *India: A History* (2000), Norman Davies's *The Isles* (1999), Mark Mazower's *The Balkans* (2001), or thematic volumes such as Linda Colley's *Captives: Britian, Empire and the World 1600–1850* (2003) or Roy Porter's *Enlightenment: Britain and the Creation of the Modern World* (2000). The increase in the number of volumes devoted to the history of Israel, particularly in the 1980s, did not signal a growing confidence in the genre, but reflected a crisis of confidence in the historian's ability to reconstruct Israelite history. This is not a self-confident genre but one beset by self-doubts. The apologetic nature of these so-called histories of Israel, despite confident claims to the contrary, illustrates that the utilization of the biblical texts for historical reconstruction is not a straightforward or simple matter.[3]

One response to this crisis—what some have termed 'the death of biblical history'—has been to call for an end to scepticism and a renewed faith and optimism in the biblical texts as historical documents which allow the historian to write a history of Israel.[4] The recent volume by Provan, Long, and Longman (2003)

---

[1] He added that 'Hebrew history, however, gathers its material from other sources as well as from the Bible', and claimed that 'to one who recognizes in that unique history the unique revelation of God to man, it is the history of all histories' (Kent 1896: 5, 6).

[2] The rhetoric of the debate is interesting, 'commonsense', 'rationality', and 'reason' being key words in assessing the work of those with whom one disagrees. Yet, as William Hazlitt remarked, 'reason, with most people, means their own opinion' (cited in Porter 2000: p. xxiii).

[3] See Provan, Long, and Longman 2003: 10–18 for a detailed treatment of key volumes in response to my pronouncement of the death of 'biblical history' (Whitelam 1996: 69).

[4] Provan, Long, and Longman (2003: 44) view the crisis as 'an invitation to revisit some fundamental questions about epistemology' that gives a proper place to philosophy and tradition. 'This', they say, 'inevitably involves questioning the rationality of the principled suspicion of tradition, and ultimately (if not initially) of philosophy, that lies at the heart of Enlightenment thought about the past' (2003: 44). They wish to attack and dismiss what they see as the 'scientific' method of historiography that emerges from the Enlightenment. This is strange, since it is normally some post-modernist thinkers who question Enlightenment notions of rationality.

represents an extended response to this loss of faith in the use of the Hebrew Bible as a source particularly for early periods of Israelite history. After a lively opening section which addresses some of the methodological issues raised in current debates, the second section is presented as 'a biblical history of Israel' which 'sets the biblical texts at the heart of its enterprise' (Provan, Long, and Longman 2003: 98). This is meant to indicate that the Hebrew Bible can and should be used as a trustworthy source for the reconstruction of the history of Israel from the time of Abraham until the Exile and after.

However, despite its confident pronouncements on the trustworthiness of the biblical traditions for historical reconstruction, it fails to deliver a synthetic treatment of Israelite history. For example, the opening chapter ('Before the Land') of this section is little more than a rehash of well-known problems that concerned historians particularly in the 1950s and 1960s: the setting of the patriarchal narratives and Near Eastern texts, the identification of the four kings in Genesis 14, and the date and route of the exodus. Despite its claim to take the 'testimony of the biblical texts seriously' (2003: 128), a large part of the volume is taken up with prolegomena rather than a reconstruction of the history of the region and its inhabitants.[5] It is difficult to see how this is an advance on the treatment of the patriarchal and exodus traditions offered by Soggin and Miller and Hayes, who are so heavily criticized by Provan, Long, and Longman for their inconsistencies and lack of nerve in utilizing the biblical traditions. Although it might be said to be another example of 'midrashic historiography', in which the biblical text is supplemented with rationalistic glosses (Davies 1991: 14), it represents a very significant departure from the standard histories of Israel which emerged from the 1980s. Its rejection of much critical scholarship of the twentieth century and its appeal to biblical 'testimony' represent a move back to pre-critical practices rather than an advance in the study of the history of ancient Israel. Yet, despite its confident pronouncements, it illustrates that the reconstruction of Israelite history and

---

[5] They acknowledge that extra-biblical sources tell us nothing about 'the migration of an obscure family' from Ur to Palestine, and so 'we are almost entirely dependent on the Bible itself for our information about the Israelites "before the land" ', particularly Genesis to Deuteronomy (2003: 108). They claim that 'we are dealing with the genre of history' (2003: 111) or 'theological history'. Although the text appears to come from a later period, they do not accept that it is possible to unravel the possible sources of the Pentateuch. Nor is there any internal information within Genesis that would allow us to assign an absolute date to the period of the Patriarchs (2003: 112), not even Gen. 14. They then use the biblical chronology to place the exodus in the fifteenth century and place the Patriarchs in the first half of the second millennium BCE (2003: 113). They note that the information is not unambiguous, and then go on to discuss the Nuzi and Mari texts. Yet their claim that the symbiosis of pastoral nomadism and village life is consistent with the picture in the Mari texts (2003: 118–19) ignores the fact that this is true of considerable periods of time in Palestinian history, including into the modern period. The kinds of detail they describe in the Joseph narrative offer little more than verisimilitude as the test of historical authenticity. Notice that Pitard (1998: 75) remarks that this mode of life was not restricted to the second millennium BCE and cannot be used to argue for the authenticity of the narratives as historical documents.

society using the biblical traditions is not as straightforward as the common-sense approach suggests.[6]

EVALUATING SOURCES

The debate on the starting-point of Israelite history—which has moved from the Patriarchs, exodus, and conquest to the early monarchy and beyond—has been a debate about how to evaluate the biblical traditions as historical sources. Coogan (1998: p. x) claims, for instance, that some dismiss the Bible as 'a credible witness' because the narratives were written centuries after the time they purport to describe, and without independent contemporaneous confirmation the events and characters in the Bible are thought to be suspect or purely fictional. In the face of this crisis of confidence, in order to counter what is seen by some as extreme scepticism in the treatment of the biblical text, it has become common to assert that the historian of Israel must use 'all available evidence'. However, this has become a means of short-circuiting the discussion of the nature of the biblical traditions and their role in historical reconstruction and of asserting the priority of the biblical text. To suggest that scholars do not use all the available evidence, or to claim that they systematically avoid the biblical texts (Provan, Long, and Longman 2003: 51–4), is misleading, to say the least. As Jordanova (2000: 96) notes, 'to call something evidence implies that the case for its relevance has been made— evidence bears witness to an issue'. There is a significant difference between sources and evidence. Since the source materials are so restricted, to biblical and extra-biblical texts and archaeological data—it is not that particular scholars ignore one class of material or another, but that they assess them differently as to their value as evidence. As Bloch (1954: 110) noted many years ago, 'At the bottom of nearly all criticism there is the problem of comparison.' While the biblical texts have *the potential* to bear on a historical problem, this has to be demonstrated. Whybray's (1966: 72) remark that the biblical text, 'however liable to correction', provides the foundation for a history of Israel, raises the crucial issue of the extent to which such 'corrections' undermine the reliance upon the text and what we can know about large parts of this history.

A volume such as *The Oxford History of the Biblical World* (Coogan 1998) illustrates the pitfalls of historical reconstruction when relying upon the biblical

---

[6] Redmount (1998: 119), who argues for a historical core to the exodus narratives, is forced to conclude that 'a study of the Exodus narrative raises many questions about the historicity and historical setting of the Exodus events, but provides few definitive answers'.

traditions. The various authors of the volume are said 'to share that methodo-logical conviction as well as a commitment to the historical enterprise—the reconstruction of the past based on the critical assessment of all available evidence' (Coogan 1998: p. xi). However, the editor is forced to admit that 'it is impossible to correlate with any certainty the events described in the first books of the Bible with known historical realities' (Coogan 1998: p. ix). The use of all 'available evidence' has raised serious questions about the historicity of the biblical narratives, for this period. This is not to systematically ignore the narratives, but rather to assess them critically in light of available information. Nor does it devalue them theologically, since they are illustrations of trust and faith in the deity.

In the same volume, Pitard (1998: 36–7) admits that there are many reasons to be sceptical of the patriarchal narratives, causing the historian to proceed with great caution (Pitard 1998: 37). Although, he claims, there are fascinating hints that suggest that genuine memories have been preserved in these stories, they 'provide modem historians with few data to reconstruct the historical, cultural, and socio-logical developments from which the Israelite nation arose' (Pitard 1998: 38). The long-running debate on the starting-point of Israelite history illustrates the same problems as are inherent in attempts to reconstruct later periods. Thus, despite the positive comments about using all the available evidence and setting the biblical text at the heart of the enterprise, the historian is faced with overwhelming difficulties in reconstructing the early history of Israel when relying upon these texts. This problem is not something peculiar to so-called minimalists or revision-ists, but faces anyone trying to reconstruct the history of Israel. A close analysis of histories of ancient Israel reveals that they offer comparatively little positive reconstruction in comparison to the space devoted to the problems of understand-ing and utilizing the biblical texts.

The historian is severely hindered by the lack of context—the inability to place the texts in chronological sequence or in their social and political context. Even documents whose provenance and date are not in question—and there are pre-cious few of those in the Hebrew Bible—have to be treated with considerable circumspection. It is not that so-called eyewitness accounts necessarily provide better access to the past than later sources. Both have to be treated carefully: eyewitness accounts suffer from myopia, while much later accounts may have distorted the past they are trying to portray. Jordanova's (2000: 97) caveat on the utilization of written sources provides an important warning to those who wish to claim that the biblical traditions offer direct access to Israel's past. Many of our documents, particularly the Hebrew Bible, 'pass through human agents, who select, alter, and make mistakes; they transform, translate, and they may also deceive' (Jordanova 2000: 98). Verisimilitude is no guarantee of historical accuracy or reality: the skilled story-teller creates an 'authentic' universe into which the reader can enter and participate. Do the stories of David refusing to kill Saul with his own spear despite the urgings of his own troops provide evidence of historical events that should form part of any history of Israel? Do we devalue them if we read them as carefully crafted elements in a complex literary narrative which employs considerable irony to illustrate that no one should threaten YHWH's anointed?

It is also incorrect to assume that because a text is dated late (in the Persian or Hellenistic periods) it is removed as a source for the historian. Even if it does not provide direct evidence for the events it purports to describe, it may reveal the past in ways which the author of the document did not intend. For instance, Bloch (1954: 63) points out that the various accounts of the lives of saints in the Middle Ages reveal little about the people they purport to describe, but a great deal about the way of life or thought peculiar to the time in which they were written. As such, they are invaluable sources for the historian, but not in the ways in which they were intended by those who wrote them. Emmanuel Le Roy Ladurie (1980) utilized the detailed Inquisition register of Jacques Fournier, bishop of Pamiers, later Pope Benedict XII, in a way in which the compilers of the register never intended. The register provides a very detailed account of the interrogation of the whole village of Montaillou on suspicion of adherence to Catharism, which had been proclaimed heretical by the Roman Catholic Church. Ladurie skilfully uses the register to reveal fascinating details about the previously unknown mental, emotional, and sexual world of village and peasant life in the thirteenth century. It is a classic illustration of Paul Veyne's (1971: 265) point that the historian constantly struggles against the perspective imposed by the sources.

Similarly, many of the texts in the Hebrew Bible provide important evidence of much broader processes in the history of the region: the problem of famine, the rhythms of nature, and beliefs about controlling the impersonal forces which threaten the livelihood and lives of the indigenous population. They are important historical sources, but not in the conventional way in which they have been used as part of the pursuit of political histories of the individual and the unique events which characterize histories of Israel. The great poem to time in Ecclesiastes (3: 1–8) along with the Gezer calendar are important historical sources which convey the rhythmic nature of existence which dominated the patterns of life in the region. Such texts and inscriptions which have emerged from the soil of ancient Palestine provide a striking illustration of an economy dominated by the rhythms of agrarian life. It is these patterns which dominate the history of ancient Palestine, not the great men, their kingdoms and empires, which are the subject of so many history books.[7] The simple, basic needs of life remained paramount for the inhabitants of Palestine. The variety of its material culture, as well as its literature, particularly the Hebrew Bible, express a love of nature and beauty, a sensitivity to aesthetics, which

---

[7] The works of Hopkins (1985) on agriculture and King and Stager (2001) on various aspects of everyday life in Palestine are good illustrations of the way in which biblical texts can be utilized to illustrate the realities of life in the Iron Age, rather than as treatments of great men and unique events. McNutt (1999) provides a comprehensive treatment of the problems in reconstructing Israelite society.

can still be seen in the pleasures of shape and form of its pottery or the fine craft work of jewelry or weaponry which have been found at sites throughout Palestine over many centuries.

EVIDENCE AND THE FALSIFICATION PRINCIPLE

The crisis of confidence in reconstructing Israelite history by relying principally on the Hebrew Bible has been brought about by a convergence of factors: the lack of agreement on the dating of biblical texts and a consequent lack of agreement on the social production of this literature and its reception, the increasing archaeological data, the impact of the social sciences on the study of the Bible, and the increasing influence of literary studies of biblical narratives. This has led to a situation in which Provan, Long, and Longman (2003: 51) claim that scholars 'feel the need to justify the acceptance, rather than justify the rejection, of biblical testimony *in particular*'. They ask:

Why should not ancient historical texts rather be given the benefit of the doubt in regard to their statements about the past unless good reasons exist to consider them unreliable in these statements and with due regard (of course) to their literary and ideological features? In short, why should we adopt a verification rather than a falsification principle? Why should the onus be on the texts to 'prove' themselves valuable in respect of history, rather than on those who question their value to 'prove' them false? (Provan, Long, and Longman (2003: 55)

It is this principle of falsification, allied strongly with the claim that 'absence of evidence is not evidence of absence', which distinguishes their attempts to write a 'biblical history of Israel' from standard volumes of the 1980s and onwards. Thus the complete lack of archaeological evidence for Jerusalem in the tenth century BCE is not allowed to undermine the biblical picture of this as the capital of David's and Solomon's kingdom. The employment of the falsification principle and the claim that absence of evidence is not evidence of absence means that there is nothing which can count against the 'testimony' of the biblical traditions about David. However, the counter-claim that Jerusalem was little more than a small rural town in the tenth century and that the traditions in Samuel do not offer a reliable picture of the past is falsifiable. If archaeologists reveal extensive tenth-century levels, pottery, monumental architecture, or even texts, then historians who currently question the standard picture of an extensive Davidic monarchy or even 'empire' will be forced to re-evaluate their conclusions. However, on the basis of the present state of knowledge, with clear evidence for occupation before and after the early Iron Age, the silence is very significant and cannot be dismissed as some form of prejudice against the biblical traditions. It is an important factor in weighing the biblical sources as evidence for the period.

The acceptance of the double principle—the principles of falsification and absence—means that the historian must accept the testimony of the *Iliad* or *Odyssey* in writing a history of Greece or of the *Bhagavad Gita* when producing a history of ancient India unless it is possible to falsify their claims. What evidence could be produced to falsify the story of the Trojan horse, the death of Achilles, or the fantastic tales of the *Bhagavad Gita*? It is difficult to see what evidence could be produced to falsify the claim that Balaam's ass could talk (Num. 22: 23–30). Any number of non-talking donkeys could be produced, only to be refuted by the mantra that 'absence of evidence is not evidence of absence'. Thus the ancient text would have to be given the benefit of the doubt. For, as they claim, 'there is no good reason to believe, either, that an account which describes the unique or unusual is for that reason to be suspected of unreliability' (Provan, Long, and Longman 2003: 70). This is important for Provan, Long, and Longman, since they wish to leave space for the surprising, including divine action within history.

The adoption of this double principle leads to an even more disturbing situation. Suppose that historians in the future, due to some cataclysmic event in the past, are left only with the writings of David Irving on the Second World War and the Holocaust. Are they to be condemned to accepting his accounts of Hitler, the Nazis, and the Holocaust because they could not be falsified?[8] History, however, is about comparison and probabilities, not the certainties of verification and falsification. Elton (1983: 100) made the point that all history writing is contingent and open to revision as more evidence is found, questions are reformulated, and adjacent areas undergo development. Major historical problems do not reach definitive solutions, 'and this is because a term like verification has virtually no usable meaning in history'. It is this problem of contingency and revision which is at odds with a theology of divine action in history and certainty.

The key question for the historian is how to judge between the competing claims of various sources. Provan, Long, and Longman (2003: 53) assert that 'we "know" what we claim to know about the history of Israel, we assert here, by listening to testimony, to interpretation, and by making choices about whom to believe'. Yet how are these judgements to be made? Their assertion is that the ancient texts should be accepted unless they can be falsified. Yet they appear to confuse verifica-

---

[8] See Evans (2001) on the use of archive materials in order to challenge Irving's accounts in the famous libel case brought against Deborah Lipstadt. The judge accepted that Irving had manipulated the documentary evidence. Evans argues strongly that the central issue in the trial was the way in which historians find out about the past through the critical examination of the evidence. All history is about comparison and judgement.

tion with certainty, and claim that those they label as sceptics are looking for certainty. However, as Bloch (1954: 124) pointed out half a century ago:

For doubt to become the tool of knowledge it is necessary, in each particular case, that the degree of probability of coincidence can be weighed with some exactitude. Here the path of historical research, like that of so many other disciplines of the mind, intersects the royal highway of the theory of probabilities.

THE BIBLE AND ARCHAEOLOGY

The results of archaeological investigations in many areas of the world have had a dramatic impact upon the study of history by calling into question previously text-based reconstructions. Barraclough (1979: 107) remarked some time ago that

the most significant and lasting result of archaeological discovery, however, is to have broken the historian's traditional reliance upon written records, and, in some instances at least, to have demonstrated the unreliability and mythical character of the information those records convey. Both in Anglo-Saxon England and in India for example, archaeo-logical evidence indicates a radically different pattern of settlement from that put forward in popular traditions and literary texts.

This has been the case for many periods of Israelite history. It is not simply the case that evidence does not exist to support the claims in the narrative, as some critics assert, and that without this supporting evidence the texts are dismissed as fictional. The major problem for the historian is that in many cases the picture drawn from an *independent* analysis of the archaeological remains is at variance with the picture put forward in text-based reconstructions. The most spectacular shift in recent years has taken place in the reconstruction of the emergence of Israel in the Late Bronze–Iron Age transition, where it is generally accepted that the archaeological evidence points to a largely indigenous development for the high-land villages that traditionally have been associated with the emergence of Israel. Leaving aside the contentious question of how to identify Israelite material remains and the debate on ethnicity, most scholars are in general agreement that on the basis of the material remains the demographic changes taking place in the Late Bronze–Iron Age transition were largely indigenous. This is in striking contrast to the biblical traditions which emphasize Israel's external origins in the exodus and conquest traditions.

In such a situation, it is incumbent on the historian to try to explain the disparity between the two different pictures. There are numerous cases throughout the world where origin traditions have been shaped by later communities and then been treated as historical facts by historians (see Whitelam 1989). Such traditions often play a crucial role in the construction of identity at later periods. As such, they are important sources for the historian, but as witnesses to the thought peculiar to the time at which they were written, rather than necessarily the events which they describe. Japhet (1979) drew attention to the fact that the Chronicler offers an alternative tradition of origin, which suggests that Israel was always in the land. A comparison of the various traditions throughout the Hebrew Bible suggests that they offer competing claims to the land by those who were 'returning' from exile and those who had remained in the land. The problem with trying to write the history of the period from such narratives, as though they are a straightforward reflection of historical events, is that this privileges particular information, a particular perception of the past and its ideology. 'The lines of national belonging', as Raphael Samuel (1989) remarks, 'so far from being instinctual, were constantly being withdrawn.' Comparisons of Ezra–Nehemiah with Chronicles suggests competing notions of identity and competing representations of the past. The acceptance of the fossilized accounts in Ezra 2 and Nehemiah 9 or the genealogies of 1 Chronicles 1–9 as the definition of the post-exilic community privilege an exclusivist claim to the past. The danger is that because of the constant assertion that these are the principal or sole sources for this period, their notions of identity and belonging become the totality of lived experience for our histories. Groups which are not part of these texts do not then form part of the history.

The myth of the empty land, explored by Carroll (1992) and Barstad (1996), provides a classic example of the way in which the past is used to legitimitize the 'new Israel' through direct continuation with the 'old'. Like many modern accounts, it presents 'a myth of unchanging national identity' (Samuel 1989: 17). The construction of the past and its retelling, in oral or written form, is the way in which particular groups define identity and their relationship to the present (Plumb 1969; Hobsbawm and Ranger 1983; Le Goff 1992).[9] Any people, groups, or events which do not conform to or contribute to the progression of this history are ignored. Where are the pastoral communities of Palestine, which throughout its history have been demographically and politically significant? As noted above, the transformation of Iron Age Palestine, which gathered momentum throughout the period, eventually leading to the revival of the towns with increasing fortification at some sites, began in the countryside as a response to the recession of the Late Bronze Age. How far it was the result of internal population displacement, external movements, or internal demographic growth is a matter of considerable debate. However, it is a process which has only become apparent as it is viewed over two to three centuries. The reordering of the countryside has been spectacularly revealed

---

[9] Barstad (1997: 57) notes that 'this theological story does not tell us what Israel's history *really* looked like *in* ancient times'; nor does it allow the systematic study of the history of ancient society in all its 'complexity and multifaceted reality'.

by the series of regional surveys conducted by Finkelstein, Ofer, Herzog, and many others. It is these surveys which have helped to revolutionize the study of the history of the Palestine in the Iron Age and undermine previous biblically based reconstructions. Although the surveys have revealed considerable regional variation, it was from within the delicate balance and continuum between peasants and pastoral groups that the revival began, leading over centuries to the transformation and realignment of Iron Age Palestine.[10] This continuum between town, countryside, and pastoralism, a constant in the history of Palestine through the ages, is hidden in our biblical sources for the Persian and Hellenistic periods. Again, biblically based reconstructions have tended to focus upon the plight of Jerusalem and its immediate environs. Barkay (1992: 372) acknowledges that the effects were localized, with material continuity in many areas of Palestine outside the confines of Jerusalem and its immediate vicinity. The fact that such regional variation has become apparent only relatively recently again illustrates the concentration of attention on a small sub-region due to the overwhelming interest in the Hebrew Bible. Recent studies by Carter (1999) and Hoglund (1992) have revealed important regional variation in response to the events of the sixth century, with a reordering of the countryside, particularly in Judah. While biblically based constructions focus upon the glare of political events in and around Jerusalem, the results of recent archaeological surveys reveal something of a silent world which suggests an alternative understanding of the history of the period. At some points it complements the biblical traditions, but at others it offers a significant challenge to them.

The historian in using 'all available evidence' is constantly forced to make comparisons and critical judgements. The nature of the sources means that it is not possible to offer definitive reconstructions: historical reconstruction is a process of constant revision and re-analysis. Bloch (1954: 62–3) points out the importance of sources, such as archaeology as well as written sources, which were not designed to influence posterity:

Indeed, without their aid, every time the historian turned his attention to the generations gone by, he would become the inevitable prey of the same prejudices, false inhibitions, and myopias that plague the vision of those same generations. For example, the medievalists would accord but a trivial significance to communal development, under the pretext that the writers of the Middle Ages did not discuss it freely with their public. In a word, to resort to a favorite figure of Michelet's, history would become less the ever-daring explorer of the ages past than the eternally unmoving pupil of their 'chronicles'.

Provan, Long, and Longman (2003: 6) ask the pertinent question: 'Even though accounts of the past are invariably the products of a small elite who possess a

---

[10] See Lemche (1985) and Coote and Whitelam (1987) for the complexities of the social continuum in ancient Palestine and the complex interrelationships between pastoral and agricultural communities. The pastoral sector never disappears completely, since the economy of urban and nomad populations is interconnected, and the two coexist at all times (Naaman 1994: 233).

particular point of view, can these accounts not inform us about the past they describe *as well as* the ideological concerns of their authors?' It is entirely possible that this may be the case. However, where we have clear evidence that this is not the case, as in the traditions of Israel's origins, then the historian is forced to consider alternative explanations. It is precisely when the historian utilizes all 'available evidence'—and that includes reading widely within the history of other times and other cultures—that it is possible to offer as comprehensive a picture as possible. Otherwise, we are restricted to the world and the world-view of the few who produced the texts on which we are reliant for the past.

BIBLIOGRAPHY

BARKAY, G. 1992. 'The Iron Age II–III'. In A. Ben-Tor, ed., *The Archaeology of Ancient Israel*, New Haven: Yale University Press, 302–73.

BARRACLOUGH, G. 1979. *Main Trends in History.* New York: Holmes and Meier.

BARSTAD, H. M. 1996. *The Myth of the Empty Land: A Study in the History and Archeology of Judah during the 'Exilic' Period.* Oslo: Scandinavian University Press.

—— 1997. 'History and the Hebrew Bible'. In L. Grabbe, ed., *Can a 'History of Israel' be Written?*, Sheffield: Sheffield Academic Press, 37–64.

BLOCH, M. 1954. *The Historian's Craft.* Manchester: Manchester University Press.

CARROLL, R. P. 1992. 'The Myth of the Empty Land'. *Semeia*, 59: 79–93.

CARTER, C. E. 1999. *The Emergence of Yehud in the Persian Period: A Social and Demographic Study.* Sheffield: Sheffield Academic Press.

COLLEY, L. 2003. *Captives: Britain, Empire and the World 1600–1850.* London: Pimlico.

COOGAN, M. D. 1998. *The Oxford History of the Biblical World.* Oxford: Oxford University Press.

COOTE, R. B., and WHITELAM, K. W. 1987. *The Emergence of Early Israel in Historical Perspective.* Sheffield: Sheffield Academic Press.

DAVIES, N. 1999. *The Isles: A History.* London: Macmillan.

DAVIES, P. R. 1991. 'Sociology and the Second Temple'. In P. R. Davies, ed. *Second Temple Studies*, i: *Persian Period*, Sheffield: Sheffield Academic Press, 11–19.

DAVIES, S. 2003. *Empiricism and History.* Basingstoke: Palgrave Macmillan.

ELTON, G. R. 1983. 'Two Kinds of History'. In R. W. Fogel and G. R. Elton, eds., *Which Road to the Past? Two Views of History*, New Haven: Yale University Press, 71–121.

EVANS, R. J. 2001. *Lying about Hitler: History, Holocaust, and the David Irving Trial.* New York: Basic Books.

HOBSBAWM, E., and RANGER, T. 1983. *The Invention of Tradition.* Cambridge: Cambridge University Press.

HOGLUND, K. G. 1992. *Achaemenid Imperial Administration in Syria-Palestine and the Missions of Ezra and Nehemiah.* Atlanta: Scholars Press.

HOPKINS, D. 1985. *The Highlands of Canaan: Agricultural Life in the Early Iron Age.* Decatur, Ill.: Almond.

IGGERS, G. G. 1997. *Historiography in the Twentieth Century: From Scientific Objectivity to Postmodern Challenge.* Hanover: Wesleyan University Press.

JAPHET, S. 1979. 'Conquest and Settlement in Chronicles'. *JBL* 98: 205–18.

JENKINS, K. 1991. *Re-thinking History.* London: Routledge.

—— 1995. *On 'What is History?': From Carr and Elton to Rorty and White.* London: Routledge.

—— 1999. *Why History?: Ethics and Postmodernity.* London: Routledge.

JORDANOVA, L. 2000. *History in Practice.* London: Arnold.

KEAY, J. 2000. *India: A History.* London: HarperCollins.

KENT, C. F. 1896. *A History of the Hebrew People: From the Settlement in Canaan to the Division of the Kingdom.* London: Smith, Elder, & Co.

KING, P. J, and STAGER, L. E. 2001. *Life in Biblical Israel.* Louisville, Ky.: Westminster/John Knox Press.

LEMCHE, N. P. 1985. *Ancient Israel: A New History of Israelite Society.* Sheffield: JSOT Press.

LADURIE, E. LE ROY 1980. *Montaillou: Cathars and Catholics in a French Village 1294–1324.* London: Penguin Books.

LE GOFF, J. 1992. *History and Memory.* New York: Columbia University Press.

MAZOWER, M. 2001. *The Balkans.* London: Phoenix Press.

McNUTT, P. M. 1999. *Reconstructing the Society of Ancient Israel.* London: SPCK.

NAAMAN, N. 1994. 'The "Conquest of Canaan" in the Book of Joshua and in History'. In I. Finkelstein and N. Naaman, eds., *From Nomadism to Monarchy: Archaeological and Historical Aspects of Early Israel,* Jerusalem: Israel Exploration Society, 218–81.

PITARD, W. 1998. 'Before Israel: Syria-Palestine in the Bronze Age'. In Coogan (1998), 33–77.

PLUMB, J. H. 1969. *The Death of the Past.* London: Macmillan.

PORTER, R. 2000. *Enlightenment: Britain and the Creation of the Modern World.* Harmondsworth: Penguin Books.

PROVAN, I., LONG, V. P., and LONGMAN, T. III. 2003. *A Biblical History of Israel.* Louisville, Ky.: Westminster/John Knox Press.

REDMOUNT, C. A. 1998. 'Bitter Lives: Israel in and out of Egypt'. In Coogan (1998), 79–120.

SAMUEL, R. 1989. *Patriotism: The Making and Unmaking of British National Identity,* i: *History and Politics.* London: Routledge.

VEYNE, P. 1971. *Comment écrit l'histoire: Esai d'épistémologie.* Paris: Éditions du Seuil.

WHITELAM, K. W. 1986. 'Recreating the History of Israel'. *JSOT* 35: 45–70.

—— 1989. 'Israel's Traditions of Origin: Reclaiming the Land'. *JSOT* 44: 19–42.

—— 1996. *The Invention of Ancient Israel: The Silencing of Palestinian History.* London: Routledge.

WHYBRAY, R. N. 1966. 'What Do We Know about Ancient Israel?' *ET* 101: 71–4.

CHAPTER 15

ISRAEL TO THE END OF THE PERSIAN PERIOD: HISTORY, SOCIAL, POLITICAL, AND ECONOMIC BACKGROUND

J. W. ROGERSON

Where should a history of Israel, including its social, political, and economic background, begin, and how should it proceed? Forty years ago this question was answered in one of two ways. A history of Israel began either with the Patriarchs (Abraham, Isaac, and Jacob) or with the coming into being of Israel as a tribal confederacy in ancient Palestine in the thirteenth century BCE (so Bright 1960 and Noth 1950, respectively). If there was disagreement over the starting-point, there was unanimity about the continuation: a history of Israel would follow the main outline presented in the books of Judges and Samuel to 2 Kings, and Chronicles, Ezra, and Nehemiah. Depending on where it ended, it would also utilize the books of Maccabees and Josephus, among other later sources. There was plenty of scope for disagreement within the consensus part of the answer—for example, over the length and extent of the reign of Saul, over whether Sennacherib campaigned once or twice against Hezekiah, and the dates of the work of Ezra and Nehemiah (see the differing treatments in Bright and Noth)—but the general approach—namely, that of following the biblical account—was not questioned.

Today the situation is quite different. While the question of where a history of Israel should begin would be answered in terms closer to Noth than to Bright (without accepting Noth's theory that Israel was a tribal confederacy with shared sacred traditions), the burning question has become whether it is possible to proceed by following the biblical outline. The main reason for this is that recent archaeological work has indicated that the kingdoms of Israel, Moab, Ammon, and Edom did not become established until the ninth century BCE, with Judah following suit a century later (Bienkowski 1992). These indications have put a question mark against the biblical account of the 'united monarchy' of Saul, David, and Solomon, not to mention the biblical account of a Davidic-Solomonic empire. This, in turn, has suggested that the beginning date for a history of Israel should be moved back to the time of the Israelite king Omri (*c.*880 BCE), or that the reign of Hezekiah, king of Judah (*c.*727–698 BCE) should be seen as the period during which the biblical tradition began to be composed. Both kings are mentioned in Assyrian sources.

There are several difficulties with moving the starting-point of Israel's history back to points in the biblical narrative that seem to be more historically 'secure'. The first is the possibility that each 'secure' point will be undermined by new archaeological findings. There will be a series of 'retreats' until nothing 'secure' remains. Secondly, there is the principle of what Whitelam has called 'the tyranny of a historical paradigm over the data' (Whitelam 2000: 387), by which he means the prior acceptance of the biblical picture as the framework according to which all other evidence should be interpreted and organized.

There is a simple way out of this dilemma, and that is to accept that the purpose of the biblical narratives is to inform us about the religion of ancient Israel and not about its history—history as understood in a modern sense. This would be to treat the history-like narratives of the Old Testament in the same way that scholars now handle narratives that contain Israelite beliefs about the physical structure of the universe, or the geographical distribution in the world of the peoples with whom Israel came into contact or about whom they had traditions (e.g. in Genesis 10). Whereas it was once accepted that Genesis 1 and 10 provided reliable physical and geographical material about the origin of the world and the distribution of its inhabitants, discoveries from the sixteenth century onwards made it clear that this information could not be preferred to the discoveries of astronomers and of naval explorers. It was, after all, Calvin who said of Genesis 1: 'he who would learn astronomy, and other recondite arts, let him go elsewhere' (Calvin 1965: 79)

There is, however, a difference between the history-like narratives of the Old Testament and what it has to say about physics and geography, and that is that the history-like narratives may well contain material that a modern historian can use with caution, in conjunction with extra-biblical texts, archaeological findings, and anthropological models. If it is accepted that the main purpose of the Old Testament is to witness to the religious faith that was held in ancient Israel, it is then possible to see what can be surmised about the history of the people(s) among whom the religious faith arose, without feeling that a rearguard action must somehow be fought on behalf of the Old Testament by salvaging as much historical 'truth' from it as possible. The value for theology of the opening chapters of Genesis does not depend upon the accuracy of its astronomy or prehistory (although many fundamentalist groups would argue that it does), and the same could be true of its history-like narratives. Freed from the need to defend 'the tyranny of a historical paradigm over the data', it will be easier to acknowledge how little is in fact known about the history of ancient Israel in the light of our present knowledge.

This brings us to another important subject: namely, how we understand the term 'Israel'. There are a number of possible ways in which the term can be used. First, there is that of the non-Israelite outsider describing or naming an entity that is viewed in opposition to itself. Such reference can be geographical (as when by 'Israel' people today mean a particular location in the Middle East), or it can be to a people, as in the Egyptian Merneptah stele (*c.*1207), where the Egyptian writing system apparently makes this explicit. Second, there is the usage of the insider, of someone or some group needing to define themselves in opposition to 'outsiders'. Third, there is a religious usage which sees 'Israel' not as a political or geographical entity, but as a people called by God to obey his laws and to witness to what he has made known of himself. This third 'Israel' is an ideal construct which, in the Old Testament, is often in conflict with the actual Israel of the first two usages. Those parts of the Bible that deal in various ways with this conflict not only dominate the history-like traditions; they are probably of more interest to theologians than to historians.

In what follows, an attempt will be made to say something about the social, political, and economic background of Israel in the first two senses given above, to the end of the Persian period. The attempt will be based upon extra-biblical texts, archaeological discoveries, and anthropological models. Where appropriate, reference will be made to Old Testament material, not in order to vindicate its historical 'truth' through the back door, but to suggest ways of looking at it in the light of the historical and social reconstruction.

The earliest extra-biblical references to Israel and events connected with it are the Merneptah inscription of *c.*1207, the so-called house of David inscription from Dan, dated to the ninth century, and the monumental remains relating to the expedition of the Egyptian pharaoh Sheshonk I to Palestine in the late tenth century. The Merneptah inscription is too cryptic to reveal any information about the nature, location, or constitution of an entity called 'Israel', and the hidden agendas surrounding its interpretation have usually concerned whether or not the inscription supports biblical claims about the presence of an Israel somewhere in thirteenth-century Canaan. I shall return to the other inscriptions later, but will focus now upon a fourth early extra-biblical source, the Mesha inscription, which is usually dated to the end of the first half of the ninth century BCE. Erected in ancient Dibon by Mesha, king of Moab, it contains the following narrative:

Omri [was] king of Israel and he afflicted Moab many days [i.e. years], because *kmš* was angry with his land. And his son succeeded him and he also said 'I will afflict Moab'... And Omri possessed the land of *mhdba*. And [Israel] dwelt therein, his days and half the days of his son, forty years... Now the men of Gad had dwelt in the land of '*trt* from of old; and the king of Israel built for himself '*trt*. And I fought against the city and took it. (For a standard translation see Pritchard 1955: 320, and cf. the study by Smelik 1992)

From this we learn of an Israelite king Omri who, together with his son, occupied two areas east of the Jordan, one of them an area inhabited by people (the men of Gad) presumably related or allied in some way to Omri. Even if the period of forty years of occupation of the area of *mhdba* is not taken literally, it represents a generation (say, of twenty to twenty-five years), and indicates more than an ephemeral exercise of occupying power. The Bible says nothing of Omri's military prowess at 1 Kgs. 16: 15–24, although he is described as a commander of the army, who seized power in a *coup d'état* and won the resulting civil war. His being credited with building a new capital in Samaria is supported by archaeological work at the site of ancient Samaria (Kenyon 1971: 73–82); and other significant public works, e.g. the water system at Megiddo, have been assigned to the time of Omri or his son Ahab.

These facts raise two questions. What was the nature and extent of Omri's kingdom? And what can be deduced from this about what preceded Omri's rise to power? In answering the first question, it is important not to read back into the situation of the ancient world modern ideas of the nation-state with its sovereignty being exercised within defined and defensible borders (see Giddens 1985: 52–3). The evidence of the Samaria Ostraca and the research of Niemann (1993) indicate that the effective exercise of power by Omri and his successors was confined to the immediate area around Samaria. His is best described as a segmentary state (Sigrist and Neu 1997: 9; cf. also Giddens 1985: 52: 'Traditional states are... fundamentally segmental in character') in which effective power outside the central authority is considerably diluted (Southall 1997: 78–9). If it is asked how Omri could, in this case, have 'afflicted Moab many days', the probable answer is that he established garrisons in several towns in Trans-Jordan which controlled their immediate surroundings, and which were a thorn in the flesh for Moabite leaders until Mesha ejected them.

What social and other circumstances preceded Omri's rise to power? Segmentary states are fragile and unstable, and because they rely upon dominant groups and their leaders, they can be subject to shifting alliances and seizures of power. That Omri's kingship was preceded by two *coups*, according to 1 Kgs. 15: 27 and 16: 9–10, fits this pattern well; but the prerequisite for such shifts in power was the existence of groups or individuals that had accumulated property and/or power over individuals that placed them in a position to vie for the most instances of power and authority. Neu (1997: 18–19) draws attention to individuals in the biblical record such as Nabal (1 Samuel 25), David, Abimelech (Judges 9), and Jephthah (Judges 11) as examples of people who are portrayed as possessing wealth and/or military power, and while this evidence must be used with caution (the name Nabal means 'fool' in Hebrew, and the narrative emphasizes Nabal's folly in not supporting David), it provides a plausible picture of the kind of conditions that existed in Palestine of the late eleventh and tenth centuries.

The 'house of David' inscription from Dan was discovered in 1993, and has been dated to the ninth century BCE. Written in Aramaic, it is very fragmentary but appears to say (lines 8–9):

> ... the king of Israel. And (I) slew (... the kin)
> g of the house of David. And I put ...

(see Lemche 2003)

Arguments about the authenticity and interpretation of this fragment have as their subtext the question of whether it does or does not support the biblical accounts of David's empire in 1 Samuel. If the view taken here is correct, that the social organizations that existed in tenth-century Palestine were segmentary states, then the inscription can be taken at face value. A ruler of a segmentary state could certainly establish a dynasty, even if the creation of an 'empire' in the modern sense was impossible. From a biblical angle, the most interesting material about David is the list of his heroes in 2 Sam. 23: 8–39. Commentators have noted that the locations of the heroes are confined to Judah and the territories immediately adjacent to the north, and that what might be called an 'early core' comes from towns within a narrow radius of Bethlehem (McCarter 1984: 500–1). If this material is authentic, it confirms the impression given in 1 Samuel that David was a kind of freebooter, whose power was invested in the loyalty of his followers, some of whom were alienated from their families and kin networks. The 'Nabal' incident of 1 Sam. 25, despite its obviously highly elaborated present form, may well indicate that David's group existed by offering 'protection' in return for food and other items. David's alliance with the Philistines (surely not an invented episode) can be seen as an instance of a change of allegiance for convenience's sake, typical of the situations in which segmentary states exist. Indeed, if 1 Sam. 27: 8–12 can be believed, David continued his freebooting under Philistine auspices. Again, his subsequent defeat of the Philistines was another instance of a shifting power balance within and between segmentary states, as were the revolts of Absalom and Sheba ben Bichri against David himself (Sigrist and Neu 1997: 9). The biblical claims that David defeated surrounding peoples such as Moab, Zobah, Ammon, and Edom (2 Sam. 8: 1–12) could mean that he set up garrisons in some or all of those territories. The garrisons would have been small (up to 300 men), and would amount to a legal claim over territory, which, however, was in no way controlled. As in the case of Omri's activities in Moab, an energetic military commander with a determined and loyal group of followers could capture and temporarily garrison key towns in neighbouring regions.

So far, the discussion has concentrated on the extra-biblical information about Omri, and on what may have preceded his rise to power. Is it possible to go further back?

In 1979 Norman Gottwald published a massively researched study which, expanding on a suggestion first made by G. E. Mendenhall (1962), argued that Israel emerged as the revolt of an egalitarian society against the power of the Canaanite city-states in the Early Iron Age. Mendenhall's contribution was an attempt to break the deadlock between the Albright theory that there had been an Israelite conquest and the Alt theory that the Israelite occupation of Canaan had been one of peaceful settlement. Mendenhall's proposal was that the 'occupation' had been an internal revolt. Gottwald's work was characterized by the attention he paid to social anthropology, including the development of 'tribal' systems in 'colonial' situations. A feature of it that captured some areas of scholarly imagination was its view that Israel had been formed as an egalitarian society, and that its God YHWH was seen as a God of liberation. The subsequent emergence of kingship was a development that denied the impulses that had led to Israel's formation. The idea of Israel as an egalitarian society was taken up in various ways, and parallels were drawn with segmentary societies, societies which lacked major centres of power, which had been found among African peoples (see Rogerson 1986). Mendenhall and Gottwald also raised the important question of whether the groups from which Israel was formed were indigenous, or whether they had invaded or settled peacefully from outside (as the book of Joshua proposed, at least with regard to invasion).

Gottwald's reconstruction presupposed acceptance of Noth's theory that there had been an Israelite amphictyony in the period of Judges—a view that today finds little support. It has also been overtaken by discussion of the results of archaeological site surveys undertaken after 1967. These surveys have revealed a striking decrease in the number of settlements in Canaan at the end of the Late Bronze Age and a striking increase in the number of small settlements in the Early Iron Age. The interpretation of this evidence has centred on two main questions: whether those who founded these settlements were indigenous or 'outsiders', and whether they can be identified as Israelites or proto-Israelites. A related question is whether the development that led to the formation of Israel from those settlements was evolutionary, in the sense of predictable social responses to environmental and external factors, or whether conscious decisions were taken to constitute a group or people in contradistinction to other groups or people in the region. With regard to the latter possibility, it has to be asked what mechanisms would enable collective decisions about the people's specific identity to be taken.

Two differing approaches to the above questions can be found in the work of Israel Finkelstein (1988; Finkelstein and Na'aman 1994) and William Dever (2003). According to Finkelstein, the settlements were largely the result of re-sedentarization from Palestine to Trans-Jordan at the end of the Late Bronze Age; in other words, they came largely from outside. Finkelstein doubts whether the settlers can be called Israelites. Dever's view is that the settlements are the result of an agrarian reform movement in which indigenous occupants of the land withdrew to the frontiers. He is certain that they can be called proto-Israelites (see most recently Dever 2003: 194–200), and also argues that the settlements exhibit a remarkable homogeneity of material culture and evidence for family and clan social solidarity (2003: 185).

The exhaustive study of selected villages in central Palestine of the Early Iron Age by Zwingenberger confirms Dever's view that the villagers were indigenous rather than 'incomers' (2001: 549), but is agnostic about whether there was a distinctive culture or some kind of decision to form an identifiable people (2001: 550–1). The evidence indicates that the social and cultural *realia* of each settlement were determined by their geographical location and environmental conditions. Survival was the main preoccupation; and during the early Iron Age villages experienced fluctuating fortunes, ending with the abandonment of some and the enlargement of others. This latter phenomenon may indicate a stage along the path to the emergence of a segmentary state. More favourable environmental conditions and the initiative or enterprise of particular individuals could enable such individuals to develop power in the sense of gaining *de facto* control over the use and benefits gained from particular areas of land. Their families would benefit, and begin to establish hierarchical and inheritable power. Such families would not control the whole of the country; some, perhaps many, villages could remain effectively outside their sphere of influence, and retain this comparative independence through into the period of the monarchy. It was sufficient that powerful families and their leaders could create the conditions for the establishment of segmentary states such as are found in the cases of David and Omri.

In the present state of our knowledge, it is impossible to answer the question about the origins of Israel, in the sense of a group self-consciously identified as a people and recognized as such by other ethnic groups (cf. also Zwingenberger 2001: 550). Israel must in some way have emerged from the villagers who established the settlements in the Palestine of the thirteenth century and onwards, and may even have existed in some form or other at the time of Merneptah's invasion (*c*.1207). However, the evidence allows no final conclusions to be drawn. The same is true of the theory of Gottwald and others regarding the egalitarian nature of early Israel. The villagers (or some of them) *may* have attempted to be an egalitarian society or a reform movement, but the evidence of archaeology does not permit such conclusions to be drawn. The same is also true of the religion of the villagers. Dever (2003: 128) sums up the situation as follows: 'our only material evidence of early Israelite beliefs and cultic practices provides additional, corroborative evidence for continuity with Canaanite religion—nothing whatsoever here that is new or revolutionary.... *Archaeologically* Yahweh is as invisible in Iron I villages as he was said to be later in biblical Israel.' The quotation expresses, of course, Dever's view that among the villagers were those who could be called Israelites or proto-Israelites, a view about which I am agnostic.

To sum up the position reached so far, the earlier evidence is of the likely emergence of individuals and families who were in a position to establish segmentary states by around the middle of the eleventh century. Some, at least, of the traditions contained in the book of Judges may reflect this situation (the lists of so-called minor Judges in 10: 1–15, 12: 8–15, certainly describe men and families with considerable localized power). The consolidation and expansion of power by the Philistines at the end of this period would have constituted a threat to such leaders and families, leading to resistance led by a figure such as Saul. The survival in the tradition of the saying 'Is Saul also among the prophets?' (1 Sam. 10: 12, 19: 24) and the role ascribed to Samuel in supporting Saul has an interesting anthropological parallel in the role of Nuer prophets in the face of colonial pressure (Evans-Pritchard 1940: 185). It is not impossible that confrontation with the Philistines was an important factor in the development of Israelite self-awareness, and that religious allegiance to YHWH, as fostered by prophetic groups, was a further ingredient in the shared conventions of that self-identity.

It has already been suggested that David was most likely the freebooting leader of a resourceful and determined group of fighters, who first allied himself with the Philistines and then broke their power (see Halpern 2001 for a recent detailed study of David). This enabled him to establish a segmentary state with garrisons in neighbouring territories. Whether his capital city of Jerusalem was occupied prior to David's capture of it has become a matter of fierce debate (see Auld and Steiner 1996). The biblical traditions about his son Solomon, with their picture of him ruling over a small empire and engaging in massive building projects, probably date from the time of Hezekiah in the eighth century (see Wälchli 1999), although they may contain older archival material. Fierce debate has raged over the dating of walls and entrance gates at Megiddo, Hazor, and Gezer. Scholars who believe that they were the work of Solomon (e.g. Mazar 1990: 380–7) see them as evidence for Solomon's establishment of a centralized state in which public buildings were erected in key administrative towns. Other experts (e.g. Finkelstein and Silberman 2001: 135–42) date these finds to the early ninth century, thus questioning the nature and extent of Solomon's rule.

The earliest extra-biblical inscription which correlates with information in the Bible is the triumphal inscription which the Egyptian pharaoh Shoshenq I caused to be inscribed on the wall of the temple at Karnak. It is a list of some 150 towns and villages which Shoshenq claimed to have captured during a campaign in Palestine around 926 BCE (for a survey of the data in the list see Kitchen 1973: 432–42). The biblical account states that Shishak came up against Jerusalem in the fifth year of Rehoboam (the king of Judah) and took away all the treasures and gold from the temple and the royal palace, and that Rehoboam replaced the gold shields that were taken with bronze ones (1 Kgs. 14: 25–8). 1 Chr. 12: 4 adds that Shishak 'took the fortified cities of Judah and came as far as Jerusalem'. Correlating Shoshenq's inscription with the biblical material illustrates nicely the problems facing any historian of ancient Israel. The Egyptian inscription is a list of cities, and any attempt to reconstruct the course of Shoshenq's campaign involves scholarly conjecture based upon knowledge of the topography of Palestine and Egyptian military tactics. Inevitably, experts have not been completely unanimous in their reconstructions (see Kitchen 1973: 442–6 for a review of several reconstructions). A particular difficulty is that Jerusalem is not itself mentioned among the towns captured (Kitchen 1973: 298), a fact that can be explained in more than one way. Kitchen's view is that Shoshenq encamped at Gibeon, a few miles to the north of Jerusalem, and from there successfully demanded Rehoboam's submission and payment of tribute. According to Herrmann (1973: 55–79), it was a task force rather than the main army that went to Gibeon to demand Rehoboam's submission. The biblical record is almost certainly derived from an archive that detailed the fate of the temple and palace treasures, and in itself provides a valuable correlation with the Egyptian material. The interpretation of the correlation is not so straightforward, as the explicit claim in 1 Kgs. 14: 25, that Shishak 'came up against Jerusalem', is not directly confirmed by the inscription.

Another problem raised by Shoshenq's campaign is directly related to the argument about the nature of Solomon's kingdom. On the assumption that Solomon had established a centralized state with fortified cities and public buildings, such as those deemed to be Solomonic at Hazor, Gezer, and Megiddo, Shoshenq directed his blows against the fortified cities of the two kingdoms of Judah and Israel that had come into being following the death of Solomon, with the blow falling most heavily upon the northern kingdom Israel (see Herrmann 1973: 247). It could be further argued that the civil war that led to the emergence of Omri as king of Israel c.880 was the result of the aftermath of Shoshenq's campaign, as the weakness that it effected was exploited by the growing power of Damascus under Ben-hadad (Noth 1950: 239). A quite different view is found in Finkelstein and Silberman (2001: 162). According to them, Shoshenq's campaign destroyed the last vestiges of power of the Canaanite city-states and created the conditions that later brought Omri to power, and to the establishment of the Israelite kingdom which extended its power into Moab, as stated in the Mesha inscription. The biblical narrative of 1 Kgs. 15: 1–16: 24 which records warfare between the kings of Judah (supported by Damascus) and the kings of Israel can be taken to provide an accurate, if necessarily very incomplete, picture of the fifty years or so from

Rehoboam's reign to the time of Omri. It makes a big difference, however, whether it is understood in terms of the breakup of a once powerful Solomonic state or in terms of a struggle for dominance of emerging segmentary states.

If it were not for extra-biblical sources, all that would be known about Omri (apart from the fact that he was wicked in the eyes of the biblical editors) was that he removed his capital to the virgin site of Samaria and that he showed might (1 Kgs. 16: 24, 27). Excavations at Samaria have confirmed the biblical information; but discoveries such as the Mesha inscription have greatly enlarged the picture, and something of the impact made by Omri on the neighbouring world of his day is indicated by the fact that some 150 years after his death, Israel was still referred to in Assyrian annals as the house or land of Omri (Pritchard 1955: 284).

That Omri and his successor Ahab were able to mobilize considerable amounts of manpower to build cities such as Samaria and Jezreel, as well as to complete such projects as the water system at Megiddo, is shown by the archaeological record. If we had only the biblical record to go by, we would have no idea of the development of Israel's military strength under Ahab, or of the growing threat to the region from the emerging strength of Assyria. More space is devoted to Ahab's reign in 1 Kings than to any monarch other than Solomon, but this is because of the opposition to his rule led by Elijah, and the space devoted to Elijah's exploits (1 Kgs. 17–19, 21). 1 Kings 20 and 22 record battles between Ahab and the Syrian king Ben-hadad, but it has long been suspected that this material may originally have been connected with Ahab's son Jehoram and reapplied to Ahab because of the hostility of the biblical editors to Ahab. Indeed, the biblical record of Ahab's reign is another classical instance of the way in which archaeological discoveries complicate the interpretation of biblical history-like narratives rather than confirm them.

The whole subject is too complex to be discussed adequately here, but the following points can be made. The order of the names of the kings of Damascus in the biblical account differ from those given in Assyrian records (Pritchard 1955: 280; see the useful presentation of the evidence in Miller and Hayes 1986: 263–4). In the same records (Pritchard 1955: 278–9) Ahab and the Syrian king are allies against Shalmaneser III at the battle of Karkara (853 BCE), with Ahab contributing the largest number of chariots; yet 1 Kings 20: 23–5 gives the impression that Israel was weak in chariots compared with Syria. The alliance of Ahab and the Syrian king must have come at the end of Ahab's reign (usually reckoned as c.873–853), yet Ahab is killed in battle by the Syrian king, according to 1 Kings 22. It is not impossible to reconcile the biblical and non-biblical materials by assuming, for example, that the biblical name for the Syrian king (Ben-hadad) is a throne-name, or allowing that Ahab's alliance with the Syrian king was born of necessity in the face of a common enemy, and that their natural enmity reasserted itself once the common threat had passed. However, it is difficult not to feel sympathy for the conclusion of Miller and Hayes (1986: 262) that the accounts of the battles with Ben-hadad (1 Kgs. 20, 22) belong to a later reign, and that the Israelite kingdom enjoyed friendly relations with Damascus at least until the reign of Jehoram. Indeed, if this adjustment is made, the state of affairs described in 2 Kings 5–10, one in which Israel suffered grievously at the hand of Syria (2 Kgs. 10: 32–3), makes sense in the light of extra-biblical evidence. It can be conjectured that the encounter with the Assyrian army at Karkara at the end of Ahab's reign weakened Israel more than Damascus. This weakness provided the opportunity for Mesha, king of Moab, to remove the Israelite garrisons from his territory (assuming that the reference to Omri's son is to his grandson, Jehoram), and ushered in a period of Syrian dominance over Israel, which created the conditions for a *coup d'état* in which Jehu overthrew the house of Omri and Ahab (2 Kgs. 9: 1–10: 18). Assyrian records state that as a result of Shalmaneser's fifth campaign to the west in 841, Jehu the son of Omri (!) paid tribute to the Assyrian king.

Of the remainder of the ninth century, until the power of Damascus was crushed by Assyria round about 800 BCE, nothing is known for certain, although it can be surmised that Israel struggled under Syrian domination and that Judah also began to seek its independence. The biblical narratives of 1 Kings 22 and 2 Kings 3 describe Judah as allied to Israel; and Athaliah, who was queen of Judah (c.840–835), was a daughter or granddaughter of Omri (2 Kgs. 8: 26). It is even possible that Jehoram, king of Israel, was also the king of Judah of that name (Miller and Hayes 1986: 280–2). The biblical evidence is confirmed indirectly by the fact that Judah is not mentioned in the Assyrian annals of the mid-ninth century. It is therefore likely that Judah was effectively part of Israel for much of the ninth century, but that as the century ended, attempts were made by Amaziah of Judah (unsuccessfully, according to 2 Kgs. 14: 8–22) to defeat Israel.

The first half of the eighth century was dominated by two kings who enjoyed long and prosperous reigns, according to the biblical record. They were Jeroboam II of Israel (c.782–747) and Azariah (Uzziah) (c.767–739). The dates can only be approximate. Little has been preserved in the archaeological record to inform us about these reigns. Finkelstein and Silberman (2001: 212) mention ivory plaques which decorated the royal palace in Samaria in the eighth century, and the Samaria Ostraca—receipts for consignments of wine to the capital from neighbouring villages. It is usual to link the strictures of Amos against the luxury of the ruling classes and the oppression of the poor (Amos 3: 9–11, 4: 1–4, 6: 1–7) with this period. Finkelstein and Silberman comment that it is under Jeroboam II's reign that the full complement of the criteria of statehood in the northern kingdom can be identified: 'literacy, bureaucratic administration, specialised economic production, and a professional army' (2001: 212). Even so, if Niemann (1993) is correct, such state-hood did not amount to anything like the control that the modern state has over the area defined by its borders.

For the second part of the eighth century, Assyrian records greatly amplify the biblical material. Tiglath-Pileser III (745–727) extended his empire towards Syria and Palestine, and forced both Menahem (king of Israel, 747–42) and Hoshea (king of Israel, 731–722) to pay tribute (Pritchard 1955: 283–4; 2 Kgs. 15: 19–20). Indeed, the Assyrian king claims to have placed Hoshea on the throne. The fact that Israel had six kings and three *coups d'état* from *c*.747 to 722/1 is best understood as the outcome of pressure from Assyria.

In 722/1 the Assyrian king Sargon captured Samaria, deported 27,290 of its inhabitants, and repopulated the city with peoples from conquered countries (Pritchard 1955: 284; 2 Kgs. 17: 1–6, 24). Assyrian policy towards Israel was probably affected by the attempts of Pekah, king of Israel (*c*.740–731), and Rezin, king of Damascus, to organize a coalition against Assyria, possibly including an unsuccessful attempt to coerce Ahaz, king of Judah, to join them (2 Kgs. 16: 5; Isa. 7: 1–8). Ahaz appealed to Tiglath-Pileser for help again Rezin and Pekah, making Judah an Assyrian vassal (2 Kgs. 16: 7–18). Ahaz's successor, Hezekiah (*c*.727–698), had other ideas. Indicators of 'statehood' such as those listed by Finkelstein and Silberman for Jeroboam II become apparent for Judah of the eighth century (Jamieson-Drake 1991), and these, together with the likely increase in the population of Judah and Jerusalem as a result of refugees coming south after the fall of Samaria, emboldened Hezekiah to stand firm against Assyria. It was probably during his reign that Judah took over the role of Israel, and that the history-like narratives of the Old Testament began to be shaped into what, several centuries later, would become their extant form. Hezekiah may have been part of an anti-Assyrian coalition as early as about 715 BCE, with support from Egypt (Isa. 20: 1–6). At any rate, Sargon II attacked and captured Ashdod in 711 for its opposition to Assyrian rule (Pritchard 1955: 286). With the accession of Sennacherib (704–681), the opportunity came for Hezekiah to rebel, in league with the city of Ekron, provoking Sennacherib's compaign of 701, which is recorded not only in his annals (Pritchard 1955: 287–8), but in reliefs of his conquest of the Judahite city of Lachish. Hezekiah submitted and paid heavy tribute (Pritchard 1955: 288 lists 30 talents of gold and 800 talents of silver, among other things; 2 Kgs. 18: 13 gives the tribute as 30 talents of gold and 300 of silver). Although Jerusalem was not captured (a fact that later gave rise to belief in the inviolability of Jerusalem), Judah as a whole must have suffered grievously. Hezekiah's rebellion led to a period of Judahite subjugation to Assyria that lasted for some sixty years, until the general decline of Assyria enabled Josiah (640–609) to make a renewed bid for independence.

The period of over sixty years between Hezekiah's humiliation and the beginning of Josiah's reign is largely a blank so far as our knowledge is concerned. It was spanned by the long reign of Manasseh (*c*.698–643), to whom the Bible devotes eighteen verses in 2 Kings 21, most of which comment adversely on Manasseh's religious offences. Assyrian records from the reigns of Esarhaddon (680–669) and Ashurbanipal (668–*c*.632; see Pritchard 1955: 291, 294) mention that Manasseh provided material and military help to Assyria. Finkelstein and Silberman (2001: 264–70) believe that Manasseh tried to integrate Judah into the Assyrian economy, that the centralized administration of the country was strengthened, and that the growing population of Judah extended into the ecologically marginal areas of the land. The researches of Jamieson-Drake (1991: 146) indicate a boom in population in the seventh century in Judah, accompanied by an equal surge in wealth as indicated by luxury items. He surmises that this prosperity would not have been possible without the vital role played in the economy by Jerusalem. According to Steiner (2001), a result of Sennacherib's invasion was that Judah was devastated to the point that Jerusalem was now able to exert almost total domination over the administration and economy of the country.

Josiah came to power as an 8-year-old boy following the assassination of his father Amon (2 Kgs. 21: 19–26). He was put on the throne by 'the people of the land' (2 Kgs. 21: 24), possibly powerful landowners who saw the declining fortunes of Assyria (Nineveh would fall in 612 BCE) as an opportunity to assert Judah's independence. The long biblical account of his reign (2 Kgs. 22: 1–23: 30) is devoted entirely to his religious reforms, reforms in which cult centres other than Jerusalem were closed down and Jerusalem became the national sanctuary. Such is the paucity of external evidence that it is impossible to know whether Josiah's reform was primarily cultic or whether the Jerusalem centralization was an economic move to reorganize the taxation system and strengthen the fiscal power of the temple over the rest of the country. Possible evidence for the cult reform is provided by the findings of Keel and Uehlinger (1992), that the official seals of the period ceased to bear artistic representations connected with astral and fertility religions. On the other hand, there is no doubt that Josiah's reign made a deep impression on the formation of the biblical tradition. The so-called Deuteronomic movement, which scholars believe was responsible for major editing of considerable parts of the history-like and prophetic traditions now extant in the Bible, if it did not originate in Josiah's reign, was either given active encouragement by it or looked back to it as a model.

Josiah's achievements, whatever they were (they may have included expanding Judah's territory northwards) did not outlive his death in 609 at the hands of the Egyptian pharaoh Necho II at Megiddo. The circumstances of his death have been the subject of various theories, most of which are plausible but not demonstrable (see Finkelstein and Silberman 2001: 289–92). Judah now faced the growing might of the neo-Babylonian empire and of Nebuchadnezzar. Jerusalem was captured in 597 BCE, and its king and nobles and craftsmen were exiled to Babylon. Zedekiah, placed on the throne by the Babylonians in 597, rebelled after eight or nine years. This time, the Babylonians destroyed Jerusalem and the temple (in 587), ushering in the so-called period of the Exile.

The biblical record (2 Kgs. 25: 21: 'So Judah was taken in to exile out of its land'; according to 2 Chr. 36: 21, the land lay desolate for seventy years) creates the impression that 'exile' meant the total evacuation of the population of Judah. That there was a severe breakdown in the economic life of Judah is indicated by the researches of Jamieson-Drake (1991: 146–7). If Jerusalem had played a major economic role in sustaining towns and villages in Judah, its destruction must have made these places economically non-viable. There would have been a reversion, where possible, to locally based, self-supporting subsistence agriculture on the part of the 75 per cent of the population that remained in Judah (Finkelstein and Silberman 2001: 306). This is obviously a far cry from the picture of a land left desolate. Little more can be said with certainty about this period.

If the 'exile' is a blank period in our knowledge, the same is true of the periods of the so-called return and the domination by Persia (see most exhaustively Grabbe 2004). The decree of the Persian king Cyrus recorded in Ezra 1: 2–4, authorizing the Jews to return to Jerusalem and to rebuild the temple, is certainly consonant with Cyrus's religious policy in general, as set out in the Cyrus cylinder (Pritchard 1955: 316), whether or not the decree in Ezra is accepted as authentic or not (see Grabbe 1992: 34–5). The problems of reconciling the number of returnees—nearly 50,000 according to Ezra 2: 64–5—with the picture presented in Haggai and Zechariah 1–8 (normally dated to around 525 BCE) of a people with little or no desire to rebuild the temple, are well known. Also, there is the fact that the Persian province of Jehud, as Judah became, was much smaller than Judah when ruled by kings (see the map in Finkelstein and Silberman 2001: 309), and it is difficult to see where 50,000 returnees could have settled. It is more likely that the list in Ezra derives from a survey carried out at a later date. Scholarly debate about the Persian period has considered whether there was opposition between 'theocratic' and 'apocalyptic' groups, and whether there was serious debate about the rebuilding of the temple. Many of the arguments are based upon the interpretation of prophetic texts, which may or may not be correct. When it comes to hard evidence, the most that can be said, in the words of Grabbe, is that 'some Jews returned to the land, over a period of time; the temple was rebuilt, probably in Darius' reign, though exactly when is uncertain; the old area of Benjamin suffered some sort of destruction in the first half of the fifth century; Nehemiah repaired the wall and undertook some other reforms. Beyond that we find fewer certainties the further we go' (Grabbe 2000: 406). If it is the case that Nehemiah's reforms in the second half of the fifth century involved making Jews divorce wives who came from Ashdod, Ammon, and Moab (Neh. 13: 23–7), it must have had dire social consequences for the women involved. The Jews who had contracted such marriages were presumably not, or descended from, returnees from Babylon, but were families that had remained in the land after 587. The complaint of the people, in Neh. 5, that ordinary citizens were having to mortgage their fields and sell their children into slavery in order to live and to pay taxes, sheds a small patch of light upon part of the period. Again, if it is the case that some of the returnees found that their land had been occupied in their absence, and if they forcibly repossessed that land, then this, together with the information from Neh. 13 and 5 suggests a picture of communal strife, for at least part of the period.

CONCLUSION

Attempting to write the history of Israel to the end of the Persian period presents scholars with formidable problems. Are they to follow the biblical outline, using archaeology to fill in the gaps; or are they to put greater weight upon the non-biblical evidence? Answers in favour of the first option may be based upon a sincere, but misplaced, wish to be loyal to the 'truth' of the Bible. Yet, as I have shown here, the biblical narrative is silent on all but religious happenings for the first half of both the eighth and the seventh centuries, as well as much of the sixth to the fourth centuries. In the case of kings such as Omri, the biblical record is virtually silent on the subject of his many military achievements. It should not be concluded that the historical information in the biblical records is worthless; and, to be fair to the biblical editors, they refer constantly to the books of the chronicles of the kings of Judah and Israel as sources for further information. As Kratz has observed (1999: 405), the writings of the Old Testament are not documents of the national and religious history of Israel and Judah, but kerygmatic texts whose form is that of collections of writings within a religious canon. That is their value, and to recognize this is not to be 'disloyal' to them. If, as a result of taking this view, we discover that we know far less for certain about the history of Israel than we thought, this will be a gain for scholarly integrity rather than a loss.

BIBLIOGRAPHY

AULD, A. G., and STEINER, M. 1996. *Jerusalem I: From the Bronze Age to the Maccabees.* Cities of the Biblical World. Cambridge: Lutterworth Press.

BIENKOWSKI, P. 1992. *Early Edom and Moab: The Beginning of the Iron Age in Southern Jordan.* Sheffield Archaeological Monographs, 7. Sheffield: J. R. Collis Publications.

BRIGHT, J. 1960. *A History of Israel.* London: SCM Press; 3rd edn. 1981.

CALVIN, J. 1965. *Genesis.* Edinburgh: Banner of Truth Trust.

DEVER, W. G. 2003. *Who Were the Early Israelites and Where Did They Come From?* Grand Rapids, Mich.: Eerdmans.

EVANS-PRITCHARD, E. E. 1940. *The Nuer: A Description of the Modes of Livelihood and Political Institutions of a Nilotic People.* Oxford: Clarendon Press.

FINKELSTEIN, I. 1988. *The Archacology of the Israelite Settlement.* Jerusalem: Israel Exploration Society.

FINKELSTEIN, I. and NA'AMAN, N. 1994. *From Nomadism to Monarchy: Archaeological and Historical Aspects of Early Israel.* Jerusalem and Washington: Yad Izhak Ben-Zvi; Israel Exploration Society/Biblical Archaeology Society.

—— and SILBERMAN, N. A. 2001. *The Bible Unearthed: Archaeology's New Vision of Ancient Israel and the Origin of its Sacred Texts.* New York: Free Press.

GIDDENS, A. 1985. *A Contemporary Critique of Historical Materialism*, ii: *The Nation-State and Violence*. Cambridge: Polity.

GOTTWALD, N. K. 1979. *The Tribes of Yahweh: A Sociology of the Religion of Liberated Israel 1250–1050 B.C.E.*. Maryknoll, NY: Orbis Books.

GRABBE, L. L. 1992. *Judaism from Cyrus to Hadrian*, i: *The Persian and Greek Periods*. Minneapolis: Fortress Press.

—— 2000. 'The History of Israel: The Persian and Hellenistic Periods'. In A. D. H. Mayes, ed., *Texts in Context: Essays by Members of the Society for Old Testament Study*, Oxford: Oxford University Press, 403–27.

—— 2004. *A History of the Jews and Judaism in the Second Temple Period*, i: *Yehud: A History of the Persian Province of Judah*. London: T. & T. Clark International.

HALPERN, B. 2001. *David's Secret Demons: Messiah, Murderer, Traitor, King*. Grand Rapids, Mich.: Eerdmans.

HERRMANN, S. 1973. *Geschichte Israels*. Munich: Kaiser.

JAMIESON-DRAKE, D. W. 1991. *Scribes and Schools in Monarchic Judah: A Socio-Archeological Approach*. Social World of Biblical Antiquity Series, 9. Sheffield: Almond Press.

KEEL, O., and UEHLINGER, C. 1992. *Göttinnen, Götter und Gottessymbole: Neue Erkenntnisse zur Religionsgeschichte Kanaans und Israels aufgrund bislang unerschlossener ikonographischer Quellen*. Quaestiones Disputatae, 134. Freiburg: Herder.

KENYON, K. 1971. *Royal Cities of the Old Testament*. London: Barrie & Jenkins.

KITCHEN, K. A. 1973. *The Third Intermediate Period in Egypt (1100–650 BC)*. Warminster: Aris & Phillips.

KRATZ, R. G. 1999. 'Schrift, Heilige I'. *TRE* 30: 402–7.

LEMCHE, N. P. 2003. ' "House of David": The Tell Dan Inscription(s)'. In T. L. Thompson, ed., *Jerusalem in Ancient History and Tradition*, London: T. & T. Clark International, 46–67.

LEVY, T. E., ed. 1995. *The Archaeology of Society in the Holy Land*. Leicester: Leicester University Press.

McCARTER, P. K. 1984. *II Samuel*. AB. New York: Doubleday.

MAZAR, A. 1990. *Archaeology of the Land of the Bible, 10,000–586 B.C.E.* New York: Doubleday.

—— ed. 2001. *Studies in the Archaeology of the Iron Age in Israel and Jordan*. JSOTS.S 331. Sheffield: Sheffield Academic Press.

MENDENHALL, G. E. 1962. 'The Hebrew Conquest of Palestine'. *BA* 25: 66–87.

MILLER, J. M. and HAYES, J. H. 1986. *A History of Ancient Judah and Israel*. Philadelphia: Westminster Press.

NEU, R. 1997. 'Die Entstehung des israelitischen Königtums im Lichte der Ethnosoziologie'. In Sigrist and Neu (1997), 12–20.

NIEMANN, H. 1993. *Herrschaft, Königtum und Staat: Skizzen zur soziokulturellen Entwicklung im monarchischen Israel*. Forschungen zum Alten Testament, 6. Tübingen: Mohr Siebeck.

NOTH, M. 1950. *Geschichte Israels*. Göttingen: Vandenhoeck & Ruprecht.

PRITCHARD, J. B. 1955. *Ancient Near Eastern Texts Relating to the Old Testament*, 2nd edn. Princeton: Princeton University Press.

ROGERSON, J. W. 1986. 'Was Early Israel a Segmentary Society?' *JSOT* 36: 17–26; repr. in D. J. Chalcraft, *Social-Scientific Old Testament Criticism: A Sheffield Reader*, Sheffield: Sheffield Academic Press, 1997, 162–71.

SIGRIST, C., and NEU, R. 1997. *Ethnologische Texte zum Alten Testament, Band 2: Die Entstehung des Königtums*. Neukirchen-Vluyn: Neukirchener Verlag.

SMELIK, K. A. D. 1992. 'King Mesha's Inscription: Between History and Fiction'. In *idem, Converting the Past: Studies in Ancient Israelite & Moabite Historiography*, Leiden: Brill, 59–92.

SOUTHALL, A. 1997. 'Zum Begriff des segmentären Staates: Das Beispiel der Alur'. In Sigrist and Neu (1997), 67–92.

STEINER, M. 2001. 'Jerusalem in the Tenth and Seventh Centuries BCE: From Administrative Town to Commercial City'. In Mazar (2001), 280–8.

WÄLCHLI, S. 1999. *Der Weise König Salomo: Eine Studie zu den Erzählungen von der Weisheit Salomos in ihrem alttestamentlichen und altorientalischen Kontext*. BWANT 141. Stuttgart: Kohlhammer.

WHITELAM, K. W. 2000. 'The History of Israel: Foundations of Israel'. In A. D. H. Mayes, ed., *Text in Context: Essays by Members of the Society for Old Testament Study*, Oxford: Oxford University Press, 376–402.

ZWINGENBERGER, U. 2001. *Dorfkultur der frühen Eisenzeit in Mittelpalästina*. OBO 180. Fribourg: Universitätsverlag; Göttingen: Vandenhoeck & Ruprecht.

CHAPTER 16

ISRAEL FROM THE RISE OF HELLENISIM TO 70 CE

LESTER L. GRABBE

The Hellenistic and Roman periods belong to what is often referred to as the 'Second Temple period'. This is a self-contained historical era marked off by the Exile at one end and the fall of Jerusalem in 70 CE at the other. The Jews of the Second Temple period neither inhabited the world of the Israelite and Judean monarchies nor practised the religion of the rabbis. The Second Temple period began with the Persian empire (c.539–331 BCE), which ended with the conquest of Alexander. It is often assumed that a major break came about in Judaism with the coming of the Greeks, but recent study shows that the situation is more complex than that. First, many of the innovations that characterized Second Temple Judaism had their origins in the Persian period (though often continuing to develop in the Greek and Roman periods). Secondly, the Greeks added a new element to the culture, but the native cultures continued to flourish. This will be discussed in more detail below.

Some object to using the term 'Israel/Israelites' to refer to the Jews in the Second Temple period, as well as 'Jews' (or 'Judaeans' or the like). The term 'Israel' had originally belonged to the Northern Kingdom that came to an end about 722 BCE. Yet the literature of the Hebrew Bible, as well as early Jewish literature, often refers to the Jews by the designation 'Israel'. It is thus clear that at least some Jews—if perhaps not all—thought of themselves as Israelites. One should note, however, that this was purely an internal designation. No outsiders refer to Judah or the Jews as Israel until at least as late as Pompeius Trogus at the turn of the Common Era (*apud* Justin, *Historiae Philippicae* 36, Epitome 2. 3–4; he represents the origin of the Jews as from Damascus, one of whose kings is said to be *Israhel*). Yet even Trogus uses the common term 'Jews' for the people of his time, not Israel. The term 'Israelite' was apparently used in pre-Christian Graeco-Roman sources only to refer to members of a community on Delos associated with the cult on Mt Gerizim, i.e. the Samaritans.

After two centuries of Persian rule, Alexander's army invaded Asia in 334. Older works often assumed that the Macedonian conquest changed the ancient Near East irrevocably, with Hellenization subjugating the old Oriental cultures, but recent study has refuted this (Kuhrt and Sherwin-White 1987; Sherwin-White and Kuhrt 1993). Things did change under Greek rule—naturally—but changes had already occurred under earlier conquerors such as the Assyrians and Persians, and the developments under Greek rule were often long-term ones. Particularly important, though often overlooked, was the extent to which the conquered Near Eastern peoples and traditions transformed the habits and way of life of their Greek conquerors. Much that is characteristic of the Hellenistic kingdoms which arose in the wake of Alexander's death represents not the city-states of the classical Greek but a continuation from the old Near Eastern empires: the government was located primarily in a monarchy, which governed a large empire rather than a small city-state; private citizens were concerned mainly with private or local affairs, rather than with the politics of the state; members of the army and administration were usually professionals; and even the arts and sciences became the concern mainly of professionals (though often under royal patronage). Thus, the Orientals may have become Hellenized, but it is equally true that the Hellenes were Orientalized.

The Jews were as much affected—and unaffected—as other Near Eastern peoples. The idea that there was a natural antipathy between Hellenistic culture and Judaism has long since been dismissed (e.g. Tcherikover 1959; Hengel 1974), though one still reads such statements. Jews generally took the view that participation in Hellenistic religions was incompatible with Judaism, and our sources are firm in showing that few crossed this line. But educated Jews in an urban environment, with some wealth, evidently found Hellenistic culture attractive. Jews in the Greek diaspora generally spoke Greek as their first language and knew little or no Hebrew. The book of 1 Maccabees was quickly translated into Greek (with the Hebrew original lost), and 2 Maccabees was written in Greek. Ben Sira's grandson translated his work into Greek. But the earliest major 'Hellenization' project was the translation of the Pentateuch into Greek in the middle of the third century BCE (Fernández Marcos 2000; Dines 2004).

As with other Near Eastern peoples, the Jewish influence from and adoption of Greek customs and culture varied greatly within the community. Those living on farms and in villages probably saw their way of life little changed and continued to speak the local language. Indeed, within the Hellenistic empires the local languages (Babylonian cuneiform, Egyptian demotic, Aramaic) continued to have an important place in administration and the legal sphere. But even at lower levels, a knowledge of the Greek language would have been useful, and at higher levels it would have been essential. Already in the first part of the third century we find Jews in the administration making use of Greek, even if it was possibly via a secretary. To repeat: the Jews were as much, and as little, Hellenized as the other native peoples in the Hellenistic empires.

THE PTOLEMAIC PERIOD

As far as the Jews were concerned, the first century and a half of Greek rule is very sketchy. This is not true just of the Jews, however, because significant gaps still exist in the history of the Ptolemaic kingdom in the third century BCE. Our knowledge of the invasion of Alexander comes from Arrian. The forty years of the Diadochi ('Successors') who fought over his empire after his death are also well known through Diodorus Siculus, who has some good sources at this point. But then from about 280 BCE there are problems even in general Hellenistic history.

We have no contemporary records that mention the Jews as such during the time of Alexander or the Diadochi. We know that Alexander led his army down the Mediterranean coast in 333, taking Tyre and Gaza and wintering in Egypt. Evidently the Jews, along with all the other local peoples of Syria and Palestine, submitted, but we have no direct information. There is a story told by Josephus (*AJ* 11. 8. 1–6, §§304–45) that Alexander came to Jerusalem, bowed before the Jewish high priest, and honoured the Jews; however, most scholars recognize this as a highly stylized legend with little or no basis in events from Alexander's time. During the wars of the Diadochi (about 320 to 280 BCE) the armies must have marched and fought near, and even in, Palestine many times. One writer quoted by Josephus makes a statement to the effect that Ptolemy I captured Jerusalem at one point (*Ap*. 1. 22, §§209–11), but we cannot confirm this any more precisely.

One of the most valuable sources for the early Ptolemaic period is the account of Hecataeus of Abdera, as quoted by Diodorus Siculus (40. 3. 1–7). The following points emerge from his account:

1. The supposed origin of the Jews is their expulsion from Egypt under the leadership of Moses.
2. There is a Jewish ethnic and national community centred on Jerusalem.

3. As well as running the cult and teaching the law, the priests provide leadership and act as judges.
4. Chief authority is invested in the high priest, who is chosen for his wisdom.
5. The description of the religion gives the picture of an aniconic and most likely a monotheistic temple-based religion.
6. The Jews have a written law, and a quotation is given which closely parallels Lev. 27: 34 and Num. 36: 13.

This remarkable description was probably taken at some point from a Jewish informant with priestly views, but it differs at several points from the biblical text, while agreeing with what we know of the Jewish community in the post-exilic period. There are also some quotations, allegedly from Hecataeus, in Josephus (*Ap.* 1. 22, §§183–204), but a major question has always been whether these quotations were also authentic. B. Bar-Kochva (1996) argues that the latter are not from Hecataeus but were composed by an Egyptian Jew about 100 BCE.

A second source for the Jews in the Ptolemaic period is the Zenon papyri. Zenon was an agent of the Egyptian finance minister, and took a journey through Palestine and southern Syria in 259 BCE. He continued to correspond with a number of people whom he had met for some years afterward. The Zenon archive is therefore a treasure-trove of information relating to the region of Palestine under Ptolemaic rule. As contemporary documents, these papyri are valuable primary sources. Because of the nature of the documents, we also have first-hand information on the local economy and society. What they show is a Palestine well integrated into the Ptolemaic empire and an important source of certain products valued by the upper classes of Egypt.

Among the many documents from Zenon's archive are several letters and documents that mention Jews or relate to individuals identified as Jewish (Tcherikover, Fuks, and Stern 1957–64). One of these was a man called Tobias who was head of a military colony in what seems to have been an ancestral home on the east side of the Jordan. He appears to be a descendant of the 'Tobiah the Ammonite' mentioned in the book of Nehemiah, and also to relate to the Tobiad family whose activities later in the century are described in a section of Josephus known as the 'Tale of the Tobiads'. Tobias writes letters in Greek, not only to Zenon but to his boss Apollonius and even to the ruler Ptolemy II himself, sending gifts and speaking as one who moves in rather high circles of the Greek administration.

The story of the Tobiads told by Josephus (*AJ* 12. 4. 1–11, §§157–236) is evidently based on some sort of family chronicle. The story itself has many legendary and romantic elements. The story is that an upper-class Jew named Tobias married into the family of the Jerusalem high priest (the Oniads), went to the court of Ptolemy, and obtained the tax-farming rights to the whole region, bidding in competition with other wealthy would-be tax farmers. Through this he was able to gain wealth and power and to exercise considerable control over the region for about twenty years. He had eight sons, seven of whom sided with him, but the eighth, named Hyrcanus, rebelled and wrested the tax-farming rights away from his father. This set him against his father and brothers, but he maintained his position for many years and built a rich estate across the Jordan.

D. Gera (1990; 1998: 36–58) has written an important evaluation of the Tobiad story, concluding that the details of the account are unreliable, especially the picture of the Tobiad family as internally divided, with Joseph and his other sons against Hyrcanus. Gera's cautions are salutary. Nevertheless, it seems to tell us something about Ptolemaic Judah in the mid- to late third century BCE if used cautiously. Its main contribution is that it draws attention to a family, the Tobiads, who exercised considerable influence and leadership over a period of several generations, perhaps even centuries (Mazar 1957). It also suggests that this family made itself very much at home in Hellenistic culture and the Hellenistic world. Archaeology has confirmed the opulence of the Tobiad family home across the Jordan, though it was probably built before the time of Hyrcanus.

In sum, the picture we currently have of the Ptolemaic period is much like that of the Persian period. The sources are episodic, and information on the Jews is partial and incomplete. Yet, from a lot of different scattered bits of data, we can piece together a good deal that is interesting and significant. The high priest remains the leader of the Jewish community, even if his power appears to fluctuate over time. The Diaspora communities that we know date from as early as the Persian period (or even before?) begin to become visible. Synagogues are first attested about the middle of the third century. Powerful families such as the Tobiads, as well as the priestly Oniads, become visible. One of the most far-reaching events, though, was the translation of the Pentateuch into Greek, which was to be one of a number of developments that would be part of major changes to Judaism in transforming it from a temple-based religion to a religion of the book.

THE HASMONAEAN PERIOD

The first half of the second century BCE was a momentous time in Jewish history, yet this period is far too often misunderstood and misrepresented. It has a villain in the person of the Seleucid king Antiochus IV, yet, for all his faults, Antiochus did not differ particularly from his Seleucid ancestors or descendants except in being more able than most of them. When Antiochus the Great (III) took Palestine in 200 BCE, there were many Jews who supported the change from Ptolemaic to Seleucid rule (including, apparently, most of the Tobiad family). For the most part, the Jews seem to have had a period of calm for the first twenty-five years of Seleucid rule, apart from an alleged unsuccessful attempt to confiscate temple funds by Seleucus IV, who succeeded Antiochus III (2 Macc. 3).

When Antiochus IV Epiphanes came to the throne in 175 BCE, things changed rapidly; however, it is important to realize that Antiochus was not the one who initiated these changes. He was not the rabid 'Hellenizer' of modern scholarly legend—he had no 'mission' to bring Hellenistic culture to the native peoples, as is sometimes alleged—but he did want to expand his empire, and he needed money to do so. According to 2 Macc. 4, the Jerusalem high priest Onias III had a brother named Jason. This Jason approached Antiochus and offered him money to be given the office of high priest, which Antiochus was all too pleased to accept. Jason also asked permission to found a gymnasium in Jerusalem, which means that he was wanting to turn Jerusalem into a Greek city, or *polis*. Notice, however, that the initiative for this new state of affairs came from the Jewish side, not from Antiochus. Antiochus does not appear as a Greek ideologue but as a normal ruler interested in power and territory.

In order to understand what Jason was doing, it is important to look behind the hostile picture of 1 and 2 Maccabees (Grabbe 2002). The Jews had been part of the Hellenistic world for a century and a half by this time. As noted above, most Jews would have found Greek religion incompatible with Judaism, but many cultural aspects of Hellenism would have occasioned no problem for the Jewish way of life, and some Jews found Hellenism highly attractive. Jason was evidently one of these. If, instead of accounts hostile to Jason, we had *his* account of his 'Hellenistic Reform' (as it is often called), he would no doubt have pointed out the benefits to the Jewish people of making Jerusalem into a *polis*. For upper-class and educated individuals especially, there must have been many things about the Greek way of life that would have been alluring, not to mention opportunities to gain wealth, power, influence, and standing in the surrounding Hellenistic world. In this light, Jason's actions may have been more than just a bid for personal power and aggrandizement—they may have sprung from a strong ideological perspective about what was best for the Jews and Judaism, and perhaps even about the essence of Judaism. What becomes clear through the haze of the hostile rhetoric against Jason is that he had popular support, at least in Jerusalem.

The 'Hellenistic Reform' came to an abrupt halt after about three years, however, when an individual named Menelaus (not an Oniad, but probably a priest) outbid Jason and replaced him as high priest. Unlike Jason, who kept the temple cult and Jewish law in operation, Menelaus seems to have interfered with these. For example, it is alleged that he sold temple vessels to gain money. This rumour was believed by many from Jerusalem who rioted and killed Menelaus's brother, who had been left in charge while Menelaus was away. About the same time Antiochus invaded Egypt (c.170 BCE). He was successful, but a second invasion (168 BCE) was stopped by the Romans. Jason took the opportunity to lead an attack against

Menelaus to try to regain the high priesthood for himself. Antiochus interpreted this as a rebellion, and sent troops to put it down. For reasons which are still unclear, not only was Jerusalem subdued over the next few months, but even the practice of Judaism was prohibited.

The attempt to suppress a religion was unprecedented at the time. In a polytheistic society, all sorts of religions were normally tolerated. If a people rebelled against their imperial overlord, it would be attacked and brought back into subjection, but this did not usually affect the native religion. The later monotheistic religions did often try to suppress other religions, but for a Greek king to do so was unheard of. The possible reasons are too complicated to go into here (see Grabbe 1992: 247–56 for a discussion), but Antiochus's actions led the Jews—who had lived under foreign rulers peaceably for several centuries—to revolt against the measures. The pro-Hasmonaean books of Maccabees ascribe the revolt to the actions of the Maccabees. More likely, it began in a more complicated fashion, perhaps by the actions of several different groups, but Judas Maccabee and his brothers eventually took over the leadership.

Recent study has shown that the Maccabean Revolt was itself rather more complicated than presented in the books of Maccabees (Sievers 1990). One of the most surprising outcomes was that it succeeded; however, the alleged miraculous success of the Maccabean fighters against the Seleucid armies is actually quite explicable in terms of normal military science (Bar-Kochva 1989; Shatzman 1991). After three years the temple was retaken, ritually purified, and the cult resumed. But this was not the end of the fighting; the Jerusalem citadel was still in Seleucid hands, and the Seleucid rulers still claimed Judah as a part of their domain. Also, the Maccabees seem to have extended their original ambitions from having the religious prohibitions rescinded to the much more ambitious aim of an independent Jewish state.

Many Jews were ready to accept an accommodation with the Seleucids, and initially only a minority seemed to have supported the continuing struggle. Judas was killed about 162 BCE. His brother Jonathan took over, and eventually rallied the population behind him. But his main success came when a rival Seleucid dynasty arose to claim the throne, and Jonathan was able to play off the one against the other. He was given the office of high priest, and it was as high priests that the Hasmonaeans ruled over Judah for the next eight decades. Jonathan himself was killed in 143, to be succeeded by the last remaining Maccabee brother, Simon. In 142 BCE a major Jewish assembly acclaimed Simon as leader and formally declared its independence.

The books of 1 and 2 Maccabees are the main extant sources for the events leading up to and during the Maccabean Revolt. But after the death of Simon Maccabee in 135 BCE, Josephus becomes our main source for Jewish history. He provides the backbone on which the next 200 years of Jewish history is hung. If we did not have Josephus, our knowledge of a significant two centuries in the history of Judaism would be enormously diminished. But Josephus's very usefulness should alert us to the importance of using his works critically. One of the banes of studying Second Temple Jewish history is the extent to which Josephus is quoted without attention to his aims, bias, or sources (Cohen 1979; Grabbe 1992: 4–13).

Simon Maccabee was killed by a Jewish rival in 135 BCE, the last of the Maccabees to 'die with his boots on', and his son John Hyrcanus (I) took over. Under Hyrcanus (135–104 BCE) Jewish independence was finally achieved, and he began to expand Jewish rule into neighbouring areas. This was continued by his sons Aristobulus I (104–103 BCE) and Alexander Jannaeus (103–76 BCE). Aristobulus was apparently the first to take the title 'king', making the Hasmonaeans priest-kings. Under Alexander the Jewish kingdom probably reached its largest extent, but he was bedevilled by considerable internal opposition. Some of this opposition is alleged to have been from the Pharisees, though the extent of their influence at this time is probably exaggerated.

One of the areas of most debate in recent years is that of the major Jewish sects which seem to have arisen in this period. Although the sects are important and need to be discussed, there is a danger in that in some treatments the sects are made to dominate the whole of Judaism and Jewish worship. Most Jews were not members of sects, nor were members of sects generally the poor and oppressed, but rather those of 'middling' wealth and education (Baumgarten 1997: 47–8). Two major questions in recent scholarship are, first, the place of the Pharisees in Jewish society and, secondly, the identity of the group at Qumran. The widespread view that the Pharisees dominated Judaism by the first century CE was challenged by J. Neusner (1971, 1973) and generally supported by a number of subsequent studies (Saldarini 1988; Grabbe 1992: 467–84; 2000a: 185–99; Stemberger 1995). More recently Steve Mason has interpreted Josephus as supporting the view that the Pharisees were dominant (1991), while Lawrence Schiffman has come to somewhat similar conclusions, based on his interpretation of the Qumran scroll 4QMMT (1990b, 1990a).

Although the sources are not simple to interpret, and our knowledge of the Pharisees is actually quite limited, a careful analysis of all the sources does not show either that Pharisaic law controlled the temple and cult or that the Pharisees dominated religious practice among the people (Grabbe 1997, 1999; cf. 2000a: 185–99; 2000b). However, the view that rabbinic Judaism owes a good deal to Pharisaism seems to be correct, which means that one can say with some justification that the Pharisaic version of Judaism did come to be the most widespread form of Judaism in the centuries after the destruction of the temple.

The identity of the group at Qumran has been much debated since the discovery of the Dead Sea Scrolls in 1947, and the writers of the Scrolls have been associated with practically every Jewish group known to scholarship by some researcher or other. The most widespread identification is the Essenes, to the point that some have taken this as axiomatic; nevertheless, the Essene hypothesis has been questioned in recent years. Schiffman was one of those who doubted it, in one of his early publications (1989), and has more recently been at the forefront of those developing the view that the Qumran group was closely related to the Sadducees. The reason is 4QMMT, which is said to express a series of *halakhot* that agree with those ascribed to the Ṣĕddukîm (usually identified with the Sadducees) in rabbinic literature. In fact, of the seventeen *halakhot* in 4QMMT, only two at the most are actually parallel, while several others suggested do not in fact stand up to scrutiny (VanderKam 1992; Grabbe 1997). Also, a number of the beliefs of the historical Sadducees known to us from Josephus and other sources do not seem to agree with significant passages in either 4QMMT or 11QTorah. Thus, despite some prominent scholars who question it, the Essene hypothesis continues to dominate thinking on Qumran; but there are several versions of it. One variant is the 'Groningen hypothesis' (García Martínez 1988; van der Woude 1990), according to which the Qumran community was a breakaway group from the central Essene movement.

THE ROMAN CONQUEST AND THE REIGN OF HEROD THE GREAT

The Hasmonaeans had achieved an independent Jewish state for almost a century. When Alexander Jannaeus died, his wife, Alexandra Salome (76–67 BCE) took over. She bestowed the priesthood on her eldest son Hyrcanus (II), but the younger son Aristobulus (II) was unhappy and revolted. After Alexandra's death, the two brothers fought a civil war. Two fateful decisions happened at this time: first, Hyrcanus enlisted Antipater, the governor of Idumaea (Edom), as an advisor and aide, and, secondly, both the rival factions appealed to the Romans for support. These decisions had far-reaching consequences.

When Hyrcanus and Aristobulus appealed to Pompey, who was the legate of the Senate in the region, the latter eventually sided with Hyrcanus and his close associate, Antipater. Although Aristobulus at first resisted, he later surrendered, but his supporters in Jerusalem shut their gates to Pompey. The Romans besieged the city, which fell in the summer of 63 BCE. Hyrcanus had won, but it was a partial victory. Judah had lost its independence; Hyrcanus was high priest, but did not have the title of king. At his side was Antipater, and it became an open question as to what extent Hyrcanus was a genuine leader or only Antipater's puppet. Whatever the case, Hyrcanus and Antipater were able over time to find ways to assist the Romans and to gain their good will in return. Antipater soon brought his two sons into the administration: Phasael and Herod.

Aristobulus II's son Antigonus was allowed to return to Palestine by the Romans. About 43 BCE Antipater was poisoned by a Jewish leader, leaving his sons to carry on his legacy. Then in 40 BCE Antigonus co-operated with the Parthians in invading and occupying Palestine. The elder brother Phasael was killed, but Herod escaped to Rome, where he was made king of Judah. With Roman support he retook Jerusalem in 37 BCE, and Antigonus was executed. The Hasmonaeans had come to an end.

The first six years of Herod's rule were rather fraught ones. Although he had good relations with Mark Antony, who was in charge of the region, Cleopatra was a thorn in his side, making inroads into his territory and power. The battle of Actium in 31 BCE brought an end to both Cleopatra and Mark Antony, but was a time of danger for Herod as well. Although he had been absent from the battle, he was seen as Antony's man. However, he showed his typical courage and astuteness by confronting the victor Octavian (later Augustus Caesar) in person. Octavian evidently recognized not only his courage, but also his usefulness and, rather than punishing him, confirmed him in his office. Herod was to prove a useful ally and even (for most of the time) a good friend for the rest of his reign.

The Herodians dominated Jewish leadership during the Roman period. Herod the Great—both the man and his rule—are difficult to evaluate dispassionately. He has become one of the most notorious individuals of antiquity, but the truth is rather more complex. Although one could hardly call him benevolent by modern standards, few ancient rulers would meet our criteria. Herod was a typical petty king of the time, no worse than most of the Hasmonaean rulers and certainly no worse than many of the Roman emperors. What is clear is that he lived a Jewish life and considered himself a Jew. This is correctly recognized in the biographahy by P. Richardson (1996; cf. also Grabbe 1992: 362–6). Unfortunately, the study by N. Kokinnos (1998), although having much useful material, too often follows uncritically the bias of his sources, especially Josephus and the New Testament.

Overall, Herod's reign was good for the Jews. There is no evidence that his taxes were greater than under the Hasmonaeans, peace predominated after 31 BCE, and many Jews prospered. However, in the area of religion, Herod's reign saw a couple of significant negative developments. Under Hasmonaean rule the high priests had become monarchs, with great power. In the eyes of some, this kingly power was incompatible with the office of high priest, and the Hasmonaean court was much like the court of any other Hellenistic ruler. Thus, the deterioration of the high priestly office had already begun under the Hasmonaeans, at least in the mind of some Jews. Under Herod the power of the high priest was reduced to the opposite extreme. Herod also began the practice of removing high priests from office and replacing them by those more amenable to his views. Although those appointed were always legitimate priests from important families, it made the holder of the office to a lesser or greater extent Herod's puppet. He also had the high priestly garments locked away and made available only when they were needed for one of the festivals. The Sanhedrin also had its authority severely curtailed, with the membership decimated by multiple executions after Herod became king. All these measures can hardly have helped but cause a decline in the respect for and authority of the high priest and the temple establishment.

In the first few years of Herod's reign, he had to deal with a number of revolts, mainly instigated by support for the Hasmonaeans. But for most of his reign he kept a tight rein on opposition. As soon as he died, though, a series of revolts broke out, and had to be put down with Roman military aid. The emperor Augustus did not appoint anyone as Herod's heir, but divided the kingdom between three of the sons (Archaelaus over Judah, Idumaea, and Samaria; Herod Antipas over Peraea and Galilee; Philip over Batanaea, Trachonitis, and Auranitis). Archaelaus was not officially king, but had the title 'ethnarch', while the other two were 'tetrarchs'. Archaelaus governed approximately ten years before he was removed from office and exiled by Augustus.

THE FIRST CENTURY CE

From Archaelaus's exile in 6 CE to 66 CE, Judah was mainly under direct Roman rule. The Herodians had influence and even ruled over some of the Jews, but except for Agrippa I's brief reign (41–4 CE), Judah was under Roman governors, which created problems that eventually culminated in full-scale revolt. Some significant events took place in the Diaspora, especially in Alexandria.

Recent years have seen a new appreciation of Philo of Alexandria (c.20 BCE to c.50 CE), including a dedicated journal, the *Studia Philonica Annual* and a useful bibliographical guide (Radice and Runia 1988). As a prime example of 'Hellenistic Judaism', Philo shows how complex Judaism was. He believed that every facet of Jewish law was binding, from circumcision to the kashrut regulations, yet presented a theology that was Platonist at its core. Philo was sent on a mission to Rome because of an attack on the Alexandrian Jewish community in 38 CE. This violent response by the Greek community has commonly been associated with an agitation for citizenship on the part of some Jews. Although the issue has been much debated (cf. Grabbe 1992: 405–9), recent study has confirmed that Jews were not citizens of the Greek cities or Rome in most cases (Pucci Ben Zeev 1998).

It was while Philo was in Rome that news came of Caligula's plan to set up his statue in the Jerusalem temple (Bilde 1978). The Jewish sources and some modern scholars have presented this as caprice, prejudice, or even madness, but the reason is likely to have been more rational: a response to the Jewish destruction of a

Graeco-Roman altar in a non-Jewish area. Jews were granted certain rights to practise their religion. Contrary to frequent assertion, the Jews were not formally exempt from the emperor cult (Pucci Ben Zeev 1998), though the sacrifices in the Jerusalem temple and the many synagogue dedications served to fulfil this duty. Judaism was tolerated, but the Jews were in turn expected to tolerate the religious practices of their Greek and Roman neighbours (cf. Rajak 1984; Noethlichs 1996; Stanton and Stroumsa 1998). Caligula's plan seems to have been a response to that act of Jewish intolerance.

According to Philo and also to Josephus (the *Antiquities* but not the *War*), it was Agrippa I who interceded with Caligula to abandon his plans. Agrippa was Herod's grandson, but had been Caligula's friend in their youth. As soon as Caligula had become emperor, he had appointed Agrippa as king over Philip's old territory (Philip had died in 34 BCE). Shortly afterward, Agrippa manoeuvred the situation to have Herod Antipas removed from office and his territory also assigned to Agrippa. Under Claudius, Agrippa was given rulership over Judah itself, as Agrippa I. The brief period of his rule (41–4 CE) was seen as idyllic in retrospect, yet his rule did not differ essentially from that of his grandfather, Herod. Perhaps if he had lived longer, greater opposition would have developed. But considering the state of things when Judah reverted to direct Roman rule, it is hardly surprising that his reign would have been looked back upon with affection and nostalgia.

As the last king of Judah, Agrippa is an interesting character, though the hostile account in Acts 12 has affected his perception. The best study of Agrippa has been given by D. R. Schwartz (1990). One widespread misconception is to refer to Agrippa as 'Herod Agrippa' (D. R. Schwartz 1990: 120 n. 50, 215–16); his name was almost certainly Julius Marcus Agrippa, like that of his son. After the death of Agrippa I, one might have expected his son Agrippa II to have inherited his kingdom. However, Agrippa II was still relatively young, and for this and possibly other reasons, the emperor Claudius decided to make Judaea into a Roman province once again. This turned out to be a fateful decision. Josephus describes a 'spiral of violence' that developed in the twenty years between Agrippa I's death and the Jewish Revolt. It has been argued that this is mainly Josephus's own invention (McClaren 1998). Perhaps so, to some extent; but tensions between the Jews and the Roman occupying force would have increased as time went on. Conditions were right for Jewish opposition to Roman rule to harden at this time (Grabbe 2000a: 108–9, 283–6).

Whatever the faults of the Herodian rulers, they were decidedly preferable to direct Roman rule. Agrippa I's short reign must have raised hopes that were cruelly dashed when Judaea became a Roman province once more in 44 CE. The Roman provincial governors did not help, but used their position to pursue personal gain and objectives, often exacerbating a situation that was far from ideal. In addition, there were various groups who threatened the Roman order: revolutionaries, assassins, miracle-workers, messianic pretenders. The resistance to Roman rule by these various groups has become an area of considerable study in the past couple of decades (Horsley 1987; Horsley and Hanson 1999). The question of the 'bandits' who many now identify as 'resistance fighters' or 'social bandits' has exercised classicists as well as students of early Judaism; however, a recent study has questioned whether the term 'social bandit' is a correct one (Grünewald 1999). In any case, our sources suggest mounting unrest caused by a variety of groups, often religious in nature.

The war with Rome began in 66 CE over a couple of apparently trivial events: an incident involving the synagogue in Caesarea and the refusal of a younger temple official to offer the traditional sacrifices for the Roman emperor and his family. But if it had not been these particular events, it would have been others. It is hard to believe that it was not just a matter of time and chance before the Jews tried to throw off the Roman yoke. The discontinuing of the sacrifices for the ruler was, however, more significant than might be realized in a modern context. As already discussed above, all people in the Roman Empire were required to show their submission by engaging in the emperor cult. For the Jews the sacrifices offered daily on behalf of the emperor and his family in the Jerusalem temple were a substitute for the emperor cult. The act of refusing to offer these was unmistakably a defiance of Roman authority.

What is surprising is not that the revolt happened or that it had widespread support, but the reaction after the Jews gained some initial successes against the Romans. The Romans did not respond to the first actions of the war very effectively at all, and the Jews were able to rout two legions and drive the Roman presence from Judaea proper. The Romans could not ignore this without major consequences, but it now necessitated a massive response, involving several legions, which took time. On the Jewish side, some preparations were made, but not very extensive ones. Then, when most of Palestine had submitted and Jerusalem had been invested by 68 CE, the death of Nero and the subsequent struggle for the throne among the Romans required that the conquest of Jerusalem be put on hold. But instead of using the time to strengthen their defences and develop strategies for defeating the Romans, the different factions among the Jews in Jerusalem fought bitterly among themselves and united only when the final attack came in 70 CE.

The siege and fall of Jerusalem has received one of the fullest accounts of any such battle in history, in books 3–6 of Josephus's *War of the Jews*. As already noted above, however, Josephus's story has to be treated critically, not only because of the bias in his version of his own involvement, but also regarding who was responsible for the revolt. Two important themes of the *War* are (a) that only a few hot-headed unrepresentative no-account individuals caused all the problems on the Jewish side, and (b) that the Romans destroyed Jerusalem only reluctantly. Josephus tries to absolve both the Romans and the bulk of the Jewish people from responsibility for the revolt. This is mainly propaganda, though, like a lot of propaganda, it was done with the best of motives. The Romans reacted with military force as they did with any revolt. On the Jewish side, it was not just 'a few hotheads' who kept it going, as Josephus alleges, but widespread support among the Jews. The leadership of the revolt was in fact mainly the traditional leadership of the high priestly families, the nobility, and the Herodians, though predominantly from the younger generation, as one might expect (Price 1992).

Jerusalem fell in the summer of 70 CE; a few resisters held out for longer (e.g. Masada did not fall until 73). The Romans were not reluctant to destroy the temple, as Josephus alleges, but recognized it as a central pillar in the revolt: it was inevitable that it be razed. The reaction to the disaster seems to have varied considerably. Many Jews found accommodation with the Romans, perhaps thinking and hoping that the temple would be rebuilt and Jerusalem restored. Judging from such apocalypses as 4 Ezra and 2 Baruch written about 100 CE (cf. also the Revelation of John), some Jews evidently expected the imminent end of the world. But a few, shunning both apocalyptic and history, participated in the creation of a new religion. Creating a timeless world-view in which the eternal was mirrored in the trivia of daily lives and the observance of God's will through detailed legal regulations, rabbinic Judaism was born (Neusner 1979). A variety of pre-70 elements probably went into this synthesis, including Pharisaism, but not confined to it. Sixty years after the fall of Jerusalem, the disastrous Bar Kokhva Revolt put Jerusalem off limits to Jews, and made it clear that the temple would not be rebuilt for a long time, if ever. It was the new religious synthesis arising out of the work of a few individuals in the small coastal town of Yavneh that sustained Judaism through the dark centuries to follow.

BIBLIOGRAPHY

Much more information on most of the topics treated here, including extensive bibliography, can be found in Grabbe 1992 and 2000a.

BARCLAY, J. M. G. 1996. *Jews in the Mediterranean Diaspora from Alexander to Trajan (323 BCE–117 CE)*. Edinburgh: T. & T. Clark.

BAR-KOCHVA, B. 1989. *Judas Maccabaeus: The Jewish Struggle Against the Seleucids*. Cambridge: Cambridge University Press.

—— 1996. *Pseudo-Hecataeus, On the Jews: Legitimizing the Jewish Diaspora*. Hellenistic Culture and Society, 21. Berkeley, Los Angeles, and London: University of California Press.

BAUMGARTEN, A. I. 1997. *The Flourishing of Jewish Sects in the Maccabean Era: An Interpretation*. JSJSup 55. Leiden: Brill.

BILDE, Per 1978. 'The Roman Emperor Gaius (Caligula)'s Attempt to Erect his Statue in the Temple of Jerusalem'. *Studia Theologica*, 32: 67–93.

COHEN, S. J. D. 1979. *Josephus in Galilee and Rome: His Vita and Development as a Historian*. CSCT 8. Leiden: Brill.

DINES, J. M. 2004. *The Septuagint: Understanding the Bible and its World*. London and New York: T. & T. Clark International.

FERNÁNDEZ MARCOS, N. 2000. *The Septuagint in Context: Introduction to the Greek Versions of the Bible*, trans. W. G. E. Watson. Leiden: Brill.

GARCÍA MARTÍNEZ, F. 1988. 'Qumran Origins and Early History: A Groningen Hypothesis'. *Folio Orientalia*, 25: 113–36.

GERA, D. 1990. 'On the Credibility of the History of the Tobiads'. In A. Kasher, U. Rappaport, and G. Fuks, eds., *Greece and Rome in Eretz Israel: Collected Essays*, Jerusalem: Israel Exploration Society, 21–38.

—— 1998. *Judaea and Mediterranean Politics 219 to 161 B.C.E.* Brill's Series in Jewish Studies, 8. Leiden: Brill.

GRABBE, L. L. 1992. *Judaism from Cyrus to Hadrian*, i: *Persian and Greek Periods*; ii: *Roman Period*. Minneapolis: Fortress Press; repr. London: SCM, 1994.

—— 1997. '4QMMT and Second Temple Jewish Society'. In M. Bernstein, F. García Martínez, and J. Kampen, eds., *Legal Texts and Legal Issues: Proceedings of the Second Meeting of the International Organization for Qumran Studies, Cambridge 1995, Published in Honour of Joseph M. Baumgarten*, STDJ 23, Leiden: Brill, 89–108.

—— 1999. 'Sadducees and Pharisees'. In Jacob Neusner and Alan J. Avery-Peck, eds., *Judaism in Late Antiquity*, Part III: *Where We stand: Issues and Debates in Ancient Judaism*, i, Handbuch der Orientalistik: Erste Abteilung, der Nahe und Mittlere Osten, 40, Leiden: Brill, 35–62.

—— 2000a. *Judaic Religion in the Second Temple Period: Belief and Practice from the Exile to Yavneh*. London and New York: Routledge.

—— 2000b. 'The Pharisees—A Response to Steve Mason'. In Alan J. Avery-Peck and Jacob Neusner, eds., *Judaism in Late Antiquity, Part Three: Where We Stand: Issues and Debates in Ancient Judaism*, iii, Handbuch der Orientalistik: Erste Abteilung, Der Nahe und Mittlere Osten, 53, Leiden: Brill, 35–47.

—— 2002. 'The Hellenistic City of Jerusalem'. In John R. Bartlett, ed., *Jews in the Hellenistic and Roman Cities*, London: Routledge, 6–21.

GRÜNEWALD, T. 1999. *Räuber, Rebellen, Rivalen, Rächer: Studien zu* Latrones *im Römischen Reich*. Forschungen zur antiken Sklaverei, 31. Stuttgart: Franz Steiner.

HENGEL, M. 1974. *Judaism and Hellenism: Studies in their Encounter in Palestine during the Early Hellenistic Period*, 2 vols. Minneapolis: Fortress; London: SCM.

HORSLEY, R. A. 1987. *Jesus and the Spiral of Violence: Popular Jewish Resistance in Roman Palestine*. San Francisco: Harper.

—— with Hanson, John S. 1999. *Bandits, Prophets, and Messiahs: Popular Movements at the Time of Jesus*, 1985 edn. with new preface. Harrisburg, Pa.: Trinity Press International.

KOKKINOS, N. 1998. *The Herodian Dynasty: Origins, Role in Society and Eclipse*. Journal for the Study of the Pseudepigrapha Supplement, 30. Sheffield: Sheffield Academic Press.

KUHRT, A., and Sherwin-White, Susan, eds. 1987. *Hellenism in the East*. London: Duckworth.

McCLAREN, J. S. 1998. *Turbulent Times? Josephus and Scholarship on Judaea in the First Century CE*. JSPSup 29. Sheffield: Sheffield Academic Press.

MASON, S. 1991. *Flavius Josephus on the Pharisees: A Composition-Critical Study*. SPB 39. Leiden: Brill.

—— 1999. 'Revisiting Josephus's Pharisees'. In Alan Avery-Peck and Jacob Neusner, eds., *Judaism in Late Antiquity*, vol. 4, pt. II, HdO: Erste Abteilung, Der Nahe und Mittlere Osten, Bd. 53, Leiden: Brill, 23–56.

MAZAR, B. 1957. 'The Tobiads'. *IEJ* 7: 137–45, 229–38.

NEUSNER, J. 1971. *The Rabbinic Traditions about the Pharisees before 70*, 3 vols. Leiden: Brill.

—— 1973. *From Politics to Piety*. Englewood Cliffs, NJ: Prentice-Hall.

—— 1979. 'The Formation of Rabbinic Judaism: Yavneh (Jamnia) from A.D. 70 to 100'. ANRW II: 19. 2. 3–42.

NOETHLICHS, K. L. 1996. *Das Judentum und der römische Staat: Minderheitenpolitik im antiken Rom*. Darmstadt: Wissenschaftliche Buchgesellschaft.

PRICE, J. J. 1992. *Jerusalem under Siege: The Collapse of the Jewish State 66–70 CE*. Brill's Series in Jewish Studies, 3. Leiden: Brill.

PUCCI BEN ZEEV, M. 1998. *Jewish Rights in the Roman World: The Greek and Roman Documents Quoted by Josephus Flavius*. Texte und Studien zum Antiken Judentum, 74. Tübingen: Mohr (Siebeck).

RADICE, R., and RUNIA, D. T. 1988. *Philo of Alexandria: An Annotated Bibliography 1937–1986*. VigChrSupp 8. Leiden: Brill.

RAJAK, T. 1984. 'Was There a Roman Charter for the Jews?' *JRS* 74: 107–23.

RICHARDSON, P. 1996. *Herod: King of the Jews and Friend of the Romans*. Studies on Personalities of the New Testament. Columbia, SC: University of South Carolina Press.

SALDARINI, A. J. 1988. *Pharisees, Scribes and Sadducees in Palestinian Society: A Sociological Approach*. Wilmington, Del.: Glazier; Edinburgh: T. & T. Clark.

SCHIFFMAN, L. H. 1989. *The Eschatological Community of the Dead Sea Scrolls: A Study of the Rule of the Congregation*. SBLMS 38; Atlanta: Scholars Press.

—— 1990a. '*Miqsat Ma'aseh Ha-Torah* and the *Temple Scroll*'. *RevQ* 14: 435–57.

—— 1990b. 'The New Halakhic Letter (4QMMT) and the Origins of the Dead Sea Sect'. *BA* 53: 64–73.

SCHWARTZ, D. R. 1990. *Agrippa I: The Last King of Judaea*. TSAJ 23. Tübingen: Mohr (Siebeck).

SCHWARTZ, S. 1990. *Josephus and Judaean Politics*. CSCT 18. Leiden: Brill.

SHATZMAN, I. 1991. *The Armies of the Hasmonaeans and Herod: From Hellenistic to Roman Frameworks*. TSAJ 25. Tübingen: Mohr (Siebeck).

SHERWIN-WHITE, S., and KUHRT, AMÉLIE 1993. *From Samarkhand to Sardis: A New Approach to the Seleucid Empire*. London: Duckworth.

SIEVERS, J. 1990. *The Hasmoneans and their Supporters: From Mattathius to the Death of John Hyrcanus I*. SFSJH 6. Atlanta: Scholars.

STANTON, G. N., and Stroumsa, Guy G., eds. 1998. *Tolerance and Intolerance in Early Judaism and Christianity*. Cambridge: Cambridge University Press.

STEMBERGER, G. 1995. *Jewish Contemporaries of Jesus: Pharisees, Sadducees, Essenes*, trans. Allan W. Mahnke. Minneapolis: Fortress.

TCHERIKOVER, V. A., 1959. *Hellenistic Civilization and the Jews*. New York: Jewish Publication Society.

—— FUKS, A., and STERN, M. 1957–64. *Corpus Papyrorum Judaicarum*, 3 vols. Cambridge, Mass.: Harvard University Press; Jerusalem: Magnes.

VANDERKAM, J. 1992. 'The People of the Dead Sea Scrolls: Essenes or Sadducees?' In H. Shanks, ed., *Understanding the Dead Sea Scrolls: A Reader from the* Biblical Archaeology Review, New York: Random House, 50–62, 300–2; originally *Bible Review*, 7/2 (April 1991), 42–7.

WOUDE, A. S. VAN DER 1990. 'A "Groningen" Hypothesis of Qumran Origins and Early History'. *RevQ* 14: 521–42.

CHAPTER 17

THE LIFE AND TEACHING OF JESUS AND THE RISE OF CHRISTIANITY

CRAIG A. EVANS

The beginning of critical research into the life of Jesus is traditionally traced to the posthumous publication of seven fragments of a lengthy manuscript on 'reasonable religion' by Hermann Samuel Reimarus (1694–1768) (see Reimarus 1970). These fragments were edited by Gotthold Ephraim Lessing (1729–81). It was fragment 7, entitled *Von dem Zwecke Jesu und seiner Jünger* ('On the Aim of Jesus and his Disciples') and published in 1778, that gained most of the attention. Reimarus believed that Jesus had not anticipated his death, but had hoped to become Israel's earthly Messiah. After the crucifixion, his disciples stole his corpse, reformulated his teachings, and proclaimed his resurrection and return as triumphant King Messiah. This critical assessment of the Gospel story of Jesus inaugurated the scholarly quest of the historical Jesus.

The nineteenth-century 'Old Quest' of the historical Jesus represents the first major phase of this scholarly quest. In his *Das Leben Jesu kritisch bearbeitet* ('The Life of Jesus Critically Examined') (2 vols., 1835–6: see Strauss 1846) David Friedrich Strauss (1808–74) argued that the Gospels do not present us with history, whether embellished with supernatural elements (so the liberal rationalists), or not (so the conservatives), but present us with myth. Liberal and conservative scholars alike opposed this radical scepticism, and searched for what was then regarded as 'historical' material. For a short time the Gospel of John was viewed as the most promising source, because it lacked some of the miraculous features characteristic of the synoptics (e.g. the virgin birth, demonic exorcisms), which many scholars viewed as mythological. Ferdinand Christian Baur, however, concluded that John was written late in the second century, and brought an end to this thinking (1847), and it was then concluded that the historical Jesus would have to be found in the synoptic gospels after all. In *Die synoptischen Evangelien: Ihr Ursprung und geschich-tlicher Charakter*, a study of the origin and historical character of the synoptic gospels, Heinrich Julius Holtzmann (1832–1920) showed that a version of Mark was written first, and that Matthew and Luke used it and another source of sayings (later called 'Q'). Mark and Q became the sources from which a historical Jesus might be reconstructed (1863). Most scholars assumed that these sources were relatively free from mythological embellishment.

With the appearance of certain publications at the turn of the century, it became evident that the old quest had not been successful. In 1892 Martin Kähler (1835–1912) published a brief essay, 'The So-Called Historical Jesus and the Historic, Biblical Christ', in which he argued that the historical Jesus of the nineteenth-century quest bore little resemblance to, or had little significance for, the Christ of Christian faith (1964). That same year Johannes Weiss (1863–1914) argued that Jesus was not a social reformer, but an apocalyptic prophet who summoned people to repent because judgement was near (see Wrede 1971). In 1901 William Wrede (1859–1906) published *Das Messiasgeheimnis in den Evangelien* ('The Messianic Secret in the Gospels'), in which he argued that far from being a simple historical account, Mark's Gospel was a theologically oriented document comparable to John's Gospel (1971). Finally, the appearance in 1906 of *Von Reimarus zu Wrede* (see Schweitzer 2000), in which Albert Schweitzer (1875–1965) concluded that Jesus had died a deluded apocalyptic fanatic, led many scholars and theologians to believe that the quest of the historical Jesus was impossible (so the form critics) and perhaps even illegitimate (so many neo-orthodox theologians). Speaking as a form critic, Rudolf Bultmann (1884–1976) once stated that 'we can now know almost nothing concerning the life and personality of Jesus' (1926: 8). The popular neo-orthodox theologian Emil Brunner (1889–1966) claimed that 'the Christian faith does not arise out of the picture of the historical Jesus', and that 'the Jesus of history is not the same as the Christ of faith' (1934: 159). Moreover, the recognition, thanks largely to Schweitzer, that the lives of Jesus of the old quest reflected the issues and emphases of each generation of scholars (the major error of the old quest) led many to suppose that the objectivity necessary for a truly fair portrait of Jesus simply could not be had. Therefore, in many circles the scholarly quest was abandoned.

It was during this time that Palestinian archaeology developed. Edward Robinson (1794–1863), Charles Gordon (1833–85), Charles Clermont-Ganneau (1846–1923), Marie-Joseph Lagrange (1855–1938), Franz Cumont (1868–1947), Raymond Weill (1874–1950), and others were among the early pioneers. Excavations in and around Jerusalem and other sites began clarifying aspects of the itinerary and activities of Jesus and his followers. Although this work had little impact on Bultmann and his students, it did plant seeds that would later bear fruit.

In 1953 Ernst Käsemann (1906–98) read a paper entitled 'Das Problem des historischen Jesus' ('The Problem of the Historical Jesus'), which inaugurated a new quest of the historical Jesus among Bultmannian scholars. Käsemann argued that a new quest, one that was careful to avoid the errors of the old quest, was historically possible and theologically necessary. A link between the Christ of faith and the Jesus of history was necessary if Christianity were to avoid lapsing into a form of docetic Gnosticism. While Käsemann emphasized the recovery of certain authentic sayings of Jesus, Ernst Fuchs (1903–83) argued for the presence of certain authentic actions or attitudes.

In its time the new quest generated a great deal of excitement. The theological and apologetic orientation of most of this work, however, is quite apparent. To what extent it can even be described as 'historical' is an open question. Its failure to take into account the land of Israel, the remains of material culture, and much of the Judaic literature of late antiquity probably accounts for the minimal contribution made by this phase of research.

In the 1960s and 1970s life of Jesus research was continued, but often the emphasis was placed on Jesus as a social or political figure, rather than as one relevant for faith (as the emphasis had been during the new quest). To mention one example, Jesus became the champion of the poor and the oppressed, and as such became the inspiration for liberation theologies. Although the legitimacy of some of this work cannot be denied, one cannot help but wonder if the basic error of the old quest was recurring.

Some of the studies that appeared in the 1970s and 1980s, however, seem to represent a quest not governed primarily by theological or political agendas. Jewish scholars are now active participants in the discussion. The emphasis is on seeing Jesus against the background of first-century Palestinian Judaism. Unlike the 'new quest', which had emphasized discontinuity between Jesus and his contemporaries, the more recent studies tend to emphasize continuity and context. Scholars now speak of a 'third quest'. Others recommend eschewing 'quest' language altogether and speaking, instead, of 'Jesus research'. This phase of research has been marked by significant progress, thanks to the recent publication of many writings from late antiquity (e.g. rabbinic, targumic, and the Dead Sea Scrolls) and the investigation of Palestine (e.g. from the point of view of archaeology, history, and sociology).

1. LIFE AND TEACHING OF JESUS

1.1 Social, Political, and Economic Setting of the Life of Jesus

Ongoing archaeological and social-scientific work in Galilee has underscored the strongly Judaic character of this region, notwithstanding significant Graeco-Roman populations in certain cities and centres. The development of major cities at Tiberias, which is located on the west bank of Lake Gennesaret, and Sepphoris, which is about four miles north-west of Nazareth, where Jesus grew up, and the discovery of impressive Graeco-Roman architecture and artefacts, have led some scholars to exaggerate the extent of the Hellenization of Galilee. Accordingly, some have suggested that the Jewish people of Galilee were for the most part not strict in the observance of their faith, and that Graeco-Roman philosophies, including Cynicism, were influential even among the Jewish population. It has even been suggested that Jesus himself came under the influence of Cynic teaching, perhaps emanating from nearby Sepphoris.

However, the archaeological data do not bear out this interpretation, especially in reference to Sepphoris. Among the faunal remains that date before 70 CE archaeologists have found virtually no pig bones, which is inexplicable if we are to imagine the presence of a significant non-Jewish population. In contrast, after 70 CE and after a sizeable growth in the non-Jewish population, pig bones come to represent 30 per cent of the faunal remains. Over 100 fragments of stone vessels have been unearthed so far, again pointing to a Jewish population concerned with ritual purity (cf. John 2: 6). Consistent with this concern is the presence of many *miqvaoth*, or ritual bathing-pools. Coins minted at Sepphoris during this period do not depict the image of the Roman emperor or pagan deities (as was common in the coinage of this time). By contrast, in the second century coins were minted at Sepphoris bearing the images of the emperors Trajan (98–117 CE) and Antoninus Pius (138–161 CE) and the deities Tyche and the Capitoline triad. Indeed, in the reign of Antoninus Pius the city adopted the name Diocaesarea, in honour of Zeus (Dio) and the Roman emperor (Caesar). The discovery of a Hebrew ostracon and several lamp fragments bearing the image of the menorah (the seven-branched candelabra) and dating from the first century CE, along with the absence of structures typically present in a Graeco-Roman city (such as pagan temples, gymnasium, odeum, nymphaeum, or shrines and statues), lead to the firm conclusion that Sepphoris in Jesus' day was a thoroughly Jewish city. Finally, the distribution of Jewish and non-Jewish pottery in Galilee lends additional support to this conclusion. Whereas non-Jews purchased Jewish pottery, the Jews of Galilee did not purchase and make use of pottery manufactured by non-Jews. Accordingly, Jewish pottery that dates prior to 70 CE is found in Jewish and non-Jewish sectors in and around Galilee, whereas non-Jewish pottery is limited to the non-Jewish sectors. These patterns of distribution strongly suggest that the Jewish people of Galilee were scrupulous in their observance of Jewish purity laws.

The political dominance of Galilee (and Israel as a whole) by Rome and its client rulers, the Herodians, constitutes the essential background of Jesus' life and teaching in general, especially his announcement of the in-breaking rule of God. Proclamation of the 'kingdom of God' would have been viewed by contemporaries as a direct challenge to Roman authority, in which the Roman emperor was viewed as 'son of God' and the 'beginning', or first cause, of all good for the inhabited earth (e.g. *OGIS* no. 458. 40–2 (birthday of Augustus); *P Oxy.* 1021. 10 (accession of Nero)). The incipit of the Marcan Gospel, admittedly part of the evangelist's apologetic and evangelistic strategy, none the less captures the essence of Jesus' challenge to Rome: 'The beginning of the good news of Jesus Christ, the son of God' (Mark 1: 1). The proclamation of the rule of God amounted to a call to the end of the political establishment.

Resentment of this political dominance sometimes led to insurrection, in Galilee and in Judaea and neighbouring territories. Josephus catalogues a number of Jewish men who in one way or another attempted to exert leadership. Although it is debated, some of these men may have thought of themselves as Davidic successors, perhaps even possessing messianic qualifications. Popular prophets also appeared on the scene, including John the Baptizer, whose actions at the River Jordan were concerned with Israel's redemption.

Literary and archaeological evidence suggests that in the early decades of the first century Galilee was for the most part prosperous. Its economic base was primarily agrarian. Writing from first-hand observation, Josephus describes the soil as rich, supporting various crops and orchards (*BJ* 3. 3. 2 §§42–3), with the result that Galilee boasted more than 200 villages and small cities (*Vit.* 45, §235). Although Josephus exaggerates the fecundity of the land and the size of the populations of the villages and cities, other sources, including archaeological excavations, provide general, if somewhat more modest, corroboration. Some of the most important excavations include those at Capernaum, Sepphoris, Tiberias, Caesarea Maritima, Bethsaida, Nazareth, and Cana of Galilee.

Ongoing archaeological work in Nazareth has revealed surprising evidence of stone masonry and viticulture. Although the extent of archaeological investigation thus far is quite limited (owing to the fact that modern Nazareth is a large, inhabited city), all indications at present suggest that Nazareth of late antiquity—in close proximity to a major highway linking Caesarea Maritima in the west to Tiberias in the east—was an active and productive centre, whose inhabitants would in all probability have had no need to seek employment in outlying areas. Portraits of Nazareth as a sleepy, isolated village are the stuff of pious imagination and hagiography, not critical study.

Lake Gennesaret (or popularly the Sea of Galilee), some 13 miles in length (north to south) and 3 to 7 miles wide, is situated about 700 feet below sea level. In the time of Jesus the lake supported (and still supports) a thriving fishing industry (cf. Strabo, *Geog.* 16. 2; Pliny, *HN* 5. 15; Josephus, *BJ* 3. 10. 7, §§506–8; Mark 1: 16–20 parr.; Luke 5: 1–10; John 21: 1–11). A network of roads encouraged a modicum of commerce, especially in the case of pottery, whose production was limited to areas that possessed sufficient amounts of appropriate clay. Most of the pottery in use in Galilee was produced at Kefar Shikhin, near Sepphoris, and Kefar Hananyah, situated near the centre of Galilee.

These archaeological and geographical considerations are consistent with literary sources, which suggest that most economic activity in Israel in this period of time was agrarian, centred on the production of food, and domestic, based largely on the labour of the family. Most families owned small parcels of land, which produced vegetables, grain, grapes, and olives. Some facilities, such as presses and mills, were shared by clusters of families or by whole villages. There was some commercial farming, supported by landless peasants and labourers. Most families produced their own clothing, shoes, and furniture, though there was trade, and some men and women were artisans and tradesmen. Jesus himself was called a 'carpenter' (*tekton*) or 'son of a carpenter' (Mark 6: 3; Matt. 13: 55). There were also professionals and retainers, such as priests, physicians, scribes, stewards, and collectors (at various ranks) of tolls and taxes. There were also persons who filled various offices of authority. These included magistrates, judges, and various Roman officers, including the governor (who in Jesus' time served at the rank of *praefectus*) and centurions.

Questions of education and literacy are also important. The evidence is compelling that Jesus was formed in the context of Israel's historic faith, as mediated by the Scriptures, as read and interpreted in the synagogue. Jesus was conversant with Israel's great story and fully embraced the redemptive vision of the prophets. His message, 'the kingdom of God has drawn near' (Mark 1: 14–15), is derived from Isaiah (e.g. 40: 9: 'behold your God'; 52: 7: 'your God reigns'), as paraphrased in the Aramaic Targum: 'The kingdom of your God is revealed!' Jesus prayed the prayers of the synagogue, again probably in Aramaic. The closest parallel to the well-known Lord's Prayer (Matt. 6: 9–13 = Luke 11: 2–4: 'Our Father in heaven, may your name be sanctified, may your kingdom come . . .') is the Aramaic prayer called the Qaddish: 'May his name be magnified and sanctified . . . and may he establish his kingdom in your lifetime . . .'. These observations in turn support the widely held opinion that Jesus' mother tongue was Aramaic, the language that had dominated the eastern Mediterranean for centuries.

The evidence also strongly suggests that Jesus frequented the synagogue, and that he was Torah-observant, even if his understanding of the oral law was significantly different from the understanding of others, such as the Pharisees. The Gospels portray Jesus as frequently debating the meaning of Scripture or the legitimacy of various aspects of the oral law. How well versed in Scripture was Jesus? Could he read? The evangelists assume that Jesus in fact could read (as seen, for example, in Luke 4: 16–30).

Although there is no unambiguous evidence for the literacy of Jesus, there is considerable contextual and circumstantial evidence that suggests that in all probability he was literate. According to the Shema', which all Torah-observant Jews were expected to recite daily, parents were to teach their children Torah (cf. Deut. 4: 9; 6: 7; 11: 19; 31: 12–13; 2 Chr. 17: 7–9; Eccles. 12: 9), even to adorn their doorposts with the Shema' (Deut. 6: 9; 11: 20). According to Philo and Josephus, approximate contemporaries of Jesus, Jewish parents taught their children Torah and how to read it (cf. Philo, *Leg.* 31, §210; Josephus, *Ap.* 1. 12, §60; 2. 25 §204). Josephus declares that 'most men, so far from living in accordance with their own laws, hardly know what they are. . . . But, should anyone of our nation be questioned about the laws, he would repeat them all more readily than his own name. The result, then, of our thorough grounding in the laws from the first dawn of intelligence is that we have them, as it were, engraved on our souls' (cf. *Ap.* 2. 18, §§176, 178). Apart from the obvious exaggeration, this claim may not be too wide of the truth, for Augustine claims that Seneca made a similar remark: 'The Jews, however, are aware of the origin and meaning of their rites. The greater part of (other) people go through a ritual not knowing why they do so' (*De civ. D.* 6. 11).

The probability that Jesus was literate is supported, if not confirmed, by his recognition as 'Rabbi' (e.g. Mark 9: 5; 11: 21; 14: 45) or its Greek equivalent 'teacher' (e.g. Mark 4: 38; 5: 35; 9: 17). Jesus refers to himself in this manner, and is called such by supporters, opponents, and non-partisans. Although prior to 70 CE the designation 'Rabbi' is informal, even vague, and lacks the later connotations of formal training and ordination, which obtain sometime after the destruction of Jerusalem and the Temple, it is very probable that at least a limited literacy was assumed.

The simplest explanation of the data we have is a literate Jesus, a Jesus who could read the Hebrew Scriptures, could paraphrase and interpret them in Aramaic, and could do so in a manner that indicated his familiarity with current interpretive tendencies in both popular circles (as in the synagogues) and in professional, even élite circles (as seen in debates with scribes, ruling priests, and elders). Of course, to conclude that Jesus was literate is not necessarily to conclude that Jesus had received formal scribal training. The data do not suggest this. Jesus' innovative, experiential approach to Scripture and to Jewish faith seems to suggest the contrary.

It should also be mentioned that there is compelling evidence for the existence of synagogue buildings in the time of Jesus, where the faithful could gather (as the Greek word *synagogē* means), to read and interpret Scripture, sing Psalms, pray, and socialize. The evidence for these buildings is seen in Josephus (cf. *BJ* 2. 285–9; 7. 44; *AJ* 19. 305) and in Philo (cf. *Prob.* 81–2), as well as in the Theodotos inscription (*CIJ* no. 1404), found in Jerusalem, which thanks various persons for donating money for the building of the synagogue, and in the Berenike synagogue inscription from Cyrene (*SEG* XVII 823), which dates to the year 56 CE. Moreover, the ruins of a synagogue at Jericho have been dated to the first century BCE, and the old basalt foundation beneath the newer limestone synagogue at Capernaum probably also dates from the first century BCE.

It was in the context of village life, in the vicinity of Sepphoris, that Jesus participated in the activities of the synagogue, hearing Scripture read and interpreted, and hearing and saying prayers. It was in this context that Jesus' religious consciousness took shape, and it is in the light of this context that his preaching and activities should be studied.

1.2 The Teaching and Activity of Jesus

The admission in the Gospels that Jesus was baptized by John is one of the most certain data of the tradition (cf. Mark 1: 9–11; Matt. 3: 13–17; Luke 3: 21–2; John 1: 29–34). It suggests that Jesus was for a time a disciple of John. There are important indications that this was the case. Jesus' proclamation of the kingdom of God (Mark 1: 14–15) may very well have emerged from an eschatological understanding of Isaiah 40 held in common with John, for the latter apparently appealed to Isa. 40: 3 ('prepare the way of the Lord') while the former appealed to Isa. 40: 9 in the Aramaic ('the kingdom of your God is revealed'). John spoke of 'these stones', which may have alluded to the twelve stones (= twelve tribes of Israel) placed by the River Jordan by Joshua, on the occasion of entry into the Promised Land (cf. Josh. 4). Jesus' appointment of twelve apostles (Mark 3: 14; 6: 30; Matt. 19: 28; Luke 22: 28–30) may very well have held a similar meaning. Lastly, Jesus' implicit claim to be the one 'mightier' than the 'strong man' (i.e. Satan) in Mark 3: 23–7 in all probability answers John's anticipation of the coming of one 'mightier' than himself (Mark 1: 7). These points of coherence between Jesus and John suggest that the latter played an important role in the formation of the former.

Jesus' proclamation that 'the kingdom of God has arrived' is to be understood, as mentioned above, in reference to the Aramaic paraphrase. 'Kingdom' (*basileia/ malkuth*) refers to God's rule or power. That is, the rule of oppressive humans (such as the Romans, the Herodians, or even the priestly aristocrats of Jerusalem) has come to an end; the rule of God is now at hand.

Jesus began this proclamation in Galilee, preaching in synagogues, in private homes, and out in the open countryside. His proclamation was accompanied by exorcisms and healings, which would have been viewed by his contemporaries not only as fulfilment of prophecy (as in Isa. 35: 5–6; 61: 1–2), but as tangible evidence that the power of God was truly present in Jesus. Accordingly, Jesus affirms, in the context of controversy over the source of his exorcistic power: 'But if it is by the finger of God that I cast out demons, then the kingdom of God has come upon you' (Luke 11: 20; cf. Matt. 12: 28).

It was Jesus' success as a healer and exorcist, as much as his proclamation, that attracted crowds. The discovery and analysis of hundreds of skeletons and skeletal remains have told us much about the health and longevity of the people in Palestine in late antiquity. It gives us pause to discover that in a typical two- or three-generation burial crypt, more than half of the skeletons are of children. Indeed, in some cases two-thirds of the remains are of children. It needs to be pointed out, too, that most of these excavated tombs belonged to the affluent—that is, to those who had access to sufficient food, clothing, shelter, and physicians. From data such as these, some historical anthropologists have speculated that on any given day as many as one-fourth of the population in Jesus' time was ill, injured, or in need of medical attention. This grim speculation gives new meaning to the Gospels' notice of pressing crowds (e.g. Mark 3: 10; 4: 1; 5: 27–8).

Jesus' success in exorcism and healing evidently also provided important messianic confirmation for him and his disciples. His allusion to Isaiah 61 and to other words and phrases from Isaiah, in response to the sceptical question of the imprisoned Baptist (Matt. 11: 2–6 // Luke 7: 18–23), is almost certainly a messianic affirmation. We can say this now because of the discovery of 4Q521, which appeals to the same Isaianic words and phrases, speaking of the Messiah in the context of healing and proclaiming good news.

The parallels between 4Q521 and Jesus' exchange with John strongly suggest that Jesus did indeed see himself in messianic terms, though precisely how his messianism was defined is not certain. After Easter, his followers proclaimed Jesus Messiah of Israel. This widespread, even unanimous, tradition supports this conclusion. How this conviction altered the message of Jesus will be considered below.

Jesus also summed up his proclamation as the 'good news' (*euaggelion/besorah*) of the arrival of God's rule (cf. Isa. 40: 9; 52: 7; 61: 1). Although repentance was required (Mark 1: 15; 6: 12; Matt. 11: 20; Luke 5: 32; 13: 3, 5; 15: 7), as it had been in John's preaching (Mark 1: 4; Matt. 3: 8), Jesus proclaimed God's forgiveness and called on his contemporaries to forgive one another (Mark 2: 10; 11: 25; Matt. 6: 12; 18: 21, 35; Luke 6: 37). Indeed, Jesus even claimed to have heavenly authority to forgive sins (Mark 2: 5, 10).

Jesus' association with 'sinners', who presumably had repented and been assured of their forgiveness (outside priestly and scribal conventions), not surprisingly occasioned criticism (Mark 2: 15–17; Matt. 18–19 // Luke 7: 33–5). This association with sinners, as part of the teaching on forgiveness, formed an important component of early Christian ethics. Although Jesus did not teach the abrogation of the Jewish Law, the practice of forgiveness apart from the conventions of priest and temple, and the willingness to associate freely with those accordingly forgiven, created a theological and ethical matrix that would later facilitate Christianity's movement away from Jewish faith and practice, as they were emerging in the first century.

1.3 The Death of Jesus

Jesus' death was the result of his entry into Jerusalem, where he threatened the ruling priestly establishment. Jesus' controversial teachings regarding sabbath, purity, and forgiveness seem to have played little or no role in his arrest and execution.

Jesus' entry was probably guided by and interpreted in the light of passages from Zechariah and Psalm 118, evidently as nuanced in the setting of the Aramaic-speaking synagogue (Mark 11: 1–11; cf. Zech. 9: 9; Ps. 118: 25–6). These Scriptures continue to play a role in Passion Week, with Jesus forbidding commercial traffic in the temple precincts (Mark 11: 15–18; cf. Zech. 14: 20–1), identifying himself as the stone rejected by the builders (Mark 12: 10–12; cf. Ps. 118: 22–3), and as the shepherd struck down by God (Mark 14: 26–7; cf. Zech. 13: 7). The words of institution probably also allude to Zechariah (Mark 14: 24; cf. Zech. 9: 11). Although it is true that the later evangelists, especially Matthew, embellish these allusions, sometimes upgrading them to formal quotations (as at Matt. 21: 4–5; John 12: 14–15), their allusive presence in Mark suggests that they were part of the earliest tradition, and probably derived from the words and actions of Jesus himself.

Whether Jesus anticipated his death and resurrection remains an item of debate. His anticipation of death seems probable, for the violent fate of John the Baptist surely impressed itself on Jesus (Mark 6: 14–29; 9: 13). What is more compelling is the scene in Gethsemane, in which the frightened Jesus falls on his face, begging God to take away the cup of suffering (Mark 14: 33–6). This is not the stuff of pious fiction or dogma. Indeed, it stands in stark contrast to the serene Jesus portrayed in John 17.

Of course, if Jesus anticipated his death, it is probable that he attempted to find meaning in it. The words of institution should be interpreted in this light. In the shedding of his blood, Jesus finds guarantee of the covenant and the kingdom of God (Mark 14: 22–5). Luke's addition of 'new', as in 'the new covenant' (Luke 22: 20), is redactional, to be sure, but it probably correctly captures the sense of Jesus' words. The 'new covenant' hearkens back to the promise of Jer. 31: 31. The new covenant cannot be established until the blood of God's Son, Israel's Messiah, is shed.

The idea of the saving benefit of a righteous man's death is hardly unusual in the Jewish world, or in the Mediterranean world in general, for that matter. There are several expressions of the belief that the death of the righteous will benefit, or even save, God's people (e.g. 1 Macc. 6: 44; 4 Macc. 1: 11; 17: 21–2; 18: 3–4; *T. Moses* 9–10; Ps.-Philo, *Bib. Ant.* 18: 5). Among the most important are traditions associated with the torture and death of the Maccabean martyrs.

If our living Lord is angry for a little while, to rebuke and discipline us, he will again be reconciled with his own servants . . . I, like my brothers, give up body and life for the laws of our fathers, appealing to God to show mercy soon to our nature . . . and *through me and my brothers* to bring to an end the wrath of the Almighty which has justly fallen on our whole nation. (2 Macc. 7: 33, 37–8, emphasis added)

Similarly, Jesus believed that God was angry with his people for having rejected his message. We see this in Jesus' weeping over the city (Luke 19: 41–4; Matt. 23: 37–9 = Luke 13: 34–5) and in his ominous allusion to the shepherd in Zech. 13: 7.

If Jesus did anticipate his death, did he anticipate his resurrection as well? Had he not anticipated it, it would have been very strange, for pious Jews very much believed in the resurrection (Dan. 12: 1–3; *1 Enoch* 22–7; 92–105; *Jubilees* 23: 11–31; 4 Macc. 7: 3; 4 Ezra 7: 26–42; 2 Bar. 21: 23; 30: 2–5; Josephus, *BJ* 2. 8. 11, §154; 2. 8. 14, §§165–6; *AJ* 18. 1. 3–5, §§14, 16, 18). One is reminded of the seven martyred sons and their mother, several of whom expressed their firmest conviction of the resurrection (2 Macc. 7: 14, 23, 29; cf. 4 Macc. 8–17). Would Jesus have faced death and then, having earlier affirmed his belief in the resurrection (Mark 12: 18–27), have expressed no faith in his own vindication? Surely not. It seems probable that Jesus would have reassured his disciples (and himself) with a confident prediction of his resurrection.

The words of Jesus, 'after three days rise again' (Mark 8: 31) and—in the other gospels—'on the third day' (Matt. 16: 21; Luke 9: 22; cf. 1 Cor. 15: 4), probably allude to the oracle of Hosea that promised the renewal of Israel: 'After two days he will revive us; on the third day he will raise us up, that we may live before him' (6: 2), though, again, as refracted through the Aramaic tradition: 'He will revive us *in the days of consolations that will come; on the day of the resurrection of the dead* he will raise us up and we shall live before him' (*Tg. Hos.* 6: 2, with italicized portion indicating differences in the Aramaic). Not only has the text been paraphrased to give expression to the resurrection (which was not the original meaning of the underlying Hebrew), it has also taken on a messianic nuance with the words 'in the days of consolations' (cf. *Tg. 2 Sam.* 23: 1). The coherence of Jesus' words with the Aramaic tradition is striking.

The juridical process that overtook Jesus (arrest, interrogation by Jewish authorities, delivery to Roman authorities with recommendation of execution, interrogation by Roman authorities, scourging, execution) corresponds to what we know of other cases. Indeed, the experience of Jesus of Nazareth parallels quite closely the experience of Jesus ben Ananias, who some thirty years later uttered oracles of doom in the city of Jerusalem and in the temple precincts themselves. Like Jesus of Nazareth (Mark 11: 17; cf. Jer. 7: 11), Jesus ben Ananias alluded to Jeremiah 7, while in the vicinity of temple (Josephus, *BJ* 6. 5. 3, §§300–5; cf. Jer. 7: 34). Unlike Jesus of Nazareth, Jesus ben Ananias was not executed (despite calls from religious leaders that he be put to death), but was released.

Jesus was taken down from the cross before nightfall and was buried according to Jewish customs (Mark 15: 42–16: 4); he was put to death as a criminal, and was buried accordingly (*m. Sanh.* 6. 5; *Semahot* 13. 7). The novel suggestion that perhaps Jesus was left on the cross, unburied (as was usually the case outside Israel; cf. Suetonius, *Augustus* 13. 1–2; Petronius, *Satyricon* 111), or that his corpse was thrown into a ditch, covered with lime, and left for animals to maul, is wholly implausible. Obligations to bury the dead properly, before sundown, was keenly felt by Jews of late antiquity (Deut. 21: 22–3; Tob. 1: 18; 2: 3–9). Moreover, unburied corpses, subject to predators, would defile the land (Deut. 21: 23; 4Q285 frg. 7, lines 5–6). It is unthinkable that the bodies of Jesus and the men crucified with him would have been left unburied, just outside the walls of Jerusalem.

2. The Rise of Christianity

2.1 The Experience of the Resurrection

The Christian faith originated as a direct result of the Easter event. The death of Jesus in all probability ended his movement, at least for a short time. It is hard to see how it would not have ended it. All other Jewish movements of restoration, in late antiquity, known to us, ended with the deaths of their respective leaders. Had there been no Easter, there would have been no movement to arise that would eventually emerge as Christianity.

The evidence for this view is seen in the earliest Christian preaching. According to the Petrine tradition, as preserved in Acts, it is by the resurrection that 'God has made [Jesus] both Lord and Messiah' (Acts 2: 36)—'this Jesus God raised up . . . this Jesus whom you crucified' (Acts 2: 32, 36). Paul states essentially the same thing: Jesus was 'designated Son of God in power according to the Spirit of holiness by his resurrection from the dead' (Rom. 1: 4). Indeed, the essence of the gospel is the resurrection: 'Now I would remind you, brethren, in what terms I preached to you the gospel . . . that Christ died for our sins in accordance with the scriptures, that he was buried, that he was raised on the third day in accordance with the scriptures, and that he appeared to Cephas, then to the twelve' (1 Cor. 15: 1–5). The gospel is no longer the kingdom, or rule, of God; it is the resurrection of Jesus Messiah and the hope of forgiveness and life that individuals now have.

2.2 The Transformation of Jesus' Proclamation

The redefinition of the gospel—from the good news of God's rule, to the good news of the resurrection of Jesus, God's Son—played an important role in the rise of Christianity. With this shift, the focus on the restoration of Israel began to fade. The kingdom of God came to be understood as God's universal rule, in which his church would be vindicated, and her enemies—the Roman Empire and the Jewish temple and, later, the synagogue—would face judgement. What role Israel would play in this eschatological scenario became more open to interpretation. In some theological circles the church was understood to have replaced Israel, or become the new Israel.

Of course, the apostle Paul does not completely lose sight of the hope of Israel's restoration. He gives forceful expression to this hope in Rom. 9–11. Israel's rejection of the gospel of Jesus Messiah is temporary, brought on by spiritual obduracy that has had a long, checkered history among God's people. Paul likens his disappointing experience to that of the prophet Elijah, who though discouraged, was told that a remnant of faithful Israelites still remained (Rom. 11: 1–4; cf. 1 Kgs. 19). So it is in Paul's day: 'there is a remnant, chosen by grace' (Rom. 11: 5; cf. 9: 27–9). During the present time of Israel's obduracy (Rom. 11: 7–10; cf. Isa. 29: 10; Ps. 69: 22–3), God is mercifully drawing a host of Gentiles into his community. He is doing now what he did for apostate Israel long ago: making a people for his possession out of a people that had become a 'non-people' and a 'not-loved-people' (Rom. 9: 22–6; 10: 16–20; cf. Hos. 1: 10; 2: 23). The Gentiles are being grafted on to the saved community, as one might graft the branches of a wild olive tree on to a cultivated tree (Rom. 11: 11–24). Nevertheless, the day will come when 'all Israel will be saved' (Rom. 11: 26). This is so because of the prophecy of Israel (Isa. 59: 20–1) and because 'the gifts and the call of God are irrevocable' (Rom. 11: 29).

2.3 The Development of the Gentile Mission

Along with the redefinition of the gospel, another major development in the rise of Christianity was the Gentile mission. The seeds for this mission are found in the Scriptures of Israel themselves. According to Isa. 56, the foreigner may join himself to the Lord and will be welcomed to his holy mountain and may enter God's house of prayer (vv. 1–8). This visionary oracle may well be related to Solomon's legendary prayer of dedication for the newly built temple (1 Kgs. 8: 22–53). As in Isaiah's oracle, so also in Solomon's prayer, the foreigner will be welcome in God's house.

It was to this tradition that Jesus alluded when he cited a portion of Isa. 56: 7: 'Is it not written, "My house shall be called a house of prayer for all the nations"?' (Mark 11: 17). How much of the prophet's oracle Jesus had in mind is not clear. But his concession to the Gentile woman of Syrophoenicia (Mark 7: 24–30) is suggestive. Perhaps in his vision of the coming rule of God, Jesus foresaw the fulfilment of Isaiah's oracle and rightly saw it as consistent with the proper function of Jerusalem's famous temple. In editing the dominical tradition the way that they did, the evangelists may have got it right when at Nazareth Jesus appeals to the benefits extended to Gentiles (cf. Luke 4: 25–7) or, after Easter, on the mountain, Jesus commands his disciples to 'make disciples of all nations' (Matt. 28: 19).

2.4 The Abandonment of Jewish Law

A natural, if not inevitable, development of the Gentile mission was the weakening, redefinition, and, for the most part, abandonment of Jewish law. Paul's earlier arguments against making Jewish law a requirement for Gentile converts (esp. in Galatians) provided apostolic authority for this development. Eventually, Jewish Christians, called Ebionites, came to be regarded as heretics.

The Gentilization of the Christian church and the concomitant abandonment of Jewish law guaranteed the collapse of the mission to the Jewish people. The movement that Jesus had launched, with its focus on the rule of God, in fulfilment of the Scriptures of Israel, and the restoration of Israel, had been dramatically transformed. The result of this transformation was a theology and a communion that had great appeal to the peoples of the Roman Empire and beyond.

Of course, the Jewish heritage as a whole was not abandoned. The Christian church retained the Scriptures of Israel that the synagogue would itself retain. For the church these Scriptures became the Old Testament. Apart from these Scriptures, the writings that eventually became the New Testament could hardly be interpreted fully and accurately. The retention of Israel's Scriptures assured retention of much of Jewish morality. The Christian church also retained the basic form of worship and fellowship as practised in the synagogue. Hymns, the reading and interpretation of Scripture, exhortation, fellowship, and socializing all became part of Christian community.

2.5 The Earliest Gentile Converts

Most of the first Gentile converts were from the lower classes. Many of them were slaves. Pliny the Younger's review of the commitments of these Christians is illustrative:

They [Christians] assured me that the sum total of their guilt or their error consisted in the fact that they regularly assembled on a certain day before daybreak. They recited a hymn antiphonally to Christ as (their) God and bound themselves with an oath not to commit any crime, but to abstain from theft, robbery, adultery, breach of faith, and embezzlement of property entrusted to them. After this, it was their custom to separate, and then come together again to partake of a meal . . . (*Epistles* 10. 96 (to Trajan); c.110 CE)

The dismissive description by Cornelius Tacitus (cf. *Annals* 15. 44; c.110–20 CE) is consistent with this conclusion. Assembling 'before daybreak' probably implies meeting together before the workday gets under way. Most of the vices from which these Christians promised to abstain were the temptations that slaves in the Roman Empire would have faced, such as 'theft', 'breach of faith', and 'embezzlement of property entrusted to them'.

During the passage of time, Christian evangelization worked its way up the social, economic, and political ladder, until many of the most prominent and powerful members of Roman society had been converted to the faith. Eventually converts were numbered even in Caesar's family. With the conversion of much of the Empire and along with it formal recognition and protection, the Christian church was faced with a new set of challenges, and began a new transformation.

BIBLIOGRAPHY

BAMMEL, E., and MOULE, C. F. D., eds. 1984. *Jesus and the Politics of his Day*. Cambridge: Cambridge University Press.

BAUR, FERDINAND, C. 1847. *Kritische Untersuchungen über die kanonischen Evangelien*. Tübingen: L. F. Fues.

BECKER, J. 1998. *Jesus of Nazareth*. Berlin and New York: de Gruyter.

BOCKMUEHL, M. N. A. 2000. *Jewish Law in Gentile Churches: Halakhah and the Beginning of Christian Public Ethics*. Edinburgh: T. & T. Clark.

—— ed. 2001. *The Cambridge Companion to Jesus*. Cambridge Companions to Religion. Cambridge: Cambridge University Press.

BRUNNER, EMIL 1946. *The Mediator: A Study of the Central Doctrine of the Christian Faith*. London: Butterworth.

BRYAN, S. M. 2002. *Jesus and Israel's Traditions of Judgement and Restoration*. SNTSMS 117. Cambridge: Cambridge University Press.

BULTMANN, RUDOLPH 1934. *Jesus and the Word*. ET New York: Scribner.

CHANCEY, M. A. 2002. *The Myth of a Gentile Galilee*. SNTSMS 118. Cambridge: Cambridge University Press.

CHILTON, B. D. 1992. *The Temple of Jesus: His Sacrificial Program within a Cultural History of Sacrifice*. University Park, Pa.: Penn State University Press.

—— and EVANS, C. A. 1997. *Jesus in Context: Temple, Purity, and Restoration*. AGAJU 39. Leiden: Brill.

EVANS, C. A. 1995. *Jesus and his Contemporaries: Comparative Studies*. AGAJU 25. Leiden: Brill.

FREDRIKSEN, P. 1988. *From Jesus to Christ: The Origins of the New Testament Images of Jesus*. New Haven: Yale University Press.

FREYNE, S, 1998. *Galilee from Alexander the Great to Hadrian 323 BCE to 135 CE: A Study of Second Temple Judaism*. Edinburgh: T. & T. Clark.

—— 2000. *Galilee and Gospel: Collected Essays*. WUNT 125. Tübingen: Mohr Siebeck.

HANSON, K. C., and OAKMAN, D. E. 1998. *Palestine in the Time of Jesus: Social Structures and Social Conflicts*. Minneapolis: Fortress.

HARVEY, A. E. 1982. *Jesus and the Constraints of History: The Bampton Lectures, 1980*. London: Duckworth.

HOLTZMANN, HEINRICH J. 1863. *Die synoptischen Evangelien, ihr Ursprung und geschichtlicher Charakter*. Leipzig: Engelmann.

HORSLEY, R. A. 1987. *Jesus and the Spiral of Violence: Popular Jewish Resistance in Roman Palestine*. San Francisco: Harper & Row.

HORSLEY, R. A. 1995. *Galilee: History, Politics, People*. Valley Forge, Pa.: Trinity Press International.

—— and HANSON, J. S. 1988. *Bandits, Prophets, and Messiahs: Popular Movements at the Time of Jesus*. New Voices in Biblical Studies. Minneapolis: Winston, 1985; repr. San Francisco: Harper & Row.

DE JONGE, M. 1988. *Christology in Context: The Earliest Christian Response to Jesus*. Philadelphia: Westminster.

—— 1991. *Jesus, The Servant-Messiah*. Shaffer Lectures. New Haven and London: Yale University Press.

—— 1998. *God's Final Envoy: Early Christology and Jesus' Own View of his Mission*. Studying the Historical Jesus. Grand Rapids, Mich., and Cambridge: Eerdmans.

KÄHLER, MARTIN 1964. *The So-Called Historical Jesus and the Historic, Biblical Christ*, trans., ed., and with an introduction by Carl E. Braaten; foreword by Paul J. Tillich. (Based on the 1896 edn. of *Der sogenannte historische Jesus und der geschichtliche, biblische Christus* (Leipzig: A. Deichert; reissued Munich: Christian Kaiser Verlag, 1956).)

MCKNIGHT, S. 1999. *A New Vision for Israel: The Teachings of Jesus in National Context*. Studying the Historical Jesus. Grand Rapids, Mich.: Eerdmans.

MEIER, J. P. 1991–2001. *A Marginal Jew: Rethinking the Historical Jesus*, 3 vols. New York: Doubleday.

MEYER, B. F. 1979. *The Aims of Jesus*. London: SCM Press.

REIMARUS, HERMANN S. 1970. *Fragments*, ed. C. H. Talbert, trans. R. S. Fraser. Philadelphia: Fortress Press.

REISER, M. 1997. *Jesus and Judgment: The Eschatological Proclamation in its Jewish Context*. Minneapolis: Fortress.

SANDERS, E. P. 1985. *Jesus and Judaism*. London: SCM Press; Philadelphia: Fortress.

SCHWEITZER, ALBERT 2000. *The Quest of the Historical Jesus: A Critical Study of its Progress from Reimarus to Wrede*. London: SCM. (German original: *Vom Reimarus zu Wrede*, Tübingen, 1906; 2nd expanded edn. under the title *Geschichte der Leben-Jesu Forschung* (Tübingen, 1913).)

STRAUSS, DAVID F. 1846. *The Life of Jesus: Critically Examined*, trans. from 4th German edn. by Marian Evans (Cross). London: Chapman.

THEISSEN, G., and MERZ, A. 1998. *The Historical Jesus: A Comprehensive Guide*. Minneapolis: Fortress.

—— and WINTER, D. 2002. *The Quest for the Plausible Jesus: The Question of Criteria*. Louisville, Ky.: Westminster/John Knox Press.

WEISS, JOHANNES. 1971. *Jesus' Proclamation of the Kingdom of God*, trans., ed., and with an introduction by Richard Hyde Hiers and David Larrimore Holland. London: SCM. (German original: *Die Predigt Jesu vom Reiche Gottes* (Göttingen: Vandenhoeck & Ruprecht, 1892).)

WITHERINGTON, B. 1990. *The Christology of Jesus*. Minneapolis: Fortress.

WREDE, WILLIAM 1971. *The Messianic Secret*, trans. J. C. G. Greig. Cambridge: Clarke. (Translation of *Das Messiasgeheimnis in den Evangelien* (Göttingen: Vandenhoeck & Ruprecht, 1901).)

WRIGHT, N. T. 1996. *Jesus and the Victory of God*. Christian Origins and the Question of God, 2. London: SPCK; Minneapolis: Fortress.

INSTITUTIONS OF THE OLD AND NEW TESTAMENTS

CHAPTER 18

PRIESTHOOD, TEMPLE(S), AND SACRIFICE

ROBERT HAYWARD

INTRODUCTION

Not long after the destruction of the Jerusalem Temple in 70 CE, Josephus wrote defending his nation against anti-Jewish slanders in the following terms:

We have but one temple for the one God (for like ever loveth like), common to all as God is common to all. The priests are continually engaged in His worship, under the leadership of him who for the time is head of the line. With his colleagues he will sacrifice to God, safeguard the laws, adjudicate in cases of dispute, punish those convicted of crime. Any who disobey him will pay the penalty as for impiety towards God Himself. (*Ap.* ii. 193–4, trans. Thackeray)

Himself of priestly descent (*Ap.* i. 54; *Vit.* 1–6), belonging to the first of the twenty-four courses into which the priests of his day were divided, Josephus had explained that the constitution of the Jewish state placed sovereignty in the hands of God (*Ap.* ii. 165), and thus granted to the priests, under the supervision of the high priest, the administration and guardianship of its affairs in accordance with the Torah (*Ap.* ii. 185). His description of the priests as responsible for the service of the Temple and for the administration of civil and criminal law under the auspices of a high priest recalls Ben Sira's praise of Aaron, according to biblical tradition the first high priest. Writing around 180 BCE, Ben Sira related how God had chosen Aaron of the tribe of Levi.

To bring near whole offering and fat portions
And to offer in sacrifice a sweet-smelling savour and a memorial portion,
And to make atonement on behalf of the sons of Israel.
And He gave him authority in decree and statute
That he might teach his people the decree
And the sons of Israel the statute.

(Hebrew Ben Sira 45: 16–17 MSB)

In his eulogy of the high priest, Simon son of Johanan, Ben Sira expresses the harmony between Simon and the other priests, 'the sons of Aaron' (Ben Sira 50: 13, 16) as the Temple service proceeds. Here we are presented with an ideal order of things, the priestly service in the Temple involving 'the people' (50: 5), 'the whole congregation of the sons of Israel' (50: 20), carried out in absolute accordance with the Torah (50: 19), issuing in a twofold blessing (50: 20–1) for a people safe and secure in a city strengthened and rebuilt by the high priest himself (50: 1–4). The service includes singers, who make sweet melody as the sacrifice is consumed (50: 18): these Ben Sira had noted earlier (47: 9) as set before the altar by order of king David. They are not priests: Josephus would later speak of them as *Levites* (*AJ* viii. 176; xx. 216), although Ben Sira does not use this term to describe them. Josephus also ascribed to the Levites the duty of guarding the Temple enclosure (*AJ* ix. 155), and named them along with gate-keepers and Temple servants in his list of those who returned to Jerusalem after the exile in Babylon (*AJ* xi. 70). They too, he tells us, had been divided by King David into twenty-four divisions in a manner reflecting the twenty-four course divisions of the priests, each division, priestly and Levitical, serving in the Temple for one week in due order (*AJ* vii. 365–7).

Israel's constitution as a people under divine governance set forth in the Torah, itself guarded and administered by a high priest and his fellow priests who are responsible for the sacrificial service of the Temple, themselves assisted by Levites who act principally as Temple singers, yet whose numbers may include door-keepers and other kinds of Temple servant, is broadly in accord with the account of matters given by the author-compiler of 1 and 2 Chronicles. In particular, the ascription to King David of the organization of both priests and Levites into twenty-four divisions; the notes that the same king had a particular hand in the singing arrangements of the Levites; the importance of the high priest; and the central role played by priests in the teaching and dissemination of knowledge of the Torah, are matters of great concern to the Chronicler, who must be numbered among the latest of the biblical writers. His treatment of the priests and the Levites, their genealogy, functions, and history, is one of the most fully developed of all biblical accounts of these things, and its influence on later writers like Ben Sira and Josephus we have briefly noted. Most importantly, it represents an 'end-point' in the course of biblical tradition, being the latest extended discussion of priesthood available to us from those writings included in the canon of the Hebrew Bible. As such, it marks a convenient starting-point for this essay, since almost every aspect of the Chronicler's discussion of priests raises questions of his relationship to earlier sources, with which it is evident that he was well acquainted.

1. PRIESTS AND LEVITES ACCORDING TO THE CHRONICLER

1 and 2 Chronicles may be dated perhaps to the latter part of the fourth century BCE (Japhet 1993: 25–8), and represents a systematic attempt to present and order Israel's political and religious life in accordance with the Torah of Moses as the author understood it. When explicitly named, and this is not often, Moses appears in Chronicles specifically in relation to priestly and Levitical concerns. First, King David's transfer of the ark of the covenant to Jerusalem is performed by the Levites, 'as Moses commanded' (1 Chr. 15: 15), a clear indication that the author assumes as authoritative texts like Deut. 10: 8, which reports the separation of Levi as a tribe to carry the ark of the covenant (cf. Deut. 31: 9). The ark contains the two tables of the commandments 'which Moses put there at Horeb' (2 Chr. 5: 10), a matter also related at Deut. 10: 2, 5. Secondly, the Chronicler reminds his readers of the tent of YHWH and the altar of burnt offering which Moses constructed in the desert (1 Chr. 21: 29): in King David's day, he informs them, these were at the high place in Gibeon, a point reiterated with regard to the tent (now called the tent of meeting) and the altar at 2 Chr. 1: 3–6 in words recalling Exod. 29: 10; 31: 2, 7, 9. Thirdly, and in many respects most important, 1 Chr. 23: 13–14 notes the genealogy of Moses: his brother was Aaron the Levite (again, cf. Exod. 6: 16–20), who had been separated to be sanctified as most holy along with his sons, to burn incense before and minister to YHWH, and to bless in his name, while Moses and his sons are named among the tribe of Levi. In other words, both Moses and Aaron the first high priest are members of the same tribe of Levi which provides the singers, door-keepers, and other Temple assistants who are also named Levites (1 Chr. 23: 3–6). This last passage also speaks of 6,000 Levites as 'officers and judges' (2 Chr. 23: 4), their relationship to Moses being underscored by the remainder of the Chronicler's direct references to Moses, which speak of him as one whom God charged with 'statutes and judgements' (1 Chr. 22: 13; cf. 2 Chr. 25: 4). For the Levites, in the Chronicler's model of Israel's constitution, also function as teachers of Torah and judges (2 Chr. 17: 8–9; 19: 8–11). 'The commandment of Moses' about Sabbath, new moons, and the three pilgrimage festivals (2 Chr. 8: 13); and the two references to the Torah of Moses (2 Chr. 23: 18; 30: 16) once more make explicit commandments

relating to the Temple service, and serve to show how closely Moses is associated in the writer's mind with these same things.

The Chronicler's work, however, takes the form of a history which concerns itself chiefly, though not exclusively, with the days of the kings David, Solomon, and the monarchy of Judah. Those days differed from the time of Moses, and the writer was not unaware of the fact. For example, the Levites might well have carried the ark and the tent of meeting while Israel was unsettled or had no Temple; but once they had deposited that ark and the vessels housed in the tent in Solomon's Temple (2 Chr. 5: 4 ff.), what was there for them to do? According to 1 Chr. 23: 26–32, David addressed this issue directly. Henceforth, they were to act as Temple guards, being responsible for purity; to prepare the bread of the presence and meal offerings for the priests; and to sing. These three different duties were the responsibility of three separate groups within the Levite tribe, including now door-keepers and singers; but not one of these duties is ordered by the priestly legislation in the Pentateuch, 'the law of Moses', which the writer is otherwise so keen to invoke with his insistence on the relationship between Moses and the details of divine worship.

The Chronicler's model for addressing these matters, however, indeed derives from the Pentateuch, and from the book of Joshua. According to Exod. 25: 9, 40, God ordered Moses to make the desert sanctuary and its appurtenances according to a pattern (*tabnît*). The Chronicler informs us that David also had such a *tabnît*, which he handed over to Solomon; but this included details not only of the Temple's construction and furnishings (1 Chr. 28: 11–12), but also of 'the courses of the priests and the Levites, and for all the work of the service of the house of YHWH' (1 Chr. 28: 13). This pattern David was made to understand *in writing* from YHWH (1 Chr. 28: 19), such that the king's disposition of the priestly and Levitical functions has the force of divine law. The significance of this becomes clearer when we note how the Chronicler has deliberately modelled David's handing over of authority to Solomon on the transfer of Moses' authority to Joshua (cf. 1 Chr. 28: 20 with Josh. 1: 5–6). Solomon stands in relation to David as Joshua stood in relation to Moses: both men inaugurate new phases in Israel's life which require the application of the Torah of Moses in new circumstances: namely, settled existence after a period of wandering, on the one hand, and a permanent fixed shrine in place of a mobile tent, on the other.

Students of the Chronicler's work agree that the times in which the author was working determined much of what he wrote. In particular, his account of the priests, Levites, and the Temple service very likely reflect the practical arrangements and concerns of his own day, and certainly address practices which the Chronicler believed to be proper. Writing at a time when Israel had no king, his history none the less makes much of the relationship between the kings of the house of David and high priest, priests, and Levites; and the heavy emphasis which he places on the formal organization of the priests and Levites and their service by King David in person (1 Chr. 23–8). The following picture emerges.

(a) The High Priest

At the head of the hierarchy stands the chief priest, Amariah (2 Chr. 19: 11; 24: 11; 26: 20; 31: 10), an office whose existence is attested in writings dated to the earliest days of the Second Temple (Hag. 1: 1, 12, 14; 2: 2, 4; Zech. 3: 1; 6: 11, *hakkōhēn haggādôl*), whose exemplar is Zadok. Although the Chronicler does not style him 'chief priest' explicitly, he reports that Zadok was anointed as priest at the same time as Solomon was made king 'for the second time' (1 Chr. 29: 22). Here, he is consecrated like Aaron according to the Priestly legislation in the Pentateuch (which does not call Aaron 'high priest'), as an individual priest anointed to high office specifically to sanctify him (see Lev. 8: 12). The timing of Zadok's anointing is highly significant for the Chronicler: while David reigned, Zadok officiated along with his fellow priests 'at the tent of YHWH in the high place that was at Gibeon', offering the *Tamid* according to that same priestly law (see Exod. 29: 38–41; Num. 28: 3–8) which sanctioned his anointing (1 Chr. 16: 39–40). With Solomon's accession, the collapsible tent is replaced by the permanent Temple, which is to have a priest consecrated like Aaron. Zadok thus links the old and the new orders of things; and his anointing at the beginning of Solomon's reign suggests that it is now that the Chronicler views the priestly law (enshrined in the Torah of Moses) as becoming fully effective.

To reinforce the central role of Zadok, the Chronicler provided him with a genealogy presenting him as a direct descendant of Aaron through his son Eleazar and grandson Phineas (1 Chr. 5: 27–41; EVV 6: 1–15), and numbering among his own descendants those specifically called 'chief priest' (e.g. Amariah, 1 Chr. 5: 37; EVV. 6: 11, and 2 Chr. 19: 11), ending with that celebrated Zadokite, Jehozadak, who was to be the first high priest of the Second Temple which the Chronicler himself knew (Hag. 1: 1; Zech. 3; Ezek. 3: 2). Since Wellhausen's days, most scholars have regarded this genealogy as an artificial construct on the Chronicler's part, designed specifically to integrate Zadok into the lineage of Aaron: the text of this genealogy is not without difficulties (Japhet 1993: 149–53), and its relationship to earlier source material about Zadok is highly problematic. Thus, 2 Sam. 8: 17 names him, without preamble, as son of Ahitub along with Ahimelech son of Abiathar (as does 1 Chr. 18: 16). But 1 Sam. 22: 20 states that Abiathar was the *son* of Ahimelech, who in turn was son of Ahitub; and Abiathar is again recorded as *son* of Ahimelech at 1 Sam. 23: 6; 30: 7. Other references to Ahitub name him as the father, not of Zadok, but of Ahijah (1 Sam. 14: 3) and Ahimelech (1 Sam. 22: 9, 11, and 20, as above).

The suspicion arises from these texts that Zadok's ancestry may have been fabricated to provide an originally rootless Zadok with a respectable ancestry; and it is reinforced if suggestions that Zadok was originally a non-Israelite priest incorporated by David into his new Jerusalem politico-religious establishment have any force. The best known of these suggestions (cf. Rowley 1950) posits

Zadok as priest of *'El 'elyon* in pre-Davidic Jerusalem, the form of his name recalling Adonizedek, king of Jerusalem (Josh. 10: 1, 3) and, most significantly, Melchizedek, king of Salem and priest of *'El 'elyon* (Gen. 14: 18). This suggestion, however, lacks evidence to sustain it, and was systematically criticized by F. M. Cross (1973: 209–15), who also took issue with Wellhausen's doubts about the genealogy of Zadok as son of Ahitub noted in 1 Sam. 8: 17, by showing how the MT of that verse is the product of textual corruption. He notes that there were most likely two different priests named Ahitub, one the grandfather of Abiathar (see above, 1 Sam. 22: 20), the other the father of Zadok; and it is clear that Abiathar was descended from Eli, the priest of Shiloh (1 Sam. 14: 3; 22: 20), whereas Zadok was of a different family, being most probably the 'faithful priest' predicted in the prophecy of 1 Sam. 2: 35–6 as the replacement for Eli's sinful house. Cross also goes some way to resolving the problem of 2 Sam. 8: 17, arguing that originally it spoke of Zadok the son of Ahitub and Abiathar the son of Abimelech. The most serious difficulty in the verse is not Zadok's ancestry, but the presentation of Ahimelech as Abiathar's father, and Cross provides a reasonable explanation for the present confusion. In any event, Cross has shown that Zadok's Aaronite ancestry can no longer simply be dismissed as a fiction; and the status accorded him by the Chronicler becomes easier to understand.

The Chronicler sees succeeding high priests as central to the administration of justice, in company with the king, the other priests, and the Levites. King Jehoshaphat's appointment of judges in the cities of Judah (2 Chr. 19: 4–11) goes hand in hand with his establishment of the Levites and the priests and the head of fathers' houses in Jerusalem as a high court for difficult cases of the kind envisaged by Deut. 17: 8–13, although the latter speaks of 'the priests the Levites' in this setting (Deut. 17: 9) and makes no mention of heads of fathers' houses. This may reflect the make-up (actual, or ideal) of the court in the Chronicler's own time (Japhet 1993: 776–9); and certainly the naming of the Levites as a distinct group is typical of the Chronicler. Japhet notes that the court is charged with making the correct distinctions between different kinds of written law (2 Chr. 19: 10). Amariah, 'the chief priest', is to be over all these judges, says Jehoshaphat, 'in all matters of the LORD', while Zebadiah, the ruler of the house of Judah, presides over 'all the king's matters', and the Levites act as officers (2 Chr. 19: 11).

The high priest's officer (2 Chr. 24: 11), along with the scribe of King Joash, was responsible for emptying the box containing the sanctuary tax 'that Moses the servant of God' ordained in the desert (2 Chr. 24: 9, 11). The money raised was used for repairs to the Temple, both king and high priest being intimately involved in the work. Yet the high priest might, in certain circumstances, pass judgement on the king. Azariah discerned that King Uzziah, having illegally offered incense in the Temple, had contracted skin disease ('leprosy'), which remained with him until he died, requiring him to live apart from others (2 Chr. 26: 16–21). The priests alone, according to Lev. 13: 1–46, may declare such a person to be unclean or clean;

indeed, as we shall see presently, this is one of the most important functions of the priestly office as detailed by Pentateuchal law. In this instance, the authority of the high priest took precedence over that of the king.

The chief priest Azariah 'of the house of Zadok' (2 Chr. 31: 10) passed favourable judgement on Hezekiah's command that the people pay the priestly dues, the tithe, and the first-fruits of agricultural produce (see Num. 18: 2–24), honey (not mentioned in the Pentateuch), and the tithe of cattle and sheep (Lev. 27: 32–3). The king's concern for priestly dues required administrators, who, under the auspices of king and high priest, stored the tithes and offerings, the Levites playing a key role in the distribution of these oblations (2 Chr. 12 ff.). Quite what this tells us about the practices of the Chronicler's own day is unclear: governors appointed by the Persians may have represented the 'king' in the business of priestly and Levitical dues, as Nehemiah is reported to have done (Neh. 13: 10–14), to allow the Temple personnel sufficient economic security to devote themselves to the service and their other duties (cf. 2 Chr. 31: 10). What is evident is that the Chronicler asserted the importance of the priestly dues, envisaged an efficient method for their collection, and allotted to the high priest a key role in the process.

(b) The Priests

According to the Chronicler, priests are descendants of Aaron, of the tribe of Levi, and of his two sons Eleazar and Ithamar: they were organized into twenty-four courses, or divisions. This information is given in 1 Chr. 24: 1–19, where the heads of the priestly courses of David's times are noted without genealogical trees connecting them to Aaron himself. Both Eleazar and Ithamar are named in the Pentateuch (see e.g. Num. 20: 25–9; Deut. 10: 6 for Eleazar; Exod. 38: 21; both men named together at Exod. 6: 23; 28: 1). 2 Chr. 13: 10 calls them 'priests, the sons of Aaron' who minister (*mᵉšārᵉtîm*) to YHWH. This is explained in detail: they offer whole burnt offerings and incense each morning and evening, set the arrangement of the bread (of the presence) upon the pure table; set in order the *menorah* each evening, and blow the trumpets of the *terû'āh* (2 Chr. 13: 11–12). They alone, that is to say, legitimately have access to the holy place of the Temple where the altar of incense, the candlestick, and the bread of the presence are placed (see e.g. Exod. 40: 22–8). The Pentateuch records that the incense belongs to the class of most holy things (Exod. 30: 34–6), as does the bread of the presence (Lev. 24: 5–9); and the sons of Aaron alone may sound the trumpets (Num. 10: 1–10). All this is contrasted with the bogus cult set up by Jeroboam I, who had 'driven out the priests of YHWH, the sons of Aaron and the Levites', installing priests in the manner of other nations by consecrating anyone who turns up with the consecration offering of an ox and seven rams (2 Chr. 13: 9). The sons of Aaron alone are sanctified (*hammᵉquddāšîm*) to burn incense (2 Chr. 26: 18); they alone offer the purification offerings for the kingdom, the sanctuary, and for Judah at Hezekiah's command (2 Chr. 29: 21), and apply the sacrificial blood to the altar (2 Chr. 29: 22), as they did in the case of the victims slaughtered at Hezekiah's and Josiah's Passover celebrations (2 Chr. 30: 16; 35: 11). Hezekiah's purification offerings include seven he-goats: these the priests slaughtered as a purification offering 'to make atonement for all Israel' (2 Chr. 29: 24).

The proper condition of priests performing their ministry is a state of holiness: along with the Levites, they sanctified themselves to bring up the ark to Jerusalem (1 Chr. 15: 14; cf. 2 Chr. 5: 11) and to offer the Passover sacrifice (2 Chr. 30: 24); if not in a sanctified state, they could not minister at the altar (2 Chr. 29: 34; 30: 3). This relationship of the priests to the sphere of the holy is perhaps the most fundamental of their aspects for the Chronicler, who speaks of them *standing* in their place (2 Chr. 35: 10), *standing* in their place according to the statute (2 Chr. 20: 16) as they applied the blood of sacrifice to the altar. This is most marked at Solomon's inauguration of the Temple service, where the priests *stood* at their posts performing their ministry and sounding trumpets, with the Levites making music (2 Chr. 7: 6); all these priests were sanctified (2 Chr. 5: 11).

The Chronicler also understood that priests have a duty to teach Torah: the absence of such a priest who is a teacher (*môreh*) is lamented in the days of King Asa: his absence means that there has been no *tôrāh* (2 Chr. 15: 3). A classic example of the priests acting in their capacity as teachers of *tôrāh*, giving authoritative decisions in matters of purity, may be found at Hag. 2: 10–14. This episode, dated to the earliest days of the Second Temple, demonstrates the manner in which specific questions would be put to priests, and the kind of clear-cut response that might be expected from them. Lack of such teaching, according to the Chronicler, was remedied in the days of Asa's son Jehoshaphat, who appointed princes and Levites to teach in the cities of Judah, and with them two priests, Elisha and Jehoram (2 Chr. 17: 7–9). But the numbers of princes and Levites outnumber the priests in this duty, indicating the Chronicler's emphasis on the Levites in the overall constitution of Israel.

(c) The Levites

In the Chronicler's scheme, descendants of the Patriarch Levi other than those descended from Aaron are called 'Levites', a word which he uses virtually as a technical term to describe personnel dedicated to work in the Temple *which is not restricted to priests*. His account of David's organization of them into twenty-four divisions corresponding to the twenty-four priestly courses gives some idea of their functions: of the 38,000 listed, 24,000 were set 'to superintend the work of YHWH's house'; 6,000 were officers and judges; 4,000 were door-keepers; and 4,000 were musicians (1 Chr. 23: 3–5). This mixture of duties, in which work in the LORD's house holds first place, might suggest that he is systematizing what was, perhaps, a more complex reality; indeed, sources not far removed in time from the Chronicler's work speak of 'the Levites, the singers, the door-keepers, Nethinim, and servants of this house of God' (Ezra 7: 24; comparing also Neh. 10: 29; 7: 1; for date, see Williamson 1985: pp. xxxv–xxxvi) as if they were discrete, unrelated groups. The genealogical material for the Levites provided by the Chronicler is of great complexity; and it, too, might suggest that what were originally unrelated families and groups have been associated with one another only secondarily (1 Chr. 23: 6–24; 24: 20–30). Thus the three sons of Levi, Gershon, Kohath, and Merari, and their descendants provide personnel for 'the work of the service of the house of YHWH' under the authority of the priests (1 Chr. 23: 6–32), while 'the rest of the sons of Levi' (1 Chr. 24: 20–31) are set in a list related to the former, but clearly differing from it. Are we here confronted with evidence of different elements within the Levite groups jockeying for position? Or has the Chronicler incorporated two different lists of Levites into his work in response to the sensibilities of different groups? Has he sought to supplement his first list with an updated second list? It is difficult to tell; and the situation is further complicated by the genealogies of the musicians who descend from Asaph, Heman, and Jeduthun (2 Chr. 25), arranged in twenty-four groups in a way judged by almost all scholars to be artificial. Likewise, the activity of these Temple musicians the Chronicler describes (without further definition) as 'prophecy' (1 Chr. 25: 1, 2, 3, 5). This description is unprecedented, and at the very least suggests that the Chronicler is attempting to distinguish this group and to promote its interests. This is borne out by the prominence given to musicians at David's transfer of the ark to Jerusalem (1 Chr. 15: 16; 16: 7–37), at the inauguration of the Temple service (2 Chr. 5: 12–13), at the purification of the Temple in Hezekiah's time (2 Chr. 29: 25–6, 30), and at Josiah's Passover (2 Chr. 35: 15). The general effect of all this is to suggest that behind the ordered façade of the Chronicler's presentation of the Levites lies a history of disagreement between different groups of Temple ministers; and this impression will be confirmed as we proceed. Indeed, recent research on the place and function of the Levites in Ezra–Nehemiah suggests that re-positioning and rearrangements of the 'pecking order' between the various groups of Temple personnel continued far into the Second Temple period, and that surviving literary sources may represent several attempts to make peace between differing groups and to provide strategies for stability in administration of state and Temple (Schaper 2000: 269–302).

The main function of the Levites before the inauguration of the Temple is clear: they carry the ark (1 Chr. 15: 12–15, 26–9; 2 Chr. 5: 4) as the Pentateuch commands (Deut. 10: 8; 31: 9; Num. 4: 15). For this they need to be *sanctified*, like the priests (1 Chr. 15: 14): it is noteworthy that the Priestly legislation in the Pentateuch never uses the stem *qdš* with reference to Levites (Milgrom 1991: 519). The Levites are also ordered to sanctify themselves for Josiah's great Passover, in the course of which they also slaughter the victims (2 Chr. 35: 6; and cf. 2 Chr. 30: 16–17, where Levites slaughter the Pesah but the priests deal with the blood of the victims). Once the Temple was functioning, they were to serve from the age of 20 (1 Chr. 23: 24, 27; 2 Chr. 31: 17) as attendants on the priests, performing *ᵃbōdāh*, 'physical labour': this term never refers to ministerial service in respect of the Levites (Milgrom 1991: 7–8). They work in Temple courts and chambers, being responsible for purity arrangements; they prepare material for the bread of the presence and cereal offerings; and they *stand* to provide music for the morning and evening offerings (the *Tamid*; see also 2 Chr. 8: 14), and for sacrifices on Sabbath, new moon, and festivals (1 Chr. 23: 32). In short, they are to keep the *mišmeret*, the 'charge', of the tent, 'charge' of the holy place, and 'charge' of the sons of Aaron, 'their brothers' (1 Chr. 23: 33): this is precisely what is laid down for their duties in the Pentateuch (Num. 3: 5–9; 18: 2–7).

Although subordinate to the priests, the position of the Levites in Chronicles is far from menial: their music accompanying the sacrifices is seen as an essential part of the Temple service, and the priests are their 'brothers' (1 Chr. 23: 33). In legal matters, too, they play a decisive role: they are included in the composition of the Jerusalem high court established by Jehoshaphat (2 Chr. 19: 8) along with priests and heads of fathers' houses; and the same king sent them out into the cities of Judah to teach Torah (2 Chr. 17: 8–10), in which mission they outnumbered their priestly colleagues. Individual Levites act as prophets: Jahaziel, a singer of the Asaphite family, was seized by the spirit of YHWH and prophesied to Jehoshaphat, who prostrated himself, while the Levitical groups, the Kohathites and the Korahites, stood up to praise YHWH. While this phenomenon may represent the absorption into a formal Temple hierarchy of an older 'cultic prophecy' (Mowinckel 1967: 2, 56, 80–2, 85–99; Johnson 1962), it is equally likely that the association of the Levites with psalms, poetic compositions regarded as divinely inspired and uttered at most solemn moments (e.g. 1 Chr. 16: 7–36), and with Torah teaching, merited for them association with prophecy (Japhet 1993: 440–1).

(d) Concluding Observations

The Chronicler presents a relatively clear account of the origins and identity of the priests and the Levites, their separate duties and functions, and their status in the life of Israel as a nation under the authority of the Torah. There is a Zadokite high priest, who has a particular role in respect of the king, although not a great deal is said about him; it is the Levites in particular who loom large in the Chronicler's mind, and their relationship with the priests, the sons of Aaron, is carefully delineated. In general terms, the Chronicler attests to the situation of his own times, and some solid information about priests and Levites in late

Persian/early Hellenistic times can be derived from him. But much in his work suggests that he speaks also of an ideal order of things. Thus, his subtlety in integrating contemporary practice with earlier Pentateuchal legislation; his provision of sometimes artificial genealogies to link together groups of Temple personnel who may once have been separate; his concern to associate Temple ministers with prophecy; and above all his sense that everything should be ordered according to a *tabnit* divinely revealed to David, speak of concerns beyond the contemporary, aspirations rather than actualities.

2. EZEKIEL

The primacy so clearly accorded to Zadok by the Chronicler is adumbrated in the earlier writing of Ezekiel 40–8, a discrete subsection of the book of Ezekiel whose final redaction was probably complete before the end of the Exile in 538 BCE. In their final form, which is what will concern us here, these chapters offer a visionary account (see Ezek. 40: 2; 43: 3) of a restored Temple in Jerusalem, with forthright rulings on the status and functions of prince, priests, Levites, and other Temple personnel in the renewed sanctuary. Many of these are quite at variance with Pentateuchal laws (and with the Chronicler's work), and at least some rabbinic authorities regarded this problem as calling into question the book's status as Scripture (*b. Shabbat* 13b; *Menahot* 45a). Throughout what follows, the visionary aspects of Ezekiel's statements should not be forgotten (Zimmerli 1979: 27–8; 1983: 329–533; Gese 1957). He certainly proposes an ideal (Schaper 2000: 122–9); and he may have expected it to be realized in constitutional form (Tuell 1992). He was himself a priest (Ezek. 1: 3), who was acutely conscious of the failure of his fellow priests in allowing profanation of *sancta*, violations of purity laws, and failure to distinguish between impurity and purity. In short, they have violated the Torah (Ezek. 22: 26), and chapters 40–8 appear to be a systematic attempt to remedy these defects in the priesthood.

In this Temple of Ezekiel's vision, the first likely mention of ministers is found in MT 40: 44 with reference to a chamber of singers (*šārîm*), situated in the inner court at the north gate: nothing further is said about them, but their appearance *en passant* suggests that they were a recognized and well-established body known in Ezekiel's time. This is so if we follow the MT of this verse; but the LXX has not singers, but *two* (likely Hebrew *Vorlage*: *š*e*ttayim*) chambers, and the whole verse may refer to chambers for the priests named in the next verse, those in the south chamber who keep the 'charge', *mišmeret*, of the Temple (a duty of

Levites in the Chronicler's work) and those in the north who keep the 'charge' of the altar. These priests 40: 46 identifies as 'the sons of Zadok, who draw near to YHWH from the sons of Levi to minister to him'. This indicates that, in Ezekiel's vision, the Zadokites alone are qualified to minister to YHWH (Milgrom 1991: 577).

Chambers to north and south are specifically designated *holy* (42: 13): there, the priests who are near to YHWH shall eat and deposit the most holy things, meal offerings, purification offerings, and reparation offerings (see 44: 29; 46: 19–20; and cf. Num. 18: 5). Lev. 6: 16, 26; 24: 9, make plain that offerings in the category of the most holy be eaten in the holy place: Ezekiel specifies *exactly* where this is to be done. On entering these chambers, the priests must not go out of the holy place into the outer court without laying aside their vestments in which they minister, because these are holy (Ezek. 42: 14): to leave, they must lay them aside and put on other clothes (a general ruling based on Lev. 6: 4, 11), lest they sanctify the people with their vestments, as Ezek. 44: 19 makes clear. But there is nothing at all in the Pentateuch to correspond to this sanctification of lay persons through the priestly garments: it is a ruling of Ezekiel's which extends the list of items which make holiness contagion possible.

Ezek. 43: 19–27 sets out the ritual for consecration of the altar of burnt offering: it is to be undertaken by 'the priests, the Levites who are of the seed of Zadok, who are near to me to minister to me'. Such a re-consecration of the altar was made necessary by its previous desecration, explained in 44: 6 ff., where Israel is accused of abominations, in bringing foreigners and uncircumcised to profane the Temple and the sacrifices. In short, Israel has not kept charge (*mišmeret*) of God's holy things (44: 8), and this is related to the failure of 'the Levites' who went astray from YHWH after idols: these are to 'bear their iniquity' (44: 9), to be divinely punished for their idolatry by their removal from the priestly office, and from contact with the holy and the most holy things (44: 10, 12–13). Rather, they are to be door-keepers having charge of the sanctuary (44: 11), and they are also given the duty of slaughtering whole burnt offering and sacrifice (*ôlāh* and *zebah*) for the people. In these verses, 'Levites' apparently designates a former priestly group now debarred from priestly office and *sancta*, paying for their former failure to preserve purity in the sanctuary by being given over wholly to the maintenance of this very thing. No source other than Ezekiel speaks of Levites as opposed to priests slaughtering *ôlāh and zebah*: their slaughtering of the Pesah recorded by the Chronicler (2 Chr. 30: 16–17; 35: 6) was dictated by the necessities of the time.

The Zadokites specifically are granted priestly privileges: 44: 15 calls them 'the priests, the Levites, the sons of Zadok'; and because they are said precisely to have kept the *mišmeret* of the sanctuary when Israel went astray, they are qualified to minister to YHWH, standing before him and offering blood and fat, entering the sanctuary, approaching the altar, ministering and keeping God's charge (44: 15–16).

Ezek. 48: 11 reiterates the claim that the Zadokites kept God's charge, and did not go astray as the Levites went astray. For the future, however, Ezek. 44: 17–31 stresses certain regulations that they must observe. As we have seen, Ezekiel singles out concern for priestly vestments (44: 17–19), unlike the Pentateuch noting that these can convey holiness to lay persons; rules relating to their hair, prohibition of alcohol, mourning laws, and laws of corpse uncleanness generally follow regulations known from the Pentateuch (44: 20–2, 25–7). It is clearly stated that they are to teach the people to distinguish between unconsecrated and consecrated, impure and pure (44: 23); and they are to act as judges (44: 24). What of *sancta* they shall eat is listed: cereal offerings, purification and reparation offerings, things vowed to the sanctuary, first-fruits and *t^erûmāh* and dough offerings (44: 29–30). Perplexing is 44: 31, ruling that they should not eat *n^ebēlāh* and *t^erēpāh*: this is a command given to all Israel at Exod. 22: 31, and its reiteration here for priests puzzled the rabbis (*b. Shabb.* 13b).

In the land of Israel itself, Ezekiel's visionary programme provides for a holy portion of the land to be set apart for the priests, for their houses and the sanctuary (45: 4), special provision also being made for the Levites, 'the ministers of the house'. The land is said repeatedly to be holy (45: 1, twice, 4, 6): it therefore requires the Levites who occupy it to be in a state of purity at all times. This mention of land leads to consideration of 'the prince' (*hannāsî*'), who is also to have a portion set aside (44: 7–8). He is responsible especially for justice in weights and measures, a matter related to the precise amounts of produce to be set aside for the Temple's sacrificial dues (*t^erûmāh*) which the prince himself is to set in order for the priests to effect purgation for Israel (45: 13–17). Tuell argues that the 'prince' envisaged was the Persian governor of the region, and that the arrangements carefully described here are intended to lead to a real political and constitutional settlement between Persians and Jews, in which the holy city of Jerusalem would come to play a central role as a symbol of Jewish identity throughout the Persian empire. The prince, it will be noted, is responsible (albeit at one remove) for Israel's purgation. Whether this ideal programme would grant to a non-Israelite or to a foreign appointee such a task is not entirely clear.

This mention of purgation leads directly to Ezekiel's regulations for Passover, which differ extensively from the Pentateuchal laws: on the fourteenth day of the first month, the first day of Passover, a bull is offered for purgation (no rule of this kind is found in the Pentateuch), and then for the next seven days seven bulls and seven rams are sacrificed. This does not cohere with Num. 28: 16–25; but it does have the effect of underscoring the need for purification. The prince has no direct part in this; but the following chapter offers precise instructions as to his mode of entry into the Temple (46: 2), and his place relative to that of the priests and the people as he brings the offerings for Sabbath and new moon (46: 3–10). Unlike the Pentateuch, Ezekiel sees the prince as playing a central role in the Temple service and the provisions for it. The specification of the exact gate by which he enters the Temple (46: 2) and the detailed descriptions of his and the people's places as they bring the offerings (46: 9–10) are all laid down: there is a place for everyone and everything, and all must be in their place.

Ezekiel's regulations appear clear-cut; and many of them have the appearance of a 'tightening up' of already existing or earlier rules, of providing detail where before there had been imprecision. The sons of Zadok alone may be priests, being qualified to approach YHWH, dealing with the altar, the holy and most holy things, and acting as judges. All other Temple personnel are subsumed under the title 'Levites', a group from which the Zadokites themselves also derive; once priests themselves, they are now assigned by Ezekiel responsibility for the Temple's purity and security, and debarred from the altar. They may slaughter sacrificial beasts; but their main task is the 'charge', guard duty, of the sanctuary. Ezekiel says nothing about a 'high priest'. He does, however, legislate for a 'prince', whose duties are carefully prescribed. And all these regulations are fitted into very precise and explicit descriptions of the Temple and its architecture, its chambers, porticos, and gates, whose dimensions are meticulously recorded. No one reading these chapters can doubt that the establishing and maintenance of *purity* inform the writer at all turns; and what is said about the Zadokites, the Levites, and the prince is but part of a larger concern for guarding that holiness which the Temple and its service should guarantee. The last words of the prophecy sum up the message of chapters 40–8: the city in which this Temple is established, in due order with priests, Levites, and prince as Ezekiel understands them, will be named 'The LORD is there' (Ezek. 48: 35).

This visionary scheme, however, confronts us with many difficulties, the most serious of which turn on the identification of Ezekiel's Levites, accused by the prophet of idolatry in former times. But biblical sources almost certainly older than Ezekiel present Levites as faithful protagonists of YHWH (e.g. Deut. 33: 8–11) who were bitterly opposed to idolatry. Indeed, the Deuteronomistic History (probably complete by 560 BCE and whose final redaction may be more or less contemporary with Ezekiel) recorded of Jeroboam I, the first king of Israel who set up golden calfs at Bethel and Dan, that he appointed priests for this cult 'from among all the people who were not of the sons of Levi' (1 Kgs. 12: 28–31). This recalls the episode of the golden calf in the days of Moses: the priest Aaron is said to have appeared to condone this (Exod. 32: 1–6), but the cult was violently attacked by Levites described as being 'on the side of YHWH' (Exod. 32: 26–9). Ezekiel's picture of Levites offers such a sharp contrast with these other accounts that he may be suspected of engaging in a polemic, designed to bolster his express support for one particular subgroup of priests, the Zadokites, whose ancestor Zadok was firmly linked with the earliest days of the Jerusalem Temple and its royal patrons.

Who, then, might Ezekiel's Levites represent? Already the Deuteronomistic History had presented Zadok as part of a much wider priestly family (see above, pp. 323–4), tracing its descent from Eli, who had presided over the pre-Jerusalem shrine at Shiloh which housed the ark (2 Sam. 8: 17; cf. 1 Sam. 14: 3). Ezekiel seems to wish to exclude from priestly service any branch of the old priestly families which could not claim descent from Zadok, whom Solomon was said to have promoted to the exclusion of Abiathar (2 Kgs. 2: 35). Baudissin (1889: 106) argued that Ezekiel's Levites were descendants of Aaron's son Ithamar, now degraded to menial tasks. Better known is Wellhausen's view (1973: 121–7), that Ezekiel's Levites represent the priesthoods of the old provisional sanctuaries of Judah ('high places') abolished in Josiah's reform (2 Kgs. 23: 1–8) in accord with Deuteronomy's stipulation that there be only one sanctuary of YHWH (Deut. 12: 5). Arguing that Deuteronomy knew no such difference between 'priests' and 'Levites' as is encountered in the Chronicler, Ezekiel, and the Priestly legislation in the Pentateuch, Wellhausen urged that the tribe of Levi was simply the priestly tribe, Deuteronomy acknowledging as much by permitting Levites from the provinces to minister as priests in the single sanctuary as of right (Deut. 18: 6–8). This ruling, however, was flouted by the Jerusalem priests (2 Kgs. 23: 9), with the result that the latter claimed priesthood exclusively as their own, and reduced the former provincial priests to subservient status entrusted with menial tasks, the term 'Levite' now being used to designate such second-class functionaries.

This simple and elegant proposal has won many adherents; but it conceals many difficulties. First, recent research has shown that Deuteronomy's account of the relationship between priests and Levites cannot be represented adequately by a direct equation of the two terms: more is said of this below (pp. 339–40) Secondly, Ezekiel's programme did not demote or degrade Levites to *menial* tasks. They are debarred from priestly activity to concentrate fully on keeping the charge of the Temple: they are to *guard* it precisely because Israel did not keep charge of God's *sancta* (Ezek. 44: 18). They operate on behalf of Israel (cf. Num. 8: 19), and are concerned not only with the physical security of the Temple, but also with its *purity*, the establishment and maintenance of which is fundamental to Ezekiel's visionary scheme. Far from being menial, the Levites' duties are crucial. If they are not carried out assiduously, impurity will gain ascendancy, driving away the Divine Presence as once before, with disastrous consequences (Ezek. 10). The singling out of Zadokites for specific priestly duties at the altar and in respect of most holy things and holy things has the effect of increasing the numbers of those who, in Ezekiel's plan, should be Levites, without whose constant vigilance in respect of purity the sanctuary cannot function. Like the prince and the priests, they reside in holy territory adjoining the Temple, and in this tract of holy land, all must be pure. One would expect little else in a city whose name is to be 'YHWH is there'.

3. THE PRIESTLY LEGISLATION IN THE PENTATEUCH

(a) The High Priest

From the outset, P envisages a high priest in the person of Aaron and his son and successor Eleazar, the ancestor of Zadok. The high priest is instituted in his office by anointing, a rite which explicitly makes him holy (Lev. 8: 12) in the course of a complex ordination ceremony, a *rite de passage* designed to transfer Aaron and other priests from everyday society and to initiate them into their new status (Milgrom 1991: 566–9). Although Moses performs this rite, P does not thereby regard him as a priest, but rather as a kind of royal figure whose installation of priests may be paralleled in other ancient Near Eastern societies (Milgrom 1991: 556–7). Unlike Ezek. 40–8, where the 'prince' is firmly under the authority of the sons of Zadok in all that we hear of him, P's ruler-figure Moses takes precedence over Aaron the high priest: it is Moses to whom YHWH addresses his commands, including matters relating to priesthood and worship in the sanctuary. Only twice does YHWH address Aaron. To the high priest belong distinctive vestments: a golden plate attached to his head-dress and worn above his forehead deals with unintentional defects in Israel's offerings (Exod. 28: 38), and he himself appears as Israel's representative in the sacrificial service by bearing the names of the twelve tribes inscribed on two precious stones set upon each shoulder of his ephod (Exod. 28: 9–12). The tribal names are inscribed again, on each of twelve jewels set into 'the breastplate of judgment' to serve as a 'memorial' continually when Aaron enters the sanctuary (Exod. 28: 13–29). Into this breastplate, Moses is ordered to put Urim and Thummim, so that Aaron continually may carry the judgement of the Israelites before the LORD (Exod. 28: 30).

While it is almost universally agreed that Urim and Thummim were objects allowing priests to determine the divine will in a wide range of matters, there is no agreement on what they actually were, although LXX 1 Sam. 14: 41 suggests that they were sacred lots (e.g. Wellhausen 1963: 110). This view, however, has not gone unchallenged (Milgrom 1991: 505–11). In any event, P restricts their use to the sanctuary 'before the LORD' (Exod. 28: 30; Num. 27: 21), in contrast to their employment to enquire of God in pre-monarchic times (e.g. Judg. 20: 27–8) and during the early monarchy (e.g. by Saul, 1 Sam. 10: 22; 14: 41 ff., and by David, 2 Sam. 2: 1; 5: 23–4) outside the sanctuary. P is clear that Joshua, Moses' successor, is to stand with Eleazar *before the LORD* as the Urim and Thummim are consulted (Num. 27: 21). This verse is the only occasion in P describing the actual use of Urim and Thummim; and it is significant that their 'judgment' or decision is portrayed as necessary for Joshua's proper leadership of Israel (Num. 27: 15–23). For P, at any rate, they are part of the high priest's equipment for offering decisions, *mišpaṭ*; he is advisor to the ruler in matters of the divine will.

P certainly envisages Aaron the high priest as responsible for the most important elements in the daily worship of the sanctuary, the *Tamid* ritual—the trimming of the lamps on the *menorah*, the offering of incense at the daily sacrifices, and the weekly setting forth of the bread of the presence (Lev. 24: 1–9; Exod. 27: 20–1), a ritual complex which seems to betray a pre-Jerusalem organization and which has been associated with the shrine at Shiloh (Haran 1978: 194–204). In Second Temple times, these duties were carried out by ordinary priests; but the ceremonies of Yom Kippur remained restricted to the high priest, as they are in P. Lev. 16 makes Aaron responsible for this annual purging of accumulated impurity from himself and his family, the people Israel whom he represents, and the sanctuary, including the Holy of Holies which he alone enters on that day, sprinkling the lid of the ark with the blood of a bull offered as a purification offering. This complex, multi-layered rite shows signs of having developed over a period of time; but its essential antiquity is supported by the existence of similar (though not identical) rites in ancient Babylon, and by the obvious need for regular riddance of impurity which, if allowed to accumulate, would drive away the divine presence (Milgrom 1991: 1067–79). The central place occupied by the high priest in P's legislation has no better illustration than this.

(b) The Priests

Priestly office is reserved for male descendants of Aaron, of the tribe of Levi: Moses consecrated Aaron's sons at the same time as he consecrated Aaron as high priest (Lev. 8). They preside at sacrifices by handling the sacrificial blood and fat (YHWH's prerogatives), and consume the portions of the victims and the cereal offerings allotted to them. In P, they are never subject of the verb 'slaughter', *šḥṭ*. Rather, they send up offerings in smoke (verb *qṭr*), perform (verb *ᶜśh*) them, and bring them near to YHWH. The blood of animal sacrifices they daub on the altar to purge (verb *kippēr*) and effect purification (verbs *ṭm'* and *ṭhr*). The crucial importance of this priestly manipulation of blood is heavily emphasized in Lev. 17: 10–16, which explicitly asserts its purgative and purificatory purpose. As they carry out these duties, the priests are never made by P the subject of the verb 'say' (*'mr*). There is no suggestion, therefore, that they recite formulae of incantation, spells, or arcane utterances. They do, however, administer oaths, as in the case of the suspected adulteress (Num. 5: 16–28), and pronounce the solemn blessing which places YHWH's name upon Israel (Num. 6: 22–7).

Central to their duties is the inspection of persons suffering from skin diseases ('leprosy'). Priests alone may declare such persons pure or impure, having first carefully scrutinized them in accordance with written regulations. Clothing and houses are also susceptible to 'leprosy', and in all matters connected with this form of impurity the priests alone adjudicate, declare what is the case, and, when appropriate, pronounce the person or object to be clean, performing the prescribed ceremonies (Lev. 13–14). Priests also carry out the formal rituals purging persons rendered impure by sexual discharges, menstrual blood (Lev. 15), and childbirth (Lev. 12); and the most contagious source of impurity, corpse uncleanness, depends for its removal on a ritual involving the high priests in preparing the ashes of a red heifer to mix with lustral water, which is then administered to the unclean person by ordinary priests (Num. 19). The priests are thus deeply involved in the lives of the Israelite people at a number of different levels; and it should be noted that the priestly laws themselves are given, through Moses, not simply to Aaron, but to 'the sons of Israel'.

Knowledge of these laws, therefore, is not confined by the legislator to the priestly class, but disseminated throughout the community. If P does not explicitly demand that the priests teach, it is because it assumes that Israel has access to those laws which are designed to foster that purity necessary for the holy God to be with his people to bless them and make them holy. God's absence brings decay and death, for he is author of life. His presence means blessing and holiness and life; Israel's purity being the necessary condition for God's presence in Israel. Given this, it is evidently in the interests of the priests to ensure that non-priests are properly instructed in the laws.

(c) The Levites

All members of the tribe of Levi who do not belong to Aaron's descendants P designates 'Levites'. Levi's sons Gershon, Kohath, and Merari are regarded as the heads and ancestors of specific family divisions within this group (Exod. 6: 16–20), their primary duties being the physical labour ($^{a}b\bar{o}d\bar{a}h$, Milgrom 1991: 7–8) of setting up, dismantling, and transporting the tent and its sacred objects. The Gershonites had charge of the tent and its coverings; the Kohathites of the ark, menorah, table, and altars; and the Merarites of the tent's boards, pillars, and sockets (Num. 3: 21–9). These Levites are subordinate to Aaron and his sons, given to them out of the Israelites (Num. 3: 9), a note followed by the ominous warning that any non-priest encroaching on Aaron's priesthood shall be put to death (Num. 3: 10; cf. 3: 38; 18: 7). The Levites have the function of guarding the sanctuary.

These duties, however, are presented in an exalted setting. All first-born creatures belong to YHWH (Exod. 13: 11–16); but out of Israel God has selected the Levites in place of the first-born sons (Num. 3: 11–13, 40–51). The ritual for their formal institution to office makes it absolutely clear that they are to be devoted to purity: at the outset, they are purged of all corpse uncleanness, and they are separated from the Israelites (Num. 8: 14, 21). Purity is the watchword of their office (Num. 8: 6, 7, 21); nevertheless, P never describes them as holy (Milgrom 1991: 519). Their guarding of the tent and its sacred objects must be seen in this light. Far from being menial, their duties are essential to P's understanding of the whole of Israel as separated from impurity (e.g. Lev. 15: 31) to ensure that the tent, the place of the divine presence, might be guarded and secure from uncleanness.

Perhaps this exalted status is not unrelated to P's awareness of attempts by Levite groups to acquire priestly rank for themselves. Num. 16–18, which tells of Korah's rebellion against Aaron's authority, openly speaks of bitter disagreements between priests and Levites; and further disharmony, this time within the Levite groups themselves, may perhaps be discerned in variations in order of named Levitical groups, some claiming higher status or even the priesthood (e.g. Num. 3: 17, Gershon–Kohath–Merari, and Num. 4: 2, 22, 42, Kohath–Gershon–Merarai: so Gunneweg 1965: 171–88). While this is likely, it should not be over-pressed. Korah's group did indeed claim the priesthood, but based this claim, not on Levitical rights, but on the assertion that *the whole congregation is holy* (Num. 16: 3), over against P's repeated insistence that Israel *is to be* holy (Lev. 11: 44–5; 19: 2; 20: 7, 26). P has no animus against Levites, and in return for the work with the tent they are granted the whole of the tithe (Num. 18: 21–4), a massive economic benefit from which they are in turn to grant one-tenth to the priests (Num. 18: 26).

(d) The Date of the Priestly Legislation

Since Wellhausen (1973: 28–51), P has been conventionally assigned to a date late in exilic or early in Second Temple times, at any rate later than Ezek. 40–8, whose basic tenets regarding the priesthood it is thought to presuppose. Embedded within it is the Holiness Code (Lev. 17–26, conventionally labelled H), a separate unit thought by most to ante-date Ezekiel's work (e.g. Kaiser 1975: 113–15). This commonly accepted dating of sources yields an apparently smooth development of the offices of high priest (not apparent in H or Ezekiel; named as such in the late sixth-century prophetic books of Haggai and Zechariah; summed up in P's legislation as Aaron; and fully represented in Zadokite form by the Chronicler); of priest (all Levites being priests in Deuteronomy; then priesthood being restricted to named family groups: sons of Zadok in Ezekiel, sons of Aaron in P and Chronicles); and of Levites (acceptable as priests in Deuteronomy, demoted by Ezekiel's plans; reduced to status of *clerus minor* by P, the Chronicler; Ezra and Nehemiah following this with some variations). This historical process was accompanied by conflicts and bitter disagreements between various priestly groups (sons of Zadok, sons of Aaron, sons of Ithamar), between them and different

Levitical families (Kohathites, Gershonites, Merarites); and between other professional interest groups such as door-keepers and singers, until some more or less
stable *modus vivendi* came about in later Second Temple times, possibly as a result
of the Chronicler's work (cf. Schaper 2000).

Yet even in its own day, Wellhausen's late dating of P was not universally
accepted (Baudissin 1889); and recent advances in research point increasingly to
a pre-exilic setting for it. Its language, especially its use of key Priestly technical
terms, appears to be earlier than Ezek. 40–8 (Hurvitz 1982); two of its most
important terms, *mišmeret* and *ᵃbôdāh*, bear meanings they never had in post-
exilic times; the granting of all tithes to Levites makes little sense for a post-exilic
legislator in days when Levites were few in number (Ezra); and the social institutions it presupposes fit pre-exilic times better than post-exilic (Haran 1978: 140–8;
Polzin 1976; Rendsburg 1980). The legislation lacks any call for a single, central
sanctuary. The likelihood that P legislated for a pre-exilic world is not easily
dismissed, and it suggests that the 'classical' arrangement of a 'high' priest alongside the ruler, presiding over priests drawn from particular families or groups, and
Levites as assistants to those priests and guardians of the sanctuary, is deeply rooted
in Israel's traditions. That such may well be the case appears possible from recent
research on Deuteronomy.

4. DEUTERONOMY

The duties of priests as outlined by D appear much the same as those described in
later times. They officiate at sacrifices (21: 5), being sustained by the customary
priestly dues (since they have no land of their own) and the first-fruits (21: 5; 18:
1–5). They act as judges, especially in difficult cases (17: 8–13; 19: 17; cf. 21: 1–9), and
refusal to accept their verdict in judgement is punishable by death (17: 12). They are
entirely responsible for supervising and making decisions in matters of skin disease
(24: 8–9). They pronounce blessings in YHWH's name, and disseminate knowledge
of Torah (17: 18; 31: 9–11). Problems arise, not so much in respect of their duties, as
regarding the terminology used to speak of them.

D in its final form legislates for a single sanctuary (12: 5) at which all sacrifice is to
be offered; and some of its legislation appears to involve the accommodation of
traditional religious customs to this requirement. Since Wellhausen (1973: 76–82),
D has been associated with Josiah's reform (621 BCE) and its abolition of provincial
sanctuaries, leaving the priests of those shrines without revenue and livelihood:
these 'Levites' are thus specially provided for in carefully drafted legislation

(18: 6–8). The term 'Levite', however, is used quite precisely by D, as Gunneweg has shown (1965: 126–31). Thus the phrase 'the Levite who is within your gates' (12: 12, 18, 19; 14: 27–9; 16: 11) describes a class of person regularly associated with resident aliens, orphans, and widows, having no land or means of support. He may take part in the great festivals, and is to receive tithes of the third year: in short, the community of Israel is to provide for his needs. At the single sanctuary itself, we hear of the tribe of Levi whom YHWH has separated to stand before him, to minister to him, and to bless in his name (10: 18; 18: 5). If any Levite comes from any of the 'gates' in Israel where he is resident, and goes to the one sanctuary, he is to be accorded all the privileges of Levites already ministering there (18: 6–8).

Then we hear of 'the priests, the Levites' (*hakkōhᵃnîm hallᵉwiyyîm*), a frequent and somewhat ambiguous phrase which may suggest that some Levites are priests, while others are not; or that some priests are drawn from Levitical families, while others are not; or that we have to deal with 'Levitical priests' in a sense possibly suggested by 18: 1: namely, that the whole tribe of Levi is a priestly tribe. This last Gunneweg prefers for D; but he notes that, even if this is so, it does not mean that from the beginning all Levites were priests, or that all priests were Levites. In its present setting, 18: 1 offers a preamble to the ruling that all Levites may serve in the one sanctuary, and it is most naturally understood in the light of this ruling. Thus it would seem that for Deuteronomy the whole tribe is separated to serve the Lord (cf. 10: 8). How this worked out in practice, however, is not entirely clear.

Recent research on the word *khn* in Deuteronomy supplies a similarly complex picture (Tuell 1992: 124–32). Several verses speak of *hkhn*, 'the priest' (e.g. 10: 6; 17: 12; 26: 3), who appears to hold special rank. Though the expression 'head/chief/ high priest' is not used, the legislator is aware of Aaron's position, and of the fact that his son acted as 'the priest' when Aaron died (10: 6). Deuteronomy, therefore, may be aware of a 'chief priest' without recourse to that terminology. The Deuteronomistic Historian similarly speaks of 'the priest' at 2 Kgs. 11: 9–10 (Jehoiada), 16: 10–11 (Urijah); 22: 10, 12, 14 (Hilkiah) who evidently held a senior post within the Jerusalem Temple and had direct dealings with the king in respect of Temple organization and finances. Within the Deuteronomistic History, Tuell also notes groups within the priesthood: 'the elders of the priests' (2 Kgs. 19: 2) who act as the king's representatives to a prophet; and 'the guardians of the threshold' (2 Kgs. 12: 10; 22: 4; 23: 4, 25: 18) who are named along with 'priests of the second order' (23: 4) and 'the head priest' and 'the second priest' (25: 18). All this suggests, first, that in the Jerusalem Temple under the later monarchy there were several groups of priests, some of higher rank than others; and secondly, that Deuteronomy itself was aware of a situation outside Jerusalem in the 'provinces' where organization of priests had also been complex. In other words, a close reading of Deuteronomy strongly suggests that different ranks and offices within the priestly society were known to the legislator.

Given this, it is possible, and indeed likely in practical terms, that different groups of officials 'specialized' in different aspects of sanctuary worship, ritual, and procedure, some devoting themselves to the details of animal sacrifice, others to the precise composition of cereal and incense offerings, others to duties involving the security of the shrine. Care of sacred vessels and other dedicated property might well have been the duty of yet other groups. Deuteronomy's language, and the terminology used by the Deuteronomistic History, indicate a more complex organization than has sometimes been perceived. The division of duties envisaged by the priestly writings, where priests and groups of Levites have specific duties allotted to them, may not, therefore be lacking in Deuteronomy, though the latter uses different language to describe the situation, and eschews the technical terminology of the priestly class to define it.

5. Early Traditions

(a) Priestly Families, Levites, and Consecrated Sons

Two narratives in particular stand out from Israel's pre-monarchical traditions, which may reflect two separate, but related settings in which priests operated. The first has an 'official' character: we hear of a shrine at Shiloh, where Eli and his sons served. Since the ark was there, Israel owed particular allegiance to this shrine (1 Sam. 1: 3; 3: 1–3). The narrative speaks of it as if it were both a 'tent' (1 Sam. 2: 22) and a house (1 Sam. 3: 15), and constructions like the tent-shrine discovered in the 1970s at Timna suggest some historical basis for this description, and hint at its antiquity (Manor 1992: 555–6). The shrine appears to be well established, with widely understood sacrificial procedures in place, but Eli's sons flouted these, and were correspondingly condemned by a prophet (1 Sam. 2: 12–17, 27–36). Eli as 'priest' was evidently responsible for teaching his sons, and their failure to obey traditional rulings about the mode and manner of sacrifice is regarded as a serious failure on his part. To this shrine, pilgrims resorted annually (1 Sam. 1: 3), and its priest issued responses in YHWH's name to worshippers' petitions (1 Sam. 1: 17). The future prophet Samuel as a child was vowed, no doubt like others, to YHWH's service at this shrine (1 Sam. 1: 27–8), and it was there that he received oracles whose messages would affect the whole of Israel (1 Sam. 3: 11–21). Samuel is never styled 'priest'; but he offered sacrifice (1 Sam. 10: 8), a parade example of sacrificial activity on the part of non-priests, which is often encountered in Israel's traditions of her early days as a settled community (e.g. Judg. 6: 19–24, 26; 11: 31(!); 13: 19), and which never ceased completely in the sense that non-priests were able to slaughter their Passover sacrifices (though not manipulate the blood and fat) until the very last days of the Temple (Philo, *QE* 1: 10). Samuel's sacrificial activity, his activity as a judge (1 Sam. 7: 15–17), and his close association with a widely respected YHWH shrine at Shiloh, led later generations to regard him as a Levite, the Chronicler providing him with a Levitical genealogy (1 Chr. 6: 28, EV). The Chronicler may not, however, be so far off the mark if the term 'Levite' originally signified a profession or status (see below, p. 344), 'one dedicated to the service' of the deity, for Samuel is apparently placed in such a state by his mother (1 Sam. 1: 28).

The second narrative is more 'popular', and initially private in tone. Judg. 17 tells of one, Micah from Ephraim, who had a 'house of god(s)' replete with ephod and teraphim: the ephod appears here as a means of discovering the divine will, as also probably at 1 Sam. 14: 3; 23: 6, 9; 30: 7, although the same term can be used of a priestly vestment in these early traditions (1 Sam 2: 28; 22: 18; 2 Sam. 6: 14). This man consecrated one of his sons as priest: subsequent events show that one of the main functions of this establishment was the discovery of the divine will on particular occasions (Judg. 18: 5; ephod and teraphim as divinatory media were still consulted in the days of Hosea towards the end of the eighth century, Hos. 3: 4). A young man from Bethelehem of Judah, but described as a Levite, was seeking to reside there as a *gēr* (Judg. 17: 7–9): this recalls Deuteronomy's designation of one class of Levite who 'dwells within your gates' as a resident alien. Micah welcomed him and, in return for a stipend, urged him to become his 'father and priest' (Judg. 17: 10). To this, the Levite agreed, becoming like one of Micah's sons; so Micah 'consecrated the Levite, and the young man became his priest, and was in Micah's house' (Judg. 17: 11–12). Micah's comment on all this is revealing: since he now has a Levite as priest, he presumes that YHWH will be good to him (Judg. 17: 13). Others, like Micah's own son, may serve as priests in this early period; but the Levites apparently have a recognized, tried and tested good relationship with YHWH. Fortunate is the man who can employ one: Micah certainly had money (Judg. 17: 2–24), and evidently regarded his shrine as a sound investment. Later, the tribe of Dan on its northward migration was also to recognize the value of this shrine as an establishment for determining the divine will. Micah's Levitical priest gave them an oracle (Judg. 18: 3–6), and they persuaded him to take the ephod and teraphim and to join them as their 'father and priest'(Judg. 18: 14–21). So they founded their city of Dan, setting up there a shrine with Moses' grandson as priest (Judg. 18: 30–1). The tradition has been handed down to us replete with editorial warnings: this shrine was opposed to the (genuine) shrine at Shiloh (Judg. 18: 31); it was idolatrous (18: 30), and founded in bloodshed, a matter directly associated with Micah's priest (18: 27). Later tradents were to obscure the name of Moses, writing it as Manasseh (MT Judg. 18: 30).

Precisely because of these editorial warnings, the story is valuable, and points to a period in Israelite society when well-to-do individuals could secure the services of Levites, recognized as having a special affinity with YHWH worship: these Levites appear to have wandered about seeking employment, the individual who comes to Micah clearly not being designated as being of *the tribe* of Levi. Had he, and others, opted for the status or profession of Levite, because he had inherited no land or property (being a third or fourth son of his father?) and was seeking some respectable means of support? (Stager 1985). Another suggestive editorial note in this narrative insists that these things took place *when there was no king in Israel* (Judg. 17: 6; 18: 1; cf. 19: 1, also involving a Levite), a formula of some importance for the final compiler of Judges who repeats it as the very last verse of the book, adding, so that no one should mistake its implication, that 'every man did what was right in his own eyes' (Judg. 21: 25). This implies that, with the advent of the monarchy, some kind of order might have been imposed on a religious world which had hitherto been unorganized, or even disorganized. Whatever the status of this editorial note, it alerts us to the profound effects which monarchy would, in the course of time, exercise on priests, Levites, and sanctuaries (Rooke 2000; Gunneweg 1965).

The Deuteronomistic Historian, through narratives like the story of Micah and the Shiloh shrine, effectively produced a 'theoretical model' of how worship in Israel and the offices of priests and Levites might have operated before the monarchy; and it is difficult to 'get behind' this official history without a certain amount of discussion of types of religion represented in Israel's early traditions (cf. Miller 2000: 46–105). For example, we may ask whether Micah's shrine represents a type of 'popular religion', or 'family religion', widespread and outside the control of Jerusalem priests, and thus regarded by 'official religion' as irregular and ultimately dangerous? Or was Micah's establishment of his shrine with a Levitical priest an attempt by a man of substance to bring order to a society which was religiously fragmented, even dysfunctional? Or was his enterprise an exercise in personal power politics? All these things may be considered; but the Historian seems most concerned to point us to the shrine at Dan, with its Mosaic priesthood, a fact which it does not choose to conceal, and which must have carried with it a considerable *cachet*. Is there a homiletic purpose in the story, an illustration, perhaps, of *corruptio optimi pessima*?

Traditions of Israel's pre-monarchic days, then, present a diverse picture of priests from established families guarding objects acknowledged as sacred to YHWH (ark, lamp, bread of the presence, and ephod: 1 Sam. 3: 3; 21: 4–6; 23: 9; 30: 7), associated with well-known sanctuaries like Shiloh, where there was a tent and house of YHWH, commanding more than local allegiance. Other shrines, like Micah's, may have been served by priests appointed *ad hoc* like Micah's son, although the appearance of an itinerant Levite is presented as in no way abnormal, and indeed a bonus for Micah's project. This Levite, it should be noticed, had still to be consecrated as priest.

What is *lacking* in these early traditions of Israel's priesthood should also be noticed. The priests and Levites are not centred on vast Temple complexes, often associated with powerful rulers, as in Egypt, Babylon, and Assyria: the ark and its associated objects appear modest, humble, and rural—not even 'provincial'—and Micah's sanctuary has a 'do-it-yourself' air about it until it is shifted to Dan. It would seem that any man might qualify as a priest in a local shrine, though certain established families were regarded as peculiarly suited to the service of YHWH. Eli's was one of these; and Levites, if they can be persuaded to act accordingly, make the most desirable priests. Why this might be, so we must now investigate.

(b) Etymologies

One prominent and conventional means of attempting to acquire knowledge of priests and Levites in earliest times has been recourse to etymology. In truth, its results are somewhat disappointing, being often uncertain, and sometimes quite conjectural. None the less, there is knowledge to be gleaned; and the major etymological theories may be briefly summarized, without any attempt at an exhaustive treatment, as follows.

(i) Priest

The main biblical Hebrew word for 'priest' is *khn*, a West Semitic word represented also in Ugaritic, Phoenician, Aramaic, and Nabataean with the same meaning. Despite frequent occurrences in Ugaritic texts, we learn from those sources next to nothing about the duties, functions, or ministry of the priest. A 'chief of priests', *rb khnm*, is known; and details of which portions of sacrificial victims belong to priests are sometimes given; but beyond this little is said. Similarly, in Phoenician and Aramaic inscriptions, the term *khn* appears, but without explication. Biblical Hebrew uses *khn* alone to speak of priests of YHWH, and also uses it to describe priests of other deities (e.g. Gen. 41: 45; 1 Sam. 5: 5; 2 Kgs. 10: 19; 11: 18; Jer. 48: 7; 49: 3). It thus seems to be a general West Semitic word for 'priest'. 2 Kgs. 23: 5 uses another word, *kmr*, to describe non-YHWH priests: a cognate term is found in Aramaic, texts from Mari, and the Amarna Letters; but no light is shed from these documents on what the *kmr* did, his powers, or his precise place in the cult. The Arabic *kāhin* should also be noted: the word refers to a soothsayer, but was in early times apparently associated with the offices of *sâdin* (sanctuary guardian) and *hâjib* (door-keeper), eventually coming to refer to an exclusively mantic and non-priestly function (Cody 1969: 14–25).

Accordingly, three significant etymologies have been proposed for Hebrew *khn*:

1. Akkadian *kânu* in the š-stem, 'incline before', such that a *khn* would be one who pays homage to the deity.
2. Hebrew *kwn*, 'stand', indicating *khn* as one who stands or serves the deity.
3. Syriac *khn*, 'be a priest', with secondary meaning 'be prosperous', such as to bring 'abundance', *khnwt*.

All have reference to some aspect of priestly service; and the most probable of them may well be the third (Cody 1969: 26–9).

(ii) Levite

Proposed etymologies of the word 'Levite' are sometimes involved in the question of whether the word is indicative of a profession or function (see above, p. 341). Three main proposals have dominated research.

(1) Levite derives from Hebrew *lwh* I, 'to join'. The Bible itself explains the *name* Levi by means of this stem (Leah's third son: see Gen. 29: 34). It is apparently in mind at Num. 18: 2, 4, 6 (the Levites are to *join* Aaron). Although dismissed by Cody (1969: 29–30) as lacking solid support, it has proved attractive to some scholars, including Baudissin (1889: 74: Levites were originally military protectors of the ark and its deity); Budde (1912: 45–7, 137: Levites were joined to Moses as his supporters, as in Exod. 32: 25–9, where, however, the stem is not used to define Levites); and Dhorme (1937: 226–7: Levites were associated with the shrine of the deity).

(2) It derives from *lwh* II, 'to borrow' (*qal*), 'to lend' (*hiphil*). Minean texts from el-Ulā, biblical Dedan in Arabia, record the forms *lw'* (masc.) and *lw't* (fem.), initially defined as 'priest' and 'priestess': some suggested that these terms illuminated Hebrew 'Levite' (e.g. Hölscher 1925: 2160). But the words mean 'one pledged for a debt or vow' (Grimme 1924): this may be helpful, and Pedersen (1926: 3–4; 1940: 680), Albright (1956: 204), and Nielsen (1955: 266) have drawn on it to suggest an understanding of Levite as one pledged, dedicated, or given away for the service of the sanctuary or the deity. The Minean texts offer little: de Vaux (1961) argued convincingly that they might well have been influenced by the Hebrew term *lwh*, since Jews had been resident from early times in the region of Dedan.

(3) Levi derives from *lwh* III, 'to turn, twist', a form associated in biblical Hebrew with Leviathan, the 'twisting serpent'. The most prominent exponent of this etymology was Mowinckel, cited by Rowley (1948: 8), who suggested that Levites turned and twisted in ecstatic ritual dancing at shrines. Others saw them as representatives of worship of YHWH in the form of a snake cult, adducing the bronze serpent of Num. 21: 8, offered a cult as Nehushtan and destroyed by Hezekiah (2 Kgs. 18: 4); the snake miracle performed by Moses (Exod. 4: 3; and 'serpent' names among Levites (e.g. *šwpym* in 1 Chr. 26: 16).

While the third of these has generally been found unconvincing, the first, and especially the second, permit an interpretation of 'Levite' as signifying originally a religious profession or occupation. This must be balanced against the use of Levi as a personal name, possibly meaning a client, adherent, or worshipper of God (Weippert 1971: 43). It should be clear, however, that whatever the root meaning of the term 'Levite', the expression came quite early in Israel's traditions to be employed for personnel engaged in a number of duties and ritual actions depending on their circumstances and times—a 'catch-all term', perhaps, which might even be used at times quite generally to speak of one officiating in some capacity in the formal service of YHWH.

(c) Levi a Secular Tribe?

The notion that once there may have been a 'secular' tribe of Levi which had no connection with priesthood and sanctuaries is based on Gen. 49: 5–7; Gen. 34; and lists of Israelite tribes which include Levi along with others which have no association with priesthood. In the first of these texts, Levi and Simeon are described by their father Jacob as brothers: their cruelty on some unspecified occasion in the past merited his curse that they be 'scattered in Israel' (Gen. 49: 7). Simeon seems to have merged with Judah (Josh. 19: 1), and Levi with other tribes (Jos. 21: 1–7). The second text possibly alludes to the past actions of Simeon and Levi condemned in the first: Gen. 34 makes them responsible for a massacre at Shechem, which their father deplored (Gen. 34: 30).

Levi also appears as a son of Leah high up in tribal lists at Gen. 29: 31–30: 24; 35: 23–6; 46: 8–25; 49: 3–27; Exod. 1: 2–4; Deut. 27: 12–13; 33: 6–25, along with other tribes who do not perform sacred duties. In other lists, however, Levi's name is conspicuously absent, his place being taken by other tribal groups: see e.g. Num. 1: 5–15, 20–43; 2: 3–31; 7: 12–83; 10: 14–28; 13: 4–15; 26: 5–51; Josh. 13–19; 21: 4–7, 9–39. Was there once, then, a secular tribe of Levi which for some reason ceased to exist? And if there had been, how might it have related to the 'priestly' Levites associated with the service of YHWH? First, it should be noted that no information about territory occupied by a (hypothetical) secular tribe of Levi survives in Israel's traditional history. Levi does not feature in the military action described in Judg. 5; and the traditional records are unanimous in asserting that Levi occupied no land. There is, in addition, no compelling reason to interpret Gen. 49: 5–7 in light of Gen. 34, or vice versa: the former could refer to an incident quite unrelated to a massacre at Shechem. As for the tribal lists, it is far from clear what historical value attaches to them. Indeed, they may be largely artificial; and it is remarkable that Levi's name is absent mainly from lists occurring in the book of Numbers and those which follow it. The former contains the detailed arrangements for Levi's separation from the rest of Israel and dedication to the work of the sanctuary. The evidence is not sufficiently strong to support the theory of the one-time existence of a secular Levi tribe, which disappeared or ceased to exist (why? when?), only to be revived (how? why? when?), or to have its name reused for a tribe involved in sacred activities. From the outset, Levites seem to have been a group within Israel particularly dedicated to the formal worship of YHWH.

Such a conclusion is supported by Deut. 33: 8–11. Though difficult to date precisely, the language and poetic structure of this vignette suggest that it belongs among Israel's early traditions (Fenton 2004: 405–6), setting forth a widely held and influential description of Levitical privileges and responsibilities as part of Moses' last words to Israel. Levi is numbered among other tribes, but as a priestly society whose world is portrayed in some detail. This world is characterized by:

a. Levitical responsibility for Urim and Thummim, the mysterious means of determining the divine will, whose later history has been briefly noted (Deut. 33: 8);

b. zealous attachment to YHWH, for whose sake Levites are prepared to go to extreme lengths (33: 9);

c. the duty of teaching to Israel YHWH's *mišpaṭ* and *tôrāh* (33: 10);

d. the privilege of offering incense and whole burnt offerings (*kālîl*) on the altar of YHWH (33: 120); and

e. the expectation that Levi will encounter enemies and opposition (33: 11).

A source dating in all probability from early Second Temple times, the prophetic book of Malachi (early fifth century BCE), threatens the contemporary priests with punishment for their failures, invoking a divine covenant with Levi himself, a matter otherwise not mentioned in the Bible. Yet the terms of this covenant recall in some measure Deut. 33: 8–11, since Levi is offered life and peace in return for his reverence and devotion to YHWH and because of his fear of YHWH's name. Levi had 'the law of truth' in his mouth; he had walked with YHWH and had turned away from iniquity. The priests' duties consist first in the preservation of knowledge; people should seek Torah from a priest, because he is a 'messenger' (*mal'āk*) of YHWH of Hosts (Mal. 2: 6–7). Malachi had already given grounds for the divine threat directed towards the priests: they had breached the laws of purity, had offered beasts unfit for sacrifice upon the altar of YHWH, and had profaned that altar (Mal. 1: 6–14). Possibly the prophet envisaged these priests as having reneged on the terms of the blessing granted to them in Deut. 33: 8–11, or one similar to it.

Malachi's oracles from the period of the Second Temple, and Deut. 33: 8–11, which may be one of the oldest notes about the priesthood available to us, address differing situations in Israel's life; but they enable us to some degree to trace the broad continuity of priestly and Levitical duties. And while the question of who should serve as priest, and where they might serve, were at times matters of intense debate, there seems never to have been much doubt about what a priest of YHWH should do.

CONCLUDING REMARKS

The duties and functions of the priests in Israel included determining the will of God, sometimes through oracular means (ephod, Urim and Thummim), sometimes by their exercise of specialized knowledge; the teaching of *tôrāh*, offering explicit instruction in the manner in which YHWH is to be served; the setting upon

YHWH's altar of the blood of animal victims, and the portions allotted to the altar; the privilege of offering incense and other non-animal offerings belonging to the category of most holy things; oversight of the purity of sanctuary, sacred objects, and worshippers; the administration of oaths and the pronouncing of blessings in YHWH's name; and the pronouncing of persons suffering from skin diseases, bodily fluxes, corpse uncleanness, and other defilements as either clean or unclean. The traditional records suggest that these duties varied little from one age to another. What was often at issue, however, was the question who might perform which action. The biblical sources briefly surveyed here give differing answers to that question.

Until comparatively recently, critical scholarship for the most part accepted as well-founded and as a working model the historical development of Israel's priestly offices as put forward by Wellhausen. German scholarship generally maintains and promotes this model, which is outlined here and offers a solution to problems which has been found helpful for many years. Two quite different developments in recent research, however, cannot be ignored. The first is the appearance of historians sometimes called 'minimalists' (see e.g. Davies 1992; Whitelam 1996), whose researches lead them to believe that little of historical worth can be found in the traditions of biblical Israel, most of which were not committed to writing until the Persian, or even early Hellenistic, period. (The history of the priesthood in Second Temple times is to some degree unaffected by the minimalist position: see Vander-Kam 2004.) For those who subscribe to a 'minimalist' position, therefore, there can be little point in attempting to draw out of the biblical documents a coherent picture of the development of Israel's priesthood and related institutions, not least since such historians are likely to hold that the several texts examined here which speak of the priests are ideological writings composed often with particular political agendas in mind. Those individual text traditions have been examined separately here; and it may be noted that the various units of biblical material can be understood as presenting a coherent image of the priesthood, whose outlines are discernible in various levels of tradition. This leads to consideration of the second development in research on Israel's priests, the contribution of Jewish scholars such as Menahem Haran and Jacob Milgrom, which in many important respects calls into question both the Wellhausen 'consensus' and the historical scepticism of 'minimalists'. Their careful analysis of priestly concerns, not least matters of holiness and purity, place the priestly office at the centre of Israel's life, and call for a much broader appreciation of priestly service than historical study on its own can provide.

In particular, the results of their detailed and painstaking researches into the individual priestly rules, the relationships of these regulations one to another, their precise placement within the larger legal and narrative frameworks of the Pentateuch, and their overall symbolic significance point to the existence within ancient Israelite society of a remarkably sophisticated and homogeneous body of priestly learning, whose precise expression in our Pentateuch represents the end-product of centuries of refinement and careful thought. Anthropological researches into the same writings (e.g. Douglas 1984, 1993, 2004) point to the priestly laws, the sacrificial rituals they prescribe and order, the kinship arrangements which they sustain, and the purity system which orders and constructs the symbolic universe they represent as foundational elements in the self-understanding of the people Israel as distinct from the nations (it will be recalled that the priestly laws are addressed to all Israel, not simply to the priestly and Levitical families). The fruitful interaction of much modern Israeli scholarship with recent anthropological insights has greatly enriched our knowledge of the priestly service in Israel, and has reinforced the sense that the priesthood and its statutory duties, far from being merely the concerns of an élite within ancient Israelite society, occupied a central place in the self-definition of the people, and in the formation of that people's moral consciousness.

SUGGESTED READING

Blenkinsopp 1995 and Miller 2000.

BIBLIOGRAPHY

ALBRIGHT, W. F. 1956. *Archaeology and the Religion of Israel*, 4th edn. Baltimore: Johns Hopkins University Press.

BAUDISSIN, W. W. G. 1889. *Die Geschichte des Alttestamentlichen Priesterthums*. Leipzig: S. Hirzel.

BLENKINSOPP, J. 1995. *Sage, Priest, Prophet: Religious and Intellectual Leadership in Ancient Israel*. Louisville, Ky.: Westminster/John Knox Press.

BUDDE, K. 1912. *Die altisraelitische Religion*, 3rd edn. Giessen: J. Ricker (Alfred Töpelmann).

CODY, A. 1969. *A History of Old Testament Priesthood*. Analecta Biblica, 35. Rome: Pontifical Biblical Institute.

CROSS, F. M. 1973. *Canaanite Myth and Hebrew Epic: Essays in the History of the Religion of Israel*. Cambridge, Mass.: Harvard University Press.

DAVIES, P. R. 1992. *In Search of 'Ancient Israel'*. Sheffield: JSOT Press.

DHORME, E. 1937. *L'Evolution religieuse d'Israel*, i: *La Religion des Hébreux nomades*. Brussels: Nouvelle Société d'éditions.

DOUGLAS, M. 1984. *Purity and Danger: An Analysis of the Concepts of Pollution and Taboo*. London: Ark Paperbacks.

—— 1993. *In the Wilderness: The Doctrine of Defilement in the Book of Numbers*. Sheffield: JSOT Press.

—— 2004. *Jacob's Tears: The Priestly Work of Reconciliation*. Oxford: Oxford University Press.

FENTON, T. 2004. 'Hebrew Poetic Structure as a Basis for Dating'. In J. Day, ed., *In Search of Pre-Exilic Israel*, London and New York: T. and T. Clark International, 386–409.

GESE, H. 1957. *Der Verfassungsentwurf des Ezechiel (Kap. 40–48) traditionsgeschichtlich untersucht*. Tübingen: Mohr.

GRIMME, H. 1924. 'Der südarabische Levitismus und sein Verhältnis zum Levitismus in Israel'. *Le Muséon*, 37: 169–99.

GUNNEWEG, A. H. J. 1965. *Leviten und Priester*. Göttingen: Vandenhoeck & Ruprecht.

HARAN, M. 1978. *Temples and Temple-Service in Ancient Israel: An Inquiry into the Character of Cult Phenomena and the Historical Setting of the Priestly School*. Oxford: Clarendon Press.

HÖLSCHER, G. 1925. 'Levi'. In Pauly-Wissowa, ed., *Real-encyclopädie der classischen Altertumswissenschaft*, Stuttgart: Metzler, xiii/2. 2155–2208.

HURVITZ, A. 1982. *A Linguistic Study of the Relationship between the Priestly Source and the Book of Ezekiel*. Paris: Gabalda.

JAPHET, S. 1993. *I and II Chronicles*. London: SCM Press.

JOHNSON, A. R. 1962. *The Cultic Prophet in Ancient Israel*. Cardiff: University of Wales Press.

KAISER, O. 1975. *Introduction to the Old Testament: A Presentation of its Results and Problems*, trans. J. Sturdy. Oxford: Blackwell.

MANOR, D. W. 1992. 'Timna (Place)'. *ABD* vi. 553–6.

MILGROM, J. 1991. *Leviticus 1–16: A New Translation with Introduction and Commentary*. AB3. New York: Doubleday.

—— 2000. *Leviticus 17–22: A New Translation with Introduction and Commentary*. AB3A. New York: Doubleday.

MILLER, P. D. 2000. *The Religion of Ancient Israel*. Louisville, Ky.: Westminster/John Knox Press.

MOWINCKEL, S. 1967. *The Psalms in Israel's Worship*, trans. D. R. ap-Thomas, 2 vols. Oxford: Blackwell.

NELSON, R. D. 1993. *Raising up a Faithful Priest: Community and Priesthood in Biblical Theology*. Louisville, Ky.: Westminster/John Knox Press.

NIELSEN, E. 1955. *Shechem: A Traditio-historical Investigation*. Copenhagen: G. E. C. Gad.

PEDERSEN, J. 1926. *Israel: Its Life and Culture*, i and ii. Copenhagen: Povl Branner.

—— 1940. *Israel: Its Life and Culture*, iii and iv. London: Oxford University Press.

POLZIN, R. 1976. *Late Biblical Hebrew: Toward an Historical Typology of Biblical Hebrew Prose*. Missoula, Mont.: Scholars Press.

RENDSBURG, G. 1980. 'Late Biblical Hebrew and the Date of "P" '. *Journal of the Ancient Near Eastern Society of Columbia University*, 12: 65–80.

ROOKE, D. 2000. *Zadok's Heirs: The Role and Development of the High Priesthood in Ancient Israel*. Oxford: Oxford University Press.

ROWLEY, H. H. 1948. *From Joseph to Joshua*. London: Oxford University Press.

—— 1950. 'Melchizedek and Zadok (Gen. 14 and Psalm 110)'. In W. Baumgartner, ed., *Festschrift für Alfred Bertholet*, Tübingen: Mohr, 461–72.

SCHAPER, J. 2000. *Priester und Leviten im achämenidischen Juda*. Tübingen: Mohr-Siebeck.

STAGER, L. E. 1985. 'The Archaeology of the Family in Ancient Israel'. *Bulletin of the American Schools of Oriental Research*, 260: 1–35.

TUELL, S. S. 1992. *The Law of the Temple in Ezekiel 40–48*. Atlanta: Scholars Press.

VANDERKAM, J. 2004. *From Joshua to Caiaphas*. Philadelphia: Fortress Press.

VAUX, R. DE 1961. 'Lévites' minéens et lévites israélites'. In *Lux Tua Veritas*, Trier: Paulinus-Verlag, 265–73.

WEIPPERT, M. 1971. *The Settlement of the Israelite Tribes in Palestine*, trans. J. D. Martin. London: SCM Press.

WELLHAUSEN, J. 1963. *Die Composition des Hexateuchs und der Historischen Bücher des Alten Testaments*, 4th edn. Berlin: de Gruyter.

—— 1973. *Prolegomena to the History of Ancient Israel*. Gloucester, Mass.: Peter Smith.

WHITELAM, K. W. 1996. *The Invention of Ancient Israel: The Silencing of Palestinian History*. London: Routledge.

WILLIAMSON, H. G. M. 1985. *Ezra, Nehemiah*. Waco, Tex.: Word Books.

ZIMMERLI, W. 1979. *Ezekiel 1: A Commentary on the Book of the Prophet Ezekiel, Chapters 1–24*. trans. R. E. Clements. Philadelphia: Fortress Press

—— 1983. *A Commentary on the Book of the Prophet Ezekiel Chapters 25–48*, trans. J. D. Martin. Philadelphia: Fortress Press.

CHAPTER 19

LAW IN THE OLD TESTAMENT

GORDON WENHAM

DEFINITION

The English term 'law' covers a much narrower range of literature than the Hebrew term *torah*, or the Greek *nomos*, which are conventionally translated 'law'. Hebrew *torah* would be better translated 'instruction', and the *torah* comprises the whole of the Pentateuch, Genesis to Deuteronomy, despite the fact that these books contain a fair amount of narrative. Psalm 1: 2, inviting the reader to meditate on the *torah* day and night, seems to envisage the book of Psalms as well as the Pentateuch being the *torah*.

By 'law' the English Bible reader understands the legal rulings and moral injunctions found within the Pentateuch, such as the Ten Commandments, the farming regulations of Exodus 22, the laws on sacrifice and purity in Leviticus, and the sermons of Deuteronomy. It is 'law' in this sense that is the focus of this essay, though it could be argued that only a broader definition that understands law as *torah* does full justice to the biblical understanding of the term. This essay also considers the administration of the law, whether by king, priest, or village elders. Throughout our discussion it will be advisable to pay attention to comparable legal texts and customs from elsewhere in the ancient Near East, for in the judicial sphere Israel shared many ideas with her neighbours.

OUTLINE

Law in the Ancient Near East

Several collections of law are found in the Pentateuch, and records of legal cases are scattered throughout the OT. These invite comparison with the collections of law, so-called codes, and the tens of thousands of legal texts from the ancient Near East. Records of legal cases from many different sites in Mesopotamia and Asia Minor tell of property transactions, loans, adoptions, marriages, and all sorts of disputes. These texts give a vivid picture of how law operated in practice in biblical times.

How far the ancient 'codes' of law reflect legal practice is less certain: some hold that these codes are collections of key decisions made by judges in court, others that these codes are more theoretical, reflecting the ideological concerns of the scribes who drafted them. The oldest of these 'codes' is that of Ur-Nammu from Ur (c.2100 BCE) written, like the laws of Lipit-Ishtar (c.1930 BCE), in the Sumerian language. The most famous collection of ancient law is that of Hammurabi of Babylon (c.1750 BCE). Other collections of Mesopotamian law in Akkadian include the laws of Eshnunna (c.1770 BCE) and the Middle Assyrian Laws (c.1076 BCE) and the neo-Babylonian laws (c.700 BCE). The Hittite Laws (c.1650–1500 BCE) are in Hittite, and come from their capital city Hattusha in what is modern Turkey (for translations of these texts see Roth 1995).

Analysis of these texts has shown that it is wrong to call them 'codes', for unlike later collections of law, such as the codes of Justinian or Napoleon, these ancient oriental texts do not attempt to be a complete or comprehensive statement of legal principles. Instead, we have a variety of topics addressed, but many areas are either unaddressed or mentioned only in passing. Thus in the Babylonian collections 'one finds no cases directly dealing with arson, treason, theft of livestock, surety, barter, murder, manumission, or sale' (Greengus 1992: 243). Similarly, the biblical collections of law are by no means comprehensive: various topics that are usually discussed in oriental collections, such as leasing, hiring of labour, sale, bride-price and dowry, are not explicitly discussed, but mentioned, if at all, only in passing.

So what are the principles underlying these collections of law? Why were they drawn up? And how do they relate to the day-to-day legal records of marriage, sale, conflict, and so on? One view of these collections is that they bring together traditional case law formulated in the courts in order to illustrate key legal principles that perhaps were being questioned at the time of composition. On the other hand, sometimes the collections are suggesting innovation or reform of traditional practice. More recent study of these collections has emphasized their similarity to other scholarly treatises of the scribal schools. These covered lists of gods, professions, omens, mathematics, and so forth. Law was another area of ancient scholarship, so scribes could take a topic—e.g. bodily injury—and show how the relevant judicial principle, talion, applied in a variety of situations and cases. This was a means of showing off the draftsman's skill and legal acumen. On this view of the collections, there could be a considerable gap between their view of the law and what was actually decided in the courts. If there is dispute about the processes of drafting these 'codes', their politico-religious function is much clearer, at least in the most fully preserved collections. Hammurabi, for example, set up his stela of law in the temple of Marduk in Babylon to commemorate all his pious deeds. He mentions his victories over Babylon's enemies, but particularly his rebuilding of various cities and the restoration of their temples, thus showing his religious devotion. At the top of the stela is a carving of Shamash, the god of justice, sitting on his throne, with Hammurabi standing in front of him. The god is giving Hammurabi the rod and the ring, symbols of sovereignty and justice. In the prologue Hammurabi declares, 'I established truth and justice as the declaration of the land', while the laws that follow, by their length and thoroughness, demonstrate just how seriously he took his duty to promote the rule of law.

In Israel, too, the kings were expected to fulfil similar roles: they were to bring peace by conquering their foes, they were responsible for building and maintaining the temple, and for administering justice. As Ps. 72: 1–2 puts it: 'Give the king your justice, O God, and your righteousness to the royal son! May he judge your people with righteousness, and your poor with justice!' The story of Solomon and the prostitute's baby demonstrates the ideal of royal judicial wisdom (1 Kgs. 3: 16–28).

However, whereas the god Shamash gave Hammurabi the gift of insight into justice, and his formulation of the laws demonstrates his exploitation of that gift, in Israel the king was not seen as the source or conduit of the laws. Rather, he was to be subject to the law himself (Deut. 17: 18–20), and the collections of biblical law celebrate not the wisdom of a human lawgiver, but the wisdom of God, who entrusted these laws to Israel. 'What great nation is there, that has statutes and rules so righteous as all this law?' (Deut. 4: 8).

In the epilogue to his laws, Hammurabi invites anyone who has a grievance to come to the temple and read his laws and then apply them to his problem (48: 3–19). This might be thought a little impractical, but the numerous copies of the laws that have been found suggest that it was a well-known scribal text. But in the tens of thousands of legal documents in Mesopotamia, there seems to be only one reference to the stela in connection with a dispute about rates of pay, a topic dealt with in Laws of Hammurabi 273–4. A similar phenomenon meets us in the Bible. The historical books make very few explicit references to the laws of the Pentateuch, and allusions to the laws in the prophets are hard to spot. But it seems likely that in both cultures the respective legal collections did exercise an important influence on legal and ethical practice, even though it may not always be obvious to the modern reader.

OT Collections of Law

Within the Pentateuch three major collections of law are distinguishable:

1. The Code of the Covenant (Exod. 20: 22–23: 33)
2. The Priestly Code (Leviticus + parts of Exodus and Numbers)
3. The Deuteronomic Code (Deuteronomy 12–28)

Prefacing them all are the Ten Commandments, or Decalogue (Exod 20: 2–17//Deut 5: 6–21), which, though not exactly laws, give a profound glimpse of Israel's fundamental religious and ethical concerns. All these codes and the Decalogue are set in the context of the exodus and the ministry of Moses, which are often dated to the thirteenth century BCE. The Ten Commandments, Code of the Covenant, and Priestly Code are all said by the Bible to have been revealed by God to Moses on Mount Sinai, while the Deuteronomic Code is part of Moses' farewell speech to Israel just before he dies.

The attribution to Moses of these collections is viewed as highly problematic by historical scholarship: usually they are supposed to have originated after his days and to have been drafted later still. The Priestly Code, for example, is typically dated to the sixth/fifth century BCE. As the issues of the growth of the Pentateuch are discussed elsewhere in this volume (see pages 471–7), they are not taken up here. However, it should be said that for later readers of the Pentateuch, the association of the laws with Sinai and with Moses was of tremendous importance and underlined the authority of the laws emphatically. The biblical laws did not originate with an inspired king, but were the very words of God himself. The Ten Commandments' special status is brought out by saying that they were inscribed on the tablets of stone 'with the finger of God' (Exod. 31: 18). Conversely, the insistence that all the laws were given to Moses, who then passed them on to Israel, highlights his unique status as the archetypal prophet with whom God spoke face to face (Num. 12: 6–8; Deut. 34: 10–12).

The Code of the Covenant

The Code of the Covenant (Exod. 20: 22–23: 33), generally supposed to be the oldest biblical code, falls into three main sections (20: 22–6; 21: 1–22: 20; 22: 21–23: 19) and an epilogue (23: 20–33). The short introductory section (20: 22–6) bans the worship of idols and gives rules about worship. A long section of case law (21: 1–22: 20) provides some of the closest parallels to extra-biblical collections. The form of these laws ('If a man does X, his punishment shall be Y') and the topics (slavery, physical injury, goring oxen, theft, seduction) are characteristic of other law codes. However, it is notable that slaves are mentioned first (21: 1–11) in this biblical code, whereas in non-biblical law their treatment is typically dealt with towards the end. It seems likely that Exodus highlights the plight of slaves, because its story-line tells of the release of Israel from slavery in Egypt (20: 2; 21: 9–14). This very point is reiterated at the start of the third section (22: 21–23: 19), which is largely a set of injunctions about caring for the poor and fulfilling religious obligations, especially the celebration of the national festivals. Finally, the epilogue (23: 20–33) is a mixture of exhortations and threats to encourage obedience to the law: such themes are typical of Near Eastern legal documents, such as law codes and treaties, which typically close with a section of blessings and curses.

The Priestly Code

The Priestly Code in its widest sense consists of most of Exodus 25 to Numbers 36, but the main legal section is found in Leviticus 1–26. This is usually divided into two major sections: the ritual laws in 1–16, and the so-called Holiness Code in 17–26. Usually, the Holiness Code is considered to be earlier than the ritual law, but this has been contested in more recent work (Knohl 1995; Joosten 1996). Chapters 1–7 give rules on the conduct of sacrifice, 11–15 define uncleanness, and 16 specifies the Day of Atonement ceremonies. The Holiness Code (17–26) covers the ethics of good neighbourliness (19), sex (18, 20), sacrifice (17, 22), and festivals (23, 25), and concludes with a collection of blessings and curses.

The Deuteronomic Code

The Deuteronomic Code (Deuteronomy 12–28) forms part of the second farewell address of Moses to Israel. Deuteronomy depicts Israel on the verge of crossing the Jordan into the promised land of Canaan, which Moses himself has been forbidden to enter. So in these farewell speeches he lays down the rules which Israel must follow if they want to prosper in the land. The Deuteronomic Code often takes up rules given in the Book of the Covenant and reformulates them (e.g. Deut. 15: 1–18; cf. Exod. 21: 1–11; Deut. 24: 10–13; cf. Exod. 22: 25–7). However, the overall sequence of material within chapters 12–25 seems to follow the order of the Ten Commandments: each block of material discusses an issue raised by the Decalogue (e.g. Deut. 15–16 (Sabbath), Deut. 19–21 (murder), Deut. 22 (adultery); see Kaufman 1978–9). Like the Book of the Covenant and the Holiness Code, Deuteronomy concludes with a section of blessings and curses (Deut. 28).

However, in one important respect the Deuteronomic law is very different from other biblical collections. Whereas the latter are presented as the direct words of God to Moses, Deuteronomy is Moses preaching about the law in much the way a prophet or preacher might do. It is essentially exhorting Israel to keep the law, not just stating what the law is. Over against their Near Eastern counterparts, these biblical collections of law contain many religious regulations about worship and loyalty to YHWH. Evidently Israel made less of a distinction between the secular and religious spheres than the Babylonians: loving God with all your heart involved treating your neighbour properly just as much as offering the correct sacrifices.

TYPES OF LAW

Laws are formulated in different ways. The commonest type begins with a conditional clause, 'if a man steals an ox', and continues with a main clause stating the consequences, 'he shall repay five oxen' (Exod. 22: 2). These are often called casuistic or case laws. Other laws are formulated unconditionally: e.g. 'Remember the Sabbath day', or 'You shall not steal' (Exod. 20: 8, 15). Alt (1966) termed this type of law apodictic, and his nomenclature has been widely followed. But there is a variety of ways in which to express the law conditionally and unconditionally, which has led to much debate as to how to classify some formulations.

Alt argued that biblical casuistic law was probably borrowed from the Canaanites, whereas the apodictic law was original to Israel and was probably developed in covenant renewal ceremonies. However, modern scholars are not so sure. We do not have any Canaanite laws to compare the biblical texts with, and apodictic formulations are found in extra-biblical treaties and are very similar to proverbs in their formulation. Proverbs may well have been passed on in a family or tribal setting, so unconditional laws could have a similar context. Thus, while it may be helpful to note the syntactic form of each law, it is risky to draw too many conclusions about its origin on the basis of its form.

More pertinent to an understanding of the laws is their use of motive clauses and their setting within the Pentateuch. Many laws have clauses inserted into them to encourage compliance with them. 'You shall not wrong a sojourner... for you *were sojourners*' (Exod. 22: 21), or 'Be holy, *for I am holy*' (Lev. 11: 45). These motive clauses are rarely found in non-biblical law, but are common in the Bible. They give an insight into the fundamental values that the law is trying to protect and also into the attitudes of the implied hearers of the law, for there would be no reason to include motive clauses unless the arguments they deploy resonated with the hearers.

The biblical codes of law, whatever their earlier settings, are now part of a narrative telling of Israel's journey from Egypt to the borders of Canaan. More exactly, Exodus to Deuteronomy could be defined as a biography of Moses (N.B. his birth Exodus 1, death Deuteronomy 34). This narrative setting is often emphasized by narrative interruptions to the collections, such as Leviticus 8–10, 24, and by the repeated phrase 'the LORD spoke to Moses'. This narrative essentially has two aims: first, to encourage submission to and compliance with the law. The stories of deliverance from Egyptian tyranny and the Sinai law giving demonstrate God's power and the danger of opposing him. The stories of the golden calf and the spies show the dire consequences of breaking the law (Exodus 32–4; Numbers 13–14). Ordinary Levites, priests, and even Aaron and Moses may face the death sentence for disobedience (Lev. 10: 1–3; Num. 16; 20: 10–12; 27: 12–23). The second purpose of the narrative is to celebrate the life of Moses and the part he played in creating the nation of Israel. Despite his own lapses, he was uniquely privileged in his access to God: no one else in Israel's history was so privy to the mind of God (Deut. 34: 10–12). Thus all later Israelites should follow his teaching loyally.

SOME PRINCIPLES OF OT LAW

1. Covenant

We have noted that the laws are set within the context of the exodus from Egypt and the experience of the Sinai wilderness. Closer reading shows that the laws form part of a covenant made at Sinai, whereby YHWH took Israel to be his people and Israel pledged herself to be devoted to him (Exod. 19: 4–6). 'I will be your God, and you shall be my people' (Lev. 26: 12) sums up the essence of the covenant relationship. It has been noted that this covenant is analogous to the vassal treaties of the ancient world, in which a victorious king imposed a treaty on his conquered vassals. This treaty making was viewed, at least by the suzerain, as an act of grace, which should prompt grateful loyalty on the part of the vassal. The stipulations of the treaty express what this loyalty should mean in practice. A similar ethos pervades the biblical laws. Loving God with all one's heart should be Israel's response to their liberation from slavery and the gift of the land (cf. Exod. 20: 2). Similarly, the command to have no other gods is an expression of covenant loyalty. We have already noted the similarity in structure of biblical and extra-biblical law codes. As ancient treaties had a similar structure (historical prologue, stipulations, curses, and blessings) to law codes, this same pattern can be traced in the biblical texts, especially the Decalogue and the book of Deuteronomy.

2. Loyalty to God

Central to the covenant was the requirement of total loyalty to YHWH. This demand heads the Decalogue (Exod. 20: 3). So important is it, that worship of other gods warrants the death penalty (Exod. 22: 20; Lev. 20: 1–5; Num. 25; Deut. 13). All the biblical codes express the anxiety that when the Israelites enter Canaan, they will be tempted to follow local worship practices and desert YHWH. Intermarriage with Canaanites is feared as most likely to lead in this direction. This is why the Canaanites are to be driven out of Canaan, and no treaties are to be made with them (Exod. 23: 23–33). The story of Israel's seduction by the wily Moabites and Midianites illustrates the problem (Numbers 25), so that Deuteronomy envisages the wholesale slaughter of the Canaanites, at least if they do not surrender (Deuteronomy 7, 20).

3. Family Solidarity

The Ten Commandments divide into two tables: the first four set out duties toward God, and the last six duties towards one's fellow man. Strikingly, the first command of the second table is 'Honour your father and mother' (Exod. 20: 12). The importance of this command is shown not simply by its position, but by the severe penalties for its breach (Exod. 21: 15, 17; Deut. 21: 18–21). Laws banning sexual relations with close relatives seem also designed to promote family solidarity and harmony (Lev. 18: 6–18; 20: 10–21). On the other hand, the parents' duty to instruct their children is also stressed (Deut. 6: 7; 11: 19),

4. Protection of the Poor

The prominence of the slavery laws in Exod. 21: 1–11 has already been noted. Though moderns view slavery as entirely negative, this was not the ancient perspective. It was a way of providing a livelihood for bankrupt peasant farmers and their families (Gen. 47: 23–6). But the law is designed to give the slave an escape into freedom if he prefers it, either in the seventh year (Exod. 21: 2–6) or in the year of Jubilee. In that year mortgaged land and property were also returned to their owner without charge (Lev. 25: 8–55). Deuteronomy also contains various regulations to help the poor, including the immigrant, the widow, and the orphan, notably a special tithe for them every third year (Deut. 14: 28–9).

5. Principles of Punishment

Deut. 19: 19–20 concisely sums up some of the key principles of biblical penal theory. 'You shall do to him as he had meant to do to his brother. So you shall purge the evil from your midst. And the rest shall hear and fear and never again commit such an evil.' Three principles are mentioned here. First, the offender must receive his legal desert, a punishment that fits the crime. This is summed up in the talion formula, 'an eye for an eye, and a tooth for a tooth' ((Exod. 21: 23–5; Lev. 24:

18–22; Deut. 19: 21). This did not mean that if someone knocked someone else's tooth out, he would lose his own, but rather that the injured person would be compensated appropriately for the lost tooth (Exod. 21: 26–7). Second, punishment purges the land of evil, especially blood guilt (Gen. 4: 10; Lev. 18: 24–8). Third, punishment acts as a deterrent, 'and the rest shall hear and fear'. A fourth principle is that of restitution: a thief must return the stolen property and some more. A farmer who lets his cattle graze his neighbour's land must make the loss good from his own field or vineyard (Exod. 22: 1–6).

6. Law and Ethics

Limiting our discussion to conditional or case law, as in the previous paragraph, may easily obscure an important fact. These case laws only regulate situations where things have gone wrong; they do not define the ethical ideals of the draftsmen. These ethical principles emerge in many of the positive unconditional laws, such as 'Be holy', 'Love your neighbour as yourself', 'Love the LORD your God with all your heart' (Lev. 11: 45; 19: 18; Deut. 6: 5). If these principles were always practised, there would be no call for the case law and the negative prohibitions. The case law and the prohibitions define minimum standards of behaviour: if these are transgressed, punishment must follow to prevent society from disintegrating into blood feuds. But it is the positive, unconditional precepts that define the Old Testament's ethical ideals.

LAW ENFORCEMENT AND ADMINISTRATION

The tight-knit village society of ancient Israel was much more law-abiding than today's urban jungles. There were no police and no professional judges at the local level. So when an offence was committed or a dispute arose, it was the responsibility of the aggrieved party or his family to bring the issue to the local elders. These elders were the senior men of the families in each locality. They gathered in a square at the city gate to hear the evidence and pronounce sentence. It was then usually the responsibility of the plaintiff's family to enforce judgment (e.g. Deut. 21: 18–21). Punishment of religious offences could involve the whole community (Josh. 7: 25). If someone was unable to enforce justice himself, he could appeal to the king (1 Kgs. 3: 16–28).

The OT presupposes a supreme judge in every era. Moses, Joshua, and Samuel are all portrayed as fulfilling this role before it was taken over by the king (Exod. 18: 16; Josh. 7: 16–25; 1 Sam. 7: 16–17). However, the texts do also seem to envisage that specially appointed judges and priests will judge some cases (Deut. 17: 8–13), and Jehoshaphat is said to have established a supreme court with the high priest presiding over religious cases and a chief from Judah judging secular issues (2 Chr. 19 : 8–11). Cases that were too difficult for local village courts to resolve were passed on to the supreme court (Deut. 17: 8).

New Testament Developments

The post-exilic era saw the development of close and detailed study of the written law (Neh. 8). It seems likely that some unrecorded legal principles were passed on by word of mouth, and that traditions of interpretation expanding the scope of the written text also developed. By the New Testament era there were different schools of thought among the Jews as to the value of this oral law. The Sadducees and the Essenes rejected these traditions, but the Pharisees valued them highly. Indeed, this was a point of contention between Jesus and the Pharisees (Mark 7: 1–13). But these Pharisaic traditions were eventually enshrined in the Mishnah (c.200 CE) and the Talmud (c.500 CE), and became central to normative Judaism.

In the NT church there were great disputes about the ongoing applicability of the OT law to Gentile converts. These disputes came to a head at the Council of Jerusalem (Acts 15), where a compromise was reached specifying what was mandatory for Gentile Christians (Acts 15: 28–9), though it seems likely that Jewish Christians were still expected to fulfil the law (Acts 16: 3; 21: 19–26). The issue of the law is discussed at length in the epistles to the Galatians and to the Romans. (For further discussion see Chapter 39.)

Suggested Reading

Patrick (1985) offers a thorough historical introduction to biblical law. Roth (1995) gives a modern translation of the extant non-biblical codes. Greengus (1992) focuses on the similarities and differences between ancient oriental law and biblical law very helpfully. From a Christian perspective Wright (2004) and Lalleman

(2004) explore the intrinsic values and ongoing relevance of OT law, while Sanders (1977) and Tomson (1990) review the place of law in NT theology and practice.

BIBLIOGRAPHY

ALT, A. 1966. 'The Origins of Israelite Law'. In *Essays on Old Testament History and Religion*, Oxford: Basil Blackwell, 79–132.

BRIN, G. 1994. *Studies in Biblical Law*. Sheffield: Sheffield Academic Press.

GREENGUS, S. 1992. 'Law'. *ABD* iv. 242–52.

JOOSTEN, J. 1996. *People and the Land in the Holiness Code*. Leiden: Brill.

KAUFMAN, S. 1978–9. 'The Structure of the Deuteronomic Law'. *Maarav*, 1.2: 105–58.

KNOHL, I. 1995. *The Sanctuary of Silence*. Minneapolis: Fortress Press.

LALLEMAN, H. 2004. *Celebrating the Law? Rethinking OT Ethics*. Carlisle: Paternoster Press.

LEVINSON, B. M., ed. 1994. *Theory and Method in Biblical and Cuneiform Law: Revision, Interpolation and Development*. Sheffield: Sheffield Academic Press.

OTTO, E. 1994. *Theologische Ethik des Alten Testaments*. Stuttgart: Kohlhammer.

PATRICK, D. 1985. *Old Testament Law*. Atlanta: John Knox Press.

PHILLIPS, A. 1970. *Ancient Israel's Criminal Law: A New Approach to the Decalogue*. Oxford: Basil Blackwell.

—— 2002. *Essays on Biblical Law*. Sheffield: Sheffield Academic Press.

ROTH, M. T. 1995. *Law Collections from Mesopotamia*, 2nd edn. Atlanta: Scholars Press.

SAALSCHÜTZ, J. L. 1853. *Das Mosaische Recht*. Berlin: Carl Heymann.

SANDERS, E. P. 1977. *Paul and Palestinian Judaism*. London: SCM Press.

SPRINKLE, J. M. 1994. *'The Book of the Covenant': A Literary Approach*. Sheffield: Sheffield Academic Press.

TOMSON, P. J. 1990. *Paul and the Jewish Law*. Assen: Van Gorcum.

WATTS, J. W. 1999. *Reading Law: The Rhetorical Shaping of the Pentateuch*. Sheffield: Sheffield Academic Press.

WENHAM, G. J. 2000. *Story as Torah: Reading the Old Testament Ethically*. Edinburgh: T. & T. Clark.

WESTBROOK, R. 1988. *Studies in Biblical and Cuneiform Law*. Paris: Gabalda.

WRIGHT, C. J. H. 2004. *OT Ethics for the People of God*. Leicester: Apollos.

CHAPTER 20

SCRIBES AND SYNAGOGUES

LESTER L. GRABBE

The topics of scribes and synagogues could be treated separately, since it is a matter of interpretation as to whether they had anything to do with each other. Nevertheless, modern theories have not infrequently seen both scribes and synagogues as 'lay' institutions, over against priests and the temple. Before considering the question of their relationship, the two topics will be looked at separately.

SCRIBES

Scribes were the backbone of administration in the ancient and Hellenistic Near East. As those able to read and write, and trained in record keeping and document drafting, they were necessary in every society. When literacy and the production of writings are discussed in scholarly writings on the Bible, the place and importance of professional scribes is not always recognized.

The Hebrew Bible assumes that scribes were used in the administration of the kingdoms of Israel and Judah: David's scribes (2 Sam. 8: 17; 20: 25; 1 Chr. 18: 16; 24: 6), Solomon's scribe (1 Kgs. 4: 3), a royal scribe in the time of Jehoash (2 Kgs. 12: 11; 2

Chr. 24: 11), Shebna the scribe (2 Kgs. 18: 18, 37; 19: 2); Shaphan the scribe (2 Kgs. 22: 3, 8–10, 12; 2 Chr. 34: 15, 18, 20), the scribe of the army commander (2 Kgs. 25: 19; Jer. 52: 25). Jeremiah has a number of references to scribes: the chamber of Gemariah, son of Shaphan, the scribe in the Temple (36: 10); the chamber of the scribe in the king's palace (36: 12); Elishama the scribe (36: 12, 20, 21); Baruch the scribe plays a prominent role (36: 26, 32); Jeremiah was imprisoned in the house of Jonathan the scribe (37: 15, 20).

Levites as scribes are mentioned in a number of passages of Chronicles that have no parallel in Kings (many would argue that these passages should be dated to the Persian period and reflect the situation then): clans of scribes were said to live at Jabez (1 Chr. 2: 55); Shemaiah ben Nathanel the Levite was a scribe (1 Chr. 24: 6); the clans of the Izharites and Hebronites acted as scribal administrators (1 Chr. 26: 29–32); Jeiel the scribe mustered the army under Uzziah (2 Chr. 26: 11); some of the Levites were scribes, officials, and gatekeepers (2 Chr. 34: 13). Zadok the scribe is appointed to a panel by Nehemiah (Neh. 13: 13); his name might suggest that he is a priest, but other members of the panel are identified as a priest and a Levite while he is said only to be a scribe.

It could be debated as to how reliable the information from the Hebrew Bible is. However, we also have contemporary information beginning at least with the Persian period. Ten seal impressions from a horde sold on the antiquities market have the name 'to Jeremai the scribe' (Avigad 1976: 7–8). These do not tell us a lot beyond the title, but we have valuable data from the Jewish community at Elephantine in Egypt. A number of the documents name the scribe who copied it (e.g. *TAD* A6. 2: 28; A6. 8: 4; A6. 10: 10; A6. 11: 6; A6. 12: 3; A6. 13: 5 = *AP* 26: 28; *AD* 4: 4; 7: 10; 8: 6; 9: 3; 10: 5). 'Scribes of the province' are named alongside judges and other officials in a letter to Arsames, the governor of Egypt (*TAD* A6. 1: 1, 6 = *AP* 17: 1, 6); we also have references to 'scribes of the treasury' (*TAD* 4. 3: 13//4. 4: 12, 14 = *AP* 3: 13//2: 12, 14). An individual, whose salary had not been paid and had complained to the 'officials', was told to complain to the scribes (*TAD* A3. 3: 5 = *BM* 4: 5).

The main employers of scribes would have been the provincial administration and the temple (Grabbe 1995: 152–71). Scribes would have worked at various levels, however, all the way from high up in the administration, where they advised and supported the governor and the main offices of the provincial administration, to posts in the treasury where records of payments and even lists of taxpayers were kept, to storage warehouses for taxes and tithes, where they kept inventory of incoming produce and dispersals for approved purposes. We also know about temple scribes. For example, they are referred to in the decree of Antiochus III about 200 BCE (*AJ* 12. 3. 3, §§142). The temple scribes would have had similar record-keeping duties, but in addition they would have had the responsibility of copying any sacred writings, manuals, instruction books, lists of regulations, priestly genealogies, and the like relating to the temple administration. Some scribes were quite powerful with a high office, whereas others had rather mundane duties. Neverthelesss, the office of scribe—whether high or low—required a trained individual and was preferable to back-breaking labour for uncertain yields in the fields, vineyards, and orchards.

There is evidence that the Levites were especially drawn on for the scribal skills necessary to run the nation as well as the temple (cf. Grabbe 1995: 160–1; Schwartz 1992: 89–101). The temple personnel—both priests and Levites—were the ones who had the education and leisure for intellectual pursuits, and thus constituted the bulk of the educated and those who read, wrote, and commented on religious literature. They were also the primary teachers in religious matters. Thus, not only the cult but also a large portion of the religious activity of other sorts, including teaching and development of the tradition, took place in the temple context.

Another function carried out by some scribes—probably only a very few—was that of literary activity. The legendary scribe Ahiqar was said to be an advisor to the king of Assyria and the composer of wise sayings. In *The Words of Ahiqar* he is described as 'a wise and rapid/skillful scribe' (*TAD* C1. 1: 1; cf. line 35) and as 'the wise scribe and master of good counsel' (*TAD* C1. 1: 42; cf. lines 12, 18). In general, scribes were an important part of the intellectual scene during the Second Temple period (Schams 1998; Grabbe 1995: 152–76).

Perhaps the most famous passage on the scribe is that of Ben Sira (38: 24–39: 11, NEB):

A scholar's wisdom comes of ample leisure; to be wise he must be relieved of other tasks. How can one become wise who guides the plough . . . whose talk is all about cattle? . . . How different it is with the one who devotes himself to studying the law of the Most High, who explores all the wisdom of the past and occupies himself with the study of prophecies! He preserves the sayings of famous men and penetrates the subtleties of parables. He explores the hidden meaning of proverbs and knows his way among enigmatic parables. The great avail themselves of his services, and he is seen in the presence of rulers. He travels in foreign countries, learning at first hand human good or human evil. He makes a point of rising early to seek the Lord. . . . If it is the will of the mighty Lord, he will be filled with a spirit of intelligence; then he will pour forth wise sayings of his own and give thanks to the Lord in prayer. He is directed in his counsel and knowledge by the Lord, whose secrets are his constant study. In his teaching he will reveal his learning, and his pride will be in the law of the Lord's covenant. Many will praise his intelligence; it will never be forgotten. The memory of him will not die, and his name will live for ever and ever. The nations will tell of his wisdom, and the assembled people will sing his praise. If he lives long, he will leave a name in a thousand; when he goes to his long rest, his reputation is secure.

This is no doubt an idealized image of the scribe, which makes the scribe responsible for knowledge and study of God's law. Ben Sira's close association with the Temple (some have argued that he was himself a priest) should be kept in mind, however. It is not clear that Ben Sira was suggesting that everyone with scribal training was to be an expert in the law.

The use of the term 'scribe' in Jewish literature after the time of Ben Sira follows basically the usage already outlined: normally, 'scribe' refers to a professional:

someone trained to write, copy, keep accounts, and otherwise carry out the functions we now associate with being a clerk or a secretary. The position could vary from a rather lowly individual keeping records in a warehouse to a high minister of state whose office was an important one in the established governmental bureaucracy. The situation can be exemplified from Josephus, who makes many references to scribes: village clerks (*BJ*. 1. 24. 3, §479); the secretary to Herod (*BJ*. 1. 26. 3, §529); the secretary of the Sanhedrin (*BJ*. 5. 13. 1, §532); the scribes of the temple (*AJ*. 12. 3. 3, §142).

Here and there, however, we find hints that the term could also be used of someone learned in the divine law and looked up to as an interpreter of scripture. This might be the case in some passages, though the possibility remains that the individuals referred to were professional scribes who served in the public bureaucracy or were employed by private clients. For example, 1 Macc. 7: 12 speaks of a delegation of scribes who appeared before Alcimus to ask for terms. On the one hand, they may have represented the learned among the anti-Seleucid opposition (some would say they were the scholars among the Hasidim—v. 13); on the other hand, it is also possible that they were professional scribes (nor is it clear that they had anything to do with the Hasidim mentioned in the same general context). Similarly, 2 Macc. 6: 18–31 refers to the martyr Eleazar as a scribe. Is this because of a special knowledge of the law or because he was just an ordinary scribe? For what it is worth, 4 Macc. 5: 4 says that he was a priest.

Apart from Ben Sira, this usage of 'scribe' to mean one learned in the sacred law is best known from the NT. In some NT texts 'scribe' seems to have almost a sectarian meaning, as if they were a religious group alongside the Sadducees, Pharisees, and others. Thus, Mark 7: 1–23 mentions both Pharisees and scribes together, as does Matt. 12: 38, 23: 2, and Luke 5: 21. Is this a new and different identity for the 'scribes'? Is there now a religious sect known as 'the scribes'? The answer is not an easy one, and needs to take into account recent study of the gospel writers, their knowledge and intent. It may be that by the time Mark (usually thought to be the earliest of the evangelists) wrote, the Pharisees were the only group really known, and references to other groups were made not on the basis of proper knowledge (cf. Cook 1978). D. R. Schwartz (1992: 89–101) has noted that since the temple personnel were often drawn on for their scribal skills, the 'scribes' of the gospels may in many cases be Levites.

The key may lie in some passages that some scholars (e.g. Cook 1978) have dismissed as secondary. The most likely reading of Mark 2: 16 is 'scribes of the Pharisees', which suggests that scribes were not a separate party but certain professionals among the Pharisees. Acts 23: 9 speaks of 'scribes of the Pharisees' party'. This suggests that other parties (e.g. the Sadducees) also had their own scribes, perhaps individuals with special expertise in the law or legal interpretations of the sect in question. If so, this usage would be in line with that of Ben Sira, in which the 'ideal' of the scribe is not only one with professional knowledge and skills but also one with knowledge and understanding of God's law. Also, this explanation need not contradict D. R. Schwartz's argument, since some of the Levites may well have belonged to various of the sects extant at the time.

The question of literacy in ancient societies has been more of an emotive issue than one might expect. This is probably because for some it is linked to the question of whether the composition of biblical literature was early or late. That is, those who defend literacy at an early time in Israel tend to be those who also argue for an early origin of the text (e.g. Millard 1985). Yet most studies agree that functional literacy among the general population was low in most pre-modern societies, especially those with complicated scripts such as Egyptian hieroglyphs or Mesopotamian cuneiform. But was it any different in Israelite and Jewish society, where there was an alphabetic script, as has been argued? Recent studies have indicated that those who had an alphabetic script were not much better off, by all counts (e.g. Young 1998). Historically, having an alphabetic script does not guarantee a high rate of literacy among the general populace, as shown by studies of Greece and Rome (Street 1984; Harris 1989) or even of Jewish society in the late Second Temple period (Hezser 2001), 5 per cent being the general maximum.

A similar judgement applies to the question of schools (Grabbe 1995: 171–4). The ideal of public education is a modern concept. In antiquity the wealthy might hire tutors, and we know that in the Graeco-Roman world 'sophists' would take on pupils for payment. Greek cities also operated a 'gymnasium' for the training of citizens, but this was limited to the small number who qualified as citizens. In short, a system of schools for the general public was unknown. In the ancient Near East schools for training scribes existed in places like Egypt and Mesopotamia because their vast bureaucracies required many scribes. In ancient Israel and Judah, however, the number of scribes would have been much smaller. Scribes in the temple would have been trained by priests. There are also indications that the scribal office was often passed down from father to son, so that training could be given via a form of apprenticeship (Grabbe 1995: 160–1).

SYNAGOGUES

The question of when and where the synagogue originated has been much debated recently (Binder 1999; Fine 1997, 1999; the essays collected in Urman and Flesher 1995). It used to be taken for granted that the institution of the synagogue arose during the Babylonian exile—or possibly even earlier—and had a central role in worship and instruction throughout Jewish communities from then on. Much recent study finds this picture problematic and ultimately unconvincing. There are several reasons for this. First, no source refers to the synagogue or anything like it until the third century BCE. Secondly, for many centuries the temple seems to have been the centre of public worship, and substitution of some other form of public worship is not likely to have come about very suddenly. Thirdly, when worship outside the temple is mentioned in the sources, the references are to prayer and the like in the context of the home.

No one questions the importance that the synagogue took on for Jewish communities in the early centuries of the Common Era. The synagogue is attested both literarily and archaeologically from the second or third centuries CE as playing a central role in most Jewish communities, functioning as a centre not only of worship but also of community life, whether in Palestine, Egypt, the Graeco-Roman world, or Babylonia. The question is: when during the half a millennium or so after the Babylonian exile did the synagogue develop into this important Jewish institution?

The move to a community place of public worship seems to have taken time. The early written sources that mention Jews worshipping outside Jerusalem always picture them doing so in the privacy of their homes. In Tobit, prayer is conducted and the festivals celebrated in the home (2: 1–3); there is no hint of a community institution. Both Daniel (6: 11) and Judith (8: 36–10: 2) picture their protagonists as praying in their homes (cf. also Acts 1: 13–14). Ben Sira, 1–3 Macc., and the *Letter of Aristeas* are silent on the question of the synagogue.

The earliest material evidence for the synagogue is in the mid-third century BCE in Egypt, i.e. the Diaspora (Griffiths 1987; Hachlili 1997). At that time we start to find buildings with inscriptions that speak of a 'prayer house' (*proseuchē*) of the Jews. This is hardly surprising, because Jewish communities in the areas far away from Palestine had no easy access to the Jerusalem Temple. Pilgrims came each year in great numbers to worship at Jerusalem during the annual festivals, yet this was still only a small minority of Jews the world over. A wealthy Jew such as Philo of Alexandria mentions travelling to Jerusalem only once (*De Providentia* 2. 64). Perhaps he went more than once in his lifetime, but the impression one has is that he did not go very frequently. Thus, the Diaspora communities would have felt a need for some means of expressing their religion in a community fashion.

Nothing is found in Palestine, however, until the first century CE Theodotus inscription (Binder 1999: 104). Most accept that it is pre-70 (though H. Kee (e.g. 1990) has consistently argued that it is post-70; but see the criticisms of van der Horst 1999: 18–23; Binder 1999: 104–9). The author of the inscription states that the synagogue of the inscription goes back to the time of his grandfather and served as a place for reading the law and giving hospitality to travellers. Otherwise, it has been difficult to find pre-70 remains of synagogue buildings. Ruins of a synagogue are thought to have been found in Gamla to the north-east of the Sea of Galilee, in Herodium, and at Masada. Although not everyone is willing to concede that the archaeology is certain (Chiat 1982: 116–18, 204–7, 248–51, 282–4; there are no inscriptions identifying them, for example), most scholars are willing to accept that the synagogue is attested as an institution in Palestine by the first century CE. This is consistent with the literary sources which suggest that the synagogue was imported into Palestine after the Maccabean Revolt.

The earliest references to anything like synagogues in extant literature are found no earlier than the first century CE. The first of these is Philo of Alexandria (*proseuchē*: In *Flacc.* 47–9, 53; *Leg.* 132–4, etc.). Both Josephus and the NT make reference to synagogues in various parts of the Roman Empire. Josephus mentions synagogues in Caesarea (*sunagogē*: *BJ* 2. 14. 4, §285), Dora (*sunagogē*: *AJ* 19. 6. 3, §§300–5), as well as in Tiberias (*proseuchē*: *Vit.* 54, §277), though not elsewhere in Palestine. The NT is the earliest set of writings that specifically locates synagogues in the centre of Palestine, including Jerusalem. Many passages in the gospels and Acts describe Jesus or the early Christians attending and even speaking in the synagogues. Perhaps one of the most detailed descriptions is found in Luke 4: 16–29.

What exactly did the synagogue do? What sorts of activities went on in it? Some attempt at describing the activities can be made (cf. Binder 1999: 389–450), but the data are insufficient to give a full picture. The sources vary from primary inscriptions, to alleged official decrees and letters in literary sources, to statements in literary sources. These are not all on the same level of credibility, and Josephus's apologetic concerns make some of his data suspect. But the same broad picture tends to emerge from the various sources. Reading scripture, prayer, and teaching and homiletic activity seem to have been the main sort of activities in synagogues, but it is difficult to go beyond that with any certainty.

It has recently been argued that the synagogue had nothing originally to do with prayer or worship (McKay 1994). This position seems misplaced for two reasons (cf. van der Horst 1999: 23–37; Binder 1999: 404–15): (1) the earliest name in inscriptions is *proseuchē* '(place of) prayer, prayer (house)', which seems an odd name to give a building which had nothing to do with prayer; (2) Agatharchides of Cnidus states that the Jews 'pray with outstretched hands in the temples (*hiera*) until the evening' (quoted in Josephus, *Ap.* 1. 22, §209). Although speaking of Jerusalem, he is likely drawing on his experience of synagogues in Alexandria and elsewhere in the Diaspora.

The Theodotus inscription speaks only of the reading and study of scriptures (as well as hospitality). The reading of the Torah seems to have been carried out in many synagogues, if not in all. We have no information that would allow us to go beyond this statement. Despite the occasional argument that a biblical reading was done according to a fixed lectionary cycle, this seems unlikely; even rabbinic literature does not attest a fixed cycle until quite late (Grabbe 1988: 408–9). The same applies to the translation of the biblical readings into Aramaic. Although this translation apparently had a place in synagogue services during the rabbinic period, no evidence has so far been produced that targums or targumizing had a place in the pre-70 synagogues.

Finally, there is the question of whether there is a relationship between scribes and the synagogue. It must first be noted that the concept of scribes and synagogues being 'lay' institutions is not borne out by the facts. A number of sources suggest that priests and Levites were often involved in major roles in the synagogue (Binder 1999: 355–60). There also seems to have been a conscious imitation of the Jerusalem Temple in many of the Diaspora synagogues (see the survey in Binder 1999: 227–341). In any case, the term 'lay institution' seems inappropriate. Of the different officials attested in the various sources (Binder 1999: 343–71), 'scribes' are occasionally associated with synagogues. A rather tattered papyrus of the first century BCE, which seems to describe a meeting of a Jewish burial society in the synagogue, mentions a scribe in a broken context (Binder 1999: 447). It probably means that one or more scribes were present to assist the meeting in its business. Two passages in the gospels criticize scribes because they seek the best seats in the synagogue (Mark 12: 29//Matt. 23: 6//Luke 20: 46; cf. Luke 11: 43) and do not teach the way Jesus does (Mark 1: 21–2). This is not a very large haul of data on the subject.

What we *can* say is that scribes were needed for certain of the activities carried out in the synagogue. They would have kept records and done the other tasks relating to writing and drawing up documents. They would probably also have served as notaries or witnesses to the signing of documents. Thus, one can reasonably presume that each synagogue would have had one or more scribes employed full- or part-time. Mark 1: 21–2 also suggests that scribes had a teaching function. This would have made even more sense if the scribes were often priests or Levites. But this does not lead us necessarily to associate scribes with synagogues or to see synagogues as particularly staffed or run by scribes.

It has sometimes been suggested that the synagogue was particularly associated with the Pharisees—that the synagogue was even a Pharisaic institution. All we can say is that this is simply speculation: there is no evidence to support such a supposition. None of the inscriptions or literary sources makes such an association: the passages on the Pharisees in Josephus, the gospels, and Acts do not mention the Pharisees as in any special way connected with synagogues.

In conclusion, it seems likely that the synagogue first arose in the Diaspora to meet the needs of communities without easy access to the temple. This was probably about the third century BCE. Synagogues served as places of prayer and/ or study, but would easily develop into some sort of central community institution. Only gradually did they filter into Palestine itself, where the temple was reasonably accessible. This is likely to have happened in the post-Maccabean period, perhaps in the first century BCE or even CE.

BIBLIOGRAPHY

AVIGAD, N. 1976. *Bullae and Seals from a Post-Exilic Judean Archive*, Qedem 4, Jerusalem: Hebrew University.

BINDER, DONALD D. 1999. *Into the Temple Courts: The Place of the Synagogues in the Second Temple Period*. SBL DS 169. Atlanta: Scholars Press.

BLENKINSOPP, JOSEPH 1995. *Sage, Priest, Prophet: Religious and Intellectual Leadership in Ancient Israel*. Library of Ancient Israel. Louisville, Ky.: Westminster/John Knox.

BOWMAN, ALAN K., and WOOLF, GREG, eds. 1994. *Literacy and Power in the Ancient World*. Cambridge: Cambridge University Press.

CHIAT, M. J. S. 1982. *Handbook of Synagogue Architecture*. BJS 29. Atlanta: Scholars Press.

COOK, M. J. 1978. *Mark's Treatment of the Jewish Leaders*. NTSupp 51. Leiden: Brill.

CRENSHAW, JAMES L. 1998. *Education in Ancient Israel: Across the Deadening Silence*. AB Reference Library. New York: Doubleday.

FINE, STEVEN 1997. *This Holy Place: On the Sanctity of the Synagogue during the Greco-Roman Period*. Christianity and Judaism in Antiquity, 11. Notre Dame, Ind.: University of Notre Dame Press.

—— ed. 1999. *Jews, Christians, and Polytheists in the Ancient Synagogue: Cultural Interaction during the Greco-Roman Period*. Baltimore Studies in the History of Judaism. London and New York: Routledge.

GRABBE, LESTER L. 1988. 'Synagogues in Pre-70 Palestine: A Re-assessment', *JTS* 39: 401–10; repr. in Urman and Flesher (1995), i. 17–26.

—— 1995. *Priests, Prophets, Diviners, Sages: A Socio-historical Study of Religious Specialists in Ancient Israel*. Valley Forge, Pa.: Trinity Press International.

GRIFFITHS, J. GWYN 1987. 'Egypt and the Rise of the Synagogue'. *JTS* 38: 1–15; repr. Urman and Flesher (1995), i. 3–16.

HACHLILI, RACHEL 1997. 'The Origin of the Synagogue: A Re-assessment'. *JSJ* 28: 34–47.

HARRIS, WILLIAM V. 1989. *Ancient Literacy*. Cambridge, Mass.: Harvard University Press.

HEZSER, CATHERINE 2001. *Jewish Literacy in Roman Palestine*. TSAJ 81. Tübingen: Mohr Siebeck.

HORST, PIETER W. VAN DER 1999. 'Was the Synagogue a Place of Sabbath Worship before 70 CE?'. In Fine (1999), 18–43.

KEE, HOWARD CLARK 1990. 'The Transformation of the Synagogue after 70 C.E.: Its Import for Early Christianity'. *NTS* 36: 1–24.

MCKAY, HEATHER A. 1994. *Sabbath and Synagogue: The Question of Sabbath Worship in Ancient Judaism*. Religions in the Graeco-Roman World 122. Leiden: Brill.

MILLARD, A. R. 1985. 'An Assessment of the Evidence of Writing in Ancient Israel'. In *Biblical Archaeology Today: Proceedings of the International Congress of Biblical Archaeology, Jerusalem 1984*, Jerusalem: Israel Exploration Society, 301–12.

NIDITCH, SUSAN 1996. *Oral World and Written Word: Ancient Israelite Literature*. Library of Ancient Israel. Louisville, Ky.: Westminster/John Knox; London: SPCK.

SCHAMS, CHRISTINE 1998. *Jewish Scribes in the Second-Temple Period*. JSOTS.S 291. Sheffield: Sheffield Academic Press.

SCHWARTZ, DANIEL R. 1992. *Studies in the Jewish Background of Christianity*. WUNT 60. Tübingen: Mohr Siebeck.

STREET, B. V. 1984. *Literacy in Theory and Practice*. Cambridge Studies in Oral and Literate Culture. Cambridge: Cambridge University Press.

URMAN, DAN, and FLESHER, PAUL V. M., eds. 1995. *Ancient Synagogues: Historical Analysis and Archaeological Discovery*, i, ii. SPB 47. Leiden: Brill.

YOUNG, I. M. 1998. 'Israelite Literacy: Interpreting the Evidence'. *VT* 48: 239–53, 408–22.

CHAPTER 21

MOVEMENTS

JUDITH M. LIEU

Accounts of Judaism often start from Josephus's description of the three 'schools of thought' (*haireseis*, sometimes misleadingly translated as 'sects'), or 'philosophies', among the Jews, the Pharisees, the Sadducees, and the Essenes (*BJ* 2. 119–66; *AJ* 13. 171–3; 18. 11–22). New Testament references to the Pharisees and the Sadducees seemingly confirmed this starting-point, while the discovery of the Dead Sea Scrolls, often associated with Josephus's Essenes, apparently completed the picture, although it also did much to stimulate reconsideration of Jewish faith and practice. On the other hand, Josephus also describes the Jews as holding a remarkable unity (*Ap.* 2. 151–219), and the tension between these two claims sets the scene for the debates about 'unity and diversity' that have dominated much modern scholarship (Cohen 1987). A stress on the diversity and different positions has led to talk of Judaisms, while one on a core unity to that of 'common Judaism'. Yet, even given this starting-point, 'three' is obviously a stylized number, and the uncritical submission to Josephus in some accounts of first-century Judaism has probably led to considerable distortion. Moreover, the language of philosophies is an evident accommodation to his Greek readers and should warn us against reading his accounts as dispassionate; it is this philosophical dress that leads him to define the groups through their views on fate and human free will, categories that sit uncomfortably with the biblical tradition to which all looked. None the less, a definition of these three groups in terms of their differentiating convictions still dominates accounts, although we shall see that it can hardly prove adequate.

Following Josephus, the origins of such movements have regularly been traced to the distinctive circumstances of the second century BCE: apart from the free-floating tradition in *AJ* 18. 171–3, they first appear, already established, when the

Hasmonaean John Hyrcanus (ruled 134–104 BCE) switched allegiance from the Pharisees to the Sadducees (*AJ* 13. 288–98). Yet what was it that should cause these and other groups to emerge at this time? Do they reflect varying responses to the historical events of the period—for example, to the 'threat of Hellenism' in the supposed attempt by Antiochus Epiphanes to outlaw Jewish practice, or to the support he received internally (1 Macc. 1: 20–63), or to the power and strategies adopted by the Hasmonaeans once independence was achieved? Do they represent changes in class structure and in opportunities for individual self-expression or access to influence that were implicated in these events? Is their appearance to be linked with other changes in Judaism in this period—for example, with the growing focus on Torah, alongside but also independently of the Temple, which made possible the rise of Torah specialists from outside the priestly classes, in which case should we trace them back to Ezra 'the scribe'? Are they best labelled 'schools of thought' on a philosophical model, 'movements', a loosely-structured tendency with a wider following than the immediate core, or 'parties', suggesting a conscious membership but a willingness to work within patterns of co-operation as well as competition, or 'sects', sociologically defined by their clear self-determined boundaries and by a conscious distancing from or rejection of other claimants to power or the tradition (see Baumgarten 1997)? Such questions lie at the heart of a fundamental debate particularly regarding the Pharisees and Sadducees, as to whether they are to be defined primarily in terms of their doctrinal stance towards the 'pillars' of Jewish faith and practice, Law and Temple, or in terms of their social context and relationship to internal and external power structures. Moreover, are they to be described diachronically in terms of their social and political history, or in the more synchronic functionalist terms of their relationship with the control-ling structures of Judaism or contemporary circumstances? (See among others Saldarini 1988; Stemberger 1995).

As can be illustrated with reference to the Pharisees, much depends on the evaluation given to the explicit references (see above) and on the detection of other sources of information. The older classic view was that the Pharisees were the dominant party in late Second Temple Judaism (following Josephus (e.g. *AJ* 18. 15) and their frequency in the Gospels and Acts), and that they represented the future shape of Judaism through their heirs, the rabbis. As a consequence, rabbinic sources were mined to illustrate Pharisaic thought and practice; on the assumption of Pharisaic dominance, such sources were also held to represent 'orthodox' Judaism of the pre-rabbinic period. Here they are a 'religious' group, characterized particularly by their allegiance to the 'oral law' as the organ of their strict interpretation of Torah (as in Josephus and the NT, e.g. Mark 7: 3–4); this view might interpret their name (from the root *prš*) as emphasizing their 'accuracy' (Josephus, *BJ* 2. 162), now mirrored by their rejection in the Dead Sea Scrolls as 'Ephraim…those who seek smooth things' (4QpNahum (*Nahum Pesher*) 3–4 ii. 2) (see Baumgarten 1983). The power claimed for them, although including a social or political dimension, is here predicated on a predominantly 'religious' definition of first-century Judaism, even when it is also accepted that they despised the 'masses who did not know the law', or (important from a Christian perspective) that the minutiae of their regulations led to a burdensome and dry legalism (cf. John 7: 49; Matt. 23: 13–24). Often also assumed here is their challenge to the Temple aristocracy (the Sadducees?), whose connivance with Rome and even financial corruption supposedly distanced them from the people. (Schaper 1999 still represents elements of this picture.)

However, this picture of a Pharisaic monopoly is now widely challenged. It is already undermined by the limited explicit role that they play in Josephus's description of the events of the first century CE (Sievers 1996). In practice, the Temple continued to be the religious and political power centre until its destruction in 70 CE, and those who held most power in the Temple—*pace* Josephus, the priestly classes—would surely have most actual power (see Sanders 1992). Accordingly, some have argued that Josephus's claims and the high profile of the Pharisees in the Gospels reflect the time when all these were written, towards the end of the first century CE, when the rabbis, supposedly their successors, were coming to prominence and provided the major opposition to the nascent Christian movement. This would, for example, explain the heightened polemic against the Pharisees in Matthew's Gospel (e.g. Matt. 23) compared with his source, Mark. Here the Pharisees appear as a group, 'waiting in the wings' prior to the destruction of the Temple, still characterized by a distinctive attitude to Torah, possibly, but not certainly, with some popular following, but not the defining representatives of 'Judaism', either religiously nor politically.

Both these pictures are susceptible to a further challenge; there is little explicit evidence that the Pharisees were the direct predecessors of the rabbis. To appeal, as is sometimes done, to their prominence in Josephus and the Gospels is only to produce the proverbial circle; rabbinic sources do not use the term 'Pharisees' of their predecessors, although they do claim a few authorities, such as Gamaliel, whom other sources identify as 'Pharisees'. There are rabbinic anecdotes where *perushim* are opposed to 'Sadducees' (e.g. *m. Yadim* 4. 6–7; cf. *m. Menahoth* 10. 3, where the more common term 'Boethusians' may represent the Sadducees); but it is not clear that the rabbis always favour the former, whose label may castigate them as 'separatists' (also *prš*). This supports a view that the rabbis represent something of a coalition with a fundamentally different ideology to that of the Pharisees even if some were included within it. While it is a constant in the sources that the Pharisees interpreted Scripture on the basis of their own traditions, that these equate with the 'oral law', could be traced back to Moses, and can be unilaterally illustrated by rabbinic traditions, is not justified.

None the less, some scholars, most notably J. Neusner, have developed techniques of analysis to determine which traditions in the Mishnah can be traced back to first-century authorities, whom they then define as 'Pharisaic' (1971, 1973b). The picture which emerges from these texts emphasizes a concern for the rules of purity and for tithing, which would be expressed most clearly in eating together: according to this view, a 'table fellowship' group dominated by these concerns would be fairly narrow and exclusive ('separatists'), and would be unlikely to hold real social or political power; yet, as a voluntary group adopting rules scripturally intended for the Temple and priesthood, neither need they have despised the ordinary people who did not, and in normal daily life could not, so live; nor would they have been avid proselytizers (Matt. 23: 15). To the natural objection that this conflicts with their evident political aspirations under John Hyrcanus and still under Salome Alexandra (76–67 BCE) (*BJ* 1. 110–12), it is suggested that they subsequently withdrew from the political arena, and, by constituting an alternative form of Temple-focused society, adopted a quietism that was itself a means of rejection of the dominant political order but that resulted in a degree of self-chosen marginalization (see also Neusner 1973*a*). Critics of such a reconstruction argue that while there were such exclusive table-fellowship groups—for example, the Dead Sea community or the *haberim* ('associates') of rabbinic sources—it is unlikely that Josephus and the New Testament would have failed to notice or comment on such behaviour by the Pharisees.

However, this move away from seeing the opposition between Pharisees and Sadducees as one of Torah *versus* Temple is supported by the Dead Sea Scrolls. The absence of the Essenes from the NT and, for the most part, from independent historical records focuses attention on the exclusive claim in the Scrolls to correct interpretation of Torah, understood both halakhically and prophetically, as well as on their apparent (but perhaps not categorical or sustained) rejection of the Jerusalem Temple alongside their reproduction of Temple in their own communal ideology and practice. If this framework can be applied to each of the 'parties', we are left to seek the dynamics by which, and the social, historical, or economic context within which, Torah and Temple became controlling symbols that could generate competing and passionately defended interpretations. While a cultural or ideological perspective may stress the dual impact of the crisis of Hellenism and the nature of the Hasmonaean hegemony, a socio-economic one will attend to the economic status of those involved, who by definition valued and could practice literate skills. The model moves firmly towards one of 'sects', competing and, as self-defined, exclusive claims to the tradition, whether of an introversionist (Dead Sea Scrolls) or reformist (Pharisees) kind; it also becomes possible both to agree that a relatively small proportion of the population belonged to such groups—numerically, they were marginal in society—and yet to concede their significance—socio-economically and structurally—for the nature of Judaism in the period (Baumgarten 1997; Schwartz 2001). This need neither exclude nor affirm the allegiance of the masses to the accepted norms of Jewish belief and practice, an issue to be settled on other grounds.

The direction in which debate has moved carries with it further decisions. Older attempts to identify particular texts as 'Pharisaic', and perhaps on this basis as representing dominant belief patterns—for example, the strongly messianic *Psalms of Solomon*—are shown to lack independent justification. Similarly, the synagogue, which belongs to what might be seen as the democratization of the Law, has also been seen as a Pharisaic institution; yet there is limited evidence that explicitly ties Pharisees to the synagogue, and the synagogue is not a major concern of rabbinic literature; neither do we find many anecdotes locating the rabbis in synagogues (if, indeed, the rabbis are indicative of Pharisaic patterns). In the later period a tension between the rabbis, with their 'house of study', and the synagogue is now often posited. Study of the NT and of early 'Jewish'–'Christian' relations (e.g. in the Fourth Gospel) has yet to take this seriously into account. Although simplisitic antitheses of Pharisaic legalism over against Jesuan grace have largely been abandoned, these debates still demand considerably more sophistication in analysis of the social, political, and religious dimensions of disputes about observance of Torah in the first century.

Without any additional sources, the Sadducees have invariably been viewed in the shadow of the Pharisees; the move towards a sectarian interpretation of the Pharisees has exacerbated this lack of independent interest, for the little we know about them fits uneasily in to this model. Josephus and the New Testament agree that the Sadducees rejected the doctrine of the resurrection and of angels, both patterns of belief that developed late in the period of the Hebrew Bible; it is then supposed that they hide behind the 'Epicureans' of rabbinic polemic who deny the resurrection and the divine origin of Torah (*m. Sanhedrin* 10. 1). This makes them appear traditionalists, a more conservative party, as too does Josephus's claim that they adhere to the Law alone and rejected the (Pharisees') oral traditions. On these two foundations appears to rest the claim by early Christian writers that they accepted only the Pentateuch, a view presupposing a clearer sense of 'canon' than there was in this period and without other support. It is often suggested that all this coheres with their aristocratic status (Josephus, *AJ* 18. 17), as being particularly associated with the priesthood (cf. Acts 5: 17), their name derived from Zadok the priest. At the same time, it is also often assumed that they were more sympathetic to a pro-Hellenizing position and to the Romans, under whose oversight the High Priestly family held power. This profile thus associates them particularly with the Temple, and ascribes their disappearance to their loss of a power base following 70 CE. Whether all this is compatible with a traditionalism might be debated, although a conservative religious position might live alongside a *realpolitik*. More important, a number of elements in this common picture are founded only on supposition; the origin of their name is far from certain, and we know of priests who were not Sadducean, Josephus included. Rabbinic accounts of disputes between *perushim* and Sadducees (Boethusians?) over the interpretation of the Law indicate that they did have their own interpretative traditions, as would anyone who sought some application to the contemporary context, while even Josephus describes them as harsher in the application of penalties (*AJ* 20. 199). Links have been detected between the interpretations ascribed to the Sadducees in rabbinic sources and positions adopted in the Dead Sea Scrolls, which themselves also have a high regard for the sons of Zadok and the whole priestly tradition. This suggests that there are patterns and networks among Second Temple movements which we do not have sufficient information to unravel.

In his account of the establishment of Roman rule in Judaea (in 6 CE) Josephus introduces a so-called Fourth Philosophy (AJ 18. 23–5), the name (since there were properly 'three') designating it as neither integral nor 'from oldest time'. Although he aligns them with the Pharisees, their religious exclusivism—God alone as Lord—is for him expressed most significantly through their revolutionary aims and methods. For this reason they are usually considered in relation to the role of a revolutionary movement in the events during the first century and leading to the first revolt of 66–70 CE: Josephus implies as much in his initial reference, but does not sustain the connection in his subsequent account. Their identification with the various revolutionary groups that Josephus describes during the first revolt, in particular with those he calls the Zealots (first explicitly in 68 CE, BJ 2. 651) or with the sicarii (dagger-men: AJ 20. 186 under Festus) is much debated; on this import-ant question hangs whether or not the picture of first-century Judaism is to include a continuous revolutionary strain, always in the background if not to the fore. Josephus also speaks of the rise of brigandage prior to the revolt (AJ 20. 4–5, 131, 160–6), as well as of those whom he labels impostors and charlatans, but who appear as charismatic figures winning followers by their prophetic message or acts (AJ 18. 85–7; 20. 169–72). Here he has provoked counter-readings, attempts to discern possible relationships between these individuals or their followers, and to locate them within a religious or a socio-economic framework, in so far as such a distinction can be sustained. Although Josephus dates their rise to the Roman period, attempts to defend a religious interpretation have often appealed to the religious associations of the term 'zeal' and to an ideology traced back to the zeal of Phinehas (Num. 25: 1–15), appealed to by the Maccabees (1 Macc. 2: 54), via Elijah—a tradition willing to kill those who defied or sought to deny God's law (Hengel 1989). Socio-economic interpretations have drawn on comparative studies of 'brigandage', within the context of the economic changes of the first century, although, in the light of what we have seen above, this need not exclude moments of intersection with the controlling 'myths' of the Jewish system (Horsley 1986).

We have already seen the extent to which the discovery of the Dead Sea Scrolls has transformed our understanding of these Jewish 'movements' (see also Davies, Chapter 6 in this volume). Nowhere is this more true than with Josephus's 'Essenes', even when his account is supplemented by the highly idealized ones by Philo (*Every Good Man* 75–91) and, from an outside perspective, by Pliny the Elder (*HN* 5. 73). Although not identical, these have enough in common and provide sufficient links with the ideology of the Scrolls to lead to the early identification of the 'Dead Sea Sect' with the Essenes (Vermes and Goodman 1989). Here confidence has wavered in more recent scholarship: the Scrolls do not identify themselves as Essene, Josephus and Philo suggest that the Essenes were a widespread movement, and a number of aspects of thought and practice found in the Scrolls are either not mentioned in descriptions of the Essenes or are incompatible with them. While a mediating, and frequently adopted, position is that the Dead Sea Scrolls represent a split within the wider Essene movement, there remains the sharp contrast between the ideology of the distinctive ('sectarian') Scrolls, which rejects all other claimants to Israel's status and covenant, and Josephus's failure to mention any such tendency. Again, while any community settled at Qumran would have been too small and isolated to have attracted the attention of early Christian writers, the 4,000 Essenes agreed by Josephus and Philo (compared with 6,000 Pharisees according to Josephus) implies a more substantial movement which might be expected to have made more of a mark on the history of the first century and beyond, or at least to have shaped society in ways now lost to us. The minority position which challenges the association of the Scrolls with the remains at Khirbet Qumran, and the identification of the latter as a monastic-style settlement—as explored alsewhere in this volume—leaves open to conjecture the relation of the thought of the Scrolls, both those overtly sectarian and those not, to other strains of Jewish thought and practice in the period (see above, Chapter 6).

However, the majority position does sharpen the question of how far dissent could extend. The Scrolls most explicitly evince a rejection as members of the covenant of those who think otherwise; a similar sectarian consciousness has been claimed of other groups, and such voluntarism could be traced much earlier within the biblical tradition, with its roots in the prophetic writings. Does the presence of conflicting claims to represent the tradition lead from talk of movements to that of Judaism*s*? Against this would be the relatively limited evidence of more than verbal polemic; certainly physical violence is part of the 'memory' of the Scrolls (1QpHab (*Habbakuk pesher*) xi. 2–8) and was to become so of some parts of the early 'Christan' movement (Acts 8: 1–3; Gal. 1: 13–14), yet these may be exceptions, and, as we have seen, Josephus himself betrays no knowledge of the schismatic consequences of Essene doctrine. The presence of diverse views, for example on messianism, among the Dead Sea Scrolls acts as a warning against seeing behind every difference in doctrine a different and incompatible coherent world-view or interpretation of 'Judaism'. On the other hand, still following Josephus, the Samaritans have not been included here on the grounds that they represent an independent trajectory, if not schism, with their own institutions, although it is arguable that, given their own claim to be 'Israelites' (as witnessed by inscriptions at Delos), they represent but another point on the scale.

Undoubtedly there were other movements: Philo gives a highly idealized account of a monastic community of men and women located in Egypt whom he calls the Therapeutae (*On the Contemplative Life*). What reality lies behind his account, and whether it might have been repeated elsewhere, is disputed: many interpreters accept the connection with the Essenes suggested by Philo himself; but this might challenge an interpretation which saw a relationship with the Temple as well as with Torah as determinative in Jewish 'sectarianism' (hence, perhaps their total absence from Baumgarten 1997). Later patristic and rabbinic texts refer to a variety of other groups, and, while there is frequently a degree of stereotyping in the numbers, they may well reflect genuine memories. Among these appear to be those who practised regular bathing or ablutions, such as the 'Hemerobaptists' and 'Masbotheans' (Justin, *Dial.* 80. 4; Eusebius, *HE* 4. 22). The influence of such groups has often been found behind later Jewish-Christian groups who practised repeated washing or 'baptism' and who seem to have been associated with areas around and east of the Jordan River, and in particular behind the later Mandaeans and Elkesaites from whose midst Manichaeism was to emerge. Other figures would include the hermit Bannus, with whom Josephus spent three years after trying out the other three sects (*Vit.* 3), John the Baptist, known from Josephus and NT sources, and presumably others like them. Including these in the picture begins to put a strain on a sectarian model that requires a core within which sectarianism can flourish; yet neither should we dismiss them as mavericks.

Certainly their inclusion raises other questions: these latter groups appear not to belong only to the period before the destruction of the Temple, which, because of the dearth of later references, is often seen as signalling the end (for a while) of Jewish sectarianism (although cf. Goodman 1994), and so as confirming an interpretation founded on its existence. The vagaries of survival of references may make us ask whether it is fundamental or accidental that, with the exception of Philo, we have been speaking only of Jews within Palestine, and perhaps predominantly of Judaea: despite Paul of Tarsus and Matt. 23: 15, evidence of even Pharisees outside its borders is largely lacking. Were there no such movements among diaspora communities despite the wide variations in Hellenistic Jewish literature towards aspects of Jewish identity (which, according to some interpretations of Acts 6, could even be expressed within Jerusalem itself)? And where, then, are we to locate what was to become Christianity, itself often identified as initially a reform movement within Judaism, albeit passed over in silence by Josephus?

Breaking free from the Josephan model returns us both to the question of origins and to a wider definition of movements. Already in 1 Macc. 2: 42; 7: 13, we find references to the 'Hasidaeans' ('Hasidim') who refuse to fight on the sabbath; although often identified with or seen as the progenitors of the Pharisees and/or of the Essenes, there is nothing to establish (or disprove) this. Some have argued from references particularly in the *Damascus Document* (CD) that the earliest origins of the Essene movement lie in the community of the exiles in Babylon; others would note the distinctive stance of texts like *Jubilees* or the Enochic traditions which may be pushed before the Maccabean period. Some would argue that these may continue local traditions opposed to the Jerusalem Temple whose real power was based on political circumstance. Even further back are the traces in the later books of the Hebrew Bible of power conflicts and groups who find themselves excluded; the development of literary genres, such as apocalyptic, has also been located here. Certainly these do not appear to have generated defined parties or sects, although we may describe them as movements; whether they take us beyond the literate élites as is sometimes claimed for apocalypticism is less certain (Stone 1980). As we saw at the beginning of this essay, the Josephan model establishes movements within a prior unity; the model itself, and, even more, recent developments in the understanding of the formation of 'Judaism', provoke the question whether there was a unity within which diversity could arise, and/or how such a unity might be defined or experienced. One answer would be that unity was achieved only after 70 CE, when, supposedly, we no longer have traces of the Sadducees, Essenes, Dead Sea sectarians, or even Pharisees, so named; if it was not a unity based on coercion, it may have been founded on the containment of permissible debate and difference enshrined in the rabbinic writings. This view, too, has been challenged, partly by appeal to the references, albeit sparse, to these groups in writings later than 70 CE, including Josephus and the NT: why detail groups whose identity was by then a matter of fading memory? Such issues lie beyond the scope of this essay, although anyone interested in the earliest history of Christianity within its Jewish matrix will have to address them.

SUGGESTED READING

Cohen (1987) gives a good account of the period. For detailed discussions of the movements from different perspectives see Baumgarten 1997 and Stemberger 1995.

BIBLIOGRAPHY

ALON, G. 1977. 'The Attitude of the Pharisees to Roman Rule'. In *Jews, Judaism and the Classical World*, Jerusalem: Magnes, 18–47.

BARNETT, P. 1981. 'The Jewish Sign Prophets'. *NTS* 27: 679–97.

BAUMGARTEN, A. 1983. 'The Name of the Pharisees'. *JBL* 102: 411–28.

—— 1987. 'The Pharisaic *Paradosis*'. *HTR* 80: 63–77.

—— 1997. *The Flourishing of Jewish Sects in the Maccabean Era: An Interpretation.* JSJSup 55. Leiden: Brill.

COHEN, S. 1987. *From the Maccabees to the Mishnah.* Philadelphia: Westminster Press.

GOODBLATT, D. 1989. 'The Place of the Pharisees in First Century Judaism: The State of the Debate'. *JSJ* 20: 12–30.

GOODMAN, M. 1994. 'Sadducees and Essenes after 70 CE'. In S. E. Porter, P. Joyce, and D. E. Orton, eds., *Crossing the Boundaries: Essays in Biblical Interpretation in Honour of Michael D. Goulder*, BIS 8, Leiden: Brill, 347–56.

HENGEL, M. 1989. *The Zealots*. Edinburgh: T. & T. Clark.

HORSLEY, R. 1986. 'The Zealots: Their Origins, Relationships and Importance'. *NT* 28: 159–92.

—— and HANSON, J. 1985. *Bandits, Prophets, Messiahs*. San Fransisco: HarperRow.

KRAFT, R. 1975. 'The Multiform Jewish Heritage of Early Christianity'. In J. Neusner, ed., *Christianity, Judaism and Other Greco-Roman Cults*, SJLA 12, Leiden: Brill, Leiden, iii. 174–99.

LIGHTSTONE, J. N. 1975. 'Sadducees versus Pharisees'. In J. Neusner, ed., *Christianity, Judaism, and Other Greco-Roman Cults*, SJLA 12, Leiden: Brill, iii. 206–17.

MASON, S. N. 1991. *Josephus on the Pharisees: A Composition-Critical Study*. Leiden: Brill.

NEUSNER, J. 1971. *The Rabbinic Traditions about the Pharisees before 70*, 3 vols. Leiden: Brill.

—— 1973a. *From Politics to Piety: The Emergence of Pharisaic Judaism*. Englewood Cliffs, NJ: Prentice-Hall.

—— 1973b. *The Pharisees: Rabbinic Perspectives*. Hoboken, NJ: KTAV.

—— 1987. 'Josephus' Pharisees'. In L. Feldman and G. Hata, eds., *Josephus, Judaism and Christianity*, Leiden: Brill, 274–92.

RIVKIN, E. 1972. 'Defining the Pharisees: The Tannaitic Sources'. *Hebrew Union College Annual*, 43: 205–49.

—— 1978. *A Hidden Revolution: The Pharisees' Search for the Kingdom Within*. Nashville: Abingdon.

SALDARINI, A. J. 1988. *Pharisees, Scribes, and Sadducees in Palestinian Society: A Sociological Approach*. Wilmington, Del.: Glazier.

SANDERS, E. P. 1992. *Judaism Practice and Belief 63BCE–66CE*. London: SCM.

SCHAPER, J. 1999. 'The Pharisees'. In W. Horbury, W. D. Davies, and J. Sturdy, eds., *The Cambridge History of Judaism*, iii: *The Early Roman Period*, Cambridge: Cambridge University Press, 402–27.

SCHWARTZ, S. 1990. 'The Pharisees, and Early Rabbinic Judaism'. In *Josephus and Judean Politics*, Leiden: Brill, 170–208.

—— 2001. *Imperialism and Jewish Society 200 B.C.E. to 640 C.E.* Princeton and London: Princeton University Press.

SIEVERS, J. 1996. 'Who Were the Pharisees?'. In J. H. Charlesworth, ed., *Hillel and Jesus*, Minneapolis: Fortress, 1–22.

SMITH, M. 1971. 'Zealots and Sicarii: Their Origins and Relation'. *HTR* 64: 1–19; repr. in *idem, Studies in the Cult of Yahweh*, i. ed. S. Cohen, Leiden: Brill, 1996, 211–26.

STEMBERGER, G. 1995. *Jewish Contemporaries of Jesus*. Minneapolis: Fortress.

STONE, M. 1980. *Scriptures, Sects and Visions*. Oxford: Blackwell.

ULRICH, E., and VANDERKAM, J. 1994. *The Community of the Renewed Covenant*. Notre Dame, Ind.: University of Notre Dame Press.

VERMES, G., and GOODMAN, M. 1989. *The Essenes according to the Classical Sources*. Sheffield: JSOT Press.

SECTION 3

GENRES OF THE OLD AND NEW TESTAMENTS

CHAPTER 22

PROPHECY

DEBORAH W. ROOKE

INTRODUCTION

Which Books are 'Prophecy'?

According to Jewish tradition, the canon of the Hebrew Bible which forms the basis of the Christian Old Testament is divided into three parts: Law, Prophets, and Writings. The division known as 'Prophets' consists of the historical books Joshua, Judges, 1 and 2 Samuel, and 1 and 2 Kings (also known collectively as the 'Former Prophets') as well as the books more commonly recognized as prophetic by Christianity: that is, Isaiah, Jeremiah, and Ezekiel and the so-called Book of the Twelve, from Hosea to Malachi. These fifteen works from Isaiah to Malachi are also known collectively as the 'Latter Prophets'. However, even though prophets appear quite frequently in Joshua–2 Kings, in terms of literary genre these books are not prophecy but historiography, and so the focus of the present discussion will be on the the Latter Prophets, consisting of the three major prophets Isaiah, Jeremiah, and Ezekiel, and the twelve minor prophets from Hosea to Malachi. This list does not include Daniel, which in the eyes both of the ancients and of modern scholarship belongs in a literary context other than that of prophecy. The Hebrew/Aramaic book of Daniel is located in the division of the Hebrew canon known as the Writings rather than in the Prophets, and modern critical scholarship has pointed to features of the book that differentiate it from prophecy as traditionally understood and associate it rather with apocalyptic writings of a relatively late date.

The present discussion will attempt to give an (inevitably brief) overview of scholarly issues that pertain to the prophetic books in general, as well as highlighting issues that are particularly associated with individual books.

Prophecy as a Literary Phenomenon

When thinking about prophecy as it appears in the Hebrew Bible, it is necessary to recognize that the written deposit known as 'prophecy' is different from the socioreligious phenomenon of prophetic intermediation upon which the written deposit claims to be based. Indeed, the relationship between individuals who functioned as prophets and the books in which (some of) their words are now supposedly embedded is highly complex, not to say obscure. The prophetic books are far from being mere transcriptions of a given prophet's words; rather, they are sophisticated literary products that have undergone an extended process of development, as is evident from their content and structure.

In the first place, the presence of headings at the start of individual books, giving the name of the prophet and often some kind of date for the period of that prophet's activity, is an indication that someone other than the prophets themselves has annotated the material, perhaps in order to contextualize it or to claim for it the authority of divine inspiration. Such contextualization, whether or not it is based upon reliable factual information, inevitably affects the way in which the material is appropriated by the reader—an observation underlying the exchange between Auld (1983) and Carroll (1983) as to whether the prophets were always viewed (or viewed themselves) as prophets. Headings also punctuate the main body of some of the books, indicating that the editing process was more thoroughgoing than the simple 'labelling' involved in naming and dating the prophet whose words are supposedly contained in any given collection.

As well as headings, and alongside the oracular material that represents the prophet's own message, there are various different types of material in the body of the books that can reasonably be accounted for only as stemming from a source other than the prophets themselves. The prime example of this is third-person biographical narratives about the prophets. Such narratives occur most notably in the books of Isaiah and Jeremiah, although biographical elements are also present to a lesser extent in Hosea and Amos. The exact source of such narrative material is often unclear, and its historical reliability cannot be taken for granted. In an extreme example of this, the book of Jonah consists entirely of third-person narrative about the prophet. Some of the books also contain first-person narrative, which has traditionally been thought of as more historically reliable than third-person narrative, but, as with the third-person narrative, its historicity should not be presumed.

As well as non-oracular material that is unlikely to have originated with the prophets themselves, most if not all of the prophetic books are also thought to contain expansions and supplementations of the oracular material. More will be said about this below; but for the moment, the point is that prophetic books are not simply a straightforward record of a single prophet's words. Rather, they are elaborate literary creations, and their existence and character owes just as much, if not more, to people other than the prophet whose words they supposedly represent.

Over the last 150 years or so, critical scholarship has responded to the literary phenomenon of prophecy in two different ways broadly speaking. With the rise of so-called historical-critical methodologies in the late nineteenth and twentieth centuries, scholarship was primarily concerned to identify the particular situations to which prophetic material was addressed and to strip away the secondary accretions in the prophetic books so as to reconstruct each prophet's original words—tasks which went hand in hand with each other. However, under the influence of changing intellectual attitudes that are both more cautious about the possibility of large-scale historical reconstruction and more sensitive to the immensely complex ways in which texts function, recent scholarship is increasingly focusing on the prophetic books as they stand, in an attempt to understand them as literary entities in their own right, rather than as sources of information regarding a set of historical circumstances which are now lost to us. That is not to say that historical research on the prophetic texts has ceased; rather, that it is now being complemented by other approaches that reflect the paradigm shift taking place in biblical studies as a whole.

AREAS OF SCHOLARLY INTEREST

From Oracles to Book

Given both the dichotomy and the presumed connection between the socio-religious and the literary phenomena of prophecy, one of the perennial issues in scholarship about prophecy has been the attempt to understand the process by which a presumed body of oracular material was transformed into a prophetic book, and the relationship between the original oracles and the literary deposit in which they now rest. There are two interconnected aspects to this question.

a. Recording the Oracles

At the heart of the issue is the question of how a prophet's words would have come to be written down; and two main answers have been offered to this question. The more widespread opinion depends on a view of prophesying as fundamentally an oral phenomenon: in a society where literacy was limited to certain minority elements of the population, prophets whose messages were addressed to the populace at large would by definition have been oral preachers. Their basic form of address would have been the short poetic oracles that appear in many of the prophetic writings, since such oracles were readily composed by the skilled oral preacher and highly memorable for the audience. Given this scenario, the way that the oracles came to be transformed into written documents would have been through disciples or followers of the prophet, who not only wrote down the prophet's words but subsequently edited them into groups of sayings on similar themes. However, this model assumes that prophets were exclusively preachers rather than writers, and that all their oracles were both conceived and delivered in oral mode, assumptions that are ultimately unprovable. An alternative explanation of how prophetic oracles got into writing is therefore that the prophets themselves wrote down their words; and indeed, Haran (1977) sees this writing as part of the characteristic activity of the figures who stand behind the collections of oracles in the Latter Prophets. He argues that the reason why we have the prophetic books at all is because these people wrote down what they said, and that it is this writing activity that distinguishes them from earlier 'prophets', such as Elijah and Elisha, for whom no such literary deposit survives. More recently, too, the traditional stark dichotomy between oral and written media, and the negative value judgements inherent in the way these categories have been applied to prophecy, have been challenged by Floyd in Ben Zvi and Floyd (2000), who points out that works that are intended for oral delivery (plays, sermons, lectures, etc.) may none the less be composed in writing.

b. The Rest of the Material

However, the question of how oracles relate to book is wider than simply how prophetic messages came to be written down. As stated above, it is widely accepted in modern scholarship that the prophetic books contain a good deal of material that probably did not originate with the prophets themselves, not only in the form of biographical narratives about the prophets, but also in the form of additional oracular material. This additional oracular material is identified on the basis of criteria such as content, style, vocabulary, and disturbance of the flow of the passage in which it occurs. Such supplementation of the original prophetic message may take the form of additional phrases or verses here and there, perhaps to link an originally indefinite oracle with a specific historical situation (for example, the reference to the king of Assyria in Isa. 7: 17), or (very commonly) to add a note of hope to a prophecy of doom in the light of changed circumstances (for example, Hos. 1: 10–11; Amos 9: 11–15, both of which consist of unexpected expressions of hope and references to the kingdom of Judah in the context of prophecies of doom against the kingdom of Israel). Supplementation may also take the form of whole chapters, or even large blocks of material consisting of several consecutive chapters, added to an existing corpus of material from a named prophet. The classic example of this is the book of Isaiah, in which scholars have identified as the basis of the book at least three different prophetic traditions from different eras of Israel's history. Within these three basic traditions further substrata from a variety of sources can be identified, so that the total time period over which the book was composed is reckoned at between 300 and 500 years.

It is impossible to know for sure who was responsible for this process of oracular and biographical supplementation, or to identify with certainty the sources of the additional material. In the case of the Isaiah material, the second major block of tradition (Isa. 40–55, also known as Deutero- or Second Isaiah) displays a consistency and cogency which suggests that it probably originated largely as the work of a single anonymous individual over a relatively short period of time, usually identified as the later part of the Babylonian exile; and Williamson (1994) suggests that the same individual was also responsible for combining his own work with the existing Isaianic corpus. However, other instances of supplementation lack such large-scale cogency, and it is often unclear whether the supplementary material is drawing on pre-existing biographical and oracular traditions which may or may not have originated with the prophet himself, or whether it is a purely literary creation—perhaps scribal recording of what had become an accepted interpretation of or rejoinder to a given oracle, or even newly composed material added for polemical or ideological purposes. An example of the latter would be the so-called Zadokite stratum in Ezekiel 44, which was identified by Gese (1957), and which claims that only priests who were descended from Zadok, and not those who were Levites, should have the right to serve at the altar in the Temple in Jerusalem. It seems likely that the priests themselves or their supporters would have been responsible for this material. Similarly, it has often been supposed that those who during the Exile edited the books of Joshua to 2 Kings in conformity with the ideology expressed in Deuteronomy prepared an initial edition of the then-known prophetic books on the same basis. The book in which this editing process has been supposed to be most clearly demonstrable and far-reaching is the book of Jeremiah, and a number of specialized studies have addressed the topic, including Nicholson (1970) and Stulman (1986). Finally, different groups of people could have different ideas about what should be included and where in a prophetic book, as is shown by the Septuagint version of the book of Jeremiah, which is significantly shorter than the Hebrew version and is arranged differently in terms of content (for detailed discussion, see Soderlund 1985 and Tov 1997). Clearly it was possible for several different forms of the tradition to be in contemporaneous circulation for a considerable period of time.

The Finished Product

Having expended a good deal of energy in identifying the various strands and layers within the prophetic books, however, scholarship has more recently developed an increasing interest in the final form of the books: that is, in how each overall composition functions as a whole, and upon what principles it was given its present form (in other words, *why* it has attained its present form, as opposed to the mechanics of *how* that form might have been reached). There are a number of impulses driving this adjustment of focus. One is the recognition that the criteria used to identify secondary strata are often highly subjective, and that there is in fact no sure-fire way of determining whether or not a given block of material is 'original' or 'secondary'—and if 'original', whether it should be deemed original to the book or to the prophet. This point is very clearly indicated by the wide range of scholarly positions that are taken over the allocation of material in prophetic books to their supposed sources. Another rather obvious, but often overlooked, element is the fact that all we have are the books in their final form; despite the sometimes perplexing evidence from other ancient versions, such as the Septuagint, we do not have the books in demonstrably earlier editions that lack some of the supposed later supplementation; nor do we have the supplements as separate bodies of material. Therefore the most obvious, legitimate, and potentially fruitful object of study is the final form of the text, rather than its hypothetical sources or earlier editions.

The major positive assumption behind an approach that attempts to understand the prophetic books in their present form as complete units is that, far from being a collection of random supplementations of an original nucleus of oracular material, the finished books have been purposefully produced and crafted into their present shape. Theories such as accidental association of discrete material because of copying on to a spare space at the end of a scroll fail to account for the verbal, structural, and thematic links that can often be identified between supposedly disparate elements of a book or, indeed, between books. This is an approach to study that has come into its own in relation both to Isaiah and to the Book of the Twelve, where recent scholarship has focused increasingly on highlighting identifiable links between individual components in these two prophetic corpora. House (1990) and Conrad (1991) are examples of this type of approach to the Twelve and to Isaiah respectively, and the more recent essay collections edited by Watts and House (1996) and Nogalski and Sweeney (2000) indicate its growth in popularity. Inevitably, as with the criteria for identifying 'secondary' elements in a prophetic book, there is a degree of subjectivity involved in identifying links between components, and the approach raises the difficult issue of whether perceived links can and should be attributed to authorial/editorial intention. However, this in itself does not automatically invalidate the approach, which can provide stimulating new insights, and each individual treatment must be judged on its own merits.

Relationship between History and Prophecy

Standard scholarly approaches to the prophetic writings over the last century or so have recognized that, rather than offering disembodied predictions of the far distant future, prophecy originated as a phenomenon closely linked with its practitioners' contemporary social, religious, and political situations. In view of this, the prophetic writings have sometimes been used rather uncritically as sources of historical information about the situations to which they were addressed. However, it is now being recognized that, as in the case of the Old Testament as a whole, the relationship between text and reality is extremely complex, and that texts do not simply represent reality, but rather manipulate their readers' perception of it. For the prophetic texts, their highly rhetorical, and to that extent propagandist, nature means that they cannot simply be treated as objective or impartial historical source material presenting a faithful reflection of actual circumstances. In addition, the fact that much of the prophetic material uses poetic and metaphorical language means that it is subject to multiple interpretations, which are determined as much by the reader's perspective as by anything inherent in the text. Keefe (2001) demonstrates this principle in her study of Hosea's metaphor of Israel as an adulterous wife, where the picture of the reality behind the metaphor is changed dramatically by highlighting and changing the (often unconscious) assumptions that determine how the metaphor is understood.

Other recent debates over the historicity of the prophetic material have centred on the question of the prophets themselves as historical personages. The issue is particularly acute in the case of Jeremiah, as demonstrated by Carroll's (1981) eloquent rereading of the large amount of ostensibly biographical information in the book of Jeremiah. The major difficulty for all the prophets is the absence of supporting documentation. None of the prophets is attested in material outside the biblical text, and very few are mentioned within the biblical text outside their own book. Indeed, the only prophet for whom traditions independent of his prophetic book have been preserved in the biblical text is Isaiah, who appears in the narrative of 2 Kings 18–20 and briefly in the equivalent passages in 2 Chr. (26: 22; 32: 20, 32). These narratives are repeated in the book of Isaiah. Four other prophets are mentioned in the biblical text outside their own book: Jeremiah appears in Ezra 1: 1; 2 Chr. 35: 25; 36: 12, 21–2; and Dan. 9: 2; Micah appears once in Jer. 26: 18; and Haggai and Zechariah appear in Ezra 5: 1; 6: 14. However, all of these occurrences are dependent upon the prophetic writings, and preserve no independent information about the prophets themselves. The identity of a fifth prophet, Jonah, whose 'biography' (the book of Jonah) is clearly legendary, appears to have been borrowed from the passing reference to Jonah ben Amittai in 2 Kgs. 14: 25, who may or may not have been a historical personage. Ultimately, whether and in what sense the lack of substantiating evidence is viewed as problematic for the historicity of the prophets depends on one's view of the nature of the writings themselves, and on whether the lack of substantiating evidence for the particular historical person-ages is viewed as evidence against their existence.

However, despite the unquestionably literary character of the prophetic material in the Old Testament and the elusiveness of the individual prophets with whom it supposedly originated, the very existence of the prophetic books, and of narratives about prophets elsewhere in the Old Testament, implies a distinct phenomenon behind them, as hinted earlier. This view is supported by the existence of prophetic phenomena in other ancient Near Eastern cultures, most notably at Mari in Mesopotamia in the eighteenth century BCE. Once again, of course, the only evidence is literary—namely, collections of oracular messages in official arch-ives—and it is notable that the Mari archives contain nothing like the extended books of prophecy in Israel. Although it is unwarranted to postulate direct influence of the prophecy at Mari upon that in Israel, not least because of the enormous gap in dating and the differences in written prophetic residue between the two societies, the existence of a related phenomenon in a neighbouring area makes its existence in Israel comprehensible as part of a common religious world-view. Ringgren (1982), Malamat (1987) and Gordon (1993) offer survey treatments of the Mari material, plus additional bibliography, and the collection of essays edited by Nissinen (2000) offers a recent survey of prophetic phenomena in the ancient Near East more generally. The major problem with attempted comparisons between Israelite and other types of ancient Near East prophecy is the very small amount of information that is available about the other types. If only an incom-plete written deposit survives, it is very difficult to say anything sensible about the phenomena themselves, and the safest comparison is at the level of the texts rather than at the level of what kind of activity might have produced the texts.

The idea that prophecy in Israel can reasonably be regarded as an actual religious phenomenon as well as a literary one is also supported by modern anthropological studies documenting the existence of individuals who display 'prophetic' behav-iour; and this has led to attempts to locate the Israelite phenomenon in its appropriate social setting using sociological and anthropological models. Wilson (1980) and Petersen (1981) are good examples of this kind of approach. The major difficulties with attempting sociological analysis of prophecy on the basis of the biblical text are, first, the lack of field evidence (there are no Israelite prophets to observe or question); secondly, the incomplete and partial nature of the written biblical evidence, which cannot be assumed to be describing prophecy for its own sake; and thirdly, the enormous time and cultural differences between the Israelite setting and modern examples that might be used for comparative purposes.

Linked, although somewhat obliquely, with the issue of social location and role are the types of speech forms used by the prophets. As in other areas of biblical scholarship, the identification of the literary forms within the prophetic corpus and the recognition that particular forms originated within particular social settings tended to lead inexorably to the conclusion that the prophets must have functioned within the social spheres from which the forms in the books originated. But the existence of a given form in a literary work should not automatically be assumed to reflect a corresponding social situation. It is more than possible for forms to be used purely for rhetorical impact in contexts other than those in which they originated. Hence, the same difficulties as already noted attend this attempt to locate the prophets in a given social sphere: namely, the lack of conclusive evidence and the complex nature of the textual phenomena.

Topics of Prophecy

The basic concept of prophecy is that of a message from God which needs to be delivered either to a particular individual or (more often) to a group of people, whether that group is a subgroup of the nations of Israel and Judah or the nation(s) as a whole. Often the message is a condemnation of perceived sin that warns the group in question of the need to amend their ways if they are to avoid punishment; at other times, most famously in the book of Ezekiel, the message is an interpretation of social and political disaster in terms of punishment for sin, and thus functions as a theodicy in order to maintain and justify continued belief in God despite adverse external circumstances. The kind of sin that is condemned varies from prophet to prophet. For some it is social injustice (especially Amos and Micah), whereas others have a more religious bias and condemn idolatrous or hypocritical worship. The once popular view that the prophets were anti-cult by definition is, however, an overstatement that arose out of the view of cultic worship as a legalistic degeneration, and the desire for Protestant Christianity to see itself as the fulfilment of the prophetic ideal. There is also condemnation of alliances with foreign powers—perhaps because such alliances were seen as almost inevitably leading to religious compromise—and indeed, a persistent tradition of oracles against foreign nations, the purpose and function of which is explored by Raabe (1995).

However, not all of the prophets' messages are warnings of doom and destruction. There are also promises of hope and restoration, which in the first instance are addressed to specific situations (most clearly, in the promises of restoration after the Exile found in Isaiah 40–55 and Ezekiel), but which subsequently take on a more generalized character and point to an indefinite time in the future when God will make everything right again for his people. Thus, the phenomenon that begins as a specific response to specific circumstances gradually becomes loosened from its historical moorings, developing a vocabulary of stock images in order to portray a time of eschatological bliss.

Suggested Reading

The bibliography on prophecy is vast, and growing daily. Two recent volumes that give a helpful survey of scholarship to the date of their publication are Blenkinsopp 1996 and Clements 1996*b*. Several useful collections exist of previously published articles that illustrate particular trends in scholarship on prophecy, including Mays and Achtemeier 1987, Gordon 1995, Clements 1996*b*, and Davies 1996. Literary, feminist, and liberation-theological perspectives on the prophetic books are becoming increasingly prevalent, and Landy 1995, Brenner 1995, and Dempsey 2000 are good examples of these newer methodologies. For an introduction to issues pertinent to a given prophetic book, the Sheffield/T. & T. Clark International Old Testament Guides are very useful. Summaries of scholarship on prophecy are found in three collections of essays prepared by members of the Society for Old Testament Study at approximately ten-year intervals, and are a useful overview of how the field has developed since the late Seventies: these are McKane 1979, Carroll 1989, and Blenkinsopp 2000. An excellent discussion of issues to do with the redaction of the prophetic books, together with a survey and bibliography of relevant scholarship from around 1960 to 1992, can be found in Collins 1993.

Bibliography

AULD, A. G. 1983. 'Prophets through the Looking Glass: Between Writings and Moses'. *JSOT* 27: 3–23.

BARTON, J. 1986. *Oracles of God: Perceptions of Ancient Prophecy in Israel after the Exile.* London: Darton, Longman & Todd.

—— 1990. 'Prophets and Prophecy'. In R. J. Coggins and J. L. Houlden, eds., *A Dictionary of Biblical Interpretation,* London: SCM Press, 556–9.

BEN ZVI, E., and FLOYD, M. H. 2000. *Writings and Speech in Israelite and Ancient Near Eastern Prophecy.* Atlanta: Society of Biblical Literature.

BLENKINSOPP, J. 1977. *Prophecy and Canon.* Notre Dame, Ind.: University of Notre Dame Press.

—— 1996. *A History of Prophecy in Israel,* revised and enlarged. Louisville, Ky.: Westminster/John Knox Press.

—— 2000. 'Prophecy and the Prophetic Books'. In A. D. H. Mayes, ed., *Text in Context,* Oxford: Oxford University Press, 323–47.

BRENNER, A., ed. 1995. *A Feminist Companion to the Latter Prophets.* Sheffield: Sheffield Academic Press.

CARR, D. 1993. 'Reaching for Unity in Isaiah'. *JSOT* 57: 61–80.

CARROLL, R. P. 1979. *When Prophecy Failed: Reactions and Responses to Failure in the Old Testament Prophetic Tradition.* London: SCM Press.

—— 1981. *From Chaos to Covenant: Uses of Prophecy in the Book of Jeremiah.* London: SCM Press.

—— 1983. 'Poets, not Prophets'. *JSOT* 27: 25–31.

—— 1989. 'Prophecy and Society'. In R. E. Clements, ed., *The World of Ancient Israel*, Cambridge: Cambridge University Press, 203–25.

CLEMENTS, R. E. 1996a. 'A Light to the Nations: A Central Theme of the Book of Isaiah'. In Watts and House, (1996), 57–69.

—— 1996b. *Old Testament Prophecy: From Oracles to Canon.* Louisville, Ky.: Westminster/ John Knox Press.

COLLINS, T. 1993. *The Mantle of Elijah: The Redaction Criticism of the Prophetical Books.* Sheffield: JSOT Press.

CONRAD, E. W. 1991. *Reading Isaiah.* Minneapolis: Fortress Press.

—— 1999. *Zechariah.* Sheffield: Sheffield Academic Press.

DAVIES, E. W. 1981. *Prophecy and Ethics: Isaiah and the Ethical Traditions of Israel.* JSOTS.S 16. Sheffield: JSOT Press.

DAVIES, P. R., ed. 1996. *The Prophets: A Sheffield Reader.* Sheffield: Sheffield Academic Press.

DAVIS, E. F. 1989. *Swallowing the Scroll: Textuality and the Dynamics of Discourse in Ezekiel's Prophecy.* JSOTS.S 78. Sheffield: Almond Press.

DEMPSEY, C. J. 2000. *The Prophets: A Liberation-Critical Reading.* Minneapolis: Fortress Press.

GESE, H. 1957. *Der Verfassungsentwurf des Ezechiel (Kap. 40–48) traditionsgeschichtlich untersucht.* Tübingen: J. C. B. Mohr (Paul Siebeck).

GORDON, R. P. 1993. 'From Mari to Moses: Prophecy at Mari and in Ancient Israel'. In H. A. McKay and D. J. A. Clines, eds., *Of Prophets' Visions and the Wisdom of Sages: Essays in Honour of R. Norman Whybray on his Seventieth Birthday,* JSOTS.S 162, Sheffield: JSOT Press, 63–79.

—— ed. 1995. *The Place Is Too Small For Us.* Winona Lake, Ind.: Eisenbrauns.

HARAN, M. 1977. 'From Early to Classical Prophecy: Continuity and Change'. *VT* 27: 385–97.

HOUSE, P. R. 1990. *The Unity of the Twelve.* JSOTS.S 97. Sheffield: Almond Press.

KEEFE, A. A. 2001. *Woman's Body and the Social Body in Hosea.* JSOTS.S 338. Sheffield: Sheffield Academic Press.

LANDY, F. 1995. *Hosea.* Sheffield: Sheffield Academic Press.

McKANE, W. 1979. 'Prophecy and the Prophetic Literature'. In G. W. Anderson, ed., *Tradition and Interpretation,* Oxford: Clarendon Press, 163–88.

MALAMAT, A. 1987. 'A Forerunner of Biblical Prophecy: The Mari Documents'. In P. D. Miller, P. D. Hanson, and S. D. McBride, eds., *Ancient Israelite Religion: Essays in Honour of Frank Moore Cross,* Philadelphia: Fortress Press, 33–52.

MAYS, J. L., and ACHTEMEIER, P. J., eds. 1987. *Interpreting the Prophets.* Philadelphia: Fortress Press.

MEIN, A. 2001. *Ezekiel and the Ethics of Exile.* Oxford: Oxford University Press.

NICHOLSON, E. W. 1970. *Preaching to the Exiles: A Study of the Prose Tradition in the Book of Jeremiah.* Oxford: Basil Blackwell.

NISSINEN, M., ed. 2000. *Prophecy in its Ancient Near Eastern Context.* Atlanta: Society of Biblical Literature.

NOGALSKI, J., and SWEENEY, M. A., eds. 2000. *Reading and Hearing the Book of the Twelve.* Atlanta: Society of Biblical Literature.

ODELL, M. S., and STRONG, J. T., eds. 2000. *The Book of Ezekiel: Theological and Anthropological Perspectives*. Atlanta: Society of Biblical Literature.

PETERSEN, D. L. 1981. *The Roles of Israel's Prophets*. JSOTS.S 17. Sheffield: JSOT Press.

RAABE, P. R. 1995. 'Why Prophetic Oracles Against the Nations?'. In A. B. Beck, A. H. Bartelt, P. R. Raabe, and C. A. Franke, eds., *Fortunate the Eyes that See: Essays in Honour of David Noel Freedman in Celebration of his Seventieth Birthday*, Grand Rapids, Mich., and Cambridge: Eerdmans, 236–57.

RINGGREN, H. 1982. 'Prophecy in the Ancient Near East'. In R. Coggins, A. Phillips, and M. Knibb, eds., *Israel's Prophetic Tradition: Essays in Honour of Peter Ackroyd*, Cambridge: Cambridge University Press, 1–11.

SODERLUND, S. 1985. *The Greek Text of Jeremiah: A Revised Hypothesis*. JSOTS.S 47. Sheffield: JSOT Press.

STULMAN, L. 1986. *The Prose Sermons of the Book of Jeremiah: A Redescription of the Correspondences with the Deuteronomistic Literature in the Light of Recent Text-Critical Research*. Atlanta: Scholars Press.

TOV, E. 1997. 'Some Aspects of the Textual and Literary History of the Book of Jeremiah'. In P.-M. Bogaert, ed., *Le Livre de Jérémie*, 2nd edn., Leuven: Leuven University Press, 145–67.

WATTS, J. W., and HOUSE, P. R., eds. 1996. *Forming Prophetic Literature: Essays on Isaiah and the Twelve in Honor of John D. W. Watts*. JSOTS.S 235. Sheffield: Sheffield Academic Press.

WESTERMANN, C. 1967. *Basic Forms of Prophetic Speech*. London: Lutterworth Press.

—— 1991. *Prophetic Oracles of Salvation in the Old Testament*. Edinburgh: T. & T. Clark.

WILLIAMSON, H. G. M. 1994. *The Book Called Isaiah*. Oxford: Clarendon Press.

WILSON, R. R. 1980. *Prophecy and Society in Ancient Israel*. Philadelphia: Fortress Press.

CHAPTER 23

APOCALYPTIC

PHILIP DAVIES

INTRODUCTION

The word 'apocalyptic' is nowadays used to describe a scenario that heralds the end of the world, or at least the end of life, or civilization, as we know it. This meaning lies some distance from the original meaning. The Greek word *apokalypsis* means 'revelation', and is the title (because it is the first word) of the New Testament book of Revelation. That book contains many descriptions of future events, particularly a time of great distress and persecution, followed by one of judgement and of bliss for the faithful. A number of books of this kind, describing the end of history, were written during the Graeco-Roman period, not only by Jews and Christians, but also by Greeks, Romans, Egyptians, and Persians. These writings have also come to be known as 'apocalypses'.

A focus on the 'end-time' is a common feature of apocalypses, but in fact this ancient literary genre needs to be defined a little more widely. It conveys (as its name implies) what are claimed to be direct revelations from heaven, given usually in a vision or by angelic dictation, or by a journey to heaven. Apocalypses were often ascribed to a venerated figure of antiquity, who would foretell what would happen in that person's future, which was, in fact, the past from the perspective of the real author and the reader. A real prediction of the future, which was usually the main point, then formed the final section of this 'pseudo-prediction'. But the 'end-time' was not the only possible content of such 'revelations'. The origins of the world, or the movements of the heavenly bodies, or the meaning of history, or the geography of heaven, the names of angels, or even the appearance of God himself, all counted among the secrets that could be learned only by revelations of this kind.

The characteristics of this literary genre of apocalypse have acquired a broader sense in biblical scholarship, one that is not altogether helpful, but which cannot be overlooked. 'Apocalyptic' or 'apocalypticism' is sometimes used to describe a way of thinking, even a kind of religion, which is other-worldly and focused on some imminent moment that will bring the existing world order to an end. On other occasions, 'apocalyptic' may even be loosely used to mean 'eschatology', or 'eschatological', i.e. concerned with the end or goal of history or the cosmos. Finally, 'apocalyptic' is occasionally used of communities that are created or sustained by hope or belief that the order will soon change; and hence literary apocalypses have tended to be understood in some quarters as being the product of millenarian sects. Most citizens of the ancient Near Eastern and classical world believed in a realm of the gods from which mortals might access knowledge about this world. Apocalypses are really a refined expression of an attitude that believes in the overwhelming reality of the transcendental world and its effects on everyday life. It is not surprising that this genre was especially popular in times of uncertainty or fear of the future, though some apocalypses seem to be generated from a kind of proto-scientific attempt to get 'behind the scenes' of reality and show what makes things happen, and how.

In the Old Testament, apocalyptic literature (or simply 'apocalyptic', as the genre is often called) might not seem to occupy a prominent place. Only the book of Daniel falls into this category. Despite its poor representation in the Bible, apocalyptic literature is not a fringe activity; nor are its contents peripheral to an understanding of Judaism (or Christianity, for that matter). It was certainly a very common kind of writing from the third century BCE onwards. It would be impossible even to begin to cover the range of apocalyptic writings now known to us that date from 300 BCE to 100 CE; for this the reader can consult the two-volume *Old Testament Pseudepigrapha* (Charlesworth 1983). The last part of this chapter will focus attention on the book of Daniel, the main Old Testament exemplar, and the book of *1 Enoch*, which contains the earliest and in many respects most important Palestinian Jewish apocalypses (Enoch himself is referred to in the New Testament, in Jude 14–15). The material in this collection known as *1 Enoch* dates from the third century BCE onwards and is often simply referred to as the *Book of Enoch* (though there are other 'books of Enoch' as well).

Apocalyptic Technique

The apocalypse is a literary genre that claims to impart knowledge of heavenly secrets. In what way does an apocalypse differ from wisdom or prophecy, or law, which also claim to derive from divine revelation? The differences lie, basically, in the words 'knowledge' and 'secrets'. Prophecy is a public announcement of a message that God wishes the recipient to hear. Wisdom instruction is knowledge derived from observation and experience by a sage and passed on in his name to his disciples or a wider audience. The apocalypse pretends to offer what cannot normally be known and what is not supposed to be known, or at least widely known. Unlike prophecy and wisdom, it is not directly an exhortation to behave in a certain way. It is, rather, essentially 'privileged information', which enables the recipient to know what is 'going on'. This knowledge is the key to salvation, and is often shared among restricted groups, hence its frequent association with sects. While the 'information' given in apocalypses may be intended to affect human behaviour (for instance, to join the privileged group with the 'saving knowledge'), it often serves to confirm that the present time, however bad, has been planned, and that a better future lies ahead. The technique of apocalyptic requires that the future is knowable and therefore has been predetermined.

Naturally, since this knowledge is presumed to be confidential, the apocalypse employs devices to explain how it has been acquired. The name of the recipient of the knowledge and (pretended) author of the book is given, along with details of the experience by which his (or her) knowledge was obtained. More often than not, the 'author' is a great figure of the past—Daniel, Enoch, Moses, even Adam—and hence many apocalypses are Pseudepigrapha, i.e. given a fictitious authorship. The 'author' is often claimed to have passed the knowledge on to his children, or to have written it down in a book which the reader is to assume has remained a secret or has been published just recently. In this respect, the book of Revelation, paradoxical as this may seem, is not like other apocalypses; and actually does not call itself an apocalypse. The 'revelation' of its opening verse refers to what is described, not to the book itself—and the author actually dubs his words 'prophecy' (1: 3). Whether it is pseudepigraphic remains unclear, but the name 'John' hardly points in that direction.

Apocalypses represent the world as governed from heaven, and either imply or insist that everything is predetermined. Were it not so, the universe would not be orderly, nothing could be learned about it which would enable humans to understand it. In a way, apocalyptic literature is trying to grasp the sense that lies beneath the nonsense of the present world—or, more graphically, the sense that lies *above* it! In that respect it is very closely linked to the ethos of wisdom. In the Hebrew Bible, however, apocalyptic literature is—Daniel apart—found in the Prophets (see below). For the origins of apocalyptic writing we must go outside the orbit of biblical prophecy and wisdom and look at an aspect of religion that was prevalent throughout the ancient Near East, including ancient Israel: divination.

DIVINATION

Babylonian Mantics

Manticism is the name for a system of belief and practice in the discovery of heavenly secrets from earthly signs. The signs may be encoded in animal entrails, in anomalous births, in the movements of the heavenly bodies, and in dreams. These are collectively called 'omens', and each of these kinds of omen requires learning the decipherment appropriate to it. Omen lists are among the earliest cuneiform texts we have, and guilds of mantic specialists probably existed in Mesopotamia from almost the beginnings of monarchy.

Interpretation of omens presupposes a belief in the possibility of communication with supernatural forces—forces that encode their secrets in *signs*. Interpreting such signs reveals the intentions of the gods, and can help to avert what is projected for the future, be it for the nation or the individual. Two-way communication could sometimes be conducted through pouring oil on water or making smoke, and specific questions could also be asked about the favourability or otherwise of certain tasks at certain times, or the outcome of a proposed action. The Babylonian omen lists typically have the form of a conditional sentence: 'if...then...', listing the consequences expected to derive from certain phenomena. If the presupposition was not scientific, the procedures were, and, in the case of observing the heavenly bodies, led to astronomy as well as astrology. The key was an assumption that certain observable phenomena could be *interpreted* as signs of divine intentions.

Divination in Israel

The extensive records of Babylonian manticism raise a question: Did this sort of thing occur also in ancient Israel? Now, divination (which is what manticism deals in) was practised in Israel and Judah, but condemned in the Old Testament: 'There shall not be found among you...anyone who practises divination, a soothsayer, or an augur, or a sorcerer, or a charmer, or a medium, or a wizard, or a necromancer' (Deut. 18: 10–11).

Jeremiah condemns prophets and diviners in the same breath: 'The prophets...are prophesying to you a lying vision, worthless divination' (Jer. 14: 14; cf. 27: 9–10 and 29: 8–9).

During their exile in Babylonia the Judaeans were, of course, exposed to a religious culture dominated by manticism, and Isa. 47: 9–15 gives an eloquent condemnation of this practice, the passion of which contrasts with the patient and faithful service of the 'wise man' Daniel, who learnt the wisdom of the

Babylonians, surpassed them in his mastery of it, and rescued them from extermination (Daniel 2). He is superior to them because his God, the Most High, is the true source of all knowledge and can reveal secrets to whom he chooses. Nevertheless, deciphering writing on the wall is manticism, and the writing of pseudo-predictions of history (Daniel 11) a by-product. Daniel is a true mantic, that is all—a Jewish mantic. How has this come about?

Mantic Wisdom

In the neo-Babylonian and Persian periods Babylonian mantic traditions were known as far west as Greece; eventually they reached Rome. By the time of the first Jewish apocalypses, in the late Persian or Hellenistic periods, manticism formed part of a culture in which Judaea was inevitably immersed. In Babylonia the mantic class, who increasingly focused on astrology, came to be called 'Chaldean' (as in Daniel); the mantic priestly class of the Persians were the Magi, whose religion was Zoroastrianism, and whose speciality was interpreting dreams. But the Magi gradually became identified with the Chaldean astrologers. Thus Matthew's 'wise men from the East' (*magoi*) are guided to Bethlehem by a star, and warned in a dream to return home without seeing Herod. Other Magian beliefs and practices included the worship of Zurvan, a time-deity, and with him the notion of world epochs. Ahura-Mazda, the creator, was their chief god, and they also believed in the pre-natal and post-mortem existence of the soul in the realm of light. Such beliefs, in fact, profoundly influenced the development of Judaism.

In the period we are examining, however, manticism was no longer tied to a cult. We are talking less about priests practising manticism and more about scribes using and developing its lore. As readers and writers of ancient texts, teachers, linguists, historians, and scientists, they were also concerned with the ultimate meaning of the world and of human history. The Deuteronomistic History (the Former Prophets) offers a theory: history depends on response to the demands of the covenant. But the idea that divine behaviour could depend on human activity was problematic, for in that way prediction was always conditional. Mantics were required to deliver something more reliable. Moreover, in an age of empires, when Judah had little autonomy in political matters, how could history be determined by such a small and insignificant province? Was history, then, dictated by the great empires? Again, no: it was the Most High God who decided these things. The great promises to his chosen people were not being fulfilled; but were the chosen people really to blame? Some Judaean theologians thought yes: they were still being punished for their previous sins: others thought not. Either way, the Most High had his plans, and what would happen would happen when he had decided.

JEWISH APOCALYPSES

I now turn to the earliest Jewish apocalypses, which modern readers of the Bible often find hard to understand. The language and even the point of a lot of apocalyptic writing can seem elusive. But, after the introduction, perhaps what follows will not seem so strange. At all events, it would not have seemed strange to any ancient reader.

Enoch

Although not part of the Western Old Testament, *1 Enoch* is in the canon of some other Christian churches (such as the Ethiopic), and in any case contains the earliest known Jewish apocalypses. In fact, the book is a collection of writings attributed to Enoch. Thanks to the discovery of literary fragments among the Dead Sea Scrolls, we can now confidently date the collection (except possibly for chapters 37–71) to the pre-Christian era, and the earliest parts to the third century BCE. The four early Enoch books in this collection are the Astronomical Book (chapters 72–92), the Book of the Watchers (chapters 1–36), the Epistle of Enoch (chapters 91–105), and the Book of Dreams (chapters 83–90). They represent a body of traditions, rather than a single tradition, but all the traditions are related and suggest a more or less coherent pattern of ideas.

How did Enoch become a patron of apocalyptic literature? The biblical notice about him (Gen. 5: 18–24) is brief: he was the son of Jared and father of Methuselah; he lived 365 years and then 'walked with God'. Then 'he was not, for God took him'. It is usual to consider this tantalizing hint of something special as the origin of the Jewish Enoch tradition; his life span suggests a connection with the solar calendar, and his manner of departure suggests that he did not die. As for 'walking with God', this suggests a fairly intimate acquaintance. But the Genesis notice probably stands not at the beginning but somewhere in the middle, or even towards the end, of Enoch's development as an apocalyptic sage. Enoch is probably derived from a figure in the Sumerian King List. This is a list of rulers of Sumer (the earliest civilization of Mesopotamia) before the Flood, and is preserved in several forms, including the third century BCE historian Berossus (see Pritchard 1955: 265). Here one of the kings, often appearing as the seventh, is called Enmeduranki or Enmeduranna. He is generally associated with the city of Sippar, which was the home of the cult of the sun-god Shamash. Moreover, in other texts (see VanderKam 1984: 39 ff.) this Enmeduranki was the first to be shown by the gods Adad and Shamash three techniques of divination: pouring oil on water, inspecting a liver, and the use of a cedar (rod), whose function is still unclear. These were to be transmitted from generation to generation, and in fact became the property of the guild of *baru*, the major group of diviners in Babylon.

These details show how the biblical portrait of Enoch corresponds to Enmeduranki: he is also seventh in the list of names in which he appears; the number 365 preserves an affinity to the sun; walking with God (or perhaps, 'angels'?) suggests a special intimacy between him and the heavenly world. The final connection links him not with Enmeduranki, but with a fish-man (*apkallu*), with whom each of the first seven kings associated and from whom they learnt all kinds of knowledge. Enmeduranki's *apkallu*, called Utu'abzu, is mentioned in another cuneiform text, where he is said to have ascended to heaven. The writer of Gen. 5: 21–4 seems to be alluding briefly to a Judaean version (as Noah is a Judaean version of Utnapishtim or Ziusudra, the Mesopotamian Flood heroes) of a figure connected with the transmission of divine wisdom by divinatory means. But since, as we saw earlier, divination was frowned upon in Judah, Enoch will acquire his knowledge by other means.

1 Enoch provides us with a lot of information about the Enoch to whom Genesis alludes. In the Astronomical Book, possibly from the third century BCE, Enoch reveals to his son Methuselah what the angel Uriel had shown him of the workings of the sun, moon, and stars. Most of this book is entirely scientific, being a description of the movements of the heavenly bodies, ostensibly revealed in heaven, but obviously the result of many generations of sky watching. However, there is a brief section (chapters 80–1) which is especially important. Here Enoch also tells of the deeds of righteous and unrighteous persons, forecasting a disruption in the natural order. It is very likely that this passage is not original, but its presence shows us how a text of purely astronomical observations came to be used in the service of ethical exhortation and eschatological prediction—something closer to the usual interest of apocalyptic writers. But according to Michael Stone (1976), the origins of apocalyptic writing lie in 'lists of things revealed', including the names and functions of angels, and from there develops a focus on the origin and end of evil, on the final judgement, and on the identity of the righteous.

In the Book of the Watchers, perhaps compiled in the late third century BCE, these more ethical dimensions come to the fore. Here we find a story about the beginning and the end of the present order, particularly the origin of sin and its ultimate solution. These ethical concerns combine the 'listing of revealed things' with traditional concerns of Wisdom: right behaviour, harmony with the natural order, divine justice, the dualism of wisdom and folly, righteousness and wickedness. The Book of the Watchers opens (chapters 1–5) with a warning that moves from the observation of order in the natural world—in obeying the laws set for it by God—to the lack of order among humans. Those persons who adhere to these natural laws are righteous; those who do not are sinners. Note that righteousness and wickedness are represented as functions of *knowledge* and *understanding*, rather than of simple obedience. In *1 Enoch* (and apocalyptic generally) we find an ascendance of these wisdom categories over the categories of law and covenant. Although the Enoch corpus does not contain very much direct or indirect interpretation of Scripture, chapters 1–5 seem to draw on the story of Balaam (Num. 22–4)—though we now know that this tradition was not confined to Israel. Chapters 6–11 describe how sin first came into the world with the descent of heavenly beings called the Watchers. Here again we encounter in *1 Enoch* a fuller version of an episode that is only briefly related in the Old Testament.

The biblical episode is Gen. 6: 1–6, where the 'children of God' have intercourse with women, producing a race of *Nephilim*, 'mighty men that were of old, men of renown'. *1 Enoch* 6–11 (which actually combines two versions of the tale) describes how these heavenly beings (all of whom are named) teach the women about spells, root cutting and plants, astrology, weapons of war, and cosmetics. The women give birth to giants, who turn to cannibalism and drink blood. The earth cries out to heaven for help, and God orders the execution of the giants, the binding of the Watchers beneath the hills until the day of judgement, and thereafter in a fiery chasm. The leader according to one version, Azazel or Asa'el, is buried under a rock, until, after judgement, he is hurled into the fire.

Many scholars take the view that this story, in its various forms, is inspired by the Greek legend of Prometheus, the Titan who brought heavenly secrets to men, and that it has also developed from the Genesis story. But that very short account makes little sense except as an allusion to some fuller version. The parallels between the story of the Watchers and the story of Cain are also intriguing: bloodshed on the earth, the earth crying out, the villain cast into the desert, the acquisition of technology, and the increase of violence among descendants. The fuller *1 Enoch* story explains the ritual of the scapegoat of Leviticus 16, where a goat is sent into the wilderness 'for Azazel'. It is thus difficult to explain the Enoch story simply as an expansion of Gen. 6: 1–4. More probably it is a version of an older myth about the origin of sin, which held sin to have originated in heaven and to have been brought to earth together with illicit knowledge which enabled humanity to progress in arts and sciences. Isa. 14: 12 possibly echoes a story about a fallen rebellious angel whom it names as the morning star (= Lucifer, as he was named in later, Christian mythology).

Later in the Book of the Watchers Enoch enters the divine presence, and learns in more detail about the future. Here he is called a 'scribe of righteousness', who records the divine sentence on the Watchers. But he also intercedes for them with God. In the rest of this book, Enoch travels twice, to the west and around the world, including visits to Jerusalem, Eden, and Sheol, the abode of the dead—thus adding a knowledge of geography to his understanding of astronomy. In all this, we can see reflected in Enoch the figure of the ideal scribe whose goal is universal knowledge, gained not only by experience but also by revelation, and who hands it on to his 'children' (the disciples of the wise man).

In the remaining two books of *1 Enoch* we find two substantial apocalypses (there is also a brief third one in 83: 3–5), both dating from the first half of the second century BCE. The earlier of these, the Apocalypse of Weeks (93: 1–10 and 91: 11–17), divides Israelite history into ten periods ('weeks'), the time of the author being the seventh. This introduces us to another common feature of apocalypses: their division of history into periods—always culminating in the present time, of course, which stands on the eve of the End. This periodizing of history and the eschatological culmination may be inspired by Persian ideas, and seems to have been a common practice among the scribal classes. The Apocalypse of Weeks makes a rather clear reference to the political and religious crisis beginning around 175 BCE (see pp. 290–3), and it takes the form of pseudo-prediction of past events followed by a genuine prediction of the (real) future. Here it foresees a restoration of order and righteousness, first in Israel, then in the world, and finally in the whole cosmos, when a new heaven and a new earth will appear.

The other apocalypse in 1 Enoch is the Animal Apocalypse (chapters 85–90), which is also an example of periodized history and prediction, and acquires its name from its depiction of individuals and nations in the guise of animals (animals are another favourite device of apocalypses, as in Daniel's beasts and Revelation's Lamb and Serpent). Unlike the Apocalypse of Weeks, this periodization commences only with the Exile, and it enumerates seventy shepherds who have ruled Israel—almost certainly inspired by Jer. 25 (esp. 32 ff.). Neither of these apocalypses is concerned merely with periodizing history, however. Both are responding to problems raised by their own time, problems that raise the question of the orderliness and purpose of history as a whole.

From this overview of 1 Enoch we have been able to see how the content, form, and world-view of the apocalypse develops from a more general concern with things unseen, with ancient secrets, and their inspired revealers. But we can offer here only a sketch of apocalyptic; for it is the product of a very rich and varied culture. It is not an esoteric and intra-Jewish development, but a cosmopolitan, variegated, many-sided, cross-cultural phenomenon. And while it is often connected with sects or religious groups, this is not always so; and its authors (and readers) come from privileged, literate, and influential levels in society.

Daniel

Like 1 Enoch, the book of Daniel is a composite collection of stories and visions, not all of which have the form of an apocalypse, but it allows us to see how the apocalypse form emerges. The stories that comprise the first part of the book (chapters 1–6) portray the adventures of a Judaean youth initiated into Babylonian manticism. His gifts, which surpass those of the native Babylonians, are those of interpreting dreams and (at least on one occasion) mysterious writing on a wall. However, as a Judaean, he acquires his knowledge by direct revelation, not by any divinatory technique. But the stories also tell of persecution and how the righteous are delivered through divine intervention. In these deliverance stories Daniel's profession is important, in that it places him in a prominent position that renders him vulnerable as a victim of the idolatrous or envious designs of kings and courtiers. Daniel is required under these circumstances of persecution to show exemplary behaviour, to teach in this case by his deeds rather than by his words.

At the close of the book of Daniel, the authors reveal their own identity:

Those among the people who are wise shall make many understand, though they shall fall by sword and flame, by captivity and plunder, for some days, but when they understand, they shall be helped a little some of those who are wise shall fall, to refine and to cleanse them, and to make them white, until the time of the end, for the time appointed is yet to be. (Dan. 11: 33–5) ... Those who are wise shall shine like the brightness of the firmament; and those who turn many to righteousness like the stars for ever and ever. (Dan. 12: 3; my trans.)

The Hebrew word for 'wise' here is *maskil*, of which Daniel himself is one (1: 4). Their task, according to this passage, is both to suffer and to reach righteousness, as did Daniel (who taught a lesson to the foreign king). An obvious model for this combination of roles is the 'servant' of Second Isaiah (chapter 53, especially verse 11). The profile of Daniel as an educated 'wise man', serving at court, a political administrator (2: 48), an interpreter of the future for the king, is a profile of the scribe and learned in mantic lore. The book of Daniel is indeed the product of 'Daniels'. The book as a whole was created by appending a series of apocalyptic visions, which we can date to the mid-second century BCE, to an older cycle of stories reflecting life in the Eastern diaspora. These stories are not apocalypses themselves, but belong to the genre of court-tale (see chapter 9), but they lay a foundation for the second, apocalyptic part of the book, with its themes of knowing the future and suffering persecution.

Daniel 7–12 is an account of Daniel's visions in the first person, though from chapter 9 onwards the emphasis shifts from visions to Daniel's penitence and then to a detailed pseudo-prophecy (again with a genuine prediction attached) of the events of the writer's own time. In the first two visions (chapters 7 and 8) we find a form familiar from biblical prophetic literature, the 'symbolic vision', a literary form that constitutes the main technique for divine revelation in Jewish apocalypses.

In the simplest form of this literary device, as found in visions of Amos (7: 1–9; 8: 1–3) or Jeremiah (1: 11–19; 24), the objects seen in the vision belong to everyday life (e.g. a basket of fruit, an almond tree), and yield their meaning by metaphor or word-play. The accounts of the vision use a simple question-and-answer pattern: the prophet is asked what he sees, then the significance is given. In a second phase, represented in Zech. 1–6, the vision develops into a more elaborate narrative, with rather more unusual objects seen, and an extended dialogue between the prophet and an interpreting angel in place of the deity. In Daniel, this type of vision is used to portray the succession of earthly empires as creatures (we have encountered this device already in *1 Enoch*). The origin of the description of the beasts remains disputed, but among the possibilities are zodiacal signs and catalogues of physical anomalies, such as are included in omen lists as significant portents. The vision of judgement in Daniel 7 also borrows motifs from other scriptural writings. From Zech. 1: 18 it gets four horns, and perhaps from Zechariah or from Ezek. 40 (where the prophet is shown the future Jerusalem), it gets an interpreting angel. The heavenly scene itself is reminiscent of those in *1 Enoch*, although no precise parallel can be cited. The theme of four world empires has long been thought to reflect a widespread notion (it is found in the Greek poet Hesiod, *c.*700 BCE), but, like the phrase 'visions of his head as he lay upon his bed' (7: 1; cf. 2: 28) probably comes directly from Dan. 2.

Interpretation of Scripture is more significant in Daniel than in *1 Enoch*. Apart from those influences just mentioned, Dan. 9 shows the hero preparing for an inspired interpretation of a biblical passage in Jeremiah (25: 11–12 or 29: 10) that he cannot understand. He is given the meaning—seventy years means seventy weeks of years, i.e. 490 years—and the events of those weeks are then enumerated in a manner similar to the Apocalypse of Weeks in *1 Enoch*. Yet another example of the use of biblical prophetic texts is the quotation from Isa. 53: 11 given earlier, while Dan. 11: 17 quotes Isa. 7: 7. The use of Jeremiah is an excellent example of the mantic technique applied to biblical texts: the texts do not mean what they appear to say, but when properly deciphered contain a message about the here and now.

As in the case of the Enochic apocalypses, the Danielic historical summaries—which become more detailed in each successive vision—are designed to account for a present crisis in terms of the meaning of history as a whole. The crisis is the destruction of the altar in Jerusalem (in 167 BCE), and first appears in Dan. 8: 11. The daily offering used to take place twice a day, at sunrise and sunset, and the phrase 'evenings and the mornings' (8: 26) recurs in later visions as a reminder of how the desolation was marked by each missed offering. The visions of chapters 7–9 are reticent about exactly what will soon happen or when: but they give assurance that it will come, for God has so ordained it. (This is essentially what the stories also imply: be faithful, and God will protect you when crisis attends.) Only in chapter 12, at the end of the final vision do we find a statement of what actually is predicted to happen, and even here it is not described in much detail. There will be trouble; the angel Michael will act; some will be raised from the dead to be punished or rewarded; the wise who set the example to the people will truly reach the pre-eminence which their exemplary behaviour in this present life merits.

Like two of the Enochic apocalypses, Daniel's visions are provoked by a specific crisis. There is evidence in other Hellenistic apocalypses also of a reaction to a crisis, but not one so sharp or well-defined. The nations overcome by the eastward expansion of Hellenism used the apocalypse to foretell the end of this domination. Examples of this evidence in Egypt are the 'Demotic Chronicle' and the 'Potter's

Oracle' (Collins 1984: 94). A second burst of apocalyptic writing occurred when the Jerusalem Temple was destroyed in the Jewish Revolt (70 CE), and Christian apocalypses (starting with Revelation) react to the persecution of that new cult. The apocalypse is an ideal form for expressing hope in an imminent change to a desperate or unhappy situation. But it typically does so by a return to the past, to authoritative figures and texts that can be made to reassure present-day readers that they saw it all coming, and all will finally be well.

BIBLIOGRAPHY

CHARLESWORTH, J. H., ed. 1983. *Old Testament Pseudepigrapha*, 2 vols. New York: Doubleday.

COLLINS, J. J. 1984. *The Apocalyptic Imagination: An Introduction to the Jewish Matrix of Christianity*. New York: Crossroad.

DAVIES, P. R. 1989. 'The Social World of the Apocalyptic Writings'. In R. E. Clements, ed., *The World of Ancient Israel*, Cambridge: Cambridge University Press, 251–71.

PRITCHARD, J. R., ed. 1955. *Ancient Near Eastern Texts Relating to the Old Testament*, 2nd edn. Princeton: Princeton University Press.

STONE, M. E. 1976. 'Lists of Revealed Things in Apocalyptic Literature'. In F. M. Cross, W. E. Lemke, and P. D. Miller, eds., *Magnalia Dei: The Mighty Acts of God*, Garden City, NY: Doubleday, 414–52.

VANDERKAM, J. C., 1984. *Enoch and the Growth of an Apocalyptic Tradition*. Washington: Catholic Biblical Association of America.

VON RAD, G. 1975. *Old Testament Theology*, 2 vols. London: SCM Press, ii. 301–15.

CHAPTER 24

WISDOM

KATHARINE J. DELL

Perhaps the most famous reference to 'wise men' is that in the New Testament to the wise men who came to visit the baby Jesus, as recorded in Matthew 2. We are told that the wise men came to worship Jesus bringing with them expensive gifts, their visit the result of observation and the pursuit of a star or other heavenly body. These were *magi*, men from the East, probably from Persia, trained in the art of wisdom, which included astronomy, astrology, and other powers of divination as well as wise thoughts and actions. This reference links up with a particular brand of wisdom known as mantic wisdom—the interpretation of omens and dreams and of the future, of divination, and of astral bodies—also witnessed to in the Old Testament figure of Daniel, who possessed 'wisdom' of this type and is described amongst other young men of the court as 'versed in every branch of wisdom, endowed with knowledge and insight' (Dan. 1: 4). Daniel famously interpreted dreams which proved to be true, and so was elevated to a high position at the Persian court. This is wisdom from a particular country of the ancient Near East—that of the Persian empire—and is generally considered a sub-branch of what we know as mainstream 'wisdom' from both Israel and other ancient Near Eastern countries, but it serves to raise the question: what is this tradition of 'wisdom' to which the wise men ultimately belong? How far back do its roots go, and what literature specifically contains its insights?

COINING AND COLLECTING PROVERBS

It is common to most cultures in the world to cultivate and exchange maxims or sayings that express, in a terse and pithy way, a clever observation or experience. In the modern world we find many examples of proverbs in English, and we have a whole fund of them from Africa (Golka 1993) and China. Going further back, we might think of the sayings of the Vikings. These proverbs often circulated in a predominantly oral culture and in rather backward societies in relation to scientific advances. The ancient world was no exception to such maxim making, and we have a particularly fine collection from ancient Sumer, one of the oldest civilizations in the world, as well as our more familiar book of Proverbs. The proverb is at the heart of the wisdom enterprise—it represents the distillation of observation and experience into a short and meaningful saying, one line or more. Comparisons are often made between unlike phenomena, such as between human behaviour and the natural world—for example, Prov. 25: 23, 'The north wind produces rain, and a backbiting tongue angry looks.' But there are proverbs covering the whole range of human experience too, and of relationship with the divine—for example, Prov. 16: 7, 'When the ways of people please the Lord, he causes even their enemies to be at peace with them.'

From ancient Sumer we have proverbial collections later taken over by the emergent Babylonian culture. They reflect an agricultural background and a concern with family life. Proverbial sayings such as 'A people without a king is like sheep without a shepherd' (*Assyrian Collection*, iv. 14–15) are interspersed with short fables, religious admonitions, and rhetorical questions. We have sayings from Egypt, often forming part of longer instructions. Both these cultures go back considerably further than the Israelite period, the proverbs probably having been written any time from the ninth to the seventh century BCE. A more contemporary source to Proverbs is the *Wisdom of Ahiqar*, a seventh-century Aramaic composition which contains a similar contrast between the righteous and the wicked as in Proverbs, as well as animal proverbs, graded numerical sayings, and a possible personification of wisdom. However, perhaps the most important source of proverbs for those who are interested in the biblical genre of wisdom is contained in the book of Proverbs in the Old Testament. Proverbs 1–9 contains only patches of proverbial material—the main sayings collection begins at Proverbs 10. Here we find a whole range of subjects tackled, such as the important distinctions between the good and the wicked, the righteous and the fool in relation to good behaviour, good communication skills, making friends, dealing with family problems, striving for money through hard work and its opposite, i.e. laziness and subsequent poverty. And underlying these themes the theological assumption that life is full of choices—one can choose the smooth path or the rough one, one can fear God or trust one's own judgement. Wisdom is on offer to those who wish to choose its path by steering a way through conflicting experience and following the advice of those who have gone before.

Proverbs probably circulated around camp-fires in early Israel, in tribal nomadic circles as well as amongst settled agricultural groups. They were probably promulgated within the family and wider family group, and we have hints in Prov. 30: 1 and 31: 1 that mothers were involved in the educational process of teaching children how to behave. Learning by the experience of others was thus a major means of education, and the whole book of Proverbs is set in the context of an address to 'young men' who need educational guidance. We find sayings in other parts of the Old Testament which may relate to this tendency to produce wise words for particular occasions on which a word of experiential advice may be pertinent. However, we need to consider the proverbial enterprise on another level: that of the more elevated circles of the educated, the literary, possibly even those involved with the courts of pharaohs and kings.

Whilst a folk origin is a possibility for Proverbs (stressed again recently in the work of Westermann (1995)), their original formulation, on the one hand, and their collection and writing down, on the other, probably represent very different processes. The formation of the text of the book of Proverbs was most likely the work of an educated group, who may have put them down in a compendium for educational purposes. The preface of Proverbs 1–9 seems to indicate this educational and instructional milieu, and gives us a lens through which to regard the rest of the proverbial material. There is also the traditional association of maxim making with King Solomon, who had the reputation of being a particularly wise king (I Kgs. 3: 29–34), and there is a further reference to interest in copying proverbial collections by the 'men of Hezekiah' in Prov. 25: 1. This adds up to a picture of educated men, probably at the court, enjoying the skill and the leisure to put together these collections, possibly in the context of training young men to become courtiers and/or administrators, depending on the scope and extent of educational institutions at the time. The proverbs may simply have been used in a court school in Jerusalem, although the production of literature is rarely for one situation alone, and we don't know how widespread pockets of education were (Lemaire (1981) has repeatedly argued that schools were found throughout Israel), or how widely proverbs in written form might have been disseminated.

Many questions are raised by collections of proverbs, especially in terms of their social context(s). Much has been learned from ancient Near Eastern parallels, particularly from those drawn with Egyptian wisdom circles. It seems that there was a powerful group of court administrators who were educated and versed in wisdom at the courts of pharaohs. In fact, the particular Egyptian form of wisdom—the Instruction—reveals that the wise words of dying pharaohs that usually formed them were often copied over and over again in school contexts in the process of teaching young men. Some of the wise would perhaps have been destined to become court administrators, whilst others may have had more academic or scribal functions. We have parallels for such an educational emphasis from ancient Sumer, where wise men had an educational and scribal role, but there was less of a courtly set-up there. Can we extrapolate from such parallels to reconstruct the possibly social context of the material we have in Proverbs? We have material very similar in form, content, and context to Instruction forms in both Prov. 1–9 and Prov. 22: 17–24: 22, which provide a close parallel to the Egyptian *Instruction of Amenemope* (just how close is debated; see recently Whybray (1994) against a close relationship, and Emerton (2001) in favour). Is this evidence of cultural interchange between the two nations—even of borrowing? After all, didn't Solomon engage in riddles with the Queen of Sheba (I Kgs. 10: 1–13)? The Israelite state was not so large as the Egyptian one, and may not have needed an administrative infrastructure such as that of Egypt. However, some scholars have posited a Solomonic enlightenment at the time of King Solomon (originally von Rad (1966*a*), expanded on by McKane (1970) and Heaton (1974)), in which such a model was emulated at the court of this wise king, and have sought comparative evidence in the Egyptian context. McKane (1970) saw the parallel in relation to the need for administration and a civil service under Solomon, which, he believed, led to a desire to establish a school for the training of officials. Others have suggested that greater evidence of written material from the eighth century BCE onwards may mean that the reign of Hezekiah was more of an enlightenment in wisdom terms (Scott 1985). Uncertainty abounds as to possible historical contexts, and we can probably speak about the likelihood of court and educational contexts only once the proverbs were gathered together in literary circles.

From ancient Sumer we have evidence that those versed in wisdom also performed a scribal function (Kramer 1958). This too should perhaps come into our equation. Do we have evidence within Proverbs and elsewhere in the Old Testament of wisdom writers shaping material? This possibility of later scribal contexts—arguably extending well into the period of the fixing of canons of the biblical literature—has been recently stressed by scholars (see Davies 1998), some-times to the exclusion of acknowledging wisdom's earlier roots. Also we need to ask how separated off from the rest of society this wisdom material would have been. Israelite wisdom appears to have a quite different character from much of the rest of the Old Testament, and yet one wonders how far palace really was from law court or temple precinct. In the post-exilic wisdom books we have some evidence of a mixing of the various genres, so that the character of wisdom itself becomes increasingly eclectic.

CHARACTERIZING WISDOM

And so to turn to the genre of wisdom. How can it be defined? Is this maxim making of an experiential nature the end of the story? Where does God come into wisdom, and what picture of God do we have from this literature? Moreover, where are the boundaries of the literature and of the genre? A close analysis of Proverbs indicates that there are profound theological themes underlying the maxim making. There are presuppositions such as that the good will be rewarded by God and the wicked will be punished. But there is also the recognition that human experience by itself is often limited, and sometimes contradictory. God is not outside the realm of interest of the maxim-makers, and we find clusters of proverbs that mention God in the main collection in Prov. 10–31. In Prov. 1–9 we find more overt mention of 'the fear of YHWH' as well as the depiction of an intriguing figure of Wisdom who is described as having assisted God in the process of creation and has been the subject of much recent attention, particularly by feminist scholars (see Camp 1985). She also provides a counterpart to the Woman of Folly, who lures young men but whose path ultimately leads to death and destruction (Camp 2000). The figure of Woman Wisdom calls to the young men learning by experience to be prudent and to follow her path, however difficult that may be. She offers all the gifts of wisdom, and she then claims to have a unique relationship with the creator God (Prov. 8: 22–31). She stands at the crossroads, therefore, between the quest for understanding, undertaken by human beings across the generations, and the wisdom that ultimately comes from God, which humans cannot fully know. God is described primarily in this literature as the Creator—of humankind and also of all nature and animals (Perdue 1994). God is not described as the salvific redeemer figure with special regard for Israel of other parts of the Old Testament. Indeed, surprisingly, the nation of Israel is never mentioned in this literature, nor its heroes such as Moses or David. Rather, God is the universal creator of the world in which everything has its part. The task of the wise man is to uncover the hidden order of the world and to understand the experience of humans within that wider context. This includes societal order as well as the order found in the natural world.

The book of Proverbs is thus our starting-point when looking at the genre of wisdom in the Bible. Its major forms of saying and instruction reappear elsewhere, and provide some criteria for discerning wisdom influence on wider material. For example, when a prophet such as Amos uses proverbs, he may well be showing knowledge of experiential wisdom, whether it be the language of the learned or just simple observation (e.g. Amos 3: 3–8). The question as to how widespread this genre was is a perennial one amongst scholars. Some see it as important to define as 'wisdom' only that literary corpus that contains the wisdom genre in large measure (Crenshaw 1982), whilst others are interested in discovering lines of possible influence across the Old Testament, whether of a formative or a scribal/redactional kind (Murphy 1990; Dell 2000). We might even look for a wider range of characters or narratives influenced by wisdom, of which a chief contender is the figure of Joseph in Gen. 37–50 (a theory propounded by von Rad (1966b)). His wisdom took him to a high position at the court of Pharaoh, and not only that, the stories of him tell of his dealings with his brothers that very much reflect the qualities of self-control and fairness espoused by the wise. Narratives where human experience, observation, and even intrigue come to the fore are also contenders for the influence of the wisdom genre, such as the Succession Narrative in 2 Samuel–1 Kings 2 (Whybray 1968), which could have been composed at court within the kinds of literary groups I have described.

It should not be forgotten that there is an important theological aspect to this wisdom—even in Proverbs (Murphy 1990)—that should not be downplayed, as some have sought to do. This paves the way for our consideration of the other wisdom books —notably, in the Old Testament canon, Job and Ecclesiastes—which are much more theological in their orientation. We also need to consider in the Apocrypha, Ecclesiasticus or the Wisdom of Jesus, son of Sirach, which returns to the maxim style of Proverbs but, being a second-century BCE document contains a number of rather different emphases, and to the Wisdom of Solomon of a century later. When we get to the New Testament, we find the influence of the genre of wisdom in its pages and some interesting contemporary background material from Qumran.

Questioning the Wisdom Tradition

The book of Job famously airs one of the major issues of the wisdom genre: the reward of the righteous and the punishment of the wicked. What happens if this equation is found not to work as a result of that mainstay of the wisdom tradition itself—human experience? Job is a kind of test case—here is a man who kept himself on the path of wisdom and never strayed from it, who certainly had not sinned and who deserved only good things from God, and he is struck down by calamity, loses his family, his goods, his social status, his health, and his self-esteem. How can the exponents of traditional wisdom explain this? The main section of the book consists of a debate between friends who visit Job, who maintain traditional views about the punishment of the wicked because of deeds committed, and Job, who maintains his innocence throughout. The climax is an appearance by God in a whirlwind, ostensibly to sort the situation out and provide some answers. However, in a great display of his creative power, God does no more than raise more questions and increase the human sense of being unable to understand and control the world. This then poses a radical challenge to the wisdom world-view of finding orders and patterns in human experience of the world that provide certainty. The book of Ecclesiastes also challenges the idea of certainty in the world. Rather than crying out to God in anger and distress, as Job does, the author of this book is resigned to the uncertainty of the quest for definite answers. He espouses wisdom maxims, but sees them in relation to personal experience that often contradicts well-established principles. Death is the great leveller that makes human striving meaningless, although there are glimpses of hope for humans who have the capacity for enjoyment and happiness in between moments of despair (stressed by Whybray 1982) and recognition of the vanity of life. God again stands behind the scenes of the wisdom quest—elusive, yet worthy of praise—and ultimately the advice of the epilogue to the book states that fearing God is the only answer: 'The end of the matter; all has been heard. Fear God, and keep his commandments; for that is the whole duty of everyone' (Eccles. 12: 13).

Some have questioned whether in undermining the wisdom quest these books can really be included in the wisdom genre (see discussion in Dell 1991). Both books are probably rather later than Proverbs, coming from the fourth and third century BCE respectively. They appear to spring from the same mainspring of ideas as the wisdom quest, but it is true that they are very much wisdom plus self-critique. Job in particular contains few proverbial sayings, and can be seen to draw from a wide variety of genres, particularly those familiar to us from psalmic lament, which may suggest that this is not a narrow wisdom production, but has links with wider genres of Old Testament literature, whilst Ecclesiastes combines the citation of traditional sayings with his own commentary.

There are parallels to the kind of theological questioning that we find in both Job and Ecclesiastes in Mesopotamian literature such as the Babylonian *Dialogue between a Man and his God*, in which a sufferer is innocent of his crime and so cannot comprehend the reason for his suffering, and two texts—*I will Praise the Lord of Wisdom* and *The Babylonian Theodicy*—which radically question the theory of just retribution in a similar manner to the dialogue of Job, both giving a test case of a pious sufferer unrewarded and seemingly unjustly treated. The *Dialogue of Pessimism* is closer in sentiment to Ecclesiastes in its description of the futility of life, but it goes a step further than the biblical counterpart in deciding that suicide is the only good.

APOCRYPHAL WISDOM LITERATURE

Ecclesiasticus (second century BCE) takes the vital step of identifying wisdom and law. Once this is done, wisdom loses the universalism that had characterized it up until this point, for instead of wisdom being on offer to all, wisdom is then primarily on offer to those who keep the law, and that refers specifically to Israelite law in all its post-exilic fullness. This book resembles Proverbs in its coverage of many aspects of human experience and its use of proverbial material. Subjects include the duties of sons (e.g. Sir. 3: 1–16), attitudes towards women (which are not always favourable) (e.g. Sir. 9: 1–9), sayings on the art of government (e.g. Sir. 9: 7–10: 18), and even on table manners (e.g. Sir. 31: 12–32: 13). It also includes historical references—notably the hymn in praise of famous men in Sir. 44–50 in which wisdom is closely linked to salvation history and to the heroes of that history. In fact, allusions to the saving history are a new feature of this work, a feature curiously absent from earlier wisdom literature. It links up with more pious and prayerful genres of the Old Testament in its use of poems, prayers with a strong emphasis on the fear of God, and hymns, notably in praise of Wisdom herself. Von Rad (1972) and Crenshaw (1982) disagree over the priority of the fear of God in the thought of this author, von Rad believing it to be subordinate to the theme of wisdom, and Crenshaw seeing it as surpassing the wisdom theme and as incorporating an emphasis on the law. There are reflections on the nature of the wise man's role (see Roth 1980), not only as teacher and scribe, but also as advisor to the powerful (Sir. 39: 4), and the widening net of genres reflected in the book suggests that barriers between different groups of priests, prophets, and sages were less marked at this stage than they were earlier on (Whybray 1974). Having said that, this book is still identifiably in the genre of wisdom, even if this requires defining the genre fairly broadly.

In the first century BCE production, The Wisdom of Solomon, the personification of wisdom is taken to a higher level, with Wisdom becoming a hypostasis, a divine attribute through which creation was performed (e.g. Wisd. 7: 25: 'For she is a breath of the power of God, and a pure emanation of the glory of the Almighty'). She is thus more closely identified with the godhead, her relationship with God being of prime interest, and her portrayal as the mediator figure between God-given wisdom and human experience, as found in Proverbs 8, is quite changed. Here we find an even more eclectic work than Ecclesiasticus, in which wisdom thought is combined with historical concerns regarding the election of the chosen people and interest in salvation history as well as religious concerns such as polemic against idols. There are few proverbial sayings in this book. There is a list in Wisd. 7: 1–7 of the curriculum of the wise man, and it is clear that this includes the kind of cosmic astronomical and astrological elements that are to be found in mantic wisdom. There are genres of prayers and psalms, and the hymn to Wisdom form is highly developed. There are links with Persian dualistic ideas and with Greek thought (although the extent of its Jewishness and Greekness has been much discussed; see Winston 1979; Grabbe 1997). The links with Israelite prophecy, notably in the polemic against idols (von Rad 1972), and with salvation history mean that the book's distinctiveness as an Israelite wisdom book is much watered down. However, it is still recognizable, in particular through its interest in Woman Wisdom, as a wisdom book written in Greek, but probably composed in Egypt amongst the Jewish population there.

WISDOM'S LATER INFLUENCE

Some of the latest material to be published from the amazing archaeological find at Qumran was material that linked up with the wisdom literature. This is sporadic, but there are interesting parallels. First of all, there are manuscripts of fragments of biblical wisdom books, and second, there are documents either inherited by or composed by the Qumran community. The most extensive work is *Sapiential Work A* (see discussion in Harrington 1996), a wisdom instruction resembling Prov. 1–9 containing advice on issues such as reward and punishment, honouring parents, living in harmony with one's family, and even on paying bank loans! Interestingly, legal texts are used as a basis for instruction (e.g. Num. 30: 6–15 is used in the context of a husband's power to annul the votive offerings of his wife in 4Q416.2.4). Two emphases here depart from mainstream wisdom. One is seeing God as the source of all goodness, and the second is a preoccupation with a 'mystery that is to come', mentioned thirty times, which is unidentified and gives an eschatological air to the work, which also mentions the divine plan from creation to final judgement.

The view of Jesus as a wise man, and hence interest in how wisdom as a genre might have influenced his thought, is a long-debated issue. Jesus can be seen to have used wisdom genres in his sayings (Perdue 1986; Witherington 1994), but the content of Jesus' sayings, which largely focus on ethical matters, is somewhat different from proverbial preoccupations with hard work, communication, loose women, and such like. There is also a strong eschatological aspect to his words that, as we have seen, is an aspect of later wisdom rather than earlier. There is also the related question of wisdom influence on the writings of Paul and on the New Testament as a whole, and the most famous example is thought to be the Epistle to the Hebrews. Reflection on the New Testament brings us full circle back to those famous wise men of Matt. 2 with whom we began our consideration of the wisdom genre.

CONCLUSION

So, to conclude, we have seen that the genre of wisdom that begins with the book of Proverbs developed in a number of different directions as the canon expanded and then closed, and as the tradition continued into the Apocrypha, the Qumran documents, and the New Testament. Whilst wisdom books appear to be in a category of their own within the canon of the Old Testament, wisdom influence on other material can easily be found, even if the exchange of influence doesn't appear to have been two-way, at least in the earliest material. Later, however, that changed, and the boundaries between the wisdom genre and other genres became indistinct. The contexts in which wisdom was practised are seen to be many and various. The theological context of wisdom became increasingly important, with a significant development in Proverbs 1–9 into the realm of cosmological Wisdom, which became very significant in apocryphal material and with important theological challenges to the wisdom world-view being posed by the authors of Job and Ecclesiastes, who questioned God's justice in the world in the light of human suffering and death. Wisdom is indeed a many-faceted genre, and it continues to elicit much scholarly interest and debate.

SUGGESTED READING

Crenshaw 1982; Dell 2000; Murphy 1990; von Rad 1972.

BIBLIOGRAPHY

CAMP, C. V. 1985. *Wisdom and the Feminine in the Book of Proverbs*. Sheffield: Almond Press.
—— 2000. *Wise, Strange and Holy: The Strange Woman and the Making of the Bible*. JSOTS.S 320. Sheffield: Sheffield Academic Press.
CRENSHAW, J. L. 1982. *Old Testament Wisdom: An Introduction*. Atlanta: John Knox Press, 1981; London: SCM Press; rev. edn. Louisville, Ky.: Westminster/John Knox Press, 1998.
DAVIES, P. R. 1998. *Scribes and Schools: The Canonization of the Hebrew Scriptures*. Louisville, Ky.: John Knox Press; London: SPCK.
DELL, K. J. 1991. *The Book of Job as Sceptical Literature*. BZAW 197. Berlin and New York: Walter de Gruyter.
—— 2000. *Get Wisdom, Get Insight: An Introduction to Israel's Wisdom Literature*. London: Darton, Longman, & Todd.
EMERTON, J. A. 2001. 'The Teaching of Amenemope and Proverbs XXII.17–XXIV.22: Further Reflections on a Long-standing Problem'. *VT* 51: 431–65.
GOLKA, F. 1993. *The Leopard's Spots: Biblical and African Wisdom in Proverbs*. Edinburgh: T. & T. Clark.
GRABBE, L. L. 1997. *Wisdom of Solomon*. Guides to Apocrypha and Pseudepigrapha. Sheffield: Sheffield Academic Press.
HARRINGTON, D. 1996. *Wisdom Texts from Qumran*. London and New York: Routledge.
HEATON, E. W. 1974. *Solomon's New Men*. London and New York: Pica Press.
KRAMER, S. N. 1958. *History begins at Sumer*. London: Thames and Hudson.
LEMAIRE, A. 1981. *Les Écoles et la formation de la Bible dans l'ancient Israel*. OBO 39. Fribourg: Éditions Universitaires; Göttingen: Vandenhoeck & Ruprecht.
McKANE, W. 1970 *Proverbs: A New Approach*. OTL. London: SCM Press.

MURPHY, R. E. 1990. *The Tree of Life: An Exploration of Biblical Wisdom Literature*. New York: Doubleday.

PERDUE, L. G. 1986. 'The Wisdom Sayings of Jesus'. *A Journal of the Foundations and Facets of Wisdom Culture*, 2/3: 3–35.

—— 1994. *Wisdom and Creation: The Theology of Wisdom Literature*. Nashville: Abingdon Press.

RAD, G. VON 1966a. 'The Beginnings of Historical Writing in Israel'. In *The Problem of the Hexateuch and Other Essays*, Edinburgh and London: Oliver & Boyd, 166–204.

—— 1966b. 'The Joseph Narrative and Ancient Wisdom'. In *The Problem of the Hexateuch and Other Essays*, Edinburgh and London: Oliver & Boyd, 1966; London: SCM Press, 1984, 144–65 (German original 1953).

—— 1972. *Wisdom in Israel*. London: SCM Press (German original 1970).

ROTH, W. 1980. 'On the Gnomic Discursive Wisdom of Jesus Ben Sira'. *Semeia*, 17: 59–79.

SCOTT, R. B. Y. 1985. 'Solomon and the Beginnings of Wisdom in Israel'. In M. Noth and D. Winton Thomas, eds., *Wisdom in Israel and the Ancient Near East*, SVT 3, Leiden: Brill, 262–79.

WESTERMANN, C. 1995. *Roots of Wisdom: The Oldest Proverbs of Israel and Other Peoples*. Louisville, Ky.: Westminster/John Knox Press; Göttingen: Vandenhoeck & Ruprecht; Edinburgh: T. & T. Clark (German original 1990).

WHYBRAY, R. N. 1968. *The Succession Narrative*. SBT, 2nd ser. 9. London: SCM Press.

—— 1974. *The Intellectual Tradition in the Old Testament*. BZAW 135. Berlin and New York: Walter de Gruyter.

—— 1982. 'Qoheleth, Preacher of Joy'. *JSOT* 23: 87–98.

—— 1994. 'The Structure and Composition of Proverbs 22:17–24:22'. In S. E. Porter, P. Joyce, and D. E. Orton, eds., *Crossing the Boundaries: Essays in Biblical Interpretation in Honour of Michael D. Goulder*, Leiden: Brill, 83–96.

WINSTON, D. 1979. *The Wisdom of Solomon*. Garden City, NY.: Doubleday.

WITHERINGTON, B. III 1994. *Jesus the Sage: The Pilgrimage of Wisdom*. Edinburgh: T. & T. Clark.

CHAPTER 25

NOVELLA

ERICH S. GRUEN

DEFINITIONS

The ancients had no word for 'novella', or 'novel'. The construct is a strictly modern one. That may cause some misgivings right away. The labelling or categorizing of literary works is always a hazardous procedure—especially so when the genre is one of our own making. This need not prevent the grouping of works with similar forms, motifs, themes, modes of expression, even values and objectives, so as to provide reciprocal illumination. As a heuristic device, it can certainly help to reconstruct an intellectual atmosphere and to probe a cultural setting or tradition within which authors (even of different periods) may have engaged. But it is important to bear in mind that the constructed collectivity is artificial, and that the authors themselves need not have consciously produced works in a genre that we perceive or conceive (cf. Pervo 1987: 102–14; Wills 1994).

This is certainly true for the Jewish 'novella'. However one defines it, the examples are diverse, and the category can be expanded indefinitely. I employ here a conservative and tentative definition: prose fiction narrating the experiences of individuals or groups, composed for entertainment but also communicating values, ideas, or guidance. The classification encompasses works as diverse as the religious fables of the book of Daniel, the morality tale of Susanna, the historical fantasy of 3 *Maccabees*, and the romantic/adventure story of *Joseph and Aseneth*. Almost all the writings traditionally clustered under this heading fall within the Hellenistic period, from the second century BCE through the first century CE, a time of considerable experimentation in literary forms and a time when Jewish writers were part of a broader Graeco-Roman cultural environment from which they benefited and which they adapted to their own ends. At the same time, they engaged with biblical themes, with traditional folk-tales, legends, and edifying stories of admirable figures caught in perilous situations and emerging triumphant.

The term 'novella' (a little novel) is a modern invention which refers in part to the length of the narrative—somewhere between a short story and a novel. The first focuses on a single episode, the latter on a more sprawling set of events. But this does not supply a perfect fit. The story of Susanna, commonly labelled a novella, is as short as any short story. Judith and Tobit are of a size comparable to one another, yet the one concentrates upon a single incident, the other on a number of different, though associated episodes. *Joseph and Aseneth* encompasses two quite separate stories. The tales in Daniel 1–6 are mini-narratives with little connective tissue. In general, no uniform pattern can be found, and none should be imposed.

Similarly, there exists no canonical list of Jewish novellas. If ancients did not acknowledge the category, they could hardly have assembled a collection to pack it. Any select group would be arbitrary. Reference is made here to eleven texts that fall within the definition outlined above, yet offer a variety and range to give a sense of the span covered by the imaginative fiction composed by Jews in the late Persian, Hellenistic, and Roman periods: Esther, Daniel, Tobit, Judith, Susanna, the *Tales of the Tobiads*, *3 Maccabees*, *Joseph and Aseneth*, the *Testament of Abraham*, the *Testament of Job*, and the writings of Artapanus.

Resemblance to Greek romances has often been remarked upon (Pervo 1987: 119–21; Wills 1995: 16–28). But the standard works in that category, those of Chariton, Xenophon of Ephesus, Longus, Achilles Tatius, and Heliodorus, tend to follow a consistent design with modifications. They narrate the separation of lovers, their numerous adventures or misadventures, whether kidnapping, shipwrecks, or the amorous designs of third parties, and then a happy ending that reunites them (Hägg 1983; Anderson 1984; Reardon 1991). One can find different elements of this general scheme in certain Jewish texts. But the only Jewish novella that approximates the pattern is *Joseph and Aseneth*, for it contains erotic elements and a union of separated lovers (West 1974; Pervo 1991; Chesnutt 1995: 85–93; Humphrey 2000: 38–46). But the separation was their own doing; and the narrative otherwise diverges rather sharply from the pattern. Moreover, uncertainties about the chronology of both the Greek and the Jewish texts make it quite probable that most of the latter preceded the former. There may or may not have been mutual influence. What matters is that they both partook of the same cultural milieu.

VARIETIES

Jewish novellas come in assorted packages, following no single model and dependent on no blueprint. Some invent heroes or heroines, placing them in an ostensibly historical setting of the distant past, but one shaped to bring out the qualities, characteristics, or experiences of the central figures rather than to shed any genuine light on the past. This holds, for instance, in the case of Tobit, conceived as dwelling in the Assyrian empire, Susanna in the Babylonian exile, Esther under Persian rule, Daniel straddling the Babylonian and Persian periods, and Judith in Palestine contending with the forces of Nebuchadnezzar, who is labelled an Assyrian! The texts aim for verisimilitude rather than history. The remoteness of the constructed past is helpful on that score. But other texts depict recent eras and familiar monarchs, drawing on the recognizable circumstances of the Hellenistic age. So, the *Tales of the Tobiads*, recorded by Josephus but based on much earlier sources, present an elaborate family saga of intrigue, escapade, and adventure set in the reigns of the Ptolemies and Seleucids. The narrative makes explicit reference to historical personages and certifiable situations, but it owes more to echoes of the biblical Joseph than to events of the Hellenistic period. Similarly, the so-called *Third Book of Macabees* (which has nothing to do with the Maccabees themselves) records specific incidents in the specific reign of Ptolemy IV, placed in its proper historical context, but delivers a fanciful fable in which angelic figures rescue terrified Jews from the inebriated elephants of the king.

Still other prose fictions, in diverse forms, reach back into the Bible itself, taking celebrated figures of the tradition and spinning new yarns about their escapades or accomplishments. The imaginative writer Artapanus revamped the story of Moses, making him the teacher of Orpheus, the author of most Egyptian institutions (including animal worship!), and the victor in a ten years' war against the Ethiopians (Tiede 1972: 146–77). The *Testament of Abraham* is no testament at all, but a wholly original tale of the patriarch that bears little resemblance to the scriptural account. The anonymous author has Abraham dodge death by manufacturing excuses and devising a multitude of schemes to delay the inevitable. Abraham's evasiveness and procrastination through a series of episodes keeps God, his representatives, and the day of judgement at a distance until the end (Ludlow 2002: 48–72). The *Testament of Job* concocts a very different set of scenes. Although much closer in theme and narrative to the biblical version, it injects numerous novelties, sparring between Job and Satan, melodramatic confrontations with Job's wife, his servants, and his friends, and the substitution of an engrossing narrative for a morality play (Gruen 2002: 193–201). In still another quite distinctive mode, *Joseph and Aseneth* picks up on just a few phrases in Genesis that have Pharaoh present Joseph with Aseneth, daughter of a priest, as his wife, who then bore him two children. The author blows this up into a full-scale romance and adventure story that employs some characters from the biblical account but creates a complex, occasionally mysterious, and captivating new version.

A number of these texts blur the boundaries between history and fiction. Indeed, fictionality itself is a slippery concept when applied to works that provide a plausible historical setting, include historical figures, and frame their narrative with historical events. For some scholars, that mode of discourse simulates reality in order to have readers buy the presentation as history (Fox 1991: 148–50). But the guise should not be confused with disguise. Neither deception nor credulousness is at play here. The works often signalled their fabrication by outrageous claims and comic exaggerations that could leave no alert reader deceived on the matter of historicity. The book of Esther opens with Ahasuerus conducting a banquet that endures for 180 days, thus tying up all the officialdom of the realm for half a year. Mordecai is described as a victim of the Babylonian Captivity, which would make him an advanced centenarian at the time of King Ahasuerus (Xerxes). The book of Judith designates Nebuchadnezzar as king of Assyria, a designation that any Jewish audience would instantly recognize as absurd. The author of Tobit confuses the sequence of Assyrian kings and makes a hash of Mesopotamian geography. The buffoonish Ptolemaic king in 3 *Maccabees* has to drug a whole herd of elephants to punish the Jews, and then forgets his own orders and countermands his own officials. *Joseph and Aseneth*'s transformation of Joseph into an actual ruler of Egypt clearly abandons the scriptural tradition well known to its readers. These are not inadvertent errors or clumsy chronological confusion, let alone an effort to deceive. They announce the fictionality of the narrative (Wills 1995: 217–24; Johnson 2004: 9–55, 182–216). And they disclose the mutual consent between author and audience to suspend disbelief. The historical novel conveys verisimilitude, but does not engage in fraud.

MESSAGES

Jewish novellas are not pure entertainment. They regularly deliver religious or moral messages. Judith and Daniel exemplify piety and trust in the Lord, who elevates them above their peers and grants them success against foes. Job's devoutness in the *Testament of Job* eclipses the doubts and defiance that characterize the canonical Job. Tobit maintains faith in adversity and adheres to the teachings of his fathers. Aseneth's sincere and intense turn to the god of Joseph converts her from an arrogant and aloof idolator to a devoted wife and warm-hearted figure. But these features can also be tempered by developments that compromise the principles and modify the virtues of the principals. Judith gains her ends by guile and wiles as well as by divine aid. Tobit's piety amounts to pompous sanctimoniousness. Abraham in the *Testament of Abraham* engages in craft and cunning to side-step God and cheat death. In other texts, the divine aspect is subordinate or missing, and the moral element is suspect. The Tobiads depend on shrewdness and calculation to gain the favour of Hellenistic monarchs and entrench their own power. Susanna's promenades in the garden roused (perhaps not innocently) the passions of the lechers. God makes no appearance in the book of Esther. And the rescue of Jews by Esther and Mordecai results in a massacre of Gentiles at Jewish hands. The messages are mixed.

The novellas are notable for the placement of women as central figures in a number of the narratives. They outstrip men in courage, virtue, or accomplishment. They drive the plot, or it pivots about them. In a society where women's privileges were circumscribed and their status subordinated to that of husbands or fathers, there was little opportunity to exercise leadership or achieve positions of authority. Yet women like Judith, Esther, Aseneth, and Susanna hold centre stage in the tales in which they appear. Does the depiction of memorable heroines represent a critique of gender hierarchy, a subversive treatment of societal norms (cf. La Cocque 1990: 71–2; Pervo 1991)?

The narratives themselves are, in fact, more subtle and nuanced. The dynamic Judith serves as a vehicle to denounce the inadequacies of community leaders rather than as a representative of female emancipation (for feminist readings of the text, see Milne 1993; Otzen 2002: 114–18). Judith's exploits, far from overturning the traditional structure, restore to it a stability, order, and relationship to the divine that its timid elders had allowed to collapse. Judith herself then retires to her estate, maintains her widowhood, and chooses to be buried, many decades later, in the tomb of her husband. In effect, she reverted voluntarily, in the last two-thirds of her life, to the position of marginality that she had occupied before.

The figure of Esther upsets certain stereotypes, but reinforces others. She entered the corridors of power, as queen to the Persian ruler, played a principal role in causing the downfall of the villain Haman, reversing the royal decree of genocide for the Jews, and gaining authorization for the slaying of their own enemies. But Esther does not stray far beyond the conventional boundaries. For much of the novella she takes instructions from her male cousin, Mordecai, who directs her behaviour and actions. And, even after she acts in her own right, she resorts to tears and pleas, conventional womanly tactics, to win the favour of Ahasuerus for her people. In the end it is Mordecai who acquires the property of Haman and the signet ring of the king, thus to be his right-hand man, clad in royal purple and a golden crown, while Esther disappears from the scene (to return to the harem?). Here again the traditional order is reinforced. Esther never usurps the role occupied by ascendant males (Wyler 1995; Laniak 1998: 164–5; but see White 1989; Fox 1991: 196–211).

Aseneth is a still more complex character (cf. Humphrey 2000: 64–79). Her arrogance, disdain, disobedience of her parents, and virginal superiority represent all that male Jews found threatening and repugnant in women. With the arrival of Joseph, however, Aseneth's hard exterior, cockiness, and contemptuousness vanish. She becomes subservient and self-abasing. She humbly welcomes her marriage, accepting her role as handmaiden to her bridegroom. Aseneth's former assertiveness could be undone only by degradation. *Joseph and Aseneth* reaffirms the suitable demeanour of women: deference to parents and submissiveness to husbands.

Susanna is virtue itself from the outset of her tale: a prim, modest, faithful matron, properly brought up by her parents in the law of Moses. Her very innocence, however, renders her vulnerable to the wicked elders, who present her with a fateful choice. Susanna chooses the lesser evil: an unfair trial rather than the loss of her virtue. The decision only underscores her helplessness. She suffers further humiliation at the trial, even stripped naked in public mortification. The rescue comes, to be sure, as do the reversal of judgement and vindication of the matron. But not through any action of her own. The heroine of the tale is hardly heroic. Susanna lacks the weight to resist the mighty, and lets her fate be decided by others. At the conclusion, she returns meekly to the household of her husband (Glancy 1995; Levine 1995; Sered and Cooper 1996). Women figured prominently in these fictional compositions. But the inventive constructs of fertile writers largely reasserted the values of their society and the place of women within it.

A number of the novellas depict Jews abroad, the setting of the Diaspora. The location is not accidental. For many scholars these works constitute 'diaspora novels', composed to comfort, reconcile, encourage, or entertain Jews dwelling in alien circumstances and under Gentile governance (Humphreys 1973; Fox 1991: 145–8; Beal 1997: 119–22; Berlin 2001: pp. xxxiv–xxxvi).

The 'court tales' would seem to fit this description (Wills 1990). The vignettes (hardly even novellas) in Daniel 1–6 portray the Israelite wise man at the court of successive Near Eastern monarchs, gaining the confidence of the Gentile king, acquiring a position of authority, and overcoming the machinations of enemies in the royal entourage (Wills 1995: 40–52; Johnson 2004: 20–5). The devout interpreter of dreams demonstrates again and again the power and foresight of his God, whose supremacy is ultimately acknowledged by the rulers themselves. The tales portray conflict within the inner circles, but accept the authority of alien rule, stressing collaboration between the Israelite courtiers and Gentile kings. The sympathetic portrayal even of Nebuchadnezzar underscores the point. Comparable messages issue from the book of Esther (cf. White 1989; Klein 1995; Levenson 1997: 14–17; Johnson 2004: 16–20). The Jewish queen and Mordecai thwart the wicked schemes of the Grand Vizier through access to the Persian ruler, manipulating the monarch, establishing their own authority, and winning royal favour for their people. Similarly, the *Tales of the Tobiads* represent Jewish leaders who ingratiated themselves with the Ptolemaic dynasty, rose to positions of high prominence in the realm, and emphasized collaboration between the crown and its Jewish subjects. The Tobiads gained their ends through their wits and resourcefulness, earning ascendancy by manoeuvring the pliant king and outsmarting his advisors. The motifs can be traced to the biblical version of Joseph in Egypt (Gera 1990; Johnson 2004: 76–93). Jews presented themselves as loyal subjects of the Gentile ruler, and thus prosperous and successful in the Diaspora.

Even the narrative of 3 *Maccabees*, though it portrays a madcap monarch who nearly annihilates the Jews of Alexandria by loosing drugged elephants upon them, produces a parallel conclusion. Ptolemy's plans are blocked by the angels of the Lord, the elephants trample his own troops, and the newly enlightened king turns on his courtiers and proclaims the power of YHWH. The text underlines throughout the consistent allegiance of the Jews to Hellenistic authority and, in return, the obeisance of the king to the majesty of God, thus recognizing the special place of Jewish worship within the kingdom. Similar implications may be found in *Joseph and Aseneth*. The initial confrontation of the two principals suggests a rigorous separation of Hebrews and Egyptians, a stark dichotomy between the faithful and the idolators. But the plot softens and overcomes the conflict. The wedding of Joseph and Aseneth takes place under the auspices of Pharaoh (who does not need to convert). The enemies of the faithful were forgiven, harmony and reconciliation followed. All the narratives place their stress on concord rather than antagonism.

Tobit and Susanna also set their narratives in the Diaspora. Tobit dwells in Nineveh, in the heartland of the Assyrian empire, where Israelites have been deported, and Susanna finds herself in Babylon, evidently as part of the Jewish community in the 'Babylonian exile'. Tobit suffered external misfortunes and domestic discord, and Susanna faced the prospect of unjust disgrace and death. Yet, in so far as the tales have a bearing on Jewish life in the Diaspora, they certainly do not paint an unrelievedly dismal picture. Tobit experiences some rough times, but even in the darkest days he has money stashed away, relatives galore, and friends and family who can move without hindrance through the Assyrian empire. The text celebrates the maintenance of Jewish identity in a Diaspora context, but Tobit's final prayer also offers a broader vision that encompasses Jew and Gentile alike. The Babylonian Jews in the tale of Susanna constitute a self-sustained community. They seem unencumbered by exile status or anxiety about external oppression. Indeed, no Gentiles enter the story. The Jews have their own leadership and populace, their own officialdom, their own élite, and their own institutions. The household of Susanna, moreover, enjoys particular esteem within that community. The flaws and lapses belong to the Jews alone, not a consequence of oppression by Gentile overlords. In short, if the novellas reflect conditions of the Diaspora, they temper any notion of anxiety or hazard with a sense of accomplishment and self-assurance.

ENTERTAINMENT

Another feature of these texts leaves a corresponding impression: the frequent recourse to wit, humour, and mockery, even self-mockery. The novellas, whatever overt or subliminal messages they may contain, aimed to entertain their readers.

The book of Esther stands out in this regard, its comedic aspects unmistakable (Greenstein 1987; Radday 1990; Whedbee 1998: 171–90; Berlin 2001: pp. xv–xxii). The witless Persian king Ahasuerus prompts ridicule from the start. The pronouncement he issued throughout his realm directing that wives should respect the authority of their husbands and that men be masters in their own homes only gave empire-wide publicity to his personal embarrassment for having failed to control his own wife. The compliant and absent-minded Ahasuerus is subsequently manipulated by his vizier, Haman, forgetful both about those who had benefited him and about his own decisions, leaving matters in the hands of others, taking action on the basis of gross misconceptions, and too dense to realize that he rejoiced in the slaughter of his own loyal Persians. The text is filled with hyperbole and comic exaggeration, like a 180-day banquet for every civil and military official in the land, 127 satrapies, a gallows set 50 cubits in the air, and a full year's cosmetic treatment for contestants who seek the king's hand. Diaspora existence is a source less of humility than of hilarity (Gruen 2002: 137–48).

The misadventures recorded in the book of Tobit create their own share of amusement (Wills 1995: 68–92; McCracken 1995). Tobit's self-righteousness and pomposity engender a bizarre retribution: bird droppings seal his eyes when he takes a nap. And the cure for his blindness carries an analogous whimsicality: the wrestling of a fish to submission, in order to procure its gall, to be smeared on Tobit's eyelids so that they could be peeled off. The parallel tale in this text, that of the luckless Sarah who has lost seven successive bridegrooms through the intervention of a demon prior to the wedding night, communicates an equally comic situation. When the eighth suitor arrives, Sarah's father prepares a grave site in advance to bury the victim before his neighbours notice, only to have this young man survive, thus causing the father to scramble madly and fill in the ditch to avoid even greater humiliation. The author's travesty has Jews themselves as targets (Gruen 2002: 148–58).

The ostensibly terrifying tale in *3 Maccabees*, where the Jews of Egypt faced annihilation under thundering herds of elephants, is actually more comedy than tragedy. The buffoonish king Ptolemy reverses his plan to crush Jews three times, either falling into a stupor or suffering from sudden amnesia. And the scheme was once frustrated when scribes, who had been instructed (for no obvious reason) to inscribe the names of all victims, ran out of pen and papyrus. The very idea of inebriated pachyderms as executioners, of course, adds a touch of the absurd. Entertainment of the readership seems a prime ingredient (Gruen 1998: 234–6).

Comic elements exist also in the story of Susanna. The spectacle of the two lechers parting company in the garden and then ignominiously bumping into each other when each had hoped to sneak back unperceived borders on slapstick. So does the scene in which they and Susanna shout at each other at the top of their lungs and one of the elders races frantically to open the garden gate in order to make his fraudulent allegation of a fleeing lover stand up. Events in the courtroom have their own jocular quality, as the bumbling defendants contradict one another's testimony, displaying an ineptitude that mocks their own lofty public status. The outcome of the trial serves less to point a moral than to provide amusement (Gruen 2002: 170–4).

The fragments of Artapanus indicate that his re-creation of the exodus story indulged in some humour as well. He assigns to Moses the authorship of a host of Egyptian institutions, including division of the state into nomes, the use of hieroglyphics, hydraulic and building devices, even the apportioning of divinities, and, most strikingly, animal worship itself. He exploits Hellenic, Near Eastern, and Egyptian legends to link Moses to Hermes, Mousaios, Sesostris, or Thot. And he has Moses teach circumcision to the Ethiopians, prompt the consecration of Apis, escape prison when the doors flew open, and cause Pharaoh to keel over in a dead faint. Artapanus's capricious transformation of familiar traditions must have brought pleasure to his readers (Tiede 1972: 146–77; Gruen 1998: 155–60; 2002: 201–11).

The *Testament of Abraham* is comedy throughout. Abraham emerges as master manipulator, exploiting his advantages with the divine, and prolonging his mortal existence again and again through a range of delaying tactics. The author pokes fun at the feckless archangel Michael, who shoots back and forth between heaven and earth unable to sway Abraham and repeatedly seeking new instructions, while confused about his own blend of human and angelic traits. And he indulges in further sport by having the figure of Death engage Abraham in a topsy-turvy game of dialogue, disguise, and reversal. The wit eclipses any weighty messages that might be found in the text (Wills 1995: 249–56; Gruen 2002: 183–93; Ludlow 2002: 28–47).

AUDIENCE

To whom were such narratives addressed? On the face of it, they would appear to belong to 'popular culture', a form of literature that appealed beyond the élite and the sophisticated. Yet, although they may have contained some folk-tales and traditions that originated in oral form, the texts themselves took shape as writings, transmitted, rewritten, and circulated over the generations. And literacy in the ancient world was not high. But a dichotomy between élite and popular culture is too simplistic. The texts can work on several planes, and they appeal to a diverse readership.

Joseph and Aseneth serves as an example. The entertainment value of the novella is high: a dramatic transformation of the two chief figures from bristling antagonists to a loving couple, and the adventure story that has the 'good' brothers of Joseph prevail over the wicked sons of Leah and the nefarious plots of Pharaoh's son. But more serious and complex elements prompt a deeper probing: matters of Jewish/Gentile relations in the Diaspora, the nature of 'conversion' and the mystical symbols involved in Aseneth's encounter with the angel. Different audiences would have different reactions.

Similarly, the tale of Susanna straddles a highbrow/lowbrow divide. The story of the wise youth outsmarting the wicked elders, or the innocent woman victimized but vindicated, has numerous folk-tale features and certainly carried wide appeal. For most audiences the good yarn, the happy ending with virtue rewarded and villains punished, would have sufficed. But on a more nuanced reading, the text not only depicts the elders as corrupt and immoral, but portrays the populace that rendered hasty judgement on Susanna as compliant, easily swayed, and not very bright. The husband and family of Susanna are more concerned with their reputations than with supporting the defendant. And even the victorious Daniel succeeds not as a devout adherent of the faith but as a crafty prosecuting attorney. All the characters in this plot—the wicked, the inept, and the flawed—are Jews, which would prompt some self-reflection. The fable carried import at more than one level, and could have resonance with more than one stratum of society.

The book of Judith as a narrative of Jewish success against heavy odds, a triumph of piety over villainy, has a strong hold on popular imagination. But here too currents of a less distinct and more subterranean character come into play. Judith is an ambivalent figure, an adherent of law and ritual who does not hesitate to practice deceit. She is both more devout and more ruthless than the males in her society. Reversals and surprises abound in the text, thus subverting a simplistic reading. The text plays with chronology and geography, turns history into fantasy, casts doubt upon Jewish leaders' grasp of their own precepts and traditions, both asserts and questions religious values, and confuses gender roles.

These works and others operate at more than one level. The idea that they could be appreciated only by either a 'popular' mentality or by a sophisticated élite breaks down upon examination. Folk-tales and romances are regularly transformed through retelling over time, with a range of readers or auditors. Populace and intelligentsia alike could take pleasure both in their narrative charm and in their subversive character.

SUGGESTED READING

Brenner 1995; Gruen 1998, 2002; Hägg 1983; Wills 1995.

BIBLIOGRAPHY

ANDERSON, G. 1984. *Ancient Fiction: The Novel in the Graeco-Roman World*. London: Croom Helm.

BEAL, T. K. 1997. *The Book of Hiding: Gender, Ethnicity, Annihilation, and Esther*. London: Routledge.

BERLIN, A. 2001. *Esther*. Philadelphia: Jewish Publication Society.

BRENNER, A. 1995. *A Feminist Companion to Esther, Judith, and Susanna*. Sheffield: Sheffield Academic Press.

CHESNUTT, R. D. 1995. *From Death to Life: Conversion in Joseph and Aseneth*. Sheffield: Sheffield Academic Press.

FOX, M. V. 1991. *Character and Ideology in the Book of Esther*. Columbia, SC: University of South Carolina Press.

GERA, D. 1990. 'On the Credibility of the History of the Tobiads'. In A. Kasher, U. Rappaport, and G. Fuks, eds., *Greece and Rome in Eretz Israel*, Jerusalem: Yad Izhak Ben-Zvi, 21–38.

GLANCY, J. A. 1995. 'The Accused: Susanna and her Readers'. In A. Brenner, ed., *A Feminist Companion to Esther, Judith and Susanna*, Sheffield: Sheffield Academic Press, 288–302.

GREENSTEIN, E. L. 1987. 'A Jewish Reading of Esther'. In J. Neusner, B. A. Levine, and E. S. Frerichs, eds., *Judaic Perspectives on Ancient Israel*, Philadelphia: Fortress, 225–43.

GRUEN, E. S. 1998. *Heritage and Hellenism: The Reinvention of Jewish Tradition*. Berkeley: University of California Press.

—— 2002. *Diaspora: Jews amidst Greeks and Romans*. Cambridge, Mass.: Harvard University Press.

HÄGG, T. 1983. *The Novel in Antiquity*. Berkeley: University of California Press.

HUMPHREY, E. M. 2000. *Joseph and Aseneth*. Sheffield: Sheffield Academic Press.

HUMPHREYS, W. L. 1973. 'A Life Style for the Diaspora: A Study of the Tales of Esther and Daniel'. *JBL* 92: 211–23.

JOHNSON, S. R. 2004. *Historical Fictions and Hellenistic Jewish Identity*. Berkeley: University of California Press.

KLEIN, L. R. 1995. 'Honor and Shame in Esther'. In A. Brenner, ed., *A Feminist Companion to Esther, Judith and Susanna*, Sheffield: Sheffield Academic Press, 149–75.

LA COCQUE, A. 1990. *The Feminine Unconventional: Four Subversive Figures in Israel's Tradition*. Minneapolis: Fortress.

LANIAK, T. S. 1998. *Shame and Honor in the Book of Esther*. Atlanta: Scholars Press.

LEVENSON, J. D. 1997. *Esther: A Commentary*. Louisville, Ky.: Westminster/John Knox.

LEVINE, A.-J. 1995. 'Hemmed in on Every Side: Jews and Women in the Book of *Susanna*'. In Brenner 1995: 303–23.

LUDLOW, J. 2002. *Abraham Meets Death: Narrative Humor in the Testament of Abraham*. Sheffield: Sheffield Academic Press.

McCracken, D. 1995. 'Narration and Comedy in the Book of Tobit'. *JBL* 114: 401–18.

Milne, P. J. 1993. 'What Shall We Do with Judith? A Feminist Reassessment of a Biblical "Heroine"'. *Semeia*, 62: 37–58.

Otzen, B. 2002. *Tobit and Judith*. Sheffield: Sheffield Academic Press.

Pervo, R. I. 1987. *Profit with Delight*. Philadelphia: Fortress.

—— 1991. 'Aseneth and her Sisters: Women in Jewish Narrative and in the Greek Novels'. In A.-J. Levine, ed., *'Women Like This': New Perspectives on Jewish Women in the Greco–Roman World*, Atlanta: Scholars Press, 145–60.

Radday, Y. T. 1990. 'Esther with Humour'. In Y. T. Radday and A. Brenner, *On Humour and the Comic in the Hebrew Bible*, Sheffield: Sheffield Academic Press, 295–313.

Reardon, B. P. 1991. *The Form of the Greek Romance*. Princeton: Princeton University Press.

Sered, S., and Cooper, S. 1996. 'Sexuality and Social Control: Anthropological Reflections on the Book of Susanna'. In E. Spolsky, ed., *The Judgment of Susanna: Authority and Witness*, Atlanta: Scholars Press, 43–56.

Tiede, D. L. 1972. *The Charismatic Figure as Miracle Worker*. Missoula, Mont.: Scholars Press.

West, S. 1974. 'Joseph and Asenath: A Neglected Greek Novel'. *CQ* 68: 70–81.

Whedbee, J. W. 1998. *The Bible and the Comic Vision*. Cambridge: Cambridge University Press.

White, S. A. 1989. 'Esther: A Feminist Model for Jewish Diaspora'. In P. L. Day, ed., *Gender and Difference in Ancient Israel*, Minneapolis: Fortress, 161–77.

Wills, L. M. 1990. *The Jew in the Court of the Foreign King*. Minneapolis: Fortress.

—— 1994. 'The Jewish Novellas'. In J. R. Morgan and R. Stoneman, eds., *Greek Fiction: The Greek Novel in Context*, London: Routledge, 223–38.

—— 1995. *The Jewish Novel in the Ancient World*. Ithaca, NY: Cornell University Press.

Wyler, B. 1995. 'Esther: The Incomplete Emancipation of a Queen'. In Brenner, ed., 1995: 111–35.

CHAPTER 26

GOSPELS

RICHARD A. BURRIDGE

1. INTRODUCTION

It might be thought that a basic question such as what the gospels actually are from a literary point of view would have been one of the first things for biblical scholars to sort out and agree about. Yet the history of the last century or more of critical study is one in which the pendulum has swung back and forth—from a biographical approach to the gospels to considering them to be unique, and then back to biography again.

In order to answer the question of the genre of the gospels properly, it is necessary to understand two key areas: the critical theory of genre and the kinds of literature contemporary with the gospels within the Graeco-Roman and Jewish worlds around the first century. Therefore, we shall look first at genre theory and then sketch a brief historical overview of scholarly approaches to the gospels; this will lead to the recently developing consensus that the gospels are a form of ancient biography and some current issues of debate and future directions of research.

2. GENRE AS THE KEY TO INTERPRETATION

A proper understanding of genre is central to the interpretation of any text—or indeed, any communication. Communication theory looks at the three main aspects of transmitter, communication, and receiver, or encoder, message, and decoder. In written works, this becomes author or producer(s), text, and audience or reader(s). Immediately the importance of discerning the kind of communication becomes clear. If the sender is transmitting Morse code, but the receiver can only understand semaphore, there will be problems in communication! Both parties must use the same code or language, and so correct interpretation depends on a correct identification of the kind of communication or genre. One does not listen to a fairy-story in the same way as to a news broadcast; each has its own conventions, expectations, and rules.

Thus genre is a key convention guiding both the composition and the interpretation of writings. Genre forms a 'contract', or agreement, often unspoken or unwritten, or even unconscious, between an author and a reader, by which the author writes according to a set of expectations and conventions, and we agree to interpret the work using the same conventions, providing an initial idea of what we might expect. Genre is identified through a wide range of 'generic features', which may be signalled in advance through a notice or preface; however, they are also embedded within the work's formal and structural composition (often called 'external features') and its content, style, mood, and character ('internal features'). When taken all together, such generic features communicate the 'family resemblance' of a group of works and thus enable us to identify the genre of a given text and interpret it accordingly.

3. Approaches to Reading the Gospels

Therefore, before we can read or interpret the gospels, we have to discover what kind of books they might be and how they compare with other texts from the same time period and location. Differing understandings of their genre will have differing implications for the interpretation of the gospels. Clearly, we will approach a text differently if we consider it to be history rather than legend; similarly, drama needs to be received differently from, say, myth.

a. Readings through History

For much of the ancient and medieval periods, the gospels, like the rest of the Bible, could be interpreted on several levels: the literal meaning would provide facts about what actually happened, while an allegorical interpretation could apply any text to the story of redemption; the use of Scripture for moral purposes would provide direct instruction for behaviour, and an anagogical or mystical reading would relate the text to the reader's own spiritual pilgrimage. This can be summed up in Nicholas of Lyra's rhyme:

> littera gesta docet
> quid credas allegoria
> moralis quid agas
> quo tendas anagogia

('The literal teaches what was done, the allegorical what you should believe, the moral what you should do, and the anagogical where you are headed'.)

The Reformers rejected all levels of reading except for the literal, and on this basis the gospels were interpreted as history—the stories of Jesus, even sometimes being seen in terms of biographies. This led later to their being used as a basis for the production of romantic 'Lives' such as Ernest Renan's *Life of Jesus* (1863). However, during the nineteenth century, biographies began to explain the character of a great person by considering his or her upbringing, formative years, schooling, psychological development, and so on; furthermore, the subject would be set within the context of the main events of their time. With their relatively shorter length and narrower focus, the gospels began to look unlike such biographies.

b. Unique Works?—Form-critical Approaches

During the 1920s, scholars like Karl Ludwig Schmidt (1923) and Rudolf Bultmann (1921) rejected any notion that the gospels were biographies: the gospels have no interest in Jesus's human personality, appearance, or character; nor do they tell us anything about the rest of his life, other than his brief public ministry of preaching, teaching, and healing. Furthermore, the extended concentration on his death was thought to overbalance any attempt to depict his life. Instead, the gospels were seen as popular folk literature, collections of short stories ('pericopae') handed down orally over time. Far from being biographies of Jesus, the gospels were described as 'unique' forms of literature, *sui generis* (see Bultmann 1972: 371–4). For Bultmann and Schmidt, this unique genre had theological implications about God's unique revelation of his Word in Jesus Christ.

Furthermore, such development of 'form-critical' approaches to the gospels meant that they were no longer interpreted as whole narratives. Instead, they concentrated on each individual pericope, and the focus for interpretation moved more to the passage's *Sitz im Leben* in the early church. Meanwhile, the author was regarded as little more than a mere stenographer, recording the stories at the end of the oral tunnel. Questions about both the literary form and genre of the work and about the author's intentions were thus not possible.

c. Gospel Communities and Redaction Critics

The rise of 'redaction criticism' half a century later led to more interpretation of each gospel's theological interests. Careful study of how Matthew and Luke edited Mark reveals something of their theology, purposes, and methods. *Redaktor* is German for 'editor' (often used of newspaper editors), and the classic redaction studies were undertaken by Bornkamm (1948), on Matthew's revision of Mark for use within the new religious community of the church, and Conzelmann (1954), on Luke's understanding of the events of Jesus taking place 'in the middle of time' between Israel and the church.

Such redaction-critical approaches led to the development of theories about the sorts of communities which produced the gospels. The gospels were seen as a type of 'community' document, within which the story of the community is overlaid upon the story of Jesus and the first disciples, giving a 'two-tier' approach to reading them. Therefore, interpretation began to focus upon the development of groups like the Matthean community (through the work of K. Stendahl (1968)) or the Johannine community (see e.g. the writings of R. E. Brown (1979) and J. L. Martyn (1979)).

However, the fact that redaction critics saw the writers of the gospels as individual theologians with particular purposes brought back questions about authorial intention and literary aspirations. The development of new literary approaches to the gospels viewed their authors as conscious writers or artists, and attention began to be given to their techniques of composition and narrative skills, such as plot, irony, and characterization, through the work of D. Rhoads and D. Michie (1982), J. D. Kingsbury (1988) and R. C. Tannehill (1986, 1990). This made it possible once again to consider the question of the genre of the gospels and their place within the context of first-century literature, and scholars like Stanton (1974), Talbert (1977), and Aune (1987) began to treat the gospels as ancient biographies.

4. The Gospels and Ancient Biography

a. Ancient Lives

In order to determine whether the gospels are a form of ancient biography, it is necessary to examine the generic features shared by ancient 'lives', or *bioi*—the word *biographia* does not appear until the ninth-century writer Photius of

Constantinople (*Bibliotheca*, 181 and 242; see Momigliano 1971: 12). From the formal or structural perspective, they are written in continuous prose narrative, between 10,000 and 20,000 words in length—the amount on a typical scroll of about 30–35 feet in length. Unlike modern biographies, Graeco-Roman lives do not cover a person's whole life in chronological sequence, and have no psychological analysis of the subject's character. They may begin with a brief mention of the hero's ancestry, family, or city, his birth and an occasional anecdote about his upbringing; but usually the narrative moves rapidly on to his public début later in life. Accounts of generals, politicians, or statesmen are ordered more chronologically, recounting their great deeds and virtues, while lives of philosophers, writers, or thinkers tend to be more anecdotal, arranged topically around collections of material to display their ideas and teachings. While the author may claim to provide information about his subject, often his underlying aims include apologetic, polemic, or didactic. Many ancient biographies cover the subject's death in great detail, since here he reveals his true character, gives his definitive teaching, or does his greatest deed. Finally, detailed analysis of the verbal structure of ancient biographies reveals another generic feature. While most narratives have a wide variety of subjects, it is characteristic of biography that attention stays focused on one particular person, with a quarter to a third of the verbs dominated by the subject, while another 15 to 30 per cent occur in sayings, speeches, or quotations from the person (see Burridge 1992: 261–74; 2004: 308–21).

b. The Gospels as Lives of Jesus

Like other ancient biographies, the gospels are continuous prose narratives of the length of a single scroll, composed of stories, anecdotes, sayings, and speeches; thus they share the same 'external' generic features. Their concentration on Jesus' public ministry, from his baptism to his death, and on his teaching and great deeds is not very different from the content of other ancient biographies. Similarly, the amount of space given to the last week of Jesus' life, his death, and the resurrection reflects that given to the subject's death and subsequent events in works by Plutarch, Tacitus, Nepos, and Philostratus. Verbal analysis demonstrates that Jesus is the subject of a quarter of the verbs in Mark's Gospel, with a further fifth spoken by him in his teaching and parables. About half of the verbs in the other gospels either have Jesus as the subject or are on his lips: like other ancient biographies, Jesus' deeds and words are of vital importance for the evangelists' portraits of Jesus. Therefore, these marked similarities of form and content demonstrate that the gospels have both the external and the internal generic features of ancient biographies.

My comparison (Burridge 1992) of the gospels with Graeco-Roman *bioi* or Lives demonstrated this generic relationship, refuting the previous *sui generis* approach of the form critics. This has been confirmed subsequently by the similarly detailed work of Frickenschmidt (1997), and the biographical hypothesis has now become the accepted scholarly consensus. It has been queried by Collins (1995), who also rejects the unique approach but prefers to see Mark at least as historical mono-graph. Wills (1997) and Vines (2002) have compared the gospels with early novels, especially those from a Jewish background, but without great success or acceptance (see Chapter 25 above). Increasingly, gospel scholars and commentators now take the biographical genre of the gospels as their starting-point, while the debate has moved on to the implications of this for their interpretation (see Burridge 2004: 252–88).

5. DIRECTIONS FOR CURRENT AND FUTURE RESEARCH

a. Literary Relationships of the Gospels

The first implication of even a brief consideration of the generic features shared by the gospels with Graeco-Roman biography is that all four canonical gospels are examples of the same genre. This is important to stress, given the fact that some gospel scholars stress the differences between them, especially that of the Fourth Gospel. While such variations may be apparent when only these four texts are studied, consideration of other, non-canonical, gospels and wider reading of contemporary literature demonstrates how closely related these four are. There-fore, any suggestions that Matthew is a manual of church discipline or Luke a historical monograph, while John and Mark belong to the same genre as each other betrays a lack of understanding of how genres function. The canonical gospels have as much in common with Graeco-Roman lives as they have with each other, and therefore belong to that genre. However, within their sub-genre, there is develop-ment, which may be a further argument for the priority of Mark: in the same way as Matthew and Luke improve Mark's Greek style (see the often quoted example of the shift from *kai* to *de*), so they also conform his genre closer to ancient biography by additions such as the infancy narratives.

One area of continuing debate concerns the genre of Luke–Acts. Aune's stress that 'Luke and Acts *must* be treated as affiliated with *one* genre' leads to his odd conclusion that Luke cannot be the same biographical genre as the other three gospels, but is a form of ancient historiography (Aune 1987: 77–80). Similar arguments are made by Sterling (1989) and Cancik (1997). Alternatively, Talbert

(1977) argued that Luke–Acts forms a biographical succession narrative, with the gospel as the 'life of the founder' followed by an account of his successors. I accepted this possibility but also suggested that Acts could be a *bios* of the church in the manner of the *Life of Greece* written in the fourth century BCE by Dicaearchus of Messene; however, the two volumes could belong to the closely related *genera proxima* with Luke as *bios* and Acts as historical monograph (Burridge 1992: 245–6; 2004: 237–9). Talbert has subsequently argued for a combination of these proposals (Talbert 1996: 70).

The fragmentary nature of some non-canonical gospels makes their genre difficult to determine. It is possible that some early Jewish-Christian gospels (such as those of the *Nazarenes*, or *Ebionites*) may have exhibited sufficient of these generic features to be also included within ancient *bioi*. However, sayings gospels like the *Gospel of Thomas* lack any narrative necessary for biography, and thus belong more with *logia* or *memorabilia*; most reconstructions of Q suggest a similar genre. On the other hand, works such as the *Book of Thomas* or the *Dialogue of the Saviour* are more like revelatory discourse after the resurrection than any attempt to recount a life. Thus there may be an argument from genre both for the choice of the four canonical gospels and for the later dating of developments into of other genres like discourse or commentaries.

b. Christological Interpretation

First and foremost, the gospels are portraits of a person, and they must be interpreted in this biographical manner. Given that space is limited to a single scroll—ranging from Mark's 11,250 words to Luke's 19,500—every story, pericope, or passage has to contribute to the overall picture of Jesus according to each evangelist. Thus Christology becomes central to the interpretation of the gospels. Each evangelist builds up their account of Jesus through the selection, redaction, and ordering of their material. The key question for the interpretation of any verse or section is what this tells us about Jesus and the writer's understanding of him. Thus the motif of the failure of the disciples to understand Jesus in Mark is not to be interpreted in terms of polemic against differing groups and leaders, with 'traditions in conflict' inside the early church (see Weeden 1971), as often happens as a result of a more form-critical approach to the gospels. Instead, it is part of Mark's portrayal of Jesus as hard to understand and tough to follow—and there-fore readers should not be surprised to find the Christian life difficult sometimes. Interpretation of the gospels thus requires a thorough understanding of the Christology of each of the evangelists, while each section must be exegeted in the context of its place in the developing narrative as a whole. I (Burridge 1994) have attempted to describe the particular Christology of each gospel narrative through the traditional gospel symbols. Drawing upon Irenaeus's comment that these are 'images of the disposition of the Son of God' (*Adv. Haer.* 3. 11. 8–9), I use the lion to describe Mark's enigmatic 'beast of conflict', while Matthew's account shows the human face of the Teacher of Israel who is rejected; the image of the ox reflects Luke's narrative of the burden-bearing Saviour, and the high-flying, all-seeing eagle symbolizes John's account of the divine incarnation in Jesus.

c. Plurality and the Fourfold Gospel

The fact that the early church fathers chose to keep four separate accounts in the canon, despite the problems of possible conflict between them, also raises interesting issues, as noted by Cullmann (1956). The decision not to follow Marcion's choice of using only one gospel nor Tatian's so-called harmony of the gospels in the *Diatessaron* demonstrates that the four gospels were recognized as coherent single accounts of Jesus, yet which belong together. Stanton (1997) and Hengel (2000) have provoked renewed interest in the idea of the 'fourfold gospel' and its theological implications for their interpretation. It has even been suggested that the early church's preservation of four gospels together may have stimulated the development of the codex in preference to the use of single scrolls. This fourfold diversity also raises interesting theological questions about plurality within the limits of the canon. Morgan (1979) sees these four canonical portraits as offering both a 'stimulus' to produce more 'faith images of Jesus', as well as acting as a 'control' upon them.

d. Theological Implications of the Absence of Jewish Biography

Furthermore, it is significant that Jesus seems to have been the only first-century Jewish teacher about whom such *bioi* were written. It is quite common to compare individual gospel pericopae with stories and anecdotes preserved in rabbinic material. Thus the question about the greatest commandment in Mark 12: 28–34 and parallels may be studied in the light of the famous story from the Babylonian Talmud, *Shabbat* 31a, of the differing reactions of Shammai and Hillel when asked to teach the whole law to a Gentile enquirer standing on one leg. If the gospels are seen merely as a collection of such stories strung together like beads on a string, we might expect similar works to be constructed about Hillel, Shammai, or other rabbis. Yet this is precisely what we do not find. Both Neusner

(1984, 1988) and Alexander (1984) have explored various reasons why there is nothing like the gospels in the rabbinic traditions. Although the rabbinic material is more anecdotal than are the gospels and some ancient Lives, it still contains enough biographical elements (through sage stories, narratives, precedents, and death scenes) to enable an editor to compile a 'life of Hillel' or whoever. Such an account would have been recognizable as ancient biography, and could have looked like Lucian's *Demonax*. Literary or generic reasons alone are therefore not sufficient to explain this curious absence of rabbinic biography. I have argued elsewhere that to write a biography is to use a genre which concentrates upon a person centre stage; however, for the rabbis, this is where only the Torah should be (Burridge 2000: 155–6; 2004: 338–40). Therefore the biographical genre of the gospels is making an explicit theological claim about the centrality of Jesus—the Christological statement that God is revealed in the life, death, and resurrection of this person.

e. Social Setting and Communities

Furthermore, the biographical genre of the gospels has implications for their function and social setting, which is different from that of other genres, such as letters to particular groups, like Paul's churches. As already noted, form-critical approaches stressed the gospels' *Sitz im Leben*, while redaction criticism led to the development of theories about the communities within which and for which the gospels were produced (e.g. Martyn 1979; Weeden 1971). Further study of the way in which ancient Lives functioned across a wide range of social levels in the ancient world cautions against too limited a view of the gospels' audiences. This has led Bauckham (1998) to argue that such 'community' approaches rest upon a genre mistake and treat the gospels like letters; instead, ancient biographies were written for broader audiences—and the gospels were also intended for such wider circulation around the early churches. Equally, the gospels may well have been read aloud in large sections, or even in their entirety, at meetings or in worship at the eucharist in a manner similar to the public reading of Lives at social gatherings or meal times in Graeco-Roman society. The previous scholarly consensus about the uniqueness of the gospels' genre saw them as a communication produced 'by committees, for communities, about theological ideas'! I have argued instead that their biographical genre means that they must be interpreted as 'by people, for people, about a person' (Burridge 1998: 115, 144). As biographies, they are composed by one person, the evangelist, with a clear understanding of Jesus that he wishes to portray to a wide range of possible readers. Thus, once again, genre is the key to interpretation—and the biographical genre of the gospels has implications for their social function, setting, and delivery.

f. Using the Gospels in Ethics

The final area to which we want to apply the biographical genre of the gospels concerns New Testament ethics. The biographical-narrative approach to the gospels reminds us that the gospels are not just collections of Jesus' sayings like the *Gospel of Thomas* or Q; nor are they letters containing teaching material, as in Paul. However, many approaches to the ethics of Jesus treat the canonical gospels as though they were like sayings or letters, and just concentrate on his teaching and words. Central to all ancient biography is that the picture of the subject is built up through both their words *and* their deeds. So, to find the heart of Jesus' ethic, we need to consider both his ethical teaching *and* his actual practice. Jesus' ethical teaching is not a separate and discrete set of maxims, but is part of his proclamation of the kingdom of God. It is intended primarily to elicit a response from his hearers to live as disciples within the community of others who also respond and follow. In his appeal for the eschatological restoration of the people of God, Jesus intensified the demands of the Law with his rigorous ethic of renunciation and self-denial in the major human experiences of money, sex, power, violence, and so forth. However, such teachings are set within the context of a biographical narrative about his central stress on love and forgiveness, which opened the community to the very people who had moral difficulties in these areas. Hence he was regularly accused of being 'a glutton and a drunkard, a friend of tax collectors and sinners' (Matt. 11: 19; Luke 7: 34).

Ancient biographies held together both words and deeds in portraying their central subject, often for exemplary purposes. Thus Xenophon described Agesilaus as a paradigm for others to follow to become better people (*Agesilaus* 10. 2). Similarly, Plutarch provides examples for the reader to imitate the virtues and avoid the vices described to improve moral character (*Pericles* 1; *Aemilius Paulus* 1). Equally in the gospels, the readers are exhorted to follow Jesus' example in accepting and welcoming others (Mark 1: 17; Luke 6: 36). Paul also stresses the theme of imitation: 'be imitators of me, as I am of Christ' (1 Cor. 11: 1; Phil. 3: 17; 1 Thess. 1: 6), following the 'example to imitate' (2 Thess. 3: 7, 9). Therefore, as befits a biographical narrative, it is not enough just to outline the main points of Jesus' teaching; New Testament ethics must also include the call to follow his example.

CONCLUSION

Genre is central to the interpretation of the gospels, as much as to any other form of communication. The scholarly consensus about the unique nature of the gospels which prevailed for much of the twentieth century has come under severe scrutiny in recent decades, as arguments for the biographical genre of the gospels have become part of a new consensus. Out of these debates, a number of areas for further study have arisen, especially concerning the Christological implications of the biographical genre of the gospels, as well as for their literary relationships, their setting within Graeco-Roman society, and their relationship to Jewish literature, especially the rabbinic material. These areas are now likely to be the focus for further research about the implications and consequences of the biographical genre of the gospels.

SUGGESTED READING

The standard introduction to Graeco-Roman biography is Momigliano (1971). For a full discussion of the biographical genre of the gospels, see Burridge (2004). The classical texts cited can be found with English translations in the Loeb Classical Library editions.

BIBLIOGRAPHY

ALEXANDER, P. S. 1984. 'Rabbinic Biography and the Biography of Jesus: A Survey of the Evidence'. In C. M. Tuckett, ed., *Synoptic Studies: The Ampleforth Conferences of 1982 and 1983*, JSNTS.S 7, Sheffield: JSOT Press, 19–50.

AUNE, D. E. 1987. *The New Testament in Its Literary Environment*. Philadelphia: Westminster.

BAUCKHAM, R., ed. 1998. *The Gospels for All Christians: Rethinking the Gospel Audiences.* Grand Rapids, Mich.: Eerdmans; Edinburgh: T. & T. Clark.

BORNKAMM, G. 1948. 'The Stilling of the Storm in Matthew'. In *idem*, G. Barth and H. J. Held, eds., *Tradition and Interpretation in Matthew*, London: SCM, 1963, 52–7.

BROWN, R. E. 1979. *The Community of the Beloved Disciple*. London: Geoffrey Chapman.

BULTMANN, R. 1921. *Die Geschichte der synoptischen Tradition*. ET: *The History of the Synoptic Tradition*, rev. edn. with supplement, trans. John Marsh. Oxford: Blackwell, 1972.

BURRIDGE, R. A. 1992. *What are the Gospels? A Comparison with Graeco-Roman Biography.* SNTSMS 70. Cambridge: Cambridge University Press.

—— 1994. *Four Gospels, One Jesus? A Symbolic Reading.* London: SPCK; Grand Rapids, Mich.: Eerdmans; rev. updated edn., 2005.

—— 1998. 'About People, by People, for People: Gospel Genre and Audiences'. In Bauckham (1998), 113–45.

—— 2000. 'Gospel Genre, Christological Controversy and the Absence of Rabbinic Biography: Some Implications of the Biographical Hypothesis'. In C. M. Tuckett and D. G. Horrell, eds., *Christology, Controversy & Community: New Testament Essays in Honour of David Catchpole*, Leiden: Brill, 137–56.

—— 2004. *What are the Gospels? A Comparison with Graeco-Roman Biography*, rev. updated edn. Grand Rapids, Mich.: Eerdmans.

CANCIK, H. 1997. 'The History of Culture, Religion and Institutions in Ancient Historiography: Philological Observations concerning Luke's History'. *JBL* 116: 673–95.

COLLINS, A. Y. 1995. 'Genre and the Gospels'. *JR* 75. 2: 239–46.

CONZELMANN, H. 1954. *Die Mitte der Zeit: Studien zur Theologie des Lukas*. ET: *Theology of St. Luke*, trans. G. Buswell. London: Faber & Faber, 1960.

CULLMANN, O. 1956. 'The Plurality of the Gospels as a Theological Problem in Antiquity'. In *idem*, *The Early Church: Studies in Early Christian History and Theology*, ed. A. J. B. Higgins, Philadelphia: Westminster Press, 37–54.

FRICKENSCHMIDT, D. 1997. *Evangelium als Biographie: Die vier Evangelien im Rahmen antiker Erzählkunst*. Tübingen: Francke Verlag.

HENGEL, M. 2000. *The Four Gospels and the One Gospel of Jesus Christ: An Investigation of the Collection and Origin of the Canonical Gospels*. London: SCM.

KINGSBURY, J. D. 1988. *Matthew as Story*, 2nd edn. Philadelphia: Fortress.

MARTYN, J. L. 1979. *History and Theology in the Fourth Gospel*. Nashville: Abingdon.

MOMIGLIANO, A. 1971. *The Development of Greek Biography*. Cambridge, Mass.: Harvard University Press.

MORGAN, R. 1979. 'The Hermeneutical Significance of Four Gospels'. *Interpretation*, 33. 4: 376–88.

NEUSNER, J. 1984. *In Search of Talmudic Biography: The Problem of the Attributed Saying*. BJS 70. Chico, Calif.: Scholars.

—— 1988. *Why No Gospels in Talmudic Judaism?* Atlanta: Scholars Press.

RENAN, E. 1863. *Life of Jesus*. ET: London: Kegan Paul, 1893.

RHOADS, D., and MICHIE, DONALD 1982. *Mark as Story: An Introduction to the Narrative of a Gospel*. Philadelphia: Fortress Press.

SCHMIDT, K. L. 1923. 'Die Stellung der Evangelien in der allgemeinen Literaturgeschichte'. In Hans Schmidt, ed., *EUCHARISTERION: Studien zur Religion und Literatur des Alten und Neuen Testaments*, Göttingen: Vandenhoeck & Ruprecht, ii, FRLANT, n.s. 19. 2: 50–134. ET: *The Place of the Gospels in the General History of Literature*, trans. Byron R. McCane, Columbia, SC: University of South Carolina Press, 2002, with an introduction by John Riches.

STANTON, G. N. 1974. *Jesus of Nazareth in New Testament Preaching*. SNTSMS 27. Cambridge: Cambridge University Press.

—— 1997. 'The Fourfold Gospel'. *NTS* 43: 347–66.

—— 2004. *Jesus and Gospel*. Cambridge: Cambridge University Press.

STENDAHL, K. 1968. *The School of St Matthew*. Philadelphia: Fortress Press.

STERLING, G. E. 1989. 'Luke–Acts and Apologetic Historiography'. In *SBL 1989 Seminar Papers*, Society of Biblical Literature, Atlanta: Scholars Press, 326–42.

TALBERT, C. H. 1977. *What is a Gospel? The Genre of the Canonical Gospels*. Philadelphia: Fortress; London: SPCK, 1978.

—— 1996. 'The Acts of the Apostles: Monograph or Bios?' In Ben Witherington III, ed., *History, Literature, and Society in the Book of Acts*, Cambridge: Cambridge University Press, 58–72.

TANNEHILL, R. C. 1986, 1990. *The Narrative Unity of Luke–Acts: A Literary Interpretation*, 2 vols. Philadelphia and Minneapolis: Fortress Press.

VINES, M. E. 2002. *The Problem of the Markan Genre: The Gospel of Mark and the Jewish Novel*. Atlanta: SBL.

WEEDEN, T. J. 1971. *Mark: Traditions in Conflict*. Philadelphia: Fortress Press.

WILLS, L. M. 1997. *The Quest of the Historical Gospel: Mark, John and the Origins of the Gospel Genre*. London: Routledge.

CHAPTER 27

LETTERS

JUDITH M. LIEU

The development and influence of the letter-form is one of the most striking characteristics of the New Testament: twenty-one of the NT writings are labelled letters from early in the manuscript tradition, although whether appropriately so may be disputed in some cases (Hebrews; 1 John). This sets a pattern that is consciously continued in the early Church (as already by the letters of Ignatius), and which, by the networks created and by the implicit claims to and recognition of authority, can be seen as crucial to the development of what was to become early Christianity. Although there are letters embedded within books of the Hebrew Bible, there are no books that themselves take the form of letters; however, the letters that prefix 2 Maccabees and the Letter of Jeremiah in the LXX also testify to the attraction of the genre in the Hellenistic period. Study of biblical letters, therefore, belongs to and contributes to broader debates, such as how NT literary forms are related to those of the wider Jewish or Graeco-Roman world; how their distinctiveness is to be identified and explained; and the hermeneutical problem of reading, and within the Christian tradition of treating as possessing authority, texts originally written for a specific readership and situation now accessible only through them.

ANCIENT LETTERS

The long history of the letter-form, its general stability, and its utility for a range of purposes has long been recognized. A major turning-point, with a particular impact on the study of NT letters, was the discovery and publication from the end of the nineteenth century of thousands of letters on papyrus discovered in Egypt— a geographical restriction whose disadvantages are now becoming more obvious; from the rubbish heaps of small communities, these predominantly represent the ephemeral dealings of private and public life, letters to family and friends, commercial or legal documents, appeals to local officials, etc. Alongside the evidence that they offer for the language, vocabulary, and style of *koinē* Greek in the Hellenistic period, and for multiple aspects of daily life, they also illustrate the tradition-bound conventions of epistolary practice reproduced extensively in the mundane transactions of every level of society over several centuries. For a while, at least, they turned attention away from the letters of the literary élite, of Cicero, Pliny, or Seneca; in particular, they reinforced the immediacy of the Pauline letters and the consequent inappropriateness of treating them as repositories of a systematic theology (see Deissmann 1901, 1927). They did not, however, displace the tendency to turn, first, to the letters of Paul, and only then to the others in the NT.

This sudden wealth of resources prompted explorations of the origin and evolution of epistolary conventions. The letter originated in the oral address of the messenger/ bearer, in Greek letters resulting in the distinctive third person and infinitive greeting formula, 'A to B, greeting (*chairein*)'; although this appears only in Jas. 1: 1 and Acts 15: 23 among NT letters (cf. Acts 23: 26), it dominates Greek letters from the third century BCE to the third century CE, often with subtle modifications according to the context and the status of the parties (Exler 1923). Other epistolary formulae, particularly within the outer framework of the letter, together with a broadly consistent structure, remain equally stable, enabling detailed studies of particular types of letters, such as introductions, recommendations, or petitions, and of fixed phrases or devices within the letter, such as the health wish, thanksgivings, transitional formulae, greetings to other parties, and the closing 'farewell' (see esp. Exler 1923; White 1971, 1972*a*, 1972*b*; Kim 1974, 1975; Doty 1973).

Despite their distinctive greeting formula ('grace to you and peace from God...'), Paul's letters do illustrate many of these conventions, and their identification has been used to expose the structure of his letters, the deliberate effect of the vocabulary and phraseology, and the expectations implicit in them, as well as to investigate questions such as the independence and integrity of Romans 16 (Gamble 1977). The most thorough attempt to locate the language, style, and strategy of the Pauline letters among the papyri letters of the period must be the Papyrologische Kommentare zum Neuen Testament, whose first volume is on Philemon (Arzt-Grabner 2003); this enterprise, in its emphasis on the search for parallels, can only complement more traditional exegetical analyses. However, even Philemon exceeds the normal restrictions of length imposed by the size of a sheet of papyrus—which, within the NT, could encompass only 2 or 3 John. Inevitably, beyond the use of standard formulae and modes of transition, the body of any letter is bound to be less convention-bound than the formulaic framework; in the case of the NT letters it is the extent of the body that most distinguishes them from the papyri letters with which they have been compared, and so an epistolary analysis can only begin to address their production or the way they were received. Concentration on the formal characteristics of the letter-genre leads to an unproductive separation between shape and content.

LITERARY LETTERS

Hence, any attempt to exclude from the picture the literary self-conscious production of the NT letters was bound to prove unworkable. Such an attempt is best exemplified by A. Deissmann's contrast between 'the letter', natural, impromptu, written with no eye to posterity—among which he included Paul's letters, no different from the papyri letters except in their authorship—and 'the epistle', artificial, designed for a wider and subsequent public, and consequently of inferior value, exemplified by the later ('catholic') epistles (1901); the history-of-religions proclivities in this approach are self-evident. Behind an attempt at such a distinction lies the fact that the letter-form was used in the Hellenistic world not only for actual communication but also as a favoured mode of literary expression, often with self-conscious references to and manipulation of the genre: many letters, even though sent, were written with an eye to eventual publication (such as those of Cicero, Pliny, and Fronto); there also circulated collections of letters, often of dubious or certainly fictional authorship, ascribed to significant figures of the past, including philosophers (such as Demosthenes, Epicurus, Isocrates, Plato, or the Cynics); moreover, a minimalistic letter-form could be adopted for a variety of purposes, such as the poetic *Epistles* of Horace; purely fictional letters appear prolifically either within narratives or to create a quasi-narrative as a novelistic device (including the imaginary letters of Alciphron or the heavenly letters of Lucian's *Saturnalia*), but can also be found extensively among the magical papyri (see Costa 2001; Rosenmeyer 2001).

Such a range renders the simple categorization of 'epistle' in contrast to 'letter' of little heuristic value. Others have proposed a distinction between 'real' and 'unreal' letters; this would put the focus on the intention to send, and so bracket out purely fictional letters, including those employed for magical or cultic purposes. Here the Pauline letters would be 'real', while we might be more uncertain about the seven letters in Rev. 2–3, but this again would not illuminate the distinctive adoption of the genre in the early Christian context. Another type of differentiation would be between 'official' letters belonging to local, provincial, or imperial organizations and government, for which there was a skilled chancellery, and 'unofficial' letters written by private individuals. However, this too can be used in different ways: despite the marginal status of sender and recipients, it has been argued that Paul's letters, with their note of authority and the assumption of public reading in the community, are closer to 'official' letters—which were sometimes preserved for the public and posterity through inscription—than to 'unofficial' letters (Stirewalt 2003).

Yet, even with regard to Graeco-Roman letters, each of these contrasts proves hard to sustain: for those who conducted their lives in public, their letters, too, however 'personal' and real, belonged to their self-presentation, which itself was shaped by convention and by rhetoric (see below); even in other circles, 'real' 'family letters' envisaged a less 'private' hearing. Moreover, almost as old as our knowledge of the practice of letter writing is our knowledge of its association with the literary tradition of the (philosophical) dialogue (see Peter 1901), for the genre lent itself to encouragement, direct address, responses to (real or imagined) questions, 'case studies', and the dissemination of ideas among established networks of associates bound by friendship—hence the particular association of letters with philosophical schools. In addition, there was a body of theory about letter writing, including such *topoi* as the letter as half a conversation, as rooted in and aimed at maintaining friendship between the parties, as rendering the writer 'as if present' in their absence, or as inviting an appropriate style and brevity; such themes are to be found in the literary theorists (e.g. Demetrius, *On Style* 223–35), who, alongside the handbooks of epistolary practice, such as those by Ps.-Demetrius and Libanius which classify types of letters, offer us another source for our knowledge of ancient letter writing (some of these are usefully collected by Malherbe 1988). These same themes are reflected, with varying degrees of sophistication, in the more immediate letters of those who relied on a local scribe to send an inarticulate attempt at contact with a distant friend or family member. Yet they are also employed by the literary élites, whether in the fictitious uses of the genre or, for example, by Seneca, who wrote 'moral letters' (or essays) to a purported, but perhaps imaginary, friend, Lucilius, thus avoiding the systematization or abstraction of a treatise (see Thraede 1970; Koskenniemi 1956).

This suggests that we should locate the types and uses of letters on a spectrum without value judgements about epistolary authenticity. It also allows attention to focus on other formal aspects, including the modes of argumentation adopted.

RHETORIC

As we have seen, a Deissmann-like delight in Pauline simplicity had to give way before the self-evident length and complexity of thought of Romans and the Corinthian correspondence, and the attraction of setting these alongside the use of letters in philosophical circles. Perhaps more than those of Isocrates (perhaps genuine) or of Demosthenes (spurious), it is those of Epicurus, whose influence is shown by the survival of fragments among the Herculaneum papyri and by their erection in an inscription by Diogenes of Oenoanda in Lycia in second century CE, which combine the functions of authoritative text, specific address, and availability to a wider audience (de Witt 1964). In terms of argument, however, the apologetic letter tradition—which might invite autobiographical elements—brings us to the impact of the study of rhetoric in the ancient world on reading Paul's letters (Kremendahl 2000).

That Paul was aware of the skills in persuasive speech that were so highly valued in, and indeed fundamental to, all public discourse in the Graeco-Roman world is evident (1 Cor. 1: 18–25). That he also employed such skills, even if only sometimes to reverse the values they stood for, has become increasingly averred. As we have seen, what marks most of the Pauline letters, in contrast to the Egyptian papyri, is both their length and their argumentation. Galatians, in particular, but also Romans, have been seen as inviting analysis, both in their overall structure and in their strategies, in terms of contemporary prescriptions and practice regarding forms of persuasive rhetoric (Betz 1975, 1979). This also recognizes that these letters are often far from sounding like 'half a conversation': they come closer to speech or to diatribe (Probst 1991; Schnider and Stenger 1987). Rhetoric belonged to the classical education, but it was also pervasive in society, and might have been absorbed by many who had never studied it, from public declamations and from the style of city debate. Certainly there is a problem that is still not always addressed sufficiently rigorously: namely, how far the rules of rhetoric, an art designed for public oral performance, can be applied to the analysis of letters, an intrinsically literary form: imposed too rigidly, the analysis of Galatians into the component elements of a rhetorical address (Kremendahl 2000) threatens to obscure rather than to heighten the passion of the letter. Moreover, although official needs, particularly from the Hellenistic period, would demand that epistolography be part of education, its place in rhetorical training is not evident: although mentioned in Theon, *Progymnasmata* (hence as belonging to preliminary studies), it is absent from many other rhetorical guides. On the other hand, we have already noted the flowering of the use of the letter-form in the Second Sophistic for a variety of literary purposes; the self-conscious attempt to create a real or fictional character from the past means that letters often deal with similar themes to those conventionally practised in rhetorical declamations (Costa 2001). While this is hardly what Paul's letters are doing, it does act as a reminder of the fluidity of any genre classification and of the need to recognize the dynamic of multiple influences. Is it possible to retain an awareness of Paul's letters as letters while also analysing them as rhetorical artefacts?

OTHER MODELS

Despite the impact of the study of classical letters on those of the NT, there are evidently other genres represented within the latter, including liturgical and catechetical materials, and extended passages which have sometimes been linked to the diatribe or to the synagogue homily. How far are these of greater influence than the formal epistolary conventions? For example, are the liturgical echoes and passages, such as benedictions and doxologies (e.g. Rom. 11: 36; 15: 13, 33; 16: 25–7), merely formal, or would they have shaped the gathered congregation's experience as they listened to the public reading of the letter (Col. 4: 16)? Some have suggested that the innovative 'grace' greeting is dependent on earlier liturgical tradition (Lohmeyer 1927), although the absence of certain parallels probably do point to Pauline creativity; Robinson (1964) argued that the distinctive thanksgivings that follow (e.g. 1 Cor. 1: 4–9) owe more to the prayer and hymnic than to the epistolary tradition. Others have drawn attention to the uncompromising claim to authority with which Paul prefaces his letters, as well as to the use of the letter-form in other literature within the Jewish and early Christian tradition, including the Testament (cf. 2 Pet. 1: 12–15) and the Apocalypse (cf. *Apocalypse of Baruch* 78–87; Rev. 1–3); this focuses attention on the character of the letter as fixed, authoritative address, rather than on its being sent, and may be able to encompass the presence of other literary elements, including thanksgiving, affirmation, and paraenesis. From this perspective, what defines the Pauline letter is Paul; the 'apostolic letter' becomes a distinct genre related most closely to the apostle's conception of himself and his task, with roots more in a religious tradition than in the epistolary format (Berger 1974).

Certainly, when we extend our view to other NT letters, the Jewish framework becomes unmistakable. 1 Peter's greeting, a wish that 'grace and peace . . . *be multiplied*' has biblical precedent in Dan. 3: 31 (Eng. 4: 1); 6: 26; the same form is found in the letters of Gamaliel in *b. San.* 11b. The circular address 'to the elect exiles of the diaspora' evidently adopts a Jewish perspective. *1 Clement*, written from and to a 'sojourning' church, uses the same greeting formula. It has been argued that behind this language, and the writing of a letter to a number of communities, or, in the case of *1 Clement*, from one community to another, stands the distinctive tradition of the 'Jewish diaspora letter'. Actual evidence for this is sparse, appealing to a few rabbinic exempla, mainly concerning calendrical matters (letters of Gamaliel and of Simon b. Gamaliel in *b. San.* 11b; *Midrash Tannaim* Deut. 26: 1), to the practice implied by the letter from the Jerusalem community in Acts 15: 22–9, and to the assumptions of texts like the Syriac *Apoc. Baruch* 78–87, fictitiously written to the nine and a half tribes. Building on the earlier work of Peterson (1959), Andresen has used this and similar traditions, including the letters prefacing 2 Maccabees, to explain the combination of encouragement and exhortation in a context of suffering found in *1 Clement,* and again in the *Martyrdom of Polycarp* and in the Letter of the Churches of Vienne and Lyons (Eusebius, *HE* 5. 1), each of which take the form of letters sent from and to communities, and which use the language of 'sojourning' and similar greetings formulae (Andresen 1965). A Jewish Diaspora letter tradition remains poorly attested, although not improbable, and further research is required here. The value of this sort of approach is that it is able to combine genre, language, context, and function of what are clearly carefully and consciously constructed texts.

THE FUNCTION OF NT LETTERS

Certainly, the emphasis on Paul as a writer of letters (and not of treatises) has been invaluable, as too has been the recognition that the NT authors were not creating a totally new (and so, perhaps, unreadable) type of literature, however multiple influences are detected. Yet the way in which Paul or other NT authors, like any author, not only reflect but also manipulate the recognized conventions may offer greater insights. For example, Paul's greetings both highlight his claim to be 'apostle' and consciously avoid the 'secular' greeting (Lieu 1985 and below); he continues to assert his apostolic authority in a variety of ways, reinforcing it in the closing paragraphs (Gal. 6: 11–17); the dynamics of absence and promised presence, and of the letter as the representation of the person, fundamental to the letter genre, acquire a particularly important resonance in this regard, even combining with the eschatological tone of his sense of the present (1 Cor. 5: 3–5; 2 Cor. 12: 14–13: 10; see Funk 1967). Letters also marked and maintained patterns of relationship, whether between equals or between those of different status. Study of the Pauline letters can expose how he too manipulates the patterns of superiority and subordination, of friendship, or of client relations, through his language and expectations (Stowers 1986). Letters might also be used in competing attempts to gain influence (2 Cor. 3: 1–3). Therefore, increasingly, attention has focused on the function of the Pauline letters and on their distinctive role within his self-understanding and strategy. On the other hand, the non-Pauline NT letters are not to be dismissed as in some way secondary ('epistles'), but should also be understood with attention to their distinctive place within the tradition; for example, the reasons for the survival of 2 and 3 John and their relation to, and even role in the preservation or authority claims of, the Johannine corpus remain unresolved.

It is within this context that it becomes significant that in the ancient world pseudonymity was particularly closely related to the epistolary genre; a number of early Christian letters are ascribed to a significant figure who was almost certainly not their author, a feature that should be problematized not only under the label of falsification.

More recently, the hermeneutical question has been raised of how a letter functions beyond its intended readership, and how the reader who is not the addressee can read it (Panier 1999). Although this is true of any text, it is exacerbated by the I/you structure of the letter.

HEBREW AND ARAMAIC LETTERS

So far this review has reflected the emphasis in biblical study on Greek letters. The letters embedded in the historical books of the Hebrew Bible have received less attention, although the increasing frequency of such in the later books (Ezra; cf. 1 Maccabees) perhaps reflects contemporary historiographical conventions of including such text-forms, real or fictitious. Fewer non-biblical Hebrew or Aramaic letters survive, and those that do belong firmly in the category of the 'real' (Fitzmyer 1974; Pardee 1982; Lindenberger 2003). Such surviving Jewish letters from the time of the Hebrew Bible—for example, those from Elephantine—offer glimpses into a way of life and practice at which we would not otherwise guess. Again, an epistolographical tradition of conventional structure and terminology can be traced in both Hebrew and Aramaic letters from that period, through the mid-second century CE letters from the camp of Bar Kochba (including, notoriously, one in Greek, which seems to explain the unwarranted use of this language), and into those embedded in rabbinic literature noted above (see Alexander 1984).

WRITING, SENDING, AND COLLECTING LETTERS

Study of ancient letters has also directed attention towards the mechanics and material *realia* of letter writing and sending. In an age of limited literacy, the agency of the scribe was indispensable, and the papyri themselves reveal vast differences in skill even among such scribes. Still debated is the degree of freedom allowed a scribe, whether one who worked to standard models in a village or the highly educated and trusted amanuensis of a Cicero or Seneca. What control did the sender retain over the final version of a missive he (*sic*) may only have sketched out, or swiftly, but not always coherently, dictated (Rom. 16: 22; see Richards 1990, 2004)? How far can stylistic idiosyncrasies be attributed to the hand of the amanuensis without detracting from the preservation of authorial intention—a question of much significance for letters whose Pauline authorship is often challenged on grounds of style or thought, such as Colossians or Ephesians, or for 1 Peter if its Greek can hardly be credited to the Galilean fisherman (cf. 1 Pet. 5: 12, 'through Silvanus'). In this light, authorial summaries and assertions of authentication (Gal. 6: 11–18; Col. 4: 18) also become more significant (Bahr 1966; Stirewalt 2003); but so too does the role of co-senders and the question of their contribution to the content (1 Cor. 1: 1; 2 Cor. 1: 1, etc.).

Also of interest is the means of delivery in a world with no postal service, usually through a traveller on the criss-crossing paths of trade or military service in the Mediterranean world (cf. 1 Cor. 1: 11). This points us back to the distinctive networks not just presupposed by, but also reinforced by, the exchange of letters which shaped the early Christian movement. Furthermore, descriptions by authors such as Cicero, but also actual exemplars among the papyri, provide evidence of the collection, copying, and storage of letters, which might give some sense of the origins and development of the Pauline and other corpora (cf. Col. 4: 16; 2 Pet. 3: 15–16).

THE INFLUENCE OF THE NT LETTER TRADITION

The distinctive character of the NT letters, their length and complexity, but also their authoritative claim, was to prove decisive in early Christian formation. Whatever it was in Paul's mission or self-understanding that drove him to write, his churches circulated, preserved, and eventually collected together his letters; they also imitated them, in *3 Corinthians* if not, as most would claim, in the Pastoral Epistles. The seven-letter collection in Rev. 2–3, although not using epistolary formulae, as well as the opening 'grace' formula (Rev. 1. 4–5), probably already betrays Pauline influence. The invocation of apostolic or similar authority continues in the prescripts of nearly all the NT letters, as too does the use of a closing benediction, and even the anticipation of an imminent visit (2 Pet. 1: 1; 3: 18; 3 John 1, 10, 13; Rev. 22: 21). The Petrine (1 Pet. 1: 2; 2 Pet. 1: 2) greeting reflects, as we have seen, a Jewish/Semitic influence, but we may suspect that the introduction of 'grace' (which has no certain Jewish parallels and is absent in Jude) is due to Pauline influence. This formula and the extended audience is, as noted above, continued in the later martyrological tradition. Although Ignatius claims to write in 'apostolic style' (*Trallians*, preface), he reverts to the Greek *chairein* greeting, as do most later ecclesiastical writers; and the collection of Ignatius's letters was itself pseudonymously expanded in the fourth century. Ultimately, the letter-form was to be developed within the Christian tradition to an extent unparalleled among contemporary non-Christian writers: it continues to be used to establish and to maintain networks of power, while it also becomes a preferred medium for theological reflection.

Suggested reading

Collections of Aramaic and Hebrew letters can be found in Lindenberger (2003). For Graeco-Roman papyri letters a useful older collection can be found in A. S. Hunt and C. C. Edgar, eds., *Select Papyri*, i–ii. LCL. London: Heinemann, 1932–4. Editions of the literary Greek and Latin letters discussed can be found under the relevant authors in the LCL. For introductions to the topic see Stirewalt (2003) and Stowers (1986).

Bibliography

ALEXANDER, P. S. 1978. 'Remarks on Aramaic Epistolography in the Persian period', *JSS* 23: 155–70.

—— 1984. 'Epistolary Literature'. In M. Stone, ed., *Jewish Writings of the Second Temple Period*, Assen: Van Gorcum, 579–96.

ANDRESEN, C. 1965. 'Zum Formular früchristlicher Gemeindebriefe'. *ZNW* 56: 233–59.

ARZT-GRABNER, P. 2003. *Philemon*. Papyrologische Kommentare zum Neuen Testament, 1. Göttingen: Vandenhoeck & Ruprecht.

BAHR, G. J. 1966. 'Paul and Letter Writing in the 1st Century'. *CBQ* 28: 465–77.

BERGER, K. 1974. 'Apostelbrief und apostolische Rede: zum Formular frühchristlicher Briefe'. *ZNW* 65: 190–231.

BETZ, H. D. 1975. 'The Literary Composition and Function of Paul's Letter to the Galatians'. *NTS* 21: 353–79.

—— 1979. *Galatians: A Commentary on Paul's Letter to the Churches in Galatia*. Hermeneia. Philadelphia: Fortress.

COSTA, C. D. N. 2001. *Greek Fictional Letters: A Selection with Introduction, Translation and Commentary*. Oxford: Oxford University Press.

DE WITT, N. W. 1964. *Epicurus and his Philosophy*. Minneapolis: University of Minnesota Press.

DEISSMANN, G. A. 1901. *Bible Studies*. Edinburgh: T. & T. Clark.

—— 1927. *Light from the Ancient East*, rev. edn. London: Hodder & Stoughton.

DOTY, W. 1966. 'The Classification of Epistolary Literature'. *CBQ* 31: 183–99.

—— 1973. *Letters in Primitive Christianity*. Philadelphia: Fortress.

EXLER, F. X. 1923. *The Form of the Ancient Greek Letter: A Study in Greek Epistolography*. Washington: Catholic University of America Press.

FITZMYER, J. A. 1974. 'Some Notes on Aramaic Epistolography'. *JBL* 93: 201–25.

FRIEDRICH, G. 1955. 'Lohmeyers These über "Das paulinische Briefpräskript" kritisch beleuchtet'. *ZNW* 46: 272–4.

FUNK, R. W. 1967. 'The Apostolic *Parousia*: Form and Significance'. In W. Farmer *et al.*, eds., *Christian History and Interpretation: Studies presented to John Knox*, Cambridge: Cambridge University Press, 249–68.

GAMBLE, H. 1977. *The Textual History of the Letter to the Romans*. Studies & Documents, 42. Grand Rapids, Mich.: Eerdmans.

KIM, C.-H. 1974. *Form and Structure of the Familiar Greek Letter of Introduction*. SBL DS 4. Missoula, Mont.: Scholars Press.

—— 1975. 'Papyrus Invitation'. *JBL* 94: 391–402.

KOSKENNIEMI, H. 1956. *Studien zur Idee und Phraseologie des griechischen Briefes bis 400 n. Chr*. Helsinki: Annales Academicae Fennicae.

KREMENDAHL, D. 2000. *Die Botschaft der Form: Zum Verhältnis von antiker Epistolographie und Rhetorik im Galaterbrief*. NTOA 46. Göttingen: Vandenhoeck & Ruprecht.

LIEU, J. 1985. 'Grace to You and Peace: The Apostolic Greeting'. *BJRL* 86: 161–78.

LINDENBERGER, J. 2003. *Ancient Aramaic and Hebrew Letters*, 2nd edn. Atlanta: SBL.

LOHMEYER, E. 1927. 'Probleme Paulinischer Theologie: I Briefliche Grußüberschriften'. *ZNW* 26: 158–73.

MALHERBE, A. J. 1988. *Ancient Epistolary Theorists*. Atlanta: Scholars Press.

MULLINS, T. Y. 1968. 'Greeting as a New Testament Form'. *JBL* 87: 418–26.

PANIER, L., ed. 1999. *Les Lettres dans la Bible et dans la Littérature: Actes du colloque de Lyons (3–5 jeuillet 1996)*. Centre pour l'analyse du discours religieux. Lectio Divina, 187. Paris: Les Éditions du Cerf.

PARDEE, D. 1978. 'An Overview of Ancient Hebrew Epistolography'. *JBL* 97: 321–46.

—— 1982. *Handbook of Ancient Hebrew Letters*. Chico, Calif.: Scholars Press.

PETER, H. 1901. *Der Brief in der römischen Literatur*. Leipzig.

PETERSON, E. 1959. 'Das Praescriptum des 1 Clemens-Briefes'. In *Frühkirche, Judentum und Gnosis*, Rome: Herder, 129–36.

PROBST, H. 1991. *Paulus und der Brief: Die Rhetorik des antiken Briefes als Form der paulinischen Korintherkorrespondenz (1 Kor 8–10)*. WUNT 2. 45. Tübingen: Mohr.

RICHARDS, E. R. 1990. *The Secretary in the Letters of Paul*. WUNT. 2. 42. Tübingen: Mohr.

—— 2004. *Paul and First-Century Letter Writing: Secretaries, Composition and Collection*. Downers Grove, Ill.: InterVarsity Press.

ROBINSON, J. M. 1964. 'Die Hodajot-Formel in Gebet und Hymnus des Frühchristentums'. In W. Eltester and F. H. Kettler, eds., *Apophoreta: Festschrift Ernst Haenchen*, BZNW 30, Berlin: Töpelmann, 194–235.

ROLLER, O. 1933. *Das Formular der paulinischen Briefe*. BWANT 4. 6. Stuttgart: Kohlhammer.

ROSENMEYER, P. 2001. *Ancient Epistolary Fictions: The Letter in Greek Literature*. Cambridge: Cambridge University Press.

SCHNIDER, F., and STENGER, W. 1987. *Studien zum neutestamentlichen Briefformular.* NTTS 11. Leiden: Brill.

SCHUBERT, P. 1939a. 'Form and Function of the Pauline Letter'. *JR* 19: 365–77.

—— 1939b. *Form and Function of the Pauline Thanksgiving.* BZNW 20. Berlin: Topelmann.

STIREWALT, M. L. 1993. *Studies in Ancient Greek Epistolography.* Atlanta: Scholars Press.

—— 2003. *Paul, The Letter Writer.* Grand Rapids, Mich.: Eerdmans.

STOWERS, S. K. 1986. *Letter Writing in Greco-Roman Antiquity.* Library of Early Christianity. Philadelphia. Westminster.

THRAEDE, K. 1970. *Grundzüge griechisch-römischer Brieftopik.* Zetemata, 48. Munich: Beck.

WEICHERT, V., ed. 1910. *Demetrii et Libanii qui ferunter* τυποι επιστολικοι *et* επιστολιμαιοι χαρακτηρες. Leipzig: Teubner.

WELLES, C. B. 1934. *Royal Correspondence in the Hellenistic Period.* London: Oxford University Press.

WHITE, J. L. 1971. 'Introductory Formulae in the Body of the Pauline Letter'. *JBL* 90: 91–7.

—— 1972a. *The Body of the Greek Letter.* SBL DS 2. Missoula, Mont.: Scholars Press.

—— 1972b. *The Form and Structure of the Official Petition.* SBL DS 5. Missoula, Mont.: Scholars Press.

—— ed. 1981. *Studies in Ancient Letter Writing.* Semeia, 22. Chico, Calif.: Scholars Press.

CHAPTER 28

THE GROWTH OF THE OLD TESTAMENT

REINHARD G. KRATZ

1. THE ISRAELITE-JUDAEAN SCRIBAL CULTURE

The growth of the Old Testament presupposes the Israelite-Judaean scribal culture. From it the biblical tradition took over the practices, knowledge, and literary remains of the scribes. At the same time they pioneered with what they took over, or produced independently on the basis of it, a very particular way that was also unique in the whole of the ancient Near East. The genre and the content of the biblical books burst the limits of the usual praxis of the scribes. From the scribes developed the scribal scholars, and from the Israelite-Judaean scribal culture they developed the Jewish tradition in the Old Testament. In order to describe this development, it is necessary first to make clear the literary-historical presuppositions.

1.1 Scribes and Scribal Schools

As in the whole of the ancient Near East, the scribal culture in Israel and Judah developed with the rise of the monarchy. The economy of the court and the temple, as well as that of trade, made the establishment of a bureaucracy necessary. As well as priests, prophets, those skilled in the law, and soldiers, it needed scribes, who practised their trade within and outside the court. Among their tasks belonged the following: bookkeeping and correspondence, as well as the writing, recording, and archiving of important political, legal, economic, and religious documents, as well as literary compositions.

There is a good deal of evidence for the view that schools were established in order to educate scribes. These dealt with not only reading and writing, but offered the widest possible education, which enabled those who completed it to undertake service in the court or the temple. The would-be scribes were made familiar with the traditions and literatures of their culture and educated in the correct behaviour in relation to themselves and others. The content of their education was collected and passed on in the context of so-called Wisdom.

It is difficult to say to what extent the scribal or wisdom schools worked in broader circles and educated other members of the upper class in addition to those who would be future servants of the state. This must be assumed, however, at least for trade and legal matters, that were not entirely centrally organized. Nevertheless, the ability to read and write as the basis for a broad education was confined to a small minority of professional scribes and other professional groups. It must be assumed that the dissemination of literature was similarly limited.

There is evidence in inscriptions for the existence of professional scribes both before and after the Exile, and some are known by name. The composition of inscriptions found in Israel and Judah as well as in the Diaspora can be attributed to them and to those like them. However, the fact that scribes copied, wrote, or even themselves composed biblical books (cf. Jer. 36; Baruch 1: 1 ff.) is never mentioned outside the Bible itself or the literature influenced by it. The reason presumably lies in the fact that scribes were trained in schools, and as a rule were active in state positions, whereas the biblical writings are somewhat reserved in their view of the court and the temple. The likely conclusion is that the authors and copiers of biblical books consisted of people who came from the scribal schools and the higher ranks of administration, but who had distanced themselves either privately or publicly from these and had gone their own ways.

The same conclusion can be drawn from the comparison of two Jewish archives that have been preserved archaeologically: those at Elephantine and Qumran. Neither the municipal archive of Jedaniah nor the private family archive of the Jewish colony from Elephantine from the fourth century BCE contain any mention of biblical books. On the contrary, the literature that was read here confines itself, so far as can be seen, to the Aramaic version of the well-known Behistun inscription of the Persian king Darius I and the book of the scribe Ahikar, a non-Israelite Wisdom writing which has left its traces in the apocryphal book of Tobit (1: 21–2; 2: 10; 11: 18; 14: 10). As, over against this, there are, with the exception of Esther, fragmentary copies of all the books of the Hebrew canon and related literature at Qumran and other places near the Dead Sea. Here, a Jewish community lived since the second century BCE, which had separated itself from the cult of the temple in Jerusalem and had founded its own scribal institutions. In the scribal chamber at Qumran and in other settlements the literary activity of the everyday life of the community and its correspondence was undertaken, but also numerous copies were made of biblical and related books, and their own writings were composed. At what point biblical books also began to be kept in the archive of the temple in Jerusalem as well as in the synagogues of the motherland and the Diaspora, we do not know. The first indications of a broader dissemination are the Greek translation of the Jewish law, the Torah, presumably from the middle of the third century BCE (the Letter of Aristeas), and the evidence for the three parts of the later canon—Torah, prophets, and additional writings—in the book of Sirach (Ecclesiasticus) (44–51 and its prologue 1: 8–10: 24–5) as well as in the instructional writing 4 QMMT (4 Q397 fr. 14–21, line 10 = 4Q398 fr. 14–17, line 5).

1.2. Script and Writing Materials

During the first half of the first millennium scribes used the old Hebrew script, a local variant of the Phoenician alphabetic script, which had developed in the transition from the late Bronze Age to the Iron Age. The first known example of the old Hebrew alphabet is on the stele of the Moabite king Mesha, and afterwards this alphabet is also met in inscriptions from Israel and Judah from the eighth century. In the second half of the first millennium it was displaced by the Aramaic square script, which was a further development of the old Aramaic variant of the alphabetic script.

The oldest biblical manuscripts that we possess, the fragments from the Dead Sea (Qumran and its neighbourhood), are mostly written in the Aramaic square script, which is still in use today. A few manuscripts, legends on coins, and the writing of the divine name in old Hebrew letters in both Hebrew and Greek manuscripts show, however, that the old Hebrew alphabet was not entirely superseded even well into post-Christian times, although it was by then something of a curiosity. In the tradition of the Samaritan Pentateuch it lives on even today.

The writing materials used were stone, ceramic, wood, metal, papyrus, and leather. The choice of materials was dependent upon the reason for writing and what it was possible to use. Stone was suitable above all for monumental and tomb inscriptions. In daily life ceramic was widespread. Ceramic vessels, handles, and bullae were inscribed—before or after firing—according to their function, while ostraca served for commercial matters and correspondence. Wood was used for dictation or instruction, in the form of a tablet covered with wax. Inscription upon metal was mostly for decorative purposes.

In the second half of the first millennium BCE papyrus and leather (later velum) established themselves as the most important writing materials, on which the text was written with ink. Like the other writing materials, papyrus had also been in use for a long time. However, up to now only one ancient Hebrew papyrus is known, a palimpsest from the seventh century (Wadi Murabba'at). Ceramic bullae, which were used for fastening and had a seal on the one side and a reproduction of a papyrus on the other, are an indirect proof for the use of this writing material in the pre-exilic period. Papyrus and leather were suitable both for use in daily life as well as for archiving and disseminating. Smaller texts like treaties or letters were written on single sheets, while longer compositions, in particular literary works, were written upon rolls in which the leaves were fastened (glued or sewn) together. The pages were divided into columns, and lines which were drawn by the scribes beforehand and then written upon.

Papyrus and leather are also the materials upon which the biblical books were written. From the pre-exilic period no biblical manuscripts have been preserved. The oldest witnesses known to us are the fragments from the Dead Sea, which date from between the third century BCE and the second century CE. They are mostly written upon leather. This material was preferred because of the length of the texts. A roll had an average length of eight to ten metres, but could also be shorter or longer. As a rule, a roll at Qumran contained one biblical writing or group of writings (e.g. the Twelve Prophets and possibly also the Pentateuch). From the time after Qumran fragments of Hebrew manuscripts are known from the sixth to the eighth centuries CE (the Cairo Geniza), and complete copies are known from the ninth century onwards. These are mostly no longer on rolls but, as in the case of the text of the Bible in Greek, written in the form of a codex. Unlike the majority of the written documents of the first millennium BCE, which are found on stone, ceramic, wood, metal, or also papyrus and leather, the biblical books and the related texts with religious content, which were found in Qumran or have come to us in other ways, exist in many, sometimes divergent, copies which have been carefully looked after by scribes by way of improvements to the text or the materials. While the other writings have been forgotten, the biblical manuscripts have been continually produced.

1.3. The Literary Evidence

Only a few examples of the Israelite-Judaean scribal culture have survived. These include the Hebrew and Aramaic inscriptions that have been found in Palestine and elsewhere, as well as the literary remains that found their way into the biblical tradition. The first are authentic witnesses of the Israelite-Judaean scribal culture, whereas the latter can be reconstructed only hypothetically by means of literary analysis, the criterion for this being obtained from the authentic witnesses.

As might be expected, the inscriptions deal mostly with *documents of the economy and administration*: accounts, lists, and letters (from Samaria, Arad,

Elephantine), as well as seals, stamps, and weights which are widely distributed as to time period and geographical region (Davies 1991: 118–263; Gibson 1971: 59–70). Such documents coming from daily life are hardly, if at all, attested in the Old Testament. Only in the case of certain lists, such as those of the sons of David (2 Sam. 3: 2–5; 5: 14–16), of David's officers (2 Sam. 8: 15–18), or of the administrative districts of Solomon (1 Kgs. 4: 1–19) may old traditions lie at their basic core, or have served as examples. All in all, the biblical tradition is far removed from everyday affairs.

More attention has been paid to the *administration of justice* in the Old Testament. As can be concluded from the petition of a labourer on the ostracon from Yavne Yam (Davies 1991: 77 f.; Gibson 1971: 26–30), law was administered at a particular place; by the 'elders' at an assembly of the full citizens 'at the gate' or, as here, by a royal official. The labourer has been deprived of his outer garment by his employer and pleads his case to a higher authority: 'let my lord, the commander, hear my case!'. Cases like these were decided on the basis of simple legal principles, the law of parity (*ius talionis*) or the principle of appropriate compensation, and it was used as a precedent. As time passed, there developed a sophisticated casuistry which was written down in collections of legal statements according to the scheme 'if—then'. An example of such a collection, for which there are also examples in the ancient world, is found in the so-called Book of the Covenant (Exod. 21: 1–22: 19). In it, cases from civil law are collected together and, in particular, laws dealing with compensation and bodily injuries in neighbourly common life, and relationships with 'neighbours' are dealt with. However, this collection remained the exception. Normally, the practice of law depended upon customary usage, and thus can be deduced only from particular cases. The family archive at Elephantine offers a view into covenant law dealing with marriage and exchange of property.

The only extant ancient collection of Israelite legal sentences in the Book of the Covenant was either collected for the purposes of education or, as in the Codex Hammurabi, put together to give honour to the king as the divinely commissioned highest defender of law and justice. In the context of the biblical tradition, in which Moses was advanced to the position of lawgiver *par excellence* and the corpora of laws were multiplied, law lost its *Sitz im Leben*. It was promoted to the rank of divine revelation, and was correspondingly ordered theologically. In consequence of this, the legal case of the labourer on the ostracon from Yavne Yam gained new meaning. The question was now no longer whether the labourer had had his cloak taken justly or unjustly. The question was that of his social status. God himself will hear the complaint of the poor so that he receives his cloak back before the sun sets (Exod. 22: 25 f.; Deut. 24: 12 f.).

In the general area of *religion*, it is above all *tomb and votive inscriptions* that have survived (Hirbet el Qom, Kuntillet 'Ajrud, Silwan, Hirbet Bet Lei). They display a quite different theological profile of the religion of Israel and Judah compared with that in the Old Testament, and in particular in relation to the First Commandment. In addition to YHWH the chief god, who is differentiated according to different places, they recognize Ashera as a divine force that gives blessings, and several other gods (El, Baal) who were worshipped alongside YHWH. One sees in the inscriptions evidence of popular religion that differed from the official or traditional religion of YHWH. There is no reason to marginalize the epigraphic evidence. The dominant position of YHWH, which is also expressed in personal names of the eighth and seventh centuries BCE and in many formulae such as those of the Aaronic blessing (Num. 6: 24–6) in one of the inscriptions from Kuntillet 'Ajrud (Davies 1991: 81, 8. 021) and the two (later) silver amulets from Ketef Hinnom (Davies 1991: 72 f.), suggests another conclusion. The boundaries between temple theology and the popular religion of the people in the pre-exilic monarchy and, if one thinks of Elephantine, also later, were fluid. The separation of orthodoxy and heterodoxy in the biblical tradition which expects blessing from YHWH alone (cf. Gen. 12: 1–3), comes from later theological construction.

Formulae of blessing and curse in inscriptions and amulets touch on a further area of religion: *magic* and *manticism*. Belief in hidden divine powers and the possibility of influencing them by means of magic can be recognized in many ways in the epigraphic and iconographic remains. However, the functionaries who presided over the art of magic and the closely connected practice of foretelling the future—namely priests and prophets—are only seldom mentioned in the inscriptions. They existed also in Israel and Judah.

In the Lachish Ostracon number 3, a letter sent from the battlefield by a lower-ranking person to his superior (Davies 1991: 1 f.; Gibson 1971: 38–41), a letter written by a royal official is referred to which mentions a prophet. In the tense situation of the siege of Jerusalem by the Babylonians (around 597 BCE), the anonymous prophet speaking no doubt in the name of the national god YHWH had counselled caution: 'be careful!', whether to warn the king against a hostile attack (cf. 2 Kgs. 6: 9), or whether because he was full of anxiety and wanted to secure the help of YHWH against his enemies (cf. Isa. 7: 4). Although this evidence is not clear, it fits best into the picture that one gets from parallels in the ancient Near East (the Mari Letters, neo-Assyrian prophecies, and the Zakur inscription). According to this, prophets were cult officials who worked in the name of the national god for the ruling king, who advised him in political, military, cultic, or ethical matters, and whose messages were conveyed in letters, and in this and in other ways were retained in archives. In the ancient Orient and also in the kingdoms of Israel and Judah, prophecy was a means of politics and propaganda.

The prophets, indeed, did not always have only good news to announce. From the closer circle of Israel come the words of Balaam, the son of Beor the seer of the gods from Deir 'Alla in the land Gilead (TUAT ii. 1: 138–48). He is none other than the Balaam of the Bible (Num. 22–4), but one meets him here in his original setting and in his time around 700 BCE, before he was taken over into the biblical tradition in connection with Israel. The inscription was written with red and black ink upon a whitewashed wall. Balaam, as Germans say, had painted the devil on the wall: a shocking catastrophe decreed by the gods, which he related to his people with tears. From the badly preserved remains it is not possible to say what caused the proclamations of disaster and curse, or the intention with which they were written down. At best they can be understood as a warning and a threat about improvements needed to appease the angry gods Shagar and Ashtar, El and the gathering of the Shaddin (cf. Num. 24: 4, 16!). The inscription recalls the old oriental science of omens, and other forms of manticism, which is concerned with the recognition and meaning of good and bad signs.

In the Old Testament not only the genres and methods of speech, but also the remains of old Israelite and Judaean prophecy, have been preserved. The *prophetic legends* in the books of Samuel and Kings stand closest to the phenomenology of the classical old oriental prophecy. Here one meets king-makers and political-military advisors of the king (Samuel in 1 Sam. 9–10; Nathan in 1 Kgs. 1–2; Elisha in 2 Kgs. 3: 11 ff.; Isaiah in 2 Kgs. 18–20), as well as the wonder-workers who are clothed with magical powers (Elijah and Elisha in 1 Kgs. 18: 41–6; 2 Kgs. 4). However, not all the narratives in Samuel and Kings have an old literary kernel which goes back to the time of the monarchy. Some were composed later, under the influence of the older material. They were all later reworked in the sense of redactions, which gave them their present forms in the books of Samuel and Kings.

The words of the prophets are collected in the books of the prophets, but here also only a few authentic words can be discerned which can be attributed to the heritage of the Israelite-Judaean scribal culture. From the time of the so called Syro-Ephraimite war around 730 BCE come the oracles of salvation of the prophet Isaiah, who prophesied the demise of the enemies of Judah in the north—namely, Aram and Israel (Isa. 7: 4, 7–9; 8: 1–4; 17: 1–3)—and just as a hundred years later, Nahum prophesied the demise of the Assyrians. Words from both sides of the Syro-Ephraimite war seem to appear in Hos. 5: 8–11. The authentic speech of the prophet Hosea, however, is in Hos. 6: 8–7: 7, and deals with the threatened demise of the kingdom of Israel, which became true in 722 BCE. The parables and woe-oracles of the prophet Amos in chapters 3–6 (Amos 3: 12; 5: 2, 3, 19; 5: 18; 6: 1 ff.; cf. 3: 12bβ; 4: 1, 5: 7) have the same purpose, in that they present the downfall of Samaria as inevitable, whether (from an Israelite perspective) these prophetic words are originally intended to induce regret and perhaps even avert this or (from the perspective of Judah), to welcome it and to some extent wish to influence it. Unambiguously spoken from the point of view of those affected are the words of the prophet Jeremiah in the form of laments about the imminent demise of Judah in the years 597–587 BCE, which erupt from the deep sympathy felt by the prophet in his innermost being (Jer. 4: 7, 11, 13, 19–21; 6: 1, 22–3). In the laments it is Jeremiah who speaks, not YHWH. He is deeply shocked by what he hears and sees about what is to come. What it is, he only hints at, but this much is clear: it is not YHWH who punishes Judah and Jerusalem for their sins, but a monstrous war machine that marches towards them—the ominous 'foe from the north'. The laments of Jeremiah can be compared with the words of Zephaniah concerning the 'day of YHWH' (Zeph. 1: 14–16), that is reminiscent of the perverted world of Balaam's presentiments of disaster from Deir 'Alla.

After all this had taken place, and the kingdoms of Israel and Judah no longer existed, the prophets lost their social setting and, with it, their meaning. Several prophets none the less uttered words here and there. Some adhered to the end to the received tradition and proclaimed a victory over the enemies in the name of YHWH (Jer. 27–8). Others made their voices heard when it became clear who would rule the land in the future and take over the custody of the temple. Two oracles have been preserved under the date of the second year of Darius I which call for the rebuilding of the temple and proclaim the entry of the glory of YHWH (Hag. 1: 1, 4, 8 and 1: 15b/2: 1, 3, 9a). From the time of the Second Temple we hear practically nothing more about prophets, which does not mean that they did not exist (Neh. 6: 7, 10–14; Zech. 13). However, the prophetic spirit was active no longer in the prophets themselves, but in the written tradition which circulated in their names and gained strength in the time of the Second Temple.

The epigraphic finds unfortunately afford us no view of the literary activity of the priests in the temples of Israel and Judah. On the basis of parallels from the ancient world, one would expect them to consist of lists of gods, rituals of sacrifices, liturgical calendars, hymns, and prayers, as well as myths about the gods. However, nothing has remained to this day except several inscriptions on cult objects. Thus one has to look to the Old Testament.

It can be assumed that behind the laws concerning sacrifices in Leviticus 1–7 and the decrees about purity in Leviticus 11–15 are the *traditions of the priests*. Also, the law of the altar in Exod. 20: 24–6 and the cultic calendar in Exod. 23: 14–16 could well rest upon older pre-exilic traditions.

Hymns and *prayers* can be found in the psalter. The old hymns such as Psalms 29 or 93 indicate that they are such because they stand in an unbroken line of tradition with Canaanite texts and represent the myth of the kingdom of God in a short poetic version. The hymns are close to the declarations of property in one of the inscriptions from Hirbet Bet Lei, to the phrase in the cave inscription from Ein Gedi, and to a description of a theophany in the old Phoenician wall inscription from Kuntillet 'Ajrud. The YHWH of Samaria and the YHWH of Jerusalem are no different from the Baal of Ugarit and the Baal or Hadad of the Phoenicians and the Aramaeans. Old prayers are the lament (e.g. Ps. 13) and the thanksgiving of the individual (cf. Ps. 118: 5, 14, 17–19, 21, 28). They are part of the liturgy that accompanied the ritual of sacrifice, which is hinted at in the text of the thanksgivings, but about which we know nothing further. Also for these prayers, the Canaanite mythology gave the inspiration, in so far as the divinity constantly conducts the supplicant from death into life. In the Ugaritic Baal epic, death (in

Hebrew Mot) is the second foe after the sea-god Yam, with whom the weather god Baal struggles for the kingship.

A particular case is *Hebrew narrative*. Myths about the gods—that is, stories from the sphere of the gods, which explain conditions upon earth, as in the Baal cycle in Ugarit or Atram Hasis and Enuma Elish in Mesopotamia—are not preserved in the Old Testament. The nearest things to myths from the ancient Orient are the narratives that underlie the primal history in Genesis 1–11: the Canaanite anthropogony in Genesis 2–4, the account of the Flood in Genesis 6–9, and the Noachite table of nations in Genesis 10. Rather, the Hebrew narrative culture stood closer to the north-west Semitic tradition of hero legends, as one knows them from the epic of Gilgamesh, and concentrated upon relationships in various social milieux, such as the family (Genesis), the tribe (Judges), or the royal court (Samuel and Kings). Only later were the individual stories brought together in larger narrative wholes and overarching historical accounts, in the course of which they were transformed into the myth of the history of God with his people Israel.

With the exception, perhaps, of the primal history, the Hebrew narrative tradition was situated not in the priestly milieu but in that of the court. The scribes who were active there had, in addition to their daily world of which the ostraca from Samaria, Arad, and Lachish are indications, first and foremost a concern with *royal annals*. From them appear to be taken the information about changes of rule and length of reign upon which the chronology of the books of Kings rest. In connection with this, as was common in such royal chronicles, other happenings were occasionally mentioned, such as military undertakings and building works. These episodes are the point of departure for historical narratives which originally arose separately and which were later incorporated into the annalistic scheme of the books of Kings (e.g., 1 Kgs. 20 and 22, 2 Kgs. 3 and 9–10). It is possible to study the transition from the one to the other in three inscriptions: the stele of King Mesha (Gibson 1971: 71–83; Pritchard 1955: 320 f.; which is the Moabite version of 2 Kgs. 3), the inscription from Tell Dan (TUAT Suppl. 2001, 176–9; which is the Aramaic version of 2 Kgs. 9–10), and the Siloam inscription (Davies 1991: 68; Gibson 1971: 21–3), the only epigraphic remains of old Hebrew prose and an episode in which neither the king nor YHWH plays a role.

Closely connected with the court was *wisdom*, the spiritual home and school of the scribes. Here the various traditions and sources of knowledge of Israelite and Jewish culture were written down, edited and taught, in so far as they were not the preserve of specialists such as chroniclers, priests, and prophets. Here, the individual stories were collected and put together into a literary form.

As the example of the Aramaic version of Ahikar, which was read at Elephantine, shows, Wisdom understood its function to be that of narrating as well as putting things into poetic form. In polished proverbs and various poetic genres, the phenomena and orders of nature as well as of human conduct and its psychology are analysed and brought to expression. Examples can be found in the ancient collections of the book of Proverbs (10: 1–22: 16; 22: 17–24: 22 and 24: 23–32; 25–9), of which Proverbs 22: 17–24: 22 possesses an Egyptian parallel (Pritchard 1955: 421 ff.). The portrayal of nature in the divine speeches of the book of Job (38–41) also stands in this tradition.

Didactic stories such as the story of Ahikar are examples of wisdom as practised and woven into the life of an exemplary sage at the end of a successful career. In the Old Testament this genre is represented by the fable of Jotham in Judg. 9 and the story of Joseph in Genesis 37–50. In addition, there are later representatives of this genre, in which the exemplary sage has become the exemplary pious believer, and increasingly, the suffering of the wise believer in God and wisdom is taken into account (Daniel, Job). Indeed, in the old narratives which come from other milieux, the narrative art of wisdom is often also at work.

2. THE BIBLICAL TRADITION

The biblical tradition was not born with Israel and Judah; but without it the two kingdoms would have disappeared like their neighbours. With the end of their political existence, they would have disappeared along with their scribal culture and fallen into oblivion, until the accident of archaeology brought one or the other to light. So it is rather astonishing that Israel and Judah have survived to this day in their memory in the biblical tradition. The transformation of the scribal culture of Israel and Judah into the biblical tradition is like a transformation into another kind, and grounds the Jewish tradition in the Old Testament. The phenomenon can barely be explained historically. By means of the differences between the epigraphic and the literary remains of the ancient scribal culture, one can none the less identify the stages by which the moves to the growth of the Old Testament were made.

2.1. From Prophets of Salvation to Prophets of Disaster

The main difference in relation to the scribal culture consists of the picture of God in the Old Testament. It bears the marks of a religion of revelation, and comes from theological reflection: YHWH has chosen Israel to be his people, and requires from Israel a conscious decision for or against him. This means that the relationship is not self-evident, but was specially established and is connected with conditions. Out of the natural symbiosis of YHWH and his worshippers in Israel and Judah, which are indicated by the remains of the ancient scribal culture, there has come in the Old Testament an exclusive relationship with God grounded upon faith and confession. As far as we can see, this picture of God has its roots in the prophetic tradition.

The transformation can be seen in the theological interpretation of the prophetic oracles. This interpretation brought about a change in the picture of God, in that it declared YHWH, the national God of Israel and Judah, to be the enemy of the two monarchies, and turned the previous court or cult prophets into prophets of disaster, who were committed not to God and to the king, but solely and only to YHWH.

Thus the oracles of salvation of the prophet of Judah, Isaiah (Isa. 7: 4, 7–9; 8: 1–4; 17: 1–3), were reformulated as oracles of disaster in a literary context, first in the so-called memorandum of Isaiah (Isa. 6–8). Just as destruction is prophesied for Judah's enemy, the kingdom of Israel (and Aram), so now the destruction of Judah is itself prophesied, a destruction that has been provoked by the people's lack of faith in God and decreed by YHWH himself. Both the nations, Israel and Judah, will suffer the judgement with which YHWH has threatened his own people (Isa. 6; 7: 9b; 8: 5–8). The memorandum in chapters 6–8 was the starting-point for the book of Isaiah: for the ring-formed composition of 'the vision' or, more precisely, the words concerning Judah and Jerusalem (Isa. 1: 1; 2: 1) in Isa. 1–12, as well as for the so-called Assyrian cycle, Isaiah 28–32, which centres on the fate of Zion, and for the oracle against the nations of Isaiah 13–23, and the scenario of the judgement of the world in Isaiah 24–7 and 33–5.

In the same way the words of Hosea in Hosea 4–9 and of Amos in Amos 3–6 were collected together and given their theological meaning. From the announcement of coming disaster for Israel come declarations of the divine judgement. Out of the complaints come charges and grounds for the judgement, out of the bemoaned shortcomings and the denounced bad behaviour, come sins against God. And in all this, the political barriers between the monarchies of Israel and Judah are removed. Israel stands for the whole of the people of God, which implicitly or explicitly also includes Judah. The destruction of both kingdoms means that YHWH has decreed the end of the people Israel. In both books, Hosea and Amos, the tradition thinks intensively about this end. The theological reflection has left its mark above all in the framework parts that were added later, in the stories of marriage and the historical-theological reflections in Hosea 1–3 and 9–14, as well as the oracles against the nations and cycles of visions in Amos 1–2 and 7–9 (cf. also Amos 4: 6 ff.).

The consequences for the picture of God are obvious. YHWH is no longer the national god of the two monarchies, only locally different from the YHWH in Samaria and the YHWH of Jerusalem. He is seen much more as the one God of the one people of God, who reveals his true nature and will in judgement. It is the end of Israel that makes clear the past and future of the relationship with God: what in the theological meaning of the prophets has led to the break is the standard by which the people of God have been guided in the past, and by which they must be guided in the future. The restoration of the broken relationship with God presupposes the repentance of the people.

The cause of this theological new interpretation of the prophetic oracle is not difficult to discern from the prophecy of disaster. It is the destruction of Samaria and the kingdom of Israel in 722 BCE which also threatened Judah at least in 701, and caused the guardians of the tradition to think of the relationship between YHWH and Israel beyond the limits of merely political concerns. The same situation repeated itself about a hundred years later in connection with the fall of Jerusalem in 597 to 587 BCE. The laments of prophet Jeremiah (Jer. 4: 7, 11, 13, 19–21; 6: 1, 22–3) were, according to the example of the older tradition, retrospectively rewritten as predictions of the divine judgement upon (Israel and) Judah (Jer. 4–6; cf. especially 4: 5–6 with 6: 1, 22). Also, here, a core tradition, the poems concerning the 'foe from the north' in Jeremiah 4–6 constituted the point of departure for the literary development of the book: for the addition of further sayings material, the symbolic actions, and the prose speeches, the stories of the suffering and the personal confessions of the prophet, and not least the extensive oracles against the nations which in the Greek version of the book stand in the middle, as also with Isaiah, but which come at the end of the Hebrew version.

In general the prophetic tradition inserts authentic oracles with a theological new interpretation of them in the sense of prophecies of judgement. In spite of the political reverses, those who passed on the tradition held fast to YHWH as the God of Israel and gave up for it the people and the God of the kingdoms of Israel and Judah. In place of the rival national gods came the God of 'both houses of Israel' (Isa. 8: 14) and in place of the two kingdoms of Israel and Judah came Israel the people of God. In all books a process of interpretation and actualization followed the understanding of the destruction of Israel and Judah as God's punishment. The extensive rewritings paint the judgement in various colours and present ever new grounds for the turning away of YHWH from his people. With time oracles against the nations and oracles of salvation for Israel were added which in many books won the upper hand (Isa. 40–66; Hag. 1–2; Zech. 1–8). They take up the old, pre-exilic tradition of the prophecy of salvation or recent oracles of that old nature (e.g. Hag. 1: 1, 4, 8 and 1: 15b/2: 1, 3, 9a) but thoroughly presuppose the destruction of both kingdoms and the literary tradition of the prophecy of judgement.

In this fashion the books of the three great prophets and that of the twelve Minor Prophets gradually came into being. They cannot be ascribed definitely to a particular epoch, because they grew over the course of centuries, until the rewriting within the books (apart from small details) came to an end at the beginning of the second century BCE. Only the beginning of the tradition can be identified according to its content. It was the end of the kingdom of Israel under Assyria at the end of the eighth century BCE that was the trigger for the prophetic tradition in the books of Isaiah, Hosea, and Amos. The end of the kingdom of Judah under Babylon set a second wave in motion, which began with the tradition in the book of Jeremiah and there, as also in the book of Ezekiel, continued a kind of midrash concerning the prophetic tradition. The next turning-point was the building of the Second Temple in Jerusalem (520–515 BCE), which was the impulse for the tradition in the books of Haggai, Zechariah, and Malachi. Between these times Joel, Obadiah, Jonah, Micah, Nahum, Habakkuk, and Zephaniah are situated, prophetical books which reflect the end of the kingdoms of Israel and Judah and await the end of the world. For the main part they come from the Persian-Hellenistic time, in which the other books were also considerably edited and received their extant forms.

2.2. From Secular Nation to the People of God

The idea of the people of YHWH is connected with the picture of God of the prophetic tradition. The prophetic tradition sees the mixed population, which was kept together in the kingdoms of Israel and Judah by means of the monarchy, united as standing under the judgement of God. Thus there emerged the higher unity of 'Israel', the people of God, an ideal entity which crosses the political boundaries and represents a theological claim. This claim was never realized in historical reality, but rather in the biblical literature. On the basis of the prophetic message about the end of the relationship with God was reconstructed the beginning of this relationship, the foundation story of the people of God, in order to gain a positive perspective for the future. For this purpose various single traditions were collected from diverse areas of the population in Israel and Judah, and these were formed into narrative cycles and historical narratives, which related the history of God with his people, the saving history of Israel. In this way the myths were born of the original unity of the two monarchies and of pre-monarchic Israel.

The development began in the pre-exilic period, between the end of Samaria in 722 and the fall of Jerusalem in 597/587 BCE. From this time come three literary works, each of which in its way offers a legend of the origin of Israel and at the same time indicates the relation to Judah: they are the legend about the beginning of the kingship and the kingdom of David in 1 Samuel–1 Kings 2, the Yahwistic primal history and history of the Patriarchs in Genesis 2–35, and the story of the Exodus in Exodus 2–Joshua 12.

1 Samuel–1 Kings 2 refers back to the beginnings of the kingship. This composition has been put together from old sources, which for their part have behind them a long period of growth: a tradition from the house of Saul in 1 Samuel 1–14 and that of the succession to the throne of David in 2 Samuel 11–1 Kings 2. By means of the hinge verse 1 Samuel 14: 52 and the linking narrative in 1 Samuel 16–

2 Samuel 5: 8–10 David and Saul are brought together for the first time, and the house of David, the southern kingdom, Judah, is declared to be the legitimate heir of the house of Saul, the northern kingdom, Israel. In this way Israel and Judah become a unity under the roof of the dynasty of David both on the political plain and also as a people. The Yahwistic primal history and history of the Patriarchs in Genesis 2–35 refer back to the beginnings of the people. They have been put together from various originally separate traditions of a sub-national and family milieu. They are woven together by means of genealogy and geography, and they are given a national identity and united with the national God of Israel and Judah, YHWH, in order to establish the unity of Israel and Judah. A preliminary step to this is provided by the old composition Genesis 26–35, which comes from a joining of the south Palestinian Isaac/Esau tradition in Genesis 26–7 with the north Palestinian Jacob/Laban tradition in Genesis 29: 16–32: 2. This was the example for the redaction which made Jacob into the eponymous ancestor of Israel (Gen. 32: 28 f.) and the father of Judah (Gen. 29: 35), and which in the form of family history described the genesis of the Syrian-Palestinian small nations. The turning- and crucial point of this redaction is the hinge passage Gen. 12: 1–3, which sets up a narrative arch from the primal history to the story of Jacob, and formulates the main perspective which sees the people Jacob/Israel that comes from Abraham in relation to Judah and the other neighbouring countries after 720 BCE.

Similarly, the story of the exodus in Exodus 2–Joshua 12 refers back to the origins of the people. However, in opposition to the two above-mentioned cases, it represents an exclusively Israelite standpoint. The nucleus of the composition are the Israelite and Benjaminite narratives about war (Exod. 14; Josh. 6 and 8) which honour God as the God of war, as does also the Song of Miriam in Exod. 15: 20 f. Through the insertion of the call of Moses in Exodus 2–4 and the bridging traditions about a wandering through the wilderness, there arose the story of the exodus of Israel from Egypt and the occupation of the land under Moses, Miriam, and (by means of the literary connection of Num. 25: 1a/Deut. 34: 5–6*/Josh. 2: 1 ff.; 3: 1 ff.) Joshua. The redactional plan is determined by the view that what has become Israel, the people of YHWH which is stateless and homeless, has come into the land from outside and is thus something very special. The Israelites of the exodus story do not feel themselves 'related' to Judah and the other neighbouring peoples, as opposed to what comes in the primal history and the patriarchal stories in Genesis, but they stress their independence. The Exodus creed was first applied after 587 to the brother nation which had now become stateless.

All three literary works, which react to the demise of the Israelite monarchy, remain situated within the parameters of the pre-exilic scribal culture in Israel and Judah. What distinguishes them from it is not so much their content as the situation that the conditions of life and the ideas that they portray have lost their institutional framework and therefore their validity. What was previously taken for granted now requires a particular grounding and legitimation in a historical context. And what grounds and legitimates does not simply relate to one of the two monarchies, but binds Israel and Judah together into a unity without political existence. The unifying bond is no longer the monarchy but the idea of the one God which absolutizes the practice of monolatry within the former national cult and which ascribes transcendent aspects to the former national God.

As in the case of the books of the prophets, these three narrative works were permanently revised and enlarged in the course of the seventh century, and above all after the fall of Jerusalem in 597/587 BCE. The most far-reaching alterations that affected them were the successive incorporations of the legal collections in the area of the Pentateuch (the Book of the Covenant in Exod. 20–3, Deuteronomy, the Ten Commandments, and the holiness laws) and the redactions that were inspired by them in the books of Joshua to Kings, which together formed the diverse legends of the origin of the kingship (Samuel to Kings) and the people of Israel (Genesis, Exodus to Joshua) into one single large narrative story (see below section 3).

This great historical narrative story served in its turn as the basis for further accounts of the history of the people of Israel as well as of the kingdoms in Israel and Judah. These date from the Persian and Hellenistic periods. The origin of the people, so far as it is recounted in Genesis to Joshua, is the content of the so-called Priestly Writing. In a strict form, structured through programmatic divine speeches (Gen. 1, 17, etc.), genealogies (Gen. 5, etc.) and itineraries (Gen. 12: 4b–5; 13: 6, 11b–12; 19: 29, etc.), it recounts the primal history, the patriarchal history and the story of the exodus, originally from the creation of the world (Gen. 1) to the founding of a sanctuary at Sinai (Exod. 24: 15b–18; 25–40) which is the prototype and ideal of the Second Temple at Jerusalem. The 'law' of Genesis–Kings is here replaced by the 'covenant': the covenant with Noah, who guaranteed the survival of the world population (Gen. 9), and the covenant with Abraham and Sarah which guaranteed YHWH's being for Israel (Gen. 17; Exod. 6: 7) and which is experienced and ritually mediated in the sanctuary (Exod. 25: 8; 29: 45 f.; 40: 34). Only later was the law (in Lev. and Num.) integrated, as also in the opposite way the law in Exodus–Kings was designated 'covenant' (Exod. 24; 34; Deut. 28: 69, etc.). These and other instances of harmonization stem from the fact that the Priestly Writing, which was conceived originally as an independent composition, was incorporated into the non-priestly account of the origin of Israel.

What remained independent was the new account of the history of the kingdom in the books of Chronicles, which recapitulates the history from Adam to Saul in genealogies (1 Chr. 1–9) and afterwards takes excerpts from the books of Samuel and Kings, which it then interprets. In the basic account the material is composed as the history of the kingdom of (Davidic) Judah, and is formed into the cult legend of the Jerusalem sanctuary by means of various insertions and particular traditions in a priestly sense. The work finds its continuation in the history of Judah and the Second Temple under Persian rule in the books of Ezra and Nehemiah, which, together with 1 and 2 Chronicles constitute the so-called Chronicler's History.

With these two literary works, the Priestly Writing and the Chronicler's History, we meet in the Old Testament with the phenomenon of the 'rewritten Bible' that is widespread outside the Hebrew Bible, in the Apocrypha and the Pseudepigrapha.

2.3. From Secular Law to Divine Law

With the picture of God in the prophetic tradition, not only has the role of Israel altered but so has the will of YHWH. The decision to end the relationship with God because Israel has become guilty in relation to its God implies a will of YHWH, the fulfilment of which makes the difference between the life and death of the people of God. In the prophetic tradition it is made clear above all what YHWH does not desire. The social and cultic criticism of the prophets mentions conditions, including misdemeanours, which have happened at all times but which became the basis for the divine judgement of sin against God. In the call to repentance the will of God can be discerned: do good and not evil (Amos 5: 14 f.); devotion and the knowledge of God are preferable to sacrifices and burnt offerings (Hos. 6: 6; cf. Mic. 6: 8). But the will of God is found in no book. In order to fulfil God's will in the future, and thereby to avoid judgement, there is required the positive execution and fixing of that which is good in the eyes of YHWH, and in which devotion and knowledge of God can be concretely expressed. This gap was filled with the law, whose codification as the divine revelation of God's will goes back to YHWH himself and the mediation of Moses, and which thus in a theologically qualified sense has become divine law. It is not the secular law that has been theologized and become divine law, but rather the prophets who are the origin of the divine law and the theologizing of secular law.

The origins of the theologizing of the secular law probably occurred in the seventh century BCE following on from the prophetic and narrative tradition, in the editing of the old collection of legal sentences (*Mishpatim*) in Exod. 21: 1–22: 19 and its inclusion in the story of the exodus in Exodus 2–Joshua 12. The editing added social and cultic laws to it, following the social and cultic criticism of the prophets, and put the whole into a new framework. At its head stands the law of the altar (Exod. 20: 24–6) and at the end the cultic calendar (Ex. 23: 14–17). A particular hallmark of this edition is its stylization as a speech of YHWH and the use of the second person singular by which the nation and every member of it is addressed. As for the content, it contains nothing new. What is new is the paraenetic style which expresses the legally regulated solidarity with one's neighbour and the usual cultic obligations to YHWH as divine law. Its inclusion in the story of the exodus contributes to a new understanding of this story in the following way: the revealed divine law which Israel receives on the divine mountain in the wilderness of Sinai, an intermediate station on the way from Egypt to the promised land, stamps the original legend of Israel's origin with the stamp of the divine law. The law book, which is called the Book of the Covenant on the basis of Exod. 24: 4–8, thus to some extent becomes the foundation document of the chosen people of God.

The next step on the way to the development of divine law took place in Deuteronomy, a rewriting of the Book of the Covenant (Exod. 20–3), which stylistically and in its content follows the redaction in the second person singular. The original version in Deuteronomy 12–26 is completely dominated by the idea of the centralization of the cult and wishes to know nothing about the proliferation of cultic places sanctioned by the stories of the Patriarchs in Genesis and by the law of the altar in the Book of the Covenant in Exod. 20: 24 and was usual in the pre-exilic period both in Israel and in Judah. The central place of Judah, the royal seat and the temple in Jerusalem, which was lost in 587 BCE, was replaced by the 'place which YHWH will choose', in order to warn people about the threatened destruction of what held the people together. The framework in Deut. 6: 4–6 ('Hear, O Israel') and 26: 16 adds to the oneness of the cultic place in Judah the oneness of YHWH as well as the oneness of the people of God, consisting of Israel and Judah, by the address 'Israel'. As with the Book of the Covenant, so also Deuteronomy is taken up into the story of the exodus. This latter makes possible its historicization, which can still be heard in the election formula for the 'place which YHWH will choose' and introduces Moses as a spokesman. Deuteronomy finds its literary place between the arrival in Shittim (Num. 25: 1a), where Moses begins to speak (Deut. 5: 1aα^1 + 6: 4–6; 12: 13 ff. to 26: 1 ff., 16) and the death of Moses, which is followed by the exit from Shittim under the leadership of Joshua (Deut. 34: 1a, 5f*; Josh. 2: 1 ff.; 3: 1 ff.). Moses makes the people familiar with the law in the land of Moab immediately before the crossing of the Jordan and the occupation of the land, the law that YHWH has revealed on the holy mountain, and adds the alterations that were considered to be necessary.

The Decalogue led to further alterations in the late Babylonian or early Persian period. Following the example of 'Hear, O Israel' in Deut. 6: 4–5 as the prologue to the collection of laws in Deuteronomy 12–16, it was added in Exodus 20 as the prologue to the Book of the Covenant, and then later added in Deuteronomy 5. In the same way that the Book of the Covenant is codified into being the will of God, the formulation of the Decalogue draws upon prophetic sources (cf. Hos. 4: 2) as well as a legal source: namely, the theologically edited Book of the Covenant itself. From now on it was not simply the unity of the cult (Deut. 12: 13 ff.) or just the oneness of YHWH (Deut. 6: 4), but the First Commandment and the exclusiveness of YHWH which was the chief commandment of the Old Testament law. It was then just a small step to the monotheistic confession that developed in the post-exilic period and received explicit expression in Isaiah 40–55. Belief in the one and only God not only forbade the worship of 'other gods' but denied their existence.

The development of the Book of the Covenant via Deuteronomy to the Decalogue is presupposed again in the account of the law giving in the Priestly Writing.

Just as Deuteronomy is a rewriting of the Book of the Covenant, so is the so-called Holiness Law in Leviticus 17–26 a rewriting of Deuteronomy under the sign of the First Commandment and the priestly idea of holiness. The Holiness Law and other laws were probably added to what was already an independent Priestly Writing. In the process a leading idea was not only the category of holiness but the idea of propitiation. The whole sacrificial cult, from which the rituals and the prescriptions come, was interpreted as a propitiatory cult in the context of the Priestly Writing. With the incorporation of the Priestly Writing in the non-priestly narrative, the giving of the law was enlarged in Leviticus and Numbers and also stretched over the older laws—Decalogue, Book of the Covenant, and covenant renewal at Sinai in Exodus 20–4; 32–4, as well as Deuteronomy in the land of Moab. It was revised and expanded in many ways in a mixture of Deuteronomistic and Priestly language. In this way there came into being the over-large Sinai pericope in Exodus 19–Numbers 10 which, according to the historical fiction, was recapitulated in Deuteronomy and which drew after it the law giving in the wilderness (Num. 15, 18, 19) as well as the plains of Moab (Num. 26–36). With the separation of the Pentateuch as the Torah of Moses or the Torah of YHWH—that is, the part of the canon later known as the Torah—the process of the theologizing of the law in the Old Testament came to an end.

This process affected not only the Pentateuch but also the other narrative books in Joshua–Kings. On the basis of the original form of Deuteronomy and its main commandment, the command for centralizing the cult, there was composed a first version of the so-called Deuteronomistic History in 1 Samuel 1–2 Kings 25. It was put together from the older narrative about the beginnings of the kingship in 1 Samuel 1–1 Kings 2 and the synchronistic chronicle of the kings of Israel in Judah in 1–2 Kings which the first Deuteronomist had taken from the annals of the kings of Israel and Judah and had commented upon in the sense of Deuteronomy. Against the background of the original unity of the kingship under David, the divided kingship which existed until 720 BCE is taken as an infringement of the command to centralize the cult. The division of the kingdom and of the unity of the cult is described as the 'sin of Jeroboam'. The 'sin of Jeroboam' leads Israel first of all to its downfall by making it guilty *per se*, followed by the downfall of Judah caused by its 'high places'.

After the introduction of the Decalogue into the law (Exod. 20, also Deut. 5), the First Commandment became the yardstick by which the people of God, 'Israel', consisting of Israel and Judah, was to be measured. This had far-reaching literary and theological-historical consequences. Under the sign of the First Commandment, the foundation legend of the people of Israel, (the story of the exodus in Exod. 2–Josh. 12) was bound into one continuous narrative sequence with the history of the kingship, the basic narrative of the Deuteronomic History in 1 Samuel 1–2 Kings 25. The book of Judges served as the connecting narrative, a collection of old heroic stories whose oldest redaction can also be called Deuteronomistic, but which presupposes the First Commandment and is thus younger than the original Deuteronomy and the first Deuteronomistic redaction in the books of Samuel and Kings. Out of the once independent literary work in (Genesis) Exodus–Joshua and 1 Samuel–2 Kings came the overall story of the history of Israel. From now on and following the incorporation of the Priestly laws and the priestly laws in Genesis–Numbers, there took place the secondary later, or post-Deuteronomistic, redactional activity in the area of Genesis–Kings over a long period, in many ways influenced by Priestly redactions. It continued until the overall narrative was divided into individual books and into the parts of the canon called the Torah (Genesis–Deuteronomy) and the Former Prophets (Joshua–Kings).

2.4. From Divine Kingship to the Kingdom of God

Although hymns and prayers, as much as the oracles of prophets and the old legal sentences, belong to the earliest body of the literature of Israel and Judah, the biblical tradition adopted them at a comparatively late period. The decisive moves in the origin of the Old Testament were taken, as we have seen, after the end of the kingdom of Israel, first of all in the prophetic traditions and, later, in the narrative and legal traditions. The appropriation of the hymns and prayers into the biblical tradition first occurred, as far as one can see, after the end of the kingdom of Judah and the destruction of the Jerusalem temple. This appropriation can be observed above all in those psalms in which an ancient core has remained. The examples are not very numerous; neither is criticism in this area very well advanced. Of the hymns, it is the group of YHWH royal psalms (29, 47, 93–5) that have been well researched. After that, Psalms 29 and 93 can be taken as fairly intact representatives, which praise YHWH as king and mighty victor over chaos. In addition, both hymns have undergone a few significant additions. The additions bring the people of God (Ps. 29: 10–11) and the law (Ps. 93: 5) into play, and add to the myth of the kingship of God the character of a personal (Ps. 92: 2) or national confession (Ps. 29: 11).

One can presume the existence of the old myth also behind the remaining examples of the YHWH royal psalms as well as some others, the closely related hymn of the theology of Zion which underwent much stronger revision. The revisions go in various directions: they declared the former weather-god, the lord of the whole earth and the king of the gods, to be the creator and sustainer of the world (Ps. 104), the saviour of Israel, and the judge of all nations (Pss. 48, 96, 98); they include the history of Israel and Judah (Pss. 47, 95, 99) or they allow only a selection of people in Israel to participate in the salvific actions of the royal God (Ps. 97; cf. Pss. 24: 3–6; 104: 35); the representative of the heavenly king upon earth, the earthly (Davidic) king, is stylized to be the messiah or the example of pious believers (Pss. 2; 18; 21: 8; 72). The revisions live from citations or allusions to the

other biblical literature and can be classified under the key words of universalization, nationalization, individualization, and the eschatologizing of the basic myth
of the kingship of God.

The same tendencies have been disclosed by the form and tradition history of the
laments and the psalms of thanksgiving. The old scheme of thanksgiving in Psalm
118 (vv. 5, 14, [15–16], 17–19, 21, 28) in verses 1–4 and 29 as well as 22–7 was
collectivized, and in verses. 6–13 individualized, and in verses 15a and 20 connected with a group of the righteous. The rescue of the psalmist from the threat of
death and action of enemies had become an example that is only told in the public
offerings of thanks (vv. 17, 19), but affects the assembled temple community itself.
The ritual of lament and thanksgiving, as it was originally practised at the temple, is
transcended in two ways: the individual psalmist and his fate stand on the one hand
for the history of suffering of the people of God, Israel itself, and on the other hand
for every just and pious believer in Israel.

Both tendencies have left their trace not only in the editing of older material but also
in the creation of new genres and new types of psalm. The collectivization of lament
and thanksgiving found expression in the new genre of the lament of the people. The
national catastrophe of 587 BCE becomes the occasion for lament and request (Pss. 44,
74, 137; cf. Lam. 1 f.). God's presence and help are no more sought in the (destroyed)
temple but in the recalling of the history of God with his people Israel (Ps. 74: 2–3).
The historical remembering results in reflection on the guilt of the people at its
destruction (Pss. 78, 79, 106) but is also a warning and something that brings new
hope (Pss. 77, 81); sometimes it has realized itself in the pure praise to God in the
historical psalms (Pss. 68, 105, 114, 135–6). In these psalms the history of salvation has
come in the place of the old myth of the kingship of God or has united with it.

The other tendency, the individualization or making interior (spiritualization)
of the lament and thanksgiving of the individual moves the personal relationship to
God into the foreground. Here the mythological pictures and images of the old
hymns and prayers become theological metaphors for the existence of the pious
individual. For the upright, the godless both within and outside Israel are the
enemies. His distress is opposition, while his deliverance is the certainty of faith.
Several marks of the genres of the lament and thanksgiving psalms gain a particular
meaning and come to expression in new compositions. In the dispute with the
enemies, the godless, forensic language becomes more frequent. The pious believer
protests his innocence and pleads for a just sentence (Ps. 26). On the other hand,
there is greater awareness of having sinned against God. The psalmist confesses his
sins, is prepared to repent, and prays for the forgiveness of his sins (Ps. 51). Both
protesting the innocence and confessing the sins are grounded in deep trust in God
that is expressed in the song of confidence, an exaggeration of the respective
elements, the acknowledgement of confidence, within the psalms of lament
(cf. Pss. 13: 6; 23). The relationship to God is formed in this text in immediate
fashion; in other psalms it is mediated through the Torah (Pss. 1, 119).

Collectivization (nationalization) and individualization are based upon the universalization of the myth of the kingdom of God, which is met not only in the hymns but also in the individual prayers (cf. Pss. 22, 103). The universalization has come to be expressed in revision of older material, as well as in new compositions. There exist Psalms that are not just single texts, but which were created for the literary context of the Psalter, which is characterized over wider areas by the universalization of the idea of God. According to the Torah, which is referred to right at the beginning of Psalm 1, the Psalter is divided into five books by concluding doxologies (Pss. 41: 14; 72: 18; 89: 53; 106: 48), and the fourth and fifth books are structured through doxological formulae as well as Toda and Hallelujah psalms. In this structure is mirrored the long history of development of the Psalter. Individual psalms and their revision led to small collections and then, by means of various steps, to the extant Psalter. One of these stages was the addition of the collection of YHWH royal psalms 93–9, to the basic collection of Psalms 2–89. In the redactional conclusion to this collection, in Psalm 100, is expressed the theocratic concept which rules the composition of the Psalter from there on through diverse caesurae and conclusions in Pss. 103–6/7; 117/18; 135/6 to the end. The kingship of God over all gods, all peoples, Israel, and the righteous finds its culmination in the kingdom of God in which all creatures are cared for and the pious are heard and protected (Ps. 145, also Pss. 146–50).

2.5. From Wise to Pious

Like the hymns and prayers, the proverbs of the wise and wisdom instruction stories found their way into the biblical tradition comparatively late. One speaks here also, as in the case of law, of a continuous theologizing of Wisdom, a term which is also applicable to many areas of tradition: prophets, narratives, law, sacrificial rituals, cult lyrics, as well as wisdom. The process of theologizing can be seen in the comparison of the writings that are taken into the Old Testament: Proverbs, Job, and Ecclesiastes. It can also be observed in the proverbs, and indeed not only in the relation of the old collections from chapter 10 to the younger instruction sentences in Proverbs 1–9, but in the transmission of the sayings themselves. As with the Psalter, criticism is not very well developed in its attempt to distinguish the older proverbial material from the younger theological commentary.

The knowledge and ideals of old wisdom are brought together in the proverbial collections in Prov. 10: 1–22: 16; 22: 17–24: 22 and 24: 23–32; 25–9. Like the old collection of laws, the *Mishpatim* in Exodus 21–2, such proverbial collections originated in the pre-exilic period for educational purposes in the wisdom schools of the scribes. The passage into the biblical tradition begins with theological glossing of these collections of proverbs. In the process, at least three tendencies become clear. The first is the connection of Wisdom with the fear of God. Prov. 24: 21 teaches that the fear of God, next to the fear of the king, is a wisdom virtue among many. This view of old Wisdom is the starting-point for later additions, which declare that the fear of God and trust in God are the basis of the older wisdom rules of life (cf. Prov. 15: 33 with 18: 12, 2: 4 with 21: 21), which substitute other standards with religious maxims (cf. Prov. 14: 26 f. with 13: 14; 23: 17 f. with 24: 13 f.) and in this way make belief in God the basic principle of wisdom (cf. also 10: 27; 16: 20; 20: 22; 21: 30 f.; 28: 5, 25; 29: 25 f.).

A second tendency can be seen in the introduction of the contrast between the righteous and the godless. The starting-point is the many oppositions which are expressed in the proverbs of old Wisdom, particularly the contrast between rich and poor. Out of the social conflict there comes, in the later proverbs, a religious opposition, which relativizes in a theological way the ideal of old wisdom (cf. Prov. 10: 16 with 10: 15; 11: 18 f. with 11: 16 f.). At the end the 'poor' is the righteous person (cf. Ps. 37), and the rich person is the evil-doer (cf. Ps. 49). But this religious antagonism is connected also to other themes, such as the broader field of correct speech and silence (cf. Prov. 10: 11 with 10: 10; 10: 20 with 10: 19; 15: 28 with 15: 23) or the central connection of deed and consequence, which is expounded as an appropriately just reward (cf. 11: 23 with 13: 12; 11: 30 f.; 12: 7 with 11: 29).

Finally, comes the third tendency, the problematizing of the human capacity for knowledge. In the old Wisdom the possibility of knowledge in spite of unpleasant surprises (Prov. 14: 12) is assumed as self-evident (cf. Prov. 20: 5). In a series of proverbs a gap appears between the ways and plans of God in visible phenomena and the human capacity for knowledge (Prov. 16: 19; 19: 21; 20: 24). The proverbs seem to say more or less the same thing according to the motto: humankind thinks, God directs. On closer inspection, it is possible to see particular variations which prepared the way for the scepticism of later Wisdom. At the end there is just the divine leading, which humankind is not in a position to understand.

The three tendencies in the theological editing of Proverbs reveal problems which were broadly dealt with in the younger Wisdom writings from the Persian or Hellenistic periods. Thus the didactic speeches in Proverbs 1–9 set out from the fear of God as the beginning and basis of Wisdom (Prov. 1: 7; 2: 1 ff.). With the personalization of Wisdom in Proverbs 8, they make the first attempt to solve the problem of mediation (cf. also Job 28; Sir. 4). Creation as such and the visible phenomena within it are no longer adequate. It is not possible to speak of a self-revelation of the creation.

The keeping of the fear of God and the affliction of the just through the experience of personal suffering are reminiscent of various theological (and literary) levels and their expression in the story of Job in Job 1–2 and 42 as well as the dialogue of the book of Job. In the legend of Job the idea of the fear of God is presented by God himself in a pact with Satan in the context of a difficult test. In the dialogues the theological ideas of the scribal schools begin to become shaky. They are relativized through the appearance of God and his answers to Job's complaints in the divine speeches of Job 38–41. Both Job, the righteous sufferer, and also his friends, the comforters and representatives of pure wisdom teaching, are put in their place.

In Ecclesiastes, finally, everything follows in the path of doubt: the fear of God, just retribution, and the possibility of knowledge. Qohelet's attempt to unite the biblical picture of God with the Hellenistic belief in fate takes him to the limits of Jewish piety and theology. As the result of his spiritual attempts to justify what happens under the sun, he commends the principle of *carpe diem* (Eccles. 9: 7 ff.), not because there is no God but because he removes himself from human understanding. Against this serene, not unpious but critical position of Qohelet, there is not only a loud protest in the book itself (Eccles. 12: 9–14). The book of Sirach (Ecclesiasticus) can be read as an anti-Qohelet book which failed to gain access to the Hebrew biblical canon only because the prologue of the Greek translation names the name of the author, and because he did not live between the time of Moses and Artaxerxes, but clearly lived and worked later. Here the ideals of older Wisdom come to life again shored up by a Jewish piety which has developed from the biblical tradition: Wisdom and Torah become united (Sir. 24) and are for Sirach revealed both in the creation and in scripture.

The latest book of the Hebrew canon, the book of Daniel, is not so straightforward. It has come from the old didactic wisdom stories of Daniel 1–6, which demonstrate in an exemplary way how Jewish wisdom and steadfast piety are preserved in the Diaspora. At the same time this concept did not entirely withstand the developing Hellenization and the threat to Judaism through the attacks of the Seleucid rulers, particularly during the religious crisis under Antiochus IV in the middle of the second century BCE. The visions in Daniel 7–12, which were added successively, transfer the solution of the problem to the end-times, in which what is promised in the scripture and which has long since been decided in heaven will be realized upon earth. Instead of being satisfied with resignation and the principle of *carpe diem*, or referring to the current teachings of the schools and scripture, the pious in the book of Daniel have a long path of suffering before them, and reach their goal only in the resurrection at the general judgement (Dan. 12: 1–3).

3. THE BOOKS OF THE OLD TESTAMENT

3.1. The Law (Torah)

The growth of the Old Testament is a process which took centuries, from the end of the eighth century till the second century BCE or, more precisely, about 100 CE, when the Hebrew canon in all its parts was almost completely fixed (4 Esdras 14; Josephus, *Ap.* 4. 1: 37–41; *b. Baba Bathra* 14b–15a). The choice and division of the three parts of the canon indicate the end of the history of the development of the literature which, as far as we know, extended well into the Hellenistic period and continued after that into the literature of Jewish and Christian tradition.

The earliest collection which received recognizable authoritative value was the part known as the Torah. It includes the five books of Moses, the so-called Pentateuch (Genesis, Exodus, Leviticus, Numbers, and Deuteronomy). The 'Torah of Moses' or 'the Torah of YHWH (God)' is already introduced into the biblical books as a reference point, although it is not always certain whether one is to understand by it the whole Pentateuch. On the basis of external witnesses (Septuagint, Samaritan Pentateuch, Sirach, the letter of Aristeas, the Qumran writing 4QMMT, Apocrypha, and Pseudepigrapha), it is possible to conclude that this was the case from the Hellenistic period and that the separation of the Pentateuch as Torah thus must have taken place in the late Persian period.

The division is artificial. As we have seen, the narrative threads of salvation history go from the creation of the world in Genesis 1 to the end of the kingdom of Judah in 2 Kings 25. This constitutes the so-called Enneateuch (Genesis, Exodus, Leviticus, Numbers, Deuteronomy, Joshua, Judges, 1 and 2 Samuel, 1 and 2 Kings). It came into being through the combination of the two older literary works of the Hexateuch (the primal history and the patriarchal narrative in Genesis as well as the story of the exodus in Exodus–Joshua) and the Deuteronomistic History (1 Samuel–2 Kings), which were linked together by the book of Judges and expanded in Genesis–Numbers by the addition of the Priestly Writing. The genetic series is thus Hexateuch—Enneateuch—Pentateuch.

As opposed to the usual view of the growth of the Pentateuch, we have not so far mentioned the well-known documentary hypothesis, according to which the Pentateuch was put together from four sources: the three parallel narrative works of the Yahwist (J), the Elohist (E), and the Priestly narrative (P) in Genesis–Numbers, and Deuteronomy (D). More recent research on the Pentateuch indicates that only for the Priestly Writing and Deuteronomy can one suggest a sure textual basis that is capable of gaining a consensus. Everything else, the non-Priestly text in Genesis–Numbers, which is usually designated as J, E, and JE, is open to further investigation. In them we find a composition that has been put together from a redactional narrative story (theme) and additions of all kinds, individual traditions as well as pre- and post-Deuteronomistic and pre- and post-Priestly additions.

As one can learn from the history of interpretation, it is not possible to apply the source hypothesis to the non-Priestly textual tradition, and to separate the two sources J and E and their redaction together (JE) cleanly. Neither are the arguments convincing which maintain that this textual remainder is a literary unity which can, as a whole, be ascribed to a late or post-Priestly 'Yahwistic' redactor. It is preferable, in dealing with the non-Priestly text of Genesis–Numbers, to distinguish between old individual traditions, their first redactional shaping into one narrative theme, and later supplements. In addition, it seems doubtful that the redaction which is responsible for the composition of the primal history and the patriarchal history in Genesis is identical with the redaction of the story of the exodus. The exodus tradition is not confined to the books of Exodus and Numbers, as has often been supposed since the work of Martin Noth, but includes the occupation of the land in the book of Joshua, which is the natural end of the story, as was assumed before the work of Noth and also by Julius Wellhausen and others.

It is the most recent literary additions that comprehend the whole context from Genesis, Exodus–Joshua, Judges, and Samuel–Kings, that is, the Enneateuch. But they are also responsible for separating the books. As a rule, the books gained at the end of the productive phase of textual production a framework that marked the beginning and ending, yet also gave indications beyond the book to the larger narrative context (cf. Gen. 50/Exod. 1; Num. 36: 13/Deut. 1–3; Deut. 31–4/Josh. 1; Josh. 24/Judg. 1–2; Judg. 17–21, especially 21: 25/1 Sam. 1–3; 2 Sam. 21–4/Kings). From there on it was possible to transmit the individual books on separate scrolls without the connection being lost.

In this way the separation of the Pentateuch as Torah also occurred. Deut. 34: 10–12 takes the death of Moses as the reason to declare him and his story as unique. The reference to the promises to the Patriarchs (Deut. 34: 4) also indicates that the whole Pentateuch, with the inclusion of Genesis, is in view. It thus gains its own particular value, even when the appointment of Joshua (Deut. 31: 1 ff.; 34: 9) points to the continuation of the history of Israel beyond the Torah. Moses becomes the epitome of an epoch that stretches from the creation to the borders of the promised land. It is only logical that he should be regarded as the author of the primal history and the stories of the Patriarchs in the book of *Jubilees*, which is a rewriting of Genesis 1–Exodus 15. In this 'Mosaic' epoch everything which will be valid for the whole of the future is instituted by YHWH. This shows itself in the continuation of the history of Israel up to and with the destruction of Judah, in which Israel founders on the claims of the Torah. But at the same time it is meant for all times, by which the 'Mosaic' epoch in the Pentateuch becomes the basis of Judaism and the further history in Joshua–Kings, the Former as well as the Latter Prophets, and the other Writings.

3.2. The Prophets (Nebiim)

The separation of the Pentateuch as Torah consequently isolated the books of Joshua–Kings. In the Hebrew canon they appear as the Former Prophets, after which follow, as the so-called Latter Prophets, the prophetic books of Isaiah,

Jeremiah, Ezekiel, and the Book of the Twelve. This arrangement presupposes the theory of the Chronicler, which is also shared by Josephus (*Ap.* I. 37–41), that each epoch had its prophets, and that the prophets were the chroniclers of their time. Thus the history writers were declared to be prophets, and the prophets to be history writers. In the so-called Praise of the Fathers in Sirach (Sir. 44–51) which comes from the early second century BCE, there is evidence for the part of the canon known as the prophets as a history of saints. The prologue of the Greek translation of Sirach, the didactic writing 4QMMT, and the New Testament, name it explicitly.

Since the work of Martin Noth, the Former Prophets have been seen as part of the so-called Deuteronomistic History that is contained in the books Deuteronomy–2 Kings and which, according to more recent research, was subject to various stages of growth, consisting of the putting together of blocks of material or horizontal additions, or both at once. The hypothesis assumes that there were originally two accounts of the occupation of the land, with one of which the sources of the Tetrateuch (Genesis–Numbers) came to an end, and to the other of which the Deuteronomistic History in Deuteronomy–Joshua began, before the two literary wholes were brought together, whereby the story of the occupation of the land was lost to the Tetrateuch without a trace. The matter looks quite different if the dogma of the documentary hypothesis is disregarded, and the tradition as we have it is looked at more carefully. It will be possible to recognize the redactional connection of Num. 25: 1a and Josh. 2: 1 ff.; 31 ff., which is bridged by the simple notice of the death of Moses after the fashion of Deut. 34: 5 f.* and becomes the framework for the oldest account of the exodus. If one takes further into account that the oldest Deuteronomistic redaction, the one orientated on Deuteronomy and the standard of cult centralization, is apparent only in the books of Samuel–Kings, it becomes self-evident that it is necessary to distinguish between the traditions of the Hexateuch and the Deuteronomistic basic tradition in Samuel–Kings (which is dependent on Deuteronomy), which linked the book of Judges and the secondary Deuteronomistic editing into the Enneateuch.

After the artificial separation of the Torah, the books Joshua–Kings were united by the literary links in Josh. 1: 7 f. and Mal. 3: 22 with the prophetic books in that part of the canon called the Prophets, and under this new sign were again connected with the Torah of Moses. Former and Latter Prophets are considered no longer as prophetic, inspired writers of the sacred history, but are also understood as teachers of the law, who summoned the people of Israel to obedience to God and his commandments, the Torah of Moses, and warned about the consequences of disobedience.

Like the Former Prophets, the Latter Prophets also had their own history before they became the second part of the Hebrew canon together with the historical books. The prophetic books were initially transmitted individually. However, literary cross-connections between the individual books enable us to conclude that they originated in proximity to each other, and that with time they were brought into line with each other. Literary composition took place first in the book of Isaiah, which was put together from two books, that of the First Isaiah in chapters 1–39, and the Second Isaiah in chapters 40–66 and in the Book of the Twelve Prophets which, for its part, came together from partial collections, as for example the series Hosea, Amos, Micah or Haggai, Zechariah, Malachi. The prophetic books Isaiah, Jeremiah, and Ezekiel and the Book of the Twelve together build up the *corpus propheticum.*

The number of prophetic books is hardly an accident, and would not be higher than what is found today in the Old Testament. Not without reason the *corpus propheticum* consists of three large and twelve small Prophets which makes one think immediately of the three Patriarchs and the twelve tribes of Israel. In addition, the books of the *corpus propheticum* are connected to each other by means of a clearly devised system of headings. Twice, once in the three great and once in the twelve minor prophets, the time of King Uzziah in the eighth century BCE to the time of the Second Temple at the end of the sixth century BCE is referred to: Isa. 1: 1/Hos. 1: 1; Amos 1: 1, and Mic. 1: 1 (from Uzziah to Hezekiah; Jer. 1: 1–3// Zeph. 1: 1) (from Josiah to Zedekiah); Ezekiel//Haggai and Zechariah (Exile and Second Temple).

Read by itself, the *corpus propheticum* thus covers the most important epochs of the history of Israel, from the Assyrian period to the Persian period, with glances back to earlier epochs from the creation to the time of the prophets, and forward looks to the end of the world. In many parts the whole is always in view: the totality of Israel, the people of God, as well as the totality of the peoples of the world. Of both it is said what God has to do with them and what he desires from them. The unity of God guarantees the unity of his diverse and sometimes contradictory action both for the unity of the changeable history which he guides, and its completion of the aim which he purposes.

The system of headings and the prophetic view of history which is bound up with it makes the *corpus propheticum* a proper complement to the historical books of Joshua–Kings, while the epochs partly intersect, so that there are textual correspondences in the Former and Latter Prophets (2 Kgs. 18–20//Isa. 36–9; 2 Kgs. 24 f.//Jer. 52). Through the literary link of Josh. 1: 7 f./Mal. 3: 22 f. and references to the 'Torah' in the books of the prophets, the *corpus propheticum,* in the context of that part of the canon called the 'Prophets', is brought into the realm of the law.

3.3. The Writings (Ketubim)

The third part of the canon, the Writings, does not have any clear order, but is a collection of books which, in accordance with the Jewish theory of canon, were chosen from the mass of writings from the Hellenistic-Roman period. It consists of books which, either according to their own claims or corresponding traditions, originated in the time between Moses and the Persian king Artaxerxes (Ezra/Nehemiah; Josephus, *Ap.* I. 40). The prologue of the Greek translation of Sirach speaks already at the end of the second century BCE of 'other books' alongside the Torah and the Prophets, and thus indicates a third group of 'canonical' books. However, it was not until the first century CE that there was any kind of unanimity about its content. The heart of the third part of the canon is the Psalter, which is ascribed in many titles to David, and in 4 QMMT and in the New Testament (Luke 24: 44) is mentioned along with the Law and the Prophets. Like the part of the canon 'the Prophets', the Psalter is connected to the Torah through Psalm 1 and the quotation from Josh. 1: 7 f. in Ps. 1: 2 f. After the prophets as the teachers of the law, there follows in the third part of the canon the teaching of the law for a life which is in accordance with Torah.

In this sense there were taken into the canon after the Psalter the Wisdom writings, Job, Proverbs, and Ecclesiastes, as well as the books of Ruth, Esther, and Daniel. Proverbs and Ecclesiastes recommended themselves in addition through their Solomonic authorship, which was also responsible for the inclusion of the Song of Songs. The choice of Ruth was assisted by the genealogy of David in 4: 17–22. With the book of Lamentations, which the tradition attributes to the prophet Jeremiah, and the books of Daniel, Ezra, Nehemiah, and Chronicles, the history of the first and second temples of Jerusalem were dealt with, which [i.e. the history] as in the second part of the canon, the 'prophets', followed the norms of the Torah. Between those books which teach the way of life (Psalms and the Wisdom writings, Job, and Proverbs) and the historical books (Daniel, Ezra, Nehemiah, and Chronicles), the remaining books constitute the group of the so-called Megillot, five scrolls which are related to particular festivals on which they were ordered to be read: Ruth (eighth day of Passover), Song of Songs (third day of the Feast of Weeks), Ecclesiastes (third day of the Festival of Tabernacles), Lamentations (ninth day of Av in memory of the destruction of the temple), and Esther (Purim).

3.4. Apocrypha and Pseudipigrapha

Up to now this chapter has confined itself to the Hebrew canon of the Old Testament and its origin. The Old Testament is, however, transmitted also in a Greek version, the so-called Septuagint (LXX). Its history began with the translation of the Torah, which, according to the legend of the Letter of Aristeas, was undertaken at the request of the king Ptolemy II Philadelphos (286–246 BCE), and through the mediation of the high official Aristeas, by a delegation of seventy-two priests from Jerusalem, six from each of the twelve tribes of Israel, the translation being completed in seventy-two days for the library in Alexandria.

Whatever one may think about the historical value of the legend, it must contain an element of truth. The spread of Greek language and culture in Egypt as well as in Syria and Palestine made a translation of the Holy Scriptures of the Jews into Greek necessary. And by these Holy Scriptures one understood first and only the Torah. Its translation was, and remained, an example for the translation of the remaining books, which followed by and by in a long process which extended into the first century CE. The oldest manuscript witnesses, Greek fragments of the books of the Pentateuch and the roll of the Twelve Prophets, come from Qumran and its surroundings. In the second century CE the Septuagint became the Bible of Christians, and from that point is also known from Christian manuscripts.

The Septuagint is distinguished through a different order and enlarged content of the biblical books. The three parts of the Hebrew canon are reversed and the books are divided anew: in the first part, all the historical books consisting of the Torah and the Former Prophets and the Writings are put together (Genesis–Joshua, Ruth, Samuel–Kings = 1 to 4 Kingdoms, Chron = Paralipomena, Ezra-Nehemiah = 2 Esdras, and Esther). In second place stand the poetic Writings (Psalms, Proverbs, Ecclesiastes, Song of Songs, and Job); at the end come the prophetic books (the Latter Prophets, Lamentations, and Daniel). In addition there come in the first part the books of 1 Esdras (3 Ezra), Judith, Tobit, 1 and 2 Maccabees (and in some manuscripts also 3 and 4 Maccabees) as well as the prayers and other additions to the book of Esther. In the second part come the Wisdom of Solomon and Sirach (Ecclesiasticus), in some manuscripts also the Odes of Solomon and the Psalms of Solomon. In the third part comes the book of Baruch, the Letter of Jeremiah (Baruch 6), as well as the additions to the book of Daniel (Susanna, Bel and the Dragon, and the two prayers in Daniel 3).

The additional writings and textual supplements either go back to an Aramaic or Hebrew original, or were originally written in Greek and dependent on the writings of the Hebrew canon. They are rewritings or imitations of biblical books or additions to them which accorded with the demands and the taste of the Hellenistic period. They indicate the variety of Jewish literature in the Hellenistic-Roman period, to which, in addition to those books that were included in the Septuagint and the many other apocryphal and pseudepigraphic books, are also to be reckoned the Jewish-Hellenistic authors as well as the writings from Qumran.

The Hebrew Bible also belongs in this broad stream of Jewish literature. If, originally, this stream of tradition was quite small and limited to a minority, it found in the Hellenistic period much greater circulation and inspired further literary production. As the many copies found at Qumran, and the literary references particularly to the Torah and the Prophets but also to the Psalms show, these established themselves very soon as the basic content for an authoritative Jewish tradition. Only in the case of the 'other Writings' was a selection made which could vary and which, in some cases were for a long time in dispute, both in rabbinic and Christian discussion. The third part of the Hebrew canon, the writings, and the enlarged content of the Septuagint, represent two divergent ways in which the growth of the Hebrew Bible or of the Old Testament came to an end.

BIBLIOGRAPHY

DAVIES, G. I. 1991. *Ancient Hebrew Inscriptions*. Cambridge: Cambridge University Press.

GIBSON, J. C. L. 1971. *Textbook of Syrian Semitic Inscriptions*, i: *Hebrew and Moabite Inscriptions*. Oxford: Oxford University Press.

HENGEL, M. 1994. 'Die Septuaginta als "christliche Schriftensammlung" ihre Vorgeschichte und das Problem ihres Kanons'. In *idem* and A. M. Schwemer, ed., *Die Septuaginta zwischen Judentum und Christentum*, WUNT 72, Tübingen: Mohr Siebeck, 182–284.

JAMIESON-DRAKE, D. W. 1991. *Scribes and Schools in Monarchic Juda: A Socio-Archaeological Approach*. JSOTS.S 109. Sheffield: Almond Press.

KRATZ, R. G. 2000. *Die Komposition der erzählenden Bücher des Alten Testaments*. Göttingen: Vandenhoeck & Ruprecht, 2000. ET: *The Composition of the Narrative Books of the Old Testament*. London: T&T Clark/Continuum, 2005.

—— 2003. *Die Propheten Israels*. Munich: Kaiser Verlag.

—— 2004. 'Reste hebräischen Heidentums am Beispiel der Psalmen'. Nachrichten der Akademie der Wissenschaften zu Göttingen (Philologisch-Historische Klasse 2), 25–65.

LEVIN, C. 2001. *Das Alte Testament*. Munich: Beck Verlag, 2nd edn. 2003. ET: *The Old Testament: A Brief Introduction*. Princeton: Princeton University Press, 2005.

NOTH, M. 1943. *Überlieferungsgeschichtliche Studien*. Halle: Schriften der Königsberger Gelehrten Gesellschaft, Geisteswissenschaftliche Klasse 18. Repr. Tübingen: Max Niemeyer Verlag, 1957. Partial English trans. of pp. 3–110, in *The Deuteronomistic History*, Sheffield: JSOT Press, 1981; 2nd edn. 1991.

—— 1948. *Überlieferungsgeschichte des Pentateuch*. Stuttgart: Kohlhammer Verlag; repr. 1960. ET: *A History of Pentateuchal Traditions*. Englewood Cliffs, NJ: Prentice-Hall, 1972.

PRITCHARD, J. B., ed. 1955. *Ancient Near Eastern Texts Relating to the Old Testament*. Princeton: Princeton University Press.

SCHAMS, C. 1998. *Jewish Scribes in the Second-Temple Period*. JSOTS.S 291. Sheffield: Sheffield Academic Press.

STECK, O. H. 1988. 'Der Kanon des hebräischen Alten Testaments: Historische Materialien für eine ökumenische Perspektive'. In J. Rohls and G. Wenz, eds., *Vernunft des Glaubens: Wissenschaftliche Theologie und kirchliche Lehre: Festschrift für W. Pannenberg*, Göttingen: Vandenhoeck & Ruprecht, 231–52.

WELLHAUSEN, J. 1905. *Prolegomena zur Geschichte Israels*. Berlin: de Gruyter. ET: *Prolegomena to the History of Ancient Israel*. New York: Harper Torchbooks, 1957.

—— 1963. *Die Composition des Hexateuchs und der historischen Bücher des Alten Testaments (1876–1878)*, 4th edn. Berlin: de Gruyter. 3 edn. 1899.

CHAPTER 29

THE GROWTH OF THE APOCRYPHA

ALISON SALVESEN

INTRODUCTION

The term 'apocrypha' is derived from Greek, and means 'hidden away'. It is applied to those books of the Bible that Judaism as a whole and also many Christians do not regard as part of the canon of Scripture. It can apply to books outside the New Testament canon, but it is most commonly used of those writings not included in the Hebrew Bible/Old Testament. Some churches do accept them, but often consider them to be less authoritative than the canonical books, even though they may be edifying on a secondary level. For instance, in the Roman Catholic Church the term 'deutero-canonical' is used, instead of 'apocryphal'. Most Protestants are barely aware of the existence of apocryphal books, and they are virtually unknown among Jews (see Orlinsky 1974). Yet other churches, such as the Ethiopian Orthodox Church, embrace them as part of the canon.

There are other, similar books that are commonly known as the pseudepigrapha because they tend to be attributed to or associated with major figures in the Bible. These have never been seriously considered part of even a secondary canon, usually because of suspicions concerning their teaching or authorship, though they have sometimes enjoyed a limited circulation.

This account implies that drawing the boundary lines between canonical, apocryphal, and deutero-canonical works was a straightforward process, when in fact there was much debate and lack of clarity for many centuries, and the status of these books still varies widely. The present article will discuss those books included in the NRSV version of the Apocrypha and also 1 *Enoch*, which is accepted in the Ethiopic church.

There are various possible reasons for the lack of canonical status of apocryphal books, not always explicitly stated by their critics in antiquity. None of the works is early, though in some cases the presumed date of composition is more or less contemporaneous with other books that do appear in the canon, such as Daniel or Esther. Attribution to an important figure in the Bible is a common phenomenon, as in the case of 1 *Enoch*, the Prayer of Manasseh, Psalm 151 (David), 1 Baruch, Letter of Jeremiah, Wisdom of Solomon, and 2 Esdras (Ezra). However, such pseudo-nymity was not necessarily successful if it was suspected that the work was written long after they lived, or if the facts did not fit the biblical account. The historicity of other books such as Tobit and Judith is problematic because of the glaring errors of chronology they display. Where canonical books provided shorter versions, as with the additions to Esther and Daniel, some prefer the more concise and older Hebrew version. 1 Esdras is a composite form of the end of 2 Chronicles, Ezra, and Nehemiah 8, but a new story has been rather awkwardly inserted in the middle for tendentious reasons. 1 Maccabees had a Hebrew original, and its contents were known and accepted by the Jewish writer Flavius Josephus (*c.*90 CE), but as history not Scripture. Josephus's criterion that a book had to be written by a prophet in order to be inspired, and that the exact succession of the prophets had ceased long ago (*Ap.* I §§37–41) excluded books such as 1 Maccabees from the canon of Scripture. For Jews in the rabbinic period, Scripture represented those writings that were traditionally recited in the liturgy or studied in the community. There are virtually no citations of apocryphal books in the New Testament, but allusions to them have been detected, and certainly the religious outlook of the first Christian writers often shows marked affinities with their ideas.

The evidence for early attitudes towards these books is found in the way they are cited in apologetic and exegetical works of Christian writers, used in the lectionary cycles of the various churches, and are occasionally referred to in rabbinic litera-ture. As the church expanded and became predominantly Greek-speaking, it made much use of Jewish religious writings that had been written in or survived in Greek. But already in the second half of the second century Melito, Bishop of Sardis, was aware that Palestinian Jews had a more restricted canon of Scripture: the list he obtained even excludes Esther. In the mid-third century Origen's letter to Julius Africanus shows that a few Christian intellectuals were querying the authorship and details of some works. At the beginning of the fifth century Jerome advised some pious parents that although their young daughter should be conversant with the scriptures, she should beware of all apocryphal books, unless she reads them very selectively (Ep. 107: 12). His attitude was shaped not merely by the questionable content of some of the writings, which did not contribute to church doctrine, but by his increasing respect for the Jewish canon represented by extant Hebrew texts. By contrast, the apocryphal writings did not seem to have Hebrew originals for their Greek forms. Jerome translated Tobit and Judith into Latin from Aramaic under pressure from his patrons, but did not render any other books that he considered apocryphal. However, he accepted the edifying value of Wisdom and Ecclesiasticus.

The use of apocryphal books varies enormously between churches. Wisdom and Ecclesiasticus appear frequently in a number of different lectionaries, and far more often than the canonical book of Leviticus. This shows that often it was the nature of the passage that determined its popularity, rather than its canonicity. Thus exhortations about wisdom, passages extolling the sacrifice of martyrs, descriptions of the restoration of the Temple, and penitential prayers are most likely to feature. But in general, churches in the Latin West have employed more readings from the Apocrypha than, say, the Syriac or Armenian churches. The comparative lack of interest in the Apocrypha among the Syriac writers and churches may be due to the influence of the Jewish canon on their concept of scriptural authority, whereas other churches had a more inclusive approach. The Church of England's lectionary includes readings from the Apocrypha, but usually only as options.

Both apocryphal and pseudepigraphical works are increasingly studied at an academic level for what they reveal of the religious preoccupations of their writers and the communities which first received them. The apocryphal writings in particular are a valuable witness to the many strands of Judaism during the period when the Second Temple stood in Jerusalem, spanning roughly the time period between the composition of the Hebrew Bible and the writings of the New Testament. Altogether the apocryphal writings discussed here cover several differ- ent genres, sometimes even within the same book. These include wisdom literature, which gives advice for right conduct and a successful life, linked to a religious outlook; apocalyptic writing, offering hope of momentous supernatural interven- tion at the end of history in order to save the people of God (see Grabbe 1989), sometimes through the agency of an anointed one or 'Messiah' (Oegema 1998; Horbury 1998); historiography or writing that purports to be history; edifying stories which are essentially folk-tales with a religious message (Wills 1990, 1995); rewritten Bible, where a familiar story from Scripture is retold with different emphases; prayers and psalms which may have had a liturgical or devotional function. The books are treated separately below because of the considerable differences between them, but some commonly occurring features do emerge, such as the dependence on and allusion to older Scripture, polemic against idolatry, and the Deuteronomistic view that God punishes his people for their sin but will vindicate them if they are faithful to his commands.

1 ESDRAS

The name '1 Esdras' goes back to the Greek name of the book, Esdras A (Esdras B corresponds to Hebrew Ezra and Nehemiah). It is a reworking of 2 Kings 23–4, 2 Chronicles 35–6, Ezra 1–10, and Nehemiah 8: 1–13, and may be based on an Aramaic or Hebrew original, now lost. It was probably translated into Greek in the second century BCE. The narrative commences with Josiah's celebration of the Passover. Though based on 2 Chronicles, it adds more explicit praise of Josiah in 1 Esd. 1: 21, 31, stressing the virtues of Josiah's kingship. 1 Esd. 5: 7–9: 36 follows Ezra 4–10 fairly faithfully.

The main feature of 1 Esdras is the insertion of the Story of the Three Youths (1 Esd. 3–5: 6), in which three young bodyguards hold a competition in front of King Darius in order to decide what is strongest. The first argues that wine is strongest, and the second youth says that the king is strongest. The third, who is at this point identified as Zerubbabel, says that women rule both wine and the king, but that ultimately it is truth that prevails over all. The winner is judged to be the third youth. He reminds the king of a previous royal vow to rebuild Jerusalem and its Temple and to restore the captured temple vessels, and as his prize he asks the king to fulfil this vow.

The insertion into the biblically based material of the Story of the Three Youths seems designed to enhance the status of Zerubbabel, who is already known from the books of Ezra, Nehemiah, Haggai, and Zechariah as a leader of the first wave of returned exiles. Talshir (1999: 270) believes that this is in fact the *raison d'être* of the entire book, though De Troyer (2002: 55) goes further and sees Zerubbabel portrayed as a kind of Solomon *redivivus*. The Story of the Three Youths has been clearly influenced by Neh. 2: 1–9. Here Nehemiah is the Persian king's cupbearer, whose downcast looks the king notices. The king ascertains that Nehemiah is distressed over Jerusalem, and allows him to return there to rebuild the city. The motif of a high-ranking, trusted official close to the king receiving royal authorization and backing to return to Jerusalem is found in both Nehemiah and 1 Esdras. But in the Story of the Three Youths, the bodyguard Zerubbabel wins a public contest before the king through his own wisdom, and so appears a more worthy recipient of the king's favour. Zerubbabel's Davidic ancestry (cf. 1 Chr. 3: 19 and Hag. 2: 21–3) is also stressed in 1 Esdras. Zerubbabel's name is also added in 1 Esd. 6: 18 (cf. Ezra 5: 14), so that he and Sheshbazzar share the honour of having returned the temple vessels to Jerusalem. So altogether, Zerubbabel's role in 1 Esdras eclipses and replaces that of Nehemiah, who, moreover, goes unmentioned in the book: compare the otherwise similar verse Neh. 8: 9 with 1 Esd. 9: 49, where only Ezra appears.

This must surely reflect a debate within early Judaism concerning the relative merits of the various leaders of the exiles. Talshir (1999: 55–7) points out that in

Sir. 49: 13, 2 Macc. 1: 18, and Josephus (*AJ* XI §§165, 169), Ezra is ignored and Nehemiah developed, whereas the rabbis prefer Ezra and denigrate Nehemiah (e.g. *b. Sanh.* 93b). The rabbis even identify Nehemiah with Zerubbabel. 1 Esdras makes Ezra the chief priest (1 Esd. 9: 39, 40, 49), whereas in the corresponding part of the book of Nehemiah, he is merely a priest and scribe (Neh. 8: 1, 2, 9). So, overall, in 1 Esdras, the figures given prominence are Josiah, Zerubbabel, and Ezra.

Another area of study is the relationship of 1 Esdras to Ezra–Nehemiah. Böhler (1997) argues that the biblical Nehemiah memoir was not known to the author of 1 Esdras, and that he therefore provides an independent and sometimes more accurate account. Most others would say that 1 Esdras is a tendentious reworking of Ezra–Nehemiah (see Williamson 1996).

Other biblical parallels apparent in 1 Esdras include Daniel and Joseph, who also prove their wisdom in royal courts. However, the wisdom of Joseph and Daniel consists of being able to interpret correctly the king's dreams, whereas the concept of wisdom in 1 Esdras is more philosophical, appropriately enough for the Hellenistic period. There are also similarities with the symposium scene in the Letter of Aristeas.

Whether the Story of the Three Youths was created for 1 Esdras is debatable. It is strange that none of the three youths is described as being Jewish, and that the third youth is identified as Zerubbabel only once, when he begins to speak in the contest (1 Esd. 4: 13), in a three-word phrase which looks very much like an insertion. Without it, the narrative in 1 Esd. 3: 1–4: 42, ending at the point where the king promises to honour the winning youth, could easily be a self-contained story. Zerubbabel's name in fact serves as the only point of contact with the rest of the book. If the story ever existed on its own, the climax would surely be the humorous reference to the king's concubine Apame, whose teasing and irreverent treatment of him only makes him fawn on her the more. A more serious note is struck by the praise of truth. This may also represent a later, non-Jewish layer in the original story, since the reference to God seems rather to be tacked on at the very end.

From the modern point of view 1 Esdras does not hang together well because of its anachronisms and inconsistencies. For instance, Cyrus is king in 1 Esdras 2; the Story of the Three Youths takes place under Darius (3: 1–5: 2); but then Cyrus seems to be king again in 5: 71, 73, before the mention of Darius's accession in 5: 73. But despite the chronological oddities, the book seems to be stressing the continuity between pre-exilic and post-exilic Judaism (deSilva 2002: 164), and begins and ends with the celebration of a major festival in Jerusalem.

Josephus seems to prefer 1 Esdras to Ezra–Nehemiah, and several early Christian writers cite the book, though Jerome rejected it (Myers 1974: 17–18). However, most of these citations refer not to the narrative parts of the book but to the praise of truth and God (1 Esd. 4: 35–41).

2 ESDRAS

The book known as 2 Esdras has nothing in common with 1 Esdras except for the figure of Ezra. The book's Latin title is 4 Ezra; in Slavonic it is 3 Esdras. Since it is in fact a composite work comprising three different documents, these are sometimes known as 5 Ezra (chapters 1–2), 4 Ezra (3–14), and 6 Ezra (15–16). The book as a whole is preserved only in Latin translation, but there are partial versions in several languages, all of them renderings of a lost Greek text. Citations from the book are found in several early writers from Clement of Alexandria onwards, but as in other cases, it was rejected by Jerome as apocryphal (Longenecker 1995: 110–11).

The core and earliest part of 2 Esdras (4 Ezra) consists of chapters 3–14. The original language was probably either Hebrew or Aramaic. The author was a Jew writing around the beginning of the second century CE. Scholarly attention is focused mainly on the theodicy of this section, its messianism, its date, and the social setting that gave rise to it.

The structure of these chapters is based on the dialogue between Ezra, portrayed as a visionary prophet, and the angel Uriel. Ezra is distressed by the misfortunes of his people, and receives revelations through angels to answer his many questions about God's justice in the world and the reasons for evil and suffering. The spirit of the replies is similar to that of Job 38–42 and Isaiah 40: God's ways are unknowable, since humans are corrupt and unable to comprehend even the natural world, but there will be a reward for the righteous and punishment for the wicked in the end (see Tiller 2000). Evil is the result of Adam's sin (3: 7, 20–2, 26; 4: 30; 7: 11; 7: 116–18/ 46–8), in contrast to the theology of another apocryphal book, *1 Enoch* (see below). There are several descriptions of the imminent end-times, in typical apocalyptic language. Ezra's revelations concern the resurrection of the soul alone, a last judgement that consigns the righteous to paradise and the wicked to Gehenna (7: 32–44, 78–99). There is a clear statement that after judgement, the prayers of the righteous for the ungodly have no effect (7: 102–5): these verses appear in a long section that may have been deliberately excised in a number of Christian manuscripts. Other important themes are God's love for creation and for his people, the existence of free will rather than predestination (8: 56–60), and the importance of repentance (9: 11). One keenly debated issue is the dating of the eagle vision (11: 1– 12: 39), strongly influenced by the visions of Daniel 7–12. The eagle's several heads and wings represent emperors, but it is unclear which ones, though most scholars consider that they refer to the Flavian dynasty at the end of the first century CE. The lion that prophesies to the eagle (11: 37 ff.) represents the Messiah, the son of David (12: 32), who comes as leader of the remnant of his people and as a destroyer of the nations. However, it is stated in 7: 28–9 that the Messiah will die. (Manuscript readings referring to the Messiah in chapters 7–13 as 'my son' or 'Jesus' are Christian interpolations.)

Chapter 14 provides a contrast to the preceding visions. In a scene that consciously refers to the career of Moses, Ezra asks God to inspire him and dictate to
him the Law that has been burned. During forty days apart from the people, he
dictates ninety-four books to five scribes. Twenty-four of them, corresponding to
the Jewish canon, are to be made public, and the other seventy to be reserved for
those who are wise among the people. In this chapter, the querulous Ezra has
become a confident scribe who communicates directly with God, and this is
one reason why some scholars consider that chapters 3–14 represent disparate
source material put together by an editor, though others (e.g. Stone 1989) argue
for their unity.

Overall, the message of chapters 3–14 is one of hope in the face of incomprehensible suffering, and the importance of the Scriptures. This is probably why the
Christian authors of the first two and last two chapters chose to 'sandwich' it with
their own compositions. Chapters 1–2 depict Ezra as a prophet who tells the Jewish
nation of their sin and consequent rejection by God, who has replaced them with
another people. There are allusions to the book of Revelation in 2: 39–48; the
resurrection of the dead is mentioned in 2: 23, and Gehenna in 2: 29. At the end of
the passage the Son of God is depicted, crowning the righteous (2: 46–7). It is
generally dated to the mid-second century CE, and may have been written in either
Greek or Latin, but survives only in Latin. Chapters 15–16 are strongly apocalyptic,
and seem to have been written in the face of persecution, perhaps as late as the mid-
third century CE, in order to encourage believers to stand firm because God will
punish their oppressors.

TOBIT

The study of Tobit was considerably enhanced by findings at Qumran. Although
the book was known in both a long and a short form in Greek, Latin, and other
languages, in 1952 one Hebrew and four Aramaic fragments were discovered among
the Dead Sea Scrolls, covering one-fifth of the text. This discovery tallies with
Jerome's remark that he produced his Latin version from an Aramaic text that a Jew
translated into Hebrew for him. Medieval Hebrew and Aramaic versions of Tobit
are renderings of the Greek and Latin forms.

Tobit is a God-fearing Israelite in Nineveh who keeps God's commandments at
risk to his own life, yet becomes blind. His family is reduced to penury, so he sends
his son Tobias on a long journey to collect some money entrusted to a friend in
Rages. Tobias does not suspect that his hired guide is the angel Raphael, who leads

him to the household of a relative in Ecbatana whose daughter Sarah is possessed by a demon which has killed all seven of her bridegrooms on their wedding night. Tobias marries Sarah and drives away the demon by burning the entrails of a fish that tried to swallow him in the course of his journey. Raphael fetches the money owed to Tobit, and he returns with Tobias and Sarah to Nineveh. The gall of the fish restores Tobit's sight, and Raphael reveals his true identity.

Thus, in terms of genre, the book is an edifying tale of Israelites in the Eastern Diaspora, whose piety delivers them from their troubles. The structure and use of irony are quite sophisticated, and the human interest and folklore elements have assured its appeal over the centuries: it has been popular in art and formed the basis for a successful modern novel, *Miss Garnett's Angel*, by Salley Vickers (2000). Tobit's advice to his son in chapter 4 and Raphael's to Tobias and Tobit in 12: 6–10 is akin to wisdom literature. Significant in this respect is the appearance of that paragon of Near Eastern wisdom, Ahiqar, as Tobit's Israelite relative (1: 21–2; 11: 18; 14: 10). Apart from the change of first person to third person by the end of chapter 3, necessitated by the narrative, the story shows some literary sophistication. It draws parallels between Tobit's family, affected by the consequences of his blindness, and Raguel's, through the demon that caused the death of his daughter's bridegrooms. In spite of their piety and integrity, Tobit and Sarah suffer reproach even within their own households. At a pivotal point in the story (3: 16–17) they each pray to God in their distress, pleading their innocence and asking to die. Their prayers are heard simultaneously, and God sends Raphael in disguise to heal them both and to marry Sarah to Tobias. As Sarah and Tobit leave their place of prayer simultaneously, unbeknown to them the answer is already at hand.

The book's message is that faithfulness to God in exile is rewarded, in this instance by the marriage alliance and the recovery of Tobit's sight and fortunes. There are echoes of the marriages of Isaac and Rebekah, and of Jacob and Rachel, and Anna's reproach to Tobit and his desire to die remind one of the book of Job. Amos and Nahum are cited explicitly, and there are several allusions to other books. The ethical teaching is in line with that of Sirach/Ecclesiasticus.

The date of Tobit's composition is generally thought to be between 225 and 175 BCE, because of its allusions to older books of the Bible, the lack of references to the problems of Hellenization, and lack of hostility to non-Jews (xenophobia would suggest the Maccabean period). Though it was apparently well known at Qumran, there is no evidence for a sectarian origin, and none of the apocalyptic or messianic thought associated with the sect. It does teach that matches are foreordained, the importance of burial of the dead and of almsgiving, which delivers from death. However, there are no traces of a belief in an afterlife. Tobit's provenance is much harder to determine. Most favour either the Eastern Diaspora because of the book's setting (though the geography is very peculiar!), or Palestine because of its interest in the homeland and the restoration of the Temple. Some research has stressed the links with ancient Near Eastern folklore, but though analysing Tobit as a folk-tale has proved fruitful, it is difficult to prove its dependence on other, non-Jewish stories because of the difficulties in dating such supposed sources.

Though many Christian writers accepted Tobit, both Origen and Jerome knew that Tobit was not part of the Jewish canon. Orlinsky (1974: 284) suggests that it was rejected because it did not conform to rabbinic rules for writing the marriage document. The rabbis may also have had reservations about the book's interest in demons, magic, and angelology, an interest shared by other apocryphal and pseudepigraphical works of that era such as *Jubilees* and *1 Enoch*. They may have objected also to its Israelite rather than Jewish protagonists. Its dubious status for Jerome explains why his Latin translation is rather free and introduces some of his own notions, such as sexual abstinence for prayer. In his defence, some believe that he may have been using a text influenced by the Essenes, though the Qumran fragments we have do not cover this portion.

JUDITH

The very opening chapter of the book of Judith reveals the fictitious nature of the work. Nebuchadnezzar is said to be the king of the Assyrians, and Arphaxad (cf. Gen. 11: 10–13) is ruler of Ecbatana; and the Assyrian army is about to attack Jerusalem, where the Temple has recently been rededicated following the return from exile. This should not deter the reader: though the author is evidently stronger on piety than history, the book has captured the artistic imagination for centuries, and now receives a good deal of attention from feminist scholars in particular because of its treatment of the issues of gender, sexuality, religion, and violence (Brenner 1995; Stocker 1998). However, the book and its heroine are highly ambiguous: some consider that the author may even have been female (van Henten, in Brenner 1995: 224–52), while others such as Milne (1993) are more pessimistic about her suitability as a feminist heroine.

Judith is a rich, beautiful, and pious widow, who delivers her town Bethulia and consequently Jerusalem itself from the Assyrian army by beguiling and then killing the enemy commander Holofernes. She does not make an appearance, however, until the beginning of chapter 8. The first seven chapters describe the political and military preparations for war against Judea. By accentuating the seemingly insuperable danger facing the Jews, they serve to highlight God's deliverance through the hands of just one woman. This is a 'rescue-story' typical of the Bible (Otzen 2002: 68): Judith's pivotal role in the salvation of her people is akin to that of Esther, especially in the embellished, Greek version of that book. Judith is also consciously modelled on figures in the book of Judges. She leads the people like Deborah (Judg. 4: 4–10), beguiles the enemy general with implicit sexual promise, slays him in his sleep like Jael (Judg. 4: 17–22; 5: 24–7), and retreats back into domestic life like her supposed ancestor Gideon (Judith 8: 1; Judg. 8: 22–8: see Levine, in Vanderkam 1992: 17–30). There are also points of contact with Abigail in 1 Sam. 25: 18–19, taking food to appease the leader of a hostile force (Judith 10: 5), and the loyalty and boldness of heroines like Tamar (Genesis 38) and Ruth. White (in VanderKam 1992: 5–16) observes that Jael, Deborah, and Judith all have husbands who are either absent from the scene or dead, so the women's identity arises from their own actions and not those of their husbands or sons.

Others have pointed out that Judith's name means 'Jewish woman', and therefore to some extent she symbolizes the entire Jewish nation, beautiful but widowed Zion (Levine, in Brenner 1995: 210).

The book has been assigned various dates. However, it seems clear from the narrative that it was written at a time of national crisis, under a foreign threat, and of consciousness of personal religious observance (note Judith's private prayers and careful adherence to dietary law). This is most likely to be the Maccabean period (160s BCE) when Antiochus IV Epiphanes threatened Jerusalem and the Jewish way of life (Otzen 2002: 132–5). Therefore, 'Assyria' is a cipher for Syria, and Nebu-chadnezzar would represent Antiochus IV, and Holofernes his general, Nicanor. A later date has been suggested by others, notably Ilan (1999), who suggests that three late books with key female protagonists, Judith, Esther, and Susanna, were all written in support of the reign of Queen Salome (Shelamzion) Alexandra (78–69 BCE), who in spite of opposition succeeded her husband Alexander Jannai at a time of national crisis. She was supported by the Pharisees, and Pharisaic tendencies have been detected in both the book of Judith and that of Susanna (q.v.: but see Craven 1983: 121). Other theological features include the phenomenon of the full voluntary conversion (including circumcision) of Holofernes' Ammonite counsellor Achior (see Roitman, in VanderKam 1992: 31–46). However, the book shows no interest in the afterlife or martyrdom.

The original language of the book is likely to have been Hebrew, though Jerome claims that his Latin translation was based on an Aramaic text. However, the main witness is now the Greek text, and Camponigro argues that the book was originally composed in Greek, on the basis of apparent allusions to Herodotus (in Vander-Kam 1992: 47–60). If that is the case, it would explain why it was not accepted into the Jewish canon, though this hesitation may have been for other reasons. Its absence from Qumran may be explained by its pro-Hasmonaean stance (Moore, in VanderKam 1992: 61–72).

The many depictions of the story usually involve Judith in the act of cutting off the head of Holofernes, or carrying it in a bag, accompanied by her maid (Stone, in VanderKam 1992: 73–93; Bal, in Brenner 1995: 253–85), and reveal a great deal about the society, the artists, and the patronage that produced the work.

SIRACH

Somewhat confusingly, this work regularly goes under three different names: Ecclesiasticus (Latin), Sirach (Greek), and Ben Sira (Hebrew). For once among the apocryphal books, we know the author's name, Jesus ben Eleazar ben Sira. Two slightly different Greek versions circulated in the Church, and over the last century a number of Hebrew fragments have been discovered at Qumran, Masada, and in the Cairo Geniza, covering over two-thirds of the original Hebrew text. The correspondence between the Greek and Hebrew texts is not always very precise, however (see Wright 1989). The Syriac translation depends on the Hebrew, while those in other languages are from the Greek. The original Greek translator was the author's own grandson, who tells us in the prologue that he came to Egypt in the thirty-eighth year of Ptolemy Euergetes (i.e. 132 BCE) and translated the book there. The Hebrew original is thought to have been written sometime between the death of the high priest Simon ben Onias in 196 and the Maccabean crisis after 170 BCE.

The book belongs to the genre of wisdom literature, but though it contains many aphoristic proverbs similar to those in the biblical book of Proverbs, as well as a passage praising Wisdom (ch. 24) that depends on Proverbs 8, it is rather more reflective in style. As in modern self-help manuals, there is much advice on how to conduct one's family life, friendships, and professional life, and on psychology, health, and spirituality. There is a strong emphasis on ethics and community, and on religion as philosophy: the connection between Wisdom as synonymous with Torah and reverence for God is stated many times (e.g. 1: 1, 14, 28; 15: 1; 24: 23).

One interesting feature is the book's attitude to the heroes of canonical Scripture in the Praise of the Ancestors (chs. 44–50; see Goshen-Gottstein, in Egger-Wenzel 2002: 235–67). Ben Sira's remarks concerning Enoch, Joseph, Shem, Seth, and Adam (49: 14–16) foreshadow their importance in pseudepigraphical literature. The roles of the priests Aaron and Phineas are enhanced, but Ezra is omitted (cf. 1 Esdras). For Ben Sira, the righteous kings are David, Josiah, and Hezekiah, but Solomon's many wives defiled the Davidic line (47: 20). The list of famous men reaches a climax in 50: 1–21, where the Hasmonaean high priest, Simon son of Onias, receives extravagant praise for fortifying the Temple and Jerusalem, deeds for which Josiah and Hezekiah are also commended (Aitken 2000). Himmelfarb (2000) notes the lack of nostalgia for kingship in Ben Sira; instead, Simon represents the apogee of both royalty and priesthood, though he is not depicted as an eschatological messiah figure (Xeravits 2001). Sir. 17: 27–8 seems to indicate that Ben Sira did not believe in an afterlife, and, like the book of Proverbs, he teaches that one receives the consequences for one's actions in this life (e.g. 27: 25–7): there is no final judgement to right wrongs and reward virtue.

Ben Sira's negative attitude towards women has frequently been noted, particularly in contrast to the female personification of Wisdom in his book (Trenchard

1982; Coggins 1998: 85–91). The androcentric bias is undeniable, but since Ben Sira was writing as a man for the education of other men, in an age when misogyny was the norm, this is not so surprising. Other reflections of his society are found in the different types of skill displayed by the physician, the scribe, and the artisan (ch. 38), though the student of Torah surpasses them all (38: 34–39: 11; Rollston 2001).

Unlike other apocryphal books, Ben Sira is sometimes quoted in the Talmuds and later rabbinic literature, though usually only the proverbs are cited. Rabbinic opinion on the status of the book varied markedly, from considering it virtually part of Scripture to warning that it endangers the soul (see Levene, in Egger-Wenzel 2002: 305–20).

WISDOM OF SOLOMON

The attribution to Solomon is based on an inference from the content of chapters 7–9, where a royal first person narrator describes his appeal to God for wisdom. However, the original language of the book is clearly Greek, because of the level of its style and vocabulary. In genre it has some similarities with Ben Sira, but it is much less practical in bent, and the hypostasization of Wisdom goes much further. The book is a kind of meditation on the history of God's people and the role that Wisdom has played in it, but one has to know the biblical account well in order to pick up the allusions. That such Wisdom could be, and frequently was, identified with the Holy Spirit or the Logos, explains the book's popularity with Christian writers in antiquity, even though some expressed doubts concerning its Solomonic authorship (McGlynn 2001: 237–43).

Sections from the consolatory passage on the sufferings of the righteous at the hands of the wicked, their eventual glorious vindication, and the confounding of the ungodly (2: 12–5: 23) appear often in lectionaries for feasts commemorating the saints and martyrs. These chapters strongly suggest a belief in a final judgement and immortality (see especially 5: 15–16), which tend to be indicators of a late date. Some of the words used also indicate a date of composition during the Roman period, i.e. from the latter half of the first century BCE. It is usually assumed that the book was written in Alexandria during a period of persecution of the large Jewish community there, reflected in its treatment of the exodus story, and it may even reflect the ethnic riot of 38 CE (Cheon 1997). Wisd. 12: 24–13: 19 is a diatribe against idolatry (cf. *Let Jer*) and the worship of animals as gods, which would also support an Egyptian context. Part of the same passage also suggests the thought of Rom. 1: 18–25: the influence of the book of Wisdom on Paul has often been noted.

However, with the rise of the rabbinic movement, in which Scripture had to be in Hebrew, and perhaps to a lesser extent because of the popularity of the Wisdom of Solomon in the Church, the book fell into disuse in later Judaism.

1   ENOCH

1 Enoch is recognized as Scripture only within the Ethiopian Orthodox Church, but nevertheless influenced early Christianity (VanderKam 1996). The discovery of a number of Aramaic fragments at Qumran has demonstrated the antiquity of the oldest layers of the book and helped to stimulate a revival of interest in the work as a whole. Nevertheless, there is still little agreement at the present time about some fundamental issues. At the outset it should be noted that 1 Enoch is in fact composed of five different documents, dating from different periods. Chapters 1–36 are known as the Book of the Watchers, and date from the third century BCE; chapters 37–71 constitute the Book of Similitudes, or Parables of Enoch, but are dated to the first century BCE or CE; chapters 72–82 are called the Astronomical Book, and were written sometime in the third century BCE; chapters 83–90 constitute the Book of Dreams, dating to the second century BCE; and chapters 91–108 are called the Epistle of Enoch, also from the second century BCE. Even within these five documents there are further layers. Most recent research has been on the oldest documents, the Astronomical Book and the Book of Watchers, for what they may reveal about trends within Second Temple Judaism of the pre-Maccabean period, especially with regard to theology, the calendar, and the priest-hood (Boccaccini 2002).

The book as a whole now exists only in Ethiopic, but we do have large parts of the Book of Watchers and the Epistle of Enoch in Greek, along with a passage from the Book of Dreams. Aramaic fragments representing all parts except the Simili-tudes have been discovered at Qumran, sometimes copied on to the same scroll, along with a related work known as the Book of Giants (Nickelsburg 2001: 7–16).

Although there are points of contact with Mesopotamian myths, the exact relationship of the Book of the Watchers to the Hebrew text of Gen. 6: 1–4 is keenly debated. Some (e.g. Bedenbender, in Boccaccini 2002: 39–48) believe that each represents a parallel development of a similar story, reflecting the contemporary tension between 'Enochic' and Mosaic Judaism. Others more convincingly argue that the Book of the Watchers is a reworking of the biblical text, and that it therefore post-dates it (Dimant 2002; Stuckenbruck, in Boccaccini 2002: 99–106; VanderKam 1995: 17–25). Certainly the ambiguities of the Hebrew of Gen. 5: 24 must have given rise to Enochic traditions: there Enoch is said to have walked with *ha-'elohim*, who took him so that he 'was not'. *Ha-'elohim* can be understood either as 'God' (with most translators) or as 'divine beings'. The *Book of the Watchers* portrays Enoch as being taken temporarily to the heavenly realms by angels, thus reflecting an alternative but legitimate understanding of the Hebrew.

The Hebrew text, however, may allude to an earlier association of Enoch with the solar calendar, when it states that he lived for 365 years (Gen. 5: 23). Boccaccini (2000) argues that the Astronomical Book supports a calendar in which the four intercalary days should be fully integrated into the year as days of the months and as equinoxes and solstices, against the reckoning of the Zadokite group who controlled the Temple. Differences over the calendar, which affected the celebration of festivals at the correct time, are also reflected in the later book of *Jubilees*, and would become a factor in the schism in Judaism that led to the formation of the Qumran community.

The theology of the Book of Watchers appears to place responsibility for earthly evil on the fallen angels who marry human women and beget violent giants (*1 En.* 6–11; cf. Gen. 6: 1–4), rather than with Adam (Elliott and Sacchi, in Boccaccini 2002: 63–75, 77–85). Alternatively, the origin of evil may commence when the angels teach humankind the arts of weapon making and personal adornment (*1 En.* 8). Several scholars believe that the sins of the fallen angels symbolize the perceived short-comings of Jerusalemites, perhaps their failure to act as intermediaries between God and the people, or illicit marriages (Himmelfarb and Suter, in Boccaccini 2002: 131–5, 137–42), or the departure of some priests from Jerusalem (heaven) to Samaria (earth) (Tigchelaar, in Boccaccini 2002: 143–5). The lack of allusions to the Law of Moses in *1 Enoch* has been seen as indicating the existence of a different type of Judaism (Kvanvig, in Boccaccini 2002: 207–12) that teaches obedience to the laws of God on the basis of the existence of the laws of nature, rather than on the Mosaic covenant (Collins and Argall, in Boccaccini 2002: 57–62, 169–78).

The documents in *1 Enoch* dating from the second century BCE, the Book of Dreams and the Epistle of Enoch, contain three apocalypses and an epistle. The Apocalypse of Weeks (93. 1–10; 91. 11–17) divides history into periods of 'weeks', rather as in Dan. 9: 24–7. Another apocalypse, in chapters 83–4, is Enoch's revela-tion to his son Methuselah of a vision concerning God's judgement that he saw in his own youth, and he tells how he prayed to the Lord to leave a righteous remnant. This of course will be accomplished through the preservation of Noah and his family. The Animal Apocalypse (85–90) presents the figures of biblical history as animals: good characters are presented as white animals, and bad characters as black ones. The entry of sin and evil into the world is not deemed to start with Adam in the events of Genesis 3, but with the murder of Abel by Cain in Genesis 4. As in the Book of Watchers, the author of the Animal Apocalypse is interested in the descent of the angels in Genesis 6 (*1 En.* 86. 1–4), and even ties the narrative to the events described in the Book of Watchers, where Enoch is taken into the heavenly places and judgement is decreed against the evil angels and giants (*1 En.* 87. 3–4). In contrast to the Book of Watchers and the Apocalypse of Weeks, however, the Animal Apocalypse shows some interest in Moses and the exodus narrative, though the Law is passed over, and the priesthood (symbolized as shepherds) is criticized for failing the people (*1 En.* 89. 59–90. 27). There is an allusion to the Maccabean Revolt in *1 En.* 90. 10 ff., which, as the last event described, would place the Apocalypse just after 164 BCE. However, the revelation ends with the birth of a white bull, representing the Messiah. The Epistle of Enoch (*1 En.* 91–105) is an exhortation to Enoch's children to pursue righteousness, for after death their spirits will live in bliss, and warnings of judgement for the wicked. At the end, the birth of a miraculous child is described, who is Enoch's great-grandson, Noah (*1 En.* 106–7). The passage is strongly reminiscent of part of the Genesis Apocryphon from Qumran (Gen. Apoc. cols. 2–5; see VanderKam 1995: 96).

The longest and latest section of *1 Enoch* is the Similitudes (*1 En.* 37–71). It describes three parables or similitudes that Enoch saw, concerning the end-times and final judgement. They show the influence of Daniel 7 and 10 and are similar in tone to Revelation, most notably in the appearance of a figure called the Son of Man and the role of angels, including Michael. The Son of Man is also known as the Chosen One or Righteous One, and there has been some debate over whether he is a single, messianic figure or represents the righteous people as a whole (Collins 1998: 183–91; Oegema 1998: 140–7; Nickelsburg, in Neusner *et al.* 1987: 49–68). Current consensus takes the former line, though VanderKam (1995: 140–2) argues that in *1 En.* 70–1 Enoch himself is identified with the Son of Man.

1 Enoch is first attested in Christian writings in the early second century, but doubts set in as early as Origen in the mid-third century (Pearson 2000). Since early Christians believed that the first scriptures were written by Moses, they may have been sceptical about the authenticity of books that claimed to pre-date him. But *1 Enoch* continued to play a role in the Coptic and then the Ethiopic churches. As for Judaism, the figure of Enoch the visionary was seen as a threat to the pre-eminence of Moses the lawgiver, and the fact that there is no trace of Hebrew copies of any part of *1 Enoch* must be linked to its non-canonical status in Judaism.

BOOKS OF THE MACCABEES

Although the Maccabean Revolt (166–160 BCE) falls outside the explicit historical scope of both Old and New Testaments, it was a defining period for the Jewish religion and nation. The book of Daniel, which most scholars believe to be contemporaneous with it, alludes to the crisis over Hellenization in the revelations given to Daniel in chapters 7–12. In 169 BCE the Seleucid king Antiochus IV Epiphanes plundered the Temple in Jerusalem, and subsequently attempted to force Greek customs on Judaea. Many Jews supported him (cf. 1 Macc. 1: 11–15, 43; 6: 21–7), but others resisted, under the leadership of Judas Maccabaeus. The resulting Hasmonaean dynasty ruled Judaea from 142 to 63 BCE. The story in its various forms was popular with both Jews and Christians for its portrayal of faith resisting tyranny. The origins of the Jewish celebration of Hanukkah, the festival of the rededication of the Temple by Judas Maccabaeus, can be seen in the accounts in 1 Macc. 4: 42 ff. and 2 Macc. 10: 1 ff., etc.

1 Maccabees

The book covers events between 176 and 135 BCE. It describes how King Antiochus IV Epiphanes desecrates the Temple and forces the Jews to abandon their religious practices on pain of death. Out of zeal for the Law, Mattathias of Modein and his five sons refuse to yield and organize resistance. On his father's death, his third son, Judas Maccabaeus, takes command and defeats Antiochus's army. Judas is able to cleanse and rededicate the Temple, and fortify Mount Zion, before embarking on a number of successful military campaigns against the surrounding peoples. Internal dissent among the Seleucids following the death of Antiochus leads the Syrian commander to withdraw from battle with the Jews, and to make peace with them. Over the next few years there is a protracted power struggle in Judaea between the party of the Hellenizing 'renegades', represented by the high priest Alcimus, and the followers of Judas Maccabaeus. When Judas dies in battle, his youngest brother Jonathan takes over as leader and becomes high priest. He takes advantage of further internal Seleucid rivalries to strengthen his position against his Jewish opponents, to renew an old alliance with the Romans, and a new one with the Spartans. On his death, his brother Simon becomes commander, ethnarch, and high priest of the Jews, but he is treacherously slain, and is succeeded by his son John (Hyrcanus).

Though the book is often biblical in style, God plays no direct part in 1 Maccabees. Rather, the book glorifies the deeds of the family of Mattathias against the backdrop of contemporary Near Eastern politics, possibly as a reaction to criticism of the Hasmonaean dynasty during the reign of John Hyrcanus and Alexander Jannaeus. Yet no figure, however heroic, is portrayed in messianic terms; nor are the events seen in an apocalyptic light, leading some to conclude that the book is a reaction to the way the crisis is depicted in the book of Daniel (Goldstein 1976: 42–54; Goldstein, in Neusner *et al.* 1987: 69–96). Martyrdom (as in 1 Macc. 1: 29–38) is not applauded, and this may be related to the author's apparent lack of belief in an afterlife (for this reason some have suggested that the author was a Sadducee: Bartlett 1998: 28–34). There is considerable hostility towards foreigners, especially the local Semitic peoples, but on the other hand, the Maccabeans are shown as happy to make alliances with powerful nations who will support them (Schwartz 1991).

The extent to which the author depended on outside sources, including Seleucid ones, or wrote independently, is still debated. He must have completed his work between the reign of John Hyrcanus and before the Roman invasion of Judaea in 63 BCE (which is not mentioned), and a date towards the end of the second century BCE is most likely. The testimony of both Origen and Jerome suggests that the book was originally written in Hebrew, and it is certainly both Semitic and biblical in style. It was then translated into Greek, and from Greek into Syriac, Latin, and Armenian. The Jewish historian Flavius Josephus used 1 Maccabees as a source for his *Jewish Antiquities* (93–4 CE).

2 Maccabees

This book covers roughly the same period and events as 1 Maccabees, and was written at about the same time. However, it is difficult to harmonize the chronologies of the two books (Bartlett 1998: 44–5), and their interpretation of history differs sharply. 1 Maccabees is strongly biased towards the entire Maccabean family, depicted as saviours of Israel, and the Hasmonaean dynasty that followed. 2 Maccabees focuses on Judas Maccabaeus, alone of his family, and Temple matters (van Henten 1997: 54–5).

There are two quite separate parts of 2 Maccabees. The opening of the book, 1: 1–2: 18, takes the form of letters sent by the Jews in Jerusalem and Judaea to those in Egypt, apparently in 124 BCE (2 Macc. 1: 9), concerning the celebration of a Feast of Booths and another of the rededication of the Temple under Nehemiah. The rest of the book claims to condense the longer account of the Maccabees written by Jason of Cyrene, and is therefore known as the Epitome. It starts at an earlier point than 1 Maccabees, with Heliodorus's demand for the money deposited in the Temple, and ends with the death of the enemy general, Nicanor.

In contrast to the perspective of 1 Maccabees, the author of 2 Maccabees attributes the deliverance of Israel not to human bravery but to divine intervention and the faith of the Jewish martyrs. Both the miracles and the martyrdoms are described in detail, and reveal the purpose of the work to be primarily didactic rather than historiographical. The theology is Deuteronomistic: the people of Israel are chastened by God for their sins, but will be rewarded for their faithfulness (2 Macc. 6: 12–16; 7: 32–3), and the nations who oppose God will be punished. There are also several clear references to a belief in the afterlife (e.g. 7: 9, 14) and bodily resurrection (7: 11; 14: 46).

In spite of the book's anti-Hellenism, it was written originally in Greek, not Hebrew, and so could not be included in the rabbinic Jewish canon. However, the content of the book has had an influence on the celebration of Hanukkah, which commemorates Judas Maccabaeus's rededication of the Temple. Early Christian martyr Acts show strong influence from the accounts of the martyrdoms of Eleazar and the woman and her seven sons (2 Macc. 6: 18–7: 42).

3 Maccabees

3 Maccabees has no relation to the other books of Maccabees except for the theme of foreign threats to the people and religion of Israel. Its setting is Egyptian, and the wicked king is Ptolemy IV Philopator, who reigned half a century before the Maccabean Revolt. The style of the book is vivid and effective (Alexander 2001: 326). When Ptolemy tries to enter the sanctuary in Jerusalem, God sends physical affliction on him. On his return to Egypt, he decides that the Jews there can only be citizens if they accept Greek religion. Those who refuse will be reduced to the status of slaves, and those who resist will be killed. Though some Jews betray their faith, the majority stand firm, but this infuriates the king, who arranges for all of them to be rounded up and trampled to death by drug-crazed elephants. As they face certain death, the elderly priest Eleazar beseeches the Lord for them, and the elephants turn on Ptolemy's soldiers instead. The king repents, and blames his counsellors for what has happened. He institutes a seven-day feast for the Jews, who purge the apostates from their midst. It may be that the book originated as an explanation for the origins of this feast in a deliverance of Jews from tyranny, as a rival to the feast of Purim in the book of Esther, and is an attempt to reconcile and interpret various local sources (Alexander 2001: 327–35).

3 Maccabees shares with 2 Maccabees a strong interest in the sanctity of the Temple, in supernatural intervention as a response to prayer, and in the idea that those who devise cruelty against the Jews will be punished by God. Alexander (2001: 332–3) believes that 3 Maccabees may be an Egyptian attempt to emulate the Palestinian 2 Maccabees. However, there are no martyrdoms in 3 Maccabees, and no mention of an afterlife. 1 and 2 Maccabees detail the horrors of Hellenization (1 Macc. 1: 11–15, 41–50; 2 Macc. 4: 11–17), while 3 Maccabees emphasizes foreign hostility to Jewish worship and dietary restrictions (3 Macc. 3: 1–7), which was something of a *topos* in anti-Jewish polemic, particularly in the volatile political and ethnic atmosphere of Ptolemaic Egypt (deSilva 2002: 315–20). The tone of the book is often said to be anti-Gentile (e.g. 3 Macc. 4: 1), yet it is certainly positive towards the Greeks who are favourably disposed towards the Jews (3 Macc. 3: 8–10; deSilva 2002: 318).

The date of the book is hard to ascertain. Some believe that it points to actual historical events, Modrzejewski (1995: 141–57) to a possible census under Ptolemy Philopator, Collins (2000: 126) to the reign of Caligula. However, the reference to a detail of a Greek addition to the book of Daniel (3 Macc. 6: 6: Azariah and the Three, v. 27) places the composition in the late second century CE at the earliest. There are similarities to 2 Maccabees in vocabulary as well as in style and outlook, and also to the Letter of Aristeas and the Greek additions to Esther.

4 Maccabees

Like 2 Maccabees, on which it probably depends, 4 Maccabees describes the martyrdoms of Eleazar and the mother and her seven sons, for refusing to renounce their Jewish faith by eating pork. However, the narrative takes the form of a eulogy of the martyrs, and is placed within the framework of a philosophical discourse (Greek *diatribe*) on reason and the mastery of the emotions. Judaism is portrayed not as a religion in the cultic sense but as a philosophy expressed in self-restraint. Its dietary restrictions teach restraint of the appetite (4 Macc. 1: 34), and the heroes of Scripture are examples of self-control in the face of temptations to lust and anger (chs. 2–3). This introduces the narrative itself, prefaced by the description in chapter 4 of the attempt to seize the monies in the Temple deposit, the removal of Onias as high priest, and the forced Hellenization programme. The martyrdoms are a demonstration of 'temperate reason' (4 Macc. 3: 19), and though the descriptions are close to those in 2 Maccabees, there is more gore and more philosophy. A new element is the atoning value of the deaths for the Jewish people (4 Macc. 6: 28–9, spoken by Eleazar, and 17: 21: see van Henten 1997: 150–2, 156–63), and a eulogy of the mother, who is said to be more noble and courageous than men for her willingness to let her sons die and to watch their torture before throwing herself into the fire (Moore and Anderson 1998). The martyrdom is described as a contest, and the martyrs as athletes (4 Macc. 11: 20; 12: 14; 16: 16; 17: 15–16), who win the prize of immortality (4 Macc. 17: 12; 18: 23), though unlike 2 Maccabees, this may involve a spiritual rather than a bodily resurrection.

The book was written in Greek for a Jewish readership (4 Macc. 18: 1–2), and its late vocabulary and apparent dependence on 2 Maccabees place it at least in the first century CE. Some have even suggested a connection to the Jewish revolt in the Diaspora against the Emperor Trajan in 115–17 CE, or to the Hadrianic persecution and Second Jewish Revolt in 130–5 CE. It may originate in the area of Antioch, where the cult of the Maccabean martyrs was strong, or in Cilicia, because of similarities with Jewish funerary inscriptions (van Henten 1997: 79–81).

ADDITIONS TO DANIEL

The Book of Daniel was written in Hebrew and Aramaic, and is found in two slightly different Greek forms: the Old Greek and Theodotionic translations. Both Greek versions contain additional material, which may derive from an alternative Semitic version of Daniel, now lost, though the Theodotionic text presents a longer version of the stories. In Daniel 3 there are three extra passages inserted between verses 23 and 24 (NRSV). These embellish the story of Daniel's three friends in the furnace of blazing fire: the Prayer of Azariah in the furnace, a short prose narrative describing the intervention of an angel to save the youths from the flames, and the Song of the Three Jews (elsewhere: Three Children), which is a canticle praising creation that proved popular in the churches. At the end of the Greek book of Daniel there are three further stories involving Daniel: the story of Susanna (ch. 13 in NRSV), the story of Bel (14: 1–22), and the story of the Dragon (14: 23–42).

The story of Susanna is a folk-tale set in the exiled Jewish community in Babylon. Susanna is the beautiful and God-fearing wife of a rich Jewish leader. Two wicked elders who have been appointed as judges try to force her to sleep with them by threatening to bring a charge of adultery against her. She refuses to yield to them, so they testify that they saw her embracing a young man in her husband's garden. In despair Susanna appeals to God. As she is led off to execution, a young lad called Daniel is stirred up by God to save her. When he questions the two elders separately, their stories do not tally, and Susanna is acquitted, while the elders receive the same punishment they had destined for her. It is to this story that Shylock refers in Shakespeare's *Merchant of Venice*: 'A Daniel come to judgement!'

As mentioned above, Tal Ilan (1999) argues that the books of Judith and Esther and the story of Susanna were all written as propaganda to support the rule of Queen Salome Alexandra (76–67 BCE). Clanton (2003) further refines this idea by suggesting that the attitude to perjury in Susanna reflects the position of the Pharisees, who were the dominant party during Salome Alexandra's reign. Moreover, there is a questioning of the assumption that male leaders are good and wise: Susanna's husband plays no role at all, and the two elders are not fit to be judges, while it is Susanna who is righteous and the youth Daniel who is wise. Others see it as a response to the wrongful execution of the son of the Pharisee Simon ben Shetah, a victim of perjured testimony, or as based on the two adulterous prophets mentioned in Jer. 29: 21–3, or even the Jewish form of a secular folk-tale (see Halpern-Amaru, in Spolsky 1996: 21–34). Like the book of Judith, the story of Susanna invites feminist, anthropological, and narratological analysis (Sered and Cooper, in Spolsky 1996: 43–55; Steussy 1993). There are also studies of its portrayal in art (Boitani and Spolsky, in Spolsky 1996: 7–10, 101–17). It was interpreted by early Christians as a parable of martyrdom, and though it was rejected by the rabbis, it was retranslated and 're-Judaized' in an interpolation to the tenth-century Hebrew work *Sefer Yosippon*.

Daniel uses his forensic skills again in the story of Bel, when he proves that it is not the idol Bel, but the priests and their families, who eat the food and wine put out for Bel each night. When the king tries to make him worship a great dragon revered by the Babylonians, Daniel kills it by feeding it cakes of pitch, fat, and hair. The Babylonians therefore throw Daniel into the lions' den, where he is fed by the prophet Habakkuk, who has been miraculously transported from Judaea. After a week the king rescues Daniel and throws his enemies to the lions instead. Both stories parody idolatry and the worship of animals, and the latter feature has led some to suppose that the work must have been written in Egypt where zoolatry was common (Roth 1975: 43; cf. Steussy 1993: 47).

The authority of the additions to Daniel was being queried among Christians by the early third century, but largely due to Susanna's popularity, it was upheld by all but Jerome (Halpern-Amaru, in Spolsky 1996: 21–34).

1 BARUCH

Baruch appears in the book of Jeremiah as that prophet's scribe (e.g. Jer. 36), and thus is an intermediary between Jeremiah and the people. As in the case of Ezra, there are other pseudonymous works attributed to him, and this phenomenon may reflect the increasing importance of scribes in Second Temple Judaism. The book of 1 Baruch is a composite work, incorporating three different documents. The first part (1: 1–3: 8) purports to be the words of a book that Baruch wrote in Babylon for the Jewish exiles, who send money to Jerusalem with instructions to make a communal confession and make offerings on the exiles' behalf. This narrative section is followed by a poetic part (3: 9–4: 4) in praise of Wisdom and her identity with 'the book of the commandments of God' (1 Baruch 4: 1; cf. Sir. 24: 23; see Harrelson 1992). The final part is also poetic in form, a consolatory exhortation to the people of Israel, placed in the mouth of Zion. Superficially the three different parts have little in common, but they do address the problem of faith in the Jewish diaspora in different ways. However, they are also quite similar to, and even derivative of, other works such as Daniel, Jeremiah, and Sirach.

It is likely that the first part of 1 Baruch was written in Hebrew originally. There is more debate about the original language of the second two parts, though Greek seems most likely (but see Burke 1982). The date of the earliest layer of the book may be as early as the second century BCE, but citations of the book in its present form do not appear until Christian writers of the late second century CE. 1 Baruch 3: 37 was especially popular with Christians, as an allusion to the Incarnation: 'Afterward she [or, he: gender is not represented in Greek verbs] appeared on earth, and lived with humankind.' This alone would have ensured the book's preservation in the churches: there are versions in several different languages, all derived from the Greek.

LETTER OF JEREMIAH

This short work is essentially a satire on idolatry, in the form of a letter supposedly sent by the prophet Jeremiah to Babylon. Thus it became associated with the canonical book of Jeremiah, along with Lamentations and Baruch. It may have taken its inspiration from Jer. 10: 11 (Moore 1977: 326). The original language must have been Hebrew or Aramaic (see Hurowitz 1999), since at times the Greek makes sense only if we assume that a mistranslation from a Semitic language has occurred. A small fragment in Greek from the Dead Sea Scrolls may relate to vv. 43–4, and has been dated palaeographically to c.100 BCE. There also seems to be an allusion to the Letter of Jeremiah in 2 Macc. 2: 1–3. In terms of content, the work is even more derivative than the book of Baruch, being dependent upon passages in Psalms, Jeremiah, and Deutero-Isaiah, and it is not often mentioned by Christian writers.

ADDITIONS TO ESTHER

There have been several recent studies of the two Greek texts of Esther, known respectively as the Septuagint text and the Alpha-Text, which have focused mainly on the relationship of the Greek versions to each other and to the extant Hebrew text. The six Greek additions themselves (A–F) have been accorded less attention. Unlike the additions to Daniel, they were intended to be an integral part of the Greek Esther story.

The first addition (A) prefaces the first chapter of the canonical book. In the manner of Daniel, Mordechai dreams of two dragons in combat, and a tiny spring that becomes a river. He then overhears two eunuchs plotting to kill the king, and he is rewarded for saving the king's life. Addition B gives the text of the edict described in Esther 3: 14, giving the reason for the annihilation of the Jews as their inability to assimilate and their hostility towards the government (cf. 3 Macc. 3: 13–29; Moore 1973: 384). Addition C consists of lengthy prayers by Mordechai and Esther, a feature that was perhaps felt to be lacking in the Hebrew Esther. Notably, Esther emphasizes her unhappiness in the harem, her abhorrence for her diadem and for the bed of the uncircumcised king, and her avoidance of foreign food and wine. Addition D replaces Esther 5: 1–2 and describes in much more dramatic detail Esther's entrance into the king's court and how God changes the king's anger to concern. Addition E is another full text of a royal edict, which besides counter-manding the previous one and allowing the Jews to defend themselves, blames Haman's malevolence for the king's former policy towards the Jews, and accuses him of treachery (cf. 3 Macc. 7: 3–9). In the final addition, F, Mordechai reflects on his earlier dream and its fulfilment. There is also a short colophon recording that the book was translated in Jerusalem and brought to Egypt in the fourth year of Ptolemy and Cleopatra (i.e. probably in 78/7 BCE). Josephus used the text of Greek Esther in his *Jewish Antiquities*, and Esther's prayer in addition C was popular in the Church, but otherwise the Greek form was not much regarded (deSilva 2002: 126).

Compared with Hebrew Esther, the Greek texts and additions give a more 'religious' feel to the book in terms of the dream, God's interventions, and the prayers. Moreover, the distinctive life-style of Jews and Gentile antipathy towards them are both strongly emphasized. However, the additions may well have been composed in different languages and at different times (Moore 1973). It is almost certain that B and E (the edicts) were written in Greek, but the other material may go back to Semitic originals.

Prayer of Manasseh

Manasseh is known from 2 Kgs. 21: 1–17 and 2 Chr. 33 as one of the most ungodly of the kings of Judah, who shed innocent blood, followed all kinds of idolatrous practices, and led the nation astray as well. However, while the account in 2 Kings ends with his death in a presumably unrepentant state, 2 Chr. 33: 10–13 tells how Manasseh was taken captive by the Assyrians and taken to Babylon, where he humbled himself before the Lord and prayed. God therefore restored him to his royal position in Jerusalem: 'Then Manasseh knew that the Lord indeed was God.' 2 Chr. 33: 18–19 also mentions that his prayer was written in the annals of the kings of Israel. This earlier Hebrew form has not survived, if indeed it ever existed, but a Prayer of Manasseh is known in both Greek and Syriac, and was translated into other languages used by Christians. The Prayer continues to be used in several churches as a canticle. The only specific allusion to Manasseh as he appears in the text of Chronicles occurs in the Prayer of Manasseh v. 10, which refers to his fettered state and his idolatry.

PSALM 151

The canonical Hebrew Psalter contains 150 psalms, but both at Qumran and in early Christianity additional psalms were found. Psalm 151 is preserved in the Greek Septuagint, but is related to two separate Hebrew psalms found among the Dead Sea Scrolls, known as Psalms 151A and 151B. Psalm 151A describes in the first person David's youth as a shepherd, his praise of God, and how he was chosen from his brothers and anointed as ruler of his people. 151B is more fragmentary, but speaks of David's encounter with Goliath. Both depend on details in 1 Samuel 15–18 and some Hebrew superscriptions of canonical psalms that refer to David. The type of Hebrew used is quite late, so the psalms could have been written as late as the first century BCE. The superscription to the Greek Psalm 151 indicates that early on it was recognized as being outside the main collection of 150. The Hebrew version is longer, but there is disagreement over whether it represents a reworking of a shorter original composition (see Smith 1997 and Haran 1988), or whether the Greek is based on an abbreviated form. Since the Greek cannot be easily understood without the Hebrew, the latter seems more likely.

BIBLIOGRAPHY

General

COLLINS, J. J. 1998. *The Apocalyptic Imagination: An Introduction to Jewish Apocalyptic Literature*, 2nd edn. Grand Rapids, Mich., and Cambridge: Eerdmans.

—— 2000. *Between Athens and Jerusalem: Jewish Identity in the Hellenistic Diaspora*. Grand Rapids, Mich.: Eerdmans.

DESILVA, D. A. 2002. *Introducing the Apocrypha: Message, Context, and Significance*. Grand Rapids, Mich.: Baker Academic.

GRABBE, L. L. 1989. 'The Social Setting of Early Jewish Apocalypticism'. *Journal for the Study of the Pseudepigrapha*, 4: 27–47.

HARRINGTON, D. J. 1999. *Invitation to the Apocrypha*. Grand Rapids, Mich., and Cambridge: Eerdmans.

HORBURY, W. 1998. 'Messianism in the Old Testament Apocrypha and Pseudepigrapha'. In J. Day, ed., *King and Messiah in Israel and the Ancient Near East: Proceedings of the Oxford Old Testament Seminar*, JSOTS.S 270, Sheffield: Sheffield Academic Press, 402–33.

NEUSNER, J., GREEN, W. S., and FRERICHS, E. S. 1987. *Judaisms and their Messiahs at the Turn of the Christian Era*. Cambridge: Cambridge University Press.

NICKELSBURG, G. W. E. 1989. 'Social Aspects of Palestinian Jewish Apocalypticism'. In D. Hellholm, ed., *Apocalypticism in the Mediterranean World and the Near East*, Tübingen: Mohr [Siebeck], 641–54.

OEGEMA, G. S. 1998. *The Anointed and his People: Messianic Expectations from the Maccabees to Bar Kochba*. Journal for the Study of the Pseudepigrapha Supplement Series, 27. Sheffield: Sheffield Academic Press.

ORLINSKY, H. M. 1974. 'The Canonization of the Bible and the Exclusion of the Apocrypha'. In *Essays in Biblical Culture and Bible Translation*, New York: KTAV, 257–86.

ROTH, W. 1975. ' "For life, he appeals to death" (Wisd 13:18): A Study of Old Testament Idol Parodies'. *CBQ* 37: 21–47.

VANDERKAM, J. C., and ADLER, W. 1996. *The Jewish Apocalyptic Heritage in Early Christianity*. CRINT. Assen: Van Gorcum; Minneapolis: Fortress Press, esp. 1–31.

WILLS, L. 1990. *The Jew in the Court of a Foreign King: Ancient Jewish Court Legends*. Harvard Dissertations in Religion. Minneapolis: Fortress Press.

—— 1995. *The Jewish Novel in the Ancient World*. Ithaca, NY, and London: Cornell University Press.

1 and 2 Esdras

BÖHLER, D. 1997. *Die heilige Stadt in Esdras a und Esra-Nehemia*. Freiburg and Göttingen: Vanderhoeck & Ruprecht.

DE TROYER, K. 2002. 'Zerubbabel and Ezra: A Revived and Revised Solomon and Josiah? A Survey of Current 1 Esdras Research'. *Currents in Biblical Research*, 1/1: 30–60.

DITOMMASO, L. 1999. 'Dating the Eagle Vision of 4 Ezra: A New Look at an Old Theory'. *JSP* 20: 3–38.

LONGENECKER, B. W. 1995. *2 Esdras*. Sheffield: Sheffield Academic Press.

MYERS, J. M. 1974. *I and II Esdras: Introduction, Translation and Commentary*. AB 42. Garden City, NY: Doubleday.

STONE, M. E. 1989. *Features of the Eschatology of IV Ezra*. HSM 35. Atlanta: Scholars Press.

TALSHIR, Z. 1999. *1 Esdras: From Origin to Translation*. SBL SCS 47. Atlanta: Scholars Press.

TILLER, P. 2000. 'Anti-apocalyptic Apocalypse'. In R. A. Argall, B. A. Bow, and R. A. Werline, eds., *For a Later Generation: The Transformation of Tradition in Israel, Early Judaism, and Early Christianity*, Harrisburg, Pa.: Trinity Press International, 258–65.

WILLIAMSON, H. G. M. 1996. 'The Problem with First Esdras'. In J. Barton and D. J. Reimer, eds., *After the Exile: Essays in Honour of Rex Mason*, Macon, Ga.: Mercer University Press, 201–16.

Tobit

FITZMYER, J. 2003. *Tobit*. CEJL. Berlin and New York: Walter de Gruyter.

MILLER, J. A. 1991. The Redaction of Tobit and the Genesis Apocryphon. *JSP* 8: 53–61.

MOORE, C. A. 1989. 'Scholarly Issues in the Book of Tobit before Qumran and After: An Assessment'. *JSP* 5: 65–8.

—— 1996. *Tobit.* AB 40A. Garden City, NY: Doubleday.

OTZEN, B. 2002. *Tobit and Judith.* Sheffield: Sheffield Academic Press.

Judith

BRENNER, A. 1995. *A Feminist Companion to Esther, Judith and Susanna.* The Feminist Companion to the Bible, 7. Sheffield: Sheffield Academic Press.

CRAVEN, T. 1983. *Artistry and Faith in the Book of Judith.* SBL DS 70. Atlanta: Scholars Press.

ILAN, T. 1999. ' "And Who Knows Whether You have not Come to Dominion for a Time Like This?" (Esth 4.14): Esther, Judith and Susanna as Propaganda for Shelamzion's Queenship'. In *Integrating Women into Second Temple History*, TSAJ 76, Tübingen: Mohr Siebeck, 127–52.

MILNE, P. J. 1993. 'What Shall We Do with Judith: A Feminist Reassessment of a Biblical "Heroine" '. *Semeia* 62: 37–55.

MOORE, C. A. 1985. *Judith.* AB 40B. Garden City, NY: Doubleday.

OTZEN, B. 2002. *Tobit and Judith.* Sheffield: Sheffield Academic Press.

STOCKER, M. 1998. *Judith, Sexual Warrior: Women and Power in Western Culture.* New Haven and London: Yale University Press.

VANDERKAM, J. C., ed. 1992. *'No One Spoke Ill of Her': Essays on Judith.* SBL, Early Judaism and its Literature, 2. Atlanta: Scholars Press.

Sirach

AITKEN, J. K. 2000. 'Biblical Interpretation as Political Manifesto: Ben Sira in his Seleucid Setting'. *JJS* 51/2: 191–208.

COGGINS, R. J. 1998. *Sirach.* Sheffield: Sheffield Academic Press.

EGGER-WENZEL, R. 2002. *Ben Sira's God: Proceedings of the International Ben Sira Conference, Durham—Ushaw College 2001.* BZAW 321. Berlin and New York: Walter de Gruyter.

HIMMELFARB, M. 2000. 'The Wisdom of the Scribe, the Wisdom of the Priest, and the Wisdom of the King according to Ben Sira'. In R. A. Argall, B. A. Bow, and R. A. Werline, eds., *For a Later Generation: The Transformation of Tradition in Israel, Early Judaism and Early Christianity*, Harrisburg, Pa.: Trinity Press International, 89–99.

MATTILA, S. L. 2000. 'Ben Sira and the Stoics: A Reexamination of the Evidence'. *JBL* 119/3: 473–501.

ROLLSTON, C. A. 2001. 'Ben Sira 38:24–39.11 and the *Egyptian Satire of the Trades*'. *JBL* 120/1: 131–9.

TRENCHARD, W. C. 1982. *Ben Sira's View of Women: A Literary Analysis.* BJS 38. Chico, Ca.: Scholars Press.

WRIGHT, B. G. 1989. *No Small Difference: Sirach's Relationship to its Hebrew Parent Text.* SBL SCS 26. Atlanta: Scholars Press.

XERAVITS, G. 2001. 'The Figure of David in the Book of Ben Sira'. *Henoch*, 23/1: 27–38.

Wisdom of Solomon

CHEON, S. 1997. *The Exodus Story in the Wisdom of Solomon.* Journal for the Study of the Pseudepigrapha Supplement Series, 23. Sheffield: Sheffield Academic Press.

GRABBE, L. L. 1997. *Wisdom of Solomon.* Sheffield: Sheffield Academic Press.

McGLYNN, M. 2001. *Divine Judgement and Divine Benevolence in the Book of Wisdom.* WUNT 2. 139. Tübingen: Mohr Siebeck.

1 Enoch

BOCCACCINI, G. 2000. 'The Solar Calendars of Daniel and Enoch'. In J. J. Collins and P. W. Flint, eds., *The Book of Daniel: Composition and Reception,* Leiden, Boston and Cologne: Brill, ii. 311–28.

—— ed. 2002. *The Origins of Enochic Judaism: Proceedings of the First Enoch Seminar, University of Michigan, Sesto Fiorentino, Italy, June 19th–23rd, 2001. Henoch,* 24/1–2.

DIMANT, D. 2002. '1 Enoch 6–11: A Fragment of a Parabiblical Work'. *JJS* 53/1: 223–37.

NICKELSBURG, G. W. E. 2001. *1 Enoch 1: A Commentary on the Book of 1 Enoch, Chapters 1–36; 81–108.* Hermeneia. Minneapolis: Fortress Press.

PEARSON, B. A. 2000. 'Enoch in Egypt'. In R. A. Argall, B. A. Bow, and R. A. Werline, eds., *For a Later Generation: The Transformation of Tradition in Israel, Early Judaism and Early Christianity,* Harrisburg, Pa.: Trinity Press International, 216–31.

VanderKam, J. C. 1995. *Enoch: A Man for All Generations.* Columbia, SC: University of South Carolina Press.

—— 1996. '1 Enoch, Enochic Motifs, and Enoch in Early Christian Literature'. In *idem* and W. Adler, eds., *The Jewish Apocalyptic Heritage in Early Christianity,* Assen: Van Gorcum; Minneapolis: Fortress Press, 33–101.

1 Maccabees

BARTLETT, J. R. 1998. *1 Maccabees.* Sheffield: Sheffield Academic Press.

GOLDSTEIN, J. A. 1976. *1 Maccabees.* AB 41. Garden City, NY: Doubleday.

SCHWARTZ, S. 1991. 'Israel and the Nations Roundabout: 1 Maccabees and the Hasmonean Expansion'. *JJS* 42: 16–38.

WILLIAMS, D. S. 1999. *The Structure of 1 Maccabees.* CBQ MS 31. Washington: Catholic Biblical Association of America.

2 Maccabees

GOLDSTEIN, J. A. 1983. *2 Maccabees.* AB 41A. Garden City, NY: Doubleday.

VAN HENTEN, J. W. 1997. *The Maccabean Martyrs as Saviours of the Jewish People: A Study of 2 and 4 Maccabees.* Leiden, New York, and Cologne: Brill.

3 Maccabees

ALEXANDER, P. S. 2001. '3 Maccabees, Hanukkah and Purim'. In A. Rappoport-Albert and G. Greenberg, eds., *Biblical Hebrew, Biblical Texts: Essays in Memory of Michael P. Weitzman,* JSOTS.S 333, Sheffield: JSOT Press, 321–39.

MODRZEJEWSKI, J. M. 1995. *The Jews of Egypt from Ramses II to Emperor Hadrian.* Edinburgh: T. & T. Clark.

TROMP, J. 1995. 'The Formation of the Third Book of Maccabees'. *Henoch,* 17/3: 311–28.

4 Maccabees

DESILVA, D. A. 1998. *4 Maccabees.* Sheffield: Sheffield Academic Press.

MOORE, S. D., and ANDERSON, J. C. 1998. 'Taking it Like a Man: Masculinity in 4 Maccabees'. *JBL* 117/2: 249–73.

VAN HENTEN, J. W. 1997. *The Maccabean Martyrs as Saviours of the Jewish People: A Study of 2 and 4 Maccabees*. Leiden, New York, and Cologne: Brill.

Additions to Daniel

BRENNER, A. 1995. *A Feminist Companion to Esther, Judith and Susanna*. The Feminist Companion to the Bible, 7. Sheffield: Sheffield Academic Press.

CLANTON, D. W. Jun. 2003. '(Re)dating the Story of Susanna: A Proposal'. *JSJ* 34/2: 121–40.

DiLELLA, A. A. 2001. 'The Textual History of Greek Daniel'. In J. J. Collins and P. W. Flint, eds., *The Book of Daniel: Composition and Reception*, Leiden, Boston, and Cologne: Brill, ii. 586–607.

MOORE, C. A. 1977. 'Additions to Daniel'. In *Daniel, Esther and Jeremiah: The Additions*. AB 44. Garden City, NY: Doubleday, 23–149.

SPOLSKY, E., ed. 1996. *The Judgment of Susanna: Authority and Witness*. SBL, Early Judaism and its Literature, 11. Atlanta: Scholars Press.

STEUSSY, M. J. 1993. *Gardens in Babylon: Narrative and Faith in the Greek Legends of Daniel*. SBL DS 141. Atlanta: Scholars Press.

1 Baruch

BURKE, D. G. 1982. *The Poetry of Baruch: A Reconstruction and Analysis of the Original Hebrew Text of Baruch 3.9–5.9*. SBL SCS 10. Chico, Ca.: Scholars Press.

HARRELSON, W. 1992. 'Wisdom Hidden and Revealed According to Baruch (Baruch 3.9–4.4)'. In E. Ulrich, J. W. Wright, R. P. Carroll, and P. R. Davies, eds., *Priests, Prophets and Scribes: Essays on the Formation and Heritage of Second Temple Judaism in Honour of Joseph Blenkinsopp*, JSOTS.S 149, Sheffield: Sheffield Academic Press, 158–71.

MOORE, C. A. 1977. 'I Baruch'. In *Daniel, Esther and Jeremiah: The Additions*, AB 44. Garden City, NY: Doubleday, 257–316.

STECK, O. H. 1993. *Das apokryphe Baruchbuch: Studien zu Rezeption und Konzentration 'kanonischer' Überlieferung*. Göttingen: Vandenhoeck & Ruprecht.

Letter of Jeremiah

HUROWITZ, V. 1999. 'An End to Flying Cats—Epistle of Jeremiah 22 Reconsidered'. *Journal for the Study of the Pseudepigrapha*, 20: 93–5.

MOORE, C. A. 1977. 'Letter of Jeremiah'. In *Daniel, Esther and Jeremiah: The Additions*, AB 44, Garden City, NY: Doubleday, 317–30.

TOV, E. 1975. *The Book of Baruch, also called I Baruch (Greek and Hebrew)*. SBL Texts and Translations, 8, Pseudepigrapha Series, 6. Missoula, Mont.: Scholars Press.

Additions to Esther

MOORE, C. A. 1973. 'On the Origins of the LXX Additions to the Book of Esther'. *JBL* 92: 382–93.

—— 1977. 'Additions to Esther'. In *Daniel, Esther, and Jeremiah: The Additions*, AB 44, Garden City, NY: Doubleday, 153–252.

Psalm 151

HARAN, M. 1988. 'The Two Text Forms of Ps 151'. *JJS* 39: 171–82.

SANDERS, J. A. 1984. 'A Multivalent Text: Psalm 151: 3–4 Revisited'. *HAR* 8: 167–84.

SMITH, M. S. 1997. 'How to Write a Poem: The Case of Psalm 151A (11QPs^a 28.3–12)'. In T. Muraoka and J. F. Elwolde, eds., *The Hebrew of the Dead Sea Scrolls and Ben Sira: Proceedings of a Symposium held at Leiden University, 11–14 December 1995*, Leiden: Brill, 182–208.

STRUGNELL, J. 1966. 'Notes on the Text and Transmission of the Apocryphal Psalms 151, 154 (= Syr. II) and 155 (= Syr. III)'. *HTR* 59: 257–72, 278–81.

CHAPTER 30

THE GROWTH OF THE NEW TESTAMENT

JOHN M. COURT

INTRODUCTION

To speak about the growth of the New Testament essentially acknowledges the fact that here is no single, unitary, and static text, but rather an emerging and developing assemblage, or library, of texts. When we speak in this way, we recognize the need to reconstruct a historical perspective, from such resources as may be available, within which individual texts are identified, and their movements and possible interactions are charted. Even in the present age of critical study of the Bible, when literary rather than historical readings are favoured, the broadest kind of historical perspective is still a prerequisite for this particular topic.

But it is this historical perspective which actually constitutes the problem for us, because different reconstructions can identify the important constituent texts quite differently. For instance, in 1792 Edward Evanson identified *ten* New Testament books as belonging to the earliest period, the apostolic age: Luke–Acts, 1 and 2 Corinthians, Galatians, 1 and 2 Thessalonians, 1 and 2 Timothy, and Revelation (chs. 4–22). Forty years later, Ferdinand Christian Baur of Tübingen would ascribe to the apostolic period only *five*: namely, Romans, 1 and 2 Corinthians, Galatians, and Revelation. By contrast, E. Earle Ellis (1998: 87) stated that 'there are strong arguments for dating the composition of the New Testament writings, with the exception of the Gospel and letters of John, during the first Christian generation, say, about A.D.50–70'—so *twenty-three* out of a possible total of twenty-seven.

'The wellspring of the New Testament was a fountain of collective memory that found its origin in the life and teachings of Jesus. Papias called it "a voice that lives and abides" ' (Baird 2002: 11). This is the voice which, for example, J. Arthur Baird sought to identify, in written memoir and underlying oral communication, within the material of the gospels and early Christian tradition. He sought to demonstrate a trajectory which leads from the teachings of Jesus, moving outwards to narratives about Jesus. The central layer of the message is the 'holy Word', on top of which are other levels represented by narrative, gospel, and traditions. Theological changes ('shifts') are involved at each level, as ultimately the Word is applied to doctrinal, ethical, and ecclesiastical concerns. Baird did not regard these changes as sinister and manipulative, but rather as a natural evolution of the message in relation to the changing needs and circumstances of the Church, and effectively therefore a witness to continuity.

A broadly similar emphasis on these salient features of the situation in which the New Testament grew historically was provided by Rowan Williams (2001: p. xxviii, writing in the different context of a comment on Richard Hooker): 'The Bible is a book always *being read* by a historical community, whose corporate sense of what Scripture says, and skills in "translating" scriptural doctrine into new situations, must equally be taken with theological seriousness' (my emphasis).

Already we can identify certain fundamental questions which must be addressed, in order that the origins and development of the New Testament can be discussed, on the basis of evidence for what we know, rather than on what we assume we know:

1. In its most significantly formative stages, is the New Testament to be regarded as an oral tradition or as a set of written documents?
2. What would constitute a quotation from this tradition, whether oral or written, so that it would be widely recognized?
3. Does the concept of growth and development in this material entail an identifiable and indeed quantifiable period of time that must elapse for this to take place?
4. Is a cultural transition, a movement from one world to another, necessarily involved in this process of development, so as to be its causal factor? Is the so-called 'parting of the ways', between Judaism and Christianity, in this way a significant aspect of the growth of the New Testament?
5. Would it be correct, as Baird suggested, to accord temporal priority to the teaching of Jesus, and to see this as moving logically to a biographical and explanatory interpretation of Jesus in the form of narrative?
6. Do any observations, which we may have, about the current shape of the canon of the New Testament, provide indicators of the shapes and likely priorities in earlier forms of the tradition? Can we do an archaeology of the text, on the basis of its present structure?

A BRIEF DISCUSSION OF THESE QUESTIONS

1.   *Orality*   As the first volume in a trilogy on *Christianity in the Making* by James D. G. Dunn, *Jesus Remembered* (2003*b*) seeks to provide fresh perspectives both on the impact made by Jesus and on the traditions about Jesus, regarded as fundamentally *oral* tradition, and so justifying the use of the title *Jesus Remembered*. The characteristic features of that tradition are analysed, comprising the tradition of John the Baptist, the motif of the kingdom, the call to discipleship and its nature, what Jesus' audiences thought of him, what might be known of what he thought of himself, the reasons why he was crucified, and how and why belief in Jesus' resurrection began. The impressions made within such an oral tradition may well be contradictory, since it is usually the editorial processes associated with a written tradition that seek to impose consistency.

The literary mindset ('default setting') of modern Western culture prevents those trained in that culture from recognizing that oral cultures operate differently. The classic solution to the Synoptic problem, and the chief alternatives, have envisaged the relationships between the Gospel traditions in almost exclusively literary terms. But the earliest phase of transmission of the Jesus tradition was without doubt predominantly by word of mouth. (Dunn 2003*a*: 139)

It is vital to recognize the impact of orality in the way it was used in an ancient culture. It is equally important to seek to be sure where the dividing line comes between the oral tradition and the written text. In the growth of the New Testament this boundary line is crossed; or it may be more strictly accurate to say that the transitions from oral to written, and back again, take place on several occasions. When working backwards from the finished product, it is not always easy to identify the signs of these transitions.

2.   *Quotations*   After we have raised and discussed the question of orality, this next question runs the risk of lapsing back into a literary mode. Burton Mack offers a colourful but anachronistic description of Mark as a New Testament author (1988: 322–3):

Mark's gospel . . . was composed at a desk in a scholar's study lined with texts and open to discourse with other intellectuals. In Mark's study were chains of miracle stories, collections of pronouncement stories in various states of elaboration, some form of Q, memos on parables and proof texts, the scriptures, including the prophets, written materials from the Christ cult, and other literature representative of Hellenistic Judaism.

A much more realistic scenario of writing in the first century CE is depicted by Raymond Brown when he describes the creation of the *Gospel of Peter* (Brown 1994: ii. 1336):

GPet was not produced at a desk by someone with written sources propped up before him but by someone with a memory of what he had read and heard (canonical and non-canonical) to which he contributed imagination and a sense of drama.

This could apply equally well to the writers of the canonical texts of the New Testament.

The ancients lacked rigorous protocols for quoting and acknowledging, as opposed to manipulating and often 'cutting and pasting', their predecessors' work.... Ancient scholars were not thereby condemned to being necessarily derivative; they were engaged in a fluid, ongoing process of recomposing and re-evaluating their cultural past.

This acknowledged quotation (Halliwell 2003: 11) accurately illustrates the contrast between ancient and modern practice, showing the fluidity in the interpretive use of writing throughout the classical world. Having acknowledged this different ethos, modern commentators are naturally still interested in the sources of ideas and the processes involved in recycling and developing thoughts. So the modern scholar will seek to apply strict (or more flexible) criteria in the recognition of quotations. The position of the New Testament texts and their 're-scripturing' is analogous in this respect to the critical questions raised about the use of the Old Testament in the New Testament (see Court 2002).

Outside the New Testament, the field of study is among the fathers of the early church. Echoes of a New Testament text in e.g. Clement of Rome's first letter to the Corinthians (*c*.95 CE), or the correspondence of Ignatius of Antioch with chosen churches on his road to martyrdom (*c*.110–15 CE), can supply important evidence for the distribution of such a text at this period, and perhaps also its authority in the church. Fairly strict criteria need to be applied in identifying a quotation, in terms of distinctive words, or a number of words in matching order, especially when no indication of the source is given by the church father. So Clement is said to know Paul's letter to the Romans and 1 Corinthians, but reminiscences of the sayings of Jesus cannot be attributed to a particular gospel source. Ignatius probably writes from memory on his journey; he is aware of the status of Paul's letters, and seems to know Matthew's Gospel (Matt. 3: 15 in Ignatius, *Smyrnaeans*, 1. 1) and possibly also John's Gospel. A good case can be made for dependence by the *Didache* on the traditions of Matthew's Gospel (see Court 1981, but also Garrow 2004; Gregory and Tuckett 2006*a*, *b*).

The other dimension of this question concerns the internal evidence within the New Testament for literary dependence and the possibilities of intertextuality. The principal data of scholarship here are the researches of recent centuries on the synoptic problem. While there may be a significant majority view, if not a consensus, for the dependence of Matthew and Luke upon Mark, further debates are far from resolved both about a literary relationship between Matthew and Luke (a reconstructed document known as Q), or an alternative explanation in terms of oral tradition, and also on the question of whether the author of the Fourth Gospel knew any of the texts of the other three gospels (as opposed to the traditions of Jesus). Some have argued that John knew Luke, or perhaps Mark, but in this area the pendulum has swung violently from positive to negative and back again. The criteria for identifying quotations are at their most specific in these debates, involving combinations of agreement in vocabulary, word order, and syntax, as well as matching ideas and contexts.

3.   *Development*   Textual and literary critics of the New Testament in nineteenth-century Germany had constructed a theoretical framework to explain the development of the gospel stories about Jesus. There was considerable agreement that the text of the Gospels must have taken a couple of centuries to evolve, before the point at which it was written down. One indication of this was the fact that the earliest of the great manuscripts, Codex Sinaiticus and Codex Vaticanus, dated from the fourth century. After so many centuries, it must have seemed unlikely that there were any earlier manuscripts which could have survived.

But counter-indicators soon emerged. In 1888 an Arabic translation was discovered of the *Diatessaron* compiled by Tatian. He had been a disciple of Justin Martyr (the church father who had referred to the gospels as the 'memoirs/ remembrances' of the apostles). Tatian's *Diatessaron* assembled a collage of quotations from the four gospels into a single narrative (see Petersen 1994). The fourth-century church historian Eusebius said that Tatian had compiled this work before 172 CE. No full copy of the original text in Greek had (or has) been found, although a Greek fragment was found at Dura Europos in Syria, which attested to its circulation prior to the conquest of Dura in 256 CE. The absence of a full manuscript of the text inevitably led to some scepticism about its existence or character. But the discovery of the Arabic version was at least an important indicator of the date by which the texts of the individual gospels must have been fully in circulation. More evidence was forthcoming by the end of the nineteenth century, in the discovery of manuscript fragments on papyri at Oxyrhynchus, to the west of the Nile, during archaeological investigations by Oxford University. One triangular fragment, which was acquired by the library in Manchester set up in memory of John Rylands, carries text from the Gospel of John, namely 18: 31–3, 37–8, including the context of Pilate's question, 'What is truth?'. This fragment (Rylands 457 = P^{52}) is dated to approximately 125 CE.

Such findings indicate the strong possibility that the date of composition for such texts can be pushed back into the first century CE, although it is unlikely that actual manuscripts will be forthcoming to provide external evidence. To establish any indications of date and early provenance for particular texts of the New Testament will then involve internal investigation of the contents of the text. Source criticism may focus on the dating of early elements included in a later process of composition. As J. A. T. Robinson expressed it, when he reopened the question in the 1970s:

[I]n New Testament chronology one is dealing with a combination of absolute and relative datings. There are a limited number of more or less fixed points, and between them phenomena to be accounted for are strung along at intervals like beads on a string according to the supposed requirements of dependence, diffusion and development. (Robinson 1976: 1)

Development, the last of these requirements, may well prove to be the most contentious. Much depends upon what yardstick is employed, in order to determine how long it takes for the germ of an idea to develop into an acknowledged concept or doctrine. John Robinson argued that the whole of Paul's extant correspondence could be fitted into a period of nine years:

This gives us some objective criterion of how much time needs to be allowed for developments in theology and practice.... The whole of Jesus' teaching and ministry (which I believe to have involved at least three fundamental shifts in the way he saw his person and work) occupied at most three or four years. And the whole development of early Christian thought and practice up to the death of Stephen and the conversion of Paul, including the first Hellenistic statement of the gospel, took place within something like the same period. Indeed [Martin] Hengel [1972]...argues strongly that the crucial stage in the church's basic understanding of Christ and his significance was represented by the four to five 'explosive' years between 30 and 35 [CE]. (Robinson 1976: 84–5)

Whereas an earlier generation had been characteristically pessimistic about New Testament history and chronology—there is safety in dating as late as possible—Hengel and Robinson, armed with their optimistic yardstick of development, were able to argue for a fast and accelerated growth of the New Testament. The truth may well lie somewhere between—or is that also a measure of caution?

4. *Cultural transition* The early church lost touch with its Jewish roots in or before 70 CE. Various passages in the NT suggest that Christians were excommunicated from the synagogue before the NT canon was completed, and certainly before 70 CE. This marked the beginning of the loss of Jewish culture within the church. A few Christian groups such as the Nazarenes and the Ebionites continued to follow Jewish customs, but these soon died out. The church very quickly forgot its Jewish roots, and thereby lost contact with much of the Jewish background of the NT writings. (Instone-Brewer 2002: 238)

An alternative angle on this:

...the question of why the Judaeo-Christians, the first of Jesus' followers, withdrew so relatively fast from the main body of the church.... the most likely reason was that the Ebionites became convinced that they were witnessing in the Hellenistic communities a fatal misrepresentation of Jesus, a betrayal of his ideals, and their replacement by alien concepts and aspirations. (Vermes 2003: 24)

Both of these viewpoints represent entrenched conclusions, seeing the original relationship between the family of Judaism and nascent Christianity as essentially severed. Judaism resembles a dysfunctional family, and the hostility involved in the breakdown renders the situation irreparable, at least in those days. The result in Christian terms was an attitude of anti-Judaism or anti-Semitism, reflected strongly in some texts of the New Testament itself.

As Judith Lieu (1996: 1) observed:

It has, in recent years, become something of a truism to assert that in order to construct *her own* identity, early Christianity had to construct for herself the identity of the '*other*', of Judaism within which she was born, of 'paganism' from which before very long most Christians came. Whereas the latter exercise has caused little anxiety, the process by which the former becomes synonymous with Christian anti-Judaism or antisemitism has justifiably provoked searching analysis.

The original picture is likely to have been quite complicated: 'the discovery of a relentless and endemic Christian anti-Judaism has been succeeded by the detailed mapping of the complex interplay of individual personalities, situations, theological traditions and literary forms which make up the early Christian responses to and constructions of Judaism' (Lieu 1996: 1). At the very least, one should speak not of a single parting but of a pluralist process of partings of the ways.

'The authors and addressees of the New Testament scriptures all lived in the Roman empire' (Stegemann and Stegemann 1999: 2). It would be surprising, then, if these circumstances did not have some effects (however varied) on their descriptions of Christianity. The most striking effects are to be seen in the two-volume work Luke–Acts, and in the book of Revelation. Since the Christian church was apparently going to continue its earthly existence within the political context of the Roman Empire, there were two opposite courses of reaction to the situation: a total withdrawal, damning society to an apocalyptic hell; or some measure of accommodation to the political, cultural, social, and economic context, for the sake of further expansion of the church. In the book of Revelation there is a selective (rather than total) critique of what Rome represented, attacking the structures of power, of trade, and of emperor worship, that were seen as at variance with Christian ideals.

Luke's choice of the second course of action, in an attitude of positive thinking and creative theological accommodation, is evident throughout his two-volume work. For example, Luke (unlike the Jewish historian Josephus) takes a positive view of the Augustan census associated with the time of Christ's birth:

Organized government had at last come to Judaea.... The beginning of a new order for the holy land under Caesar Augustus also marks the beginning of a new order for the holy people under Jesus Christ. Luke had no intention of positing an affinity between the rise of the Zealots and the birth of Jesus, nor of challenging the ideal of *pax Augusta*. Rather the 'world-wide' decree which Luke records united the world under a universal politic of peace, and it provided a fitting birth announcement for him who would found a universal religion of peace. (Walaskay 1983: 27–8)

Luke seeks to present simultaneously two faces of an apologetic within his narrative. He seeks to demonstrate the essential continuity of Christianity with Israel as heir to the promises of salvation history. At the same time he needs to distance Christianity from Israel for the benefit of politically sensitive readers. Unlike the Judaism which brought about the costly Jewish War, Luke represents Christianity as neither rebellious nor legalistic. He claims that it was widely recognized as normal and supportive of good government, for Christians did not set themselves up as critics of Rome's political supremacy. In Luke's narrative, both Jesus and Paul were declared by Roman administrators to be totally innocent.

5. *Priority of teaching* Baird (2002) seemed to claim an objectivity for his own reconstructed paradigm of development (not absolute, but 'sufficiently' certain). But what he regarded as his primary evidence, based on the statistics of vocabulary use and the association of terms (patterns of word usage taken as characteristic of Jesus' teaching, or alternatively of the process of redaction—see Baird 1969) may well be deceptive in this respect. It is only by actually presupposing a certain kind of movement, from the oral and recorded basis of teaching to the biographical and explanatory interpretation of narrative, that one can accord any historical objectivity to this reconstructed version of events. Alternatively, someone who advocates the primacy of story-telling as the heart of the kerygma, and as the basis of narrative theology, would take a different order of priorities. Word-thinking, or such a focus on the ultimate source of teaching, could be either a primary instinct of faith or a theological refinement (a kind of movement of 'back to basics'). The use of a particular vocabulary to express this may actually be formulated to reflect the later realizations, as in Logos doctrine, just as readily as (or more so than) it can express a fundamental instinct.

6. *Shape of the canon* According to its present appearance, the New Testament clearly prioritizes the four gospels. This can be reflected in common usage, as when, for example, Libby Purves writes in *The Times* (10 July 2003) : 'The later strictures of St. Paul are, I think, less binding than what we find in the true core of the Bible, the four Gospels.' There is in the New Testament a substantial collection of letters written to various churches, but these might seem to be subordinated (like an extended appendix of documentary evidence) to the narrative account of the mission of the early Christian church, to be found in the Acts of the Apostles. The book of Revelation comes last, either because its subject-matter concerns the trials and final triumph of Christianity in the ultimate cataclysm at the end of time, or because this book is a reluctant addition to the canon, rather like Daniel among the category of Writings at the end of the Hebrew Bible. None of these empirical observations of the appearance of the New Testament throughout the majority of the Christian centuries seems to be accurate or helpful when it comes to determining how the New Testament actually grew.

Just as we may need to adjust the priorities in, or deductions about, the contents of the New Testament canon, it may also be appropriate to ask about the other early Christian writings which were ultimately excluded from that canon. For this reason some recent writers on the New Testament, with Dominic Crossan (1991: Prologue) as a notable example, have insisted on using the widest range of data and establishing their independent critical methods in doing so. There is then no a priori reason why one should exclude evidence, for example, from the *Gospel of Thomas* in this enquiry. It is necessary to set every work in a historical context, establishing its provenance, and being prepared to distinguish between the earliest context and the later contexts of use or disuse.

A SUGGESTED RECONSTRUCTION OF THE GROWTH OF THE NEW TESTAMENT

1. First Impressions

The starting-point of the reconstruction is the personal encounter between Jesus and another individual. The woman at the well of Samaria (John 4), or Zacchaeus climbing the sycamore tree (Luke 19), might serve as examples of the stereotype, admittedly a theologically enhanced description of just such an event. In the Jewish context established by Geza Vermes (2003), as his contribution to the quest for the historical Jesus, we are encouraged to think of Jesus as a charismatic figure, a miracle-worker and holy man (*Hasid*) from Galilee, who dispenses health and forgives sins. Vermes' comparison is with Honi (in the first century BCE) and Hanina ben Dosa (in the first century CE), who were such charismatic *Hasidim*. Jesus, whether because of his origins, coming from Galilee, or because of what he actually did, was not appreciated by the Pharisaic party in Jerusalem, even though there were identifiable resemblances in his teaching to that of the eminent rabbi Hillel.

First impressions are concerned with what Jesus did and also with what he said. As for his words, the best indication of the style of Jesus' teaching may well be in the briefest of parables, those which have been identified by the techniques of form criticism, or referred to as 'one-liners' (on analogy with one-line jokes) in the description by Bernard Brandon Scott (1981: ch. 3). A good example would be the parable of the mustard seed (Mark 4: 30–2 and parallels). In this way the picture conveyed by the classic film by Pier Paolo Pasolini, *The Gospel According to St. Matthew* (1964), of Jesus striding through the countryside, uttering his teaching to the disciples who follow him, may well preserve quite an accurate first impression.

The point about first impressions is that they comprise the way in which different people react 'from cold' to such an encounter with someone new. For some people the emphasis may be on what Jesus does, for others what Jesus teaches, and for others again what kind of person Jesus is. It is also important that any representative cross-section of responses should include the impact of negative reactions and criticism. Some observers and hearers will not like what they see of Jesus. Others, again, may respond positively, perhaps because they, or someone they know well, have been beneficiaries of a miracle of healing; but they in turn may be the object of interrogation or scrutiny by the religious leadership. A good example may then be the treatment of the man blind from birth and of his parents in John 9. It is important to take into the calculation of first impressions what effect the official Jewish reaction may have had on those Jesus touched. Those involved may find themselves caught up into a defensive argument, where ultimately all that can be said is a denial of the counter-arguments, an expression of amazement and a simple statement of belief. This kind of first impression and reaction to criticism marks the beginnings of what subsequently develops into religious apologetic.

2. The Forms of Remembering

Any recollections will assume a formal shape, even if the person remembering is not too conscious of any attempt at structuring. The simplest forms will be those most appropriate to the application of what is remembered. So the person who is, for example, good at telling jokes will gather material into the memory in forms, probably triggered by cue-words, for the most effective recollection and communication of the humorous anecdote. In New Testament studies the classic works of the form critics (after the First World War and in the 1920s) still provide us with good guidelines. Their classifications were based on an analysis of the numerous independent units (pericopes or paragraphs) found, for example, in Mark's gospel.

More recent work in narrative theology and comparative literary studies has enriched the understanding and importance of the process of telling stories. The basic formal category is that of the tale, referring to stories pure and simple. Their purpose may be just to attract attention, to interest or entertain. In the first place they did not necessarily possess a theological moral or edificatory motive. Such tales could be full of incidental, even trivial, details: these may be based on actual recollections, or may be included to enhance interest; in the long run many such details become lost in the later processes of tradition, as unusual features are smoothed out.

The miracle stories associated with Jesus provide striking examples of such tales. The form critics made comparisons with the style of miracle stories in the Hellenistic world:

Accounts of miraculous healing run as follows: first, the condition of the sick person is depicted in such a fashion as to enhance the magnitude of the miracle. In this connection it is frequently said that the sickness had lasted a long time. Occasionally it is stated that many physicians had attempted in vain to cure the sick person. Sometimes the terrible and dangerous character of the sickness is emphasised. . . . After the introductory description of the illness comes the account of the healing itself. The Hellenistic miracle-stories often tell of unusual manipulations by the miracle-worker; the Gospel accounts, however, seldom mention this trait (Mark 7: 33; 8: 23). The Gospels, however, do retain other typical items. They narrate that the Saviour came near to the sick person—perhaps close to his bed—that he laid his hands upon the patient and took him by the hand and then uttered a wonder-working word. . . . The Gospels occasionally reproduce this wonder-working word in a foreign tongue, as for example 'Talitha cumi' (Mark 5: 41) and 'Ephphatha' (Mark 7: 34) . . . The close of the miracle-story depicts the consequences of the miracle, frequently describing the astonishment or the terror or the approval of those who witnessed the miraculous event. In other cases the close of the narrative shows the one who is healed demonstrating by some appropriate action that he is entirely cured. (Bultmann 1926)

The very naturalness of the narrative pattern revealed by this comparative study itself limits the conclusions that can be drawn by historians: either this is how it happened, or this is how such stories were always told.

The form critics identified a mixed form which they called a paradigm or pronouncement story. Here the significance of the story was not in the event or episode described, but in the saying which comes as the climax to the narrative. Typical examples are the controversy about the Sabbath in Mark 2: 23–8 and the episode of the demon-possessed child in Mark 9: 14–29. Sometimes the setting and the action of the story may seem little more than a foil to the significant saying. The critics disputed among themselves how such a mixed form might have originated: was the paradigm created from the story by the addition of the saying? or was the story specially constructed as a context for the saying? or is the mixed form itself original? The narrative of the healing of the paralysed man (Mark 2: 1–12) could well have existed as a separate story, while Mark 10: 13–16 (where the children are brought to Jesus) looks more like a natural foil for the saying.

It is clear that the sayings of Jesus could have been collected, apart from the stories, for their own significance. The formal category of separate sayings is a broad one: it has been subdivided into distinct groupings, such as parables and similes, proverbial sayings and aphorisms, and conversations where the saying of Jesus fits in a context of controversy. Each of these groups may have been created and maintained for its own reasons. The parable, or specially constructed story, goes beyond the tale in its function as a teaching vehicle, with its focus in a single moral or statement of truth (the similitude), or perhaps a coded message making a controversial comment on a current situation (the allegory). The proverb serves as a widely remembered jewel of wisdom, available for use as a slogan or watch-word. The comments of Jesus on an issue of controversy, such as the relation of his teaching to that of Judaism, could well be preserved within a context of debate, simply because that controversy was still relevant to Jesus' followers at a later stage.

The modern biography seems incomplete without a pen-portrait of what its subject looked like—and probably descriptions of parents and grandparents as well. By contrast, there is no evidence that those who preserved recollections of Jesus were concerned to record his physical appearance. Possibly a good analogy is with the enigmatic references to, and lack of any description or identity of, the Teacher of Righteousness in the Dead Sea Scrolls. The earliest Christian representations of Jesus worked with stereotypes—a fact which is scarcely surprising in an age when even high-born Romans could be content with conventional images rather than personal portraits. But there were forms of recollecting the person and personality of Jesus, if not his appearance. It was a matter of attaching to him an appropriate or approximate label: master/teacher, messiah, even worker of miracles or magician. To ascribe a role-label to him was to attempt a classification of what the experience of him had meant. It was still a long way from the later investment in titles for Jesus, in the earlier or later stages of a Christological formulation. But perhaps the first step in this direction was to recollect the use of a term of honour and respect, the Greek word *kyrios*, simply translated as 'Sir' but in its ambiguity opening up the possibilities of honouring a teacher, revering a superhuman personality, or building a connection to the term used for the unique deity of the Hebrew Bible. We should come back to this starting-point of Christological thinking at a later stage.

It is likely that the earliest form of recollection of Jesus was an attempt at explaining what went wrong with his ministry and why he died. For those who believed in him, this was a matter of the utmost urgency, to show why they still held to, or had recovered, their belief in him. There was need for an account of Jesus' last days from the Christian standpoint, to tell the story in such a way as to confront criticism, to demonstrate Jesus' innocence of the charges brought against him by Jews or Romans, and to explain the events as the fulfilment of prophecy. So aspects of the story of Jesus' trial and death began to be assembled into a narrative. The much later development of this story within Mark's gospel illustrates two of the major motives which drove this recollection; this account emphasizes Jesus' innocence (e.g. 14: 48–9, 56; 15: 14) and the way prophecy has been fulfilled (e.g. 14: 18; 15: 24, 26). Again it will be necessary to revisit this basic recollection, to see how it evolves in the later stages (3 and 4 below).

A final category of recollection, for which there is also some evidence preserved in the New Testament, is the attempt to describe the experiences of Jesus' resurrection and the post-resurrection experiences of him. The tradition seems to move in these two directions that are potentially divergent. The shortest (and probably most original) ending of Mark's gospel, breaking off at 16: 8, offers an enigmatic, restrained, but powerful statement of the circumstances of the empty tomb.

Another way of looking at the experience is in terms of the sequence of revelatory visions listed in Paul's First Letter to the Corinthians at chapter 15. Here the cumulative witness of Christians, to their own individual or collective encounters with Jesus after his crucifixion, is brought together to attest the weight of Christian tradition, in the face of Corinthian difficulties with the concept of resurrection, with which Paul is wrestling at a later stage.

3. Putting Recollections to Use

Already there are hints of the various purposes of recollection, given the occasions and the format for doing so. It is possible to be more precise about some of these applications, at an early stage of religious self-awareness among the first Christians.

The earliest form critics (in the first decades of the twentieth century) emphasized particularly the need to preach the *kerygma*—the good news about Jesus—as a missionary activity to attract converts. So the kerygmatic principle almost became a slogan in this understanding of New Testament growth. It became highly controversial, as other scholars contested the underlying idea of the uniqueness of the earliest form of gospel preaching, questioning whether it was actually unparalleled in the Jewish or Graeco-Roman worlds. Some New Testament scholars rediscovered the idea of the gospels as biographies and drew analogies in the neighbouring cultures. Other scholars asserted the importance of other principles which shaped early Christian communication, and suggested that these were more important than the kerygmatic principle. But the idea of the *kerygma* deserves to be retained, even as one of several principles shaping the tradition. The New Testament gospel material is not biographical, at least not in the way in which the modern or the ancient world understood biographies. One form critic preferred the term 'pseudo-biographical' as doing justice to the skeletal framework of a life of Jesus—almost from birth to death—but also emphasizing the inadequacy of the classical 'lives of Jesus' as a way of understanding the gospel. To return to the kerygmatic principle as important for the growth of the gospels does not mean that all the early Christian groups were by definition equally evangelistic, or even evangelical. The New Testament texts can be used to demonstrate different theories of mission, including the internal mission to existing members.

The form critics, and many others since, have wanted to speak of the first Christians as a group gathered for worship. By reading between the lines of various New Testament texts, it is possible to reconstruct the situations and the particular forms and intentions of worship, without too much anachronistic reference to later church practice and liturgies. One of the best examples of this kind of reconstruction can be found in a slim book by Walter J. Hollenweger, entitled *Conflict in Corinth* (1982). The form critics employed the skills of detective work to identify the poetic forms of hymns within the writings of the New Testament, and argued that such materials were designed to meet the needs of the group for worship.

There is considerable scope for disagreement here in particular reconstructions. Would one expect the early Christians to worship in the Jewish tradition, or to break out into more classical forms of poetry, or even to operate with a bilingual form of liturgy such as has been detected in the early chapters of the book of Revelation (e.g. *nai amēn*, 'so be it, amen', 1: 7)? But even with such disagreements, scholarship has made considerable gains: one can identify an underlying structure of a hymn in Paul's Letter to the Philippians (2: 6–11) and make a good case for Paul's deliberate adaptation of a familiar and regularly used worship-text, in order to make significant corrections to Philippian belief and ethical practice. In modern terms it is only possible to imagine this working effectively where a pastor has a close relationship with his or her congregation and knows the importance to them of the words in their worship-book.

Another clue as to early Christian practice of worship may be found in Paul's First Letter to the Corinthians, referring in chapter 11 to the commemoration of the Last Supper. It is possible to read verse 26 ('as often as you eat this bread and drink the cup, you proclaim the Lord's death until he comes') as evidence for the repetition of an account of Christ's passion at a celebration of the Eucharist ('you tell the story of the Lord's death'). Evidence such as this is an important step towards the literary form of the Passion narrative as a fundamental part of the gospel, as will be seen in the next section (4).

In the previous section (2) the ambiguity inherent in the term of respect and role label *kyrios* ('Sir') was cited as possibly marking the starting-point in a movement towards defining the person of Christ. The suggestions conveyed by this term in both Greek and Hebrew thought worlds would be followed up, measured against the experience of the first disciples, and complemented by an experimental range of other terms and titles. The field of possibilities opens up to messianic terms developed from the Hebrew Bible. It is probable that the significant and mysterious term 'Son of Man' is first developed by early Christians operating within a Jewish tradition and seeking to match their exegesis of texts such as Daniel 7 with their experiences of Jesus' ministry as representative of humanity and at the same time an enigmatic revelation of an elusive presence. As the Church preached about the cross of Jesus (as in the Passion story just mentioned), so the cross seems to have become the symbol—not the stumbling-block (1 Cor. 1: 23–4)—in the argument for Jesus' messiahship. Understanding the death and understanding the person of Jesus become mutually interactive tasks.

As well as attempting a definition of Christ, the early Christian was beginning to define what it meant to be a follower of Christ. This was partly an extension of a process of apologetic (glimpsed in section 2 as the defence of Jesus' innocence in the fulfilment of prophecy) which entailed defending what one does in following him, against the accusations or derision of one's adversaries. It also involved the development of a pattern of ethical practice appropriate for a follower of Christ. In Hellenism and in Hellenistic Judaism there were formulated instructions as to what the individual should do in his or her particular station in life (as husband and wife, children and parents, masters and slaves). The Christian community in turn adopted such traditional instructions and formulae, while developing the exhortations and empowering them as directions which received their authority 'in the Lord'. This process of Christian adoption and adaptation of traditional patterns of behaviour can be seen in what are known as the Household Codes (*Haustafeln*). The basic form is visible in Col. 3: 18–4: 1 and elaborated in Eph. 5: 22–6: 9, and elsewhere (cf. 1 Pet. 2: 13–3: 12).

4. The Transition from Oral to Written Materials

The fact is sometimes overlooked that the letters of Paul are among the first writings of the New Testament. In this way the simple order of the books can be misleading. Paul's First Letter to the Thessalonians is probably the oldest written text in the whole collection. But equally it needs to be remembered that Paul's letters are not just literary deposits; they are real letters, written to particular churches, at a certain time, to meet a particular situation. They are occasional documents, written by someone with a passionate concern and a pastoral care. While one must always make allowances for the differences between oral and written communications, it can still be said that Paul wrote (or dictated to a secretary) what he would probably have uttered directly if he had been present. The practice among Christian communities of reading the latest letter of Paul in the context of their meeting for worship would have enhanced the sense of direct authority, as well as anticipating the later practice of liturgical reading.

A similar desire for a directly authoritative text would lie behind the wish to preserve the actual words of Jesus' teaching. Evidence bearing on the process of collecting Jesus' individual sayings seems to have become more substantial in recent years. There are two main reasons for this. One is the consolidation of academic reconstructions of the synoptic sayings source, usually referred to as Q, being the initial letter of the German word *Quelle* or 'source'. Earlier reconstructions were highly subjective and impressionistic. Later versions, while still reconstructions, and often reflecting individual preferences, have achieved a measure of academic collaboration and agreement, resulting in the critical edition produced by Robinson, Hoffmann, and Kloppenborg (2000). The other reason is the recognition of possibly analogous collections of sayings in extant manuscripts, which can demonstrate what an alternative collection to the synoptic source actually looked like. The *Gospel of Thomas*, significant in other ways as a Gnostic text, has grown in importance as such an organized collection of sayings. The early

Christian work, the *Didache*, or Teaching of the Twelve Apostles, also demonstrates the development of the process of a collection of sayings in the further stages of interpretation and application to the needs of a religious group.

There is a Jewish process whereby the sayings of individual celebrated rabbis are remembered and preserved; but their system here is thematic, relating such sayings by different rabbis to a particular scriptural text or doctrinal theme. In the Christian process the sayings are remembered, because they are sayings of Jesus himself, and in addition because they have a direct relevance to the needs of his followers. Recent studies of analogous texts such as the *Didache* and the *Gospel of Thomas* have tended to focus on how they serve the needs of the believing community. In the same way, for example, Burton Mack (1993), in his reconstruction of Q, took special account of its community orientation. Similarly Richard Valantasis (1997) in his reading of the *Gospel of Thomas*, and in a proposed commentary on Q, seeks to show how such texts have an 'ascetical use, as a means of forging an alternative subjectivity, defining alternative social relationships, and constructing an alternative symbolic universe'. These are texts which function, not so much as a window on the teaching of the historical Jesus, but as a constructive and catechetical influence on the religious individual and group.

On two previous occasions there have been references to the significant function of the story of Jesus' death. The importance for both *kerygma* and worship in the early Christian community can be symbolized by the strategic position and scale of the Passion Narrative in the gospel of Mark, as well as its theological development in the later tradition. Chapters 14 and 15 of Mark stand apart because of their extended and firm narrative thread, contrasted with the separate units of narrative elsewhere in the gospel. The cohesion of these chapters is largely due to its longer period of existence as a set narrative, because of the definitive significance of its contents and the frequency of its use.

Paul refers to the credal importance of this summary of faith in the opening verses of 1 Corinthians 15. These summary statements set the pattern for a literary development of the *kerygma* of the death and resurrection 'of the Son of God and Lord, proclaimed in the word and present in the cult of the Church—the Lord who is at the same time the Rabbi and Prophet Jesus of Nazareth' (Bornkamm 1957: 750). Paul Winter (1961: 5) described the process of literary development:

The Gospel grew backward; the end was there before the beginning had been thought of.... Only later, when the Gospel had grown, was the story of Jesus' Passion prefaced, as it were, by reminiscences of events in his life. The point at which the Gospel begins was traced back from the time of his death to the time of his baptism; later to his birth; and finally—to begin with the very beginning—to the Word that was with God.

Other reactions could be far more radical and urgent, among some more fanatical religious adherents, in a process which was committed to developing a text for the *kairos* (the opportune time or critical moment) interpreted as now. 'Not only the Jews but the whole world had to begin all over again. This existing world had gone wrong. It was a world of injustice and oppression, exploitation and anxiety. It would perish because of its own transgressions in a great divine judgment. But then a new world would begin' (Theissen 1987: 23).

As an example, following Theissen who uses an edited version of this text, one can take *Sibylline Oracles* 3: 767–95, from a Jewish section in this book of oracles, probably written in the second century BCE, which was circulated widely in antiquity. The themes of this particular text are built up from the prophecy of Isa. 11: 1–9.

> And then, indeed, he will raise up a kingdom for all
> ages among men, he who once gave the holy Law
> to the pious, to all of whom he promised to open the earth
> and the world and the gates of the blessed and all joys
> and immortal intellect and eternal cheer. . . .
> (for mortals will invoke the son of the great God)
> [This line is an explicitly Christian interpolation].
> Wolves and lambs will eat grass together in the mountains.
> Leopards will feed together with kids.
> Roving bears will spend the night with calves.
> The flesh-eating lion will eat husks at the manger
> like an ox, and mere infant children will lead them
> with ropes. For he will make the beasts on earth harmless.
> Serpents and asps will sleep with babies
> and will not harm them, for the hand of God will be upon them.

A similar kind of development of prophecies, in a continuing exposition of an underlying text, can be found in the use of Daniel 7 in 4 *Ezra* 11. The clearest example within the gospels of this kind of writing is the so-called 'Little Apocalypse' in Mark 13. Often associated with the threat of the Roman emperor Gaius (Caligula) to interfere with the Holy of Holies in the Jerusalem Temple, and if so to be dated to the years after 40 CE, this text itself provides a scheme of apocalyptic expectation which was developed in subsequent writing (see Court 1982).

A different kind of reason for seeking to develop a written text would be to lay down rules for social living (in what time might remain). It might seem very obvious that followers of Jesus should follow his example in behaviour, and accordingly should formulate guidelines of Christian practice. But the academic evidence offered surprises by its paucity, perhaps for two reasons: ethical questions often receive lightweight treatment in New Testament introductions; and some issues are further complicated because of textual difficulties. To give one example of the latter, the episode of the woman taken in adultery may be found at the beginning of John 8, but is not thought to belong to this gospel. Given its textual problems, what weight should be attached to the story when considering the prototypes for Christian ethics?

An earlier section (3) has already referred to the Household Codes as formulae from the ancient world which could be applied in this new Christian context.

To these codes could be added the stereotypical lists of virtues and vices, to be found in the same context in Colossians (3: 5–17) and Ephesians (4: 2–3, 17–24). The new setting is the authority given 'in the Lord' to such examples of practice. But there are more distinctive aspects of New Testament ethics which must be acknowledged. These include the example of Jesus Christ himself in grace and humility (e.g. 2 Cor. 8: 9; Phil. 2); the teaching of Jesus (in the sermons of Matthew and Luke, in the parable of the Good Samaritan, and in the love command of John's gospel and its demonstration in the foot washing of John 13); the distinctive contribution made by Paul (e.g. in the working out of the relationship of faith and obedience in Galatians); and finally, but still pervading the rest, for reasons that we have seen, the context of eschatological urgency and challenge (e.g. 1 Cor. 7: 28–31).

5. The Invention of the Gospel

On reflection, it is no accident that the first words of Mark's Gospel speak of the 'beginning of the gospel'. In the first place the word 'gospel' denotes something more dynamic (kerygmatic) and less literary than our immediate understanding; it is also the case that the syntax of Mark's opening verses is debated—is this 'beginning' the appearance of John the Baptist or the substance of the Old Testament proof-text? But whatever the immediate interpretation, it seems reasonable to hold the view that Mark (or at least an early form of Mark) is—to the best of our knowledge—the prototype of the gospel form. But even if Mark is credited rightly with the first shaping of this preaching and teaching about Jesus, arising from the twin facts of Jesus' death and resurrection, it is still appropriate to ask about the special characteristics and theological emphases of Mark's own composition. The provocative proposals of Wrede's classic work of 1901, concerned with the messianic secret (that Jesus was indeed the Messiah but wanted it kept secret) as a leading characteristic of Mark's gospel, and suggesting that it was more a theological device than a historical fact, still deserve to be taken seriously.

The new invention identified in the structure of Mark's Gospel is the combination of the Passion narrative with a range of other materials, many of them reflecting the controversies faced by the early Christians. This includes the challenge regarding Jesus' identity and power represented by the miracle stories, and the other kinds of challenges in the teaching of Jesus, particularly in the shock tactics of the parables. Given such challenges, the rationale of any gospel is to suggest a response from Christian experience to the awkward questions and theological implications about Jesus. It is almost inevitable that a small group of Christians in a particular place are the ones grappling with these problems and working out their solutions in the ways that suit their group context and worship practice.

Missionary teachers, such as Paul and Peter, are seen to travel between centres. Inevitably comparisons are made, and insights adopted from other Christian groups. But the starting-point will be with local questions and answers. An important book, edited by Richard Bauckham in 1998, sought to challenge widely held assumptions about gospel origins: that gospels were produced for particular communities and express the characteristic theology developed in those groups; and that inevitably they reveal at least as much about the social context of those communities as they do about Jesus. Scholars need to be challenged to face up to the pervasive nature of their theories and the dangers of the circular argument. But Bauckham's challenge, though timely, was inconclusive. The scholarly basis is far from flimsy, given the reality of the differing but synoptic strands of the gospel tradition, which invite the comparative analysis and identification of local pressures and concerns that biblical theologians have recognized.

In the broadest way one needs to acknowledge the fact of a gospel defined for a community: for example, to distinguish in early Christianity between the Jewish communities connected with the historical Jesus and the Gentile communities confessing the risen Christ. To quote from the Stegemanns' distinction, based on sociological principles:

Under the concept *followers of Jesus* we include the actual Jesus movement, the so-called early Jerusalem church, and the messianic groups in the land of Israel that in our view are represented by the Gospels of Matthew and John.... By contrast, the Christ-confessing communities outside Israel—even with all their affinities with Jewish religious tradition— are no longer a phenomenon of Judaism, above all for sociological reasons. (Stegemann and Stegemann 1999: 4)

In the absence of precise geographical references, to assign any of the canonical gospels to a particular place in the tradition is almost bound to be controversial. Whereas in the first half of the twentieth century John's gospel was regarded primarily as reflecting Hellenistic culture, thereafter a new look at this gospel revealed a fairly introvert, Jerusalem-orientated community, firmly built on Jewish principles, on analogy with the evidence from the Dead Sea Scrolls about the Qumran sect. The battleground was frequently the relationship with Judaism, given the proliferation of variants on the Jewish tradition in the first century CE, revealing a situation as complex as modern Jewry in its secular and varied religious aspects. While Paul crossed and re-crossed the boundaries of Judaism and Gentile life, Matthew's account of the teaching of Jesus is firmly related to the Jewish law. This evangelist's interpretation is modelled on the work of the scribe 'trained for the kingdom of heaven' (13: 52). The fierce criticism of 'scribes and Pharisees' in chapter 23 is no contradiction of this view, but a natural consequence, given the Jewish traditions of active debate. The greatest contrast is provided by the evangelist who is believed to have followed Paul on at least some of his journeys into the Gentile world. Luke's is the gospel for a wider audience, and the sequel to this gospel, the Acts of the Apostles, supplies the reader with such a wider context, in its missionary activity to the heart of the Roman Empire.

6. The Partings of the Ways

Since this larger question has already been considered at the outset, its impact can be described in summary at this point in the reconstructed story. The variety of relationships between Judaism and the early Christian groups can be illustrated by examples from inside and on the boundaries of the New Testament. In a situation which is almost impossible to define with any precision—either early in the story, or much later in some backwater—is the work known as the *Didache* (or Teaching of the Twelve). This provides an important continuity with traditional Judaism in several aspects: the delineation of the two ways (life and death) as a scheme of ethical teaching, the presentation in an eschatologically charged apocalyptic context, and the depiction of the Christian mission in terms of wandering charismatics in the traditions of Old Testament prophecy and priesthood.

It has just been noted that the Gospel of John stands in the Jewish messianic tradition, analogous in some ways to the Dead Sea Scrolls. But this gospel also contains explicit references to the fractured relationship between Christian believers and the synagogue (John 9: 22; 12: 42; 16: 2). Was this break the actual catalyst which produced the gospel? Or are these additions to the original text which bear witness to the developing historical experience of the parting of the ways? According to one reconstruction, the harsh strictures against the Jews in chapter 8 referred originally to those Jewish disciples of the historical Jesus who defected because his teaching proved too demanding (8: 31; cf. 6: 60). Subsequently, after the Council of Jamnia excommunicated the 'Heretics', this became, in Christian experience, a condemnation of Jewish informers against the Christians (see Martyn 2003, although other scholars differ).

A further stage, when the newly erected boundaries are actually crossed, could be represented by the theological essay known as the Letter to the Hebrews. The censure on apostasy in Hebrews 6 bears comparison with what we have just seen in John 8. In the same way, the language of Old Testament ritual comes close to the treatment of such themes in the extra-canonical *Epistle of Barnabas*. To use the language of the Jewish tradition here does not mean that one's theology is defined by it. On the contrary, the 'word of exhortation' (Heb. 13: 22) is a drive to Christian earnestness in moral and spiritual terms which should go beyond and transcend the pattern of Jewish faith and practice out of which Christianity has emerged.

These movements could be called descriptions of a journey which at different points have led to a parting of the ways. As the texts witness to groups who act in certain ways, they are open, as has been indicated, to the possibilities of sociological analysis. It should also be remembered that there are great developments taking place here in theological and Christological terms. If the first impressions of Jesus evoked awe and respect, the later developments sought to use role-labels, many of them from Judaism, while at the same time wrestling at the sublime end of the spectrum with the problems posed by Jewish monotheism. At the stage represented in Hebrews, there is a preference for the mystical language of the heavenly Son of Man rather than for Jewish messiahship. And the priestly/sacramental/sacrificial dimension has its focus on the mysterious figure of Melchizedek and does more than merely suggest the inferiority of the Old Testament system of sacrifice.

7. Towards the Theological Definition of the Church

In sociological terms, the Christian groups come to a recognition of their separate existence. This experience entails an attempt to redefine their group identity. At this stage the theological agenda includes the important item of ecclesiology. The available terminology comes from Jewish and Graeco-Roman sources, and, as with the first steps in defining Jesus, these moves towards defining the religious grouping can take advantage of existing ambiguities. This group has a sense of vocation, but for what purpose exactly is it summoned?

There are three New Testament books—of rather different kinds—which contribute in the longer term to this task of group self-definition. They are the Acts of the Apostles, the Letter to the Ephesians, and the book of Revelation. Despite their obvious differences, their tasks can be seen as complementary to each other, within the ultimate structure of the New Testament canon.

The broadly historical narrative of Acts reveals an organization which moves from the smallest beginnings to a public witness at the heart of the Roman Empire. Although various figures move across the narrative, there is a concentration on two figures, Peter and Paul, who are presented as a definition of apostolic ministry. They share the church, as the pair of Roman consuls would share the classical ideals of the Republic. There is no sign here of the controversy surrounding Paul's apostleship, which he declares honestly in his letters; instead, Paul takes the major role, and his apostolic commissioning is reinforced by the threefold repetition of the Damascus experience. The authority of the church is clear, as is its direction in mission. What are much less clear from these pages are the answers to the subsidiary questions about church orders and ministries, or the relationship between water and spirit baptisms as the initiation into church membership. On the other hand, the 'breaking of bread' is a clear symbol of belonging, and of participation in the experience of revelation, ever since the two walked to Emmaus in Luke 24: 13 ff.

As with Hebrews, it might be better to describe the Letter to the Ephesians as a theological essay. It probably dates to the last quarter of the first century, and seeks to expound some of the ideas of Pauline theology particularly in relation to the church, its unity in the Holy Spirit, and its future development in salvation history. The structure of the exposition is systematic and complex, matched by its expression in long complex sentences. The theory of the church expounded here is universal, rather than localized, founded by the apostles in the past (2: 20). The historical perspective is balanced by a sense of development, in which the church is God's new creation in an eschatological programme that was inaugurated by Christ's resurrection (2: 1–10). The promise that the Gentiles will be incorporated into the church is here fulfilled (2: 11–19). The process of evolution in the church is both practical and theoretical: it is made concrete in the structure of the household of God, identified as the body of Christ; it is also an evolution with a sense of mystery as it moves to its ultimate 'omega point'.

Historical evolution and theological structure are complemented, in the third place, by the visionary dimension of the potential and responsibilities of the church in the book of Revelation. Various symbols assist in inspiring the reader with this vision. The Christian experience is authorized at the outset by the risen Lord, Christ himself; he communicates not only to the seer, but also to the seven angels or spirits of God who represent the church in its symbolic totality and equally in its local actualization (seven representative church communities). The church plays its part in the visions of heaven in the form of the worshippers, the twenty-four elders, the martyrs, the representatives sealed from the twelve tribes of Israel, the two prophetic witnesses of Revelation 11, perhaps even the woman clothed with the sun in Revelation 12. Pre-eminently there is the new Jerusalem figure, the bride adorned for the messianic marriage, who forms a bridge between earth and heaven. The visionary inspiration for the church members, confronted by all kinds of trial and suffering, is to be found in the promises made to the one who is victorious (chapters 2 and 3), promises fulfilled in membership of the New Jerusalem (chapters 21 and 22). With this vision of Revelation, then, we find the culmination and climax of the process of growth of the New Testament.

RETROSPECT

This suggested reconstruction has proceeded with the benefit of hindsight and a number of scholarly hypotheses. Although an account of growth almost automatically carries with it a sense of chronological development, in this case it is important to emphasize that not all early Christian communities will have trodden the same path through these same progressive stages. Some groups will have by-passed some stages, or seen this or that step as irrelevant to them. It is not necessary to conclude that all Christians will have arrived at the same climax of religious experience as is seen in the vision of Revelation.

The New Testament can be defined (as at the outset in this article) as an assemblage, or in other words 'a collection of documents in diverse forms written by a number of different individuals both named and unnamed to an assortment of churches and individuals living in different areas, or with few or no hints as to their addressees, and for a variety of reasons' (Achtemeier *et al.* 2001: 4). But the New Testament, viewed holistically, also 'represents the collective experience and under-standing of the Christian community during the formative years of its existence' (Achtemeier *et al.* 2001: 608). So even if one begins by recognizing fragments of religious experience, it is almost inevitable that one will end up with the phenom-enon of the church, its disciplines, doctrines, and ethics, and the canon of Scripture finally closed (see Chapter 43 below).

The story of the movement in the first centuries towards the canon of the New Testament has three particularly significant historical features, or catalysts, and three literary aspects. A collection of texts becomes self-limiting, and effectively closed, both to protect what is within the collection and to guard against unwel-come additions. The historical catalysts just mentioned are identified as, first, the existence in the first centuries of groups with alternative Christian philosophies, often labelled 'Gnostic'; if their rationale is too different, they need to be held at a distance. Secondly, there is the influence, in the mid-second century, of Marcion, whose programme was to exclude both the Old Testament texts and any elements that echoed the Old within the New Testament. And thirdly there was a second-century movement known as Montanism which emphasized the elements of prophecy, continuing charismatic inspiration, and a revolutionary view of the future. The canon originated, at least in part, in reaction to these pressures within and without.

The three significant literary aspects concern the gospels, the epistles, and the other texts with apostolic associations. Towards the end of the second century, particularly as defended for symbolic reasons by the church father Irenaeus (*Adv. Haer.* 3. 1. 1; 3. 11. 8), the gospel texts, earlier referred to as the recollections or memoirs of the apostles, were seen as authoritative by virtue of their being four in number. At this stage other gospel texts are known to have existed. Secondly, a collection of letters has been assembled, believed to have been written to newly founded churches and other contacts by apostolic missionaries such as Paul. The significant aspect here is the way in which the Pauline letter collection achieves a primacy and is the model for future collections. Thirdly, the other texts (besides gospels and epistles) are included in the collection as well. The Acts of the Apostles fulfils a supportive function in relation to the letter collection: in both Paul is pre-eminent. Other essays, like Ephesians and Hebrews amplify the theological discussion. And the Apocalypse, or book of Revelation, from first to last is a disturbing presence in the collection, and is liable to rejection for reasons of language, Old Testament ethos, theology, or ethics. But for its champions, Revelation is the culmination of the church's self-understanding and the climax of the process of growth of the New Testament.

Suggested Reading

This chapter covers the New Testament ground in a rather different way from many books, which specialize in either the historical or the literary aspects. A broadly based introduction to the New Testament materials has been co-written by Achtemeier, Green, and Thompson 2001. An unusual presentation of the earliest stages of the process of experiencing Jesus is offered in Theissen 1987 (and more recent reissues). A Jewish perspective on the New Testament materials is Geza Vermes, *The Changing Faces of Jesus* (New York: Viking; Harmondsworth: Penguin, 2001). Two other substantial treatments of particular angles on the critical questions are Gerd Theissen's analysis, in Religious Studies terms, of the symbolic system of early Christianity, *A Theory of Primitive Christian Religion* (London: SCM Press, 1999); and a study of Christianity from the aspect of worship (particularly baptism and the Eucharist), Étienne Nodet and Justin Taylor, *The Origins of Christianity: An Exploration* (Collegeville, Minn.: Liturgical Press, 1998).

Bibliography

ACHTEMEIER, PAUL J. 2001. *Introducing the New Testament, its Literature and Theology*, ed. in association with Joel B. Green and Marianne Meye Thompson. Grand Rapids, Mich.: Eerdmans.

BAIRD, J. ARTHUR 1969. *Audience Criticism and the Historical Jesus*. Philadelphia: Westminster Press.

—— 2002. *Holy Word: The Paradigm of New Testament Formation*. JSNTS.S 224. Sheffield: Sheffield Academic Press.

BAUCKHAM, RICHARD 1998. *The Gospels for all Christians: Rethinking the Gospel Audiences*. Grand Rapids, Mich.: Eerdmans.

BORNKAMM, GUNTHER 1957. 'Evangelien'. In *Religion in Geschichte und Gegenwart*, ii, Tübingen: Mohr.

BROWN, RAYMOND E. 1994. *The Death of the Messiah*. London: Geoffrey Chapman.

BULTMANN, RUDOLF 1926. 'The New Approach to the Synoptic Problem'. *JR* 6: 337–62.

COURT, JOHN M. 1981. 'The Didache and St. Matthew's Gospel'. *SJT* 34: 109–20.

—— 1982. 'Paul and the Apocalyptic Pattern'. In M. D. Hooker and S. G. Wilson, eds., *Paul and Paulinism: Essays in Honour of C. K. Barrett*, London: SPCK, 57–66.

—— 2002. *New Testament Writers and the Old Testament: An Introduction*. London: SPCK.

CROSSAN, JOHN DOMINIC 1991. *The Historical Jesus: The Life of a Mediterranean Jewish Peasant.* San Francisco: Harper.

DUNN, J. D. G. 2003*a.* 'Altering the Default Setting: Re-envisaging the Early Transmission of the Jesus Tradition' (Presidential Address at Durham meeting of *Studiorum Novi Testamenti Societas,* August 2002). *NTS* 49: 139–75.

—— 2003*b. Christianity in the Making,* i: *Jesus Remembered.* Grand Rapids, Mich., and Cambridge: Eerdmans.

ELLIS, E. EARLE 1998. 'New Directions in the History of Early Christianity'. In T. W. Hillard, R. A. Kearsley, C. E. V. Nixon, and A. M. Nobbs, eds., *Ancient History in a Modern University,* ii, Grand Rapids, Mich.: Eerdmans, 71–92. (Lecture first delivered at Abilene Christian University in 1993.)

GARROW, ALAN 2004. *The Gospel of Matthew's Dependence on the Didache.* JSNTS.S. London: Continuum and T. & T. Clark International.

GREGORY, ANDREW, and TUCKETT, CHRISTOPHER, eds. 2006*a. The Reception of the New Testament in the Apostolic Fathers.* Oxford: Oxford University Press.

—— —— 2006*b. Trajectories through the New Testament and the Apostolic Fathers.* Oxford: Oxford University Press.

HALLIWELL, STEPHEN 2003. A review of Craig A. Gibson, *Interpreting a Classic* (University of California Press, 2002). *Times Literary Supplement,* 14 Feb. 2003, p. 11.

HENGEL, MARTIN 1972. 'Christologie und neutestamentliche Chronologie'. In H. Baltensweiler and B. Reicke, eds., *Neues Testament und Geschichte: Oscar Cullmann zum 70. Geburtstag,* Zürich and Tübingen: Theologischer Verlag, 43–67.

HOLLENWEGER, WALTER J. 1982. *Conflict in Corinth.* New York: Paulist Press.

INSTONE-BREWER, DAVID 2002. *Divorce and Remarriage in the Bible.* Grand Rapids, Mich.: Eerdmans.

LIEU, JUDITH M. 1996. *Image and Reality: The Jews in the World of the Christians in the Second Century.* Edinburgh: T. & T. Clark.

MACK, BURTON L. 1988. *A Myth of Innocence: Mark and Christian Origins.* Philadelphia: Fortress Press.

—— 1993. *The Lost Gospel: The Book of Q and Christian Origins.* Shaftesbury: Element Books.

MARTYN, J. LOUIS 2003. *History and Theology in the Fourth Gospel,* 3rd edn. Louisville, Ky.: Westminster/John Knox Press.

PETERSEN, WILLIAM L. 1994. *Tatian's Diatessaron: Its Creation, Dissemination, Significance and History in Scholarship.* VigChrSupp. Leiden: Brill.

ROBINSON, JAMES, M., HOFFMAN, PAUL, and KLOPPENBORG, JOHN S. eds. 2000. *The Critical Edition of Q: Synopsis.* Leuven: Peeters.

ROBINSON, J. A. T. 1976. *Redating the New Testament.* London: SCM Press.

SCOTT, BERNARD BRANDON 1981. *Jesus, Symbol-Maker for the Kingdom.* Philadelphia: Fortress Press.

STEGEMANN, E. W. AND STEGEMANN, W. 1999. *The Jesus Movement: A Social History of its First Century.* Minneapolis: Fortress Press.

THEISSEN, GERD 1987. *The Shadow of the Galilean.* London: SCM Press.

VALANTASIS, RICHARD 1997. *The Gospel of Thomas.* New Testament Readings. London: Routledge.

VERMES, GEZA 2003. *Jesus in his Jewish Context.* London: SCM Press.

WALASKAY, P. W. 1983. *And So We Came to Rome: The Political Perspectives of St. Luke* SNTSMS. Cambridge: Cambridge University Press.

WILLIAMS, ROWAN 2001. General Introduction to G. Rowell, K. Stevenson, and R. Williams, eds., *Love's Redeeming Work: The Anglican Quest for Holiness*. Oxford: Oxford University Press.

WINTER, PAUL 1961. *On the Trial of Jesus*. Studia Judaica, i. Berlin: W. de Gruyter.

WREDE, W. 1971. *The Messianic Secret*. London and Cambridge: James Clarke. ET of German original of 1901.

CHAPTER 31

AUTHORS, BOOKS, AND READERS IN THE ANCIENT WORLD

ALAN MILLARD

1. OLD TESTAMENT TIMES

(a) Mesopotamia

Authors

Putting one's name to a written text may indicate presence as a witness, or agreement as a party to a deed, ownership of the text, responsibility for accuracy, or authorship. Each of these is attested in the Old Testament world. Authorship is necessarily admitted in letters and related to letters are prophetic communications. Numerous examples of prophecies from Mari in the eighteenth century BCE and from Assyria in the seventh century include or are accompanied by the names of those who spoke the oracles (Nissinen in Nissinen *et al.* 2003). Clearly there would be value in knowing which prophet's words proved to be true. Inscriptions celebrating a king's military prowess or building works were usually composed as if the monarch was speaking, 'I am . . .', but the authors were the royal scribes, all of whom remain unknown, with the exception of the writer of the formal letter to the god Ashur, 'Sargon's Eighth Campaign' (Luckenbill 1926–7: ii. 99, §178). Kings also declared their responsible rule by proclaiming laws, asserting that they did so at divine command. Earliest are the Sumerian 'Reforms of Uru-inimgina' (formerly read Urukagina), c.2350 BCE (Hallo 2000); then there are the 'Laws of Ur-Namma', c.2100 BCE, and of Lipit-Ishtar, c.1930 BCE (Roth 2000a, b). In Babylonia the name of the author of Laws of Eshnunna is uncertain, but Hammurabi proudly enacted his laws shortly after, c.1760 BCE (Roth 2000c, d). Later law collections do not retain their authors' names (Roth 2000e, f). Authorship is less commonly displayed in works of literature; indeed, the most extensive range of literary compositions from the Old Testament world, the Sumero-Babylonian, is largely anonymous. The authors of major compositions, such as the Epics of Creation, of Gilgamesh, of Atrahasis, and of the Descent of Ishtar to the Netherworld, are unnamed, as are those of the stories about Sargon of Akkad and other famous kings. No authors are known for the many Sumerian literary works preserved mainly in copies of the early second millennium BCE, with the exception of the hymns to Inanna (Ishtar) spoken by Enheduanna, the daughter of Sargon of Akkad, c.2300 BCE, whom he installed as high-priestess of the moon-god at Ur. Modern opinion accepts the attribution, making her 'the first non-anonymous and non-legendary author in history' (Hallo 1997: 519). An author who may be classed as 'legendary', is Shuruppak, who gives advice on life and behaviour to his son, Ziusudra, the Babylonian Noah, in 'The Instructions of Shuruppak'. This 'wisdom' composition already existed among the oldest surviving Sumerian literary manuscripts copied about 2600 BCE at Abu Salabikh and lived on for another millennium or more, when there was a Babylonian translation (Alster 1974). Another sage whose advice to his son was copied in Hattusha and at Ugarit in the Late Bronze Age was the otherwise unknown Shube-Awilim (Foster 1996: 330–4). In some Babylonian works the authors reveal themselves obliquely through acrostics, where the first syllable of each line, read in sequence, spells out the name and profession, as is the case in the wisdom poem known as 'The Babylonian Theodicy' (Foster 1996: 790–8). In the 'Poem of the Righteous Sufferer', or 'The Babylonian Job', the speaker is named in the course of the text, although whether he was the author, or not, cannot be decided (Foster 1996: 306–23). Hymns and prayers to the gods from the third millennium BCE onwards were written in the names of kings who uttered them in rituals (e.g. Foster 1996: 68–71, 240–3, 724–44) and there are a few examples in the names of other individuals (Foster 1996: 486–94), with the names occasionally hidden in acrostics (Foster 1996: 610–11, 704–9). While those individuals may have composed the poems, it is impossible to tell whether the kings had or not; some indications may suggest that they could have done so (e.g. Foster 1996: 231, 697). The clearest statement of authorship in Babylonian texts is given at the end of the Epic of Erra: 'The composer of its text was Kabti-ilani-Marduk, of the family of Dabibi. He (the god) revealed it to him at night, and when he spoke it while he was waking, he omitted nothing at all, not one line did he add. When Erra heard it he approved', and uttered a blessing on everyone who recited or heard about his feats (Foster 1996: 759–89).

Beside the names occurring in the texts, Babylonian scribes in the first millennium BCE had traditions about authorship, associating gods and humans with particular works (Lambert 1962). Thus Ea, the god of wisdom, was credited with some incantations, rituals, and omen compendia, the early third millennium BCE king Enmerkar with a hymn about the date-palm, and a series of cultic personnel with a range of works including hymns and prayers, and the Theodicy whose author's name is given in an acrostic in the text itself (see above). Several identifiable poems, introduced as 'The series of' Gilgamesh, Etana, etc., are credited to specific individuals. The name given for the Gilgamesh Epic is Sin-leqe-unninni. That belongs to a name-type current in the second half of the second millennium BCE, so cannot be the name of the primary author, for copies of the epic survive from earlier in the millennium. The best conclusion is that this man edited older texts to produce the version that became widespread in the first millennium (George 2003: 28–33).

Analysis of some Babylonian works and the existence of manuscripts of different dates for some compositions disclose the activities of editors over the centuries. While some writings were handed down for generations unaltered, as the Laws of Hammurabi were for more than 1,000 years, changes ranging from single words through phrases to whole episodes occur in others (e.g. the Atrahasis Epic (Foster 1996: 160–203); Nergal and Ereshkigal (Foster 1996: 410–28)). There is a tendency for later copies to expand earlier texts, as in the Great Prayer to Ishtar, which 'provides an excellent case study in how a Mesopotamian literary text could evolve or expand and still remain true in its essentials to the intentions of the original author' (Foster 1996: 503–9, esp. 503). The changes that took place in the various manuscripts of the Gilgamesh Epic written between c.1800 and 180 BCE have been discussed extensively (Tigay 1982; George 2003: 39–47). However, a truly consistent pattern is hard to see. Having only an early second millennium copy, it would be difficult, if not impossible, to predict what changes might appear in a copy made eight or ten centuries later; nor could a second millennium version be reconstructed with any confidence at all on the basis of a first millennium copy alone. A short composition about the futility of life is preserved in Sumerian and in a Babylonian translation, in copies dating from c.1800 to 650 BCE found in Babylonia, Syria, and Nineveh which reveal 'creative recensions' (Lambert 1995: 37–42). Some compositions could be used in more than one of the extensive rituals, and older liturgical texts could be modified to be applied to new situations (e.g. a prayer to Shamash that had a place in a royal purificatory rite also served in the dedication of a statue (Seux 1976: 220–3); various Sumerian prayers (Cohen 1981: 36–9) or the same hymn may be addressed to one deity in one copy and to another in a second (e.g. Gula and Belet-ili (Foster 1996: 576–7)). That scribes might recognize how they were changing texts handed down to them is indicated in one case by the notation 'Addition' at the end of one Sumerian hymn in an extensive collection (Sjöberg and Bergmann 1969: 8, 24). The colophons of some copies of established works made in the first millennium indicate more than one exemplar, and there are commentaries which sometimes note variant readings, signs that scribes were aware of the vagaries of textual history.

Books

The usual physical form of the book in Babylonia was the clay tablet, normally of a size convenient to hold in the left hand while the right impressed the cuneiform signs with a reed stylus. Larger tablets were laid on a flat surface for inscription, and were often ruled in vertical columns. The cuneiform signs appear to hang from horizontal lines, and those are physically ruled on some tablets. Scribes were concerned that their work should be intelligible to the readers, and usually avoided splitting a word between two lines, either crowding the signs into one line, or carrying them over two lines, usually leaving a space in the middle rather than at the end of a line. In letters scribes would include glosses on words they thought obscure—well-known examples occur in the El-Amarna Letters—but explanatory notes can be found in narrative texts also, and are clearly not added later to the compositions (Krecher 1969). From early in the second millennium onwards, Akkadian translations of Sumerian works were made, sometimes in interlinear form. Literary tablets which survive from the third and early second millennia BCE are mostly the products of pupil-scribes, copied as exercises in language, style, and accuracy. Attention to the accuracy is plain in the occasional notations 'broken' or 'new break' showing where the exemplars were defective. At the end of Sumerian compositions a title is given, 'Hymn to X', or an indication of the genre of song, prayer, or lament, and frequently those and other works end with a note 'Praise the god(dess) X' (e.g. Safati 1997; Cohen 1981). The copyists rarely added their own names to Sumerian works, but fuller information is given for three tablets of the Babylonian Epic of Atrahasis produced by a student *c.*1635 BCE, forming a classic colophon: name of the composition, number of the tablet if more than one, number of lines on the tablet with the total on the last tablet, scribe's name, date (Lambert and Millard 1969: 31–2). Similar colophons indicating who was responsible for the copy appear later in the second millennium and in the first, sometimes adding the name of a second scribe who collated the copy. Extra lines may state that the tablet was made for an individual or for a specific library, for reciting, singing, or reading (Pearce 1993). There may also be a note of ownership; Ashurbanipal's name and title were stamped on some tablets made for his library at Nineveh, and a curse might be added on anyone who stole the tablet (Hunger 1968).

Beside clay tablets, cuneiform was written on wax-covered wooden boards (*le'um*) which could be joined by hinges into pairs or longer sets. They were in use from the end of the third millennium BCE and were primarily intended for running accounts, registers, and similar administrative records. However, these boards could also contain compositions of a more literary type, and the colophons of some clay tablets state that they had been copied from writing boards. Actual examples of writing boards survive only from the first millennium: the ivory specimens from Nimrud which held the omen series *Enuma Anu Enlil* extending to some 5,000 lines, wooden fragments from Nimrud, and a wooden board from Assur (Wiseman 1955; Klengel-Brandt 1975).

Readers

The complexity of the cuneiform script meant that reading was a skill confined to those trained in scribal schools, some of whom may have progressed from the scribal profession to take other offices in temples and royal courts. Where colophons give the names of the owners of tablets, they were often professionals engaged in religious or semi-religious functions (exorcists, singers, diviners) as well as priests and scribes (Hunger 1968). Contrary to often repeated statements, books were not the prerogative of temples and palaces, a deduction made partly from the recovery of Ashurbanipal's 'library' at Nineveh in the earliest days of Near Eastern archaeology. Continuing excavations throughout Mesopotamia have recovered numerous collections of clay tablets from private houses of all periods, which, while mostly comprising business and legal documents, sometimes include literary works (Pedersén 1998). The tablets were stored in baskets, jars, or on shelves, and labels from such containers list literary compositions that were once in them (Hoffner 2002). Some of the householders belonged to the professions noted already; some were scribes who made their homes into schools, where they taught their craft to apprentices. Sumerian essays describe the experiences of such apprentices, their curriculum and stages of progress (Tinney 1999). They not only copied existing works, they also made up their own, for schooling involved the creation of didactic works, like the Sumerian 'debates' (Vanstiphout 1997).

An author's words, written by himself or by a scribe, would remain unknown unless they were copied or read by others. How a work reached an audience, or who that audience might have been, is not clear. Rituals required texts that would be recited regularly and precisely, and cultic changes could demand new texts, of which the Babylonian Creation Poem is a prime example, resulting from the pre-eminence given to Marduk late in the second millennium BCE (Foster 1996: 350–401). Individual scribes might compose hymns or prayers of personal piety for themselves or for clients; some prayers have a space left for an individual's name to be inserted, or the words 'So and so'. How and why the major Babylonian literary works came to be composed, and then written, is obscure; there is no way to tell whether the written forms were the end result of lengthy oral traditions, or the compositions of individual scribes who put them into writing immediately (Vogelzang and Vanstiphout 1992). The praise of particular gods may have been one purpose of the Epic of Atrahasis, a story which explains how Babylonian society came to be (Atrahasis III. viii. 9–18; Foster 1996: 185). The Epic of Gilgamesh tells a good tale with a variety of characters and adventures, aiming to give the lesson that man is mortal (George 2003: 33–9). Questions about the cycle of life and life after death may lie behind the stories of deities descending to the underworld and either remaining there (Nergal and Ereshkigal), or supplying a substitute (The Descent of Ishtar). Unhappy historical circumstances in Babylon are apparently explained by the Erra Epic, and tales about kings of the past, like Sargon of Akkad (Foster 1996: 103–8, 251–7, 803–4), may have carried a sense of nostalgia. Some lines recur in two or more compositions (Reiner 1985: 32–3), and scribes sometimes quoted lines from standard works in letters; but who, apart from them, would recognize such allusions remains unknown. Most of the Sumerian compositions recovered are products of the schoolroom in the Old Babylonian period, but whether they had their origin there or were copied from tablets written in other contexts is unknown.

(b) Egypt

Authors

Most of ancient Egyptian writing is anonymous. Accounts of the pharaohs' achievements were composed at royal command by chosen, but unnamed, scribes for carving on temple walls and other monuments. To celebrate Ramesses II's famous battle with the Hittites at Qadesh (c.1275 BCE), a lengthy poem was created with the king as narrator, supplemented by a more prosaic, third-person narrative, both accompanying the pictorial presentation. The whole has been judged Ramesses' inspiration, carried out by his best scribes and artists to produce 'a unique phenomenon in Egyptian literature' (Gardiner 1960: 46, 47, 53; Kitchen 2000).

From early in the Sixth Dynasty, c.2300 BCE, come private tomb memorials relating notable deeds in the lives of the deceased, written in prose with some poetic passages, and these continue until the end of ancient Egyptian history (see Kitchen 1999). Undoubtedly the majority were composed by scribes on the basis of personal information provided. Most famous among these 'autobiographies' is the story of Sinuhe, the account of an exile's life in Canaan and eventual return to honour in Egypt in the twentieth century BCE. The oldest manuscripts of this text were copied about a century after the time of the setting of the story (Lichtheim 1997a). No tomb of Sinuhe has been found, so debates continue about the nature of the narrative, whether it is a straightforward tomb inscription, an adaptation of one to promote political interests, or a piece of fictional propaganda, the last appearing unlikely in view of the accuracy with which life in Canaan is portrayed (see Posener 1956; Parkinson 1997; Kitchen 1996b). Similarly, the report of Wenamun (Lichtheim 1997c) has been characterized as a factual, first-person account of a journey to Byblos to procure cedar wood c.1075 BCE (Čzerny 1952), but some

Egyptologists treat it as a 'novelistic' composition (see Gardiner 1961: 306; Eyre 1996). The New Kingdom has provided a number of small funerary stelae set up by individuals which include 'psalms' praising the deity, pleading for favour and even suffering punishment from the god for sin and being rescued by him. In some cases there are clearly personal circumstances which imply either custom-made composition by a scribe or creation by the individual himself (examples in Kitchen 1999: 269–314).

The books for which authors are regularly named are the books of 'wisdom', for effective instruction requires authority, and 'wisdom' requires personal authority. Significantly, a thirteenth-century BCE scribe who lauds the immortality that authorship confers by saying that authors' names live on in the books they made, then cites eight names, four from the Old Kingdom and four from the Middle Kingdom (Wilson 1955). Two of the former are the authors of surviving 'wisdom' books, Ptahhotep and Hardedef (Wilson 1955), one, Kaires, may have been the father whose name is missing from the Instruction for Kagemni (Lichtheim 1973–80 : i. 59–61), and the fourth was the polymath Imhotep, to whom no extant books can be attributed. Two of the Middle Kingdom names are attached to 'books of instruction': The Prophecy of Neferti and The Complaints of Khakheperre-Sonb (Shupak 1997). One was said to be the author of the Instruction of Amenemhat (Lichtheim 1997b) and the fourth name has been associated with the Loyalist Instruction (Posener 1976). These authors' names were probably known because their works were copied in scribal schools (Lesko 1994: 138–43). The names of other authors are preserved in their works: Ipuwer, Amenemope, Amennakht, Dua-Khety, Any, Ankh-sheshonqy, mostly, again, known from the copies made by pupil-scribes, sometimes very corrupt. How far these names truly represent the authors of the works is debated. The Middle Kingdom language of Ptahhotep and Kagemni has led some to the conclusion that they are pseudepigrapha, although reflecting the Old Kingdom period (Lichtheim 1973–80: i. 6–7). Other scholars see no reason to doubt these attributions, the writers having held posts at various levels, some in the royal court, others as teachers (see Kitchen 1998: 346–9). When a king is said to have composed instructions for his son, as in the case of the Teaching for Merikare (the father's name is damaged; the date is a little before 2000 BCE), it may be assumed that the book was written at the king's behest; the extent of his own contribution cannot be known, but the fact that there is evidence for literate kings (see below) suggests they could have involved themselves in creating such works. Beside the 'wisdom' works, some Egyptologists identify a specific genre,the 'Königsnovelle', narratives in which the king is hero, solving an awkward problem, although its existence may be doubted (Loprieno 1996b; Leprohon 2001; contrast Redford 2001a; for a list of the Egyptian texts, see Redford 1992: 374–7).

Editorial activity can be seen or assumed within scribal circles. The copy of the Maxims of Ptahhotep, made about 2000 BCE, is written in Middle Kingdom Egyptian, not the language of the Old Kingdom, as Hardjedef is, and so, assuming the book is an Old Kingdom composition, the language has been modernized. By the thirteenth century BCE that version was so archaic that a thoroughly revised text was created (Lichtheim 1973–80: i. 61–80). In other cases modernization of language is evident when New Kingdom expressions replace Middle Kingdom ones or old ritual texts are rephrased in later language. Some of these substitutions may have been made unconsciously, but most will have been deliberate. Sufficient knowledge is now available about the history of the Egyptian language from a wide range of texts to enable such distinctions to be made.

Books

The availability of stone in Egypt meant that multitudes of texts were carved in tombs, on rock surfaces, and on stelae. They are mainly royal inscriptions or funerary memorials, the latter often containing prayers and sometimes biographical narratives. Books were written on rolls of leather or, more commonly, papyrus; the oldest papyrus roll known is a blank one, buried in a tomb for the owner's use c.3000 BCE. The papyrus sheets were made from strips of pith peeled from the papyrus reed and laid side by side with a second layer on top at right angles to the first. The two layers were pressed or hammered together, the sap forming a glue, then the surfaces polished with a smooth stone. Writing was normally done along the horizontal fibres. The sheets were approximately 30 × 20 cms. (11 × 8 in.), glued side by side to make rolls on average 4 m. long, but extra sheets could be added at will, and one roll is 40.5 m. (133 ft.) long. The full height of the sheet was not often used for literary texts; rolls were bisected or cut even shorter, down to 10 cm. (4 in.). Excerpts from books were copied on ostraca, or wooden tablets, probably as writing exercises, so that some compositions are represented by many manuscripts of varying extent and quality. The texts were written with black ink made from soot and gum, with headings, opening phrases, and rubrics in red ink, made from red ochre. Exercise texts sometimes have red dots to show division of phrases or accentuation. Not all owners cared for their books. When papyrus was not readily available, the roll might be turned over and its back used for something else, or the ink washed off, or pieces might be cut from a roll and reused.

Besides the 'wisdom' works with named authors (see above), there is as great a variety of Egyptian literature as of Babylonian. The books range from technical treatises on topics such as mathematics, medicine, dream interpretation, and magic spells, through love poems and wisdom literature, to matter-of-fact narratives like Sinuhe and Wenamun, to fantastic tales like Cheops and the Magicians and the Shipwrecked Sailor up to myths about the gods and hymns to them. (For a catalogue of surviving Egyptian literary manuscripts, see Quirke 1996.) Absent from Egypt are collections of laws, perhaps because, in theory, the pharaoh's word could not be challenged, although records of lawsuits survive, and there were archives of past cases which could be consulted. Also absent are continuous chronicles of events covering more than one reign, distinct from individual kings' annals, the 'demotic chronicle' for the third century BCE being exceptional (Spiegelberg 1914).

Readers

In Egypt most scribes were occupied with administrative tasks; tomb models and tomb paintings show them listing deliveries, estimating yields, or ready to record their masters' orders. The able or well-connected might leave behind such mundane tasks as they rose through the hierarchy to positions where they employed secretaries of their own. The highest in the land might claim scribal skills: Ramesses II's monuments report that he 'researched in the office of archives and unrolled the writings', and his son Merneptah was described as 'the Royal Scribe with skilled fingers' (Kitchen 1996a: 183, 214). Tutankhamun's tomb was furnished with many imitation writing palettes, but a real one, gold-plated, from early in his reign and an ivory one from a later year bear his name and had been used, presumably by the boy-king (Carter 1933: 79, 80). Literary compositions present kings as able to read and write as a matter of course: e.g. the Middle Kingdom Prophecy of Neferti 15 ff., in which the king writes the words of the sage (Shupak 1997: 107).

Scribes were trained in 'the house of life' attached to temples or administrative offices in larger towns, and perhaps simply by following professional scribes in smaller places. When they graduated, they might copy books for patrons, for temples and for themselves. The activity of one scribe who composed five short poems and a brief 'wisdom book' in the twelfth century BCE has been traced, together with the work of some of his pupils (Bickel and Mathieu 1993). It seems to be the personal copies that have been recovered, and in a relatively few cases their provenance and treatment are known. Books might be placed in tombs for the delectation of the dead in the afterlife—copies of several classic literary works are thought to have been found in the Twelfth Dynasty tomb of their Theban owner (Parkinson 1997: 1). One letter tells of depositing papyri in an ancestor's tomb in the twelfth century BCE, although it is not clear whether that was for the benefit of the dead, or simply for safe-keeping (Pestman 1982: 156–7). Those papyri would have been kept in their owners' houses with the letters and papers of daily business, as found in the Twelfth Dynasty workmen's village at Lahun (Collier and Quirke 2002: pp. x–xiii) and in the Nineteenth and Twentieth Dynasty tomb-builders' village at Deir el-Medineh. The latter collection, accumulated within one family for over 100 years, included technical compositions (medical and magical prescriptions, a book of dream interpretations) and literary works, among them the Contendings of Horus and Seth, the Hymn to the Nile, and love poetry (Pestman 1982). In addition, hundreds of ostraca found in and around the village bear extracts from literary writings, the products of scribes amusing themselves, practising or quoting texts, or, most commonly, the exercises of their pupils. The papyri and ostraca together, the books from Deir el-Medineh, it has been said, 'represent most of the literature surviving from ancient Egypt' (Lesko 1994*a*: 133). Whether this collection would have been duplicated widely in other settlements in the Nile Valley, or only in major towns, is impossible to say, just as it is impossible to know how widely the literature was known outside scribal circles. While it has been said that although '99% of the documentation from the most important of Egypt's cities, towns, temples, and other work sites is missing—jar labels etc. indicate literacy extended to household servants' (Lesko 1994*a*: 134), most ancient Egyptians, if they were familiar with the contents of any of their civilization's literature, had learnt it from oral presentations.

(c) The Levant

Scripts and Texts

Sumero-Babylonian texts were copied at Ebla in north Syria *c.*2300 BCE and at many sites during the Middle and Late Bronze Ages. There was probably a scribal centre at Aleppo in the eighteenth century BCE disseminating Babylonian traditions so that secretaries in several towns as far south as Hazor read and wrote cuneiform (Wiseman 1962). In the Late Bronze Age cuneiform was current across the region for diplomatic and local affairs. (For cuneiform texts found in Palestine, see Horowitz, Oshima, and Sanders 2002.) The El-Amarna archive from Egypt has letters from dozens of rulers of Levantine towns, and includes some copies of Babylonian books used for teaching Egyptian scribes to write in Babylonian. That was probably the purpose, too, of the fragment of the Epic of Gilgamesh found at Megiddo. Beside these imports, there is no native, 'Canaanite' literature written in cuneiform. One Egyptian legend seems to echo a Canaanite myth (Ritner 1997), but it is unlikely that Canaanite scribes used Egyptian for writing their own stories. If scribes were writing out literary compositions in Late Bronze Age Canaan, they were probably using the infant alphabet, developed during the previous centuries, but writing in ink on papyrus or leather rolls or on wooden boards, which have not survived. This supposition arises from the situation at Ugarit. There, scribes schooled to use Babylonian language and script learnt of the Canaanite alphabet and created a cuneiform alphabet on its pattern, for writing on clay tablets. Examples of their work include several books: the Epic of King Keret, the Story of Aqhat, the Ba'al cycle of myths, and the myth of Dawn and Dusk (Pardee 1997). With the fall of the Late Bronze Age towns of the Levant, this script disappeared. The tablets from Ugarit demonstrate the existence of an indigenous literature in coastal north Syria beside the Mesopotamian cuneiform repertoire. These tablets date from the thirteenth century BCE, evidence for the existence of any local written literature at earlier dates has not been found (Millard 1999).

The Aramaean kingdoms of the first millennium BCE adopted the alphabet, but inevitably the only lengthy texts available today are the royal monuments on stone. The earliest is the Tell Fekheriyeh Statue, *c.*840 BCE, which is unusual in being largely a translation from an Assyrian original (Millard 2000*a*). The three Sefire stelae (*c.*750 BCE; Fitzmyer 2000) preserve the terms of a treaty with curses on the oath-breaker which evidently continue old and widespread forms. About 800 BCE someone at Tell Deir 'Alla in the Jordan Valley copied a column of a book roll on to the plaster of a wall. The script is Aramaic, each word is separated from the next by a point, and certain phrases are written in red ink. A word omitted by haplography could be inserted above the line (Millard 1982: 148). The language is a local dialect related to Aramaic. The opening words serve as the title, 'The Book of Balaam, son of Beor'. Here is the oldest example of a book in a West Semitic language written with the alphabet, and the oldest piece of Aramaic literature. It narrates visions of catastrophe given by the gods to Balaam (Levine 2000). The next piece of Aramaic literature, chronologically, is a badly damaged composition written on the walls of a tomb at Sheikh Fadl in Egypt in the fifth century BCE. The passages that can be read include references to rulers of the seventh century BCE, religious expressions, and declarations of love (Lemaire 1995). By this time the words are simply separated by spaces. From about the same time come the papyri from a colony of Aramaic speakers on Elephantine Island in the Nile, near Aswan. Apart from small pieces, there are two major compositions, one a version of the 'Behistun Inscription' of Darius I, the other the Wisdom of Ahiqar. Each was contained on a papyrus roll, the Ahiqar text being written on the back of an old account book which was about 13.5 m. long, although Ahiqar itself occupied only twenty-one columns or so, needing about 5.6 m. This is the oldest example of a West Semitic book roll (Porten and Yardeni 1993: C 1–2).

Authors

Some of the Ugaritic literary tablets concerning Ba'al, Keret, and Aqhat have an initial note *lb'l, krt, l'qht*. While similar to the notes in the headings of some Hebrew psalms, these are not to be treated as notes of authorship; they simply designate the composition they belong to (Pardee 1997: 241 n. 4; 268 n. 241). Similarly, the Tell Deir 'Alla text opens with 'The book of Balaam' (*spr bl'm*), but there is no indication that he was reckoned its author, unlike Ahiqar, which starts, 'These are the words of Ahiqar' (Porten and Yardeni 1993: 26–7).

Readers

Among the literary tablets from Ugarit, a few end with colophons naming the scribe Ilumilku, a highly placed official in the royal court during the last days of Ugarit (Millard 1979: 613; Dalix 1999: 15). Whether he wrote them for reading to his master, or for some other purpose, is unknown. Who would read the Balaam text, or in what context, is not clear, for the nature of the building where it stood is uncertain, and the purpose of the Sheikh Fadl text is equally obscure. The Ahiqar and Behistun papyri were presumably copied by scribes or people able to write for their own education and delectation, perhaps for reading aloud to others.

Hebrew

(a) *Extra-biblical*   The existence of Israelite literature much earlier than the seventh century BCE—indeed, of any extensive written texts in Israel—has been denied (Thompson 1992: 391; Blenkinsopp 2001: 41), but the epigraphic evidence from excavations there and the consistent testimony from other cultures contradicts that. A few fragments on potsherds and wall plaster imply the production of longer texts which would have been written on perishable papyrus or leather (Millard forthcoming).

(b) *Biblical*   The Hebrew Bible is unrivalled as a collection of books from a single culture in the ancient Near East. No other culture is known to have created continuous historical narrative, a unified account of the nation's origins and establishment, such lengthy compilations of prophets' words, or so large an anthology of hymns. At the same time, the Hebrew books share forms and patterns which were current in other ancient Near Eastern societies. The books of the Hebrew Bible were produced over a long period and show great variety of content and differences of style (see Part IV in this volume).

Authors

The attachment of personal names to several biblical books has given the mistaken impression that those persons wrote the books bearing their names. In most cases nothing in the texts supports such a claim; the names indicate *the*, or *a*, major actor in the book: e.g. the books of Joshua, Samuel, Job, on the same pattern as the books of Kings. The ascription 'Books of Moses' is no different; Moses is the key figure in the Pentateuch. Just as the notations on Ugaritic tablets indicate their subject-matter, so the headings of many Psalms, 'of David' (*ldwd*) may celebrate him, although they may equally well signify authorship. Where individual authorship may be claimed is in books of wisdom and prophecy which are, significantly, the same types of composition for which authors are named in Babylonia and Egypt. In Wisdom literature the Proverbs of Solomon is a prime example, giving the king's name both in the initial sentence (1: 1) and at the head of chapter 25, where additions were made in Hezekiah's reign. As with Egyptian instructional works especially, the name need not denote the originator of every sentence, but rather that the collecting was done at his behest or in his honour. That does not mean that he had no part at all in the composition.

Prophetic collections indicate the speaker of the oracles: e.g. 'The words of Amos', without requiring him to be the author. Habakkuk was told to write his vision (2: 2), and Isaiah was ordered to write his unborn son's name and to seal a text (Isa. 8: 1, 16), and one of his visions is described as 'words sealed in a scroll' (29: 11), suggesting that prophets may have recorded their messages themselves. However, Jeremiah may not have been the only prophet who used a secretary (Jer. 36, etc.).

Nehemiah's first-person memoir, unique in the Hebrew Bible, may be compared with the Egyptian 'autobiographies' usually found on statues and in tombs (see above and, for the Persian period, the inscription of Udjahorresne, Lichtheim 1973–80: iii. 36–41).

Books

Within the Hebrew Bible the first reference to writing in a book is Moses' record of the Amalekite war (Exod. 17: 14). Thereafter books are integral to Israel's culture, for religious and secular purposes (e.g. the Book of the Law, Josh. 1: 7–8; the Book of Jashar, 2 Sam. 1: 18; 'the books of the chronicles of the kings of Israel' and 'of Judah', 1 Kgs. 14: 19, 29, etc.). There is no reason to doubt the production of books throughout the history of Israel, written in the limited alphabet inherited from the Canaanites. Leather or papyrus rolls could contain books of any length, and the epigraphic evidence is sufficient to demonstrate the presence of writers from the days of the conquest onwards (Millard 1998a, forthcoming). The inscriptions show that the Old Hebrew script was normally written with a point separating each word from the next, but with no compunction about splitting a word between two lines (Millard 1970). When the Aramaic writing practices of the Persian Empire were adopted, resulting in the 'square' script, spaces were used to separate words, and words were not split across lines.

Intense analyses of the Hebrew books which attempt to discover sources and literary forms have been conducted within the texts, without external controls—that is, with relatively little attention to the abundant literature of the ancient Near East. Yet the Hebrew books conform in many ways to the customs known from elsewhere in the ancient Near East, although the books themselves are not attested in their present forms earlier than the second century BCE (the Dead Sea Scrolls). The lack of earlier copies renders any attempt to trace stages in a history of composition wholly hypothetical; that has proved possible for some Babylonian and Egyptian books only when manuscripts of different dates are available (see above). When the compositions in Egyptian and in cuneiform are taken into account, the Hebrew works can be objectively understood as arising from the same milieu, created in similar ways, and sharing similar features. Written accounts of political or military events, or prophetic utterances, could be made at the time they occurred and might be made simultaneously in prose and in poetry, as with

Ramesses II's Qadesh narrations (see above) and for Tukulti-Ninurta I's conquest of Babylon (Grayson 1972: 108–34; Foster 1996: 211–29). Literary forms have analogies elsewhere (e.g. the Psalms; Gunkel and Begrich 1926; Gunkel 1967), and whole genres are clearly comparable to those in Egypt (Proverbs, Song of Songs; see also Chapter 5 above), while within the books, *inclusio* and chiasm, for example, mark discontinuity, and resumption of nouns etc., continuity (e.g. Baker 1983). At the same time, there are significant differences, notably in the continuous story of Israel from the exodus to the exile, with which the Babylonian Chronicle is only partly comparable, unlike the first-person records left by individual kings, and principally in the consistent theological perspective of history, hymnody, wisdom, and prophecy.

Discussion of the relationship between oral and written tradition is inconclusive. The existence of oral tradition throughout biblical history is certain, reaching to the 'tradition of the elders' in the Gospels (see Mark 7). There can be no conclusive identification in the written texts of passages that may have originated orally, for supposedly oral forms within the written text can do no more than point to an oral origin for those forms; a scribe could incorporate them in a new written composition without the necessity of any oral precursor. The weight given to written texts throughout the ancient Near East implies that oral versions carried less authority. Spoken words could be put into writing immediately in almost every circumstance, as is especially evident for prophecy (see Nissinen *et al.* 2003), and there would not be many places in Israel which lacked someone able to read or write. (See Niditch 1997 with Millard 1998*b*.)

Readers

According to the biblical texts, public reading of the Law took place at Sinai (Exod. 24: 3, 4, 7; 34: 32), was expected every seven years once Israel was settled in the Promised Land (Deut. 31: 9–13), was envisaged in the prescription for the monument on Mount Ebal, fulfilled after the conquest (Deut. 27: 1–8; Josh. 8: 32–5) and was reported on various occasions (2 Kgs. 23: 2; 2 Chr. 17: 9; Neh. 8). Jeremiah's prophecies were read to officials and to people in the temple (36: 10, 13–15). Two occasions are reported when books were read to a king and his court: the 'book of the Law' read to Josiah (2 Kgs. 22: 10) and Jeremiah's prophecies read to Jehoiakim (Jer. 36: 21–4). Xerxes, king of Persia, sleepless, had the records of his reign read to him, either to induce sleep or to occupy his mind (Esther 6: 1). The Israelite king was expected to provide himself with his own copy of the Law and to read it himself (Deut. 17: 18, 19). Other examples of individuals reading are rare, but Isaiah speaks of presenting a sealed scroll to one who can read and to one who cannot (29: 11–12). Whether or not credence is given to the biblical texts, they carry the assumption of their various authors that writing was accessible at the moments they describe. Although reading and writing were largely confined to the élite, the twenty-two-letter script was not hard to learn, and the epigraphic evidence, notably the graffiti, again suggests that there were people who could read scattered across the land, not confined to palaces and religious centres (Millard forthcoming).

2. NEW TESTAMENT TIMES

Authors

Alexander the Great's conquests brought Greek literature and literary conventions to the Near East, among them the wider use of authors' names. Thus the account of Egyptian history in Greek is known by its writer's name, Manetho, and that of Babylonian history by Berossus's name. In the first century Josephus proudly attached his name to his books aimed at Roman audiences. However, despite the adoption of this custom by Jewish writers using Greek, it does not seem to have become common in religious circles. The 'wisdom' book Ecclesiasticus, includes its author's name, Jesus son of Sirach (50: 27), Baruch transmits a letter, but other books are named after their heroes (Judith, Tobit, Maccabees). Numerous works claiming to report words of men of ancient times were written in the Hellenistic and Roman periods, and so are known by their names, although claims to authorship by those named are not universal (compare the opening of the *Testament of Job*, 'The book of the words of Job' with the 'Psalms of Solomon' in which the king's name does not appear; Spittler 1983; Wright 1985). Their authors were religious people aiming to instruct, to inculcate particular doctrines, or to provide information that the biblical books noted briefly or not at all. The debate over pseudepigraphy needs to keep these points in view (see Baum 2001). The Dead Sea Scrolls have disclosed the continued custom of writing anonymously, even in documents which carry authority, like the Community Rule, although in several cases the beginnings are missing (as in the Temple Scroll and the halachic document known as MMT; Martinez 1994: pp. xxv–xxvii, 3, 154, 77).

The New Testament writings follow the traditional patterns. The letters declare their senders' identities, although not always by name (1–3 John), with the exception of Hebrews, and the single prophetic work makes its author clear (Rev. 1: 1, 4, 9). The historical narratives, the Gospels and Acts, are anonymous, the attributions to Matthew, Mark, Luke, and John being first reported in the mid-second century by Irenaeus (*Adv. Haer.* iii. 1. 1–2), but the dedication of the Third Gospel and the Acts of the Apostles to the same man, Theophilus, is taken to demonstrate their common authorship, the writer being hidden behind the 'we' passages in Acts.

Books

The roll of papyrus or leather remained the standard form of book throughout the Hellenistic period and well into Roman times. Thousands of papyrus fragments from Egypt, the carbonized rolls from Herculaneum and the Dead Sea Scrolls demonstrate that. The Dead Sea Scrolls, hidden about 67 CE, scrolls left at Masada a few years later, and those from caves used during the Second Revolt (132–5) illustrate the shape of biblical books in the first century. The texts were set out in columns, sometimes ruled at both margins, the lines ruled horizontally; there was little attempt to justify the left-hand side of the columns, but spaces were used to indicate divisions in texts. Errors were corrected by writing correct words above the lines, occasionally running down the left margins. The roll continues to be the vehicle for the Scriptures read in synagogues today, often in larger formats than were used in biblical times. However, by the first century wax-coated wooden tablets, long known in the Near East, widely used for memoranda, continuing records, and school exercises, were apparently imitated in papyrus or parchment. The result was the codex, the book with pages. In Rome, the poet Martial commended this form of book as more convenient than the roll for a traveller to read. He had copies of works by Homer and Virgil, among others, in this form (Martial, *Epigrams* I.2, XIV, 183 ff.; Shackleton Bailey 1993). No examples are known among the manuscripts preserved in Egypt or anywhere else from the first century, but literary manuscripts dated to the second century CE do include about twenty works in codex form, beside more than 850 on rolls. The situation in Egypt may not represent the situation across the Roman world; scribes are inherently conservative, and the innovation that Martial welcomed may have spread slowly at first. Intriguingly, almost half of the second-century codex books are Christian products, copies of New Testament books, books of the Septuagint, and apocryphal gospels. Why Christians adopted this novel shape of book is uncertain; it may be related to the indications in the manuscripts that many of them were not made by professional book copyists but by clerks in the administration accustomed to writing notes in notebooks or on wax tablets. Unlike the standard Greek books, the Christian ones have numerals written as ciphers, not as words, and common terms such as Jesus, Lord, Christ, God, abbreviated to their first and last letters, rather than the first two or three letters, as in Greek book rolls, signs that they were not the products of professional copyists. The codex was more economical than the roll, as both sides of the writing material were used; it was also easier to make cross-references from one page to another. By the fourth century the codex had replaced the roll to become the normal form of book for all Greek and Latin literature, and existing works on rolls were either jettisoned or re-copied into codices which could hold much greater amounts of text, even to the complete Christian Bible, as the great codices Vaticanus and Sinaiticus show. (For this paragraph see Millard 2000*b*.)

Readers

Jewish tradition required males to be able to read the Torah, and there were schools throughout Palestine from the first century BCE according to rabbinic sources, borne out by Josephus (Millard 2000*b*: 157). Luke depicts Jesus reading from Isaiah in the synagogue at Nazareth (4: 16) as a matter of course, from which it may be deduced that synagogues held collections of books which may have been available to anyone who wanted to read them or hear them read. In his addresses Jesus makes an interesting distinction between the Jewish teachers whom he assumes could read the Scriptures and the larger audiences whom he expected to have heard the Law (e.g. Mark 2: 25; 12: 10; Matt. 5: 2 ff; John 12: 23; see Millard 2000*b*: 158).

The owners of the Dead Sea Scrolls were zealous Bible students who believed that Scripture was written specifically for their situation. Accordingly, they tried to apply it to their circumstances through commentaries, which applied ancient names to current events (e.g. the Kittim of Cyprus denoted the Romans), and used variant readings and word-play. (On the biblical texts at Qumran, see Chapter 6 above.) In the course of their studies they copied books of the Bible whole and also made extracts, copying chapters or sections on different rolls or juxtaposing separate verses. If the owners of the Scrolls were Essenes, Josephus's report that Essenes were to be found in the towns and villages of Judaea, whether totally or only partially true, suggests that copies of the books of the Hebrew Bible and of those basic to the sect, such as the Community Rule, might be found in their homes. The Rule required continual reading of the Law in the community (6. 7–8; Martinez 1994: 9).

That the early Christian communities similarly included members able to read is demonstrated by the despatch of letters to them by Paul and others. Note Paul's request that his Letter to the Colossians be read to the Laodicean church, and vice versa (Col. 4: 16). The apostle owned books (2 Tim. 4: 13), and he is unlikely to have been unique in this respect. The Gospels, too, were directed to Christian communities for instruction and for use in proselytizing (Bauckham 1998).

That ancient Israel settled as a nation in a land where the early alphabet was current, and that the Christian church arose in a region where Aramaic and Greek were widely written and read, can be seen as providential: literacy has proved essential to the survival of both Judaism and Christianity.

SUGGESTED READING

The most extensive recent collection of Babylonian texts in translation is Foster 1996; CoS i–iii provide a wide range of texts from the whole of the ancient Near East, supplemented by the older collection, Pritchard 1969. *Ancient Near Eastern*

Texts Relating to the Old Testament. Princeton: Princeton University Press, which contains some relevant texts not in CoS.

BIBLIOGRAPHY

ALSTER, B. 1974. *The Instructions of Shuruppak: Mesopotamia*, ii. Copenhagen: Akademisk Forlag.

BAKER, D. W. 1983. 'Diversity and Unity in the Literary Structure of Genesis'. In Millard and Wiseman 1983: 197–215.

BAUCKHAM, R. 1998. *The Gospels for All Christians*. Edinburgh: T. & T. Clark.

BAUM, A. D. 2001. *Pseudepigraphie und literarische Fälschung im frühen Christentum*. Tübingen: Mohr.

BICKEL, S., and MATHIEU, B. 1993. 'L'écrivain Amennakht et son enseignement'. *Bulletin de l'Institut français d'archéologie orientale au Caire*, 93: 31–51.

BLENKINSOPP, J. 2001. 'The Social Roles of Prophets in Early Achaemenid Judah'. *JSOT* 93: 39–58.

CARTER, H. 1933. *The Tomb of Tut-ankh-amen*, iii. London: Cassell.

CHARLESWORTH, J. H., ed. 1983, 1985. *The Old Testament Pseudepigrapha*, i, ii. New York: Doubleday.

COHEN, M. E. 1981. *Sumerian Hymnology: The Eršemma*. Hebrew Union College Annual Supplements, 2. Cincinnati: Hebrew Union College.

—— SNELL, D. C., and WEISBERG, D. B. 1993. *The Tablet and the Scroll: Near Eastern Studies in Honor of William W. Hallo*. Bethesda, Md.: CDL Press.

COLLIER, M., and QUIRKE, S. 2002. *The UCL Lahun Papyri: Letters*. BAR International Series, 1083. Oxford: Archaeopress.

ČZERNY, J. 1952. *Paper and Books in Ancient Egypt*. London: H. K. Lewis.

DALIX, A.-S. 1999. 'Suppululiuma (II?) dans un Texte alphabétique d'Ugarit et la Date d'Apparition de l'Alphabet cunéiforme'. *Semitica*, 48: 5–15.

DAY, J., GORDON, R. P., and WILLIAMSON, H. G. M., eds. 1995. *Wisdom in Ancient Israel: Essays in Honour of J. A. Emerton*. Cambridge: Cambridge University Press.

DEMARÉE, R. J., and JANSSEN, J. J., eds. 1982. *Gleanings from Deir el-Medina*. Leiden: Nederlands Instituut voor het Nabije Oosten.

EYRE, C. J. 1996. 'Is Egyptian Literature "Historical" or "Literary"?' In Loprieno, 1996a: 415–33.

FITZMYER, J. A. 2000. 'The Inscriptions of Bar-Ga'yah and Mati'el from Sefire'. In *CoS* iii. 213–17.

FOSTER, B. R. 1996. *Before the Muses*, 2nd edn. Bethesda, Md.: CDL Press.

GARDINER, A. H. 1960. *The Kadesh Inscriptions of Ramesses II*. Oxford: The Griffith Institute, Ashmolean Museum.

—— 1961. *Egypt of the Pharaohs*. Oxford: Clarendon Press.

GELLER, M. J., GREENFIELD, J. C., and WEITZMAN, M. P., eds. 1995. *Studia Aramaica: New Sources and New Approaches. Journal of Semitic Studies Supplement* 4. Oxford: Oxford University Press.

GEORGE, A. R. 2003. *The Babylonian Gilgamesh Epic*. Oxford: Oxford University Press.

GRAYSON, A. K. 1972. *Assyrian Royal Inscriptions*, i: *From the Beginning to Ashur-resha-ishi L*. Wiesbaden: Harrassowitz.

GUNKEL, H. 1967. *The Psalms: A Form-Critical Introduction*, trans. T. H. Hooker. Philadelphia: Fortress Press.

—— and BEGRICH, J. 1926. *Einleitung in die Psalmen*. Göttingen: Vandenhoeck & Ruprecht.

HALLO, W. W. 1997. 'The Exaltation of Inanna'. In *CoS* i. 518–22.

HALLO, W. W. 2000. 'Reforms of Uru-inimgina'. In *CoS* ii. 407–8.

—— and YOUNGER, K. L., eds. 1997, 2000, 2002. *The Context of Scripture*, 3 vols. Leiden: Brill; abbreviated *CoS*.

HERRMANN, A. 1938. *Die ägyptischen Konigsnovelle*. Leipziger Ägyptologische Studien, 10. Glückstadt: J. J. Augustin.

HOFFNER, H. A. 2002. 'Archive Shelf Lists'. In *CoS* iii. 67–9.

HOROWITZ, W., OSHIMA, T., and SANDERS, S. 2002. 'A Bibliographical List of Cuneiform Inscriptions from Canaan, Palestine, Philistia, and the Land of Israel'. *Journal of the American Oriental Society*, 122: 753–66.

HUNGER, H. 1968. *Babylonische und assyrische Kolophone*. Alter Orient und Altes Testament, 2. Kevelaer: Butzon & Bercker.

IZRE'EL, S., SINGER, I., and ZADOK, R., eds. 1998. *Past Links: Studies in the Languages and Cultures of the Ancient Near East: Essays in Honour of Anson Rainey*. Israel Oriental Studies, 18. Winona Lake, Ind.: Eisenbrauns.

KITCHEN, K. A. 1996a. *Ramesside Inscriptions Translated and Annotated: Translations*, ii: *Ramesses II, Royal Inscriptions*. Oxford: Blackwell.

—— 1996b. 'Sinuhe: Scholarly Method versus Trendy Fashion'. *Bulletin of the Australian Centre for Egyptology*, 7: 55–63.

—— 1998. 'Biblical Instructional Wisdom: The Decisive Voice of the Ancient Near East'. In Lubetski, Gottlieb, and Keller 1998: 346–63.

—— 1999. *Poetry of Ancient Egypt, Documenta Mundi: Aegyptiaca 1*. Jonsered: Paul Aströms Forlag.

—— 2000. 'The Battle of Qadesh'. In *CoS* ii. 32–40.

KLENGEL-BRANDT, E. 1975. 'Eine Schreibtafel aus Assur'. *Altorientalische Forschungen*, 3: 169–71.

KRECHER, J. 1969. 'Glossen'. In Von Soden *et al.* 1969: iii. 431–40.

LAMBERT, W. G. 1962. 'A Catalogue of Texts and Authors'. *Journal of Cuneiform Studies*, 16: 59–77.

—— 1995. 'Some New Babylonian Wisdom Literature'. In Day, Gordon, and Williamson 1995: 30–42.

—— and MILLARD, A. R. 1969. *Atrahasis: The Babylonian Story of the Flood*. Oxford: Clarendon Press.

LEMAIRE, A. 1995. 'Les inscriptions araméennes de Cheikh-Fadl (Egypte)'. In Geller, Greenfield, and Weitzman 1995: 77–132.

LEPROHON, R. J. 2001. 'Encomia'. In Redford 2001b: i. 470–1.

LESKO, L. H. 1994a. 'Literature, Literacy, and Literati'. In Lesko 1994b: 131–44.

—— ed. 1994b. *Pharaoh's Workers: The Villagers of Deir el Medina*. Ithaca, NY: Cornell University Press.

LEVINE, B. A. 2000. 'The Deir 'Alla Plaster Inscriptions'. In *CoS* ii. 140–5.

LICHTHEIM, M. 1973–80. *Ancient Egyptian Literature: A Book of Readings*, 3 vols. Berkeley: University of California Press.

—— 1997*a*. 'Sinuhe'. In *CoS* i. 77–82.

—— 1997*b*. 'Amenemhet'. In *CoS* i. 66–8.

—— 1997*c*. 'Wenamun'. In *CoS* i. 89–93.

LOPRIENO, A., ed. 1996*a*. *Ancient Egyptian Literature: History and Forms*. Leiden: Brill.

—— 1996*b*. 'The "King's Novel" '. In Loprieno 1996*a*: 276–95.

LUBETSKI, M., GOTTLIEB, C. and KELLER, S., eds. 1998. *Boundaries of the Ancient Near Eastern World: A Tribute to Cyrus Gordon*. Sheffield: Sheffield Academic Press.

LUCKENBILL, D. D. 1926–7. *Ancient Records of Assyria and Babylonia*. Chicago: University of Chicago Press.

MARTINEZ, F. G. 1994. *The Dead Sea Scrolls Translated: The Qumran Texts in English*, trans. W. G. E. Watson. Leiden: Brill.

MILLARD, A. 1970. '*Scriptio Continua* in Early Hebrew: Ancient Practice or Modem Surmise?'. *Journal of Semitic Studies*, 15: 2–15.

—— 1979. 'The Ugaritic and Canaanite Alphabets: Some Notes'. *Ugarit-Forschungen*, 11: 613–16.

—— 1982. 'In Praise of Ancient Scribes'. *BA* 45/3: 143–53.

—— 1998*a*. 'Books in the Late Bronze Age in the Levant'. In Izre'el, Singer, and Zadok 1998: 171–81.

—— 1998*b*. Review of Niditch (1997). *JTS* 49: 699–705.

—— 1999. 'The Knowledge of Writing in Late Bronze Age Palestine'. In Van Lerberghe and Voet 1999: 317–26.

—— 2000*a*. 'Hada-yith'i'. In *CoS* ii. 153–4.

—— 2000*b*. *Reading and Writing in the Time of Jesus*. Sheffield: Sheffield Academic Press.

—— Forthcoming. 'Books in Ancient Israel'. In Roche *et al.*, Forthcoming.

—— and WISEMAN, D. J., eds. 1983. *Essays on the Patriarchal Narratives*. Winona Lake, Ind.: Eisenbrauns.

NIDITCH, S. 1997. *Oral Word and Written Word: Orality and Literacy in Ancient Israel*. London: SPCK.

NISSINEN, M., with contributions by Seow, C. L., and Rittner, R. K. 2003. *Prophets and Prophecy in the Ancient Near East*. Writings from the Ancient World, 12. Atlanta: Society of Biblical Literature.

PARDEE, D. 1997. 'Ugaritic Myths and Epic'. In *CoS* i. 241–83, 333–56.

PARKINSON, R. B. 1997. *The Tale of Sinuhe and other Ancient Egyptian Poems 1940–1640 B.C.* Oxford: Clarendon Press.

PEARCE, L. E. 1993. 'Statements of Purpose: Why the Scribes Wrote'. In Cohen, Snell, and Weisberg 1993: 184–93.

PEDERSÉN, O. 1998. *Archives and Libraries in the Ancient Near East 1500–300 B.C.* Bethesda, Md.: CDL Press.

PESTMAN, P. W. 1982. 'Who were the Owners, in the "Community of Workmen", of the Chester Beatty Papyri'. In Demarée and Janssen 1982: 155–72.

PORTEN, B., and YARDENI, A. 1993. *Textbook of Aramaic Documents from Egypt*, iii: *Literature, Accounts, Lists*. Winona Lake, Ind.: Eisenbrauns.

POSENER, G. 1956. *Littérature et politique dans l'Egypte de la xiie dynastie*. Paris: Bibliothèque de l'École des Hautes Etudes, 307. Paris: Libraire ancienne Honoré Champion.

PRITCHARD, J. B. ed. 1955. *Ancient Near Eastern Texts Relating to the Old Testament*, 2nd edn. Princeton: Princeton University Press.

QUIRKE, S. 1996. 'Archive'. In Loprieno 1996*a*: 379–401.

REDFORD, D. B. 1992. *Egypt, Canaan and Israel in Ancient Times*. Princeton: Princeton University Press.

—— 2001*a*. 'Historical Sources: Textual Evidence'. In Redford 2001*b*: ii. 105–6.

—— ed. 2001*b*. *Oxford Encyclopedia of Ancient Egypt*. New York: Oxford University Press.

REINER, E. 1985. *Your Thwarts in Pieces, Your Mooring Rope Cut: Poetry from Babylonia and Assyria*. Ann Arbor, Mich.: University of Michigan Press.

RITNER, R. K. 1997. 'The Legend of Astarte and the Tribute of the Sea'. In *CoS* i. 35–6.

ROCHE, C. *et al.*, eds., forthcoming. *Du Sapounou au Saphon: sur les routes des peuples du Levant*. Paris.

ROTH, M. 2000*a*. 'The Laws of Ur-Namma (Ur-Nammu)'. In *CoS* ii. 408–10.

—— 2000*b*. 'The Laws of Lipit-Ishtar'. In *CoS* ii. 410–14.

—— 2000*c*. 'The Laws of Eshnunna'. In *CoS* ii. 332–5.

—— 2000*d*. 'The Laws of Hammurabi'. In *CoS* ii. 335–53.

—— 2000*e*. 'The Middle Assyrian Laws'. In *CoS* ii. 353–60.

—— 2000*f*. 'The Neo-Babylonian Laws'. In *CoS* ii. 360–1.

SAFATI, Y. 1997. 'Love Poems'. In *CoS* i. 540–3.

SEUX, M.-J. 1976. *Hymnes et Prières aux Dieux de Babylonie et d'Assyrie*. Littératures anciennes du Proche-Orient, 8. Paris: Éditions du Cerf.

SHACKLETON BAILEY, D. R. 1993. *Martial: Epigrams*. Loeb Classical Library, Cambridge, Mass.: Harvard University Press.

SHUPAK, N. 1997. 'The Complaints of Khakheperre-Sonb, The Prophecies of Neferti'. In *CoS* i. 104–10.

SJOBERG, A. W., and BERGMANN, E. 1969. *The Collection of Sumerian Temple Hymns*. Texts from Cuneiform Sources, 3. New York: J. J. Augustin.

SPIEGELBERG, W. 1914. *Die sogenannte demotische Chronik*. Leipzig: J. C. Hinrichs.

SPITTLER, R. P. 1983. 'Testament of Job'. In Charlesworth 1983: 829–68.

THOMPSON, T. L. 1992. *Early History of the Israelite People from the Written and Archaeological Sources*. Leiden: Brill.

TIGAY, J. H. 1982. *The Evolution of the Gilgamesh Epic*. Philadelphia: University of Pennsylvania Press.

TINNEY, S. 1999. 'On the Curricular Setting of Sumerian Literature'. *Iraq*, 61: 159–72.

TOV, E. 2004. *Scribal Practices and Approaches Reflected in the Texts Found in the Judean Desert*. STDJ 54. Leiden: Brill.

VAN LERBERGHE, K. and VOET, G., eds. 1999. *Languages and Cultures in Contact: At the Crossroads of Civilizations in the Syro-Mesopotamian Realm*. Proceedings of the 42th RAI. Leuven: Peeters.

VANSTIPHOUT, H. L. J. 1997. 'Disputations, School Dialogues'. In *CoS* i. 575–93.

VOGELZANG, M. E., and VANSTIPHOUT, H. L. J. 1992. *Mesopotamian Epic Literature: Oral or Aural?* Lewiston, NY: Edwin Mellen Press.

VON SODEN, W., *et al.*, eds. 1969. *Reallexikon der Assyriologie*, iii. Berlin: de Gruyter.

WILSON, J. A. 1955*a*. 'The Instruction of the Vizier Ptah-hotep'. In Pritchard 1955: 412–14.

—— 1955*b*. 'The Instruction of Prince Hor-Dedef'. In Pritchard 1955: 419–20.

—— 1955*c*. 'In Praise of Learned Scribes'. In Pritchard 1955: 431–2.

WISEMAN, D. J. 1955. 'Assyrian Writing Boards'. *Iraq*, 17: 3–13.

PART V

METHODS IN BIBLICAL SCHOLARSHIP

CHAPTER 32

ARCHAEOLOGY

JOHN R. BARTLETT

THE ARCHAEOLOGICAL TASK

Archaeology makes an important contribution to biblical scholarship; but to understand and evaluate that contribution, it is important to understand what are the general aims of archaeologists, and how they approach their task. R. Braidwood defined archaeology as 'The study of things men made and did in order that their whole way of life may be understood' (Daniel 1967: 17). Renfrew and Bahn (1996: 11) more fully defined it as 'partly the discovery of the treasures of the past, partly the meticulous work of the scientific analyst, partly the exercise of the creative imagination . . . But it is also the painstaking task of interpretation so that we come to understand what these things mean for the human story.' This approach has been seen as too limited; we should not isolate ancient history from present experience. Hodder therefore sees archaeology as a continual process, and the material past as 'part of the present experience through which we come to understand ourselves' (Hodder 1999: 178). We may reverse that view, and admit that we cannot interpret the past without incorporating our experience of the present, and that each historian and archaeologist may be open to the accusation of bias in presentation. We must also note particular concerns: for example, earlier archaeologists allowed the biblical account of the conquest of Israel to determine the site and scope of their excavations, while more recent archaeologists have aimed at reconstructing from archaeological evidence alone the nature of Iron Age I society in the hill country.

OBSERVATION OF STRATA

Archaeologists may have differing aims from one generation to the next, but there is an increasing consensus on good practice and scientific method applicable to archaeology in the Holy Land, as everywhere else. Archaeology begins from simple observation on the ground. Thus in England John Aubrey (1626–97) observed, described, and planned such large ancient monuments as Avebury, and concluded that they were pre-Roman; in Scandinavia C. J. Thomsen (1788–1865) demonstrated from examination of tombs that the ancient classical distinction of Stone, Bronze, and Iron Ages was correct, and that Bronze succeeded Stone, and Iron, Bronze. John Frere (1740–1807) in England and Boucher de Perthes (1796–1860) in France observed human-made implements in gravel strata below strata containing bones of extinct animals and evidence of marine deposits (see Greene 2002: 21–30). Such observations, and the growing understanding in the early nineteenth century of geological stratification, prepared the way both for a revised view of antiquity totally undermining the biblical dating of creation some 2,000 years before Abraham reached Canaan and for the archaeological excavations of the late nineteenth and early twentieth centuries which themselves led to further revision of the biblical history. The all-important factors were the observation and growing grasp of the principles of stratification and, equally, the recognition of the possibility of dating objects by cross-linkages between one culture and another.

BASIC ARCHAEOLOGICAL PRACTICE

1. Field Surveying

Archaeological observation began with observation and recording of ancient monuments and with the surveying and mapping of the surface of the land. In the nineteenth century it moved into excavation, but excavation has the serious disadvantage that it destroys the evidence as fast as it produces it. In the later twentieth century, archaeologists, before contemplating any excavation, developed the practice of surveying systematically the complete surface of the land and recording everything visible on the surface—small sites of human activity, settlements, monuments, artefacts, types of soil, and vegetation—primarily to assess the historical development of the area. Smaller areas might be studied intensively by use of a marked-out grid. Features below the surface may be revealed by ground shadows observed at low sunlight, by crop marks and soil marks (often seen with the help of aerial photography), and in particular by modern geophysical surveying: magnetometers detect magnetic variations in the subsoil, indicating previous human activity; resistivity surveying reveals different levels of conductivity, so locating buried walls and ditches; ground penetrating radar (GPR) can reveal the shape and position of underground objects. The content of soil or buried containers—phosphates, foodstuffs, organic wastes, all indicative of the nature of local human activity—can be analysed chemically. Mapping of areas and location of sites has been revolutionized by the use of the Global Positioning System (GPS) and the databases of Geographical Information Systems (GIS). With GPS the archaeologist can position a site almost immediately on the map within a metre, without the need for the old systems of ground measurement and triangulation; with GIS the archaeologist can store, analyse, and manipulate archaeological and environmental data in order to answer a variety of questions about the 'environmental signature' of a site. Thus the modern archaeologist, in Israel/Palestine, as elsewhere, can amass an enormous amount of information about an area or site before contemplating the labour and expense of excavation.

Field surveys of recent decades have made important contributions in particular to the major historical question of the settlement of early Israel. Nelson Glueck's early surveys of Transjordan and the Negeb in the 1930s revealed the presence of Early Bronze, Middle Bronze, and Iron Age settlements and the comparative absence of Late Bronze settlements in southern Transjordan, and initiated historical research on ancient Edom, Moab, and Ammon. Y. Aharoni's surveys in Galilee and the Negev revealed new unwalled Early Iron I settlements which, coupled with the lack of evidence for destruction at Late Bronze Age sites, led him to support Alt's theory of a peaceful Israelite infiltration of Canaan (Aharoni 1957). From his survey of the land of Ephraim (1980–6) Israel Finkelstein (1988) argued for the peaceful settlement of the central hill country at the end of the Late Bronze Age by settlers from a pastoral background within Canaan. Such surveys provide a large new database for investigating historical and environmental issues. Large areas (including Jerusalem, Judah and Samaria, and the Negeb) have been surveyed in great detail by the Israel Antiquities Authority; east of the Jordan, recent surveys have covered the east Jordan valley, the Hesban region, the Kerak plateau, the Wadi el-Hasa, and other areas.

2. Excavation

Surveys are non-invasive, non-destructive, and relatively inexpensive means of acquiring information; excavation is invasive, destructive of the stratigraphical evidence it seeks, and relatively expensive. Excavation, therefore, is reserved for the investigation of particular problems for which survey work is inadequate, such as the detailed history of a particular site. Such sites are chosen with care, for their importance for current research purposes or their particular public interest; some sites are excavated because threatened with total destruction by building programmes ('rescue digs'). In recent years excavation has taken place at well-known 'biblical' sites such as Tel Dan, Hazor, Lachish, Gezer, and et-Tell (Bethsaida), but there has been particular interest in some lesser-known Persian period sites (e.g. Tel Megadim, 'Ein Hofez, Shoham, Yavneh Yam), in Philistine sites (T. Miqne/Ekron, T. Batash/Timnah), and in Phoenician sites (Horvat Rosh Zayit/Cabul). Recently excavated sites of the biblical period in Jordan include T. es-Sa'idiyeh, T. Deir 'Alla, the Amman citadel, Hesban, 'Umeiri, Sahab, Balu', and Tell Mudeibhi.

Excavation methods have developed over the last century. The earliest archaeologists were primarily interested in finding and recording interesting artefacts, and their successors in revealing the architecture. The developing understanding of stratigraphy through the nineteenth century led to improved excavation techniques. Mortimer Wheeler developed a disciplined, systematic method of excavation that would mitigate the destructive aspect of digging and extract the utmost information from the ground. Seeing stratigraphy as the key to interpreting the site, Wheeler used a box-pattern of excavated squares, leaving the baulks between the squares as a record of the stratigraphy. These baulks were accurately drawn; the relationships between walls, floors, foundation trenches, pits, collapse-debris, and so on, were fully recorded; similarly, the pottery and individual artefacts were located and recorded within the stratigraphical framework. Thus a full vertical picture of the site could be put together, though this system was less suitable for recording the horizontal dimension. Wheeler's pupil Kathleen Kenyon developed this system at Jericho and Jerusalem, and it became known as the Wheeler–Kenyon system. However, the need to reveal the full horizontal extent of a site or stratum of a site could not be denied, especially where there was much public interest in biblical sites, and American and Israeli archaeologists modified the Wheeler–Kenyon methods to allow for this, dispensing with baulks where necessary after appropriate recording, or even sometimes adopting total open-area excavation (which is, as Wheeler knew, sometimes completely appropriate). Also important in American–Israeli practice is the 'locus', which is a definable unit such as a wall, a floor, an oven, or a pit. Whatever method is used, the recording of relationships between walls, floors, foundations, pits, etc., and the successive strata, in vertical 'section drawings' as well as horizontal plans, remains vital for the overall comprehension of the site, and the early twentieth century system, by which a complete tell might be removed stratum by stratum (as attempted at Megiddo in the 1920s and achieved at Tell el-Kheleifeh in 1938), leaving nothing by which a later excavator can check the findings of predecessors, is a thing of the past.

3. Methods of Dating

For early archaeologists of Palestine, the dating framework was provided primarily by the Bible, assisted by Josephus and by the classical writings. Later, as scholars learned to translate hieroglyphic and cuneiform texts, cross-reference could be made to historical writings from Assyria, Babylonia, and Egypt. Written texts, seen as the prime source of historical knowledge and reconstruction, were used to date archaeological findings. However, appreciation of the importance of stratigraphy made it possible for archaeologists to date their findings at least relatively, if not absolutely. At Tell el-Hesi, Flinders Petrie developed 'sequence dating', relating groups of material to strata on the site, and at Tell Beit Mirsim W. F. Albright (1926–32) established a 'ceramic index' and a pottery chronology for Palestine that still stands virtually unaltered; these tools reduced the archaeologist's total dependence on biblical dating, establishing the possibility of an independent source for chronology. Comparison of pottery from successive strata and different sites allowed archaeologists to observe the development of shapes and forms, and so to establish 'typologies', from which in turn other pottery could be identified. Such typologies can be subjective or over-refined, not allowing sufficiently for the whim of an ancient potter, but the modern technique of thermoluminescence can date pottery, from a few decades to a nearly a million years old, basically by measuring the amount of radioactivity absorbed by the pot from trace minerals present in it and from its surrounding soil since it was first fired (see Greene 2002: 171–3).

The age of pottery in a particular stratum can also be checked by the use of radio-carbon dating on organic material found in the same stratum; in this technique, first developed by William Libby in 1948, one can calculate the time that has elapsed since the material died (i.e. ceased to absorb radio-active carbon 14 from the atmosphere) by comparing the strength of the remaining ^{14}C with the assumed original strength, given that ^{14}C has a half-life of 5,730 years (i.e. a piece of wood 5,730 years old has a concentration of ^{14}C which is half its value at formation) (Greene 2002: 161–8; Aitken 1997: 113–14). Subsequent research has adjusted upwards dates previously set pre-6000 b.p. (before present); radio-carbon dates are converted into calendar dates by the use of a calibration curve.

Another potentially important dating tool for archaeology in Israel/Palestine is dendrochronology (tree-ring dating)(Greene 2002: 156–9). The age of a tree when felled is known from the annual growth rings, whose thickness varies with the climatic conditions experienced. The sequence of annual weather change can be seen in the sequence of tree-rings. Specimens taken from bristle-cone pines in California give a sequence going back to c.4000 BCE; evidence from oak-trees in Europe yields a sequence extending beyond 8000 BCE. Ring sequences in trees over about 50 years old can be identified in the longer sequences, and so dated precisely. Dendrochronology can also, within its chronological limits, provide a check on radio-carbon dating.

The Contribution of Archaeology
to Biblical Scholarship

Biblical scholarship needs the archaeologist, as it needs the anthropologist, epig-raphist, the philologist, the Assyriologist, the classical scholar, the student of Qumran, the rabbinic scholar, and others for the interpretation of the biblical writings. Archaeology is not so much a *method* of biblical scholarship, as an intellectual discipline and practice, incorporating many methods and subject to many methodologies, assisting the modern interpretation of the Bible. The nature of its assistance is disputed, for several reasons: professional archaeologists reject the old view of archaeology as a handmaid to biblical scholarship or as a prop for belief, and biblical scholars sometimes find archaeologists naïve in their treatment of biblical evidence (and vice versa). It is important to be clear what archaeology can and cannot do for biblical scholarship.

(a) Illustrating General Cultural Background

Certainly archaeological work has vividly illustrated the material culture visible in the biblical writings—the ancient city with its walls, fortifications, gates, palaces, water systems, store-rooms, houses, streets, and general planning; the religious cult with its temples and local shrines, its altars and cultic furniture, the *mikvaoth* (ritual baths) in houses; agricultural life with its tools, buildings, livestock, and produce; military installations and weapons; evidence of administration and trade from written *ostraca*; monumental inscriptions and private letters; personal cos-tume and jewellery; tombs and burial practices, etc. Archaeology can reconstruct both daily life in ancient Israel and Roman Judaea (see especially King and Stager 2001), and the wider economic and social scene (see especially Levy 1995), setting Israel and early Christianity in their wider historical contexts.

(b) Direct Biblical Connections

Archaeology, however, has produced less evidence that connects directly with the biblical narrative. The pool of Gibeon (2 Sam. 2: 13) may be the pool discovered at el-Jib by J. B. Pritchard. The present pool of Siloam, and the Siloam tunnel and in-scription (rediscovered 1880), connect with the 'pool and conduit' mentioned in 2 Kgs. 20: 20; cf. Isa. 7: 3, Sir. 48: 17). The tomb inscription of '[. . .]yhw 'aser'al habbayit' in Silwan may be that of 'Shebna who is over the household' described in Isa. 22: 15.

The stele of Mesha found in Diban certainly testifies to King Mesha (2 Kgs. 3) and to the Israelite Omri and his son (Ahab, though not named), but fits uneasily with the narrative of 2 Kings 3. A broken Aramaic stele from Tel Dan certainly refers to Hadad of Syria and, tantalizingly, to 'the house of David' and, less certainly, to the Israelite and Judaean kings '[Jo]ram, son of [Ahab]' and '[Ahaz]yahu son of [Jehoram]'. Assyrian records refer to several kings of Israel and Judah, and Babylonian records to Jehoiachin (cf. 2 Kgs. 24: 12); the Assyrian capture of Lachish (701 BCE) is vividly portrayed on surviving limestone slabs from the Assyrian palace at Nineveh, now in the British Museum, but this event is not mentioned in the Bible. For the New Testament scholar, archaeology has produced an inscription at Caesarea naming Pontius Pilatus as prefect of Judaea, and an inscription from Delphi naming Gallio as proconsul of Achaia (probably for the year 51–2 CE, thus providing a useful peg for Pauline chronology: see Murphy-O'Connor 1983: 141–52). Such evidence at least confirms that the biblical texts speak of real people and actual events.

(c) New Evidence for the Historian

However, while archaeological evidence may illumine the cultural background, and confirm (especially from inscriptions) some details of the biblical record, it can produce problems for the scholarly historian. The archaeologist's account of the Middle Bronze Age in Palestine no longer offers a secure background for the patriarchal stories of the book of Genesis, as was earlier assumed (see Dever and Clarke 1977). The archaeological evidence for the Late Bronze–Early Iron I Canaan no longer supports the picture of an Israelite military conquest of Canaan given in the book of Joshua (see Finkelstein 1988; Dever 2003; Chapter 3 above). The archaeological evidence for a flourishing Solomonic tenth-century BCE city of Jerusalem is virtually absent, for whatever reason, and the attribution of the six-chambered gateways and attached walls at Gezer, Megiddo, and Hazor (cf 1 Kgs. 9: 15) to the work of Solomon in the tenth century BCE (Yadin 1958; Holladay 1995; Dever 1997, 2001) is now strongly challenged (Finkelstein and Silberman 2001: 135–45, 340–4). While the Deuteronomistic History, for reasons of its own, makes little of the Israelite kings Omri and Ahab, the archaeological evidence from Iron IIB (c.900–700 BCE) makes clear that it is their age, the ninth century BCE, that saw the establishment of the kingdom of Israel and its relative prosperity and independence through the eighth century until its destruction by Assyria in 722 BCE. The Deuteronomistic History explains the Assyrian destruction of Samaria by underlining Israelite religious apostasy (2 Kgs. 17: 7–18), and explains Jerusalem's preservation from like destruction by King Hezekiah's prompt political submission (2 Kgs. 18: 14) and religious penitence in time of crisis (2 Kgs. 19); but the Deuteronomist does not openly mention the brutal destruction of the city of Lachish so vividly presented by excavations at Lachish and by the reliefs at Sennacherib's palace in Nineveh (see Ussishkin 1997). The biblical writers convey the impression that when Nebuchadnezzar's army took Jerusalem in 587/586 BCE, the destruction of Jerusalem and Judah and the exile of the people to Babylon were total; archaeological evidence is limited, but while Jerusalem and sites in the south—Engedi, Lachish, Arad, and Beth-hakkerem (Ramat Rahel)—suffered destruction, there is some archaeological evidence that life at more northern towns—including Mizpah (T. en-Nasbeh), Gibeon (el-Jib), Bethel, and Gibeah (T. el-Ful)—continued as usual (see Barstad 1996). And finally, archaeology has given us visible evidence of religious and cultic practices condemned by the Deuteronomistic Historian; at Tel Dan in northern Israel, Biran has excavated a large cult site (cf. 1 Kgs. 12: 29; Biran 1994), and at Kuntillet 'Ajrud (south of Kadesh Barnea) and Khirbet el-Qom (near Hebron) inscriptions suggest that the goddess Asherah was worshipped alongside YHWH as a consort (see Dever 1994: 149–51; 2001: 183–7; *contra* Mayes 1997: 63). The archaeological evidence for Solomon's Temple, however, remains indirect; see Dever 2001: 144–57, 172–98.

(d) Limitations of Archaeology

Archaeology thus certainly supplements the contribution of the historical texts to our knowledge of the history, culture, and religion of ancient Israel and early Christianity. Archaeology can present the physical history of a site and clarify the cultural context of a particular stratum of that site; but without written material, whether derived from literature, monumental or more ephemeral inscriptions, or from public or private documents written on papyri or leather, archaeology is limited. For example, it might offer vivid evidence for the life and destruction of a small Iron Age country town, but remain silent on the ethnicity or nationality of its occupants; to tell us that we need some human written record or oral tradition. It might present a stratum rich in artefacts, but remain silent about the length of time covered by that stratum; to tell us that we need some method of cross-dating with evidence from another site. Some scholars argue that an independent, objective history of Israel should be written on the basis of archaeological evidence alone, but there are important objections to this approach. First, any such history would be no more 'objective' than the scholars who wrote it; all archaeological discoveries need interpretation, and their interpretation will depend upon the historical presuppositions and concerns of the interpreter. Second, archaeological evidence always has gaps and is never complete; surveys do not see everything, excavation is necessarily selective, and in any case much of the evidence has already suffered human or natural destruction. There is no doubt that the historian should draw upon all available sources, whether literary or artefactual. The only serious question is how they should be used.

'BIBLICAL ARCHAEOLOGY'

In the mid-twentieth century the accepted practice was 'biblical archaeology'. W. F. Albright described biblical archaeology as that archaeology which covered all lands mentioned in the Bible. His pupil G. E. Wright identified biblical archaeology as 'a special "armchair" variety of general archaeology', and the biblical archaeologist as one who 'studies the discoveries of excavations in order to glean from them every fact that throws a direct, indirect, or even diffused light upon the Bible . . . His chief concern is not with methods or pots or weapons in themselves alone. His central and absorbing interest is the understanding and exposition of the scriptures' (Wright 1962: 17; cf. Wright 1971); in 1938 Wright founded a journal named *The Biblical Archaeologist*. W. G. Dever rejected this approach strongly, seeing it as rooted in a conservative and archaeologically amateurish religious concern to demonstrate the truth of the Bible. Dever advocated 'Syro-Palestinian archaeology', a term which indicated an area of professional archaeological activity (Dever 1985; 1992; 2001: 61 attributes the term to Albright); Dever wished to underline the 'specialist, professional and secular' nature of archaeology (2001: 62), and was rightly concerned that archaeology in Palestine/Israel should be conducted according to international professional standards, concerned with fields ranging well beyond 'biblical' history. Dever wanted Syro-Palestinian archaeology to be independent of biblical studies; J. M. Miller countered that radical separation was neither realistic nor advisable, and that scholars crossing the disciplinary lines 'should respect the procedures, warrants, and limitations of the different kinds of evidence they draw upon'. But Miller demanded that 'for the specifics of history, we must depend primarily on written records' (Miller 1987: 58; cf. Miller 1991). Other scholars continued to defend the legitimacy of 'biblical archaeology' as a 'subspecies of biblical studies' (Lance 1982: 100; cf. Glock 1986); but in practice archaeology in the Levant has become the responsibility of professional archaeologists who are archaeologists first and biblical scholars second, if at all; in 1998 Wright's *Biblical Archaeologist* became (after much discussion) *Near Eastern Archaeology*.

ARCHAEOLOGY, BIBLE, AND HISTORY

Morton Smith observed in his 1968 Presidential Address to the Society of Biblical Literature that 'for a correct history of the Israelites we must have the archaeological facts determined quite objectively and independently by competent archaeologists, and the biblical texts likewise by competent philologians, and then we can begin to compare them' (Smith 1969: 34). Similarly, Dever has recently concluded, arguing for dialogue between texts and artefacts (and those who interpret them), that these two sources 'must be interpreted separately and similarly, and then compared' (2001: 79; cf. Bartlett 1997: 14).

The main problem of 'biblical archaeology' was that it was one-sided, attempting to fit archaeological evidence into the mould set by biblical historians. 'Syro-Palestinian archaeology' was in equal danger of subordinating biblical evidence to an archaeological framework. Dialogue is necessary; the resources of texts and artefacts must be combined. However, there are difficulties here, because 'literature and archaeology just do not meet' (Knauf 1991: 39). Knauf also reminds us that 'facts' are theoretical constructs (a point which surely applies to archaeological 'facts' as much as to written information). What the archaeologist offers the historian is interpretation of artefacts; similarly, what the biblical scholar offers the historian is interpretation of texts. Knauf reminds us that 'history' is always 'someone's history of something' (1991: 37), that 'every history is the creation of a human mind' (1991: 27); that 'we do not find knowledge, we make it' (1991: 29); and he warns us that 'only ideologists are always right; scholars know that everything they say is potentially wrong' (1991: 31). Such words are important for archaeologists and biblical historians alike.

SUGGESTED READING

For modem archaeological principles and methods, see Greene 2002; for archaeological methods in Israel/Palestine see R. Moorey, *Excavation in Palestine* (Guildford: Lutterworth Press, 1981), and *A Century of Biblical Archaeology* (Cambridge: Lutterworth Press, 1991). On the relationship of biblical and archaeological studies, see J. C. H. Laughlin, *Archaeology and the Bible* (London and New York: Routledge, 2000); also Dever 2001. See also Chapter 3 above.

BIBLIOGRAPHY

AITKEN, M. J. 1997. 'Dating Techniques'. In E. M. Meyers, ed., *The Oxford Encyclopedia of Archaeology in the Near East*, New York and Oxford: Oxford University Press, i. 113–17.

BARSTAD, H. M. 1996. *The Myth of the Empty Land*. Symbolae Osloenses Fasc. Suppl. 28. Oslo: Scandinavian University Press.

BARTLETT, J. R. 1997. 'What has Archaeology to do with the Bible—or vice versa?'. In J. R. Bartlett, ed., *Archaeology and Biblical Interpretation*, London and New York: Routledge, 1–19.

BIRAN, A. 1994. 'Tel Dan: Biblical Texts and Archaeological Data'. In M. D. Coogan, J. Cheryl Exum, and L. E. Stager, eds., *Scripture and Other Artifacts*, Louisville, Ky.: Westminster/John Knox Press, 1–17.

DANIEL, G. 1967. *The Origins and Growth of Archaeology*. Harmondsworth: Penguin.

DEVER, W. G. 1985. 'Syro-Palestinian and Biblical Archaeology'. In D. A. Knight and G. M. Tucker, eds., *The Hebrew Bible and its Modern Interpreters*, Philadelphia: Fortress Press, 31–74.

—— 1992. 'Archaeology, Syro-Palestinian and Biblical'. In *ABD*, i. 354–7.

—— 1994. 'The Silence of the Text: An Archaeological Commentary on 2 Kings 23'. In M. D. Coogan, J. Cheryl Exum, and L. E. Stager, eds., *Scripture and Other Artifacts*, Louisville, Ky.: Westminster/John Knox Press, 143–68.

—— 1997. 'Archaeology and the 'Age of Solomon': A Case-study in Archaeology and Historiography'. In L. K. Handy, ed., *The Age of Solomon: Scholarship at the Turn of the Millennium*, Leiden: Brill, 217–51.

—— 2001. *What Did the Biblical Writers Know and When Did they Know it?* Grand Rapids, Mich.: Eerdmans.

—— 2003. *Who were the Early Israelites and Where did they Come From?* Grand Rapids, Mich.: Eerdmans.

—— and CLARKE, M. 1977. 'The Patriarchal Traditions: Palestine in the Second Millennium BCE: The Archaeological Picture'. In J. H. Hayes and J. M. Miller, eds., *Israelite and Judean History*, London: SCM Press, 70–120.

FINKELSTEIN, I. 1988. *The Archaeology of the Israelite Settlement*. Jerusalem: Israel Exploration Society.

—— and SILBERMAN, N. A. 2001. *The Bible Unearthed: Archaeology's New Vision of Ancient Israel and the Origin of its Sacred Texts*. New York: The Free Press (Simon & Schuster).

GLOCK, A. E. 1986. 'Biblical Archaeology: An Emerging Discipline'. In L. Geraty and L. G. Herr, eds., *The Archaeology of Jordan and other Studies*, Berrien Springs, Mich.: Andrews University Press, 85–101.

GREENE, K. 2002. *Archaeology: An Introduction*, 4th edn. London and New York: Routledge.

HODDER, I. 1999. *The Archaeological Process: An Introduction*. Oxford: Blackwell.

HOLLADAY, J. S. jun. 1995. 'The Kingdoms of Israel and Judah: Political and Economic Centralization in the Iron IIA–B (ca. 1000–750 BCE)'. In T. F. Levy, ed., *The Archaeology of Society in the Holy Land*, New York: Facts on File, 368–98.

KING, P. J. and STAGER, L. E. 2001. *Life in Biblical Israel*. Louisville, Ky., and London: Westminster/John Knox Press.

KNAUF, F. A. 1991. 'From History to Interpetation'. In D. V. Edelman, ed., *The Fabric of History: Text, Artifact and Israel's Past*. JSOTS.S 127, Sheffield: Sheffield Academic Press, 26–64.

LANCE, H. D. 1982. 'American Biblical Archaeology in Perspective', *BA* 45/2: 97–101.

LEVY, T. E., ed. 1995. *The Archaeology of Society in the Holy Land*. London: Leicester University Press.

MAYES, A. D. H. 1997. 'Kuniillet 'Ajrud and the History of Israelite Religion'. In J. R. Bartlett, ed., *Archaeology and Biblical Interpretation*, London and New York: Routledge, 51–66.

MILLER, J. M. 1987. 'Old Testament History and Archaeology'. *BA* 50/1: 55–63.

MILLER, J. M. 1991. 'Is it Possible to Write a History of Israel without Relying on the Hebrew Bible?' In D. V. Edelman, ed., *The Fabric of History: Text, Artifact and Israel's Past*, JSOTS.S 127, Sheffield: Sheffield Academic Press, 93–102.

MURPHY-O'CONNOR, J. 1983. *St Paul's Corinth: Texts and Archaeology.* Wilmington, Del.: Glazier.

RENFREW, C., and BARN, P. 1996. *Archaeology: Theories, Methods and Practice.* London: Thames & Hudson.

SMITH, N. M. 1969. 'The Present State of Old Testament Studies'. *JBL* 88: 19–35.

USSISHKIN, D. 1997. 'Lachish'. In E. M. Meyers, ed., *The Oxford Encyclopedia of Archaeology in the Near East*, New York and Oxford: Oxford University Press, iii. 317–23.

WRIGHT, G. E. 1962. *Biblical Archaeology*, 2nd edn. Philadelphia: Westminster Press; London: Duckworth.

—— 1971. 'What Archaeology Can and Cannot Do'. *BA* 34/3: 70–6.

YADIN, Y. 1958. 'Solomon's City Wall and Gate at Gezer'. *IEJ* 8: 80–6.

CHAPTER 33

TEXTUAL CRITICISM

ARIE VAN DER KOOIJ

1. REASONS

Modern editions of the Hebrew Bible, the Old Testament, are based on manuscripts which date to the tenth and eleventh centuries CE—the codex of Aleppo and the codex Leningradensis. The former is used in the edition of *The Hebrew University Bible*, whereas the latter forms the basis of the third edition of the *Biblia Hebraica* edited by R. Kittel, and of the *Biblica Hebraica Stuttgartensia*, as will also be the case with the forthcoming *Biblia Hebraica Editio Quinta*. Unlike the modern editions of the Greek New Testament, those of the OT do not offer a text which is the outcome of a critical assessment of the available data, but represent the text of a particular MS. That is to say, they are editions of the diplomatic type, not critical editions in the strict sense of the word.

The two MSS just mentioned are the most important witnesses of the so-called Masoretic text (MT). Although in matters of details such as vocalization, accentuation, and delimitation, Masoretic MSS show some variety, they do represent—particularly as far as the *ketib* is concerned—a text of the Hebrew Bible which testifies to a standardized text tradition.

Since, as is generally assumed, the biblical books in Hebrew (and Aramaic) go back to a period of a much earlier date—that of the seventh to the second centuries BCE—the question suggests itself as to whether the text of the biblical books has been transmitted, through the ages up to its attestation in the early Middle Ages, accurately, or not. It is the task of textual criticism to examine the text's reliability from the perspective of the transmission history. One has to reckon with errors and deliberate changes in the text, in the course of time. Moreover, early Jewish sources bear witness to the latter category of intentional changes, as they provide lists of theological corrections in the text, the so-called *tiqqune sopherim* (McCarthy 1981).

The idea that the reliability of the MT should not be taken for granted came up in the sixteenth and seventeenth centuries when scholars realized that the Hebrew text, as it was attested in the editions of the time (*Biblia Rabbinica*), was not the only text of the Hebrew Bible. Study of the Samaritan Pentateuch and of the Septuagint (LXX) led to a great deal of textual comparison. It became apparent that there are quite a number of variant readings which require evaluation. The same realization prompted B. Kennicott and G. B. de Rossi, in the eighteenth century, to publish the many variant readings extant in a range of medieval manuscripts.

Thus textual criticism started with textual comparison based on the evidence available at that time. Later on, since the nineteenth century, it was extended to cases where the text was considered to be 'difficult' or corrupt, and where in a number of cases no variants were attested. The picture that emerges from commentaries and from the editions of *Biblica Hebraica* (edited by R. Kittel, BHK 1 (1905–6), 2 (1912), 3 (1937)), is that of numerous 'problems' in the MT, including morphological, syntactical ones, as well as matters of style (e.g. *metri causa*) and literary-critical issues (e.g. glosses). In a large number of instances, these difficulties in the MT were viewed as being due to scribal errors. It is interesting to note, though, that, unlike many exegetes, grammarians of the time, like W. Gesenius, F. Böttcher, and E. König, were less inclined to state that a given reading in the MT is to be seen as 'incorrect' Hebrew.

The reason why textual criticism is needed has become fully clear since the remarkable finds in the Judaean desert in the years 1947–56. A great number of biblical texts were found at Qumran, Masada, Nahal Hever, and Wadi Murabba'at. Most of these texts are written in the language of the Hebrew Bible, i.e. Hebrew or Aramaic, thus representing a 'direct' witness, in contrast to 'indirect' witnesses such as the ancient versions (translations). The biblical texts of the Dead Sea region (hereafter Qumran) are very important, as they date from the earliest period in which the biblical text is attested: viz. the third century BCE to the second century CE. In comparison to the other witnesses of this period (LXX and Samaritan Pentateuch), the Qumran texts have an additional value in that they constitute manuscript evidence that goes back directly to this period, and not indirectly (i.e. via a reconstruction of the text on the basis of manuscripts of a later date, such as in the case of the LXX). On the other hand, it is frustrating that the Qumran evidence is so fragmentary, except in the case of the 'great' scroll of Isaiah (1QIsa-a). Nevertheless, these findings have proved beyond any doubt the need and importance of textual criticism. The Qumran material provides clear evidence that the MT represents a very old textual tradition, but it also offers a large number of variant readings in comparison to the MT (variants, pluses, and minuses), as well as cases of remarkable differences pertaining to clauses, sentences, and pericopes.

2. MEANS

The critical examination of the MT should be carried out, in principle, on the basis of all the evidence available. This concerns:

a. The ancient witnesses to the biblical text, both the Hebrew texts (Qumran, SamPent.) and the ancient versions, translations of a parent text in Hebrew (LXX, Targumim, Peshitta, Vulgate, and others; daughter versions are usually left out of consideration). For more information about the ancient versions, the reader is referred to Chapter 12 above.
b. The quotations in Hebrew, both in Qumran documents and in rabbinic writings.
c. The Hebrew manuscripts dating to the (late) Middle Ages.

In practice, however, the three sets of sources just mentioned are not considered of the same value from the text-critical point of view. As to (C), some scholars (e.g. Borbone 1990) are of the opinion that, in line with Kennicott and De Rossi, these MSS should be taken into consideration. Most scholars, however, share the view of Goshen-Gottstein (1967) that, except in a few cases, these MSS have no value at all for the quest of an early text tradition. Regarding the second group (B), the quotations in Qumran documents are certainly of interest (on methodological issues involved, see e.g. Lim 2002), but the difficulty with rabbinic sources is that in most cases the literature concerned is not (yet) available in critical editions.

Thus one is mainly left with the first group (A) as a means of text-critical research. But even in this case, some differentiation is involved. As appears from text critical studies, the focus is to a large extent on the evidence from the earliest period of manuscript documentation, viz. the third century BCE to the first century CE. Most attention is paid, in practice, to the evidence of Qumran, the LXX, and the SamPent (as far as the Pentateuch is concerned). Why is this so? The underlying idea is that the witnesses of later date belong to a period which is marked by the presence and dominance of a Hebrew text that actually is very similar to the MT, and which therefore is termed as 'proto-masoretic'. An important witness in this respect is the Twelve Prophets scroll from Wadi Murabba'at (first half of second century) which shows remarkable agreement, including specific spellings of words, with the later MT (*ketib*). Consequently, the later versions—Aquila, Symmachus, Targumim, Peshitta, Vulgate—are considered less significant for text-critical research, as sources for variant readings which might turn out to be earlier or even better readings than in the MT. They are nevertheless of great value in other respects, for they widen the text-historical horizon in the following ways:

a. They show a variety of styles of translation, which is helpful for the study of the LXX (which also displays a variety of types of translations).

b. They are very important from the perspective of the history of 'reading' and interpretation of the Hebrew text, because in this respect they can shed light, at least by analogy, on variant readings in the early witnesses (Qumran, LXX).

c. The later versions, specifically the Targumim, may be useful in clarifying the phenomenon of literary creativity in the early texts. It would be interesting to study the cases of reworked and expanded versions in Qumran documents and in the LXX in the light of similar cases in the Targumim.

But still, in practice the focus of text-critical study is on the Qumran texts and the LXX, because they testify to a period of textual fluidity and pluriformity (for more information of this important matter, see Chapter 12 above).

3. PURPOSE

Generally speaking, textual criticism aims at the recovering or reconstruction of the original wording of a given literary work by evaluating the text as attested in several, diverging manuscripts. This is the main object of textual criticism, which also applies to the study of the Old Testament text. From the outset of text-critical study of the OT, the aim was to establish the original wording of a particular biblical book, later on designated the 'archetype' or 'Urtext'. As from the twentieth century, most exegetes preferred to use the expression 'the final redaction' of a given book. The difficulty with this term, however, is that it was associated with the idea of standardization and canonization of a given book (sometime in the Persian period), which has been criticized in recent years on good grounds. It is therefore more appropriate to take the term in the sense of what it actually means: i.e. the literary completion of the primary text of a biblical book.

Scholars have argued, however, that the idea of one original text does not recommend itself. They argue that, since there are different readings that are equally valid, one should assume that from the outset different pristine versions of biblical books were circulating, which were regarded as of equal status. This view has been criticized, rightly so, by Tov: 'One's inability to decide between different readings should not be confused with the question of the original form of the biblical text' (Tov 2001: 174).

In the first edition of his well-known introduction *Textual Criticism of the Hebrew Bible*, Tov himself argued that it is the task of the text critic 'to aim at that literary composition which has been accepted as binding (authoritative) by Jewish tradition' (Tov 1992: 317). He has in mind the edition 'that was later to become M' (p. 316): i.e. the proto-masoretic text. In his view, large-scale differences pertaining to a textual tradition which is earlier than proto-MT—as in the case of the book of Jeremiah (see also below)—are part of the literary history of a book, and therefore not to be seen as belonging to the transmission history, thus as falling outside the scope of textual criticism. In the second edition of his work Tov revised his view on the matter, since 'such thinking ... attaches too much importance to the canonical status of M, disregarding the significance of other textual traditions which at the time must have been as authoritative as M was at a later stage' (Tov 2001: 177). He now advances the view that in case of consecutive 'original editions', the previous edition—in the case of Jeremiah, Edition I (4QJer-b,d; LXX)—should be taken into account for the reconstruction of elements in the original text. But, as he puts it, 'such a reconstruction does not pertain to elements which the editors of consecutive literary editions would or could have changed ... but it does pertain to readings created by the vicissitudes of textual transmission, often visible in textual corruptions' (2001: 180).

Here we touch upon the issue of the relationship between textual criticism and literary criticism (in the sense of redaction criticism). This issue concerns biblical texts attested by versions either in Hebrew (Qumran) or in Greek (LXX) which differ markedly, particularly in a quantative manner, from (proto-)MT. According to Tov and other scholars, these texts—the prime example being the book of Jeremiah—represent an earlier stage in the literary, or redaction, history of a given book. Since textual criticism has to do with the transmission history of a given text, and redaction criticism with the literary history of it, the earlier text, or edition, which is regarded as belonging to the literary history of a given book, does not belong to the field of textual criticism. This view underlies his just quoted remark.

However, the question arises as to why one should limit the reconstruction of the original text in the way stated by Tov. The crucial matter is whether an earlier text is to be seen as a stage in the literary growth of a given book. Alternatively, one could argue that the earlier text, which might be labelled 'pre-MT', should be regarded as the final redaction of the primary text of a given book. This seems to be more likely, as the reworkings involved are comparable to reworkings in texts which are regarded as 'subsequent to M' (Tov 1992: 316): i.e. reworked texts (e.g. SamPent.; LXX Esther) which presuppose proto-MT. It would mean that in some cases the proto-MT itself represents a reworked edition of an earlier, primary text (pre-MT), while in other cases this applies to texts which are the result of a reworking of a proto-MT type.

Thus, it seems best to consider all available textual data, including differences of a literary (scribal) type, as pertaining to the transmission history. This is not something exceptional. An interesting example is the textual history of the *Life of Adam and Eve* that is marked by different 'editions' (including sizeable differences) which actually represent several stages in the transmission history of an underlying primary text (Tromp 2002). The task of textual criticism then is to try to account for all these data in order to recover, as far as this is possible, the original wording of a text, or, to put it another way, the wording of a text which lay at the basis of attested differences between the witnesses, including different 'editions' of a given passage, or of the book concerned. One should go as far back as the textual evidence allows and requires.

A final remark in this section on the purpose of textual criticism is in order. It is interesting to note that there is a tendency in the field of Old Testament studies to date the redactional completion of biblical books later than was done by scholars in the past. Consequently, the distance between these datings and the first period of textual (manuscript) documentation is becoming smaller. To give an example: if scholars are correct in dating the first complete edition of the book of Isaiah to somewhere in the third century BCE (e.g. Steck 1991), it is plausible to assume that the 'original' text was still available in the temple of Jerusalem in the second and first centuries BCE; that is to say, in the period in which LXX Isaiah and several Isaiah texts from Qumran were produced.

4. METHOD

We now turn to the issue of methodology: how to realize the goal of textual criticism. We will deal with this matter both on a theoretical level and on a practical one by providing a few examples which may be illustrative.

It can not be denied that in practice the above-stated purpose will not be achieved in every instance in a convincing way, as there are many obstacles, such as the fact that the number of ancient witnesses in Hebrew is very limited indeed. Surely, we now have an impressive number of biblical texts from the Dead Sea area, but for most books this material is of a fragmentary nature. Besides, there are cases which are complicated, and cases which in the end are difficult to decide as to which reading or wording might have been the (more) original one. All this means that textual criticism can be carried out only by trial and error, including, as is usual in textual and historical research, an element of subjectivity.

To reach one's goal as a textual critic, there are roughly speaking two steps to be taken:

1. First, one should collect the relevant data in a case, or in a group of cases, and analyse these data, each in its own context.
2. Second, the evidence has to be evaluated in view of the question of which reading may be the preferred one, in the sense of the (more) original one.

As has been indicated above (sect. 1), the reason behind the first step may be either the availability of one or more variant readings in a case, or the idea that a reading or passage in the MT may be 'corrupt', or both. In the case of a difficulty, or supposed corruption, it may be that variant readings are not available (i.e. all ancient witnesses support MT, at least concerning its *ketib*). In such a case, one may consider a conjectural emendation.

The collection of the relevant data (first step) concerns the issue of variant readings (variant, plus, or minus) in a case. These readings are to be noted, be it in Hebrew in the case of a Hebrew witness, or in the language of one or more ancient translations. It may be useful to compare the witnesses involved with the help of a synoptic overview of a given passage (verse, or pericope). Having done so, the relevant data should be analysed, each variant reading in the context (verse, or pericope) of the witness involved against the background of the characteristics of a given witness. The purpose of this analysis is to find out whether one has to do with a variant reading which is not due to a translator, or scribe, but may reflect an ancient reading. However, in cases in which it turns out to be difficult to reach such a decision, the question should be left open, and the evidence should be treated as a virtual variant in the second step, when the data are to be evaluated in view of the question as to which reading may be the (more) original one.

In the next, and final section, of this paragraph I will address some aspects of method, illustrated by a few examples of cases in which variant readings are attested. (For a discussion of 'conjectural emendation', including examples, see Tov 2001: 351–69.)

As to the weighing of the evidence, several factors are involved, which may differ from case to case, such as linguistic, philological, exegetical, literary, and cultural considerations. As a rule, one factor will not be sufficient for an evaluation of a case. This also applies to the well-known rule *lectio difficilior potior*.

This rule may do in some cases, such as the following one: Gen. 17: 16. The MT reads: 'I will bless *her*, and *she* shall be to nations; kings of peoples shall come from *her*'; cf. Targ. However, the other witnesses—LXX, Pesh., Vulgalte, and SamPent. (partly)—read 'him' (i.e. Isaac), 'he', 'him'. The MT is likely to offer the more difficult reading in the sense of the preferable one.

The rule of the more difficult reading can thus be helpful, but in many instances one needs additional arguments or considerations. For example, Gen. 2: 2:

MT: God stopped his work 'on the seventh day'; cf. Targ., Vulg.;
LXX: 'on the sixth day'; cf. SamPent.; Pesh. (see also *Jubilees* 2. 16).

This is a well-known case of what might be considered a good example of *lectio difficilior potior*: the reading 'seventh' is clearly the more difficult one since, from the narrative context, one would expect 'sixth'. Thus, the reading 'seventh' should be the preferred one. However, the reading 'sixth' is the reading which seems to make more sense, while the reading 'seventh' could be explained as due to a scribal error, triggered by the next clause in the verse (Hendel 1998: 33). Yet, as an additional factor, or consideration, one may point to the fact that, as the section about the sixth day (Gen. 1: 24–31) ended at v. 31, one would not expect a reference to that day afterwards, the more so since Gen. 2: 2–3 is about the seventh day. This is in favour of the reading 'seventh' as the original one. The idea of v. 2 may well be that, as soon as the seventh day began, God stopped working, and rested from his work during that day.

Another additional argument may be the rule that the non-harmonized reading is to be preferred to the harmonized one: for example, Deut. 34: 1–3. In this case, the MT contains a fairly detailed description of the promised land, which Moses was allowed to see; cf. LXX, Targ., Pesh., Vulg.; SamPent., on the other hand, offers a text which is much shorter than the MT: 'from the land of Egypt to the great river, the river Euphrates, and to the Western Sea'. Since it represents a case of harmonization (see Gen. 15: 18), it can not be regarded as reflecting the more original text.

Or an additional argument may be of a linguistic nature: for example, Isa. 45: 2 as far as the reading הרורים in the MT is concerned. The other witnesses offer the following readings and renderings: 1Qa הררים, 1Qb הרורים, LXX ὄρη, Targ. 'the walls', Pesh 'rocky place' (cf. 40: 4 for MT העקב), Vulg. *gloriosos* ('notables'). Hebrew הדורים presents a difficulty, since its meaning is uncertain and disputed ('spiral roads', 'uneven places'?). Scholars have therefore argued that the variant reading attested by 1Qa and LXX (and 1Qb?), 'mountains', is to be preferred, as this makes good sense in the context. However, the difficulty with this solution is that the reduplicated plural (הררים) does not occur in biblical Hebrew in the absolute state (Koole 1997: 435). As has been argued by other scholars, MT *Ketib* may well represent the original reading if taken in the sense of 'the walls', in line with Akkadian *dūru* (cf. Targ.) (Southwood 1975: 802). Contextually, this would fit even better because of the 'doors of bronze' and 'bars of iron' in the rest of the verse.

An important matter concerns the characteristics of the witnesses involved, including the MT itself. For instance, for the weighing of variant readings, it is important to know that a text like 1QIsa-a represents a witness which, from a linguistic point of view, displays many readings of a secondary nature in comparison to the MT. However, although an overall view of a witness may help us in weighing the evidence, this is not to say that it is decisive in every case. On the contrary, although a text such as 1QIsa-a contains many readings which, linguistically speaking, are of a secondary nature, one should not exclude the possibility that this scroll also offers readings which are very significant and which may be preferred to MT. So, in principle, each case should be treated in its own right.

A good example of such a reading is found in Isa. 19: 18, where 1QIsa-a offers a variant (החרס, '[city of] the sun'; cf. 4QIsa-b) which is likely to be regarded the original reading, whereas the reading of the MT (ההרס, '[city of] destruction') is of a secondary nature. (The variant reading of the LXX—ἀσεδεκ—is due to influence from Isa. 1: 26.) Another interesting case is the plus of אור 'light' in

Isa. 53: 8, attested in 1QIsa-a and in 1QIsa-b, 4QIsa-d, and the LXX as well, over against the MT and the other, later, witnesses (Targ., Pesh., Vulg.). The fact that this variant is found in all the available early witnesses favours the idea that this reading represents an older text tradition than the MT. This is the more probable since 1QIsa-b, a conservative type of text, joins the other texts.

Another interesting case concerns the book of Jeremiah. The text of this book is attested in two versions, a longer one (MT, 4QJer-a, Theod., Aq., Sym., Targ., Pesh., Vulg.), and a shorter one (LXX, 4QJer-b). Many scholars are of the opinion that the shorter version represents the older one, whilst others hold the opposite view. Whatever theory one adheres to, also in this case each case should be treated, first of all, as an individual. For example, in Jer. 31: 39–40 a remarkable difference between the MT and the LXX concerns the beginning of v. 40 (MT): 'the whole valley of the dead bodies and the ashes', which is not found in the LXX (38: 39–40). It may well be that this phrase was not present in the parent text of LXX, but even then the question remains as to whether it represents a secondary addition, or whether it was left out for one reason or another. In the text attested by MT (cf. Targ., Pesh., Vulg.) the phrase about the dead bodies and the ashes is part of a context in which the city (Jerusalem) is described as a territory 'sacred to the Lord'. Since a place with dead bodies and ashes (graves?) in Jerusalem as holy city creates serious difficulties for reasons of purity, it is easier to imagine that this phrase was left out than that it was added at a later date. As we know from Jewish sources of the Hellenistic era (4QMMT, Temple Scroll), the issue of the purity of Jerusalem as holy city was a matter of serious concern, particularly after the dramatic events in the seventies and sixties of the second century BCE (profanation of the temple).

Interestingly, LXX-Jeremia presents a version according to which the sacred area has been interpreted as 'sanctuary' (ἁγίασμα). Hebrew קרש has been taken here in the sense of 'sanctuary', and not as 'sacred (to the Lord)' as e.g. in LXX-Zech. 14: 20, 21 (ἅγιον). The ending of v. 39 in Greek which, unlike MT, refers to an encircling wall of precious stones (καὶ περικυκλωθήσεται κύκλῳ ἐξ ἐκλεκτῶν λίθων) is in line with this interpretation. It seems that a particular wall is meant here, viz. the περίβολος, the enclosing wall of the temple, just as in LXX-Isa. 54: 12: καὶ τὸν περίβολόν σου λίθους ἐκλεκτούς. Whether one would consider the translator the one who left out the phrase in v. 40, or not, it is clear that this phrase does not fit the interpretation of the text as attested by the LXX.

The rule that each case should be treated in its own right is an important one, but at the same time it is a rule which does not apply to every case. There are also text-critical cases which do not stand on their own, but are related to other cases in a book, or collection of books. An interesting example is Deut. 32: 8, which seems to be part of a network consisting of Deut. 32: 43, Gen. 46: 20, 27, and Exod. 1: 5 (Barthélemy 1978; Van der Kooij 1994).

Finally, I will deal with another aspect of method: viz. that of the relationship between text-critical and literary-critical methods. This has become a major issue in modern text-critical research, mainly in view of the issue of different 'editions' as far as attested by textual evidence (MT, Qumran, LXX). Methodologically speaking, one might argue that textual criticism should come first, and literary (or redactional) criticism next. In theory this makes good sense, but in practice it does not work. Considering the complexities involved in both types of research, it seems better to apply both approaches, each in its own right, that is to say, in interaction with each other, as will be illustrated in the following two examples.

(1) Joshua 20. The Old Greek of Joshua 20, the chapter about the cities of refuge, is much shorter than the MT (= Targ., Pesh., Vulg.): vv. 4–5, most of v. 6, and one expression in v. 3 ('unintentionally') are not attested in this version. The latter (LXX) reflects a text of Joshua 20 which is fully in line with the related passage in Num. 35: 11–12. This might evoke the idea of a harmonization, but since both texts belong to the same stratum, viz. the Priestly one (P), this is not plausible. As has been pointed out by scholars, from a literary-critical point of view, the pluses in MT are of a secondary nature (Cortese 1990: 79 f.). If so, the text atttested by LXX corresponds to the results of a literary-critical analysis of MT.

As to the pluses in MT Joshua 20, the question arises as to whether they are part of a stratum, or layer, in the book. Rofé (1985: 145) and Tov (1992: 330) regard these pluses as 'Deuteronomistic'. According to the latter, '[t]he layer of additions ... in Joshua contains words and sections from Deuteronomy 19 which are meant to adapt the earlier layer to Deuteronomy—an assumption which is not surprising regarding the book of Joshua, whose present shape displays a deuteronomistic revision elsewhere in the book' (Tov 1992: 330). However, the pluses actually contain elements from D (Deut. 19) and P (in v. 6, compare Num. 35: 25, 28) as well. Consequently, the reworking of the text is of a late date when P and D elements were easily combined (as e.g. is the case in the book of Chronicles, or in the Temple Scroll). It is therefore not plausible to assign the pluses in Joshua 20 to a stratum such as a 'Deuteronomistic' redaction of the book. Moreover, if this were the case, one would expect that LXX would attest at other 'Deuteronomistic' places in Joshua a pre- or proto-Deuteronomistic text, which actually is not the case, at least not in terms of sizeable differences. The pluses of Joshua 20 seem to have more of an occasional character than part of a redaction of the book as a whole.

(2) 1 Samuel 17. The text-critical issue concerning 1 Samuel 17, the story of David and Goliath, represents another most interesting example in terms of the relationship between textual criticism and literary criticism. The text of this story is attested in two versions, a longer one, MT (58 verses) and a shorter one, LXX (32 verses; the larger minuses are 17: 12–31, 41, 48b, 50–8). It is a well-known theory that the latter reflects the earlier version of the text, whereas the longer version (MT) is the result of a later expansion (Lust, and Tov, both in Barthélemy et al. 1986; for the opposite view, see Barthélemy, and Gooding, also both in Barthélemy et al. 1986). The crucial question is whether a literary-cricital analysis of the longer version would confirm, as in the case of Joshua 20, the idea that the shorter version may

well be considered as the (more) original form of the text. There is reason to believe that such an analysis does not support the idea that the version reflected by LXX would converge with a source component of the MT version (Van der Kooij 1992; Aurelius 2002). This would imply that the LXX attests a version of the story which belongs to the history of reception and not to that of the redaction of the book.

SUGGESTED READING

KOOIJ, A. VAN DER 2001. 'Textgeschichte/Textkritik der Bibel, i: Altes Testament'. In: *TRE* xxxiii. 1/2. 148–55.

—— 2002. 'The Textual Criticism of the Hebrew Bible Before and After the Qumran Discoveries'. In E. D. Hiebert and E. Tov. eds., *The Bible as Book: The Hebrew Bible and the Judaean Desert Discoveries*, London: The British Library and Oak Knoll Press, 167–77.

TOV, E. 1997. *The Text-Critical Use of the Septuagint in Biblical Research*, 2nd edn., revised and enlarged. Jerusalem: Simor.

—— 2001. *Textual Criticism of the Hebrew Bible*, 2nd rev. edn. Minneapolis: Fortress Press; Assen and Maastricht: Van Gorcum. orig. 1992.

TREBOLLE BARRERA, J. 1998. *The Jewish Bible and the Christian Bible: An Introduction to the History of the Bible*, trans. W. G. E. Watson. Leiden: Brill; Grand Rapids, Mich.: Eerdmans.

WÜRTHWEIN, E. 1995. *The Text of the Old Testament: An Introduction to the Biblica Hebraica*, 2nd edn., revised and enlarged, trans E. F. Rhodes. Grand Rapids, Mich.: Eerdmans.

BIBLIOGRAPHY

AURELIUS, E. 2002. 'Wie David ursprünglich zu Saul kam (1 Sam 17)'. In C. Bultmann, W. Dietrich, and C. Levin, eds., *Vergegenwärtigung des Alten Testaments. Beiträge zur biblischen Hermeneutik. Festschrift für Rudolf Smend zum 70. Geburtstag*, Göttingen: Vandenhoeck & Ruprecht, 44–68.

BARTHÉLEMY, D. 1978. 'Les tiqquné sopherim et la critique textuelle de l'Ancien Testament. In *idem*, *Études d'histoire du texte de l'Ancien Testament*, OBO 21, Fribourg: Éditions universitaires; Göttingen: Vandenhoeck & Ruprecht, 91–110.

—— GOODING, D. W., LUST, J., and TOV, E. 1986. *The Story of David and Goliath: Textual and Literary Criticism: Papers of a Joint Research Venture*. OBO 73. Fribourg: Éditions Universitaires; Göttingen: Vandenhoeck & Ruprecht.

BORBONE, P. G. 1990. *Il libro del Profeta Osea: Edizione critica del testo ebraico*. Quaderni di Henoch, 2, Turin: Zamorani.

CORTESE, E. 1990. *Josua 13–21: ein priesterschriftlicher Abschnitt im Deuteronomistischen Geschichtswerk*. OBO 94. Freiburg: Éditions Universitaires; Göttingen: Vandenhoeck & Ruprecht.

GOSHEN-GOTTSTEIN, M. H. 1967. '*Hebrew Biblical Manuscripts: Their History and their Place in the HUBP Edition*'. *Biblica* 48: 243–90.

HENDEL, R. S. 1998. *The Text of Genesis 1–11: Textual Studies and Critical Edition*. New York and Oxford: Oxford University Press.

KOOLE, J. L. 1997. *Isaiah, Part 3, Volume 1: Isaiah 40–48*. HCOT. Kampen: Kok Pharos.

KOOIJ, A. VAN DER 1992. 'The Story of David and Goliath: The Early History of Its Text'. *ETL* 68: 118–31.

—— 1994. 'The Ending of the Song of Moses: On the Pre-Masoretic Version of Deut 32:43'. In F. García Martínez, A. Hilhorst, J. T. A. G. M. van Ruiten, and A. S. van der Woude, eds., *Studies in Deuteronomy in Honour of C. J. Labuschagne on the Occasion of his 65th Birthday*, Leiden: Brill, 93–100.

LIM, T. H. 2002. 'Biblical Quotations in the Pesharim and the Text of the Bible—Methodological Considerations'. In E. D. Herbert and E. Tov, eds., *The Bible as Book: The Hebrew Bible and the Judaean Desert Discoveries*, London: The British Library and Oak Knoll Press, 73–9.

MCCARTHY, C. 1981. *The Tiqqune Sopherim and Other Theological Corrections in the Masoretic Text of the Old Testament*. OBO 36. Freiburg: Universitätsverlag; Göttingen: Vandenhoeck & Ruprecht.

ROFÉ, A. 1985. 'Joshua 20: Historico-Literary Criticism Illustrated'. In J. H. Tigay, ed., *Empirical Models for Biblical Criticism*, Philadelphia: University of Philadelphia Press, 131–47.

SOUTHWOOD, C. H. 1975. 'The Problematic *hadurim* of Isaiah xlv 2'. *VT* 25: 801–2.

STECK, O. H. 1991. *Studien zu Tritojesaja*. BZAW 203. Berlin: de Gruyter.

TOV, E. 1992. *Textual Criticism of the Hebrew Bible*. Minneapolis: Fortress Press; Assen and Maastricht: Van Gorcum.

—— 2001. *Textual Criticism of the Hebrew Bible*, 2nd rev. edn. Minneapolis: Fortress Press; Assen and Maastricht: Van Gorcum.

TROMP, J. 2002. 'The Textual History of the Life of Adam and Eve in the Light of a Newly Discovered Latin Text-form'. *JSJ* 33: 28–41.

CHAPTER 34

FORM, SOURCE, AND REDACTION CRITICISM

JOHANNES P. FLOSS

FORM CRITICISM

1. Presuppositions

Form criticism, like source criticism, literary criticism, and redaction criticism, is a scientific method of interpreting the texts of the Old Testament. Before the method and its procedures are described, its presuppositions will be stated: first, in relation to its subject-matter (the texts of the Old Testament); second, in relation to its objectives (interpretation); and third, the qualified sense in which it is scientific.

1.1 The Priority of the Original Languages

The original languages of the texts of the Old Testament, Hebrew and Aramaic, demand the strictest attention. The only working basis for a methodical interpretation is the Hebrew/Aramaic text. Not even a translation that aims to reproduce the syntax of the Hebrew/Aramaic is a satisfactory basis for a scientific interpretation. This stems from the fact that the languages of the Bible are 'dead': that is, since antiquity there have been no native speakers of these languages, and thus there are no competent informants. Israeli speakers of modern Hebrew cannot count as such (Kutscher 1984: 243: 'Israeli Hebrew is a New Entity', and against Buss 1999: 75: 'Jews had known since biblical times how to speak Hebrew'; cf. Kahle 1927 [1967]: 23). This lack of linguistic competence cannot be compensated for by Hebrew philology, because the knowledge of the language by philologists is second-ary, and is influenced by the theoretical assumptions of Western grammars and the language systems of European languages (Richter 1978: 6). An additional problem arises from the two successive periods of the transmission process of the text of the Old Testament: that of the consonantal text, which ended at the beginning of the first century CE, and that of the vocalization of the consonantal text, which followed it from the early seventh to the tenth centuries CE. While the form of the pure consonantal text contains the structures of the words and the structures that bind the words together (morphology and morphosyntax) as well as the syntax, the aim of the vocalization is to make the text readable for the purposes of worship and study. The construction of vowels and syllables thus has a primarily phonetic aim. The vowels of classical Hebrew are retained only partially in the vocalized text (i.e. the Masoretic Text, from the technical term *massora*, meaning 'tradition'), and their structural (phonemic) reconstruction is thus possible on the basis of a knowledge of the Masoretic laws of sounds and syllables (see the morphemic reconstruction of the texts of the Old Testament in *Biblia Hebraica transcripta*, edited by Richter 1991–3). The morphemic reconstruction of the Old Testament makes possible a functional analysis of the different text levels (the levels relating to sound, word, phrase, sentence, and sentence connection). The functional analysis does not confer any linguistic competence in classical Hebrew, but can be understood as a partial substitute for such competence. Above all, it serves as a control and restraint upon the subjective contributions of interpreters. Functional analysis makes pos-sible the transparency, intersubjectivity, and critical examination of interpretation. In addition to the Old Testament texts being written in dead languages, it has to be taken into account that the extant remains of biblical Hebrew/Aramaic are frag-mentary (Richter 1978: 9 notes Ullendorf's comment that biblical Hebrew is 'no more than a linguistic fragment'). This inevitably has a not inconsiderable detri-mental effect on grammatical, morphological, and syntactic analysis.

1.2 Categorizing the Term

Form criticism, like source, literary, and redaction criticism, is deliberately subor-dinated to the general term 'interpretation'. Corresponding to the breadth of its meanings in Latin (*interpretatio* can mean 'clarification', 'interpretation', 'meaning', 'translation', 'understanding', while the Greek verb *hermeneuo* similarly has a wide range of meanings), this term integrates not only the methods described in this chapter, but also the most diverse methodological approaches to determining the meaning of a text. Further, the term has the capacity to unite the various specialisms within Old Testament scholarship, and those who represent them. This unity, which results from the subject of research, is in no way endangered by necessary disagreements about hypotheses and methods. One such is the recently advocated supposed opposition between understanding and elucidating the final form of the text and the exposition of the genesis of the text (Dohmen 2001: 91, 104). Such pseudo-oppositions imply that there is only one method appropriate to a text (understanding and elucidating), as opposed to the allegedly inappropriate method of elucidating its literary genesis. To the latter is accorded the stigma of atomizing the text, and it is often branded as being untheological. But the inappropriateness of such an opposition is indicated by the emphasis on the term 'final form'. This indicates, by definition, that a text has experienced successive forms of literary genesis. The illumination of the literary genesis of the final form of a text is thus an integral part of its elucidation and its understanding.

1.3 Indicators of the Scientific Nature of a Method

While it is impossible here to enter into a theoretical discussion of models of scholarship and science that are current in the philosophy of science (e.g., 'deduct-ive-a priori' or 'inductive-verificatory' models), it is necessary at least to mention the generally acknowledged indicators of what is meant by 'scientific'. The first characteristic is that of the argumentation context. The knowledge gained from research on the texts of the Old Testament, and the conclusions drawn from them, need a systematic context of argumentation. This context is above all that of the text itself, and only to a very limited extent, extra-textual data. Another characteristic relates to the making of hypotheses. If a hypothesis comprehensively explains all the relevant factors, it can count as verified, and thus as a theory. If there are details that it does not explain, it has only a greater or lesser degree of probability. The possibility of being verified is a third, and indispensable, characteristic. Statements can be called scientific only if they prove comprehensible and verifiable. Verifi-ability, in turn, constitutes the pre-condition for intersubjectivity, which is an indispensable aspect of scientific method.

2. Definition of Form Criticism

To begin with, the two elements of the term (form and criticism) need each to be redefined separately.

2.1 Form

The first element, which is used in different senses in linguistics and literary criticism, is understood here as the form of a linguistic sign. As part of a language system, each linguistic sign of this system must assume a form. All linguistic signs of all linguistic levels are by necessity constituted as a form (see 1.1 on text levels). This view of the form goes back to F. de Saussure: 'la langue est une forme et non une substance' (1968: 276). Because of the lack of linguistic competence (Fr. *langage*) for the biblical languages and the termination of any recent actual language use (Fr. *parole*), attention to the form of the linguistic signs receives the highest priority.

2.2 Criticism

The second element of the term, criticism, indicates the analysis of the form as defined in 2.1. Correspondingly, it is also possible to speak of form *analysis*. Because the term 'criticism' has been used as a term or part of a term for methods of the scientific interpretation of texts since the Renaissance and the Enlightenment in dependence upon antiquity, it will be employed here (Bormann and Tonelli 1976: 1249–66; Kraus 1982: 65–70; Buss 1999: 92–155). However, the general term 'form criticism' requires to be distinguished from similar definitions of the same term.

2.3 Delimitation

Because 'form criticism' is frequently used interchangeably with 'form history' (German *Formgeschichte*; cf. Meurer 1999: 82 f.: 'Form criticism ... goes ... back to the work of Hermann Gunkel'. Meurer even speaks of 'form or genre criticism as an instance of the diachronic methods of interpretation'. See also Soulen and Soulen 2001: 61: 'The term *form criticism* is a translation of the German word *Formgeschichte*'), more precise delimitations are urgently needed.

2.3.1 *Formgeschichte* according to M. Dibelius

Formgeschichte as understood by M. Dibelius (who was inspired by Hermann Gunkel's research into genre criticism and its further development and alteration into the criticism of forms by Franz Overbeck and Eduard Norden) was adapted for research on the gospels, and did not mean the linguistic analysis of a specific text. 'Specifically, he defined *Formgeschichte* as a study of the "laws which make the rise of these small genres understandable"' (1919: 3; Buss 1999: 288). Dibelius thus investigated the written individual forms as found in the transmitted text from the point of view of their conditions of origin in the pre-literary oral phase of transmission. On the basis of structural elements, he drew conclusions about the history of the oral genesis of these forms. As a result, he dispensed (necessarily) with the synchronic analysis of individual forms, in order to deal with their diachronic history. However Dibelius's contribution may be judged (see the very informative observations of Buss 1999: 287–308), the adoption by Old Testament scholars of the term as determined by Dibelius, together with the tacit acceptance of the *alteration* in the meaning of the term has not always led to methodological clarity, as the quotation from Meurer above indicates. It is also necessary to note other delimitations.

2.3.2 *Formgeschichte* according to K. Koch

Koch (1989) requires the form-*critical* investigation of literary units that are isolated from their context; but this procedure is for him a *historical* investigation. This conclusion results for Koch from his definition of *Formgeschichte* as a general term for all exegetical methods (which contain the element 'criticism' or 'historical' *geschichtlich*). Even though Koch's understanding of the term agrees with that of Dibelius only verbally, it is quite different from the view of form criticism that is described in this chapter.

2.3.3 *Formgeschichte/Form criticism* according to H. Barth and O. H. Steck

For Barth and Steck (1987) the form-historical aspect also concerns the linguistic shaping of a text. The description of this linguistic shape, however, is confined to the ascertainment of first-hand results, which are even then qualified as 'provisional'. In the subsequent genre analysis these results would then be shown to be either corroborated, or in need of correction, or even eventually false. However, this raises the question of how a written linguistic sign can be provisional in relation to the various text levels. Of course, the understanding of the content of a text and the decision of an interpreter can be provisional. The consequences of an assumed closer connection between form and content are evident here, which is maintained against Richter (1971; Barth and Steck 1987: 58 n. 84). Later, it will be shown, in furtherance of the views of Richter, how methodologically indispensable it is to distinguish between form and content, on the one hand, and the function of this distinction, on the other. The 'indissoluble connection between form and content' that is claimed by Barth and Steck (1987: 58 n. 84), which undoubtedly exists and which, incidentally, has never been disputed by Richter, can also be explained from the notion of form that is maintained in this chapter. Additional proof is needed, however. Mere assertion ('the linguistic utterance in its extant contoured form ... includes the formed content': Barth and Steck 1987: 57 n. 84) is no substitute for proof.

2.3.4 Biblical form criticism according to M. Buss

In his study published in 1999, Buss understands form criticism as genre criticism. 'The study of literary (including oral) forms, or form criticism can be defined as the study of patterns of speech' (Buss 1999: 15). Referring to Gunkel, the designation of form criticism is explicitly commented on : 'in fact, it properly denotes a holistic design of speech, including its perceptible (physical) phenomena, its (referential) content and its (socio-psychological) role' (1999: 16). The *Handbook of Biblical Criticism* by R. N. and R. K. Soulen also understands form criticism as genre criticism, as indicated by the observations under the entry 'form criticism'. Irsigler (1995) offers a brief summary of the origin, subject aims, and the altered understanding of *Formgeschichte*, as opposed to form criticism.

3. Form Criticism according to W. Richter

3.1 *Methodological Breakthrough*

The separation of the terms 'form' and 'genre' is indispensable, according to Richter, because form has to do with a single text, whereas genre concerns a text type: that is, a number of individual texts with comparable, similar, or identical structural elements. The individual text that is to be analysed for its form must, according to Richter, be available in its original extent. If this original extent is not available, it has to be investigated by means of literary criticism ($\rightarrow$Source/literary criticism). In that the literary unit that is to be the object of *form*-critical analysis is isolated by *literary* criticism, this methodological step (form criticism) necessarily presupposes literary criticism. Richter also acknowledges the possibility of form-critically analysing an individual text that has not been investigated by literary-critical means. Such form criticism will then, however, in his view, describe only the 'last edited state': i.e. the final form of the text (cf. the quotation summing up the preceding discussion at Richter 1971: 72). The narrowing of the investigation of form to the individual text, as well as the small literary units, yields their *synchronic* quality. Whereas *Formgeschichte* (form *history*) proceeds mainly diachronically, form *criticism* is strictly synchronic. Herein lies the most important difference between the view of form criticism that is adopted in this chapter and those referred to above in 2.3.1–4. Richter must take the credit for being the first scholar to offer terminological and methodological clarity. He divides form criticism into the analysis of the form and the function of the form. By means of the criteria for analysing the form ('ornamental' and 'structural' form), Richter delineates the procedure of form criticism. Weight is put unmistakably on the analysis of the structural forms (the procedures concerning ornamental forms are dismissed fairly quickly, because the indices of ornamental forms—sound, rhythm, rhyme, etc.— provide very little significant data in texts transmitted by writing). The structural form is further divided by Richter into 'outer' and 'inner' form. While the analysis of the outer form embraces the description of the syntax (on the levels of sentence and word) and statistics, attention to the inner form provides clues to the 'deep' structure of the unit. This is indicated by the semantic fields of the words and word groups, the alternation of action and speech, their position and movement in the text, as well as the semantic classes of the verbs. The occurrence of characters and the scenes, as well as scene changes, also indicate the deep structure of a text. In the process of illuminating the structural form, special attention is paid to the fixed expressions which, after all, conditionally offer criteria for deciding 'whether a unit is a literary composition or was transmitted in a pre-literary manner' (1971: 99; translation by author). Richter outlines his analysis of forms on the basis of nine examples of forms (1971: 104–13). Under the heading 'Functions of the Forms', Richter discusses the question of the purpose of a unit. Revealing a unit's structure by means of form-critical analysis makes it possible to answer the question of its purpose, which in turn reveals what the unit states or intends. It is important to discover whether this purpose is contained in the unit itself, or whether it refers to something beyond itself. In the latter case it is presumably part of a larger literary complex. In the context of this investigation the fixed expressions, formulae, and schemata may also enable larger contexts to be identified, whether their quality derives from originally literary or redactional activity. Richter makes use here of the term 'horizon', which was introduced by Eissfeldt in 1927 (Richter 1971: 117 n. 142). If all the information given in a unit can be understood from the unit itself, then the horizon will be limited by the beginning and end of the unit. If, however, in order to be understood, information from the unit needs additional details, either from the context preceding or that following the unit, these additional details indicate its wider horizon (forwards, backwards, or in both directions). The unit enables a wider horizon to be recognized in addition to its own horizon as defined by its beginning and end.

3.2 Further Developments and Procedures

Form criticism as understood by Richter obviously presupposes grammar, and in particular a linguistically based grammar, because the description of the various text levels in form criticism cannot be undertaken without their grammatical definition. Richter is well aware of this as his *Grundlagen einer althebräischen Grammatik* (Foundations of a Grammar of Ancient Hebrew) begun in 1978 shows, together with the additional volumes published in 1979 and 1980. In his methodological programme published in 1971, Richter gives only a brief account of the relationship between literature and structural linguistics (pp. 29–30). The methodology advocated by Fohrer and others (1973, cited here according to the 6th edn. of 1993), which in many aspects agrees with that of Richter (e.g. in the operation and aims of literary criticism) pays particular attention to linguistic prerequisites. This expresses itself in the designation of the second methodological step after the literary criticism which he puts under the heading of 'linguistic analysis', and not form criticism. Above all, the point is emphasized that the texts of the Old Testament are 'ossified linguistic events' (Fohrer *et al.* 1993: 59). For this reason the linguistic signs divided into their particular levels receive special attention. The term 'form criticism' is then deliberately avoided, because, as Richter shows, it goes beyond the methodological separation of the two aspects and *in fact* divides form and content, and thus creates the impression that 'formal analysis can be undertaken with the deliberate neglect of the aspect of meaning' (Fohrer *et al.* 1993: 65). The objection, which is not expressed as strongly as that of Barth and Steck cited above, is not all that convincing, especially since in further procedures of linguistic analysis except for semantic analysis Fohrer *et al.* agree extensively with Richter (1993: 76–8). In this way the attempt is made to come nearer to the level of meaning, starting from the lexical morphemes. Utzschneider and Nitsche also prefer the term 'text analysis' to form criticism (2001: 59–112). R. Knierim (1985) provides an informative overview of the development of the discussion about form up to 1985 (pp. 136–8). His question as to whether the analysis of the structure of a text belongs to literary criticism or form criticism must be answered in favour of form criticism. Form criticism according to Richter's intention and to some extent in the sense of Fohrer *et al.*'s linguistic analysis first became possible on the basis of Richter's foundational Hebrew grammar (see above). Richter's grammatical description of the morphology, morphosyntax, and sentence syntax on the basis of the categories of linguistics made possible a form criticism based on the linguistic levels of a text. I have developed a 'level-specific analysis in order to present the structure of the plane of expression (*Ausdrucksseite*)'. By means of metalinguistic categories of description, the data of each text level from word to sentence connection levels is registered in ascending order, and evaluated in regard to their effect in each immediately superior text level. In a syntactic synthesis the networks connecting the four levels are described. Through the syntactic synthesis of all the signs *qua* means of expression, the uncovering of the semantic function of the expression plane (*Ausdrucksseite*) in a semantic matrix is achieved, which in turn serves as the basis for an analysis of the structure of the content plane (Floss 1982: 88–178; for the procedure, Floss 1991: 691–2). Form criticism as the level-specific analysis of modes of expression was taken up and further developed by Seidl (1982) and Irsigler (1984). Along with bringing greater precision to the criteria and procedures of analysis, Irsigler, going beyond Floss and Seidl, has integrated aspects such as lexis, stylistics, and text typology into form criticism. The result is designated by Irsigler as 'criticism of the text-structure' (1984: 140).

4. Form Criticism as an Impetus for Research into Old Testament Texts and Language

Form criticism, as expounded by Richter, carries many traits of provisionality. It is a component of 'An Outline of an Old Testament Theory of Literature and Methodology'. Outlines are provisional, and not forever. Their purpose is to provoke, and not to legislate. Although books of method following Richter have appeared (unaltered) in a number of editions, as though there had been no advance in research, there were no further editions of *Exegese als Literaturwissenschaft*

(Exegesis as the Study of Literature). Richter's first 'outline' drew attention to gaps in scholarship: for example, the lack of a foundation Hebrew grammar. While at the end of the twentieth century interpreters of the Old Testament were still indebted to the grammars of the nineteenth (Gesenius and Kautzsch) or the first quarter of the twentieth century (Bergsträsser, Joüon, Brockelmann), and while authorities such as de Saussure and Chomsky seemed to be unknown to members of the scholarly guild, Richter was swimming against the (sluggish) current and writing a foundation grammar based on linguistics. The form criticism that was continued on this basis by Richter's students consisted in discovering further gaps. The morphemic transcription of the often uneven Masoretic Text in respect of orthography, phonemics, and syntax may have seemed completely superfluous to the mainstream of Old Testament research; but it challenges each interpreter 'before ascending into the realm of spiritual dimensions to grapple with the small matters of grammar, lexicon, text and writing' (Richter 1983: 2). Richter's publication entitled 'Transliteration and Transcription', from which this quotation is taken, not only offers the possibility of such 'grappling'; it also provides the basis for the already mentioned *Biblia Hebraica transcripta* (*BHt*) published under Richter's editorship in 1991–3. Its use enables time-consuming attention to the 'small matters of grammar' to be considerably reduced, in so far as such questions are in any case of interest to interpreters. Those who look further than their noses will immediately recognize the value of *BHt* for computer-based text analysis (see further below). Form criticism as level-specific 'analysis of the expression plane' (Floss) or as 'criticism of the text structure' (Irsigler) uncovered further gaps in scholarship. How do verbs function? What valency do they possess? Attention has focused especially upon the syntax of verbal clauses, concerning which there has hitherto been scarcely any extensive information in the grammatical literature, so that 'the Hebrew verbal clause appears as an accidental linguistic form' (Richter 1985: 2). Richter's investigations into the valency of Hebrew verbs published in 1985 spear-headed the advance of form criticism of the 'outline' of 1971. Following up the investigation of 1985 into valency were the works of Richter (1986), Seidl (1997), and Häusl (1997). Nissim's 2000 publication provides an investigation of the valency of all ancient non-agentive Hebrew verbs. Valency research has revealed further desiderata for the descriptive syntax which is part of form criticism. Gross investigated in 1987 'the pendens construction of biblical Hebrew', and thus provided syntactic elucidation for one of the most frequent and important aspects of style in biblical Hebrew. In 1995 Rechenmacher presented a concise but convincing investigation of the attributive sentence in which he went beyond observations on syntax to treatment of modes of speech typology. Gross, with the assistance of Disse and Michel, dedicated to Richter in 1996 an exhaustive investigation concerning the order of constituents in the verbal clause of Old Testament prose, which opened up further avenues for research. All these advances, which were the result of the impetus to research provided by the 1971 'outline', eventually led Richter with the *Biblia Hebraica transcripta* to the decision to make use of computers for the interpretation of Old Testament texts, because only by means of analyses based upon computation could the interpretation of Old Testament texts be carried out with greater precision and success. Eckhardt, a member of Richter's circle, published in 1987 a 'computer-based analysis of ancient Hebrew texts', and thereby established a programme of the 'algorithmic recognition of the morphology'. He was followed in 1990 by Specht's 'knowledge-based analysis of ancient Hebrew morphosyntax', which he named 'the AMOS expert system'. Richter devoted his time and energies exclusively to the basic research initiated by his form criticism. The subtitles of the 'materials for a data bank of ancient Hebrew' can be briefly mentioned in the order of their year of publication: 'Personal names in biblical Hebrew and Aramaic analysed morphologically and syntactically' (1996), 'Nominal forms' (1998), 'Phrases (2000), 'Verbal forms (2002). These materials were produced with the assistance of Rechenmacher and Riepl, as was 'the transcription of ancient Hebrew inscriptions' (1999).

5. The Problem of Form and Content

5.1 *De Saussure's Theory of Signs and the Model of Semiological Constructivism*

The notion of form was defined above (sect. 2.1) according to de Saussure's definition of the language system (*langue*). This in no sense means, as Barth and Steck allege of Richter's understanding of form, that form has no content. When de Saussure ascribes form *to* a language system but *denies* its substance, this is to be understood on the basis of his theory of the sign. Linguistic signs are realized for de Saussure in two 'states of matter', analogous to the solid and the liquid, as Jäger puts it (Jäger 1997: 205 n. 25): namely, first as elements of semiological consciousness. De Saussure calls the linguistic sign in this state a *parasème*. The second aggregate condition he calls an *aposème*. De Saussure describes the aposeme metaphorically as an 'envelope de sème' or even as a 'cadavre de sème' (Jäger 1997: 205 n. 25). The metaphorical description of the aposeme enables it to be recognized as the linguistic sign of *expression*.

5.2 *'Paraseme' and 'Aposeme' as Key Terms in the Form–Content Problem*

The structural division of the linguistic sign (*sème*) by de Saussure and Jäger's model of semiological constructivism, built upon Saussure and W. von Humboldt, can contribute to the elucidation of the form–content problem. Parasemes are:

individual sediments of communication experiences; as such they are preserved picked up in the absent/present network structure of psychological systems ('parasemies'). On the other hand they just as well appear as present entities in discourse, as aposemes, as 'shells' of the paraseme with no meaning in themselves . . . Above all in the state of presence the structural dichotomy, which is absolutely constitutive of the linguistic sign, is clear: aposemes are both expressions of the speech intentions of speakers in the course of making themselves understood and thus tied to the parasemic sense horizon and at the same time interpretation stimuli for the meaning-seeking procedures of the comprehending hearer, who thus activates his parasemic sense horizon. (Jäger 1997: 205; translation here and in subsequent quotations from Jäger by author)

There are two reasons for this long quotation. First, its makes clear the *difference* between form (= aposeme) and content (= paraseme), as well as their *indivisible* connection in the linguistic sign. On the other hand, the priority of noting and describing the form in 'dead' languages becomes immediately apparent. The indispensable attempts at mutual understanding between speaker and hearer according to the model of semiological constructivism are entirely lacking for texts in 'dead' languages. But does it follow that no use whatever can be made of a model that explains 'living' languages to grasp the meaning of texts in 'dead' languages? Too hasty an affirmative answer would yield grave consequences. It would never then be possible to grasp the meaning of texts in dead languages, because the parasemic sense horizon of the speaker (= the author of the texts) has long since become defunct, and thus there can be 'no mode of familiar communication' (Jäger 1997: 205) with present-day readers of these texts. A less hasty decision, however, raises the question of which elements from de Saussure's theory of linguistic signs and Jäger's account of semiological constructivism can be taken over for grasping the meaning of texts in 'dead' languages. This question gains its legitimacy from the fact that the 'dead' languages were once 'living' languages, linguistic systems to which de Saussure's theory of signs and the model of semiological constructivism would have been applicable. A further question is *whether* and *how* the parasemic sense horizon of the speaker or author that once existed and which has undoubtedly left its traces in the text can be grasped from the text. An answer to this question would be a great gain for settling the long-running argument about form and content in Old Testament scholarship.

5.3 *Limits, Possibilities, and Conditions of the Appropriation*

De Saussure's theory of the linguistic sign and the epistemological, semiotic, and communication-theoretical assumptions of semiological constructivism presuppose, as already indicated, the existence of spoken languages and recent speakers. If even a partial appropriation is to prove valid, the texts in the 'dead' language must enable text signals to be found which show conclusively whether the epistemological, semiotic, and communication-theoretical bases of semiological constructivism find confirmation even in a text in biblical Hebrew. I have recently

(Floss 2005) tested the limits and possibilities of this appropriation on the basis of Psalm 77 and formulated the conditions thereof.

5.3.1 Epistemological assumption

If, according to the basic epistemological assumptions of Jäger's account of semiological constructivism (also building on W. von Humboldt and taking further the work of Antonio Damasio), 'self-awareness … can only develop in the course of a somatic self-perception of the spirit' (Jäger 1997: 203), it must be possible also in a text in a 'dead' language (in this case, Psalm 77) to rediscover signals of a (religious/believing) consciousness. As I (Floss 2005: 161–81) show in a detailed manner, the rediscovered *topoi* of the religious/believing traditions of Israel in the psalm have left a trace that cannot be overlooked or overheard. Also the genre of Psalm 77, that of the individual lament, leaves unmistakable traces that indicate that the self-aware religious/believing individual constituted through 'somatic self-address' (Damasio) and semiological interaction (Humboldt; Jäger 1997: 204) has not, in the extant text, faded into unrecognizability.

5.3.2 Semiotic assumption

As emphasized above, only a partial appropriation is possible: namely, the relevant part of the second 'aggregate condition'. For today's reader/hearer of biblical texts, the interlocutor who constructs the meaning is lacking. In his grammar, Richter (see sect. 4 above) has supplied the prerequisites for making the functional analysis of the expression plane of a text in such a precise form, that they 'can almost take on the role of a competent speaker' (1978: 8). In relation to the terminological inventory of Jäger's semiotic assumption, this means that the linguistic signs that are found *materially* in the Hebrew text in the form of aposemes are observed according to indices which can indicate the communicative intention of the author and his parasemic horizon of meaning. Of course, this will not provide absolute clarity concerning the communicative intention of the original speaker/author. How will that be possible, when even in a contemporary linguistic interchange 'no factor that transcends the discourse, no other criterion, exists other than that both partners in the discourse have learned the semanticisation of the aposemes interactively in similar speech games?' (Jäger 1997: 205).

5.3.3 Communication—theoretical assumption

According to everything just said about the epistemological and semiotic assumptions of semiological constructivism, Jäger's communication-theoretical assumption cannot serve as the model for linguistic communication seen as a process of the transfer of information (from sender to receiver). For, as has been shown, the common stock of signs between informant and addressee relates within the same linguistic system only to the aposemes. The parasemes, because of the individual communicative experiences between informant and addressee, are no longer congruent. Between a ('dead') biblical Hebrew text and a contemporary reader/hearer there exists an even less common stock of signs. The aposemes are indeed accessible through philological studies. But the 'efforts at mutual understanding which become a communicative site at which the partners in the discourse participate in establishing in a specific way that is constitutive of the communicated meaning' presumed by Jäger for 'living' languages (Jäger 1997: 207) simply do not exist between a biblical text and its contemporary readers/hearers. The central element of Jäger's communication-theoretical assumption can, however, be utilized, and is decisive for the solution of the form–content problem. If this element consists 'in working out the modality of the aposeme' (Jäger 1997: 208), and an aposeme functions as 'a structured expression' of a semantic intention, then the aposeme in texts of a 'dead' language can be understood 'as the interpretable mediating entity of the communicative interaction of the partners to the discourse' (Jäger 1997: 208) in so far as the contemporary partners in the discourse (the readers/ hearers of the biblical text) undertake the above-mentioned functional analysis and so to some extent become a substitute for the interlocutor who is no longer directly available. For the use of the basic assumptions of semiological constructivism as outlined in 5.3.1–2 see now Floss 2005).

Source/Literary Criticism

1. The Ambiguity of the Terms

1.1 Source

The term 'source' as used in connection with a transmitted text of lesser or greater extent connotes, first—as in the everyday meaning of the term 'source'—the aspect of the origin/provenance of the material in a general way. Specifically, this aspect of 'source' is concretized in many and different ways. A 'source' for a historian may be a single written document which is chosen as the object of research in order to shed light on the origin/provenance and contexts of past historical events and/or people. For Rendtorff, 'the Old Testament is the single source from which we learn something about the course and context of [Israel's] history' (1988: 1). In accordance with Rendtorff, it is possible to understand the whole Old Testament in practice as a 'source' in the restricted sense of a source for Israel's history, and in an unrestricted sense as a source for Jewish and Christian belief. According to A. Alt (1968: 183) it is necessary before historical questions are addressed to the biblical text to clear up the literary foreground for the historical field of work. As a part of the notion of source criticism, 'source' is understood differently again. This understanding has its roots in the rediscovery of ancient conceptions of history at the time of the Renaissance and humanism, and the resultant attention to ancient sources. The attempt was made to study these in their original languages. Biblical scholarship was also not unaffected by the modern movement *ad fontes*. The critical study of the Bible, led by Hebrew philology, noted duplications and contradictions in the Old Testament text, above all in that of the Pentateuch. In the search for the reasons for such duplications, etc., theories were developed. In connection with the term 'source criticism' the term 'source' came to designate written documents of greater or smaller length whose subsequent inclusion in, and addition to, the final text could have caused the duplications and contradictions that had been observed. By isolating such sources, for which terms such as *documents* or *fragments* were also employed, it was expected that light would be shed on the literary composition of the texts, and insights would be gained into the history, faith, and religion of Israel (cf. Kraus 1982: 25–8, 242–59).

1.2 Literary Criticism

The method by means of which the isolation of sources was attempted was first called 'literary criticism', and then simply 'source criticism'. It was originally confined to the study of the Pentateuch. Its results culminated in the 'newer documentary hypothesis' formulated by Graf, Kuenen, and Wellhausen. Its further development (by Eissfeldt, Fohrer, and others) was called 'the latest documentary hypothesis'. In fact, all these modifications to the documentary hypothesis, which have continued to the most recent times, indicate the weakness of literary criticism, in so far as it has been understood and practised as *source* criticism. For attempts to isolate literary elements have not led in many parts of the Pentateuch to the discovery of one or more sources. Additionally, there are often great differences in results despite the use of the same method (e.g. cf. in Gross 1974: 419–28 the variegated results of the literary analyses of the prose in Numbers 22–4). These divergences presumably have their origin in methodological criteria that are differently defined and employed. Nevertheless, literary criticism serves to establish the unity or lack of unity of a text (cf. also Gross 1974: 143–7). Literary criticism thus constitutes the first methodological step on the path to seeking the origin and the provenance of a text. Further steps (including form criticism and redaction criticism) must follow later, in order to place a stratum or source in its proper place within a larger textual whole where possible (cf. Richter 1971: 50). Here, the term 'literary criticism' is used rather than 'source criticism'. It goes without saying that with this narrowing of the term no option for or against the documentary or source hypothesis, which to this day is disputed or challenged, is implied (see Zenger 2001: 113–18 for the present state of the discussion).

2. Subject, Definition, Aim

Prior to the description of criteria, their use, and the appraisal of their demonstrative ability, it is necessary to consider the subject, definition, and aim of literary criticism. The order in which they are considered follows from the context in which they are grounded.

2.1 Subject

The subject, in the broadest sense, is the text that is transmitted in writing in the Hebrew/Aramaic Bible, to the extent that its literary unity is not immediately self-evident. Since this evidence of unity is the exception rather than the rule, every Old Testament text which lacks this evidence must be investigated in the context of a scientific literary-critical interpretation. In the narrower sense, every literary complex can be seen as the subject of literary criticism to the extent that this single text or text-complex lacks evidence of literary unity (cf. Richter 1971: 49; Barth and Steck 1987: 13; Fohrer *et al.* 1993: 45–6; Kaiser 1975: 23; Schmidt 1991: 211; Gross 1995: 648–9; Utzschneider and Nitsche 2001: 233–5). An opposite view is found in Dohmen, who, referring back to B. Jacob (1928 and 1930) is sceptical about the process of isolating literary sources, at any rate of that which is understood as source criticism. When he says that 'the value of such analysis' must be measured by the 'plausibility of the (methodologically) necessary synthesis', it is necessary to take notice. Is not this synthesis also agreed upon by all the writers just mentioned? The breadth with which Dohmen cites Jacob's opinion (2001: 89–92) evokes the suspicion that by this synthesis he means the 'final form' of the text, since he shares Jacob's scepticism about discovering any possible literary growth of the text.

2.2 Definition

Literary criticism is understood here as the method by which the literary integrity of a text is examined by means of a number of criteria that are relevant to the subject (i.e. a written text). At each stage of its procedure it is a synchronic method. Both the use of the criteria and the establishing of the lack of unity of a text in each case, as well as the resulting determination of the relation of the parts of the text to each other (relative diachrony) have to take place strictly at the level of the text under investigation, i.e. in the domain of synchrony. Literary criticism understood as synchronic is thus distinct from conventional *source* criticism, which improperly mixed synchrony and diachrony and was connected with the search for sources always according to their age and their subsequent redactional incorporation.

2.3 Aim

The aim of literary criticism comes from the definition of this term within its methodology. It lies in answering the question of whether the text that is being analysed is a literary unity or whether there are indications that it is composite. If the latter is the case, the aim of the literary-critical investigation is expanded to embrace the relative diachrony of the various elements of the text. Synchronically, an answer to the question is sought as to which textual element (or elements) is (or are) the presupposition for other textual elements. At this stage of the analysis the decision is confined to determining the original unit (*Ausgangseinheit*). Richter calls this 'the older unity' (1971: 70). Although he understands 'older' in a relational sense, the term 'original unity' will be used instead of 'older' in order to avoid misunderstanding.

Richter (1971: 70–2) gives (as examples) three cases which make possible the reaching of a decision. (1) Larger unit versus a single sentence or sentences: because the latter can hardly have existed as isolated cases, they are allocated to a later stage in the relative diachrony than the larger unit. The decision can be firmed up in so far as these single sentences indicate that they are additions (through such things as repetitions) to the greater unit. In addition, there are also more extensive insertions, which presuppose the original unity (compare the examples and their evaluation at Richter 1971: 70–1). (2) The original unit has been enlarged either at its beginning and/or at its end: these parts of the text then prove to be a frame for the original unit. These framing parts thus presuppose the unit which they frame (cf. the examples from Judges, Richter 1971: 71). (3) Two small units have been worked into each other: in this case each must have existed previously as a separate entity. Determining their relative diachrony is then not possible. This, however, could still be achieved if 'one was composed in the view of the other' (Richter 1971: 71).

3. The Criteria

Richter 1971 set the standards for the criteria of the method, its certainty, and its utility. Otto Eissfeldt, one of the old masters of classical literary criticism, according to Knierim (1985: 129), replied to G. von Rad's request in the early 1950s for a guide to literary criticism for students with a reference to his own introductory handbook. Richter (1971: 51 nn. 5–7) also referred to the 'arguments' of Eissfeldt and other scholars occasionally mentioning criteria. Richter can be credited with establishing and grounding the ranking order of the criteria, their certainty, and their utility. They are (1) duplications and repetitions, (2) contradictions (3) further observations, and (4) parallels to other parts of the text (for copious examples cf. Richter 1971: 51–62). The first criterion has the greatest weight. This weight becomes less with a rise in the number of criteria. 'Certainty in a decision is scarcely possible with a single one of these indicators' (Richter 1971: 62). It is not only the cumulation of criteria that increases the certainty. A decision is most certain when all criteria are present, although this is seldom enough. Arneth (2002: 389) sees the 'common indices for the presence of literary growth taken from the data'. From those that are indicated, only doublets, syntactic breaks, and contradictions are included here.

'Differences in terminology', 'differences in style', 'peculiarities of speech', 'elements typical of a genre', occasion further analytical steps: for example, form criticism. As in the case of form criticism, Richter's methodology has produced 'disciples'. Fohrer and others (1993: 45–58) do not deviate essentially from Richter. Also, Barth and Steck (1987: 34–8) agree to a considerable extent with Richter concerning the aim (examining the literary integrity) and the necessity of literary criticism. Also, even though in a modified way, they agree about the limiting of the criteria. As opposed to Richter, Barth and Steck deal with the question of the greater literary contexts and strata as well as their identification and historical ordering on the level of literary criticism, although they admit that further methodological steps are eventually necessary. Dohmen (2001) interprets this requirement quite liberally. He deals with the list of well-known repetitions and contradictions in the story of the Flood by means of arguments drawn from semantics, narrative logic, and narrative technique, and 'on the basis of the rich treasury of ancient oriental stories of the flood' (p. 101). Gen. 6: 9 ('these are the generations of Noah ...'), 'which inserts a midrashic type of addition' (p. 101), allegedly interrupts the context of Gen. 6: 5–8. These exclusively noetic arguments possess neither literary nor redaction-critical weight. Regarding the appropriateness, utility, and certainty of the criteria, and with them the method in general, note must be taken of the very important monograph of G. Vanoni, 'Literary Criticism and Grammar'. In the course of his investigation of the repetition and contradictions in 1 Kings 11–12, Vanoni draws attention not only to the necessity of literary criticism as the very first step of analysis (1984: 18–21). He is able to demonstrate the priority of textual criticism initially within a *single* strand of the transmitted text (e.g. only in the strand of MT) in its positive consequence for literary criticism. By the textual criticism of several strands of tradition (e.g. the MT strand and the LXX strand at the same time), relevant literary critical indices may often, he says, be clarified in the course of textual criticism. A text thus 'cleared up' might possibly appear as a unit, while the MT in itself must be regarded as composite (cf. 1984: 269). 'An examination that integrates the textual and linguistic features as much as possible has been valuable for literary criticism' (1984: 169). The innovative function which literary criticism acquires through grammar, and which Vanoni convincingly expounds, can be explained again through the impetus which came from Richter's methodology in 1971.

REDACTION CRITICISM

1. Methodological Categorization

The last step for analysing the content of a text is, according to Richter's method (1971), 'to explain the literary fusion and editing of the individual units and compositions' (1971: 165). This analytical step presupposes the following obligatory operations: (1) literary criticism, in which the parts of the texts have been established and placed in their relative diachrony; (2) form criticism, in which the textual contexts and texual horizons and the units that are eventually formed are recognizable; (3) genre criticism, which makes it possible 'to establish the upper limits, namely, the transition from pre-existing units to literary compositions' (1971: 166). As in these preceding operations, redaction criticism concerns itself with form and not with content. Composition and redaction are, according to Richter, to be distinguished through the intensity of editorial work. Composition can be recognized by a more intensive engagement with the units and the way that they are fitted together and built into episodes to achieve a desired end. Redaction tends to put the individual texts next to each other, but in an uncoordinated way (cf. Richter 1971: 166 n. 4). Because both composition and redaction concern the editorial working of pre-existing literary units, both are subjects for redaction criticism. Barth and Steck differ from Richter in methodological procedure. Indeed, they make literary criticism precede redaction history rather than form criticism, in whose place comes tradition history (1987: 50–3). According to Weimar (2001: 302), redaction criticism absolutely presupposes literary criticism as a synthetic procedure. In the process he does not mention form criticism and genre criticism expressly as further prerequisites. Prematurely opposed to redaction criticism, because he is diverted by a concern for the content, he makes redaction criticism inquire after the 'establishment of the literary theological profile' of the redactional interventions. Fohrer *et al.* adhere closely not only to Richter's methodological procedure, but also to his terminological and practical separation of composition and redaction (1993: 139–42). Kratz also seems to require as a prerequisite for redaction criticism 'the determining of the literary and factual unevenesses' (1997: 368), but avoids the term 'literary criticism' in this connection. This he wants to confine to 'alterations in the course of the genesis of the text on the written level'. Against this he distinguishes the *Vorlage* (source text) from the redaction (1997: 367). However, *Vorlage* (source text) is in this connection as much open to misunderstanding (as also used in other senses) as 'genesis of the text on the written level'. A redactionally edited small unit already documents in its original version a textual origin on the written level. These unclarities of terms in Kratz's exposition are no isolated instance. Dohmen lists a whole series of composition and redaction-critical attempts in connection with the narrative of the Flood (2001: 92–5). Because of their divergence, he regards them as well as the traditional source criticism as inadequate to shed light on the genesis of the narrative of the Flood. In view of Kratz's terminological unclarity, it is difficult to avoid the suspicion that the divergences in the redaction-critical and redaction-historical investigations of the narrative of the Flood which Dohmen has pointed out are to be traced back to a deficit in method and methodology (cf. Meurer 1999 and also Utzschneider and Nitsche 2001: 213–85). Under the general term 'history of the text' one can find in the latter work 'combining methods' and 'mutation'). As a result in what follows, the term, the criteria, and the function of redaction criticism must be established precisely.

2. The Term

Redaction (from *redigere* in the transferred meaning of 'to make something in some form of composition, to bring or make or turn it into a state or condition', compare Georges 1962 *sub voce*) is understood here as the last editorial stage of a written text. Its result marks the final text. Regardless of whether this editorial work is compositional activity or indicates a looser joining together of given texts, it aims to produce a whole. Redaction *criticism* is the methodological step which seeks to uncover and indicate the prerequisites for the course of redaction which have been named above in section 1 (cf. Richter 1971: 167–8; Barth and Steck 1987: 51 n. 73; Fohrer *et al.* 1993: 142; Kaiser 1975: 24; Weimar 2001: 302).

3. The Criteria

The initial criteria are provided by the *small* units and their diverse *formal construction*, as well as their *aims* and *horizons*. On the basis of these initial criteria, further criteria of *given* and *constructed* units can be distinguished. The examination of their relationship to each other indicates a further point of difference. This yields information about whether it is a case of *compositional intentions* or merely *unconnected juxtapositions*. In the case of *self-sufficient units* ('traditions'), questions are asked about the nature of their editing (enlarged or framed through an addition or additions). From form criticism (aim and horizon) the criteria are obtained for ordering the parts of the text or the editing. With such criteria it is possible to distinguish composition from looser redaction (cf. Richter 1971: 167 f.) and also but with different emphasis Fohrer *et al.* 1993: 143–7). Units without context can be of various kinds (additions, interpolations, glosses).

4. Function

The assembling and designation of criteria is not sufficient for a redaction-critical evaluation. The function that can be read from them goes further. Information about this is given by the structures into which the individual elements determined by form criticism have been edited. If these structures are now examined in connection with the putting together of the parts of the text through redaction, it becomes apparent 'that not only each unit, but also each composition, stratum and redaction indicates a structure' (Richter 1971: 170). The whole structure presents itself either as unique or refers to parallels. In the latter case it is possible, as in form criticism, to look for fixed expressions which possibly belong to a genre. Out of the complete structure it is further possible to discern the aim or an intention. 'With them it is possible to determine the *Sitze im Leben* (basis in reality) of the compositions and redactions, and their authors and redactors. Thus at *end of redaction criticism* [my emphasis] it is possible to recognise the various sociological and intellectual historical backgrounds of the individual works and redactions and their authors right down to the final hand' (Richter 1971: 172).

5. The Mutation of Terms and Methods

The lack of clarity of terms which has been described in section 1 above, as well as the presumed deficits in methods and methodology are connected with the main point about the various attempts to explain the origin of the Pentateuch either through modifications of the 'newer documentary hypothesis' or by means of 'an extensive new analysis of the Pentateuchal narrative fund' (von Rad 1972: 362). Such concerns are understandable and necessary for large areas of the Pentateuch, the clarification of whose origin can hardly, if at all, be supplied by the documentary hypothesis. The great divergences in the results of the literary-critical analysis as source criticism undermine the high regard in which this hypothesis is held. An extensive new analysis has been undertaken above all by R. Rendtorff (1977) and E. Blum (1984 and 1990). The high-profile publications of these two scholars cannot here be given an appropriate evaluation. They are, however, symptomatic of the aforementioned mutation of terms and methods. Factually, remarks about Rendtorff and Blum are pertinent in an essay on redaction criticism to the extent that they use terms and criteria which to some extent touch upon redaction criticism and to some extent upon form and genre-critical aspects. The 'tradition-historical problem of the Pentateuch' leads Rendtorff to a solution in which he sees the great 'tradition complexes' as comprehensively edited (1977: 42–57). If one considers these greater complexes of tradition which are obtained by the content-orientated criterion of 'the narrative substance' (1977: 69 and frequently), these themes are *de facto* only obtained from the postulated content. For the 'editing' of these themes, 'formulaic expressions' (1977: 43 and frequently), are presumed. Since these expressions are mostly components of divine speeches (as promises), they are ascribed the main function for the 'composition of the patriarchal narratives' and are compared with 'a theological editing of the text corpus'. 'Formulaic expressions', a term from form and genre criticism, is mutated here to a criterion for editorial work. What editorial work?! The term 'composition' makes it possible to suppose that what is meant is a stage in the redaction on the way to a written final text. But this is in fact not so, since what is meant is the editing of themes (traditions). Both Blum's monographs contain in the title the term 'composition' as a key concept. As in the case of Rendtorff, this term is not meant as an object of redaction criticism, even if Blum wishes to go further than Rendtorff by 'leaving open the limits of the transmitted units' (1984: 1). Through many detailed analyses, Blum follows his own postulate. He deliberately does not follow the analytical steps of Richter, Barth and Steck, Fohrer *et al.*, Gross, and many others, but pursues further the line of Rendtorff. Apart from the fact that Blum is concerned primarily with the *content* ('narrative substance', 1984: 34), he makes no secret of his individual mutation of methods, when he understands literary criticism as a possible aspect of 'tradition-historical analysis' (1984: 2 n. 3). In the 1990 monograph Blum pursues this path even more consistently. 'Methodologically it is necessary ... as I understand it, to undertake the attempt ... to combine holistic experience of text and interpretation with a kind of diachronic relief description' (1990: 4). This 'relief description' is not only again determined primarily by *content*, but remains methodologically *un*defined. The term cannot be subject to verification and falsification, according to Karl Popper (1984: 26–8, 47–59) the most important criteria for the scientific nature of a hypothesis. Compare on this the reservations of Zenger (2001: 117). Whether one can accept the comparison of Blum grounds of inadequate verification and falsification with regard to the Blum hypothesis, is questionable (Dohmen 1996: 354). Without question, the 'newer documentary hypothesis', which Wellhausen was substantially involved in developing, did indeed fulfil Popper's criteria.

BIBLIOGRAPHY

ALT, A. 1968. *Kleine Schriften zur Geschichte Israels,* i. Munich: Beck.

ARNETH, M. 2002. 'Literarkritik der Bibel'. *RGG* v. 389–90.

BARTH, H., and STECK, O. H. 1987. *Ein Arbeitsbuch für Proseminare, Seminare und Vorlesungen,* 11th edn. Neukirchen-Vluyn: Neukirchener Verlag.

Biblia Hebraica transcripta, ed. W. Richter. ATSAT 33. 1–33. 13. St Ottilien: Verlag Eos, 1991–3.

BLUM, E. 1984. *Die Komposition der Vätergeschichte.* Neukirchen-Vluyn: Neukirchener Verlag.

—— 1990. *Studien zur Komposition des Pentateuch.* BZAW 189. Berlin and New York: Walter de Gruyter.

BORMANN, C. VON, and TONELLI, G. 1976. 'Kritik'. In *Historisches Wörterbuch der Philosophie (HWP)*, Basel: Verlag Schwabe, iv. 1249–66.

BUSS, M. J. 1999. *Biblical Form Criticism in its Context*. JSOTS.S 274. Sheffield: Academic Press.

DIBELIUS, M. 1919. *Die Formgeschichte des Evangeliums*. Tübingen: Mohr Verlag.

DOHMEN, C. 1996. *Schöpfung und Tod: die Entfaltung theologischer und anthropologischer Konzeptionen in Gen 2/3. Aktualisierte Neuauflage von 1988*. Stuttgart Biblische Beiträge, 35. Stuttgart: Verlag Kath. Bibelwerk.

—— 2001. 'Untergang oder Rettung der Quellenscheidung? Die Sintfluterzählung als Prüfstein der Pentateuchexegese'. In A. Wénin, ed., *Studies in the Book of Genesis: Literature, Redaction and History*, Leuven: Leuven University Press, 81–104.

ECKHARDT, W. 1987. *Computergestütze Analyse althebräischer Texte: Algorithmische Erkennung der Morphologie*. ATSAT 29. St. Ottilien: Verlag Eos.

FLOSS, J. P. 1982. *Kunden oder Kundschafter? Literaturwissenschaftliche Untersuchung zu Jos 2, i: Text, Schichtung, Überlieferung*. ATSAT 16. St. Ottilien: Verlag Eos.

—— 1991. 'Formkritik'. In M. Görg and B. Lang, eds., *Neues Bibel-Lexikon*, i, Zürich and Düsseldorf: Benzinger, 691–2.

—— 2005. ' "Aber Deine Spuren wurden nicht bekannt": Bibelhebräische Psalmenlektüre nach dem Konzept des semiologischen Konstruktivismus'. In Gisela Fehrmann *et al.*, eds., 'Spuren, Lekturen': *Praktiken des Symbolischen: Festschrift für Ludwig Jäger*, Munich: Verlag Wilhelm Fink, 167–81.

FOHRER, G. *et al.* 1993. *Exegese des Alten Testaments: Einführung in die Methodik*, 6th edn. Uni(versitäts)-Taschenbücher, 267. Heidelberg and Wiesbaden: Verlag Quelle & Meyer.

GEORGES, K. 1962. *Ausführliches Lateinisch-Deutsches Wörterbuch*, ii, 11th edn. Basel: Verlag Benno Schwabe & Co.

GROSS, W. 1974. *Bileam—Literar- und formkritische Untersuchung der Prosa in Num 22–24*. Studien zum Alten und Neuen Testament. Munich: Kösel-Verlag.

—— 1987. *Die Pendenskonstruktion im Biblischen Hebräisch: Studie zum althebräischen Satz*, i. ATSAT 27. St. Ottilien: Verlag Eos.

—— 1995. 'Literarkritik'. In M. Görg and B. Lang, eds., *Neues Bibel-Lexikon*, ii, Zürich and Düsseldorf: Benzinger, 648–9.

—— 1996. *Die Satzteilfolge im Verbalsatz alttestamentlicher Prosa: Untersucht an den Büchern Dtn, Ri und 2Kön*. Forschungen zum Alten Testament, 17. Tübingen: Mohr.

HÄUSL, M. 1997. *Bedecken, Verdecken, Verstecken*. ATSAT 59. St. Ottilien: Verlag Eos.

IRSIGLER, H. 1984. *Psalm 73—Monolog eines Weisen: Text, Programm, Struktur*. ATSAT 20. St. Ottilien: Verlag Eos.

—— 1995. 'Formgeschichte, Formkritik'. *LThK*, iii. 1353–6. Freiburg im Breisgau: Herder.

JÄGER, L. 1997. 'Die Medialität der Sprachzeichen'. In Maria Lieber and Willi Hirdt, eds., *Kunst und Kommunikation: Betrachtungen yum Medium Sprache in der Romania*, Festschrift zum 60. Geburtstag von Richard Baum, Tübingen: Verlag Stauffenberg, 199–220.

KAHLE, P. 1927 [1967]. *Massoreten des Westens*, i/ii. Hildesheim: Georg Olms.

KAISER, O. 1975. 'Die alttestamentliche Exegese'. In Gottfried Adam *et al.*, eds., *Einführung in die exegetischen Methoden*, 5th edn., Munich: Verlag Kaiser, 9–60.

KNIERIM, R. 1985. 'Criticism of Literary Features, Form, Tradition, and Redaction'. In D. A. Knight and G. M. Tucker, eds., *The Hebrew Bible and its Modern Interpreters*, Philadelphia: Fortress Press, 123–200.

KOCH, K. 1989. *Was ist Formgeschichte? Methoden der Bibelexegese: Fünfte, verbesserte Auflage mit einem Nachwort: Linguistik und Formgeschichte.* Neukirchen: Verlag des Erziehungsvereins.

KRATZ, R. 1997. 'Redaktionsgeschichte/Redaktionskritik'. *TRE* xxviii. 367–78. Berlin and New York: Walter de Gruyter.

KRAUS, H.-J. 1982. *Geschichte der historisch-kritischen Erforschung des Alten Testaments,* 3rd edn. Neukirchen: Verlag des Erziehungsvereins.

KUTSCHER, E. Y. 1984. *A History of Hebrew Language,* ed. Raphael Kutscher, 1st edn. 1982; 2nd corr. edn. 1984. Jerusalem: The Magnes Press, The Hebrew University.

MEURER, T. 1999. *Einführung in die Methoden alttestamentlicher Exegese.* Münsteraner Einführungen—Theologische Arbeitsbücher—3. Münster, Hamburg, and London: LiT-Verlag.

NISSIM, U. 2000. *Die Bedeutung des Ergehens: Ein Beitrag zu einem Biblisch-Hebräischen Valenzlexikon am Beispiel von Ergehensverben.* ATSAT 65. St. Ottilien: Verlag Eos.

POPPER, K. R. 1984. *Logik der Ferschung,* 8. weiter verbesserte und vermehrte Auflage. Tübingen: Mohr Verlag.

RAD, G. VON 1972. *Das erste Buch Mose: Genesis,* 9th edn. Göttingen: Vandenhoeck & Ruprecht.

RECHENMACHER, H. 1995. *Der Attributsatz: Beobachtungen zu Syntax und Redetypik.* ATSAT 46. St. Ottilien: Verlag Eos.

RENDTORFF, R. 1977. *Das überlieferungsgeschichtliche Problem des Pentateuch.* BZAW 147. Berlin and New York: Walter de Gruyter.

—— 1988. *Das Alte Testament: Eine Einführung,* 3rd rev. edn. Neukirchen: Verlag des Erziehungsvereins.

RICHTER, W. 1971. *Exegese als Literaturwissenschaft: Entwurf einer alttestamentlichen Literaturtheorie und Methodologie.* Göttingen: Vandenhoeck & Ruprecht.

—— 1978. *Grundlagen einer althebräischen Grammatik, A: Grundfragen einer sprachwissenschaftlichen Grammatik; B: Die Beschreibungsebene, i. Das Wort (Morphologie).* ATSAT 8. St. Ottilien: Verlag Eos.

—— 1979. *Grundlagen einer althebräischen Grammatik: Die Beschreibungsebenen, ii: Die Wortfügung (Morphosyntax).* ATSAT 10. St. Ottilien: Verlag Eos.

—— 1980. *Die Beschreibungsebenen, iii: Der Satz (Satztheorie).* ATSAT 13. St. Ottilien: Verlag Eos.

—— 1983. *Transliteration und Transkription: Objekt- und metasprachliche Metazeichensysteme zur Wiedergabe hebräischer Texte.* ATSAT 19. St. Ottilien: Verlag Eos.

—— 1985. *Untersuchungen zur Valenz althebräischer Verben, i: 'RK.* ATSAT 23. St. Ottilien: Verlag Eos.

—— 1986. *Untersuchungen zur Valenz althebräischer Verben, ii: GBH, CMQ, QSR II.* ATSAT 25. St. Ottilien: Verlag Eos.

RICHTER, W. 1995. *Materialien einer althebräischen Datenbank: Die bibelhebräischen und aramäischen Eigennamen morphologisch und syntaktisch analysiert.* ATSAT 47. St. Ottilien: Verlag Eos.

—— 1998. *Materialien einer althebräischen Datenbank. Nominalformen.* ATSAT 51. St. Ottilien: Verlag Eos.

—— 1999. *Althebräische Inschriften transkribiert.* ATSAT 52. St. Ottilien: Verlag Eos.

—— 2000. *Materialien einer althebräischen Datenbank: Wortfügungen.* ATSAT 53. St. Ottilien: Verlag Eos.

RICHTER, W. 2002. 'Materialien einer althebräischen Datenbank Verbalformen'. In Hubert lrsigler, ed., *WER DARF HINAUFSTEIGEN ZUM BERG JHWHS?—Beiträge zu Prophetie and Poesie des Alten Testaments—Festschrift für SIGURDUR ÖRN STEINGRÍMSSON zum 70. Geburtstag,* ATSAT 72. St Ottilien: Verlag Eos.

SAUSSURE, F. DE 1968. *Cours de linguistique général,* critical edn., ed. Rudolf Engler, i. Wiesbaden: Verlag Otto Harrassowitz.

SCHMIDT, L. 1991. 'Literarkritik I'. In *TRE* xxi. 211–22.

SEIDL, T. 1982. *Tora für den "Aussatz"- Fall: Literarische Schichten und syntaktische Strukturen in Levitikus 13 und 14.* ATSAT 18. St. Ottilien: Verlag Eos.

—— 1997. *Untersuchungen zur Valenz hebräischer Verben: 3. ṬHR, "Rein sein".* ATSAT 57. St. Ottilien: Verlag Eos.

SOULEN, R. N., and SOULEN, R. K. 2001. *Handbook of Biblical Criticism,* 3rd edn, prev. and expanded. Louisville, Ky.: Westminster/John Knox Press.

SPECHT, G. 1990. *Wissensbasierte Analyse althebräischer Morphosyntax: Das Expertensystem AMOS.* ATSAT 35. St. Ottilien: Verlag Eos.

UTZSCHNEIDER, H., and NITSCHE, S. A. 2001. *Arbeitsbuch literaturwissenschaftliche Bibelauslegung: Eine Methodenlehre zur Exegese des Alten Testaments.* Gütersloh: Kaiser.

VANONI, G. 1984. *Literarkritik und Grammatik: Untersuchung der Wiederholungen und Spannungen in 1Kön 11–12.* ATSAT 21. St. Ottilien: Verlag Eos.

WEIMAR, P. 2001. 'Redaktionskritik'. In M. Görg and B. Lang, eds., *Neues Bibel-Lexikon,* Zürich and Düsseldorf: Benzinger, iii. 302.

ZENGER, E. 2001. *Einleitung in das Alte Testament,* 4th edn. Stuttgart: Kohlhammer.

CHAPTER 35

RHETORICAL AND NEW LITERARY CRITICISM

MARGARET M. MITCHELL

At first glance this chapter seems to be faced with an impossible task, or at the very least to have been assigned a kind of grab-bag of interpretive approaches, in the very pairing of 'rhetorical criticism' with 'new literary criticism', and in the fact that there is no scholarly consensus about what each of those two 'methods' in itself does or should include. Add to that the reality that these methodological approaches have some distinct applications in the Hebrew Bible and in the New Testament, and one seems to be in the position of trying to herd cats. But there is some commonality, and the labels do refer to recognizable shifts on the landscape of biblical scholarship in the second half of the twentieth century.

A usual way of justifying this collocation is the claim that what these interpretive stances essentially share is a quasi-, non-, or even anti-historical perspective in the face of the colossal, impervious mountain of historical-critical biblical scholarship seen as the default setting against which these interpretive modes are 'the other'. This conception of things (from which I will seek to demur in this essay) is indeed not merely externally imposed, for some modern 'rhetorical' and 'literary'-critical approaches to New Testament texts do have in common with one another (and, ironically, with the 'historical-critical method' itself) an originating rhetoric, dating to the 1970s and 1980s, of liberation from a range of Babylonian captivities from which biblical studies required an exodus:

(a) 'biblical texts [being] valued less for what they actually were than for what they told us about other putative texts or events to which there was no direct access'. (Alter and Kermode 1978: 4)

(b) 'from a dogmatist, historical-scientistic or culturally relativist paradigm of interpretation to a critical rhetorical-emancipating paradigm'. (Schüssler-Fiorenza 1999: 57; 1987: 9)

(c) 'out of an increasingly confining captivity, exile or dispersion imposed by the dual hegemony of traditional science and traditional philosophy'. (Wuellner 1987: 462)

(d) 'liberat[ing] biblical narrative from scholars and specialists and giv[ing] it back to nonspecialized readers by emphasizing plot, characterization, and theme'. (West 1992: 424)

(e) 'out of the ghetto of an aesthetizing preoccupation with biblical stylistics which has remained for centuries formalized, and functionless, and contextless'. (Wuellner 1987: 462)

(f) de-centring 'the authority of an author as a "canonical", "elitist", or "privileged" source of knowledge'. (Thiselton 1992: 472, who himself critiques this position)

Equally ironically, these 'new methods' have actually found a large measure of acceptance within 'mainstream' biblical scholarship (such that no *Handbook*, such as this, could bypass them). Yet their precise definitions, responsibilities, and relationship to 'historical-critical' exegesis remain in a process of negotiation and ongoing development.

The present essay will provide one sketch of some historically significant moments in the emergence of these interpretive approaches, and give some methodological pointers and resources for those who seek to comprehend and exercise them. But we should be clear at the outset about expectations: none of these methodologies should be taken as a simple three-point programme for the 'right' reading, or even necessarily an improved one; but each forefronts a different set of questions and resources which an astute reader may profitably bring into play in her or his readings of various biblical texts. Nor should these methodologies be treated as professions; one should not aspire to *be* solely a 'rhetorical critic' or a 'literary critic'. Pluralism in interpretive approaches is no passing modernist or post-modernist fad; it is here to stay, and informed readers should be prepared to hear and (perhaps even) to speak in many tongues, even as they have distinct preferences and proclivities that deserve to be honoured.

The basic assumption informing the present essay is a simple one: texts worth not only reading but rereading, not just for ephemerally pertinent information, but for continual human formation, scrutiny, criticism, and inspiration, when encountered by inquisitive readers (the best kind!), occasion a plurality of questions. Critical methodologies are means whereby experienced readers have learned to follow up those questions fruitfully to reach some answers, or at least insights, into the questions they pose. Many readers of biblical texts are confronted immediately by a range of historical questions: the who, what, when, and where of the ancient contexts denoted and connoted in the texts cry out for explication. And it has been the work of centuries of historiographical investigation, which of course continues at this very moment, to amass, interpret, and judiciously correlate the body of historical data (textual, artefactual, archaeological) with the texts in question. It would be needlessly restrictive (as well as practically impossible) for any reader to bracket off completely *any* whole set or type of question from any consideration, just as it would be uncivil (and unwise) to refuse to grant that other readers may wish to focus their energies in different places from oneself. Given this rationale, rather than taking as a starting-point an inherited dichotomy between clearly demarcated 'historical' and 'ahistorical' methodologies (in agreement with Barton 1998: 18), I would suggest instead that what unites the different methodological approaches I shall cover in this chapter is a pair of somewhat paradoxical values: a shared commitment *to a close reading of the exact wording and inner working of the text*, and an understanding of *the text as in some sense dynamic* rather than static or fixed. One may inculcate these two principles in approaches that emphasize the text's ancient origins, or in those which seek to focus on its modern readers. Most readings meet somewhere in the middle.

RHETORICAL CRITICISM

'Rhetorical criticism' understands a text as dynamic in the sense that it is an instance of communicative persuasion, 'a set of means chosen and organized with an eye to an audience rather than to self-expression or pure making' (Sternberg 1985: 282). If texts are not just denotative of meaning in some cool or dispassionate way, but seek to convince their readers or change their readers' perspectives, that raises the question of *how* they encode that persuasive purpose and how readers (from varying contexts) participate in that reality as they read a text which is meant to (or simply does) elicit certain responses. 'Rhetorical criticism' or, less strictly, interpretations that focus on rhetorical techniques and effects of biblical texts, have been a major part of the interpretive landscape in biblical studies from the mid-1970s to the present. Biblical scholars who talked about rhetoric in the late twentieth century (and the next) did so against two different backdrops: 'the classical rhetorical tradition' (variously represented) and 'the new rhetoric' associated with Kenneth Burke, Chaim Perelman and L. Olbrechts-Tyteca, Wayne Booth, and others which emerged in the 1960s and 1970s. The possible combinations of interface between these disparate sources and the particularities and peculiarities of 'biblical literature' have unsurprisingly brought rather varied results (see the panoply of approaches in such essay collections on 'rhetorical criticism' as Porter 1997, Porter and Stamps, 2002, Hester and Hester [Amador] 2004; a variety reflected in study of rhetoric throughout the humanities, as shown, e.g., by Jost and Olmsted 2004). In general it may be said that 'rhetorical criticism' of the Hebrew Bible and the New Testament overlap most when it comes to their approaches to narrative texts (which are found in both corpora), but diverge in regard to the other major genre characteristic of each one, but not the other—poetry in the Hebrew Bible, and argument-bearing epistles in the New Testament.

Rhetorical Criticism of the Hebrew Bible

'Rhetorical criticism' of the Hebrew Bible is usually said to have been inaugurated in James Muilenberg's 1968 Presidential Address to the Society of Biblical Litera-ture, which beckoned scholars to 'venture beyond the confines of form criticism into an inquiry into other literary features which are all too frequently ignored today' (Muilenberg 1969: 4). What Muilenberg meant was an attention to stylistic features and elements of literary aesthetics on the level of the particularity of the text in question (thus moving against the grain of the accent on the typical in form criticism), grounded in an insistence upon the inseparability of form and content. He urged scholars to attend to the text as an integrated literary unit, a work of art with an internal logic and set of interacting features, which can best be appreciated through a close reading focusing on its beginning and ending, repeated motifs and patterns. His clarion call—not to reject form criticism, but to supplement it with 'rhetorical criticism'—bore fruit among many, such as Phyllis Trible, who exem-plified this approach of heightened literary sensibility to the inner workings and seductive strategies in narratological texts in the corpus of documents making up the Hebrew Bible (Trible 1978, 1984). The interchangeability of 'rhetoric' and 'literary' in the titles of these early books illustrates the direction and thrust that Old Testament rhetorical criticism would take in the decades after Muilenberg. From early on it became a watershed for a whole range of non-historical ap-proaches to biblical texts, 'on their own terms', apart from literary history (form and source criticism) or intense attention to elements of the external historical context as interpretive tools. This move led to an increasing number of 'rhetorical' readings of biblical narratives that were, to all intents and purposes, identical with 'literary readings' (see the contents of Watson and Hauser 1994; further discussion below), and 'rhetorical' studies of Hebrew poetry (e.g. van der Lugt 1995) that focus more strictly on grand structure, strophic patterns, and formal features regarded as 'analytical patterns' of Semitic poetry (West 1992). Though claiming the same methodological moniker ('rhetorical criticism'), the approaches of Trible on Jonah, for instance, and van der Lugt on Job (to cite two recent examples) differ considerably. The latter is an almost classic instance of stylistic analysis of an old and venerable type, if analytically more fine-tuned (for the long history of this approach, see Meynet 1998). The former is marked by its 'snow-balling' of a whole range of interpretive perspectives and influences (classical rhetoric, literary critical theory, literary study of the Bible, form criticism) into a force field of general 'guidelines' which Trible offers for rich reading (Trible 1994: 101–6):

1. Read and reread the text.
2. Read a range of scholarly works, not only 'literary analyses'.
3. '[S]urround the study of the text with background knowledge to give depth and perspective'.
4. '[A]cquaint yourself with rhetorical terms'.
5. Pay attention to these textual 'features':
    1. the beginning and ending of the text
    2. repetitions
    3. discourse types (direct and indirect)
    4. design and structure
    5. plot development
    6. character portrayals
    7. syntax
    8. particles
6. Replicate the structure of the original in a translation that follows the Hebrew word order and employs 'formal or literal correspondence' in lexicographic choices.
7. '[T]ranslate so as to retain not only the Hebrew syntax but also the original number of words'.
8. '[D]evise a series of markers (for your own text) to indicate prominent features of the text, particularly repetition'.
9. '[D]escribe in clear prose what the structural diagram shows and interpret both diagram and description'.
10. '[C]orrelate your discoveries'.

What this list contains is a set of guidelines from a skilled reader of texts of some of the things she looks for as she works, digs, frowns, laughs, and puzzles over both the biblical text and her own commentarial writing on it (as Trible exemplifies in her subsequent reading of the book of Jonah). This list can help school readers in the art of 'close reading', but it is questionable whether it constitutes a 'method' that should claim the title 'rhetorical criticism', especially given that only (4) specifically mentions 'rhetoric', and even that statement does not stipulate how the 'acquaintance' with rhetorical terminology should or even might affect exegesis. The subsequent attention to translation may be a hint that for Trible the language of the Greek and Latin rhetoricians serves as an alternative language of translation of the text which creates arresting images for ongoing conversation. But the question remains as to why or if 'rhetorical criticism' is the umbrella category, or whether 'literary criticism' should be given that place, with 'rhetorical criticism' a specially spiced sub-variant (the problem is illustrated in Watson and Hauser 1994: 4 and *passim*).

In addition to the models of Hebrew Bible 'rhetorical criticism' as stylistic analysis or narrative criticism, one should also note that Muilenberg himself called for continued engagement with parallel ancient Near Eastern literature as an essential element of 'rhetorical criticism'. Although it has not been a major part of his legacy, this practice has been endorsed as a key aspect of the method of 'rhetorical criticism' by Roland Meynet, who offers a few brief examples of Ugaritic and Babylonian texts employing such similar stylistic techniques that Meynet can speak of a 'rhetorique semitique' (1989: 312–14, 316–18). We can glimpse here the fault line among works of 'rhetorical criticism', as to whether they seek universal patterns of persuasion (either argued or merely assumed), or seek to reconstruct the specific conventions active and operative in the historical moments of composition of the texts in question. In a sense the issue is *which dynamic moment* (in a history of many) the rhetorical analysis seeks to analyse. This emphasis on the historically and culturally conditioned quality of rhetorical discourse leads us into the emergence of 'rhetorical criticism' in New Testament scholarship.

Rhetorical Analysis of the New Testament

In the early years of the twentieth century, German scholars like Johannes Weiss and Rudolf Bultmann investigated the style and composition of the Pauline letters by comparison with ancient rhetorical figures and fashions, such as the diatribe. This practice, which goes back to patristic exegesis (book 4 of Augustine's *De doctrina christiana* is often and rightly cited), was extended in the 1970s to a study, not just of the rhetorical style of Paul's letters, but also of their rhetorical species and arrangement. The commentary on Galatians by Hans Dieter Betz, published in the Hermeneia series in 1979, put these questions at the forefront of Pauline scholarship, and set the agenda for the next two decades. Betz argued that Paul's letters show influences of the rhetorical tradition, not just in their forms of expression (*lexis*, or 'style', one of five 'works of a rhetor'), but also in their argumentative logic (what in rhetorical theory is called *heuresis*, 'invention') and arrangement (*taxis*) (Aristotle, *Rhetoric* 3.1). In particular, Hellenistic theory retained from Aristotle's time the distinction among three *genē*, or 'species' of rhetoric: forensic (arguments of accusation or defense), deliberative (of persuasion and dissuasion to a future course of action), and epideictic (of praise or blame for a given subject). Aristotle largely favoured a simple arrangement of proposition (*prothesis*) and proof (*pisteis*), to which an introduction (*prooimion*) and conclusion (*epilogos*) could be added (*Rhetorica* 3.13); in the later Hellenistic rhetorical textbooks the *moria logou*, or 'parts of a speech', become even more atomized, with sections for division (between one's view and one's opponents), enumeration of proofs, etc. separated out. Aristotle also differentiated three types of 'artificial proofs' (as opposed to the given evidence, such as documents, witnesses, etc.), each of which focuses on one of the three parts of the communicative moment: *ēthos* (the character of the speaker), *pathos* (the emotional impact on the hearer), and *logos* (the cogency of the argument itself) (Aristotle, *Rhetoric* 1.2.3). Betz, who began his studies of Pauline rhetoric with the ways in which Paul's rhetoric of *apologia* in 2 Corinthians 10–13 stood in the tradition of Socrates' self-defence (Betz 1972), identified Galatians as a forensic argument of defence, and then provided a detailed analysis of the flow and logic of the argumentation of the letter carried out in direct conversation with the rhetorical handbooks that specify general rules for rhetorical composition, especially the master-work of the late first-century Roman rhetorical teacher Quintilian (Betz 1979). In the years to come, scholars disputed both Betz's designation of the rhetorical species of Galatians, with some taking it to be more a deliberative argument on the question: should we or should we not become circumcised? (see Aune 2004: 191–4), and particulars of his analysis of the subsections and sub-arguments. Yet most who did so employed his same procedure and set of sources.

A few, however, have questioned the enterprise of rhetorical investigation of Paul's letters in principle, either on the grounds of Pauline biography, doubting that Paul, if he were trained at Jerusalem at the feet of Gamaliel could have had a Greek rhetorical education, or by claiming that those who should know best whether Paul's letters employed Graeco-Roman rhetorical techniques—i.e. the well-educated patristic exegetes—completely denied Paul any such proficiency (Anderson 1999; Kern 1998; Classen 2000, though less categorically). But neither of those assertions constitutes a significant rebuttal, because the Lucan portrait of Paul's 'rabbinic' education (Acts 22: 3; appealed to by Anderson 1999) is hardly a historically reliable datum of greater weight than the evidence of the letters themselves, and the latter claim is based upon a selective and uncritical reading of patristic use of the famous and ubiquitous 'unlettered orator' *topos* for the apostles (see Mitchell 2001; 2000: 240–5, 278–91). Such denials that Paul or other New Testament authors employed rhetorical techniques either knowingly or unknowingly (a distinction often invoked but of dubious analytical value) echo an apologetic line that the early church fathers inherited from a tradition as old as Plato—of insisting on the independence of philosophy (and hence truth) from rhetoric (see e.g. *Gorgias*, 459C).

It is incontestable that Paul's letters seek to persuade their audiences to adhere to his own contested and controversial positions, and do so using intricate proofs. The question remains for all Pauline interpreters: how are these rhetorical strategies to be recognized and accounted for in the process of interpretation? The place to start, I would suggest, is not the memorization of a five-point procedure, though some can be found, such as the following:

1. 'a determination of the rhetorical unit to be studied', which 'must have a beginning, a middle, and an end';
2. definition of the rhetorical situation (i.e. the rhetorical 'exigence', as defined by Bitzer 1968; cf. Aune 2004: 422–5);
3. determination of the rhetorical species (forensic, deliberative, epideictic);
4. consideration of 'the arrangement of material in the text';
5. a final move 'to look back over the entire unit and review its success in meeting the rhetorical exigence and what its implications may be for the speaker or audience' (Kennedy 1984: 33–8).

Such steps may be useful up to a point, but they have significant limitations, as Kennedy himself recognizes when he says (like Trible) that they should be regarded as more a 'circular process' than a mere sequence (Kennedy 1982: 33). None the less, his own emphasis rests securely on getting to the identification of structural divisions (step 4), since the first three are treated as 'preliminary matters' (Kennedy 1984: 37). The danger is that this heavy emphasis on defining the *moria logou*, or 'parts of the speech', can lead to an overly wooden approach to 'rhetorical criticism' as a quest to 'divide and conquer' the text by segmentation and labelling (where is the *narratio*?). Structure is surely a key to meaning, but structure must be discerned from a more supple and nuanced interplay between inner textual features and *any* external model (especially since the handbooks themselves show variety on the parts of a speech and their appropriateness in different kinds of arguments). It is also problematic to engage in 'rhetorical criticism' of a part of a text (*pace* Kennedy 1984: 33) as though it were a speech or argument independent of the composition and rhetorical *skopos* ('goal') of the whole (Mitchell 1991: 6, 16–17; also Aune 2004: 418).

It is in my view more illuminating to view historical-rhetorical criticism not as a set of formulaic procedures, but rather, first and foremost, as *a sensibility and set of resources* that skilled readers may wish to bring to a study of early Christian texts, composed in Greek, which contain argumentation and small narrative forms (*chreiai*). This means that long before one can 'identify a rhetorical unit' anywhere in the New Testament, one must first become acquainted more broadly with the ancient *paideia* through which those who were literate in Greek and Latin were educated. To do this, students must read the ancient rhetorical handbooks themselves (the *Rhetorica ad Herennium*, attributed to Cicero, is a good entrée) and then engage in comparisons among them (the major works to be mastered early on are Aristotle, *Ars rhetorica*, and the handbook the *Rhetorica ad Alexandrum*, Cicero, *de Inventione*, and then the more encyclopaedic and conservative work of Quintilian, *Institutiones oratoriae*, as well as the late antique handbook of epideictic rhetoric by Menander Rhetor (Russell and Wilson 1981)). Other *technai* ('rhetorical handbooks'), especially those containing the *progymnasmata*, or 'school exercises', long known to scholars in the venerable Spengel and Walz collections, are increasingly being translated (Hock and O'Neil 1986, 2002; Kennedy 2003; Dilts and Kennedy 1997), which should increase access and use of these singularly important works which show us, not only how ancient students were trained, but what kinds of situations they were expected to be able to handle, and with what kinds of examples they conventionally dealt. These and other primary sources should be read also in relation to the history of rhetoric (Kennedy 1980, 1994; articles throughout Aune 2004 on many topics) and ancient literary criticism in general (useful collections and analysis in Russell 1981; Russell and Winterbotham 1989). Secondary compendia and systematizations of ancient rhetoric (e.g. Lausberg 1998) are less useful, especially when one has never read for oneself the works they harmonize into a modern system; more valuable once one has read broadly in the ancient sources are studies that help probe the significance of the differences among the handbooks (such as Anderson 2000; Aune 2004, with further literature). There are also major investigations which will help students to feel the culture of ancient *paideia* and its place in the ancient *polis* (Kaster 1988; still essential is Marrou 1956). But even this is not enough, for the handbooks are the 'recipes', but one does not know what good food tastes like just by looking at a list of ingredients and recommendations for their combination. Hence those who seek to read the New Testament in the light of its rhetorical setting need to read widely e.g. in the speeches of Demosthenes (crucial because of his prominence in rhetorical education down into late antiquity), Dio Chrysostom, Aelius Aristides, those found within historical works like Polybius and Dionysius of Halicarnassus, and treatises by Lucian, as well as epistolary arguments as found in the Platonic epistles, those of Seneca, and many others. Without this kind of broad education in the *ars rhetorica*, interpreters are left to set up narrow comparisons between individual lines of selected handbooks and isolated portions of Pauline letters—comparisons that will always remain speculative and yield meagre interpretive insights. Historical rhetorical criticism as I am defining it here (also Mitchell 1991: 6–17, which sketches five 'mandates' for such study) requires equal contextualization on both sides of the comparison; it is not just a procedure, but an awareness about ancient literary culture that one brings to the reading of any individual piece. It is an attempt to meet ancient *paideia* with modern *paideia*.

With a historical imagination thus furnished by broad reading in ancient sources, one turns to the Pauline letters with a sensitive appreciation for Paul's outspoken dilemma of preaching the gospel in linguistic forms that would communicate in his culture, while also (like most rhetoricians) claiming that he does not use (merely) the 'wisdom of words' to persuade his audiences (1 Cor. 2: 1–5). Paul, whose rhetorical proficiency was challenged by his detractors (2 Cor. 11: 6), was in the uncomfortable position of having to show that his letters—conceded even by his disparagers to be 'weighty' documents! (2 Cor. 10: 10)—were not merely persuasive in a human way. But he needs to persuade them of that fact using *some* language! Hence, the first step in historical rhetorical analysis of the Pauline letters, in my judgement, is an appreciation of the dilemmas of *logos* in early Christian discourse from the fifth verse of the earliest extant letter (1 Thess. 1: 5). Next, one needs to engage in the task of historical reconstruction to seek to comprehend the setting of any given Pauline letter (or letter fragment), and to attempt to determine what are the issues at stake. At this point a crucial step is needed: to try to catch Paul at his *heuresis*—that is, how Paul himself determined what was *to krinomenon*, 'the point to be adjudicated', and what were the propositions of which he sought to persuade his readers. The emphasis on *heuresis* is crucial here, for otherwise one will imagine that Paul and his readers viewed things the same way, which they frequently did not, which is often why he had to write in the first place.

But, above all, one must recognize that Paul does not respond directly to the historical situation *we* reconstruct, but, rather, he responds *to the situation as he diagnoses it*. The relationship between historical reconstruction and Pauline rhetoric is always extremely tenuous (given that we must depend largely on his rhetoric for the former task), but rhetorical criticism must seek to keep the two independent; otherwise it runs the risk of granting Paul his arguments too readily or uncritically. The analysis of the propositions that Paul wishes to prove must be embedded in a compositional analysis of the epistle itself. Very often Paul sets his *hypotheseis*, 'hypothesis', 'thesis statements', at the outset of a letter (e.g. Rom. 1: 16–17; 1 Cor. 1: 10); he also uses subsidiary propositions throughout his arguments (e.g. 1 Cor. 8: 1; Gal. 1: 11–12; 2: 16). He constructs ingenious arguments which draw upon a range of appeals (to written evidence, usually 'scripture', to human experience, both particular and general, to syllogistic logic, especially the logic of contraries, and to an array of *paradeigmata*, or 'rhetorical examples', both positive and negative, *sugkriseis*, 'comparisons', and *prosōpopoiia*, 'personification'), as well as commonplaces like 'then and now' and 'from the lesser to the greater' (for these and other forms, see Aune 2004; Samply 2003). Rhetorical analysis in this mode seeks to recreate the dynamic interplay between Paul and his earliest audiences by reconstructing the expectations they shared about what might (and might not) constitute a persuasive argument in service of a given point.

Other New Testament scholars have found the 'new rhetoric' of modern philosophers and literary critics useful in seeking to understand Pauline argumentation. For example, Wuellner (1991) offered a reading of Romans as epideictic rhetoric (according to the definition of Perelman and Olbrechts-Tyteca 1969) as a way to resolve the stalemate in scholarship on the 'theological' or 'historical' setting of that massive and yet contextually puzzling Pauline missive. Wire (1990) also drew on the 'New Rhetoric' in her search for the voice of the 'Corinthian women prophets' to whom Paul addressed his arguments. Both readings provide illuminating insights, and could be taken as a kind of '3D chess game' arrangement, which sets Paul's rhetoric in conversation with ancient rhetorical conventions as seen through the refracted synthesis of the 'New Rhetoric'. There is some room for confusion, however, when labels such as 'epideictic rhetoric' have varied meanings in the different periods, which may be effaced.

A historical-rhetorical critical perspective can also be useful for other parts of the New Testament (Mack 1990), but in more carefully circumscribed ways, depending upon the genres represented. For instance, analysis of the rhetoric of historiographical prefaces has been a major element of Luke–Acts research (e.g. Moessner 1999), even as the speeches in that same work have rightly been considered, analysed, and better understood in the light of their rhetorical forms, structure, placement, and function within the narrative (Aune 2004: 285–8). A rhetorical-critical approach also lends a hand in gospel genre studies, for biography and *encomium* were closely allied forms in antiquity (Aune 1987: 29–37; Burridge 2004). However, 'narrative' in the rhetorical handbooks is not quite what we find in the gospels, since it is largely treated as a sub-form of the larger compositional unit of a speech (usually a forensic one). But valuable insights have come from an application of the theory of the *chreia*, or 'pronouncement story', in the rhetorical exercises which have come down to us (called the *progymnasmata*), which have much in common with many individual units of the gospel tradition (see Mack 1990: 43–7, 78–87), and even show how students were taught ways to embed existing stories into new grammatical and literary contexts, an important procedure behind the gospels and Acts.

Historical-rhetorical criticism seeks to understand one moment of the dynamic life of an ancient text as a persuasive act made by an author toward recipients within his or her literary culture. Detailed investigation seeks to provide a good understanding (and it is always only partial) of the specific and general rhetorical contexts for which the text was composed. One need not, and should not, declare the results of such an enterprise either certain (who can constrict all ancient readers into one paradigm of reading, no matter how plausibly documented?) or as having authority or veto power over all subsequent readings (as would be necessary to sustain the broad-brush critique of Schüssler-Fiorenza 1999: 88, against such work). Methodological approaches should be evaluated according to their stated goals and their results. One can engage in historical-rhetorical analysis without eschewing or repudiating interest in how the dynamic power of an ancient text operates on modern persons according to modern rhetorical expectations, and how it contributes to or thwarts ethical practices.

Yet there remains a key issue of method. How is 'rhetorical criticism' related to other forms of interpretation? At present three different models have been set forth: that rhetorical criticism is an interdisciplinary complement to other methods (Mack 1990: 93); that it is a creative supplement and co-ordinating agent among them (Robbins 1996 and many other works of 'socio-rhetorical criticism'); or that rhetorical criticism is the critical alternative to all other modes of reading, which redefines the very ethical task of interpretation (Schüssler-Fiorenza 1999: 91 and *passim*). Almost twenty years ago Wuellner stipulated that rhetorical criticism stood at a 'crossroads' 'between two competing versions of rhetorical criticism: the one in which rhetorical criticism is identical with literary criticism, the other in which rhetorical criticism is identical with practical criticism' (Wuellner 1987: 453). But who is to say readers may not (with apologies to Robert Frost) double back and take the other road on occasion?

'Literary Criticism'

We do so now, and turn to 'the odd and rather artificial category of "literary readings" of the Bible' (Jasper 1998: 23). One reason why the term 'literary criticism' can confuse is that the classical post-Enlightenment methods of 'historical criticism' were in fact largely 'literary' (Jasper 1998: 22). In particular, the search for the sources or strands of a text that could be reconstructed (such as J, D, E, and P in the Pentateuch, or Q or Special Matthean material in the gospels) was at one time called 'literary criticism' (now more usually 'source criticism'). But another type of 'literary-critical' study of the Bible emerged in the 1970s and 1980s when biblical scholars reacted against what they regarded as the atomistic excesses of precisely those 'literary' procedures of form and source criticism, and when notable literary critics, such as Frank Kermode (1979), Robert Alter (1981), Northrop Frye (1982), and Meier Sternberg (1985) published works of biblical interpretation (including the compendium volume, Alter and Kermode 1987). The movement to understand the Bible as literature drew many to seek to read the 'final form' of the text as a single, unitary piece of literary art, and to see how it (in translation, as well as in the original language that was the focus of biblical scholarship) created a 'story world' which the reader could enter and understand 'on its own terms'. This scholarship (like 'rhetorical criticism', which it often overlaps, as we have noted above) involves a close reading of precise details of the text viewed as a unity (deflecting overemphasis on historical context or the historical information to be gained from it when treated as a source), and appreciates especially *the dynamism of the world inside the text*, as a system of complex and meaningful interactions among its constituent parts.

It is sometimes claimed that narrative criticism came about when biblical scholars (who knew little about 'literature', since they were all trained as 'historians') peered over the fence into English departments and learned from those more able critics to jettison their adolescent romance with historical context, and focus instead on 'the text in itself'. Usually the inhabitants of the world on the other side of the departmental divide are identified with the 'New Critics', who in the 1950s and 1960s countered the psycho-biographical focus of Romanticism by insisting that texts should be interpreted 'on their own terms' and apart from external data meant to 'explain' them, including appeals to authorial identity and intention. There was some common ferment, around the problematic conception of 'authorial intention', and through the influence of the French structuralists such as Lévi-Strauss on linguistic and cognitive polarities (see Patte 1990), but not contemporaneity or precise complementarity of concerns. As Stephen Moore cogently demonstrated, there is no exact neighbour on the other side of the fence whose authority as a 'real literary critic' can be invoked by New Testament scholars using this method, for the kind of work that biblical scholars are doing with narrative is not precisely like *any* form of literary criticism then (or now) current (Moore 1989: 11). But even if the 'secular critic' who valorized this enterprise was a bit of a fabrication (or at least a strangely imbricated composite robot), with the aid of 'toned-down theory' (paraphrasing Moore 1989: 54–5) that has a populist appeal for its comprehensibility and accessibility, scholars did something different in seeking to read entire gospels in a 'holistic' way. Reading the Bible as literature meant paying careful attention to things that matter to its internal life, such as its plot, characters, internal tensions, and poetic and metaphorical forms (recall that these are included in Trible's methodology for 'rhetorical criticism').

This type of literary criticism was especially congenial to the narrative portions of the Hebrew Bible (the Pentateuch, the Deuteronomistic History), and the gospels and Acts. Viewing the text, regardless of its origins, as a creative composition of an author, scholars sought to investigate the point of view from which the narration ensued, and hence the 'implied author' (the authorial presence in the voice of the text) and 'implied reader' (one who brings to the task of reading a knowledge of the cultural codes that the author presumed she or he shared with the readers) for whom it seems to have been intended. Such literary criticism seeks to understand the consciously designed plot that animates biblical texts, and the cast of characters who develop (or not) and interact in the course of events, as well as the style and set of rhetorical features with which the story is told, like metaphor, allegory, or irony (Gunn and Fewell 1993; Struthers-Malbon, in Anderson and Moore 1992: 23–49; Powell 1990). Readings like Trible 1978, 1984, 1994, and Berlin 1983 (on the David cycle in 1 and 2 Samuel and the book of Ruth) exemplify the lively possibilities in this approach, as does Kugel 1981, on parallelism in biblical poetry. In the New Testament, the gospels and their individual portraits of Jesus, when seen as narrative constructs, were readily understood as having intricate plots wrapped around such devices as secrecy and disclosure (especially in Mark) and conflict, both between Jesus and his disciples and with religious and political authorities that led to his death (Rhoads *et al.* 1999: 73–97; Kelber 1979). To some degree this work spilled over from earlier redaction-critical studies, which emphasized the redactor's work as that of a theologian who shaped his inherited materials into a narrative creation that embodied in literary form his portrait of Jesus. What distinguish narrative or literary readings, theoretically, from redaction-critical ones are two main considerations: their choice to leave the historical redactor out of the equation, in favour of the text, since the focus is on what is intrinsic to the narrative itself, independent of the intentionality of any author or editor, and a substitution of 'the character of Jesus' for the traditional holy grail of 'the evangelist's theology' (however, often the former once found is considered to be the latter). One significant outcome of this scholarship has been an exponential increase in interest in the Gospel of Mark, rescued once by historical critics in the eighteenth century for its possible historical value, and now re-rescued from a reputation for clumsiness by many readings respectful of the enigmatic earliest gospel for its raw emotional power, carefully crafted irony, and its clipped ending, which could now be regarded and interpreted as thoroughly intended for profound literary and theological effect (Kermode 1979; Anderson and Moore 1992; Rhoads *et al.* 1999). Matthew and John have received similar investigation (e.g. Kingsbury 1988; Culpepper 1983; full literature in Aune 2004: 297–300, 243–9), but to different effect, given their long monologues by Jesus, which can be emplotted and understood according to various meaningful structural outlines. Luke–Acts has increasingly, due to such an approach, been treated as a single literary work with one coherent plot line and unfolding narrative (Tannehill 1986–90; questioned by Parsons and Pervo 1993). As with 'rhetorical criticism', the question of which literary theories and sources should inform reading has arisen, leading to mixtures of modern literary approaches with studies of ancient fiction (Pervo, Tolbert) for instance, historiography (discussion in Aune 2004: 280–8), and social-scientific methodologies (Kingsbury 1997; Robbins 1996). There remains much latitude and variety today as to the degree to which literary-critical readings of biblical narrative wish to interact with what can be known about ancient literary culture, depending upon which audience construct (ancient or modern, real or implied) is at the forefront. And the question always haunts the enterprise: is the unity of the text that these readings celebrate one created by the reader, or found there?

AN INTERMEDIARY TERM—THE HISTORY OF INTERPRETATION AND EFFECTS

Methodological plurality and combination are possible as long as neither text, reader, author, nor *any single context* is claimed as the totality of meaning or singular focus of interest. For many interpreters (including myself), it is the history of interpretation itself (and *Wirkungsgeschichte*, 'the history of effects') that helps to integrate the art of biblical interpretation, old and new. First off, those who take seriously the history of interpretation know readily and emphatically that it is an empirical fact that the biblical texts cannot be locked into any single meaning. Second, patristic exegetes are terrific reading partners for those interested in rhetoric in biblical texts, since their reading practices were thoroughly conditioned by their rhetorical education (Young 1997; Clark 1999; Mitchell 2001). Third, perhaps not entirely independent from trends in biblical studies, recent research into early biblical interpretation has in turn been demonstrating the plurality of reading strategies used by Christians and Jews in late antiquity (Young 1997; Clark 1999; Kugel and Greer 1986). Fourth, the traditional ancient divide between 'literal' and 'allegorical' readings, which is in some degree replayed in contemporary discourse about a hermeneutical divide between historical and 'ahistorical' approaches, has increasingly been undermined by recent research (Young 1997) and shown to be itself part of rhetorical practice (Mitchell 2005). Lastly, attention to rabbinic and patristic biblical interpretation reveals the ancient preoccupation with close reading (the frequent term for this among the early Greek authors was *akribeia*, 'accurate attention' to the details of the text so prized in modern rhetorical and literary analyses). We should not overly romanticize early exegesis as somehow more 'pure' than modern or post-modern biblical scholarship (do we really want to cancel the advances of historical and philological research—send the Dead Sea Scrolls back to the hills, and better biblical manuscripts back to oblivion?). But it does no harm, and perhaps much good, to see ourselves, like biblical interpreters of all times, as curious readers whose interpretive work follows up insistent questions posed by diligent examination of the text, attuned to its own rhetorical dimensions and narrative logic, while also attending carefully to the ways in which we, like they, create forms of rhetorical commentary and explication that fashion worlds in turn.

Suggested Reading

A thoughtful introduction to a range of critical methods and possibilities for their interaction may be found in Barton 1998. For a flavour of the various types of literary readings of the Hebrew Bible, see Trible 1994, and many other works listed in Watson and Hauser 1994. An indispensable resource for rhetorical and literary criticism of the New Testament is the comprehensive dictionary by Aune (2004).

Bibliography

ALTER, R. 1981. *The Art of Biblical Narrative*. New York: Basic Books.
—— and KERMODE, F. 1987. *The Literary Guide to the Bible*. Cambridge, Mass.: Harvard University Press.

ANDERSON, J. C., and MOORE, S. D., eds. 1992. *Mark and Method: New Approaches in Biblical Studies*. Philadelphia: Fortress.

ANDERSON, R. D. 1999. *Ancient Rhetorical Theory and Paul*. Louvain: Peeters.

—— 2000. *Glossary of Greek Rhetorical Terms Connected to Methods of Argumentation, Figures, and Tropes from Anaximenes to Quintilian*. Louvain: Peeters.

ARISTOTLE, *The "Art" of Rhetoric*. 1926. J. H. Freese, trans. Loeb Classical Library. Cambridge, Mass.: Harvard University Press.

AUNE, D. E. 1987. *The New Testament in its Literary Environment*. Philadelphia: Westminster.

—— 2004. *The New Testament and Early Christian Literature and Rhetoric*. Louisville, Ky.: Westminster/John Knox.

BARTON, J., ed. 1998. *The Cambridge Companion to Biblical Interpretation*. Cambridge: Cambridge University Press.

BERLIN, A. 1983. *Poetics and Interpretation of Biblical Narrative*. Sheffield: Almond.

BETZ, H. D. 1972. *Der Apostel Paulus und die Sokratische Tradition: Eine exegetische Untersuchung zu seiner "Apologie" 2 Kor 10–13*. Beiträge zur historischen Theologie, 45. Tübingen: Mohr Siebeck.

—— 1979. *Galatians: A Commentary on Paul's Letter to the Churches in Galatia*. Hermeneia. Philadelphia: Fortress.

BITZER, L. 1968. 'The Rhetorical Situation'. *Philosophy and Rhetoric*, 1: 1–18.

BURRIDGE, R. A. 2004. *What Are the Gospels? A Comparison with Graeco-Roman Biography*, rev. edn. Grand Rapids, Mich.: Eerdmans.

CICERO, *De Inventione, de optimo genere oratorum, topica*. 1949. H. M. Hubbell, trans. Loeb Classical Library. Cambridge, Mass.: Harvard University Press.

[CICERO], *ad C. Herennium de ratio dicendi*. 1954. H. Caplan, trans. Loeb Classical Library. Cambridge, Mass.: Harvard University Press.

CLARK, E. A. 1999. *Reading Renunciation: Asceticism and Scripture in Early Christianity*. Princeton: Princeton University Press.

CLASSEN, C. J. 2000. *Rhetorical Criticism of the New Testament*. WUNT 128. Tübingen: Mohr Siebeck.

CULPEPPER, R. A. 1983. *Anatomy of the Fourth Gospel: A Study in Literary Design*. Philadelphia: Fortress.

DILTS, M. R., and KENNEDY, G. A., trans. and eds. 1997. *Two Greek Rhetorical Treatises from the Roman Empire*. Mnemosyne Supplementum 168. Leiden: Brill.

DOZEMAN, T. B. 1992. 'Rhetoric and Rhetorical Criticism, OT Rhetorical Criticism'. In *ABD* v. 712–15.

FRYE, N. 1982. *The Great Code: The Bible and Literature*. New York: Harcourt Brace Jovanovich.

GUNN, D. M., and FEWELL, D. N. 1993. *Narrative in the Hebrew Bible*. Oxford: Oxford University Press.

HESTER, J. D., and HESTER, J. D. (Amador) eds. 2004. *Rhetorics and Hermeneutics: Wilhelm Wuellner and his Influence*. New York: T. & T. Clark International.

HOCK, R. F., and O'NEIL, E. N., trans. and eds. 1986. *The Chreia in Ancient Rhetoric*, i: *The Progymnasmata*. SBLTT 27. Atlanta: Scholars.

—— trans. and eds. 2002. *The Chreia and Ancient Rhetoric*, ii: *Classroom Exercises*. Writings from the Greco-Roman World. Atlanta: Society of Biblical Literature.

JASPER, D. 1998. 'Literary Readings of the Bible'. In Barton 1988: 21–34.

JOST, W., and OLMSTED, W., eds. 2004. *A Companion to Rhetoric and Rhetorical Criticism*. Blackwell's Companions to Literature and Culture, 22. Malden, Mass.: Blackwell.

KASTER, R. A. 1988. *Guardians of Language: The Grammarian and Society in Late Antiquity*. Berkeley: University of California Press.

KELBER, W. H. 1979. *Mark's Story of Jesus*. Philadelphia: Fortress.

KENNEDY, G. A. 1980. *Classical Rhetoric and its Christian and Secular Tradition from Ancient to Modern Times*. Chapel Hill, NC: University of North Carolina Press.

—— 1984. *New Testament Interpretation through Rhetorical Criticism*. Chapel Hill, NC: University of North Carolina Press.

—— 1994. *A New History of Classical Rhetoric*. Princeton: Princeton University Press.

—— 2003. *Progymnasmata: Greek Textbooks of Prose Composition and Rhetoric*. Writings from the Greco-Roman World. Atlanta: Society of Biblical Literature.

KERMODE, F. 1979. *The Genesis of Secrecy: On the Interpretation of Narrative*. Cambridge, Mass.: Harvard University Press.

KERN, P. H. 1998. *Rhetoric and Galatians: Assessing an Approach to Paul's Epistle*. SNTSMS 101. Cambridge: Cambridge University Press.

KINGSBURY, J. D. 1988. *Matthew as Story*, 2nd edn. Philadelphia: Fortress.

—— ed. 1997. *Gospel Interpretation: Narrative-Critical and Social-Scientific Approaches*. Harrisburg, Pa.: Trinity Press International.

KUGEL, J. L. 1981. *The Idea of Biblical Poetry: Parallelism and its History*. New Haven: Yale University Press.

—— and GREER, R. A. 1986. *Early Biblical Interpretation*. Philadelphia: Westminster.

LAUSBERG, H. 1998. *Handbook of Literary Rhetoric: A Foundation for Literary Study*, trans. and ed. D. E. Orton and R. D. Anderson. Leiden: Brill.

MACK, B. L. 1990. *Rhetoric and the New Testament*. Guides to Biblical Scholarship. Minneapolis: Fortress.

MARROU, H. I. 1956. *A History of Education in Antiquity*, trans. G. Lamb. New York: Sheed & Ward.

MEYNET, R. 1998. *Rhetorical Analysis: An Introduction to Biblical Rhetoric*. JSOTS.S 256. Sheffield: Sheffield Academic Press.

MITCHELL, M. M. 1991. *Paul and the Rhetoric of Reconciliation: An Exegetical Investigation of the Language and Composition of 1 Corinthians*. Hermeneutische Untersuchungen zur Theologie, 28. Tübingen: Mohr Siebeck; repr. Louisville, Ky.: Westminster/John Knox, 1993.

—— 2000. *The Heavenly Trumpet: John Chrysostom and the Art of Pauline Interpretation*. Hermeneutische Untersuchungen zur Theologie, 40. Tübingen: Mohr Siebeck; repr. Louisville: Westminster/John Knox, 2001.

—— 2001. 'Reading Rhetoric with Patristic Exegetes: John Chrysostom on Galatians'. In A. Y. Collins and M. M. Mitchell, eds., *Antiquity and Humanity: Essays on Ancient Religion and Philosophy Presented to Hans Dieter Betz on His 70th Birthday*, Tübingen: J. C. B. Mohr/Paul Siebeck, 333–55.

—— 2005. 'Patristic Rhetoric on Allegory: Origen and Eustathius Put 1 Samuel 28 on Trial'. *JR* 85: 414–45.

MOESSNER, D. P. 1999. *Jesus and the Heritage of Israel: Luke's Narrative Claim upon Israel's Legacy*. Harrisburg, Pa.: Trinity Press International.

MOORE, S. D. 1989. *Literary Criticism and the Gospels: The Theoretical Challenge*. New Haven: Yale University Press.

MUILENBERG, J. 1969. 'Form Criticism and Beyond'. *JBL* 88: 1–19. Repr. in P. R. House, ed., *Beyond Form Criticism: Essays in Old Testament Literary Criticism*, Sources for Biblical and Theological Study, 2, Winona Lake, Ind.: Eisenbrauns, 1992, 49–69.

PARSONS, M. C., and PERVO, R. I. 1993. *Rethinking the Unity of Luke and Acts*. Minneapolis: Fortress.

PATTE, D. 1990. *Structural Exegesis for New Testament Critics*. Guides to Biblical Scholarship. Minneapolis: Fortress.

PERELMAN, C., and OLBRECHTS-TYTECA, L. 1969. *The New Rhetoric: A Treatise on Argumentation*, trans. J. Wilkinson and P. Weaver. Notre Dame, Ind.: University of Notre Dame Press.

PORTER, S. E., ed. 1997. *Handbook of Classical Rhetoric in the Hellenistic Period, 330 B.C.– A.D. 400*. Leiden: Brill.

—— and STAMPS, D. L., eds. 2002. *Rhetorical Criticism of the Bible*. JSNTS.S 195. Sheffield: Sheffield Academic Press.

POWELL, M. A. 1990. *What is Narrative Criticism?* Guides to Biblical Scholarship. Minneapolis: Fortress.

QUINTILIAN. *Institutiones oratoriae. ET: The Education of an Orator*. 2001. D. A. Russell, trans., 5 vols. Loeb Classical Library. Cambridge, Mass.: Harvard University Press.

RHOADS, D., DEWEY, J., and MICHIE, D. 1999. *Mark as Story: An Introduction to the Narrative of a Gospel*, 2nd edn. Minneapolis: Fortress.

ROBBINS, V. K. 1996. *The Tapestry of Early Christian Discourse: Rhetoric, Society and Ideology*. London and New York: Routledge.

RUSSELL, D. A. 1981. *Criticism in Antiquity*. Berkeley: University of California Press.

—— and WILSON, N. G., trans. and eds. 1981. *Menander Rhetor*. Oxford: Clarendon Press.

—— and WINTERBOTTOM, M. 1989. *Ancient Literary Criticism: The Principal Texts in New Translation*, rev. edn. Oxford: Oxford University Press.

SAMPLEY, J. P., ed. 2003. *Paul in the Greco-Roman World: A Handbook*. Harrisburg, Pa.: Trinity Press International.

SCHÜSSLER-FIORENZA, E. 1988. 'The Ethics of Biblical Interpretation: Decentering Biblical Scholarship'. *JBL* 107: 3–17.

—— 1999. *Rhetoric and Ethic: The Politics of Biblical Studies*. Minneapolis: Fortress.

STERNBERG, M. 1985. *The Poetics of Biblical Narrative: Ideological Literature and the Drama of Reading*. Indiana Studies in Biblical Literature. Bloomington, Ind.: Indiana University Press.

TANNEHILL, R. C. 1986–90. *The Narrative Unity of Luke–Acts: A Narrative Interpretation*, 2 vols. Philadelphia: Fortress.

THISELTON, A. 1992. *New Horizons in Hermeneutics*. Grand Rapids, Mich.: Zondervan.

TRIBLE, P. 1978. *God and the Rhetoric of Sexuality*. Philadelphia: Fortress.

—— 1984. *Texts of Terror: Literary-feminist Readings of Biblical Narratives*. OBT 13. Philadelphia: Fortress.

—— 1994. *Rhetorical Criticism: Context, Method, and the Book of Jonah*. Minneapolis: Fortress.

VAN DER LUGT, P. 1995. *Rhetorical Criticism and the Poetry of the Book of Job*. Oudtestamentische stüdien, 32. Leiden: Brill.

WATSON, D. F., and HAUSER, A. J. 1994. *Rhetorical Criticism of the Bible: A Comprehensive Bibliography with Notes on History and Method*. Biblical Interpretation, 4. Leiden: Brill.

WEST, M. 1992. 'Reflections on the Current and Future Status of Biblical Hebrew Poetry'. In P. R. House, ed., *Beyond Form Criticism: Essays in Old Testament Literary Criticism*, Sources for Biblical and Theological Study, 2, Winona Lake, Ind.: Eisenbrauns, 423–31.

WIRE, A. C. 1990. *The Corinthian Women Prophets: A Reconstruction through Paul's Rhetoric*. Minneapolis: Fortress.

WUELLNER, W. 1976. 'Paul's Rhetoric of Argumentation in Romans'. *CBQ* 33: 330–51.

—— 1987. 'Where is Rhetorical Criticism Taking Us?' *CBQ* 49: 448–63.

—— 1991. 'Paul's Rhetoric of Argumentation in Romans: An Alternative to the Donfried–Karris Debate over Romans'. In K. P. Donfried, ed., *The Romans Debate*, rev. edn. Peabody, Mass.: Henrickson, 128–46.

YOUNG, F. M. 1997. *Biblical Exegesis and the Formation of Christian Culture*. Cambridge: Cambridge University Press.

CHAPTER 36

FEMINIST CRITICISM AND RELATED ASPECTS

MARIE-THERES WACKER

FEMINIST *CRITICISM* OR *FEMINIST* CRITICISM?

Following Dorothee Sölle, feminism can be defined as 'the emergence of women from a state of submission for which they themselves were responsible or which others had attributed to them'. Feminist exegesis is correspondingly a scientific engagement with the Bible with the intention of contributing to the emancipation, liberation, and empowering of women. Feminist exegesis is thus not simply a *method* of biblical interpretation in the sense of a particular technique for analysing texts, but a *critical hermeneutic* of engagement with the Bible and in this sense feminist *criticism*. It employs already existing methods of biblical scholarship, but also subjects these methods to a feminist critique, and in that way contributes to the development of methods.

The adjective 'feminist' has in any case not been regarded as a suitable description for their activity by all those who have sought to contribute to the emancipation, liberation, and empowering of women in their scholarly work. It suggests a limitation to the problems of white, West, Christian, heterosexual middle-class women. Therefore, there are currently quite a number of alternative approaches. There is 'Womanist' biblical criticism as practised by black American women; there is the approach of the 'mujeristas', the women of Central and Latin America, as well as the Bible readings of Asian 'women theologians' or the approach of African women. Christian feminist exegesis has other procedures and thematic concerns compared with a Jewish feminist engagement with the Bible; and criticism of society, politics, and the economy is not carried out with the same sharpness by all of these. Lesbian and queer (gender-confusing) exegetical approaches bring in yet other perspectives. The designation 'queer' indicates in addition the debate about the deconstruction of 'gender' which, from its side, also brings pressure to define afresh the contours of 'feminist' theology and exegesis. The following discussion deals first with basic hermeneutical questions (I) and then turns to methodological perspectives (II).

I. Feminist Hermeneutics

1. Biblical Criticism by Christian Women before the Beginning of the Feminist Movement of the Twentieth Century

For women who understand themselves as believing Christians and wish to relate themselves to Christian tradition, the Bible presents a particular challenge. On the one hand it is regarded as Holy Scripture, which remains normative for the teaching and practice of the churches. On the other hand, in the history of Christianity women have always suffered from particular gender-specific limitations, indeed discriminations, which have been based upon this Holy Scripture. These have been found particularly in the area of marriage, which stood under patriarchal law (cf. Genesis 2–3 and Ephesians 5) and in the area of public speech (cf. 1 Cor. 14: 33b–5; 1 Tim. 2: 8 ff.). With Hildegard of Bingen in Germany (twelfth century) and Christine de Pizan in France (fifteenth century), two learned Christian women can be named by way of example, who already in the High Middle Ages and in the early modern period had, in their different ways, raised objections to such an androcentric claim of the Bible and who developed counter-readings in the interest of a much greater area of action for women or against a much more positive view of women (for the period 1500 and 1920 cf. Selvidge 1996). At the end of the nineteenth century in the USA, Elizabeth Cady Stanton, an abolitionist and fighter for women's rights took, with her 'Woman's Bible', the step of accepting the Bible as a sacred text only to the extent that it agreed with a critical reason which recognized woman as made in the image of God the creator in the same way as man. However, it was only in the 1970s that the biblical criticism of Christian women which aimed to break these texts as instruments of patriarchy and to use them in a new way as sacred texts also for women, began to find broad acceptance, first in America and then in Western Europe.

2. Feminist Beginnings: From Women of the Bible to Criticism of 'Systemic Androcentrism'

Initially it was, on the one hand, the women characters in the Bible and, on the other, the female presentations of God in the Bible which stood at the centre of Christian feminist interest.

The well-known women characters—above all, the matriarchs in the Old Testament and the women who accompanied Jesus—were reassessed in a woman-centred way. With amazement and also indignation at the fact that that they featured so little in traditional Christian teaching, attention was then also paid to the many lesser-known female figures in the Bible. The expectation was aroused that their way of faith could be made fruitful for women today, through identification with these 'distant sisters'. Attention was drawn to the biblical presentation of God as mother and the Holy Spirit as feminine (Schüngel-Straumann 1992) and these insights were developed into impulses for new language for prayer and theology. The hope of feminist theologians directed itself to the possibility of constructing from the many traces of women in the biblical texts a sufficient counterweight to make possible the option of women standing on their own in God's presence.

However, it became increasingly clear that it was not simply the Christian interpretation of the Bible that had turned the sacred text into an instrument for discrimination against women, but that the Bible itself had to be seen as a document of patriarchy. The text has been transmitted, redacted, and composed by learned men, and also the world of biblical women is one dominated by men and centred on men. Women in their limited social world, and the female metaphors used in language about God, stand in the context of a 'systemic androcentrism'; that is, they mirror only the places and values that were allowed for women in a world dominated by androcentric values. Thus, early on, feminist engagement with the Bible had to tackle the critical question of finding a hermeneutic which would be in a position to break up this systemic frame if the holy scriptures were to fulfil the task for Christians of being God's liberating word for *all* human beings.

3. First Hermeneutical Approaches

At the beginning of the 1980s, the Catholic New Testament scholar Elisabeth Schüssler-Fiorenza set out a basic feminist hermeneutic for the New Testament

(Schüssler-Fiorenza 1983, 1984). Biblical interpretation in the interests of women becoming subjects before God is to be undertaken in the four steps of a hermeneutics of *suspicion*, which uncovers the 'systemic androcentrism' of Scripture, a hermeneutics of *remembrance* which pushes back to the women at the beginnings of the Jesus movement; a hermeneutics of *proclamation*, which interprets the Bible consciously as a document of liberation for women and which silences those texts which oppose this; and a hermeneutic of *creative actualization*, which provides space for an individual and methodologically freer approach to the Bible. This concept is based essentially upon the impression that in the origins of the Jesus movement—the interaction of men and women with each other, their hopes and their images of God with their astonishingly strong accent on wisdom as feminine —are characterized by an egalitarian impetus, and that the Jesus movement can therefore be described as a 'discipleship of equals'. By joining this historic 'primal rock' with the modern and contemporary desire of women for all-embracing justice, including political justice, a hermeneutical criterion is obtained with the help of which the history of primitive Christianity (beginning with Paul!) and continuing through the remainder of Christian history can be traced in a feminist critical way. In a similar way, but less emphatically grounding her criteria in contemporary feminist challenges and claims, Rosemary Radford Ruether provided a critical approach in the field of Christian interpretation of the Old Testament. For her, an orientation critical of power as found above all in the writings of the prophets (and then also in the Jesus movement) is decisive, and elevates into a criterion for a feminist rereading of the Bible as well as into new notions of God which deliberately embrace the bi-gendered term 'god/dess' (Radford Ruether 1983).

Over against this 'egalitarian feminist' paradigm in feminist theology and biblical criticism, which centred on the equality of men and women and adopted basic methods and perspectives of liberation theology, there stood in the 1980s a 'gynocentric paradigm'. It assumed for human history in general, but also for that of Early Israel, a primal religion of the great goddess, which expressed itself in women-centred social forms, and which was destroyed by patriarchal forces (so-called matriarchal feminism or goddess feminism). The Hebrew Bible was read as a document of the oppression of this religion, and at the same time as a source for its reconstruction (in Germany cf. Weiler 1984/9; in the USA, Teubal 1984).

4. Christian anti-Judaism—Jewish Feminism

It was above all about this type of feminist biblical criticism that a debate arose in West Germany from the middle of the 1980s in respect of anti-Judaism in Christian feminist theology, a debate which had already begun in the USA at the end of the

1970s. Jewish feminists maintained that where the charge of 'murdering the goddess' was brought against patriarchal Israel, this was nothing other than a repeat of the Christian anti-Jewish cliché of the 'murder of God'. They also made it quite clear that Christian feminist reconstruction of the woman-friendly Jesus movement ran the danger of presenting the Judaism of that time in a negative way, thus giving new impulses to anti-Jewish prejudices (particularly Plaskow 1978, 1990). The debate about a sometimes not even conscious feminist anti-Judaism on the part of women writers who had imbibed Christian attitudes particularly coloured these years, and contributed to the attempt to become more sensitive to, and aware of, the various mechanisms of attributing guilt, in the light of the history of traditional Christian anti-Judaism (Schottroff and Wacker 1996). Feminist Christian theologians are much more resolved as a result to examine self-critically what they say in relation to Judaism, and to take account of the various formulations of Jewish feminism within the Jewish denominations. In so far as the criticism of the *Bible* is concerned, it becomes clear that Jewish feminist criticism has a different set of priorities for a feminist critical revision of Jewish identity compared with that of Christian women, particularly Protestants with their Bible-centred tradition. However, a crucial area shared by Jewish and Christian women alike is that of the use of the Bible in worship and the connected question of the gender-sensitive language of liturgy, particularly in connection with names for God and the address of the congregation to God. In universities, both Jewish and Christian feminists work on texts and themes of the Hebrew Bible. In North America there are also Jewish feminists who are experts in the study of New Testament texts (Reinhartz 1991, 2001; Kraemer 1992; Kraemer and D'Angelo 1999; Levine and Bickenstaff 2001 ff.).

5. Womanist Interpretation of the Bible

Womanist theology and biblical interpretation have assumed clear contours since the 1980s. The term 'womanist' was coined by the black American author Alice Walker, and was introduced into feminist theological discourse by Katie Cannon in 1985. Black American women criticized the feminist movement as racist, since it absolutized the perspective of white, Western-formed middle-class women. A pertinent case was feminist historiography, which mentioned the nineteenth-century Elizabeth Cady Stanton with her 'Woman's Bible' but which forgot the name of Sojourner Truth, who stands for all black women fighting in the nineteenth century for the abolition of slavery and for the rights of women, with particular reference to the Bible. Womanist theology and biblical interpretation is particularly concerned to analyse, as entangled together, a threefold discrimination on the grounds of (black) colour of skin, economic hierarchy (slavery), and (female) gender. In this the Bible is seen much more as a source of critical strength against oppression than as a document of the oppressors. A notable example is the womanist engagement with the biblical character of Hagar. Because, as an Egyptian and as a slave, ethnically and economically, she did not belong to the powerful, she is particularly suited to be an identification figure, who receives sympathy from narratives in the Bible which also do not leave relations of power uncriticized. The best-known womanist biblical scholar to date, Renita Weems, works in her particular way to articulate biblical visions for her community; but neither does she ignore themes which require a critical engagement with biblical texts (Weems 1988, 1995; cf. 2003).

6. The Dynamics of Sex/Gender Distinction

At the beginning of the feminist movement, a general 'we-consciousness' of women and an 'essence of the feminine' were assumed mostly without question. The debates about racism and anti-Judaism led decisively to the recognition of the many and deep differences among women, and made possible a breakthrough in biblical interpretation which distinguished between (biological) sex and (cultural) gender, with the help of which it became possible to analyse both biological similarities and cultural differences. Beginning with its 'discovery' in social anthropology (Rosaldo and Lamphere 1974), the distinction between sex and gender made another critical point, whose wide-ranging implications seemed to become clear only in the 1990s. The distinction made it possible to expose the supposedly unalterable 'natural' features which were actually the product of historical growth or were cultural givens in the context of a dominant sex/gender system. Instead of focusing on the supposedly always similar experience of being a woman, for example in the realm of motherhood, attention could be drawn to the historically very different bodily experiences of women, or valuations of women as mothers. Most recently, lesbian and gay biblical hermeneutics have followed this line, which has both analysed critically the appropriation of the Bible for discrimination against same-sex sexuality and has also developed its own constructive forms of reading biblical texts (Brooten 1996; Nissinen 1998; Stone 2001).

7. Thematic Variety

In the 1990s the thematic spectrum of feminist biblical scholarship became increasingly specialized and diversified. The exegesis of texts concerned with female biblical characters as well as the biblical books about women remained, as before, an important field. However, more clearly than previously, a distinction was made between the textual construction of these figures (the literary level), the reality of women in the biblical period (the historical level), and connections with the present experience of exegetes (the theological and political level). The feminist-theological options which were connected with this new profile of biblical female characters affected internal debates such as those concerning the question of women in ecclesiastical offices, but also current feminist political discussions including those about health and sickness, disability and 'normality' (Fontaine 1996), motherhood, the participation and speaking of women in public affairs, and especially the theme of sexual violence against women and girls (Müllner 1997). All these have become themes which bind women together globally in suffering and hope. At present, exchange women around the globe is possible, especially with the founding of the European Society of Women in Theological Research (ESWTR) in 1986, which during the 1990s had a strong influx of women theologians from many of the lands of Eastern Europe, as well as the Ecumenical Association of Third World Theologians (EATWOT) in Latin America, Africa, and Asia, which has formed new associations of feminist theologians.

In the universities the question of the worship of goddesses in Ancient Israel has been tackled by feminist exegetes, advancing in their own ways the current debates in Old Testament scholarship on biblical monotheism and the history of religions (Wacker 2004). The figure of divine wisdom, as developed in the wisdom writings of Early Judaism and which can be seen in the wisdom Christology of the New Testament, has awakened particular interest among feminist exegetes (Camp 1985; Schroer 2000). Complementary to it was work on female metaphors in biblical writings, particularly the metaphor of the true or unfaithful wife for the people of Israel (Vieira Sampaio 1999) and the metaphor of sexual power especially in the prophetic accounts of the relationship between God and his people (Baumann 2000). If, at the beginning of feminist criticism, it was the figure of Jesus which stood at the centre of concern, now it was much more the figure of Paul, or, better, he was de-centred in favour of his time and of his communities (Janssen 2001). The concern of feminist exegesis was broadened to the early Jewish and Christian writings which lay outside the canon (cf. the corresponding contributions e.g. on the Acts of Thecla or the Book of Joseph and Aseneth in Schüssler-Fiorenza 1993/4 and Schottroff and Wacker 1999/2006) and to the historical neighbouring areas of biblical scholarship such as Ancient Near Eastern studies, the Christian orient, classical archaeology, and comparative religion, but also decisively to modern literary and cultural criticism, particularly art and film (cf. Exum 1996). Bound up with this has been the question of the authority of the Bible, or a feminist theological concept of 'Women's Sacred Scriptures' (Kwok and Schüssler-Fiorenza 1998). In many biblical commentaries the attempt has been made meanwhile not only to remain with individual figures or themes specific to women, but to undertake feminist rereadings of all biblical texts and to broaden the definition of what is 'relevant' to feminism (Newson and Ringe 1992; Schüssler-Fiorenza 1993/4; Schottroff and Wacker 1999/2006). Along the same lines have been attempts to consider afresh from feminist points of view the 'classical' themes of biblical theology such as creation (Keel and Schroer 2002), the image of

God (Frettlöh 2002), the cross (Janssen 2000), and the resurrection (Sutter Rehmann *et al.* 2002). The *Feminist Companion to the Hebrew Bible* edited by Athalya Brenner brings together in two ten-volume series the feminist discussions of central biblical themes and figures of the 1990s (Brenner I, 1993–6; Brenner II, 1998 ff.). In the meantime a companion project for the New Testament has been completed (Levine and Bickenstaff 2001 ff.).

8. Hermeneutical Specifications

From the hermeneutical point of view, the debates about the variety of the contexts of the life of women and their many forms of oppression, but also possibilities of action, have been translated into a new, clarified concept of 'patriarchy', which seeks to analyse the historical and situated structures of power, as well as economic, educational, colour-specific, and age-determined factors, as well as those belonging to sexual orientation, and last but not least also specific religious circumstances. Elisabeth Schüssler-Fiorenza has suggested the term 'Kyriarchate' as a description of this system of multiple interdependencies (Schüssler-Fiorenza 1992) and has broadened her hermeneutic to a seven-step 'hermeneutical dance' (Schüssler-Fiorenza 2001). A separate hermeneutical step is now devoted to an analysis of the (dominant) *context* of the exegete as well as to the designation of her *experiences*, in order to do justice to the variety of life contexts. The 'hermeneutics of suspicion' is directed particularly to the rhetorical constructions of the Bible itself, which, in a 'hermeneutics of *critical evaluation*', are counter-read in respect to their cultural and specific theological implications. Particular stress is thus laid on a critical constructive altercation with the power of the text. '*Creative imagination*' is reserved not only for actualization, but becomes also part of the process of '*remembering and reconstruction*', and does so not only because it cannot be excluded from the hermeneutical circle, but also because it is a necessary authority against the rhetorical power of the texts. All these stand in the service of a 'hermeneutics of *transformative action for change*'. The motif of 'dance' signals the openness of the hermeneutical movement and the interdependence of the steps, whose sequence is not strictly determined, but which can be followed in all directions, as well as the aesthetic components of such scholarly work.

9. Challenges for the Third Millennium

I see the situation of feminist exegesis at the beginning of the third millennium as characterized by a number of challenges, which can be summed up under the (interconnected) keywords 'post-colonial', 'post-feminist', and 'post-Christian'.

A *post-colonial* interpretation of the Bible is demanded by theologians and exegetes from the Southern Hemisphere, whose countries of origin largely became acquainted with Christianity through missions sent from Europe only, a type of Christianity often associated with exploitation and the alienation of the indigenous culture. Consequently, post-colonial rereadings of the Bible have taken two main directions. On the one hand, biblical texts and themes are often linked in such readings with the traditions of the indigenous culture, whether they be myths of oppressed folk cultures or the sacred scriptures of the culture's high religions. On the other hand, there is, in these readings, a critical concern with colonial structures in the Bible itself, including the colour symbolism, which devalues what is dark (and thus also dark skin) as well as the polarization between opponents, particularly on the ethnic and political levels. The demonstration of such colonial or colonializing tendencies in the Bible, however, can be placed by, and joined to, critical voices within the Bible itself. Structurally similar to classical feminist hermeneutics, a 'hermeneutics of suspicion' against the Bible can be opposed to a 'hermeneutics of trust' in that 'de-colonializing' readings are supported by the Bible itself (cf. in general Sugirtharajah 2001, 2002; for the African context Dube 2000, 2001, 2003; for East Asia Kwok 1995: for the quite different Korean context cf. Lee 2003; You-Martin 2004).

The term *post-feminist* is sometimes understood as pointing to the deconstructive turn in feminism. In a narrower sense, deconstruction aims at the dominant sex/gender system with its binary assignations of gender roles, in order to 'trouble' or 'queer' gender identity. As over against a reading of the Bible as a historical document from the perspective of a world which presupposes and affirms the two sexes, the deconstructive approach entails an exciting search for traces of figures or metaphors which shatter the gender indications or which overcome them. This can begin with the nouns of Hebrew which grammatically have two genders, such as 'ruach'/spirit or 'shemesh'/sun. This approach, however, has implications reaching much further. Under the sign of deconstruction—that is, without any assumption of stable notions of essence, subject, or identity—the characterization of what can be termed 'feminist', especially in its global perspective, becomes more difficult. For feminist exegesis this means recognition of a variety of possibilities of interpretations and options, without an a priori common denominator of what is 'feminist'. However, in connection with the approach of a post-colonial exegesis, the necessity becomes clear that sight must not be lost of the concrete material structures of global injustice.

The climate, at any rate in German-speaking contexts, is *post-Christian* in so far as familiarity with the traditions and daily practice of Christianity, and above all knowledge and life with the Bible, are rapidly disappearing. In this situation feminist exegesis can no longer rely, as it did twenty-five years ago, on general and similar experiences of suffering of Christian women about and with the Bible. Correspondingly there is no longer simply 'the' liberating exegesis, but new ways of creative reading must be developed—a task which has also arisen through the deconstructive turn. In this connection troubling inequalities, particularly at the global level, must be noticed. Alongside an increasing 'secularization' there is, in the Northern Hemisphere, perhaps indeed world-wide, an increasing fundamentalism also within Christianity. On the other hand, as previously, Christianity with its traditions has an important significance as a liberating (and thus often persecuted) religion, which in many parts of the world seeks to question the structures of political and economic injustice. Another aspect of the 'post-Christian' situation is the growing awareness that the great religions of the world can overcome the global tasks of our present world (including the respect of the human rights of women as taught and lived out) by working not against, but with each other. As a result, they need to work out a strategy not of separation from each other but of paying attention to what they have in common. Feminist engagements with the Bible must find a way between awareness of their own particularity and the search for common perspectives.

II. Methods of Feminist Biblical Interpretation

The concerns of feminist exegesis are met with the help of all the scholarly methods currently practised in biblical scholarship; but because feminist theology and biblical exegesis try to come close to human experiences, the boundaries between the methods that have been traditionally practised in biblical criticism and those employed in the fields of the practical use of the Bible, are fluid. The following sketch concentrates mostly upon scholarly exegetical methods in the narrower sense: namely, historical criticism and new impulses from literary criticism, and, given this limitation, can only offer some typical examples of the use of feminist methods and criticism (cf. also Wacker in Schottroff *et al.* 1998).

A. Historical-Critical Methods

The historical-critical methods are concerned above all with the production processes of biblical texts and the world 'behind' the texts. These approaches are also relevant to feminist exegesis, in that they promise information about the historical changes in the literary depiction of female characters and in the concrete life of women, as well as insight into different sex/gender constructions in biblical literature and into the actual forms of community life of the sexes in biblical times.

1. Textual Criticism

In the area of New Testament textual criticism, the 'rehabilitation' of Junia as a female apostle (Rom. 16: 7) is the most prominent example of a feminist critical undertaking (Brooten 1977). Previously, a gender-biased scholarship driven by dogmatic prejudices could only recognize Junia as a man.

Old Testament textual criticism in the last two decades has been less concerned with rediscovering the 'original texts' and more concerned with comparing the ancient versions and their interpretation in particular historical contexts. From a feminist perspective, such comparison of versions is particularly fruitful where very different textual traditions exist. Thus, in her text-critical study of the book of Esther, Kristin de Troyer has undertaken a detailed comparison of the closing chapters of the three versions (de Troyer 2000). Her text-critical thesis, that the second Greek version of Esther (the A text) is a free reworking of the Septuagint version, implies the assumption that the figure of Esther is pushed into the background to the benefit of the figure of Mordechai. Thus the A text, which, according to de Troyer, dates from the first Christian century, is one among other early Jewish witnesses (also including some books of the New Testament) with the tendency to downgrade women. The two important, continuing translation projects of the Septuagint in Germany and France raise hopes that our knowledge not only of the translation techniques of the Greek editors but also the horizon of their world will be deepened, especially in regard to their views of the world of women and, where possible, this world itself.

2. Source Criticism/Literary or Redaction Criticism/Composition Criticism

In Old Testament scholarship classical source criticism has currently been replaced by a number of competing models for the origins of the Pentateuch. A burning feminist theme which enables feminists to take part in this discussion, and which in its results distances it from the classical view, is the literary role of Miriam in the Pentateuch, and consequently the historical meaning of this symbolic figure for prophecy in general, and for women as prophetesses in particular. Ursula Rapp (2002) shows in her monograph on Miriam that the Miriam traditions in the Pentateuch as well as in Mic. 6: 3–4 belong to the Persian era and can be read as evidence of a dispute about the authority of Moses or the Torah. In the area of the New Testament, Helgar Melzer-Keller (1997) argues, on the basis of the two-source theory, that Jesus' contact with women was less 'friendly' than was supposed at the beginning of the feminist Christian discovery of Jesus. In regard to recent trends in the investigation of the historical Jesus, Elisabeth Schüssler-Fiorenza (2004) warns against new hermeneutical restrictions.

3. Form Criticism

Fokkelien van Dijk-Hemmes and Athalya Brenner, building on the classical methods of form criticism and taking this further in the direction of new literary criticism, have developed the concept of 'gendering texts', which asks about female voices in biblical texts and holds that it is possible to draw conclusions about the historical spaces of women (Brenner and van Dijk-Hemmes 1993). A 'classical' example is the Song of Songs. The greater the concentration on the text as text, the more do such correlations of text and context become methodologically questionable; it becomes important to look for extra-biblical evidence for spaces of men and women in societies such as those in Ancient Israel. Here, valuable insights can be gained by the findings of gender-sensitive research in social anthropology.

4. History/Social History/History of Religion

The reconstruction of a history of women in the biblical period is bound up with many great difficulties in the pre-Hellenistic periods, because the dating of biblical texts as well as the assessment of their value as sources is at present very controversial, and extra-textual material is restricted. Phyllis Bird (1997) has contributed methodological clarity by outlining the likely places of women in the society of Ancient Israel. Silvia Schroer has attempted a first longitudinal sketch of a history of women in Israel (Schroer in Schottroff *et al.* 1998) and has also contributed to the religious history of Israel from the point of view of the iconography of the ancient world (cf. Schroer 1989 and 2000). For the period of the Second Temple, a notable contribution has been made by Tal Ilan with her trilogy on traces of women in the Hellenistic and, above all, the Roman period (Ilan 1995, 1997, 1999). The investigation of Ross Sh. Kraemer spans several religions by investigating female cults in Graeco-Roman times (Kraemer 1992; Kraemer and D'Angelo 1999). In the field of New Testament scholarship, Luise Schottroff and her students have been working on a feminist social history of Early Christianity. New Testament texts are read against the background of the deep political-economic antagonisms in the Roman Empire, and interest is focused upon everyday life and the resistance particularly of marginalized women such as Lydia, the despised seller of purple (Schottroff 1995), and the two elderly women Elizabeth and Hannah (Janssen 1998), or also upon themes such as birth and marriage, with their institutional as well as biographical individual aspects and their ambivalent meanings for women (Sutter Rehmann 1995, 2002). New Testament, rabbinical, and pagan texts can illuminate each other mutually in such an opening-up of women's history. This approach is not closed up in academic concerns, but rather, a feminist reformulation of liberation theology: with its focus on women who have suffered injustice, it draws attention to present-day injustice. Important also for this approach is the confrontation with anti-Jewish tendencies in Christian exegesis. Luise Schottroff deals with them by assuming that the movement which related to the risen Christ should be understood in the context of the pluriformity of Judaism before 135 CE, and that anti-Jewish polemic in the New Testament is a 'quarrel among brothers and sisters' which only later became a conflict between religions (Schottroff in Schottroff and Wacker 1996).

5. An Exegesis of Gender Justice

In dispute with classical historical-critical literature but reaching far beyond, Irmtraud Fischer has developed an approach of 'gender justice' in exegesis. She demonstrates, on the one hand, where unexamined and preconceived norms were decisive in previous scholarly discussion of the analysis of texts about women or, to put it another way, where research was conducted on an unenlightened 'gender-biased' basis. On the other side, she makes clear which viewpoints are possible for approaching biblical texts when one is freed from one's own prejudices in the perception of gender relationships in the ancient world. The matriarchs of Israel can be released from their 'only wife and mother' roles and become fellow builders of Israel. The book of Ruth no longer needs to be reduced to being merely an idyll, but can be seen as a document in post-exilic Israel that is concerned with a just interpretation of the law in connection with foreigners. The prophetesses of Israel can be seen as preachers of God's will, who, like their male colleagues, are involved in the disputes about prophecy in the exilic and post-exilic periods (Fischer 2000/2005, 2001, 2002).

B. Literary Methods

The exegetical reception and adaptation of literary methods has become enormously differentiated in the last two decades. As the smallest common denominator, an interest in the 'functioning' of the biblical text in its extant form may be noted, an interest that concerns itself with the internal structure of the text as well as the communicative act between the text and those who receive it (some approaches include the question of the production of the text). In feminist biblical scholarship a broad spectrum of literary-critical methods can be found, with differing main points in the way in which the text is perceived. What is 'feminist' is articulated, on the one hand, almost entirely as a gender-sensitive ideological critical approach to biblical texts, while, on the other hand, it takes differing forms of affirmative rereadings.

Currently, the terms and indeed the exact definitions of the newer exegetical methods are not unified (cf. Wacker 1998 and the observations in this Handbook). In particular, the term 'new literary criticism' used as an umbrella term covers a whole spectrum of differing methods which are also combined (Exum and Clines

1993; Struthers-Malbon and McKnight 1994). The following attempt to distinguish these approaches examines, first, varying schools, second, lines of development, and lastly, recognizable material preferences.

1. Structuralist Interpretation/Narratology and Beyond

In critical allegiance to the tradition of French structuralism (esp. G. Genette) the literary and cultural critic Mieke Bal has developed a narratological methodology which has been tested on a series of biblical texts and has concentrated on feminist critical issues, in that it connects every aspect of analysis with the question of the gender-specific division of power in a text. In addition to her work on the book of Judges (Bal 1988a, b), a concern with 'femmes imaginaires' of the Hebrew Bible has stood at the centre of her interest (Bal 1986/7; cf. also her contributions to various volumes of the *Feminist Companion* (Brenner I and II)). In the context of a wide-ranging engagement with the work of Rembrandt in which her methods of textual reading have been developed further according to the standards of cultural criticism (Bal 1991), she has newly interpreted a number of his representations of biblical women in dialogue with the biblical text.

2. Rhetorical Criticism

The term 'rhetorical criticism' describes, on the one hand, an approach to biblical interpretation which uses a kind of close reading to detect compositional structures of a text decisive for its meaning. This line is followed by Phyllis Trible with her two well-known monographs on various concepts of female sexuality in the Hebrew Bible (Trible 1978) and on 'texts of terror', i.e. texts about violence against women which initiate not only sadness at such misused power but resistance against it (Trible 1984). This perspective has been taken up by Angela Bauer in her monograph on the book of Jeremiah (1998).

At the same time Elisabeth Schüssler-Fiorenza has described her approach since the beginning of the 1990s as a *rhetorical* model of feminist critical analysis. This definition starts from an understanding of biblical texts as rhetorical constructs emerging from and responding to political-ethical conflicts in a very precise way. Thus, methods of textual analysis and methods focusing upon the analysis of the historical context must be carried out together; but, more basically, feminist rhetorical biblical criticism must be understood as a practical political science. Given the present situation of the irreducible multivocality of women themselves, its concern cannot be to discover the *one* meaning of the text, the less so since, from the textual theoretical point of view, doubt may be cast on whether there is such a thing. Feminist rhetorical criticism is much more concerned with discussing the multiplicity of interpretations in the democratic 'ecclesia of women' and enabling it to enter into the general political-ethical debate (Schüssler-Fiorenza 1992, 2001).

The monograph on Miriam by Ursula Rapp (2002) works with Schüssler-Fiorenza's approach to rhetorical criticism in order both to trace the rhetorical shaping of
the figure of Miriam in the biblical texts and to show how an alternative feminist
critical rhetoric can enable the Miriam fragments to be read.

3. Inter-textual Analysis

By inter-textuality is meant the interrelatedness of texts, whereby the choice of texts
taken into consideration can be narrow or much wider. From a feminist perspective
the interconnectedness of texts marked by gender is particularly productive. For
the inner-biblical textual area Klara Butting (1999) has shown that the figure of
Esther is presented as a female Joseph, and that it is therefore a retelling of the
biblical story of Joseph with its main theme of the Jewish man at the court of a
foreign ruler, in a manner sensitive to gender issues and in reflection on ancient
enmity to Jews. Similarly, Claudia Rakel (2003) somehow sees the figure of Judith
as the textual incarnation of an original interpretation of the Torah. This type of
approach can focus on the historical chronology of the texts to point out how, in
the Hellenistic period, female figures were included in a positive manner to depict
the struggle for Jewish identity at that time. This approach can also be used to listen
to the polyphony of the canon, which possesses sufficient critical potential for a
feminist reception, or as a reference to hitherto undiscovered relationships between
biblical texts, which can lead to the conclusion that 'these letters will be amazed'
(Butting 1994). In a wider sense the concept of inter-textuality broadens the view to
the whole area of the reception history of the Bible, or better, its critical interruptions through creative new alliances with texts or text-analogous structures. In this
sense the post-colonial joining of biblical texts or traditions with African folk
stories or with texts of the Asiatic high religions can be embedded in the methodological concept of inter-textuality.

4. New Literary Criticism

If the 'new' of 'new literary criticism' consists in widening the narrow view of pure
text-immanent structures as carriers of meaning to external circumstances that
constitute the meaning of a text (cf. Exum and Clines 1993: 17), then all approaches
of feminist literary-critical biblical interpretation belong to it by definition in so far
as they reflect the feminist interest as something which is determinative for
interpretation. Several authors only are mentioned here who, along with specific
feminist perspectives, consider significant for their exegesis other external factors
which determine the meaning of texts.

   Cheryl Exum's (1992) monograph on the dimension of tragedy in the books of
Samuel still stays rather close to the structures immanent in the text. In her more

recent interpretation of the book of Judges (Exum 1997) she employs psychoana-
lytical categories in order to show the basic lines of thought responsible for
the devaluation of the female figures in this biblical book, and in a further
monograph she draws on representations from the history of art and films about
the Bible to open up and deconstruct biblical texts and their images of women
(Exum 1996).

Athalya Brenner asks about female voices or employs the perspective of inter-
textuality (Brenner and van Dijk-Hemmes 1993), reflects on the basis of reader-
response criticism upon her presuppositions and expectations as a reader, and
further corrects or indeed deconstructs her own references (cf. her various interpretations of the Song of Songs: Brenner in Schottroff and Wacker 1998; Brenner in
Companion to the Song of Songs, II). A particular methodological line found in her
work is that of 'gendering texts': that is, the gender-specific unlocking of biblical
texts in regard to particular themes (cf. the study of a gender-specific analysis of
sexuality and desire in the Hebrew Bible: Brenner 1997 and her collected volume on
biblical humour, Brenner 2003).

The New Testament scholar Tina Pippin has engaged in various publications
with the world of metaphors of the Apocalypse of John (cf. Pippin 1992 and in
Schüssler-Fiorenza 1993/4). The gender rhetoric of this last book of the Christian
Bible is for her irredeemably misogynist, and her reaction as a female reader to its
pictures of war and power is one of abhorrence and defence. She is ready, though,
to question her own way of reading through the perspective of non-Western
women who stress the motives of hope and the establishment of justice, and thus
hold to a colonial-critical characterization of the Apocalypse in so far as this is
employed against the great power of Rome in the name of a persecuted minority.
Besides this, the Apocalypse of John is for Tina Pippin an occasion for seeing the
Bible as fantasy literature, or, for the perception of what is fantastic in the Bible
(Pippin and Aichele 1998).

It is to be hoped that the many impulses of Bible reading from the perspective of
feminists will bear their fruits in all those communities of believers which relate to
the Bible!

Suggested Reading

1. *Introductions to feminist exegesis*

Bach 1999; Brenner and Fontaine 1997; Schottroff *et al.* 1998; Schüssler-Fiorenza 2001.

2. *Feminist commentaries on the Bible*

Newson and Ringe 1992/8; Schüssler-Fiorenza 1993/4; Schottroff and Wacker 1999/2006. See
    also Brenner I and II; Levine and Bickenstaff 2001.

BIBLIOGRAPHY

BACH, ALICE, ed. 1999. *Women in the Hebrew Bible: A Reader.* New York: Routledge.

BAL, MIEKE 1986/7. *Femmes imaginaires: l'ancien testament au risque d'une narratologie critique.* Utrecht: Hes Publishers. Abridged English edition: *Lethal love.* Bloomington, Ind.: Indiana University Press.

—— 1988a. *Death and Dissymmetry: The Politics of Coherence in the Book of Judges.* Chicago: University of Chicago Press.

—— 1988b. *Murder and Difference: Gender, Genre, and Scholarship on Sisera's Death.* Bloomington, Ind.: Indiana University Press.

—— 1991. *Reading Rembrandt: Beyond the Word–Image Opposition.* Cambridge: Cambridge University Press.

BAUER, ANGELA 1998. *Gender in the Book of Jeremiah.* New York and Frankfurt: Lang.

BAUMANN, GERLINDE 2000. *Liebe und Gewalt: Die Ehe als Metapher für das Verhältnis JHWH Israel in den Prophetenbüchern.* Stuttgarter Biblische Beiträge 185. Stuttgart: Katholisches Bibelwerk.

BIRD, PHYLLIS 1997. *Missing Persons and Mistaken Identities: Women and Gender in Ancient Israel.* Minneapolis: Fortress Press.

BRENNER, ATHALYA, ed. 1993–6. (Brenner I)/1998 ff. (Brenner II). *A Feminist Companion to the Hebrew Bible,* 1st and 2nd series. Sheffield: Sheffield Academic Press.

—— 1997. *The Intercourse of Knowledge: On Gendering Desire and "Sexuality" in the Hebrew Bible.* BIS 26. Leiden: Brill.

—— ed. 2003. *Are We Amused? Humour about Women in the Biblical Worlds.* JSOTS.S 383. London: T. & T. Clark.

BRENNER, ATHALYA, and FONTAINE, CAROLE, eds. 1997. *Reading the Bible: Approaches, Methods and Strategies.* Sheffield: Sheffield Academic Press.

—— and VAN DIJK-HEMMES, FOKKELIEN 1993. *On Gendering Texts: Female and Male Voices in the Hebrew Bible.* Leiden: Brill.

BROOTEN, BERNADETTE 1977. 'Junia... Outstanding among the Apostles'. In Leonard and Arlene Swidler, eds., *Women Priests,* New York: Paulist Press, 141–4.

—— 1996. *Love between Women: Early Christian Responses to Female Homoeroticism.* Chicago and London: University of Chicago Press.

BUTTING, KLARA 1994. *Die Buchstaben werden sich noch wundem: Innerbiblische Kritik als Wegweisung feministischer Hermeneutik.* Berlin: Alektor.

—— 1999. 'Esther: A New Interpretation of the Joseph Story in the Fight Against Anti-Semitism and Sexism'. In Athalya Brenner, ed., *A Feminist Companion to Ruth and Esther,* Sheffield: Sheffield Academic Press, 239–48.

CAMP, CLAUDIA 1985. *Wisdom and the Feminine in the Book of Proverbs.* Sheffield: Almond Press.

—— 2000. *Wise, Strange and Holy: The Strange Woman and the Making of the Bible.* Sheffield: Sheffield Academic Press.

CANNON, KATIE G. 1985. 'The Emergence of Black Feminist Consciousness'. In Letty Russell, ed., *Feminist Interpretation of the Bible,* Philadelphia: Westminster Press, 30–40.

CARDOSO PEREIRA, NANCY 2003. 'Changing Seasons: About the Bible and Other Sacred Texts in Latin America'. In Schroer and Bietenhard 2003: 48–58.

DE TROYER, KRISTIN 2000. *The End of the Alfa-Text of Esther.* SBL SCS 48. Atlanta: SBL.

DUBE, MUSA 2000. *Postcolonial Feminist Interpretation of the Bible*. St Louis: Chalice Press.

—— 2001. *Other Ways of Reading: African Women and the Bible*. Atlanta: SBL.

—— 2003. 'Jumping the Fire with Judith: Postcolonial Feminist Hermeneutics of Liberation'. In Schroer and Bietenhard 2003: 60–76.

EXUM, J. CHERYL 1992. *Tragedy and Biblical Narrative*. Cambridge: Cambridge University Press.

—— 1996. *Plotted, Shot, and Painted: Cultural Representations of Biblical Women*. JSOTS.S 215. Sheffield: Sheffield Academic Press.

—— 1997. *Was sagt das Richterbuch den Frauen?* Stuttgarter Biblische Beiträge 169. Stuttgart: Katholisches Bibelwerk.

—— and CLINES, DAVID J. A., eds. 1993. *New Literary Criticism and the Hebrew Bible*. JSOTS.S 143. Sheffield: JSOT Press.

FISCHER, IRMTRAUD 2000/2005. *Woman who Wrestled with God. Biblical Stories of Israel's Beginnings*. Collegeville: Liturgical Press. 2nd Generation edn. translated.

—— 2001. *Rut*. Herders Theologischer Kommentar AT. Freiburg: Herder.

—— 2002. *Gotteskünderinnen: Zu einer geschlechterfairen Deutung des Phänomens der Prophetie und der Prophetinnen in der Hebräischen Bibel*. Stuttgart: Kohlhammer.

FONTAINE, CAROLE R. 1996. 'Disabilities and Illness in the Bible: A Feminist Perspective'. In Athalya Brenner, ed., *A Feminist Companion to the Hebrew Bible in the New Testament*, Sheffield: Sheffield Academic Press, 286–300.

FRETTLÖH, MAGDALENE L. 2002. *Wenn Mann und Frau im Bilde Gottes sind...: Über geschlechtsspezifische Gottesbilder, die Gottesbildlichkeit des Menschen und das Bilderverbot*. Wuppertal: Foedus-Verlag.

ILAN, TAL 1995. *Jewish Women in Greco-Roman Palestine: An Inquiry into Image and Status*. TSAJ 44. Tübingen: Mohr.

—— 1997. *Mine and Yours are Hers: Retrieving Women's History from Rabbinic Literature*. AGAJU 41. Leiden: Brill.

—— 1999. *Integrating Women into Second Temple History*. TSAJ 76. Tübingen: Mohr.

JANSSEN, CLAUDIA 1998. *Hanna und Elisabeth—zwei widerständige alte Frauen in neutestamentlicher Zeit: Eine sozialgeschichtliche Untersuchung*. Mainz: Grünewald.

—— ed. 2000. *Erinnern und aufstehen—antworten auf Kreuzestheologien*. Mainz: Grünewald.

—— ed. 2001. *Paulus: Umstrittene Traditionen—lebendige Theologie. Eine feministische Lektüre*. Gütersloh: Gütersloher Verlagshaus.

KEEL, OTHMAR, and SCHROER, SILVIA 2002. *Schöpfung: Biblische Theologien im Kontext altorientalischer Religionen*. Göttingen: Vandenhoeck & Ruprecht.

KRAEMER, ROSS SHEPARD 1992. *Her Share of the Blessings: Women's Religions among Pagans, Jews, and Christians in the Greco-Roman World*. New York: Oxford University Press.

—— and D'ANGELO, MARY ROSE, eds. 1999. *Women and Christian Origins*. New York: Oxford University Press.

KWOK, PUI LAN 1995. *Discovering the Bible in the Non-Biblical World*. Maryknoll, NY: Orbis Books.

—— and SCHÜSSLER-FIORENZA, ELISABETH, eds. 1998. *Women's Sacred Scriptures*. Conclium 34/3. London: SCM Press; Maryknoll, NY: Orbis Books.

LEE, KYUNG-SOOK 2003. 'The Biblical Hermeneutics of Liberation from the Perspective of Asian Christian Women: Recovering the Liberation-Tradition of Early Christianity in Korea'. In Schroer and Bietenhard 2003: 164–70.

LEVINE, AMY-JILL, with BICKENSTAFF, MARIANNE, eds. 2001. *A Feminist Companion to the New Testament*. Sheffield: Sheffield Academic Press.

MELZER-KELLER, HELGA 1997. *Jesus und die Frauen: Eine Verhältnisbestimmung nach den synoptischen Überlieferungen*. Freiburg: Herder.

MÜLLNER, ILSE 1997. *Gewalt im Hause Davids: Die Erzählung von Tamar und Amnon (2 Sam 13, 1–22)*. Freiburg: Herder.

NEWSOM, CAROL A., and RINGE, SHARON H., eds. 1992/8. *The Women's Bible Commentary*. 2nd, expanded edition, London: SPCK; Louisville, Ky.: Westminster/John Knox Press.

NISSINEN, MARTTI 1998. *Homoeroticism in the Biblical World: A Historical Perspective*. Minneapolis: Fortress Press.

PIPPIN, TINA 1992. *Death and Desire: The Rhetoric of Gender in the Apocalypse of John*. Louisville, Ky.: Westminster/John Knox Press.

—— and AICHELE, GEORGE, eds. 1998. *Violence, Utopia, and the Kingdom of God: Fantasy and Ideology in the Bible*. London and New York: Routledge.

PLASKOW, JUDITH 1978. 'Christian Feminism and Antijudaism', *Cross Currents*, 33: 306–9.

—— 1990. 'Feministischer Antijudaismus und der christliche Gott'. *Kirche und Israel*, 5/1: 9–25.

RADFORD RUETHER, ROSEMARY 1983. *Sexism and God-Talk*. Boston: Beacon Press.

RAKEL, CLAUDIA 2003. *Judit—über Schönheit, Macht und Widerstand im Krieg: Eine feministisch-intertextuelle Lektüre*. BZAW 334. Berlin: de Gruyter.

RAPP, URSULA 2002. *Miriam: Eine feministisch-rhetorische Lektüre der Miriamtexte in der hebräischen Bibel*. BZAW 317. Berlin: de Gruyter.

REINHARTZ, ADELE 1991. 'From Narrative to History: The Resurrection of Mary and Martha'. In Amy-Jill Levine, ed., *'Women Like This': New Perspectives on Jewish Women in the Greco-Roman World*, Atlanta: Scholars Press, 161–84.

—— 2001. *Befriending the Beloved Disciple: A Jewish Reading of the Gospel of John*. New York: Continuum.

ROSALDO, MICHELLE Z., and LAMPHERE, LOUISE, eds. 1974. *Women, Culture and Society*. Stanford, Calif.: Stanford University Press.

SCHOTTROFF, LUISE 1995. *Lydia's Impatient Sisters: A Feminist Social History of Early Christianity*. Louisville, Ky.: Westminster/John Knox Press.

—— SCHROER, SILVIA, and WACKER, MARIE-THERES 1998. *The Bible in Women's Perspective*. Philadelphia: Augsburg Fortress Publishers.

—— and WACKER, MARIE-THERES, eds. 1996. *Von der Wurzel getragen: Christlich-feministische Exegese in Auseinandersetzung mit Antijudaismus*. Leiden: Brill.

—— —— eds. 1999/2006. *Kompendium Feministische Bibelauslegung*. Gütersloh: Gütersloher Verlaghaus. Amercian translation, Grand Rapids, Mich.: Eerdmans.

SCHROER, SILVIA 1989. 'Die Göttin auf den Stempelsiegeln aus Palästina/Israel'. In Othmar Keel, Hildi Keel-Leu, and Silvia Schroer, *Studien zu den Stempelsiegeln aus Palästina/Israel*, ii, OBO 88, Fribourg and Göttingen: Universitätsverlag und Vandenhoeck & Ruprecht, 89–207.

—— 2000. *Wisdom has Built her House: Studies on the Figure of Sophia in the Bible*. Collegeville, Minn.: Liturgical Press.

—— and BIETENHARD, SOPHIA, eds. 2003. *Feminist Interpretation of the Bible and the Hermeneutics of Liberation*. Sheffield: Sheffield Academic Press.

SCHÜNGEL-STRAUMANN, HELEN 1992. *Rûah bewegt die Welt: Gottes schöpferische Lebenskraft in der Krisenzeit des Exils*. Stuttgarter Biblische Beiträge 151. Stuttgart: Katholisches Bibelwerk.

SCHÜSSLER-FIORENZA, ELISABETH 1983. *In Memory of Her: A Feminist Critical Reconstruction of Christian Origins.* New York: Crossroads.

—— 1984. *Bread Not Stone: The Challenge of Feminist Biblical Interpretation.* Boston: Beacon Press.

—— 1992. *But She Said: Feminist Practices of Biblical Interpretation.* Boston: Beacon Press.

—— ed. 1993/4. *Searching the Scriptures,* 2 vols. New York: Crossroad.

—— 2001. *Wisdom Ways: Introducing Feminist Biblical Interpretation.* Maryknoll, NY: Orbis Books.

—— 2004. 'Die Grenzen wissenschaftlicher Jesusforschung aufzeigen: Wer sagt, wer Jesus wirklich war?'. In *idem, Grenzen überschreiten: Der theoretische Anspruch feministischer Theologie,* Theologische Frauenforschung in Europa, 15, Münster: Lit-Verlag, 203–15.

SELVIDGE, MARLA J. 1996. *Notorious Voices: Feminist Biblical Interpretation 1500–1920.* Sheffield: Continuum.

STONE, KEN, ed. 2001. *Queer Commentary and the Hebrew Bible.* Sheffield: Continuum.

STRUTHERS-MALBON, ELIZABETH, and MCKNIGHT, EDGAR V. 1994. *The New Literary Criticism and the New Testament.* JSNTS.S 109. Sheffield: Sheffield Academic Press.

SUGIRTHARAJAH, RASIAH S. 2001. *The Bible and the Third World: Precolonial, Colonial and Postcolonial Encounters.* Cambridge: Cambridge University Press.

—— 2002. *Postcolonial Criticism and Biblical Interpretation.* Oxford: Oxford University Press.

SUTTER REHMANN, LUZIA 1995. *Geh, frage die Gebärerin: Feministisch-befreiungstheologische Untersuchungen zum Gebärmotiv in der Apokalyptik.* Gütersloh: Gütersloher Verlagshaus.

—— 2002. *Konflikte zwischen ihm und ihr: Sozialgeschichtliche und exegetische Untersuchungen zur Nachfolgeproblematik von Ehepaaren.* Gütersloh: Kaiser, Gütersloher Verlagshaus.

—— et al., eds. 2002. *Sich dem Leben in die Arme werfen: Auferstehungserfahrungen.* Gütersloh: Gütersloher Verlagshaus.

TAMEZ, ELSA 1993. *The Amnesty of Grace: Justification by Faith from a Latin American Perspective.* Nashville: Abingdon Press.

TEUBAL, SAVINA J. 1984. *Sarah the Priestess: The First Matriarch of Genesis.* Athens, Oh.: Swallow Press.

TRIBLE, PHYLLIS 1978. *God and the Rhetoric of Sexuality.* Philadelphia: Fortress Press.

—— 1984. *Texts of Terror: Literary-Feminist Readings of Biblical Narratives.* Philadelphia: Fortress Press.

VIEIRA SAMPAIO, TANIA MARA 1999. *Movimentos do corpo prostituído da mulher: Aproximações da profecia atribuída a Oséias.* São Paulo: Edições Loyola.

WACKER, MARIE-THERES 1998. 'Bibelkritik 1: Methoden der Bibelkritik im Alten Testament'. In H. D. Betz, D. S. Browning, B. Janowski, and E. Jüngel, eds., *Religion in Geschichte und Gegenwart,* 4th edn., Tübingen: Mohr, I. 1474–80.

—— 2004. *Von Göttinnen, Göttern und dem einzigen Gott: Studien zum biblischen Monotheismus aus feministisch-theologischer Sicht.* Theologische Frauenforschung in Europa, 14. Münster: Lit-Verlag.

WEEMS, RENITA 1988. *Just a Sister Away: A Womanist Vision of Women's Relationships in the Bible.* San Diego: Lura Media.

WEEMS, RENITA 1995. *Battered Love: Marriage, Sex and Violence in the Hebrew Prophets*. Minneapolis: Fortress Press.

—— 2003. 'Re-Reading for Liberation: African American Women and the Bible'. In Schroer and Bietenhard 2003: 19–32.

WEILER, GERDA 1984/9. *'Ich verwerfe im Lande die Kriege...': Das verborgene Matriarchat im Alten Testament*. Munich: Frauenoffensive; third edition under the title *Das verborgene Matriarchat im Alten Israel*. Stuttgart: Kohlhammer.

YOU-MARTIN, CHOON-HO 2004. *Frauenbewegung und Frauentheologie in Südkorea*, posthumously edited by Marie-Theres Wacker and Hermes A. Kick. Theologische Frauenforschung in Europa, 16. Münster: Lit-Verlag.

CHAPTER 37

SOCIAL, POLITICAL, AND IDEOLOGICAL CRITICISM

CHRISTOPHER ROWLAND

This essay explores ways in which ideological criticism may contribute to biblical studies. The discussion is rooted in the central role that the critique of ideology has within the Marxist tradition (McLellan 1987) and the ways in which that rich tradition of discussion can serve biblical exegesis and theology. I will give two specific examples of the way in which there has been a challenge to dominant ideologies. First of all, the emergence of liberationist hermeneutics (linked as it is with both feminist and 'Black' theologies; Rowland 1999) has posed questions to a dominant, 'First World', biblical hermeneutics and its idealist presuppositions, in which the history of ideas have taken precedence over their relationship to their social formation. Secondly, there have been throughout the history of Christianity alternative patterns of biblical interpretation, with different priorities and with the interests of readers, from below other than the élites of the day (West 1998). The essay closes with some consideration of the historical dimension of ideological criticism in which different doctrinal and practical priorities have emerged within readings of the Bible which have emerged apart from the dominant ideological contexts.

IDEOLOGY AND THE STRUGGLE FOR POWER

One of the great contributions of Enlightenment criticism was the analysis of society and its individuals, not that the social critique had been absent in the centuries before that (on which see below), but with the analysis of social forces at work, the understanding of society and the relationship between wealth and power attained a new level of sophistication. The pioneering work of Weber, Durkheim, and Marx on the ways in which texts and ideas relate to their social contexts only slowly infiltrated the world of biblical studies, dominated as it has been by the history of ideas and in particular the history of the development of the religious themes of particular communities (Giddens 1996). The different perspectives offered by the three great social scientists have begun to make their mark on the interpretation of the Bible. While there remains an exegesis which is primarily philological and theological, the social significance of theological ideas is now an accepted part of the study of biblical texts. There has been less immediate impact from the Marxist tradition, though, arguably, indirectly, in the study of ideology this has been equally pervasive though not always recognized (Kautsky 1925; Kyrtatas 1987; de Ste Croix 1982). The situation is very different with sociological and anthropological study, however. The sociology of religion, itself much influenced by the study of the way in which a charismatic Christian sect became an institution (Troeltsch 1931), more than any other discipline has transformed the way in which biblical texts are studied. The growing concentration on the importance of the role of the texts and their witness to the identity of communities and the way in which ritual, life, and ideas functioned one with another in enabling individuals and groups to discern their place in the world has led to a more holistic approach to biblical texts than has been the case hitherto when there was more concern with the way in which doctrines emerged and developed, largely independent of their socio-economic context.

The character of the study of ideology has tended to focus almost exclusively on the ancient texts themselves, and there has been surprisingly little hermeneutical reflection on the importance of the sociological critique on the interpreters themselves. There has been less evidence of scrutinizing the interests of the biblical interpreters and the understanding of the interaction between text and reader which has taken place at different periods of history. The work on *Wirkungsgeschichte* (the history of the effects of the biblical texts) has begun to help greatly, for studying the effects of a text will of necessity demand that one engages in a contextual approach as the particular moment of engagement with the text is explored.

Ideology is not something which belongs exclusively to those who use the Bible in their political struggles, for it is also at work in the products of those who claim to be engaging in 'scientific' methods of biblical study, not least among dominant élites which affirm that what they study is 'normal' and 'objective' (Eagleton 1991). A critical interpretation must manifest an awareness of its own approach to the text, but also the understandable constraints that this method imposes and the necessity of openness to other interpretative methods as both checks and a stimulus to change. 'Ideology' is a word which is widely used and whose meaning in its different contexts always needs to be monitored. It can be used in a general sense as a way of describing a system of ideas. It may also be used as a term of abuse in political discourse, when a position is dubbed 'ideological' because it is attached to narrow, doctrinaire positions. In the Marxist tradition, however, it has been linked with illusory belief or false consciousness, where people have the true state of social and economic affairs hidden from them by sets of ideas, which effectively prevent injustice from being made apparent. In this there is sometimes a contrast between the ideological and the scientific, the latter indicating the true state of affairs in human society. The Marxist tradition, which has offered the most purchase on the word, claims that the ideological concerns the ways in which language and meaning are used, whether deliberately or not, to legitimate the prevailing, usually unequal power relations in society (Hall 1985; McLellan 1987). Ideology thus functions in the interests of the wielders of power (often termed 'hegemonic groups'), who have an interest in maintaining things as they are and the interpretation of the world as it is, thereby enabling the economic interests of those with most wealth and influence to continue to wield that influence. This means that particular social arrangements and their justification are presented as if they were governed by social laws as unchangeable as the laws of physics and so impossible to change. So the study of ideology is to see how ideas and systems of thinking and belief function in a society in such a manner that the way people think and the ruling groups appear to be 'natural' and 'just'. Though these interests are not always compatible with the interests of the rest of the community, as the powerful groups are merely sectional in their interests, the way in which the language and systems of ideas function is to make it appear that they are in fact in the interests of all. Thereby the fact that society functions to benefit the interests of the powerful more than the weak is obscured. The critique of ideology involves the exposure not only of overt ways in which sectional interests are supported, but especially of the covert ways in which dominant interests are served. It involves laying bare the contradictions in society and the habit which the dominant groups have of neutralizing their potential for resistance and change, for example, by co-opting some of the ideas into the dominant ideology.

If we examine components of Christian doctrine, we can see them functioning as means of legitimating the interests of the powerful. Simple requests to accept the example of Christ as a paradigm of patient suffering can have the effect of leaving the world very much as it is. A very different understanding of the example of

Christ emerges in the way in which the cross is seen as either an act of rebellion or as the means whereby the interests of the powerful are challenged. According to the second approach, when Jesus told his followers to take up their cross, he was advocating the path of rebellion. The death of Jesus in the Gospel of Mark, for example, is a sign of the revolutionary potential of martyrdom as the ideological system based on the temple is challenged as its veil is torn in two from top to bottom (Myers 1988; Belo 1981; Clevenot 1985; Horsley 2001).

All works may be viewed as ideological, and have a relationship to vested interest in relation to social formations (Jameson 1981; Williams 1977). Texts are going to relate to very particular social situations as well as wider social and economic movements whose history is far bigger than the immediate situation in which a text is written (Hall 1985). Thus, as well as representing the narrow confines of the struggles and language of a particular group, the text is an individual representative of the struggles between social classes and the contradictions of human existence. Doing justice to the way in which texts form part of the struggles for power and survival depends to a large extent on knowledge of the particular social situation and general social trends of which they are a part. The paucity of information about the peculiar circumstances which might have determined, wholly or partly, the symbolic constellation or narrative of an ancient text makes ideological criticism a difficult task, to ascertain what precisely were the factors which helped form the text as we now have it. Biblical scholars have resorted to a significant amount of imaginative reconstruction in order to offer answers to the question: in what kind of situation and as part of what sort of social struggle did people write this kind of text in this kind of way? There has been an ongoing attempt to assemble sufficient information to form some picture of the social formation.

Texts' relationships to the world are never straightforward, as they both reflect and refract social reality. The texts are complex artefacts whereby the tensions of society are expressed. They can be means of expressing hope in a situation where insurmountable constraints mean that the fulfilment of that hope is impossible immediately. They are, therefore, channels of escape in which resolution of the contradictions and frustrations of the world takes place in the aesthetic realm. In other words, texts and rituals can offer solutions which satisfy the imagination of readers and offer solace when the real world seems to offer no resolution whatsoever. The story which ends happily ever after, the glorious conclusion to a religious service, contrasts with a world in which conflict is the order of the day.

In a situation of conflict, those who exercise power will seek to do so not only in terms of control of wealth creation but also in terms of the ideas which can justify and support the way in which the world is run. The recognition of this process and the way in which those who refuse to accept the dominant understanding of the way the world is forms a central part of the investigation of ideology. A text must be interpreted as part of a struggle between different class interests, in which a ruling class ideology seeks to offer itself as 'common sense' or 'normality', and all else as deviant and irrational. A ruling class ideology will offer strategies of legitimation, while an oppositional culture or ideology will often in covert ways seek to contest and to undermine the dominant value system. In the latter there is a process of reappropriation and neutralization by the dominant ideology. Equally, there is always an attempt by the powerful to pick the best ideas of the opposition and use those, thereby minimizing their potency and the strength of the opposing groups who introduced them. Thus care is needed when we speak of the Christian tradition, as it is easy to identify it with those parts of it which have been accepted by those who have wielded power. A text will not usually produce a particular ideology in a 'pure' form, whether it be supportive of the *status quo* or not. Accordingly, however loud the note of protest in a text, it is going to be shot through with the ambiguities of being part and parcel of a world that is itself full of contradiction and pain. Any text's relation to that struggle will not necessarily stand firmly on one side or another. Sometimes it will manifest the voice of the oppressor and his ideology in the process of seeking to articulate that subversive memory. It is part of the task of interpretation to lay bare the ambiguities and contradictions that are inherent in all texts. A critical examination of the Bible suggests that texts which have in the subsequent history of religion had a radical impact, such as Second Isaiah, were in their original production means of reinforcing the ideas of the ruling élite who were transported into exile and then sought to establish their God-given right to lead on their return (Mosala 1989). In order to understand fully such a text, it is necessary to enquire into the nature of the mode of production, the constellation of groups, and their different ideas and interests. Biblical books are made up of contradictory themes, which reflect something of the competing ideas and interests in the society of the time when it was given its final form, rather than when the oracles were uttered originally. Only with difficulty is it possible to retrieve from the biblical text an alternative perspective to the dominant ideology which has so permeated the text.

This approach is part and parcel of the hermeneutics of suspicion which has been such a feature of modern biblical scholarship. The difference is that contradictions in the text are interpreted politically and economically rather than merely in terms of ideas. It is a way of reading which recognizes the diversity both religiously and politically within one text. Texts do include the dominant ideology either by way of reaction or specific espousal alongside its witness to other less conformist traditions. Even what may appear to us to be the most reactionary texts may surprise us by offering what Jameson (1981: 288) calls a 'utopian impulse'. Criticism has a role in helping lay bare that impulse, but the task of retrieval is not its only, or even its main, function.

EARLY CHRISTIAN TEXTS, IDEOLOGY
AND SOCIAL CONTEXT

With regard to early Christian writings, part of the task of Christian literary production in its earliest phase was to position itself over against the dominant ideology,
whether it be a dominant form of Judaism or the ideologies of the wider Graeco-
Roman world (Wengst 1985; Esler 1984; Mosala 1989). An example of the ambiguity of
an early Christian text may be detected in the Gospel of Luke, which at times seems to
evince a greater concern to convince and perhaps even placate the influential and
important rather than be a mouthpiece for the oppressed. Luke wrote in order to
present an acceptable religion which conformed to Jewish tradition, offered hope to
the penitent rich and mighty, and did not frighten the powerful segments of Roman
society. The reader of the gospel is left in little doubt about the appropriate response to
those like Lazarus, however. Luke, like his contemporary Flavius Josephus, enables us
to catch a glimpse of another dimension to the story of Second Temple Judaism than
what appears to have been the one preferred by him (Rowland 1993).

History is rarely the memory of the poor and insignificant, which is frequently
lost for ever from our view. This is an important point to bear in mind when a
facile choice of texts like the Lucan beatitudes may be seen as an indication of
'history from below' (Hall 1985; cf. Scott 1990; Bradstock and Rowland 2002;
Rowland 1988; West 1998). Its retrieval is the task of the critics of another age
sympathetic to the voiceless and the marginalized. The focus of interest in Luke is
different from a modern grass-roots story of popular protest. This has Christology,
albeit in narrative form at the centre of their presentation, and this towers over all
other concerns. The poor and the outcast are incidental to that dominant concern.
But that Christological perspective privileges the orientation of Christ towards the
outcasts and rejects, and so, in the process of convincing Theophilus of his version
of the story of Jesus, Luke at least ensured that the story was written. The writing of
the tradition about Jesus was a formative moment for the antique world in its focus
on the relatively insignificant life of a Galilean peasant. The story was thus fixed in
the midst of genres which were largely the prerogative of those who served the
interests of the politically powerful. Luke to some extent falls into the category of a
book which seeks to set down a story which might hardly merit a record in the
annals of the ancient world, and in so doing includes a glimpse of those poor and
insignificant people who were the beneficiaries of the gospel.

Paul as a Social Actor

Sociological approaches to Paul (Horrell 1999; Meggit 1998; Meeks 1983; Theissen
1999) have attended to the social function of the doctrine rather than the origin of

particular ideas like the righteousness terminology. In such an approach, the way in which ideas are intended to effect social change is examined. So, Paul's activity as a communities organizer is served by ideas whose purpose is to establish a community with enough sense of common endeavour that they can survive as distinct, and viable, groups in the social contexts. Justification by faith alone is less an article of faith than a technique of social cohesion used to weld disparate ethnic and social groups together. The maintenance of social identity is enabled by strategies of ideological polemic. Ancient traditions are appropriated and reinterpreted in favour of the new group. So the Abraham story functions as legitimating story not of the election of the Jewish nation but for those who espouse the law-free gospel (Watson 1986).

In this approach to the Pauline letters, ideological criticism is used to analyse the role of doctrines in the context of a social strategy determined by a socio-economic context. In addition, there is the elucidation of the power struggles at work and the reasons for this. Such a task is as old as the modern study of the New Testament, when F. C. Baur pointed to the life and death struggles between Paul and the representatives of the Jerusalem church. The difference in modern social and ideological criticism is twofold, however. First, it is less related to personalities, except as they are embedded in particular patterns of social change. Paul represents a particular trend in the emerging movement (charismatic, sitting loose to received wisdom) and to a degree continues a liberal attitude to the ancestral custom which is found in Pharisaism. James, on the other hand, is more respectful and attached to the contemporary interpretation of the ancestral religion. Secondly, there is a wider socio-economic context in the Roman Empire, in which protest movements of the politically marginalized find in religion some degree of fulfilment in a situation where they are cut off from real political power (Meeks 1983; Holmberg 1978).

APOCALYPSE: SUBVERSION, PROTEST, OR FANTASY?

Similar texts can be used in the service of vastly different causes, as the history of European religion down the centuries has shown. Of no text is this truer than the Apocalypse, the book of Revelation. It has probably been used more often in the service of those who have set about subverting the contemporary social order, but has also been a corner-stone of political quietism (as with the Jehovah's Witnesses) and political reaction (as with modern fundamentalists; Kovacs and Rowland 2004). Apocalyptic symbolism, therefore, has never been the sole preserve of the oppressed and the poor. Even in post-exilic Israel, in the very years when eschatological hope was being formed, there was a common stock of images which two sides in a struggle for power used to achieve pre-eminence for their own positions. It can be found buttressing the projects of those whose quest for utopia is firmly rooted in conventional values and the nostalgic yearning for a golden age of moral perfection based on hierarchy and subservience. Here apocalyptic symbolism serves to undergird a view of the world which supports the conviction of a comfortable elect that they will ultimately be saved.

Revelation's stark contrasts and uncompromising critique have appealed to those who find little hope in compromise with the powers that be and demand something more than a meek acceptance that the way the world is, is what God intended. In this reading it gives little comfort to the complacent church or the powerful world. For the powerful and the complacent it has a message of judgement and doom, whereas for the powerless and oppressed it offers hope and vindication. The characterization of contemporary society in the apocalyptic symbolism of Beast and Harlot is a denunciation of the ideology of the powerful, by which they seek to legitimize their position by persecution and economic exploitation. A critique of the present is effected by the use of a contrast between the glories of the future and the inadequacies of the present. The process of unmasking involves an attempt to delineate the true character of contemporary society and the superhuman forces at work in the opposition to God's righteousness in the world. Revelation seeks to persuade its readers that the present moment is a time of critical importance. Although it often comes close to drawing its readers into an escape into fantasy, the readers of the Apocalypse are not allowed to dream about millennial bliss without being brought face to face with the obstacles which stand in the way of its fulfilment and the costly part to be played by them in that process.

A text will not usually produce a particular ideology in a 'pure' form whether it be supportive of the *status quo* or not. The apocalyptic outlook could be appropriated and neutralized by its incorporation into the dominant ideology (as, for example, the way in which the Augustinian dualistic world-view in *The City of God*, a work so dependent on the Apocalypse, offers an implicit resistance to an impetus to social change). Religions in particular offer excellent examples of the way in which this process of domestication can take place. Movements of protest born as the way of keeping alive ideas and aspirations contrary to the dominant culture can in the course of time lose their cutting edge and become part of a diffused cultural phenomenon incorporated into the needs of the dominant economic system. Accordingly, however loud the note of protest in a text, it is often going to be shot through with the ambiguities of being part and parcel of a world that is itself full of contradiction and pain. Any text's relation to that struggle may well be ambiguous. Sometimes it will manifest the voice of the oppressor and his ideology in the process of seeking to articulate that subversive memory. It is part of the task of interpretation to lay bare the ambiguities and contradictions that are inherent in all texts.

Nowhere is this more true than in the attitude to women in the Apocalypse. There is a real problem for modern readers of Revelation because of its negative attitude to women (Pippin 1992; Schüssler-Fiorenza 1993). The book's images of women are of either whores or brides, active Jezebels or passive wives and mothers. Women are viewed in terms of a patriarchal culture and its attendant economy. Women are either idealized or demonized in Revelation, using conventional tropes. Whatever its radical politics and subversive attitude towards empire, in terms of gender it presents huge ideological problems—yet another reminder of the complex nature of a text's ideological position. Yet, paradoxically, as a prophetic book, Revelation has offered space for women as well as men to enable their spirituality to flourish and for them to emerge as characters in their own right, created in God's image, in the midst of a society permeated by patriarchy. The prophets and the mystics have found in Revelation an inspiration to explore the inner life and to exercise a ministry denied by much else in Scripture and tradition. They found in this allusive text a licence to resist received religion and practice precisely because a canonical text opened a door for an experience of God which enabled them to transcend the boundaries imposed by what was conventionally possible. The problem is that the medium can detract from its message, so that far from rubbing our noses in the reality of our world, the unpalatable character of its imagery becomes an obstacle.

Apocalyptic symbolism strikes us as bizarre today. It represents a powerful form whereby the oppressed can keep alive the oppressed culture in the face of a dominant and powerful ideology. The apocalyptic imagery and cosmology themselves betoken a view of the world where protest and resistance to compromise are the order of the day. Walter Benjamin wrote of the necessity of 'brush[ing] history against the grain', in order to rescue tradition from the conformity imposed upon it by the powerful: 'In every era the attempt must be made anew to wrest tradition away from a conformism that is about to overpower it' (Benjamin 1978: 248). The Apocalypse has certainly served this social purpose down the centuries.

THE CONTRIBUTION OF LIBERATIONIST HERMENEUTICS

Christopher Columbus reached the Americas in 1492, and opened a significant era in the mission of the Church. The conquest of the Americas, destructive as it was, soon included the raising of important questions about the discovery of America. For example, Bartolomé de Las Casas, the ex-slave-owner who became a Dominican, asserted that indigenous people possessed equal dignity in the sight of God (Gutiérrez 1994). As a young priest, he prepared a homily on Ecclus. 34: 21–7; the words 'Like one who kills before his father's eyes is a person who offers a sacrifice from the property of the poor' crystallized a sense of the injustice of the economic system of which he was a part, which exploited indigenous peoples. The rest of his life was devoted to obtaining rights for indigenous peoples from the Spanish crown and showing that they therefore had equal rights to life, liberty, and full development. Las Casas influenced Spanish legislation and affected the *encomienda* system by which grants of land included all the Indians settled on them. He became a bishop who acted as 'the voice of the voiceless'. Figures like Las Casas provided the inspiration for the movement which arose in the last decades of the twentieth century known as liberation theology.

Like the Marxist tradition with which it has affinities and has from time to time been influenced, liberation theology rejects the notion that humans think first and act on the basis of rational thought. Rather, the latter emerges out of specific contexts, and is determined by those contexts and the human interests at work in them. Talk about God, therefore, is always potentially ideological, and needs to be examined within the power relations at work in a particular social context.

Liberation theology developed in the context of the emergence of the Basic Ecclesial or Christian Communities, the CEBs. In the CEBs an alternative space opened up to reflect on the way of Christ over against prevailing ideology, thus empowering people to share in the task of bringing the transforming power of the gospel to every part of an unjust world. Understanding the Bible takes place in the dialectic between the literary memory of the people of God and the issues of the contemporary world (Mesters 1989). So, the emphasis is not on the text's meaning in itself, but rather on the meaning the text has for the people reading it. It is an interpretation which challenges a widespread view that exegesis is primarily about letting the text speak for itself, unencumbered by contexts and contemporary issues. Among grass-roots communities the Bible has become a catalyst for the exploration of pressing contemporary issues relevant to that community, and offers a language so that the voice of the voiceless may be heard. The biblical tradition becomes a catalyst for new thought and action related to the circumstances of everyday commitments. Connections between contemporary demands are made with the experience set out in the stories of biblical characters. Educational programmes enable the Bible to be a resource in which the experience of life is illumined. This can take various forms. It can be Bible study which goes straight to the text with no concern to ask questions about its original historical context. This method Clodovis Boff (1987:146–9) describes as an example of 'correspondence of terms', in which persons or events function in a kind of typological relationship with scriptural analogies. Alternatively, popular education also includes outlines of historical and social contexts, so that the interpretation of Scripture involves a dialectic between insights from the contemporary struggle of the people of God:

the experience of poverty and oppression (often termed 'life' or 'reality') and the text as witness to the people of God at another time and place engaging in their struggle for justice (Sugirtharajah 1992).

Liberationist hermeneutics demands a break with the hermeneutical assumptions inherited from Western theology, which have been assumed unquestioningly by much liberation theology. Commitment to the struggle for justice is certainly a key hermeneutical factor, but one also needs to probe the nature of the struggle behind and beneath the biblical texts. In this, insights emerge when readers are involved in the contemporary struggle for justice to which the canonical text bears witness. The primary basis for an examination of the biblical issue is the experience of the contemporary world and the insight that the perspective of the 'underside of history' of the struggle may offer. It becomes essential to understand something of the culture, in the widest sense of that term, out of which the struggle for power comes and in which the biblical interpreter is located. In this she or he is not just a passive observer, but part of that conflict of interests and concerns which engulf the individual in an increasingly global capitalism.

Liberation theologians insist that all theology is inevitably contextual and conditioned by the environment and activity in which the theologians are themselves engaged. The practice of the life of discipleship itself throws up understanding of texts which would only with difficulty have emerged in the calm reflection of academy or church. The implication is that academic endeavour might not, in some instances at least, offer us the best or most appropriate understanding of a text, and that one who is engaged in 'applied or practical theology' might, in certain circumstances, capture the spirit of the text better. This is absolutely central to liberationist hermeneutics, and explains the belief in the epistemological privilege of the poor and the marginalized.

Unsurprisingly, one of the most hard-hitting challenges to theology has come from the recognition of the 'ideological' character of theology and its role within a complicated political struggle within the churches to maintain the ascendancy of certain positions. The emphasis on the contextual nature of all theology has led liberation theologians to question the absolute character of theological pronouncements from the past as well as the present and to a theological unmasking of the reality. One needs, therefore, to ask: What is the connection between a particular theological theme and a particular set of historical circumstances? Who is helped by a particular theme or a particular type of Christology? What interests does it represent, and what concrete projects does it support? The issue is summarized in a typically pungent way by the Brazilian theologian Leonardo Boff:

Theologians do not live in clouds. They are social actors with a particular place in society. They produce knowledge, data, and meanings by using instruments that the situation offers them and permits them to utilize.... The themes and emphases of a given christology flow from what seems relevant to the theologian on the basis of his or her social standpoint.... In that sense we must maintain that no christology is or can be neutral.... Willingly or unwillingly christological discourse is voiced in a given social setting with all the conflicting interests that pervade it. That holds true as well for theological discourse that claims to be 'purely' theological, historical, traditional, ecclesial and apolitical. Normally such discourse adopts the position of those who hold power in the existing system. If a different kind of christology with its own commitments appears on the scene and confronts the older 'apolitical' christology, the latter will soon discover its social locale, forget its 'apolitical' nature, and reveal itself as a religious reinforcement of the existing status quo. (L. Boff 1980: 265)

The contributions of liberation theologians form a small part of a long debate within Christianity, both modern and ancient, about appropriate attitudes and responses to the poor and vulnerable, and the Church's relations with the political powers. Liberation theologians are engaged in mediation between the poor, Church teaching, and appropriate 'secular' wisdom which contributes to understanding the reality of a life of suffering and facilitates theological reflection, though with a clear commitment to the poor, rather than being neutral theological brokers. Their own theological emphases are on the gospels, rather than Paul, and the exodus, rather than the accounts about the settlement in Canaan (Gottwald 1980). They have shown up the unease felt by mainstream Christianity with more revolutionary parts of the canon. But liberation theology has reminded us that the prophetic strand, with its daring convictions about a new order in this world, open to abuse and disappointment, has continued throughout the history of Christianity to be a potent resource for those who have been unwilling to cope with the demands of the kingdom by confining its demands and its impacts to a sacred sphere whether in the life of the ecclesia or the soul of the individual. Liberation theology has reminded us, if nothing else, that when viewed from the underside of history, by the poor and the marginalized, the message of Jesus looks rather different from the way in which it has been portrayed by those who have had the power to write the story of the Church and formulate its dogmas and its social concerns.

In writing influenced by liberation theology there has been an attempt both to trace the radical currents in the Bible and the influence they have had in movements down the centuries. As far as the Hebrew Bible is concerned, an influential theory has been that associated with Norman Gottwald (1980), in which the God of the Hebrews is a God who sides with the oppressed and downtrodden and who liberates slaves and offers hope for a new type of religion. That utopian project with its egalitarian characteristics is chosen by an Egyptian prince who in the words of the Letter to the Hebrews 'chose rather to share ill-treatment with the people of God than to enjoy the fleeting pleasures of sin' (Heb. 11: 25). That option for the poor and the marginalized is found in traces throughout the prophetic literature, as appeal is made to that original vision for Jewish polity embodied in the legislation of Deuteronomy and Exodus. It is this which undergirds Jesus' proclamation of

God's kingdom, not as some other-worldly hope but as a this-worldly possibility. That egalitarian strain is reflected in the community of goods practised by the earliest Christians in Judaea and even reflected in the extraordinary project of mutual support instigated by the apostle Paul.

Such radical strands are at odds with those which either propound some notion of support for civilization or seek some kind of compromise with the surrounding society. In the settlement of Jews in Canaan, the links with the surrounding culture, the subject of severe critique from many of the biblical prophets as diverse as Samuel, Elijah, and Jeremiah, provide an interface between distinctiveness and difference and conformity with the cosmopolitan culture of the time. This interface was itself the very dynamic of the emerging religion of the Jewish people as the extent of compromise and difference was negotiated (Pixley 1981).

There is a parallel development within early Christianity, as the Jesus movement, made up in its earliest days of wandering radicals, interacted with more settled patterns of life whether based in Judaea or in the emerging Christian communities in the cities of the Eastern Mediterranean. It is not too difficult to see a very different religious ethos emerging in the Pauline communities. Nevertheless, despite the tenuous links with the radicalism of the Jesus tradition, the Pauline letters indicate that the new converts did have to learn a degree of accommodation, albeit laced with subtle differences in its ethos, with the world as it was, and yet there are echoes of the call to discipleship of the teacher from Nazareth. Paul, the radical innovator and founder of the Gentile church, sowed the seeds of the acceptability of the world order as it is and passivity towards it. Nevertheless, there is at the heart of the emerging Christian identity a distinctive identity in which élite goods and privileges (wealth, power, holiness, and knowledge) ceased to be the prerogative merely of an élite but were open to all within the common life of the Christian communities (Theissen 1999).

The Alternative, Radical Tradition in Christianity as a Challenge to the Dominant Ideology

Deviant faith and practice have by the consent of the powerful been excluded and branded as unfit for proper ecclesiastical consumption. In some cases we can see why such decisions may have been necessary. But this does not by any means always apply. There awaits a task of rediscovering bits of the tradition which have become submerged by dominant ideologies. The canon in one sense is a domestication of awkward ideas, but in another sense, in the very process of domestication, it contains within it the minority opposition ideas. The formation of a dominant ideology involves the incorporation of the opposition ideas—which means that they are not completely lost and are available. So their very presence continued to provide a basis for the rediscovery of social and ecclesiastical alternatives. The importance of the retrieval of an 'alternative story' has been a significant component of feminist biblical interpretation as well as projects influenced by the theology of liberation (Rowland 1999; Bradstock and Rowland 2002). The liberation theology perspective on the story of the Church likewise seeks to activate that present concern with the story of the people's struggle by attempting to recover that story down the centuries. This will mean giving less time to the writings of the great men and more attention to popular religion as carriers of that subversive memory. It is these different, and frequently forgotten, traditions that kept alive the alternative horizon which protested at the language of the victors.

There is indeed a remarkable 'hinterland' of radical themes in the Christian tradition (Bradstock and Rowland 2002). As a convenient way of describing the writings in the collection put together by Andrew Bradstock and myself, one may use the word 'radical' as a collective description. Of course, 'radical' is one of those words which has become extremely flexible in its usage. Yet there is often an appeal to the roots: to Jesus and the early church as paradigms of what Christian polity and action should be about. Occasionally there is a more violent dimension: being so convinced of the godlessness of contemporary culture and institutions, radical theologians consider it necessary to uproot them by force, though there are many who protest against violence in the way exemplified by Jesus himself, resistance even unto death (Cohn 1957).

One theme pervades many of these radical sources: a strong sense of vocation, such that writers believe that they are called to an activity which is explicitly contrary to received wisdom and practice, as they see their own activity in the light of the struggle between the forces of light and the forces of darkness. Alongside this, there is often an intense awareness of God's presence and a conviction that God or Christ indwells and empowers. The divine indwells the human as well as the process of history, and there is often an intimacy of interaction between the human and the divine in enabling the understanding of God's purposes to be known. This is often linked with the doctrine of the Spirit and the conviction that the believer is closely identified with Christ.

Throughout many of the radical texts there is a heartfelt hope for a new world, echoing prophetic texts and the hope for the New Jerusalem in the Apocalypse. Nevertheless this hope differs quite markedly from the character of hope within other areas of Christian tradition. In many of the radical texts we are concerned with a hope for *this* world rather than some transcendent realm. The coming reign of God is not merely an article of faith for the future, but is in some sense already present, either in the life of the prophetic group, called to implement or proclaim, or as a phenomenon within the historical process which demands a response and interpretation—what is known as 'reading the signs of the times'. So the present is the decisive moment in the divine purposes, exhibiting what Karl Mannheim termed the 'chiliastic mentality', where the present moment is one of utmost significance within the whole gamut of history (Mannheim 1931: 193–213).

A frequent theme is that theology is a matter not just of abstract reflection, but of exposition of understandings which are based on an active engagement to see another kind of order at work in the world, the realization of God's kingdom on earth. There is an approach to the Bible in which interpreters refuse to be content with the letter, but pierce to the real meaning of the text. This attitude may manifest itself as a rejection of the priority of Scripture and a subordination of it to the inner understanding which comes through the Spirit. The meaning of Scripture and tradition is subordinated to experience as a prior datum which must be the necessary condition of the way in which Scripture is read. There is an emphasis on the ability of all those open to the Spirit of God to understand the meaning of Scripture, and so a hermeneutical egalitarianism. This can come without access to the wisdom of the experts.

We see an oblique relationship with the Scriptures in which the words become the catalyst for discernment of the divine way in the present. What counts is not so much what the text meant to Isaiah, Jesus, or Paul, but what import these words may have in the circumstances of the present. The claim to be able to understand the Scriptures without recourse to learned divines is a repeated theme. Patterns of biblical exegesis which have emerged in parts of Latin America over the last twenty years offer a more recent example of the way in which the practical faith of the non-professional reader can be resourced by a mode of reading of the Scriptures which does not need (even if it was often supported by) sympathetic intellectuals (West 1998).

The messianic and millenarian proclivities of early Christianity and parts of ancient Judaism indicate that there were strands of thought which reflected difference and hoped for something better. Of course, such ideas can easily lapse into other-worldly fantasy, but the potential of future hopes for illuminating the disjunction between the group and wider society should not be underestimated. This is brilliantly captured by Walter Benjamin in his last work. He emphasized that the cultural monuments celebrated by official history could not be understood outside the context of their origins, a context of oppression and exploitation (Benjamin 1978: 258). Incorporated into the tradition of conventional history, they were no more than booty carried in the triumphal procession of the victors. Just as the cultural object itself will never be free from barbarity, 'so neither is the process of handing down by which it is passed from one to the next'. He spoke of the need to capture a memory 'as it flashed past in a moment of danger' (Benjamin 1978: 257). It was the 'involuntary memory of a redeemed humanity' which contrasted with convention and false tradition. It was necessary to 'brush history against the grain' (Benjamin 1978: 259). According to Benjamin, the task of each generation was to rescue tradition from the conformity which the powerful seek to impose upon the subversive—thereby neutralizing it and making it part of the dominant ideology.

BIBLIOGRAPHY

AICHELE, G. et al. 1997. The Postmodern Bible. The Bible and Culture Collective. New Haven: Yale University Press.

BARR, J. 2000. History and Ideology in the Old Testament: Biblical Studies at the End of a Millennium. Oxford: Oxford University Press.

BELO, F. 1981. A Materialist Reading of the Gospel of Mark. Maryknoll, NY: Orbis.

BENJAMIN, W. 1978. 'Theses on the Philosophy of History'. In Illuminations, ed. H. Arendt, London: Collins Fontana, 245–55.

BOFF, C. 1987. Theology and Praxis. Maryknoll, NY: Orbis.

BOFF, L. 1980. Jesus Christ Liberator. London: SPCK.

BRADSTOCK, A., and ROWLAND, C. 2002. Radical Christian Writings: A Reader. Oxford: Blackwell.

CASTELLI, E. A., MOORE, S. D., PHILIPS, G. A, and SCHWARZ, R., eds. 1995. The Postmodern Bible. New Haven: Yale University Press.

CLEVENOT, M. 1985. Materialist Approaches to the Bible. Maryknoll, NY: Orbis.

COHN, N. 1957. The Pursuit of the Millennium. London: Paladin.

CROIX, G. E. M. de Ste 1982. The Class Struggle in the Ancient Greek World. London: Duckworth.

EAGLETON, T. 1991. Ideology: An Introduction. London: Routledge, Chapman and Hall.

ESLER, P. 1984. Community and Gospel in Luke–Acts. Cambridge: Cambridge University Press.

GIDDENS, A. 1996. Capitalism and Modern Social Theory: An Analysis of the Writings of Marx, Durkheim and Weber. Cambridge: Cambridge University Press.

GOTTWALD, N. K. 1980. The Tribes of Yahweh. London: SCM.

—— and HORSLEY, R. The Bible and Liberation, rev. edn. Maryknoll, NY: Orbis.

GUTIÉRREZ, G. 1988. A Theology of Liberation, rev. edn. London: SCM.

—— 1994. Las Casas in Search of the Poor of Jesus Christ. Maryknoll, NY: Orbis.

HALL, S. 1985. 'Religious Ideologies and Social Movements in Jamaica'. In R. Bocock and K. Thompson, eds., Religion and Ideology, Manchester: Manchester University Press, 269–96.

HENNELLY, A. T., ed. 1990. Liberation Theology: A Documentary History. Maryknoll, NY: Orbis.

HOLMBERG, B. 1978. Paul and Power. Philadelphia: Fortress.

HORRELL, D. 1996. The Social Ethos of the Corinthian Correspondence: Interests and Ideology from 1 Corinthians to 1 Clement. Edinburgh: T. & T. Clark.

—— 1999: Social-scientific Approaches to New Testament Interpretation. Edinburgh: T. & T. Clark.

HORSLEY, R. A. 2001. Hearing the Whole Story: The Politics of Plot in Mark's Gospel. Louisville, Ky.: Westminster.

JAMESON, F. 1981. *The Political Unconscious.* London: Methuen.

JOBLINE, D., PIPPIN, T., and SCHLEIFER R. 2001. *The Postmodern Bible Reader.* Oxford: Blackwell.

KAUTSKY, K., 1925. *The Foundations of Christianity: A Study in Christian Origins.* London: Orbach and Chambers.

KOVACS, J., and Rowland, C. 2004. *Revelation: The Apocalypse of Jesus Christ.* Blackwell Bible Commentaries. Oxford: Blackwell.

KYRTATAS, D. 1987. *The Social Structure of the Early Christian Communities.* London: Verso.

McLELLAN, D. 1987. *Marxism and Religion: A Description and Assessment of the Marxist Critique of Christianity.* Basingstoke: Macmillan.

MANNHEIM, K. 1931. *Ideology and Utopia.* London: Routledge, Kegan and Paul.

MEEKS, W. 1983. *The First Urban Christians.* New Haven: Yale University Press.

MEGITT, J. 1998. *Paul, Poverty and Survival.* Edinburgh: T. & T. Clark.

MESTERS, C. 1989. *Defenseless Flower.* Maryknoll, NY: Orbis.

MOSALA, I. 1989. *Biblical Hermeneutics and Black Theology in South Africa.* Grand Rapids, Mich.: Eerdmans.

MYERS, C. 1988. *Binding the Strong Man.* Maryknoll, NY: Orbis.

PIPPIN, T. 1992: *Death and Desire: The Rhetoric of Gender in the Apocalypse of John.* Philadelphia: Fortress.

PIXLEY, G. 1981. *God's Kingdom.* London: SCM.

ROWLAND, C. 1985. 'The Theology of Liberation and its Gift to Exegesis'. *New Blackfriars,* 66: 157–72.

—— 1988. *Radical Christianity: A Reading of Recovery.* Cambridge: Polity.

—— 1993. 'In Dialogue with Itumeleng Mosala: A Contribution to Liberation Exegesis'. *JSNT* 50: 43–57.

—— ed. 1999. *The Cambridge Companion to Liberation Theology.* Cambridge: Cambridge University Press.

SCHÜSSLER-FIORENZA, E. 1993. *Revelation: Vision of a Just World.* Edinburgh: T. & T. Clark.

SCOTT, J. 1990. *Domination and the Arts of Resistance: Hidden Transcripts.* New Haven: Yale University Press.

SEGUNDO, J. L. 1976. *The Liberation of Theology.* Maryknoll, NY: Orbis.

SUGIRTHARAJAH, R. 1992: *Voices from the Margins.* London: SPCK.

THEISSEN, G. 1978. *The First Followers of Jesus.* London: SCM.

—— 1982. *The Social Setting of Pauline Christianity.* Edinburgh: T. & T. Clark.

—— 1999. *A Theory of Primitive Christian Religion.* London: SCM.

TROELTSCH, E. 1931. *The Social Teaching of the Christian Churches.* London: Allen and Unwin.

WATSON, F. 1986. *Paul, Judaism and the Gentiles.* Cambridge: Cambridge University Press.

WENGST, K. 1985. *'Pax Romana' and the Peace of Jesus Christ.* London: SCM.

WEST, G. 1998. *The Academy of the Poor: Towards a Dialogical Reading of the Bible.* Sheffield: Sheffield Academic Press.

WILLIAMS, R. 1977. *Marxism and Literature.* Oxford: Oxford University Press.

PART VI

THE INTERPRETATION OF THE BIBLE

CHAPTER 38

OLD TESTAMENT THEOLOGY

WALTER BRUEGGEMANN

The discipline and practice of Old Testament theology is a more complex and problematic enterprise through the twentieth century than the name itself may indicate.

I. THE MODERN PREOCCUPATION WITH 'HISTORY'

Old Testament study, through 200 years of Enlightenment rationality, largely eschewed primal theological claims and assertions, and for the most part was preoccupied with historical questions, including (a) the historical events pertaining to Israel's life, (b) the history of developing traditions and eventually documents, and (c) the history of religious ideas and practices. The acceptance of such a perspective on study slowly gelled into a more-or-less consensus hypothesis about the 'development' of Israel's religion that clusters into the so-called documentary hypothesis that came to be associated with the name of Julius Wellhausen, a great German interpreter at the end of the nineteenth century.

It is important to recognize that the rise of such 'historical-critical' preoccupations under the aegis of the rational autonomy of Enlightenment philosophy was itself a response to the scholastic 'hardening of the arteries' of Protestant orthodox theology in Europe (especially in Germany) in the seventeenth century. Thus historical-critical studies undertaken by university professors (largely in Germany and exclusively Protestant Christians) were an attempt to stake out a zone of emancipated scholarly reasoning that did not need to conform to the dogmatic requirements of restrictive church theology. The long-standing tension between church and academy—and by inference the disputatious settlement of issues of 'faith and reason'—eventuated in a Protestant mode of scholarship that long dominated the academic field of Old Testament interpretation.

In retrospect, it is clear that such an academic enterprise was powerfully shaped by the 'evolutionary' assumption of a culture rooted in Hegel and articulated by Charles Darwin in the latter part of the nineteenth century; consequently, the 'religion of Israel' and the articulation of the God of Israel were understood in 'evolutionary' categories that moved characteristically from primitive to sophisticated, from polytheism to monotheism, and from cultic procedures to ethical insistences. The import of such an 'evolutionary' notion, however, caused every 'phase' of the development to be context-specific in Israel's culture, and therefore quite relative to a particular time and place. The inescapable consequence of such an assumption is that every 'faith claim' given in the text is relative; as a result, no 'faith claim' could be, or needed to be, regarded as normative, either in any ancient community of the text or in any contemporary reading community. The contemporary reading community itself—in Enlightenment modes—characteristically prized intellectual autonomy and had no wish to submit to any authority beyond reason, textual, interpretive, or otherwise. By such an interpretive procedure, deeply informed by cultural and philosophical assumptions in the nineteenth century, Old Testament theology as a normative discipline became an intellectual impossibility through the nineteenth century in an academic environment.

II. The Break with Historical Relativism

The thralldom of theological interpretation of the Old Testament to questions of 'history' was definitively and decisively broken by the spectacular commentary on the book of Romans by Karl Barth in 1919 (Barth 1968). At the time, Barth was a little-known Swiss Calvinist pastor. He came to recognize through the First World

War that theological 'liberalism'—committed as it was to evolutionary developmentalism—had reduced biblical 'faith claims' to contextual relativism that provided no intellectual grounding for bold theological stands or courageous ethical decision making. In a frontal assault on the assumptions of such developmental relativism, Barth initiated a theological programme that was destined to become the definitive articulation of evangelical Christian faith in the twentieth century. It is impossible to overstate the revolutionary import of Barth, who insisted upon the *normative* theological claims of the Bible that broke free of *relativizing, descriptive studies* in the history of Israelite religion. It is hardly an overstatement to say that Barth opened the way for an entirely new enterprise in Old Testament theology, a study of *normative* theological claims of the Bible that would fund the critical thought and ethical action of faith communities and that would, derivatively, inform and infuse public issues in societies still roughly attentive to a biblical inheritance.

III. A Fresh Beginning beyond Historicism

As Karl Barth opened the way for the *normative* study of 'faith claims' in the Bible, the period around the Second World War witnessed important new initiatives in Old Testament theology. Two studies are especially prominent in shaping the ensuing discussion. In the 1930s, Walther Eichrodt, a Calvinist scholar at the University of Basel (also Barth's university), published a two-volume work on Old Testament theology organized around the single dominant theme of 'covenant' (Eichrodt 1961, 1967). In his reading, Eichrodt made covenant—a long-standing Calvinist theme—the 'constant' of Old Testament theology, an affirmation that the God of ancient Israel is characteristically *in relationship*, and practices that relationship with Israel and with the world in freedom and in fidelity. Other scholars followed Eichrodt in articulating Old Testament theology around a single motif or claim.

The second and more influential study was the two-volume work of Gerhard von Rad, a Lutheran scholar eventually situated at the University of Heidelberg (von Rad 1962, 1965). While von Rad published his work in the 1950s, its roots are clearly in the 1930s, when Eichrodt published his work and when Barth's influence had become immense in the European church. In understanding von Rad's work, it is important to note that in 1934, the 'Confessing Church' in Germany took a dramatic stand against Hitler and National Socialism by publishing the Barmen Declaration, a manifesto largely authored by Karl Barth. At that time Gerhard von Rad was a young Lutheran pastor. In 1936, only two years after the Barmen Declaration, von Rad published an early article declaring that 'in genuine Yahwistic belief the doctrine of creation never attained to the stature of a relevant, independent doctrine' (von Rad 1966: 142). Thus von Rad insisted that the Old Testament was preoccupied with YHWH's 'acts in history'. In retrospect, it is clear that von Rad's thesis was aimed against the 'fertility religion' (= creation theology?) of National Socialism. Von Rad's proposal became a thesis that was to dominate Old Testament study for more than a generation. The focus of von Rad's study concerned historical actions that were confessed to be acts of YHWH.

In 1938, again two years later, von Rad published his extended essay, 'The Form-Critical Problem of the Hexateuch', in which he laid out the argument that was to become the plot for his later publication of *Old Testament Theology*, volume i (von Rad 1966a). In that article von Rad argued that Israel's earliest statement of faith was a 'credo' that recited and responded to God's decisive saving deeds in the history of Israel. The examples to which von Rad characteristically appealed were found in Deut. 6: 20–4, 26: 5–9, and Josh. 24: 2–13. Von Rad regarded these three recital passages as quite early, and at the beginning of Israel's theological trajectory. It is clear that von Rad formulated his argument in the environment of the German church's struggle over the Barmen Declaration; his formulation of a 'credo' stands close to the 'credal' confession of Barmen, so that Israel's confession against 'Canaanite fertility religion' is to be seen in close proximity to the German church's struggle against National Socialism. This is an unmistakable example of the way in which social circumstance informs scholarly articulation. Von Rad's 'Theology of Recital' came to regard God's saving deeds as normative for Israel's faith, a confessed truth upon which the community of faith could take its stand and risk its life. Von Rad soon published a second volume of *Old Testament Theology*, in which he showed how the later prophetic traditions reused the normative historical memory in later historical-theological crises. Thus von Rad, like Eichrodt, is, in the manner of Barth, completely committed to the normative character of the historical recital of Israel's faith. (The same arguments were made in the USA at the same time by G. Ernest Wright, no doubt the most important theological interpreter of the Old Testament in that country during this period (Wright 1944, 1950).)

Von Rad definitively enacted in Old Testament study the kind of normative claim that Barth had initiated in dogmatic study. At the same time, however, it is also clear that von Rad continued to be committed to 'history' as the dominant category of Old Testament interpretation, an assumption that he shared with the older 'liberal' scholarship that was dominant in the German universities. At mid-century, then, Old Testament theology in general, and von Rad in particular, held together the long-established *historical-critical* assumptions that remained unquestioned in the field and the *normative theological claims* for the text that were his real interest. These matters were held in some tension, even though it was a tension seldom recognized and for a long time not critiqued, because the terms of the conversation were kept imprecise. The middle years of the century featured an *emerging study of Israel's normative faith* that did not trouble to break with *historical liberalism*. At the same time, it is clear that von Rad himself knew with some uneasiness about keeping these matters together, a combination to some extent achieved by a rhetorical sleight of hand:

> Thus there is a clear tension between the account actually given in the narrative and the intention of the narrator, whose aim was, with the help of this material, to describe the conquest of the land by all Israel, and who, in so doing, asked too much of it. In the end this conception was most succinctly given in the narrator's words that under Joshua Israel took possession of the whole land 'at one time' (*Hebrew* Josh. x.42). This was the rounding off of the construction of that magnificent picture made by later Israel of Jahweh's final saving act. Beyond it no further unification was really any longer possible. But our final comment on it should not be that it is obviously an 'unhistorical' picture, because what is in question here is a picture fashioned throughout by faith. Unlike any ordinary historical document, it does not have its center in itself; it is intended to tell the beholder about Jahweh, that is, how Jahweh led his people and got himself glory. In Jahweh's eyes Israel is always a unity: his control of history was no improvisation made up of disconnected events: in the saving history he always deals with all Israel. This picture makes a formidable claim, and actually in the subsequent period it proved to have incalculable power to stamp affairs. How this came about is quite interesting. Israel made a picture of Jahweh's control of history on his people's behalf whose magnificence far surpasses anything that older and more realistic accounts offered. Faith had so mastered the material that the history could be seen from within, from the angle of faith. What supports and shapes this late picture of Israel's taking possession of the land is a mighty zeal for and glorification of the acts of Jahweh. (von Rad 1962: 302)

In any case, the enterprise of von Rad, after his work was translated into English in the 1960s, along with the work of Wright, had an immense impact upon the interpretive scene in the USA. It funded new programmes of education in US churches and, breaking with older formulations of Old Testament faith, it gave lay people access to scripture study. An important by-product was the recruitment of a generation of younger scholars into Old Testament study, which gave fresh energy and impetus to Old Testament theology in the United States.

IV. Beyond the Mid-Century 'Settlement'

The uneasy combination of historical criticism and normative claim dominated the field through the 1960s, but was then rendered largely ineffective in the 1970s. The collapse of that synthesis made Old Testament study exceedingly complex and somewhat amorphous. As a consequence, a variety of contextual factors, some of which are perhaps not visible to us yet today, impacted study in the 1970s and evoked quite fresh initiatives. In general, this decade of reformulation featured a move away from the single-minded, completely accepted dominance of historical-critical methods that offered not only a consensus in method, but along with the method something of a consensus in substantive interpretation. The outcome of this move away from a single, dominant perspective resulted in a much more diverse, pluralistic, and variegated field of study that still pertains today. Among the factors that caused this change are the following:

- A remarkably abrupt awareness that the formulation of 'the acts of God' that had been central in von Rad's approach was recognized as an exceedingly problematic notion, the content and claim of which were not clear (Brueggemann 1997: 120–6).
- The move of Claus Westermann, close associate of von Rad, and Frank Cross, a close associate of G. Ernest Wright, to recover the theme of creation that had been squeezed out in a focus on 'history' (Westermann 1971, 1978, 1982; Cross 1973). Westermann articulated a theology of blessing that was grounded in the fecundity of creation, and Cross suggested that even 'historical narratives' were shaped by antecedent 'myths' of cosmic order. It is more than a little ironic that in both cases, of von Rad and of Wright, it was a near associate and colleague (Westermann and Cross respectively) who opened new vistas of interpretation alongside the foremost advocates of a 'historical' approach.
- The emergence of newer methods, which challenged the complete domination of historical-critical methods. The newer methods that quickly gained broad usage included especially rhetorical criticism, as advocated by Phyllis Trible (1978, 1994), and sociological analysis, as advocated by Norman Gottwald (1979). These methods suggested that there is more than one legitimate way in which to read texts, so 'historical questions' need not be the only questions to which scholarship attended. These newer perspectives, in turn, quickly generated new journals in the field that provided rich alternative interpretive possibilities. These included the *Journal for the Study of the Old Testament, Horizons in Biblical Theology*, and *Biblical Interpretation*.
- New voices joining the interpretive enterprise outside the standard scope of academic, Western, white, mostly male interpreters (Felder 1991; Dube 2000). These emerging voices represented especially a fresh feminist hermeneutic and Third World articulations of a liberation hermeneutic. It is clear in these latter cases that such interpretive enterprises were, in quite explicit ways, acts of advocacy that arose from quite particular social contexts. This new acknowledgement and recognition of contextual impact upon interpretation, moreover, had the effect of making clear that even the older, more 'scientific', and more 'objective' scholarship that had dominated the field was to some extent advocacy,

and therefore less 'scientific' and 'objective' than had been claimed or imagined. The new environment of interpretation thus created a much more open picture of contestation in the field, so that the old 'assured results' in the discipline have had to be reconsidered and renegotiated. This new recognition pertains not simply to theological interpretation, but also to the long assumed 'historical' backgrounds upon which theological interpretation was said to be based (Dever 2001; Finkelstein and Silberman 2000).

• The recognition that, because scholarship never happens in a vacuum but always in a funding environment, these newly emergent realities in the study of the Old Testament arose as a part of a larger social reality in the 1970s. This is the period that dramatically began 1968 with the assassinations of Martin Luther King Junior and Bobby Kennedy, the Democratic Convention in Chicago, and, most spec- tacularly, the student revolts in Paris that required a startling response from the French government. These events were harbingers of what was to come in terms of the Vietnam War protests, Watergate, and the Civil Rights Movement, all of which together constituted a systemic upheaval in social relationships. In my judgement, there can be little doubt that the broadly based challenge to historical criticism in Old Testament study with its rather one-dimensional approach to texts was part of this larger critique of old, established certitudes. Thus, by the end of the 1970s, much of the perspective that had dominated Old Testament study since the initial contribution of von Rad had now been placed deeply in question.

It is to the astonishing credit of von Rad himself that in 1970, just prior to his death, he published his remarkable book *Wisdom in Israel.* That book shows von Rad himself moving beyond the 'historical' issues that long preoccupied him, now addressing new issues of creation and cosmic order. It is as though that book is a harbinger of what is to happen in the coming period of Old Testament theology. It is fair to say that with the demise of the consensus of the mid-century—a consensus that had established an uneasy settlement between *historical-critical methods* and *confessional claims*—the task of Old Testament theology became exceedingly problematic, as the field became diffuse and without a consensus picture of critical assumptions that heretofore had served theological interpret- ation so well. Thus with the 1970s we witness a considerable reorientation in the field, a reorientation nicely chronicled in 1994 by Leo Perdue (1994). The 'collapse' of the synthesis led to a move away from the old foundationalism that appealed to 'universal' presuppositions and a new emergence of contextual approaches and confessional presentations that were content to make interpretative claims without the necessity of bringing the entire field of study along with them. The loss of 'universal objectivity' in such interpretative claims was of course severely felt in some quarters. For the most part, however, interpreters came to recognize the legitimacy and appropriateness of interpretation that belonged to and served a sub-community of interpretation, confessional or contextual.

V. FRESH FOCI IN THE 1970S

By the 1970s, with the widespread abandonment of the dominant paradigm of the mid-century—the affirmation of 'God's mighty deeds in history'—we are able to identify emerging new accents in the field, of which I shall mention four.

1. The 'crisis' of 'the historical'. We have seen that the paradigm of von Rad and G. Ernest Wright depended upon an uneasy combination of 'real history' and 'salvation history'. That uneasy combination pertained to a 'recital' of saving miracles that had happened in Israel's past, transformative interventions in the life of the world that were credited to YHWH and that were given normative liturgical and literary form. Indeed, one of Wright's most important books was entitled, *God Who Act* (Wright 1952). 'Real history', conversely, referred to a more-or-less scientific reconstruction of what 'actually happened' in the ancient world. This sort of research through mid-century was especially important in the United States under the leadership of William Foxwell Albright and his influential students (Albright 1957). The outcome of such research—reflected in John Bright's *A History of Israel* (1959)—confirmed the deep and broad 'historical reliability' of Israel's reportage on the past. Even so, of course, what the archaeologists meant by 'history' and what von Rad meant by 'saving history' were not at all the same.

In the 1970s, beginning with the work of Thomas Thompson and John van Seters, scholarly judgements began to accumulate toward the conclusion that the Old Testament presentation of 'history' was, especially in the early period, not reflective of what 'actually happened' (Thompson 1992, 1999; van Seters 1975). A new impetus in scholarship led a number of scholars to argue that 'Old Testament memory' is in fact an ideological construct, and not reliable reportage (see Dever 2003: 245). Up until today, it is generally held that the Old Testament is rooted in Near Eastern culture and social history, but the connections are not at all precise and one-to-one, as had been earlier assumed. While Old Testament theology is inescapably drawn to an ancient Near Eastern linkage, the nature of that linkage is now uncertain, and cannot be counted upon in any simple or innocent way, as had been assumed heretofore.

2. A counter-move that seeks freedom from such a cultural connection is the new appreciation of 'confessional' reading that had been precluded in the 'object-ive', 'foundationalist' approaches prior to Karl Barth. While the older scholarship had been committed to objective claims that were universally credible, one new mode of interpretation recognizes that the Bible is *formed* and is *to be read* as a confessional statement of faith by a concrete community of worship and practice that intentionally advocates a certain set of 'truth claims' that are insisted upon in the face of other, competing truth claims. This mode of partisan advocacy is already implicit in von Rad's notion of 'credo', but by the 1970s had taken on new significance in the field.

We may divide this subject of confessional readings into two quite distinct parts. First, a number of scholars—of whom Brevard Childs, Ronald Clements, and James A. Sanders are the foremost—saw that the Old Testament itself was shaped by an intentional 'canonizing' interpretive activity that over time took random memories and religious resources far from Near Eastern culture and formed them into a coherent traditioning process (Childs 1979; Sanders 1972; Clements 1996). That process eventuated in a canon, that is, a normative teaching literature for an intentional community of faith, namely, Israel. It is agreed that the work toward a canon is essentially a product of emerging Judaism in the sixth and fifth centuries BCE, whereby the dominant teachers and interpreters among the Jews in exile and just after the exile transposed the residue of the faith of pre-exilic Israel into an authoritative platform for a Judaism that was now without the conventional supports that had been offered by city, king, and temple. (There were in this period, of course, the re-established city of Jerusalem and the rebuilt temple, but neither of these refounded institutions exercised the powerful supportive force and symbolic authority that had been the case prior to the destruction of 587 BCE.) What became the Old Testament is thus a self-conscious reconstruction of the past (a reconstruction featured in the 'documentary hypothesis' of the nineteenth century) that was bound to 'what happened', but committed to a new theological construal on which the community was to stake its life.

Brevard Childs most conspicuously has insisted that it is impossible and inappropriate to try to 'go behind' this intentionally constructed textual tradition to 'what happened' (Childs 1970). Such a manoeuvre is impossible and inappropriate, because the makers of the canon were engaged not in reportage but in confessional construction. Thus the proper goal of Old Testament theology is to try to understand this theological intentionality and its impact upon the ongoing community of faith and practice. A case in point is the remarkable article of Ronald Clements (1977) concerning the prophetic books. While the prophetic books consist in collections of oracles uttered by spectacular personalities, and while the prophetic books are witnesses to a long, complicated traditioning process, the important point to 'the final form of the text'—whatever the initiating persons may have said—is characteristically a document organized in *judgement* and *hope*, the themes that correlate with Israel's *descent into exile* and *Jerusalem's emergence* as a new community of hope. The canonizing process characteristically overrides the claims of older material with this powerful interpretive intentionality. It is the merit of Sanders (1976) to insist that while there was indeed such a propensity in the canonizing process, it was not a fully comprehensive achievement. Consequently, even the canonically constructed theological statement of the text is not free of older, quite odd residues of earlier sources that continue to be present in the text alongside, and sometimes in tension with, more obvious gains of canonical intentionality.

It is to be noticed that while this *identification of intentionally constituted canonical claims* serves Old Testament theology well, the same data in the traditioning process can well be read in another way. Thus scholars who affirm and appreciate the canonical process tend to be committed to 'church theology'. Conversely, scholars who look askance at 'church theology', and who for personal and/or intellectual reasons read 'against the grain', tend to view this canonical intentionality as ideological imposition upon the text that distorts it in order to serve power élites who control the canonizing process. While a commitment to Old Testament theology inclines scholars to appreciate this canonizing process, there is no obvious reason why a positive assessment of canon has any privilege over a negative assessment of ideology. Or conversely, there is no obvious reason why a negative assessment of ideology has any privilege over a positive assessment of canon. This matter of *canon and ideology,* a major enterprise in the field since the 1970s, is of particular interest, because it evidences the decisive impact of a scholar's location and predilection upon interpretive outcomes. Neither *an appreciation of canon* nor *a critique of ideology* can be said to be innocent and neutral; in each case the judgement is a committed and often passionate advocacy. 'Canonists' characteristically insist that they are echoing the advocacy of the text itself, and so 'canonical interpretation' is congruent with the text. Critics of ideology tend to view the canonizing process suspiciously, and so sense themselves obligated as critical scholars to 'expose' such canonizing imposition. It is important to recognize, in my judgement, that neither passionate verdict can claim 'a free ride'; in each case, rather, attention must be paid to the axe that the scholar wants to grind. I suggest that in every case the 'grinding' that yields interpretive passion is likely to be found in quite personal history. It may be noted that the context between *fideists* who affirm the canonical and *skeptics* who find ideological imposition likely replicate the old seventeenth century dispute between orthodox church theologians and academics who rallied to 'history' as a zone of emancipated scholarship.

The 'confessional dimension' of Old Testament theology may be traced a step further, as we acknowledge that this scholarly venture now removes the Old Testament text from its originary environment of the ancient Near East and treats the Old Testament text in more recent venues of interpretation. On the one hand, Brevard Childs in his more recent work, as he seeks to break the connection of the Old Testament to ancient Near Eastern history, draws the Old Testament decisively toward the New Testament (Childs 1992). (Of course, the connection of Old Testament to New Testament is a long-standing issue for Christian Old Testament scholars.) Thus Childs, in his important book of 1992, proposes that the Old Testament and the New Testament are 'two witnesses to Jesus Christ'. In this articulation Childs, of course, intends to situate interpretation in the Church and to treat the Old Testament as a resource singularly pertinent to the life and faith of the Church. Indeed, Childs goes further than any conventional connection between the Old Testament and the New Testament to insist that the Old Testament must be read according to the Christian 'rule of faith' (Childs 1992: 63–8). This is an immense interpretative leap away from all preoccupation with historical matters and with any ancient Near Eastern context. The notion of a 'rule of faith' is, it seems likely, a second-century Christian formulation that subsequently came to refer to the Christian dogmatic articulation of the doctrines of the Trinity and the Church's Christology of incarnation (but see the qualifications in Polk 1997). In Childs's most advanced argument, the Old Testament text is to be read and interpreted according to the most foundational affirmations of the Church, affirmations that were not fully formulated until the third and fourth centuries of the Christian era. Thus Childs intends Old Testament theology to be in the direct service of the Church's dogmatic tradition; in this, he has of course deliberately moved well beyond whatever might have been meant by the 'canonizing tendency' of the Old Testament, for such doctrinal commitments in the Church could not have been on the horizon of the canon-makers. The implication of Childs's work is to undo the entire project of modern historical criticism, even though Childs himself is a most skilful practitioner of those disciplines. In his recent Isaiah commentary, moreover, Childs goes so far as to judge that Old Testament texts 'coerce' readings toward the new (Childs 2001: 5, 58, 94, 102, 216, 422). It is clear that Childs's work is an immense contribution to the field, but one that is in some quarters judged as deeply problematic.

On the other hand, alongside the confessional perspective of 'canonical' approaches, the emancipation of scholarship from the domination of 'the historical project' has permitted and legitimated a good deal of *contextual theological interpretation.* That is, particular communities of faith and practice read the text as though its proper matrix for meaning were not the ancient Near East nor even the canonizing process of emerging Judaism, nor even the large claims of Christian doctrine, but rather the immediate circumstances of a particular community of faith in all of its contemporary reality. This contextual contemporaneity has been particularly important in the oppressed communities of the Third World and, to a lesser extent, also in a feminist hermeneutic (see Branson and Padilla 1986; Ukpong *et al.* 2002). Thus, for example, the ancient narrative text of the exodus has been taken up by George Pixley (1983) as a warrant for contemporary social analysis and a social environment of extreme and oppressive wealth and its accompanying poverty and disempowerment. A more recent example is the interpretation of Luke 2: 1–20 by Elsa Tamez (2002), who contrasts the 'peace of Augustus Caesar' and the 'peace of Jesus of Nazareth'. In her exposition she understands the 'peace of Augustus Caesar' to be the tyrannical dictatorships that are faced throughout Central and South America, and understands the promise of the gospel to be a public social alternative to those exploitative regimes. Thus Tamez is an excellent example of the way in which the text becomes immediately contemporary.

Such immediately contextual readings, of course, have little interest in ancient Near Eastern settings and little more interest in the great dogmatic claims of the Church. These readings, rather, in their urgent need and passion, move past whatever 'historical distance' may be suggested by the ancient text, and take the text with immediate and poignant contemporaneity. Such contextualism is not at all what Childs has in mind in his canonical-confessional proposal, but such readings in their own way do indeed treat the text as canonical: that is, as authoritative and defining for the truth of life in urgent contemporary practice. On both counts, *the confessional-canonical* and the immediately *contextual,* it is breathtaking to notice how far our reading practices have moved in a short time from the older 'objective' stance that was preoccupied with historical questions and that relegated contemporaneity of interpretation to other disciplines, as though contemporaneity was not at all the mark of Old Testament theology. The new interpretative possibilities introduced in the 1970s have opened up the field of Old Testament theology in a lively and disputatious way, for the Old Testament is now a venue for vigorously contested readings without many 'assured results' of critical perspective.

My own work is fully appreciative of the canonical thrust of the work of Childs, Sanders, and Clements, which represents a decisive move away from historical-critical retrieval and from any assured bases in 'history'. At the same time, my intention is to pay more attention than the 'canonists' do to the way in which the 'utterance' of the text itself—in its canonical intentionality that only partly succeeded in its passionate intentional advocacy—participates in immense contestation in the text itself that in turn funds the contestation of contemporary interpreters among various interpretative communities (Brueggemann 1997: 317–403). My own work tries to find a way to attend to the disputes that are present in the canon itself and, consequently, to allow for the funding of contestation as a characteristic way in which this text functions in particular communities of faith and practice. To that end, I have tried to explore the rhetorical practice of the Old Testament in its vigorous contestation without allowing the edge of the rhetoric to be shaved or toned down by what is judged to be historically possible or dogmatically acceptable. My presentation seeks, in the best way I know, to take seriously non-foundational commitments, refusing censorship of either a certain view of history or a certain view of doctrine (Thiel 1994; Grenz and Franke 2001). The outcome of such a reading, of course, shows the text to be openly ended disputatious, more open-ended than is tolerable for most settled interpretations when the text is measured by 'history', or by 'reason', or by 'canon' (Brueggemann 2002).

3. It will have been noticed that the course of Old Testament study since the seventeenth century that I have traced is largely a Protestant enterprise, and almost exclusively a Christian enterprise. Roman Catholics, for the most part, were not able to enter the critical discussion until after Vatican II, but since then have made important contributions. The matter has been much more complex concerning Jewish scholarship in a field dominated by Christian questions and a Christian agenda.

It is important to remember that modern critical study of the Bible arose in 'Christian Europe', and specifically 'Christian Germany', at a time when Jews were

distinctly 'outsiders' to the dominant cultural enterprise of scholarship and interpretation, even though the Jewish community in its own rabbinic modes continued
vigorous interpretative work. Thus the horizon of church and even university
interpretation was decisively Christian and unchecked by the presence of any
'other' who would expose the interests and limits of partisan interpretative interest.
In Old Testament studies, the dominant Enlightenment hypothesis of interpretation was an evolutionary notion of the religion of Israel that presented the Torah
preoccupation with purity—a primary accent of Jewish faith—as ignoble and
inferior to Christian ethical concerns. The dominant evolutionary hypothesis,
moreover, hurried along to the New Testament, where was found a 'superior'
religion (Soulen 1996). Thus the dominant assumptions of Old Testament theological interpretation were supersessionist—that is, the governing assumption was
that Judaism has been superseded by a superior Christian faith—and therefore
intrinsically anti-Jewish in articulation. Jon Levenson has traced the way in which
Old Testament theology—an exclusively Christian project—was vigorously anti-
Semitic well into the twentieth century. The evidence Levenson (1993) cites is
beyond refutation for scholarship of that period.

Given such an exposé, it is fair to conclude that the end of the twentieth century
has seen a change in these dynamics of interpretation, and has seen the entry of
Jewish interpreters into the mainstream of biblical theological interpretation
(Levenson 1988; Goshen-Gottstein 1987; Barr 1999: 286–311). Consequently, the
new situation has permitted and required Christian interpretation to proceed
with greater awareness of confessional assumptions that heretofore had passed as
'objective'. Thus the new circumstance of Christian interpretation in the presence
of and alongside Jewish interpreters has permitted Christian interpreters themselves to see how confessionally motivated much interpretation characteristically
has been.

The move from 'objective' historical-critical study to *confessional, contextual*
study has been, as Levenson (1993) has shown, an immense gain. It is a gain
because confessional, contextual self-awareness has lured many scholars away
from the unexamined practice of treating Christian interpretation—so long hegemonic—as objective and neutral. That is, Jews have no objection to biblical
interpretation by Christians that is validly and manifestly done in a Christian
community according to Christian categories. Such a stance, of course, acknowledges the legitimacy of parallel work in the Jewish interpretation done in Jewish
community, so that Jewish and Christian interpreters—with much in common,
together with decisive differences—can proceed in parallel fashion as legitimate
twinned readings of Scripture (Brueggemann 2001). Such a stance, relatively new in
mainstream interpretation, is very different from the older conventional interpretation that was totalizing and that proceeded as though it had a monopoly upon
interpretation. Thus the move from historical-critical methods is not only a change
in method; it is also a recognition that interpretation is situated in something of an

immediate context that makes interpretation partial and likely partisan, never objective and never interpretatively neutral. The turn to the twenty-first century has seen an opening to the possibility of Jewish biblical theology that is validly Jewish, an interpretative enterprise alongside Christian biblical theology that is validly Christian. Such an approach precludes any hegemonic claims on the part of Christian scholarship and is the reason why Levenson, a determinedly Jewish interpreter, can welcome the Christian project of Childs (Levenson 1993: 79–81).

We may identify two aspects of the entry of Jews into the practice of biblical theology. First, a number of scholars, of whom Levenson is the most prominent, are now able to contribute to ongoing work of theological interpretation, and may do so with full acknowledgement of a Jewish perspective. Levenson has made major contributions to the ongoing discussion, and I will mention three of his most important essays.

Interpreters are increasingly aware of anti-Semitism in the New Testament, an anti-Jewish polemic that is best understood as an intra-Jewish dispute before Christians left the synagogue and before Christianity was recognized as a distinct religious community. Levenson has with great discernment shown how anti-Canaanite polemic in the Hebrew Bible is of the same ilk as anti-Jewishness in the New Testament (Levenson 1985). I presume that Levenson would be quick to point out, none the less, that while the two are parallel, they are dissimilar in that there is no enduring Canaanite community to receive an endless, echoing textual polemic, as is the case with Jews in the New Testament polemic.

In a quite polemical essay Levenson has railed against 'liberation theologians', who have by attentiveness to the exodus narrative disregarded the Jewishness of the tradition and that treated the narrative as a universally applicable narrative of emancipation (Levenson 1993: 127–59). The appropriation of the tradition in a liberation hermeneutic, moreover, has focused on liberation without reference to the sequence that led to Sinai and Torah obedience. Levenson polemicizes against the attempt to take this explicitly Jewish tradition and make it universally applicable in other venues. J. Pixley (2000) has responded vigorously to Levenson and defended his usage. I take this exchange, albeit one with some acrimony, to be an opening for the way in which Jewish and Christian interpreters may disputatiously engage texts that belong in quite different ways to more than one ecclesial reading community.

Levenson (1996) has considered the way in which the explicit theological claims of Israel and other peoples of the world are juxtaposed in the Hebrew Bible. He of course takes as a given the priority of Israel in the theological understanding of the Hebrew Bible. He will not, however, permit that priority to cancel out the abiding attentiveness of the God of the Hebrew Bible to other peoples. Levenson's judicious discussion focuses upon an increasingly urgent issue in Old Testament theology: namely, the relationship of God the creator to those parts of the creation that lie beyond Jewishness.

Second, it should not be imagined that an opening to Jewish biblical theologians is a possibility simply contained in the community of biblical scholars. Rather, it is clear that the matter opens up much larger issues of cultural anti-Semitism, the acute barbarism of the *Shoah* under National Socialism, and the ongoing life of Judaism with particular reference to the State of Israel. Seen in larger scope, few matters can function as a more encouraging harbinger for the future beyond anti-Semitism in Old Testament theology than the manifesto, *Dabru Emet*, a statement issued by a number of theologically serious Jewish scholars. That statement urged that there has been an important recent development in Jewish–Christian relations and that it is no longer the case that all Christians are anti-Semitic. Thus it is proposed that Jews may with some confidence approach the whole matter of Jewish–Christian relations with some greater assurance of fair treatment and a fair hearing. Indeed, the statement operates on the assumption that the community of theologically serious Jews and the community of theologically serious Christians are appropriate dialogue partners and have much about which to interact.

This statement is of immense importance, even if greatly disputed by other Jewish interpreters. It suggests that as Christian interpreters are honestly Christian interpreters without assuming long-standing Western hegemonic authority, serious Christian biblical theologians and serious Jewish biblical theologians may read together a great deal of the way; when such common reading reaches a point where it is no longer possible to read together, reading differently with respect and with the possibility of mutual instructiveness is important. Such a stance signifies an immense change from a practice of alienation and fear in the asymmetrical relationship between Christians and Jews that prevailed only a couple of generations ago.

Congruent with the issuance of *Dabru Emet*, Peter Ochs has emerged as a leader in a new movement of interpretation now termed 'textual reasoning' (Ochs 2000; Frymer-Kensky 1998; Kepnes 1996). That interpretive enterprise is currently exploring fresh, imaginative initiatives in Jewish biblical interpretation that may have counterparts in Christian reading, once Christian reading has ceased to be imperialistic and hegemonic. The enterprise is greatly instructed by the contribution of David Weiss Halivni, who has considered the ways in which sub-communities of faith and interpretation, within the framework of consensus teaching, may make specific extrapolations in 'pragmatic' ways in the service of a particular sub-community (Halivni 1991, 1998). Such a distinction of sub-communities makes way for the legitimate particularity of communal interpretation, not only Jewish but also Christian; the import of Halivni's argument is important for Christians, for Christian Old Testament theology must now be acknowledged to be the work of a sub-community within the larger interpretative enterprise.

4. The above-named features of recent Old Testament theology—(1) the 'collapse' of the hegemony of 'the historical', (2) the emergence of confessional and contextual interpretations, and (3) the entry of Jewish interpreters into the ongoing conversation—have all conspired to push Old Testament theology (and its Jewish

counterpart, theology of Hebrew Scripture) in the direction of the normative. That is, all of these emergents are enacted in specific communities of faith wherein the Bible is received as a primal teaching, witnessing authority. It is important in light of such a development to notice that there continues to be an important role for descriptive study that takes the form of the history of Israelite religion. The relationship between *normative* theological interpretation and *descriptive* presentations of the religion of Israel is not an obvious one. James Barr has suggested that the difference is that history of Israelite religion seeks to take into account all of the textual data, whereas theological interpretation selects certain data that serve the particular community of faith (Barr 1999: 133). While that may be an accurate characterization of bygone practices, it is my expectation that responsible theological interpretation of the Old Testament in time to come must take into account increasing portions of the biblical text. The reason for such an expansive repertoire of texts for theological interpretation is that in order to be credible, theological interpretation must have in purview all of the textual data; clearly a selection of texts that is too careful and limited makes the outcomes of theological interpretation manipulative and consequently inescapably suspect.

In any case, the theological interpretation of the Old Testament has benefited from two recent presentations of the history of Israelite religion. Rainer Albertz (1994), has presented such a history, and has vigorously made the argument that the religion of the Old Testament is profoundly pluralistic. In making this compelling argument, Albertz clearly flies in the face of the older, historical-critical synthesis that imagined Israelite religion to be a singularly, unilaterally evolutionary phenomenon. Such a judgement about pluralism concerning the history of Israelite religion would in turn preclude any theology of the Old Testament that is excessively reductionist and simplistic and inattentive to the complexity of the data. More recently, Erhard Gerstenberger (2002) has published a most interesting and somewhat complex history of the religion of the Old Testament. He has identified five distinct social communities in ancient Israel—family, clan, village, tribe, and state—and has sought to identify the particular articulations of God that arise from and are appropriate to each of these social communities. Thus Gerstenberger's work is a historical-sociological study, but with an opening to theology or, as his thesis requires, 'theologies' in the Old Testament. Specifically, Gerstenberger opines that village faith produced an intimate God who was not fierce or strong, but always attentive to the needs of the community; conversely, state religion produced a God who was powerfully sovereign but noticeably short on compassion and tenderness. It may readily be doubted whether one can so closely correlate social community and theological claim, as Gerstenberger has done. In any case, Gerstenberger suggests a way to do descriptive study that in his presentation readily becomes normative. It is clear in my judgement that theological interpretation depends upon, and is informed by, the kind of historical studies that are offered by Albertz and Gerstenberger. No doubt in time to come the twin developments of the history of Israelite religion and theological interpretation will continue to develop in parallel fashion, informing and correcting each other.

VI. Prospects

As we anticipate next developments in Old Testament theology into the twenty-first century, it is reasonable to anticipate that the lines of interpretation reported here will continue to be primary trajectories. Beyond that, of course, no one can foresee what twists and turns will emerge in ongoing interpretative work. It is clear, however, that there is currently great energy and dynamism in the field; it is likely that new developments will soon be under way from a younger generation of scholars and practitioners who have been, perhaps, not so enthralled by old issues of historicism. At least, the following seem likely.

1. Particular communities of faith will understand themselves more intentionally as 'peoples of the Book'. This in turn will evoke, I anticipate, a variety of confessional and contextual appeals to, and reliance upon, the text tradition of the Old Testament. Thus I anticipate that across the spectrum of Protestant Christianity there will be a return to the text in a fresh engagement with 'the strange new world' that is offered there. While there will continue to be disputatious studies of the history of Israelite religion (as indicated above), it is less likely that there will be programmatic presentations of Old Testament theology that are situated outside and 'above' particular communities of faith and practice. That is, the older modernist approaches that seek to appeal to 'universal' claims in a foundationalist way, I believe, have no promising future. The work, rather, will be undertaken to find the self-identity and self-understanding of communities engaged in faithful practice. Such a direction of course runs the risk of sectarianism; that, however, seems to me now the inescapable risk, even as a kind of self-deceptive 'objectivism' was the risk in an earlier modernist era. Such confessional and contextual efforts at their best will need to answer to the critical expectations of the larger interpretative community, but not in a way that precludes distinctive interpretative ventures. If such an expectation comes to fruition, it assures that Old Testament theology will in the future be rich, complex, and vibrant, precisely because it will live close to the faith and practice of concrete communities. The one future in Old Testament theology is that such interpretive enterprises will live close to communities and missional praxis.

2. Confessional and critical readings of course run the risk of filtering the text tradition to serve the interests of the moment. (But that propensity is evident and was operative even in the magisterial work of Eichrodt and von Rad as they sought grounding in the face of the threat and alternative of National Socialism.) A counterpoint to such confessional and contextual readings will be that such specific communities of confession and context will do their work in a larger horizon and will inescapably recognize that the text offers a comprehensive vista well beyond any particular community of faith and interpretation, including the one that is at the moment operative in interpretation.

Old Testament theology in time to come will be done in an environment of religious and cultural pluralism that makes confessional and contextual claims complex. There can be, in such a context, no more myopic scenarios of Old Testament theology that refuse acknowledgement of the 'other' who is present in text and in context.

Old Testament theology will be done in time to come, I anticipate, for the sake of a 'people of the Book', mindful of the other 'peoples' of the Book. Thus Christian Old Testament theology will be done by reading the text in the presence of Jews, with some attentiveness to the different readings of the text by serious Jews. In time to come, moreover, the same awareness will surely be extended to serious Islamic readers of the text, who are also among the 'peoples of the Book'.

Beyond these several communities of the *children of Abraham*, in time to come more attention is likely to be given to the other *children of Noah*. The rabbis, of course, have long since recognized the covenant of Noah, and have urged that other peoples, in a very different kind of covenant, are also commanded by YHWH in the Noachide commandments. Thus the peculiar claim of the elect community (Israel and eventually for Christians, 'New Israel') will be much more explicitly affirmed in the presence of other faith communities and other faith claims:

The Noachic covenant legitimates *God's* structures of creation for humankind, precisely those that belong to the natural world's capacity to sustain the matrix of history. The covenantal benefit, however, includes nature itself and not just humankind. That is, we tend to make a distinction between nature incorporating the material world and the creatures inhabiting it, leaving history to refer to the realm of human life and activity. The Noachic covenant views matters differently. The natural environment is secured in covenant with human and natural creatures. The covenant with Noah restores and secures the creation for the benefit of the creatures, animal and human. Human treatment of the natural world, therefore, is a matter not only of the attitude toward the creation, but also how humankind receives the promise, which it shares with the animal world. . . . The Noachic covenant is a guarantee of the created order on God's part but not a license for violence and corruption on the part of the human creature. For such corruption can threaten the creation and its order. Rendtorff has called attention to the phrase in Gen 8:22, 'As long as the earth endures, seedtime and harvest, cold and heat, summer and winter, day and night, shall not cease,' and suggested that we can so disturb the earth in lasting fashion that the alternation of day and night, summer and winter, is broken by the permanent night and the permanent winter, what we call 'nuclear winter,' and the alternation of cold and heat is broken by the 'warming' of the plant, so that the fundamental conditions for God's promise in the Noachic covenant, 'so long as the earth remains,' are altered.... But the contrast between the universal/creation and the particular/covenant that is suggested there does not fully reflect the complexity of the way(s) creation and covenant meet in the OT, and especially with regard to Israel and the nations. Here again, the Noachic covenant needs to be taken into account.

The nations are a part of the created order, the outcome of the blessing of God in the completion of creation. The restoration of the creation after the Flood involves also the restoration of humanity as a part of that creation and of the renewal of the blessing (Gen 8:17; 9:1, 7) through the lineage of Noah (Gen 9:19). So also the establishment of covenant with Noah is an establishment of covenant with all of humankind. The text makes this point repeatedly and thus with much emphasis. The universal covenant with humankind as a way of perpetuating and maintaining the creation incorporates the nations of which Israel is a single part.

The nations, therefore, are susceptible to the same divine *blessing, mercy, and redemption* as is Israel.

The covenant with Noah, therefore, has incorporated the whole creation, including the nations, in the blessing, the compassion, and the redemption of God arising out of the promise to maintain the creation. Mosaic covenant does not stand against that or mark out a special place for Israel. That raises the question, quite naturally, of what that covenant does mean for Israel if the Noachic covenant is the larger framework that both establishes a natural order as the matrix of human and historical existence, and creates the conditions for God's compassionate and redemptive activity to become available for 'every living creature'. (Miller 1995)

The matter is freshly on the docket among us and requires fresh critical thought that will move beyond conventional ecclesial thinking among Christians. Gerstenberger has made an effort in this direction, though I think not a very effective one. The confessional and contextual Old Testament theology cannot any longer settle for hegemonic or monopolistic assumptions, because the text makes clear that the God-given promise of the 'other' characteristically de-absolutizes every absolutizing theological temptation.

3. For all the difficult and potentially disputatious interaction that Christian Old Testament theology may have with other peoples of the Book and with other communities comprehended in the Noachide Covenant, the key issue for time to come, I anticipate, is that all those who find truth mediated through this textual tradition—among them Christians, Jews, and Muslims—will together attest to the mystery of God's holy presence in a world that increasingly understands itself and presents itself in profane ways. That is, sectarian interpretation in any reading community is an ill-afforded luxury when in fact all of these communities of faith that are grounded in the biblical text share kinship that is contrasted with the predominant metanarrative of the emerging world that is marked by technological,

therapeutic, military, consumerist values that empty the world of abiding meaning and risky fidelity. Thus Old Testament theology in time to come may be understood as an exposition of a metanarrative—one that is, to be sure, complex and disjunctive—that subverts and offers an alternative to the dominant ideological trajectory of the global economy.

I propose, then, that Old Testament theology be undertaken as a subversive alternative to the dominant, even hegemonic metanarrative of our time. In such a perspective we may usefully recognize that each of the great theological affirmations of the Old Testament is indeed a radically countercultural offer in a flattened world of anti-neighbourly social arrangements:

- An affirmation of the *Holiness of God* who is present in and for the life of the world is a subversive claim against a sociology that imagines a profane world without ultimate meaning beyond human construction.
- An affirmation of YHWH as *creator* who governs, loves, and summons the world is a subversive claim against a world understood mechanically or profanely. Creation faith attests to the hidden, but decisively defining, providential care of God for the world, a claim against an 'empty sky' without a giver who gives life beyond our inventiveness.
- An affirmation of *wisdom* as a force for the ordering of the world with its gifts, choices, and limits is a subversive claim against a modern world of self-invention or a post-modern world that lives close to nihilism, a practice that either way evolves without restraints into self-destructiveness and death in the myriad modes of foolishness.
- An affirmation of *covenant* with its stipulations and requirements is a subversive claim against a world of autonomy in which relationships are sustained only by convenience, and not fidelity, in which duty and responsibility are overridden in self-indulgence that devours self, neighbour, and environment.
- An affirmation of *prophecy* with its imaginative power to conjure alternatives in judgement and hope is a subversive claim against the world that has stilled dissent, silenced the poets, and reduced the social processes to monologues among the privileged and powerful.

On all these counts—plus many others that could be added—Old Testament theology in the time to come must attend to a world that is 'strange and new', so strange that it will not fit our conventional expectations, so new that its coming is profoundly destabilizing and abrasive. In time to come, the task of Old Testament theology may well be undertaken especially by 'organic intellectuals'—that is, by those who are concerned to fund and enact the bold practices of specific communities of faith. In so far as that will be the nature of such work in time to come, it is clear that the discipline has moved a long way from any complacent 'objectivity'. That move, however, will be congruent with the disruption voiced by Karl Barth, who gave impetus and permit for the vigour and ferment of the twentieth-century discipline. As the human community becomes increasingly under threat in the twenty-first century, the urgency of the task critically, canonically, confessionally, and contextually is immense; it awaits fresh and venturesome practitioners.

BIBLIOGRAPHY

ALBERTZ, R. 1994. *A History of Israelite Religion in the Old Testament, Period I and II*. OTL. Louisville, Ky.: Westminster/John Knox Press.

ALBRIGHT, W. F. 1957. *From the Stone Age to Christianity: Monotheism and the Historical Process*. Baltimore: Johns Hopkins University Press.

BARR, J. 1999. *The Concept of Biblical Theology: An Old Testament Perspective*. Minneapolis: Fortress Press.

BARTH, K. 1968. *The Epistle to the Romans*, 6th edn. New York: Oxford University Press.

BRANSON, M. L., and RENE PADILLA, C., eds. 1986. *Conflict and Context: Hermeneutics in the Americas*. Grand Rapids, Mich.: Eerdmans.

BRIGHT, J. 1959. *A History of Israel*, 1st edn. Philadelphia: Westminster Press.

BRUEGGEMANN, W. 1997. *Theology of the Old Testament: Testimony, Dispute, Advocacy*. Minneapolis: Fortress Press.

—— 2001. 'Dialogue between Incommensurate Partners: Prospects for Common Testimony'. *Journal of Ecumenical Studies*, 38: 383–98.

—— 2002. 'The ABC's of Old Testament Theology in the US'. *Zeitschrift für die alttestamentliche wissenschaft*, 114: 412–32.

CHILDS, B. S. 1970. *Biblical Theology in Crisis*. Philadelphia: Westminster Press.

—— 1979. *Introduction to the Old Testament as Scripture*. Philadelphia: Fortress Press.

—— 1992. *Biblical Theology of the Old and New Testaments*. Minneapolis: Fortress Press.

—— 2001. *Isaiah: A Commentary*. OTL. Louisville, Ky.: Westminster/John Knox Press.

CLEMENTS, R. E. 1977. 'Patterns in the Prophetic Canon'. In George W. Coats and Burke O. Long, eds., *Canon and Authority: Essays in Old Testament Religion and Theology*, Philadelphia: Fortress Press, 42–55.

—— 1996. *Old Testament Prophecy: From Oracles to Canon*. Louisville, Ky.: Westminster/ John Knox Press.

CROSS, F. M. 1973. *Canaanite Myth and Hebrew Epic: Essays in the History of Israelite Religion*. Cambridge, Mass.: Harvard University Press.

DEVER, W. G. 2001. *What Did the Biblical Writers Know & When Did They Know It? What Archaeology Can Tell Us abut the Reality of Ancient Israel*. Grand Rapids, Mich.: Eerdmans.

—— 2003. *Who Were the Early Israelites and Where Did They Come From?* Grand Rapids, Mich.: Eerdmans.

DUBE, M. W. 2000. *Postcolonial Feminist Interpretation of the Bible*. St Louis: Chalice Press.

EICHRODT, W. 1961, 1967. *Theology of the Old Testament*, 2 vols. OTL. Philadelphia: Westminster Press.

FELDER, C. H., ed. 1991. *Stony the Road We Trod: African American Biblical Interpretation*. Minneapolis: Fortress Press.

FINKELSTEIN, I., and SILBERMAN, N. A. 2000. *The Bible Unearthed: Archaeology's New Vision of Ancient Israel and the Origin of its Sacred Texts.* New York: Free Press.

FRYMER-KENSKY, T., ed. 2000. *Christianity in Jewish Terms.* Boulder, Colo.: Westview Press.

GERSTENBERGER, E. S. 2002. *Theologies in the Old Testament.* Minneapolis: Fortress Press.

GOSHEN-GOTTSTEIN, M. H. 1987. 'Tanakh Theology: The Religion of the Old Testament and the Place of Jewish Biblical Theology'. In Patrick D. Miller Jun. *et al.*, eds., *Ancient Israelite Religion: Essays in Honor of Frank Moore Cross*, Philadelphia: Fortress Press, 617–44.

GOTTWALD, N. K. 1979. *The Tribes of Yahweh: A Sociology of the Religion of Liberated Israel, 1250–1050 B.C.E.* Maryknoll, NY: Orbis Books.

GRENZ, S. J., and FRANKE, JOHN R. 2001. *Beyond Foundationalism: Shaping Theology in a Postmodern Context.* Louisville, Ky.: Westminster/John Knox Press.

HALIVNI, D. W. 1991. *Peshat & Derash: Plain & Applied Meaning in Rabbinic Exegesis.* Boulder, Colo.: Westview Press.

—— 1998. *Revelation Restored: Divine Writ & Critical Responses.* Boulder, Colo.: Westview Press.

KEPNES, S. 1996. *Interpreting Judaism in a Postmodern Age.* New York: New York University Press.

—— OCHS, PETER, and GIBBS, ROBERT 1998. *Reasoning after Revelation: Dialogues in Postmodern Jewish Philosophy.* Boulder, Colo.: Westview Press.

LEVENSON, J. D. 1985. 'Is There a Counterpart in the Hebrew Bible to New Testament Antisemitism?' *Journal of Ecumenical Studies*, 22: 242–60.

—— 1988. *Creation and the Persistence of Evil: The Jewish Drama of Divine Omnipotence.* San Francisco: Harper & Row.

—— 1993. *The Hebrew Bible, the Old Testament, and Historical Criticism: Jews and Christians in Biblical Studies.* Louisville, Ky.: Westminster/John Knox Press.

—— 1996. 'The Universal Horizon of Biblical Particularism'. In Mark G. Brett, ed., *Ethnicity and the Bible*, Leiden, E. J. Brill, 143–69.

MILLER, P. D. 1995. 'Creation and Covenant'. In Steven J. Kraftchick, Charles D. Myers, jun., and Ben C. Ollenburger, eds., *Biblical Theology Problems & Perspectives: In Honor of J. Christiaan Beker*, Nashville: Abingdon Press, 165–8.

OCHS, P., ed. 2000. *Reviewing the Covenant: Eugene B. Borowitz and the Postmodern Renewal of Jewish Theology.* Albany, NY: SUNY Press.

PERDUE, L. G. 1994. *The Collapse of History: Reconstructing Old Testament Theology.* OBT. Minneapolis: Fortress Press.

PIXLEY, G. V. 1983. *On Exodus: A Liberation Perspective.* Maryknoll, NY: Orbis Books.

PIXLEY, J. 2000. 'History and Particularity in Reading the Hebrew Bible: A Response to Jon D. Levenson'. In Alice Ogden Bellis and Joel S. Kaminsky, eds., *Jews, Christians, and the Theology of the Hebrew Scriptures*, Atlanta: Society of Biblical Literature, 231–7.

POLK, T. H. 1997. *The Biblical Kierkegaard: Reading by the Rule of Faith.* Macon, Ga.: Mercer University Press.

RAD, G. VON 1962, 1965. *Old Testament Theology*, 2 vols. San Francisco: Harper & Row.

—— 1966a. 'The Form-Critical Problem of the Hexateuch'. In *The Problem of the Hexateuch and Other Essays*, New York: McGraw-Hill, 1–78.

—— 1966b. 'The Theological Problem of the Old Testament Doctrine of Creation'. In *The Problem of the Hexateuch and Other Essays*, New York: McGraw-Hill, 131–43.

—— 1972. *Wisdom in Israel*. Nashville: Abingdon Press.

SANDERS, J. A. 1972. *Torah and Canon*. Philadelphia: Fortress Press.

—— 1976. 'Adaptable for Life: The Nature and Function of Canon'. In Frank Moore Cross et al., eds., *Magnalia Dei: The Mighty Acts of God: Essays on the Bible and Archaeology in Memory of G. Ernest Wright*, Garden City, NY: Doubleday & Co., Inc., 531–60.

SETERS, J. VAN 1975. *Abraham in History and Tradition*. New Haven: Yale University Press.

SOULEN, R. K. 1996. *The God of Israel and Christian Theology*. Minneapolis: Fortress Press.

TAMEZ, E. 2002. 'Reading the Bible under a Sky without Stars'. In Walter Dietrich and Ulrich Luz, eds., *The Bible in a World Context: An Experiment in Contextual Hermeneutics*, Grand Rapids, Mich.: Eerdmans, 3–15.

THIEL, J. E. 1994. *Nonfoundationalism*. Minneapolis: Fortress Press.

THOMPSON, T. L. 1992. *Early History of the Israelite People from the Written and Archaeological Sources*. Leiden: E. J. Brill.

—— 1999. *The Mythic Past: Biblical Archaeology and the Myth of Israel*. New York: Basic Books.

TRIBLE, P. 1978. *God and the Rhetoric of Sexuality*. OBT. Philadelphia: Fortress Press.

—— 1994. *Rhetorical Criticism: Context, Method, and the Book of Jonah*. Guides to Biblical Scholarship. Minneapolis: Fortress Press.

UKPONG, J. S. *et al.* 2002. *Reading the Bible in the Global Village: Cape Town*. Atlanta: Society of Biblical Literature.

WESTERMANN, C. 1971. *Creation*. Philadelphia: Fortress Press.

—— 1978. *Blessing in the Bible and in the Life of the Church*. OBT. Philadelphia: Fortress Press.

—— 1982. *Elements of Old Testament Theology*. Atlanta: John Knox Press.

WRIGHT, G. E. 1944. *The Challenge of Israel's Faith*. Chicago: University of Chicago Press.

—— 1950. *The Old Testament against its Environment*. Studies in Biblical Theology, 2. London: SCM Press.

—— 1952. *God Who Acts: Biblical Theology as Recital*. SBT 8. London: SCM Press.

CHAPTER 39

NEW TESTAMENT THEOLOGY

JAMES D. G. DUNN

WHAT IS NEW TESTAMENT THEOLOGY?

The concept of 'New Testament theology' is more contested than is often appreciated. By convention, 'theology' denotes not only talk of God as such, but the corollaries of an active belief in God, including the understanding of the world as 'created', of human living as responsible before this God, of divine revelation and redemptive purpose, and so on. So 'New Testament theology' could mean simply a description of the beliefs on such subjects as adduced from the writings of the New Testament (NT). But that simple definition at once raises a variety of questions which need at least to be posed if the task of 'NT theology' is to be adequately appreciated.

For example, is NT theology only a *descriptive* exercise, an exercise in historical literary archaeology—the task of merely grouping and sequencing various pronouncements on such topics in the NT? Or is the real task to search out principles and teachings which can be argued to be of continuing relevance and importance for the twenty-first century, a *prescriptive* rather than a descriptive exercise? In other words, is what is envisaged the task of *reporting* NT thought or of *doing* theology by drawing on NT thought? Or again, is NT theology the province of the historian or literary scholar, or only that of the Church which historically recognized these writings as New Testament and for whom the NT by definition is Scripture?

Another set of questions arises from the lack of clarity as to whether the subject-matter of NT theology is what the writers of the NT themselves *believed* or simply what they *wrote*. Is it to be assumed that the writers in each particular instance were drawing on a larger well or fountain-head of theology, which can (and should) be deduced from the particular language of each text? Or should the concern be only with the text itself? Either way, the further question cannot be ignored: to what extent does our understanding of the particular text depend on our knowledge of the contexts from which and to which it was directed? And even if we eschew the attempt (or possibility) to enquire behind a text to the mind of its author, what weight should be given to the allusions and echoes in the texts themselves—echoes of other texts, allusions to issues not fully elucidated in the texts themselves?

Then there are the implications of using the qualifier 'New Testament' in talking of 'New Testament theology'. Few would want to claim that there is a single, uniform theological teaching on any subject within the NT writings. These writings certainly form a unified body of texts, united above all by their common focus on and devotion to Jesus Christ. But round that common core there is considerable diversity. Consequently, it is rarely wise to talk simply of 'the NT teaching' on any particular subject. For in some cases the teaching referred to is to be found in only one or two of the NT writings, attitudes to homosexuality being a case in point. And in other cases, there is a marked tension between the different views expressed on a particular theme, as for example, in attitudes to the (Jewish) law. Or should we go down the road of 'canonical criticism' and insist that, as part of 'the New Testament canon', individual texts should be read only canonically—that is, within the context of the canon as a whole? Here the unifying factor—that just these texts came to be reckoned as canonical, as 'the New Testament'—would become in effect the perspective of the fourth-century Christian church which dubbed just these and rejected others as 'canonical'. And the scope for recognizing a prickly individualism, such as Paul's theology could be said to have evinced, might then be closed down, and important theological input be devalued.

Questions like these have constantly bubbled up in modern scholarship, particularly in the last 100 years. What is known as the History of Religions school in Germany at the end of the nineteenth and beginning of the twentieth centuries was in large part a reaction against treating religion as merely theology. The NT should not be seen as simply a repository of doctrine. Rather, it bears witness to religious experience and to early Christianity's interaction with other religious movements of the time. For example, William Wrede in 1897 argued that we should abandon the name 'New Testament theology' and speak instead of 'early Christian history of religion', or 'the history of early Christian religion and theology'. And Wilhelm Bousset's famous study of 1913 of the development of early Christology (understanding of Christ) took its point of departure from the practice of the early community's worship.

The middle decades of the twentieth century saw a reassertion of theology—the NT as in some important sense speech *from* God and not merely *about* God. Here the names of Rudolf Bultmann and the most influential Bultmannian of the following generation, Ernst Käsemann, command attention. And latterly the debate has diverged in several directions, with some insisting that the NT texts should be read primarily as historical sources, others concerned more with the literary and aesthetic appeal of the texts, others emphatic that the texts can be properly understood only within the Christian tradition itself. Within the resulting confusion the possibility and desirability of NT theology has become something of an open question.

All that being said, however, if theology is a viable exercise, then a role for the NT within that exercise certainly cannot be excluded or ignored. For the NT is the primary witness to the beginnings of Christian theology, and remains a primary source for Christian theology in all ages. Indeed, it can be fairly argued that the NT writings define and provide the subject-matter for Christian theology, on which all subsequent Christian theologizing is ultimately commentary. And even if some would regard that last statement as something of an overstatement, it nevertheless remains an inescapable fact that the NT writings provide the literary basis for all Christian theology. So, despite the difficulties of defining the objects and scope of NT theology, some attempt to describe the theological contribution of the NT is unavoidable.

New Testament Theology

A critical element in determining the character and content of NT theology is the fact that the writings which provide its subject-matter are described as the *New* Testament. That is, they are defined by their relation to the writings known as the *Old* Testament. NT theology, in other words, is determined in part at least by its character as *new*, over against the theology which is characterized as *old*. To be noted at once is the fact that the terms 'old' and 'new' are themselves not neutrally descriptive; on the contrary, they already express the perspective of the new—the 'old' so described only by contrast with the 'new', the 'new' in contrast with the 'old'.

At the same time, the two phrases share a term in common—'testament', from the Latin *testamentum*. The Latin translates the Greek *diathēkē*, 'last will and testament, compact, contract, covenant', and the Hebrew *běrît*, 'pact, compact, covenant'. It is in this last sense, 'covenant', that the word has carried most theological freight. For in Jewish and Christian Scriptures the term 'covenant' denotes the promises made to Israel's patriarchs in Genesis 12–17 (Exod. 2: 24; Lev. 26: 42–5; Deut. 4: 31) and the resulting formal agreements made between YHWH and Israel at Mt Sinai (Exod. 19: 5–6), and in the plains of Moab (Deut. 29–31). These were the promises and agreements (notably the Torah) which formed the core of Israel's self-understanding as the people of YHWH. The phrase 'new testament' itself is drawn directly from NT references to 'the new covenant', particularly in Luke 22: 20; 1 Cor. 11: 25; 2 Cor. 3: 6; and Heb. 9: 15. These texts all express the claim that the ancient prophecy of a 'new covenant' (Jer. 31: 31) has been fulfilled in what Christ achieved through his mission, death, and resurrection. It is no accident, then, that the same phrase came to denote the writings which bear most immediate testimony of and to that claim—the New Testament.

The very phrase 'New Testament theology', therefore, immediately presents its primary agenda: the NT claims about Christ, not just in themselves, but as fulfilment of the old covenant's hopes and expectations. But, of course, such an agenda cannot be pursued without asking equally fundamental questions. Is the new testament/covenant to be understood (theologically) as essentially in continuity with the old? Or rather, should it be regarded as superseding the old and rendering the old covenant/testament null and void? The latter option is posed by the Letter to the Hebrews (particularly Heb. 8: 13), and gave rise to a whole 'supersessionist' theology—Christianity as having sucked all that was good from the old covenant and left it as an empty husk—which dominated Christian attitudes towards Israel and Jews for centuries, indeed, until the last few decades. Alternatively posed, are the New Testament and Christianity to be seen as a wholly new revelation which determines how all earlier revelation should be evaluated? Is the New Testament to be understood as the goal of the Old—goal in the double sense of 'end', of climax and completion? Such questions, of course, pose challenges particularly for articles on 'the Old Testament' and 'Old Testament theology'. But their implications for the stuff and thrust of 'New Testament theology' can hardly be ignored.

In short, if the fundamental task of NT theology is to analyse what the New Testament brings to theology or how the New Testament determines the subject-matter and weighting of Christian theology, then its character both as *testament* and as *new* needs to be kept in focus throughout. New *Testament* theology deals with the NT writings as testimony of a compact made by God with human beings. *New* Testament theology starts with the perspective that the NT writings represent (or constitute) a new phase in the relationship between God and human beings, in comparison or even contrast with the older phase expressed by the Old Testament.

If, then, the primary task of NT theology is determined by its character as *New Testament* theology, this suggests that its main subject-matter has to be the principal themes which both unite the Testaments as *testament* and distinguish the NT from the OT as *new*. These themes are fourfold: God, the people of God, the saving purpose of God, and the people's response.

GOD AS SUBJECT

In a memorable sentence, Nils Dahl described 'God' as 'The Neglected Factor in New Testament Theology' (1991: 153–63). He was referring to the fact that 'God' is the great unstated *axiom* and *assumption* of the NT writers. They did not need to expound or argue for a belief in God. All their readers knew (or thought they knew) who or what the word referred to. 'God' was uncontroversial, a semiotic sign of immeasurable significance, but so familiar that the significance rarely needed to be unpacked. In fact, the term 'God' is one of the most frequently recurring words in the NT, well ahead of 'Jesus' and 'Christ', for example. But reference is to God as a constant presence and primary factor in human existence, which is so pervasive as not to require any further or fuller articulation.

Consequently, a NT theology of God, *theology* in the narrow sense, has to work in the interstices and between the lines, to spell out what was so obvious to the NT writers that it need not be stated, to write out the earliest Christians' A, B, C with what would have seemed to many of them pedantic tautology. A NT theology of God has perforce to work with the allusions and inferences of the text, whether at an inter-textual level or as an attempt to illuminate the theology of the writers themselves. This also means that a NT theology of God needs to fill out the allusions and assumptions by reference to the earliest Christians' own definitive Scriptures—subsequently known as the Old Testament. On this subject NT theology is dependent on and begins as OT theology. That God is creator of all, has revealed himself in different ways, including through inspiration and creation, and will exercise final judgement over his creation is simply taken over as a basic conviction taught by the Law, the Prophets, and the Writings, and too obvious for most NT writers to require any elaboration. The assumptions, controversial for other religious traditions and for modernist Christianity, and their taken-for-granted nature are clear enough from such texts as Matt. 6: 30; Heb. 1: 1, and Rom. 3: 6.

The most striking feature of the first Christians' *theological* heritage was the further axiomatic feature of Jewish belief that God is one—expressed in the classic and fundamental Jewish creed, the Shemaʿ: 'The Lord our God is one Lord' (Deut. 6: 4). In a typically polytheistic ancient Near East, this was the most distinctive feature of OT *theology*. Whether or not 'monotheism' is the most accurate description of early Jewish belief, the belief that God is 'one', or that there is (only) one God, was evidently taken equally as bedrock by the NT writers (e.g. Mark 12: 29; Rom. 3: 29–30; 1 Tim. 2: 5; Jas. 2: 19). It is at this point, however, that we stumble upon the first problematic of NT *theology*: that several NT writers seem to want to redefine their monotheism to make room for Jesus.

As already observed, it is the common focus on and devotion to Jesus Christ which gave the NT its unifying identity. This included, of course, the memory of

Jesus' mission, preserved in the traditions of what Jesus did and said in the Gospels. Included also is the fundamental assertion that Jesus was/is the Christ, the one who fulfilled Jewish hopes of an anointed figure who would 'restore the kingdom to Israel' (Acts 1: 5). The earliest necessity to make this apologetic case, that one who had been crucified was none the less God's anointed, is still echoed in Matthew's 'fulfilment quotations' (e.g. 1: 22–3; 2: 15; 8: 17; 12: 17–21; 21: 4–5) and Luke's portrayal in Luke 24: 25–7, 44–6, and Acts (e.g. 8: 32–5; 17: 11). But already in the Pauline letters the argument is assumed to be as good as won, and 'Christ' is already more or less a proper name—Jesus Christ. So despite the awkwardness of asserting the messiahship of one executed by crucifixion (1 Cor. 1: 23), there is nothing here to disturb the heritage of OT *theology*.

More challenging was the conviction, again a fundamental unifying feature of NT theology, that God had raised Jesus from the dead. But that disrupted the time-frame more than the God-frame of earliest Christian perception (see further below). The implications for *theology* only begin to become clear when the further conviction is taken into account—that God had exalted the risen Jesus to his right hand. Here the theological dynamic seems to have been twofold: first, the influence of the key OT passage, Ps. 110: 1 in particular—'The Lord says to my lord: "Sit at my right hand, till I make your enemies your footstool" ' (Mark 14: 62; Acts 2: 34–5; 1 Cor. 15: 25; Heb. 1: 3; 1 Pet. 3: 22)—and second, the impact of earliest Christian experience, presumably particularly in worship, understood in terms of the Spirit of God active in their hearts (e.g. Phil. 3: 3; John 4: 23–4), but also as the risen and exalted Christ active in their midst (in Acts 3–4 through his name). The most obvious expressions of this are Paul's characteristic talk of being 'in Christ', plus passages like Rom. 8: 9–10 and Gal. 2: 20, and John's equally characteristic imagery of mutual indwelling (classically John 15: 1–10).

Here again, these claims to be experiencing in the present what OT prophets had longed for might not have been so disturbing to Israel's belief in God as one. After all, the OT included accounts of Enoch and Elijah being taken to heaven (Gen. 5: 24; 2 Kgs. 2: 11–12), and later reflection gave them exalted roles in heaven. And neither Jesus nor Paul had any difficulty in envisaging the disciples/saints sharing in the final judgement—as judges (Matt. 19: 28; 1 Cor. 6: 2). But in addition, across a broad front, we see the NT writers pressing to express their faith in Jesus Christ in terms which seem to go beyond anything which had previously been expressed in regard to someone who had recently died.

Matthew does not hesitate to express the significance of Jesus in terms of divine presence: Jesus is to be called 'Emmanuel, God with us' (Matt. 1: 23); he promises to be in the midst of any gathering of two or three of his disciples (18: 20); he has been given 'all authority in heaven and on earth', and will be with his disciples always (28: 18–20).

John frames his Gospel with a twofold confession that Jesus is God: the creating Word who is God, who became flesh in Jesus, the only God (the best reading) in the bosom of the Father (John 1: 1, 14, 18); the confession of Thomas as the climax of the Gospel—'my Lord and my God' (20: 28). John makes no attempt to deny the charge levelled against the Johannine Jesus: that he made himself equal with God, that he made himself God (5: 18; 10: 33).

Hebrews likewise does not hesitate to cite a psalm as addressed to Jesus as 'God' (Heb. 1: 8), and the Revelation of John famously portrays the Lamb sharing the throne of God (Rev. 7: 17; 22: 1, 3).

But in many ways the most striking language is to be found in Paul's letters. He includes Christ with God in his prayers and benedictions. Grace and peace come from 'God our Father and the Lord Jesus Christ' (e.g. Rom. 1: 7; 1 Cor. 1: 3; Gal. 1: 3). He refers texts which speak of YHWH as 'Lord' to Jesus, most notably the emphatically monotheistic affirmation of Isa. 45: 21–3 in Phil. 2: 10–11. The OT 'day of the Lord', referring to the expectation of divine judgement (e.g. Amos 5: 18–20; Joel 2: 1–2, 11, 31), is now, without any sense of inappropriateness, 'the day of our Lord Jesus Christ' (e.g. 1 Cor. 1: 8; 1 Thess. 5: 2; Phil. 1: 10). The Spirit of God is now referred to, again without any sense of inappropriateness, as the Spirit of Christ, the Spirit of the Son (Rom. 8: 9; Gal. 4: 6; Phil. 1: 19); the risen Christ can be identified with 'the life-giving Spirit' (1 Cor. 15: 45).

Most striking of all however is the formula Paul crafts, or even quotes, in 1 Cor. 8: 5–6:

> Even if there are so-called gods, whether in heaven or on earth,
> as indeed there are gods many and lords many,
> yet for us there is one God, the Father,
> from whom all things and we for him,
> and one Lord Jesus Christ,
> through whom all things and we through him.

Here we see clearly taken up the Shema', Israel's confession of God as one, as one Lord, over against all convictions of polytheistic neighbours. But most astonishing is what can hardly be anything other than a conscious reshaping of that fundamental assertion of Israel's monotheism. In this version, the Shema is enlarged (what is the best word to use?) to include Christ within it—the oneness of God as Lord confessed now as embracing both the Father and Jesus Christ.

It is at such a point that the debate becomes relevant as to how NT theology, rightly so called, is to be defined. A definition in terms of a historical description of what the NT writers thought and/or intended to write will tend to focus on how such language could and did emerge, and on how it was understood within the limited horizons of the conceptualities of the day. In the case of Paul, in particular, it becomes appropriate to ask whether he intended to convey what subsequent generations heard him to say. Did he, for example, refrain from speaking of Jesus as 'God'?—the punctuation of Rom. 9: 5 is a famous crux. How significant is it that he never addressed the normal prayer terms (*deomai, deēsis*) to Christ, but only to God? Similarly in Paul, where the normal worship terms appear, only God is worshipped; only God gives the Spirit; thanks are delivered to God through Christ. How significant is it that the Paul who can refer OT YHWH texts to Christ can also speak of 'the *God*...of our *Lord* Jesus Christ' (e.g. Rom. 15: 6; 2 Cor. 1: 3; 11: 31)? Perhaps most noteworthy of all is the absence of any hint that the language reviewed in the previous two paragraphs caused any surprise or offence among Shema-confessing Jewish members of the churches to which Paul wrote (in contrast to the later John 5: 18 and 10: 33).

It would appear, then, that the task of NT theology in its role of trying to explicate how the distinctives of Christian theology (in this case Christology) emerged has to proceed with great care. What seem to be obvious implications, with the benefit of hindsight, may need to be reckoned, initially at least, as the hyperbole of worship or the flourish of rhetoric, and seen as such when they were *initially* set down in writing.

NT theology as canonical theology, on the other hand, can pay less attention to any reserve Paul may have expressed, since worship of Jesus as God seems to be less inhibited elsewhere, in John's Gospel and the Revelation of John. And when NT theology is seen as the initial statement of and first contribution to Christian theology, the Wisdom/Logos Christology of passages like John 1: 1–18; Col. 1: 15–20; and Heb. 1: 1–4 becomes important as pointing the way forward for the developing Christology of the second and third centuries, just as the NT's Father–Son language and the subordinationist language of 1 Cor. 15: 24–8 become fundamental in the structure of the classic Christology of the creeds and subsequent confessions.

Whatever the refinements of the debate about the function of NT theology, it remains clear that earliest Christian belief regarding Christ is what gave definitive shape to Christianity and its New Testament. It was NT Christology which above all proved incapable of being held within the framework of Christianity's parent religion, the religion of Israel, Judaism, or, alternatively expressed, of OT theology seen in its own right and not simply as a tributary of NT or Christian theology. And it is this feature of Christian theology, in its refined form as Trinitarian theology, God as one but three, which remains the chief stumbling-block in inter-faith dialogue, with Judaism and Islam especially. However defined, then, Christology forms the distinctive heart of NT theology.

THE PEOPLE OF GOD

The other most distinctive feature of OT *theology* is the belief in the God of *Israel*. Not that such a belief was strange in the ancient Near East: belief that each nation had its own god was a standard religious prescription. What made Israel's belief stand out is that it was precisely belief that the *one* God is *Israel*'s God. Whether this was originally little more than chauvinist triumphalism, or defiant faith in the face of catastrophe, or exceptional revelation granted to Israel's prophets, need not distract us now. More to the point is the fact that Israel's election was at the heart of its peculiar faith, and so also of OT theology. YHWH, the God over all, had chosen Israel to be his own. In the classic words of the song of Moses, the Most High had allotted the nations their inheritance, but had kept Israel for himself (Deut. 32: 8–9).

This fundamental conviction created a tension within OT theology, particularly with respect to the relationship between Israel and the (other) nations (Gentiles). On the one hand, we read of horrific slaughter visited on the other peoples of the land, as in Gen. 34: 25; Josh. 6: 21; and 1 Sam. 15: 3, apparently with YHWH's approval. Set-apartness to God was seen to require set-apartness from the peoples, a separateness marked by the laws of clean and unclean, with the implication that the other peoples as such were themselves unclean and a threat to Israel's holiness (Lev. 20: 22–6). A strand of Israel's expectation for the future entertained no doubt that the lot of the nations, Israel's enemies, was destruction and devastation at the hand of the Lord (e.g. Ps. 2: 8–9; Isa. 47: 3; Zeph. 2: 9). On the other hand, Abraham was offered the prospect of being a blessing to the nations (Gen. 12: 3). Israel's provision for the resident alien and stranger was a striking feature of its social legislation (e.g. Deut. 10: 19; 14: 29; 24: 14). Again, the Servant of YHWH, Israel itself (Isa. 49: 3), was commissioned to be a light to the nations (49: 6). Jonah was sent unwillingly to bring a message of hope to pagan Nineveh. And the stronger hope for the future was that Gentiles would come in pilgrimage to Zion ('eschato-logical proselytes') to pay tribute or to worship God there (e.g. Ps. 22: 27–8; Isa. 2: 2–4; 45: 14; Zeph. 3: 9–10; Hag. 2: 7–9).

NT theology finds itself caught in a similar tension. On the one hand, no one could think to dispute on the basis of the NT accounts that Jesus himself was other than a Jew. He is remembered as pursuing a mission limited to Israel: 'I was sent only to the lost sheep of the house of Israel' (Matt. 15: 4; similarly 10: 5–6). A characteristically Jewish attitude dismissive of Gentiles is echoed not only in Matthew ('Gentile and taxcollector'—18: 17), but also in Paul ('Gentile sinners'—Gal. 2: 15) and Ephesians ('having no hope, without God in the world'—Eph. 2: 12). And it is little surprise that Babylon, responsible for Israel's faith-threatening exile, is still the image of demonic and cosmic opposition to God in Rev. 17: 5 and ch. 18.

At the same time, a totally astonishing new contrast is readily apparent in the NT—astonishing for anyone coming to it from an OT or Jewish perspective. For the NT contrast to Jewish hostility to Gentiles is not just Jewish openness to and concern for Gentiles, but *Gentile* hostility to *Jews*: most notably in the tendency of the Gospel writers to put the blame for Jesus' death primarily, it would seem, on the heads of the Jewish participants in the events leading up to the execution of Jesus (by the Romans). All the people accept the responsibility: 'His blood be on us and on our children' (Matt. 27: 25). The charge is clearest in Luke's account of the earliest Christian preaching: 'you crucified and killed him' (Acts 2: 23; 3: 14–15; 10: 39); and through the latter half of Acts 'the Jews' feature regularly as closed-minded opponents of the gospel (13: 45; 14: 19; 17: 5; 18: 12; etc.). In John's Gospel the antithesis is still sharper: 'the Jews' are implacably opposed to Jesus and seek to kill him during his ministry (John 5: 16–18; 7: 1; 10: 31); and Jesus returns the compliment with apparently equal venom—offspring of the devil (8: 44; similarly Rev. 2: 9— 'synagogue of Satan'). Even Paul (see below) speaks in not dissimilar vein, when he attributes the death of Jesus to the Jews and consigns them to the wrath of God (1 Thess. 2: 14–16).

It is precisely at this point that NT theology cannot claim to be merely descriptive (without responsibility for the way in which the description is heard) or as straightforwardly prescriptive (the NT tells Christians how to regard the Jews). For such NT texts—Matt. 27: 25 and John 8: 44 in particular—have resonated down through the history of Christianity and been used to justify countless pogroms and persecutions of Jews. The question posed to NT theology cannot, dare not, be ignored: 'Does the NT provide any warrant for anti-Judaism or anti-Semitism?' At which point it becomes imperative that such texts are not read as though they were timeless dogmas, a situationless word applicable to all situations. NT theology must insist that its subject-matter (the NT) is read historically. The particular situation of a new, still small (Christian) sect in the face of a dominant national and state-recognized religion has to be appreciated, as also the fierceness of rhetoric and vituperation which characterized mutual hostility and polemic between groups in those days, not to mention the sharp critique and rebuke of the OT prophet directed against his own people. A New Testament theology which disregards historical context is a recipe for bigotry and intolerant sectarianism.

The main thrust of the NT writings drives between the two extremes. Matthew brings his Gospel to its resounding climax with 'the great commission' to 'Go and make disciples of all nations' (Matt. 28: 19). Luke, in one of the canticles which was soon to become permanently lodged in Christian liturgy, already strikes the balance which is to characterize his description of the early Christian mission: a salvation 'prepared in the presence of all peoples, a light for revelation to the Gentiles and for glory to your people Israel' (Luke 2: 30–2). To the same effect, the text which more than any other points to the resolution of the Jew/Gentile tensions afflicting the earliest mission, where James speaking in the Jerusalem Council quotes Amos 9: 11– 12: 'After this I will return, and I will rebuild the dwelling of David which has fallen ... and I will set it up, so that all other peoples may seek the Lord—even all the Gentiles over whom my name has been called' (Acts 15: 16–17). And Paul, it is clear, saw his mission not as a turning his back on his people, but as a fulfilment of Israel's own commission as the Servant of YHWH to be a light to the nations (Gal. 1: 15, echoing Isa. 49: 1, 6), his gospel as fulfilling the promise that Abraham would be a blessing to the Gentiles (Gal. 3: 8).

The issue which this thrust of NT theology poses to Christianity has not been sufficiently acknowledged or resolved inadequately. The issue is the identity of Israel and the continuity of the Church with Israel. The fact that the very term 'church' (*ekklēsia*), used for the Christian assembly already in Matt. 16: 18 and 18: 15–17, but consistently from Acts onwards, is evidently influenced by the use of the same term in the Greek OT for the assembly of Israel, 'the church of God' (as in Gal. 1: 13), calls for more attention than it has received. What does James imply when he writes his letter to Christians as 'the twelve tribes in the Diaspora' (Jas. 1: 1), or Peter similarly to 'the exiles of the Diaspora' (1 Pet. 1: 1)? And what is the full force of Paul's image of the olive-tree (Israel) from which branches (unbelieving Israel) have been broken off and wild branches (believing Gentiles) grafted in, with the prospect of the broken branches being restored (Rom. 11: 17–24)? An image *not* of the old tree uprooted and replaced by another. In all these cases there is a sense of Israel redefined, not in ethnic terms but in terms of God's call (Rom. 9: 6–9), an Israel which includes not Jews only but also Gentiles (9: 24–6). This more nuanced understanding of Israel does not give warrant to traditional Christian supersessionism, but what it means for Christian self-understanding and for Christian relationships with Jews becomes a major item for a Christian theology in which NT theology reflects the complexity of the issue but ultimately proffers to serve as a moderator and arbiter. Who are the people of God? If the OT demonstrates that Gentiles posed troubling questions to the identity of Israel, we should not be surprised if the NT demonstrates that Jews pose not dissimilar questions to the identity of Christians. Such is the grist which provides the grain of NT theology.

How God Saves

A third fundamental strand of NT theology has to deal with human salvation. The presupposition of all religions is that humans need God, above all to save them from the dangers of natural calamity and human folly, of war and disaster, of disease and death. Here again the NT writers inherited a whole theological schema embodied in cultic ritual from their Jewish forebears. The starting-point was, as above, the divine initiative: God had chosen Israel to be his own people, and had instructed them in the ways of worship and sacrifice to express their gratitude and their repentance and as a means of atonement and forgiveness. All this forms a massive backdrop to NT theology, a huge taken-for-granted presupposition in determining key features and emphases in Christian soteriology (teaching on salvation), without which large tracts of NT teaching would be meaningless and metaphors would lose their power to evoke new insight. Apart from anything else, the temple in Jerusalem and its cult provide an extensive subtext running through the accounts of Jesus' mission and the writings of the first generation of Christianity and beyond, without which so much of the NT text cannot be adequately understood.

Over against all this, but also understood as the climax to it, stands one central feature of the NT and its theology: the death of Jesus. As *Jesus* is what made the NT necessary and provides the central, defining distinctive of NT theology, so it is the *death* of Jesus which marks the distinctive feature of the NT understanding of salvation. The cross of Jesus, Christ crucified, became *the* symbol for Christianity because from the first and throughout the NT the cross of Jesus is the key that unlocks the mystery of how God saves for the NT writers.

A standard definition of the Gospels is of 'passion narratives with extended introductions'. That definition catches the character of the Gospels well. For however much they are interested in the pre-passion mission of Jesus, as of course they are, it is nevertheless the steady drive towards and mounting anticipation of Jesus' betrayal and crucifixion which provides the connecting thread and motivation for the whole: so, for example, in the early foreshadowings in Mark 2: 20; 3: 6, 19; and 6: 14–29, 41; prior to the turning-point of 8: 27–33 ('the Son of Man must suffer many things, and be rejected …'), from which time on the shadow of the cross becomes ever clearer. In Luke a similar effect is achieved by the prophecy of Simeon ('a sign that will be opposed'), the final prophecy of the birth narratives (Luke 2: 35), and the long travel narrative which enfolds so much of Jesus' mission within the fateful last journey to Jerusalem (9: 51–19: 28). More effective is John's reference to the salvation climax of Jesus' mission by the several-stranded theme of 'glorification' and 'being lifted up' (most notably John 12: 23–33), and the steady drum beat of the approaching climax in his talk of his coming 'hour' (2: 4; 7: 30; 8: 20; 12: 23, 27; 13: 1; etc.).

Somewhat surprisingly, the sermons in Acts focus on the death of Jesus more as a foil to Jesus' vindication than as a saving act (Acts 2: 23–4; 3: 15; 4: 10; etc.), but there are echoes of Jesus seen as the suffering servant of Isa. 52: 13–53: 12 (Acts 3: 13, 26; 4: 27, 30), as well as the explicit exposition of Isa. 53 in 8: 32–5, and 20: 28 includes a powerful, if somewhat obscure reference to the church of God 'obtained through the blood of his own'. The suffering servant of Isaiah 52–3 certainly had a powerfully explanatory force for the first Christian contemplation of the death of Jesus, as clearly evidenced in the NT—most notably in 1 Pet. 2: 22–5. And at the heart of the Revelation of John stands the lamb slaughtered to provide a ransom (Rev. 5: 6–12), and as such, the key which both unlocks and effects the saving purpose of God.

It is in Paul's letters that the centrality of the cross of Jesus to the new Christian gospel becomes most clear. We were enemies to God, but reconciled by the death of his Son (Rom. 5: 10). Despite its blatantly counter-intuitive and shocking character (that God has worked his saving purpose through an executed felon), Paul's preaching centres four-square on 'Christ crucified ... the power of God and the wisdom of God' (1 Cor. 1: 23–4). His urgent compulsion is motivated by the conviction that 'one has died for all, therefore all have died' (2 Cor. 5: 14). For Paul salvation is secured by becoming identified with Christ in his death (Rom. 6: 3–4; Phil. 3: 10), and he lives his life now by faith in the Son of God, who loved him and gave himself for him (Gal. 2: 20). God's purpose was 'to reconcile to himself all things, whether on earth or in heaven, by making peace through the blood of his [Christ's] cross' (Col. 1: 20). The confession of Jewish monotheism is now supplemented by the confession of 'one mediator between God and human beings, the human being Christ Jesus, who gave himself a ransom for all' (1 Tim. 2: 5–6).

Within the variety of images used to describe the effectiveness of Jesus' death, the metaphor of cultic sacrifice stands at the centre. The Last Supper, foreshadowing Jesus' death, is understood as a passover meal, his blood 'poured out for many' (Mark 14: 24), the lamb of God that takes away the sins of the world (John 1: 29). One of the earliest Christian confessions is that 'Christ died for our sins in accordance with the scriptures' (1 Cor. 15: 3), where the sacrificial overtones are almost self-evident. Paul speaks of 'the redemption which is in Christ Jesus' as an 'expiation (*hilastērion*) in his blood' (Rom. 3: 25), where the reference is to the 'mercy seat' within the Holy of Holies where the blood of the sin-offering was sprinkled on the day of atonement (Lev. 16). The theme of Jesus' death as the day of atonement sin-offering, taking away sin once and for all, dominates the Letter to the Hebrews (climaxing in Heb. 9: 23–10: 18).

One of the tantalizing features of NT theology at this point is the degree of ambiguity which remains in the attitude of the NT writers to the cult. Jesus is not explicitly recalled as denouncing the cult, though many assume that a supersessionist inference should be drawn from the Last Supper and from the report that the curtain shutting off the Holy Place to all but priests, or the innermost Holy of Holies to any but the High Priest, was torn in two from top to bottom at the death of Jesus (Mark 15: 38). But Luke evidently had no qualms about reporting Peter and John going up to the Temple at the time of, and presumably to attend, the evening sacrifice (Acts 3: 1). And presumably Paul could only invoke the Day of Atonement as a means of understanding the efficaciousness of Christ's death if he had believed the Day of Atonement to be efficacious (Rom. 3: 25). It is Hebrews which puts the issue beyond doubt in its sustained argument that the old cult only foreshadowed the new, that the old sacrifices were inefficient (they had to be repeated), and that since Christ's sacrifice was effective for the forgiveness of sins, there was no further need of sacrifice (Heb. 9–10).

Here again the enterprise of NT theology has to take stock. Does it regard the author of Hebrews as the spokesperson for NT theology on this issue? Does it attempt to resolve the tensions between the variety of metaphors and attitudes by detecting a selective or eclectic consistency? How, for example, does an Abraham being justified by faith prior to and independent of the cult, or a prodigal son finding re-acceptance by the Father without the intervention of a Jesus figure, fit with a soteriology of redemption through sacrificial blood?

The potential anomalies stretch further. Christians soon seem to have turned their backs on the Jerusalem Temple; for the seer of Revelation there was no need for a temple in the heavenly Jerusalem, since the presence of God and of the Lamb made a temple unnecessary (Rev. 21: 22). And there is a consistent tendency in the NT to spiritualize the old insistence on ritual purity, necessary if one was to enter the Temple (e.g. Mark 7: 14–23; 1 Cor. 6: 11; Titus 2: 14; 1 Pet. 1: 22). But there is also a clear recognition that the priestly role of offering sacrifice has been transmuted into the obligations of the gospel (Rom. 12: 1; 15: 16; Phil. 2: 25), and that, given the immediate access to God now opened up, there is no further need for a special order of priesthood (Rom. 5: 2; 1 Pet. 2: 5; Rev. 5: 10; Heb. 9–10). And yet a trend began in the Apostolic Fathers to reclaim the structures of priesthood and sacrifice for Christianity, at just the time that rabbinic Judaism resolved the problem of the Temple's destruction by transferring the central religious role from the priest to the rabbi (teacher). Ironically, Judaism pursued the logic of the NT writers at this point more closely than did the direct heirs of the NT writers. Here, more than anywhere else, NT theology finds itself caught uncomfortably between an OT theology which it has left behind and a Christian theology which has left it behind.

How God's People Should Live

There is no doubt as to the OT answer to the question, How should God's people live? The OT *is* the answer. Or, to be more precise, the canonical heart of the OT, the Torah, the Law of Moses, is the answer, with the Prophets and the Writings indicating, *inter alia*, what obedience to the law should mean in practice. The law is, as it were, the other side of God's covenant love in choosing Israel to be his people and in providing means for Israel's salvation. The law indicates the human response appropriate to the divine initiative: 'I am the Lord your God, who brought you out of the land of Egypt, out of the house of slavery; you shall have no other gods before me' (Exod. 20: 2–3). There is no doubt that the law was given to be obeyed, and in Deuteronomy, 'the book of the law', it is made clear that Israel's prosperity and length of days in the land was dependent on that obedience (Deut. 28–30). The law served also to ensure Israel's holiness/set-apartness to God by marking out its difference and separation from others—circumcision, sabbath, and food laws in particular (Gen. 17: 9–14; Exod. 31: 12–17; Lev. 20: 24–6).

Here too an adequate appreciation of NT ethics can be achieved only when this background is borne in mind. Much of Jesus' teaching is remembered as dealing with issues of how the law should be interpreted and lived, and there are fascinating tensions between Matthew's and Mark's portrayals of Jesus at this point (cf. e.g. Matt. 5: 17–20 with Mark 7: 19—the laws of clean and unclean set aside!). If Jesus' call to 'Love your neighbour as yourself' can be described as the sum of Christian ethics, as it obviously can be (Mark 12: 31; John 15: 12–17; Gal. 5: 14; Jas. 2: 8; 1 John 4: 7–12), then we need to recall that it draws directly on a specific commandment of the law (Lev. 19: 18) and is presented as the sum of the law (Rom. 13: 9). James seems to assume that the teaching of Jesus and the law cohere in 'the perfect law', the royal 'law of liberty' (Jas. 1: 25; 2: 8, 12). And for Paul too, despite all the negative things he says about the law, the Law remains 'holy and just and good' (Rom. 7: 12). It still provides a rule for life: 'Obeying the commandments of God is everything' (1 Cor. 7: 19, NRSV).

The distinctives (and problems) of NT theology at this point are caused by two factors. One is the initial Christian claim that they were experiencing the fulfilment of ancient hopes, a fulfilment which could previously be envisaged only for those who were wholly faithful to the covenant God and his law. The claim is remembered in the Gospels as being put forward by Jesus' message of the kingdom of God already present in a real sense through his ministry (Matt. 11: 2–6; Luke 11: 19–20) and in his table fellowship with tax-collectors and sinners (Matt. 11: 19; Mark 2: 17). The contradiction which the execution of Jesus seemed to constitute to this claim was wholly countermanded by the conviction that Jesus had been raised from the dead, or, more precisely, that the end-time resurrection had already begun in Jesus—a fulfilment, in other words, of the climactic hope which people and martyrs had previously cherished as the final act of God's saving purpose. And it was further strengthened by the early Christian experience of the Spirit of God poured out as long ago promised for the age to come (classically Acts 2: 16–21). The problem (if that is the right word) is that an indwelling Spirit had been seen as the key to successful law obedience (particularly Ezek. 36: 26–7), and still in Rom. 8: 3–4, but that now it seemed to make much of the law unnecessary (Rom. 2: 28–9; 14: 17; Phil. 3: 3); obedience was to be determined by the Spirit (Gal. 5: 16–18), not as 'works of the law' which could be said to quench the Spirit (Gal. 3: 2–5).

Here we need to give full weight to the much abused term 'eschatological'. For it was this sense of fulfilled hopes, that what had hitherto been expected only for the age to come (or the end of historical time) was already happening, which explains so much of the tension between NT and OT attitudes to the law, as indeed the tension *within* NT attitudes to the law. Much of this can, of course, be put down to the first flush of charismatic enthusiasm of a new sect. But the point for us is that this eschatological spirit suffuses the theology of the NT, and NT theology cannot be adequately appreciated, or drawn into wider theologizing, without taking it into account. What Christian theology does with an eschatology which has been 'realized' for nearly two millennia, and which still awaits the eschaton or end is a problem which can hardly be resolved apart from the eschaton! And what Christianity does with a law whose goal has already been reached in Jesus and his resurrection and in the outpouring of the Spirit remains a theological conundrum.

The other factor which both distinguishes NT from OT theology and problematizes the former in its relation with the latter is the fact that the gospel of or about Jesus spread so quickly among Gentiles. Here too Gentiles who received the Spirit and evident grace of God, without crossing any of the boundaries which the law had set to keep Israel separate from its pagan neighbours, quickly posed (and resolved) the question of whether such boundary markers needed to be preserved (Gal. 2: 7–9). Acts provides the classic precedent in chapter 10, with Peter applying the lesson learned in his vision (Acts 10: 11–16) directly to the Gentile Cornelius (10: 28), despite Lev. 20: 24–6, and readily accepting the outpouring of the Spirit on his uncircumcised hearers (10: 44–8); the precedent ensured the acceptance of Gentile converts without circumcision in the first Christian Council (15: 7–9). And it was evidently in this context, of Gentiles receiving the Spirit without works of the law, that Paul initially formulated his most famous theological formula, that 'a person is justified not by works of the law but through faith in Jesus Christ' (Gal. 2: 16).

The problems caused to NT theology in consequence have been unending. Does Paul's formulation of justification by faith and not law effectively dispense with the law as having any part in the salvation process, the law which is so fundamental to OT theology? Does the Spirit render the law superfluous in Christian ethics? Or is the problem resolved by making some distinctions within the law, as traditionally between moral law and ritual law, or more recently between the law as rule for life and the law as separating Israel from the nations? Some sort of balance has to be achieved, equivalent in OT theology to the balance between God's covenant initiative and Israel's response of obedience. For the NT not only speaks of gospel and grace, of Spirit and faith, but also demands a response. Obedience is also required of believers (Rom. 1: 5; 15: 18; 1 Pet. 1: 2). Final judgement will be 'according to works' (Rom. 2: 6–11; 2 Cor. 5: 10)—how to distinguish justification 'not by works' from final justification 'according to works'? Paul as well as Matthew look for 'fulfilment' of the law (Matt. 5: 17–20; Rom. 8: 4). Imagery of reward for achievement or good deeds (works) is not lacking (e.g. Matt. 6: 1–6; 10: 41–2; 25: 34–40; 1 Cor. 3: 14; 9: 24–5; Phil. 3: 14). Salvation (eternal life) is in some degree conditional on faithfulness (e.g. Mark 13: 13; Rom. 8: 13; 1 Cor. 15: 2; Heb. 6: 4–6). There is a tension in NT soteriology and ethics almost as severe as in OT soteriology. Or should we rather say, given the former's realized eschatology, a tension still more severe than in the OT?

New Testament theology, then, is a challenging enterprise, as it seeks to bring into fruitful dialogue the NT's own interaction with its OT heritage and assumptions, the texts in the historical contexts which determined their lasting shape, and the ongoing questions, old as well as new, which continue to call for theological response in the present. The existential sharpness of many of the questions involved is unlikely to permit the task to be merely and dispassionately descriptive. But how NT theology speaks to such questions requires an openness to be addressed by the NT text which is, sad to say, increasingly rare.

SUGGESTED READING

Balla 1997; Dunn 1998; Marshall 2004; Strecker 2000; Stuhlmacher 2006. The New Testament Theology series (Cambridge: Cambridge University Press) consists of studies of the individual New Testament writings.

BIBLIOGRAPHY

BALLA, P. 1997. *Challenges to New Testament Theology*. Tübingen: Mohr Siebeck.
BARTH, M. 1983. *The People of God*. JSNTS.S 5. Sheffield: JSOT Press.
BAUCKHAM, R. 1998. *God Crucified: Monotheism and Christology in the New Testament*. Carlisle: Paternoster Press.
BOUSSET, W. 1970. *Kyrios Christos*. Nashville: Abingdon Press. orig. pub. 1921.
BULTMANN. R. 1952–3. *Theology of the New Testament*, 2 vol. London: SCM Press.
CAIRD, G. B. 1994. *New Testament Theology*. Oxford: Clarendon Press.
CARROLL, J. T., and GREEN, J. B. 1995. *The Death of Jesus in Early Christianity*. Peabody, Mass.: Hendrickson.
CHILDS, B. S. 1992. *Biblical Theology of the Old and New Testaments*. London: SCM Press.
DAHL, N. A. 1991. *Jesus the Christ: The Historical Origins of Christological Doctrine*. Minneapolis: Fortress Press.
DUNN, J. D. G. 1989. *Christology in the Making*, 2nd edn. London: SCM Press.
—— 1991. *The Partings of the Ways between Christianity and Judaism*. London: SCM Press.
—— 1998. *The Theology of Paul the Apostle*. Edinburgh: T. & T. Clark.
—— 2005. *The New Perspective on Paul*. Tübingen: Mohr Siebeck.
HAYS, R. B. 1996. *The Moral Vision of the New Testament*. San Francisco: HarperCollins.
HENGEL, M. 1981. *The Atonement: The Origins of the Doctrine of the Atonement in the New Testament*. London: SCM Press.
—— 1995. *Studies in Early Christology*. Edinburgh: T. & T. Clark.
HOOKER, M. D. 1994. *Not Ashamed of the Gospel: New Testament Interpretations of the Death of Christ*. Carlisle: Paternoster Press.
HURTADO, L. W. 2003. *Lord Jesus Christ: Devotion to Jesus in Earliest Christianity*. Grand Rapids, Mich.: Eerdmans.
KÄSEMANN, E. 1964. *Essays on New Testament Themes*. London: SCM Press.
—— 1969. *New Testament Questions of Today*. London: SCM Press.
LOHSE, E. 1991. *Theological Ethics of the New Testament*. Minneapolis: Fortress Press.
MARSHALL, I. H. 2004. *New Testament Theology*. Downers Grove, Ill.: InterVarsity Press.

RÄISÄNEN, H. 1990. *Beyond New Testament Theology.* London: SCM Press.

RICHARDSON, P. 1986. *Anti-Judaism in Early Christianity,* i: *Paul and the Gospels.* Waterloo, Ontario: Wilfrid Laurier University Press.

SCHRAGE, W. 1988. *The Ethics of the New Testament.* Edinburgh: T. & T. Clark.

SLOYAN, G. S. 1995. *The Crucifixion of Jesus: History, Myth, Faith.* Minneapolis: Fortress Press.

STRECKER, G. 2000. *Theology of the New Testament.* Berlin: de Gruyter; Louisville, Ky.: Westminster/John Knox.

STUHLMACHER, P. 2006. *Biblical Theology of the New Testament.* Grand Rapids, Mich.: Eerdmans.

WESTERHOLM, S. 1988. *Israel's Law and the Church's Faith.* Grand Rapids, Mich.: Eerdmans.

WILSON, S. G. 1995. *Related Strangers: Jews and Christians 70–170 C.E.* Minneapolis: Fortress Press.

WREDE, W. 1973. 'The Task and Methods of "New Testament Theology" (1897)'. In R. Morgan, ed., *The Nature of New Testament Theology,* London: SCM Press, 68–116.

ZIESLER, J. 1990. *Pauline Christianity,* rev. edn. Oxford: Oxford University Press.

CHAPTER 40

BIBLICAL THEOLOGY

BERND JANOWSKI

The purpose of the following observations is to give an overview of various basic problems in biblical theology from the point of view of how they have developed since the beginnings of biblical theological work in the seventeenth century and how they appear today. This sketch of the problems will therefore concern itself less with a discussion of details than with major trends and contexts. After a definition of the term 'biblical theology' (1) and a brief outline of the history of interpretation (2) there follows a sketch of those problems which are at present most intensively discussed (3). In accordance with the aspects of the work on which I myself have concentrated, the main emphasis will be on the Old Testament and its significance for a theology of the whole Bible.

1. The Term 'Biblical Theology'

'Biblical theology' has more than one meaning. It means either *theology which is in accordance with scripture* or *theology that is contained in the Bible*. In the first case, 'biblical theology' is a normative term, whereas in the second case it is an historical term.

In the one case, 'biblical theology' indicates the correct way or method of theology completely; the other case concerns a particular historical expression of theology. In the one case the term 'biblical theology' concerns theology in its essence, in the other case it is concerned only partially with various factors within theology, namely, a particular theological discipline. In the one case, 'biblical theology' concerns the dogmatic theologian, in the other case it concerns the historian among the theologians. Even if this distinction is really only a provisional one, it is also clear that we cannot be content with this straightforward distinction between the two meanings of 'biblical theology'. (Ebeling 1955: 70; ET 1963: 80)

The question is how the two forms of biblical theology relate to each other and what mutual influence between them exists. Depending upon how the relationship is accented, the term 'biblical theology' can be contoured in various ways (see Barr 1986):

> If the accent is upon 'biblical' in opposition to 'dogmatic', then biblical theology is descriptive and historical, but not normative.
>
> If the stress is upon 'theology' in opposition to 'history of religion', then the Bible will be read not only from the point of view of the history of religions— that is, as a source for the religion of Israel or of early Christianity—it will be seen from the point of view of its theology, that is, as a witness to God's speaking.
>
> If the stress is upon the difference between the Bible and its surrounding world—Mesopotamia, Egypt, Asia Minor, Ancient Syria, Persia, the Graeco-Roman world, etc.—then biblical theology is concerned with the special characteristics of the Bible (the so called Proprium), in spite of similarities with these neighbouring worlds.
>
> If, finally, priority is given to the inner connections of the Bible—the 'unity of scripture'—in opposition to the varied nature of its traditions, then biblical theology will stand in contrast to the theology of the Old and New Testaments or to the theology of particular biblical writings or traditions (prophetic, apocalyptic, Pauline, or Johannine theology. See, for the New Testament, Hahn 1994; Stuhlmacher 1995; Reumann 1998).

Apart from the clarification of the relationship between historical and dogmatic encounter with the Bible, a designation of the relationship between *genesis* (the origin of the varied traditions) and *normativeness* (the binding nature of the Bible) belongs to the chief tasks of a biblical theology. It has to account for the 'understanding of the Bible as a whole, that is above all of the theological problems that arise from the fact that the multiplicity of the witnesses in the Old and New Testament are expounded in the context of their backgrounds' (Ebeling 1955: 88). The search for an answer to the question of how this relationship can be grounded, and whether biblical theology is thus a discipline within theological fields, whether it is an interdisciplinary theological programme or whether it simply functions as a regulative leading idea in formulating a theology in accordance with the Bible, belongs to the future tasks of theology (Welker 1998a).

2. ASPECTS OF THE HISTORY
OF INTERPRETATION

The *terminus a quo* for the origin of the term 'biblical theology' is the modern separation of historical and systematic theology, which began at the time of rationalism. The coining of 'biblical theology' sounds very reformed, because Holy Scripture from a reformed point of view is both a source and a guideline for teaching (*doctrina*) but it was not used by the reformers. At the time of its origin in the first half of the seventeenth century (Ebeling 1955: 75 n. 8), it was the solution for a theological programme of reform, which was concerned neither with the content of orthodox dogmatics nor with the form of systematic theology as such, but which was critical of certain excesses such as the domination of 'naïve' biblical statements by the 'presumptuous subtleties' (Spener 1675; see Ebeling 1955: 74–6) of dogmatics. However, the *formal criticism* of the gulf between the Bible, on the one side, and the dominant form of theology and its dogma of inspiration, on the other side, which was conducted in the name of 'biblical theology' gave rise to the *hermeneutical problem* that reflected upon the tension between text and interpretation and how theology could be tied to Scripture. In this connection strenuous attempts were made to put together the various dogmatic loci *dicta probantia* from the Bible. In Catholic circles it was also done from texts from the church fathers (Walter 1994; Schmidt 1671, 1676) in order to tie theology back to its basis in Scripture.

The consequences of this procedure, which meant that biblical theology was nothing more than a subsidiary discipline of dogmatics, became clear first of all in the eighteenth century, as Protestant theologians of the Enlightenment devoted themselves to the task of a biblical theology and step by step developed this into a competitor of dogmatic theology. The decisive breakthrough to a self-standing, historical-critical discipline alongside dogmatics is connected with Johann Philipp Gabler, who, in his inaugural lecture in the University of Altdorf, *De iusto discrimine theologiae biblicae et dogmaticae regundisque recte utriusque finibus* ('On the Correct Distinction of Biblical and Dogmatic Theology and the Correct Distinguishing of the Aims of them both') delivered on 30 March 1787, made a programmatic distinction between biblical theology as a historical discipline and dogmatic theology as a didactic discipline (German translation in Merk 1972: 273–84; English translation in Sandys-Wunsch and Eldredge 1980). The bridge to dogmatics is therefore worked out from the basic biblical ideas that come from 'a pure biblical theology':

Biblical theology possesses historical character: transmitted, concerned with what the sacred writers thought about divine things. Dogmatic theology on the other hand possesses a didactic character: teaching, what each theologian philosophised over divine things by means of his ability and/or in accordance with the conditions of the time, the age, the place, the sects, the schools and other similar things of this type. The former, because it argues historically is, considered in itself, always similar (although according to the system of teaching by which it is worked out, it will differ from others that are worked differently). The latter, like the rest of human disciplines, is subject to many alterations, as is abundantly proved by careful observation of what has happened in many centuries.... This must not be understood as though I were saying that everything in theology must be taken for uncertain and doubtful. However, the point I am making with these words is that we must carefully distinguish the divine from the human; that we must make a certain distinction of biblical and dogmatic theology after we have distinguished what, in Holy Scripture, is directed to all times and all human beings: that only these pure ideas should underlie our philosophical views about religion which divine providence has made valid for all places and times, and in this way to have a clearer idea of the divine and human areas of wisdom. Thus at the end, our theology will be more certain and more firm and will have much less to fear from the fiercest assault of the enemy. (Gabler, in Merk 1972: 275–6)

If the idea of biblical theology was originally thought of only as a reform of systematic theology, its emancipation from dogmatics and the assumption of its methodological and material independence had a considerable back-working effect upon dogmatics. At the same time, the conception of biblical theology as a historical discipline resulted in a new explanation of its basis both in general considerations of the nature of history or historical consciousness and in the interpretation of sources. The attempts at writing a biblical theology that followed, based on these premises, were to some extent affected by contrary tendencies, which will be sketched briefly in what follows.

2.1 Biblical Theology and Historical Criticism

Out of the historical-critical direction of biblical theology were drawn first of all the consequences of a separate presentation of the theology of the Old and the theology of the New Testaments (Georg Lorenz Bauer). In addition, the *methodological instrumentarium* of Gabler was further developed (by Wilhelm Martin Leberecht de Wette, Ferdinand Christian Baur, Daniel Georg Conrad von Cölln, and others; see Merk 1980). In Ferdinand Christian Baur's *Vorlesungen über neutestamentliche Theologie* (1864), the programmatic viewpoints of Gabler and Baur—that is, the interconnection of historical reconstruction and theological interpretation—were brought to the highest point of critical investigation so far. With them, perspectives became visible which reached well into the era after Baur, but which belonged to the most insoluble problems of a biblical theology of the New Testament until the end of the nineteenth century (Holtzmann 1911; Merk 1980: 459–61).

2.2 History of Religion versus Biblical Theology

The conception of biblical theology as a historical discipline developed in the context of a growing historical consciousness, but at the same time in acknowledgement of the relevance of Holy Scripture for Christian faith. The result was the double insight, that biblical theology as a historical discipline is bound not only to the historical setting of the experiencing subject, but also to the conception which the subject has of Christian faith. Depending upon the weight placed upon one or other of these aspects, a further spectrum of possible variations becomes apparent. The position of the history of religions school would have many rich consequences in this connection, a school which made the appreciation of historical distance into a principle of knowledge, and which came to expression in William Wrede's programmatic writing *Über Aufgabe und Methode der sogenannten Neutestament-lichen Theologie* (1897).

The name 'biblical theology' means originally not a theology which is contained in the Bible, but a theology which has biblical character, which is created from the Bible. This cannot be to us a matter of indifference. (Wrede 1897: 79; Ebeling 1955: 69–70)

As a result of this, biblical theology of the Old and New Testaments took on more and more the character of a history of the religion of Israel or of early Christianity. [1]

2.3 Biblical Theology versus History of Religion

Simultaneous with the arrival of dialectical theology there were, in the 1920s and 1930s, reactions against the results of historical-critical scholarship which reached a climax in the charge of *analytical confusion,* of *historical relativism* and *deficient theological interpretation.*[2] In reaction to this, theologies of the Old Testament and

---

[1] Hermann Gunkel expressed a view programmatically on this problem in 1927: 'if one looks deeper and tries to recognise the last grounds of these inadequacies of biblical theology, one notices that these are dominated by the old church view of inspiration. According to this the whole of the biblical material must work at one level and the unity of thought which the Bible is believed to possess can be systematically ordered in a united disposition. If this procedure is contradicted in present time, this means in the last analysis that the spirit of historical research has entered into this discipline. The phenomenon that our generation has experienced, according to which biblical theology has been substituted by the history of Israel's religion, can also be understood that in the place of the theory of inspiration, the spirit of historical research has begun to enter' (Gunkel 1927; emphasis original). On the present discussion of the relationship between the history of Israelite religion and/or the theology of the Old Testament see sect. 2.3.

[2] See already Martin Kähler 1897: ii. 691: 'Historical research seeks to establish past reality and to understand its historical development. In the process it loses the unity of the Bible, and the Bible simply becomes a collection of devalued accounts and documents. The majority of readers of the Bible on the other hand seek in its smallest parts a word of God, which can be applied to each in his circumstances of life. Over both exaggerations, which seem to stand in irreconcilable opposition, a

of the New Testament were written which sought to correct the previous presentations of the 'history of the religion of pre-Christendom' through their demonstration of the *similarities* between the historically transmitted materials of the Christian Bible and the *differences* compared with its neighbouring world. Also in view was the structural unity of religious belief of the Old Testament and its connection with the New Testament (Walther Eichrodt, Ludwig Köhler; see Kertelge 1994). At the same time, some scholars attempted a compromise by trying to write a 'history of Israelite religion' alongside a theology of the Old Testament (Eduard König, Ernst Sellin, also Georg Fohrer; see Albertz 1992: 20–4). The current discussion is (once more) characterized by the alternative of the 'history of Israelite religion' versus 'theology of the Old Testament' and by the plea for a new orientation in the light of the history of interpretation (Albertz 1995, 2001: 3–24; see the essays in Janowski and Lohfink 1995, 2001). That these alternatives offer no relevant answer to the continuing basic questions is shown by the most recent contributions to the theme, although they seek to bring arguments for an integrative perspective: that is, for the material connection between history of religion and *theology* (Köckert 1998; Hermisson 2000; Keel 2001; Janowski 2003; Jeremias 2003. For a similar discussion regarding the New Testament see von Bendemann 2003).

A future biblical theology will consequently ignore neither the literature nor the history of Israelite religion or early Christianity, even though it will be concerned with concrete happenings in history. In the matter of history of religion, the old questions about the relationship between *genesis* and *normativeness* reappear: how can the unity of the Old and New Testaments or of the Christian Bible be spoken about when at the same time the *diversity* of their religious traditions is taken into account? And is the question of the uniqueness of faith in YHWH excluded by concentration on the social-historical background of religious sayings and theological concepts of the Old and New Testaments? Or are both aspects connected with each other in the context of an integrative model? How such a model might look is a matter of considerable controversy in present research (see, with various options, Welker 1998*a*; Herms 1997; Barth 1998; Hübner 1998; and the criticism by Welker 1998*b*).

2.4 Biblical Theology and the Canonical Approach

A new approach in the discipline was initiated first by Gerhard von Rad who, in his epoch-making attempt, conceived of a theology of the Old Testament as the exegesis of the Old Testament texts in the context of their history of transmission, and raised

sober consideration of the facts can help, that these many single pieces of scripture throughout their putting together into a Bible have won a new value over and above their original meaning and that this Bible in its workings through the centuries has an abiding present rather than simply being a monument of a great past.'

the question of the correlation between revelation and history to its hermeneutical principle (see Oeming 2001). Building on this initiative, stress was laid partly on the *event structure of belief in YHWH* (Claus Westermann, Horst-Dietrich Preuss), and partly on the idea of the 'uniqueness of YHWH' as the *centre of the Old Testament* (Walther Zimmerli; see Janowski 1999*a*: 273–81). In the English-speaking realm, following on from the 'biblical theology movement', there was the search for a 'new 'biblical theology' for which Brevard S. Childs with his *biblical theology of the Old and New Testaments* provided a significant canonically orientated impulse (Childs 1992; German translation 1994–6. See Rendtorff 1994; Barth 1998). The canonical approach to the theology of the Old Testament, represented above all in Germany by Rolf Rendtorff (1999; cf. Rendtorff 1991), bases itself not only on the canonical form of the Hebrew Bible, but also makes 'the text itself in its extant canonical form the starting point of the presentation' (Rendtorff 1999: 1). However, in common with the historical criticism that it criticizes, it is dependent on sometimes quite far-reaching hypotheses (see Jeremias 2003: 40–2).

3. CONTEMPORARY PROBLEMS

The short sketch of the history of interpretation has made the problem of 'biblical theology' clear in so far as the unity not only of the Bible but also of the Old and of the New Testaments has become questionable (Ebeling 1955: 82–7). Since the oft-quoted concluding section to the second volume of Gerhard von Rad's *Theology of the Old Testament*, this problem has become ever more burdensome and at the same time an attempt at solving it has been undertaken (Barth 1998: 384). According to von Rad,

a much further aim of our concern is whether a 'biblical theology' is possible in which the dualism between a limited and particular theology of the Old and of the New Testament can be overcome. How such a biblical theology would then be presented is very difficult to conceive. It is, however, encouraging that today the need for it is ever more stressed. (von Rad 1993: 447).

That was more than forty years ago. In view of the continuing task of a biblical theology which makes possible the investigation of the *diversity* of the biblical traditions in their *context*, as well as 'an understanding of the Bible as a whole' (Dohmen 1995), four aspects of the problem need to be examined and in what follows will be sketched: the question of the 'centre' of Scripture, the question of the continuum of revelation, the fact that the Christian Bible is divided into two, and the meaning of biblical canon.

3.1 The 'Centre' of Scripture

The search for a 'centre' of Scripture is currently (again) in discredit, because it allegedly follows an apologetic need to lay out an overarching unity which diminishes the diversity of the biblical traditions and flattens their contradictions (Janowski 1999*a*: 251–5, 273–81). The difficulty in determining from a particular term such as 'covenant', 'justice', or the 'kingship of God' the centre of the Old Testament lies in its execution. This played a central role in the related controversy between Gerhard von Rad and Walther Zimmerli (see Reventlow 1982: 138–47; Preuss 1991: 25–7; Levenson 1991; Albertz 1995, 2001: 11–12; Janowski 1999*a*). It can, however, be met with a reference to the difference between text and subject. Not the terminologically fixable centre of a pluriform *collection of texts* (the Old Testament), but the fact of a *happening* (the relationship between Israel and YHWH) is to be seen as the centre of the Old Testament. This can be explained with the help of the so-called covenant formula, *locus classicus* in Deut. 26: 17–19 (YHWH the God of Israel—Israel the people of God; see Smend 1986*a* and Janowski 1999*a*: 278 n. 135) or with the help of the understanding of Torah (Kaiser 1993: 329–53, on which see Spieckermann, 1997). In spite of the problematic relationship of the Old and New Testaments, it can also be used in the New Testament and precisely so that 'YHWH the God of Israel, Israel the people of God' is the internal, and 'Jesus Christ' the external, centre of the Old Testament, whereby 'the external centre may not be separated from the internal, because "Jesus Christ" in his meaning cannot come to expression without the relationship of YHWH and Israel' (Hermisson 1997: 232; somewhat differently, Merk 1980: 471–2). Thus the question of the connection between the Old and the New Testaments is posed afresh.

3.2 The Continuum of Revelation

The question of how the continuum of the revelatory happening which is testified to in the canonical unity of the Old and New Testaments can be made precise has been answered in recent times either in terms of *tradition history* or *revelation history* (Hartmut Gese, Peter Stuhlmacher) or in terms of *canonical history* (Brevard S. Childs). The relationship of the two Testaments, which are bound together through their witness to the one God and his saving action *vis-à-vis* Israel and the world, does not come in the form of an unbroken continuity that springs over historical and theological tensions, but as a 'contrastive unity' (Zenger 2004). In the horizon of a complete biblical theology, this event, which finds its complete outworking in the self-disclosure of God in Jesus Christ, takes the form of an *eschatologically* directed and, in its dynamic, essentially open *history of salvation* (Haag 1994; Hermisson 1997: 227–33; Kertelge 1994: 433). The unity of the revelation of God, which wins its eschatological clarity in Jesus Christ, includes the diversity of the words which previously went 'to the fathers through the prophets' (Heb. 1: 1–2) and integrates these in the expectation of a coming judging and saving action of God *vis-à-vis* Israel and the world.

3.3 The Christian Bible as Two-Part Scripture

An attempt at a biblical theology has thus to begin from the existence and the recognition of a Christian biblical canon that arises from both Testaments. The extent to which the fact of the canon is relevant for a whole biblical theology follows from the fact that a distinctive theological relationship of both Testaments together was the presupposition for the origin of the Christian canon. By looking back to the Bible that came into existence in Israel (Tanach/Old Testament), on which the form of the Christian Bible was based, the authors of the New Testament proceeded from an understanding of the Christ event as an 'ultimate and decisive act of God in accordance with the scriptures' (Zenger 2004: 14)—that is, that the God of Israel had revealed himself anew in Jesus Christ and, at the same time, had remained true to his promise. The primitive Christian hermeneutic of the Old Testament belongs thus to the origin of Christian theology, and is not something that was later attached to it (examples in Kertelge 1994: 432–3 and Janowski 1999a: 261–4). In this connection it becomes clear that the New Testament, which sets out from its own hermeneutic of Scripture, is not a reading of the Old Testament as an independent canon that is then added on to a complete Old Testament, but that together with that first part, which is later and indeed on the grounds of this procedure called the Old Testament, becomes the one, two-part Christian Bible.

3.4 The Meaning of the Canon

Decisive for the growth of the Christian biblical canon is finally the fact that Old Testament texts are the multi-vocal expression of experiences of God, which first of all entered into the communicative memory of Israel and Judah in a weakly developed form (*Mündlichkeit*), before they were consolidated into the context of more complex processes of decision and selection and institutionalized mnemonics (*Schriftlichkeit*), and finally constituted as fixed elements of the identity of the biblical and post-biblical beliefs in YHWH (*Kanonbildung*; see Schwienhorst-Schönberger 2000: 362). To the relevant aspects for the growth of the Old Testament as canon belong, thus, the discursive character of the tradition, the synthesis of what has come into being, and the coherence of the canon.

3.4.1 The Discursive Character of the Tradition

In the Old Testament, the coming into being of the tradition forms itself as *an explication of speaking about God* which is an essential function of theology. This explication of speaking about God is an explanation of faith which, since Deuteronomy (seventh century BCE) increasingly adopted a discursive form and used technical terms, building didactic sentences, tended towards argumentation, and used scribally informed interpretations (Janowski 2003: 337). In accord with this definition, I agree with the formulation of Christof Hardmeier in terms of 'the discursive character of biblical tradition' (Hardmeier 1995, 2001, esp. 113; on Old Testament 'discourse hermeneutics' see Zenger 2002)—that is, from the fact that the various and in part contradictory statements about YHWH and Israel are to be understood as aspects of a 'systematic of speech utterances' which 'concentrate attention on the various addresses about and to God in the transmitted texts themselves, and which thinks through these speeches as symbolic interactive relational events' (Hardmeier 1995, 2001: 112–13).

This variety of speech about God has its ground in the structure of the Old Testament experience of God and its significant various forms rooted in everyday reality. If one understands a description of God as a culturally minted *explication of experiences of transcendence*, these explications appear in the Old Testament in great polyphony and rich metaphoric. YHWH is, to name only one example, the creative, the hallowing, the rescuing, the besought, the judging, the forgiving, or the almighty God, and he is the shepherd, the king, the father, the mother, the warrior, the lion, or the physician. This *polyphony of Old Testament speech about God* is a mirror of the unity of God in the manifold of his expressions, and indeed expressions which are always culturally formed. To understand the biblical revelation thus means to understand a *culturally minted connection of forms*.

3.4.2 The Synthesis of What has Come into Being

Decisive for the process of building the canon is the further observation that the biblical texts were not simply collected, but were chosen, commented upon, and supplemented. Because this *process of redaction* is of theological significance for the growth of the Old Testament as a collection of scripture, it is necessary to pay particular and careful attention to those 'interfaces'[3] which, like Deuteronomy, the Deuteronomistic History, or the Priestly writing, have become decisive for the redaction of the Old Testament as well as the process of becoming canon.

---

[3] On the term 'interface' (German *Schnittstellen*) see Waschke 2001: 257. The period of the seventh/sixth century BCE was probably such an 'interface' for the growth of the Old Testament, and with it for the formation of Old Testament theology in the sense of a theology of the Old Testament. See Smend 1986b: 111–15; Janowski 2003: 343; and Jeremias 2003: 30–1.

Thus the central *notion of redaction* means the 'editing of a given text in the context of a written tradition and its transformation into a new whole' (Kratz 1997: 367). As opposed to the *reconstruction of preliminary phases*, which is typical of the history of religions and the history of traditions approaches, redaction criticism, which is concerned with 'the process of the growth of the text in its literary and factual dimension' (Kratz 1997: 367) leads to *a synthesis of what has come to be*, in that it follows the growth of the text from its beginnings via various literary stages to its final form (*Endgestalt*), and at every stage asks about the historical, religious, and social-historical implications. None of these possible preliminary stages is transmitted unaltered, and all have been revised from a later, mostly exilic or post-exilic point of view. Redaction means not the deleting of older texts or conceptions, but the reformulation of their original sense under new conditions of understanding (Kratz 1997: 370).

3.4.3 *The Coherence of the Canon*

If redaction history brings to light the *diversity of the biblical traditions* in their literary and factual dimensions, the unavoidable question arises as to how this is to be reconciled with the thesis of *canon as a coherent construction of sense*. Does the canon, and it alone, give rise to this sense, or does it merely present it, in that it makes visible an enrichment of sense and nuances that are either already existing or made apparent through the history of redaction? This question contains several different aspects (Janowski 2003: 345–8), of which the fluid passage from the origin of the canon to its completion is particularly relevant for our enquiry.

The ending of the canon is an act through which texts receive their normative form and function, and from that point on can no longer be added to or revised or interpreted externally (Zenger 2001, following Assmann 1992: 93–7). As a literary and cultural memory, canon is a complex construction. It '*seals*' a historically grown sense of a pluriform collection of writings, and at the same time *newly completes* them. It is, of course, closed from outside through the enclosure of what has been chosen and the exclusion of what has been rejected, but it is also open to new sense constructions on the grounds of its inner multi-vocality and the complex architecture of its parts. The old texts or text levels, therefore, do not function simply as presuppositions of understanding for the final forms that have come into being through redactions, but they possess theological significance in themselves (Gross 2001: 139–40). As a collection of texts whose relevant sense can be compared, the canon builds the 'context in which these different voices can find expression', but it does not 'intrude on their place' (Gross 2001: 129–44; Waschke 2001: 263–5). A leading factor is the insight that the canon is a complex whole, something like a 'contrastive unity' (Zenger 2004: 19–20). In this way it corresponds to the polyphony of Old Testament speech about God, which is a mirror of the unity of God in the diversity of his expressions.

If the question of the biblical canon as a coherent construction of senses is discussed, prudent account must be taken of this multiplicity of aspects. This must be done at the *level of the individual texts and larger contexts*, through the reconstruction of its implications for the history of religion, the history of tradition, and the history of theology, at the *level of the books and parts of the canon*, through the bold attempt at 'thinking things together' (Saebø 1998; Janowski 2003: 344–8), and on the *level of the completed canon* through the grasping of the polyphonous and contrastive language of God, which is ever afresh the address of God to humankind (Waschke 2001: 261). It must also be followed in situations which are the expression of plurality and which correspondingly make possible a variety of interpretations. The fact that pluralism must not be confused with the post-modern 'do as you please', but must be understood much more as a coined connection of forms (Welker 2003), is assisted by the biblical canon and the completion of its inner structure.

4. Conclusion

The above sketch has by no means exhausted the current problems. Among the future tasks of a biblical theology, that of the relationship of biblical theology to Jewish–Christian dialogue, stands alongside the question of the relationship between biblical theology and dogmatics. The not yet fully explained relationship between a religious and historical methodology and the normative claims of the Bible plays a role also in the context of Jewish–Christian dialogue. This is not only because the question of the 'centre' of the Old Testament is a specifically Christian concern (see the contributions in Janowski and Lohfink 1995, 2001, also Janowski 1999*b*), but because the total biblical perspective contains a 'kernel of anti-Judaism' (Levenson 1991 and Janowski 1999*a*: 251–5, 273–81), and to this extent is not suitable for Jewish–Christian dialogue. The fact, however, that the 'Bible of Israel' as the Old Testament is the common Scripture of Jews and Christians to which both communities of faith relate in different ways without monopolizing it, gives grounds for hope, and to both sides if one looks beyond ideological closed minds.

In spite of these open questions, which can be multiplied, there can be general agreement that who ever is concerned with basic questions of a biblical theology is motivated by the wish to contribute to the specific character of Christian faith. The double task of defining our Christian identity without disregarding that Bible which is common to Jews and Christians (Tanach/Old Testament), while at the same time affirming the unity of Scripture (Old and New Testaments) belongs to the central tasks of all theological disciplines in the future. For, the biblical traditions which are connected with each in many ways and which have been bound to each other in many ways build a construction that drives the experience of the work of God among human beings, the living memory of that and the expectation of this action drama and which makes possible historical, cultural and ecclesiastical learning and growing in this knowledge. (Welker 1998a: 1552)

This sketch can be ended by saying that scripture is a self-authenticating witness as a living whole, in that it indicates, in many perspectives, the divine action upon and in the creation, and that it is itself a living source for the present (cf. Luther 1897: 7. 97, 24–5).

BIBLIOGRAPHY

ALBERTZ, R. 1992. *Religionsgeschichte Israels in alttestamentlicher Zeit.* GAT 8/1–2. Göttingen: Vandenhoeck & Ruprecht.

—— 1995, 2001. 'Religionsgeschichte Israels statt Theologie des Alten Testaments! Plädoyer für eine forschungsgeschichtliche Umorientierung'. In Janowski and Lohfink 1995, 2001: 3–24.

ASSMANN, J. 1992. *Das kulturelle Gedächtnis: Schrift, Erinnerung und politische Identität in frühen Hochkulturen.* Munich: Beck.

BARTH, G. 1998. 'Biblische Theologie: Versuch einer vorläufigen Bilanz', *EvTh* 58: 384–99.

BARR, J. 1986. 'Biblische Theologie 1'. In *EKL*, i. 488–94.

BAUR, F. C. 1864. *Vorlesungen über neutestamentliche Theologie (1863)*, ed. Ferdinand Friedrich Baur. Leipzig: Fues.

BENDEMANN, R. VON 2003. ' "Theologie des Neuen Testaments" oder "Religions-geschichte des Frühchristentums?" '. *VuF* 48: 23–8.

CHILDS, B. S. 1992. *Biblical Theology of the Old and New Testaments.* London: SCM Press. German translation: *Die Biblische Theologie der einen Bibel*, i: *Grundstrukturen*, trans. Christiane Oeming, Freiburg: Herder, 1994; ii: *Hauptthemen*, trans. Christiane Oeming, Freiburg: Herder, 1996.

DOHMEN, C. 1995. 'Probleme und Chancen Biblischer Theologie aus alttestamentlicher Sicht'. In Christoph Dohmen and Thomas Söding, eds., *Eine Bibel—zwei Testamente: Positionen Biblischer Theologie*, Uni-Taschenbücher 1893, Paderborn: Schöningh, 9–16.

EBELING, G. 1955. 'Was heißt "Biblische Theologie"?'. In *Wort und Glaube*, i, 3rd edn., Tübingen: Mohr Siebeck, 1967; ET: 'The Meaning of Biblical Theology', in *Word and Faith*, London: SCM Press, 79–97.

GABLER, J. P. 1787. *De iusto discrimine theologiae biblicae et dogmaticae regundisque recte utriusque finibus.* German translation in Merk 1972: 273–84. ET in Sandys-Wunsch and Eldredge 1980: 133–58.

GROSS, W. 2001. 'Ist biblisch-theologische Auslegung ein integrierender Methodenschritt?' In Frank-Lothar Hossfeld, ed., *Wieviel Systematik erlaubt die Schrift? Auf der Suche nach einer gesamtbiblischen Theologie*, Quaestiones Disputatae, 185, Freiburg: Herder, 110–49.

GUNKEL, H. 1927. 'Biblische Theologie und biblische Religionsgeschichte'. In *RGG*, 2nd edn, i. 1090.

HAAG, E. 1994. 'Biblische Theologie IIA'. In *LThK*, 3rd edn., 428–30.

HAHN, F. 1994. 'Vielfalt und Einheit des Neuen Testaments'. *BZ* 38: 161–73.

HARDMEIER, C. 1995, 2001. 'Systematische Elemente einer Theo-logie (*sic*) in der Hebräischen Bibel: das Loben Gottes—ein Kristallisationsmoment biblischer Theologie (*sic*)'. *JBTh* 10: 111–27.

HERMISSON, H.-J. 1997. 'Jesus Christus als externe Mitte des Alten Testaments'. In Christof Landmesser *et al.*, eds., *Jesus Christus als die Mitte der Schrift: Studien zur Hermeneutik des Evangeliums: Festschrift für Otfried Hofius*, BZNW 86, Berlin: Walter de Gruyter, 199–233.

—— 2000. 'Alttestamentliche Theologie und Religionsgeschichte Israels'. *ThLZ*, ser. 3, 199–233.

HERMS, E. 1997. 'Was haben wir an der Bibel? Versuch einer Theologie des christlichen Kanons'. *JBTh* 12: 99–152.

HOLTZMANN, H. J. 1911. *Lehrbuch der neutestamentlichen Theologie*, 2 vols., 2nd edn., ed. Adolf Jülicher and Walter Baur. Tübingen: [Mohr Siebeck].

HÜBNER, H. 1998. 'Fundamentaltheologie und biblische Theologie'. *ThLZ* 123: 443–58.

JANOWSKI, B. 1999*a*. 'Der eine Gott der beiden Testamente: Grundfragen einer Biblischen Theologie'. In *Die rettende Gerechtigkeit: Beiträge zur Theologie des Alten Testaments*, ii, Neukirchen-Vluyn: Neukirchener Verlag, 249–84.

—— 1999*b*. 'Die "Kleine Biblia": Zur Bedeutung der Psalmen für eine Theologie des Alten Testaments'. In *Die rettende Gerechtigkeit: Beiträge zur Theologie des Alten Testaments*, ii, Neukirchen-Vluyn: Neukirchener Verlag, 125–64.

—— 2003. 'Theologie des Alten Testaments: Plädoyer für eine integrative Perspektive'. In *Der Gott des Lebens: Beiträge zur Theologie des Alten Testaments*, iii. Neukirchen-Vluyn: Neukirchener Verlag, 315–50.

—— and LOHFINK, N., eds. 1995, 2001. *Religionsgeschichte Israels oder Theologie des Alten Testaments?*, *JBTh* 10.

JEREMIAS, J. 2003. 'Neuere Entwürfe zu einer "Theologie des Alten Testaments" '. *VuF* 48: 29–58.

KÄHLER, M. 1897. 'Bibel'. In *RE*, 3rd edn., ii. 686–91.

KAISER, O. 1993. *Der Gott des Alten Testaments: Theologie des Alten Testaments*, i: *Grundlegung*. Uni-Taschenbücher 1747. Göttingen: Vandenhoeck & Ruprecht.

KEEL, O. 2001. 'Religionsgeschichte Israels oder Theologie des Alten Testaments?' In Frank-Lothar Hossfeld, ed., *Wieviel Systematik erlaubt die Schrift? Auf der Suche nach einer gesamtbiblischen Theologie*, QD 185, Freiburg: Herder, 88–109.

KERTELGE, K. 1994. 'Biblische Theologie IIB'. In *LThK*, 3rd edn., ii. 430–3.

KÖCKERT, M. 1998. 'Von einem zum einzigen Gott: Zur Diskussion der Religionsgeschichte Israels'. *Berliner Theologische Zeitschrift*, 15: 135–75.

KRATZ, R. G. 1997. 'Redaktionsgeschichte/Redaktionskritik I'. In *TRE*, xxviii. 367–78.

LEVENSON, J. D. 1991. 'Warum Juden sich nicht für Biblische Theologie interessieren', *EvTh* 51: 402–30.

LUTHER, M. 1897. *D. Martin Luthers Werke: Kritische Gesamtausgabe*, ed. J. F. K. Knaake *et al.* Weimar: Hermann Böhlau.

MERK, O. 1972. *Biblische Theologie des Neuen Testaments in ihrer Anfangszeit: Ihre methodischen Probleme bei Johann Philipp Gabler und Georg Lorenz Bauer und deren Nachwirkungen*. Marburger theologische Studien, 9. Marburg: Elwert.

—— 1980. 'Biblische Theologie II'. In *TRE* vi. 455–77.

OEMING, M. 2001. 'Gesamtbiblische Theologien der Gegenwart: Das Verhältnis von AT und NT in der hermeneutischen Diskussion seit Gerhard von Rad'. In *Das Alte Testament als Teil des christlichen Kanons? Studien zu gesamtbiblischen Theologien der Gegenwart*, Zürich: Pano Verlag, 51–62, 71–125.

PREUSS, H. D. 1991. *Theologie des Alten Testaments*, i: *JHWHs erwählendes und verpflichtendes Handeln*. Stuttgart: Kohlhammer.

RAD, G. VON 1993. *Theologie des Alten Testaments*, ii: *Die Theologie der prophetischen Überlieferungen Israels*, 10th edn. Munich: Chr. Kaiser.

RENDTORFF, R. 1991. 'Theologie des Alten Testaments: Überlegungen zu einem Neuansatz'. In *Kanon und Theologie: Vorarbeiten zu einer Theologie des Alten Testaments*, Neukirchen-Vluyn: Neukirchener Verlag, 1–14.

—— 1994. 'Rezension B. S. Childs, Biblical Theology of the Old and New Testaments'. *JBTh* 9: 359–69.

—— 1999. *Theologie des Alten Testaments: Ein kanonischer Entwurf*, i: *Kanonische Grundlegung*. Neukirchen-Vluyn: Neukirchener Verlag.

REUMANN, J. 1998. 'Profiles, Problems, and Possibilities in Biblical Theology Today I–II'. *Kerygma und Dogma*, 44: 145–69.

REVENTLOW, H. GRAF 1982. *Hauptprobleme der alttestamentlichen Theologie im 20. Jahrhundert*. Erträge der Forschung, 173; Darmstadt: Wissenschaftliche Buchgesellschaft.

SAEBØ, M. 1988. 'Vom "Zusammen-Denken" zum Kanon: Aspekte der traditionsgeschichtlichen Endstadien des Alten Testaments'. *JBTh* 3: 115–33.

SANDYS-WUNSCH, J., and ELDREDGE, L. 1980. 'J. P. Gabler and the Distinction between Biblical and Dogmatic Theology: Translation, Commentary and Discussion of his Originality'. SJT 33: 133–58.

SCHMIDT, S. 1671, 1676. *Collegium biblicum in quo dicta Veteris et Novi Testamenti iuxta seriem locorum communium theologicorum explicandur*. Argentorati.

SCHWIENHORST-SCHÖNBERGER, L. 2000. 'Gottesbilder des Alten Testaments', *ThPQ* 148: 358–68.

SMEND, R. 1986a. 'Die Mitte des Alten Testaments (1970)'. In *Die Mitte des Alten Testaments: Gesammelte Studien*, i, BEvTh 99, Munich: Chr. Kaiser, 73–82.

—— 1986b. 'Theologie im Alten Testament'. In *Die Mitte des Alten Testaments: Gesammelte Studien*, i, BEvTh 99, Munich: Chr. Kaiser, 104–17.

SPENER, P. J. 1675. *Pia Desideria*.

SPIECKERMANN, H. 1997. 'Die Verbindlichkeit des Alten Testaments: Unzeitgemäße Betrachtungen zu einem ungeliebten Thema'. *JBTh* 12: 25–51.

STUHLMACHER, P. 1995. *Wie treibt man Biblische Theologie?* Biblisch-theologische Studien, 24. Neukirchen-Vluyn: Neukirchener Verlag.

WALTER, P. 1994. 'Biblische Theologie I'. In *LThK*, 3rd edn., ii. 426–8.

WASCHKE, E.-J. 2001. 'Zur Frage einer alttestamentlichen Theologie im Vergleich zur Religionsgeschichte Israels'. In *Der Gesalbte: Studien zur alttestamentlichen Theologie*, BZAW 306, Berlin: Walter de Gruyter, i. 253–66.

WELKER, M. 1998a. 'Biblische Theologie II'. In *RGG*, 4th edn., i. 1549–53.

—— 1998b. 'Sozio-metaphysische Theologie und Biblische Theologie: Zu E. Herms "Was haben wir an der Bibel?" '. *JBTh* 13: 309–22.

—— 2003. 'Sola Scriptura? The Authority of the Bible in Pluralistic Environment'. In Brent A. Strawn and Nancy R. Bowen, eds., *A God So Near: Essays on Old Testament Theology in Honor of Patrick D. Miller*. Winona Lake, Ind.: Eisenbrauns, 375–91.

Wrede, W. 1897. *Über Aufgabe und Methode der sogenannten Neutestamentlichen Theologie*. Göttingen: Vandenhoeck & Ruprecht.

Zenger, E. 2002. 'Exegese des Alten Testaments im Spannungsfeld von Judentum und Christentum'. *Theologische Revue*, 98: 357–66.

—— 2004. 'Heilige Schrift der Juden und der Christen'. In *Einleitung in das Alte Testament*, 5th edn., Kohlhammer-Studienbücher Theologie, 1.1, Stuttgart: Kohlhammer, 11–33.

—— 2004. 'Die Tora/der Pentateuch als Ganzes'. In *Einleitung in das Alte Testament*, 5th edn., Kohlhammer-Studienbücher Theologie, 1.1, Stuttgart: Kohlhammer, 60–73.

CHAPTER 41

THE BIBLE IN ETHICS

ERYL W. DAVIES

A. METHODOLOGICAL ISSUES

i. The Old Testament

Anyone who has been concerned to examine the ethics of the OT has had to contend with the fact that they are engaged in a difficult and highly complex enterprise. The main problem arises from the sheer amount of material that needs to be analysed. Moral considerations feature prominently in Israel's laws, and are clearly evident in the denunciations levelled by the prophets against their compatriots. Many of the narratives contained in the historical books raise profound ethical questions, and moral issues frequently recur in the sayings of the wise and in various passages in the Psalms. Thus those attempting to write a volume on OT ethics are immediately faced with the perplexing problem of deciding precisely where to begin.

Some scholars—especially those writing in the nineteenth and early part of the twentieth century—opted for a chronological approach to the biblical material, and sought to trace the ethical values of the OT from the patriarchal period down to the exilic and post-exilic age, often with the aim of demonstrating how Israel's morality gradually developed from crude and primitive beginnings to the more enlightened and sophisticated insights of later times (cf. Mitchell 1912; Smith 1923). Other, more recent, scholars have preferred to focus on particular literary genres, such as the biblical narratives (Janzen 1994; Wenham 2000), or the legal (Harrelson 1980), prophetic (E. W. Davies 1981), or wisdom (Blenkinsopp 1983) traditions. Still others have favoured a thematic approach, and have sought to examine the teaching of the

OT concerning such matters as wealth and poverty, war and violence, marriage and divorce, land and inheritance (Rodd 2001). But whichever method is adopted, there is now general agreement among scholars that ethics deserves to be treated as a distinct discipline within biblical studies, and that the subject should be studied in its own right and not subsumed under the broader category of 'biblical theology', as was once the common practice (cf. e.g. Eichrodt 1967: 316–79).

A further problem that faces those attempting to write a volume on the ethics of the OT is to decide on the methodological approach that best suits the subject-matter under discussion. Some biblical interpreters have opted for a historical-critical analysis of the biblical material (cf. Otto 1994), while others have preferred to adopt a literary-critical approach (cf. Mills 2001). Those who favour the former tend to focus on the moral beliefs and ethical principles embraced by the people of Israel and Judah, in so far as these can be reconstructed from the biblical texts. In effect, the OT is regarded as a window through which the perceptive reader can observe the social world and daily experiences of the ancient Israelites and thus come to some understanding of the manners and mores of the peoples of biblical times. The task of the biblical scholar, according to this approach, is to describe the type of community that produced the ethical norms found in the biblical text and to illuminate the historical and social context in which those norms were originally formulated.

The historical-critical method, however, is not without its difficulties, for the task of describing the ethical values embraced by the people of ancient Israel is by no means as straightforward as might initially be supposed. In the first place, serious reservations have been expressed concerning the possibility of reaching behind the biblical text in an attempt to describe the moral norms of a people who can no longer be observed or questioned at first hand. The task is made all the more daunting by the fact that ancient Israel consisted of diverse groups that probably adhered to a wide variety of ethical ideals, and these ideals were inevitably changed, modified, and refined from one period to another. Any comprehensive account of the ethics of ancient Israel would thus need to include the distinctive moral insights represented by various groups in various periods of Israel's history; but since the requisite evidence needed to carry out such a study is not available, the picture of ancient Israelite ethics must, of necessity, remain fragmentary and incomplete (cf. Barton 1983: 118–19; Knight 1995b: 4–5).

Moreover, the OT writings probably reflect, at least for the most part, the 'official' religion of Israel, and the biblical interpreter must constantly be aware of the possible dissemblance between the thoughts and perspectives of the 'ordinary Israelites' and those who had a hand in producing the biblical canon. It is often tacitly assumed, for example, that religion was *the* decisive influence in moral matters for the people of Israel, but due allowance must be made for the fact that the OT is largely a body of religious documents produced by a people for whom religion was presumably a dominant interest. Of course, Israel's ethic appears to demand a religious interpretation, but this is only because it has already been given one in the documents at our disposal (cf. McKeating 1979: 70). This leads to an important observation, the implications of which have not always been fully appreciated: the ethics of the OT and those of ancient Israelite society do not necessarily coincide, and the former may not always be an accurate representation of the latter (cf. Barton 1978). As a result, many studies that purport to be an examination of the ethics of ancient Israel have, in fact, proved to be little more than descriptions of the 'official' religion advocated in the OT.

In view of the difficulties inherent in the historical-critical approach, some scholars have favoured adopting a literary analysis of the biblical material. Adherents of this approach do not necessarily minimize the importance of past efforts to understand the original historical setting of the ethical teaching contained in the OT; they merely believe that such research has probably taken us as far as we are able to go, and that it is now time to move on and explore the text from a different perspective. The literary approach involves a close reading and detailed exposition of specific biblical texts that raise issues of ethical concern, and a careful analysis is then conducted of the language, structure, and genre of the passage in question. For example, the story of David's adultery with Bathsheba and Nathan's parable of the poor man's ewe-lamb (2 Samuel 11–12) is viewed primarily as a literary composition that was intended to stimulate the reader to reflect on human behaviour when faced with particular moral choices (cf. Gunn 1978: 87–111). Whether the narrative reflects an actual occurrence in the lives of the individuals concerned is regarded as a secondary (and perhaps even irrelevant) consideration. Rather, the narrative is read primarily as a literary composition that gives concrete form to abstract ethical issues, and which challenges its readers to reassess their own values and to reconsider their own moral principles accordingly.

Of course, the literary approach, like the historical-critical approach, is not without its difficulties, for the ethical material in the OT is preserved in books which date from different periods and which have often been subjected to a long process of collating and editing. Consequently, the ethical principles that they contain are not always self-consistent, and scholars who have attempted to analyse the subject in any depth have inevitably been confronted with the unresolved tensions that exist between various ethical demands. Moreover, some of the key ethical terms that appear in the OT, such as 'righteousness' and 'holiness', have a wide variety of connotations, and what such concepts mean in one literary context may be quite different from what they mean in another. Any attempt to study the subject of OT ethics from a literary-critical point of view must therefore be carefully nuanced, for biblical interpreters are faced with the difficult balancing act of recognizing the rich diversity of the ethical principles of the OT, on the one hand, and upholding the essential unity of biblical thought, on the other.

Thus, whether OT scholars opt for the historical-critical or the literary-critical approach, it is clear that they are faced with numerous methodological problems. This may well be the reason why the subject of ethics has, for some considerable time, remained a much neglected area of OT research. Fortunately, the tide is now beginning to turn, and the current resurgence of interest in the field of OT ethics is warmly to be welcomed, notwithstanding the reservations expressed by some scholars that the writing of an 'ethics of the OT' may well ultimately prove to be an impossible task (cf. Rodd 1990: 208–9).

ii. The New Testament

Many of the methodological problems confronting scholars of the OT have also had to be addressed by their NT counterparts. Here, too, the sheer amount of ethical material that has to be analysed is so great that it is difficult to know how it can be organized and presented in a coherent and systematic way. Some scholars, aware that an exhaustive treatment of all the relevant NT material would probably occupy several volumes, have limited their research to a particular passage (e.g. Matthew 5–7; cf. Strecker 1988; 1 Corinthians 5–7; cf. Rosner 1999), book (e.g. Mark; cf. Via 1985), or author (e.g. Paul; cf. Sampley 1991) within the NT canon. But those who have attempted to write a full-blown account of the 'ethics of the NT' have been faced with the problem of deciding where to begin. Many have opted to start with the ethical teaching of Jesus before moving on to discuss the ethical traditions reflected in the epistles of Paul and in other NT writings (cf. Schnackenburg 1965; Sanders 1975; Schrage 1988). Others prefer to begin with Paul, partly because his letters represent the earliest extant Christian writings and partly because, of all the NT authors, it is Paul who offers the most profound and extensive wrestling with major ethical issues (cf. Houlden 1973). Many NT interpreters, however, have preferred to adopt a synthetic approach to the biblical material and have sought a unity of ethical perspective within the rich diversity of the canonical writings. Sometimes this has been done by focusing on a single principle (such as love; cf. Furnish 1972) or on a cluster of central images (such as 'cross', 'community', and 'new creation'; cf. Hays 1996a) that might provide an interpretative framework in which the ethical material of the NT could be explored.

Scholars who have adopted the historical-critical approach to the NT writings have largely been concerned to reconstruct the moral teaching of the historical Jesus and the ethical values embraced by members of the early church. Attempts have also been made to describe the distinctive character and 'ethos' of the communities within which those values developed, and the ways in which the early Christians absorbed the ethical traditions of the surrounding nations (Meeks 1987; McDonald 1998). Such studies have undoubtedly shed much light on the background of Jesus' teaching and on the social context and community setting of Paul's ministry. Yet, the historical, or 'diachronic', approach to NT ethics has its limitations. As is well known, attempts to reconstruct the 'Jesus of history' are beset with difficulties, and there remain many uncertainties as to which ethical pronouncements can be traced back to Jesus himself and which are the product of later tradition. Similarly, it is difficult to obtain a clear picture of the ethical beliefs and social organization of the earliest Christian communities, since scholars are forced to rely primarily on the idealized description of the early church in Acts, and on a tentative reconstruction of pre-Pauline traditions in Paul's epistles.

In view of these difficulties, many scholars have preferred to focus on the NT texts themselves, rather than on the social reality to which those texts are supposed to bear witness. In this regard, many useful studies have appeared which illuminate the ethical perspective of the individual evangelists or the moral teaching encountered in the Johannine writings or in the Pauline and deutero-Pauline epistles. The problem arises, however, when the interpreter attempts to discover a moral coherence within the NT canon, for there are sometimes significant differences between the biblical authors regarding particular ethical issues (cf. Hays 1990: 44–5). One need only compare, for example, the treatment of divorce in Matthew (5: 31–2; 19: 3–12) and Paul (1 Cor. 7: 10–16), or the radically different assessments of the relationship of the Christian community to the Roman Empire reflected in such texts as Romans 13 and Revelation 13. Such differences serve as a salutary reminder that one cannot properly speak of *the* ethics of the NT (any more than one can speak of *the* ethics of the OT), for what we have is a variety of ethical perspectives that sometimes complement and sometimes contradict one another. The task facing the biblical interpreter is to ensure that each individual voice is heard, and that the tensions between different texts regarding moral issues be allowed to stand. Of course, the diversity of moral viewpoints within the NT raises a profound hermeneutical problem, for one is inevitably left wondering how the NT documents can serve as a reliable guide to faith and practice if its writings are not internally consistent. The hermeneutical problems faced by the biblical interpreter will be discussed below; here it is sufficient to note that any attempt to provide a clear, systematic account of the ethics of the NT is bound to prove a complex and challenging task.

B. The Basis of Old Testament Ethics

i. Law

Scholars who have examined the basis of the ethical teaching contained in the OT have generally focused their attention primarily on the traditions of the law and the covenant. YHWH's commands were proclaimed as binding for the people of Israel, and those commands were expressed in concentrated form in the Decalogue (Exod. 20: 1–17). One of the chief motivations for obedience was that God had acted to liberate his people from their bondage, and Israel's readiness to observe his commandments was regarded as a fitting response to YHWH's initiative. Significantly, the commands of the Decalogue begin with a reminder that 'I am the LORD your God who brought you out of the land of Egypt' (Exod. 20: 2), and the theology of Deuteronomy is predicated on the assumption that God's sovereign action in history demanded a reciprocal response from the people of Israel, which is to take the form of obedience to the divine will.

Recent studies, however, have suggested that the law does not necessarily provide an adequate picture of the generally accepted norms of behaviour embraced by the people of ancient Israel, for Hebrew legislation probably contained only the minimum standards of conduct required of every morally decent person (E. W. Davies 1995: 45–6; Wenham 2000: 79–87). Precepts safeguarding life, marriage, and property, such as those found in the Decalogue of Exodus 20, were never intended to provide a complete system of rules governing all aspects of human behaviour. On the contrary, such stipulations contained only the basic minimum of God's requirements of his people, and since such demands usually involved only some measure of forbearance on their part, they must have been regarded as precepts that could easily have been obeyed. To refrain from killing another person, for example, was a duty which was presumably regarded as easy to discharge, requiring no extraordinary moral heroism. Such laws as those contained in the Decalogue defined merely what ancient Israelite society regarded as the minimum conditions for a tolerable social life. Even though the stipulations of the law were binding, and any infringement of them would be duly punished, it was the voluntary participation of the people in acts which they themselves believed to be good, right, and proper that ultimately made it possible for the social order to function equitably.

Certainly, many of the practices against which the eighth-century prophets inveighed came within that area of moral action that was not regulated by law. For example, as far as is known, Israel had no sumptuary laws, and if this was so, Amos's condemnation of the people's extravagance and luxury (Amos 6: 4–6) cannot have been rooted in Israel's legal tradition. Similarly, the law did not concern itself with sobriety, and consequently Isaiah's polemic against drunkenness (Isa. 5: 11, 22) could have had no basis in any legal stipulation. Further, it is unlikely that the prophetic condemnation of pride, self-gratification, and vanity (Isa. 3: 16; 5: 21) was rooted in the law, for it is difficult to see how such attitudes of mind could have been effectively controlled through legislation. In such cases, conduct must be governed by mutual trust and respect, rather than by strict compliance with defined obligations.

Thus, although the law has largely dominated ethical discussions of the OT, it is important to recognize that Hebrew legislation cannot be regarded as a full or comprehensive statement of the ethical imperatives incumbent upon the people of

Israel. The fact is that Israelite laws 'set a floor for behaviour within society', but they do not necessarily 'prescribe an ethical ceiling' (Wenham 2000: 80). In view of the inadequacy of the law to regulate all aspects of human behaviour, the possibility needs to be considered that the ethics of the OT may be based on factors apart from obedience to the express will of God. In this regard, scholarly attention has recently focused in particular on the concepts of 'natural law' and 'imitation of God'.

ii. Natural Law

The idea that a 'natural law' type of ethic may be found in the OT was mooted over fifty years ago by Friedrich Horst (1950–1), although, at the time, his arguments met with little response in the scholarly world. More recently, however, scholars such as James Barr (1993) and John Barton (1979) have been prepared to consider afresh the possibility that a 'natural law' ethic may be found in some of the writings of the OT canon. It has, of course, long been recognized that some such ethic undergirds much of the wisdom literature of the OT, but Barr finds traces of the concept also in the Law, the Prophets, and the Psalms (1993: 81–101). By his own admission, Barr started out as one who was instinctively 'distrustful of the entire box of tricks that makes up traditional natural theology' (1993: 103); but upon closer examination of the evidence he was forced to concede that the phenomenon was more prominent in the OT than he had hitherto supposed, and he concluded that it formed a continuous tradition which could be traced from OT times down to the period of the post-NT church.

But what are the criteria to indicate that a 'natural law' type of ethic is operative within a particular passage? Barton (1979: 9–14) suggests that one possible clue is that the passage in question may well indicate that the punishment for a particular offence will correspond to the crime. Those who offend against the norms of society will receive their just deserts, for a kind of 'poetic justice' is regarded as operative in the world. A good example of this retributive justice is found in Isa. 5: 8–10, where the prophet condemns those who dispossess the poor of their property. The punishment that awaits those who 'join house to house' is that 'many houses shall be desolate'; the punishment in store for those who add 'field to field' in an attempt to increase their crops is that the expected produce will be drastically reduced: 'ten acres of vineyard shall yield but one bath, and a homer of seed shall yield a mere ephah'. If such an ethic can be shown to exist in the prophetic literature, then its appeal to the prophets is easy to comprehend, for it was a system of law that presupposed the notion of an immutable justice. Its precepts could not be altered, repealed, or abolished, and there would be little point in resorting to casuistry in order to escape its obligation, for its principles were binding at all times and in all places.

The possibility that a 'natural law' type of ethic undergirds some of the biblical material may well open up significant new perspectives in our understanding of OT ethics, and it may force us to question some of the presuppositions which have hitherto been regarded as axiomatic. For example, the tendency to regard the ethics of the OT as exclusively revelational may need to be reconsidered, for it may well be that Scripture bears witness to principles of right conduct that are discoverable rationally. Moreover, the view, often adumbrated, that the type of ethic evinced in the wisdom literature is to be regarded as something of an aberration within the OT may need to be revised, for the ethic of the sages may well have been more orthodox and normative than has hitherto been allowed.

iii. Imitation of God

The significance of the notion of imitating God for the ethics of the OT was suggested by Martin Buber in an article published as long ago as 1926; however, until comparatively recently, the concept has been regarded as of only marginal significance in discussions of OT ethics. But there is some evidence to suggest that scholars are now prepared to recognize that the notion is more prevalent in the OT than was previously thought, and that the moral norms encountered in the Hebrew Scriptures arise out of imitation of God's character as well as out of obedience to God's will (cf. E. W. Davies 1999).

The clearest expression of the principle of *imitatio Dei* in the OT is to be found in Lev. 19: 2, which forms part of the so-called Holiness Code: 'You shall be holy, for I the LORD your God am holy' (cf. Lev. 11: 44; 20: 7, 26; 21: 8). God is here presented not so much as the source of ethical commands but as the pattern of ethical behaviour. Although at first sight it might appear that the command to be holy represents a utopian and abstract ideal, the principle underlying the law—that people must emulate the character and actions of God—is found in various legal enactments in the Pentateuch. Thus, male and female slaves, and the resident alien in Israel, were to be given rest on the sabbath because God himself had ceased from his work of creation on the seventh day (Exod. 20: 8–11; cf. 31: 12–17). Further, the divine partiality shown towards the poor and needy was to provide an example for a similar concern to be exhibited by the Israelites (cf. Deut. 10: 17–19; 15: 13–15). The frequent exhortations in Deuteronomy to 'walk in the ways of the LORD' (Deut. 8: 6; 10: 12; 11: 22; 26: 17; 28: 9) similarly suggest that Israel was destined to travel on a journey in which God was to lead the way as a guide and example for the people to follow.

The notion of *imitatio Dei* also underlies many of the prophetic utterances, for some of the characteristics postulated of God in the OT are precisely those that were considered by the prophets as the most noble expressions of human behaviour. The prophets conceived of God as possessing certain moral qualities, and they believed that these same qualities should be reflected in the behaviour of the Israelites towards one another. Thus, for example, Isaiah, at the time of his call, encountered the holy God in the sanctuary (Isaiah 6), and this encounter set the tone of much of his subsequent preaching and determined the way in which he was to interpret God's demands. God's holiness was the central standard by which Israel's life would be judged, and the iniquities that were present in Judah were largely due to the fact that the people had neglected the presence of the holy God in their midst (Isa. 1: 4; 30: 9–11; 31: 1).

While the notion of imitating God is not particularly prominent in the Psalms, the concept is implied in the way in which God's character and deeds are presented as the basis on which the pious should model their lives. The frequent descriptions of God's justice, mercy, and compassion in the Psalms (cf. 25: 6; 33: 5; 37: 28; 119: 156) were clearly designed to inculcate the same ethical values in the worshipper, for God's character was regarded as the foundation upon which the believer's life should be based. The extent to which the Psalmist viewed human virtues as a reflection of the divine is particularly well illustrated in the twin acrostic Psalms 111 and 112, for the attributes of God set forth in the former are regarded in the latter as being reflected in the life of the true believer. In fact, Psalm 112 may be understood as an elaborate way of saying that the characteristics of the pious mirror those of God himself, and that an element of conformity exists between the acts of the faithful and those of the God whom they worship.

The biblical narratives are also important in this regard, for it was through them that the basic character and nature of God were established. After all, if the Israelites were to emulate YHWH, it was clearly vital that they should have some knowledge of the divine nature and attributes, and it was through stories relating God's encounters with his people that such knowledge was mediated to them. The manner in which God was portrayed in the narratives was thus of profound significance, for the depiction of the divine character was to become the basis for subsequent ethical reflection. If God could be shown to have acted with justice and compassion, it was surely incumbent upon his people to act likewise; if he had identified himself with the weak and oppressed, it was surely imperative that his people should do the same. The character and actions of God were not presented as morally neutral observations; rather, they were designed to inculcate a sense of duty and moral responsibility in the people and to provide them with a model of the type of behaviour that should be mirrored in their own lives (cf. Birch 1991: 125).

The above discussion of the basis of OT ethics suggests that a reappraisal is needed of the way in which its ethical teaching is often viewed. It has been customary for those discussing the ethics of the OT to focus on the revealed will of God, and the common perception of OT morality is that it is framed in the language of command and obedience. However, the presence in the biblical documents of concepts such as 'natural law' and 'imitating God' should serve as a salutary reminder that there is far more to OT ethics than the mere observance of prescribed rules.

C. NEW TESTAMENT ETHICS

i. Jesus and the Law

One of the central questions concerning Jesus' ethical teaching revolves around his attitude to the law of Moses. Did he accept and endorse the law, or did he intend to abrogate it in the light of his own mission and preaching concerning the coming of the kingdom of God? There are certainly passages in the gospels that imply a negative appraisal of the law on the part of Jesus. His actions and words were often at variance with the demands of the law: he healed on the sabbath (Mark 3: 1–6), enjoyed table fellowship with tax-collectors and sinners (Mark 2: 15–16), and broke down the traditional barriers between clean and unclean (Mark 5: 25–34; 7: 1–23). At one point Jesus suggests that divorce, though sanctioned by the law (Deut. 24: 1), was in conflict with the original will of God the creator (Matt. 19: 3–12; cf. Gen. 1: 27; 2: 24), and in the antitheses of the Sermon on the Mount ('you have heard it said . . . but I tell you'; Matt. 5: 21–48) Jesus implies that he is providing an entirely new and radical understanding of God's will. Other passages also suggest that the coming kingdom of God could not but set the law in a new light (cf. Mark 2: 21–2), and in Luke 16: 16 there is an explicit contrast between the law and the prophets, on the one hand, and the kingdom of God, on the other.

At other times, however, Jesus appears to reaffirm some of the commandments of the OT and to regard them as suitable guidelines for proper ethical conduct. For example, he endorses the provisions concerning loving God (Mark 12: 29–30; cf. Deut. 6: 4–5), loving one's neighbour (Mark 12: 31; cf. Lev. 19: 18), and honouring parents (Matt. 15: 4; Mark 7: 10; cf. Exod. 20: 12; 21: 17). Moreover, when the rich young man asked Jesus what he must do to inherit eternal life, Jesus pointed to some of the commands of the Decalogue (Mark 10: 19). Such passages suggest that Jesus was deeply rooted in the moral teaching of his people, and that he regarded the continuing validity of the law as important.

The ambivalence in Jesus' attitude to the law was probably due to the fact that he was opposed, not to the law *per se*, but to a misapprehension of its purpose and significance, such as that exhibited by the Pharisees. They had given detailed attention to trifling matters of the law, such as the tithing of herbs from the garden, but had neglected its weightier demands, such as the need for justice, mercy, and faithfulness (Matt. 23: 23). Their rigid interpretation of the law is well exemplified in their attitude towards the sabbath. According to the Pharisees, it was forbidden on the sabbath to pluck grain from the cornfields or to heal any disease that was not immediately life-threatening; on the other hand, Jesus approved of both (Mark 2: 23–3: 6), and he justified his actions by stating that 'the sabbath was made for humankind, not humankind for the sabbath' (Mark 2: 27). The point that Jesus makes here is that God did not create the Sabbath—and, by implication, the law— to be an intolerable burden upon the people; nor was it intended to be a constraint upon human activities; on the contrary, the law was given as an act of kindness, and was to be regarded as a gift and an opportunity. To fulfil the law did not entail observing this or that commandment or embracing all its requirements; rather, it meant carrying out its intent, for what mattered to Jesus above all was the inward disposition of the individual. Nowhere is this more evident than in Jesus' statement that the content of the law could be summarized in the dual command to love God and to love one's neighbour (Mark 12: 28–31).

For Jesus, the command of love (Greek *agapē*) was the absolute norm to which all other commandments were secondary. Love was the fundamental, all-encompassing attitude that must always be exhibited in the lives of his followers. Jesus' emphasis on the primacy of love did not, of course, mean that all the other commandments were null and void, but love was to be regarded as the quintessence of all God's commandments and was to form a principle by which those commandments could be judged. Yet, the love demanded by Jesus was not an emotional or mystical relationship with God; nor was it a vague, abstract love for humanity in general; rather, it entailed concrete involvement and personal action, as Matt. 25: 31–46 makes clear.

ii. Jesus and Eschatology

NT scholars have generally recognized that Jesus' ethical teaching was profoundly influenced by his belief in the imminence of the kingdom of God (cf. Schrage 1988: 13–40). The significance of eschatology for Jesus' ethical teaching was long ago recognized by Albert Schweitzer, who argued that Jesus' world-view—like that of his contemporaries—was dominated by apocalyptic eschatology. The present was merely a time of preparation for the coming of the kingdom, and Jesus' ethical instruction, as exemplified in such passages as the Sermon on the Mount, was intended as an 'interim ethic' (*Interimsethik*), relevant only for the very brief interval between the proclamation of the kingdom and its imminent advent (Schweitzer 1910: 364; cf. McDonald 1993: 82–5). Even scholars who expressed considerable reservations concerning Schweitzer's interpretation of the kingdom in purely futuristic terms recognized that a link existed between his eschatological outlook and his ethical teaching. Thus, for example, C. H. Dodd, who argued in favour of a 'realized eschatology' (1938: 50–1), believed that Jesus' ethical teaching was intended to serve as a guide for positive moral action on the part of those who had already received the kingdom. Jesus' call for appropriate conduct was predicated on the assumption that 'the zero hour in which decisive action is called for' had already come (Dodd 1951: 60).

Although more recent scholars have tended to modify both Schweitzer's thoroughgoing eschatology and Dodd's 'realized eschatology', there is, nevertheless, general recognition that Jesus' ethical teaching cannot be divorced from his eschatological outlook. In Jesus' teaching, the eschaton, with its implied judgement, provided a powerful motivation for proper ethical conduct, as is evident from the so-called crisis parables (e.g. Luke 12: 54–6), and from Jesus' pronouncement that all would have to appear before God's judgement-seat and account for every careless word uttered (Matt. 12: 36–7) and every unjust action performed (Mark 12: 40). It was because the kingdom was imminent that Jesus issued his call to repentance: since God was about to make the final intervention in human affairs, the only appropriate response was for the people to abandon their sinful ways (Mark 1: 15). The call to repentance did not mean merely a change of attitude; rather, it involved a total reorientation that was to affect every sphere of life. But those who heeded Jesus' call to repent would reap abundant rewards, for they would partake in the blessings of the kingdom. Thus, in addition to the threat of judgement, the promise of reward also belongs among the eschatological motifs in Jesus' ethical teaching, although it is emphasized that such rewards are a gift of God's grace and are not to be regarded as a human claim upon God (cf. Schnackenburg 1965: 144–67). Indeed, the point of some of Jesus' parables (such as the parable of the master and servant in Luke 17: 7–10) was to dispense with all speculative calculation of reward and to emphasize that humans cannot put God in their debt. Those who will be rewarded will be those who seek no reward, for their actions will be based on love, and love cannot be motivated by any selfish concern.

Of course, the eschatological perspective does not determine the entire corpus of Jesus' ethical teaching in the Gospel tradition, and it is important to recognize other influences at work in the proclamation of Jesus' message. Some of Jesus' exhortations—such as the command to love God and one's neighbour (Mark 12: 29–31)—do not seem to have been directly affected by his expectation concerning the end of the present world order and the imminent advent of the new age. Moreover, his observations that humans cannot extend their life span by anxiety (Matt. 6: 25–34), and that taking a neighbour to court may prove to be a costly and futile exercise (Matt. 5: 25) appear to be based on common sense and rational insight, and such sayings are redolent of the type of sentiments expressed in the wisdom traditions of Judaism (cf. Winton 1990). Yet, it is important to recognize that many of the sayings concerning wisdom and folly in Jesus' preaching are imbued with an eschatological significance: thus the foolishness against which Jesus warns in the parable of the rich fool (Luke 12: 16–21) is the folly of those who do not heed his warning concerning the approach of the eschatological hour; similarly, the prudence commended by Jesus in the parable of the shrewd steward (Luke 16: 1–9) consists in recognizing the imminence of God's judgement and acting accordingly.

iii. The Background of Paul's Ethics

Much attention has been given in discussions of Paul's ethics to the basis and background of his moral teaching (cf. Furnish 1968: 25–67). Were his moral norms grounded in the gospel proclaimed by Jesus, or was the apostle appealing to broader, common-sense standards of morality and decency? Did the OT and Jewish traditions influence his ethical pronouncements, or was he drawing upon the general moral wisdom enshrined in Hellenistic popular philosophy? Of course, these alternatives are not necessarily mutually exclusive, and various sources probably contributed to Paul's moral outlook.

Clearly, the traditions concerning Jesus influenced his ethical teaching, at least to some degree (cf. Dunn 1998: 649–58). Although there are only three explicit citations of the sayings of Jesus in the letters of Paul which are generally regarded as authentic (1 Cor. 7: 10–11; 9: 14; 11: 23–5), there are occasional echoes of the gospel tradition in Paul's letters, such as his teaching concerning retaliation (Rom. 12: 14; cf. Matt. 5: 44; Luke 6: 27–8), defilement (Rom. 14: 14; cf. Matt. 15: 11; Mark 7: 15) and the importance of living in peace with others (1 Thess. 5: 13; cf. Matt. 5: 9; Mark 9: 50). The apostle also occasionally refers to sayings of the Lord where no clear parallels from the gospel tradition can be found (e.g. 1 Cor. 14: 37; 1 Thess. 4: 15). Yet, of far greater significance for Paul's ethics than the explicit citations or vague echoes of Jesus' teaching was the concept of 'imitating Christ' (*imitatio Christi*), which was a fundamental element in the apostle's vision of the moral life (cf. Tinsley 1960). In 2 Cor. 4: 10 Paul speaks of the life of Christ 'made visible in our bodies', and in other letters he provides concrete examples of how that should happen. In Rom. 15: 1–3, Paul implores the strong not to assert their rights, but to put the interests of others before their own, in imitation of Christ, and in the famous Christological hymn in Phil. 2: 5–11 the example of Christ's obedience, humility, and selfless service becomes the ground for Paul's appeal for mutual concern for others. Sometimes, Paul offers his own apostolic conduct as a model for imitation, in the knowledge that he himself has been an 'imitator of Christ' (cf. 1 Cor. 4: 16–17; 11: 1; 1 Thess. 1: 6–7). The Christian community was called upon to follow in the way of Christ's suffering, and the love that Christ manifested was to serve as the criterion of Christian conduct.

Any discussion of the background of Paul's ethics must also give due regard to the influence of his Jewish heritage. Although some scholars have questioned the extent of Paul's indebtedness to the OT (e.g. von Harnack 1928), there can be little doubt that the apostle, in his moral teaching, was much influenced by the Hebrew Scriptures (Holtz 1981; Hays 1996b). He frequently applied the moral lessons of the OT to his congregations, and saw the events of Israel's history as paradigmatic for the life of the church. Israel's sin with the golden calf (Exod. 32: 6) is cited in 1 Cor. 10: 6 as a warning to members of the Corinthian church of the dangers of idolatry, and in 2 Cor. 8: 1–15 Paul encourages the church to contribute to the collection for the relief of the poor in Jerusalem by referring to Israel's experience of God's provision of manna in the desert (v. 15; cf. Exod. 16: 18). In Rom. 4: 1–25, Paul refers to Abraham's exemplary faith (cf. Gen. 15: 6), and applies it to Christian believers in his own age, and in Gal. 3: 6–14 he argues, on the basis of the same passage of Scripture, that Gentiles were included in God's plan of salvation.

Paul was also indebted to the Jewish legal tradition for his moral instructions, although his attitude to the law of Moses is highly ambivalent (cf. Rosner 2003: 214–15). On the one hand, the apostle could claim that the law was written 'for our instruction' (Rom. 15: 4; cf. 1 Cor. 10: 11) and that it was 'holy, just and good' (Rom. 7: 12), and in Rom. 13: 9–10 he proceeds to list the prohibitions of the Decalogue concerning adultery (Exod. 20: 14), murder (Exod. 20: 13), theft (Exod. 20: 15), and covetousness (Exod. 20: 17). In appealing for financial support for the ministry (1 Cor. 9: 3–12) Paul quotes from Deut. 25: 4, and his condemnation of incest in 1 Cor. 5: 1 suggests that his view of the issue was guided and informed by the law (cf. Lev. 18: 8). Yet, paradoxically, Paul could state that 'now faith has come we are no longer under the supervision of the law' (Gal. 3: 25), and in Col. 2: 14 he claims that God has 'cancelled the written code with its regulations'. The apostle sometimes felt able to set aside some of the explicit commandments of the law, such as those relating to circumcision (1 Cor. 7: 17–20), and he could even claim that the effect of the law was to stimulate and intensify sinful passions (Rom. 7: 5). The reason for the apparent contradiction, however, is that in Paul's view the believer now understands the content and force of the law in a new way: through the ministry of Jesus, the law's intention had been decisively revealed, and it no longer has a value as a norm independent of the believer's new life in Christ.

In addition to the OT, Paul's ethical teaching appears to have been influenced by traditions emanating from rabbinic Judaism (cf. Segal 2003). The apostle uses midrashic techniques characteristic of rabbinic exegesis to support his Christian arguments, and he was clearly familiar with various rabbinic ideas and modes of thought. While it may be going too far to call the apostle a 'Christian Rabbi' (W. D. Davies 1955: 145; cf. Furnish 1968: 38–42), he was clearly ready to deploy his rabbinic exegetical skills to demonstrate the power and truth of the gospel.

Paul's ethical teaching was also influenced by sources from the Hellenistic world. At one point, the apostle cites the Greek poet Menander ('Bad company ruins good morals'; 1 Cor. 15: 33), although it is not clear whether Paul was here quoting directly from a literary source, or whether the words were an everyday proverb in common use. The term 'conscience' (Greek *suneidēsis*), which plays an important role in Paul's ethical teaching (cf. Rom. 2: 15; 9: 1; 13: 5; 1 Cor. 8: 7–13; 10: 25–30; 2 Cor. 1: 12; 4: 2), was evidently borrowed by the apostle from the Greek world (the word having no Hebrew equivalent), and his condemnation of 'greed' (Greek *pleonexia*; cf. Rom. 1: 29; 2 Cor. 9: 5; Col. 3: 5) and his commendation of 'self-control' (Greek *enkrateia*; Gal. 5: 22–3; cf. 1 Cor. 7: 9; 9: 25) would also have found a resonance in Greek philosophical ethics. Further, the catalogues of vices and virtues that Paul sometimes cites (cf. Rom. 1: 29–31; 13: 13; 1 Cor. 6: 9–10; Gal. 5: 22–3; Phil. 4: 8; Col. 3: 12) are entirely consistent with those encountered in the writings of the Greek moral philosophers of his day, and the so-called Household Codes (*Haustafeln*), reflected in such passages as Col. 3: 18–4: 1, were evidently in common use in many circles in the ancient world (cf. Longenecker 1984: 56).

Clearly, then, Paul's ethical teaching reflects the fusion of two cultures, and his ideas and vocabulary are drawn from both his Jewish and his Hellenistic background. It would be invidious, however, to try to compare the extent of the Greek as opposed to the Jewish influence on the apostle. The boundaries between the two were fluid in the first century CE, and in the Hellenistic society that formed the setting of Paul's ministry, various movements and traditions interpenetrated one another to such an extent that it is not always easy to identify the specific background of particular ethical pronouncements. All that can be concluded is that Paul was influenced by two very different, and sometimes opposing, cultures, and it would be misconceived to emphasize one at the expense of the other.

iv. Paul's Christology and Eschatology

There is widespread agreement among NT scholars that Paul's ethical pronouncements are integrally related to both his Christology and his eschatology. Paul's interpretation of the significance of Christ's death and resurrection was determinative for his understanding of the Church's ethical responsibility. The confession of Christ as the crucified and risen Lord brought with it an obligation for Christians to live out their lives in a way appropriate to their faith, for God's eschatological act of salvation in Christ was the basis and prerequisite for all Christian conduct. To be sure, there is, in Paul's letters, a tension between what Schrage (1988: 168) calls the 'indicative of assurance' ('you have been set free from sin'; Rom. 6: 22) and 'the imperative of ethical admonition' ('let not sin reign'; Rom. 6: 12); and attempts to resolve the dichotomy have not always proved particularly convincing (cf. Parsons 1988). Older scholars sought to distinguish between the 'ideal' (the indicative) and the 'actual' (the imperative), arguing that the imperative served as a corrective to the apostle's idealism. More recent scholars, however, have tended to adapt and refine the type of approach advocated by Bultmann (1924; 1952: 332–3), who argued that in Paul's thinking the imperative proceeds naturally out of the indicative, so that the apostle is saying, in effect, 'become what you are'. According to this interpretation, the indicative and the imperative are to be regarded as complementary rather than contradictory, for the former is the necessary presupposition of the latter. What Christ has done is the basis of what the believer must do, and in this sense, the imperative may be viewed as the outworking of the indicative.

Paul's ethical judgements are also worked out in the context of his eschatological beliefs. In Rom. 13: 11–14, Paul urges his readers to dissociate themselves from the present age and to refrain from drunkenness, debauchery, licentiousness, and jealousy in the knowledge that 'the hour has come' and the end is near. An appeal to eschatology as an incentive to moral earnestness is also encountered in 1 Thess. 5: 1–11, 23; indeed, it is the very imminence of the end that often gives to Paul's moral exhortations their urgency. Further, the expectation of future judgement and future reward provides an eschatological motivation for Christian obedience and an incentive for moral action. Those who judge others will themselves be judged when they appear before God, to whom they are accountable (Rom. 2: 1–16; 14: 10; 2 Cor. 5: 9–10); on the other hand, the reward of eternal life is promised to those who do not regard their good works as an end in themselves (Rom. 2: 7). For Paul, the sense of the nearness of the coming of the Lord, far from instilling in the people a sense of resignation and passivity, was intended to encourage them to pursue all the more anxiously the tasks of love and mutual service (cf. Hays 1996a: 19–27).

D. HERMENEUTICAL ISSUES

The use of the Bible in contemporary moral decision making is a complex hermeneutical issue, and there are conflicting views among biblical scholars even as to the role and status of Scripture in arriving at ethical decisions. For some, the Bible represents the absolute and sole authority for the Christian, and provides the solution to moral problems encountered in all areas of life, ranging from economic practices to family obligations, from one's duty to the state to one's duty towards one's neighbour. For others, however, the Bible constitutes merely one factor (albeit an important and perhaps primary factor) in the adoption of ethical positions; according to this view, other sources of authority (reason, conscience, experience, tradition, etc.) must also be allowed to play a role in the formation of normative judgements. Still others argue that the ethical provisions of the Bible are so alien and foreign to contemporary society that its statements, principles, and practices are of little use in the formation of a Christian social consciousness (cf. Sanders 1975: 130).

Most biblical interpreters incline towards the second position, the first being generally regarded as too simplistic, while the third is viewed as too extreme. To regard the Bible as the only source of authority in ethical decision making overlooks the fact that decisions reached concerning moral dilemmas are often the product of subconsciously internalized norms that reflect the values of the culture in which the individual has been nurtured. On the other hand, to dispute the legitimacy of using the Bible at all in the formation of a Christian consciousness appears strange, for any system of social morality that claims to be Christian must surely be guided and informed by the ethical teaching contained in Scripture.

But if the Bible is to function as a source of moral authority for the Christian, the question remains: how is it to be used? The question arises because the application of the Bible to modern decision making is by no means as straightforward as might be supposed. In this regard, two problems in particular call for comment. The first concerns the so-called culture gap that separates contemporary communities of faith from the communities to whom the texts were originally addressed. The biblical authors expressed their insights in terms appropriate to the time in which they were writing, and they inevitably reflect the attitudes, outlooks, and beliefs of the people of their age. As a result, many of the provisions recorded in the Bible can no longer be regarded as binding in our own secular, pluralist society. The other side of this coin is that many issues that might feature prominently on *our* moral agenda (such as sexual equality or care for the environment) hardly feature at all in the Bible, and many ethical dilemmas facing people today (such as nuclear war or genetic engineering) simply did not exist in biblical times. The problem caused by the historical and cultural distance between the biblical world and our own is therefore twofold: on the one hand, many of the laws and customs of the Bible no longer seem relevant to contemporary communities of faith; on the other hand, many problems which do arise in the complex, technological age in which we live are such that the Bible offers no guidance or direction by which they can be resolved.

The second problem is that several passages in the Bible (especially in the OT) appear to advocate moral standards that seem, to the contemporary reader, to be offensive and unacceptable (cf. Kaiser 1983: 247–304; Rogerson 2001: 31–2). Many of the laws contained in the OT (such as those that require the death penalty for adultery; cf. Lev. 20: 10; Deut. 22: 22) appear, by our standards, to be harsh, cruel, and intolerably vindictive, and even some of the motives given for right conduct in the laws (riches, honour, long life) seem morally suspect. Moreover, several of the narratives recorded in the Hebrew Bible (such as those which describe the massacre of the Canaanites by the Israelites in Josh. 11: 16–23) relate acts of extreme violence and bloodshed, and—to make matters even worse—such acts are often performed at the express command of God himself (v. 20; cf. Deut. 7: 1–2; 20: 16–18). Even some of the Psalms, so often regarded as the high-water mark of Israel's faith, frequently breathe a spirit of unbridled revenge and malice, and exhibit an attitude of exclusivism and provincialism that smacks of the worst type of xenophobia (cf. Pss. 109, 137).

The problem caused by the temporal gap between us and the peoples of biblical times is often resolved by seeking out the underlying principles contained in the biblical texts and reapplying them in appropriate ways to issues of contemporary concern (cf. Wright 1983: 40–5; 1995: 57–66). For example, the institution of animal sacrifice in the OT may appear to be completely irrelevant as it stands; yet the principle that underlies the institution may be entirely applicable in so far as it serves as a reminder of the gravity of sin and the human need for forgiveness (cf. Bright 1967: 148–9). Similarly, in the NT, the practice of the early Christian community of sharing all possessions in common (Acts 2: 44–5; 4: 32–7) may appear to be highly impractical if applied literally to members of the contemporary church, but the principle underlying the custom is entirely relevant if it serves as a challenge to Christians to reconsider in a radical way their attitude towards their own material wealth (cf. Hays 1996a: 302–3). Such an interpretative strategy is not without its problems (cf. Longenecker 1984: 3–5), but it is argued that by rooting out the underlying principles of Scripture, the reader can remain true to the spirit of the biblical text while at the same time making it relevant and applicable to the modern world.

The difficulty encountered by the morally dubious passages of Scripture has been resolved in a variety of ways (see E. W. Davies 2005), but the presence of such passages in the Bible should serve as a reminder that its readers have an ethical duty to evaluate its norms and to resist those elements in its teaching that appear to be destructive, harmful, or detrimental to human well-being. Instead of tacitly accepting the standards of judgement established in the text and capitulating uncritically to its demands, they must be prepared to challenge its assumptions, question its insights, and (if necessary) discredit its claims (E. W. Davies 2003). Of course, some are bound to feel uneasy about applying an ethical critique to the Bible on the ground that such a procedure will inevitably impugn its authority as Scripture. However, an ethical critique of Scripture can be justified on inner-biblical grounds, for the biblical authors themselves often exercise a critical role, questioning past beliefs and querying past judgements. The Bible comes to us bearing clear traces of its own critique of tradition, and this may be regarded as providing the contemporary reader with a warrant to dissent from its teachings and to question some of its more dubious ethical pronouncements.

SUGGESTED READING

With regard to OT ethics, the volumes by Birch (1991), Otto (1994), and Rodd (2001) cover the subject with commendable detail. John Barton has written extensively on the subject, and many of his articles have now been collected together in a single volume (2003). C. J. H. Wright, writing from a broadly conservative perspective, has also made a valuable contribution to this area of research (1983, 1995, 2004). Shorter studies worth consulting include those by McKeating (1979), P. R. Davies (1995), Rogerson (2000, 2001, 2004), and the articles in the volume edited by Knight (1995a).

There are many excellent expositions of the ethical teaching of the NT that provide a good foundation for understanding the biblical material. Mention may be made in particular of the volumes by Schnackenburg (1965), Schrage (1988), Lohse (1991), Marxsen (1993), McDonald (1993, 1998), Hays (1996a), and Matera (1996). For excellent discussions of Paul's ethical teaching, readers should consult Furnish (1968) and Sampley (1991), and several important articles on Paul's ethics have been collected in Rosner (1995). Those interested in hermeneutical issues should consult Birch and Rasmussen (1976), Longenecker (1984), and Ogletree (1984), and for further discussion of the importance of an ethical critique of Scripture, see E. W. Davies (2003).

BIBLIOGRAPHY

BARR, J. 1993. *Biblical Faith and Natural Theology*. Oxford: Clarendon Press.

BARTON, J. 1978. 'Understanding Old Testament Ethics'. *JSOT* 9: 44–64; repr. in Barton 2003: 15–31.

—— 1979. 'Natural Law and Poetic Justice in the Old Testament'. *JTS*, n.s. 30: 1–14; repr. in Barton 2003: 32–44.

—— 1983. 'Approaches to Ethics in the Old Testament'. In J. Rogerson, ed., *Beginning Old Testament Study*, London: SPCK, 113–30.

—— 2003. *Understanding Old Testament Ethics: Approaches and Explorations*. Louisville, Ky., and London: Westminster/John Knox Press.

BIRCH, B. C. 1991. *Let Justice Roll Down: The Old Testament, Ethics, and Christian Life*. Louisville, Ky.: Westminster/John Knox Press.

—— and RASMUSSEN, L. L. 1976. *Bible and Ethics in the Christian Life*. Minneapolis: Augsburg Publishing House.

BLENKINSOPP, J. 1983. *Wisdom and Law in the Old Testament*. Oxford: Oxford University Press.

BRIGHT, J. 1967. *The Authority of the Old Testament*. London: SCM Press.

BUBER, M. 1926. 'Nachahmung Gottes'. *Morgen* 1: 638–47; repr. in Buber, *Kampf um Israel: Reden und Schriften [1921–1932]*, Berlin: Schocken Books, 1933; trans. G. Hort, 'Imitatio Dei', in *Israel and the World: Essays in a Time of Crisis*, New York: Schocken Books, 1948, 66–77.

BULTMANN, R. 1924. 'Das Problem der Ethik bei Paulus'. *ZNW* 23: 123–40; trans. as 'The Problem of Ethics in Paul', in Rosner 1995: 195–216.

—— 1952. *Theology of the New Testament*, i, trans. K. Grobel. London: SCM Press; German original 1948.

CHILTON, B., and MCDONALD, J. I. H., eds. 1987. *Jesus and the Ethics of the Kingdom.* London: SPCK.

DAVIES, E. W. 1981. *Prophecy and Ethics: Isaiah and the Ethical Traditions of Israel.* Sheffield: JSOT Press.

—— 1995. 'Ethics of the Hebrew Bible: The Problem of Methodology'. In Knight 1995*a*: 43–53.

—— 1999. 'Walking in God's Ways: The Concept of *Imitatio Dei* in the Old Testament'. In E. Ball, ed., *In Search of True Wisdom: Essays in Old Testament Interpretation in Honour of Ronald E. Clements*, Sheffield: Sheffield Academic Press, 99–115.

—— 2003. *The Dissenting Reader: Feminist Approaches to the Hebrew Bible.* Aldershot: Ashgate Publishing Limited.

—— 2005. 'The Morally Dubious Passages of the Hebrew Bible: An Examination of Some Proposed Solutions'. *Currents in Biblical Research*, 3/2: 197–228.

DAVIES, P. R. 1995. 'Ethics and the Old Testament'. In J. W. Rogerson, M. Davies, and M. Daniel Carroll, eds., *The Bible in Ethics: The Second Sheffield Colloquium*, Sheffield: Sheffield Academic Press, 164–73.

DAVIES, W. D. 1955. *Paul and Rabbinic Judaism.* London: SPCK.

DODD, C. H. 1938. *The Parables of the Kingdom*, rev. edn. London: Nisbet & Co. Ltd.

—— 1951. *Gospel and Law.* Cambridge: Cambridge University Press.

DUNN, J. D. G. 1998. *The Theology of Paul the Apostle.* Edinburgh: T. & T. Clark.

EICHRODT, W. 1967. *Theology of the Old Testament*, ii, trans. J. A. Baker. London: SCM Press; German original, 5th edn. 1964.

FURNISH, V. P. 1968. *Theology and Ethics in Paul.* Nashville and New York: Abingdon Press.

—— 1972. *The Love Command in the New Testament.* Nashville and New York: Abingdon Press.

GUNN, D. M. 1978. *The Story of King David: Genre and Interpretation.* Sheffield: JSOT Press.

HARNACK, A. VON 1928. 'Das Alte Testament in den paulinischen Briefen und in den paulinischen Gemeinden'. In *Sitzungsberichte der Preussischen Akademie der Wissenschaften zu Berlin*, 124–41; ET: 'The Old Testament in the Pauline Letters and in the Pauline Churches', in Rosner 1995: 27–49.

HARRELSON, W. 1980. *The Ten Commandments and Human Rights.* Philadelphia: Fortress Press.

HAYS, R. B. 1990. 'Scripture-Shaped Community: The Problem of Method in New Testament Ethics'. *Interpretation*, 44: 42–55.

—— 1996*a*. *The Moral Vision of the New Testament: A Contemporary Introduction to New Testament Ethics.* Edinburgh: T. & T. Clark.

—— 1996*b*. 'The Role of Scripture in Paul's Ethics'. In E. H. Lovering and J. L. Sumney, eds., *Theology and Ethics in Paul and his Interpreters*, Nashville: Abingdon Press, 30–47.

HOLTZ, T. 1981. 'Zur Frage der inhaltlichen Weisungen bei Paulus'. *ThLZ* 106: 385–400; ET: 'The Question of the Content of Paul's Instructions', in Rosner 1995: 51–71.

HORST, F. 1950–1. 'Naturrecht und Altes Testament'. *EvTh* 10: 253–73; repr. in H. W. Wolff, ed., *Gottes Recht: Gesammelte Studien zum Recht im Alten Testament*, Munich: C. Kaiser, 1961: 235–59.

HOULDEN, J. L. 1973. *Ethics and the New Testament*. Harmondsworth: Penguin.

—— 1990. 'Ethics (New Testament)'. In R. J. Coggins and J. L. Houlden, eds., *A Dictionary of Biblical Interpretation*, London: SCM Press; Philadelphia: Trinity Press International, 205–8.

JANZEN, W. 1994. *Old Testament Ethics: A Paradigmatic Approach*. Louisville, Ky.: Westminster/John Knox Press.

KAISER, W. C. 1983. *Toward Old Testament Ethics*. Grand Rapids, Mich.: Zondervan Publishing House.

KNIGHT, D. A., ed. 1995a. *Ethics and Politics in the Hebrew Bible*. Semeia, 66. Atlanta: Scholars Press.

—— 1995b. 'Introduction: Ethics, Ancient Israel, and the Hebrew Bible'. In Knight 1995: 1–8.

LOHSE, E. 1991. *Theological Ethics of the New Testament*, trans. M. E. Boring. Minneapolis: Fortress Press; German original 1988.

LONGENECKER, R. N. 1984. *New Testament Social Ethics for Today*. Grand Rapids, Mich.: Wm B. Eerdmans Publishing Company.

McDONALD, J. I. H. 1993. *Biblical Interpretation and Christian Ethics*. Cambridge: Cambridge University Press.

—— 1998. *The Crucible of Christian Morality*. London and New York: Routledge.

McKEATING, H. 1979. 'Sanctions against Adultery in Ancient Israelite Society, with some Reflections on Methodology in the Study of Old Testament Ethics'. *JSOT* 11: 57–72.

MARXSEN, W. 1993. *New Testament Foundations for Christian Ethics*, trans O. C. Dean jun. Edinburgh: T. & T. Clark; German original 1989.

MATERA, F. J. 1996. *New Testament Ethics*. Louisville, Ky.: Westminster/John Knox Press.

MEEKS, W. 1987. *The Moral World of the First Christians*. London: SPCK.

MILLS, M. E. 2001. *Biblical Morality: Moral Perspectives in Old Testament Narratives*. Aldershot: Ashgate Publishing Limited.

MITCHELL, H. G. 1912. *The Ethics of the Old Testament*. Chicago: University of Chicago Press.

OGLETREE, T. 1984. *The Use of the Bible in Christian Ethics*. Oxford: Blackwell.

OTTO, E. 1994. *Theologische Ethik des Alten Testaments*. Stuttgart: Kohlhammer.

PARSONS, M. 1988. 'Being Precedes Act: Indicative and Imperative in Paul's Writing'. *EQ* 88: 99–127; repr. in Rosner 1995: 217–47.

RODD, C. S. 1990. 'Ethics (Old Testament)'. In R. J. Coggins and J. L. Houlden, eds., *A Dictionary of Biblical Interpretation*, London: SCM Press; Philadelphia: Trinity Press International, 208–10.

—— 2001. *Glimpses of a Strange Land: Studies in Old Testament Ethics*. Edinburgh: T. & T. Clark.

ROGERSON, J. 2000. 'Old Testament Ethics'. In A. D. H. Mays, ed., *Text in Context: Essays by Members of the Society for Old Testament Study*, Oxford: Oxford University Press, 116–37.

—— 2001. 'The Old Testament and Christian Ethics'. In R. Gill, ed., *The Cambridge Companion to Christian Ethics*, Cambridge: Cambridge University Press, 29–41.

—— 2004. *Theory and Practice in Old Testament Ethics*, ed. M. Daniel Carroll R. JSOTS.S 405. London: T. & T. Clark International.

ROSNER, B. S., ed. 1995. *Understanding Paul's Ethics: Twentieth-Century Approaches*. Grand Rapids, Mich.: Wm B. Eerdmans Publishing Company; Carlisle: Paternoster Press.

—— 1999. *Paul, Scripture and Ethics: A Study of 1 Corinthians 5–7*. Grand Rapids, Mich.: Baker.

—— 2003. 'Paul's Ethics'. In J. D. G. Dunn, ed., *The Cambridge Companion to St Paul*, Cambridge: Cambridge University Press, 212–23.

SAMPLEY, J. P. 1991. *Walking between the Times: Paul's Moral Reasoning*. Minneapolis: Fortress Press.

SANDERS, J. T. 1975. *Ethics in the New Testament*. London: SCM Press.

SCHNACKENBURG, R. 1965. *The Moral Teaching of the New Testament*, trans. J. Holland-Smith and W. J. O'Hara from the 2nd rev. German edn. 1962. London: Burns & Oates; Freiburg: Herder.

SCHRAGE, W. 1988. *The Ethics of the New Testament*, trans. D. E. Green. Edinburgh: T. & T. Clark; original German edn. 1982.

SCHWEITZER, A. 1910. *The Quest of the Historical Jesus*, trans. W. Montgomery. London: Adam & Charles Black; original German edn. 1906.

SEGAL, A. F. 2003. 'Paul's Jewish Presuppositions'. In J. D. G. Dunn, *The Cambridge Companion to St Paul*, Cambridge: Cambridge University Press, 159–72.

SMITH, J. M. P. 1923. *The Moral Life of the Hebrews*. Chicago: University of Chicago Press.

STRECKER, G. 1988. *The Sermon on the Mount: An Exegetical Commentary*, trans. O. C. Dean jun. Nashville: Abingdon; German original 1985.

TINSLEY, E. J. 1960. *The Imitation of God in Christ*. London: SCM Press.

VIA, D. O. 1985. *The Ethics of Mark's Gospel: In the Middle of Time*. Philadelphia: Fortress Press.

WENHAM, G. J. 2000. *Story as Torah: Reading the Old Testament Ethically*. Edinburgh: T. & T. Clark.

WINTON, A. P. 1990. *The Proverbs of Jesus: Issues of History and Rhetoric*. Sheffield: Sheffield Academic Press.

WRIGHT, C. J. H. 1983. *Living as the People of God: The Relevance of Old Testament Ethics*. Leicester: InterVarsity Press.

—— 1995. *Walking in the Ways of the Lord: The Ethical Authority of the Old Testament*. Leicester: Apollos.

—— 2004. *Old Testament Ethics for the People of God*. Leicester: InterVarsity Press.

CHAPTER 42

JEWISH INTERPRETATION OF THE BIBLE

JONATHAN MAGONET

DEFINITION

Certain problems of definition of the term 'Jewish' need to be clarified in order to address this subject. The work, in particular, of Michael Fishbane (1985) has emphasized the way in which even within the Hebrew Bible itself there is evidence of 'interpretation', whereby earlier materials are reworked in later passages for specific purposes. Where this activity is a post-exilic exercise, it may be possible to speak of it as being 'Jewish' biblical interpretation, though the subject of inner-biblical developments is outside the remit of this chapter: Similar problems of definition arise with the works of Philo and the pseudepigraphical writings and, for that matter, the New Testament itself. All of them operate within a Jewish context, but were marginal to, or departed from, what was to become mainstream Judaism. Again, they are treated separately within this Handbook.

Thus for the earliest period of Jewish interpretation we will confine ourselves to such translations, interpretations, and commentaries as emerged out of and served the needs of Jewish communities. (The Septuagint and Targums, as Jewish translations, will be addressed elsewhere.)

At the other end of the historical spectrum, with the rise of modernity, particularly after the emancipation of European Jewry, definitions of 'Jewishness' itself and questions as to what constitutes a particularly 'Jewish' approach to the interpretation of the Hebrew Bible are not easily resolved (Magonet 1995). Thus today Bible study *per se* is most actively pursued within the various synagogue-based Jewish religious movements and an emerging secular/humanist movement. However, an overlapping but different orientation can be found within the State of Israel, where the Hebrew Bible is additionally studied and interpreted as a national treasure and cultural artefact, as well as a 'political' document. The Hebrew Bible is also studied as an academic discipline within universities and seminaries. Here it may be taught by scholars who happen to be Jewish but who may have little commitment to their Jewish identity, and hence to its implication for their approach to the Bible, and varying degrees of access to or interest in classical Jewish methods of exegesis. I will address the question of what might constitute contemporary Jewish approaches in the final part of this study.

HISTORICAL OVERVIEW

Since the Jewish people have passed the major part of their post-biblical existence as minorities within Christian or Muslim societies, and have been considerably affected by their relationship to the dominant culture, a brief overview of this history will help establish the framework for the forms of Jewish interpretation that emerged.

After Jewish national life was destroyed by the Romans in 70 CE, Jews were widely dispersed (Diaspora), though the process had already begun in the wake of the destruction of the First Temple in 586 BCE. Large Jewish communities existed as far apart as Babylon/Persia, Syria, Antioch, Rome, Athens, and Alexandria. At the height of the Roman Republic communities could also be found in Spain, France, and Germany. Following the Arab conquest in the seventh century, communities in the Middle East and Mediterranean came under the sway of Islam. The Jewish community in Spain experienced a golden age, in a symbiotic relationship with a flourishing Islamic culture, only to come under persecution at the hands of the Almohades at the end of this period. Those who took refuge in Christian Spain were subsequently to experience the Inquisition and ultimately expulsion in 1492. The refugees found a home in the Ottoman Empire, but also gathered in new communities in Amsterdam, London, and other European cities. These groups, preserving their Judaeo-Spanish language and customs, were known as Sephardim.

The other major Jewish grouping, the Ashkenazim, lived in Germany and Eastern Europe under Christianity. From the time of the First Crusade in the eleventh century, they experienced successive expulsions and massacres, one result being a massive flight of German Jews to the Polish provinces. Yet, despite this overall negative picture, under constant pressure to give up their faith and accept Christianity, particular times and circumstances enabled communities and individuals to flourish, and dialogue to take place across the boundaries, particularly amongst scholars.

In the period preceding and following the American and French revolutions, Jews gradually acquired equal citizenship rights. The price that was paid for this opportunity for the individual was the loss of the coherent, self-regulating, collective Jewish identity that had preceded it. Different religious and secular ideologies struggled to retain the loyalty of individual Jews to Judaism as a faith or to the Jewish people. The destruction wrought upon one-third of the total Jewish population of the world by the Holocaust, and the subsequent emergence of the State of Israel, introduced radically new issues that are central to any Jewish self-understanding today.

All these different historical and geographical experiences of almost 2,000 years of Diaspora existence have coloured the Jewish response to the Hebrew Bible, the one document common to all Jewish experience. The continuing process of reinterpretation of the Bible was one of the mechanisms that helped the Jewish people to understand the meaning of their existence and develop strategies for survival. It is against these often radically different backgrounds that the rich variety of approaches to biblical interpretation evolved.

Some Underlying Assumptions

The basis of rabbinic Judaism is the view that alongside the 'written Torah', the 'five books of Moses', given by God to Moses on Mt Sinai, there was a verbal teaching from God to accompany it, the 'oral Torah'. This was to enable the Jewish people to apply the teachings and legal precepts of the 'written Torah' to new or changing circumstances. (The term 'Torah', from a root meaning to shoot arrows at a target, hence also indicate a direction, is used in a narrow sense in the Hebrew Bible for an individual legal precept and more broadly for the generality of laws and teachings of divine origin (Psalms 19, 119). Thus the frequently used translation as 'law' is too restrictive for a term that, in Judaism, came to embrace law and lore—indeed, all teachings ultimately derived from the study of traditional sources.)

The commandment in Deuteronomy (4: 2; 13: 1) that one should neither 'add to nor subtract from' the words of Torah, effectively sealed the text of the Pentateuch, and ultimately the entire scriptural canon. Yet precisely this closure inevitably opened the doors to the process of interpretation. Such exercises in reading the text of Scripture so as to understand the contemporary situation and determine one's actions became the common activity for all the different Jewish groups and communities competing for authority as the legitimate heirs of the biblical tradition.

The precise origins of the materials that came to make up the 'oral Torah' is unknown. They were compiled and edited about 200 CE in a collection known as the Mishnah, the work being attributed to Rabbi Yehudah Ha-Nasi, the 'patriarch', the political and spiritual leader of the Diaspora communities. The term 'Mishnah' means 'repetition' and presumably reflects the method whereby the oral tradition was memorized, studied, and handed on through oral repetition to others. It has six divisions, or 'orders', divided into 'tractates' and subdivided into chapters. Over the following two to five centuries the rabbis undertook a major examination of the contents of the Mishnah, in part seeking to relate them to the appropriate legal passages from the 'written Torah'. This activity led to two enormous compilations of comment and discussion: the Palestinian Talmud (edited in about the fourth century) and the Babylonian Talmud (edited by the seventh century). (The term 'talmud' derives from the Hebrew root meaning to 'study' or to 'teach'.) The former shows evidence of incompleteness, probably because of the deterioration of Jewish life in Palestine. The latter became the central source of study, both for the purpose of deriving new laws and practices for the community and for its own sake as a spiritual task.

The materials in the two Talmuds are orientated around the Mishnah; nevertheless, they contain considerable numbers of examples of biblical exegesis. The other great collections of rabbinic materials, that are known under the title 'Midrash', are structured around the biblical materials as commentaries on individual books or under the name of the eponymous author.

Considerable scholarly debate surrounds the meaning of two crucial terms that underlie the rabbinic approach to exegesis. *Peshat*, literally 'to strip off', is used to clarify the 'plain meaning', which is not always to be equated with the literal meaning of a text. Rimon Kasher defines it as 'an exegetical method that seeks *to expose the meaning of scripture by considering its context, using philological insights and with historical "awareness"* ' (Kasher 1988: 553; emphasis original). He describes the difficulty of defining midrashic interpretation thus:

A cursory glance at the scholarly research on midrashic literature suffices to indicate the incredible number of conceptions, definitions and characterizations. Some emphasize the purpose (religious, educational or social), some focus on the function of midrashic literature in Jewish society, others attempt to characterize the midrash by its literary genre, while still others emphasize techniques and methods. It seems to me that we ought to define midrashic by referring to the definition of *peshat*. In other words, an interpretation which does not fit the criteria for *peshat* will be considered as *midrash/derash*.

Peshat consists of two principal elements: 1. Exposing the original or contextual meaning of the text through a historical awareness and 2. use of methods based mainly on context and philology. Thus, a *midrash* does not always fulfil both requirements: it does not always seek to reveal the original or contextual meaning of scripture, nor is it always a response to legitimate problems of interpretation. Moreover, even when the *midrash* does answer to the first requirements of *peshat*, the difference between the method of the *midrash* and of the *peshat* is particularly striking. *The midrash completely ignores both the context and the rules of biblical language.* (Kasher 1988: 560; emphasis original)

David Weiss Halivni warns against making a value judgement on the rabbinic approach to exegesis.

It is my contention that the rabbis did not share our devotion to the simple literal meaning. Exegesis is 'timebound'. Each interpretive state of mind has its own system of exegesis, and the rabbis' interpretive state of mind did not dictate to them that the simple, literal meaning was inherently superior to the applied meaning. Although they generally began their interpretations of the Bible with the simple, literal meaning of the text, they did not feel committed to it. The slightest provocation, most often an apparently superfluous word or letter, moved them to abandon it.

This position is difficult for a modem exegete to grasp. The modem state of mind demands a greater faithfulness to the simple, literal meaning (to the peshat), and a greater obligation to preserve it. Only in the face of virtually insurmountable problems is this approach abandoned. The presence of an extra word, letter, or even an entire phrase can be easily seen as a stylistic peculiarity. Peshat, from this point of view, is synonymous with exegetical truth, and one does not abandon truth lightly. But to the rabbis of the Talmud, deviation from peshat was not repugnant. Their interpretative state of mind saw no fault with an occasional reading in. It was not against their exegetical conscience, even though it may be against ours. (Halivni 1991: 8–9)

We will examine the Midrash further in the next section, after addressing the more general issue of some of the assumptions underlying rabbinic interpretation.

Given that the Hebrew Bible is seen as the word of God, and thus the potential source of all knowledge, wisdom, and practice, there are nevertheless two broad divisions in the approach to interpretation, though they may overlap and be expressed in different forms and terminologies in different periods. One approach seeks to be rational, and insists on the plain meaning of the text as being the prime source of information about the will of God. Nevertheless, there is considerable debate about what constitutes the 'plain meaning' in any given context. This approach is characterized by the Talmudic axiom that occurs three times: *dibra tora kil'shon b 'nei-adam*, 'The words of Torah are expressed in human language' (*Berakhot* 31b; *Sanhedrin* 85a; *Nedarim* 3a). In these contexts are sentences wherein certain words are repeated, and the axiom asserts that these repetitions are simply conventional forms of expression in biblical Hebrew. The intention is to counter the approach, commonly found in the Midrash, that is not bound by the plain meaning and seeks in every seemingly redundant word or even letter a hint of a further concealed truth. An example would be the way an interpreter addresses the particle *et*, which simply indicates that the word that follows is the object of the verb. Those who follow the teachings of Rabbi Aqiba would seek in each use of *et* additional elements to be governed by the particular law.

A second axiom mediates between the two approaches: *ein miqra yotzei middei peshuto*, 'no biblical verse ever loses its plain meaning' (*Shabbat* 63a). That is to say, whatever midrashic interpretations may be found, the plain meaning remains and must be reckoned with. The distinction between *peshat* and *derash* is not universally made in the early rabbinic materials, but became more directly addressed in the medieval rabbinic commentaries.

The same rational tendency can be seen at work in the formulation of hermeneutic rules to govern the modes of interpretation of legal matters. Thirteen such rules are attributed to Rabbi Ishmael, a text to be found in standard editions of Jewish daily liturgy, and other collections exist. They seek to provide a consistent and logical methodology: for example, the argument from minor to major, the comparison of two passages because of the appearance of a common word in both, or how to treat cases in the Bible where a general rule is followed by a detailed example, and vice versa. Such principles are not always followed, nor do they account for all the exegetical methods employed by the rabbis. Nevertheless, they do point to the desire to find a rational basis to the interpretation and application of the law.

The tension between these approaches, which we might term 'rational' and 'mystical', can be seen in the different ways in which the rabbis approached the chronology within the Hebrew Bible. The question arises as to who wrote the last verses of the book of Deuteronomy that record the death of Moses. One view conforms with the rational approach: 'Moses wrote his own book and the section [in Numbers 22–4] about Balaam, as well as the Book of Job. Joshua wrote his own book and the last eight verses of the Book of Deuteronomy' (*Baba Bathra* 14b). This view is given in the name of Rabbi Joshua or Rabbi Nehemiah, but is challenged by Rabbi Simeon: ' "Could the scroll of the Torah be short of even a single word?! Yet it is written: Take this book of the Torah (Deut 31: 26). Rather, from here onwards [i.e. the last eight verses of Deuteronomy] the Holy One, blessed be He, dictated and Moses wrote it down with tears in his eyes" ' (*Baba Bathra* 15a). Rabbi Simeon's view, that divine inspiration, or human imagination, transcends the limitations of chronology, became the dominating approach in 'Aggadic' Midrash. (The term 'Aggadah', literally 'narrative', designates all the material not of a legal ('Halakhic') character in the Midrash.) The Torah thus becomes a document that transcends time and space. Biblical characters and events become alive and actual in any contemporary situation, a constant source of inspiration and guidance.

One final feature of rabbinic discourse, common to Talmud and Midrash, needs to be noted: namely, the acceptance of a plurality of views on the possible meaning of an individual passage standing alongside one another, and seemingly given equal weight. How could it be otherwise, the argument seems to run, when the words of Scripture are those of an all-powerful and all-knowing God, and thus could not possibly be contained within a single meaning. It is articulated in the rabbinic phrase that there are 'seventy faces to the Torah' (*Otiyyot d'Rabbi Aqiba* 8a). The Midrash describes its own activity in precisely these terms in a justly celebrated image: 'Someone from the school of Rabbi Ishmael transmitted: "[Is not My word like fire, said the Lord] and like a hammer that shatters the rock?"' (Jer 23:29). Just as each blow of a hammer strikes forth many sparks, so a single verse unfolds into many senses (*Sanhedrin* 34a). Naturally when it comes to the need for a decision in a legal matter which has practical consequences, within the Talmud or the subsequent legal codes, one opinion will be chosen as binding, but the other opinions are preserved for possible future re-evaluation. When no conclusion could be reached in a celebrated debate between the schools of Hillel and Shammai, a heavenly voice intervened and declared: 'Both these and these are the words of the living God, but the law follows the school of Hillel' (*Erubin* 13b). Why was Hillel's judgement preferred? Because he would quote the opinions of his opponent as well as his own. Apart from the legitimacy given to both sides of such a debate, the passage suggests that if there is no debate conducted with integrity and honesty between scholars, then God is no longer 'living'!

MIDRASH

The term 'Midrash' is used both for the process of exegesis itself and for the various collections of rabbinic materials. It is conventional to divide rabbinic Midrash into two types: *midrash halakhah* (legal midrash)—for example, *Mekhilta, Sifra,* and *Sifre*—and *midrash aggadah* (non-legal midrash)—for example, *Genesis* or *Exodus Rabbah.* However, all these collections contain materials of both sorts. Some collections offer a running commentary on the biblical text, or sections of it, whereas others, described as 'homiletic', are built around a variety of texts and are related to festival days, possibly representing the material used in sermons.

The approach of Midrash is illustrated by Jay M. Harris, focusing on Deut. 14: 16: 'Fathers shall not be put to death for sons, nor sons for fathers; a man shall be put to death for his own sin.' He writes:

A modem reader...will have no difficulty understanding the simple meaning (*peshat*) of this verse. It means that each individual will be held accountable for his or her own actions, and that only he or she may suffer the ultimate punishment, if appropriate. Guilt is not hereditary, nor is it visited upon ancestors.... None of these readers is likely to be overly troubled by the verse's verbosity and redundancy....

Those with some legal training, aware of the importance of statutory construction, may, however, be troubled by these features. They may seek to tease more meaning from the verse or they may simply attribute the verbosity to different legal standards, or perhaps, to sloppy construction.... But what if the option of sloppy construction were not available? What if one took for granted that the author was incapable of sloppy construction, indeed, incapable of less than perfect construction? One would then be forced to find in each of the clauses a distinct statement that eliminates the redundancy, and, indeed, that is precisely what the *darshan* (the author of a piece of Midrash) ... does with this verse. (Harris 1995: 8)

Harris's approach focuses on the triggering factor within a scriptural verse that leads to the need to interpret. Jacob Neusner, examining the broader purpose, notes that Midrash is

how 'our Sages of blessed memory' wrote with Scripture.... For the Holy Scriptures were transformed by the Judaic sages. Thus Midrash works in three dimensions: first, as explanation of meaning imputed to particular verses of Scripture; second, as a mode of stating important propositions, syllogisms of thought, in conversation with verses or sustained passages of Scripture; and, third, as a way of retelling scriptural stories in such a way as to impart to those stories new immediacy. (Neusner 1995: 94)

Because of the variety of ways in which the term 'Midrash' is applied, including to virtually any rewriting of biblical material today, a helpful definition is furnished by Gary Porton: 'Midrash is a type of literature, oral or written, which has its starting point in a fixed canonical text, considered the revealed word of God by the midrashist and his audience, and in which this original verse is explicitly cited or clearly alluded to' (Porton 1992: 819). Neusner notes that what are important in Porton's definition are three elements: (1) exegesis (2) starting with Scripture and (3) ending in community (Neusner 1995: 96).

As indicated above, scholars are divided on a number of issues regarding how to read Midrash. Daniel Boyarin points to one of the problems:

I wish to discredit the opposition between reading which is value-free and concerned with the difficulties of the biblical text and that which is unconcerned with those difficulties and speaks to the needs of the moment. It is clear then that I am not denying the reality of ideological concerns on the part of the rabbis nor that these ideological concerns may have often had an effect on the interpretive choices they made. I am asserting that we will not read midrash well and richly unless we understand it first and foremost as *reading*, as hermeneutic, as generated by the interaction of rabbinic readers with a heterogeneous and difficult text, which was for them both normative and divine in origin. (Boyarin 1990: 5)

Boyarin bases his approach on inter-textuality, which for him has three important dimensions:

[T]he first is that the text is always made up of a mosaic of conscious and un-conscious citation of earlier discourse. The second is that texts may be dialogical in nature—contesting their own assertions as an essential part of the structure of their discourse—and that the Bible is a pre-eminent example of such a text. The third is that there are cultural codes, again either conscious or unconscious, which both constrain and allow the production (not creation) of new texts within the culture. (Boyarin 1990: 12)

It is helpful to cite Boyarin further as the argument regarding the nature of midrashic reading offers an approach to the interpretative methods and schools of later periods.

Rather than seeing midrashic departures from what appears to the 'simple' meaning of the local text as being determined by the needs of rhetoric and propaganda and rooted in the extratextual reality of the rabbinic period, or as being the product of the creative genius of individual rabbis wholly above time and social circumstance, I suggest that the intertextual reading practice of the midrash is a development (sometimes, to be sure, a baroque development) of the intratextual interpretive strategies which the Bible itself manifests. Moreover, the very fractured and unsystematic surface of the biblical text is an encoding of its own intertextuality, and it is precisely this which the midrash interprets. The dialogue and dialectic of the midrashic rabbis will be understood as readings of the dialogue and dialectic of the biblical text. (Boyarin 1990: 15)

MEDIEVAL JEWISH EXEGESIS

Saadiah Ibn Joseph Al-Fayyumi (882–942) was the head (*Gaon*) of the rabbinic academy of Sura. He was the first rabbinic scholar to introduce the use of philology into the study of the Hebrew Bible, the author of a lexicon of Hebrew grammar and an Arabic translation of the Bible. His major philosophical work, *Book of Beliefs and Opinions*, was part of a struggle against the influence of the Karaites, who rejected the rabbinic concept of the Oral Torah. His approach revolutionized Jewish Bible exegesis and ushered in what Wilhelm Bacher characterized as 'the period of the Peshat' (1903: 166).

The impact of these new directions was particularly felt in Muslim and Christian Spain, which saw the development of Hebrew grammar and lexicography. Menachem ben Saruk (*c.*960) composed his *Machberet* (Dictionary) in Hebrew, beginning the research that led to the recognition of the triliteral theory of Hebrew roots developed by his opponent Dunash ibn Labrat (*c.*920–90) and completed by Judah ben David Hayyuj (*c.*945–*c.*1000), writing in Arabic, and subsequently Jonah Ibn Janah (eleventh century) in his Hebrew *Book of Roots*. Hayyuj's studies were translated into Hebrew by Moses ibn Gikatilla (eleventh century), whose observations were to influence the most significant Spanish biblical exegete of the period,

Abraham Ibn Ezra (c.1092–1167). Born in Tudela, Spain, Ibn Ezra was a typical representative of the learned figure of the time, a poet, philosopher, and grammarian, who wrote books on astronomy, astrology, and mathematics. He spent the latter part of his life travelling, including extended periods in Italy, France, and England, composing commentaries to most books of the Hebrew Bible. His style is succinct, and thus at times obscure, leading to a multiplicity of super-commentaries being composed on his writings within his lifetime. Though firmly within the tradition, he noted what he saw as glosses added to the Pentateuch and hinted that Isaiah 40 was written by a different author.

Ibn Ezra is clearly to be located within the rational trend within Jewish exegesis indicated above. In his introduction to his commentary on Genesis he provides a snapshot of the methods used by his contemporaries with whom he is in disagreement: 1. Those who introduce an excess of extraneous matter into their commentary—a critique of the methods used by the Geonim, the spiritual leaders of Babylonian Jewry. 2. Those who entirely reject tradition and rely solely on their own reasoning—the Karaites, whom he calls 'Sadducees'. 3. Those who delight in mysticism and reject the literal sense of the text—this probably applies to the Christians, who, he writes elsewhere, treat the laws of the Pentateuch as allegories. 4. Those who value the peshat but mistakenly give preference to midrashic explanations that were only meant to be understood figuratively—though not named here he seems to mean those like Rashi (see below) who profess to be concerned with the *peshat* but whose commentaries are largely Midrash. (In his commentary on Lamentations he compares the *peshat* to the body and the Midrash to the clothing, adding that some of the latter are like fine silk, while others are like thick sackcloth!) Ibn Ezra considers himself to belong to a fifth class of commentator, who explains the grammatical form of every word and pays attention to the traditional explanation of the laws even when his own reasoning leads him to a different conclusion (based on Friedländer 1877: 120–2). (For a detailed investigation of the approaches of Saadiah, the Karaites, Moses Ibn Gikatilla, and Abraham Ibn Ezra to the Psalms, see Simon 1991.)

To illustrate Ibn Ezra's approach, in the longer of his two commentaries on Exodus he includes an excursus on the two versions of the Ten Commandments. The problem of the different wordings of the sabbath commandment ('Remember the sabbath day' (Exod. 20: 8) and 'Keep the sabbath day' (Deut. 5: 12)) had been resolved in rabbinic tradition with the statement that they were expressed 'in a single utterance'. Ibn Ezra takes issue with those who take this rabbinic saying literally on the basis that God might be able to say two things simultaneously, though no human being could understand them! He argues that in the Deuteronomy version Moses explains elements that are not clear in the Exodus version. As to the occasional differences in wording (and cases where the same word is spelt slightly differently), he argues that this is not significant provided the different words express the same idea, for 'the words are like the body, but the meaning is like the soul'. In an excursus on Ecclesiastes he tackles the apparent contradictions within the book: 'no sage would write a book and contradict himself within it!' He dismisses the view that it was a collective work compiled by the teacher's students and tries to reconcile the contradictory statements with reference to the inner struggle within the soul.

While the rich Islamic culture with its scholarly and intellectual traditions nourished Ibn Ezra and his contemporaries, the most celebrated and beloved Jewish exegete Rashi (Rabbi Solomon ben Isaac, Ra[bbi] Sh[elomo] I[tzhaki], 1040–96) lived in the very different climate of Christian Europe. Born in Troyes, he studied in Worms, which, alongside Mayence and Speyer, were centres of Talmudic learning from the tenth century. Returning home, he established his own school in the city that was a major centre of Christian scholarship. Little is known about his life, though he probably earned a living from viticulture. His three daughters married Talmudic scholars, and his grandson, Rabbi Samuel ben Meir (Rashbam, c.1085–1158), also wrote biblical commentaries in which he debated with his grandfather.

Rashi is rightly renowned for his commentary on the Talmud, which became an essential tool for studying the often difficult text. His commentary on most of the Bible had a very special appeal to the Jewish masses, and his commentary on the Pentateuch was the first Hebrew work whose place and date of printing are known, Reggio in 1475. His commentaries had a significant influence on Christian scholars who sought the plain meaning of the Hebrew. Erwin Rosenthal notes:

[H]e was aptly called by Reuchlin *ordinarius Scripturae interpres*. Nicholas of Lyra quoted him so often that Reuchlin remarked that not many pages would remain over if one took away references to 'Rabi Salomon' from Nicholas's *Postillae*. His exegesis figures largely in the Latin translation of Sebastian Münster, who so decisively influenced the Puritan scholars and translators. Rashi's comments can be detected in Tyndale, Coverdale and the Genevan and Bishop's Bibles, important forerunners of the King James Version, whose chief architect, John Reynolds, refers to him—as Reuchlin had—as 'the author of their ordinary gloss' in his commentaries on Haggai and Obadiah. (Rosenthal 1969: 261–2)

What characterizes Rashi's commentary is the mixture of *peshat* and *derash*, the precise significance of which has been the subject of scholarly debate. In a detailed study of Rashi's use of the terms, Sarah Kamin concluded that they were not used by him as exegetical categories. Rashi accepted both the rabbinic view that the text contained many possible meanings, but also that the 'plain' meaning had to be retained. Thus in places where the text contained features that invited a number of interpretations he would select the traditional one that best fitted the context and linguistic features. He thus created a comprehensive view of the text as a whole, integrating the rabbinic understanding into what he regarded as the 'plain' meaning. It was his grandson, Rashbam, who distinguished clearly between *peshat* and *derash*, who 'limited himself to the text itself, interpreting it according to its vocabulary, syntax and context, in relation to biblical parallels, according to the common sense as well as *derekh eretz* (what is customary). Unlike Rash, Rashbam did not integrate Biblical text and Midrash' (Kamin 1980: 32).

Rashbam, in a celebrated remark, characterizes the openness of his grandfather as a scholar:

And Rabbi Solomon, my maternal grandfather, the light of the eyes of the Diaspora, who commented on the Torah, the Prophets and the Writings, devoted himself to explaining the Peshat of the scriptures; and I, Samuel son of Meir, his son-in-law (may the name of the righteous one be a blessing), debated with him and before him, and he confessed to me that if he had had the leisure, he would have had to have provided other explanations according to the plain meanings (Peshat) that suggest themselves anew every day. (Rashbam commentary to Gen. 37: 2)

Rashi introduced grammatical comments when appropriate, basing himself on the work of Menachem ben Saruk and made particular use of Targum Onqelos. Because he often provided a translation of a particular word, his writings are a valuable source for the study of old French. It is evident that among his concerns, something even more emphasized in the commentaries of the grammarian and exegete Rabbi David Kimchi (Radak, *c*.1160–*c*.1235), were the ongoing debate with Christianity and the eschatological hopes of Jewish contemporaries. Thus Rashi explains Ps. 22: 27, 'the humble shall eat and be sated', as, 'at the time of our redemption in the days of our Messiah'. The 'suffering servant' of Isaiah 52–3 he explains as the Jewish people as a collectivity suffering at the hands of the nations. In his commentary to Ps. 2: 12, Radak explicitly refutes the Christian view that the opening phrase, translated as 'Kiss the son', refers to Jesus, arguing that all such language as 'the mouth of the Lord, the eyes of the Lord' and 'the son of God' or 'the Sons of God', must be understood figuratively.

This internal strengthening of Jewish self-understanding through the commentaries, sometimes expressed through hints alone because of the fear of Christian censorship, was clearly needed. One public manifestation of the pressure to abandon their faith was in the forced public 'Disputations' (Paris, 1240; Barcelona, 1263, and Tortosa, 1413–14). The third great Bible commentator of this early medieval period, alongside Rashi and Ibn Ezra, Moshe ben Nachman (Nachmanides, Ramban, 1195–1270), represented the Jewish people in the Barcelona disputation before King James of Aragon. Hyam Maccoby describes the background:

The fact that the disputation was held at all was a sign that the position of the Jews of Spain was beginning to deteriorate; yet enough remained of the confidence and *élan* of the Jewish 'golden age' to make it into a real occasion, when Jewish attitudes towards fundamental matters such as the meaning of the Messiah, the scope of Original Sin, and the semantics of Biblical and Midrashic exegesis, were expounded in the manner of one giving instruction and enlightenment, not, as at Tortosa, in desperate self-defence. Even Nachmanides was forced to some extent to take a defensive role, as he himself complained; for he was not allowed to put questions against Christianity, but only to answer questions put to him by his Christian opponent. (Maccoby 1982: 12)

Born in Gerona, Nachmanides studied with teachers reflecting the different centres of Jewish learning of his time, 'the glory of the Babylonian academies of which he is the heir, together with the philosophical grasp of the school of Maimonides and the subtlety of the French school of Rashi—not to mention the esoteric mysticism of the Kabbalah [see below], which had recently achieved a new development in Spain, and of which he was a master' (Maccoby 1982: 13). His commentary on the Pentateuch frequently begins by citing the comments of Rashi and Ibn Ezra before taking issue with them. He debates the rationalistic approach of Maimonides, the greatest Jewish medieval philosopher, who sought in his *Guide for the Perplexed* to reconcile biblical teachings with Aristotelian philosophy. For example, Nachmanides challenges Maimonides on the view that all scriptural references to people seeing angels should be understood as prophetic visions rather than as actual events (commenting on Gen. 18: 1–15).

The Hebrew term 'Kabbalah' refers to tradition that has been handed down, and was used in a general sense before being applied to Jewish mysticism. Though present from earlier periods (*Hekhalot* (Palaces) and *Merkavah* (Chariot) literature date from the time of the Talmud and Midrash), there was a new impetus at the end of the twelfth century in Provence and in Spain. The principal text that emerged at the end of the thirteenth century was the *Zohar* (Book of Splendour), the composition of Moses de Leon, which he claimed contained ancient midrashim with interpretations and homilies on the Scripture from the hand of the second-century Palestinian rabbi Shimon bar Yohai. Composed in Hebrew and Aramaic, it is a commentary on the Pentateuch which addresses selective verses from the weekly portion read in the synagogue and creates homilies, stories, and dialogues amongst the sages familiar from the Talmud. This collection of writings exerted an extraordinary power over the Jewish mind, by the sixteenth century sharing pride of place alongside the Bible and the Talmud. (For an introduction to Kabbalah and further reading, see Fine 1984, and for an anthology of *Zohar* texts, Tishby, and Lachower 1989).

For completeness, it is important to mention other medieval commentators whose works were regularly published and studied in Jewish circles, though there is no space here to examine their individual contributions: the mystical approach of Hazzekuni (thirteenth century, France) and Bahya ibn Asher (Rabbenu Bahya, d. 1340, Spain); Jacob ben Asher (Baal ha-Turim, fourteenth century, Spain), whose commentary was devoted to Gematria, the use of the numerical value of Hebrew letters; Levi ben Gershon (Gersonides, Ralbag, 1288–1344), who summarized at the end of each biblical section the philosophical lessons; Isaac Arama (born in Spain, d. 1494 in Naples), who used Talmudic, kabbalistic, and philosophical authors to create a coherent account of different biblical sections; Don Isaac ben Judah Abravanel (born in Spain, 1437, died in Venice, 1508) who introduces each section of his commentary on the Pentateuch with questions addressed to the text which he answers with reference to wide-ranging areas of knowledge; Obadiah ben Jacob

Sforno (Italy, d. 1550), author of a philosophical commentary on the Pentateuch and the teacher of Johann Reuchlin, the Christian defender of Jews and Jewish literature. (An introduction, commentary, and sampling of the above and other 'traditional' commentators till the nineteenth century can be found in Jacobs (1973) and through comparative citations of different biblical verses in Leibowitz (1976). For further studies of the commentaries of, among others, Rashi and Ibn Ezra, see Sarna (2000).)

THE MODERN PERIOD

Writing in his *Tractatus Theologico-Politicus*, published in 1670, Spinoza virtually defines the approach of modern historical criticism of the Bible:

The history of Scripture should consist of three aspects: 1. an analysis of the Hebrew language; 2. the compilation and classification of the expressions of each of the books of the Bible; 3. research as to the origins of the biblical writings as far as they can still be ascertained i.e. concerning the life, the conduct and the pursuits of the author of each book, who he was, what was the occasion and the epoch of his writing, whom did he write for, and in what language. Further it should inquire into the fate of each book: how it was first received, into whose hands it fell, how many different versions there were of it, by whose advice was it received into the Canon, and lastly, how all the books now universally accepted as sacred, were united into a single whole.

If Spinoza was to have a direct influence on the subsequent development of biblical criticism, his excommunication by the rabbinic authorities of Amsterdam cut him off from any immediate impact on the Jewish community. Instead, it was Moses Mendelssohn (1729–86) a century later in Germany who was to open up to the Jewish world the new realm of biblical scholarship. As part of an attempt to encourage the Jewish community to reject Yiddish and learn German, he set about translating the Bible into German, transliterating the text into Hebrew characters, and adding a commentary, the *Biur*. Though it too received massive condemnation from Orthodox authorities, it helped open the way for many Jews to enter German society and explore the delicate balance between the two components of their identity.

Whereas Mendelssohn's Bible commentary remains within the traditional framework, it is Shmuel David Luzzato (1800–65), known by the acronym Shadal, who is the first to debate with the modern Bible critics in his commentaries on the Pentateuch and Isaiah. He was lecturer in Bible at the rabbinical seminary in Padua, established in 1829. Though traditional in his own views of the Bible, alongside

Rashi and the other medieval commentators, he quotes the opinions of contemporary scholars ranging from Isaac Newton to Gesenius.

His contemporary, Samson Raphael Hirsch (1808–88) reflects instead just how the divide was beginning to emerge in the Jewish world, and how it was reflected in the approach to Scripture. The foremost exponent of Orthodoxy in the nineteenth century, throughout his life he was in a struggle with the newly emerging Reform movement. He served as Rabbi in Frankfurt for thirty-seven years, where he developed his concept of modern Orthodoxy, *torah im derekh eretz*, strict adherence to traditional Judaism combined with playing a full role in contemporary life. He translated the Pentateuch and the book of Psalms into German, trying to keep as close as possible to the Hebrew original, and as such was to influence the translation of Franz Rosenzweig and Martin Buber a century later. The accompanying commentary, which shows his mastery of rabbinic sources and his creative use of philology, remains a source book for the modern Orthodox community.

Of a quite different order, however, are the writings of Benno Jacob (1862–1945). Also the product of an Orthodox education, the rabbinical seminary, and the University of Breslau, he served as an Orthodox rabbi before retiring in 1929 to devote himself to exegesis. Though not a fundamentalist, he came to a denial of modern Bible criticism because of flaws he found in its methodology and assumptions. He found the textual emendations of Higher Criticism to be arbitrary and unscientific, since their only purpose was to validate the prior assumptions of the scholars. He also saw in the school of Higher Criticism anti-Semitic trends and prejudice against Judaism. Tragically, his major work, *Das Erste Buch der Torah: Genesis, übersetzt und erklärt*, was published in 1934 and was burnt by the Nazis. Thus his thought, until very recently, never entered into the scholarly debate within Germany about the Documentary Hypothesis.

Along the same trajectory from rabbinic training to scholarly engagement with the text of the Bible stands Umberto Cassuto (1883–1951). Born in Florence, he served briefly there as a rabbi before devoting himself to scholarship, first in the field of the history of the Jews of Italy, but later as a Bible scholar, where his studies in Ugaritic were of great significance. In place of the Graf–Wellhausen theory, which he subjected to a devastating critique in his book *The Documentary Hypothesis* (1961b), he found evidence of an oral tradition and a number of poetic epics. But he was particularly sensitive to the literary construction of the texts of the Pentateuch, noting especially the use of number symbolism and the repetition of key words. He is thus one of the bridging figures to the contemporary literary examination of the biblical texts.

Two figures stand out in the Orthodox circles of Eastern Europe who uniquely focused on biblical commentary: Rabbi Meir Leib ben Yechiel Michael, the Malbim (1809–79) (Poland and Russia), in his own struggle against the Reformers, sought to show that the Oral and Written Torah were inseparable; and Rabbi Naftali Tzvi Yehudah Berlin, the Netziv (1817–93) (Poland), the beloved head of the yeshivah of

Volozhin, the spiritual centre of Russian Jewry, sought to explain how the Talmudic comments on the Bible clarified its plain meaning. These approaches express two contrasting emphases within Orthodoxy. To oversimplify somewhat, the one seeks to explain Scripture in terms of the tradition, the other to explain the tradition in terms of Scripture.

The nineteenth-century movement for the *Wissenschaft des Judentums*, the scientific study of Judaism, was part of a programmatic attempt to bring Jews into their full place within Western society. Moreover, Judaism was to enter the same respectable academic framework as other disciplines, through applying the contemporary values of reason, scholarly objectivity, and historical perspective to the traditions and values of the past. Leopold Zunz, who is considered the father of this new movement, did pioneering work on Rashi, collecting and comparing the different manuscripts of Rashi's Bible commentaries, and from them deriving historical information on the man himself, his family, his studies, the languages he knew, and the sources available to him. Zunz's writings and the methodology he applied influenced an entire generation of Jewish scholars, in Western and Eastern Europe. They in turn began to explore the classic Jewish writings and figures, thus transforming the study of the Bible, the midrashic tradition of commentary, and the medieval Jewish exegetes, making them accessible and significant in a new way, geared to the needs of post-emancipation Jewish society.

The *Wissenschaft* movement found a home in the newly created rabbinic seminaries, but also in the lectureships and chairs in Jewish Studies that began to be established in universities. In this latter context, however, a different emphasis prevailed to that of the seminaries: the secular, even anti-religious, one of academia. Jewish scholars in such departments, apart from their thorough knowledge of post-biblical rabbinic sources and mastery of Hebrew, were often indistinguishable in their work from their academic counterparts who were often religiously uncommitted Christians. Thus we have a real problem in attempting to define what, if anything, can be claimed as being particularly Jewish in their work. It may be that in their private life such Jewish scholars had a religious commitment of some sort, but this was not allowed to colour the supposed objectivity of their scholarly labours.

Yet the end of the twentieth century has seen a renewal of Jewish scholarly interest in the Hebrew Bible, particularly in the area of literary studies. The biblical articles of Franz Rosenzweig and Martin Buber, in conjunction with their monumental German translation of the Bible, introduced an attempt at a 'close reading of the text'. This synchronic approach, while acknowledging the value of the historical critical and other schools, starts with the final form of the biblical text that presents itself to the reader. Through studying individual passages, examining the use of language, the inner structure, the conventions of narrative composition and rhetoric, these newer approaches to the biblical text have triggered a revolution in biblical exegesis, particularly evident over the last decades of the twentieth century. What is fascinating in this context is the extent to which Jewish scholars have made major contributions in this field, and comparison with the commitment to 'close reading' and the quest for meaning of the composers of Midrash and the medieval Jewish scholars is inevitable. The following is a list of some of the better-known scholars in this ever-growing field: Robert Alter, Yaira Amit, Shimon Bar-Efrat, Adele Berlin, Chanan Brichto, Michael Fishbane, Edward L. Greenstein, Gabriel Josipovici, Jonathan Magonet, Samuel Sandmel, Jack Sasson, George W. Savran, Meir Steinberg, Meir Weiss, and Avivah Gottlieb Zornberg, in the field of narrative, and Robert Alter, Adele Berlin, Marcia Falk, Robert Gordis, Harold Fisch, in the field of poetry.

Individual Jews have contributed to areas in which biblical ideas are being challenged or reassessed. Martin Walzer's *Exodus and Revolution* (1985) makes an important contribution to the development of liberation theology. Moshe Greenberg (1995) has explored in particular biblical law. Judith Plaskow's *Standing Again at Sinai: Judaism from a Feminist Perspective* addresses a number of biblical issues, as do the writings of Athalya Brenner, Tamara C. Eskenazi, Tikva Frymer-Kensky, Llana Pardes, and Rachel Adler. Classics in the relatively small field of Jewish theology are two studies of biblical prophecy: A. J. Heschel's *The Prophets* and Andre Neher's *The Prophetic Existence*. No survey can exclude the many biblical writings of Martin Buber and those of his collaborator in translating the Bible, Franz Rosenzweig. Erich Fromm explores the struggle with idolatry in *You Shall be as Gods* (1966). Arthur Waskow rereads biblical narratives and festivals in terms of contemporary issues in his challenging book *Godwrestling* (1978).

A radical approach is taken by the philosopher and theologian Emil L. Fackenheim (1990). In criticizing the apparently seamless continuity of theological thinking, in the Christian and Jewish worlds alike, despite the enormity of the Shoah, he calls for a radical rereading of the Bible. Thus he can no longer share the stance of the biblical narrator who criticizes the Israelites for complaining in the wilderness about the lack of water for their children. In the light of Auschwitz and the murder of the children, a different view is needed: 'The narrator takes sides with Moses, with God, and castigates the murmurers while, for their part, these murmurers invoke the children. As this is read by Jews of this generation, they perceive just how radically their religious situation has changed; they have no choice but to take sides with the mothers of the children, against the narrator, against Moses and, if necessary, against God Himself' (Fackenheim 1990: 32).

Fackenheim also proposes that a book like Esther, that has long been assigned to the rear of theological concerns, should now take centre stage, with its realistic picture of the violence of the world and the seeming absence of God. In today's post-Shoah world God's silence is no longer acceptable.

Jewish societies today are caught up in the general secular values of the West, which sets relatively little store by Scripture, or else receives it in some kind of pre-packaged and pre-digested form. Jews are also subject to the same social movements, like the return to fundamentalism, that drive some people back to their Bibles, but so as to read them in a highly selective, and often politicized, way. Jewish tradition, on the other hand, demands an engagement with the text that leaves it open to constant rediscovery and reinterpretation, and the reader open to an unlimited growth in understanding. A Jewish community that does not read and reread the Hebrew Bible is seriously impoverished. Today, however, it is well furnished with materials, classical and modern, academic and spiritual, that can open the many dimensions of the text of the Hebrew Bible to itself and others.

BIBLIOGRAPHY

ADLER, R. 1998. *Engendering Judaism: An Inclusive Theology and Ethics.* Philadelphia and Jerusalem: The Jewish Publication Society.

ALTER, R. 1981. *The Art of Biblical Narrative.* London: George Allen and Unwin.

—— 1985. *The Art of Biblical Poetry.* New York: Basic Books.

AMIT, Y. 2001. *Reading Biblical Narratives: Literary Criticism and the Hebrew Bible.* Minneapolis: Fortress Press.

BACHER, W. 1903. 'Bible Exegesis—Jewish'. In *The Jewish Encyclopedia*, New York and London: Funk and Wagnell, iii. 162–74.

BAR-EFRAT, S. 1989. *Narrative Art in the Bible.* Sheffield: Almond Press.

BERLIN, A. 1983. *Poetics and Interpretation of Biblical Narrative.* Sheffield: Almond Press.

—— 1985. *The Dynamics of Biblical Parallelism.* Bloomington, Ind.: Indiana University Press.

—— 1991. *Biblical Poetry through Medieval Jewish Eyes.* Bloomington, Ind.: Indiana University Press.

BOYARIN, D. 1990. *Intertextuality and the Reading of Midrash.* Bloomington, Ind., and Indianapolis: Indiana University Press.

BRENNER, A. 1985. *The Israelite Woman: Social Role and Literary Type in Biblical Narrative.* The Biblical Seminar, 2. Sheffield: JSOT Press.

—— ed. 1995. *Feminist Companion Series to the Bible.* Sheffield: Sheffield Academic Press.

BRICHTO, H. C. 1992. *Toward a Grammar of Biblical Poetics: Tales of the Prophets.* Oxford and New York: Oxford University Press.

—— 1996. *The Names of God.* Oxford and New York: Oxford University Press.

BUBER, M. 1946. *Moses: The Revelation and the Covenant.* New York: Harper & Row.

—— 1949. *The Prophetic Faith.* New York: Harper & Row.

—— 1968. *Biblical Humanism*, ed. N. N. Glatzer. London: Macdonald.

CASSUTO, U. 1961a. *A Commentary on the Book of Genesis*, 2 vols., trans. Israel Abrahams. Jerusalem: The Magnes Press, The Hebrew University.

—— 1961b. *The Documentary Hypothesis and the Composition of the Pentateuch*, trans. Israel Abrahams. Jerusalem: The Magnes Press, The Hebrew University.

—— 1967. *A Commentary on the Book of Exodus*, trans. Israel Abrahams. Jerusalem: The Magnes Press, The Hebrew University.

ESKENAZI, T. C. 1992. 'Out from the Shadows: Biblical Women in the Postexilic Era'. *JSOT* 54: 25–43.

FACKENHEIM, E. L. 1990. *The Jewish Bible after the Holocaust: A Re-reading*. Manchester: Manchester University Press.

FALK, M. 1982. *Love Lyrics from the Bible: A Translation and Literary Study of the Song of Songs*. Sheffield: Almond Press.

FINE, L. 1984. 'Kabbalistic Texts'. In Barry W. Holtz, ed., *Back to the Sources: Classic Jewish Texts*. New York: Summit Books.

FISCH, H. 1990. *Poetry with a Purpose: Biblical Poetics and Interpretation*. Bloomington, Ind.: Indiana University Press.

FISHBANE, M. 1979. *Text and Texture: Close Readings of Selected Biblical Texts*. New York: Schocken Books.

—— 1985. *Biblical Interpretation in Ancient Israel*. Oxford: Clarendon Press.

—— 1989. *The Garments of Torah: Essays in Biblical Hermeneutics*. Bloomington, Ind.: Indiana University Press.

FRIEDLÄNDER, M. 1877. *Essays on the Writings of Abraham Ibn Ezra*. London: The Society of Hebrew Literature.

FROMM, E. 1966. *You Shall be as Gods: A Radical Interpretation of the Old Testament and its Tradition*. Greenwich, Conn.: Fawcett Publications.

FRYMER-KENSKY, T. 1989. 'Law and Philosophy: The Case of Sex in the Bible'. *Semeia*, 45: 89–102.

GORDIS, R. 1971. *Poets, Prophets and Sages: Essays in Biblical Interpretation*. Bloomington, Ind.: Indiana University Press.

GREENBERG, M. 1995. *Studies in the Bible and Jewish Thought*. Philadelphia and Jerusalem: The Jewish Publication Society.

HALIVNI, D. W. 1991. *Peshat and Derash: Plain and Applied Meaning in Rabbinic Exegesis*. New York and Oxford: Oxford University Press.

HARRIS, J. M. 1995. *How Do We Know This? Midrash and the Fragmentation of Modern Judaism*. Albany, NY: State University of New York Press.

HESCHEL, A. J. 1962. *The Prophets*. Philadelphia: The Jewish Publication Society of America.

JACOB, B. 1934. *Das Erste Buch der Tora: Genesis*. Berlin: Schocken Verlag. Repr. Stuttgart: Calwer Verlag, 2000. ET: *The First Book of the Bible: Genesis*, abridged, ed. and trans. E. I. and W. Jacob. New York: Ktav Publishing House, 1974.

—— 1992. *The Second Book of the Bible: Exodus*, trans. with an introduction by Walter Jacob. Hoboken, NJ: Ktav Publishing House Inc.

JACOBS, L. 1973. *Jewish Biblical Exegesis*. The Chain of Tradition Series, 4. New York: Behrman House.

JOSIPOVICI, G. 1988. *The Book of God: A Response to the Bible*. New Haven: Yale University Press.

KAMIN, S. 1980. 'Rashi's Exegetical Categorization with Respect to the Distinction between Peshat and Derash; according to his Commentary to the Book of Genesis and Selected Passages from his Commentaries to other Books of the Bible'. *Immanuel*, 11: 16–32. (Based on her book *Rashi's Exegetical Categorization in Respect to the Distinction between Peshat and Derash* (Hebrew). Jerusalem: The Magnes Press, The Hebrew University.)

KASHER, R. 1988. 'The Interpretation of Scripture in Rabbinic Literature'. In Martin Jan Mulder, ed., *Mikra: Text, Translation, Reading and Interpretation of the Hebrew Bible in Ancient Judaism and Early Christianity*, Assen and Maastricht: Van Gorcum; Philadelphia: Fortress Press.

KUGEL, J. L. 1981. *The Idea of Biblical Poetry: Parallelism and its History*. New Haven: Yale University Press.

LANDY, F. 1983. *Paradoxes of Paradise: Identity and Difference in the Song of Songs*. Sheffield: Almond Press.

LEIBOWITZ, N. 1972–80. *Studies in... Bereshit (Genesis)* (1972); *Shemot (The Book of Exodus)* (1976); *Vayikra (Leviticus)* (1980); *Bamidbar (Numbers)* (1980); *Devarim (Deuteronomy)* (1980), trans. and adapted from the Hebrew by A. Newman. Jerusalem: The World Zionist Organization, Department for Torah Education and Culture in the Diaspora.

MACCOBY, H. 1982. *Judaism on Trial: Jewish–Christian Disputations in the Middle Ages*. The Littman Library of Jewish Civilization. London and Toronto: Fairleigh Dickinson University Press.

MAGONET, J. 1976. *Form and Meaning: Studies in Literary Techniques in the Book of Jonah*. Beiträge zur biblischen Exegese und Theologie. Bern and Frankfurt: Herbert Lang and Peter Lang; repr. with a Postscript, Sheffield: The Almond Press, 1983.

—— 1994. *A Rabbi Reads the Psalms*. London: SCM Press, 2nd edn.

—— 1995. 'How Do Jews Interpret The Bible Today? The Sixteenth Montefiore Lecture (17 February 1994), University of Southampton'. *JSOT* 66: 3–27.

NEHER, A. 1969. *The Prophetic Existence: A New Analysis of the Prophets of the Old Testament*, trans W. Wolf. London: A. S. Barnes; South Brunswick: Thomas Yoseloff.

NEUSNER, J. 1995. *The Classics of Judaism: A Textbook and Reader*. Louisville, Ky.: Westminster/John Knox Press.

PARDES, I. 1992. *Countertraditions in the Bible: A Feminist Approach*. Cambridge, Mass.: Harvard University Press.

PLASKOW, J. 1991. *Standing Again at Sinai: Judaism from a Feminist Perspective*. San Francisco: Harper Collins.

PORTON, G. G. 1992. 'Midrash: Palestinian Jews and the Hebrew Bible in the Greco-Roman Period'. ANRW 2/19/2: 103–38. Cited in his article 'Midrash' in *ABD* iv. 818–21.

ROSENTHAL, E. I. J. 1969. 'The Study of the Bible in Medieval Judaism'. In G. W. H. Lampe, ed., *The Cambridge History of the Bible*, ii, Cambridge: Cambridge University Press, 252–79; repr. in *idem, Studia Semitica*, i: *Jewish Themes*, Cambridge: Cambridge University Press, 1971.

ROSENZWEIG, F. n.d. *Die Schrift: Aufsätze, Übertragungen und Briefe*, ed. K. Thieme. Frankfurt am Main: Europäische Verlagsanstalt.

SANDMEL, S. 1972. *The Enjoyment of Scripture: The Law, the Prophets and the Writings*. New York: Oxford University Press.

SARNA, N. 2000. *Studies in Biblical Interpretation*. Philadelphia: The Jewish Publication Society.

SASSON, J. M. 1979. *Ruth: A New Translation with a Philological Commentary and a Formalist-Folklorist Interpretation*. Baltimore: The Johns Hopkins University Press.

SAVRAN, G. W. 1988. *Telling and Retelling: Quotation in Biblical Narrative*. Bloomington, Ind.: Indiana University Press.

SIMON, U. 1991. *Four Approaches to the Book of Psalms: From Saadiah Gaon to Abraham Ibn Ezra*. Albany, NY: State University of New York Press.

STEINBERG, M. 1987. *The Poetics of Biblical Narrative: Ideological Literature and the Drama of Reading*. Bloomington, Ind.: Indiana University Press.

TISHBY, I., and LACHOWER, FISCHEL 1989. *The Wisdom of the Zohar: An Anthology of Texts*, trans. David Goldstein. The Littman Library. Oxford University Press: Oxford.

WALZER, M. 1985. *Exodus and Revolution*. New York: Basic Books.

WASKOW, A. I. 1978. *Godwrestling*. New York: Schocken Books.

WEISS, M. 1984. *The Bible from Within*. Jerusalem: The Magnes Press.

ZORNBERG, A. V. 1996. *The Beginning of Desire: Reflections on Genesis*. New York and London: Doubleday.

PART VII

THE AUTHORITY
OF THE BIBLE

CHAPTER 43

CANON

LEE MARTIN McDONALD

I. INTRODUCTION

An examination of the origin and development of the biblical canons of both Judaism and Christianity is essentially about the processes that led to the stabilizing of fixed collections of writings that undergird the core of beliefs and religious practices of those communities. The corollary of canon formation is the belief that the writings that make up those collections have their origin in God; that is, they are inspired by God, and consequently are authoritative for worship, instruction in core beliefs, mission activity, and religious and practical conduct. While the definition of a biblical canon has more to do with the end of a process—that is, with a fixed list of sacred scriptures—the authority attributed to those writings was recognized much earlier when they were in a more fluid stage of development and were more open to adaptability or change to meet the needs of the religious community. Many factors played a role in the complex history of the formation of the biblical canon, including the origin of the notion of sacred literature, the processes that led to the recognition of that literature, and the final fixing of a closed collection of sacred literature.

There is little agreement among scholars on *when* this 'canonical activity' began, *where* it began, and especially when it was completed. Resolving such problems is made more difficult by the fact that there are no discussions of the origins, development, and recognition of biblical canons in antiquity. By all appearances, this was an unconscious process throughout most of its development. Most information on the matter is tenuous, and it is generally drawn from an investigation of a limited but familiar collection of ancient texts (referred to below). There is no evidence from the time of Jesus that either the Jews or the followers of Jesus were even remotely interested in the notion of a closed collection of sacred scriptures.

The textual form of the Scriptures was also of little serious consideration in the early stages of the canonical processes, though at various times some texts and translations did receive widespread but not universal acceptance in the Christian and Jewish communities. For example, most early churches unofficially adopted the Septuagint (LXX), or Greek translation of the Hebrew Scriptures, as its divinely inspired version, and the Jews later opted for the Masoretic Text of the Hebrew Bible, although the earliest complete witness to that text dates from 1008 CE. 'Septuagint' originally referred only to the translation of the Pentateuch, a point made forcefully, first by the author of the *Letter of Aristeas* (§§3–5, 19, 30, etc.), who was the first to call the translation a 'bible' (§316), but also by Jerome in the fifth century (cf. his introduction to *Hebraica Questiones in Libro Geneseos* I/1). The translation gradually expanded to include all of the books of the Jewish Scriptures, including several that are not part of the Masoretic tradition (often called apocryphal or deutero-canonical in the Christian tradition). It was this Greek version which was used to translate the Bible into various languages.

The relationship between canon formation and textual or translation considerations has resurfaced recently as important issues for the Church, but these were not significant matters throughout most of its history and no certain decisions were made on these matters in the patristic period (*c.* second to sixth centuries CE). The differences in the manuscripts that survive from antiquity, as well as in the variety of translations of the biblical literature, show that the Church had little concern for such matters throughout most of its history. While most scholars who produce *critical* commentaries today focus at least minimally on the history of the text of biblical books, seldom do they emphasize the significance of this for determining a *canonical text*: that is, an authoritative text for the Church. Historically, the most common assumption has been that the earliest text of the Bible is more authoritative, but recently that view has been challenged, and many textual scholars no longer believe that an original text is recoverable.

The following discussion will examine the notion of canon in antiquity and its application to the writings that eventually received canonical recognition in the Jewish and Christian communities of faith. The investigation of the Hebrew Bible and the 'First' or 'Old' Testament of the Church, as will become clear, are inextricably bound together. The lack of agreement in antiquity on the definition of a biblical canon, as well as the books that comprise it, and the inconsistency in the use of terms to describe it and its processes make any investigation of the origins and stabilization of the Bible more difficult, but some inferences and conclusions can be drawn. This examination will begin with a focus on the context of canon formation, and then proceed to what can be discerned in the ancient sources.

II. Scribes and Scriptures in the Ancient World

Scribes (Hebrew *soferim*) in the ancient world were highly esteemed, and were afforded a significant sacred status in the Jewish community. Often, whatever they wrote was considered very important, even though much of it was simply copying what others had said (Bar-Ilan 1990). Most of what was written was deemed important, and referring to it as 'it is written' came to refer to its divine authority (Davies 2002: 42–4).

The word 'fulfill' or its various forms ('fulfilled' or 'as it is fulfilled') also designates the authority and sacredness of ancient literature. All revelatory material, for example, was given special consideration. When prophets spoke, they were thought to convey the word and will of God. If they wrote down their prophecies, the writings took on the status of divine authority within the religious community. If one believed that a prophecy given earlier had been fulfilled in subsequent events, the prophecy was thereby validated, and the divine origin of the prophecy was affirmed. Prophecy-fulfilment motifs are frequently found in biblical literature, and were received as integral to authoritative sacred writings among Jews and Christians. In the New Testament, as well as in the early Christian communities, various designations were used to emphasize the sacredness of the body of literature that we now call the Old Testament by identifying it as 'it is written', 'the writings say', 'the scripture says', or 'as the scripture says' (Metzger 1987: 289–95).

The basic properties of 'Scripture', both for ancient Judaism and Christianity, appear to have included at least four essential ingredients. Generally speaking, Scripture is a written document believed to have divine origin that communicates the will and truth of God for a believing community, and it provides a source of regulations for the corporate and individual life of that community (Farley 1982: 58; Kelsey 1975: 89–94). When a particular writing was acknowledged by a religious community to be divinely inspired and authoritative, it was eventually elevated to the status of Scripture, even if the writing was not yet called 'Scripture' and even if that status was only temporary (e.g. *Eldad and Modad, Epistle of Barnabas, Shepherd of Hermas, 1 Clement, Letters of Ignatius*). There was limited discussion in the early church of such matters, and in the first two centuries there was only limited agreement on which books were acknowledged as Scripture.

Among the world's religious traditions, Judaism, Christianity, and Islam have defined themselves and their mission in terms of sacred texts. The development of a collection of Scriptures in these traditions appears to have come from a common belief in the notion of a 'heavenly book' that contains both divine knowledge and decrees from God. This heavenly book generally included wisdom, destinies (or laws), a book of works, and a book of life (Graham 1987: 49–50). This notion goes back to ancient Mesopotamia and Egypt, where the heavenly book indicated not only the future plans of God, but also the destinies of human beings. An example of this understanding can be found in Ps. 139: 15–16: 'My frame was not hidden from you, when I was being made in secret, intricately woven in the depths of the earth. Your eyes beheld my unformed substance. In your book were written all the days that were formed for me, when none of them as yet existed' (NRSV). This notion is also found in Rev. 5: 1, 3, and in the description of the opening of a book in 6: 1–17 and 8: 1–10: 11. In Rev. 20: 12, 15, books are opened before the great white throne of God in heaven, and 'another book was opened, the book of life. And the dead were judged according to their works, as recorded in the books... and anyone whose name was not found written in the book of life was thrown into the lake of fire' (NRSV). According to Exod. 32: 33, sinners will be blotted out of God's book. The same notion of a heavenly book lies behind Paul's assertion about Clement and the rest of his colleagues in ministry, 'whose names are in the book of life' (Phil. 4: 3).

This belief gave rise to the notion that divine knowledge and heavenly decrees are contained in a divine book that is symbolized in written scriptures (Graham 1987: 50–1). In the Qur'an, reference is made to a divine book of destinies in which 'no misfortune strikes on earth or in yourselves without its being [written] in a Book before we cause it to be. Truly, that is easy for God' (*Surah* 57. 22; trans. Graham 1987: 50–1). Long before the notion of a biblical canon, the Law was believed to have come directly from God. Moses proclaimed the words and ordinances of God (Exod. 24: 3), and was commissioned by God to write them down (Exod. 34: 4, 27). It was believed that God was the writer of the Decalogue, or Ten Commandments (Exod. 34: 1; Deut. 4: 13; 10: 4). The Jews came to believe that the Law of God was written and preserved in sacred writings, and this belief played an important role in the development of their notion of a revealed and authoritative scripture.

Although the belief in divinely inspired writings was widespread in Israel in late antiquity and also in early Christianity, what each group believed was scripture is not always clear. Even though ancient writers often cited written texts, this does not necessarily mean that they or their readers viewed them as sacred and inviolable scriptures. Likewise, when an ancient teacher cites a particular text *as scripture,* one cannot conclude that all teachers of that time and place considered that writing sacred. For example, Paul reportedly cited several non-biblical sources in his speaking and writings (Acts 17: 28, Epimenides and Aratus; cf. Titus 1: 12, Epimenides), but one cannot conclude that he cited them *as scripture.* Also, even though Irenaeus argued for a fourfold gospel collection, those four and no more, after him Bishop Serapion of Antioch initially allowed the *Gospel of Peter* to be read in the churches, but later, after examining its theological contents, he reversed himself on the matter. The reversal was not because of his discovery of a widely accepted closed collection of gospels, but because he subsequently became aware of its contents. Likewise, as late as the mid-fourth century, Athanasius published his twenty-seven-book list of the writings of the New Testament in his 39th Festal Letter, but it was not universally accepted in the rest of the Roman Empire, or even in Egypt itself in his generation. Widespread approval took much longer. Just because well-known church teachers cited ancient texts, one cannot conclude that such writings were a part of their biblical canons. Every citation or quote must be evaluated on its own merit before being added to someone's sacred collection.

The Church inherited its collection of Old Testament Scriptures from first-century Judaism before its separation from the synagogue. The writings that the Jews believed were sacred *before* this separation were also the same ones acknowledged in the earliest Christian churches. That collection was largely, but not completely, formed before the time of Jesus, and it included the Law and the Prophets, and an imprecise collection of other writings. It could be that these other writings were fewer than, the same as, or even more than those in the current Hebrew Scriptures. The early Christians apparently accepted several 'apocryphal' writings as 'scripture', since they cited them as such in the second and third centuries, and several of these writings appear in various biblical manuscripts in the fourth and fifth centuries as well as in various canonical lists from the same time (McDonald 1995: 108–18, 268–73). The variety in those collections diminished in time, but some diversity was present for several centuries—indeed, throughout church history. Had there been any understanding in the early church that Jesus had received and passed on to his disciples a fixed biblical canon, it is unthinkable that the early church would have considered producing another 'Testament' of sacred writings or receiving as sacred any books that Jesus had rejected. The development of a 'New' Testament in the last third of the second century CE is evidence that the church was *not* born with a *fixed* biblical canon in its hands, as some allege. How could a new collection emerge if there was already a fixed biblical canon widely acknowledged?

III. CANONS IN ANTIQUITY

Christians in the fourth century made use of a familiar Greek term, 'canon' (Greek *kanōn*), to describe a closed collection of sacred scriptures. Originally the word referred to a measuring instrument, a standard to follow, and eventually a rule or guide. The notion was applied to art, sculpturing, and architecture, such as in the perfect frame to be copied, as well as to music, where the monochord was the canon by which all other tonal relationships were controlled. It was also used by Alexandrians in reference to grammar, and they produced a canon of classical writers whose Greek was used as a model for other writers. They were connected with the famous Alexandrian library, and compiled a body of literature, even lists, that reflected the literary standards of their day (VanderKam 2000: 29–30; Pfeiffer 1968: 123–51). This example may be the context of the *Letter of Aristeas* that told of the famous Greek translation of the Hebrew Scriptures that was presented to the Pharaoh in Egypt (*c.*280 BCE). This idea may well have given rise to notions of canon in the Jewish and Christian communities, but the lines of dependence are not clear.

In the second-century church, *kanon* was employed as a 'rule of faith' (Latin *regula fidei*, Greek *ho kanōn tēs pisteōs*), and even a 'rule of truth' (Latin *regula veritatis*, Greek *ho kanōn tēs alētheias*), to designate a core of beliefs that identified the Christian community (Metzger 1987: 251–2).

In the Graeco-Roman world, Epicurus of Samos (*c.*341–270 BCE) argued that logic and method in thought stemmed from a canon (*kanōn*) or criterion (*kritērion*) by which one could measure and determine what was true or false and what was worth investigating or not. For him, philosophical inquiry enabled one to discover what was both true and false, and he wrote a treatise on the matter entitled 'Of the Standard' or 'Canon' (*Peri kriteriou; Kanōn*). Diogenes Laertius writes: 'Now in the Canon, Epicurus affirms that our sensations and preconceptions and our feelings *are the standards or truth*' (Diogenes Laertius, *Lives of Eminent Philosophers*, x. 31, 'Epicurus', (LCL, italics added); see also 27, 30; and Seneca, *Epistles*, 89. 11–12). Epictetus argued that the goal of philosophy is to determine a 'standard of judgement' and adds that whatever subject needs to be investigated, it needs to be 'subject to the standard' (*hupage autēn tō kanoni*) (*Dissertationes*, ii. 11. 13, 20; cf. ii. 23. 21). Aeschines of Athens (*c.*397–322 BCE) likewise writes:

In carpentry, when we want to know whether something is straight, we use a ruler (*kanōn*) designed for the purpose. So also in the case of indictments for illegal proposals, the guide (*kanōn*) for justice is this public posting of the proposal with accompanying statement of the laws that it violates. (*Against Ctesiphon* 199–200, trans. Danker)

This is not unlike the way that biblical scriptures have been understood and employed in the Jewish and Christian communities of faith: namely, as a standard of faith, mission, and conduct.

The works of Homer were reverently esteemed by the Greeks, and the gods referred to in his *Iliad* and *Odyssey* became the acknowledged gods of the Greeks. Unlike other ancient writings of the time, each of these books was divided into twenty-four parts or chapters, each identified by a letter of the Greek alphabet. The use of the alphabet as a sign of the divine source and importance of those works is helpful in understanding the NT reference to God and Jesus as the 'Alpha and Omega', the first and last letters of the Greek alphabet (Rev. 1: 8; 21: 6; 22: 13). Like those who revered Homer and used the alphabet to designate chapters in his works, the Jews identified the number of books in their sacred collection with the number of letters in the Hebrew alphabet (twenty-two) and later adopted the number of the Greek alphabet (twenty-four). Before that time, several psalms were divided by the twenty-two letters of the Hebrew alphabet (e.g. Pss. 25, 33, 34, 103, and especially

119, which has twenty-two sections, each beginning with a different letter of the Hebrew alphabet). Homer became 'canon' for the Greeks, and it is also interesting that Alexander the Great, under the influence of Aristotle, worshipped Homer and even founded a cult of Homer at Alexandria (see Graham 1987: 52). In other Graeco-Roman literature, 'canon' was employed as a means of determining the quality of something, whether it 'measured up' (Euripides, *Hecuba* 602; Demosthenes 18. 18, 296; Aeschines, *In Ctesiphonem* 88; Plutarch, *Consolatio ad Apollonium* 103a; Epictetus, *Dissertationes* i. 28. 28; Lucian, *Piscator* 30).

In the New Testament, *kanōn* is found only in Paul's letters where he speaks of guidelines established by God, the limits of Paul's ministry, the boundaries of another's ministry (2 Cor. 10: 13, 15, 16), and once as the standard or norm of true faith (Gal. 6: 16). Later, Clement of Rome (*c.*90 CE) uses the term in reference to the church's revealed truth, that is 'the rule of our traditions' (*1 Clem.* 7. 2). Similarly, in Irenaeus 'canon' refers to the essence or core of Christian doctrine. Irenaeus contends that a true believer retains 'unchangeable in his heart the *rule of the truth* which he received by means of baptism' (*Adv. Haer.* 1. 9. 4, ANF). Eusebius (*c.*320–30 CE) indicates that Clement of Alexandria spoke of an 'ecclesiastical canon' or 'body of truth' (*HE* 6. 13. 3). The word was also common in Jewish writings; for example, Josephus refers to Josiah's ascension to the throne (2 Kgs. 22: 1; 2 Chr. 34: 1) and says that he used King David 'as a pattern and rule (*kanoni*) of his whole manner of life' (*AJ* 10. 49; see also *Ap.* 2. 174; Philo, *Leg. All.* 3. 233; *Test. Napht.* 2. 3; 4 Macc. 7: 21; *Ep. Arist.* §2).

Athanasius (367 CE) was the first to use *kanōn* in reference to a fixed collection of sacred books, and also to identify the twenty-seven books that eventually made up the New Testament. In his Festal Letter of 367 CE, he also uses a verbal form of *kanōn* (*kanonizomenon* = 'canonized') to refer to a body of sacred scriptures. Following Athanasius, a closed list, or fixed collection, of sacred scriptures came to be referred to as a biblical 'canon'. Earlier (325 CE), Eusebius described sacred books in the church as 'covenanted' (Greek *endiathēkē*, literally, 'encovenanted') writings (*HE* 3. 25. 6), or 'recognized' (Greek *homologoumenon*) (*HE* 6. 25. 3). The word he uses for a list of sacred books is 'catalogue' (Greek *katalogos*) (*HE* 3. 25. 6; 4. 26. 13). When he uses the term *kanon*, he generally focuses on the church's rule of faith. Of the ten instances of this word in his writings, two are possible candidates for referring to an exclusive list of sacred scriptures (*HE* 5. 28. 13 and 6. 25. 3). Eusebius provides the first datable lists of recognized canonical books in the church (*HE* 3. 25. 1–7), and he presents what he claimed was Origen's collection of scriptures as follows, saying 'in the first of his [Commentaries] on the Gospel according to Matthew, defending the canon of the Church (*ton ekklesiastikon fulattōn kanona*), he gives his testimony that he knows only four Gospels' (*HE* 6. 25. 3). The only question here is whether the 'canon of the Church' refers to the rule of faith (teachings) or to a body of sacred Christian literature, a catalogue.

Eusebius cites Origen's 'encovenanted books' (*endiathēkous biblous*) as a collection of Christian scriptures (*HE* 6. 25. 1).

The writings of the prophets became authoritative both for the Jews and later also for the Christians, but initially those writings, and even their textual forms, were not yet fixed or inviolable. Early on they were welcomed as divinely inspired messages from God, but for centuries there was considerable freedom in the church to alter those writings. A NT example of altering an inspired text is found in the quotation of Ps. 68: 18 in Eph. 4: 8.

In time, these prophetic writings became known among the Jews as the *Tanakh*, a term derived from the first Hebrew letter of each division of the Hebrew Bible: *Torah*, *Nebiim*, *Ketubim* (the first two followed by a vowel), and by the end of the second century the Christians began calling them their 'Old Testament Scriptures'. At the end of that process, the writings that made up those collections were looked upon as sacred and inviolable, and they were placed in a fixed sacred collection called the Holy Scriptures. In the early and fluid stages of development, the writings were often changed or dropped out of use in churches and synagogues, but they nevertheless had an impact on the life, worship, conduct, and mission of these two communities of faith, if even for a short time. The distinctions between scripture and canon, as well as the various processes or stages of canonical development, have been variously represented in recent scholarship (Sanders 1987; Sheppard 1987; Ulrich 1999, 2002). At the beginning of the process, one can only speak of a biblical canon anachronistically, and it is difficult to find appropriate vocabulary to identify the processes of canonization. This is because the ancient religious communities showed little interest in biblical canons, and even less in telling the story that led to the final fixing of their biblical canons.

It is not unusual for scholars today to speak of 'canon' in reference to the early recognition of the authority and value of the biblical writings, but such uses did not exist in the ancient church until the fourth century CE. It is probably better to speak of a canonical 'process' or 'processes' at these early stages (Ulrich 1999). There is no precise language to describe canonical formation in antiquity, a factor that suggests little interest in the matter for several centuries. The following is a survey of the processes that led to the recognition and stabilization of the Christian Scriptures.

IV. The Beginning of the Process

Ancient recognition of the divine authority of written documents was accompanied by the repetition of a story in believing communities and the ability to tell that story in a variety of contexts to meet the needs of the community of faith and offer it hope (adaptability). The primary function of canon in a community of faith is to aid that community in its own self-definition (who are we) and its guidelines for living (what are we to do) and the order of its beliefs and hopes (what we are to believe). Those traditions that eventually became canon for ancient Israel also empowered that community for life; that is, they gave hope even in hopeless situations (the Exile) and brought life to the remnant of the nation of Israel. The literature that spoke to the needs of one generation, but was unable to be interpreted or adapted to meet the needs of another, simply did not survive in Judaism or Christianity. There are several books mentioned in the Old Testament that did not survive antiquity (2 Sam. 1: 18; 1 Kgs. 11: 41; 14: 19, 29; 15: 7, 23, 31; 16: 5, 14, 20, 27; 22: 39, 45; 2 Kgs. 1: 18; 8: 23; 10: 34; 12: 19; 13: 8, 12; 14: 15, 18, 28; 15: 6, 11, 15, 21, 26, 31, 36; 16: 19; 20: 20; 21: 17; 21: 25; 23: 28; 24: 5; 1 Chr. 27: 24; 2 Chr. 20: 34; 33: 18; Ezra 4: 15; Neh. 12: 23). These are listed more completely in McDonald 2006.

The survivability of the ancient scriptures had much to do with their ability to be interpreted afresh in new communities and new circumstances. The new interpretations were the product of hermeneutics that searched for relevance and meaning of this literature in ever new circumstances. The adaptability of this story ultimately led to its canonicity, and this became a primary characteristic of canonical material. The stabilization of the biblical text came later in the canonical process, though the church as a whole never opted for any particular text of the biblical scriptures.

The *story* that is at the heart of the earliest Jewish biblical canon is about a people who migrated from Egypt to Canaan under the guidance and protection of YHWH, who rescued them from bondage and brought them to their promised land. Other elements were added to this story, both at its beginning (the Genesis tradition) and at its ending (the prophetic tradition, wisdom literature, and the history of the fall of the nation). The earliest story did not include a Decalogue or other lists of divine commandments, but consisted essentially in telling the story of God's calling the Jewish people to a foreign land and preserving them through divine acts. They responded to these acts by recognizing YHWH as the one true God of Israel and their need to obey God's call to be a holy nation. There are many examples of this primal story in the OT Scriptures, especially in the Prophets (Amos 2: 9–11; 3: 1–2; 4: 10–11; 5: 25; 9: 7, 11; cf. also Deut. 26: 5–9 and Josh. 24), but also in the NT, where it continued to serve in establishing the true identity of God's people (Acts 7: 2–53; 1 Cor. 10: 1–11; Heb. 3: 5–19).

After the exile of Israel to Babylon, the Jews reconsidered their story from the perspective of the classical prophets whose witness to that story gave them life and hope. In the message from Ezekiel, for example, the people could, through the faithfulness of YHWH, look forward to the resurrection of the nation following its death (Ezek. 36–7). In the exilic sojourn, Ezekiel echoed the vision of Jeremiah, who spoke of the reforming of the nation (Jer. 18: 1–11).

After Israel had lost its land, national leaders, temple, and cultus in the terrible destruction of Jerusalem in 586 BCE, unlike other nations before and after them, they did not simply merge with other nations, acknowledge other gods, and become extinct as a people who served YHWH. Instead, Israel was reborn. The only thing that remained that had not been destroyed, which was also commonly available, adaptable, and transportable, was the story of God's redemption that preserved the Jews from extinction. That *story* was transported to Babylon, and there it was adapted to the new circumstances of the Jewish nation in captivity, and there its faith and hope were reborn (Sanders 1987: 18–19).

Subsequent biblical writings reflect the belief that the revelation and will of God were disclosed not only in the mighty acts of God through which YHWH invaded history, (e.g. in the exodus), but also in written materials (as in the tablets of stone that contained the Ten Commandments) and subsequently in the Pentateuch, where the writing down of God's word was an important mark of God's revelation (Exod. 24: 12; 31: 8; 32: 15, 32; 34: 1; Deut. 4: 2, 13; 8: 11; etc.). Just as Moses wrote down the commandments of the Lord (Exod. 24: 4; 34: 27), so also did Joshua (24: 26) and Samuel (1 Sam. 10: 25). In the book of Deuteronomy, the king was called upon to write down for himself a copy of the Law of God for reading all the days of his life, to remind him of the statutes of God and to be humble in his dealings with his people (Deut. 17: 18–20). The people were also called upon to write the words of God on their doorposts (Deut. 6: 9; 11: 20).

The writers of the Old Testament literature do not generally reckon with a written 'scripture' as an acknowledged authoritative feature in the life of Israel, except toward the end of that period, as in the reforms of Josiah (cf. 2 Kgs. 18: 20a with 22: 3–13; cf. Mal. 4: 4) at approximately 622–621 BCE. Those prophets who earlier said 'Thus says the Lord', were not speaking on the basis of an already existing text, but rather from their understanding of the will of God that came to them by revelation. Almost nothing in the OT suggests that there were sacred scriptures to turn to when guidance was needed. Neither David nor Solomonn nor Hezekiah spoke about sacred books that were current and normative in the life of Israel. Individuals related to God more through persons (priests and prophets) and institutions (tabernacle and temple) than through sacred writings, except toward the end of the OT period.

While it is true that some of the Psalms, especially 19 and 119, emphasize meditation on the word, law, precepts, and statutes of God (all of these are the same), most of the psalms do not date before the time of Josiah's finding of the book of the Law (probably Deuteronomy) in 621 BCE. This is not to suggest that sacred religious traditions that functioned in an authoritative manner in the life and worship of the ancient Jewish people did not exist earlier. No religious community exists without rule or authority or a sacred tradition, regardless of whether it is expressed in scriptures, creeds, liturgies, or oral traditions, and, by its nature, that which is divinely inspired can be adapted to new circumstances of life or it ceases to be canonical.

At what point was the religion of Israel governed by or built upon the Law or any written authority? It was probably not much before the reforms of Josiah

(2 Kgs. 23: 1–25; 2 Chronicles 34–5), but certainly no later than the reforms of Ezra one or more centuries later when the book of the Law was read to the people (Neh. 8: 1–8; 9: 1–3; cf. Ezra 7: 6, 10, 14; 9: 11–12). The Deuteronomic movement in Israel in the eighth to the seventh centuries BCE no doubt played a major role in effecting that change. This can be seen in the admonition not only to obey the commandments of YHWH, but also the warning against adding to them or taking away from them (Deut. 4: 2). When what was written down in Israel was later translated and explained to the people as having normative value in the life of their community (Neh. 8: 8–11), the notion of Scripture was present in Judaism.

During the Exile a remnant of Jews remembered the message of the prophets who had accurately predicted what would happen to the nation. As the truthfulness of the prophets' message of warning and judgement was remembered, that remnant also recognized a message of hope that allowed Israel to survive the terrible judgements that had been inflicted upon them in their captivity. These Jews accepted the message of the prophets, took responsibility for their failure as a nation, and accepted their captivity and destruction as judgement from YHWH for their own misdeeds. The Jewish remnant remembered and repeated this message. Earlier, the pre-exilic prophets, who had warned their nation of the consequences of their disregard for their covenant with God, had been accused of being 'madmen, unpatriotic, blasphemous, seditious, and traitorous' (Jer. 29: 26), but now they were remembered because what they had predicted actually came to pass. The remnant believed that the core of this prophetic message was contained in the Torah. This message was eventually expanded to include both the Former and then the Latter Prophets (Isaiah, Jeremiah, Ezekiel, and the Twelve) and finally the Writings (Ezra–Nehemiah, Job, Psalms, Proverbs, Song of Songs, Ecclesiastes, Daniel, and 1 and 2 Chronicles). As the Jews returned from Babylon, their authoritative writings were primarily the laws of Moses, but soon this included the whole of the Pentateuch and subsequently (c.200 BCE) the Prophets also. In the repetition of this story within context (a feature of canon), the remnant of Israel discovered life and hope.

The fluidity of the transmission of this story, and its adaptability through the genius of hermeneutics, continued well into the time of Jesus when the lack of a fixed or stabilized tradition contributed to the existence of the variety of sects within Judaism (Sadducees, Pharisees, Essenes, Samaritans, and Christians) that flourished in the first century CE. After the destruction of the Temple and its cultus in 70 CE, and following the failure of the messianic movement in the Bar Kochba rebellion of 132–5 CE, rabbinic Judaism, early Christianity, and a small band of Samaritans were the only brands of Judaism that survived these traumatic events. The first of these began to restrict its sacred writings to a time when it believed that the spirit of prophecy had existed in Israel (from Moses to Ezra), and all other books were excluded, even though several other books, Wisdom of Solomon and Sirach, continued to be read by pious Jews for several centuries. By the end of the first century CE, the biblical canon of the Jews *began* to reflect for some Jews the twenty-two or twenty-four books of the Hebrew Bible. This long and complicated process began with a fluid and adaptable story in the pre-exilic period that was finally fixed for the Jews in the fourth through the sixth centuries CE.

This process was completed for the Christians at roughly the same time, but for completely different reasons and with a different collection and ordering of books. The Hebrew Bible concludes with the Chronicles telling the story of the remnant of Jews returning from bondage in Babylon to their homeland to rebuild their land, homes, and temple (2 Chr. 26: 22–3). By contrast, the Christian Old Testament ends with Malachi, the last of the Minor Prophets, which looks forward to the coming of Elijah at the end of the ages to bring both reconciliation to families and an escape from the judgement of God (Mal. 4: 5–6). The way that each scripture canon is ordered presents a significantly different message to its readers, although in both it ends on a strong note of hope.

V. Origins of the Hebrew Bible/ Old Testament

A. Important Texts in the Formation of the OT Canon

There are a number of important texts that offer guidance in tracing the processes of canonization. Each of them speaks of collections of sacred writings that are not yet clearly identified. Before this there are texts that refer to prominent individuals in Israel and some familiarity with stories preserved in written materials, but writings do not receive much attention. Sirach (*c*.180 BCE), for example, identifies in his list of famous men (Sir. 44: 1–50: 24) those who had positively influenced the nation of Israel and led them in the ways of God. There is one exception, in Sir. 49: 10, where he mentions the 'bones of the Twelve Prophets' that comforted the people of Israel—a clear reference to the collection of Minor Prophets that circulated at that time in one volume. Sirach does not identify any literature attributed to these prophets or others; rather, he emphasizes their roles as persons of God. In his focus on the Patriarchs, kings, and prophets who best influenced the nation, he shows familiarity with the Law and many of the Prophets. He praises the activities of the scribes who devote themselves to the law, prophecies, and wisdom (38: 24–39: 3), but does not identify any particular writings associated with the groups of writings or the famous men he praises. It may be instructive that Sirach's three groupings of writings (law, prophecies, and wisdom) reflect an early stage of a three-part collection of scriptures (see Luke 24: 44, discussed below), but that is not clear.

The most important ancient texts that signal a development in the canonical processes for both the Hebrew Bible and the Old Testament of the Christians include the following:

1. Prologue to Sirach   Sirach's grandson (*c.*130 BCE) moved to Egypt and translated his grandfather's work into Greek. He identifies in his prologue to that work the great teachings of the 'Law and the Prophets *and the others that followed them*' and he followed up with a reference to his grandfather, Jesus (Jesus ben Sirach), who 'devoted himself especially to the reading of the Law and the Prophets and *the other books of our ancestors*'. He does not identify the 'other books', probably because they had not yet reached a fixed form in his generation. Some scholars frequently seek to equate that collection of writings called 'others that followed them' with the third part of the Hebrew Bible (the 'Writings', Hebrew *Ketubim*, Greek *Hagiographa*), but there is nothing in the text itself that leads one to that conclusion or limits that collection to the biblical books that eventually became the Writings.

2. Jubilees 2. 23–24 (c.160–140 BCE)   This text speaks of 'twenty-two chief men from Adam until Jacob and twenty-two kinds of works were made before the seventh day'. A later text of this passage from Epiphanius's *De mensuris et ponderibus* (22), that some scholars contend pre-dates the copy found at Qumran, also lists 'twenty-two letters in the Hebrew alphabet and twenty-two sacred books', but there is no convincing evidence that shows that this reading represents an earlier tradition of a twenty-two-book collection.

3. 4QMMT   Similar to Sirach's description of sacred books is a passage found in the Qumran text, 4QMMT (or *Miqsat Ma'aseh ha-Torah*), also identified as the 4QHalakic Letter or 'the Second Letter on Works Reckoned as Righteousness'. It is a fragmentary document dating perhaps as early as 150 BCE, and the pertinent passage in it for our purposes reads: 'to you we have written that you must understand the book of Moses and the words of the prophets and of David and the annals of each generation' (4Q397, frr. 7 + 8: 10–11, Martinez trans. 84). It is possible that 'David' is a reference to psalmic literature, but it is uncertain which psalmic literature is in view. Some scholars contend that the 'annals of each generation' is a reference to the Chronicles that concluded the third section of the Hebrew Bible, but this is speculation and the precise contours and contents of the literature referred to are not identified in the text.

4. 2 Maccabees 2: 13–15   This well-known text (*c.*104–63 BCE) refers to an act that is not preserved in the biblical book of Nehemiah: namely, that Nehemiah founded a library and collected 'the books about the kings and prophets, and the writings of David, and the letters of kings about votive offerings' (on votive offerings, see Ezra 7: 15–20). The author further indicates that Judas Maccabeus 'collected all the books that had been lost on account of the war [with the Seleucid dynasty] that had come upon us and they are in our possession. So if you have need of them, send people to get them for you' (2 Macc. 2: 13–14). Earlier, when Antiochus IV profaned the temple and sought to force the Jews to sacrifice to Zeus, he also confiscated their sacred books and destroyed them: 'The books of the law that they found they tore to pieces and burned with fire. Anyone found possessing the book of the covenant, or anyone who adhered to the law, was condemned to death by decree of the king' (1 Macc. 1: 56–7, NRSV).

There is no evidence that the books that were salvaged by Judas constituted a canonizing process of selecting books received as sacred scripture among the Jews. It is valid to say that several books besides the Law were acknowledged as sacred and important to the beliefs and conduct of the Jews at that time, but nothing suggests that Judas Maccabeus was the 'canonizing force' behind the Hebrew Scriptures. There is also considerable ambiguity in terms of what was collected and preserved by the Jews. Some scholars conclude that the 'books of the law' is a reference to all of the Jewish Scriptures, not just the books of Moses (Leiman 1976: 29).

5. *Philo (c.20BCE–40 CE)*   This native of Alexandria and a contemporary of Jesus and Paul, identifies the writings of a religious Jewish sect in Egypt known as the Therapeutae who take into their sanctuary or closet, or consecrated room for study purposes, 'laws and oracles delivered through the mouth of prophets, and psalms and anything else which fosters and perfects knowledge and piety' (*Contemplative Life* 25, LCL). Later, Philo calls those writings 'Holy Scriptures' (*hierois grammasi*) (ibid. 28). Once again, there is nothing in the text that identifies the contents or books of these scriptures.

6. *Dead Sea Scrolls*   At roughly the same time, a similar but not identical religious sect from Qumran, perhaps to be identified with the Essenes, appealed to a body of literature that is larger in scope than the scriptures of the later 'canonized' Hebrew Scriptures. These additional writings included 1 *Enoch, Jubilees,* and the *Temple Scroll,* the *Psalms of Joshua,* and many others as well (VanderKam 2000: 23–4). See more discussion on Qumran below.

7. *Luke 24: 44*   As the risen Christ met with his disciples on the last day of his appearances, he told them that what had happened to him in his death and

resurrection was a fulfilment of the Scriptures that he identified as 'the law of Moses, the prophets, and the psalms' (Luke 24: 44). Normally in the NT, the Hebrew Scriptures are simply identified as 'the Law' or 'the Law and the Prophets' (see examples below). This appears to be an early reference to other writings that were advancing into the category of scripture for the church. A few scholars have tried to identify the reference to 'psalms' as a fixed collection of scriptures that made up the Writings, or third part of the Hebrew Bible. On the other hand, there is nothing from first century or before that suggests that Ezra, Nehemiah, the Chronicles, and the other poetic literature (the *Megilloth*)—the writings that eventually comprised the third part of the Hebrew Scriptures—were ever called the 'psalms' (*contra* Beckwith 1985: 438–49).

8. *Luke 11: 49 (cf. Matt. 23: 45)*   When Jesus mentions the deaths of martyrs from Abel (Gen. 4: 8) to Zechariah (2 Chr. 24: 20–4), some assume that he was referring to all of the books of the Hebrew Bible from Genesis to 2 Chronicles. This theory depends heavily on the current order of the Hebrew Bible, which cannot be demonstrated in antiquity. Even in the previous passage (Luke 24: 44), the scriptures end with 'psalms' and not Chronicles. In any event, whichever books concluded the Jewish canon, and in whatever sequence they were found, it would not affect what Jesus had to say about the final martyr (McDonald 1995: 46–8). The text merely reflects Jesus' awareness of a common tradition of his day about martyrs in Israel. Further, it cannot be shown that the 'prophets' are the same as those in the Hebrew Bible. All writers of sacred literature at that time were considered prophets (Barr 1983: 55–6).

9. Baba Bathra *14b (?c.140–180 CE).*   This is the first Jewish text that identifies the books of the Hebrew Bible. Although preserved in the Babylonian Talmud (BT), this passage is generally understood as a *baraita* ('external'; pl. *baraitoth*), that is, a tradition from the time of 70–200 CE that was not included in the Mishnah. That this *baraita* did not find a place in the Mishnah suggests that the text had not yet found widespread approval by the closure and codification of the Mishnah at the end of the second century CE. It clearly identifies the second and third parts (Prophets and Writings) of the Hebrew Bible and assumes the Law, or Torah. The Prophets (*Nebiim*) and Writings (*Hagiographa*, or *Ketubim*) are identified as follows:

Our Rabbis taught: The order of the Prophets is Joshua, Judges, Samuel, Kings, Jeremiah, Ezekiel, Isaiah, and the Twelve Minor Prophets.... The order of the Hagiographa [or 'Writings', = *Ketubim*] is Ruth, the book of Psalms, Job, Proverbs, Ecclesiastes, Song of Songs, Lamentations, Daniel and the Scroll of Esther, Ezra and Chronicles. (*b. Baba Bathra* 14b, Leiman trans.)

Following the listing of books in the Prophets and the Writings, the authorship of each book in this passage is identified (see complete text of 14b–15a). The order and books of these scriptures varied considerably for Christians until the technology used in producing writings materials in the fourth century CE had progressed sufficiently so that all of the scriptures could be included in a single large volume. When that happened, there was a greater stability in the order and specific books in the Bible. While the *Baba Bathra* text likely reflects an early understanding of the contents of the Hebrew Bible, there is no evidence that this view was widespread in the second century CE. Otherwise, it would probably have been included in the Mishnah in the early part of the third century CE.

B. The Importance of Qumran

The collection of books found near the location of the Essene community at Qumran is very important for determining the status of scripture among the Jews in the first century. It is well known that all of the books of the Hebrew Bible/Old Testament of the Protestant churches except Esther were found in the caves of Qumran. One should not make too much of the absence of Esther, however, since the failure to find a copy of Esther at Qumran may be more a matter of chance than design. Only a small fragment of the Chronicles was found at Qumran, and had there been more worms in the cave where it was found, it too might not have survived. Cross could be right in suggesting that the absence of Esther may be due to worms rather than rejection by the Essenes (Cross 1998: 225)! Nevertheless, a wide collection of non-canonical literature was also found alongside canonical literature in the eleven caves at Qumran. Remarkably, except for the books of Genesis (fifteen copies), Exodus (fifteen) Deuteronomy (twenty-five), Isaiah (nineteen), and Psalms (thirty), there were more manuscripts of several non-canonical books than most of the books in the Old Testament. For example, there are multiple copies of *1 Enoch, Jubilees,* and the *Temple Scroll.* The *Damascus Document* at Qumran cites *Jubilees* as the authority on divisions of times (CD 16. 3–4), a reference to the sacredness of that text.

C. The Rabbinic Tradition

The rabbis of the late first and early second centuries CE distinguished sacred writings from non-sacred ones by calling the former writings those 'that defile the hands' (for the use of this description for holy books see *m. Shabbath* 14a–b; *m. Pesahim* 10. 9; *m. Yadayim* 4. 5; cf. *t. Yadayim* 2. 12–13; *t. Niddah* 9. 18; *y. Sotah* 18a).

The reading of a text in public worship and teaching it in a religious community imply its sacredness, and the forbidding of that reading in worship also suggests that it was not yet or was no longer considered sacred. For several centuries the rabbis debated the merits of several books that were eventually included in the Hebrew Bible (Leiman 1976: 92–101; see examples below). To account for this phenomenon, Leiman suggests that the disputed writings were 'canonical' but not inspired (Leiman 1976: 100)! Nothing in antiquity suggests such a separation between inspiration and canon, however, and inspiration was always a corollary of canon. Later, the rabbis pronounced curses on those who read disputed or rejected books (those that did not 'defile the hands'), and they were eventually excluded. In the Tosephta (Hebrew for 'supplement'), that is, writings that were produced some time after the Mishnah (c.220 CE) and before the editing of the two Talmudim, perhaps around 300 CE, it is stated:

The gospels (GYLYWNYN) and books of heretics do not impart uncleanness to hands. And the books of Ben Sira [Sirach, or *Ecclesiasticus*] and all books written thenceforward do not impart uncleanness to hands. A. R. Simeon b. Menassia' says, 'The Song of Songs imparts uncleanness to hands, because it was said by the Holy Spirit. Qohelet [Ecclesiastes] does not impart uncleanness of hands, because it is [merely] the wisdom of Solomon'. (*t. Yadayim* 2.13–14, trans. Neusner: 1907–8)

Elsewhere in the Tosephta, another reference to the Gospels states that 'The books of the Evangelists and the books of the *minim* [heretics] they [pious Jews] do not save from a fire. But they are allowed to burn where they are, they and the references to the Divine Name which are in them'; and further, 'Said R. Tarfon, "May I bury my sons, if such things come into my hands and I do not burn them, and even the references to the divine Name which are in them" ' (*t. Shabbat* 13.5, trans. Neusner: 405). See also *b. Gittin* 45b, which states that a Torah book written by a heretic, even if it contained divine names, was to be burned on the spot, including the divine names. The usual practice of rabbinic Jews was to cut out divine names and store them in a special store-room in a synagogue (a *Geniza*) used for 'hiding' old sacred manuscripts, and to burn the rest of the scroll or book, but not in the case of heretical literature.

According to the Mishnah, those who have no part in the world to come are those who deny the resurrection of the dead, those who deny that the Law comes from heaven, and the Epicureans—that is, those who live without restraint. Rabbi Aqiba adds to that, 'Also he that reads the heretical books' [= external books, or those excluded from the Hebrew Scriptures] as well as the one who 'pronounces the Divine name with its proper letters' (*m. Sanhedrin* 10.1). In the *Midrash Rabbah* on Numbers (c.400–500 CE), those who read non-canonical writings are condemned: 'The following have no share in the World to Come: among others, he who reads uncanonical books' (*Num. Rab.* 14. 4; trans. Slotki 1983). The rejection of some of the apocryphal books may have had something to do with the influence that those books had among the Christians, who recognized them as sacred literature, but also because some believed that all books written after Ezra had no prophetic voice and so were considered heretical. What all of this suggests, of course, is that some in the Jewish community continued to read books that did not make it into the Hebrew Scriptures, and this is at a relatively late date in the rabbinic tradition (fourth to fifth century CE).

VI. The Emergence of a New Canon

As in the case of the Jewish scriptures, the New Testament also had its origins in a *story* that gave identity, hope, and clarity of mission to the early Christians. That *story* is inextricably bound to their belief in God's activity in Jesus as the central authority figure for all who believe in him. This faith in Jesus as the Lord and saviour of humankind (Rom. 10: 9) was the origin of the New Testament scripture canon. The earliest authority of the church, of course, was Jesus; that is, his life, teachings, and fate were all central to the faith of his followers. The story of and about Jesus is what first gathered the Christian community together after his death and resurrection, and gave rise to the written documents that later became its fixed collection of New Testament scriptures, read alongside its Old Testament. This story of and about Jesus was first told in preaching (Acts 2: 17–36) and teaching (1 Cor. 15: 3–8), and in time both the story and its implications for humanity were expanded and expressed in a variety of written forms (gospels, history epistles, sermons, apocalyptic).

Christians did not generally speak of a closed collection of New Testament or Christian scriptures before the fourth century CE. The first delimitation of Christian writings appears to have been with Marcion (*c.*140 CE), but his aim was not so much to put together a closed biblical canon of Christian scriptures as to sever the church from its Jewish roots. Marcion accepted only ten letters of Paul and the Gospel of Luke, but he 'expressly and openly used the knife, not the pen, since he made such an excision of the Scriptures as suited his own subject matter' (Tertullian, *Praescript.* 38.7 (ANF); cf. also *Adv. Marc.* 5. 18). He used only what suited his purposes and expunged the rest. His followers did not consider Marcion's collection closed, and later they cited other NT literature, including Matthew's gospel (see Ephrem Syrus, *Song* 24. 1).

The first clearly closed collection of Christian scriptures comes from Irenaeus (*c.*170–80 CE), who argued that there could only be four Gospels (Matthew, Mark, Luke, and John), but his view was not widely accepted in his day. The fact that he argued so strenuously, and unconvincingly, for four gospels (*Adv. Haer.* 3. 11. 8–9; cf. 3. 1. 1), suggests that his view was not universally acknowledged at the end of the second century. Indeed, other gospels continued to be read in churches, as in the case of the pseudepigraphal *Gospel of Peter.* Tatian (*c.*170 CE) authored a harmonized version of the gospels called the *Diatessaron* (lit. 'Through Four'), which may have included traditions other than those of the four canonical gospels, possibly the *Gospel of Peter.* Justin and Clement of Alexandria also used a more extensive gospel tradition, perhaps related to such a gospel harmony. The influence of the *Diatesseron* stretched from China to England and up to the fourteenth century. Ephrem (d. *c.*373) wrote a commentary on the *Diatessaron.* Eusebius (*c.*320–30 CE) also, unlike Irenaeus, simply introduced the four canonical gospels as the 'holy tetrad of the Gospels' without any defence (*HE* 3. 25. 1). By the fourth century, the four canonical gospels were widely accepted in the Church, but that was not the case at the end of the second century. Later, when the *Muratorian Fragment* lists the gospels, there is no defence of them, suggesting that in that era (*c.*350–75 CE, following Hahnemann 1992), it was no longer necessary to defend them; they were already established.

The second and third centuries CE saw the production of many pseudonymous Christian writings attributed to apostles, including gospels, acts, epistles, and apocalypses, that continued to be read in churches for several centuries. Unlike the prevailing Pharisaism, the primary form of Judaism that emerged from the first century CE, the Christians did not believe that prophecy had ceased, and they continued to produce writings that they believed were inspired by God (2 Pet. 3: 15; cf. also Rev. 22: 18–19 and 1 Cor. 7: 40). Those Christian writings were read in the churches, and no later than the mid-second century some of them were being read alongside and sometimes instead of their inherited Hebrew Scriptures, the Old Testament (see Justin Martyr, *1 Apol.* 67). Their value was almost immediately and widely recognized in the churches, but they were not generally called 'scripture' until the end of the second century. Their scriptural status in the churches was recognized following their use in proclamation, instruction, apologies, and community life.

In the early fourth century, Eusebius was the first to produce a list of those books that had obtained a scriptural (or 'enconvenanted') status in the churches (*HE* 3. 25). The criteria generally employed to identify this collection of writings included: 1. *apostolicity,* that is, if a writing was believed to have been written by an apostle, it was accepted; 2. *orthodoxy,* that is, if the writing agreed with the generally accepted 'canon of faith' (*regula fidei,* or orthodoxy), it was also seriously considered; 3. *antiquity,* if the writing was from the generation of the apostles, it was a candidate; and 4. *use,* if the writing was in wide use in the churches—and in the larger churches at that, it was more likely to be included (McDonald 1995: 228–49; McDonald and Sanders 2002: 416–39). Those writings that continued to be valued because of their ability to address the current needs and issues facing the churches, as well as offer life and hope in their circumstances, were generally approved first of all in local churches, then by local gatherings of churches, and finally by councils of churches. There are some fifteen lists or catalogues of New Testament scriptures from the fourth to the sixth century, and also several major manuscripts that identify most of the literature that comprises the current New Testament canon. No two lists are exactly alike, including the order of the books (Hahneman 1992: 133, 171–2). These include:

1. Eusebius, *HE* 3. 25. 1–7 (303–25, from Palestine/Western Syria)
2. Catalogue in Codex Claromontanus (303–67, from Alexandria/Egypt)
3. Cyril of Jerusalem, *Catech.* 4. 33 (*c.*350, from Palestine)
4. Athanasius, Festal Letter 39 (*c.*367, from Alexandria/Egypt)
5. Mommsen Catalogue (*c.*365–90, from Northern Africa)
6. Epiphanius, *Panarion* 76. 5 (*c.*374–7, from Palestine/Western Syria)
7. Apostolic Canon 85 (*c.*380, from Palestine/Western Syria)
8. Gregory of Nazianzus, *Carm.* 12. 31 (*c.*383–90, from Asia Minor)
9. African Canons (*c.*393–419, from Northern Africa)
10. Jerome, *Ep.* 53 (*c.*394, from Palestine)
11. Augustine, *De Doct. Christ.* 2. 8. 12 (*c.*396–7, from Northern Africa)
12. Amphilochius, *Iambi ad Seleucum* 289–319 (*c.*396, from Asia Minor)
13. Rufinus, *Comm. in Sym. Apost.* 36 (*c.*400, from Rome/Italy)
14. Pope Innocent, *Ad Exsuper. Tol.* (*c.*405, from Rome/Italy)
15. Syrian catalogue of St Catherine's (*c.*400, from Eastern Syria)

Along with the above, the following manuscripts are also important:

Codex Vaticanus (*c.*331–50, from Alexandria/Egypt)
Codex Sinaiticus (*c.*331–50, from Alexandria/Egypt)
Codex Alexandrinus (*c.*425, from Asia Minor)
Syriac Peshitta (*c.*400, from Eastern Syria)

The movement toward the stabilization of Christian writings that faithfully told the church's story *began* in the first century and was largely determined by the end of the fourth century. At almost the same time, the scriptures of the OT were also moving toward stabilization in the Christian community. Historically, the Church has never agreed on all of the writings in its biblical canon, especially on its Old Testament scriptures, but to some extent also in regard to its New Testament scriptures. For example, Martin Luther marginalized James, Jude, Hebrews, and Revelation.

Initially the scope of Old and New Testament scriptures was somewhat obscure, but in time that gave way to a more stable tradition. There is no question that the OT scriptures (the limits of which were not yet precisely defined in the time of Jesus) were viewed as sacred and authoritative literature in the early Christian churches (Matt. 21: 42; 22: 29; 26: 56; Luke 24: 32, 44; John 5: 39; 1 Cor. 15: 3 ff.), but the boundaries of that collection of writings was still imprecise even in the last quarter of the second century CE. Melito, Bishop of Sardis (*c.*170 CE), made a trip to the east (Jerusalem?) to determine the books that made up the (OT) scriptures and their order. What he discovered is not the same as the final form of either the Hebrew Bible or the Christian OT. His list included the Wisdom of Solomon, but excluded Esther (see *HE* 4. 26. 13–14). Nehemiah is not mentioned, but it could have been included with Ezra. This is the first known listing of the books of the Old Testament observed in the Christian community. The Wisdom of Solomon appeared in a fourth-century NT collection (*Muratorian Fragment*). Eusebius reveals the considerable uncertainty over several 'disputed' (*antilegomena*) books of the New Testament (James, Jude, 2 Peter, 2–3 John) and also expresses doubt about the authenticity of Hebrews and Revelation (*HE* 3. 25. 4–5). By the end of the fourth century, his 'doubtful' list was more widely accepted, but not without considerable hesitation in some cases, especially in regard to Hebrews, James, Jude, and Revelation.

The processes of canonization of the church's *Christian* scriptures took place in five significant stages of development, beginning in the first century CE: (1) the acknowledgement of Jesus as the central authority figure for Christian faith; (2) the recognition of the value for preaching and catechetical instruction of those writings that reflected the teachings, activity, death, and resurrection of Jesus (Gospels), and that literature that reflected the mission of Jesus (the rest of the literature of the New Testament); (3) the rise of the New Testament writings to the status of Scripture (late second century); (4) the conscious grouping of this literature into closed collections—for example, the four gospels and the epistles of Paul; and (5) the formation of a closed list of authoritative literature by the mid-fourth century CE, after which very little is added or deleted.

VII. Closing the Biblical Canon

A. Cessation of Prophecy

The belief that prophecy had ceased in Israel (1 Macc. 14: 40–1; Josephus, *Ap.* 1. 43–4) gave rise to the view that only writings produced during the time of the prophets (Moses to Ezra) were inspired, and so writings after that did not belong in the biblical canon. This position, of course, does not reflect the views of the Essenes, who believed that the Spirit of God was active in their own community as well as in their writings. For example, the author of the *Rule of the Community* says to the community at Qumran that one who spurns the decrees of the community also rejects the decrees of God. That one does not allow himself to be taught by the community counsel, and the author concludes: 'For, by the spirit of the true counsel concerning paths of man, all his sins are atoned so that he can look at the light of life' (1QS 3. 6–8, trans. Martinez). He later adds: 'these are the counsels of the spirit for the sons of truth in the world' (1QS 4. 6, trans. Martinez). The residents at Qumran believed that the presence and power of the Holy Spirit were present in their community and active through their teachings; for example, 'you [God] have graciously granted us Your Holy Spirit. Take pity on us' (4Q506 fos. 131–2: 11; for other examples, see CD 7. 4; 1QS 3. 7; 1QS 4. 21; 1QSb 2. 22 and 2. 24; 4Q213a 1. 14; 4Q287 10. 13; 4Q416 2ii. 13; 4Q418 8. 6; 4Q509 97–8i. 9).

Christians also believed that the Holy Spirit was active in their midst and that belief stands behind their production of a New Testament of scriptures. Indeed, Christians taught that the outpouring of the Holy Spirit came as a result of the activity of Jesus (John 7: 39; 20: 22; Luke 24: 49; Acts 1: 8; 2: 17–18), and that prophecy was still active among them. They recognized the gift of prophecy in their midst (Rom. 12: 6; 1 Cor. 12: 29; 14: 1, 3–5; cf. Acts 21: 4, 10–11). Paul believed that he spoke by the Spirit when he wrote his letter to the Corinthians (1 Cor. 7: 40), as did other early church writers. For example, Clement of Rome recognized that Paul wrote 1 Corinthians 'with true inspiration' (*1 Clem.* 47. 3), but adds that his own epistle was 'written by us through the Holy Spirit' (63. 2). The author of *2 Clement* introduces *1 Clem.* 23. 3 with the words, 'for the prophetic word also says' (*2 Clem.* 11. 2). The early church father Ignatius (*c.*115–17 CE) believed that he also wrote in the power of the Spirit: 'I spoke with a great voice—with God's own voice', and says that some accused him of saying this because he had previous knowledge of a situation to which he spoke, but he contends that 'the Spirit was preaching and saying this' (*Phld.* 7. 1b–2). The Montanists of the late second century argued that the prophetic voice was still alive in the church, and they produced many writings that they believed were prompted by the Spirit. Their argument was so persuasive that even the great church father and teacher Tertullian (*c.*200 CE) joined their ranks.

Of all of the references to inspiration and being filled with the Spirit in the church of the first five centuries, the only time that something said or written was not considered inspired was if the writing or message was 'heresy', that is, something contrary to the truth of God. When Bishop Serapion (*c.*200 CE) rejected the *Gospel of Peter*, he called it 'heterodox' (or 'heretical'): that is, contrary to the truth of God. He also spoke of 'pseudepigraphal' writings: that is, 'writings which falsely bear their [apostles] names' (Euseb. *HE* 6. 12. 2–3). The early Christians believed that the power of the Spirit was present and active in their midst, and therefore prophetic words were essential to their religious experience. Inspiration, at that time, was not limited to sacred writings of the past.

An eschatological perspective was at the heart of the early Christian view of the Jewish Scriptures (Hebrew Bible)—that is, the belief that the Scriptures had their primary fulfilment in Jesus (e.g. Matt. 2: 5, 17, 23; 3: 3; 4: 14; Mark 14: 49; 15: 28; Luke 4: 21; Acts 1: 16; John 17: 12; 19: 24, 28). Similarly, those at Qumran believed that the Scriptures were fulfilled in their religious community and activities. Although Paul taught that the Scriptures had fulfilment in the Christian community (Rom. 4: 23; 15: 4; 16: 26; 1 Cor. 9: 10; 10: 11), still for him the risen Christ was the primary norm for the understanding and use of the OT Scriptures in the early church (2 Cor. 3: 12–16). The early church uniformly held that the OT Scriptures were of unimpeachable authority (John 10: 35; Matt. 5: 18), and that they constituted 'the authoritative declaration of the divine will', but that its primary authority was found in its Christological fulfilment. Unlike in Judaism, the early Christians' basic stance toward the Jewish scriptures was moulded by their Christology. The Old Testament scriptures functioned as Christian scriptures for the church, because they bore witness to Christ. Both the Old and New Testament Scriptures were received as authoritative primarily because Christians believed that they pointed to God's redemptive activity in Jesus Christ.

It is important to observe that the author of Acts claims that the early church was focused on 'the apostles' teaching' and *not* on the OT Scriptures (2: 42), although there is no doubt that the teachings about Jesus and the coming of the Spirit were also presented as a fulfilment of the scriptures (2: 17–36). The book of Acts is sprinkled throughout with OT references, which were employed as sacred texts for preaching about Jesus (see Acts 2: 17–21, 25–8, 34, 35; 4: 25–6; 8: 32–3, *passim*), but one does not find any particular devotion to the study of the OT such as is found in the later post-Pauline texts of 2 Tim. 2: 15 and 3: 14–15.

B. Factors in the Selection Process

The limits of the scriptures that defined both faith and the will of God for the Jewish and Christian communities were largely fixed by the middle to late fourth century for both Jews and Christians, even though questions about some books continued for a while longer. Despite the complex and often unknown circumstances that led to the closing of the biblical canon, the available evidence allows some conclusions to be drawn.

The factors that shaped the contours of scripture collections were theological, social, and practical. In the first instance, there was a belief in Judaism that with the cessation of prophets following Ezra, the production of divine literature ceased. While the Christians did not accept that belief, they did acknowledge the scriptures they received from the Jews, but also came to the view that a new day had come and that new scriptures were also needed for their community. These scriptures were framed by a commonly accepted body of beliefs about Jesus that circulated in early Christianity. The *social*, or historical, factors that led the church to finalize its sacred collections included the Roman persecutions of the church under Decian (*c*.250–1) and Diocletian (*c*.303–13). In the latter persecution, Christians were required under threat of death to turn over their sacred writings to the authorities to be burned (see Euseb. *HE* 8. 5–6 and *Gesta apud Zenophilum* in *Corpus Scriptorum Ecclesiasticorum Latinorum* 26). These acts of violence forced Christians to decide which literature was sacred and could not be turned over to the authorities without violating conscience. Another social factor was Constantine's (*c*.314–40) push for religious conformity within the Christian communities, under the threat of banishment for those who did not comply. These factors do not appear to have influenced the scope of the Jewish biblical canon.

A third factor that surely influenced large communities of faith was Constantine's request of Eusebius to produce fifty copies of the church's scriptures to be used in the churches of the new Rome, Constantinople, which was the new centre of the Roman Empire (McDonald 1995: 182–90). The contents of whatever it was that Eusebius produced for the emperor must surely have had significant influence on many in the church in that vicinity (Greece and Asia Minor) and even further away.

As noted above, prior to the late fourth century, when the capacity of books was not sufficient to include all of the sacred writings, churches and synagogues often had unbound collections of books or manuscripts. This affected the ordering or sequence of the books, and probably also the contents of the biblical canons (Gamble 1995).

The major sects of Judaism in the first century CE (Sadducees, Pharisees, Essenes, Samaritans, and Christians) agreed that God spoke through divinely inspired writings, but they disagreed on which writings were sacred. The Sadducees accepted only the books of Moses as divine scripture, and similarly the Samaritans acknowledged a modified and enlarged Pentateuch; but the Pharisees accepted initially a much larger and undetermined collection of scriptures. By the end of the first century, they were beginning to be more limited in scope for the Jews, even though there was no universal agreement on their number. The Essenes clearly accepted a larger collection than did the Pharisees, especially the *Community Rule, Jubilees,* and the *Temple Scroll* (VanderKam 2000, 2002).

The first discussion about a fixed number of books in the Hebrew Bible came at the end of the first century CE when Josephus wrote: 'Our books, those which are justly accredited, are but two and twenty, and contain the record of all time' (*Ap.* I. 38), and describes a closed twenty-two-book collection of Hebrew scriptures that, he says, 'no one has ventured to add, or to remove, or to alter a syllable; and it is an instinct with every Jew, from the day of his birth, to regard them as the decrees of God, to abide by them, and if need be, cheerfully to die for them' (*Ap.* 1. 42, LCL). He also identifies these books by categories of Law, or the 'books of Moses', the 'prophets who wrote history, and hymns to God and precepts for the conduct of human life' (*Ap.* 1. 39–40, LCL). The reason, he says, why no one adds to them is the 'failure of the exact succession of prophets' (1. 41): that is, the belief that prophecy had ceased in Israel and that writings after that do not have the same merit since they do not have their source in God (see discussion above). Cross suggests that Josephus's collection may actually have come from Hillel as an import from Babylon (c. late first centuryBCE–early first century CE), the early *tanna'* (or teacher who repeats traditions) and his school. This suggestion may have some merit, and it answers several questions, but it is still only a theory (Cross 1998: 221–5).

At roughly the same time (c.90–100 CE), the author of 4 Ezra (= 2 Esdras) acknowledged twenty-four books that both the 'worthy and unworthy' could read, but he also mentions seventy other books that were reserved for the 'wise' because in them 'is the spring of understanding, the fountain of wisdom, and the river of knowledge' (4 Ezra 14: 45–6). That the author of 4 Ezra drew different conclusions about the scope of a fixed collection of scriptures at the same time that Josephus argues that all Jews everywhere recognized the same books. The fact that both authors pegged their scripture collections to the sacred letters of the Hebrew and Greek alphabets (twenty-two and twenty-four letters respectively), and 4 Ezra's acceptance of seventy other books may reflect another holy number: namely, the elders of Israel or the divinely inspired translators of the Law into Greek noted in the Letter of Aristeas.

In the early development of the Old Testament/Hebrew Bible, there are signs that earlier written materials were recognized as having divine origins and authority in the Jewish community (Nehemiah 8; 1 Kings 22–3; Daniel 9), but there is no record of the processes that were at work in the religious communities that gave rise to the sacred collections that emerged in Judaism and Christianity. Something of those processes, however, can be discerned in the biblical and non-canonical sources that survive antiquity (see sect. V. A above); that is, some reasonable inferences can be made, but several ambiguities remain. In the case of the Hebrew Bible, there is no evidence that all Jews either in or outside Palestine agreed on the matter even at the end of the first century CE, contrary to the opinion of Josephus (*Ap.* 1. 42). Discussions about which texts 'defile the hands' continued in Judaism for several centuries, even if most of the contents of the Hebrew Scriptures had already been largely determined. The question at this time was more one of exclusion than inclusion: namely, whether Jews should continue to read questionable books.

Certain disputed writings among the Jews were probably produced in a later period (e.g. Esther, Song of Songs, Ezekiel), but especially Sirach (Ecclesiasticus), *1 Enoch*, Wisdom of Solomon, *Jubilees*, the *Testaments of the Twelve Patriarchs*, and 1–4 Maccabees, but references to them made their way into various Christian writings. The attempts to ban some of these books in the Amoraic period (c.250–530 CE) of the rabbinic tradition (see *t. Yadayim* 2. 13; *y. Sanhedrin* 28a, 100b; *Koheleth Rabbah* 12. 12) argues, in fact, for their continued reception in the Jewish community.

The number twenty-four, the number of letters in the Greek alphabet, prevailed in the rabbinic tradition during the period of the Amoraim writing in the third to sixth centuries (see *b. Taanith* 8a; *Bemidbar Rabbah* 13. 16, 14. 4, 18; 18. 21; *Sir Ha-Shirim Rabbah* 4. 11; *Koheleth Rabbah* 12. 11, 12). Some rabbis contested the scriptural status of some of the books, and many opted for a more limited biblical collection and questioned the status of Song of Songs (*m. Eduyoth* 5. 3; *m. Yadayim* 3. 5; *b. Megillah* 7a; *t. Yadayim* 2. 14) Ecclesiastes (*b. Shabbat* 100a; see also Jerome on Ecclus. 12: 14); Ruth (*b. Megillah* 7a); Esther (*b. Sanhedrin* 100a; *b. Megillah* 7a; cf. *t. Megillah* 2. 1a;)); Proverbs (*b. Shabbat* 30b); and Ezekiel (*b. Shabbat* 13b; *b. Hagiga* 13a; *b. Menahot* 45a; for other examples, see Leiman 1976: 82–108).

Neither Josephus nor 4 Ezra identify the books in their collections, and neither speaks of the three categories that eventually identified the books of the Hebrew Bible (Law, Prophets, Writings). The author of 4 Ezra describes how Ezra was able to drink a special potion of 'something like water, but its color was like fire' (4 Ezra 14: 39), and his memory increased allowing him to remember all of the sacred writings including the twenty-four that were for general dissemination, and the seventy more that were for those who were wise (14: 46–7).

Although Josephus claims that all Jews everywhere acknowledged the same sacred books, there is no evidence of any agreement at that time on all the books that eventually belonged to their scripture collection. In fact, the surviving evidence points in the opposite direction: namely, the large collection cited by the Christians in the first and second century. For example, Jude cites as prophecy a pseudepigraphal writing (Jude 14; cf. *1 Enoch* 1. 9). An appreciation of apocalyptic books among the Jews waned following the devastating consequences of the failed messianic movement in Israel when they once again sought independence from Rome (132–5 CE). This was not so among Christians, who continued appreciation and use of such literature through much of the rest of the second century and even later.

The Essenes also had a much larger collection of scriptures than those that finally attained canonical status in rabbinic Judaism and in the Protestant church. These extra books were often called 'apocryphal' (*apocrypha* = 'hidden'), a term originally used to speak of legitimate 'hidden' texts that were read in the churches and used in theological discourse; but eventually the term was used to identify heretical teachings (Irenaeus, *Adv. Haer.* 1. 20. 1; cf. also Clement of Alexandria, *Strom.* 3. 4. 29). Jerome is the first to use this term for the 'deutero-canonical' or apocryphal writings that were eventually both marginalized and contested in the Church, but were often used in catechetical instruction (*Prologus in libro regum 365*). The pseudepigraphal writings were marginalized in the early church and eventually rejected (Euseb. *HE* 6. 12. 3).

Later, Christians also acknowledged the importance of the twenty-four letters in the Greek alphabet to enumerate the books of their OT scripture canon and, by various combinations of books, they continued to acknowledge the same sacred number, but were able to accept a variety of additional materials into their collections (Hengel 2002: 57–74).

Without question, the Law, or Pentateuch, was at the heart of all scripture collections for the Jews. The Law was followed by the Prophets (that is, the Former and Latter Prophets of the Hebrew Bible = Joshua–2 Kings and Isaiah, Jeremiah, Ezekiel, and the Twelve Minor Prophets), and eventually also by an ambiguous collection (at first) eventually called the Writings. What precisely was included in the final group is unclear until the middle to late second century CE, when its contents are listed under the name of *Hagiographa* (lit. 'sacred writings'), or called *Ketubim*. Before then, the books that were later called Writings were called Prophets. All of the Hebrew Scriptures were eventually identified by the term *Tanakh*.

In New Testament times, the most common designations for the sacred scriptures included 'the Law' (e.g. Matt. 5: 18; Rom. 8: 3–4), or 'the Law and the Prophets' (Matt. 5: 17; 7: 12; 11: 23; Luke 16: 16, 29, 31; 24: 27; John 1: 45; Acts 13: 5; Rom. 3: 21), or just 'the Prophets' (Acts 7: 42; see the only exception in Luke 24: 44 below). Initially, the rabbinic tradition also regularly spoke of 'the Law' or 'the Law and the Prophets' as designations for all scripture (*m. Rosh Ha-Shanah* 4. 6; *m. Megillah* 4. 3, 4; *t. Baba Metzia* 11. 23; *t. Terumoth* 1. 10). Only gradually (generally after the fourth to fifth centuries) are the three parts of the Hebrew Bible regularly mentioned (*t. Rosh Ha-Shanah* 4. 6; *y. Megillah* 73d) or identified. In the first century BCE–CE, and for a considerable time afterwards, 'Writings' were not a part of the *lingua franca* of either Jews or Christians.

C. Apocryphal and Pseudepigraphal Writings in Early Christianity

The early church fathers not only cited many OT and early Christian writings, they also cited apocryphal and pseudepigraphal writings, although less frequently. The earliest Christian citation of Sirach (4: 31), for instance, occurs in *Didache* 4. 5 and the *Epistle of Barnabas* 19. 9. Later Clement of Alexandria argued that Sirach was written by Solomon, who inspired the pre-Socratic Heraclitus (*Strom.* 2. 5. 17, 24). Tertullian, Origen, Cyprian, John Chrysostom, Cyril of Jerusalem, Jerome, and Augustine also cited Sirach. The ancient prophecy called *Eldad and Modad* was cited as an authoritative resource in the *Shepherd of Hermas* (*Vis.* 2. 3. 4), and the author of the *Epistle of Barnabas* cites 1 Enoch three times, twice employing scriptural designations (see 4. 3 which begins 'it was written as Enoch says' and 16. 5 citing 1 Enoch 89. 55, 66, 67 beginning with the words 'For the scripture says'). It continued to be cited well into the fourth century, but generally not by name. It appears that in the fourth century, the offence of Jude was not that he made use of 1 Enoch as other Christian writers had done, but that he referred to it specifically by name. The use of *1 Enoch* was acceptable in the church in the second century, but not in the fourth! The early church frequently cited *1 Enoch, Assumption of Moses, Jubilees, Apocalypse of Baruch, Prayer of Joseph,* and the *Testaments of the Twelve Patriarchs* (Adler 2002). Not only did many Christians read apocryphal writings, they also produced many apocryphal *Christian* writings, such as gospels, acts, and epistles, that were read in churches in the first three centuries. Writings such as the *Acts of Paul and Thecla* and others were quite popular in the early church for several centuries. Debates and doubts over this literature are well noted by Eusebius in the fourth century (*HE* 3. 25) and in the *Muratorian Fragment.*

Whatever led the church to reject the pseudepigraphal writings, they were also a part of the Jewish heritage of early Christianity, and in some cases were cited as sacred scripture (Adler 2002). The books that were accepted by the church varied 'at the fringes' for several centuries, but the core writings (the four gospels, letters of Paul, 1 Peter, and 1 John) were widely accepted and used in churches. After the fourth century, there was more focus in the church on the hermeneutics that enabled them to adapt the story of God's activity in Jesus to the ever new and changing circumstances of the church.

D. The Emergence of the *Christian* 'Old' and 'New' Testaments

Because the term 'Old Testament' is not found in the Christian community until the end of the second century CE, in the writings of Melito, Irenaeus, and Tertullian, it is premature to speak of an 'Old Testament' or a 'New Testament' before the end of the second century. Irenaeus (*c*.170–80) was apparently the first to use these terms to distinguish the two parts of Christian scriptures. He writes: 'Inasmuch, then, as in both Testaments there is the same righteousness of God [displayed] when God takes vengeance, in the one case indeed typically, temporarily, and more moderately; but in the other, really, enduringly, and more rigidly... For as, in the New Testament, that faith of men [to be placed] in God has been increased, receiving in addition [to what was already revealed] the Son of God, that man too might be a partaker of God' (*Adv. Haer.* 4. 28. 1–2). Likewise, Melito, Bishop of Sardis (*c*.170–80), speaks of 'the books of the old covenant [= testament] (*ta tēs palaias diathēkēs biblia*)'. These words are preserved in the fourth century (Euseb. *HE* 4. 26. 13 f.), but we also find similar references in Clement of Alexandria (*Strom.* 15. 5. 85), Origen (*de Princ.* 4. 11), and Tertullian (*c*.200), who states: 'If I fail in resolving this article (of our faith) by passages which may admit of dispute out of the Old Testament, I will take out of the New Testament a confirmation of our view' (*Adv. Prax.* 15).

At about 220 CE in Alexandria, Origen argues that his teachings are 'found both in the *so-called Old Testament* and in the so-called New, appears so plainly and fully' (*Comm. John* 5. 4; cf. 10. 28 and *de Princ.* 4. 11; emphasis added). The terms 'Old Testament' and 'New Testament' were originally identical not to the OT and NT canons, but rather to the biblical covenants. They are found in both the OT (Jer. 31: 31) and in the NT (Luke 22: 20; 1 Cor. 11: 25; Heb. 8: 8, 13; 9: 15; 12: 24), as well as 'first' covenant (Heb. 9: 1) for the 'old covenant', but such terms are never used in the Bible as a reference to a body of literature. These uses emerged in the second century, but they still had to be explained to the churches even in the fourth century. Eusebius (*c.*325 CE), describing Josephus's canon of scripture writes: 'he gives the number of the canonical scriptures of the so-called *Old Testament*, and showed as follows which are undisputed among the Hebrews as belonging to ancient tradition' (*HE* 3. 9. 5, LCL). Later, while speaking of the NT, he says: 'At this point it seems reasonable to summarize the writings of the New Testament which have been quoted' (*HE* 3. 25. 1, LCL). The distinctions were used by some of the church fathers in the late second century, but were not generally and regularly employed until the middle of the fourth century. In canon 59 of the Synod of Laodicea (*c.*360) we read: '[It is decreed] that private psalms should not be read in the church, *neither uncanonized books, but only the canonical [books] of the New and Old Testament* (*oude akononista biblia, alla mona ta kanonika tēs kainēs kai palaias diathēkēs*)' (emphasis added).

The notion of 'old' in antiquity did not mean the same as it does today. Then it meant good and reliable, or trustworthy. Whatever was new, religiously speaking, was unworthy of consideration. Indeed, having roots in antiquity was critically important for the mission of the early church, and the attempt by Marcion to sever the church's relations with its past in Judaism and in the scripture tradition it had received from Judaism was resolutely condemned, and he was excommunicated. The marvel for the church, then, was not that it had accepted something *old*, but rather that it had accepted something *new*!

The early Christians' acceptance of the notion of new scriptures is rooted in their fundamental belief that God has acted decisively in the activity and fate of Jesus. From the beginning, the church recognized the value of those writings that told of Jesus' life, teachings, death, and resurrection (the gospels), and they were quickly and readily used authoritatively in churches precisely because they contained the words of Jesus, the Lord of the church. The gospels were cited in the early churches from the beginning, and were used in their catechetical and apologetical mission; but they were not generally cited as 'scripture' until the end of the second century. They were cited primarily because they contained the words of Jesus. Only in the middle of the second century do they gain any other recognition, such as 'memoirs of the apostles' (Justin, *1 Apol.* 67). Their authority resided not in who wrote them, but rather in what they said about Jesus and in their reporting the words of Jesus.

The obvious value of the continuation of the story of the mission of Jesus in the church (Acts) and the call to faithful living and obedience to the mission of Jesus (the epistles) was also acknowledged and received early on in the church. This recognition, coupled with the church's belief that the authors of these writings wrote in the power of the Spirit, easily moved the church to collect and circulate these writings in their churches. Their usefulness in the church's life, worship, instruction, mission, and apology was obvious in regard to the gospels (especially Matthew) and the epistles (especially Paul's), and they circulated widely among the Christians in the first and second centuries. When the churches began to read these writings alongside the Old Testament scriptures in their worship, the process of scriptural recognition and canonization had already begun (McDonald 1995: 142–64).

VIII. Summary

The literature that survived in the religious communities of both Judaism and early Christianity, and was recognized as sacred scripture, was that which was believed by those communities to have continuing validity for their faith, identity, conduct, and mission. Both Jews and Christians saw the value of the biblical writings in their worship, instruction, and mission, but they also believed that something more than the scriptures of the First Testament were necessary to meet their needs. The Jews saw the value of codifying the oral traditions into what they called the Mishnah and what eventually became known among the rabbinic sages as the 'Oral Torah'. Almost immediately its value for faith and life in the Jewish community was recognized, and that document of sixty-three tractates began to be interpreted in the various Jewish communities. Those interpretations (*gemara*), with more scriptural support, became known as the two Talmuds (*Talmudim*) of the Jews, one from the land of Israel (*Yerushalmi*) and the other from Babylon (*Bavli*). The rabbinic sages also produced several commentaries that likewise were useful in their religious life.

Similarly, the Christians developed a New Testament collection of scriptures, but, unlike the Jews, they received their new literature as inspired and sacred 'scripture'. Like the Jews, they also produced commentaries on, and translations of, their own scriptures because they saw in them the working of God through their adaptability to the ever-changing circumstances of the church. As noted above, some of the literature that was valued earlier by the Christians did not survive the adaptability test, and was removed from sacred collections. In time, those writings that survived became inviolable—that is, canon—but the Christians have never fully agreed on the literature that comprised their biblical canon, let alone which text or translation of scripture is authoritative for the Church.

BIBLIOGRAPHY

Translations

DANBY, H. 1933. *The Mishnah*. Oxford, New York, and Toronto: University Press.

DANKER, F. W. 1989. *II Corinthians*. Augsburg Commentary on the New Testament. Minneapolis: Augsburg Publishing House.

—— ed. 2000. *A Greek–English Lexicon of the New Testament and Other Early Christian Literature*, 3rd edn., rev. and ed. Chicago: University of Chicago Press.

LEIMAN, S. Z. 1976. *The Canonization of the Hebrew Scripture: The Talmudic and Midrashic Evidence*. Hamden, Conn.: Archon Books.

MARTINEZ, F. G. 1996. *The Dead Sea Scrolls Translated: The Qumran Texts in English*, 2nd edn. Leiden, New York, and Cologne: Brill/Eerdmans.

NEUSNER, J. 2002. *The Tosefta: Translated from the Hebrew with a New Introduction*, 2 vols. Peabody, Mass.: Hendrickson Publishers.

ROBERTS, A., and DONALDSON, J. 1885/1994. *Ante-Nicene Fathers*. Peabody, Mass.: Hendrickson.

SLOTKI, J. J. 1983. *Midrash Rabbah, Numbers*, 3rd edn. London and New York: Socino Press.

Secondary Literature

ADLER, W. 2002. 'The Pseudepigrapha in the Early Church'. In McDonald and Sanders 2002: 211–28.

AUWERS, J.-M., and DE JONGE, H. J. eds. 2003. *The Biblical Canons*. Bibliotheca Ephemeridum Theologicarum Lovaniensium, 163. Leuven: Leuven University Press.

BAR-ILAN, M. 1990. 'Scribes and Books'. In M. J. Mulder, ed., *Mikra: Text, Translation, Reading and Interpretation of the Hebrew Bible in Ancient Judaism and Early Christianity*, Assen and Maastricht: Van Gorcum; Minneapolis: Fortress Press, 21–37.

BARR, J. 1983. *Holy Scripture: Canon, Authority, Criticism*. Philadelphia: Westminster Press.

BARRERA, J. T. 1998. *The Jewish Bible and the Christian Bible: An Introduction to the History of the Bible*, trans. W. G. E. Watson. Leiden, New York and Cologne: Brill and Eerdmans.

BARTON, J. 1997. *Holy Writings, Sacred Text: The Canon in Early Christianity*. Louisville, Ky.: Westminster/John Knox Press.

BECKWITH, R. 1985. *The Old Testament Canon of the New Testament Church*. Grand Rapids, Mich.: Eerdmans.

BROYDE, M. J. 1995. 'Defilement of the Hands, Canonization of the Bible, and the Special Status of Esther, Ecclesiastes, and the Song of Songs'. *Judaism* 44: 65–79.

BRUCE, F. F. 1988. *The Canon of Scripture*. Downers Grove, Ill.: InterVarsity Press.

CROSS, F. M. 1998. *From Epic to Canon: History and Literature in Ancient Israel*. Baltimore and London: The Johns Hopkins University Press.

DAVIES, P. R. 1988. *Scribes and Schools: The Canonization of the Hebrew Scriptures.* Louisville, Ky.: Westminster/John Knox Press.

—— 2002. 'The Jewish Scriptural Canon in Cultural Perspective'. In McDonald and Sanders 2002: 36–52.

ELLIS, E. E. 1992. *The Old Testament in Early Christianity: Canon and Interpretation in Light of Modern Research.* Grand Rapids, Mich.: Baker Book House.

FARLEY, E. 1982. *Ecclesial Reflection.* Philadelphia: Fortress.

GAMBLE, H. Y. 1995. *Books and Readers in the Early Church: A History of Early Christian Texts.* New Haven and London: Yale University Press.

—— 2002. 'The New Testament Canon: Recent Research and the Status Quaestionis'. In McDonald and Sanders 2002: 267–94.

GRAHAM, W. A. 1987. *Beyond the Written Word: Oral Aspects of Scripture in the History of Religion.* Cambridge and New York: Cambridge University Press.

GROSHEIDE, F. W., ed. 1948. *Some Early Lists of the Books of the New Testament,* i: *Textus Minores.* Leiden: E. J. Brill.

GUILLORY, J. 1990. 'Canon'. In Frank Lentricchia and Thomas McLaughlin, eds., *Critical Terms for Literary Study,* Chicago: University of Chicago Press, 233–49.

HAHNEMAN, G. M. 1992. *The Muratorian Fragment and the Development of the Canon.* Oxford Theological Monographs. Oxford: Clarendon Press.

HELMER, C., and LANDMESSER, CHRISTOF, eds. 2004. *One Scripture or Many? Canon from Biblical, Theological and Philosophical Perspectives.* Oxford: Oxford University Press.

HENGEL, M. 2002. *The Septuagint as Christian Scripture: Its Prehistory and the Problem of its Canon,* trans. M. Biddle. Edinburgh and New York: T. & T. Clark.

KELSEY, D. H. 1975. *The Uses of Scripture in Recent Theology.* Philadelphia: Fortress.

KOOIJ, A. VAN DER, and TOORN, K. VAN DER, eds. 1998. *Canonization and De-canonization: Papers Presented to the International Conference of the Leiden Institute for the Study of Religions (LISOR) Held at Leiden 9–10 January 1997.* SHR 82. Leiden: E. J. Brill.

KRAEMER, D. 1991. 'The Formation of the Rabbinic Canon: Authority and Boundaries'. *JBL* 110: 613–30.

LEIMAN, S. Z. 1976. *The Canonization of the Hebrew Scripture: The Talmudic and Midrashic Evidence.* Hamden, Conn.: Archon Books.

McDONALD, L. M. 1995. *The Formation of the Christian Biblical Canon,* 2nd edn. Peabody, Mass.: Hendrickson.

—— 1997. 'The First Testament: Its Origin, Adaptability and Stability'. In C. A. Evans and S. Talmon, eds., *From Tradition to Interpretation: Studies in Biblical Intertextuality in Honor of James A Sanders,* BIS 18, Leiden: E. J. Brill, 287–326.

—— 2006. *The Biblical Canon: Its Origin, Transmission, and Authority.* Peabody, Mass.: Hendrickson.

—— and SANDERS, JAMES A., eds. 2002. *The Canon Debate.* Peabody, Mass.: Hendrickson.

METZGER, B. 1987. *The Canon of the New Testament: Its Origin, Development, and Significance.* Oxford: Clarendon Press.

MEUER, S., ed. 1991. *The Apocrypha in Ecumenical Perspective,* trans. P. Ellingworth. UBS Monograph Series, 6. New York and Reading: United Bible Societies.

MOORE, G. F. 1974. 'The Definition of the Jewish Canon and the Repudiation of Christian Scriptures'. In Sid Z. Leiman, ed., *The Canon and Masorah of the New Hebrew Bible,* New York: KTAV Publishing House, Inc., 99–125.

PFEIFFER, R. 1968. *History of Classical Scholarship: From the Beginnings to the End of the Hellenistic Age.* Oxford: Clarendon Press.

RUTGERS, L. V., VAN DER HORST, P. W., HAVELAAR, H. W., and TEUGELS, L., eds. 1998. *The Use of Sacred Books in the Ancient World.* Leuven: Peeters.

SANDERS, J. A. 1987. *From Sacred Story to Sacred Text.* Philadelphia: Fortress Press.

—— 1992. 'Canon: Hebrew Bible'. In *ABD* i. 837–52.

—— 2002. 'The Issue of Closure in the Canonical Process'. In McDonald and Sanders 2002: 252–63.

SCHNIEDEWIND, W. M. 2004. *How the Bible Became a Book.* Cambridge: Cambridge University Press.

SHEPPARD, G. T. 1987. 'Canon'. In Mircea Eliade, ed. in chief, *The Encyclopedia of Religion,* New York and London: Macmillan Publishing Co., iii. 62–9.

SUNDBERG, A. C. 1964. *The Old Testament of the Early Church.* Cambridge, Mass.: Harvard University Press, 1964.

—— 2002. 'The Septuagint: The Bible of Hellenistic Judaism'. In McDonald and Sanders 2002: 68–90.

TOV, E. 2002. 'The Status of the Masoretic Text in Modern Text Editions of the Hebrew Bible: The Relevance of Canon'. In McDonald and Sanders 2002: 234–51.

ULRICH, EUGENE C. 1999. *The Dead Sea Scrolls and the Origins of the Bible.* Grand Rapids, Mich., and Cambridge: Eerdmans; Leiden: Brill.

—— 2002. 'The Notion and Definition of Canon'. In McDonald and Sanders 2002: 21–35.

VANDERKAM, J. 2000. *From Revelation to Canon: Studies in the Hebrew Bible and Second Temple Literature.* JSJSup 62. Leiden: Brill.

—— 2002. 'Questions of Canon Viewed through the Dead Sea Scrolls'. In McDonald and Sanders 2002: 91–109.

CHAPTER 44

FUNDAMENTALISM(S)

HARRIET A. HARRIS

IDENTIFYING FUNDAMENTALISM

The term 'fundamentalism' was first used in the 1920s by Protestant Christians who sought to defend the fundamental doctrines of their faith. However, the position of these first fundamentalists is best understood not as centring around particular doctrines but as wanting a fundament, or firm foundation, on which to ground faith. This remains true of Protestant fundamentalists today. They take the Bible to be the foundation of their faith, by which they mean that Scripture provides the evidence to justify faith and the data from which to build up the doctrines of their belief system. Their apologetic stance, therefore, is that we must know that the Bible is true before we can go on to say anything else concerning God. Without a reliable Bible, they fear either that they cannot get started in faith, or that their faith must surely collapse. This way of thinking is found amongst both self-proclaimed fundamentalists and a large number of evangelicals.

Since the late 1970s, so-called fundamentalist movements have been identified across the world's faiths. The term 'fundamentalism' has now become so elastic that a core definition is difficult to retain. Within Protestant fundamentalism notions of biblical authority must be understood in relation to the foundational status given to Scripture. Other religious resurgent movements around the world are foundationalist in some respect, and many select and absolutize particular interpretations of particular texts. This is so even when their host religion— for example, Hinduism—is not strongly scripturalist. Therefore analysing fundamentalism as biblical or textual foundationalism, as we will do in the following pages, will help illuminate points of comparison and contrast across the fundamentalisms of the world (cf. Harris 2002).

EARLY FUNDAMENTALISM

Coining the Term

Curtis Lee Laws, a member of the Northern Baptist Convention in the United States of America, coined the term 'fundamentalist' in an attempt to avoid the more reactionary and exclusivist connotations of words like 'conservative'. Laws was concerned about a drift within his denomination towards theological modernism, particularly the impact that Higher Criticism of the Bible was having upon faith in the authority of Scripture and upon traditional understandings of Christian doctrine. So in 1920 he convened a pre-Convention rally for all those wishing to resist these trends. There he issued this rallying cry:

We here and now move that a new word be adopted to describe the men among us who insist that the landmarks shall not be removed. 'Conservatives' is too closely allied with reactionary forces in all walks of life.... We suggest that those who still cling to the great fundamentals and who mean to do battle royal for the fundamentals shall be called 'Fundamentalists'. (Laws 1920)

The Fundamentals

Talk of the 'fundamentals' had been around in the preceding decades. A series of pamphlets known as *The Fundamentals* were produced in Chicago, probably between 1909 and 1915. These were distributed free of charge to pastors and missionaries, and were sponsored by two oil tycoons from California, Milton and Lyman Stewart. Contributors to these pamphlets ranged from highly respected scholars such as James Orr of Glasgow and B. B. Warfield of Princeton, to revivalists and premillennialists such as R. A. Torrey and Arthur T. Pierson. There were also many lesser-known writers, particularly for the later volumes, when the standard of contributions was slipping.

These pamphlets reflect both the diversity and the ethos of early fundamentalism. Contributors differed in their assessment of evolutionary theory and questions of prophecy and the return of Christ, which were major issues then as now amongst Protestant fundamentalists. But they shared what many of them expressed as a concern to defend supernatural Christianity over against naturalistic reductions of Christian faith. This involved defending the factual reality of miracles recounted in Scripture, especially those relating to the divinity of Christ. In defending biblical authority, they identified and rejected key points of liberal criticism (cf. Hebert 1958: 17–27):

- that biology, geology, and astronomy could endanger belief in God as Creator in so far as they called into question the creation account given in Genesis;
- that the new study of Comparative Religion revealed influence from surrounding pagan religions upon the religion of Israel;
- that the Pentateuch could be analysed into sources J, E, D, and P, and that the last of these could be dated during and after the Exile, so that the Pentateuch could not have been written by Moses;
- that the OT could be interpreted in terms of the general evolution of world religions, and as showing a gradual evolution towards monotheism;
- that Jesus taught ultimate religious truths concerning the fatherhood of God and brotherhood of man, and that Paul perverted his Gospel into a message of salvation from sin;
- that, given Jesus' ultimate message, it was irrelevant whether he regarded himself as the Messiah, or cast out demons, or would return in a Second Coming;
- that the universality of laws of nature rendered miracles unbelievable (except perhaps for some faith healings), and therefore that narratives of the virgin birth and Jesus' resurrection need to be interpreted non-physically.

These concerns formed the central issues of the 'fundamentalist–modernist' controversies of the 1920s, when fundamentalists sought to control their denominations or, failing that, to break away from them. The controversies took place in the northern United States, particularly in Boston, Chicago, and New York, and attracted much media interest. The respected Princeton theologian J. Gresham Machen argued on the fundamentalist side that 'liberalism', or 'modernism'—the terms were used interchangeably at the time—was a new, non-Christian religion (Machen 1923). Shailer Mathews of the University of Chicago Divinity School responded by setting out *The Faith of Modernism* (1924), to which Machen replied with *What is Faith?* (1925). He attacked modernism for trying to turn faith from an objective publicly verifiable matter into a subjective, private venture verified only by the feelings of the individual (Machen 1923, 1925). Fundamentalists believed that by defending the authority of Scripture they were protecting the objective data on which faith rests. Throughout the twentieth century their apologetic developed as one of fact over against feeling, objective certainty over against subjective judgement (Harris 1998a: 180–204). In the 1950s, during debates over fundamentalism in Britain (Harris 1998a: 53–6), James Packer argued like Machen that 'the way in which [our critics] deal with the Bible is fundamentally unchristian.... Instead of subjecting their own judgement wholly to Scripture, they subject Scripture in part to their own judgement' (Packer 1958: 140).

The 'Five Points of Fundamentalism'

During these controversies, a set of five fundamentals emerged as fundamentalist rallying points. This was not an official list issued by any particular body. In 1910 and again in 1916 and 1923 the Presbyterian General Assembly had made a similar five-point declaration, though one that posited the authenticity of the miracles rather than the literal second coming of Christ. The 'five points of fundamentalism', as they became known, were:

- the inerrancy of Scripture;
- the deity of Christ;
- his virgin birth;
- his substitutionary atonement;
- his bodily resurrection and literal second coming.

Today one might expect such a list to look slightly different: for example, to include the 'doctrine of man' in connection with creation and with concerns over homosexuality and the role of women (cf. Grudem 1994: 439–525). But what the five fundamentals tell us about the nature of fundamentalist faith is as relevant now as it was in the 1920s.

Most significantly, the inerrancy of Scripture came first, and the remaining four points were believed to follow logically from that doctrine. Noticeably the list did not include such core Christian convictions as belief in a Creator God, or in God's triune nature (cf. K. Ward 2004: 1–2), even though the doctrine of the Trinity had been challenged by Unitarians, and the traditional doctrine of creation was being modified by evolutionary biology. But then, as now, fundamentalist polemics were waged most voraciously over doctrines that reflect and bolster the fundamentalist way of reading the Bible, as giving us hard, physical facts—or in the case of a literal second coming, hard, physical predictions. The virgin birth, bodily resurrection, and literal second coming were important first and foremost to fundamentalists, not for upholding Jesus' divinity, but for maintaining the Bible's authority as able to tell us what really happened, and when we could expect Christ's return. From a fundamentalist perspective, if Scripture cannot be relied upon to give us correct facts, we can have no knowledge of Jesus' divinity and no certainty about anything (Schaeffer 1984: 46; Grudem 1994: 119–20).

Yet, fundamentalists were not of one mind on the question of evolution. Leading fundamentalist theologians, including Warfield and Machen, accepted the theory.

The anti-evolution crusades of the 1920s did not reflect fundamentalist activity, which mostly took place in the northern states, so much as the traditional southern religion which readily allied itself with fundamentalism. However, northern fundamentalists lent moral support to southern anti-evolution crusaders during the 1925 'Scopes Monkey Trial', when schoolteacher John Scopes was tried in Dayton, Tennessee, for teaching evolution. Thereafter, fundamentalism became identified in people's minds with a southern anti-intellectualism, and was assumed to be anti-Darwinian (Marsden 1980: 184–9).

It was in the 1960s, with the publication of *The Genesis Flood* (Whitcomb and Morris 1961), that creation science began to take hold. This was largely due to the development of flood geology, which encouraged moves away from day-age and gap theories that allowed the history of life on earth to span millions of years, to a doctrine that compresses earth history into no more than 10,000 years (Numbers 1993: p. xi). In a representative evangelical *Systematic Theology* from the 1990s, Wayne Grudem casts doubts on evolutionary theory that older inerrantists such as Carl Henry, James Packer, or John Stott would not have shared (Grudem 1994: 262–314).

The fifth of the five points, belief in the literal second coming, lent itself to premillennialism. This doctrine taught the imminent return of Christ and his 1000-year reign. Not all fundamentalists were premillennialists, but speculation about the end-times had wide appeal and the nineteenth-century prophetic movement was a major root of twentieth-century fundamentalism (Sandeen 1970). Watching for the 'signs of the times' has remained a fascination, as is apparent from such premillennialist bestsellers as Hal Lindsey's *The Late Great Planet Earth* (1970), and Tim LaHaye and Jerry B. Jenkins' *Left Behind* series (1995–2004). The former interprets world events in the light of biblical prophecy; the latter gives a fictional account of those left behind in the world after believers have been raptured up to Christ.

The most influential form of premillennialism, John Nelson Darby's Dispensationalism, was developed in the mid-nineteenth century. It provided a detailed schema for interpreting Scripture which involved dividing the biblical writings into seven ages, or dispensations. This is the theory at work in the *Scofield Reference Bible* (1909, sometimes written as *Schofield Reference Bible*), which was the Bible that most fundamentalists in the USA used between about 1920 and 1950. Many self-proclaimed fundamentalists in the USA today continue to use it, or its more recent sibling the *New Scofield Bible* (1967, compiled by a series of editors). Darby's system placed all of the events prophesied in the book of Revelation in the future. In Britain the historicist approach of Henry Gratten Guinness, which interpreted Revelation in the light of historical events, modified Darby's influence (Bebbington 1988: 108–9). *The Scofield Bible* defines a dispensation as 'a period of time during which man is tested in respect of obedience to some *specific* revelation of the will of God' (5 n. 4), and lists the dispensations as Innocence (Gen. 1: 28), Conscience

(Gen. 3: 23), Human Government (Gen. 8: 20), Promise (Gen. 12: 1), Law (Exod. 19: 18), Grace (John 1: 17), and Kingdom (Eph. 1: 10). According to this schema, the present age is under the dispensation of Grace which began with the death and resurrection of Christ, with the surprising result that Christ's teachings are relegated to the dispensation of Law. The *New Scofield Bible* gives Christ's teachings greater prominence, which may be an apologetical move enabling the authority of Christ to be invoked in defence of inerrancy (Boone 1989: 80). For if Jesus cited Scripture as though it were the very word of God, who are we to disagree?

This is a question commonly posed in fundamentalist apologetic (e.g. Warfield 1948: 299–348; Manley 1926; Packer 1958: 54 f.; Wenham 1972/93), though it makes the apologetic circular, since fundamentalists also argue that if we cannot first know that Scripture is reliably authoritative, we cannot affirm anything about Christ. Fundamentalists put epistemology first, as though the question 'how can we know?' needs resolving before we can have faith. The same epistemological anxiety affects much modern Christianity, and in other contexts has resulted in reason, experience, tradition, or the Magisterium in the Roman Catholic Church being given normative status (cf. Murphy 1996; Abraham 2003: 137–42). In the context of biblical fundamentalism, it has led to Scripture being treated as an epistemological norm. The Princeton theologian Benjamin Warfield, who, together with Alexander Hodge, formulated the doctrine of inerrancy, held that faith resembled knowledge, in that both 'rest equally on evidence and are equally the product of evidence' (Warfield 1932/88: 330).

This evidence-based conception of faith was crucial in the development of the doctrine of inerrancy, as we shall see in the next section. In the present section we have seen that the original fundamentalists were concerned above all to defend the authority of Scripture, which they assumed entailed its inerrancy. They also believed that all other doctrines depended on knowing that the Bible made no mistakes. They treated Scripture as the fundament, or foundation, of their faith, which is why analysing fundamentalism as a form of foundationalism helps to make sense of the phenomenon.

FUNDAMENTALISM AS FOUNDATIONALISM

Fundamentalism is a form of strong foundationalism, to use a philosophical and specifically epistemological term. Foundationalism is a particular way of modelling how our various beliefs relate to one another. It has been dominant in Western thought, and so is by no means unique to fundamentalists (Murphy 1996;

Plantinga and Wolterstorff 1983; Wood 1998). It portrays a system of beliefs as built upon foundations which are themselves self-justifying. Within a foundationalist theory of knowledge, reasoning is conceived as working predominantly in one direction: from the foundations upwards. Beliefs are inferred or deduced from the foundations, and more ramified beliefs are inferred or deduced from more foundational ones.

This is not an uncommon way of thinking, and has affected both liberal and fundamentalist Protestantism, as it has numerous strands of thought. Liberal Protestantism posits universal religious experience as foundational, and places Scripture further up the belief structure, as manifesting the religious experience of its authors. Fundamentalism treats Scripture as foundational. Hence a fundamentalist theology invariably begins with the doctrine of Scripture, because of the conviction that the Bible must be secured before we can go on to build a theology (from it) (Harris 1998b). Within this tradition, the Bible has frequently been described as the 'textbook' of theology (e.g. Packer 1958: 112; Stott 1982: 188). The dominant method for inferring doctrines from Scripture has been 'biblical induction', by which the systematician collects relevant texts on a given topic and develops from them general conclusions (Stott 1982: 183). John Jefferson Davis's book *Let the Bible Teach you Christian Doctrine* (1985) exemplifies this method. It simply quotes, with some marginal comment, all the biblical verses that Davis finds relevant to particular doctrines. The method is also practised by Wayne Grudem in his *Systematic Theology* (1994).

For Scripture to be foundational, it must have various properties which justify its status as the basis of a belief system. Each of these properties is distinctive of fundamentalist claims about the Bible.

1. It must be unmediated. The doctrine of plenary (full) verbal inspiration is crucial in this respect. According to this doctrine, the very words of the Bible are given by God. Fundamentalists carefully avoid saying that God dictated the words, but they do want to say that the words we have in Scripture, at least in the original autographs, were not tainted by any human mediation. They assume that it makes sense to speak of original autographs, as though there was a single original version of Luke's Gospel, for example, rather than numerous related documents evolving and circulating in the primitive church, all equally authoritative before (and even after) the canon took shape (cf. Bauckham 1998; L. T. Johnson 1999; Witherington III 2004). They also believe that the human scribes of these original versions worked in such co-operation with God, whether knowingly or unknowingly, that the Scriptures communicate immediately what God has willed to communicate (Warfield, in Noll 1983: 268–88; Packer 1958: 79; Stott 1996).

2. An unmediated Bible must also be perspicuous, readily accessible by everyone, with minimal need for interpretation. Interpretation undermines Scripture's

immediacy. Fundamentalists defend the 'plain sense' of the text and the ability of the 'plain man' to understand it, although in reality it is their own reading of the text that they follow. Ironically, while professing to stand under the Word, fundamentalists actually stand under the readings of their own leaders and communities (Vanhoozer 1998: 425; Boone 1989). Their suspicion of interpretation blinds them to this fact. Their assumption that Scripture teaches a doctrine of plenary verbal inspiration in 2 Tim. 3: 16 is a case in point. As Keith Ward points out, this verse teaches that all Scripture is breathed by or from God; it does not teach that all Scripture is written or spoken by God (K. Ward 2004: 4).

The fundamentalist conviction that interpretation obstructs God's clear communication is reflected well in an exchange between William Jennings Bryan and Clarence Darrow at the infamous Scopes Trial. Bryan was the prosecuting lawyer, but Darrow called him as a witness for the defence, and asked him if his readings of Scripture were not in fact interpretations:

BRYAN. I would not say interpretations, Mr. Darrow, but comments on the lesson.
DARROW. If you comment to any extent these comments have been interpretations?
BRYAN. I presume that any discussion might be to some extent interpretations; but they have not been primarily intended as interpretations....
DARROW. Do you claim that everything in the Bible should be literally interpreted?
BRYAN. I believe everything in the Bible should be accepted as it is given there.

(Scopes Trial Transcript 1925: 734–5)

More recently, the British creation scientist David C. C. Watson has argued that Scripture 'no more requires interpretation than the ... cricket scores in your morning paper' (1975, 1989: 37). If Scripture needs interpreting, the foundation of faith is shifting rather than fixed.

3. Thirdly, if Scripture is to be foundational, it must be self-justifying. To use a phrase more familiar in biblical apologetics, it must be self-authenticating—hence the circular arguments that Scripture posits its own inspiration and authority. These arguments draw most heavily, though not exclusively, on 2 Tim. 3: 16 ('All scripture is God-breathed...') and 2 Pet. 1: 20–1 ('men spoke from God as they were carried along by the Holy Spirit'), and ask us to take these verses on trust, so that from them the inspiration of the rest of Scripture can be defended (e.g. Warfield 1948; Grudem 1994: 73–7; J. J. Davis 1985: 13–18).

4. But it is not sufficient for Scripture to be immediately from God, immediately comprehensible to us, and self-authenticating. It must also be inerrant (without error); otherwise our fixed foundation is not reliable. The doctrine of inerrancy received its classic formulation in 1881 at the hands of the Presbyterian biblical scholars A. A. Hodge and B. B. Warfield. They stated:

the historical faith of the Church has always been that all the affirmations of Scripture of all kinds whether of spiritual doctrine or duty, or of physical or historical fact, or of psychological or philosophical principle, are without any error when the *ipsissima verba* of the original autographs are ascertained and interpreted in their natural and intended sense. (Hodge and Warfield 1881: 238)

Apparent contradictions in Scripture were said to be unnatural, or not in accordance with the intended sense of the passage, or based on manuscripts containing copyist errors rather than the actual words of the original manuscripts, which are no longer in existence.

Inerrancy has since been seen as the 'watershed' issue between evangelicals and others (Schaeffer 1984: 43–65). Indeed, it has been described as the 'traditional evangelical cornerstone' and 'foundational truth' (Oss 1989: 181). But the doctrine has become highly diverse since Hodge and Warfield's day. For many evangelicals it now means something akin to traditional affirmations of 'infallibility': that Scripture is a reliable guide in matters pertaining to faith and salvation. Even so, there is what James Barr calls a 'maximal conservative' tendency amongst evangelicals (Barr 1977: 85–9, 124–8) to let go of a factual reading only if the evidence against such a reading is overwhelming, as it was once thought to be in the case of six-day creation.

Inerrancy, Reason, and Evidence

To understand how arguments for inerrancy are constructed, and modified, we need to see how fundamentalists appeal to reason and evidence.

A fundamentalist apologetic uses both deductive (logical) and inductive (empirical) arguments to defend the Bible's authority. Therefore, despite the intention to subject all things to the authority of Scripture, fundamentalists in fact make reason more foundational than Scripture. Their deductive and inductive arguments, which potentially cancel one another out, reflect both the Protestant scholastic roots and the modern scientific heritage of biblical fundamentalism. On the deductive, scholastic side, fundamentalist apologetics rest upon a rational argument that Scripture is inspired by God word for word (plenary verbal inspiration), that God does not err, and therefore that Scripture cannot err: 'All Scripture is the direct product of the omnipotent and omniscient God who is not subject to error' (J. J. Davis 1985: 17 n. 20). The British evangelical theologian James Packer can conceive of no reason for asserting inspiration except to proclaim freedom from error: 'what is the cash-value of saying Scripture "inspires" and "mediates the Word of God", when we have constantly to allow for undetectable possibilities of error on the part of each biblical author?' (1979: 27). Likewise, leading American evangelical theologian Carl F. H. Henry insists that the doctrines of biblical inspiration and inerrancy are inseparably linked: 'What is errant cannot be divinely authoritative nor can God have inspired it' (Henry 1979a: 480).

On the inductive, empiricist side, fundamentalist apologetics expect that Scripture will show itself to be the Word of God, notably by its accuracy and the harmony of its various parts. For this reason, B. B. Warfield asserted that inspiration is not the first but the last claim we make about Scripture:

[W]e first prove [the Scriptures] authentic, historically credible, generally trustworthy, before we prove them inspired. And the proof of their authenticity, credibility, general trustworthiness would give us a firm basis for Christianity prior to any knowledge on our part of their inspiration, and apart indeed from the existence of inspiration. (Warfield 1948: 210)

A more recent apologist in Warfield's line argues:

[O]ne should begin with Scripture as an ancient source book and grant it a high degree of accuracy. Based on the evidence it contains, one concludes that the miracles and resurrection of Jesus Christ are highly probable, that Christ is therefore who He claimed to be, and that therefore His testimony concerning the Scripture and the accrediting of His apostles as authoritative teachers is to be trusted; the Bible is to be received as the inspired, inerrant Word of God. The highly reliable book at the beginning of the argument is discovered at the end of the argument to be the very Word of God, partaking of divine qualities that far transcend mere empiricist reliability. (D. C. Davis 1984: 376)

By the same reasoning, the divine authorship of apocryphal literature is denied on the grounds that this literature contains 'historical, chronological and geographical errors' (E. J. Young, 'The Canon of the Old Testament', quoted in Grudem 1994: 59).

This empirical line of enquiry generally finds what it is looking for, so that a fundamentalist who sets out to establish the accuracy, and thereby the divine authorship, of Scripture is likely to read, or interpret, texts in such a way that they appear as accurate or harmonious as possible. This can involve quite complex handling of biblical passages, such as John Wenham's attempts to harmonize the resurrection narratives in *Easter Enigma* (1984, 1992). It may also involve renderings that seem flatly to contravene a plain reading, as when Harold Lindsell suggested notoriously that Peter denied Jesus six times, because he could find no other way of harmonizing the passion narratives (Lindsell 1976: 175–6).

An inductive approach to inspiration is important to most inerrantists because they believe that the Bible can be shown to be reliable (i.e. error-free). But inductive arguments make the Bible vulnerable to unsympathetic findings. Hodge and Warfield recognized that a 'proved error in Scripture contradicts not only our doctrine, but the Scripture claims and, therefore, its inspiration in making those claims' (1881: 245). But they contended that the 'critical investigation must be made, and we must abide by the result when it is unquestionably reached' (1881: 242). Hodge was apprehensive about the empirical search, but Warfield persisted with the procedure because he thought that sound textual criticism was bringing critics close to unearthing the original manuscripts (Letis 1991: 180–3). The British biblical scholars B. F. Westcott and F. J. A. Hort produced an edition of the Greek New Testament, published in 1881. Influenced by their work, Warfield thought it would be possible to repristinate the autographs of biblical texts, which, he reasoned deductively, would be inerrant because verbally inspired. He expected that seeming errors would in time be proved true.

In the 1960s and 1970s Daniel Fuller, son of Charles E. Fuller, who founded the inerrantist institution Fuller Theological Seminary, shocked the evangelical world by developing a theory that the Bible is inerrant only in revelational matters (Fuller 1968, 1972, 1973). He argued that he was following Warfield in letting 'induction control from beginning to end' (Fuller 1973: 332). But both he and Warfield had ways of protecting the Bible's inerrant status. Warfield distinguished extant manuscripts from the original autographs, which he insisted must have been totally inerrant. Fuller distinguished revelational from non-revelational matters in Scripture, and reserved inerrancy for those that are revelational. His theory posed the problem of how to determine 'which biblical material is revelational and which is not' (Pinnock 1973: 334). The Canadian evangelical Clark Pinnock derisorily labelled it 'limited inerrancy' (Pinnock 1971: 79; 1973: 334).

The concept of inerrancy has become increasingly malleable (S. T. Davis 1977; Dorrien 1998: 103–52; Harris 1998a). The systematic theologian Donald Bloesch affirms inerrancy in G. C. Berkouwer's sense of undeceiving rather than impeccable (1978: 67; 1983: p. ix). New Testament scholar Robert H. Gundry means by inerrancy that the Bible commits no theological errors. He has abandoned the assumption that apparently historical narratives correspond to factual states of affairs. The Evangelical Theological Society in the USA dismissed Gundry in 1983 for applying redaction criticism to Matthew's Gospel and concluding that 'sub-tractions, additions, and revisions of order and phraseology... represent develop-ments... that result in different meanings and departures from the actuality of events' (Gundry 1982: 623). Gundry begins by attributing theological rather than historical significance to the genealogy of Jesus (1982: 13 f.). From there, he suggests that Matthew 'manipulate[s] the dominical tradition' (1982: 35 f.) regarding the birth stories, the beatitudes, and many of the works and sayings of Christ. ETS has been described as practising 'critical anti-criticism', which performs biblical study in order to protect biblical inerrancy from the conclusions of faulty criticism. Such criticism is common within fundamentalist apologetics. Gundry represents a more recent approach, which has been called 'believing criticism' (Noll 1986: 156–73). This approach allows research to overturn traditional evangelical conclusions about the Bible without necessarily undermining beliefs in the Bible's inspiration and inerrancy. But retaining the language of inerrancy reveals a continued convic-tion that Scripture is the foundation of faith and therefore needs to be 100 per cent reliable, even if not factually so.

The Tenacity of Fundamentalism

The fundamentalist doctrine of Scripture is tenacious. Even when evangelicals move away from it, it remains a standard against which they test biblical conservatism. Yet it is also the case that fundamentalist ways of thinking are currently being undermined. This is partly because foundationalism itself is being undermined, and with it the old dividing lines between conservative and liberal, and also because evangelicals are becoming increasingly charismaticized. So these two developments, discussed below, have a moderating effect on biblical fundamentalism. None the less, a fundamentalist apologetic remains within the bloodstream of central, charismaticized evangelicalism, as is apparent from the internationally influential *Alpha* course. The author of *Alpha*, Nicky Gumbel, does not vehemently defend the fundamentalist doctrine of Scripture, but he does assume it. His stance, which will also be considered below, is typical of an evangelicalism that has developed no doctrine of Scripture besides a fundamentalist one.

Challenges to Foundationalism

There have been various challenges to foundationalism in recent philosophy, and this has affected theology (e.g. Murphy 1996; Plantinga and Wolterstorff 1983; Hauerwas, Murphy, and Nation 1994). The distinction between basic and non-basic beliefs has been challenged as arbitrary. The notion that reason moves only from more basic to less basic beliefs, rather than revisiting and modifying more basic beliefs, cannot be sustained. On matters of textual interpretation, it is realized that readers bring questions from their own context, and interact back and forth with a text, such that understanding develops in a way that is more circular than linear. (Philosophical hermeneutics are discussed in a later section.) Theologically, the idea that either the Bible or experience could be foundational in any straightforward way is no longer credible. Rather, it is understood that there is a complex interaction between the two: an interaction that is affected by our cultural formation and the filters through which we interpret the world.

These developments have led to assorted trends that are incompatible with biblical fundamentalism, including narrative theology and emphases on images, metaphors and models, and symbols. These categories, over which post-conservatives and post-liberals converge, intimate journeying, imagination, experimentation, open-endedness, and mystery (e.g. Grenz 1993; Olson 1995; Phillips and Okholm 1996; Hilborn 1997; Erickson 1997/8). Readers interact with the story imaginatively in weaving an understanding of God's message, God's world, and their part in those things. The meaning derived from the story is therefore not static.

By contrast, fundamentalist interpretative methods have assumed a fixed meaning, discernible via historical study. They have attempted first to understand the meaning of the text, and then to apply that meaning in the present—as have 'liberal' historical-critical readings. Thus fundamentalism and liberalism favour a foundationalist approach. But post-conservative and post-liberal theologies both tend towards non-foundationalism or weak foundationalism. On these models, one continually returns to starting-points or foundations, and understands them differently according to changing circumstances. Reason is thereby understood to move in more than one direction. In fact, narrative, highly interactive readings have long been practised by Pentecostals, and especially black Pentecostals (Beckford 1998; Land 1993: 74–5; Hollenweger 1997: 204 ff.). They are not far removed from the way in which many evangelicals relate to and derive guidance from Scripture, but technically they undermine a fundamentalist doctrine of Scripture to which so many evangelicals subscribe.

Charismaticism

Many post-conservatives have been through charismatic renewal, and have become disillusioned with rationalistic aspects of evangelicalism (Tomlinson 1995). Charismaticism modifies fundamentalist tendencies amongst evangelicals, because it expresses faith and conviction in ways that cannot be contained in intelligible language, particularly by speaking in tongues, using the body in worship, and spiritualizing the everyday world. All of these things intimate a realm of faith that cannot be reduced to verbal propositions. Most importantly, charismatics verify Scripture's authority experientially by the way Scripture works in their lives, and not only by rational arguments in defence of Scripture. They have an affinity with the Holiness tradition, whose doctrine of assurance rests on biblical promises and the experience of life in Christ, rather than on what can be proved from the Bible.

The *Alpha* course is representative of mainstream, charismaticized evangelicalism today. It was designed by Nicky Gumbel of Holy Trinity, Brompton, an Anglican evangelical church in London, and is now used world-wide and ecumenically. In the *Alpha* material, Gumbel answers the question 'How Can I Be Sure of My Faith?' not in terms of the reliability of biblical facts, but in terms of the promises stated in Scripture and of the testimony of the Holy Spirit (Gumbel 1993: ch. 4; 1994: ch. 1). An emphasis of *Alpha* teaching is that assurance, or certainty, comes from knowing, loving, and following Jesus Christ, and being sure that God will be true to his promises (e.g. Gumbel 1994: 17–18). This is very different from an emphasis on the sure foundation-stone of Scripture.

Residual Fundamentalism

Yet there is a residual fundamentalism in *Alpha* which reflects more generally the tenacity of the fundamentalist doctrine of Scripture. Gumbel is not much exercised over the doctrine of inerrancy, and does not hold it up as a mark of true Christian identity. Nevertheless, he moves into a fundamentalist way of thinking when he tries to explain how it is that we know about Jesus. He says that becoming a Christian 'is not a blind leap of faith, but a step of faith based on firm historical evidence' (1993: 23), and for this reason he introduces Jesus by the historical evidence for his existence. He therefore needs an accurate Bible. He gets it via implicit use of the deductive argument that Scripture is verbally inspired by God. He follows a line of reasoning from B. B. Warfield, James Packer, John Stott, and others, which turns on 2 Tim. 3: 16. He endorses the dual-authorship model of inspiration (also endorsed by Warfield, Packer, and Stott), which conceives of Scripture as both '100% the work of human beings... [and] 100% inspired by God (just as Jesus is fully human and fully God)' (1993: 73–4). According to this model, the human writers are totally guided by God, but feel themselves simply to be writing human accounts based on eyewitness evidence. Although fundamentalists are frequently criticized for not doing justice to the human element of Scripture, actually they test Scripture as one would test the accuracy of any human report. They would take a proven inaccuracy to imply a flaw in the reporter, and since human reporters are fallible, they insist upon divine plenary verbal inspiration, assuming that God can be relied upon to get the facts right. 'Difficulties' and 'apparent contradictions' could, Gumbel implies, militate against claims that the Bible is inspired: 'Although some of the apparent contradictions can be explained by differing contexts, others are harder to resolve. This does not mean, however, that it is impossible and that we should abandon our belief in the inspiration of Scripture' (1993: 74–5). In other words, the doctrine of inspiration is dependent on there being no actual contradictions. If there were some actual contradictions, Scripture could not have been inspired, and the Christian faith would have no reliable basis. This is a fundamentalist apologetic.

FUNDAMENTALISM AND THE WORLD

We have defined fundamentalism theologically and philosophically as biblical foundationalism. However, scholars have suggested a wide range of defining characteristics. Prominent among these are 'militant separatism' when discussing the Protestant context, and 'political activism' when comparing fundamentalisms across the world faiths. Separatism and activism are almost contrary characteristics: one is quietist, and the other engaged in its policies towards the outside world.

Militant Separatism

Historians of Protestant fundamentalism favour militant separatism as a defining feature of fundamentalism (see esp. Marsden 1980: 4, 102–3, 141, 164–70, 228). This is because of the divergence that developed between fundamentalists and evangelicals in the USA in the mid-twentieth century.

As the fundamentalist–modernist controversies dissipated in the 1920s, the more extreme fundamentalists left their denominations. This fragmented the fundamentalist movement. By the 1940s, a second generation of fundamentalists had grown up and were beginning to question key aspects of their heritage, notably the militant schismatic tendencies and the withdrawal from political and social responsibility. A group emerged who came to call themselves 'the new evangelicals'. Billy Graham was their key evangelist, and Carl F. H. Henry and Bernard Ramm their leading theologians.

Over time, 'new evangelical' identity became simply 'evangelical' identity (Ockenga 1978). More militant conservatives retained the label 'fundamentalist'. They kept themselves separate from non-believers and from other sorts of Christians. Bob Jones, for example, withdrew his support from his former student Billy Graham, when Graham began co-operating with a wide range of Christians in evangelistic rallies. Because Graham accepted sponsorship from people who were not 'born-again' and 'Bible-believing', Bob Jones senior questioned his very belief in the Bible as the Word of God:

I cannot see how Billy Graham says he believes the Bible is the Word of God (He knows that all we know about Jesus Christ, His Virgin Birth, His Incarnation, His vicarious blood atonement, His bodily resurrection, and His coming again, is what is clearly taught in the Word of God.) [sic] and can be sponsored by preachers who do not believe these fundamentals and give to these preachers the same recognition that he gives to God's faithful, sacrificing servants who refuse to compromise. (Jones 1957: 4)

For their part, the new evangelicals regarded themselves as fundamentalist in theology but not in their attitudes towards intellectual life or social responsibility. Carl Henry delivered one of the first and most direct self-criticisms of the fundamentalist position in his book *The Uneasy Conscience of Modern Fundamentalism* (1947). In it he sought to reassure readers that he was not abandoning a fundamentalist approach to Scripture:

[T]he 'uneasy conscience' of which I write is not one troubled about the great Biblical verities, which I consider the only outlook capable of resolving our problems, but rather one distressed by the frequent failure to apply them effectively to crucial problems confronting the modern mind. It is application of, not a revolt against, fundamentals of the faith, for which I plead. (Henry 1947: preface)

He continued to uphold a doctrine of inerrancy, and has been disappointed by the modifications to that doctrine made by his evangelical colleagues over the ensuing decades (Marsden 1987; Dorrien 1998).

Political Activism

In the 1970s a large number of self-proclaimed fundamentalists in the USA modified their separatist principles in order to contribute to the efforts of the newly emerging Christian Right. Older-style, separatist fundamentalists, such as the Bob Jones dynasty, are engaged in a long-standing feud with this newer politicized breed. Bob Jones senior called them 'fudgymentalists' for fudging the scriptural command to keep oneself separate:

Scripture clearly enjoins two sorts of separation . . . ; (1) the ecclesiastical separation, which the 'fudgymentalists' ignore; and (2) personal separation from sin and the world, which they usually profess to follow. Both are enjoined by Scripture, and no man has a right to profess to obey one but to ignore the other. (Jones 1978)

Bob Jones III labelled Jerry Falwell's movement the Moral Majority 'neo-fundamentalist', meaning that it was a new and deviant form of fundamentalism that dirtied its hands by joining with 'Catholics, Jews, Protestants of every stripe, Mormons, etc., in a common religious cause' (Jones III 1980: 1).

Both old-style fundamentalists and the new, politicized fundamentalists claim Scripture as foundational for their attitudes towards politics and society. Old-style fundamentalists withdraw from political life out of the conviction that the Christian's duty is to save individual souls from sin, and that conversion of individuals is the remedy for an immoral society. Moreover, most separatist fundamentalists hold premillennialist convictions which de-motivate them politically. They expect the world to become a worse and worse place until Christ returns, and regard the immorality of the nation as a sign of the times.

Politicized fundamentalists, by contrast, treat Scripture as a source-book for political action. They seek to restructure society according to biblical principles. Pat Robertson, who superseded Falwell in Christian Right politics and founded the Christian Coalition, wrote in the early 1980s:

Once we perceive this secret [that the Bible is the Word of God], we realize anew that the Bible is not an impractical book of theology, but rather a practical book of life containing a system of thought and conduct that will guarantee success. And it will be true success, true happiness, true prosperity, not the fleeting, flash, inconsistent success the world usually settles for.

The Bible, quite bluntly, is a workable guidebook for politics, government, business, families, and all the affairs of mankind. (Robertson 1983: 44)

The Bible as textbook has been a favourite metaphor among fundamentalists and evangelicals, but it has classically been restricted to the theological application of Scripture (e.g. Lindsell 1976: 31; Manley 1925: 137; Stott 1996: 17). Robertson views the Bible as encyclopaedic in nature, offering guidance for virtually every aspect of life. This is a logical consequence of a doctrine of plenary verbal inspiration: that Scripture comprises inspired and therefore unerring statements, such that even its inferences and asides will provide at least some truths for almost every sort of theory-making enterprise (Clouser 1991: 94).

This encyclopaedic assumption extends the demands put on Scripture; that it be inerrant even in matters not directly pertaining to salvation. So Francis Schaeffer believed that scripture gives 'affirmations about that in which science has an interest' (Schaeffer 1975: 25), and Harold Lindsell claimed that 'when the writers of Scripture spoke of matters embraced in [history, science and mathematics], they did not indite error' (1976: 31). Such an outlook underlies fundamentalist educational policies. David Beck, professor of philosophy at Jerry Falwell's Liberty University, holds that a Christian institution gains its distinctiveness from 'the inclusion of the propositions of Scripture within the hard data of its instructional content' (1991: 15–16). He advocates incorporating the 'data of Scripture' (1991: 11) into the teaching of philosophy, literature, social and natural sciences, and even health and sports. It is therefore not surprising to find fundamentalists also looking to Scripture for guidance on how to run a country.

COMPARATIVE FUNDAMENTALISM AND SCRIPTURAL AUTHORITY

Jerry Falwell founded the Moral Majority in the USA in 1979, the same year as the *coup* in Iran and the return of Ayatollah Khomeini from exile. These two developments revealed mass following for conservative forms of religion that could be mobilized politically. The label 'fundamentalism' was extended from the North American context to the Iranian revolutionaries, and became associated with religio-political activism. Soon it was applied to numerous religious resurgent movements, including *Hindutva* (Hindu-ness) organizations in India and Sinhalese Buddhists in Sri Lanka. Most of these movements had been in existence for decades, and had originated as reactions to Western colonial and missionary activity. Whether they are all rightly called 'fundamentalist', or have significant features in common, are contentious matters.

The most agreed method today for finding meaning for the term 'fundamentalism' is to discern the overlapping resemblances amongst so-called fundamentalist groups (e.g. Marty and Appleby 1995; Bruce 2000). For example, Jewish 'fundamentalists' share Muslim 'fundamentalist' devotion to scriptural law, and some share the desire to build a religious state. Like Hindu and Buddhist 'fundamentalists', they identify their people by the preservation of religious practices and by religio-historical links to a particular land. None of these groups fully exhibit the Protestant fundamentalist approach to Scripture or the emphasis on right belief, but all do select particular aspects of their tradition that they absolutize and may make foundational.

Early comparative studies of fundamentalism focused on the Abrahamic religions, as 'religions of the Book'. 'Scripturalism' was identified as a key feature of fundamentalism, as a mode of believing organized around texts whose status is somehow absolute (Lawrence 1989; Hunter 1990). The Fundamentalism Project (1988–93), based at the University of Chicago and funded by the American Academy of the Arts and Sciences, studied hundreds of movements across the world's faiths, and implied in its conclusions (without explicitly stating) that scriptural absolutism is a feature of genuine fundamentalism. See point 4 in the following list of fundamentalist characteristics identified by the Project:

1. reactivity to the marginalization of religion
2. selectivity
3. moral dualism
4. absolutism and inerrancy
5. millennialism and messianism
6. elect membership
7. sharp boundaries
8. charismatic and authoritarian leadership
9. behavioural requirements

The Project found that movements most strongly reflecting these characteristics were from the Abrahamic religions, for whom scriptural revelations relating to political, moral, and social issues form the corpus of demands. It judged groups such as Ulster Protestants and Hindutva groups, who recognize true Hindus by their allegiance to the land of India, to be only 'fundamentalist-like' because they promote cultural and national purity, rather than scriptural and doctrinal purity (Marty and Appleby 1995: Part 5).

If we say that scripturalism is a central feature of fundamentalism, we must recognize that it takes different forms in different religions. The term 'scripturalism' suggests bibliolatry or a heterodox emphasis on Scripture, and one religion's heterodoxy might be another's orthodoxy. The belief that all Scripture is an immediate word-for-word communication from God is a specifically fundamentalist belief within Protestant Christianity, but not within a Muslim context. *All* Muslims, 'fundamentalist' or otherwise, hold the Qur'an to be the very words of Allah given to the Prophet Muhammad—this is an aspect of Islamic orthodoxy.

Protestant fundamentalists, we have suggested, attempt to make the Bible foundational for faith and to read it plainly. The emphasis on the 'plain sense' indicates a concern to close off rather than to open out interpretative possibilities. Realizing this, some Muslim and Jewish scholars have rejected the fundamentalist label for Muslim and Jewish groups, in so far as it implies a suspicion of the interpretation of Scripture which is peculiar to Protestant fundamentalism (Hassan 1990; Wieseltier 1990; cf. Barr 1977: 7, 182, 284–6).

Jewish 'fundamentalists' have allegiances to particular rabbinic traditions, Islamic 'fundamentalists' to particular schools of law. Both consciously reside within traditions of interpretation. 'Fundamentalism' might, in this sort of context, mean rigid adherence to practices advocated within particular interpretative traditions. It would not necessarily cancel out the possibility of vigorous reinterpretation of the fundamentals of Scripture. For example, Ayatollah Khomeini insisted that the Qur'an and Hadith cannot be understood outside of eleven centuries of Shi'a scholarship, and he developed an innovative Shi'a concept of the state as supervised by *ulama* (clergy) and religious jurists.

That said, so-called Muslim fundamentalists disagree widely over the place of interpretation, partly depending on whether they are Sunni or Shi'i Muslims. There is space here for only brief consideration of some of their differences, but the disagreements will illuminate points of comparison and contrast between Muslim and Protestant scripturalism.

Sunni and Shi'i Muslims disagree over whether the Qur'an is uncreated, as is the Sunni belief, or created. Shi'i Muslims believe it was created and came into existence in the seventh century CE. Hence they are less inclined than Sunni Muslims to believe that the Qur'an is eternally and universally valid in such a way that it does not necessarily need interpreting with reference to seventh-century Arabia. Shi'i Muslims place greater emphasis than Sunni Muslims on the need for careful exegesis and interpretation. For this reason they are sometimes described as being more 'Catholic', and Sunni more 'Protestant' in their approach to Scripture (Goddard 2002: 150). Within Shi'i Islam, *'aql* (reason) came to be considered one of the four legitimate sources of guidance, along with the Qur'an, the Hadith (Muslim tradition), and the *ijma* (consensus) of the community. Most Sunni Muslims recognize sources other than the Qur'an as legitimate for guidance, but in recent centuries a view has emerged that the earliest generation provides the supreme model, and later history is a corruption, rather than a legitimate development, of the tradition. These Sunni attitudes resemble radical elements of the Protestant Reformation, which regarded Christian history since the days of the Apostles to be a process of corruption (Goddard 2002: 154–5). This, then, is the likeliest place to look for similarities between Protestant and Sunni forms of scriptural fundamentalism.

Within Sunni Islam, the ancestry of this view can be traced back to Ahmad ibn Hanbal in the ninth century. The Hanbali legal school named after him does not accept either *ijma* or *quiyas*, and takes only the Qur'an and Hadith as sufficient authority on which to base conclusions. Descendants of this way of thinking include the eighteenth-century Wahabi movement in Arabia, and many later groups sometimes collectively known as the Salafiyya—those who base themselves on the *Salaf* (the ancestors), the first generation of Muslims (Goddard 2002: 155). They can be said to reveal a primitivism similar to that of Protestant fundamentalists. Indeed, one recent commentator likens the self-taught Salafiyya reformists to fire-breathing Protestant fundamentalists, both of whom abjure traditional scholarship, and who between them are precipitating a clash of civilizations (Ernst 2004). Muslims reflecting this Salafist approach are currently involved in separatist or violent responses to the Western world. Fifteen of the nineteen suicide hijackers of September 11, 2001, were Saudi citizens, and therefore influenced by Wahabbism.

Tariq Ramadan, grandson of Hasan al-Banna, who founded the Muslim Brotherhood in Egypt in 1927, has recently criticized his grandfather's Salafist followers. The Muslim Brotherhood called for the establishment of an Islamic state governed by *shar'ia* (divine law), as opposed to the secular Arab states governed by European laws. It today bears an influence over much of the Sunni Muslim world, though it is criticized by more radical groups, like Jama'a, for operating in mainstream politics. Several offshoots from the Brotherhood, such as Hamas in Palestine, have become separate entities. Ramadan (2004) criticizes al-Banna's present-day followers for teaching Muslims living in the West to keep themselves apart from their host cultures by, for example, adopting distinctive dress codes. Ramadan himself counteracts these Salafist tendencies by arguing that on social matters (*al-muamalati*) the divine text of the Qur'an 'almost never allows itself, alone, to lay down a universal principle'. Rather, he says: 'It is the human mind that derives both absolute and relative principles, as appropriate, from the Text and from the reality of the context in which it was revealed' (Ramadan 2004: 21). He emphasizes that 'the Revelation was elaborated in time and space, over twenty-three years, in a certain context expressed in pronouncements affected by circumstance, open to evolution, accessible to reason, in a historical setting' (Ramadan 2004: 21). He is thereby criticizing a Muslim form of militant separatism, and the use of Scripture undergirding it, reminding Salafists that when they appeal to Scripture they are always interpreting it: 'There can be no revealed Text unless there is human intellect up to the task of reading and interpreting it' (Ramadan 2004: 20).

Once the concept of 'fundamentalism' is extended to cover movements within Indian and Far Eastern religions, it cannot be said always to be organized around scriptural norms. Sinhalese Buddhist activists derive their absolute principle, a command to maintain the Buddhist purity of Sri Lanka, from a particular construction of Buddhist history that lies outside the Pali canon (Obeyeskere 1995). If they are to count as 'fundamentalist', their fundamentalism is not scripturalist. It is related to a myth which operates powerfully in the self-identity of the Sinhalese—that the Buddha visited Sri Lanka by means of supernatural powers and consecrated the land—and to histories in which aggressive defence of the land's (ethnic) purity are justified as bringing glory to the Buddhist order. This accounts for the seeming anomaly and irony that Buddhist 'fundamentalists' can perform acts of violence, whereas primary Buddhist principles derived from the Pali canon oppose violence.

There is a different kind of irony regarding Hindutva ideology, which celebrates its plurality of texts and authorities, and regards the absence of essentials as essential to Hinduism. It propounds the 'irreducibly non-fundamentalist nature of Hindu thinking' (Ram-Prasad 1993: 292; cf. Parekh 1992: 43–5; Madan 1997). At the same time, its assertion of self-identifying essentials against the encroachment of Western culture betrays some influence from Western fundamentalist patterns of thought.

Arguably fundamentalism is most at home in the Protestant context. Not only did it originate there, but its thought patterns are those prevalent in the post-Reformation, and especially post-Enlightenment, Christian West, where a particular kind of apologetic process had emerged of treating the Scriptures as providing the justifying grounds for faith. This hardened into a textual foundationalism which set the Bible up as a self-authenticating authority for faith, an immediate divine communication requiring no interpretation, 100 per cent verbally inspired and 100 per cent inerrant. Other fundamentalisms across the world's faiths are not scripturalist in quite this way, and some are not scripturalist at all. Whereas Protestant fundamentalists go 'back to the Bible' and bypass elements of tradition which seemingly deviate from the Bible's plain truth, others go back to 'the ancestors', or to teachings of a particular school of law, or to foundational myths not even enshrined in Scripture. What they have in common is a belief in some original, unconditioned teaching or pristine state. It is a mistake to regard fundamentalists as traditionalists. Traditionalists are keenly aware of the organic development of their religion. Fundamentalists are primitivist and selective, wanting to return to some unconditional origin, and ignoring parts of the religious tradition which detract from that.

PHILOSOPHICAL HERMENEUTICS

In the Protestant context, evangelical Christianity has been infused by fundamentalist ways of thinking. But it would be remiss to end this essay without noting moves by evangelicals to employ hermeneutical methods which are in principle antithetical to fundamentalism, methods which challenge a 'back to the Bible' primitivism and *naïveté*. Since the 1970s, evangelicals have taken some things on board from phenomenological hermeneutics (The Nottingham Statement, printed in Stott 1977; The Willowbank Report 1978). Phenomenological hermeneutics operates with the philosophical conviction that all phenomena, including texts, attain the meaning we attribute to them, and that readers interpret texts and the whole of life according to the contexts in which they are phenomenologically situated. Such theory undermines fundamentalist assumptions, and some evangelicals reject it precisely on the grounds that it turns the sure foundation of Scripture into the 'texture of quicksand', and makes truth 'dissolv[e] in the mists of postmodernity' (Carson 1996: 92, 91). Others claim to have moved away from fundamentalist positions when they have taken modern hermeneutical questions seriously (France 1991). Evangelical engagement with hermeneutics brings into focus concerns at the heart of biblical fundamentalism, particularly the desire to determine the meaning of biblical passages, and shows how difficult it can be even to want fully to relinquish a fundamentalist doctrine of Scripture (Harris 1998*a*: 278–312).

The popular British evangelical theologian John Stott has promoted and popularized the hermeneutical theory that Anthony Thiselton introduced to evangelicals. Thiselton, a British philosophical theologian, criticizes a 'theological conservatism' which 'simply assumes no difference between a "common sense" interpretive tradition and what the text itself says' (Thiselton 1985: 80–1). He also rejects the classic evangelical process of grammatico-historical exegesis, which implies that individual words are the primary bearers of meaning. He promotes a speech-act model which regards language uses as acts which have effects (1980: 129, 436; 1985: 100, 107–13; 1992: 16 f.). In this he has been influenced by J. L. Austin and by Wittgenstein's emphasis upon language as forming 'part of an activity' in public interaction. He thus emphasizes the functional alongside the cognitive aspect of the biblical writings: 'acts of blessing, acts of forgiveness, acts of pronouncing judgment, acts of repentance', and so on (1992: 17–18). Speech acts occur at the point of interrelation between the situation addressed by the biblical writer and the situation of the modern reader. They lead us to take into account feelings and attitudes, and not just the communication of thought.

Thiselton encourages evangelicals to think not in terms of a biblical message neatly packaged, but of the biblical impact in real life. He warns them not to assume that the meaning of Scripture is self-evident (1977: 92). The problem, as he describes it, is 'that of how the text of the Bible, written in the ancient world, can so speak to the modern hearer that it engages with his own situation and horizons without doing violence to its original purpose' (1977: 92). His solution is a combination of 'distancing' and 'fusion': distancing the assumptions of one's own background whilst reading the text, but allowing a fusion in which one listens to the text and allows it to speak. Failure to distance one's own assumptions will result in seeing the text 'through the spectacles' of one's own tradition (1977: 104).

John Stott takes Thiselton's emphasis on the fusion of the horizons and places it alongside E. D. Hirsch's dictum, 'a text means what its author meant' (Stott 1982: 221, 186). He tells evangelicals that it is an 'illusion that we come to the biblical text as innocent, objective, impartial, culture-free investigators' (1982: 185). However, his commitment to Hirsch, which is shared by other evangelical theologians and exegetes (e.g. Henry 1979b; Kaiser 1979; and see Boone 1989 for an analysis of fundamentalism in light of the hermeneutics of Hirsch), leads him to believe that one can discern the meaning of the text independently of the process of fusion between the horizon of the text and the horizon of the interpreter. Hirsch distinguishes between meaning and significance, according to which meaning lies in the author's intended sense and significance lies in the present application. He regards discernment of meaning as a process 'separate and distinct' from relating the text to a present situation (Hirsch 1967: 255–6). Thiselton insists, by contrast, that our questions and reformulated questions have a bearing on our apprehension of the text's meaning. Stott leans more towards Hirsch, and resists rendering meaning as unstable as Thiselton's hermeneutics imply. He attempts to preserve the doctrine of inerrancy at the level of meaning, and confines insights from hermeneutical philosophy to the level of significance or application. This move, made in numerous evangelical publications (cf. The Chicago Statement on Biblical Hermeneutics 1982; Packer 1984; Geisler 1984), in fact nullifies any appeal to phenomenological hermeneutics, and again reveals the tenacity of a fundamentalist doctrine of Scripture.

Few evangelical apologists have engaged hermeneutical philosophy in a way that seriously challenges fundamentalist assumptions. Some have worried that the principle of authorial intention opens 'the door wide to a kind of psychological second-guessing as replacing a sober analysis of the text' (Nicole 1983: 206), and so wish to revert to a grammatico-historical approach that seeks to be more objective (R. K. Johnson 1988: 60). Of those who have endorsed authorial intention, some have done so because they believe that it embodies the Reformation insistence that Scripture be interpreted literally rather than allegorically (Packer 1990: 49), or because appeals to authorial intention can be made in defence of inerrancy. For example, if numerical or scientific precision were not the author's primary intention, then numerical or scientific imprecision would not count against the inerrancy of a text. There is deep reluctance to see meaning itself as affected by hermeneutics. Timothy Ward (2002), writing as an academic rather than a popular theologian, has attempted to combine a speech-act theory with Warfield's doctrine of Scripture, but where tensions arise, he upholds Warfield's approach, and hence a commitment to fixed, inerrant meaning. Kevin J. Vanhoozer makes a more significant move, disputing the epistemological concern to determine the meaning of a text, but at the same time protecting the divinely authored meaning from the shifting sands of hermeneutics (Vanhoozer 2002: 286, 276).

Vanhoozer is an evangelical postmodern theologian. He interprets postmodernism as 'messianic', meaning that it is 'open to the coming of the other and the different', and, for this reason, he insists that faith, not reason, is 'endemic to the postmodern condition' (2003: 18). Hermeneutically, he develops a speech-act model whilst also following Hirsch's distinction between meaning and application (1998; 2002: 127–203, 275–308). He holds that 'the Bible may be significant in different ways to different readers who nevertheless agree that there is a single meaning in the text' (1998: 424). He introduces an eschatological dimension to the discernment of meaning, and so holds that while a text has a single meaning, our grasp of that meaning is partial and its significance incomplete (Vanhoozer 1998: 429–30). We have to wait rather than bring the final interpretive solution to a premature conclusion. Vanhoozer thereby challenges fundamentalist claims to be in possession of the truth, but he rejects the possibility of multiple meanings.

His resistance to a multiplicity of meanings is surprising, given that Vanhoozer operates with a theory of meaning as communicative act. He is interested in the efficacy of Scripture, meaning its power to produce effects (Vanhoozer 1998: 424–7), rather than the sufficiency of Scripture in giving us evidence or reasons. If meaning is related to efficacy, it is not obvious that it need be singular and unattained, rather than plural and differently attained as befits the circumstances. Vanhoozer's commitment to a single meaning reflects an ongoing fundamentalist-like anxiety about shifting ground. At the same time, his emphases on discernment, moral and spiritual formation, and the authority of the Holy Spirit are undermining of fundamentalist rationalism. He favours the term 'discernment' over 'deduction' and 'induction' for the processes involved in reading Scripture and practising theology. He tries to discern meaning through a process of 'theological interpretation' that is 'formed, informed and reformed by Christian doctrine' (2002: 286), and holds that proper discernment depends on readers developing interpretive virtues, for which the Christian community is formative. Hermeneutics, he believes, should socialize people into the Body of Christ, not aim to determine the meaning of the text or author as part of an epistemological project. Understanding requires not only reason but repentance, not only scholarship but faith (where faith means something other than rational assent to evidence) (Vanhoozer 1998: 430). He criticizes fundamentalists for assuming that one can extract the truth from Scripture without the hard discipline of living in the Christian community, and without effective acknowledgement of the role of the Holy Spirit. He agrees with the new-evangelical theologian Bernard Ramm, who argued in the 1950s that fundamentalism displays an 'abbreviated Protestant principle' (1957: 29)—'abbreviated', because its understanding of Scripture interpreting Scripture relegates the Holy Spirit to the margins. This aspect of his critique is helpful for identifying the idolatrous nature of fundamentalism. Through marginalizing the Holy Spirit, fundamentalism becomes bibliolatry—a religion of the Book—and fundamentalists come to equate the meaning of the text with their own reading of it. In a more faithful Reformed theology, 'Scripture interprets Scripture' means that God the Holy Spirit, speaking in and through Scripture, interprets Scripture. God the Holy Spirit is free and cannot be fixed.

Vanhoozer responds to fundamentalism by offering the conditions for a differently constructed theology, in which the threefold God is the ground of faith and Scripture, and the Spirit speaks through Scripture to make it efficacious. On a fundamentalist rendering, by contrast, Scripture is the ground of faith, meaning that it is the basis upon which we know anything about God, and the threefold God inspires and interprets Scripture in order to insure the sufficiency of the evidence it contains.

CONCLUDING REMARKS

Protestant fundamentalists regard the Bible as foundational for faith, and believe that if the Bible were found to be flawed, Christianity would collapse. They therefore also feel concerned at the prospect of more than one meaning to a biblical passage, for their foundation would then seem more like shifting sand than solid rock. While they believe they base Christian faith on Scripture, in practice they base it on reason, or a particular deductive and inductive process by which they require Scripture to pass stringent rational and empirical assessments (Harris 2000). Their position stems from an epistemological anxiety that we cannot know anything of Christ or God if we cannot first be sure that the Bible is (factually) reliable. They imagine that Scripture preceded the development of Christian orthodoxy, and that orthodox beliefs were extracted from it, whereas Scripture itself emerged out of the developing orthodoxy of the primitive and early church (cf. Witherington III 2004: 103; L. T. Johnson 1999: 601). They then treat the Bible as something it is not: a static source of inerrant data. While fundamentalist believers may experience faith more dynamically than their fundamentalism conveys, as a gift from God that defies rationalization, they adhere to an apologetic that puts faith at the mercy of investigations into apparent errors and inconsistencies in Scripture.

The concept 'fundamentalism' makes most sense in Protestant Christianity, where it applies to a strongly foundationalist model of biblical authority. Protestant

fundamentalists rest faith upon reason and evidence, and regard the Bible as supplying the data that justify faith. In treating Scripture as foundational, they require it
to be unmediated or fully verbally inspired, perspicuous, and not in need of interpretation, self-authenticating, and inerrant. Their rigidity over right belief and practice
is related to the foundational structure of reasoning and a *naïveté* about the plain
sense of Scripture: Protestant fundamentalists have seen themselves as reading doctrine and morality straight off from the Bible. Philosophical challenges to foundationalism, and developments in hermeneutical theory, undermine fundamentalist
assumptions about the objective nature of reason and evidence, and of their own
readings of Scripture. Post-conservative and charismatic developments both modify
fundamentalism because they bring to the fore non-verbal, non-cognitive forms of
interaction between God and ourselves. But fundamentalist notions of biblical
authority are tenacious, and make their presence felt wherever inerrancy functions
as the norm against which to gauge a person's level of conservatism. The *Alpha* course
self-consciously reflects both charismatic and what it calls postmodern trends,
and yet retains a fundamentalist doctrine of Scripture. At the same time, it does not
focus its energy on defending this doctrine. *Alpha* provides a good indicator of the
place of biblical fundamentalism amongst mainstream evangelicals at the turn of the
twenty-first century.

Suggested Reading

The authoritative history of Protestant fundamentalism, which also interprets the
phenomenon theologically and not only sociologically, is Marsden 1980. Prime
examples of fundamentalist apologetic from the early, mid-, and late-twentieth
century are Machen 1923, Packer 1958, and Grudem 1994. David Edwards and John
Stott (1988) published a helpful discussion. For critical analyses of fundamentalist
notions of biblical authority see Barr 1977, Barton 1988, and Harris 1998a. Martin E.
Marty and R. Scott Appleby (1992) provide an introductory way into reading about
fundamentalism across the world's faiths. Ramadan (2004) gives an accessible and
scholarly analysis of scripturalist issues within Islam.

Bibliography

ABRAHAM, W. J. 2003. *The Logic of Renewal*. London: SPCK.
BARR, J. 1977. *Fundamentalism*. London: SCM.
—— 1991. ' "Fundamentalism" and Conservative Scholarship'. *Anvil*, 8/2: 141–52.
BARTON, J. 1988. *People of the Book? The Authority of the Bible in Christianity*. London:
    SPCK.

BAUCKHAM, R., ed. 1998. *The Gospels for All Christians: Rethinking the Gospel Audiences.* Edinburgh: T. & T. Clark.

BEBBINGTON, D. W. 1988. 'The Advent Hope in British Evangelicalism since 1800'. *SJT* 9: 103–14.

BECK, D. W. 1991. 'Introduction: Designing a Christian University'. In D. W. Beck, ed., *Opening the American Mind: The Integration of Biblical Truth in the Curriculum of the University,* Grand Rapids, Mich.: Baker.

BECKFORD, R. 1998. *Jesus is Dread: Black Theology and Black Culture in Britain.* London: Darton, Longman, and Todd.

BLOESCH, D. 1978. *The Essentials of Evangelical Theology,* i: *God, Authority and Salvation.* San Francisco: Harper & Row.

—— 1983. *The Future of Evangelical Theology: A Call for Unity amid Diversity.* Garden City, NY: Doubleday.

BOONE, K. C. 1989. *The Bible Tells Them So: The Discourse of Protestant Fundamentalism.* Albany, NY: State University of New York Press; London: SCM.

BRUCE, S. 2000. *Fundamentalism.* Cambridge: Polity.

CAMERON, P. 1994. *Heretic.* Sydney, Auckland, Toronto, New York, and London: Doubleday.

CARSON, D. A. 1996. *The Gagging of God: Christianity Confronts Pluralism.* Leicester: Apollos.

Chicago Statement on Biblical Hermeneutics 1982; repr. in Radmacher and Preus 1984: 881–7.

CLOUSER, R. A. 1991. *The Myth of Religious Neutrality: An Essay on the Hidden Role of Religious Belief in Theories.* Notre Dame, Ind.: University of Notre Dame Press.

COHEN, N. J., ed. 1990. *The Fundamentalist Phenomenon: A View from Within; A Response from Without.* Grand Rapids, Mich.: Eerdmans.

DAVIS, D. C. 1984. 'Princeton and Inerrancy: The Nineteenth-Century Philosophical Background of Contemporary Concerns'. In J. D. Hannah, ed., *Inerrancy and the Church,* Chicago: Moody, 1984, 359–78.

DAVIS, J. J. 1985. *Let the Bible Teach you Christian Doctrine.* Carlisle: Paternoster.

DAVIS, S. T. 1977. *The Debate about the Bible Inerrancy vs Infallibility.* Philadelphia: Westminster.

DOCKERY, D. S., ed. 1995. *The Challenge of Postmodernism: An Evangelical Engagement.* Grand Rapids, Mich.: Baker.

DORRIEN, G. 1998. *The Remaking of Evangelical Theology.* Louisville, Ky.: Westminster/ John Knox.

EDWARDS, D. L., and STOTT, J. 1988. *Essentials: A Liberal–Evangelical Dialogue.* London: Hodder & Stoughton.

ERICKSON, M. J. 1997/8. *The Evangelical Left: Encountering Postconservative Evangelical Theology.* Grand Rapids, Mich.: Baker Books; Carlisle: Paternoster.

ERNST, C. W. 2004. *Following Muhammad: Rethinking Islam in the Contemporary World.* Chapel Hill, NC: University of North Carolina Press; Edinburgh: Edinburgh University Press.

FRANCE, R. T. 1991. 'James Barr and Evangelical Scholarship'. *Anvil,* 8/1: 51–64.

FULLER, D. 1968. 'Benjamin B. Warfield's View of Faith and History'. *Bulletin of the Evangelical Theological Society,* 11/2: 75–83.

—— 1972. 'The Nature of Biblical Inerrancy'. *Journal of the American Scientific Affiliation,* June: 47–51.

—— 1973. 'Daniel Fuller and Clark Pinnock: On Revelation and Biblical Authority'. *Christian Scholar's Review*, 2/4: 330–5.

GEISLER, N. L., ed. 1979. *Inerrancy*. Grand Rapids, Mich.: Zondervan.

—— 1984. 'Explaining Hermeneutics: A Commentary on the Chicago Statement on Biblical Hermeneutics Articles of Affirmation and Denial'. In Radmacher and Preus 1984: 889–904.

GODDARD, H. 2002. 'Is Islam a "Fundamentalist" Religion?' In M. Percy, ed., *Fundamentalism, Church and Society*, London: SPCK, 145–59.

GRENZ, S. J. 1993. *Revisioning Evangelical Theology: A Fresh Agenda for the 21st Century*. Downers Grove, Ill.: InterVarsity Press.

GRUDEM, W. 1994. *Systematic Theology: An Introduction to Biblical Doctrine*. Leicester: Inter-Varsity Press; Grand Rapids, Mich.: Zondervan.

GUMBEL, N. 1993. *Questions of Life*. Eastbourne: Kingsway.

—— 1994. *A Life Worth Living*. Eastbourne: Kingsway.

GUNDRY, R. H. 1982. *Matthew: A Commentary on His Literary and Theological Art*. Grand Rapids, Mich.: Eerdmans.

HARRIS, H. A. 1998a. *Fundamentalism and Evangelicals*. Oxford: Clarendon Press.

—— 1998b. 'Fundamentalism and Theology'. Farmington Papers, June 1998. Farmington Institute for Christian Studies.

—— 2000. 'A Diamond in the Dark: Abraham Kuyper's Doctrine of Scripture'. In Luis Lugo and Max Stackhouse, eds., *Religion, Pluralism and Public Life: Abraham Kuyper's Legacy for the 21st Century*, Grand Rapids, Mich.: Eerdmans, 123–44.

—— 2002. 'How Helpful is the Term "Fundamentalism"?'. In Christopher Partridge, ed., *Fundamentalisms*, Carlisle: Paternoster, 3–18.

HASSAN, R. 1990. 'The Burgeoning of Islamic Fundamentalism: Toward an Understanding of the Phenomenon'. In Cohen 1990: 151–71.

HAUERWAS, S., MURPHY, N., and NATION, M. 1994. *Theology without Foundations: Religious Practice and the Future of Theological Truth*. Nashville: Abingdon Press.

HEBERT, G. 1957. *Fundamentalism and the Church of God*. London: SCM Press.

HENRY, C. F. H. 1947. *The Uneasy Conscience of Modern Fundamentalism*. Grand Rapids, Mich.: Eerdmans.

—— 1979a. *God, Revelation and Authority*, iii: *God Who Speaks and Shows, Fifteen Theses, Part Two*. Waco, Tex.: Word Books.

—— 1979b. *God, Revelation and Authority*, iv: *God Who Speaks and Shows, Fifteen Theses, Part Three*. Waco, Tex.: Word Books.

HILBORN, D. 1997. *Picking Up the Pieces: Can Evangelicals Adapt to Contemporary Culture?* London, Sydney, and Auckland: Hodder & Stoughton.

HIRSCH, E. D. jun. 1967. *Validity in Interpretation*. New Haven: Yale University Press.

HODGE A. A., and WARFIELD, B. B. 1881. 'Inspiration'. *Presbyterian Review*, 2 (April): 225–60.

HOLLENWEGER, W. J. 1997. *Pentecostalism: Origins and Developments Worldwide*. Peabody, Mass.: Hendrickson.

HUNTER, J. D. 1990. 'Fundamentalism in its Global Contours'. In Cohen 1990: 56–72.

JOHNSON, L. T. 1999. *The Writings of the New Testament: An Interpretation*. London: SCM.

JOHNSON, R. K. 1988. 'How We Interpret the Bible: Biblical Interpretation and Literary Criticism'. In *Proceedings of the Conference on Biblical Interpretation*, Nashville: Broadman Press, 51–63.

JONES, B. sen. 1957. Letter dated March 6, explaining Bob Jones senior's withdrawal of support for Billy Graham. Archived in the Fundamentalism File at Bob Jones University.

—— 1978. 'What is "Second Degree Separation"?'. *Faith for the Family*, November: 4.

JONES B. III. 1980. 'The Moral Majority'. *Faith For the Family*, September 1: 1, 27–8.

KAISER, W. C. jun. 1979. In Giesler 1979: 117–47.

LAHAYE, T., and JENKINS, J. B. 1995. *Left Behind*. London: Tyndale Publishing House.

—— —— 2004. *The Glorious Appearing*. London: Tyndale Publishing House.

LAND, S. J. 1993. *Pentecostal Spirituality: A Passion for the Kingdom*. Sheffield: Sheffield Academic Press.

LAWRENCE, B. B. 1989. *Defenders of God: The Fundamentalist Revolt Against the Modern Age*. San Francisco: Harper & Row.

LAWS, C. L. 1920. 'Convention Side Lights'. *Watchman-Examiner*, 1 July: 834.

LETIS, T. P. 1991. 'B. B. Warfield, Common Sense Philosophy and Biblical Criticism'. *American Presbyterians*, 69/3: 175–90.

LINDSELL, H. 1976. *The Battle for the Bible*. Grand Rapids, Mich.: Zondervan.

LINDSEY, H., with CARLSON, C. C. 1970. *The Late Great Planet Earth*. Grand Rapids, Mich.: Zondervan.

McGRATH, A. E. 1996. *A Passion for Truth: The Intellectual Coherence of Evangelicalism*. Leicester: Apollos.

MACHEN, J. G. 1923. *Christianity and Liberalism*. New York: Macmillan.

—— 1925. *What is Faith?* London: Hodder & Stoughton.

MADAN, T. N. 1997. *Modern Myths, Locked Minds: Secularism and Fundamentalism in India*. Delhi: Oxford University Press.

MANLEY, G. T. 1925. 'The Inspiration and Authority of the Bible'. In J. R. Howden, ed., *Evangelicalism*. London: Chas. J. Thynne & Jarvis, 121–55.

—— 1926. '*It Is Written*'. London: Religious Tract Society.

MARSDEN, G. M. 1980. *Fundamentalism and American Culture: The Shaping of Twentieth Century Evangelicalism 1870–1925*. Oxford: Oxford University Press.

—— 1987. *Reforming Fundamentalism: Fuller Seminary and the New Evangelicalism*. Grand Rapids, Mich.: Eerdmans.

MARTY, M. E., and APPLEBY, R. S. 1992. *The Glory and the Power: The Fundamentalist Challenge to the Modern World*. Boston: Beacon.

—— —— eds. 1995. *Fundamentalisms Comprehended*. Chicago: University of Chicago Press.

MATHEWS, S. 1924. *The Faith of Modernism*. New York: Macmillan.

MURPHY, N. 1996. *Beyond Liberalism and Fundamentalism: How Modern and Postmodern Philosophy Set the Theological Agenda*. Valley Forge, Pa.: Trinity Press International.

NICOLE, R. 1983. 'The Inspiration and Authority of Scripture: J. D. G. Dunn versus B. B. Warfield'. *Churchman*, 97/3: 198–215.

NOLL, M. A., ed. 1983. *The Princeton Theology 1812–1921: Scripture, Science, and Theological Method from Archibald Alexander to Benjamin Breckinridge Warfield*. Grand Rapids, Mich.: Baker.

—— 1986. *Between Faith and Criticism: Evangelicals, Scholarship and America*. Grand Rapids, Mich.: Baker.

Nottingham Statement 1977. London: Falcon.

NUMBERS, R. L. 1993. *The Creationists: The Evolution of Scientific Creationism*. Berkeley, Los Angeles, and London: University of Caifornia Press.

OBEYESKERE, G. 1995. 'Buddhism, Nationhood, and Cultural Identity: A Question of Fundamentals'. In Marty and Appleby 1995: 231–56.

OCKENGA, H. J. 1978. 'From Fundamentalism, through New Evangelicalism, to Evangelicalism'. In Kenneth S. Kantzer, ed., *Evangelical Roots: A Tribute to Wilbur Smith*, Nashville: Thomas Nelson, 35–46.

OLSON, R. E. 1995. 'Postconservative Evangelicals Greet the Postmodern Age'. *The Christian Century*, May 3: 480–3.

OSS, D. A. 1989. 'The Interpretation of the "Stone" Passages by Peter and Paul: A Comparative Study'. *Journal of the Evangelical Theological Society*, 32/2: 181–200.

PACKER, J. I. 1958. *'Fundamentalism' and the Word of God*. London: Inter-Varsity Fellowship.

—— 1979. *God Has Spoken*, rev., enlarged edn. London: Hodder & Stoughton.

—— 1984. 'Exposition on Biblical Hermeneutics'. In Radmacher and Preus 1984: 905–14.

—— 1990. 'Understanding the Bible: Evangelical Hermeneutics'. In M. Tinker, ed., *Restoring the Vision: Anglican Evangelicals Speak Out*, Eastbourne: MARC, 39–58.

PAREKH, B. 1992. *The Concept of Fundamentalism*. London: Peepal Tee Books.

PHILLIPS, T. R., and OKHOLM, D. L., eds. 1996. *The Nature of Confession: Evangelicals & Liberals in Conversation*. Downers Grove, Ill.: InterVarsity Press.

PINNOCK, C. H. 1971. *Biblical Revelation—The Foundation of Christian Theology*. Chicago: Moody Press.

—— 1973. 'Daniel Fuller and Clark Pinnock: On Revelation and Biblical Authority'. *Christian Scholar's Review*, 2/4: 330–5.

PLANTINGA, A., and WOLTERSTORFF, N., eds. 1983. *Faith and Rationality: Reason and Belief in God*. Notre Dame, Ind.: University of Notre Dame Press.

RADMACHER, E. D., and PREUS, R. D., eds. 1984. *Hermeneutics, Inerrancy and the Bible*. Grand Rapids, Mich.: Zondervan.

RAMADAN, T. 2004. *Western Muslims and the Future of Islam*. Oxford: Oxford University Press.

RAMM, B. 1957. *The Pattern of Religious Authority*. Grand Rapids, Mich.: Eerdmans.

RAM-PRASAD, C. 1993. 'Hindutva Ideology: Extracting the Fundamentals'. *Contemporary South Asia*, 2/3: 285–309.

SANDEEN, E. 1970. *The Roots of Fundamentalism: British and American Millenarianism 1800–1930*. Chicago: University of Chicago Press.

SCHAEFFER, F. A. 1975. *No Final Conflict: The Bible without Error in All that it Affirms*. London: Hodder & Stoughton.

—— 1984. *The Great Evangelical Disaster*. Eastbourne: Kingsway.

Scofield, C. I., ed. 1909. *The Scofield Reference Bible*. New York: Oxford University Press.

Scopes Trial Transcript, 1925. Billy Graham Center Archives, Collection 244–2, Wheaton College, Illinois.

STOTT, J. R. W., ed. 1977. *Obeying Christ in a Changing World*, i: *The Lord Christ*. Glasgow: Collins.

STOTT, J. 1982. *I Believe in Preaching*. London: Hodder & Stoughton.

—— 1996. 'The Anglican Communion and Scripture'. In John Stott *et al.*, eds., *The Anglican Communion and Scripture: Papers from the First International Consultation of the Evangelical Fellowship in the Anglican Communion, Canterbury, UK, June 1993*, Carlisle: EFAC and Regnum, 13–49.

THISELTON, A. C. 1977. 'Understanding God's Word Today'. In Stott 1977: 90–122.

THISELTON, A. C. 1980. *The Two Horizons: New Testament Hermeneutics and Philosophical Description with Special Reference to Heidegger, Bultmann, Gadamer and Wittgenstein.* Carlisle: Paternoster.

—— 1985. 'Reader-Response Hermeneutics, Action Models and the Parables of Jesus'. In R. Lundin, A. C. Thiselton, and C. Walhout, eds., *The Responsibility of Hermeneutics,* Grand Rapids, Mich.: Eerdmans, 79–113.

—— 1992. *New Horizons in Hermeneutics.* London: HarperCollins.

TIDBALL, D. J. 1994. *Who are the Evangelicals? Tracing the Roots of Modern Movements.* London: Marshall Pickering.

TOMLINSON, D. 1995. *The Post-Evangelical.* London: Triangle.

VANHOOZER, K. J. 1998. *Is There a Meaning in this Text? The Bible, the Reader and the Morality of Literary Knowledge.* Grand Rapids, Mich.: Zondervan.

—— 2002. *First Theology: God, Scripture and Hermeneutics.* Downers Grove, Ill.: Inter-Varsity Press; Leicester: Apollos.

—— 2003. 'Theology and the Condition of Postmodernity'. In K. J. Vanhoozer, ed., *The Cambridge Companion to Postmodern Theology,* Cambridge: Cambridge University Press, 3–25.

WARD, K. 2004. *What the Bible Really Teaches: A Challenge for Fundamentalists.* London: SPCK.

WARD, T. 2002. *Word and Supplement: Speech Acts, Biblical Texts, and the Sufficiency of Scripture.* Oxford: Oxford University Press.

WARFIELD, B. B. 1932/88. *Studies in Theology.* Edinburgh: Banner of Truth.

—— 1948. *The Inspiration and Authority of the Bible.* Phillipsburg, NJ: Presbyterian and Reformed Publishing Co.

WATSON, D. C. C. 1975, 1989. *The Great Brain Robbery.* [n. p.]: the author.

WENHAM, J. 1984, 1992. *Easter Enigma.* Guernsey: Paternoster.

WHITCOMB, J. C. jun., and MORRIS, H. M. 1961. *The Genesis Flood: The Biblical Record and its Scientific Implications.* Philadelphia: Presbyterian and Reformed Publishing Co.

WIESELTIER, L. 1990. 'The Jewish Face of Fundamentalism'. In Cohen 1990: 192–6.

Willowbank Report, 1978, printed in *Down to Earth: Studies in Christianity and Culture: The Papers of the Lausanne Consultation on Gospel and Culture,* London: Hodder & Stoughton, 308–42.

WITHERINGTON III, B. 2004. *The New Testament Story.* Grand Rapids, Mich.: Eerdmans.

WOOD, W. J. 1998. *Epistemology: Becoming Intellectually Virtuous.* Leicester: Apollos.

CHAPTER 45

HISTORICAL CRITICISM AND THE AUTHORITY OF THE BIBLE

J. W. ROGERSON

Fifty years ago hardly anyone in academic circles doubted that the historical-critical method was the principal, if not all-sufficient, way of studying the Bible responsibly. It is true that voices from 'conservative' quarters were heard in opposition to historical criticism, and that scholarly works such as the introduction to the Old Testament by a scholar such as R. K. Harrison (1970) sought to defend traditional views about the authorship and composition of the Bible; but these voices were few compared with the opposition that had manifested itself when historical criticism in its nineteenth-century form was first encountered by the churches. In Germany the advent of 'rationalist' biblical criticism led to the founding in 1817 of an 'orthodox and church-directed seminary in Wittenberg that would train clergy for the ministry in accordance with traditional beliefs' (Rogerson 1992: 146–7). In Britain a whole commentary series known as the Speaker's Commentary was organized in order to combat the historical-critical views presented in J. W. Colenso's *The Pentateuch and Joshua* (1862–79; see Rogerson 1993: 97). In the early 1950s it seemed as though historical criticism had won an almost complete victory, in academic circles at any rate.

Today the situation is quite different, and it is possible, in Anglo-American academic circles, to hear the historical-critical method described as a product of the Enlightenment that has become as suspect as the Enlightenment project itself. This situation has not been brought about by a resurgence in conservative evangelicalism, although, as will be noted later, it has been partly driven by ecclesiastical concerns that resemble those that led to the establishment of the Wittenberg seminary in 1817. It has resulted, rather, from the revolution in biblical studies worked by contact with developments such as liberation theology, feminist criticism, and structuralism and post-structuralism. There is also another important strand in this, which is that the historical-critical method is not a monolithic and unchanging phenomenon, but an approach which has subjected itself to the self-critical scrutiny characteristic of, and necessary to, any academic discipline. The fact that *within* historical criticism many of what used to be described as 'assured results' have been challenged or overturned has looked to outsiders as though the approach itself has been discredited, which is far from the truth.

The first part of this chapter will describe some of the modifications that have occurred *within* historical criticism, before considering attacks upon the method that have been driven by ecclesiastical concerns. This will then lead to a broader consideration of the relationship between biblical criticism and the authority of the Bible, including the understanding of the Bible as 'scripture'.

Historical criticism is a blanket term covering many specialized disciplines, ranging from textual criticism (the attempt to be as close as possible to the original autographs of the biblical books, assuming that there were such autographs; see Chapters 12, 13, and 33 above), through historical and sociological studies of ancient Israel and the early church, to the study of the formation of the biblical writings, their genres, their literature, and their theology. This whole Handbook indicates the extent and complexity of the discipline, and even scholars who are critical of the historical-critical method are in fact deeply indebted to it in one or more of its forms. What has happened in practice is that historical criticism, or the historical-critical method (the two terms are often used interchangeably, whether or not this is justified), has come to be associated not only popularly, but even in academic circles, with certain particular conclusions that have dominated scholarly discussions for a century or more. On the Old Testament side, historical criticism has been closely linked to the so-called Graf–Wellhausen hypothesis, which divided the Pentateuch into the four sources J, E, D, and P, dated their composition to between the ninth and fifth centuries, in that order, and proposed a history of Israelite religion, priesthood, and sacrifice in which the institutions ascribed to Moses in Exodus, Leviticus, and Numbers were regarded as late developments in Israelite religion, rather than divine ordinances revealed to Moses at its outset. On the New Testament side, the scholarly consensus identified with historical criticism has been that which held Mark's Gospel to be the earliest, and to be the main source, along with a collection of sayings of Jesus called 'Q', for the gospels of Matthew and Luke, John's Gospel being the latest of the four to be composed.

The so-called Graf–Wellhausen hypothesis has been assailed from many quarters. A magisterial examination of the whole position was published by the Israeli scholar Yehezkel Kaufmann in the late 1950s (5th edn. 1963), but the most serious questioning of it has come from scholars such as John van Seters (1983), who have dated the J source much later than hitherto and who have questioned the view that the legislation in Deuteronomy (D) is later than and dependent on that in J and E (in the book of Exodus). Again, scholars such as Rendtorff (1976) and Blum (1984) have questioned whether the Pentateuch is made up of sources running 'horizon-tally' through Genesis to Numbers, or whether the stories of Abraham and Jacob, to take two examples, are not rather independent 'vertical' blocks of material that have been joined together. It must be stressed that these questionings of the old scholarly conclusions do not amount to a rejection of historical criticism. They are refinements that presuppose it. To people outside the discipline, these refinements and modifications may appear to discredit historical criticism, if the latter is identified solely with the views presented classically by Wellhausen. They may also provide ammunition for critics of the method in the form of the argument that if historical critics do not agree about their results, their method must be faulty. If this argument had any validity, it would have to apply to all academic disciplines from Classics to the Natural Sciences!

A more fundamental questioning of historical criticism was made in 1971 by W. Richter, in *Exegese als Literaturwissenschaft* and the work done by his pupils (see Chapter 34 above). Richter pointed out the circularity of arguments for dividing narratives into sources, and argued that much form criticism was in reality content criticism. However, Richter's aim was not to dispense with the methods of historical criticism, but to place them on a sounder scientific basis in the light of modern linguistics. The same can be said of J. Barr's pioneering *Semantics of Biblical Language* (1961), which was directed to lexical and semantic aspects of historical criticism.

The advent of literary structuralism and final form criticism in the 1970s brought the criticism that the sources postulated by historical criticism were hypothetical, whereas the final form of the text was the datum of interpretation. The study of plot structure, characterization, and literary artistry in biblical narratives also went in directions which had usually been ignored by historical criticism. The duplica-tions and apparent contradictions in narratives, which provided the clues to the discovery and reconstruction of literary sources in historical criticism, were seen quite differently by structuralists who were looking for binary opposition, or literary critics investigating plots and characterization (see Alter 1981; Bar-Efrat 1989; as well as the reservations about the notion of 'final form of the text' voiced by some contributors to Dietrich 2004). It was fair comment to say that these aspects had often been unrepresented in historical criticism. At the same time it should be noted that some structuralist and literary approaches were concerned only with the 'world of the text'; and were indifferent, or even hostile, to the question whether biblical texts were making truth claims about the world outside the text. Whatever its shortcomings, historical criticism partly took the form that it did because it was concerned with the historical and social circumstances in which the Bible had been produced, and the implications of these circumstances for the truth claims made in the Bible about God's activity in the world.

Another quarter from which the historical-critical method was assailed was that of liberation theology and feminist criticism from the 1970s (Gutiérrez 1974; Mosala 1989; Collins 1985). The criticism was not so much about methodologies as about the interests of the practitioners of historical criticism, who were undeniably overwhelmingly male, Western, and privileged. It was easy to demonstrate that, because of this, historical criticism had overlooked the needs of poor and op- pressed users of the Bible, as well as the interests of women, however these latter interests were defined. In many cases, however, liberation theology and feminist criticism did not abandon historical criticism, but used it to investigate those areas of concern that traditionally had been overlooked. For example, attempts were made to reconstruct and thus rediscover the roles of women in ancient Israel and in the early church (Meyers 1988; Schüssler-Fiorenza 1987) or to reconstruct ancient Israel's history as one in which events such as Josiah's reforms in 622 BCE had greatly disadvantaged the poor (Nakanose 1993). To the extent that these ap- proaches utilized the methods of historical criticism, they can be regarded as having broadened historical criticism rather than refuted it.

It is now time to turn to the attack on historical criticism that has been driven by the view that it has not served the needs of the churches. Whether this is a fair criticism will be discussed later. One of the most prominent advocates of this view has been Brevard Childs, and the canonical criticism that his work has inspired (see Brett 1991). Childs's arguments should probably be seen in part as a response to the failure of one of the attempts within historical criticism to assist the churches: namely, the biblical theology movement that was prominent in Britain and North America in the 1940s to the 1960s (see Barr 1999). In one of its forms, biblical theology held that God had been revealed in the saving events witnessed in the Bible, such as the Israelite exodus from Egypt and the resurrection of Jesus, and that this concern for saving history was unique to the Israelites in a world where other peoples interpreted reality mythologically (Wright 1950). Another feature of biblical theology was that the Hebrew language of the Bible was a unique vehicle for conveying truths about God's self-revelation, so that Hebrew word studies could form the basis for claims about the nature of God and the world. Both of these positions were attacked and refuted from within historical criticism (Albrektson 1967; Barr 1961), and the demise of biblical theology left an apparent vacuum in the way that historical criticism could produce results of value to the churches.

Working from within historical criticism, Childs (1979) argued that the process by which the biblical books grew to assume their final form was not an arbitrary process, but one which was guided by the intention that the final form should be scripture: that is, sacred writings believed to witness to the nature and purposes of God. If this was accepted, historical criticism as practised in academic circles had a legitimate theological aim: namely, to discover and describe the canonical processes—i.e. the editorial and redactional procedures that had aimed to produce sacred writings out of the laws, narratives, psalms, proverbs, etc. that had been transmitted down the ages. An implication was that the discovery of the canonical processes would provide clues as to how the biblical texts should be interpreted as scripture: that is, as texts that made claims about the nature of God and the world, and that made claims upon members of churches that accepted the Bible as in some sense authoritative.

There is no doubt that Childs's canonical approach has led to some interesting insights, especially in the case of the of the Psalms and the twelve so-called Minor Prophets, books in which there is internal evidence of redactional processes that were intended to express a particular theology (e.g. Wilson 1985; Saur 2004). Whether or not there is evidence of a 'canonical shaping' elsewhere is open to question. A real problem is that even if evidence can be found that shows that texts were compiled and redacted with the intention that they should be regarded as scripture, it is not clear whether, or to what extent, that intentionality can or should provide guidelines for Christian interpretation in today's world. The early church interpreted the Jewish scriptures in their Greek translation as prophecies and exemplifications of the ministry, death, and exaltation of Jesus (Rogerson 2004). In so doing, they made a break with the Jewish community's reading of their scriptures inevitable. Indeed, it has often been argued that the way in which the Old Testament is interpreted in the New Testament should be mandatory for Christian understandings of the Old Testament. A bone of contention that goes back many centuries is whether Isa. 7: 14 should be understood as an eighth-century prophecy that Judah will be delivered from her enemies before a pregnant young woman's child reaches the age of 2, or whether it is a prophecy of the birth of Jesus, as claimed in Matt. 1: 23. It is also the case that for much of its history the church allegorized the Old Testament and regarded its literal sense as less important than its deeper mystical, Christological, and spiritual senses (de Lubac 1961–4). To put it another way, if the Jewish compilers of the Old Testament consciously shaped the final form of the texts in order to express a particular theology or theologies, Christian interpretation of these texts took a quite different line, governed as it was by the belief that the Bible had to be understood in terms of the ministry and exaltation of Jesus. It is true, of course, that modern historical criticism has not regarded itself as bound by earlier centuries of Christian interpretation (but see further on this below), and that it has preferred in cases such as Isa. 7: 14 a historical explanation of the text rather than a Christological one. The question is whether the intentionality that gave the Hebrew Bible its canonical form (assuming the existence and recoverability of such an intentionality) is simply evidence of what was believed by a particular community over 2,000 years ago, or whether it is an authoritative set of guidelines for contemporary use of the Bible. Different answers will be given to this question depending on the commitments, interests, and priorities of those who choose to consider it.

A different attack on historical criticism from the angle of its supposed failure to do proper justice to the Bible as scripture has come from Watson (1994). Watson is sympathetic to feminist criticism of the historical-critical method as well as to women's issues, although he is far less amenable to literary approaches that deny that texts have any extra-linguistic reference. Part of his objection to the historical-critical method is based upon Frei's (1974) arguably idiosyncratic account of the rise of modern biblical criticism, an account that attributed it to the alleged lack of a tradition of the novel in Germany in the late eighteenth century. Watson wants to work with the final form of the text, but to subject it to a 'hermeneutic of suspicion' wherein its morality or interests are contrary to those of modern sensibilities. However, this is not an adjustment of the text to suit modern tastes. Watson argues that the narratives of creation in Genesis 1–2 envisage a created order free from gender discrimination, and that Old Testament laws are concerned with compassion for the poor and oppressed. Thus the mandate for treating with suspicion those biblical texts that offend modern readers comes from the Bible itself. Put another way, modern concerns about justice and equality make it possible to discern those imperatives in the Bible itself, and to use them as keys to the interpretation of the Bible in today's world. In this way the Bible is reclaimed as scripture and as a source of authority for the church.

There is much in Watson's approach that is commendable, although it is a pity that he is so hard on historical criticism and its supposed failures. While it cannot be denied that historical criticism can be used, and has been used, to advocate positions that deny to the Bible any credibility as a humanitarian text, let alone a text regarded as scripture, it must be emphasized that this is not a characteristic of historical criticism *per se*, but of its particular uses. The recent work of Lauster (2004, 2005) is important here, representing a serious attempt to work out a view of biblical authority that takes full account of new developments not only in critical biblical scholarship, but in literary and communication theory. The next section will indicate that there is an important strand of historical-critical scholarship that has regarded the method as an integral part of the churches' task in interpreting the Bible, and which has sought to produce biblical commentaries and other works in this light.

It must never be forgotten that the study of the Bible has always been critical, if 'critical' is understood to refer to the use of every available branch of human knowledge to determine the accuracy of manuscript and other written witnesses to the biblical texts, to enquire after the authorship and circumstances of their composition, and to assess their historical and scientific accuracy. At different times in the history of the church, different issues have been at the forefront of the discussion. In the second century, for example, there was much argument about the phrase 'he reigns from the tree' that was found in the Old Latin version of Ps. 96: 10 (Ps. 95: 10 in the Greek numbering) and which led Justin Martyr (d. 165 CE) to accuse the Jews of having removed it from the text (*Apol.* 1. 41). This, and other disagreements led Origen (185–254) to compile an enormous work of textual criticism entitled the *Hexapla*, which placed the Hebrew text of the Old Testament in a column alongside which were ranged all the Greek versions known to him. A century later, Eusebius of Caesarea (d. 339/40) quoted the opinions of earlier divines such as Papias (*c.*110) and Dionysius of Alexandria (d. *c.*255–6) about the authorship of the Gospels and the book of Revelation. These were not trivial matters. In a world in which the followers of Marcion (*c.*85–*c.*160) wanted to dispense with the Old Testament and reduce the New to Luke's Gospel and seven letters of Paul, while Gnostic teachers wished to add 'secret' teachings of Jesus to the corpus of sacred writings, it was vital to use every piece of information to establish the authorship and provenance of New Testament books (see further Reventlow 1990; Körtner 1998). Papias's view, quoted by Eusebius, that the apostle Peter, in recalling what Jesus had done and said, adapted his instructions to the needs of the moment and did not attempt to present an orderly account, and that Mark had therefore not written down Christ's words and deeds in their proper order, anticipates in a small way the conclusions of nineteenth- and twentieth-century Gospel criticism.

Controversy in the early centuries was not confined to textual criticism and authorship. A follower of Marcion named Apelles attacked the view that the Old Testament was inspired by God by arguing that the story of the ark contained many impossibilities (Stevenson 1957: 104–5). In the fifth century, Augustine had to devote space in *The City of God* to discussing questions such as what sort of light was created by God on day one in Genesis 1 before the sun and moon were created on the fourth day, whether the years of life reckoned to the patriarchs in Genesis 5 were the same as ordinary years (Methuselah lived to be 957), and whether there were really giants on the earth in ancient times, as claimed by Gen. 6: 4 (Augustine 1972: 436–7, 609–20).

Matters that would come to be regarded as the central issues of historical criticism in the nineteenth and twentieth centuries were already being discussed hundreds of years earlier. 'Post-Mosaica'—that is, verses in the Pentateuch that were unlikely to have been written by Moses, such as the account of his death in Deut. 34: 5–12 or references to him in the third person such as at Num. 12: 3—had long been noted. The Jewish commentator Abraham Ibn Ezra (d. 1158) had maintained that they were written by Joshua. Baruch Spinoza (1632–77) added a number of other passages to the traditional 'post-Mosaica' and concluded that the Pentateuch owed its final form to the work of Ezra in the fifth century BCE. The attempt by the French Catholic scholar Richard Simon (1638–1712) to answer Spinoza's criticism led to further advances in historical criticism. Simon maintained that the laws attributed to Moses in the Pentateuch had indeed been written by him, but that the remainder of the Pentateuch had been written by inspired 'public writers' whose work had continued down to the time of Ezra. These 'public writers' were responsible for making many changes and additions to the Bible, basing themselves upon records that were preserved in the archives of the nation. Glimpses of them could be seen in the books of Chronicles, which mention Samuel the seer, Nathan the prophet, and Gad the seer (1 Chr. 29: 29–30). The activities of these public writers explained, for example, why there appeared to be two accounts of the creation, in Genesis 1 and 2, and why different styles of Hebrew could be found, as well as repetitions of material (see Reventlow 2001: 87–113).

Simon's great *Histoire critique du Vieux Testament* (1678) was ordered to be confiscated and destroyed by Bishop Jacques-Bénigne Bossuet, and subsequently appeared in places outside the bishop's jurisdiction. It would be easy to conclude from this that Simon's work was done in an unbelieving spirit, but this would be a great mistake. Simon remained a devout Catholic, believed that he could justify his biblical criticism by appealing to Catholic tradition, and showed himself to be a formidable opponent of the Protestant view that the Bible alone could be the basis of Christian faith. It was commitment to his faith and to the integrity of the Bible that drove Simon to work as he did. However, it was not Simon whose views determined the Catholic and Protestant thinking about the composition of the Bible for the next century or so, but the French Benedictine monk August Calmet, whose monumental *Dictionnaire de la Bible* (1730) became the standard work on almost every aspect of the study of the Bible, and which was translated into several languages. It was marked by great learning and tolerance, and although it was traditional and orthodox in its conclusions, it addressed fairly and squarely all the moral, historical, and scientific difficulties that had been found in the Bible up to that time. Calmet insisted that all sources of learning, whether or not they were advocated by Christians or non-Christians, were relevant to the proper study of the Bible.

The main area of advance in the eighteenth century was in the field of textual criticism, especially of the Old Testament, a remarkable monument to which was the *Biblia sacra* of Charles François Houbigant (1753). Houbigant made a careful study of the ancient versions of the Old Testament, including the Samaritan Pentateuch, and, convinced that the traditional Hebrew text had suffered many corruptions, proposed some 5,000 corrections, some of which were conjectural emendations which have been accepted by modern scholarship as providing 'probable readings' of the Hebrew. His work was rewarded with two gold medals by Pope Benedict XIV, and was well received in Britain, where it was constantly referred to and followed in Bishop Robert Lowth's (1779) new translation and notes on the book of Isaiah. This interest in establishing the most accurate text of the

Bible was not the invention of Houbigant or scholars such as Benjamin Kennicott. In its most recent form it went back to the great polyglot Bibles: the Complutensian (1514–17), the Antwerp (1568–72), the Paris (1628–45), and the London polyglots (1653–57/8), works which made available not only the Hebrew, Aramaic, and Greek texts of the Bible, but also translation of them into Latin, Greek, Syriac, Aramaic, and Arabic. All this work was produced within, and published by authority of, different churches. At the same time, not everybody welcomed the work of scholars such as Houbigant. Protestant Germany, for example, was uncomfortable with what some saw as his cavalier treatment of the sacred text, with the result that his competence as a linguist was questioned and his reputation was so assailed that he became, understandably, but unjustly, an almost neglected figure in the history of biblical scholarship (Rosenmüller 1797: 500).

There is, of course, no smoke without fire, and the bad reputation which historical criticism was to gain was earned largely in the nineteenth century. In the first part of this period, tendencies and developments that had originated in the eighteenth century were synthesized and presented in ways which seemed threatening to traditional Christian faith and use of the Bible. These can be summed up under two headings: the questioning of belief in the supernatural, and the questioning of the biblical accounts of the history of Israel, and of the life of Jesus and the origins of Christianity.

The questioning of belief in the supernatural was not a denial of the supernatural or miracles as such, although it had undoubtedly become more difficult for some intellectuals in the church to accept these things in the eighteenth century. The issue was whether the biblical writers, in recording events of miracles or in describing events as supernatural, had correctly interpreted them (Rogerson 1974: 4–10). If the scientific knowledge of the biblical writers was rudimentary in comparison with that available in the eighteenth century, there was a real possibility that what they had described as supernatural or miraculous happenings would be seen as perfectly natural or explicable in a better-informed scientific age. Thus a method of biblical interpretation was developed which sought natural explanations for events described in supernatural terms in the Bible. An example is the view that the fruit that Adam and Eve ate in the garden of Eden was slightly poisonous. It did not cause death, but made the couple aware of their sexual differences and potential. A thunderstorm was then interpreted by the couple as the voice of God condemning their actions (Rogerson 1974: 4). While it is easy to make fun of what today seems to be such an absurd handling of Genesis 2–3, it is easier to overlook the important issues that such handling was addressing. Those who practised it were making a claim for the importance of the information contained in the Bible. At a time when the Bible was still believed to contain the oldest information about the origins of the human race, these early 'demythologizers' were advocating a method of biblical interpretation which upheld the value of the Bible as a historical source. They were also arguing for the necessity of interpreting its narratives in the light of its time of composition, a time when the human race had little scientific awareness and could mistake 'ordinary' occurrences for manifestations of the divine.

As applied to the New Testament, this type of approach also explained the miraculous in ordinary ways. For example, at the Feeding of the Five Thousand, the generous offer of a youth to share his loaves and fishes had shamed others present who had food with them, into sharing this with their neighbours (Luz 1996 i/ii, 397 n. 19). No doubt this line of interpretation was encouraged by difficulties in accepting that 5,000 people had been fed by the miraculous multiplication of very small resources; but the present form of the narrative was not regarded as a fabrication of the truth. The miraculous element derived from the way in which the story had been transmitted, and as 'demythologized' it still had something important to teach about mutual sharing. However, it is not surprising that such radical challenges to traditional ways of understanding the Bible should have aroused deep suspicion in both the churches and academia; and it was partly to oppose such approaches that were thought to be the products of 'rationalist' theological faculties in universities that the church seminary in Wittenberg was set up in 1817.

The questioning of the biblical accounts of the history of Israel and of the life of Jesus and Christian origins reached its high point in 1835, with the publication of W. Vatke's *Biblical Theology* and D. F. Strauss's *Life of Jesus*. The former presented a minimal view of what could be known about Israel's history before and up to the time of Moses. The latter undermined the hitherto unassailable authority of John's Gospel, as an 'eyewitness Gospel', for reconstructing the life of Jesus. Strauss argued that the miracle stories in the Gospels were attempts to represent 'ideas' in narrative form, and that they had little historical value. Twelve years later, one of Strauss's pupils, F. C. Baur, argued that the New Testament had resulted from a compromise worked out in the second century between Jewish and Gentile Christians. Only four letters of Paul were genuine, according to Baur; the other New Testament letters and the Acts of the Apostles had been composed in the second century (Kümmel 1973: 120–43).

Such historical scepticism was bound to provoke opposition in church and academy alike. In German, the Göttingen orientalist Heinrich Ewald waged an unremitting war against such views, albeit from a historical-critical position which yielded reconstructions that accorded more closely with traditional views. In Britain, the ranks of scholarship were closed against such radical opinions (Rogerson 1984: 91–103).

However, it was the content of the Bible itself, and the need to interpret it in ways that made sense to the contemporary world, that had led to the no doubt exaggerated views of scholars such as Vatke, Strauss, and Baur. The questions that the Bible provoked could not be permanently silenced, and from the 1860s they began once more to receive expression. Some of those who led the way in this were committed churchmen, who embraced historical criticism precisely because its methods promised a way of enabling the Bible to assert its authority in the situations in which they worked.

J. W. Colenso, the Bishop of Natal in the British South African colony of that name (he was bishop from 1853 to 1883), was faced with the question of what to make of biblical material about occult practices such as witchcraft. While it was true that the Bible condemned such practices, it nevertheless took them seriously, as in the account of Saul using a medium to contact the dead prophet Samuel. Colenso was convinced that science showed such beliefs to be unfounded, as well as the biblical view that Balaam's ass could speak (a passage that had long perplexed interpreters), and that Joshua had commanded the sun to stand still, to name only some of the difficulties. What was he to tell his Zulu converts, whose own culture was replete with superstitions, but who were also intelligent enough to know that animals did not speak and that the sun did not stand still? Colenso's answer was that a scientifically informed biblical criticism made it possible to distinguish what was of permanent value in the Bible from what was conditioned by the times in which it was produced. Only the former was binding upon believers today. Colenso's conviction that the love of God for all mankind as revealed in the Bible was a message of salvation and hope made him a most effective missionary, who won many converts, and who trained them to be evangelists to their own people. But Colenso's own theological training had left him completely unprepared for such matters, and his determination to understand the criticism of the Bible turned him into one the most formidable and misunderstood pioneers of British biblical scholarship in the second half of the nineteenth century (Rogerson 1984: 220–37).

In 1861 Colenso published the first volume of a monumental work that would run to seven volumes and over 3,000 pages (Colenso 1862–79). It was concerned with the biblical account of the Israelite exodus from Egypt and the wilderness wanderings, and it argued with devastating detail of facts and figures, how impossible it would have been for the 600,000 male Israelites together with their families and sheep and cattle who, according to Exod. 12: 32 and other passages, had left Egypt, to have done so and to have sojourned in the wilderness. Colenso was not the first scholar to draw attention to such difficulties (see Rogerson 1984: 25), but that an Anglican bishop had done so was seen at the time as a scandal; yet few, if any, appreciated the *pastoral* and *missionary* concerns that underlay his work.

Pastoral and evangelistic concerns also underlay the work of another pioneer of British biblical criticism, William Robertson Smith, who, in 1870, at the age of 24, became Professor of Old Testament at the Aberdeen College of the Free Church of Scotland. The Free Church was a conservative body theologically, bound to the Westminster Confession of Faith (1648), and Smith was initially cautious about biblical criticism. However, visits to Germany, where he met theologians who were able to combine an acceptance of critical methods with sincere Christian belief, convinced Smith not only that the churches had nothing to fear from biblical criticism, but that the best 'believing criticism' of his day was necessary for the churches if they were to proclaim the gospel effectively in a scientific age. Smith could have had academic careers in physics or mathematics, but he remained true to Old Testament studies, and reached independently a view of the so-called Graf–Wellhausen hypothesis, which in Smith's case used the biblical sources to reconstruct what he called a history of God's self-revelation, which was also a history of God's grace (Smith 1881: 22; see further Rogerson 1995).

In the event, both Colenso and Smith were so far ahead of their churches, when it came to recognizing the implications and value of biblical criticism for the theology of their times, that they suffered for their convictions. Colenso was tried for heresy and 'deposed' by a synod convened by Bishop Robert Gray of Capetown. Although his appeal to the Judicial Committee of the Privy Council was upheld, the Church of England nevertheless consecrated a rival bishop to take his place. Colenso remained in Natal, however, and continued his missionary work there until his death. Smith was charged with heresy and dismissed from his post in 1881, after which he moved to Cambridge, where he later became Professor of Arabic. History has been kinder to Smith than to Colenso, probably because Smith, by moving to Cambridge, more directly affected the next generation of scholars, in both Cambridge and Oxford. One of the members of the next generation, A. S. Peake, was a Primitive Methodist layman, who played a prominent part in the establishment of the Hartley Primitive Methodist College in Manchester, and who became the first Professor of Biblical Criticism in the Victoria University of Manchester in 1904. His many books breathed the same spirit as the writing of Smith, expressing the view that biblical criticism could free the Bible from methods of interpretation that were completely inappropriate in a scientific age (Peake 1913).

By the beginning of the twentieth century, biblical criticism had been accepted in the English university departments that taught theology, as well as in many of the English theological colleges in which the bulk of training for ordination was still done, especially in the Nonconformist churches. This acceptance had been prepared, among other things, by commentary series such as the Cambridge Bible for Schools and Colleges (from 1872) and the International Critical Commentary from 1891. The former series became more 'critical' as time went on; but the fact that it was intended for schools and colleges indicates how critical scholarship was seeking to reach out into the general field of education. The beginning of the twentieth century saw the launch of the Century Bible, a series of commentaries written mostly by Nonconformists, which laid before the general public the interpretation of the Bible as understood on the basis of the developing biblical criticism.

The burden of this section is that biblical criticism was never intended to be or to become an arid intellectual discipline divorced from the needs of the churches and/or necessarily damaging to Christian faith. That it was, and still is, so regarded in some quarters had (and has) to do more with dogmatic and ecclesiastical matters than with biblical studies.

Before these dogmatic and ecclesiastical matters are considered in the final section, the present section will be completed by noting further examples of critical commentaries that were designed to meet the needs of churches as well as scholars. These are the German *Biblischer Kommentar Altes Testament* and the *Evangelisch-Katholischer Kommentar zum Neuen Testament.* It would also be possible to include, among other series, the Dutch *De Prediking van het Oude Testament* and the German Catholic *Die neue Echter Bibel,* not to mention such English-speaking series as the *Word Bible Commentaries,* the *New Century Bible,* the Hermeneia series, and *The New International Greek Testament Commentary* series. The *Biblischer Kommentar* series, which must represent the largest commentary undertaking ever begun, has at the end of each piece of exposition a section headed *Ziel* (aim). The purpose of this is to articulate the permanent theological significance of what has been expounded, with connections, where appropriate, to the New Testament. While users may not always be satisfied with the results of this, it cannot be denied that here is a historical-critical enterprise that is fully aware of its theological responsibilities. The *Evangelisch-Katholischer Kommentar* goes even further. It includes sections on the *Wirkungsgeschichte* of each passage discussed (i.e. how it has been understood by Christian interpreters down the centuries), and concludes with a consideration of its 'meaning for today' in the light of the historical-critical exegesis and the history of the use of the passage.

This section will hopefully have shown that while historical criticism *can* produce results that are threatening or hostile to Christian faith, or can become so technical as to be totally irrelevant to the needs of the church, this is not an inevitable or inescapable part of its character. It has arisen from the content of the Bible itself, and was developed primarily by scholars working within the churches as they sought to discover the message of the Bible in the light of new sources of knowledge of their day.

This final section will seek to do the impossible, to describe how and in what ways the Bible is authoritative. The task is impossible because it is viewed in so many different ways by different churches, some of which stridently claim that their understanding of biblical authority is the only one that is truly 'biblical' and in accordance with 'traditional Christianity'. Such a stance is currently at the heart of the bitter dispute in the world-wide Anglican Communion about whether people who are in active partnerships with members of the same sex should be bishops, or whether people of the same sex can be married.

Before these problems are addressed in more detail, the important general question must be considered as to why the Bible (whatever is meant by that) is regarded as authoritative or as 'scripture'. Part of the answer is that decision-making bodies such as Ecumenical Councils of the Church or the Westminster Parliament in London or Synods have declared scripture (however defined) to be authoritative. Yet at the same time, such declarations have not conferred upon the Bible a status that it did not already have. The declarations have rather endorsed an intrinsic authority that the Bible was already recognized to have; and these acts of recognition have roots going back to the processes that led to the formation of the Bible in the first place (see Chapters 28 and 40 above). While it is true that the churches have never agreed about the exact extent of the Old Testament, they have all agreed that its most fundamental part is what is called the Hebrew Bible, or the Old Testament as accepted by Protestants.

With the closure, or fixing, of the sacred canon of writings, the processes of interpretation and elaboration of texts, processes that were once part of their *internal* growth, become *external* to the fixed corpus. These interpretations can take many forms, including sermons, commentaries, ethical compendia, theologies, and dictionaries. They will also diverge, depending upon the doctrinal positions taken by the various interpreters. In turn, these doctrinal positions will depend upon history and geographical situations. Some of the issues that arise will be outlined.

Reference has already been made to the Catholic scholar Richard Simon. In his controversy with Protestants of his day, Simon was accused of subordinating the Bible to the doctrinal restraints of the Church. In reply, Simon argued that if the Bible alone was to be the basis of Christian faith, the most logical position to take was that of the Aryan Socinians who denied that Jesus was consubstantial with God (Simon 1699). Simon's opponents took exception to this charge; but all that this showed was that they, too, read the Bible from the point of view of predetermined doctrines, even if they did not admit it.

This (no doubt not deliberate) 'blindness' regarding the way in which doctrinal presuppositions affect the interpretation of the Bible in different churches is no doubt at the heart of the divisions in the Anglican Communion over practising homosexual bishops. It is a danger that becomes greater, the more that a church or denomination lacks an explicit statement of doctrinal belief. For example, churches that adhere strictly to the Westminster Confession of Faith will be clearly committed to belief in the infallibility of the Bible, and to upholding traditional views about its authorship and composition. The Thirty-nine Articles of Religion of the Church of England, on the other hand, merely state that Holy Scripture contains all things necessary to salvation, and that nothing should be required to be believed that cannot be proved from Scripture. This allows a situation in which many different views of the admissibility of biblical criticism, or the ecclesiastical organization of the church, can be held, at any rate, in Britain and North America. It means that in practice, ordinary church-goers are dependent upon the theological outlook of the priest of the church they attend. Since these outlooks may range from hard-line Calvinism to extreme Catholicism via clergy who doubt the divinity or resurrection of Christ, it is no wonder that there should be sharp divisions within the Anglican Church, and uncertainty in some of its parts about how, and how much authority, is to be accorded to the Bible.

Even within those circles that accept the Bible as an infallible authority, there are, or have been, sharp divisions about how it should be interpreted. The Salvation Army has, from its beginnings, allowed women to exercise ministry alongside, and independently, of men. Some evangelical churches reject the ordination of women as being contrary to biblical teaching about male 'headship'. Some evangelical circles oppose the remarriage of divorced people in church on scriptural grounds, a practice that was allowed under certain conditions by Luther and Calvin (Phillips 1988: 45–62). The Open Brethren, with their 'dispensational' view of Scripture, traditionally opposed any charismatic phenomena such as 'speaking with tongues'. These gifts were given only to the first generation of the followers of Jesus, and their appearance in modern times was the work of Satan. On the other hand, charismatic churches would claim that their exercise of the gifts of the Spirit is a sign that they are authentically bearing witness to the Christianity of the New Testament. An issue that has divided fundamentalist Christians in the United States is whether the present age is that of the thousand-year reign of Christ foreseen in Rev. 20: 1–10, or whether we are currently living in an age dominated by Satan, an era that will be ended by the return of Christ and the inauguration of his thousand-year reign (Marsden 1980: 124–38).

An issue that has divided the Lutheran and Reform traditions is whether one should interpret scripture against scripture, or whether the Bible should be regarded as a harmonious whole free from contradictions (Ebeling 1979: 28–35). The former (Lutheran) view is based partly on the fact that the early church both accepted that Christ's death and exaltation were 'in accordance with the scriptures' and rejected the view that the legal obligations of the Old Testament were binding upon non-Jews who had become Christians (Acts 15). In other words, the acceptance of the authority of the Bible (Old Testament) by the early church was conditioned by a readiness to reinterpret it radically in the light of the Christ event. Luther's low estimation of the Epistle of James ('I refuse him a place among the writers of the true canon of my Bible' (Dillenberger 1969: 36; Luther 1974: 2455)), whether justified or not, is an example of using scripture against scripture: i.e. of judging a biblical book against a principle taken from the Bible which is regarded as having paramount authority (in Luther's case, whether the prominence of Christ is emphasized or not).

The question of a dialectical approach to scripture in opposition to scripture as a harmonious whole leads to two further matters which have divided the Lutheran and Reformed traditions (Thielicke 1978: 184–258; 1982: 177–81). The first is whether one should adopt a 'canon within the canon'—that is, privilege certain books such as Romans, or the synoptic gospels, and use their viewpoints as a standard by which to judge the adequacy of other biblical books. The alternative view would be that all parts of the Bible are equally authoritative. Closely aligned to this question is whether the coming of Christ has abolished the Old Testament law or whether Christians are obliged to obey as much of the Old Testament law as can still be applied to today's world. The differing answers to this last question are at the heart of the controversy about Christian attitudes to lesbians and homosexuals. Passages such as Gen. 2: 24, Genesis 19, and Levticus 18 and 20 are appealed to (along with several New Testament texts) by those who believe that the Bible opposes such relationships (Green *et al.* 1980). A hidden or acknowledged assumption here is that Old Testament passages are as authoritative as New Testament passages. In actual fact, whatever people and churches may claim to do, in practice they all operate with a 'canon within the canon', and the Old Testament law can be applied to today's problems only by being read very selectively and in regard to private, usually sexual, morality. However, this description would probably not be accepted by 'Bible-believing Christians' who are broadly in the Reformed tradition.

An important matter is whether it is believed that the Bible's task is to teach propositional truths about human history and God's nature, or whether the Bible's main purpose is to bring people into a relationship of faith with God. The two views are not, of course, mutually exclusive, but the belief that the Bible contains essentially propositional information, whose accuracy is guaranteed by its divine origin, has been and is at the heart of attempts to defend the accuracy of its scientific and historical statements.

One conclusion that might be drawn from the above examples of differing attitudes to the authority of the Bible is that the whole subject is a sham; that churches are lumbered with the Bible, and have to do their best to make of it what they can, and then find ways of justifying the outcomes. It might also be added that the Bible can be made to say whatever one wants it to say, and that an authoritative book that can be manipulated in this way exhibits a rather dubious form of authority. This viewpoint will hardly be accepted by people who belong to churches whose approaches might be quite different and even contradictory, but who have found a common hope in the mercy of God through their encounter with the Bible. Books such as Job, the Psalms, Ecclesiastes, and the Gospel of John can resonate with the most deeply held human hopes, fears, and doubts. On various occasions in the history of the church, it has been the reading of the Bible that has led to reformations which exposed the corruption of ecclesiastical institutions and led to sincere attempts to rediscover the basic principles of Christianity.

'The Bible bears witness to a proclamation that has taken place and is the impulse to a proclamation which is to take place . . . It has to do with reality, which it changes' (Ebeling 1966: 183–4). This minimalist definition of the authority of the Bible which, perhaps, all the differing approaches mentioned in this chapter might agree upon, is a reason why the Bible remains such an indispensable phenomenon. It is a happening—a complex happening—occasioned by many historical circumstances and embodying the insights of many people. Its resultant accumulation of human wisdom and insights makes it a unique collections of documents. Its authority for faith communities lies in the fact that it is also able to engender and sustain faith in transcendent realities. At the end of the day, the Bible defies and undermines all attempts to define its authority. It cannot be neatly pigeon-holed and classified. It is more than the sum of its parts, still able in a changing world to inspire visions, give hope, and demand the highest and most exacting standards of scholarship for its elucidation and interpretation.

BIBLIOGRAPHY AND SUGGESTED READING

ALBREKTSON, B. 1967. *History and the Gods.* Lund: Gleerup.

ALTER, R. 1981. *The Art of Biblical Narrative.* London: George Allen & Unwin.

AUGUSTINE, 1972. *Concerning the City of God against the Pagans,* trans. Henry Bettenson. Harmondsworth: Penguin.

BAR-EFRAT, S. 1989. *Narrative Art in the Bible.* Sheffield: The Almond Press.

BARR, J. 1961. *The Semantics of Biblical Language.* Oxford: Oxford University Press.

—— 1977. *Fundamentalism.* London: SCM Press.

—— 1999. *The Concept of Biblical Theology: An Old Testament Perspective.* London: SCM Press.

BLUM, E. 1984. *Die Komposition der Vätergeschichte.* WMANT 57. Neukirchen-Vluyn: Neukirchener Verlag.

BRETT, M. G. 1991. *Biblical Criticism in Crisis? The Impact of the Canonical Approach on Old Testament Studies.* Cambridge: Cambridge University Press.

CALMET, A. 1730. *Dictionnaire historique, critique, chronologique, géographique et littéral de la Bible,* 2nd edn. Geneva.

CHILDS, B. S. 1979. *Introduction to the Old Testament as Scripture.* London: SCM Press.

COLENSO, J. W. 1862–79. *The Pentateuch and Joshua Critically Examined.* London.

COLLINS, A. Y. 1985. *Feminist Perspectives on Biblical Scholarship.* Chico, Calif.: Scholars Press.

DIETRICH, W., ed. 2004. *David und Saul im Widerstreit—Diachronie und Synchronie im Wettstreit. Beiträge zur Auslegung des Ersten Samuelbuches.* OBO 206. Fribourg: Academic Press; Göttingen: Vandenhoek & Ruprecht.

DILLENBERGER, J. 1969. *Martin Luther: Selections from his Writings.* New York: Doubleday.

EBELING, G. 1966. *The Nature of Faith,* trans. from *Das Wesen des christlichen Glaubens.* London: Collins Fontana.

—— 1979. *Dogmatik des christlichen Glaubens,* i. Tübingen: Mohr Siebeck.

FOWL, S. E., ed. 1997. *The Theological Interpretation of Scripture: Classic and Contemporary Readings.* Oxford: Blackwell.

FREI, H. W. 1974. *The Eclipse of Biblical Narrative: A Study in Eighteenth and Nineteenth Century Hermeneutics.* New Haven and London: Yale University Press.

GOLDINGAY, J. 1994. *Models for Scripture.* Grand Rapids, Mich.: Eerdmans; Carlisle: Paternoster.

—— 1995. *Models for Interpretation of Scripture.* Grand Rapids, Mich.: Eerdmans; Carlisle: Paternoster.

GREEN, M., HOLLOWAY, D., and WATSON, D. 1980. *The Church and Homosexuality: A Positive Answer to the Current Debate.* London: Hodder & Stoughton.

GUTIÉRREZ, G. 1974. *A Theology of Liberation.* London: SCM Press.

HARRISON, R. K. 1970. *Introduction to the Old Testament*. London: Tyndale Press.

HOUBIGANT, C. F. 1753. *Biblia sacra*, 4 vols Paris.

KAUFMANN, Y. 1963. *Tol^edot ha^emunah hayisraelit*, 8 vols., 5th edn. Jerusalem and Tel Aviv: Musad Bialik/D^evir. Abridged translation: *The Religion of Israel: From the Beginnings to the Babylonian Exile*. Chicago: University of Chicago Press; London: George Allen & Unwin, 1960.

KAYE, E. 1999. *For the Work of Ministry: A History of Northern College and its Predecessors*. Edinburgh: T. & T. Clark.

KÖRTNER, U. H. J. 1988. *Papiasfragmente: Schriften des Urchristentums*, iii: *Papiasfragmente, Hirt des Hermas*. Darmstadt: Wissenschaftliche Buchgesellschaft.

KÜMMEL, W. J. 1973. *The New Testament: The History of the Investigation of its Problems*. London: SCM Press.

LAUSTER, J. 2004. *Princip und Methode: die Transformation des protestantischen Schrift-prinzips durch die historische Kritik von Schleiermacher bis zur Gegenwart*. Hermeneutische untersuchungen zur Theologie, 46. Tübingen: Mohr Siebeck.

—— 2005. *Religion als Lebensdeutung: Theologische Hermeneutik heute*. Darmstadt: Wissenschaftliche Buchgesellschaft.

LOWTH, R. 1779. *Isaiah: A New Translation; with a Preliminary Dissertation and Notes, Critical, Philological and Explanatory*. London.

LUBAC, H. DE 1961–4. *Exégèse Médiévale: les Quatre sens de l'Écriture*. Paris: Aubier.

LUTHER, M. 1974. *Die ganze Heilige Schrifft*, iii. Munich: Deutscher Taschenbuch Verlag.

LUZ, U. 1996. *Das Evangelium nach Matthäus (Mt. 8–17): Evangelisch-katholische Kommentar zum neuen Testament*, 1/2. Solothurn and Düsseldorf: Benzinger; Neukirchen-Vluyn: Neukirchener Verlag.

MARSDEN, G. M. 1980. *Fundamentalism and American Culture: The Shaping of Twentieth Century Evangelicalism 1870–1925*. New York and Oxford: Oxford University Press.

MEYERS, C. 1988. *Discovering Eve: Ancient Israelite Women in Context*. New York: Oxford University Press

MOSALA, I. J. 1989. *Biblical Hermeneutics and Black Theology in South Africa*. Grand Rapids, Mich.: W. B. Eerdmans.

NAKANOSE, S. 1993. *Josiah's Passover: Sociology and the Liberating Bible*. Maryknoll, NY: Orbis Books.

PEAKE, A. S. 1913. *The Bible: Its Origin, its Significance and its Abiding Worth*, 2nd edn. New York and London: Hodder & Stoughton.

PHILLIPS, R. 1988. *Putting Asunder: A History of Divorce in Western Society*. Cambridge: Cambridge Univesity Press.

RENDTORFF, R. 1976. *Das überlieferungsgeschichtliche Problem des Pentateuch*. BZAW 147. Berlin: de Gruyter.

REVENTLOW, H. Graf 1990. *Epochen der Bibelauslegung*, i: *Vom Alten Testament bis Origenes*. Munich: C.H. Beck

—— 2001. *Epochen der Bibelauslegung*, iv: *Von der Aufklärung bis zum 20. Jahrhundert*. Munich: C. H. Beck.

ROGERSON, J. W. 1974. *Myth in Old Testament Interpretation*. BZAW 134. Berlin: W. de Gruyter.

—— 1984. *Old Testament Criticism in the 19th Century: England and Germany*. London: SPCK.

—— 1992. *W. M. L. deWette, Founder of Modern Biblical Criticism: An Intellectual Biography*. JSOTS.S 126. Sheffield: Sheffield Academic Press.

—— 1993. 'British Responses to Kuenen's Pentateuchal Studies'. In P. B. Dirkson and A. Van der Kooij, eds., *Abraham Kuenen (1828–1891): His Major Contributions to the Study of the Old Testament*, OS 29, Leiden: E. J. Brill, 91–104.

—— 1995. *The Bible and Criticism in Victorian Britain: Profiles of F. D. Maurice and William Roberson Smith*. JSOTS.S 201. Sheffield: Sheffield Academic Press.

—— 2004. 'The First Christian Writings'. In G. R. Evans, ed., *The First Christian Theologians: An Introduction to Theology in the Early Church*, Oxford: Blackwell, 15–23.

ROSENMÜLLER, E. F. K. 1797. *Handbuch für die Literatur der biblischen Kritik und Exegese*, Göttingen.

SAUR, M. 2004. *Die Königspsalmen: Studien zur Entstehung und Theologie*. BZAW 340. Berlin: de Gruyter.

SCHÜSSLER-FIORENZA, E. 1987. *In Memory of Her: A Feminist Theological Reconstruction of Christian Origins*. New York: Crossroad.

SETERS, J. VAN 1983. *In Search of History: Historiography in the Ancient World and the Origins of Biblical History*. New Haven and London: Yale University Press.

SIMON, R. 1678. *Histoire critique du Vieux Testament*. Paris.

—— 1699. *De l'inspiration des Livres Sacrez (sic): avec une Réponse au livre intitulé Defense des Sentiments de quelques Theologiens de Hollande sur l'Histoire Critique du Vieux Testament*. Rotterdam.

SMITH, W. R. 1881. *The Old Testament in the Jewish Church: Twelve Lectures on Biblical Criticism*. Edinburgh.

STEVENSON, J. 1957. *A New Eusebius: Documents illustrative of the history of the Church to A.D. 337*. London: SPCK.

STRAUSS, D. F. 1835. *Das Leben Jesu, kritisch bearbeitet*. Tübingen.

THIELICKE, H. 1978. *The Evangelical Faith*, ii: *The Doctrine of God and of Christ*. Edinburgh: T. and T. Clark.

—— 1982. *The Evangelical Faith*, iii: *Theology of the Spirit*. Grand Rapids, Mich.: W. B. Eerdmans.

VATKE, W. 1835. *Die biblische Theologie*, i: *Die Religion des Alten Testaments*. Berlin.

WATSON, F. 1994. *Text, Church and World. Biblical Interpretation in Theological Perspective*. Grand Rapids, Mich.: W. B. Eerdmans.

WILSON, G. H. 1985. *The Editing of the Hebrew Psalter*. SBLDS 76. Chico, Calif.: Scholars Press.

WRIGHT, G. E. 1950. *The Old Testament against its Environment*. SBT 2. London: SCM Press.

Index of Subjects and Names

Index of References

HEBREW BIBLE–OLD TESTAMENT

OLD TESTAMENT APOCRYPHA
AND PSEUDEPIGRAPHA

NEW TESTAMENT

MIDRASHIM